Register Your Book

at ibmpressbooks.com/ibmregister

Upon registration, we will send you electronic sample chapters from two of our popular IBM Press books. In addition, you will be automatically entered into a monthly drawing for a free IBM Press book.

Registration also entitles you to:

- Notices and reminders about author appearances, conferences, and online chats with special guests
- Access to supplemental material that may be available
- Advance notice of forthcoming editions
- Related book recommendations
- Information about special contests and promotions throughout the year
- Chapter excerpts and supplements of forthcoming books

Contact us

If you are interested in writing a book or reviewing manuscripts prior to publication, please write to us at:

Editorial Director, IBM Press
c/o Pearson Education
800 East 96th Street
Indianapolis, IN 46240

e-mail: IBMPress@pearsoned.com

Visit us on the Web: ibmpressbooks.com

Understanding DB2®
Second Edition

Understanding DB2®
Second Edition
Learning Visually with Examples

Raul F. Chong
Xiaomei Wang
Michael Dang
Dwaine R. Snow

IBM Press
Pearson plc

Upper Saddle River, NJ • Boston • Indianapolis • San Francisco
New York • Toronto • Montreal • London • Munich • Paris • Madrid
Capetown • Sydney • Tokyo • Singapore • Mexico City

ibmpressbooks.com

IBM Press Program Managers: Tara Woodman, Ellice Uffer
Cover design: IBM Corporation
Associate Publisher: Greg Wiegand
Marketing Manager: Kourtnaye Sturgeon
Publicist: Heather Fox
Acquisitions Editor: Bernard Goodwin
Managing Editor: John Fuller
Project Editor: Lara Wysong
Copy Editor: Plan-it Publishing
Indexer: Barbara Pavey
Compositor: codeMantra
Proofreader: Sossity Smith
Manufacturing Buyer: Anna Popick

Published by Pearson plc
Publishing as IBM Press

IBM Press offers excellent discounts on this book when ordered in quantity for bulk purchases or special sales, which may include electronic versions and/or custom covers and content particular to your business, training goals, marketing focus, and branding interests. For more information, please contact:

U.S. Corporate and Government Sales
1-800-382-3419
corpsales@pearsontechgroup.com.

For sales outside the U.S., please contact:

International Sales
international@pearsoned.com

This Book Is Safari Enabled

The Safari® Enabled icon on the cover of your favorite technology book means the book is available through Safari Bookshelf. When you buy this book, you get free access to the online edition for 45 days. Safari Bookshelf is an electronic reference library that lets you easily search thousands of technical books, find code samples, download chapters, and access technical information whenever and wherever you need it.

To gain 45-day Safari Enabled access to this book:

- Go to http://www.ibmpressbooks/safarienabled
- Complete the brief registration form
- Enter the coupon code CQE9-VLXD-FHEY-DFDM-CQHL

If you have difficulty registering on Safari Bookshelf or accessing the online edition, please e-mail customer-service@safaribooksonline.com.

Library of Congress Cataloging-in-Publication Data

Understanding DB2 : learning visually with examples / Raul F. Chong ... [et al.]. — 2nd ed.
p. cm.
Includes bibliographical references and index.
ISBN-13: 978-0-13-158018-3 (hardcover : alk. paper)
1. Relational databases. 2. IBM Database 2. I. Chong, Raul F.

QA76.9.D3U55 2007
005.75'65—dc22

2007044541

Pearson Education, Inc
Rights and Contracts Department
501 Boylston Street, Suite 900
Boston, MA 02116
Fax (617) 671-3447

ISBN-13: 978-0-13-158018-3
ISBN-10: 0-13-158018-3

Text printed in the United States on recycled paper at RR Donnelley in Crawfordsville, Indiana.
First printing, December 2007

Raul would like to thank his wife Jin for her understanding, support, and love. Her insightfulness, patience, and beautiful smile kept him going to complete this second edition of this book. Raul would also like to thank his parents, Elias and Olga Chong, for their constant support and love, and his siblings, Alberto, David, Patricia, and Nancy for their support.

Xiaomei would like to thank her family—Peiqin, Nengchao, Kangning, Kaiwen, Weihong, Weihua, and Chong, for their endless love and support. Most of all, Xiaomei wants to thank Chau for his care, love, and understanding when she spent many late nights and weekends writing this book.

Michael would like to thank his wonderful wife Sylvia for her constant support, motivation, understanding, and most importantly, love, in his quest to complete the second edition of this book.

Dwaine would like to thank his wife Linda and daughter Alyssa for their constant love, support, and understanding. You are always there to brighten my day, not only during the time spent writing this book, but no matter where I am or what I am doing. Dwaine would also like to thank his parents, Gladys and Robert, for always being there.

All the authors of this book would like to thank Clara Liu, coauthor of the first edition, for helping with this second edition. Clara was expecting a second child at the time this book was being written, and decided not to participate for this reason.

Contents

Chapter 2 DB2 at a Glance: The Big Picture 33

Chapter 3 Installing DB2 85

Chapter 5 Understanding the DB2 Environment, DB2 Instances, and Databases 189

Chapter 6 Configuring Client and Server Connectivity 231

Chapter 10 Mastering the DB2 pureXML Support 453

Chapter 11 Implementing Security 543

Chapter 12 Understanding Concurrency and Locking 603

Foreword

What a difference two years make. When the first edition of this book came out in 2005, DB2 Universal Database® (UDB) for Linux®, UNIX®, and Windows® version 8.2 was the hot new entry on the database management scene. As this book goes to press, DB2 9.5 is making its debut. While this latest DB2 release builds on the new features introduced in 8.2, it also continues along the new direction established by DB2 9: native storage and management of XML by the same engine that manages traditional relational data.

Why store and manage relational and XML data in the same data server, when specialized management systems exist for both? That's one of the things you'll learn in this book, of course, but here's the high-level view. As a hybrid data server, DB2 9 makes possible combinations of relational and XML data that weren't previously feasible. It also lets companies make the most of the skills of their existing employees. SQL experts can query both relational and XML data with an SQL statement. XQuery experts can query both XML and relational data with an XML query. And both relational and XML data benefit from DB2's backup and recovery, optimization, scalability, and high availability features.

Certainly no newcomer to the IT landscape, XML is a given at most companies today. Why? Because as a flexible, self-describing language, XML is a sound basis for information exchange with customers, partners, and (in certain industries) regulators. It's also the foundation that's enabling more flexibility in IT architecture (namely service-oriented architecture). And it's one of the key enabling technologies behind Web 2.0. That's the high-level view. This book's authors provide a much more thorough explanation of XML's importance in IT systems in Chapter 2, DB2 at a Glance: The Big Picture, and Chapter 10, Mastering the DB2 pureXML™ Support.

DB2 9.5 addresses both changes in the nature of business over the past two years as well as changes that are poised to affect businesses for years to come. XML falls into both categories. But XML isn't the only recent change DB2 9.5 addresses.

A seemingly endless stream of high-profile data breaches has put information security front and center in the public's mind—and it certainly should be front and center in the minds of companies that want to sell to this public. Not only do security controls have to be in place, but many companies have to be able to show in granular detail which employees have access to (and have accessed) what information. Chapter 11, Implementing Security, covers the DB2 security model in great detail, including detailed instructions for understanding and implementing Label-Based Access Control (new in DB2 9), which enables row- and column-level security.

When new business requirements come onto the scene, old concerns rarely go away. In fact, they sometimes become more important than ever. As companies look to become more efficient in every sense, they're placing more demands on data servers and the people who support them. For that reason, performance is as important as it has ever been. Chapter 17, Database Performance Considerations, covers DB2 tuning considerations from configuration, to proper SQL, to workload management, and other considerations. It also explains some of DB2's self-managing and self-tuning features that take some of the burden of performance tuning off the DBA's back.

Though thoroughly updated to reflect the changes in DB2 in the last two years, in some important ways, the second edition of this book isn't vastly different from the first. Readers loved the first edition of this book for its step-by-step approach to clarifying complex topics, its liberal use of screenshots and diagrams, and the completeness of its coverage, which appealed to novices and experts alike. Browsing the pages of this second edition, it's clear that the authors delivered just what their readers want: more of the same, updated to cover what's current today and what's coming next.

—Kim Moutsos

Editor, *DB2 Magazine* and DB2mag.com

Preface

In the world of information technology today, it is more and more difficult to keep up with the skills required to be successful on the job. This book was developed to minimize the time, money, and effort required to learn DB2 for Linux, UNIX, and Windows. The book visually introduces and discusses the latest version of DB2, DB2 9.5. The goal with the development of DB2 was to make it work the same regardless of the operating system on which you choose to run it. The few differences in the implementation of DB2 on these platforms are explained in this book.

Who Should Read This Book?

This book is intended for anyone who works with databases, such as database administrators (DBAs), application developers, system administrators, and consultants. This book is a great introduction to DB2, whether you have used DB2 before or you are new to DB2. It is also a good study guide for anyone preparing for the IBM® DB2 9 Certification exams 730 (DB2 9 Fundamentals), 731 (DB2 9 DBA for Linux, UNIX and Windows), or 736 (DB2 9 Database Administrator for Linux, UNIX, and Windows Upgrade exam).

This book will save you time and effort because the topics are presented in a clear and concise manner, and we use figures, examples, case studies, and review questions to reinforce the material as it is presented. The book is different from many others on the subject because of the following.

1. **Visual learning:** The book relies on visual learning as its base. Each chapter starts with a "big picture" to introduce the topics to be discussed in that chapter. Numerous graphics are used throughout the chapters to explain concepts in detail. We feel that figures allow for fast, easy learning and longer retention of the material. If you forget some of the concepts discussed in the book or just need a quick refresher, you will not need to read the entire chapter again. You can simply look at the figures quickly to refresh your memory. For your convenience, some of the most important figures are provided in color on the book's Web site (www.ibmpressbooks.com/title/0131580183). These figures in color can further improve your learning experience.
2. **Clear explanations:** We have encountered many situations when reading other books where paragraphs need to be read two, three, or even more times to grasp what they are describing. In this book we have made every effort possible to provide clear explanations so that you can understand the information quickly and easily.
3. **Examples, examples, examples:** The book provides many examples and case studies that reinforce the topics discussed in each chapter. Some of the examples have been

taken from real life experiences that the authors have had while working with DB2 customers.

4. **Sample exam questions:** All chapters end with review questions that are similar to the questions on the DB2 Certification exams. These questions are intended to ensure that you understand the concepts discussed in each chapter before proceeding, and as a study guide for the IBM Certification exams. Appendix A contains the answers with explanations.

GETTING STARTED

If you are new to DB2 and would like to get the most out of this book, we suggest you start reading from the beginning and continue with the chapters in order. If you are new to DB2 but are in a hurry to get a quick understanding of DB2, you can jump to Chapter 2, DB2 at a Glance: The Big Picture. Reading this chapter will introduce you to the main concepts of DB2. You can then go to other chapters to read for further details.

If you would like to follow the examples provided with the book, you need to install DB2. Chapter 3, Installing DB2, gives you the details to handle this task.

A Word of Advice

In this book we use figures extensively to introduce and examine DB2 concepts. While some of the figures may look complex, don't be overwhelmed by first impressions! The text that accompanies them explains the concepts in detail. If you look back at the figure after reading the description, you will be surprised by how much clearer it is.

This book only discusses DB2 for Linux, UNIX, and Windows, so when we use the term DB2, we are referring to DB2 on those platforms. DB2 for i5/OS®, DB2 for z/OS®, and DB2 for VM and VSE are mentioned only when presenting methods that you can use to access these databases from an application written on Linux, UNIX, or Windows. When DB2 for i5/OS, DB2 for z/OS, and DB2 for VM and VSE are discussed, we refer to them explicitly.

This book was written prior to the official release of DB2 9.5. The authors used a beta copy of the product to obtain screen shots, and to perform their tests. It is possible that by the time this book is published and the product is officially released, some features and screenshots may have changed slightly.

CONVENTIONS

Many examples of SQL statements, XPath/XQuery statements, DB2 commands, and operating system commands are included throughout the book. SQL keywords are written in uppercase bold. For example: Use the **`SELECT`** statement to retrieve data from a DB2 database.

XPath and XQuery statements are case sensitive and will be written in bold. For example:
`/employee/DEPT/Id`

DB2 commands are shown in lowercase bold. For example: The **list applications** command lists the applications connected to your databases.

You can issue many DB2 commands from the Command Line Processor (CLP) utility, which accepts the commands in both uppercase and lowercase. In the UNIX operating systems, program names are case-sensitive, so be careful to enter the program name using the proper case. For example, on UNIX, **db2** must be entered in lowercase. (See Appendix B, Use of Uppercase versus Lowercase in DB2, for a detailed discussion of this.)

Database object names used in our examples are shown in italics. For example: The *country* table has five columns.

Italics are also used for variable names in the syntax of a command or statement. If the variable name has more than one word, it is joined with an underscore. For example: **CREATE SEQUENCE *sequence_name***

Where a concept of a function is new in DB2 9, we signify it with the follwing icon:

When a concept of a function is new in DB2 9.5 we signify it with the following icon:

Note that the DB2 certification exams only include material of DB2 version 9, not version 9.5

Contacting the Authors

We are interested in any feedback that you have about this book. Please contact us with your opinions and inquiries at udb2book@ca.ibm.com.

Depending on the volume of inquires, we may be unable to respond to every technical question but we'll do our best. The DB2 forum at `www-128.ibm.com/developerworks/forums/dw_forum.jsp?forum=291&cat=81` is another great way to get assistance from IBM employees and the DB2 user community.

What's New

It has been a while since we've updated this book, and there have been two versions of DB2 for Linux, UNIX, and Windows in that time. This section summarizes the changes made to the book from its first edition, and highlights what's new with DB2 9 and DB2 9.5.

The core of DB2 and its functionality remains mostly the same as in previous versions; therefore, some chapters required minimal updates. On the other hand, some other chapters such as Chapter 15, The DB2 Process Model, and Chapter 16, The DB2 Memory Model, required substantial changes. Chapter 10, Mastering the DB2 pureXML Support, is a new chapter in this book and describes DB2's pureXML technology, one of the main features introduced in DB2 9.

We have done our best not to increase the size of the book, however this has been challenging as we have added more chapters and materials to cover new DB2 features. In some cases we have moved some material to our Web site (www.ibmpressbooks.com/title/0131580183).

There have been a lot of changes and additions to DB2 and to this edition of the book. To indicate where something has changed from the previous version of the book, or was added in DB2 9 and/or DB2 9.5, we have used the icons shown below.

V9.5

The following sections will briefly introduce the changes or additions in each of these new versions of DB2.

DB2 9

DB2 9 introduced a few very important features for both database administrators as well as application developers. Developers have been most interested in pureXML, DB2's introduction of a native data type and support for XML documents. This allows you to store, index, and retrieve XML documents without the need to shred them, or store them in a CLOB and do unnatural things to access specific elements in the document. In addition, you can use SQL or XQuery to access the relational and XML data in your tables. The new developer workbench is a development environment that is integrated into the eclipse framework. It helps you to build, debug, and test your applications and objects such as stored procedures and UDFs.

From the DBA's point of view, there are a number of enhancements that came in DB2 9 that made life easier. Automatic storage allows you to create paths that your databases will use, and then create table spaces in the database that will automatically grow as data is added in these table spaces. Automatic self-tuning memory provides you with a single memory-tuning knob. You can simply tell DB2 to "manage yourself" and DB2 will adjust the memory allocations based on the system configuration and the incoming workload, and it will adapt to changes in the workload automatically.

Table or range partitioning allows you to logically break up your tables for easier maintenance and faster roll in and roll out of data. This, combined with MDC and DB2's database partitioning, provides the ultimate in I/O reduction for large, data-intensive queries. Data compression automatically replaces repeated strings, which can even span multiple columns with a very small symbol, resulting in even more I/O reduction. When you add data compression on top of the data partitioning, you get much smaller databases, with much faster performance than ever before possible. In DB2 9, the compression dictionary, where the symbols and the values they replace are stored, must be built offline using the REORG tool. This dictionary is then used for subsequent inserts and updates, but it is static, meaning new repeated values are not added automatically.

Another important feature of DB2 9 that we discuss in detail in this book is Label Based Access Control, or LBAC. LBAC allows you to control access to the rows and columns of data in your tables so that you can comply with both business and regulatory requirements.

DB2 9.5

If you were excited by DB2 9, you are going to be even more excited about DB2 9.5. One thing those of you running on Linux or UNIX will notice immediately is that DB2 9.5 uses a threaded engine, not a process-based engine as in previous versions. This will help to increase performance and make administration even easier. Because there is only one main engine process now, the memory configuration task has been simplified. The default **AUTOMATIC** setting on most memory-related configuration parameters makes memory management much easier, and much more efficient. You will not have to worry about those pesky db2 agent processes any more. DB2 9.5 is also introducing a new locking mechanism so that readers do not block writers.

While DB2 9 introduced automated statistics gathering, DB2 9.5 takes that a major step further. If there has been a significant amount of changes to the table since the last **RUNSTATS** was run, DB2 will automatically run a **RUNSTATS** before it optimizes a new access plan that hits that table. Along the same vein, if you have a table which has been enabled for compression, DB2 will now create a dictionary, or update the existing dictionary as data is added to, or updated in the table, and if you are **LOAD**ing data into the table. You no longer have to run a **REORG** or **INSPECT** to get a dictionary, and it is no longer a static dictionary.

If you tried HADR with DB2 V8.2, or DB2 9, it is now even easier, and that is saying something. You no longer have to worry about setting up the scripts and the clustering software to automatically detect server failures and manage server failovers. This setup is now done for you automatically when you set up HADR.

Roles are another important feature added in DB2 9.5. Roles allow you to mimic the job functions within your organization, and grant privileges or rights to roles instead of to specific users or groups. This makes the management of who can see what data much easier and more intuitive since it provides a single point of security and privilege management.

Both of these new versions of DB2 include features and functions that will make your life easier. We hope that we have described them in a manner that is easy to understand, and that shows you how and when you might want to take advantage of the new features of the different versions of DB2.

Acknowledgments

Raul, Xiaomei, Michael, and Dwaine would like to thank Liam Finnie, Matthias Nicola, Philip Gunning, Denis C. F. de Vasconcelos, Robert Bernard, Hassan A Shazly, Sylvia Qi, and Ilker Ender for their review of the book.

Susan Visser provided guidance and invaluable help throughout the whole process of planning, writing, and publishing the book. Without her help, this book would never have been completed as smoothly as it has been.

About the Authors

Raul F. Chong is the DB2 on Campus Program Manager based at the IBM Toronto Laboratory. His main responsibility is to grow the DB2 Express community, helping members interact with one another and contributing to the forum. Raul is focusing on universities and other educational institutions promoting the DB2 on Campus program. Raul holds a bachelor of science degree in computer science from the University of Toronto, and is a DB2 Certified Solutions Expert in both DB2 Administration and Application Development. Raul joined IBM in 1997 and has held numerous positions in the company. As a DB2 consultant, Raul helped IBM business partners with migrations from other relational database management systems to DB2, as well as with database performance and application design issues. As a DB2 technical support specialist, Raul has helped resolve DB2 problems on the OS/390®, z/OS, Linux, UNIX, and Windows platforms. Raul has also worked as an information developer for the Application Development Solutions team, where he was responsible for the CLI guide and Web services material. Raul has taught many DB2 workshops, has presented at conferences worldwide, has published numerous articles, and has contributed to the DB2 Certification exam tutorials. Raul summarized many of his DB2 experiences through the years in the first edition of *Understanding DB2: Learning Visually with Examples* (ISBN 0131859161) for which he is the lead author. He has also coauthored the book *DB2 SQL PL Essential Guide for DB2 UDB on Linux, UNIX, Windows, i5/OS, and z/OS* (ISBN 0131477005). In his spare time, Raul is an avid tennis player (though 90% of his shots go off the court!). He also enjoys watching basketball and hockey, traveling to interesting places, and experiencing new cultures. Raul is fluent in Spanish as he was born and raised in Peru, but he keeps some of the Chinese traditions from his grandparents. He also enjoys reading history and archeology books.

Xiaomei Wang is a technical consultant for IBM Discovery & Enterprise Content Management (ECM) based at the IBM Toronto Laboratory. Her current assignment is assisting business partners with integrating IBM Discovery and ECM products into their solutions. Xiaomei has more than eight years of DB2 UDB experience via various positions with IBM. As a DB2 Advanced Support IT Specialist, Xiaomei handled critical DB2 customer situations worldwide, exploiting her expertise in both non-partitioned and partitioned database environments. She spearheaded the DB2 Problem Determination and Trouble Shooting education activities across IBM DB2 support centers worldwide and has helped to establish the DB2 L2 Support Centers in AP countries. Her other experiences include working as the IBM Greater China Group Business Development manager to increase DB2 presence on non-IBM hardware platforms. Following that, Xiaomei also worked as a worldwide pre-sales IT specialist for IBM Information Management to drive incremental DB2 revenue on partner platforms (i.e., Sun and HP). Xiaomei has presented at conferences worldwide, and has written a number of articles, and coauthored the redbook *SAP Solutions on IBM DB2 UDB V8.2.2 Handbook*. Xiaomei is an IBM Certified Solution Experts (Content Manager, FileNet P8, DB2 UDB Database

Administration, DB2 UDB Application Development, DB2 UDB Advanced Technical Expert, and Business Intelligence), and also a Red Hat Certified Technician.

Michael Dang is a DB2 technical sales specialist. He currently works in the IBM Techline Americas organization, whose main focus is to provide quality technical presales support to help the IBM sales force sell and win solutions. In this role, Michael specializes in solution design, database sizing, product licensing, and Balanced Warehouse configurations. Prior to this, Michael has also worked as a DB2 support analyst, and as a DB2 database administrator for more than seven years. In those roles, Michael provided in-depth technical support to resolve customer DB2 problems, and managed production databases for many major companies. Michael has contributed to numerous articles and is an IBM Certified Advanced Technical Expert.

Dwaine R. Snow is a senior product manager for DB2 for Linux, UNIX, and Windows, and focuses on ensuring that DB2 is the best data server for our customers and partners. Dwaine has worked with DB2 for the past 17 years as part of the development team focusing on the database engine and tools, the development of the DB2 Certification program, and as part of the lab-based consulting team. Dwaine has presented at conferences worldwide, contributed to the DB2 tutorial series, and has written a number of articles and books on DB2. Book credits include *Understanding DB2®: Learning Visually with Examples*, *Advanced DBA Certification Guide and Reference for DB2® Universal Database for Linux, UNIX, and Windows*, *DB2® UDB for Windows*, *The DB2 Cluster Certification Guide*, and the second edition of the *DB2® Certification Guide for Linux, UNIX, and Windows*. Dwaine helps write and review the product certification tests, and holds all DB2 certifications.

A.0.1 Author Publications

Chong, Raul. "Getting Started with DB2 for z/OS and OS/390 Version 7 for DB2 Distributed Platform Users." www.ibm.com/software/data/developer. July 2002.

______. "Leverage Your Distributed DB2 Skills to Get Started on DB2 UDB for the iSeries® (AS/ 400®)." www.ibm.com/software/data/developer. October 2002.

______. "Backup and Recovery: DB2 V8.1 Database Administration Certification Prep, Part 6 of 6." www.ibm.com/software/data/developer. May 2003.

______. *DB2 SQL PL, Second Edition: Essential Guide for DB2 UDB on Linux, UNIX, Windows, i5/OS, and z/OS.* Upper Saddle River, N.J.: Prentice Hall, 2005.

Wang, Xiaomei. "DB2 UDB OLTP Tuning Illustrated with a Java™ Program." www.ibm.com/software/data/developer. August 2005.

______. "SAP Solutions on IBM DB2 UDB V8.2.2 Handbook." www.redbooks.ibm.com/abstracts/sg246765.html. October 2005.

______. "IBM Classification Module for WebSphere® Content Discovery Server and Classification Workbench Installation Guide." www.ibm.com/software/data/developer. September 2006.

______. "Add Advanced Search to Your WebSphere Commerce Store with OmniFind™ Discovery Edition." www.ibm.com/software/data/developer. May 2007.

Dang, Michael. "DB2 9 DBA Exam 731 Prep, Part 7: High Availability: Split Mirroring and HADR" www.ibm.com/software/data/developer. July 2006.

______. "The DB2 UDB Memory Model." www.ibm.com/software/data/developer. June 2004.
______. "DB2 Universal Database Commands by Example." www.ibm.com/software/data/developer. June 2004.
Snow, Dwaine. *DB2 Universal Database Certification Guide, Second Edition.* Upper Saddle River, N.J.: Prentice Hall, 1997.
______. *DB2 UDB Cluster Certification Guide.* Upper Saddle River, N.J.: Prentice Hall, 1998.
______. *The Universal Guide to DB2 for Windows NT.* Upper Saddle River, N.J.: Prentice Hall, 1999.
______. *Advanced DBA Certification Guide and Reference for DB2 Universal Database V8 for Linux, UNIX, and Windows.* Upper Saddle River, N.J.: Prentice Hall, 2004.

CHAPTER 1

Introduction to DB2

DATABASE 2 (DB2) for Linux, UNIX, and Windows is a data server developed by IBM. Version 9.5, available since October 2007, is the most current version of the product, and the one on which we focus in this book.

In this chapter you will learn about the following:

- The history of DB2
- The information management portfolio of products
- How DB2 is developed
- DB2 server editions and clients
- How DB2 is packaged for developers
- Syntax diagram conventions

1.1 Brief History of DB2

Since the 1970s, when IBM Research invented the Relational Model and the Structured Query Language (SQL), IBM has developed a complete family of data servers. Development started on mainframe platforms such as Virtual Machine (VM), Virtual Storage Extended (VSE), and Multiple Virtual Storage (MVS). In 1983, DB2 for MVS Version 1 was born. "DB2" was used to indicate a shift from *hierarchical* databases—such as the Information Management System (IMS) popular at the time—to the new *relational* databases. DB2 development continued on mainframe platforms as well as on distributed platforms.[1] Figure 1.1 shows some of the highlights of DB2 history.

1. Distributed platforms, also referred to as **open system platforms,** include all platforms other than mainframe or midrange operating systems. Some examples are Linux, UNIX, and Windows.

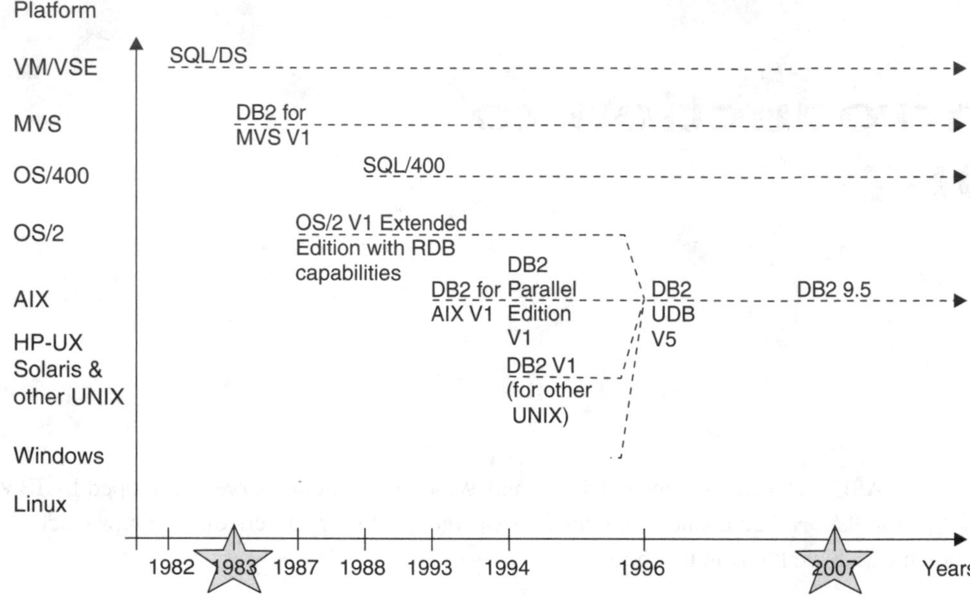

Figure 1.1 DB2 timeline

In 1996, IBM announced DB2 Universal Database (UDB) Version 5 for distributed platforms. With this version, DB2 was able to store all kinds of electronic data, including traditional relational data, as well as audio, video, and text documents. It was the first version optimized for the Web, and it supported a range of distributed platforms—for example, OS/2, Windows, AIX, HP-UX, and Solaris—from multiple vendors. Moreover, this universal database was able to run on a variety of hardware, from uniprocessor systems and symmetric multiprocessor (SMP) systems to massively parallel processing (MPP) systems and clusters of SMP systems.

Even though the relational model to store data is the most prevalent in the industry today, the hierarchical model never lost its importance. In the past few years, due to the popularity of e**X**tensible **M**arkup **L**anguage (XML), a resurgence in the use of the hierarchical model has taken place. XML, a flexible, self-describing language, relies on the hierarchical model to store data. With the emergence of new Web technologies, the need to store unstructured types of data, and to share and exchange information between businesses, XML proves to be the best language to meet these needs. Today we see an exponential growth of XML documents usage.

IBM recognized early on the importance of XML, and large investments were made to deliver pureXML technology; a technology that provides for better support to store XML documents in DB2. After five years of development, the effort of 750 developers, architects, and engineers paid off with the release of the first hybrid data server in the market: DB2 9. DB2 9, available since July 2006, is a hybrid (also known as multi-structured) data server because it allows for storing relational data, as well as hierarchical data, natively. While other data servers in the market, and previous versions of DB2 could store XML documents, the storage method used was not ideal for performance and flexibility. With DB2 9's pureXML technology, XML documents are stored internally in a parsed hierarchical manner, as a tree; therefore, working with XML documents is greatly enhanced. In 2007, IBM has gone even further in its support for pureXML, with the release of DB2 9.5. DB2 9.5, the latest version of DB2, not only enhances and introduces new features of pureXML, but it also brings improvements in installation, manageability, administration, scalability and performance, workload management and monitoring, regulatory compliance, problem determination, support for application development, and support for business partner applications.

NOTE The term "Universal Database" or "UDB" was dropped from the name in DB2 9 for simplicity. Previous versions of DB2 database products and documentation retain "Universal Database" and "UDB" in the product naming.

Also starting in version 9, the term *data server* is introduced to describe the product. A data server provides software services for the secure and efficient management of structured information. DB2 Version 9 is a hybrid data server.

NOTE Before a new version of DB2 is publicly available, a code name is used to identify the product. Once the product is publicly available, the code name is not used. DB2 9 had a code name of "Viper", and DB2 9.5 had a code name of "Viper 2". Some references in published articles may still use these code names.

Note as well that there is no DB2 9.2, DB2 9.3 or DB2 9.4. The version was changed from DB2 9 directly to DB2 9.5 to signify major changes and new features in the product.

DB2 is available for many platforms including System z (DB2 for z/OS) and System i (DB2 for i5/OS). Unless otherwise noted, when we use the term DB2, we are referring to DB2 version 9.5 running on Linux, UNIX, or Windows.

DB2 is part of the IBM information management (IM) portfolio. Table 1.1 shows the different IM products available.

Table 1.1 Information Management Products

Information Management Products	Description	Product Offerings
Data Servers	Provide software services for the secure and efficient management of data and enable the sharing of information across multiple platforms.	IBM DB2 IBM IMS IBM Informix IBM U2
Data Warehousing and Business Intelligence	Help customers collect, prepare, manage, analyze, and extract valuable information from all data types to help them make faster, more insightful business decisions.	DB2 Alphablox DB2 Cube Views DB2 Warehouse Edition DB2 Query Management Facility
Enterprise Content Management & Discovery	Manage content, process, and connectivity. The content includes both structured and unstructured data, such as e-mails, electronic forms, images, digital media, word processing documents, and Web content. Perform enterprise search and discovery of information.	DB2 Content Manager DB2 Common Store DB2 CM OnDemand DB2 Records Manager FileNet P8 and its add-on suites OmniFind
Information Integration	Bring together distributed information from heterogeneous environments. Companies view their information as if it were all residing in one place.	IBM Information Server integration software platform, consisting of: - WebSphere Federation Server - WebSphere Replication Server - WebSphere DataStage - WebSphere ProfileStage - WebSphere QualityStage - WebSphere Information Services Director - WebSphere Metadata Server - WebSphere Business Glossary - WebSphere Data Event Publisher

1.2 The Role of DB2 in the Information On Demand World

IBM's direction or strategy is based on some key concepts and technologies:

On-Demand Business
Information On Demand (IOD)
Service-Oriented Architecture (SOA)

Web Services
XML

In this section we describe each of these concepts, and we explain where DB2 fits in the strategy.

1.2.1 On-Demand Business

We live in a complex world with complex computer systems where change is a constant. At the same time, customers are becoming more demanding and less tolerant of mistakes. In a challenging environment like this, businesses need to react quickly to market changes; otherwise, they will be left behind by competitors. In order to react quickly, a business needs to be integrated and flexible. In other words, a business today needs to be an on-demand business.

An **on-demand business,** as defined by IBM, is "an enterprise whose business processes—integrated end to end across the company and with key partners, suppliers and customers—can respond with speed to any customer demand, market opportunity, or external threat."

IBM's on-demand business model is based on this definition. To support the on-demand model, IBM uses the e-business framework shown in Figure 1.2.

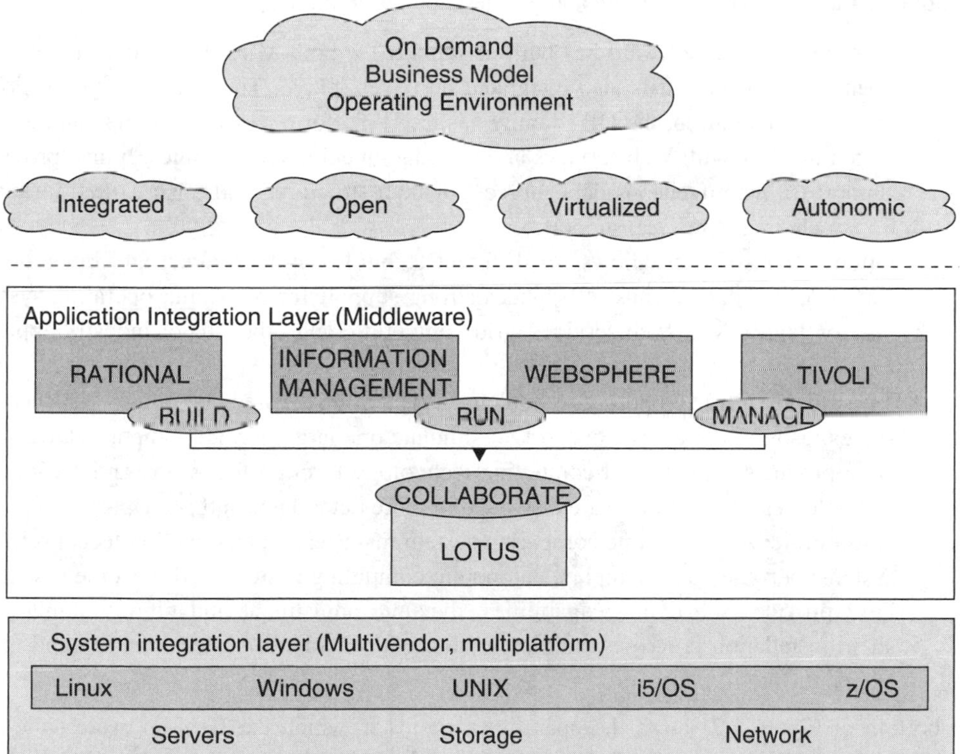

Figure 1.2 The IBM e-business framework

In Figure 1.2 the dotted line divides the logical concepts at the top with the physical implementation at the bottom. Conceptually, the IBM e-business framework is based on the on-demand business model operating environment, which has four essential characteristics: It is integrated, open, virtualized, and autonomic. These characteristics are explained later in this section.

The area below the dotted line illustrates how this environment is implemented by the suite of IBM software products.

- Rational is the "build" software portfolio; it is used to develop software.
- Information Management (where DB2 belongs) and WebSphere are the "run" software portfolios; they store and manipulate your data and manage your applications.
- Tivoli is the "manage" software portfolio; it integrates, provides security, and manages your overall systems.
- Lotus is the "collaborate" software portfolio used for integration, messaging, and collaboration across all the other software portfolios.

The IBM DB2 software plays a critical role in the on-demand operating environment. All elements of the Information Management portfolio, including DB2, are developed with the four essential characteristics of the on-demand business model in mind.

- **Integrated:** DB2 software has built-in support for both Microsoft and Java development environments. It is also integrated into WebSphere, Tivoli, Lotus, and Rational products. In addition, the DB2 family has cross-platform capabilities and can be integrated natively with Web services and message-queuing technologies. It also provides support for heterogeneous data sources for both structured and unstructured information, including pureXML support.
- **Open:** DB2 software allows for different technologies to connect and integrate by following standards. Thus, it provides strong support for the Linux operating system and for Java, XML, Web services, grid computing, and other major industry applications.
- **Virtualized:** Grid computing technology, a type of distributed computing, collects and shares resources in a large network to simulate one large, virtual computer. DB2 software products support grid computing technology through federation and integration technologies. Both of these are discussed in more detail later in this chapter.
- **Autonomic:** An autonomic computing system manages, repairs, and protects itself. As systems become more complex, autonomic computing systems will become essential. DB2 provides self-tuning capabilities, dynamic adjustment and tuning, simple and silent installation processes, and integration with Tivoli for system security and management.

The bottom of Figure 1.2 shows the operating systems in which the IBM software suite can operate: Linux, UNIX, Windows, i5/OS, and z/OS. Below that, the servers, storage, and network represent the actual hardware used to support the framework.

An on-demand business depends on having information available on demand, whenever it is needed, by people, tools, or applications. Information On Demand is discussed in the next section.

1.2.2 Information On Demand

Information On Demand, as its name implies, is making information available whenever people, tools, or applications demand or request it. This can be made possible by providing information as a service. IBM commonly uses the illustration in Figure 1.3 to explain what "information as a service" means. Let's use the following example to explain this concept in a more interesting way. Assume you are the general manager of a supermarket, and your main goal is to make this business profitable. To accomplish this, you must make good decisions, such as how to display items on shelves so that they sell more. In order to make good decisions, you need to have up-to-date, reliable information.

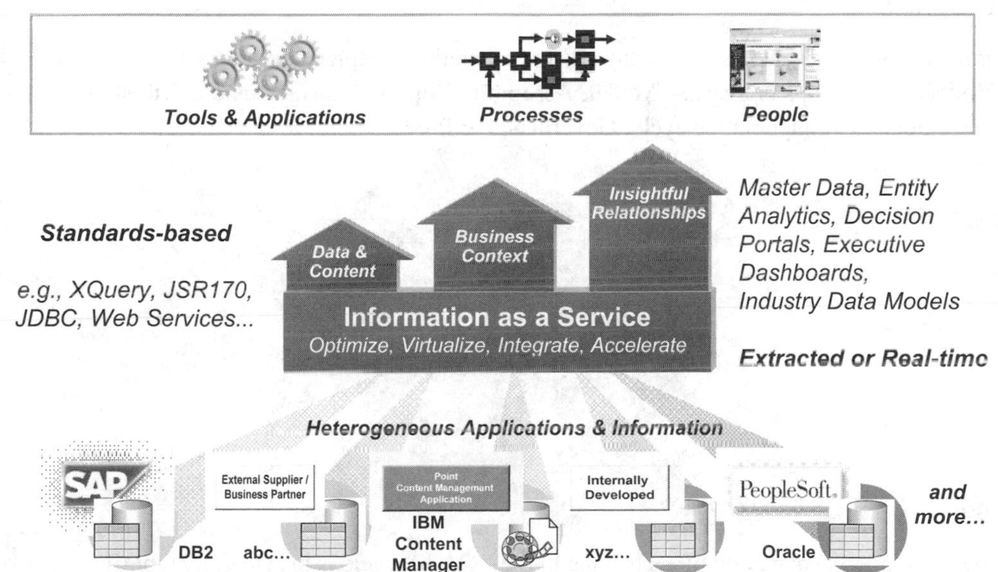

Figure 1.3 Information as a service

As depicted at the bottom of Figure 1.3, many businesses today have a large number of heterogeneous sources of information. For this particular example let's assume your suppliers use SAP and DB2, your sales department uses an internally developed application, your smaller supermarket clients use Peoplesoft, and Oracle, and so on. Thus, you see several heterogeneous applications with semi-raw data, which will only be valuable to you if you can integrate them all. In order to integrate the data, it needs to be provided as a service, and this is possible through the use of standards such as JDBC and ODBC, and wrapping each of these applications as a Web service. Once the data are integrated, you may come up with decisions that might not have been logical otherwise, such as putting beer and diapers in the same aisle in order to sell more of both products.

With the data integrated you can further massage it to perform some additional analysis and get insightful relationships. This further massaging of the data can be performed by other software, such as entity analytics, master data, and so on as shown on the right side of the figure. Finally, this integrated data can be passed to other processes, tools and applications, and people for further analysis.

1.2.3 Service-Oriented Architecture

Service-Oriented Architecture (SOA), as its name implies, is an architecture based on services—mainly Web services. SOA is not a product, but a methodology, a way to design systems that allow for integration, flexibility, loosely coupled components, and greater code reuse. With this architecture, business activities are treated as services that can be accessed on demand through the network.

Figure 1.4, which is also used in many IBM presentations, depicts the SOA lifecycle. It consists of four iterative steps or stages—Model, Assemble, Deploy, Manage—and a fifth step that provides guidance throughout the cycle: Governance & Processes.

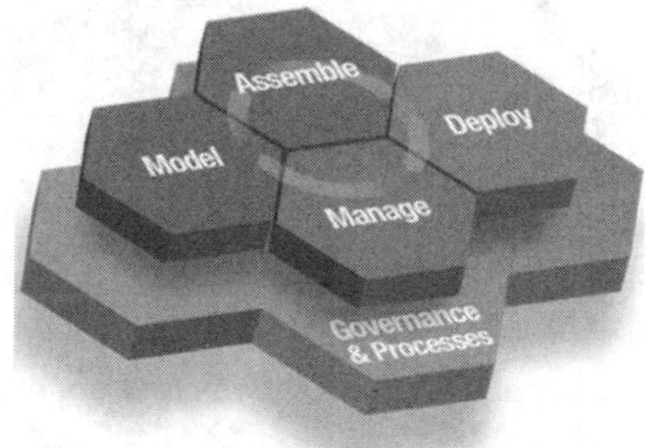

Figure 1.4 The SOA Lifecycle

A more detailed explanation of each stage in the SOA lifecycle is provided in Table 1.2.

Table 1.2 The SOA Lifecycle Stages

SOA stage	Description	IBM Tools That Can Be Used
Model	This stage is used to model and optimize your business processes. It is also used to determine the kinds of services needed and the type of data these services would access.	WebSphere Business Integration Modeler Rational Software Architect

Table 1.2 The SOA Lifecycle Stages *(Continued)*

SOA stage	Description	IBM Tools That Can Be Used
Assemble	This stage is about building new services and/or reusing existing ones, and assembling them to form composite applications.	WebSphere Integration Developer Rational Application Developer
Deploy	In this stage your services and applications are deployed into a secure environment that integrates people, processes, and information within your business.	WebSphere Process Server WebSphere Message Broker WebSphere Partner Gateway WebSphere Portal WebSphere Everyplace Deployment Workplace Collaboration Services WebSphere Information Integrator WebSphere Application Server
Manage	In this stage, you need to manage and monitor your system, find and correct inefficiencies and problems, deal with security, quality of service, and general system administration.	WebSphere Business Monitor Tivoli Composite Application Manager for SOA Tivoli Identity Manager
Governance	Governance underpins all the lifecycle stages. It ensures that all the services from inside and outside the organization are controlled so the system does not spin out of control. Governance provides both direction and control.	N/A

1.2.4 Web Services

A Web service, as its name implies, is a service made available through the Web. A more formal, but still simple definition states that a Web service is a way for an application to call a function over the network; however, there is no need to know

- The location where this function will be executed
- The platform in which the function will run (for example Linux, UNIX, Windows, the mainframe, Mac OS/X, etc.)
- The programming language in which the function was created (for example Java, Cobol, C, etc.)

Web services are powerful because they allow businesses to exchange information with minimal or no human intervention. Let's go back to the supermarket example to see the power of Web services in a more realistic scenario:

Let's say you order 100,000 cookies from a supplier, expecting all of them to be sold in one month. After the month passes only 60,000 are sold, so you are left with 40,000. Because these are cookies of a special kind, they will spoil in two weeks. You need to act fast and sell them to other smaller supermarkets or Internet companies such as Amazon.com or eBay. You can grab the phone and spend an entire morning calling each of the smaller supermarket clients, offering them as many cookies as they would want to buy from you; or you could take a more "technical" approach and develop a simple application that would do this for you automatically. Assuming each of these smaller supermarket clients provide Web services, you could develop an application (in any programming language) that allows you to SQL insert overstocked items, such as the 40,000 cookies, into a DB2 database table *overstock*. You could then define a trigger on this table which invokes a DB2 stored procedure (more about triggers and stored procedures in Chapter 7, Working with Database Objects) that could consume Web services provided by the Internet companies or the smaller supermarket clients. This scenario is depicted in Figure 1.5.

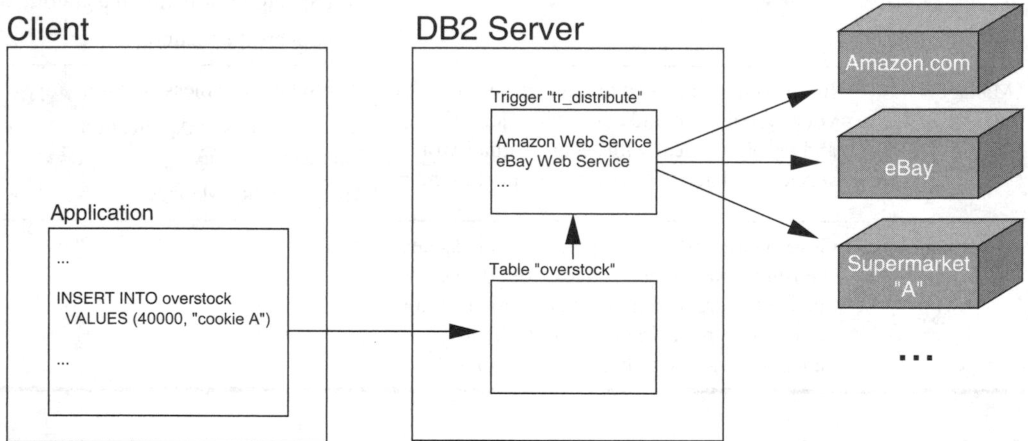

Figure 1.5 Using a Web service

As you can see from Figure 1.5, the simple act of inserting 40,000 cookies through your application into the table *overstock* in the DB2 server allows the systems of many smaller supermarkets and Internet companies, through the use of their Web services, to make the cookies available on their systems quickly, opening new sales channels. In Figure 1.5, DB2 is behaving as a Web service consumer, because it is using or "consuming" the Web services, while the smaller supermarket clients and Internet companies are behaving as the Web service providers, because they are making these Web services available for others to use. For simplicity purposes, we have omitted in Figure 1.5 the call to a stored procedure. This scenario shows the power of Web services: business-to-business exchange of information using applications. There is no need for human intervention. DB2 and Web services will be discussed in more detail in Chapter 10, Mastering the DB2 pureXML Support.

1.2.5 XML

XML stands for e**X**tensible **M**arkup **L**anguage. XML's popularity and use has grown exponentially in the past few years, as it is a core component of many new technologies. The easiest way to understand how XML works is by comparing it to HTML, given that many people today are familiar with HTML. Let's take a look at the following line in an HTML document:

```
<b>Raul</b>
```

In the above line, the tag **<b>** indicates the way you would like to *display* the text, in this case, **Raul** in bold. Now Let's take a look at the following line in an XML document:

```
<name>Raul</name>
```

In the above line, the tag **<name>** *describes* the text **Raul.** The tag is saying that **Raul** is in fact a name. See the difference? In HTML, tags are used to indicate how you would like to display the data; in XML, tags are used to actually describe the data. Table 1.3 describes the characteristics of XML.

Table 1.3 Characteristics of XML

XML Characteristic	Description
Flexible	XML is a flexible language because it is easy to modify or adapt. XML is based on a hierarchical model, which is most appropriate to store unstructured types of information such as financial information, life sciences information (for example Genome, DNA), and so on.
Easy to extend	XML is easy to extend; that is, you can create your own tags. For example, in addition to the **<name>** tag in the example above, you could create new tags such as **<address>, <email>, <phone>,** and so on. This means you can create your own language or protocol based on XML.
Describes itself	XML can describe itself; another document called an XML Schema (which itself is an XML document) is used to provide rules and descriptions as to what each of the tags in a document mean and restrict the type of data the tags can contain. An older method, but still widely used today, is to use DTD documents. In the above example, an XML Schema or DTD document can indicate that the tag **<name>** can only be used to store characters.
Can be transformed to other formats	XML can be transformed to other formats like HTML, using Extensible Stylesheet Language Transformations (XSLT), a language used for the transformation of XML documents.
Independent of the platform or vendor	XML is independent of the platform or vendor; after all, XML documents can be stored in text files containing tags. Text documents are supported everywhere.
Easy to share	XML is easy to share with other applications, businesses, and processes given that it can be stored as a text document. Because it is easy to share, it's appropriate as the core of Web services.

XML is also at the core of Web 2.0 development technologies. Web 2.0, as defined in Wikipedia.org "refers to a perceived second generation of web-based communities and hosted services—such as social-networking sites, wikis, and folksonomies—which facilitate collaboration and sharing between users". Wikis, blogs, mash-ups, RSS or atom feeds, and so on, which are part of Web 2.0 development technologies, are all based on or related to XML. This makes DB2 9.5 the ideal data server platform for Web 2.0 development. Table 1.4 describes the different technologies that are part of Web 2.0.

XML is discussed in more detail in Chapter 10, Mastering the DB2 pureXML Support.

Table 1.4 Web 2.0 Technologies

Web 2.0 Technology	Description
AJAX	Asynchronous Javascript and XML: A technique for creating interactive Web applications, which can update parts of a Web page without refreshing the entire page.
AdSense	This is an advertisement serving program where Web site owners can enable text, image, and video advertisement on their site, and ads will appear based on the Web site content, the user's geographic location, and other factors.
Blog	Also known as a Web log, this is a Web-based publication of periodic articles in journal style displayed in chronological order. It is often used to provide personal commentaries on a subject or as personal online diaries.
Mashup	This is a Web application hybrid, that is, a Web site or application that is derived by aggregating components or services from other sources such as RSS or atom feeds, and JavaScript.
REST	Representational State Transfer: An architectural style for distributed hypermedia systems like the World Wide Web.
RSS and Atom	RSS (Really Simple Syndication) and Atom are XML file formats for Web syndication, which provides a way to distribute information.
Tagging	Bookmarks that provide a way to attach keywords to pages or images on the Web, helping categorize and making things easier to find (i.e, metadata).
Wiki	A type of Web site that allows for community authoring (add/delete/edit content).

1.2.6 DB2 and the IBM Strategy

Now that you understand the key concepts of the overall IBM strategy, you may be asking yourself, how do these concepts relate to each other? Where does DB2 fit in the overall strategy? To answer these questions, let's take a look at Figure 1.6.

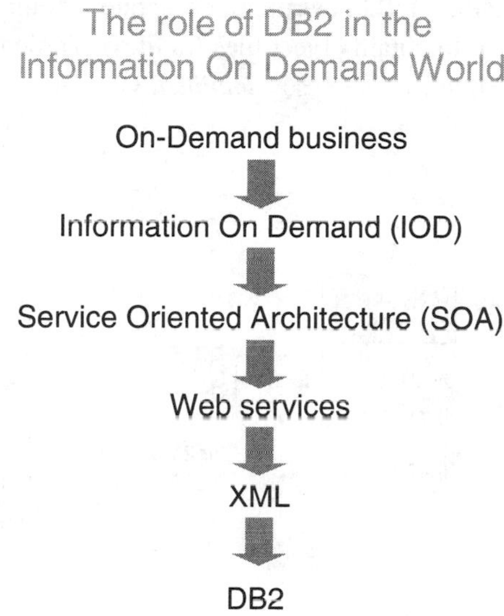

Figure 1.6 The role of DB2 in the IBM strategy

As shown in Figure 1.6, an on-demand business depends on Information On Demand, which depends on Service-Oriented Architecture, which depends on Web services, which depends on XML. The figure shows why XML is so important: XML is at the base of all of these concepts; without it, they would be hard to implement.

XML documents need to be stored in a safe place that allows for storing, managing, and retrieving large volumes of these documents. Persistency, scalability, security, recovery, and good performance are all important features to consider when selecting a repository for your XML documents. All of these features have already been provided for many years in databases; therefore, a database is probably the best repository for XML documents. DB2 has been providing support to work with XML documents for several years. Starting in version 9, as described earlier in this chapter, pureXML technology is made available, which greatly enhances performance by internally storing XML documents in a parsed-hierarchical manner, as a tree. Thus, in summary, the role of DB2 in the Information On Demand world is to be *the* repository of XML documents. This is why DB2 is shown at the bottom of the figure, supporting all the other technologies.

1.3 DB2 Editions

DB2 for Linux, UNIX, and Windows (sometimes referred to as **LUW**) is developed using the C/C++ language. More than 90 percent of the code is common among these platforms. The remaining code is unique to take full advantage of the underlying platform architecture; however, the database functionality on all of these platforms is the same.

Like any other C/C++ application, DB2 is written in separate modules—.c/.C source files—that have been separately compiled to obtain object files (.o files). These object files are later linked to obtain an executable file. Figure 1.7 shows a *simplified* view of how each edition is built.

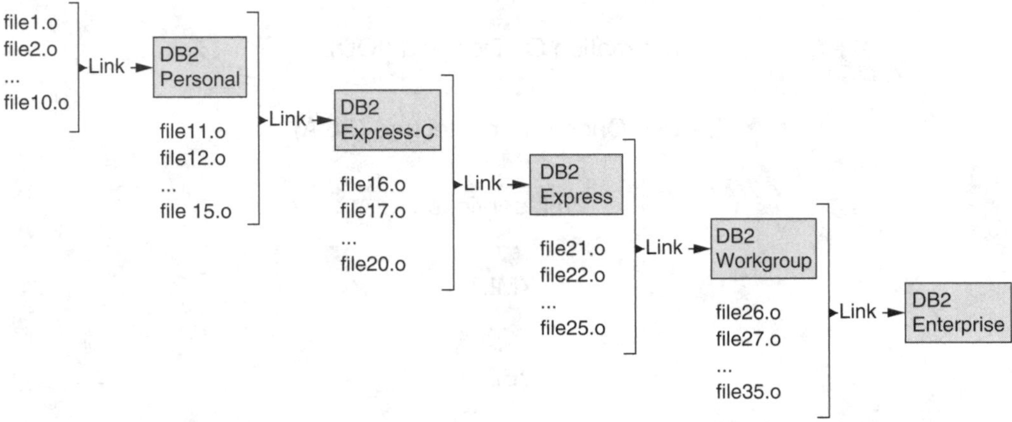

Figure 1.7 How DB2 editions build on top of each other

As you can see in Figure 1.7, each edition (other than DB2 Everyplace, which is not shown in the figure) builds on top of the other by linking modules or object files that contain additional functionality. The core of the DB2 code is common across all editions, which greatly benefits application development. For example, if you are developing an application for DB2 Personal, this application will also work on DB2 Express-C, DB2 Express, DB2 Workgroup, and DB2 Enterprise on any of the supported platforms.

From the above explanation, it should be clear that the DB2 LUW editions are mainly packaging and licensing distinctions that let you choose the appropriate features or functions you need for the right price. The underlying technology is always DB2, so choose the appropriate edition based on the features and functions you need.

> **NOTE** DB2 for z/OS, DB2 for VM/VSE, and DB2 for i5/OS use a different code base from that used by DB2 LUW. Note, however, that the Linux operating system extends across all of IBM's servers: System x, System p, System i, and System z. DB2 for Linux on all of these server platforms is the same. Thus, DB2 for Linux on System z uses the same code base and is licensed in the same way as DB2 for Linux on a System x (Intel) platform.

NOTE Refer to Appendix C, IBM Servers, for a description of the System x, p, i, and z servers.

Figure 1.8 illustrates the different editions and the types of servers they typically run on. By default, DB2 takes advantage of all the processing power it is given. The figure also shows that DB2 is a scalable product. With the exception of DB2 Everyplace, the functions, features, and benefits of an edition shown on the bottom of the figure are included in each subsequent edition as you move up the figure. The following sections provide more detail on the functionality of each edition.

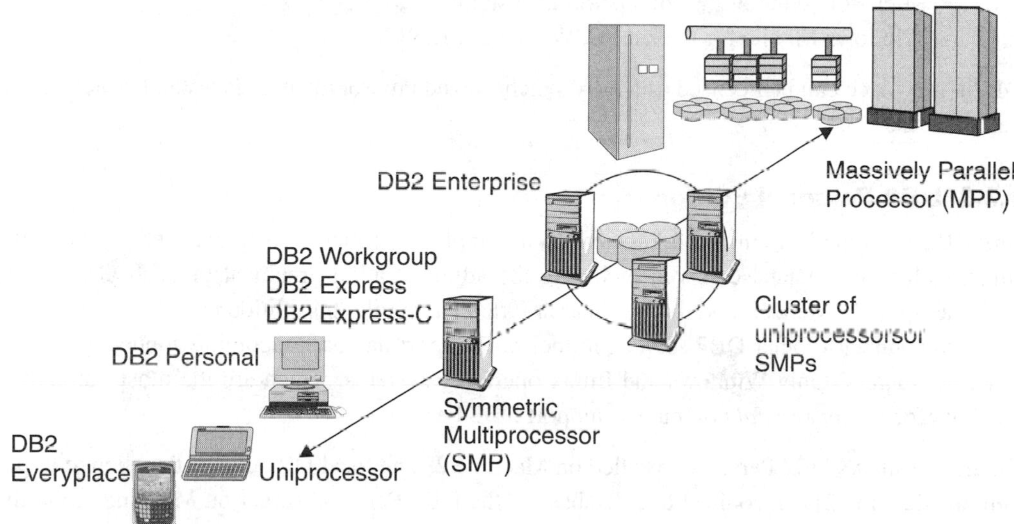

Figure 1.8 DB2 editions

1.3.1 DB2 Everyplace Edition

As its name implies, the DB2 Everyplace edition (DB2 Everyplace) can run anywhere, anytime, and in all kinds of small devices, such as personal digital assistants (PDAs), handheld computers, embedded devices, and laptops. DB2 Everyplace, though only about 350K in size, is a true relational database that uses a subset of the DB2 server SQL functionality. If you know how to code an application for a DB2 server edition, you know how to code for DB2 Everyplace. Applications can be developed using ODBC, CLI, JDBC, and .NET.

Typically, users of DB2 Everyplace store information in the mobile database and later replicate it to a back-end database server using the DB2 Everyplace Sync Server installed on another machine.

This edition supports the following operating systems that run on mobile devices:

- Embedded Linux
- Linux distributions
- J2ME devices
- Palm OS
- QNX Neutrino
- Symbian OS
- Microsoft Windows 32-bit operating systems
- Windows Mobile for Pocket PC, Windows CE.NET

DB2 Everyplace can be licensed as a fully synchronized environment or as a standalone embedded database.

1.3.2 DB2 Personal Edition

The DB2 Personal Edition (DB2 Personal) is a complete product for a single user. It has all the functionality of a database server, including the administration graphical tools. It also comes with the Spatial Extender, and the Net Search Extender. While this edition can also be used as a client to connect to other DB2 servers, it does not support database incoming connections from other computers. Only Windows and Linux operating systems, which are the most commonly used platforms in *personal* computers, support DB2 Personal.

Figure 1.9 shows DB2 Personal installed on Machine 2. The local DB2 client (the client component of Machine 2) can connect to a database in the DB2 Personal server on Machine 2, but the remote DB2 client in Machine 1 cannot connect to a database in the server on Machine 2 because DB2 Personal does not accept remote (inbound) connections. The figure also shows DB2 Personal on Machine 2 as the remote client to other DB2 server editions installed on machines 3, 4, and 5.

> **NOTE** A DB2 data server is considered a server when it can accept inbound client connections for data retrieval purposes. Hence, DB2 Personal is not considered a DB2 server.

1.3.3 DB2 Express-C

DB2 Express-C is a version of the DB2 Express edition for the community. Businesses developing an application that needs to connect to a data server can use DB2 Express-C for free. Note that we refer to it as a version: It is not an edition of DB2 because it is free. Also note that the core code of DB2 Express-C is the same as the other DB2 editions as shown in Figure 1.7. DB2

Express-C can be used in production or in a commercial setting. In addition, businesses can embed and distribute DB2 Express-C as part of their application also for free. DB2 Express-C does not impose limits on the database size, the number of instances per server, or the number of users.

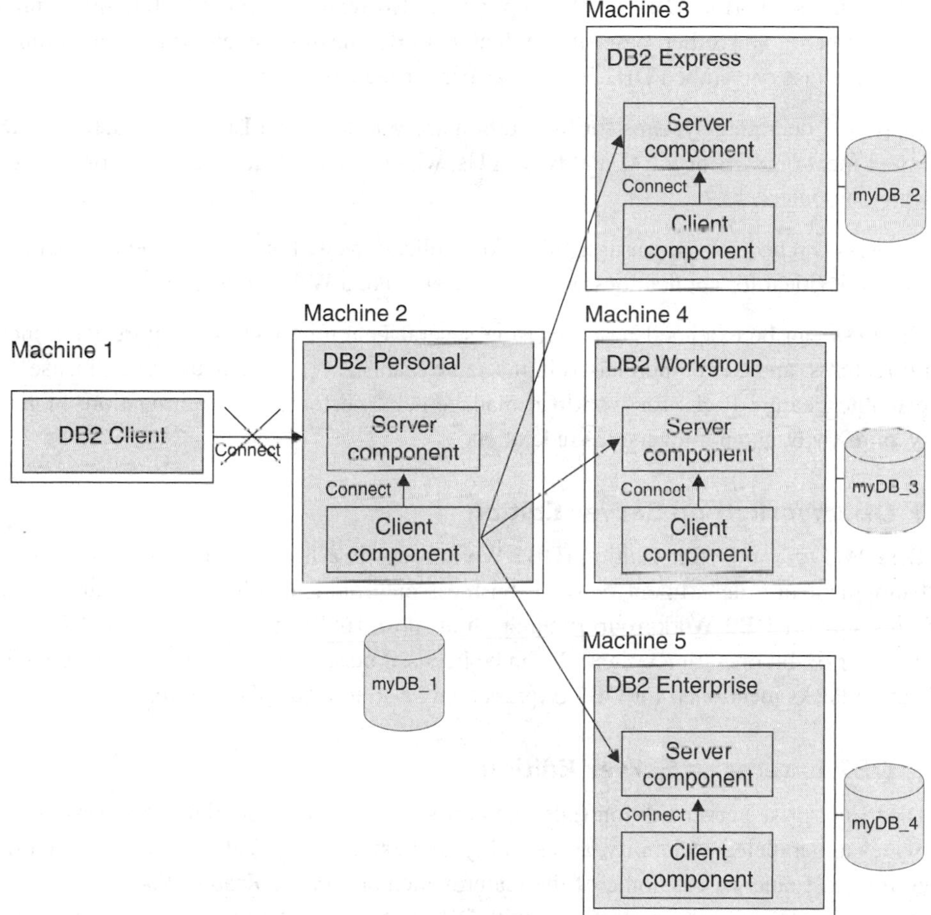

Figure 1.9 DB2 Personal as a (local) server and a remote client

The supported operating systems for this version are Windows and Linux (on Intel and AMD), running on a system with any amount of processors and memory, however the total resource utilization by all instances of DB2 Express-C on a given system cannot exceed 2GB of RAM and 2 processor cores on 32- or 64-bit SMP hardware computers. An optional renewable 12-month subscription license can be purchased for DB2 Express-C to obtain IBM DB2 Technical support (24/7), and also support for the SQL replication and the High Availability and Disaster Recovery (HADR) feature. This subscription edition of DB2 Express-C is licensed to run on up to two dual-core processors and no more than 4GB of memory. Without this license, the product is free but without the mentioned features, and with support provided only through a free community-based online forum. For further details, refer to the DB2 Express Web site: www.ibm.com/db2/express.

1.3.4 DB2 Express Edition

The DB2 Express Edition (DB2 Express), a low-cost, full-function data server, is ideal for a business that requires a database, but has minimal in-house database skills. This edition provides the same support as DB2 Workgroup, but it also features simple installation, enhanced self-management, and other ease-of-use features. Businesses developing applications that require a database can embed DB2 Express as part of their solution.

The supported operating systems for this edition are Windows and Linux (on Intel and AMD), running at most on 4GB of RAM and two CPUs, which can be dual core on 32- or 64-bit SMP hardware computers.

DB2 Express can be licensed per user (ideal for applications with just a few users) or per processor value unit (ideal for applications with many users, like a Web application).

DB2 Express can be extended by purchasing several Feature Packs. A Feature Pack includes several features, and can be purchased in the same manner as a DB2 data server license. There are available Feature Packs for workload management, performance optimization, high availability, pureXML, and homogeneous federation.

1.3.5 DB2 Workgroup Server Edition

The DB2 Workgroup Server Edition (DB2 Workgroup) is a full-function data server designed for deployment in a department or small business environment. Linux, UNIX, and Windows platforms support DB2 Workgroup running on at most 16GB of RAM and four CPU servers with a 32- or 64-bit operating system. It can be licensed per user or per processor value unit. All the Feature Packs mentioned for DB2 Express apply also to DB2 Workgroup.

1.3.6 DB2 Enterprise Server Edition

The DB2 Enterprise Server Edition (DB2 Enterprise) is the most complete data server offering. It provides unparalleled scalability, accessibility, and extensibility features, and is the edition of choice for most enterprises. Some of the features included in the Feature Packs available with DB2 Express or DB2 Workgroup are free with DB2 Enterprise. DB2 Enterprise has its own Feature Packs as well. For example, to use the database partitioning feature (DPF) you need to purchase the Feature Pack "Database Partitioning Feature for DB2 Enterprise." DPF allows you to partition your data within a single server or across multiple servers running the same operating system. This means that your databases can grow to sizes that are limited only by the number of servers available.

DB2 Enterprise can be used in SMP systems, and DB2 Enterprise with DPF can be used in either SMP or clustered server systems. The supported operating systems are Linux, UNIX, and Windows.

Table 1.5 obtained at the time of publication from the DB2 for Linux, UNIX, and Windows main Web page at http://www-306.ibm.com/software/data/db2/9/, provides a comparison of the DB2 server editions.

Table 1.5 Comparing the DB2 Editions

Find the DB2 9 edition that meets your needs

	DB2 Express	DB2 Workgroup	DB2 Enterprise
Function	DB2 Express is a full-function hybrid data server, which provides very attractive entry-level pricing.	Includes all of the features of DB2 Express with scalability to larger servers.	Includes all of the features of DB2 Workgroup plus features required to provide the scalability to handle high user loads and provide 24x7x365 availability, including: High Availability Disaster Recovery (HADR)
	Simple installation including silent installation capability		Tivoli System Automation
	Self managing		Table Partitioning
	Optimized interfaces and tools for application developers		Multi-dimensional data clustering
	Supports wide array of development paradigms		Materialized Query Tables
	Minimal disk space requirements		Full intra-query parallelism
	Worldwide 24x7 Service and Support		Connection concentrator
Customizable	Expandable with pureXML and optional enterprise class features to preserve and improve performance, workload management, and high availability	Expandable with pureXML and optional enterprise class features to preserve and improve performance, workload management, and high availability	Expandable with pureXML and advanced features like storage optimization, performance optimization, advanced access control, scale-out clustering, geodetic data, and more
Scalable	2 CPUs / 4GB RAM maximum (may run on machines with more than 4GB)	4 CPUs / 16GB RAM maximum	Unlimited
Platforms	Linux, Solaris x86 and Windows	Linux, UNIX, and Windows	Linux, UNIX, and Windows
Pricing Metrics	Authorized User (Min. 5 per server), or Per Processor	Authorized User (Min. 5 per Server), or Per Processor	(Authorized User (Min. 25 per CPU) or Per Processor

1.4 DB2 Clients

To connect from a client to a DB2 data server database, you usually need to install DB2 client software on the client machine. This isn't always required; for example, this isn't necessary for a JDBC application using the Type 4 driver running on the client machine. We provide more detail about connectivity scenarios in Chapter 6, Configuring Client and Server Connectivity.

A DB2 client installed on a different machine than the DB2 server is known as a **remote client**. A remote client can establish communication to the server using TCP/IP or Named Pipes (Windows only).

If the DB2 client is installed on the same machine as a DB2 server, then it is known as a **local client,** and it connects to the server using inter-process communication (IPC). Note that since all DB2 servers come with a local client component, you don't need to install the DB2 client separately after installing a DB2 server. Figure 1.10 shows local and remote clients. Client Machine 1 and 2 are remote clients with the DB2 client code installed and are accessing Server Machine A, which has a DB2 server installed. The DB2 server has a client component that is the local client.

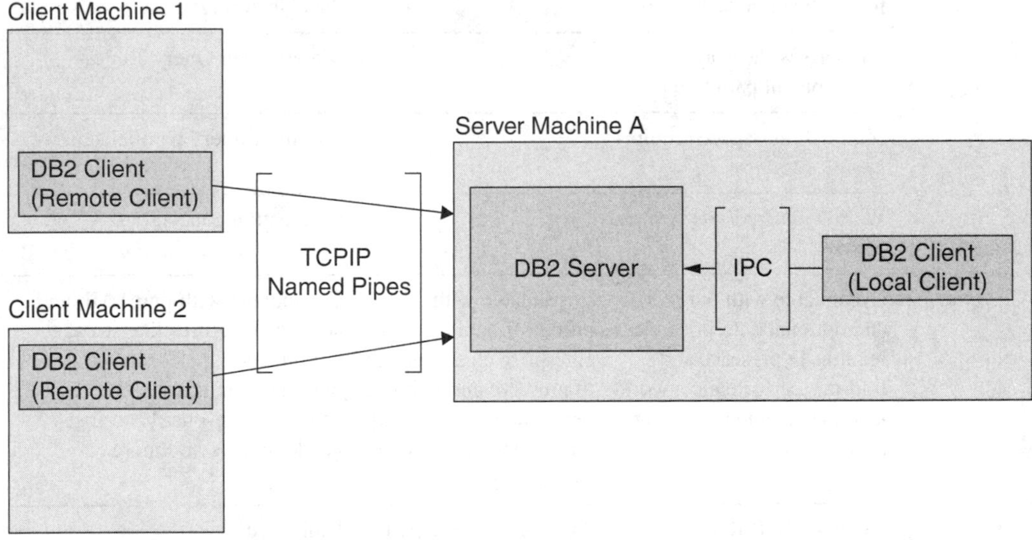

Figure 1.10 Local and remote clients

V9.5 There are three types of clients in DB2:

- Thin client
- IBM Data Server Runtime client
- IBM Data Server client

and there are two drivers:

- IBM Data Server Driver for JDBC and SQLJ
- IBM Data Server Driver for ODBC, CLI, and .NET (DSDRIVER)

A **thin client,** also known as a **dumb terminal,** is a machine with no operating system or DB2 client code. A thin client has to first get from another machine all the libraries and modules it requires to fulfill a request. Figure 1.11 shows an example of thin clients, where the thin client first requests, and then gets the libraries and modules it needs and the code of the DB2 client from the Data Server Client machine on the left side of the figure. This can only work on Windows platforms and will not work if the machine on the left side of the figure was an IBM Data Server Runtime client. It must be an IBM Data Server client.

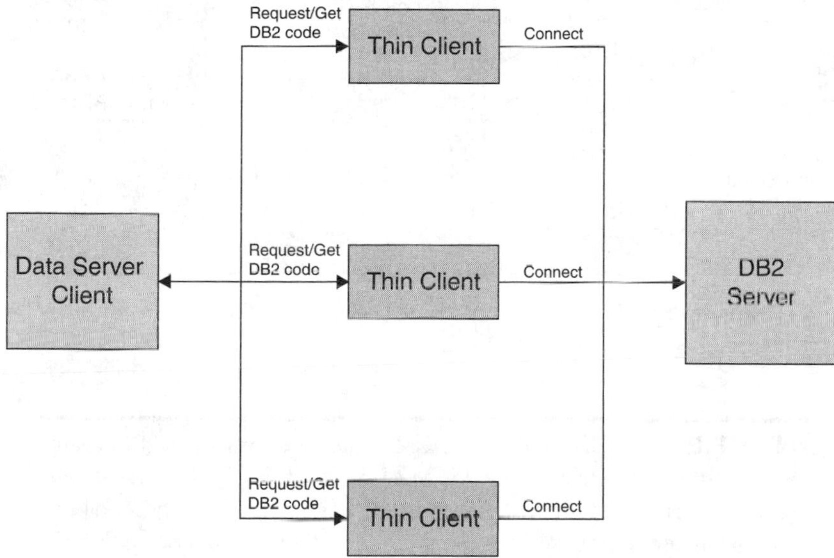

Figure 1.11 A thin client

The **IBM Data Server Runtime client** has the minimum basic requirements to connect to DB2 databases and to provide basic client functionality. It includes the drivers for ODBC, CLI, .NET, PHP, Ruby, Perl-DB2, JDBC, and SQLJ. There are also IBM Data Server runtime client merge modules for Windows, which allow you to add IBM Data Server runtime client functionality to any product that uses the Windows installer. The **IBM Data Server client** comes with everything the IBM Data Server Runtime client has, plus graphical administration tools and development tools and libraries.

Prior to DB2 9, the drivers for ODBC, CLI, JDBC, and SQLJ could only be obtained by downloading and installing a DB2 client. With DB2 9, the **IBM Data Server Driver for JDBC and SQLJ** was introduced as a separate downloadable image. Now with DB2 9.5, the **IBM Data Server Driver for ODBC, CLI and .NET (DSDRIVER)** client is introduced to deploy drivers for applications to access remote IBM data servers. It includes support for PHP, Ruby, and

Perl-DB2 as well. Both drivers are free and can be redistributed. Figure 1.12 illustrates the client progression.

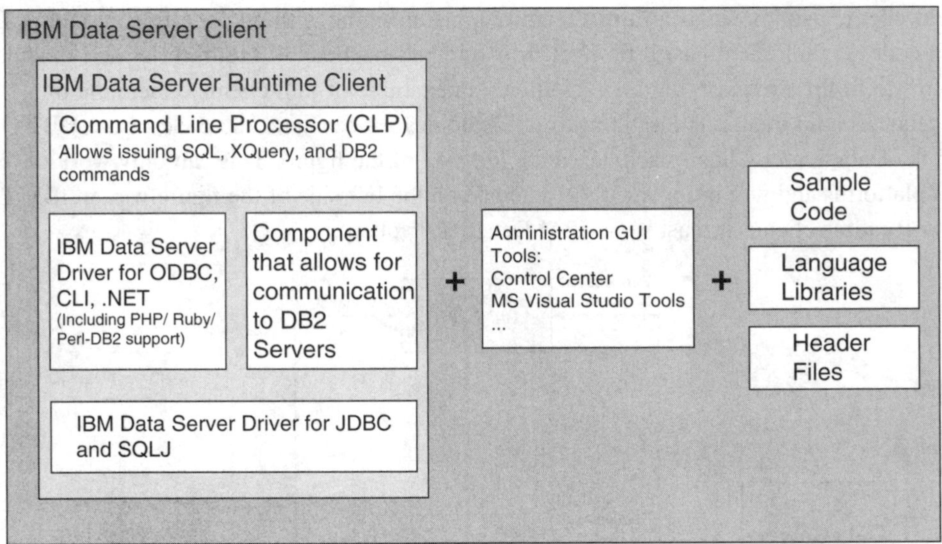

Figure 1.12 Client progression

> **NOTE** The DB2 9 Runtime Client has been renamed IBM Data Server Runtime Client starting in DB2 9.5. The DB2 9 Client has been renamed IBM Data Server Client starting in DB2 9.5. These name changes reflect changes in the client code, as these clients not only can connect to DB2 data servers, but can also connect to Informix data servers.

1.5 Try-and-Buy Versions

A DB2 9.5 Try-and-Buy version allows you to try DB2 for an evaluation period of 90 days. DB2 will stop working after the 90 days unless you buy and apply the full license. Other than this time limitation, the Try-and-Buy version contains all the features of a fully licensed version. During or after the Try-and-Buy period you can buy a permanent license by calling 1-800-IBM-SERV. An IBM representative will direct you to the License Key Center. Once you receive the license file, you can use it to upgrade the Try-and-Buy version to the fully licensed product level without reinstalling it. Use the following command from a command-line window to install the license file:

```
db2licm -a file_name
```

where ***file_name*** stands for the name of the license file, which normally has a .lic extension.

Issuing the **db2licm -l** command lists the software products installed on your machine and the current license. After adding a full license, the Expiry Date field will have a value of *Permanent*. Chapter 3, Installing DB2, discusses more about the **db2licm** command and the License Center.

> **NOTE** Licensing policies, as well as the evaluation period, are subject to change. The information in this section is accurate as of the time of publication.

1.6 Host Connectivity

DB2 Connect is a software product containing the license files required to communicate from a DB2 distributed client, also known as the **DRDA Application Requester,** to a host DB2 server, a **DRDA Application Server.** (DRDA—Distributed Relational Database Architecture—is the standard that defines formats and protocols for providing transparent access to remote data.) Host DB2 servers include DB2 for z/OS and OS/390, DB2 for VM/VSE, and DB2 for i5/OS. DB2 Connect also includes an IBM Data Server Runtime client.

> **NOTE** DB2 Connect software is only required when connecting from DB2 LUW to a host DB2 server, such as DB2 for z/OS; it is *not* required in the other direction, for example, when DB2 for z/OS behaves as the client, and DB2 LUW is the server.

DB2 Connect comes in two main editions. Other editions not listed below refer to licensing options:

- The Personal Edition supports the direct connection of one DB2 client to multiple host DB2 servers.
- The Enterprise Edition supports the connection of multiple DB2 clients to multiple host DB2 servers via a DB2 Connect server.

1.7 Federation Support

Federation allows you to query and manipulate data stored on other servers and in other data servers. When you issue an SQL statement in a federated environment, you may actually be accessing information from multiple databases and potentially multiple data servers (see Figure 1.13).

Federated support is included in DB2 when the other databases being accessed are part of the IBM DB2 family, that is, another DB2 database or an Informix database. For accessing databases from other vendors, refer to the IBM WebSphere Federation Server product described in Section 1.9.

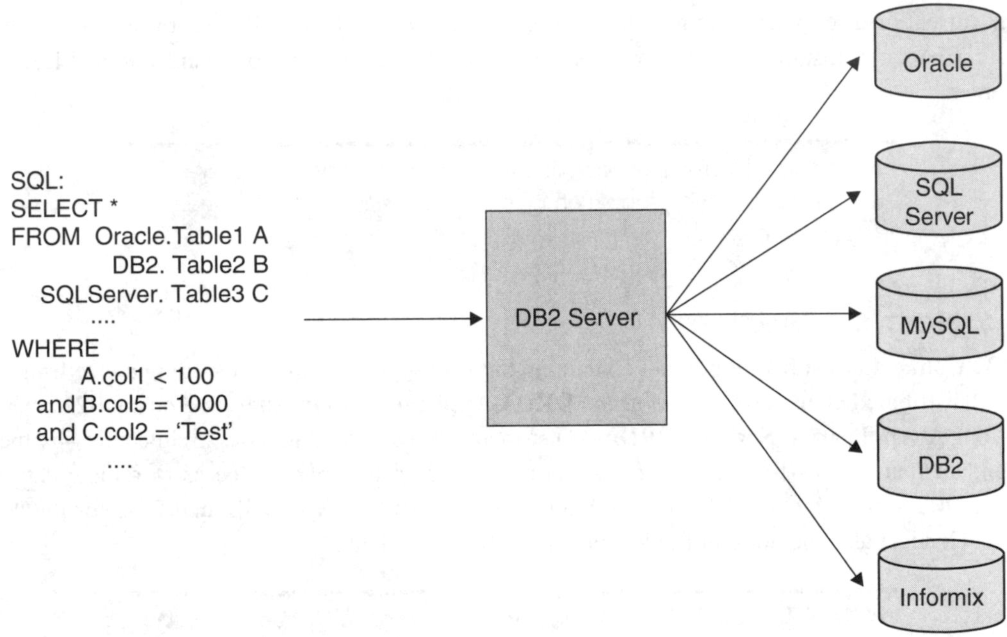

Figure 1.13 DB2 federation

1.8 Replication Support

Replication lets you propagate data to different servers to keep multiple databases synchronized. This can be useful in situations where a single server is used for day-to-day transaction operations, and where issuing reporting queries at the same time would be costly for performance. By replicating the data to another server, this second server could be used for reporting without disturbing the first server. Figure 1.14 illustrates how the data changes captured at one server are later applied to another (target) server. In the figure, the first box shows the source server and the fourth box shows the target server. The second and third boxes contain the "capture" and "apply" components, respectively.

DB2 has built-in support for replication when source and target databases are part of the IBM family, which includes Informix. For databases from other vendors, such as Oracle or SQL Server, the IBM WebSphere Replication Server software is required.

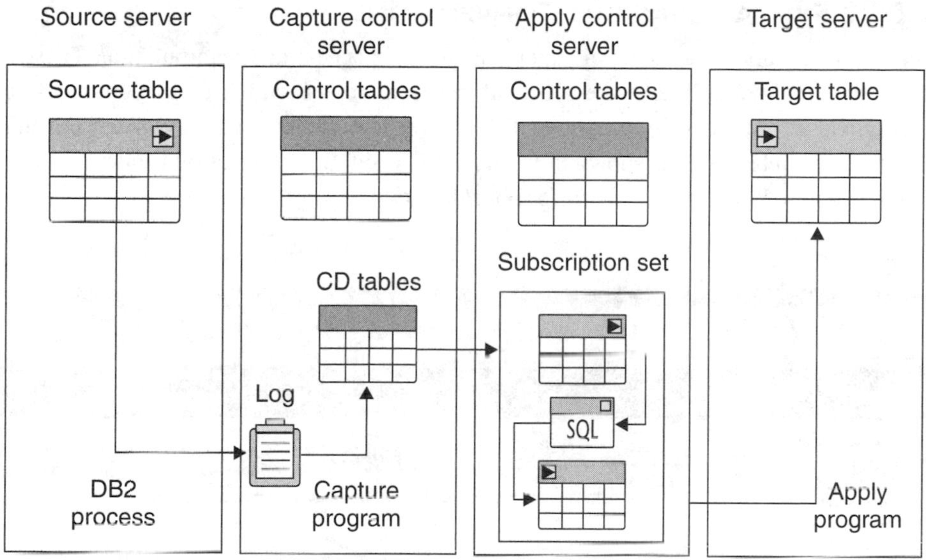

Figure 1.14 DB2 replication environment

1.9 IBM WebSphere Federation Server and WebSphere Replication Server

IBM WebSphere **Federation Server** provides federated support by making remote data sources from IBM or different vendors appear as if they were part of the same database. The Federation server uses wrappers to communicate with and retrieve data from those other data sources; it encapsulates any conversions required from the source database and presents them to the target database as tables.

IBM WebSphere **Replication Server** provides replication support from one data server to another, even if they are not part of the IBM family. Replication Server includes both Q-replication and SQL replication (SQL replication is free with DB2 Enterprise).

IBM WebSphere Federation and Replication server software were formerly called WebSphere Information Integrator.

1.10 Special Package Offerings for Developers

The Database Enterprise Developer's Edition (DEDE) provides developers with a package that includes several DB2 editions and features, Informix products, and DB2 Connect. This package is offered at a reduced price, and is restricted to the development, evaluation, demonstration, and testing of application programs. The package is licensed on a per developer basis.

1.11 DB2 Syntax Diagram Conventions

DB2 supports a comprehensive set of statements for data access and manipulation. These statements are documented online in the DB2 Information Center, which gives you access to all information about DB2 as well as major DB2 features and components. It can be conveniently accessed by using a browser, as shown in Figure 1.15. The DB2 Information Center is also available at http://publib.boulder.ibm.com/infocenter/db2luw/v9r5/index.jsp.

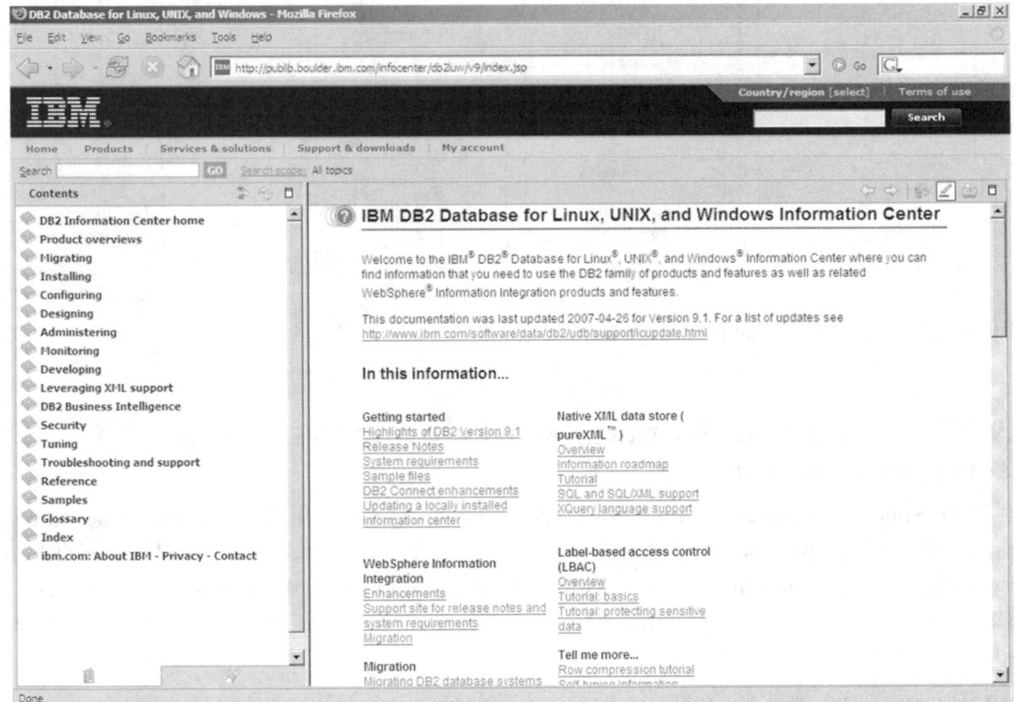

Figure 1.15 The DB2 Information Center

You can find the syntax of any commands or statements we introduce in this book in the DB2 Information Center. Understanding how to read the syntax diagrams will help you use the numerous options available with many of the statements.

Syntax diagrams are all read from left to right and top to bottom, following the path of each line. Table 1.6 summarizes a few of the most commonly used symbols in a syntax diagram.

Table 1.6 Summary of Some Symbols Used in Syntax Diagrams

Symbol	Description
`>>---`	Indicates the beginning of a syntax diagram.
`--->`	Indicates that the syntax is continued on the next line.
`>---`	Indicates that the syntax is continued from the previous line.
`---><`	Indicates the end of a syntax diagram.

When a mandatory field is required, it appears on the horizontal line (the main path) like this.

```
>>-mandatory_field----------------------------------------><
```

Optional fields appear below the main path.

```
>>-mandatory_field--+-----------------+-------------------><
                    '-optional_field-'
```

If an optional field appears above the main path, it means that it is the default option.

```
                    .-default_field-.
>>-mandatory_field--+----------------+-------------------><
                    '-optional_field-'
```

If two or more mandatory choices are available, one of the mandatory choices will appear in the main path, and the rest will appear in a stack. You must choose one of these options.

```
>>-mandatory_field--+-mandatory_choice1-+----------------><
                    '-mandatory_choice2-'
```

An arrow returning to the left, above the main line, indicates an option can be repeated. In this example, repeated options are separated by one or more blanks.

```
                     .-----------------.
                     V                 |
>>-mandatory_field----repeatable_field-+-----------------><
```

If the repeat arrow contains a comma, you must separate repeated items with a comma.

```
                     .-,---------------.
                     V                 |
>>-mandatory_field----repeatable_field-+-----------------><
```

You should now feel comfortable reading syntax diagrams in the DB2 documentation. Browse through the DB2 online documentation and review some examples there.

1.12 Case Study

John recently graduated from Pennsylvania State University, where he learned DB2 as part of the IBM Academic Initiative program, a program that provides DB2 and other IBM software for free to teach database skills.

While at school, he worked with a DB2 Enterprise Server Edition installed on a System p machine at the university computer lab. He was given SYSADM authority, and was able to see connections from many different clients to all created databases using the **`list applications`** command. John wanted to develop a Java application using the JDBC Type 4 driver, so he downloaded and installed on his laptop the 90-Day Try-and-Buy version of DB2 Personal Edition. With this edition, he was able to build, test, and run his application and connect to the database created on his laptop. Since the client and data server were both on his laptop, he was dealing with a local client connection.

John wanted to test whether his application would work as a remote client, so he used the client software that comes with DB2 Personal Edition to test his application against the database he had created earlier on the university's System p machine. This also worked, and John was feeling like a DB2 guru.

Eager to show his program to his colleagues, he e-mailed the executable to his friend Peter, who had just bought a new laptop with Microsoft Windows Vista installed. Peter detached the file and tried to run the application against John's database on the University's pSeries server. After spending a few hours trying to figure out why he couldn't, he dropped by John's place. John realized that Peter had to download and install either an IBM Data Server Runtime client, an IBM Data Server client, or just the IBM Data Server JDBC and SQLJ driver, as he needed the JDBC Type 4 driver on his laptop. Given that Peter was neither going to develop a new program nor administer a database, John asked Peter to download just the IBM Data Server JDBC and SQLJ driver from the IBM Web site, and after installation, voilà!, the program successfully ran. Peter then asked John to perform the test from his laptop against the database on John's laptop, but John said it would not work because he had installed DB2 Personal Edition, which is not a database server, and it cannot accept inbound remote client connections.

After the graduation ceremony, John received a PDA as a gift from his dad. His dad had heard John praise DB2, so he had had DB2 Everyplace installed on the PDA. Since John was going to take six months off to travel before looking for a job, John decided to take his PDA with him rather than his laptop. John's account at the university was going to be active for the next eleven months, so while he was traveling he could connect to his "old" database on the System p server and use his application (which he had installed on his PDA) to transfer information about all the friends he met and places he visited during his trip. This way he was able to save information in another place should he lose his PDA.

After his trip, John applied for a position at a medium-sized company in his hometown. To prepare for his interview, John again tested the program he had written against his laptop database, but the Try-and-Buy evaluation period had expired. John figured that he would always need DB2 on his laptop, so he decided to buy the permanent license. When John received the license file after the purchase, he installed it on his laptop with the command **`db2licm -a`** ***`filename`*****.** Once this problem was resolved, John demonstrated his program during the job interview and was immediately hired.

Company ABC, which was using DB2 Workgroup Server Edition, asked John to modify his application so that it would connect to a DB2 for z/OS host machine. John responded that he did not need to make any modifications, but since DB2 Workgroup Server Edition does not come with the DB2 Connect software component, the company could purchase this software, or get the Database Enterprise Developer Edition (DEDE), as it would be cheaper and has most of the software for all DB2 editions. DEDE is licensed per developer, and this company did not have that many developers, so DEDE was good for them. If Company ABC wanted to use DB2 in a production environment, they would not be able to use DEDE, but would have to buy the appropriate edition and license.

Company ABC was also interested in the DB2 Express-C Edition, because it was free, and one of their applications needed a database to be embedded as part of their solution. Other than John, there were not many skilled DB2 personnel in the company, so DB2 Express-C was also ideal because of its ease-of-use features. John indicated that whilst DB2 Express-C was free, it would not have 24/7 IBM support unless the 12-month subscription license was purchased. Without this license, questions could be posted in a free community-based forum, but community participation was voluntary.

Three months after John was hired, he was promoted. John is well on his way to a very successful career with DB2!

1.13 Summary

This chapter introduced DB2 and its history. IBM pioneered relational database management systems and invented SQL. IBM's technology in the relational database management system area has been around for more than twenty years. Its legacy is visible in the Information Management product line that includes database management software, data warehousing and business intelligence software, enterprise content management and discovery software, and information integrator software.

This chapter also discussed the types of clients and servers available with DB2. Although different editions are available to provide varying functionality, the core DB2 product is the same; therefore, application development on any edition will work on all editions. The various editions allow you to choose the functions that best suit your needs.

In addition, the chapter explained federated support, replication, the WebSphere Federation Server, the WebSphere Replication server, and packaging options available for application developers. These packaging options allow developers to obtain DB2 software at a reduced price.

1.14 Review Questions

1. IBM added the term "Universal" to the DB2 name with Version 5 of the product. Why was this term added?
2. Which five software brands support the IBM on-demand strategy?
3. Can an application developed for DB2 Personal Edition work with DB2 Enterprise Server Edition?
4. Is DB2 Connect required to connect from a DB2 for z/OS client to a DB2 for Linux, UNIX, and Windows server?
5. What is the term used to describe DB2 9's unique support for XML?
6. Is IBM WebSphere Federation server required to set up a federation environment between a DB2 server and an Informix server?
7. Provide an example when replication support may be required.
8. Does DB2 for Linux, UNIX, and Windows have one single file that is used for installation in any of these platforms?
9. What does the Database Partitioning Feature (DPF) allow you to do?
10. What should you do when your Try-and-Buy license period expires and you would like to buy a permanent license?
11. Which of the following products is the minimum required on the Windows client to *run* a DB2 application accessing a DB2 database on UNIX?
    A. DB2 Enterprise
    B. DB2 Personal Edition
    C. DB2 Connect
    D. IBM Data Server Runtime Client
12. Which of the following products is the minimum required to *run* a DB2 application using JDBC Type 4?
    A. IBM Data Server Client
    B. IBM Data Server Runtime Client
    C. Data Server Driver for JDBC and SQLJ
    D. Data Server Client
13. Which of the following products does not allow applications to connect to its databases from remote clients?
    A. DB2 Express
    B. DB2 Personal Edition
    C. DB2 Enterprise Server Edition
    D. DB2 Workgroup
14. Which of the following products is *not* considered a DB2 server?
    A. DB2 Workgroup Server Edition
    B. DB2 Express-C
    C. DB2 Personal
    D. DB2 Enterprise

15. Which of the following DB2 clients provide the DB2 graphical administration tools?
    A. Thin client
    B. IBM Data Server client
    C. Thick client
    D. IBM Data Server Runtime client
16. Which of the following DB2 editions is the most appropriate for sales personnel who need a basic database to store contacts and business leads made during business trips?
    A. DB2 Everywhere
    B. DB2 Satellite Edition
    C. DB2 Everyplace
    D. DB2 Personal Edition
17. A software development company would like to test an application that connects to both DB2 for LUW as well as DB2 for z/OS. Which of the following would suit its needs the best?
    A. DB2 Enterprise Server Edition
    B. DB2 Workgroup Server Edition
    C. DB2 Connect Enterprise Edition
    D. DEDE
18. Which of the following data servers can run on a System z server?
    A. DB2 for Linux, UNIX, and Windows
    B. DB2 for iSeries
    C. DB2 Connect
    D. IBM Websphere Information Integrator
19. Which of the following products allows ten clients to connect from DB2 LUW to DB2 for z/OS?
    A. Database Enterprise Developer's Edition
    B. DB2 Universal Developer's Edition
    C. DB2 PE
    D. DB2 LUW
20. Which of the following products can be used to collect, prepare, and analyze your data to allow you to make better business decisions?
    A. DB2 Content Manager
    B. DB2 Warehouse Manager
    C. IBM DB2 WebSphere Federation Server
    D. DB2 LUW

CHAPTER 2

DB2 at a Glance: The Big Picture

This chapter is like a book within a book: It covers a vast range of topics that will provide you with not only a good introduction to DB2 core concepts and components, but also an understanding of how these components work together and where they fit in the DB2 scheme of things. After reading this chapter you should have a general knowledge of the DB2 architecture that will help you better understand the topics discussed in the next chapters. Subsequent chapters will revisit and expand what has been discussed here.

In this chapter you will learn about the following:

- SQL statements, XQuery statements, and DB2 commands
- DB2 tools
- The DB2 environment
- Federation
- The Database Partitioning Feature (DPF)

You interact with DB2 by issuing SQL statements, XQuery statements, and DB2 commands. You can issue these statements and commands from an application or you can use DB2 tools. The DB2 tools interact with the DB2 environment by passing these statements and commands to the DB2 server for processing. This is shown in Figure 2.1.

2.1 SQL Statements, XQuery Statements, and DB2 Commands

SQL is the standard language used for retrieving and modifying data in a relational database. An SQL council formed by several industry leading companies determines the standard for these SQL statements, and the different relational database management systems (RDBMSs) follow these standards to make it easier for customers to use their databases. Recent additions to the standard include XML extension functions. These are also refered to as SQL/XML extension functions. This section introduces the different categories of SQL statements and presents some examples.

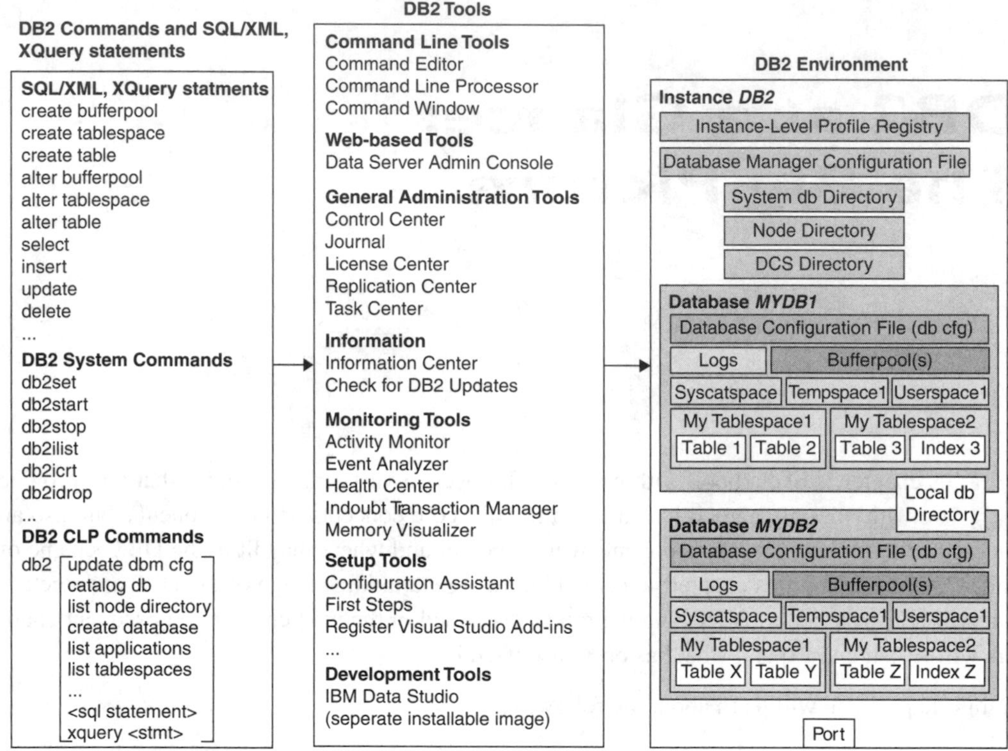

Figure 2.1 Overview of DB2

The XML Query Language (XQuery) specification is a language used for querying XML documents. XQuery includes the XML Path Language (XPath), which is also used to query XML documents. The XQuery specification is managed by W3C, a consortium formed by several industry leading companies and the academia. The specification has not been fully completed; however, several of the working drafts of the specification have now reached W3C "Candidate Recommendation" status, bringing the specification as a whole much closer to "Final Recommendation." In this section we will provide a few simple XQuery and XPath examples.

DB2 commands are directives specific to DB2 that allow you to perform tasks against a DB2 server. There are two types of DB2 commands:

- System commands
- Command Line Processor (CLP) commands

> **NOTE** SQL statements and DB2 commands can be specified in uppercase or lowercase. However, in Linux or UNIX some of the commands are case-sensitive. XQuery statements are case sensitive. See Appendix B for a detailed explanation of the use of uppercase versus lowercase in DB2.

2.1.1 SQL Statements

SQL statements allow you to work with the relational and XML data stored in your database. The statements are applied against the database you are connected to, not against the entire DB2 environment. There are three different classes of SQL statements.

- **Data Definition Language (DDL)** statements create, modify, or drop database objects. For example

```
CREATE INDEX ix1 ON t1 (salary)
ALTER TABLE t1 ADD hiredate DATE
DROP VIEW view1
```

- **Data Manipulation Language (DML)** statements insert, update, delete, or retrieve data from the database objects. For example

```
INSERT INTO t1 VALUES (10,'Johnson','Peter')
UPDATE t1 SET lastname = 'Smith' WHERE firstname = 'Peter'
DELETE FROM t1
SELECT * FROM t1 WHERE salary > 45000

SELECT lastname
 FROM patients
 WHERE xmlexists ($p/address[zipcode=´12345´]
       passing PATIENTS.INFO as p)
 AND salary > 45000
```

- **Data Control Language (DCL)** statements grant or revoke privileges or authorities to perform database operations on the objects in your database. For example

```
GRANT  select ON employee TO peter
REVOKE update ON employee FROM paul
```

> **NOTE** SQL statements are commonly referred to simply as "statements" in most RDBMS books. For detailed syntax of SQL statements, see the *DB2 SQL Reference* manual.

2.1.2 XQuery Statements

XQuery statements allow you to work with relational and XML data. The statements are applied against the database you are connected to, not against the entire DB2 environment. There are two main ways to work with XML documents in DB2:

- **XPath** is part of XQuery. Working with XPath is like working with the Change Directory (`cd`) command in Linux or MS-DOS. Using the `cd` operating system command, one can go from one subdirectory to another subdirectory in the directory tree. Similarly, by using the slash (/) in XPath, you can navigate a tree, which represents the

XML document. For example, Figure 2.2 shows an XML document in both serialized format and parsed hierarchical format.

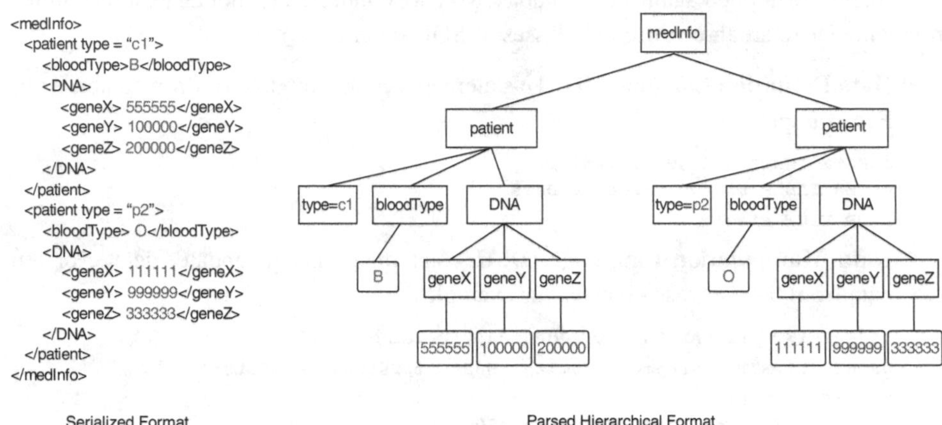

Figure 2.2 An XML document in serialized and parsed hierarchical format

Table 2.1 shows some XPath expressions and the corresponding values obtained using the XML document in Figure 2.2 as input.

Table 2.1 Sample XPath Expressions

XPath expression	Value to be returned
/medInfo/patient/@type	c1 p2
/medInfo/patient/bloodType	<bloodType>B</bloodType> <bloodType>O</bloodType>
/medInfo/patient/DNA/geneX	<geneX>555555</geneX> <geneX>111111</geneX>

- XQuery FLWOR expression. FLWOR stands for:

  FOR: Iterates through an XML sequence, binds variables to items
  LET: Assigns an XML sequence to a variable
  WHERE: Eliminates items of the iteration; use for filtering
  ORDER: Reorders items of the iteration
  RETURN: Constructs query results; can return another XML document or even HTML

```
xquery
for $g in db2-fn:xmlcolumn('GENOME.INFO')/medInfo
let $h := $g/patient[@type="cl"]/DNA/geneX/text()
return
   <geneXList>
   {$h}
   </geneXList>

which would return:
   <geneXList>
   555555
   </geneXList>
```

For example, using the XML document as shown in Figure 2.2, an XQuery expression could be XPath and XQuery will be discussed in more detail in Chapter 10, Mastering the DB2 pureXML Support.

2.1.3 DB2 System Commands

You use DB2 system commands for many purposes, including starting services or processes, invoking utilities, and configuring parameters. Most DB2 system commands do not require the instance—the DB2 server engine process—to be started (instances are discussed later in this chapter). DB2 system command names have the following format:

```
db2x
```

where **x** represents one or more characters. For example

```
db2start
db2set
db2icrt
```

> **NOTE** Many DB2 system commands provide a quick way to obtain syntax and help information about the command by using the **-h** option. For example, typing **db2set –h** displays the syntax of the **db2set** command, with an explanation of its optional parameters.

2.1.4 DB2 Command Line Processor (CLP) Commands

DB2 Command Line Processor (CLP) commands are processed by the CLP tool (introduced in the next section). These commands typically require the instance to be started, and they can be used for database and instance monitoring and for parameter configuration. For example

```
list applications
create database
catalog tcpip node
```

You invoke the Command Line Processor by entering **db2** at an operating system prompt. If you enter **db2** and press the Enter key, you will be working with the CLP in interactive mode, and you can enter the CLP commands as shown above. On the other hand, if you don't want to work with the CLP in interactive mode, precede each CLP command with **db2.** For example

```
db2 list applications
db2 create database
db2 catalog tcpip node
```

Many books, including this one, display CLP commands as db2 *CLP_command* for this reason. Chapter 4, Using the DB2 Tools, explains the CLP in greater detail.

NOTE On the Windows platform, **db2** must be entered in a DB2 Command Window, not at the operating system prompt. The DB2 Command Window and the DB2 CLP are discussed in detail in Chapter 4, Using the DB2 Tools.

NOTE A quick way to obtain syntax and help information about a CLP command is to use the question mark (**?**) character followed by the command. For example

```
db2 ? catalog tcpip node
or just
db2 ? catalog
```

For detailed syntax of a command, see the *DB2 Command Reference* manual.

2.2 DB2 Tools Overview

Figure 2.3 shows all the tools available from the IBM DB2 menu. The IBM DB2 menu on a Windows system can be typically displayed by choosing **Start** > **Programs** > **IBM DB2.** On a Linux or UNIX system, the operating system's graphical support needs to be installed. DB2's graphical interface looks the same on all platforms. This section briefly introduces the tools presented in the IBM DB2 menu. Chapter 4, Using the DB2 Tools, covers these tools in more detail, but for now simply familiarize yourself with them.

2.2.1 Command-Line Tools

Command-line tools, as the name implies, allow you to issue DB2 commands, SQL statements, and XQuery statements from a command-line interface. The two text-based interfaces are the Command Line Processor (CLP) and the Command Window. The Command Window is available only on Windows, while the CLP is available on all other platforms.

The Command Editor is a graphical interface tool that provides the same functionality as the text-based tools—and more. It also has the ability to invoke the Visual Explain tool, which shows the access plan for a query.

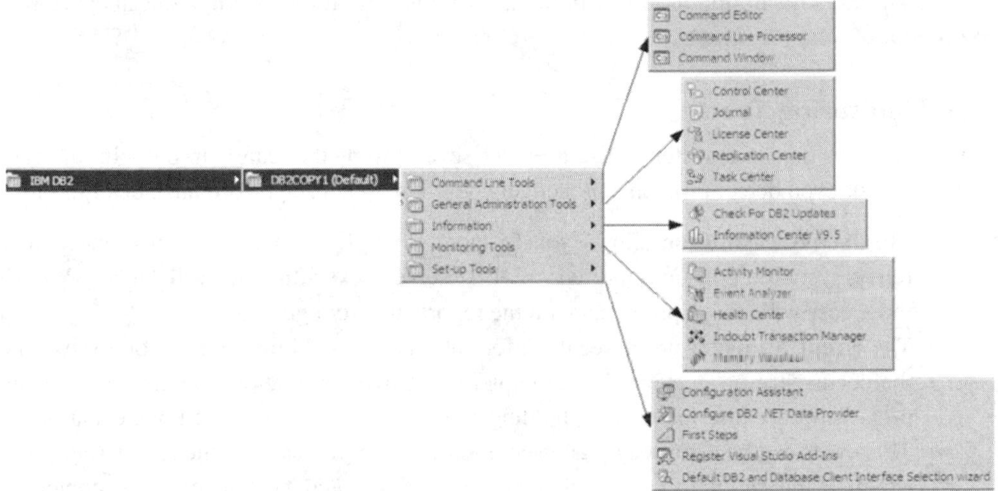

Figure 2.3 The IBM DB2 menus

2.2.2 General Administration Tools

The general administration tools allow database administrators (DBAs) to manage their database servers and databases from a central location.

- The **Control Center** is the most important of these tools. Not only does it support the administration of DB2 database servers on the Linux, UNIX, and Windows platforms, but also on the OS/390 and z/OS platforms. From the Control Center, database objects can be created, altered, and dropped. The tool also comes with several advisors to help you configure your system more quickly.
- The **Journal** tool can help investigate problems in the system. It tracks error messages and scheduled tasks that have been executed.
- The **License Center** summarizes the licenses installed in your DB2 system and allows you to manage them.
- The **Replication Center** lets you set up and manage your replication environment. Use DB2 replication when you want to propagate data from one location to another.
- The **Task Center** allows you to schedule tasks to be performed automatically. For example, you can arrange for a backup task to run at a time when there is minimal database activity.

2.2.3 Information Tools

The Information menu provides easy access to the DB2 documentation. The **Information Center** provides a fast and easy method to search the DB2 manuals. You can install the Information Center locally on your computer or intranet server, or access it via the Internet. Use the **Check**

for DB2 Updates menu option to obtain the most up-to-date information about updates to the DB2 product.

2.2.4 Monitoring Tools

To maintain your database system, DB2 provides several tools that can help pinpoint the cause of a problem or even detect problems proactively before they cause performance deterioration.

- The **Activity Monitor** allows you to monitor application performance and concurrency, resource consumption, and SQL statement execution for a database. You can more easily diagnose problems with the reports this tool generates.
- The **Event Analyzer** processes the information collected by an event monitor based on the occurrence of an event. For example, when two applications cannot continue their processing because the other is holding resources they need, a deadlock event occurs. This event can be captured by an event monitor, and you can use the Event Analyzer to examine the captured data related to the deadlock and help resolve the contention. Some other events that can be captured are connections to the database, buffer pool activity, table space activity, table activity, SQL statements, and transactions.
- The **Health Center** detects problems before they happen by setting up thresholds, which when exceeded cause alert notifications to be sent. The DBA can then choose to execute a recommended action to relieve the situation.
- The **Indoubt Transaction Manager** can help resolve issues with transactions that have been prepared but have not been committed or rolled back. This is only applicable to two-phase commit transactions.
- The **Memory Visualizer** tool lets you track the memory used by DB2. It plots a graph so you can easily monitor memory consumption.

2.2.5 Setup Tools

The Setup tools help you configure your system to connect to remote servers, provide tutorials, and install add-ins to development tools.

- The **Configuration Assistant** allows you to easily configure your system to connect to remote databases and to test the connection.
- **Configure DB2 .NET Data Provider** allows you to easily configure this provider for .NET applications.
- **First Steps** is a good starting point for new DB2 users who wish to become familiar with the product. This tool allows you to create a sample database and provides tutorials that help you familiarize yourself with DB2.
- The **Register Visual Studio Add-Ins** menu item lets you add a plug-in into Microsoft Visual Studio so that DB2 tools can be invoked from Visual Basic, Visual C++, and the .NET development environment. In each of these Microsoft development tools, the add-in inserts the DB2 menu entries into the tool's View, Tools, and Help menus. These

add-ins provide Microsoft Visual Studio programmers with a rich set of application development tools to create stored procedures and user-defined functions designed for DB2.

- **Default DB2 and Database Client Interface Selection Wizard** (Windows only) allows you to choose the DB2 installation copy to use as the default. Starting with DB2 9 multiple DB2 installations are possible on the same machine, but one of them should be chosen as the default copy. Multiple DB2 copy installation is described in Chapter 3, Installing DB2. This tool will also help you choose the default IBM database client interface (ODBC/CLI driver and .NET provider) copy.

2.2.6 Other Tools

The following are other DB2 tools that are not invoked directly from the DB2 menus.

- **Visual Explain** describes the access plan chosen by the DB2 optimizer, the brain of DB2, to access and retrieve data from tables.
- **SQL Assist** aids new users who are not familiar with the SQL language to write SQL queries.
- The **Satellite Administration Center** helps you set up and administer both satellites and the central satellite control server.
- The **IBM Data Studio** provides an integrated data management environment which helps you develop and manage database applications throughout the data management lifecycle. Data Studio can be used for design and prototype of projects and queries using Data Modeling diagrams. It comes with an Integrated Query Editor that helps you build SQL and XQuery statements more easily. You can also use it to develop and debug stored procedures, user-defined functions, and Web services. IBM Data Studio supports most IBM Data Servers including Informix. This is a separate, downloadable image based on the Eclipse Integrated Development Environment (IDE). It replaces the Development Center used in previous DB2 versions.
- The **Data Server Administration Console** (DSAC) is a Web-based tool that allows you to perform about 80 percent of your administrative tasks. It can be used to manage hundreds of IBM data servers from different platforms such as DB2 for Linux, UNIX and Windows, DB2 for z/OS and IDS. It is fast, simple but powerful, and task based. Web-based tools such as the DSAC represent the new generation of tooling that will replace existing tools in the near future.

2.3 The DB2 Environment

Several items control the behavior of your database system. We first describe the DB2 environment on a single-partition database, and in Section 2.6, Database Partitioning Feature (DPF), we expand the material to include concepts relevant to a multipartition database system (we don't want to overload you with information at this stage in the chapter).

Figure 2.4 provides an overview of the DB2 environment. Consider the following when you review this figure:

- The figure may look complex, but don't be overwhelmed by first impressions! Each item in the figure will be discussed in detail in the following sections.
- Since we reference Figure 2.4 throughout this chapter, *we strongly recommend that you bookmark page 43*. This figure is available for free in color as a GIF file (Figure_2_4.gif), on the book's Web site (www.ibmpressbooks.com/title/0131580183). Consider printing it.
- The commands shown in the figure can be issued from the Command Window on Windows or the operating system prompt on Linux and UNIX. Chapter 4, Using the DB2 Tools, describes equivalent methods to perform these commands from the DB2 graphical tools.
- Each arrow points to a set of three commands. The first command in each set (in blue if you printed the figure using a color printer) inquires about the contents of a configuration file, the second command (in black) indicates the syntax to modify these contents, and the third command (in purple) illustrates how to use the command.
- The numbers in parentheses in Figure 2.4 match the superscripts in the headings in the following subsections.

2.3.1 An Instance(1)

In DB2, an instance provides an independent environment where databases can be created and applications can be run against them. Because of these independent environments, databases in separate instances can have the same name. For example, in Figure 2.4 the database called *MYDB2* is associated to instance *DB2*, and another database called *MYDB2* is associated to instance *myinst*. Instances allow users to have separate, independent environments for production, test, and development purposes.

When DB2 is installed on the Windows platform, an instance named *DB2* is created by default. In the Linux and UNIX environments, if you choose to create the default instance, it is called *db2inst1*.

To create an instance explicitly, use

```
db2icrt instance_name
```

To drop an instance, use

```
db2idrop instance_name
```

To start the current instance, use

```
db2start
```

To stop the current instance, use

```
db2stop
```

When an instance is created on Linux and UNIX, logical links to the DB2 executable code are generated. For example, if the server in Figure 2.4 was a Linux or UNIX server and the instances *DB2* and *myinst* were created, both of them would be linked to the same DB2 code. A logical

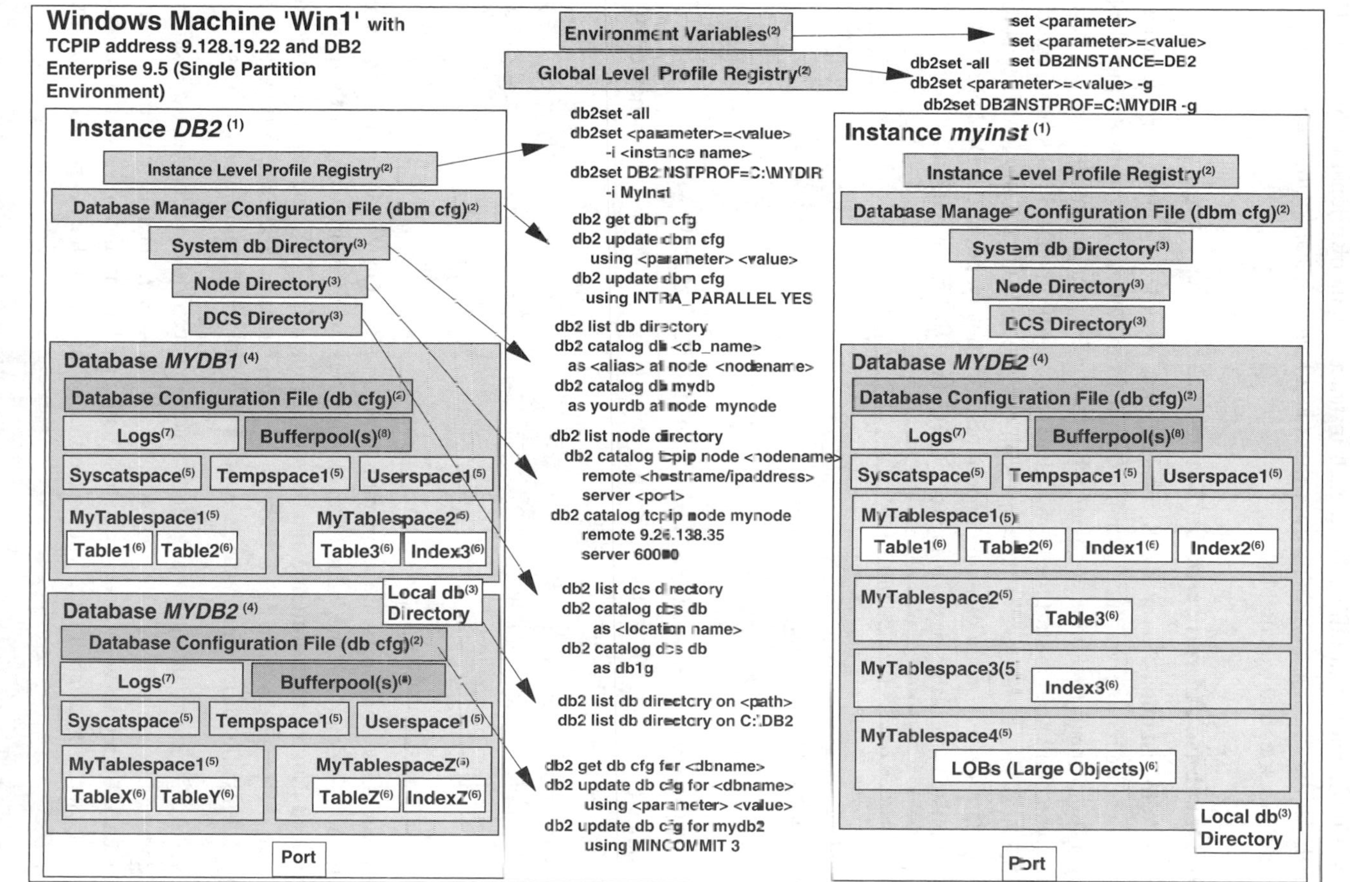

Figure 2.4 The DB2 environment

link works as an alias or pointer to another program. For non-root Linux and UNIX installations as we will see in Chapter 3, Installing DB2, each instance has its own local copy of the DB2 code under the sqllib directory. On Windows, there is a shared install path, and all instances access the same libraries and executables.

2.3.2 The Database Administration Server

The Database Administration Server (DAS) is a daemon or process running on the database server that allows for remote graphical administration from remote clients using the Control Center. If you don't need to administer your DB2 server using a graphical interface from a remote client, you don't need to start the DAS. There can only be one DAS per server regardless of the number of instances or DB2 install copies on the server. Note that the DAS needs to be running at the data server you are planning to administer remotely, not at the DB2 client. If you choose to administer your data servers using the DSAC, the DAS is not required.

To start the DAS, use the following command:

```
db2admin start
```

To stop the DAS, use the following command:

```
db2admin stop
```

2.3.3 Configuration Files and the DB2 Profile Registries(2)

Like many other RDBMSs, DB2 uses different mechanisms to influence the behavior of the database management system. These include

- Environment variables
- DB2 profile registry variables
- Configuration parameters

2.3.3.1 Environment Variables

Environment variables are defined at the operating system level. On Windows you can create a new entry for a variable or edit the value of an existing one by choosing **Control Panel > System > Advanced Tab > Environment Variables.** On Linux and UNIX you can normally add a line to execute the script **db2profile** (Bourne or Korn shell) or **db2cshrc** (C shell) (provided after DB2 installation), to the instance owner's .login or .profile initialization files.

The DB2INSTANCE environment variable allows you to specify the current active instance to which all commands apply. If DB2INSTANCE is set to *myinst*, then issuing the command **CREATE DATABASE mydb** will create a database associated to instance *myinst*. If you wanted to create this database in instance *DB2*, you would first change the value of the DB2INSTANCE variable to *DB2*.

Using the Control Panel (Windows) or the user profile (Linux or UNIX) to set the value of an environment variable guarantees that value will be used the next time you open a window or session. If you only want to change this value temporarily while in a given window or session, you can use the operating system **set** command on Windows, or **export** on Linux or UNIX. The command

set DB2INSTANCE=DB2 (on Windows)

or

export DB2INSTANCE=DB2 (on Linux and UNIX)

sets the value of the DB2INSTANCE environment variable to *DB2*. A common mistake when using the command is to leave spaces before and/or after the equal sign (=)—no spaces should be entered.

To check the current setting of this variable, you can use any of these three commands:

echo %DB2INSTANCE% (Windows only)

set DB2INSTANCE

db2 get instance

For a list of all available instances in your system, issue the following command:

```
db2ilist
```

2.3.3.2 The DB2 Profile Registry

The word "registry" always causes confusion when working with DB2 on Windows. The DB2 profile registry variables, or simply the DB2 registry variables, have no relation whatsoever with the Windows Registry variables. The DB2 registry variables provide a centralized location where some key variables influencing DB2's behavior reside.

> **NOTE** Some of the DB2 registry variables are platform-specific.

The DB2 Profile Registry is divided into four categories:

- The DB2 instance-level profile registry
- The DB2 global-level profile registry
- The DB2 instance node-level profile registry
- The DB2 instance profile registry

The first two are the most common ones. The main difference between the global-level and the instance-level profile registries, as you can tell from their names, is the scope to which the variables apply. Global-level profile registry variables apply to all instances on the server. As you can see from Figure 2.4, this registry has been drawn outside of the two instance boxes. Instance-level profile registry variables apply to a specific instance. You can see separate instance-level profile registry boxes inside each of the two instances in the figure.

To view the current DB2 registry variables, issue the following command from the CLP:

```
db2set -all
```

You may get output like this:

```
[i] DB2INSTPROF=C:\PROGRAM FILES\SQLLIB
[g] DB2SYSTEM=PRODSYS
```

As you may have already guessed, **[i]** indicates the variable has been defined at the instance level, while **[g]** indicates that it has been defined at the global level.

The following are a few other commands related to the DB2 Registry variables.

To view all the registry variables that can be defined in DB2, use this command:

```
db2set -lr
```

To set the value of a specific variable (in this example, DB2INSTPROF) at the global level, use

```
db2set DB2INSTPROF="C:\PROGRAM FILES\SQLLIB" -g
```

To set a variable at the instance level for instance *myinst*, use

```
db2set DB2INSTPROF="C:\MY FILES\SQLLIB" -i myinst
```

Note that for the above commands, the same variable has been set at both levels: the global level and the instance level. When a registry variable is defined at different levels, DB2 will always choose the value at the lowest level, in this case the instance level.

For the **db2set** command, as with the **set** command discussed earlier, there are no spaces before or after the equal sign.

Some registry variables require you to stop and start the instance (**db2stop/db2start**) for the change to take effect. Other registry variables do not have this requirement. Refer to the *DB2 Administration Guide: Performance* for a list of variables that have this requirement.

2.3.3.3 Configuration Parameters

Configuration parameters are defined at two different levels: the instance level and the database level. The variables at each level are different (not like DB2 registry variables, where the same variables can be defined at different levels).

At the instance level, variables are stored in the Database Manager Configuration file (dbm cfg). Changes to these variables affect all databases associated to that instance, which is why Figure 2.4 shows a Database Manager Configuration file box defined per instance and outside the databases.

To view the contents of the Database Manager Configuration file, issue the command:

```
db2 get dbm cfg
```

To update the value of a specific parameter, use

```
db2 update dbm cfg using parameter value
```

For example

```
db2 update dbm cfg using INTRA_PARALLEL YES
```

Many of the Database Manager Configuration parameters are now "configurable online," meaning the changes are dynamic—you don't need to stop and start the instance. From the Control Center, described in Chapter 4, Using the DB2 Tools, you can access the Database Manager (DBM) Configuration panel (right click on the desired instance, and choose Configure Parameters), which has the column "Dynamic" that indicates whether the parameter is configurable online or not. In addition, many of these parameters are also "Automatic," meaning that DB2 automatically calculates the best value depending on your system.

At the database level, parameter values are stored in the Database Configuration file (db cfg). Changes to these parameters only affect the specific database the Database Configuration file applies to. In Figure 2.4 you can see there is a Database Configuration file box inside each of the databases defined.

To view the contents of the Database Configuration file, issue the command:

```
db2 get db cfg for dbname
```

For example

```
db2 get db cfg for mydb2
```

To update the value of a specific variable, use

```
db2 update db cfg for dbname using parameter value
```

For example

```
db2 update db cfg for mydb2 using MINCOMMIT 3
```

Many of these parameters are configurable online, meaning that the change is dynamic, and you no longer need to disconnect all connections to the database for the change to take effect. From the Control Center, described in Chapter 4, Using the DB2 Tools, you can access the Database Configuration panel (right click on the desired database, and choose Configure Parameters), which has the column "Dynamic" that indicates whether the parameter is configurable online or not. Many of these parameters are also "Automatic," where DB2 configures the parameter for you.

2.3.4 Connectivity and DB2 Directories(3)

In DB2, directories are used to store connectivity information about databases and the servers on which they reside. There are four main directories, which are described in the following subsections. The corresponding commands to set up database and server connectivity are also included; however, many users find the Configuration Assistant graphical tool very convenient to set up database and server connectivity.

Chapter 6, Configuring Client and Server Connectivity, discusses all the commands and concepts described in this section in detail, including the Configuration Assistant.

2.3.4.1 System Database Directory

The system database directory (or system db directory) is like the main "table of contents" that contains information about all the databases to which you can connect from your DB2 server. As you can see from Figure 2.4, the system db directory is stored at the instance level.

To list the contents of the system db directory, use the command:

```
db2 list db directory
```

Any entry from the output of this command containing the word *Indirect* indicates that the entry is for a local database, that is, a database that resides on the data server on which you are working. The entry also points to the local database directory indicated by the *Database drive* item (Windows) or *Local database directory* (Linux or UNIX).

Any entry containing the word *Remote* indicates that the entry is for a remote database—a database residing on a server other than the one on which you are currently working. The entry also points to the node directory entry indicated by the *Node name* item.

To enter information into the system database directory, use the **catalog** command:

```
db2 catalog db dbname as alias  at node nodename
```

For example

```
db2 catalog db mydb as yourdb at node mynode
```

The **catalog** commands are normally used only when adding information for remote databases. For local databases, a catalog entry is automatically created after creating the database with the **CREATE DATABASE** command.

2.3.4.2 Local Database Directory

The local database directory contains information about databases residing on the server where you are currently working. Figure 2.4 shows the local database directory overlapping the database box. This means that there will be one local database directory associated to all of the databases residing in the same location (the drive on Windows or the path on Linux or UNIX). The local database directory does not reside inside the database itself, but it does not reside at the instance level either; it is in a layer between these two. (After you read Section 2.3.10, The Internal Implementation of the DB2 Environment, it will be easier to understand this concept.)

Note also from Figure 2.4 that there is no specific command used to enter information into this directory, only to retrieve it. When you create a database with the **CREATE DATABASE** command, an entry is added to this directory.

To list the contents of the local database directory, issue the command:

```
db2 list db directory on drive / path
```

where **drive** can be obtained from the item *Database drive* (Windows) or **path** from the item *Local database directory* (Linux or UNIX) in the corresponding entry of the system db directory.

2.3.4.3 Node Directory

The node directory stores all connectivity information for remote database servers. For example, if you use the TCP/IP protocol, this directory shows entries such as the host name or IP address of the server where the database to which you want to connect resides, and the port number of the associated DB2 instance.

To list the contents of the node directory, issue the command:

```
db2 list node directory
```

To enter information into the node directory, use

```
db2 catalog tcpip node node_name
    remote hostname or IP_address
    server service_name or port_number
```

For example

```
db2 catalog tcpip node mynode
    remote 192.168.1.100
    server 60000
```

You can obtain the port number of the remote instance to which you want to connect by looking at the SVCENAME parameter in the Database Manager Configuration file of that instance. If this parameter contains a string value rather than the port number, you need to look for the corresponding entry in the TCP/IP services file mapping this string to the port number.

2.3.4.4 Database Connection Services Directory

The Database Connection Services (DCS) directory contains connectivity information for host databases residing on System z (z/OS or OS/390) or System i (OS/400) server. You need to have DB2 Connect software installed.

To list the contents of the DCS directory, issue the following command:

```
db2 list dcs directory
```

To enter information into the DCS directory, use

```
db2 catalog dcs db dbname as location_name
```

For example

```
db2 catalog dcs db mydb as db1g
```

2.3.5 Databases[4]

A database is a collection of information organized into interrelated objects like table spaces, tables, and indexes. Databases are closed and independent units associated to an instance. Because of this independence, objects in two or more databases can have the same name. For example, Figure 2.4 shows a table space called *MyTablespace1* inside the database *MYDB1* associated to instance *DB2*. Another table space with the name *MyTablespace1* is also used inside the database *MYDB2*, which is also associated to instance *DB2*.

Since databases are closed units, you cannot perform queries involving tables of two different databases in a direct way. For example, a query involving *Table1* in database *MYDB1* and *TableZ* in database *MYDB2* is not readily allowed. For an SQL statement to work against tables of different databases, you need to use *federation* (see Section 2.4, Federation).

You create a database with the command **CREATE DATABASE.** This command automatically creates three table spaces, a buffer pool, and several configuration files, which is why this command can take a few seconds to complete.

> **NOTE** While **CREATE DATABASE** looks like an SQL statement, it is considered a DB2 CLP command.

2.3.6 Table Spaces(5)

Table spaces are logical objects used as a layer between logical tables and physical containers. **Containers** are where the data is physically stored in files, directories, or raw devices. When you create a table space, you can associate it to a specific buffer pool (database cache) and to specific containers.

Three table spaces—SYSCATSPACE (holding the Catalog tables), TEMPSPACE1 (system temporary space), and USERSPACE1 (the default user table space)—are automatically created when you create a database. SYSCATSPACE and TEMPSPACE1 can be considered system structures, as they are needed for the normal operation of your database. SYSCATSPACE contains the catalog tables containing **metadata** (data about your database objects) and must exist at all times. Some other RDBMSs call this structure a "data dictionary."

> **NOTE** Do not confuse the term "catalog" in this section with the **catalog** command mentioned earlier; they have no relationship at all.

A system temporary table space is the work area for the database manager to perform operations, such as joins and overflowed sorts. There must be at least one system temporary table space in each database.

The USERSPACE1 table space is created by default, but you can delete it. To create a table in a given table space, use the **CREATE TABLE** statement with the **IN table_space_name** clause. If a table space is not specified in this statement, the table will be created in the first user-created table space. If you have not yet created a table space, the table will be created in the USERSPACE1 table space.

Figure 2.4 shows other table spaces that were explicitly created with the **CREATE TABLESPACE** statement (in brown in the figure if you printed the softcopy version). Chapter 8, The DB2 Storage Model, discusses table spaces in more detail.

2.3.7 Tables, Indexes, and Large Objects(6)

A **table** is an unordered set of data records consisting of columns and rows. An **index** is an ordered set of pointers associated with a table, and is used for performance purposes and to ensure uniqueness. Non-traditional relational data, such as video, audio, and scanned documents, are stored in tables as large objects (LOBs). Tables and indexes reside in table spaces. Chapter 8 describes these in more detail.

2.3.8 Logs[7]

Logs are used by DB2 to record every operation against a database. In case of a failure, logs are crucial to recover the database to a consistent point. See Chapter 14, Developing Database Backup and Recovery Solutions, for more information about logs.

2.3.9 Buffer Pools[8]

A **buffer pool** is an area in memory where all index and data pages other than LOBs are processed. DB2 retrieves LOBs directly from disk. Buffer pools are one of the most important objects to tune for database performance. Chapter 8, The DB2 Storage Model, discusses buffer pools in more detail.

2.3.10 The Internal Implementation of the DB2 Environment

We have already discussed DB2 registry variables, configuration files, and instances. In this section we illustrate how some of these concepts physically map to directories and files in the Windows environment. The structure is a bit different in Linux and UNIX environments, but the main ideas are the same. Figures 2.5, 2.6, and 2.7 illustrate the DB2 environment internal implementation that corresponds to Figure 2.4

Figure 2.5 shows the directory where DB2 was installed: H:\Program Files\IBM\SQLLIB. The SQLLIB directory contains several subdirectories and files that belong to DB2, including the binary code that makes DB2 work, and a subdirectory that is created for each instance created on the server. For example, in Figure 2.5 the subdirectories DB2 and MYINST correspond to the instances *DB2* and *myinst* respectively. The DB2DAS00 subdirectory corresponds to the DAS.

At the top of the figure there is a directory H:\MYINST. This directory contains all the databases created under the H: drive for instance *myinst*. Similarly, the H:\DB2 directory contains all the databases created under the H: drive for instance *DB2*.

Figure 2.6 shows an expanded view of the H:\Program Files\IBM\SQLLIB\DB2 directory. This directory contains information about the instance *DB2*. The db2systm binary file contains the database manager configuration (dbm cfg). The other two files highlighted in the figure (db2nodes.cfg and db2diag.log) are discussed later in this book. For now, the description of these files in the figure is sufficient. The figure also points out the directories where the system database, Node, and DCS directories reside. Note that the Node and DCS directories don't exist if they don't have any entries.

In Figure 2.7, the H:\DB2 and H:\MYINST directories have been expanded. The subdirectories SQL00001 and SQL00002 under H:\DB2\NODE0000 correspond to the two databases created

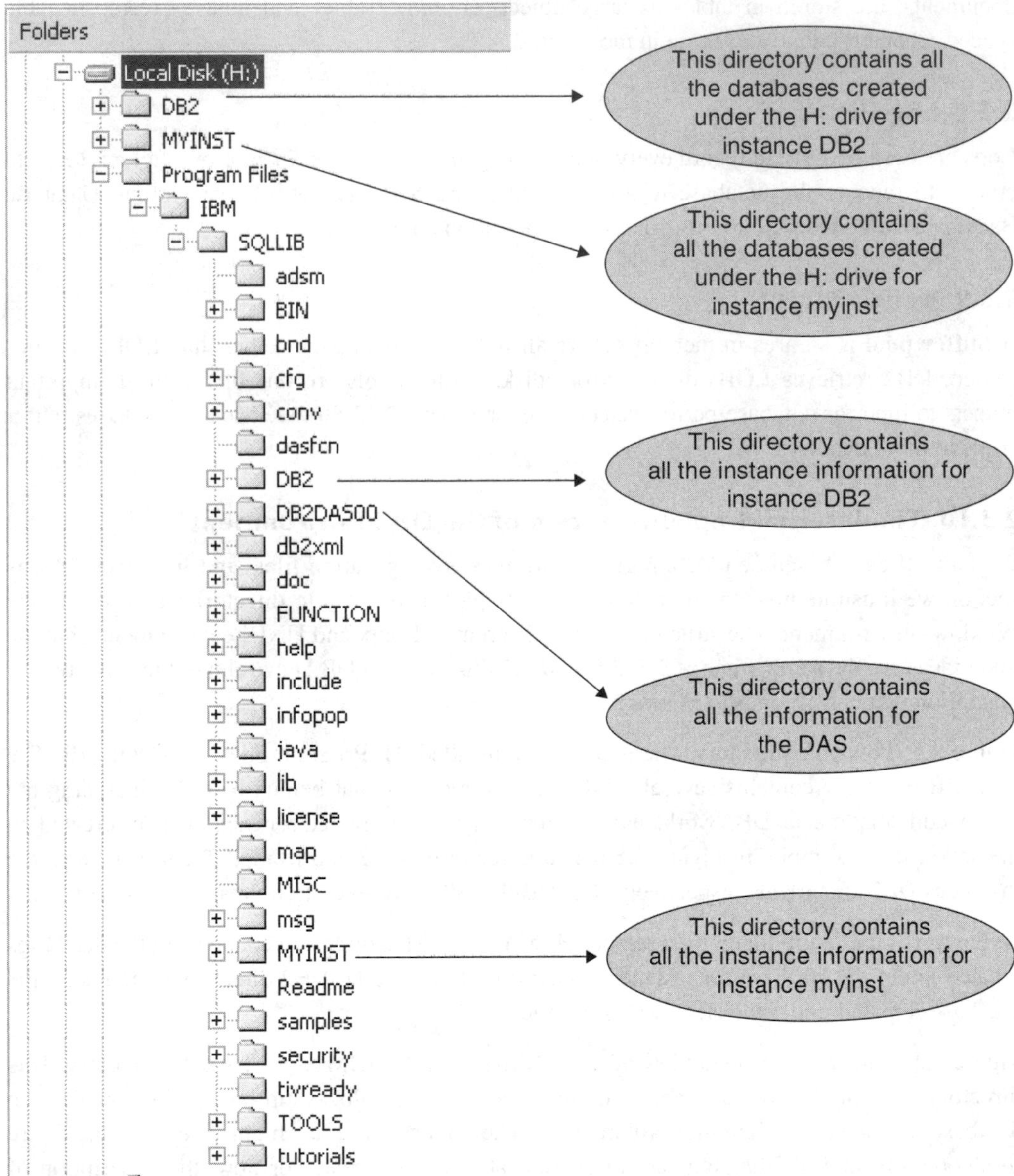

Figure 2.5 The internal implementation environment for DB2 for Windows

under instance *DB2*. To map these directory names to the actual database names, you can review the contents of the local database directory with this command:

```
list db directory on h:
```

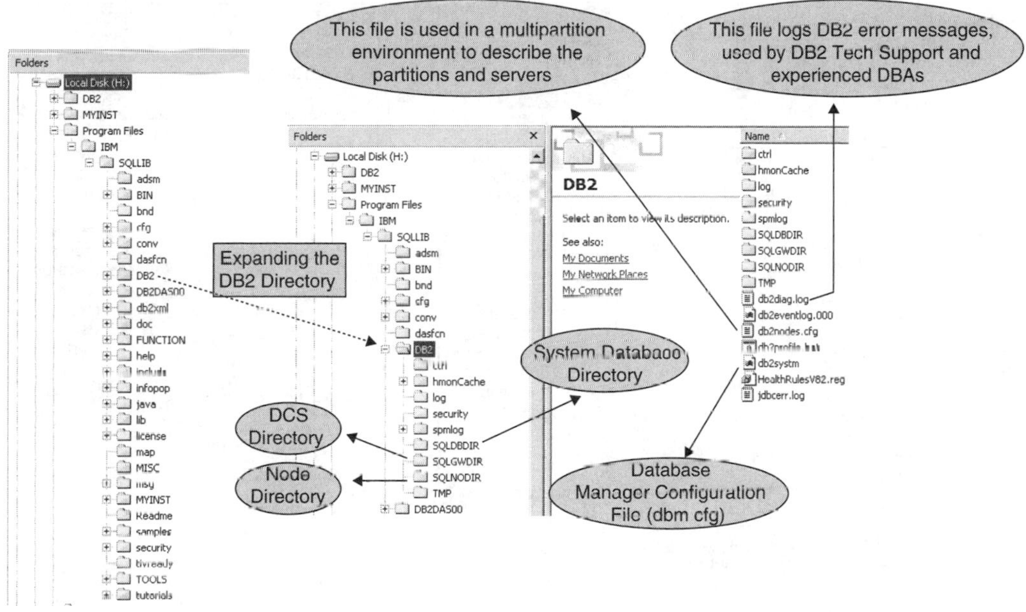

Figure 2.6 Expanding the DB2 instance directory

Chapter 6, Configuring Client and Server Connectivity, shows sample output of this command. Note that the local database directory is stored in the subdirectory SQLDBDIR. This subdirectory is at the same level as each of the database subdirectories; therefore, when a database is dropped, this subdirectory is not dropped. Figure 2.6 shows two SQLDBDIR subdirectories, one under H:\DB2\NODE0000 and another one under H:\MYINST\NODE0000.

Knowing how the DB2 environment is internally implemented can help you understand the DB2 concepts better. For example, looking back at Figure 2.4 (the one you should have printed!), what would happen if you dropped the instance *DB2*? Would this mean that databases *MYDB1* and *MYDB2* are also dropped? The answer is no. Figure 2.5 clearly shows that the directory where the instance information resides (H:\Program Files\IBM\SQLLIB\DB2) and the directory where the data resides (H:\DB2) are totally different. When an instance is dropped, only the subdirectory created for that instance is dropped.

Similarly, let's say you uninstall DB2 at a given time, and later you reinstall it on the same drive. After reinstallation, can you access the "old" databases created before you uninstalled DB2 the first time? The answer is yes. When you uninstalled DB2, you removed the SQLLIB directory, therefore the DB2 binary code, as well as the instance subdirectories, were removed, but the databases were left untouched. When you reinstall DB2, a new SQLLIB directory is created with a new default DB2 instance; no other instance is created. The new DB2 instance will have a new empty system database directory (db2systm). So even though the directories containing the database data were left intact, you need to explicitly put the information in the DB2 system

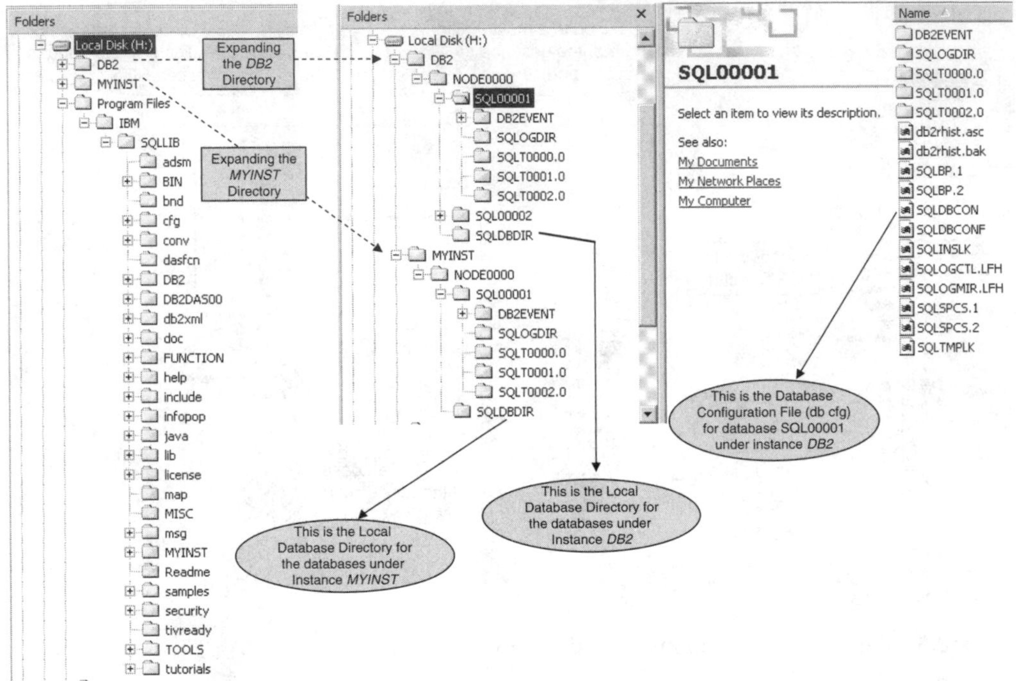

Figure 2.7 Expanding the directories containing the database data

database directory for DB2 to recognize the existence of these databases. For example, if you would like to access the MYDB1 database of the *DB2* instance, you need to issue this command to add an entry to the system database directory:

```
catalog db mydb1 on h:
```

If the database you want to access is MYDB2, which was in the *myinst* instance, you would first need to create this instance, switch to the instance, and then issue the **catalog** command as shown below.

```
db2icrt myinst

set DB2INSTANCE=myinst

catalog db mydb2 on h:
```

It is a good practice to back up the contents of all your configuration files as shown below.

```
db2 get dbm cfg > dbmcfg.bk

db2 get db cfg for database_name > dbcfg.bk

db2set -all > db2set.bk

db2 list db directory > systemdbdir.bk

db2 list node directory > nodedir.bk

db2 list dcs directory > dcsdir.bk
```

Notice that all of these commands redirect the output to a text file with a .bk extension.

> **CAUTION** The purpose of this section is to help you understand the DB2 environment by describing its internal implementation. We strongly suggest that you *do not tamper with the files and directories discussed in this section.* You should only modify the files using the commands described in earlier sections.

2.4 Federation

Database federated support in DB2 allows tables from multiple databases to be presented as local tables to a DB2 server. The databases may be local or remote; they can also belong to different RDBMSs. While Chapter 1, Introduction to DB2, briefly introduced federated support, this section provides an overview of how federation is implemented.

First of all, make sure that your server allows federated support: The database manager parameter FEDERATED must be set to YES.

DB2 uses NICKNAME, SERVER, WRAPPER, and USER MAPPING objects to implement federation. Let's consider the example illustrated in Figure 2.8.

The DB2 user *db2user* connects to the database *db2db*. He then issues the following statement:

```
SELECT * FROM remote_sales
```

The table **remote_sales,** however, is not a local table but a **nickname,** which is a pointer to a table in another database, possibly in another server and from a different RDBMS. A nickname is created with the **CREATE NICKNAME** statement, and requires a SERVER object (*aries* in the example) and the schema and table name to be accessed at this server (*csmmgr.sales*).

A SERVER object is associated to a WRAPPER. A wrapper is associated to a library that contains all the code required to connect to a given RDBMS. For IBM databases like Informix, these wrappers or libraries are provided with DB2. For other RDBMSs, you need to obtain the IBM Websphere Federation Server software. In Figure 2.8, the wrapper called *informix* was created, and it is associated to the library *db2informix.dll.*

To access the Informix table *csmmgr.sales*, however, you cannot use the DB2 user id and password directly. You need to establish a mapping between the DB2 user id and an Informix user id that has the authority to access the desired table. This is achieved with the **CREATE USER MAPPING** statement. Figure 2.8 shows how the DB2 user *db2user* and the Informix user *informixuser* are associated with this statement.

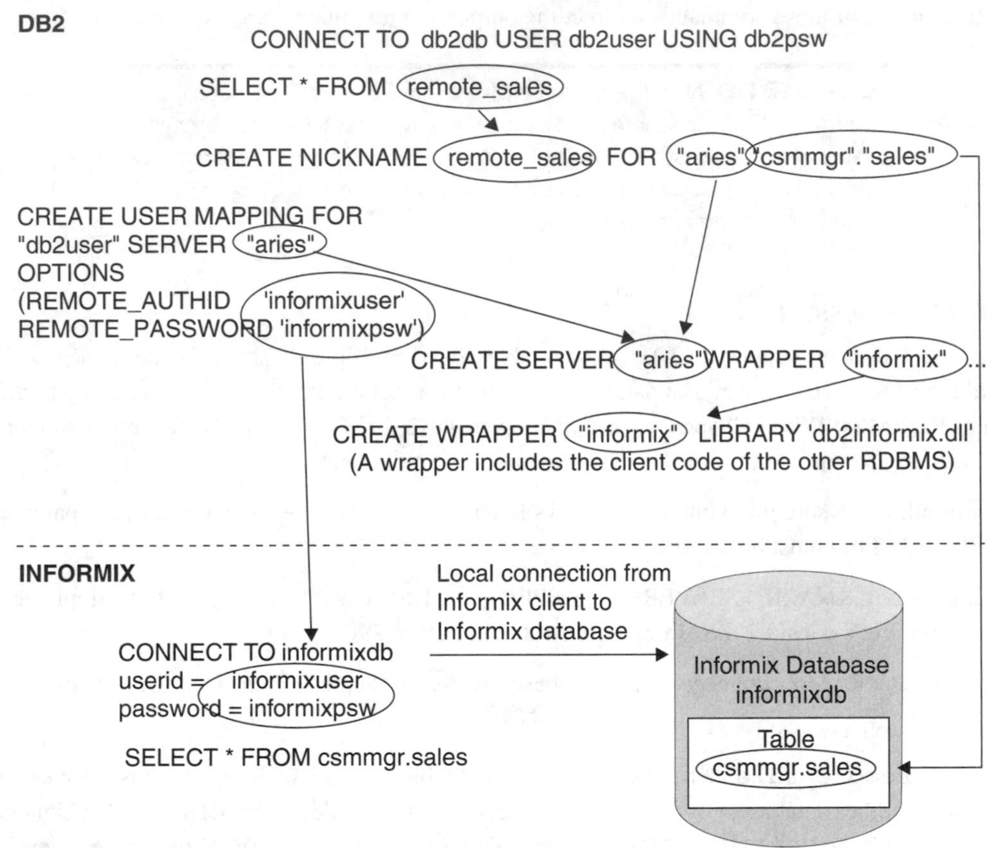

Figure 2.8 An overview of a federation environment

2.5 Case Study: The DB2 Environment

> **NOTE** Several assumptions have been made in this case study and the rest of the case studies in this book, so if you try to follow them, some steps may not work for you. If you do follow some or all of the steps in the case studies, we recommend you use a test computer system.

You recently attended a DB2 training class and would like to try things out on your own laptop at the office. Your laptop is running Windows Vista and DB2 Enterprise has been installed. You open the Command Window and take the following steps.

1. First, you want to know how many instances you have in your computer, so you enter `db2ilist`

2. Then, to find out which of these instances is the current active one, you enter

```
db2 get instance
```

With the **db2ilist** command, you found out there were two instances defined on this computer, *DB2* and *myinst*. With the **db2 get instance** command, you learned that the *DB2* instance is the current active instance.

3. You would now like to list the databases in the *myinst* instance. Since this one is not the current active instance, you first switch to this instance temporarily in the current Command Window:

```
set DB2INSTANCE=myinst
```

4. You again issue **db2 get instance** to check that *myinst* is now the current instance, and you start it using the **db2start** command.

5. To list the databases defined on this instance you issue

```
db2 list db directory
```

This command shows that you only have one database (*MYDB2*) in this instance.

6. You want to try creating a new database called *TEMPORAL*, so you execute

```
db2 create database temporal
```

The creation of the database takes some time because several objects are created by default inside the database. Issuing another **list db directory** command now shows two databases: *MYDB2* and *TEMPORAL*.

7. You connect to the *MYDB2* database (**db2 connect to mydb2**) and check which tables you have in this database (**db2 list tables for all**). You also check how many table spaces are defined (**db2 list tablespaces**).

8. Next, you want to review the contents of the database configuration file (db cfg) for the *MYDB2* database:

```
db2 get db cfg for mydb2
```

9. To review the contents of the Database Manager Configuration file (dbm cfg) you issue

```
db2 get dbm cfg
```

10. At this point, you want to practice changing the value of a dbm cfg parameter, so you pick the INTRA_PARALLEL parameter, which has a value set to NO. You change its value to YES as follows:

```
db2 update dbm cfg using INTRA_PARALLEL YES
```

11. You learned at the class that this parameter is not "configurable online," so you know you have to stop and start the instance. Since there is a connection to a database in the current instance (remember you connected to the *MYDB2* database earlier from your current Command Window), DB2 will not allow you to stop the instance. Enter the following sequence of commands:

```
db2 terminate (terminates the connection)
db2stop
db2start
```

And that's it! In this case study you have reviewed some basic instance commands like **`db2ilist`** and **`get instance.`** You have also reviewed how to switch to another instance, create and connect to a database, list the databases in the instance, review the contents of the database configuration file and the database manager configuration file, update a database manager configuration file parameter, and stop and start an instance.

2.6 Database Partitioning Feature

In this section we introduce you to the Database Partitioning Feature (DPF) available on DB2 Enterprise. DPF lets you partition your database across multiple servers or within a large SMP server. This allows for scalability, since you can add new servers and spread your database across them. That means more CPUs, more memory, and more disks from each of the additional servers for your database!

DB2 Enterprise with DPF is ideal to manage large databases, whether you are doing data warehousing, data mining, online analytical processing (OLAP), also known as Decision Support Systems (DSS), or working with online transaction processing (OLTP) workloads. You do not have to install any new code to enable this feature, but you must purchase this feature before enabling the Database Partitioning Feature. Users connect to the database and issue queries as usual without the need to know that the database is spread among several partitions.

Up to this point, we have been discussing a single partition environment and its concepts, all of which apply to a multipartition environment as well. We will now point out some implementation differences and introduce a few new concepts, including database partitions, partition groups, and the coordinator partition, that are relevant only to a multipartition environment.

2.6.1 Database Partitions

A **database partition** is an independent part of a partitioned database with its own data, configuration files, indexes, and transaction logs. You can assign multiple partitions across several physical servers or to a single physical server. In the latter case, the partitions are called **logical partitions,** and they can share the server's resources.

A single-partition database is a database with only one partition. We described the DB2 environment for this type of database in Section 2.3, The DB2 Environment. A **multipartition database** (also referred to as a **partitioned database**) is a database with two or more database partitions. Depending on your hardware environment, there are several topologies for database partitioning. Figure 2.9 shows single partition and multipartition configurations with one partition per server. The illustration at the top of the figure shows an SMP server with one partition (single-partition environment). This means the entire database resides on this one server.

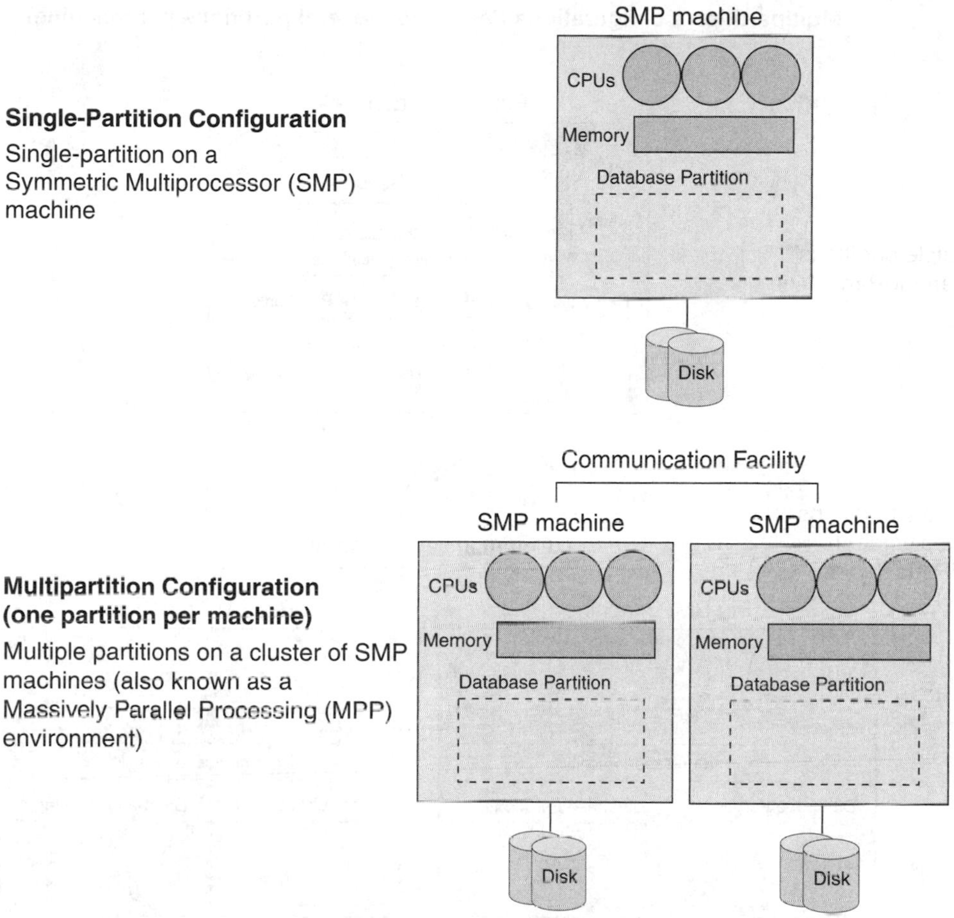

Single-Partition Configuration

Single-partition on a Symmetric Multiprocessor (SMP) machine

SMP machine

CPUs

Memory

Database Partition

Disk

Multipartition Configuration (one partition per machine)

Multiple partitions on a cluster of SMP machines (also known as a Massively Parallel Processing (MPP) environment)

Communication Facility

SMP machine

CPUs

Memory

Database Partition

Disk

SMP machine

CPUs

Memory

Database Partition

Disk

Figure 2.9 Database partition configurations with one partition per server

The illustration at the bottom shows two SMP servers, one partition per server (multipartition environment). This means the database is split between the two partitions.

> **NOTE** In Figure 2.9, the symmetric multiprocessor (SMP) systems could be replaced by uniprocessor systems.

Figure 2.10 shows multipartition configurations with multiple partitions per server. Unlike Figure 2.9 where there was only one partition per server, this figure illustrates two (or more) partitions per server.

To visualize how a DB2 environment is split in a DPF system, Figure 2.11 illustrates a partial reproduction of Figure 2.4, and shows it split into three physical partitions, one partition per

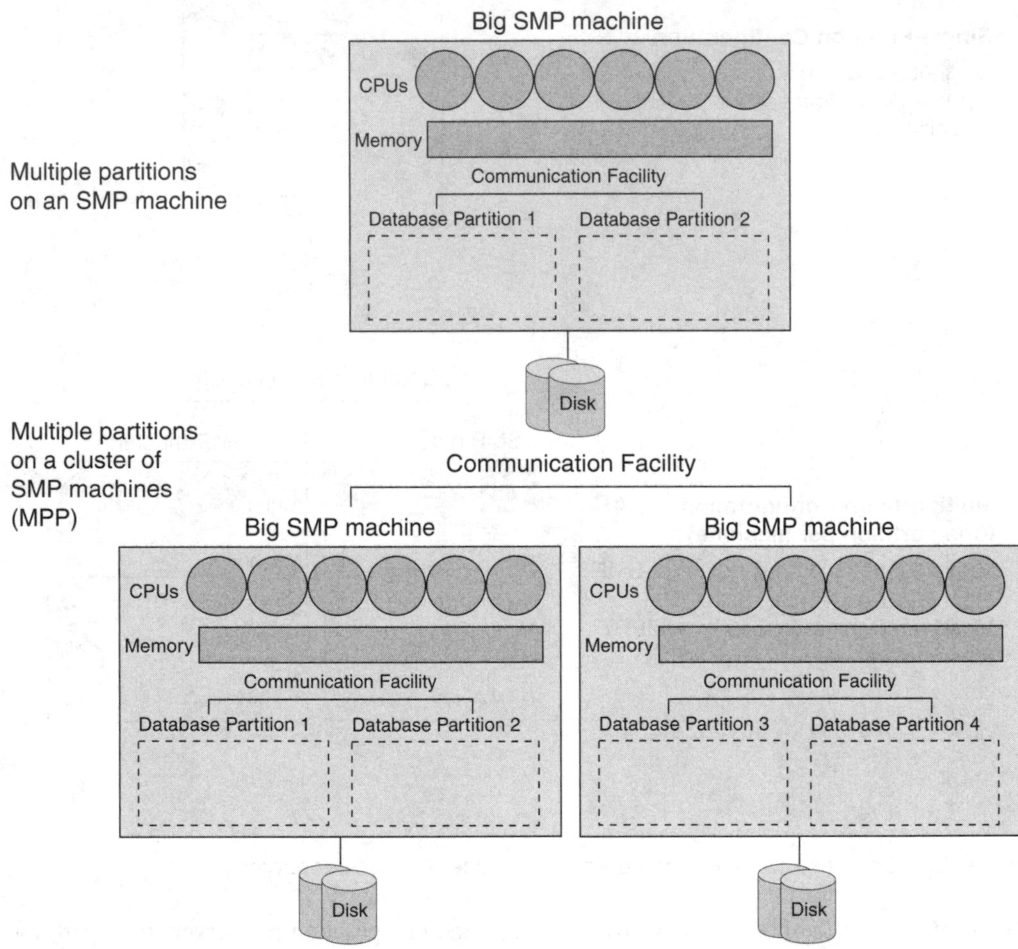

Figure 2.10 Database partition configurations with multiple partitions per server

server. (We have changed the server in the original Figure 2.4 to use the Linux operating system instead of the Windows operating system.)

> **NOTE** Because we reference Figure 2.11 throughout this section, *we recommend that you bookmark page 61.* Alternatively, since this figure is available in color on the book's Web site, www.ibmpressbooks.com/title/0131580183 (Figure_2_11.gif), consider printing it.

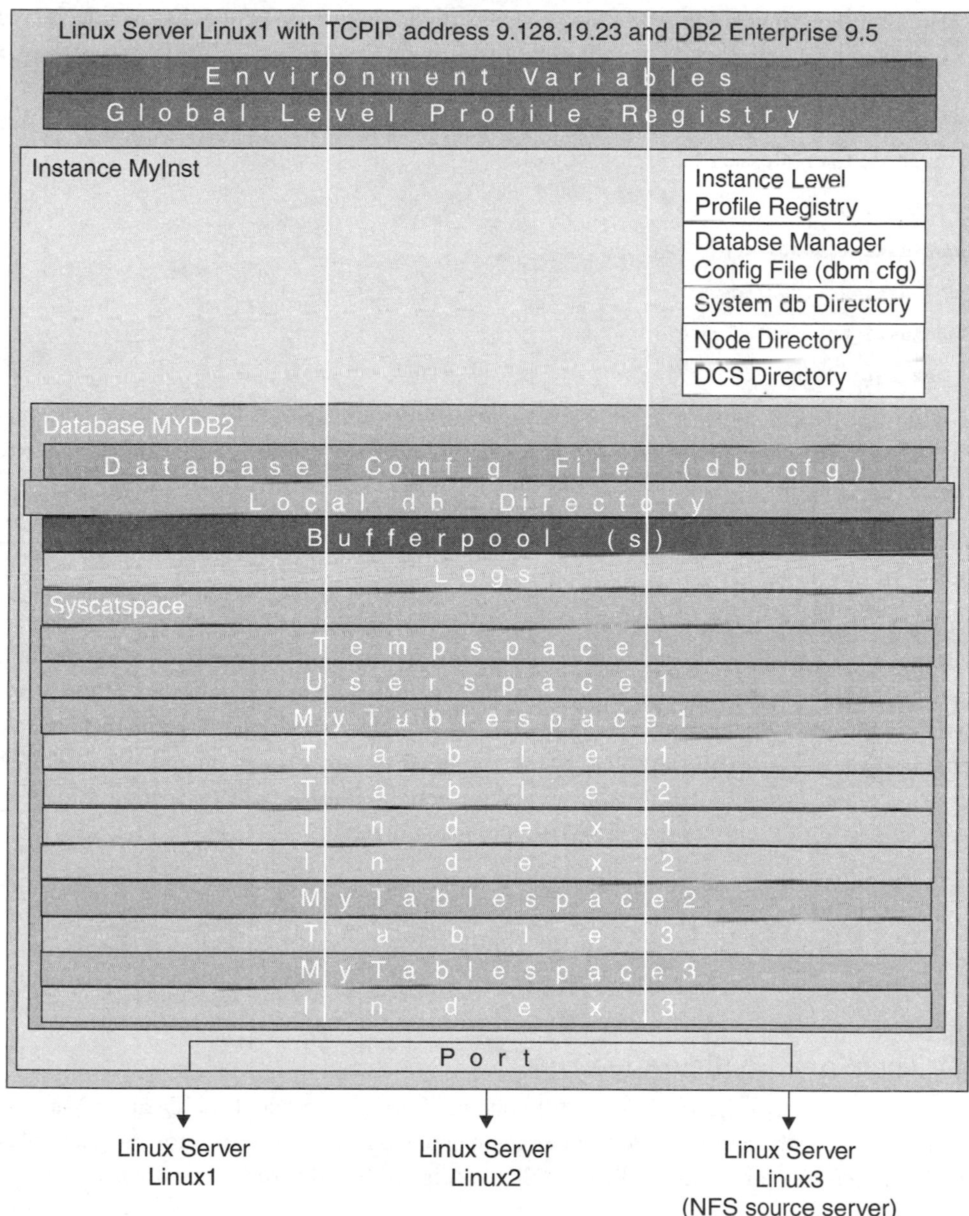

Figure 2.11 The DB2 environment on DB2 Enterprise with DPF

In Figure 2.11, the DB2 environment is "split" so that it now resides on three servers running the same operating system (Linux, in this example). The partitions are also running the same DB2 version, but it is important to note that different Fix Pack levels are allowed. This figure shows where files and objects would be located on a new installation of a multipartition system.

It is also important to note that all of the servers participating in a DPF environment have to be interconnected by a high-speed communication facility that supports the TCP/IP protocol. TCP/IP ports are reserved on each server for this "interpartition" communication. For example, by default after installation, the services file on Linux (/etc/services) is updated as follows (assuming you chose to create the *db2inst1* instance):

```
DB2_db2inst1 60000/tcp

DB2_db2inst1_1 60001/tcp

DB2_db2inst1_2 60002/tcp

DB2_db2inst1_END 60003/tcp

db2c_db2inst1 50000/tcp
```

This will vary depending on the number of partitions on the server. By default, ports 60000 through 60003 are reserved for interpartition communication. You can update the services file with the correct number of entries to support the number of partitions you are configuring.

When the partitions reside on the same server, communication between the partitions still requires this setup.

For a DB2 client to connect to a DPF system, you issue **catalog** commands at the client to populate the system and node directories. In the example, the port number to use in these commands is 50000 to connect to the *db2inst1* instance, and the host name can be any of the servers participating in the DPF environment. The server used in the **catalog** command becomes the coordinator, unless the DBPARTITIONNUM option of the **connect** statement is used. The concept of coordinator is described later in this section. Chapter 6, Configuring Client and Server Connectivity, discusses the **catalog** command in detail.

> **NOTE** Each of the servers participating in the DPF environment have their own separate services file, but the entries in those files that are applicable to DB2 interpartition communication must be the same.

2.6.2 The Node Configuration File

The node configuration file (db2nodes.cfg) contains information about the database partitions and the servers on which they reside that belong to an instance. Figure 2.12 shows an example of the db2nodes.cfg file for a cluster of four UNIX servers with two partitions on each server.

In Figure 2.12, the partition number, the first column in the db2nodes.cfg file, indicates the number that identifies the database partition within DB2. You can see that there are eight partitions in total. The numbering of the partitions must be in ascending order, can start from any number, and gaps between the numbers are allowed. The numbering used is important as it will be taken into consideration in commands or SQL statements.

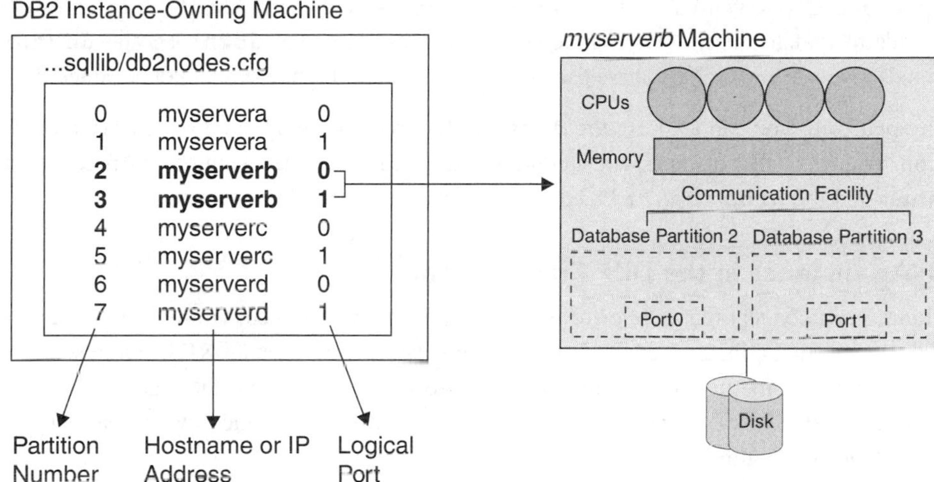

Figure 2.12 An example of the db2nodes.cfg file

The second column is the hostname or TCP/IP address of the server where the partition is created.

The third column, the logical port, is required when you create more than one partition on the same server. This column specifies the logical port for the partition within the server and must be unique within a server. In Figure 2.12, you can see the mapping between the db2nodes.cfg entries for partitions 2 and 3 for server *myserverb* and the physical server implementation. The logical ports must also be in the same order as in the db2nodes.cfg file.

The fourth column in the db2nodes.cfg file, the netname, is required if you are using a high-speed interconnect for interpartition communication or if the resourcesetname column is used.

The fifth column in the db2nodes.cfg file, the resourcesetname, is optional. It specifies the operating system resource that the partition should be started in.

On Windows, the db2nodes.cfg file uses the *computer name* column instead of the *resourcesetname* column. The *computer name* column stores the computer name for the server on which a partition resides. Also, the order of the columns is slightly different: partition number, hostname, computer name, logical port, netname, and resourcesetname.

The db2nodes.cfg file must be located

- Under the SQLLIB directory for the instance owner on Linux and UNIX
- Under the SQLLIB*instance_name* directory on Windows

In Figure 2.11 this file would be on the Linux3 server, as this server is the Network File System (NFS) source server, the server whose disk(s) can be shared.

On Linux and UNIX you can edit the db2nodes.cfg file with any ASCII editor or use DB2 commands to update the file. On Windows, you can only use the **db2ncrt** and **db2ndrop** commands to create and drop database partitions; the db2nodes.cfg file should not be edited directly.

For any platform, you can also use the **db2start** command to add and or remove a database partition from the DB2 instance and update the db2nodes.cfg file using the **add dbpartitionnum** and the **drop dbpartitionnum** clauses respectively.

2.6.3 An Instance in the DPF Environment

Partitioning is a concept that applies to the database, not the instance; you partition a database, not an instance. In a DPF environment an instance is created once on an NFS source server. The instance owner's home directory is then exported to all servers where DB2 is to be run. Each partition in the database has the same characteristics: the same instance owner, password, and shared instance home directory.

On Linux and UNIX, an instance maps to an operating system user; therefore, when an instance is created, it will have its own home directory. In most installations /home/*user_name* is the home directory. All instances created on each of the participating servers in a DPF environment must use the same name and password. In addition, you must specify the home directory of the corresponding operating system user to be the same directory for all instances, which must be created on a shared file system. Figure 2.13 illustrates an example of this.

In Figure 2.13, the instance *myinst* has been created on the shared file system, and *myinst* maps to an operating system user of the same name, which in the figure has a home directory of /home/ myinst. This user must be created separately in each of the participating servers, but they must share the instance home directory. As shown in Figure 2.13, all three Linux servers share directory /home/myinst, which resides on a shared file system local to Linux3. Since the instance owner directory is locally stored on the Linux3 server, this server is considered to be the DB2 **instance-owning server**.

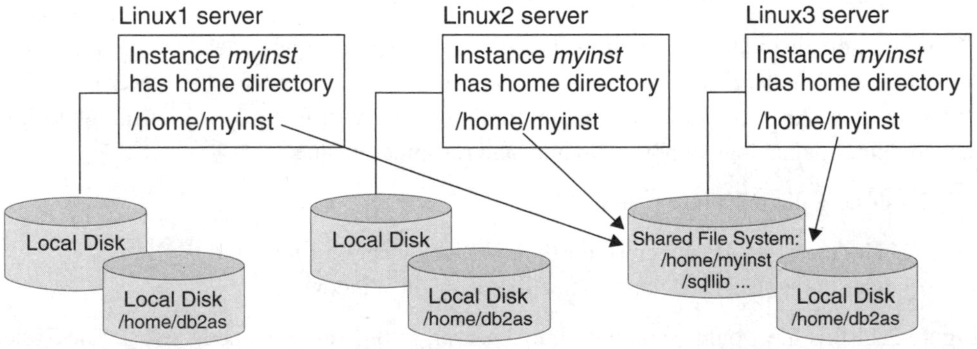

Figure 2.13 An instance in a partitioned environment

Figure 2.13 also shows that the Database Administration Server user db2as is created locally on each participating server in a DPF environment. There can only be one DAS per physical server regardless of the number of partitions that server contains. The DAS user's home directory cannot be mounted on a shared file system. Alternatively, different userids and passwords can be used to create the DAS on different servers.

> **NOTE** Make sure the passwords for the instances are the same on each of the participating servers in a DPF environment; otherwise the partitioned system will look like it is hanging because the partitions are not able to communicate.

2.6.4 Partitioning a Database

When you want to partition a database in a DPF environment, simply issue the **CREATE DATABASE** command as usual. For example, if the instance owner home directory is /home/myinst, when you execute this command:

```
CREATE DATABASE mydb2
```

the structure created is as shown in Figure 2.14.

```
/home
  /myinst
     /NODE0000
        /SQL00001
     /NODE0001
        /SQL00001
     /NODE0002
        /SQL00001
```

Figure 2.14 A partitioned database in a single file system

If you don't specify a path in your **CREATE DATABASE** command, by default the database is created in the directory specified by the database manager configuration parameter DFTDBPATH, which defaults to the instance owner's home directory. This partitioning is not optimal because all of the database data would reside in one file system that is shared by the other servers across a network.

We recommend that you create a directory with the same name, locally in each of the participating servers. For the environment in Figure 2.13, let's assume the directory /data has been created locally on each server. When you execute the command

```
CREATE DATABASE mydb2 on /data
```

the following directory structure is automatically built for you:

```
/data/instance_name/NODExxxx/SQLyyyyy
```

The /data directory is specified in the **CREATE DATABASE** command, but the directory must exist *before* executing the command. *instance_name* is the name of the instance; for example, *myinst*. NODE*xxxx* distinguishes which partition you are working with, where *xxxx* represents the number of the partition specified in the db2nodes.cfg file. SQL*yyyyy* identifies the database, where *yyyyy* represents a number. If you have only one database on your system, then *yyyyy* is equal to 00001; if you have three databases on your system, you will have different directories as follows: SQL00001, SQL00002, SQL00003. To map the database names to these directories, you can review the local database directory using the following command:

```
list db directory on /data
```

Inside the SQL*yyyyy* directories are subdirectories for table spaces, and within them, files containing database data—assuming all table spaces are defined as system-managed space (SMS).

Figure 2.15 illustrates a partitioned database created in the /data directory.

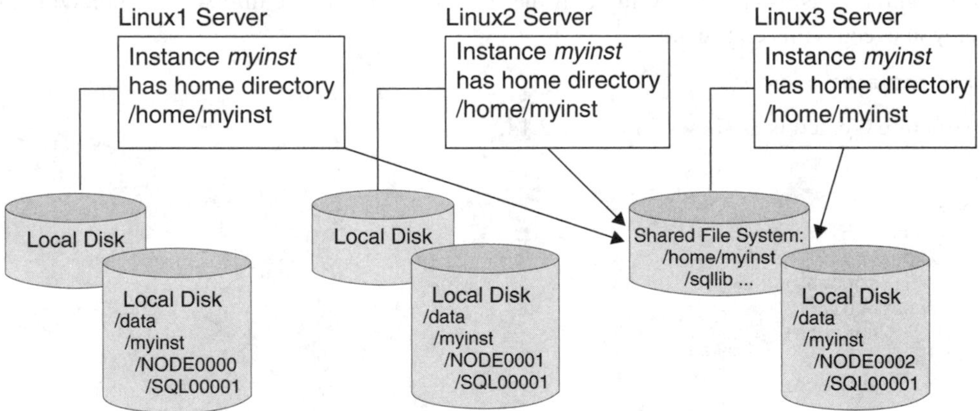

Figure 2.15 A partitioned database across several file systems

> **NOTE** Before creating a database, be sure to change the value of the dbm cfg parameter, DFTDBPATH, to an existing path created locally with the same name on each of the participating servers of your DPF system. Alternatively, make sure to include this path in your **CREATE DATABASE** command. Similarly, to create the SAMPLE database, specify this path in the command:
>
> **db2sampl** ***path***

Partitioning a database is described in more detail in Chapter 8, The DB2 Storage Model.

2.6.5 Configuration Files in a DPF Environment

As shown in Figure 2.11, the Database Manager Configuration file (dbm cfg), system database directory, node directory, and DCS directory are all part of the instance-owning server and are not partitioned. What about the other configuration files?

- Environment variables: Each participating server in a partitioned environment can have different environment variables.
- Global-level profile registry variable: This is stored in a file called default.env that is located in a subdirectory under the /var directory. There is a local copy of this file on each server.
- Database configuration file: This is stored in the file SQLDBCON that is located in the SQL*yyyyy* directory for the database. In a partitioned database environment, a separate SQLDBCON file is created for each partition in every database.
- The local database directory: This is stored in the file SQLDBDIR in the corresponding directory for the database. It has the same name as the system database directory, which is located under the instance directory. A separate SQLDBDIR file exists for each partition in each database.

CAUTION We strongly suggest you do *not* manually edit any of the DB2 configuration files. You should modify the files using the commands described in earlier sections.

NOTE The values of the global-level profile registry variables, database configuration file parameters, and local database directory entries should be the same for each database partition.

2.6.6 Logs in a DPF Environment

The logs on each database partition should be kept in a separate place. The database configuration parameter *Path to log files* (LOGPATH) on each partition should point to a local file system, not a shared file system. The default log path in each partition includes a NODE000*x* subdirectory. For example, the value of this parameter in the DPF system shown in Figure 2.11 could be:

- For Partition 0: /datalogs/db2inst1/NODE0000/SQL00001/SQLOGDIR/
- For Partition 1: /datalogs/db2inst1/NODE0001/SQL00001/SQLOGDIR/
- For Partition 2: /datalogs/db2inst1/NODE0002/SQL00001/SQLOGDIR/

To change the path for the logs, update the database configuration parameter NEWLOGPATH.

2.6.7 The Catalog Partition

As stated previously, when you create a database, several table spaces are created by default. One of them, the catalog table space SYSCATSPACE, contains the DB2 system catalogs. In a partitioned environment, SYSCATSPACE is not partitioned but resides on one partition known as the **catalog partition.** The partition from which the **CREATE DATABASE** command is issued becomes the catalog partition for the new database. All access to system tables must go through this catalog partition. Figure 2.11 shows SYSCATSPACE residing on server Linux1, so the **CREATE DATABASE** command was issued from this server.

For an existing database, you can determine which partition is the catalog partition by issuing the command **list db directory.** The output of this command has the field *Catalog database partition number* for each of the entries, which indicates the catalog partition number for that database.

2.6.8 Partition Groups

A **partition group** is a logical layer that provides for the grouping of one or more database partitions. A database partition can belong to more than one partition group. When a database is created, DB2 creates three default partition groups, and these partition groups cannot be dropped.

- **IBMDEFAULTGROUP:** This is the default partition group for any table you create. It contains all database partitions defined in the db2nodes.cfg file. This partition group cannot be modified. Table space USERSPACE1 is created in this partition group.
- **IBMTEMPGROUP:** This partition group is used by all system temporary tables. It contains all database partitions defined in the db2nodes.cfg file. Table space TEMPSPACE1 is created in this partition group.
- **IBMCATGROUP:** This partition group contains the catalog tables (table space SYSCATSPACE). It only includes the database's catalog partition. This partition group cannot be modified.

To create new database partition groups, use the **CREATE DATABASE PARTITION GROUP** statement. This statement creates the database partition group within the database, assigns database partitions that you specified to the partition group, and records the partition group definition in the database system catalog tables.

The following statement creates partition group *pgrpall* on all partitions specified in the db2nodes.cfg file:

```
CREATE DATABASE PARTITION GROUP pgrpall ON ALL DBPARTITIONNUMS
```

To create a database partition group *pg23* consisting of partitions 2 and 3, issue this command:

```
CREATE DATABASE PARTITION GROUP pg23 ON DBPARTITIONNUMS (2,3)
```

Other relevant partition group statements/commands are:

- **ALTER DATABASE PARTITION GROUP** (statement to add or drop a partition in the group)
- **DROP DATABASE PARTITION GROUP** (statement to drop a partition group)
- **LIST DATABASE PARTITION GROUPS** (command to list all your partition groups; note that IBMTEMPGROUP is never listed)

2.6.9 Buffer Pools in a DPF Environment

Figure 2.11 shows buffer pools defined across all of the database partitions. Interpreting this figure for buffer pools is different than for the other objects, because the data cached in the buffer pools is not partitioned as the figure implies. Each buffer pool in a DPF environment holds data only from the database partition where the buffer pool is located.

You can create a buffer pool in a partition group using the **CREATE BUFFERPOOL** statement with the **DATABASE PARTITION GROUP** clause. This means that you have the flexibility to define the buffer pool on the specific partitions defined in the partition group. In addition, the size of the buffer pool on each partition in the partition group can be different. The following statement will create buffer pool *bpool_1* in partition group *pg234*, which consists of partitions 2, 3, and 4.

```
CREATE BUFFERPOOL bpool_1 DATABASE PARTITION GROUP pg234
       SIZE 10000
       EXCEPT ON DBPARTITIONNUM (3 TO 4) SIZE 5000
```

Partition 2 in partition group *pg234* will have a buffer pool *bpool_1* defined with a size of 10,000 pages, and Partitions 3 and 4 will have a buffer pool of size 5,000 pages.

As an analogy, think of it as if you were issuing the **CREATE BUFFERPOOL** statement on each partition separately, with the same buffer pool name for each partition but with different sizes. That is:

- On partition 2: **CREATE BUFFERPOOL bpool_1 SIZE 10000**
- On partition 3: **CREATE BUFFERPOOL bpool_1 SIZE 5000**
- On partition 4: **CREATE BUFFERPOOL bpool_1 SIZE 5000**

Note that we use these statements only to clarify the analogy; they will not work as written. Executing each of these commands as shown will attempt to create the same buffer pool on all partitions. It is not equivalent to using the **DATABASE PARTITION GROUP** clause of the **CREATE BUFFERPOOL** statement.

Buffer pools can also be associated to several partition groups. This means that the buffer pool definition will be applied to the partitions in those partition groups.

2.6.10 Table Spaces in a Partitioned Database Environment

You can create a table space in specific partitions, associating it to a partition group, by using the **CREATE TABLESPACE** statement with the **IN DATABASE PARTITION GROUP** clause. This allows users to have flexibility as to which partitions will actually be storing their tables. In a partitioned database environment with three servers, one partition per server, the statement

```
CREATE TABLESPACE mytbls IN DATABASE PARTITION GROUP pg234
       MANAGED BY SYSTEM USING ('/data')
       BUFFERPOOL bpool_1
```

creates the table space *mytbls*, which spans partitions 2, 3, and 4 (assuming *pg234* is a partition group consisting of these partitions). In addition, the table space is associated with buffer pool *bpool_1* defined earlier. Note that creating a table space would fail if you provide conflicting partition information between the table space and the associated buffer pool. For example, if *bpool_1* was created for partitions 5 and 6, and table space *mytbls* was created for partitions 2, 3, and 4, you would get an error message when trying to create this table space.

2.6.11 The Coordinator Partition

In simple terms, the **coordinator partition** is the partition where the application connects to.

In general, each database connection has a corresponding DB2 agent handling the application connection. An **agent** can be thought of as a process (Linux or UNIX) or thread (Windows) that performs DB2 work on behalf of the application. There are different types of agents. One of them, the coordinator agent, communicates with the application, receiving requests and sending replies. It can either satisfy the request itself or delegate the work to multiple subagents to work on the request.

The coordinator partition of a given application is the partition where the coordinator agent exists. You use the **SET CLIENT CONNECT_NODE** command to set the partition that is to be the coordinator partition. Any partition can potentially be a coordinator, so in Figure 2.11 we do not label any particular partition as the coordinator node. If you would like to know more about DB2 agents and the DB2 process model, refer to Chapter 15, The DB2 Process Model.

2.6.12 Issuing Commands and SQL Statements in a DPF Environment

Imagine that you have twenty physical servers, with two database partitions on each. Issuing individual commands to each physical server or partition would be quite a task. Fortunately, DB2 provides a command that executes on all database partitions.

2.6.12.1 The db2_all command

Use the **db2_all** command when you want to execute a command or SQL statement against all database partitions. For example, to change the db cfg parameter LOGFILSIZ for the database *sample* in all partitions, you would use

```
db2_all ";db2 UPDATE DB CFG FOR sample USING LOGFILSIZ 500"
```

When the semicolon (;) character is placed before the command or statement, the request runs in parallel on all partitions.

> **NOTE** In partitioned environments, the operating system command **rah** performs commands on all servers simultaneously. The **rah** command works per server, while the **db2_all** command works per database partition. The **rah** and **db2_all** commands use the same characters. For more information about the **rah** command, refer to your operating system manuals.
>
> In partitioned environments, pureXML support is not yet available; therefore, this section does not mention XQuery statements.

2.6.12.2 Using Database Partition Expressions

In a partitioned database, database partition expressions can be used to generate values based on the partition number found in the db2nodes.cfg file. This is particularly useful when you have a large number of database partitions and when more than one database partition resides on the same physical server, because the same device or path cannot be specified for all partitions. You can manually specify a unique container for each database partition or use database partition expressions. The following example illustrates the use of database partition expressions.

The following are sample contents of a db2nodes.cfg file (in a Linux or UNIX environment):

```
0 myservera    0
1 myservera    1
2 myserverb    0
3 myserverb    1
```

This shows two servers with two database partitions each. The command

```
CREATE TABLESPACE ts2
  MANAGED BY DATABASE USING
  (file '/data/TS2/container $N+100' 5000)
```

creates the following containers:

- `/data/TS2/container100 on database partition 0`
- `/data/TS2/container101 on database partition 1`
- `/data/TS2/container102 on database partition 2`
- `/data/TS2/container103 on database partition 3`

You specify a database partition expression with the argument **$N** (note that there must be a space before **$N in** the command). Table 2.2 shows other arguments for creating containers. Operators are evaluated from left to right, and % represents the modulus (the remainder of a division). Assuming the partition number to be evaluated is 3, the value column in Table 2.2 shows the result of resolving the database partition expression.

Table 2.2 Database Partition Expressions

Database Partition Expressions	Example	Value
[blank]$N	$N	3
[blank]$N+[number]	$N+500	503
[blank]$N%[number]	$N%2	1
[blank]$N+[number]%[number]	$N+15%13	5
[blank]$N%[number]+[number]	$N%2+20	21

2.6.13 The DB2NODE Environment Variable

In Section 2.3, The DB2 Environment, we talked about the DB2INSTANCE environment variable used to switch between instances in your database system. The DB2NODE environment variable is used in a similar way, but to switch between partitions on your DPF system. By default, the active partition is the one defined with the logical port number of zero (0) in the db2nodes.cfg file for a server. To switch the active partition, change the value of the DB2NODE variable using the **`SET`** command on Windows and the **`export`** command on Linux or UNIX. Be sure to issue a **`terminate`** command for all connections from any partition to your database after changing this variable, or the change will not take effect.

Using the settings for the db2nodes.cfg file shown in Table 2.3, you have four servers, each with two logical partitions. If you log on to server *myserverb*, any commands you execute will affect partition 2, which is the one with logical port zero on that server, and the default coordinator partition for that server.

Table 2.3 Sample Partition Information

Partition	Server Name	Logical Port
0	Myservera	0
1	Myservera	1
2	Myserverb	0
3	Myserverb	1
4	Myserverc	0
5	Myserverc	1
6	Myserverd	0
7	Myserverd	1

If you would like to make partition 0 the active partition, make this change on a Linux or UNIX system:

```
DB2NODE=0
export DB2NODE
db2 terminate
```

> **NOTE** You must issue the **terminate** command, even if there aren't any connections to any partitions.

Note that partition 0 is on server *myservera*. Even if you are connected to *myserverb*, you can make a partition on *myservera* the active one. To determine which is your active partition, you can issue this statement after connecting to a database:

```
db2 "values (current dbpartitionnum)"
```

2.6.14 Distribution Maps and Distribution Keys

By now you should have a good grasp of how to set up a DPF environment. It is now time to understand how DB2 distributes data across the partitions. Figure 2.16 shows an example of this distribution.

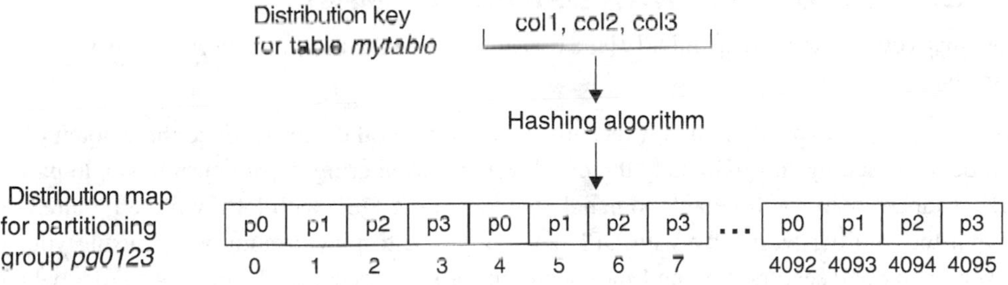

Figure 2.16 Distributing data rows in a DPF environment

A **distribution map** is an internally generated array containing 4,096 entries for multipartition database partition groups or a single entry for single-partition database partition groups. The partition numbers of the database partition group are specified in a round-robin fashion in the array.

A **distribution key** is a column (or group of columns) that determines the partition on which a particular row of data is physically stored. You define a distribution key explicitly using the **CREATE TABLE** statement with the DISTRIBUTE BY clause.

When you create or modify a database partition group, a distribution map is associated with it. A distribution map in conjunction with a distribution key and a hashing algorithm determine which database partition will store a given row of data.

For the example in Figure 2.16, let's assume partition group *pg0123* has been defined on partitions 0, 1, 2, and 3. An associated distribution map is automatically created. This map is an array with 4,096 entries containing the values 0, 1, 2, 3, 0, 1, 2, 3. . . . (note that this is shown in Figure 2.16 as p0, p1, p2, p3, p0, p1, p2, p3 . . . to distinguish them from the array entry numbers). Let's also assume table *mytable* has been created with a distribution key consisting of columns col1, col2, and col3. For each row, the distribution key column values are passed to the hashing algorithm, which returns an output number from 0 to 4,095. This number corresponds to one of the entries in the array that contains the value of the partition number where the row is to be stored. In Figure 2.16, if the hashing algorithm had returned an output value of 7, the row would have been stored in partition *p3*.

> **NOTE** Prior to DB2 9 the DISTRIBUTION MAP and DISTRIBUTION KEY terms were known as PARTITIONING MAP and PARTITIONING KEY respectively.

2.7 Case Study: DB2 with DPF Environment

Now that you are familiar with DPF, let's review some of the concepts discussed using a simple case study.

Your company is expanding, and it recently acquired two other firms. Since the amount of data will be increased by approximately threefold, you are wondering if your current single-partition DB2 database server will be able to handle the load, or if DB2 with DPF will be required. You are not too familiar with DB2 with DPF, so you decide to play around with it using your test servers: two SMP servers running Linux with four processors each. The previous DBA, who has left the company, had installed DB2 Enterprise with DPF on these servers. Fortunately, he left a diagram with his design, shown in Figure 2.17.

Figure 2.17 is a combined physical and logical design. When you validate the correctness of the diagram with your system, you note that database *mydb1* has been dropped, so you decide to rebuild this database as practice. The instance *db2inst1* is still there, as are other databases. These are the steps you follow.

1. Open two telnet sessions, one for each server. From one of the sessions you issue the commands **db2stop** followed by **db2start**, as shown in Figure 2.18.

   The first thing you note is that there is no need to issue these two commands on each partition; issuing them on any partition once will affect all partitions. You also can tell that there are four partitions, since you received a message from each of them.

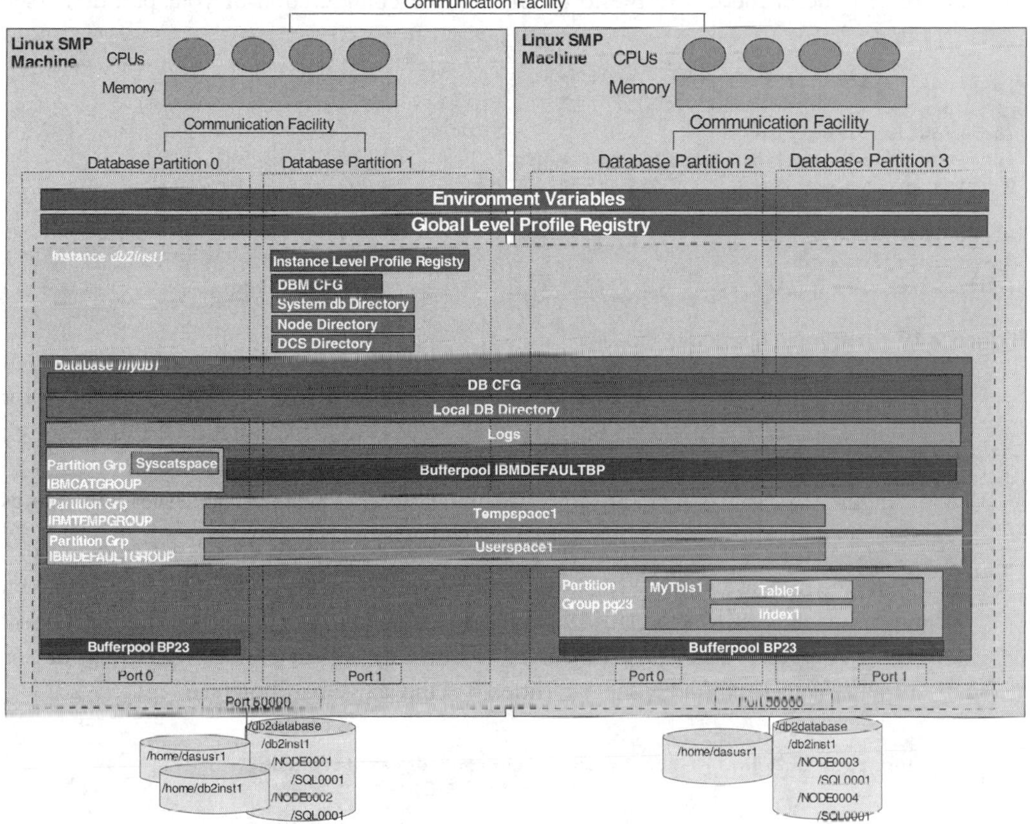

Figure 2.17 DB2 Enterprise with DPF design

```
[db2inst1@aries db2inst1]$ db2stop
10-18-2007 23:44:42     3   0   SQL1064N  DB2STOP processing was successful.
10-18-2007 23:44:43     1   0   SQL1064N  DB2STOP processing was successful.
10-18-2007 23:44:44     2   0   SQL1064N  DB2STOP processing was successful.
10-18-2007 23:44:44     0   0   SQL1064N  DB2STOP processing was successful.
SQL1064N  DB2STOP processing was successful.

[db2inst1@aries db2inst1]$ db2start
10-18-2007 23:44:51     1   0   SQL1063N  DB2START processing was successful.
10-18-2007 23:44:51     0   0   SQL1063N  DB2START processing was successful.
10-18-2007 23:44:52     3   0   SQL1063N  DB2START processing was successful.
10-18-2007 23:44:53     2   0   SQL1063N  DB2START processing was successful.
SQL1063N  DB2START processing was successful.

[db2inst1@aries db2inst1]$
```

Figure 2.18 Running the db2stop and db2start commands

2. Review the db2nodes.cfg file to understand the configuration of your partitions (see Figure 2.19).

```
[db2inst1@aries sqllib]$ pwd

/home/db2inst1/sqllib
[db2inst1@aries sqllib]$ more db2nodes.cfg
0 aries.myacme.com 0
1 aries.myacme.com 1
2 saturn.myacme.com 0
3 saturn.myacme.com 1
[db2inst1@aries sqllib]$
```

Figure 2.19 A sample db2nodes.cfg file

Using operating system commands, you determine that the home directory for instance *db2inst1* is /home/db2inst1. The db2nodes.cfg file is stored in the directory /home/db2inst1/sqllib.

Figure 2.19 shows there are four partitions, two per server. The server host names are *aries* and *saturn*.

3. Create the database *mydb1*. Since you want partition 0 to be your catalog partition, you must issue the **CREATE DATABASE** command from partition 0. You issue the statement **db2 "values (current dbpartitionnum)"** to determine which partition is currently active and find out that partition 3 is the active partition (see Figure 2.20).

```
[db2inst1@saturn db2inst1]$ db2 "values (current dbpartitionnum)"

1
-----------
          3

  1 record(s) selected.
```

Figure 2.20 Determining the active partition

4. Next, you change the DB2NODE environment variable to zero (0) as follows (see Figure 2.21):

```
DB2NODE=0
export DB2NODE
db2 terminate
```

In the **CREATE DATABASE** command you specify the path, /db2database in this example, which is an existing path that has been created locally on all servers so that the data is spread across them.

5. To confirm that partition 0 is indeed the catalog partition, simply issue a **list db directory** command and look for the *Catalog database partition number* field under the entry for the *mydb1* database. Alternatively, issue a **list tablespaces**

```
[db2inst1@saturn db2inst1]$ DB2NODE=0
[db2inst1@saturn db2inst1]$ export DB2NODE
[db2inst1@saturn db2inst1]$ db2 terminate
DB20000I  The TERMINATE command completed successfully.

[db2inst1@saturn db2inst1]$ db2 list applications
SQL1611W  No data was returned by Database System Monitor. SQLSTATE=00000

[db2inst1@saturn db2inst1]$ db2 create db mydb1 on /db2database
DB20000I  The CREATE DATABASE command completed successfully.

[db2inst1@saturn db2inst1]$ db2 connect to mydb1

   Database Connection Information

 Database server        = DB2/LINUX 9.1
 SQL authorization ID   = DB2INST1
 Local database alias   = MYDB1

[db2inst1@saturn db2inst1]$ db2 "values (current dbpartitionnum)"

1
-----------
          0

  1 record(s) selected.

[db2inst1@saturn db2inst1]$
```

Figure 2.21 Switching the active partition, and then creating a database

command from each partition. The SYSCATSPACE table space will be listed only on the catalog partition.

6. Create partition group *pg23* on partitions 2 and 3. Figure 2.22 shows how to accomplish this and how to list your partition groups. Remember that this does not list IBMTEMPGROUP.
7. Create and manage your buffer pools. Issue this statement to create buffer pool *BP23* on partition group *pg23*:

```
db2 "create bufferpool BP23 database partition group pg23 size 500"
```

Figure 2.23 shows this statement. It also shows you how to associate this buffer pool to another partition group using the **ALTER BUFFERPOOL** statement.

To list your buffer pools and associated partition groups, you can query the SYSCAT.BUFFERPOOLS catalog view, also shown in Figure 2.23.

Note that a buffer pool can be associated with any partition group. Its definition will be applied to all the partitions in the partition group, and you can specify different sizes on the partitions if required.

```
[db2inst1@saturn db2inst1]$ db2 "create database partition group pg23 on
dbpartitionnum (2 to 3)"
DB20000I  The SQL command completed successfully.

[db2inst1@saturn db2inst1]$ db2 "list database partition groups"

DATABASE PARTITION GROUP
---------------------------
IBMCATGROUP
IBMDEFAULTGROUP
PG23

  3 record(s) selected.

[db2inst1@saturn db2inst1]$
```

Figure 2.22 Creating partition group pg23

```
[db2inst1@saturn db2inst1]$ db2 "create bufferpool BP23 database partition group pg23
size 500"
DB20000I  The SQL command completed successfully.

[db2inst1@saturn db2inst1]$ db2 "alter bufferpool BP23 add database partition group
IBMCATGROUP"
DB20000I  The SQL command completed successfully.

[db2inst1@saturn db2inst1]$ db2 "select bpname, ngname from syscat.bufferpools"

BPNAME                                                      NGNAME
-------------------------------------------------------------------------------------
IBMDEFAULTBP                                                -

BP23                                                        PG23

BP23                                                        IBMCATGROUP

  3 record(s) selected.

[db2inst1@saturn db2inst1]$
```

Figure 2.23 Managing buffer pools

8. Create the table space *mytbls1*:

```
db2 "create tablespace mytbls1 in database partition group pg23
         managed by system using ('/data') bufferpool bp23"
```

9. Create table *table1* in table space *mytbls1* with a distribution key of col1 and col2:

```
db2 "create table table1 (col1 int, col2 int, col3 char(10))
            in mytbls1
            distribute by (col1, col2)"
```

10. Create the index *index1*. Note that this doesn't have any syntax specific to a DPF environment:

```
db2 "create index index1 on table1 (col1, col2)"
```

The index will be constructed on each partition for its subset of rows.

11. Test the **db2_all** command to update the database configuration file for all partitions with one command. Figure 2.24 shows an example of this.

    And that's it! In this case study you have reviewed some basic statements and commands applicable to the DPF environment. You reviewed the **db2stop** and **db2start** commands, determined and switched the active partition, and created a database, a partition group, a buffer pool, a table space, a table with a distribution key, and an index. You also used the **db2_all** command to update a database configuration file parameter.

```
[db2inst1@aries sqllib]$ db2 get db cfg for mydb1 | grep LOGFILSIZ
 Log file size (4KB)                         (LOGFILSIZ) = 1000
[db2inst1@aries sqllib]$ db2_all "db2 update db cfg for mydb1 using LOGFILSIZ 500"

DB20000I  The UPDATE DATABASE CONFIGURATION command completed successfully.
aries.myacme.com: db2 update db cfg for mydb1 using LOGFILSIZ 500 completed ok

DB20000I  The UPDATE DATABASE CONFIGURATION command completed successfully.
aries.myacme.com: db2 update db cfg for mydb1 using LOGFILSIZ 500 completed ok

DB20000I  The UPDATE DATABASE CONFIGURATION command completed successfully.
saturn.myacme.com: db2 update db cfg for mydb1 using LOGFILSIZ 500 completed ok

DB20000I  The UPDATE DATABASE CONFIGURATION command completed successfully.
saturn.myacme.com: db2 update db cfg for mydb1 using LOGFILSIZ 500 completed ok
[db2inst1@aries sqllib]$ db2 get db cfg for mydb1 | grep LOGFILSIZ
 Log file size (4KB)                         (LOGFILSIZ) = 500
[db2inst1@aries sqllib]$
```

Figure 2.24 Using db2_all to update the db cfg file

2.8 IBM Balanced Warehouse

A data warehouse system is composed of CPUs (or processors), memory, and disk. A balanced mix is the key to optimal performance. Unbalanced, ill-planned configurations will waste a lot of money if the system has

- Too many or too few servers
- Too much or too little storage
- Too much or too little I/O capacity and bandwidth
- Too much or too little memory

To help alleviate these issues, and ensure that DB2 customers build highly performing data warehouses, IBM has focused on a prescriptive and quality approach through the use of a proven balanced methodology for data warehousing. This is called the IBM Balanced Warehouse (BW) (formerly known as Balanced Configuration Unit or BCU), and is depicted in Figure 2.25.

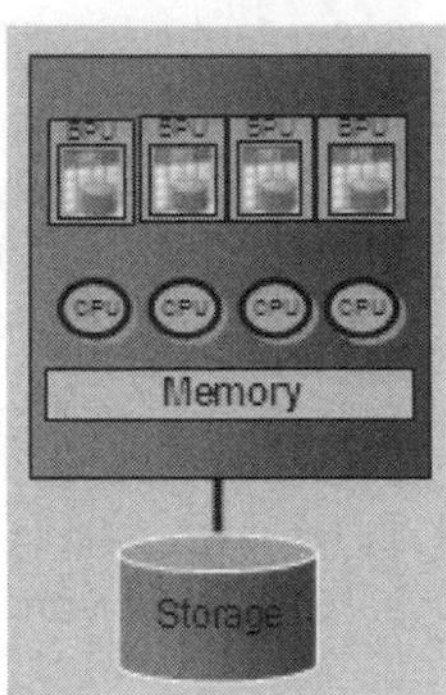

Figure 2.25 IBM Balanced Warehouse

The BW applies specifically to DB2 data warehouses. It is composed of a methodology for deployment of the database software, in addition to the IBM hardware and other software components that are required to build a data warehouse. These components are integrated and tested as a preconfigured building block for data warehousing systems. The prescriptive approach used by the BW eliminates the complexity of database warehouse design and implementation by making use of standardized, end-to-end stack tested designs, and best practices that increase the overall quality and manageability of the data warehouse.

This modular approach ensures that there is a balanced amount of disks, I/O bandwidth, processing power and memory to optimize the cost-effectiveness and throughput of the database. While you might start off with one BW, if you have a large database, you might also start off with several of these BW building blocks in a single system image. As the database grows, you can simply add additional building blocks (BWs) to handle the increased data or users as shown in Figure 2.26.

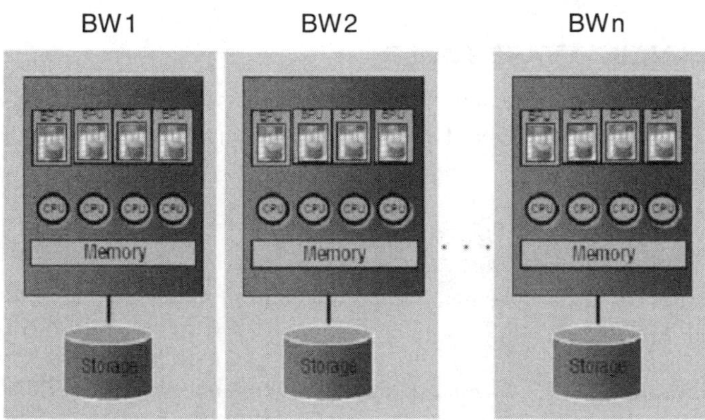

Figure 2.26 BW as building blocks

The main advantages of the BW are

- best-of-breed IBM components selected for optimum price/performance
- repeatable, scalable, consistent performance that can grow as business needs grow
- a prescriptive, fully validated and tested, successful best practices design that reduces the time and removes the risk of building a business intelligence solution

2.9 Summary

This chapter provided an overview of the DB2 core concepts using a "big picture" approach. It introduced SQL statements and their classification as Data Definition Language (DDL), Data Manipulation Language (DML), and Data Control Language (DCL) statements. XQuery with XPath and the FLWOR expression were also introduced.

DB2 commands were classified into two groups—system commands and CLP commands—and several examples were provided, such as the command to start an instance, `db2start`.

An interface is needed to issue SQL statements, XQuery statements, and commands to the DB2 engine. This interface is provided by using the DB2 tools available with the product. Two text-based interfaces were mentioned, the Command Line Processor (CLP) and the Command Window. The Control Center was noted as being one of the most important graphical administration tools, while the Data Server Administration Control was presented as the next generation of graphical administration tooling.

This chapter also introduced the concepts of instances, databases, table spaces, buffer pools, logs, tables, indexes, and other database objects in a single partition system. The different levels of configuration for the DB2 environment were presented, including environment variables, DB2 registry variables, and configuration parameters at the instance (dbm cfg) and database (db cfg) levels. DB2 has federation support for queries referencing tables residing in other databases in the DB2 family. The chapter also covered the Database Partitioning Feature (DPF) and the concepts of database partition, catalog partition, coordinator node, and distribution map on a multipartition system. The IBM Balanced Warehouse (BW) was also introduced.

Two case studies reviewed the single-partition and multipartition environments respectively, which should help you understand the topics discussed in the chapter.

2.10 Review Questions

1. How are DB2 commands classified?
2. What is a quick way to obtain help information for a command?
3. What is the difference between the Information Center tool and simply reviewing the DB2 manuals?
4. What command is used to create a DB2 instance?

5. How many table spaces are automatically created by the **CREATE DATABASE** command?
6. What command can be used to get a list of all instances on your server?
7. What is the default instance that is created on Windows?
8. Is the DAS required to be running to set up a remote connection between a DB2 client and a DB2 server?
9. How can the DB2 environment be configured?
10. How is the local database directory populated?
11. Which of the following commands will start your DB2 instance?
    A. startdb
    B. db2 start
    C. db2start
    D. start db2
12. Which of the following commands will list all of the registry variables that are set on your server?
    A. db2set -a
    B. db2set -all
    C. db2set -lr
    D. db2set -ltr
13. Say you are running DB2 on a Windows server with only one hard drive (C:). If the DB2 instance is dropped using the **db2idrop** command, after recreating the DB2 instance, which of the following commands will list the databases you had prior to dropping the instance?
    A. list databases
    B. list db directory
    C. list db directory all
    D. list db directory on C:
14. If the **list db directory on C:** command returns the following:

```
Database alias                          = SAMPLE
Database name                           = SAMPLE
Database directory                      = SQL00001
Database release level                  = a.00
Comment                                 =
Directory entry type                    = Home
Catalog database partition number       = 0
Database partition number               = 0
```

    which of the following commands must be run before you can access tables in the database?
    A. catalog db sample
    B. catalog db sample on local
    C. catalog db sample on SQL00001
    D. catalog db sample on C:

15. If there are two DB2 instances on your Linux server, *inst1* and *inst2*, and if your default DB2 instance is *inst1*, which of the following commands allows you to connect to databases in the *inst2* instance?

A. export inst2

B. export instance=inst2

C. export db2instance=inst2

D. connect to inst2

16. Which of the following DB2 registry variables optimizes interpartition communication if you have multiple partitions on a single server?

A. DB2_OPTIMIZE_COMM

B. DB2_FORCE_COMM

C. DB2_USE_FCM_BP

D. DB2_FORCE_FCM_BP

17. Which of the following tools is used to run commands on all partitions in a multipartition DB2 database?

A. db2_part

B. db2_all

C. db2_allpart

D. db2

18. Which of the following allows federated support in your server?

A. db2 update db cfg for federation using FEDERATED ON

B. db2 update dbm cfg using FEDERATED YES

C. db2 update dbm cfg using NICKNAME YES

D. db2 update dbm cfg using NICKNAME, WRAPPER, SERVER, USER MAPPING YES

19. Which environment variable needs to be updated to change the active logical database partition?

A. DB2INSTANCE

B. DB2PARTITION

C. DB2NODE

D. DB2PARTITIONNUMBER

20. Which of the following statements can be used to determine the value of the current active database partition?

A. values (current dbpartitionnum)

A. values (current db2node)

C. values (current db2partition)

D. values (current partitionnum)

CHAPTER 3

Installing DB2

Now that you have an overview of DB2, the next step is to install it. In this chapter we walk you through the DB2 installation process on the Linux, UNIX, and Windows (LUW) platforms with step-by-step instructions. For the latest information about DB2 installation system requirements, see

http://www.ibm.com/software/data/db2/9/sysreqs.html.

In this chapter you will learn about:

- The DB2 installation methods
- Non-root installation on Linux and UNIX
- The user IDs and groups required to install DB2
- Installing DB2 using the DB2 Setup Wizard
- Installing DB2 using the Silent install method
- Installing DB2 licenses
- Installing multiple DB2 copies on the same server
- Installing DB2 Fix Packs
- Migrating from DB2 Version 8 to DB2 9

3.1 DB2 Installation: The Big Picture

Table 3.1 lists the two methods for installing DB2 on Windows and the four methods for installing DB2 on Linux and UNIX.

The **DB2 Setup Wizard** provides an easy-to-use graphical interface for installing DB2. In addition to creating a DB2 instance and any required user IDs, it also sets up some initial configuration parameters. It guides you through the installation tasks listed in Figures 3.1, 3.2, and 3.3. After the installation is completed, DB2 is ready for use. We recommend that you use this installation method.

Table 3.1 Installation Methods by Operating Systems

Installation Method	Windows	Linux and UNIX
DB2 Setup Wizard	Yes	Yes
Silent install	Yes	Yes
db2_install script	No	Yes
Manual intalation of DB2 payload files	No	Yes

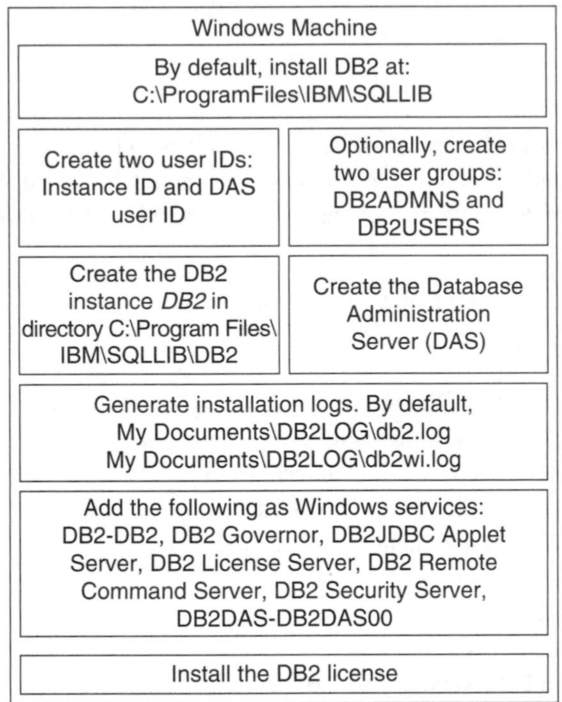

Figure 3.1 The big picture: DB2 installation on Windows

The DB2 **silent install** is a method that allows you to install DB2 without requiring user interaction. The key to this installation method is the **response file,** a text file that contains setup and configuration values. You pass this file as input to the DB2 setup program (setup.exe on Windows, and db2setup on Linux and UNIX), and the setup program installs DB2 according to the values specified in the response file. Silent install is appropriate in situations where you have to install DB2 on hundreds or thousands of machines. Rather than manually answering the prompts of an interactive installation tool like the DB2 Setup Wizard, you can have DB2 automatically get the responses to these questions from the response file. Silent install is also appropriate when you are developing an application that embeds the DB2 software. As part of your application installation, you can invoke the DB2 setup program so it transparently installs DB2 while it installs your application. Silent install will be discussed in detail in Section 3.4.

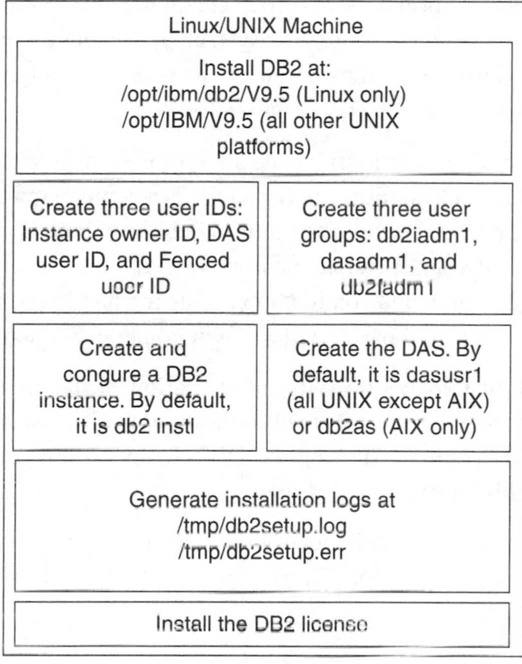

Figure 3.2 The big picture: DB2 root installation on Linux and UNIX

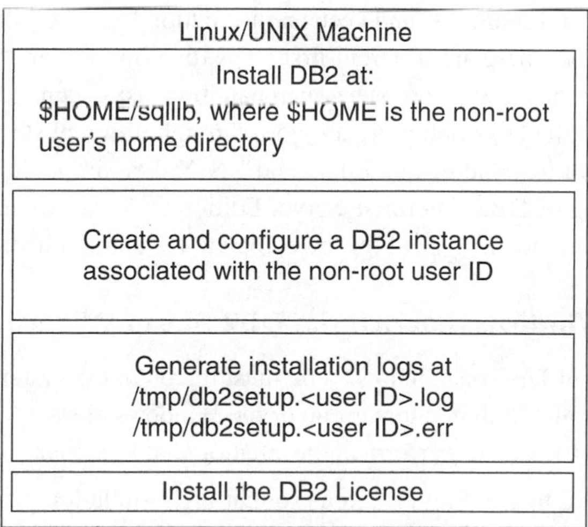

Figure 3.3 The big picture: DB2 non-root installation on Linux and UNIX

The **db2_install** script installation method (only available on Linux and UNIX platforms) uses the operating system's native installation utility to install DB2. The **db2_install** script method prompts you for a DB2 product keyword and then installs all components for the DB2 product you specify. You cannot select or deselect components or specify the language to be used. This method does not perform user and group creation, instance creation, or configuration; it simply installs the DB2 components onto your system. You might prefer this method of installation if you want to customize the instances and their configurations yourself. The **db2_install** script will be discussed in detail in Section 3.5.1.

V9 With DB2 9, you can manually install DB2 using an advanced installation method that requires the user to manually install payload files. A payload file is a compressed tarball file that contains all installation files and metadata required for an installable component. This requires advanced knowledge of both DB2 and your operating environment. You must manually perform user and group creation, instance creation, and configuration. This method is not recommended for most users. Instructions on how to install payload files can be found in Section 3.5.2.

Figures 3.1, 3.2, and 3.3 give you an overview of the various installation methods on the Windows, Linux, and UNIX platforms respectively. The figures also list the items that the DB2 Setup Wizard creates. We recommend using the DB2 Setup Wizard for all platforms, and we focus on that method in this chapter.

In particular, DB2 9.5 allows the installation by non-root users on Linux and UNIX platforms with key tasks shown in Figure 3.3. More information about non-root installation is discussed in Section 3.2.

3.2 Installing DB2 Using the DB2 Setup Wizard

The DB2 Setup Wizard uses a step-by-step method to guide you through the installation process, perform the tasks listed in Figure 3.1, and keep an installation log. The following steps highlight the main points. Note that there are different first steps for Windows and Linux and UNIX, but the procedure is mostly the same. Moreover, when handling tasks such as user and instance creation and configuration, the DB2 Setup Wizard goes through different steps in non-root installations versus those in root installations on Linux and UNIX. For simplicity, we have used screen shots from our installing of DB2 Enterprise Server Edition on Windows in this section. Refer to the documentation that comes with DB2 for the complete installation instructions.

3.2.1 Step 1 for Windows: Launch the DB2 Setup Wizard

To start the installation of DB2 on Windows, you must log on to the system with a user ID that either belongs to the local Administrators group or the Windows elevated privileges setting to allow a non-Administrator user to perform an installation that is properly configured.

- First, make sure to close all programs so that the installation program can update files as required.
- Insert the DB2 CD-ROM. If enabled, the auto-run feature automatically starts the DB2 Setup Launchpad, and the window shown in Figure 3.4 appears.

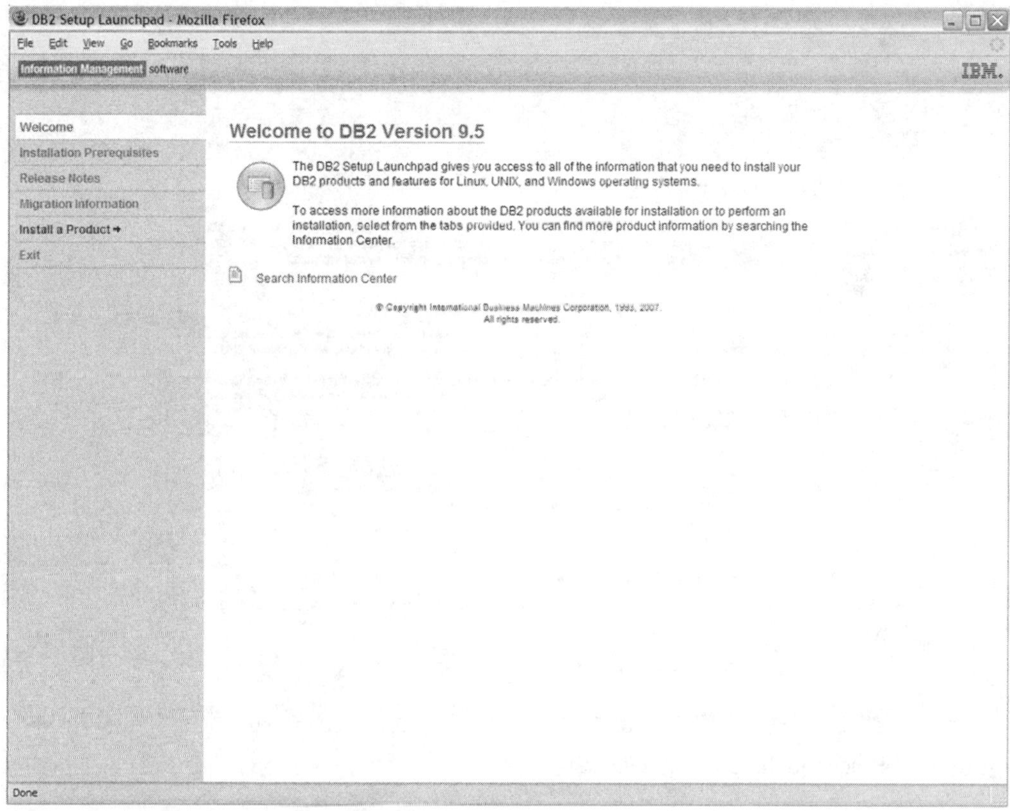

Figure 3.4 The DB2 Setup Launchpad

From the launchpad, you have the option to view the installation prerequisites, release notes, migration information, or to proceed directly to the installation. Select *Install a Product* and you will see the screen shown in Figure 3.5. Since this is a brand new installation of DB2 on this server, you have the choice to install either the DB2 Enterprise Server Edition or the IBM Data Server Client. Select *Install New* under DB2 Enterprise Server Edition.

The DB2 Setup Wizard will determine your system's language and launch the setup program in that language. If you want to run the setup program in a different language, or if the setup program fails to start automatically, you can start the DB2 Setup Wizard manually and use the **/i** option to specify a language. To start the DB2 Setup Wizard manually, change to the CD-ROM drive and double-click *setup*. Alternatively, click *Start* > *Run*. In the Open field, enter the following command:

```
x:\setup /i language
```

where:

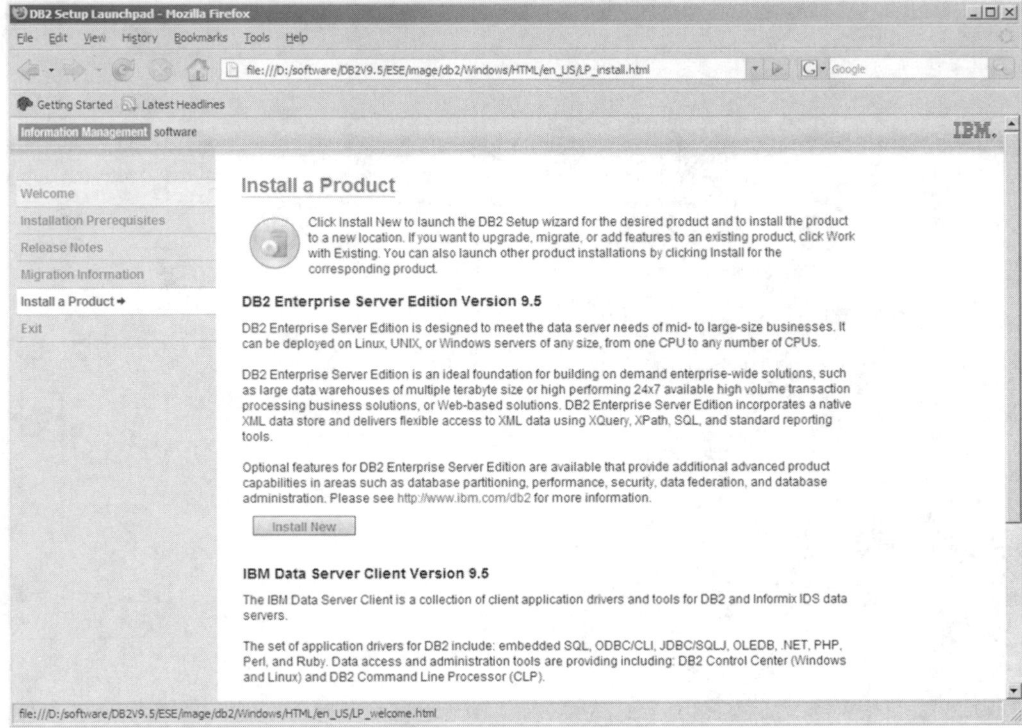

Figure 3.5 Selecting the product to install

> ***x*** represents your CD-ROM drive, and ***language*** is the territory identifier for your language (for example, **EN** for English).
>
> If the **/i** flag is not specified, the installation program will run in the default language of the operating system. You can also click *Browse*, change to the CD-ROM drive, and run *Setup*.

Hit *next* to continue, then read and accept the license agreement, and hit *next* to continue.

Continue with step 2.

3.2.2 Step 1 for Linux and UNIX: Launch the DB2 Setup Wizard

The DB2 Setup Wizard is also available on Linux and UNIX platforms. You must have X-Window software capable of rendering a graphical user interface for the DB2 Setup Wizard to run this on your machine. Do one of the following:

- To install DB2 on Linux and UNIX platforms, log on as a proper user based on the root or non-root installation type and mount the CD-ROM.
- For Solaris and AIX 5L, you need to copy the file *product name*.tar.Z, where *product name* represents the product you are installing, to a file system on the server with a size of at least 2GB. Then enter:

```
zcat product_name.tar.Z | tar -xf - ;
./product_name/db2setup
```

For example, if the product name for DB2 Enterprise Server Edition is *ese*, enter the following command:

```
zcat ese.tar.Z | tar -xf - ; ./ese/db2setup
```

You will see the same DB2 Setup Launchpad as shown in Figure 3.4. Continue with step 2.

3.2.3 Step 2: Choose an Installation Type

As shown in Figure 3.6, you can select one of three installation types.

Typical installs all required components as well as tools that are used most often, such as ODBC support and the DB2 GUI tools. The DB2 instance and the DAS will be created and customized during installation.

Compact installs only the required DB2 components plus ODBC support. The DB2 instance and the DAS will be created and customized during installation.

Custom installs all required components, but gives you the flexibility to pick and choose which tools to install. You can also choose whether to create the DB2 instance and the DAS.

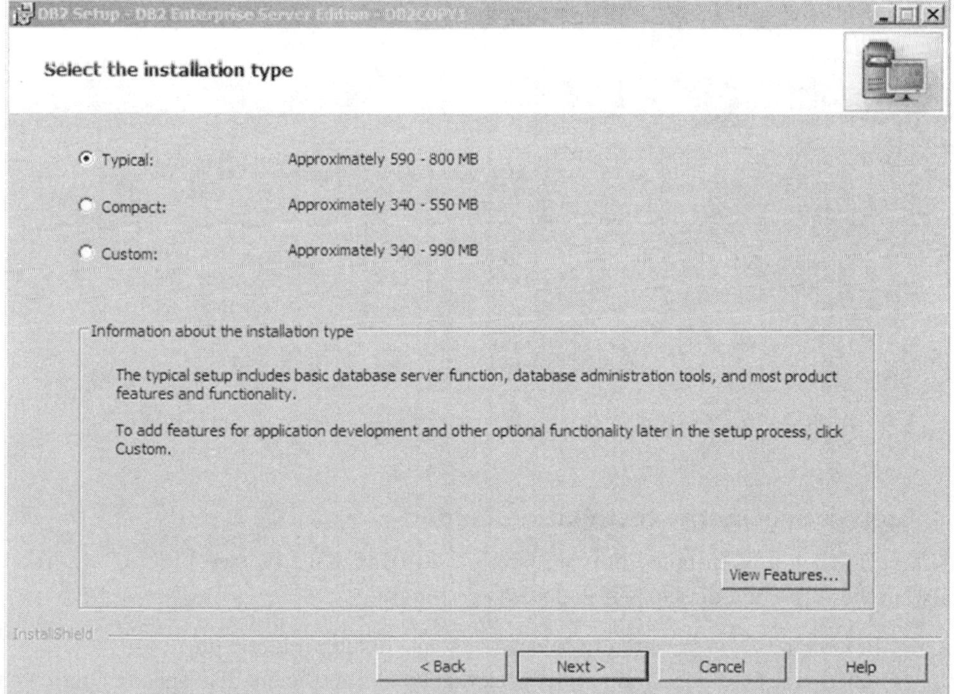

Figure 3.6 Selecting the installation type

3.2.4 Step 3: Choose Whether to Generate a Response File

As mentioned earlier, a response file allows you to perform DB2 installation on other computers in an unattended mode (refer to Section 3.5, Silent Install Using a Response File, for information on how to do this).

You can choose to either install DB2 Enterprise Server Edition on this computer, save the settings to a response file only, or both. If you need to install DB2 with the same configuration on other computers, it is a good idea to create a response file and install the DB2 code (see Figure 3.7). Note, that you can change the response file path and name, or use the default. The default is *C:\Documents and Settings\Administrator\My Documents\PROD_ESE.rsp*.

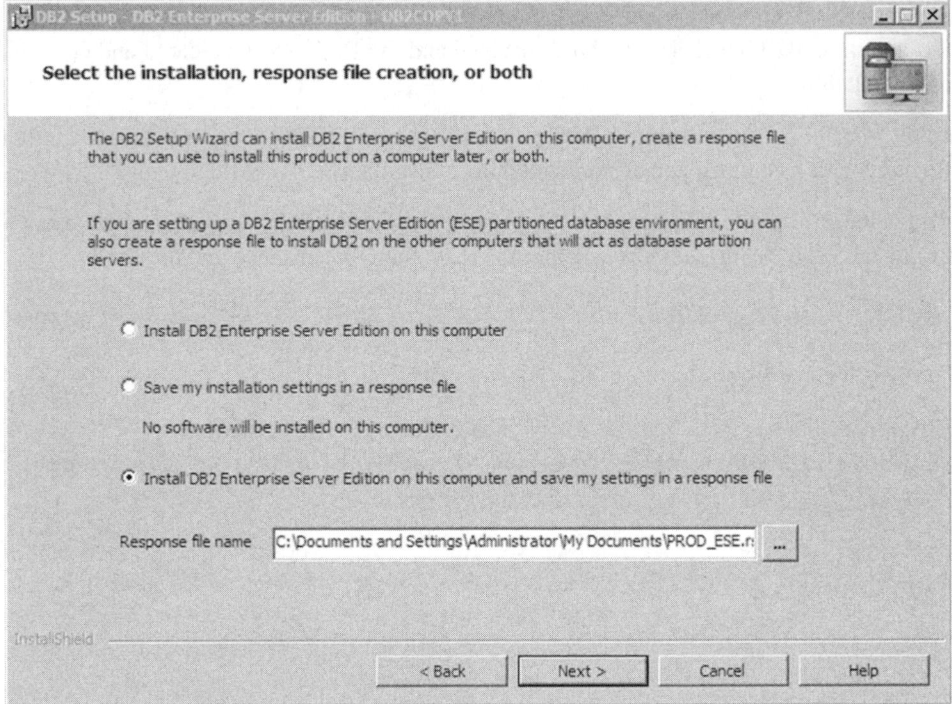

Figure 3.7 Selecting the installation action

3.2.5 Step 4: Specify the Installation Folder

By default, DB2 will be installed in C:\Program Files\IBM\SQLLIB (see Figure 3.8). You can specify another drive and directory if you wish.

- Click on the *Change* button to select a new installation folder path.
- Click on the *Disk space* button to check that there is sufficient disk space to perform the installation.

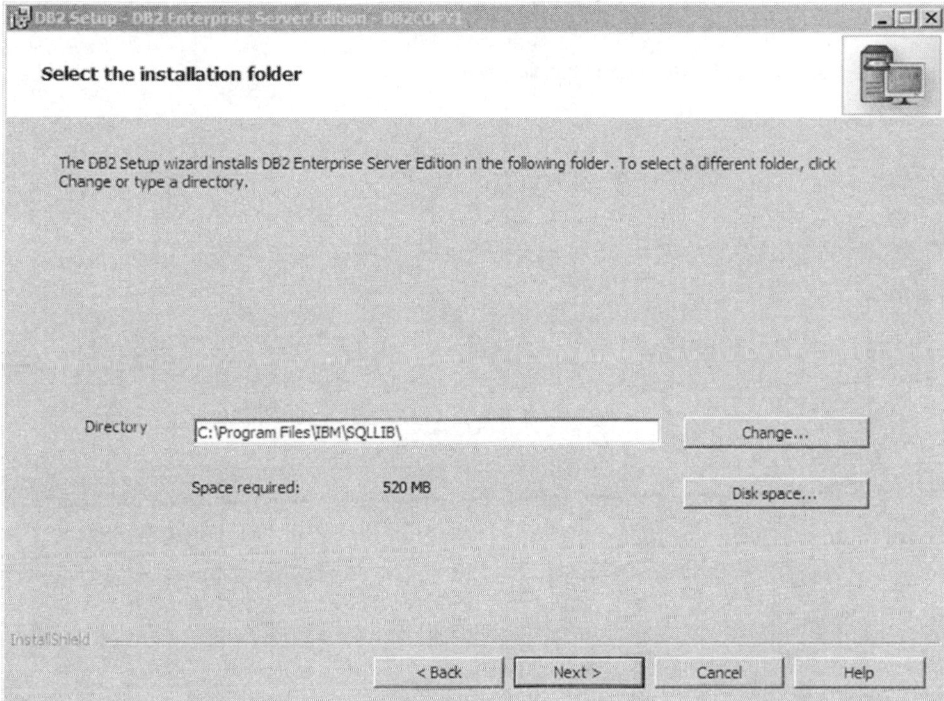

Figure 3.8 Selecting the installation folder

3.2.6 Step 5: Set User Information for the DB2 Administration Server

The DAS is a special service needed to support the DB2 graphical administration tools and assist with administrative tasks on local and remote DB2 servers. Each server can have only one DAS. During the installation the DAS is configured to start when the operating system is started.

You can specify either a local user or a domain user. If specifying a domain user, click on the *domain* drop-down list and choose the domain. Otherwise, leave it as *None – use local user account*. If the user does not already exist, it will be created and granted the appropriate rights. If the user already exists, DB2 will grant it the appropriate rights.

If you are creating a domain user, the user ID you are using for this installation must belong to the administrator group of the domain.

Click on *Next* to proceed.

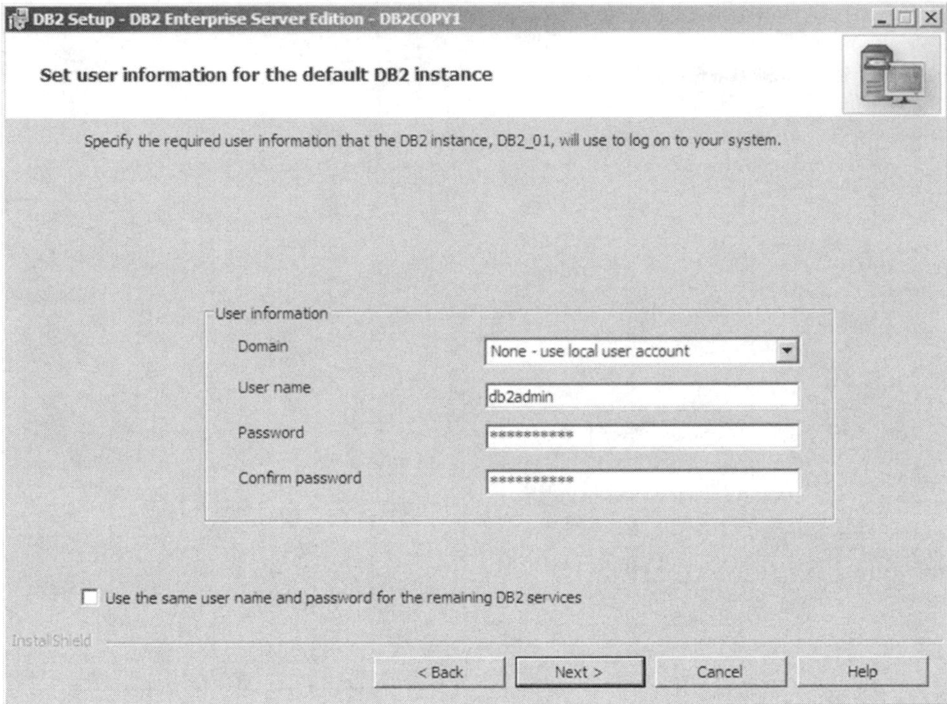

Figure 3.9 Setting DAS user information

3.2.7 Step 6: Create and Configure the DB2 Instance

By default, a DB2 instance named *DB2* will be created. The DB2 Setup Wizard automatically detects the communication protocols configured on the server and generates communication parameter values for the instance to use, for each detected protocol (see Figure 3.10).

Click the *Configure* button to display the settings for instance configuration. Figure 3.10 shows a list of the supported protocols on Windows: TCP/IP, and Named Pipes. If a protocol is installed and configured correctly, the *Configure* option will be checked. Otherwise, the *Do not configure at this time* option will be checked. You can use the default values or enter different values.

The DB2 instance needs a port number to accept connections from remote DB2 clients using TCP/IP. The clients will connect to the server through this port. If configured, the *x*:\WINNT\System32\ drivers\etc\services file will be updated, where *x* represents the Windows install drive.

The service name is the name that is associated with the port number in the services file. If you want to specify a different port number, make sure that this number does not already exist in the services file, because you cannot use the same port for two different applications.

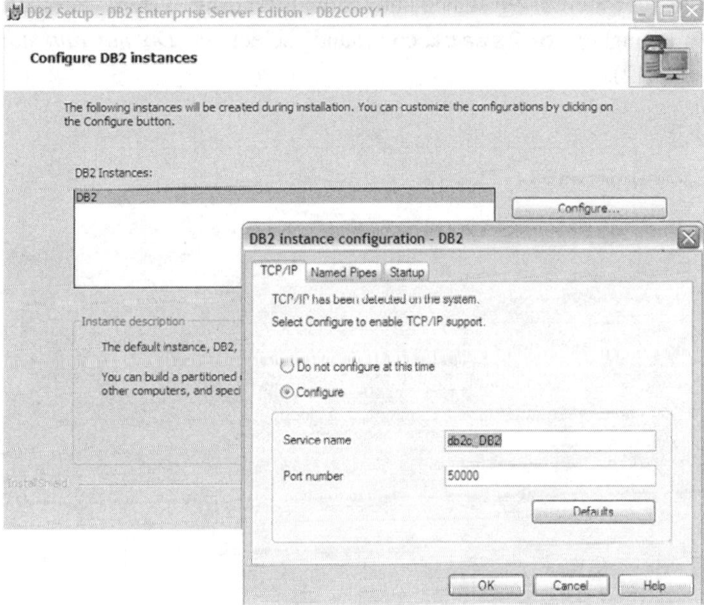

Figure 3.10 Configuring the DB2 instance and its communication protocols

Figure 3.11 shows that the Name Pipes protocol is not going to be configured.

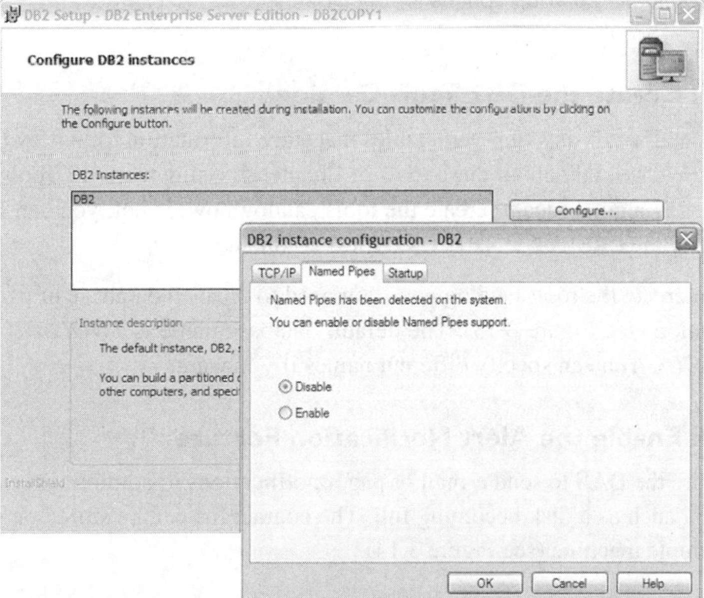

Figure 3.11 Configuring startup options for the DB2 instance

You can choose to start the DB2 instance automatically during system startup. If you prefer to start it manually (using the **db2start** command) select the *Do not autostart the instance* option (see Figure 3.12).

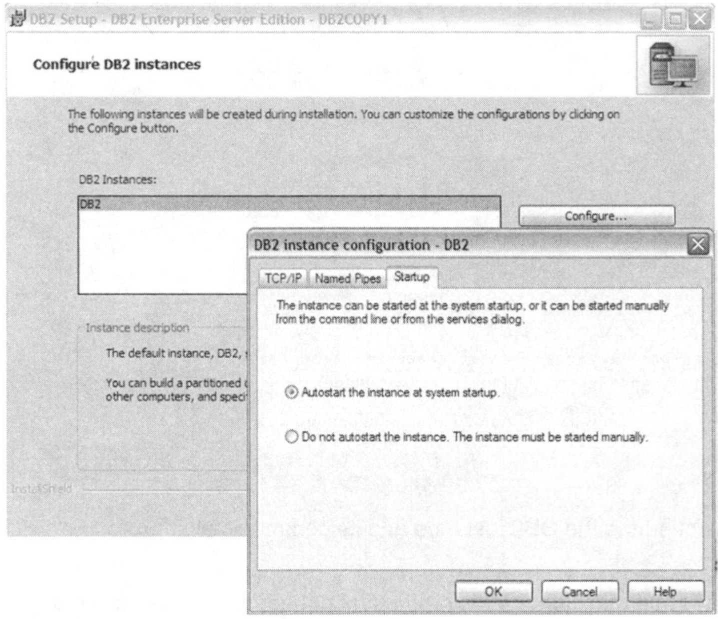

Figure 3.12 Configuring startup options for the DB2 instance

3.2.8 Step 7: Create the DB2 Tools Catalog

The DB2 tools catalog consists of several tables that store information for use by the Task Center and the Journal. We will talk about these tools in Chapter 4, Using the DB2 Tools. If you plan to use these tools, it is a good idea to create the tools catalog now; if not, you can create the tools catalog later using the **CREATE TOOLS CATALOG** command.

If you choose to create the tools catalog now, you need to create a database in which to store the catalog information (see Figure 3.13). The default database name is *TOOLSDB*, with a default schema *SYSTOOLS*. You can specify different names if you want.

3.2.9 Step 8: Enable the Alert Notification Feature

You can configure the DAS to send e-mail or pager notifications to administrators should certain conditions occur, such as a disk becoming full. The contact list can be stored on either the local machine or a remote machine (see Figure 3.14).

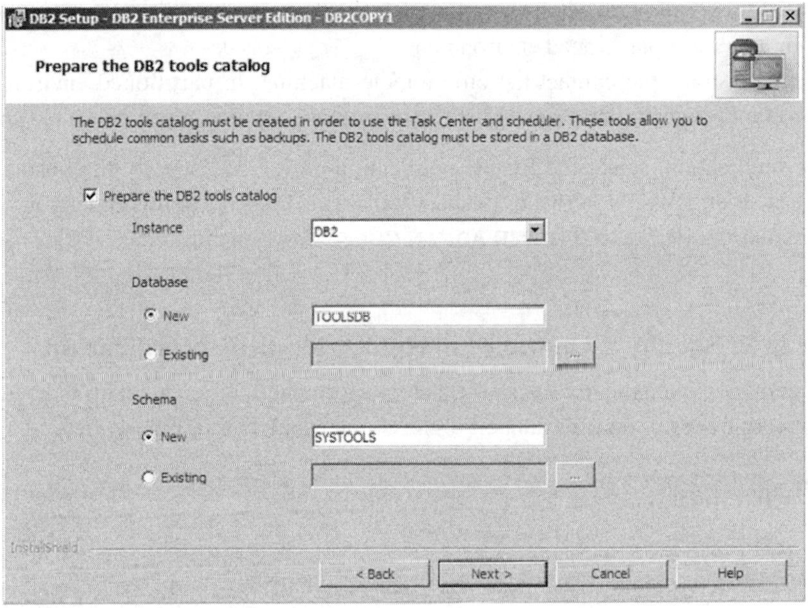

Figure 3.13 Prepare the DB2 tools catalog

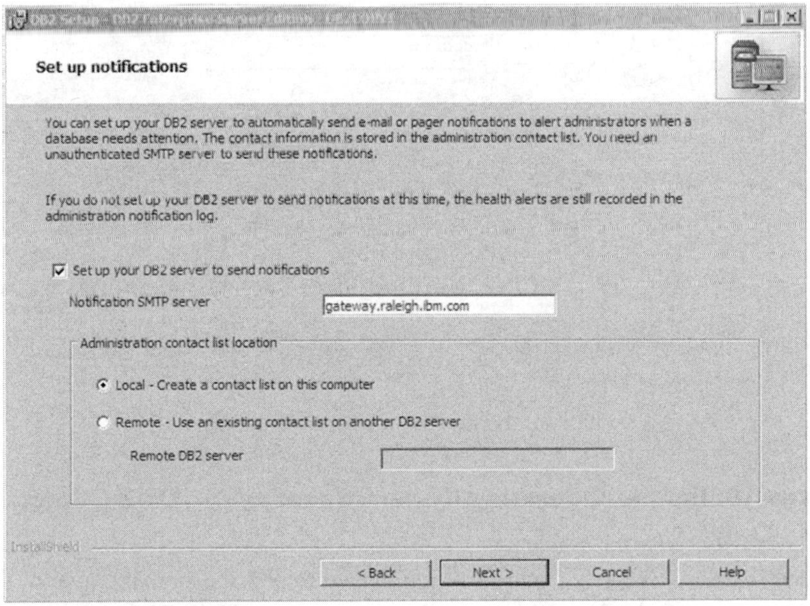

Figure 3.14 Set up notifications

- **Local** stores the contact list on the DB2 server only. This list can be used by other computers in a partitioned environment.
- **Remote** stores the contact list on a remote machine. In partitioned environments, we recommend storing the contact list on the instance-owning machine for easy access.

To send the notification, select the Enable notification option and specify the hostname of the mail (SMTP) server. If you don't want to specify the SMTP server at this time, you can do this after the installation. (Refer to **UPDATE ADMIN CONFIG** command in the *DB2 Command Reference* manual.)

3.2.10 Step 9: Specify a Contact for Health Monitor Notification

The health monitor automatically tracks database performance. When a health indicator reaches an alarm or warning level, it sends an alert to the contact specified in Figure 3.15.

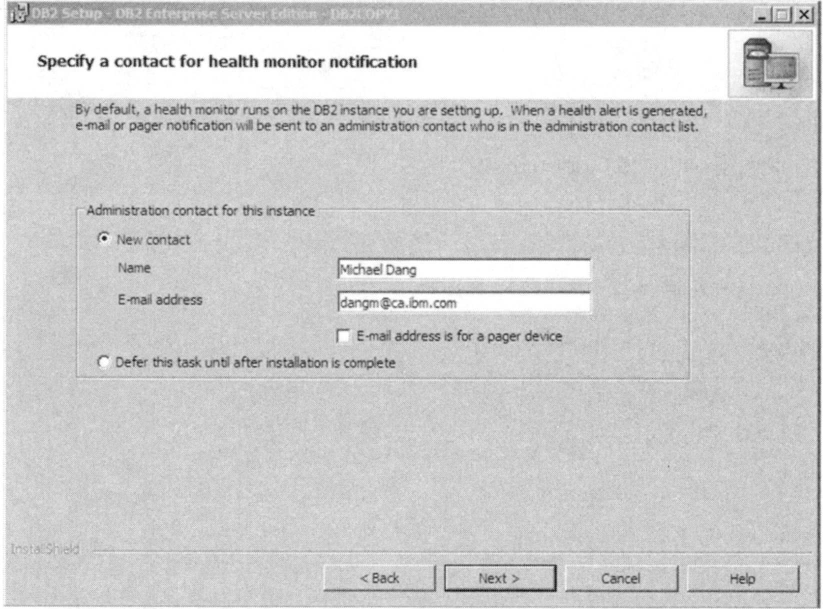

Figure 3.15 Specifying a contact for the health monitor notification

3.2.11 Step 10: Enable Operating System Security for DB2 Objects (Windows Only)

The Extended Windows security feature was introduced to provide an extra layer of security to your DB2 instances and database objects. If this feature is enabled, DB2 will create two user groups in the operating system (see Figure 3.16). Their default names are DB2ADMNS and DB2USERS. Optionally, you can specify different group names.

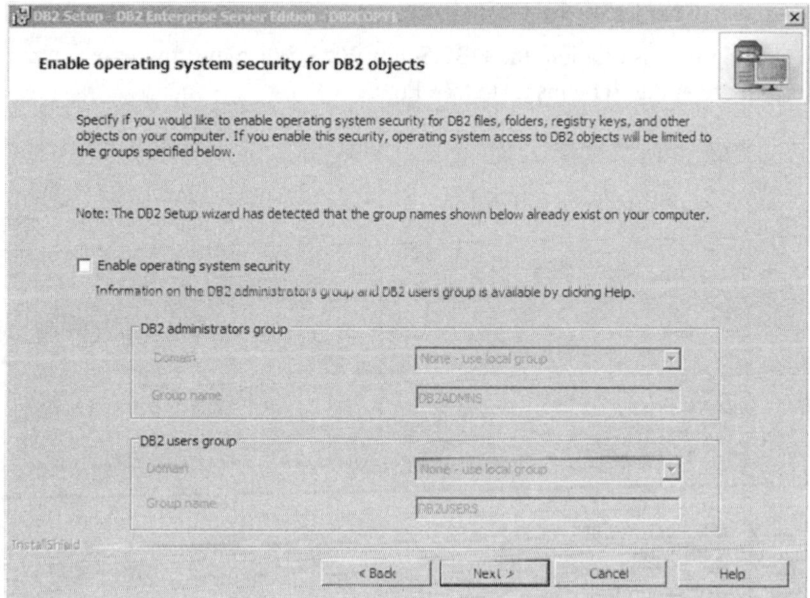

Figure 3.16 Enable operating system security for DB2 objects

After successfully completing a DB2 installation, you can add users to the DB2ADMNS or the DB2USERS groups to give them access to DB2. Users in the DB2ADMNS groups have complete control over all DB2 objects in the instance; users in the DB2USERS group have read and execute privileges only.

V9 If you choose not to enable the Extended Windows security feature now, you can still do so after the installation completes by running the **db2extsec.exe** (formerly known as **db2secv8.exe** in Version 8.2) command. Note we have unchecked Enable operating system security in Figure 3.16.

Once you enable this security feature using the **db2extsec.exe** command, you have two options for backing out. If you made *any* changes after running the **db2extsec.exe** command to the system, you *must* use the second option.

- Run the **db2extsec.exe -r** command again immediately *without* making any additional changes to the system.
- The safest way to remove the extended security option is to uninstall the DB2 database system, delete all the relevant DB2 directories (including the database directories), and then reinstall the DB2 database system without extended security enabled.

The second option can be quite tedious, so make plans to decide if it will benefit your environment before enabling.

3.2.12 Step 11: Start the Installation

Just before starting the installation, the DB2 Setup Wizard displays a window summarizing the components that are going to be installed (see Figure 3.17).

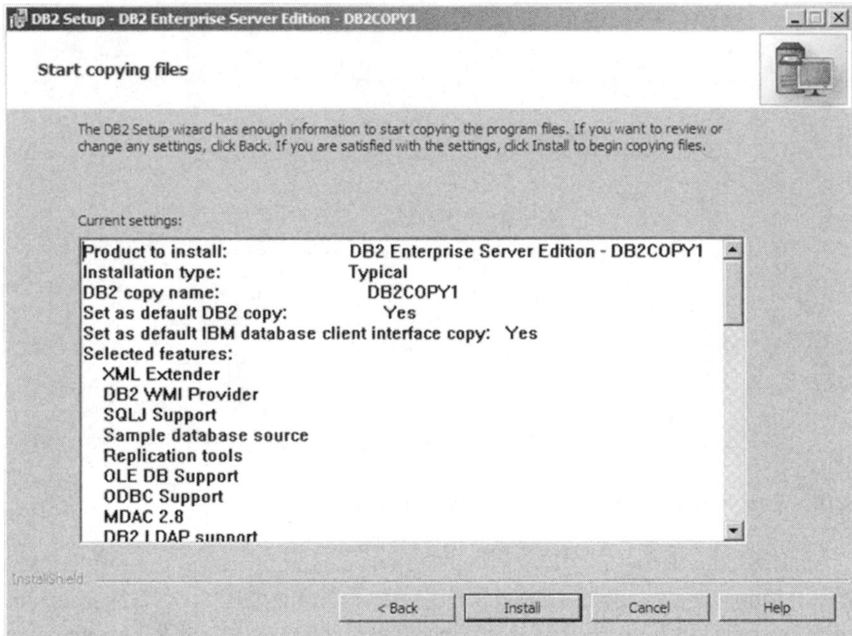

Figure 3.17 Component summary and starting the installation

If you specified in step 3 to save your setting in a response file, the file information is displayed at the end of the summary. Review this window carefully. Click *Back* to make any changes; click *Finish* to start the installation.

Figure 3.18 shows the window that displays when the DB2 installation is complete. Read the list of recommended steps, click *Next* to optionally install additional products, and then click *Finish* to exit the DB2 Setup Wizard.

When you exit the DB2 Setup Wizard after a successful DB2 installation, the DB2 First Steps dialog is automatically launched (see Figure 3.19). From this menu, you have the option to create a sample database, create your own database, create an application using various development environments, find DB2 information, check for DB2 updates, or exit First Steps. There is a wealth of information available here. It is a good idea for you to take the time to browse through First Steps.

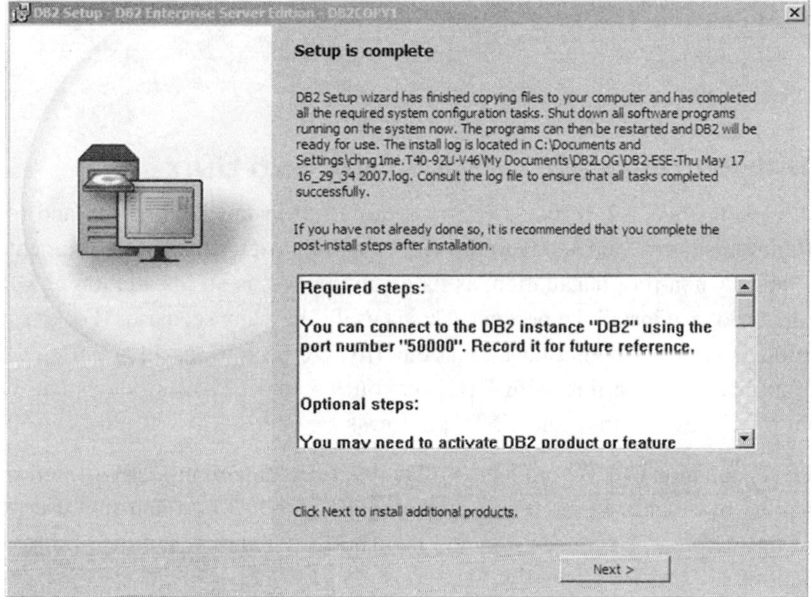

Figure 3.18 Setup complete

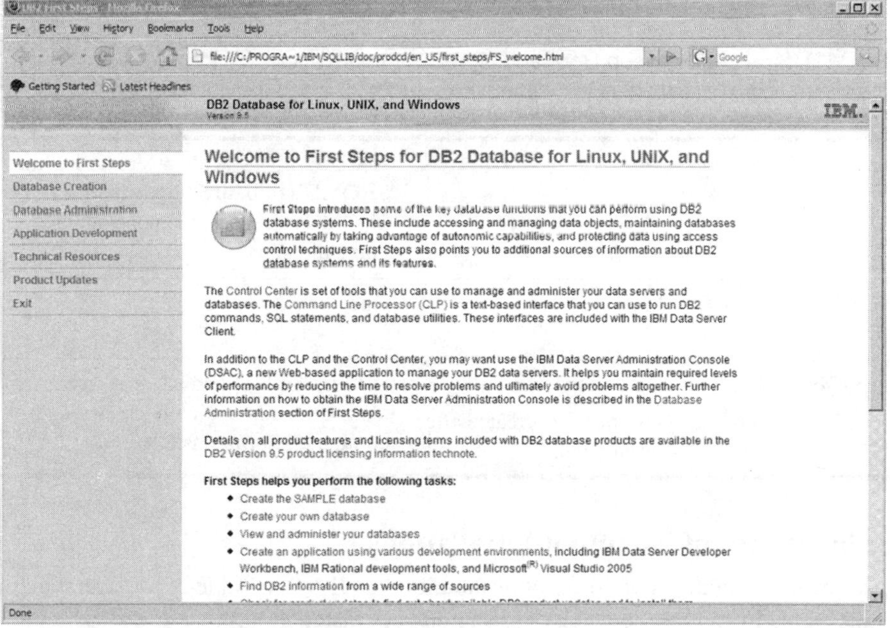

Figure 3.19 DB2 First Steps

> **NOTE** The DB2 9 First Steps provides links to the functions and documentations based on the type of user (Database Administrator or application developer). It can be used to get you started with DB2.

3.3 Non-Root Installation on Linux and UNIX

In previous versions of DB2, a root user was required to install DB2, apply and roll back fix packs, configure instances, and add features. However, in most customer environments, this may not be practical. A non-root installation, as its name implies, is an installation of DB2 where a user other than root can install the product. This is useful in many scenarios. For example, application developers typically do not have root authority, but need to install and use DB2 products to develop applications. Starting with DB2 Version 9.5, most DB2 products can be installed without root privileges on Linux and UNIX platforms.

The non-root installation of DB2 products results in a fully functioning DB2 instance with most features enabled by default. Before you install any DB2 product as a non-root user, you should be aware of the differences between root and non-root installations, and the limitations of non-root installations.

3.3.1 Differences between Root and Non-Root Installations

Table 3.2 summarizes the differences between root and non-root installations.

Table 3.2 Differences between Root and Non-Root Installations

Criteria	Root Installations	Non-Root Installations
User can select installation directory	Yes	No. DB2 image is always placed in the $HOME/sqllib directory, where $HOME represents the non-root user's home directory.
Number of DB2 instances allowed	Multiple	One
Files deployed during installation	DB2 image files only. Instances are created after installation.	DB2 image files and instance files. An instance is automatically created and configured during installation.

3.3.2 Limitations of Non-Root Installations

There are several limitations of non-root installations, as listed in Table 3.3. Understanding the limitations can help you decide when to use a non-root installation.

Table 3.3 Limitations of Non-Root Installations

Limitations	Description
Product	Some DB2 products are not supported in non-root installations: • IBM Data Server Developer Workbench • DB2 Embedded Application Server • DB2 Query Patroller • DB2 Net Search Extender Locally installed DB2 Information Center
Database Partitioning Feature (DPF)	Partitioned databases are not supported in non-root installations.
DB2 Copies	Each non-root user can have only one copy of a DB2 product installed.
Features and Tools	The following features and tools are not supported in non-root installations: • DB2 Administration Server (DAS) • Configuration Assistant • Control Center • The ability for db2governor to increase priority • The agent priority set in the Work Load Manager is ignored even though the operation is allowed.
DB2 Instance Operations	The following DB2 instance operations are not supported in non-root installations: • Automatic start of DB2 instances at system reboot • User instance commands: db2icrt, db2iupdt, db2idrop, db2imigr • DAS instance commands: dascrt, dasdrop, daslist, dasmigr, and dasupdt
Migration	Root instances cannot be migrated to a non-root instance.

3.3.3 Installing DB2 as a Non-Root User

Most DB2 products can be installed as a non-root user. Installing DB2 products as a non-root user is transparent to the non-root user. There isn't anything special required for a non-root user to install a DB2 product, other than being logged in as a non-root user.

To perform a non-root installation:

- Log in as a non-root user.
- Install the DB2 product using one of the methods listed in Table 3.1, such as the DB2 Setup Wizard.

- After the installation, you need to log in via a new login session to use the non-root DB2 instance. Alternatively, you can use the same login session if you source the DB2 instance profile (e.g., $HOME/sqllib/db2profile) in the session.

When installing a DB2 product as a non-root user, a single instance is automatically created and configured. If the non-root user instance needs to be manually configured or updated afterwards, you can use the **db2nrcfg** configuration tool, or the **db2nrupdt** update command respectively. In addition, the only way to drop a non-root user instance is to uninstall the product.

3.3.4 Enabling Root-Based Features in Non-Root Installations

Some root-based features and abilities are initially unavailable in non-root installations, but can be enabled by running the **db2rfe** command with the root authority.

The affected features and abilities are

- Operating system-based authentication
- High Availability (HA) feature
- The ability to reserve service names in the /etc/services file
- The ability to increase user data limits (ulimits) on AIX

To enable those features and abilities in non-root installations:

1. Locate the db2rfe.cfg configuration file of the **db2rfe** tool under the $HOME/sqllib/instance directory, where $HOME is the non-root user's home directory.
2. Make a copy of the configuration file for the recovery purpose.
3. Update the original configuration file accordingly.

   The example below shows an updated configuration file that will enable the following features and abilities:

   - High availability
   - Operating system-based authentication
   - DB2 Text search with a service name of db2j_db2inst1 and a port value of 55000

   ```
   INSTANCENAME=db2inst1
   SET_ULIMIT=NO
   ENABLE_HA=YES
   RESERVE_REMOTE_CONNECTION=NO
           **SVCENAME=db2c_db2inst1
           **SVCEPORT=50000
   RESERVE_TEXT_SEARCH_CONNECTION=YES
                   SVCENAME_TEXT_SEARCH=db2j_db2inst1
                   SVCEPORT_TEXT_SEARCH=55000
   ```

4. Log in as a user with root authority.
5. Run the **db2rfe** command located under the $HOME/sqllib/instance directory, using the following syntax:

```
db2rfe -f config_file
```

where **`config_file`** is the configuration file edited in Step 3.

3.4 Required User IDs and Groups

Figures 3.1 and 3.2 show that you create several user IDs and user groups that DB2 requires during the Windows install or the root installation on Linux and UNIX. This section discusses the basic requirements of those user IDs and groups, which are different for Windows and Linux and UNIX.

3.4.1 User IDs and Groups Required for Windows

In addition to requiring an **installation user ID** to install the DB2 product on Windows, to operate DB2 you need two other user IDs.

- The **Instance owner** owns and controls the DB2 instance.
- The **DB2 Administration Server** (DAS) **user** runs the DB2 administration server service on your system. The DB2 GUI tools also use this ID to perform administration tasks against the local server database instances and databases.

Table 3.4 describes these user IDs in more detail.

Table 3.4 User IDs and Groups for DB2 on Windows

	Installation User ID	Instance Owner User ID	DAS User ID
Authority of the User ID	A local or domain user account that is part of the administrator group on the server where you are installing DB2 or a non-administrative ID with elevated rights to installation. The user right "Access this computer from the network" is required. You can also use the built-in Local System account to run the installation for all products except DB2 Enterprise Edition. If you want to have the DB2 Setup Wizard create a domain user account for the Instance owner or the DAS user, the installation ID must have authority to create domain user accounts.	A local or domain user account that belongs to the administrator group on the server.	A local or domain user account that belongs to the administrator group on the machine. The built-in Local System account can also be used.

(continues)

Table 3.4 User IDs and Groups for DB2 on Windows *(Continued)*

	Installation User ID	Instance Owner User ID	DAS User ID
When to Create It	Before installation.	Before installation, or during installation by the DB2 Setup Wizard. Either way, the necessary rights will be granted during the installation process.	Same as Instance Owner User ID.
Rights Granted During Installation	• Act as part of the operating system. • Debug programs. • Create a token object. • Increase quotas. • Lock pages in memory. • Log on as a service. • Replace a process-level token.	• Act as part of the operating system. • Debug programs. • Create a token object. • Increase quotas. • Lock pages in memory. • Log on as a service. • Replace a process-level token.	Same as Instance Owner User ID.

NOTE Starting in DB2 9, the installation user no longer needs to be part of the Administrators group. You can now install DB2 using a non-administrative ID. Just make sure that a Windows Administrator configures the elevated privileges feature in Windows before installing DB2.

3.4.2 IDs and Groups Required for Linux and UNIX

For root installations on Linux and UNIX, you need to sign in as a root user to perform DB2 installation. In addition, you need three users and three groups to operate DB2.

- The DB2 **Instance owner** is created in the instance user ID home directory. This user ID controls all DB2 processes and owns all file systems and devices used by the databases contained within the instance.
- The **Fenced user** runs fenced user-defined functions (UDFs) and stored procedures. Fenced UDFs and stored procedures execute outside of the address space used by the DB2 instance and therefore cannot interfere with the execution of the instance. If you do not need this level of security, you can use the instance owner as your fenced user.
- The same as on Windows, the **DAS user** runs the DB2 Administration Server process on your system. This user ID is also used by the DB2 GUI tools to perform administration tasks against the local server database instances and databases.
- Three separate user groups must also be created for the Instance Owner, the Fenced User, and the DAS user.

Table 3.5 describes these user IDs and groups in more detail.

Table 3.5 User IDs and Groups Required for Installing DB2 on UNIX Platforms

	Instance Owner User ID	Fenced User ID	DAS User ID
When to Create It	If the system is running NIS or similar security software, and you plan to create a DB2 instance during the DB2 installation process, then you must create this ID prior to installing DB2. See Section 3.4.3, Creating User IDs and Groups if NIS Is Installed in Your Environment (Linux and UNIX Only), for more information. Otherwise: • During installation when using the DB2 Setup Wizard or Silent install. • After installation when using the **`db2_install`** script or native OS install tool.	Same as Instance Owner User ID.	Same as Instance Owner User ID.
Default User ID Created by DB2 Installer	db2inst1 If *db2inst1* already exists, the DB2 installer will then search for the user *db2inst2*. If that user doesn't exist, it will then create that user. If that user does exist, the DB2 installer will continue its search (*db2inst3*, *db2inst4*, and so on) until it finds an available user.	db2fenc1 Uses the same algorithm as Instance Owner User ID.	• db2as (AIX only) • dasusr1 (all other Linux/UNIX platforms). Uses the same algorithm as Instance Owner User ID.
Example Primary Group Name	db2iadm1	db2fadm1	dasadm1
Example Secondary Group Name	dasadm1	Not applicable.	db2iadm1

NOTE In the Data Partitioning Feature (DPF) environment, each partition of the database must have the same set of users and groups defined. If the definitions are not the same, a user may not be authorized to perform the required actions on some database partitions. Consistency across all partitions is recommended.

3.4.3 Creating User IDs and Groups if NIS Is Installed in Your Environment (Linux and UNIX Only)

NIS is a secure and robust repository of information about network entities, such as users and servers, which enables the efficient administration of enterprise client/server networks. Administration tasks such as adding, removing, and reassigning systems and users are facilitated by modifying information in NIS. **NIS+** is a more mature version of NIS with better support for security issues and very large work groups.

If you have NIS or a similar security component installed on your machine, you must create the users and groups listed in Table 3.3 *manually before* installing DB2, because the DB2 installation scripts attempt to update objects that are under the control of the security packages. NIS prevents DB2 from doing those updates.

Keep the following restrictions in mind if you are using NIS or NIS+.

- You must create groups and users on the NIS server before installing DB2.
- You must add the primary group of the instance owner to the secondary DAS group. Likewise, you must add the primary DAS group to the secondary group for the instance owner.
- On a DB2 Enterprise system, before you create an instance, you must create an entry for the instance in the etc/services file. For example, if you want to create an instance for the user *db2inst1*, you require an entry similar to the following:

```
DB2_db2inst1     50000/tcp
```

> **NOTE** These considerations hold true for any environment in which an external security program does not allow the DB2 installation or instance creation programs to modify user characteristics.

3.5 Silent Install Using a Response File

When you need to install DB2 on a number of computers, you may want to install it using a response file to reduce the amount of work involved. With a response file, you can install DB2 unattended. This installation method is available on all DB2 supported platforms.

A response file is a text file with the extension *.rsp*. It specifies configuration and setup parameters such as the destination directory (Windows only) and the products and components to install. It can also be used to:

- Create instances
- Set up global DB2 registry variables
- Set up the database manager configuration

Figure 3.20 shows a response file, *db2ese.rsp*, which can be used to perform a DB2 Enterprise Edition server installation on Windows.

```
PROD=ENTERPRISE_SERVER_EDITION
LIC_AGREEMENT=ACCEPT
FILE=C:\Program Files\IBM\SQLLIB\
INSTALL_TYPE=TYPICAL

LANG=EN
DAS_CONTACT_LIST=LOCAL

CONTACT=CONTACT

DATABASE=TOOLS_DB
TOOLS_CATALOG_DATABASE=TOOLS_DB
TOOLS_CATALOG_SCHEMA=SYSTOOLS
TOOLS_DB.DATABASE_NAME=TOOLSDB

INSTANCE=DB2

CONTACT.INSTANCE=DB2

TOOLS_DB.INSTANCE=DB2
TOOLS_DB.LOCATION=LOCAL
DB2.NAME=DB2
CONTACT.CONTACT_NAME=Michael Dang
CONTACT.NEW_CONTACT=YES
CONTACT.EMAIL=dangm@ca.ibm.com
CONTACT.PAGER=0
DEFAULT_INSTANCE=DB2
DB2.SVCENAME=db2c_DB2
DB2.DB2COMM=TCPIP
.
.
.
```

Figure 3.20 A response file excerpt (created by the DB2 Setup Wizard)

As shown in Figure 3.20, a response file consists of keywords and their values. For example, the *PROD* keyword specifies the DB2 product you are installing. The *FILE* keyword specifies the install location, and the *INSTALL_TYPE* keyword specifies whether to perform a *TYPICAL* install, a *COMPACT* install, or a *CUSTOM* install. These are the values you would have to enter interactively if you were installing DB2 using the DB2 Setup Wizard.

3.5.1 Creating a Response File

There are three ways to create a response file for your installation.

- Using the DB2 Setup Wizard to save the setup and configuration data.
- Modifying a sample response file to create a custom response file.
- Using the response file generator (Windows only).

3.5.1.1 Creating a Response File Using the DB2 Setup Wizard

If you use the DB2 Setup Wizard to install DB2, you have the option to create a response file (refer to step 3). This response file will record all the parameters you input to the DB2 Setup Wizard, and you can use this file to perform installations on other computers. The DB2 Setup Wizard created the response file excerpt shown in Figure 3.20.

3.5.1.2 Creating a Custom Response File Using a Sample Response File

You can manually edit the response file created by the DB2 Setup Wizard or the sample response files provided on the DB2 CD-ROM. Each DB2 product has sample response files. They are located at the *cd-rom*/db2/*platform*/samples directory (where *cd-rom* represents the location of the installable version of DB2 and *platform* refers to the appropriate hardware platform). Figure 3.21 shows a sample Windows response file.

```
* General Options
** ---------------
PROD                          = ENTERPRISE_SERVER_EDITION
*FILE                         = C:\Program Files\IBM\SQLLIB
** FILE determines the base install path.  If you specify a path that does not
** yet have this product, this will install a new copy.  If you specify a path
** that does have this product, this will be considered an "existing"
** install intended to install additional functionality.  This is an optional
** keyword.
```

Figure 3.21 A sample Windows response file

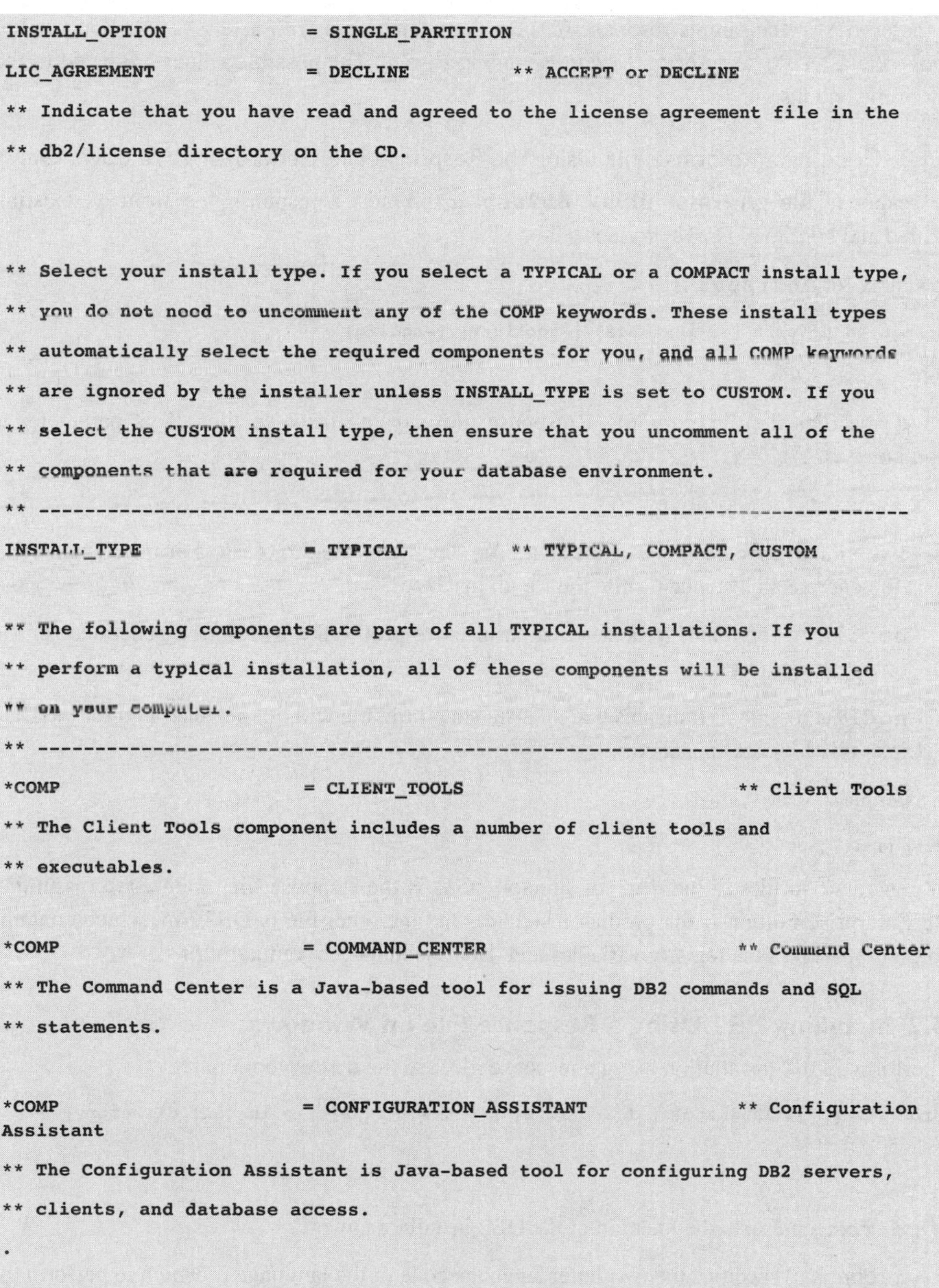

```
INSTALL_OPTION          = SINGLE_PARTITION
LIC_AGREEMENT           = DECLINE        ** ACCEPT or DECLINE
** Indicate that you have read and agreed to the license agreement file in the
** db2/license directory on the CD.


** Select your install type. If you select a TYPICAL or a COMPACT install type,
** you do not need to uncomment any of the COMP keywords. These install types
** automatically select the required components for you, and all COMP keywords
** are ignored by the installer unless INSTALL_TYPE is set to CUSTOM. If you
** select the CUSTOM install type, then ensure that you uncomment all of the
** components that are required for your database environment.
** -----------------------------------------------------------------------------
INSTALL_TYPE            = TYPICAL        ** TYPICAL, COMPACT, CUSTOM

** The following components are part of all TYPICAL installations. If you
** perform a typical installation, all of these components will be installed
** on your computer.
** -----------------------------------------------------------------------------
*COMP                   = CLIENT_TOOLS                      ** Client Tools
** The Client Tools component includes a number of client tools and
** executables.

*COMP                   = COMMAND_CENTER                    ** Command Center
** The Command Center is a Java-based tool for issuing DB2 commands and SQL
** statements.

*COMP                   = CONFIGURATION_ASSISTANT           ** Configuration
Assistant
** The Configuration Assistant is Java-based tool for configuring DB2 servers,
** clients, and database access.
.
.
```

Figure 3.21 A sample Windows response file *(Continued)*

All the entries in the sample response files are commented out with asterisks (*). You need to remove the asterisks to activate the corresponding entries. The possible values are listed to the right of the equal sign.

3.5.1.3 Creating a Response File Using the Response File Generator (Windows Only)

The **response file generator utility, `db2rspgn`,** creates a response file from an existing installed and configured DB2 product.

The syntax for **`db2rspgn`** is:

```
db2rspgn –d x:\path [-i instance] [–noctlsrv] [-nodlfm]
```

where

> **`-d`** specifies the directory for a response file and any instance files. This parameter is required.
>
> **`X`** represents the disk drive.
>
> **`-i`** (optional) specifies a list of instances for which you want to create a profile. The default is to generate an instance profile file for all instances.
>
> **`-noctlsrv`** (optional) indicates that an instance profile file will not be generated for the Control Server instance.
>
> **`-nodlfm`** (optional) indicates that an instance profile file will not be generated for the Data Links File Manager instance.

For example

```
db2rspgn d:\temp
```

will generate two files in the *d:\temp* directory. One is the response file, *db2ese.rsp* (assuming DB2 Enterprise Edition is the product installed), and the other file is *DB2.INS*, which contains information such as the registry variables and database manager configurations.

3.5.2 Installing DB2 Using a Response File on Windows

To perform a DB2 installation using a response file, use the **`setup`** command.

```
cd-rom/setup [-i language] [-l log_file] [-t trace_file] [-p install_directory] -u
response_file
```

where

> ***`cd-rom`*** represents the location of the DB2 installable image.
>
> **`-i`** (optional) specifies the two-letter language code of the language in which to perform the installation.

-l (optional) specifies the fully qualified log filename, where setup information and any errors occurring during setup are logged. If you do not specify the log file's name, DB2 names it *db2.log* and puts it in the *My Documents/db2log* folder.

-p (optional) changes the installation path of the product. Specifying this option overrides the installation path that is specified in the response file.

-t (optional) specifies the full path name of a file to trace install information.

-u specifies the full path name of the response file.

For example

```
setup -u d:\temp\db2ese.rsp
```

3.5.3 Installing DB2 Using a Response File on Linux and UNIX

To perform a DB2 installation using a response on Linux and UNIX, use the **db2setup** command (ensure that you log on with the proper user ID based on the root or non-root installation type):

```
cd-rom/db2setup [-i language] [-l log_file] [-t trace file] -r response_file
```

where

cd-rom represents the location of the DB2 install image.

response_file represents the full path name of the response file.

-i (optional) specifies the two-letter language code of the language in which to perform the installation.

-l (optional) specifies the fully qualified log filename, where setup information and any errors occurring during setup are logged. If you do not specify the log file's name, DB2 names it *db2.log* and puts it in the */tmp directory*.

-t (optional) specifies the full path name of a file to trace install information.

-r specifies the full path name of the response file.

For example

```
db2setup -r /usr/tmp/db2ese.rsp
```

3.6 Advanced DB2 Installation Methods (Linux and UNIX Only)

DB2 supports two additional methods for installing DB2 on Linux and UNIX.

- Using the **db2_install** script
- Manual installation

These two methods require a certain level of operating system knowledge. Tasks such as user and instance creation and configuration that would be performed for you by the DB2 Setup Wizard or during a response file installation must be performed after the product is installed. We do not recommend using either of these methods if you are new to DB2.

3.6.1 Installing DB2 Using the db2_install Script

The **db2_install** script is located in the root directory on your DB2 9 product CD-ROM. To perform a DB2 installation using the db2_install script, follow these steps:

1. Log in as a proper user ID based on the root or non-root installation type.
2. Insert and mount the appropriate CD-ROM or access the file system where the installation image is stored.
3. If you downloaded the DB2 product, decompress and untar the product file.
4. Change directory to the product directory.
5. Run the **db2_install** command:

```
db2_install [-b install_path] [-p product_ID] [-c image_location] [-n]
[-L language] [-l log_file] [-t trace_file]
```

where

-b (optional) specifies the path where the DB2 product is to be installed in root installations. This parameter is mandatory if the **-n** parameter is selected. The default installation path is

- for AIX, HP-UX or Solaris /opt/IBM/db2/V9.5
- for Linux /opt/ibm/db2/V9.5

-p (optional) specifies the DB2 product to be installed. Enter the keyword for the product you want to install. If you specify more than one product keyword, separate the key words with spaces in quotation marks. A list of DB2 product keywords is shown in Table 3.6, or it can be found in the file ComponentList.htm located in the /db2/*platform* directory on the CD-ROM (where *platform* is the platform on which you are installing).

-c (optional) specifies the product image location.

-n (optional) specifies non-interactive mode. If selected, you must also specify the **-b install_path** parameter.

-L (optional) specifies national language support. By default, English is always installed.

-l (optional) specifies the log file. The default log file is /tmp/db2_install.log$$, where $$ is the process ID.

-t (optional) turns on the debug mode.

For example

```
./db2_install
```

or

```
./db2_install –p ese –b /db2/newlevel -n
```

Table 3.6 Keywords Used by the db2_install Script

DB2 Product	Keyword
DB2 Client	DB2.CL
DB2 Connect Enterprise Edition, DB2 Connect Unlimited Edition, and DB2 Connect Application Server Edition	DB2.CONEE
DB2 Connect Personal Edition	DB2.CONPE
DB2 Cube Views	DB2.CUBE
DB2 Enterprise Server Edition	DB2.ESE
DB2 Express Edition	DB2.ESE
DB2 Personal Edition	DB2.PE
DB2 Query Patroller	DB2.QP
DB2 Spatial Extender	DB2.GSE
DB2 Workgroup Server Edition	DB2.WSE

3.6.2 Manually Installing Payload Files (Linux and UNIX)

To manually install payload files:

1. Log in as a proper user ID based on the root or non-root installation type.
2. Insert and mount the appropriate CD-ROM or access the file system where the installation image is stored.
3. Locate the DB2 component you want to install. The component list is shown in Table 3.5, or it can be found in the file **ComponentList.htm** located in the /db2/*platform* directory on the CD-ROM (where *platform* is the platform on which you are installing).
4. The DB2 payload file is compressed and uses the same format for all supported operating systems. You can uncompress the payload file with the following commands:

   • For AIX, HP-UX, or Solaris:

```
cd DB2DIR
gunzip -c /cd/db2/platform/FILES/filename.tar.gz
   tar -xf -
```

- For Linux:

```
cd DB2DIR
   tar xzf /cd/db2/platform/FILES/filename.tar.gz
```

where

DB2DIR is the full path name where you are installing.

- For root installations, the default path for AIX, HP-UX or Solaris is /opt/IBM/db2/V9.5
- For Linux the default path is /opt/ibm/db2/V9.5
- For non-root installations, DB2DIR must be $HOME/sqllib. This directory must be empty.

cd represents the mount point of the DB2 CD.

filename is the name of the DB2 component you are installing.

5. To ensure the embedded library search path on each DB2 executable and library file uses the installation path, enter

```
DB2DIR/install/db2chgpath
```

6. For non-root installations, run $HOME/sqllib/db2nrcfg to configure the non-root instance.
7. For non-root installations, after the DB2 product is installed, open a new login session to use the non-root DB2 instance. Alternatively, you can use the same login session if you source the DB2 instance profile (e.g., .$HOME/sqllib/db2profile) in the session.

After the product is installed, tasks such as user and instance creation and configuration will have to be performed for root installations. This method is not recommended. It is recommended that you install DB2 products, components, and features using the DB2 Setup Wizard or by using a response file.

NOTE Beginning in DB2 9, you ***cannot*** manually install a DB2 product, component, or feature using an operating system's native installation utility such as rpm, SMIT, swinstall, or pkgadd. As a result, you can no longer use operating system commands for installation. Any existing scripts that you use to interface and query with DB2 installations will need to be changed. Adjust your scripts to use the payload installation method discussed in this section.

3.7 Installing a DB2 License

Licenses are automatically installed if you installed the DB2 product using the DB2 Setup Wizard or response file. If you installed DB2 using the **db2_install** script or manually installed DB2, you need to install the licenses manually.

There are two ways you can install a DB2 license: using the GUI License Center or the **db2licm** command.

3.7.1 Installing a DB2 Product License Using the License Center

The License Center is a GUI tool you can use to display, add, remove, or change a license. To start the License Center from the Control Center, click on the icon that looks like a key and a user (see Figure 3.22).

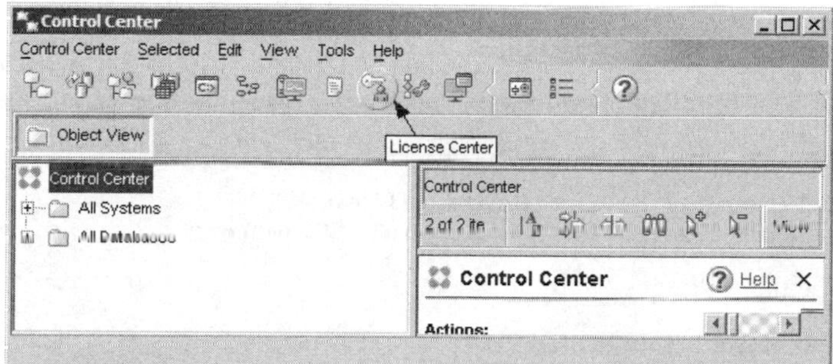

Figure 3.22 Starting the License Center from the Control Center

Figure 3.23 shows the License Center.

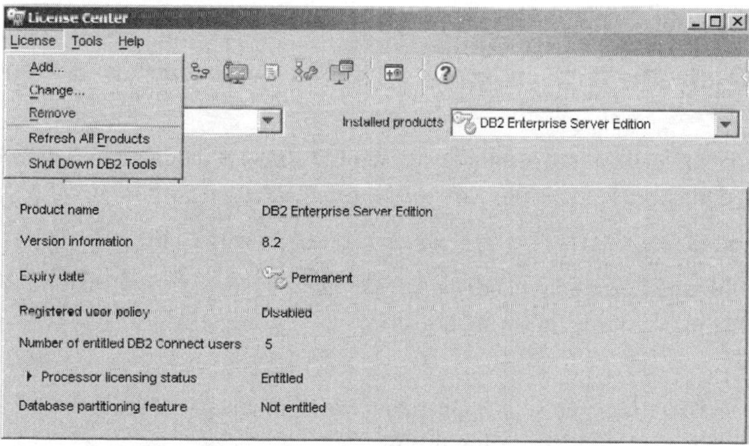

Figure 3.23 The License Center

If a license is already installed, it will be displayed. If not, you have to add a license using the **License > Add** menu option.

3.7.2 Installing the DB2 Product License Using the db2licm Command

You can also install the license by using the **db2licm** command.

You can either log in as a root user or an instance owner to install a license. In non-root installations, the only option is to install a license as the instance owner.

As an instance owner use the following:

On Linux and UNIX:

```
db2instance_path/adm/db2licm -a filename.lic
```

On Windows:

```
db2instance_path\adm\db2licm -a filename.lic
```

As a root user for root installations on Linux and UNIX, type (assume default path) the following:

```
/opt/ibm/db2/V9.5/adm/db2licm -a filename (on Linux)
/opt/IBM/db2/V9.5/adm/db2licm -a filename (on all UNIX platforms)
```

On Windows, type the following:

```
db2instance_path\adm\db2licm -a filename
```

where

> ***db2instance_path*** is where the DB2 instance was created.
>
> ***filename*** is the full pathname and filename for the license file that corresponds to the product you purchased.

The license file is located in the /db2/license directory at the root directory of the product's CD-ROM.

For example, on AIX with a root installation, if the CD-ROM is mounted in the /cdrom directory and the name of the license file is db2dlm.lic, the command to use would be

```
/opt/IBM/db2/V9.5/adm/db2licm -a /cdrom/db2/license/db2dlm.lic
```

After running the **db2licm** command, the DB2 product license key information is contained in the nodelock file in one of the following directories:

- For AIX: /var/ifor
- For HP-UX, Linux, or Solaris Operating Environment: /var/lum
- For Windows: DB2PATH/sqllib/license

3.8 Installing DB2 in a DPF Environment

In a DPF environment with multiple physical machines, each of the participating machines must have DB2 installed locally. To ease the installation of DB2 on other machines, we recommend you create a response file when you install DB2 on the first machine. Once this response file is created, you can transfer the file to the other machines and run a Silent installation (see Section 3.5, Silent Install Using a Response File, for details).

The DB2 install code from the installation CD-ROM can reside on a shared disk, from which you proceed to install DB2 locally onto each participating computer, as illustrated in Figure 3.24.

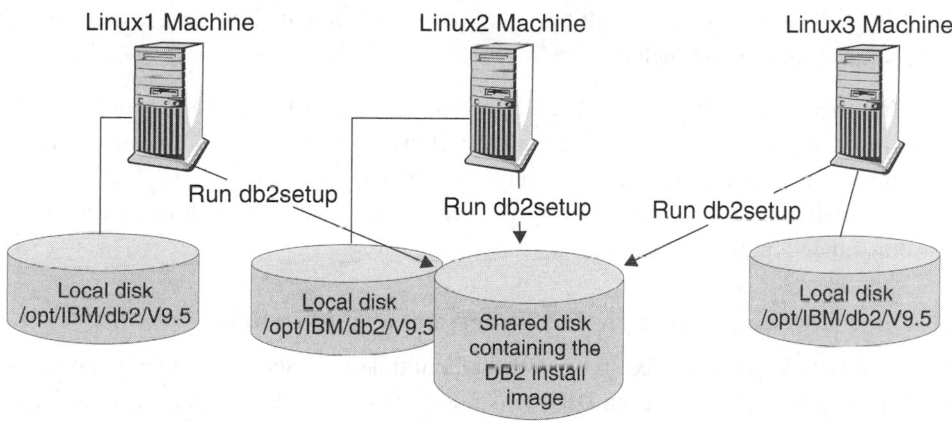

Figure 3.24 Installing DB2 in a DPF environment

The Linux2 machine in Figure 3.24 has a disk onto which the install code from the installation CD-ROM has been copied. This disk is set up so that it can be shared by the other two machines, Linux1 and Linux3. From each of the machines you can execute the **db2setup** command to install DB2 locally; therefore, each machine will have its own local directory /opt/ibm/db2/V9.5 containing the DB2 installed binaries. Installing DB2 locally on the Linux2 machine and sharing the installed binaries with Linux1 and Linux3 is not supported.

V9

> **NOTE** On Linux, the DB2 installed binaries are locally stored in directory /opt/ibm/db2/V9.5. On AIX, HP-UX or Solaris operating systems, DB2 is installed under /opt/IBM/db2/V9.5. Use the **db2level** command to determine where the installed code has been locally installed in your machine.

3.9 Installing Multiple DB2 Versions and Fix Packs on the Same Server

Imagine that you are working on a high risk project that requires a particular DB2 version and Fix Pack. The new server you ordered will not arrive for another week, and your manager is breathing down your neck asking for status updates. There is an active development server that has the minimum resources you need to run your tests, but the server is already running DB2 at a lower version and Fix Pack. Can you use the active development server to run a different version of DB2 and Fix Pack? Can you install different versions of DB2 on the same Windows machine at the same time? What if you wanted to test a particular version of DB2 on the same server as your production, and then simply migrate it after the tests are successful? Beginning in DB2 9, it is now possible to do all of the above. You can install and run multiple DB2 copies on the same computer. A **DB2 Copy** refers to one or more installations of DB2 database products in a particular location on the same computer. Each DB2 copy can be at the same or different code levels.

This is done by installing multiple DB2 product codes in different paths on the same machine. Other benefits of this feature include

- Install anywhere: You can install DB2 using any valid path that you choose.
- Install any number of times: You can install two or more copies of the same DB2 code on one machine. The code levels can be the same or different.
- Maintain each copy independently: You can update one copy without affecting any of the other copies.

3.9.1 Coexistence of Multiple DB2 Versions and Fix Packs (Windows)

Starting with DB2 9, you have the ability to install multiple DB2 server and client copies on the same machine. DB2 will install each **DB2 copy** into different installation paths and use separate registry keys. Each DB2 installation copy can either be at the same DB2 level or at a different level. During installation, a unique DB2 copy name is generated, which you can later change.

When there is only one installation of DB2, that DB2 copy automatically becomes the default DB2 copy, which works like any DB2 copy prior to DB2 9. The default DB2 copy is required for your applications to access DB2 databases through the default or native interface. In other words, any applications that have not been coded to target a specific DB2 copy, will access the databases within the default DB2 copy. When you install subsequent versions of DB2, you can choose to work with an existing copy or install a new one. Working with an existing copy allows you to update the functionality of your current DB2 copy whereas installing a new copy creates a new unique DB2 copy on the machine. Figure 3.25 shows you the Install a Product panel, indicating your choice of installation. If DB2 Version 8 already exists on the server, then you have the option to *Install New* or *Migrate* the DB2 copy.

> **NOTE** DB2 Version 8 and DB2 9 DB2 copies can coexist on the same data server; however DB2 Version 8 is always the default copy.

Figure 3.26 shows you the Select the Installation Folder panel. Take note of the installation directory. It is *C:\Program Files\IBM\SQLLIB_01*. The path name is set by DB2 for you by appending a two digit sequence to the end of the path. You can change this path to any valid path on your system.

Figure 3.27 shows you the Set the DB2 copy name panel. A default DB2 copy name is created for you by appending a two-digit sequence to the end of the default DB2 copy name. In this case, it is DB2_01. If you install a third and subsequent copies of DB2 on this server, then the default names will be DB2_02, DB2_03, and so on. You can change the DB2 copy name to any eight-character string you choose. Note also that the *Set this as the default DB2 copy on this computer* option was unchecked. If you leave this option checked, then the new DB2 copy will become your default installation copy. You need to decide if this is what you want to do and select the option appropriately. In this case, we want to leave the original installation as the default, so the option has been unchecked.

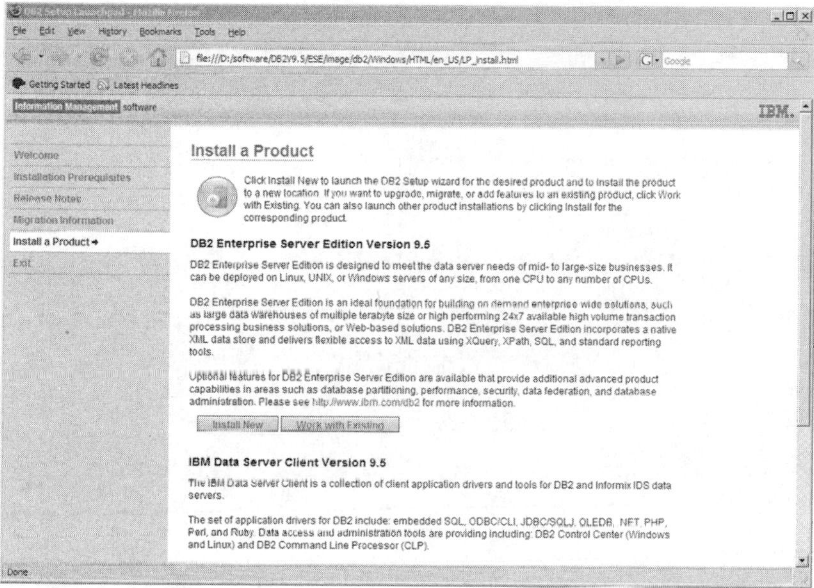

Figure 3.25 Install a Product: Install new or Work with Existing panel

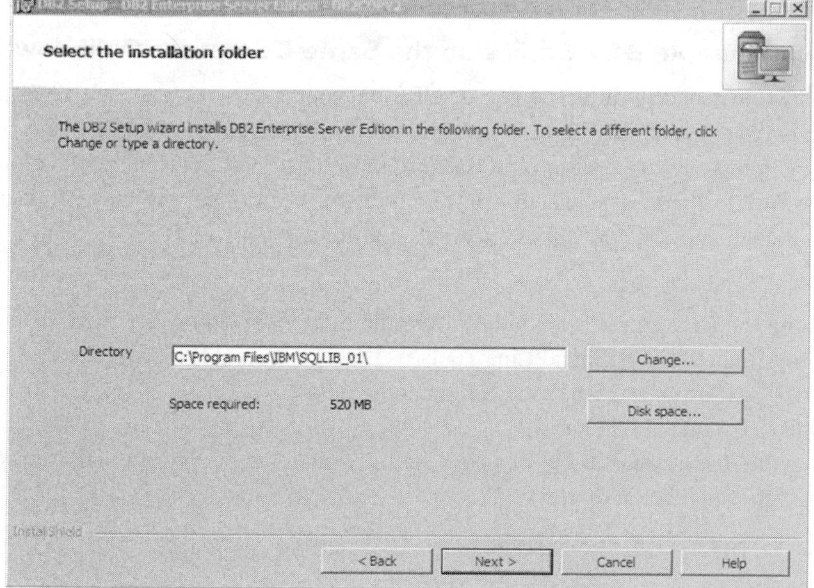

Figure 3.26 Select the Installation Folder—creating another DB2 copy path

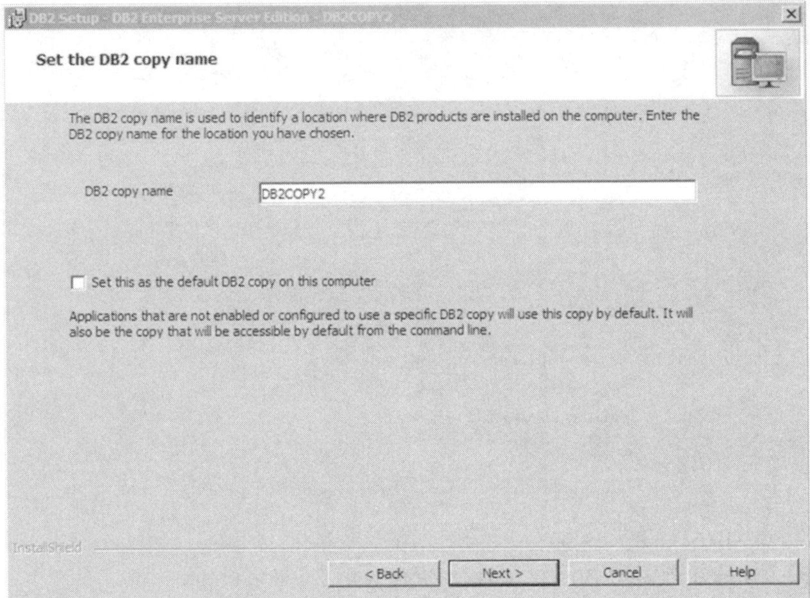

Figure 3.27 Set the DB2 copy name

3.9.2 Using Multiple DB2 Copies on the Same Computer (Windows)

After you have installed multiple copies of DB2 on your machine, you may need to change which copy is your default DB2 copy. A scenario in which you may want to do this is where you are promoting a test environment into production. In order for your current applications to connect successfully to the new production DB2 copy, you need to set the new production DB2 copy as the default copy. If you want to access a non-default copy of DB2 (for testing purposes for example), you can use the following two methods:

- Using the DB2 command window from the Start -> Programs -> IBM DB2 -> <DB2 Copy Name> -> Command Line Tools -> DB2 Command Window (see Figure 3.28).
- Using **db2envar.bat** from a command window:
- Open a command window.
- Run the **db2envar.bat** file using the fully qualified path for the DB2 copy that you want the application to use:

```
Eg. X:\DB2_01\bin\db2envar.bat
```

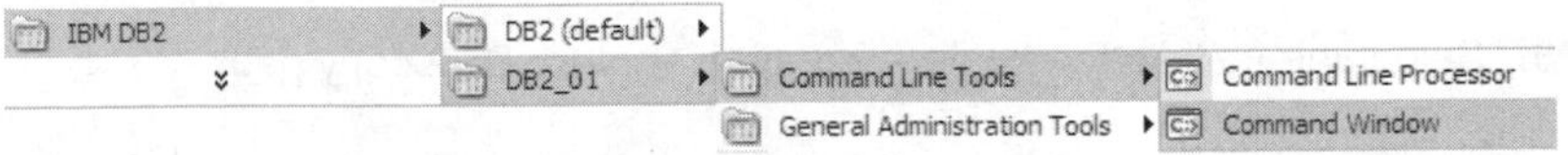

Figure 3.28 Selecting DB2 copy instance to use

You can change which copy of DB2 becomes the default DB2 copy by using the new Global Switcher, **db2swtch.exe** command. You can either launch this as a graphical interface or run it as a command. To launch the Default DB2 Selection Wizard, type **db2swtch.exe** without any arguments at the command window. Figure 3.29 shows you the welcome panel that greets you. Click *Next*.

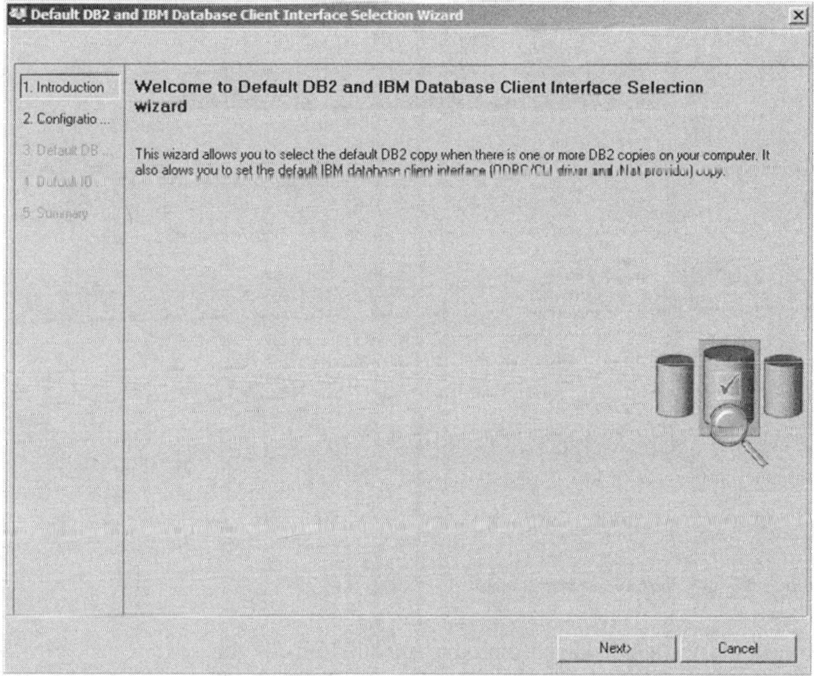

Figure 3.29 Default DB2 Selection Wizard

In Figure 3.30 you can see your current default DB2 copy and all other installation copies available on your system. We will select the DB2COPY2 DB2 copy, and make that our default DB2 copy. Highlight *DB2COPY2* and click *Next*.

You will now see that the switch of your new default DB2 copy is successful. Your new default DB2 copy is now DB2COPY2. Click *Finish* to complete the process.

> **NOTE** Chapter 4 also discusses how to select your default DB2 copy.

You can also switch the default DB2 copy by running the db2swtch.exe command with special arguments.

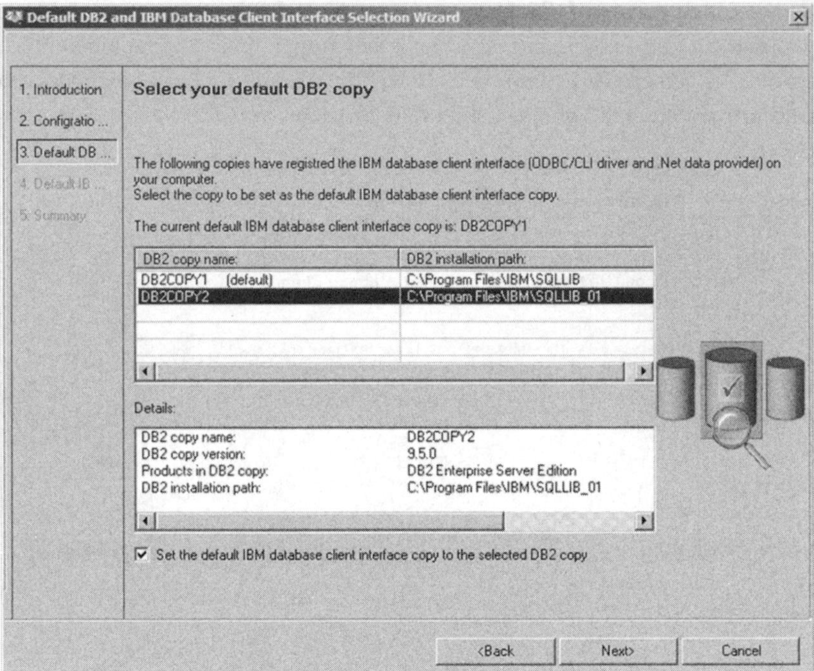

Figure 3.30 Select your default DB2 copy

```
db2swtch.exe -l -d <installation name>
```

where

-l displays a list of DB2 database product installations on the system

-d <installation name> sets the default DB2 copy.

See Figure 3.31 for an example of how to do this from the command line.

3.9.3 Coexistence of Multiple DB2 Versions and Fix Packs (Linux and UNIX)

Similar to Windows, with root installations you can install multiple versions and Fix Packs of DB2 to any location on a Linux or UNIX server. However, each non-root user can have only one copy of a DB2 product installed. During the installation or migration process, you can specify if you want to install new, migrate, or work with existing DB2 copies. Each DB2 copy can be at the same or different code levels. In DB2 9.5, the default installation path for root installations is as follows:

- /opt/IBM/db2/V9.5 for AIX, HP-UX or Solaris
- /opt/ibm/db2/V9.5 for Linux

Figure 3.31 Using the db2swtch.exe command

You can specify your desired installation path, or let DB2 specify it for you. If the default path is already used (by another DB2 copy), DB2 will use the following naming convention:

- /opt/IBM/db2/V9.5_## for AIX, HP-UX or Solaris
- /opt/ibm/db2/V9.5_## for Linux

where ## is a sequential number ranging from 01 to 99. For example, if you decide to install two copies of DB2 on your Linux machine, then by default, DB2 will install the first in /opt/ibm/db2/V9.5 and the second in /opt/ibm/db2/V9.5_01.

V9 3.9.3.1 The db2ls Command (Linux and UNIX)

A new command, **db2ls**, is used to provide information about DB2 database systems and features installed on your Linux and UNIX systems. You can use the **db2ls** command to list where DB2 products are installed on your system and list the DB2 product level for each DB2 copy. You can also list all or specific DB2 products and features in a particular installation path. The **db2ls** command is available in the */usr/local/bin* directory.

```
db2ls –q –f feature_id –a –p –b base-install-path –l logfile
```

where

-q will query the list of installed DB2 products and features. By default, only the visible components or features are displayed unless the **–a** parameter is also specified.

-f feature_id(optional) will query if the specified feature is installed on the system.

-a(optional) will list all hidden components as well as visible features.

-p(optional) will list products installed on the system only.

-b base-install-path will specify which installation directory you are querying.

-l logfile(optional) will produce a trace file for debugging purposes in the path you ran the db2ls command.

Different feature listings are obtained depending on the root versus non-root type of DB2 installation and the user running the command.

For example, to query if all DB2 database features are installed to a particular path, issue

```
db2ls –q –a –b /opt/ibm/db2/V9.1
```

> **NOTE** In Version 9 or later, the db2ls command is the only method to query a DB2 product. You can no longer query DB2 products using the native Linux and UNIX utilities such as pkgadd, rpm, SMIT, or swinstall.

3.9.3.2 DB2 Administrative Server (DAS) and Multiple DB2 Copies

You can only operate one active DAS on any given system at any given time, regardless of the number of DB2 installation copies that are installed on the machine. This is unchanged from previous versions. The DAS can be from any version of DB2 that is currently installed on the machine. If the DAS is created on DB2 9, then it can administer both DB2 Version 8 and DB2 9 instances. If the DAS is created on DB2 Version 8, then it can only administer DB2 Version 8 instances. You can choose to either drop the DB2 Version 8 DAS, migrate the DB2 Version 8 DAS to DB2 9, or create a new DB2 9 DAS to administer both version instances. You may have seen a reminder in Figure 3.29 or Figure 3.30 that you will need to run the **dasimgr** command in order to switch the DAS when you switch the default DB2 copy.

3.10 Installing DB2 Fix Packs

A DB2 **Fix Pack** provides fixes to program defects. A fix to a program defect is also known as an Authorized Program Analysis Report (APAR). APARs can be discovered during IBM testing, or reported by customers in test or production environments. Every Fix Pack is accompanied by a document known as the APAR List (APARLIST.TXT), which describes the fixes that particular Fix Pack contains.

All Fix Packs are cumulative. This means that the latest Fix Pack for any given version of DB2 contains all of the updates of the previous Fix Packs for the same version of DB2. For example, FP3 will include all the fixes present in FP1 and FP2. Fix Packs are normally available every three months. It is recommended to keep your DB2 environment running at the latest Fix Pack level to ensure a low-incident operation.

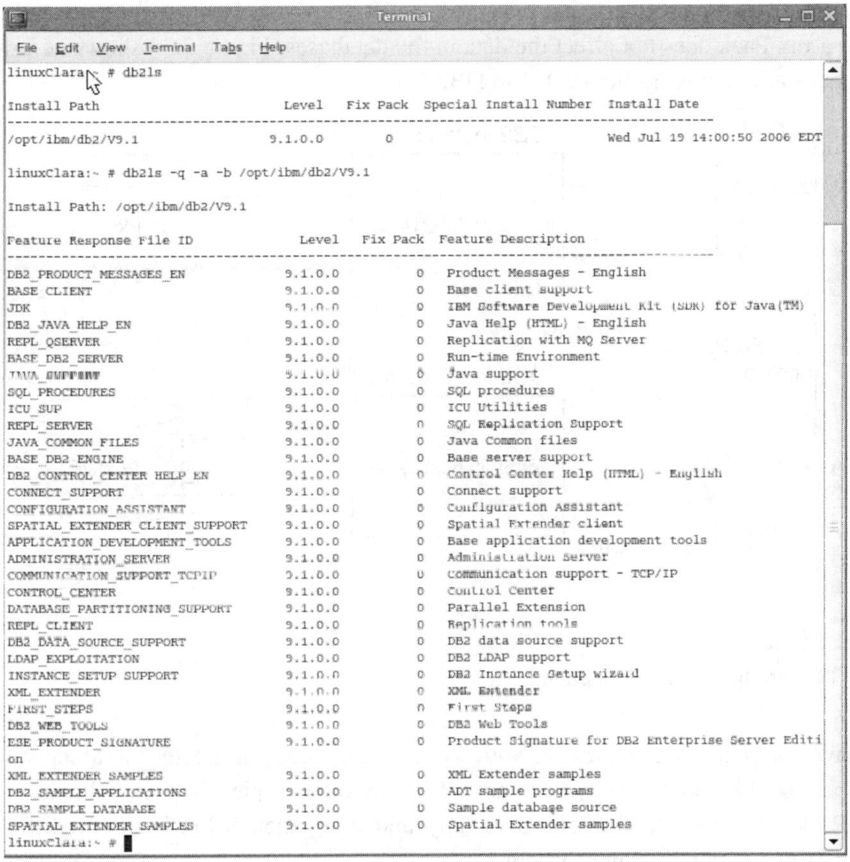

```
Terminal
File  Edit  View  Terminal  Tabs  Help
linuxClara:~ # db2ls

Install Path                        Level    Fix Pack  Special Install Number  Install Date
-----------------------------------------------------------------------------------------
/opt/ibm/db2/V9.1                 9.1.0.0        0                              Wed Jul 19 14:00:50 2006 EDT

linuxClara:~ # db2ls -q -a -b /opt/ibm/db2/V9.1

Install Path: /opt/ibm/db2/V9.1

Feature Response File ID              Level    Fix Pack  Feature Description
-----------------------------------------------------------------------------------------
DB2_PRODUCT_MESSAGES_EN             9.1.0.0         0    Product Messages - English
BASE_CLIENT                         9.1.0.0         0    Base client support
JDK                                 9.1.0.0         0    IBM Software Development Kit (SDK) for Java(TM)
DB2_JAVA_HELP_EN                    9.1.0.0         0    Java Help (HTML) - English
REPL_QSERVER                        9.1.0.0         0    Replication with MQ Server
BASE_DB2_SERVER                     9.1.0.0         0    Run-time Environment
JAVA_SUPPORT                        9.1.0.0         0    Java support
SQL_PROCEDURES                      9.1.0.0         0    SQL procedures
ICU_SUP                             9.1.0.0         0    ICU Utilities
REPL_SERVER                         9.1.0.0         0    SQL Replication Support
JAVA_COMMON_FILES                   9.1.0.0         0    Java Common files
BASE_DB2_ENGINE                     9.1.0.0         0    Base server support
DB2_CONTROL_CENTER_HELP_EN          9.1.0.0         0    Control Center Help (HTML) - English
CONNECT_SUPPORT                     9.1.0.0         0    Connect support
CONFIGURATION_ASSISTANT             9.1.0.0         0    Configuration Assistant
SPATIAL_EXTENDER_CLIENT_SUPPORT     9.1.0.0         0    Spatial Extender client
APPLICATION_DEVELOPMENT_TOOLS       9.1.0.0         0    Base application development tools
ADMINISTRATION_SERVER               9.1.0.0         0    Administration Server
COMMUNICATION_SUPPORT_TCPIP         9.1.0.0         0    Communication support - TCP/IP
CONTROL_CENTER                      9.1.0.0         0    Control Center
DATABASE_PARTITIONING_SUPPORT       9.1.0.0         0    Parallel Extension
REPL_CLIENT                         9.1.0.0         0    Replication tools
DB2_DATA_SOURCE_SUPPORT             9.1.0.0         0    DB2 data source support
LDAP_EXPLOITATION                   9.1.0.0         0    DB2 LDAP support
INSTANCE_SETUP_SUPPORT              9.1.0.0         0    DB2 Instance Setup wizard
XML_EXTENDER                        9.1.0.0         0    XML Extender
FIRST_STEPS                         9.1.0.0         0    First Steps
DB2_WEB_TOOLS                       9.1.0.0         0    DB2 Web Tools
ESE_PRODUCT_SIGNATURE               9.1.0.0         0    Product Signature for DB2 Enterprise Server Editi
on
XML_EXTENDER_SAMPLES                9.1.0.0         0    XML Extender samples
DB2_SAMPLE_APPLICATIONS             9.1.0.0         0    ADT sample programs
DB2_SAMPLE_DATABASE                 9.1.0.0         0    Sample database source
SPATIAL_EXTENDER_SAMPLES            9.1.0.0         0    Spatial Extender samples
linuxClara:~ #
```

Figure 3.32 Example of db2ls output

3.10.1 Applying a Regular DB2 Fix Pack (All Supported Platforms and Products)

Regular

Fix Packs provide cumulative fixes that are applied on top of other regular Fix Packs, or the base DB2 code, also known as the **generally available (GA)** code.

You can download the latest DB2 Fix Pack from the IBM DB2 and DB2 Connect Online Support Web Site at http://www.ibm.com/software/data/db2/udb/winos2unix/support. Each Fix Pack also contains a set of Release Notes and a Readme file. The Readme file provides instructions for installing the Fix Pack for each operating system.

When you apply a DB2 regular Fix Pack, you are in fact refreshing the DB2 code by overwriting some or all of the DB2 binaries. You then need to reestablish the links to an existing instance using the **db2iupdt** program on Linux and UNIX (this step is not required on Windows). Applying a Fix Pack does not affect the data in the databases. Figure 3.33 shows an example of what happens after applying Fix Pack 1 to DB2 9.5.

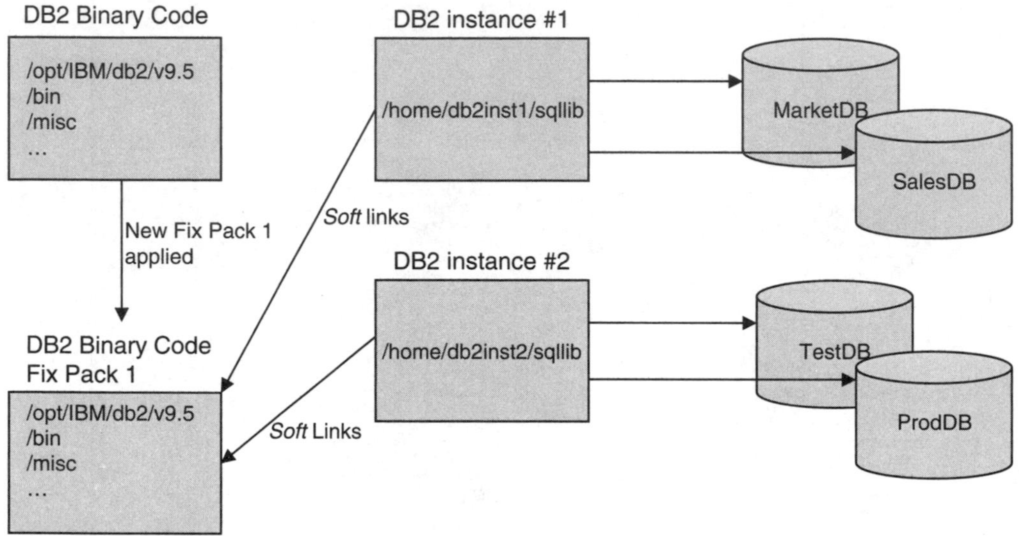

Figure 3.33 Applying a DB2 fix pack

If you have multiple DB2 copies on your system, each copy is treated as a separate entity. Applying a Fix Pack on one copy does not affect any other copies. You can choose to apply a new Fix Pack at a certain level to one DB2 copy, and apply another Fix Pack of a different level to another DB2 copy on the same system.

> **NOTE** Alternative Fix Packs provided in previous versions of DB2 are now obsolete given that DB2 9 has the ability to install multiple DB2 installation copies to multiple locations.

3.10.2 Applying Fix Packs to a Non-Root Installation

In DB2 9.5, the task of applying Fix Packs to a non-root installation on Linux and UNIX platforms is essentially the same as applying Fix Packs to a root installation with a few exceptions.

Before applying Fix Packs to a non-root installation, you must log on with the same user ID that was used to install the non-root installation. In addition, if you had root-based features enabled in your non-root installation, you should run the **db2rfe** command again as a post-FixPack operation to update and re-enable those root-based features.

3.11 Migrating DB2

If you are still running an older version of DB2, and want to migrate to a new version of DB2, then you need to perform the following migration process:

- Migrate DB2 servers—Migrate DB2 instances (Linux and UNIX only) and migrate DB2 databases.
- Migrate DB2 clients—Migrate DB2 client instances to keep the configuration of your existing DB2 clients.

> **NOTE** We will discuss the migration process for the DB2 server next.
>
> The term "migrate" is commonly used in the DB2 manuals to indicate an upgrade from one version of DB2 to another. We will follow this convention in this book, although, the term "Upgrade" would have been more appropriate.

3.11.1 Migrating DB2 Servers

Migrating DB2 servers involves upgrading your existing instances and databases so that they can run properly in DB2 9. If you are migrating from DB2 Version 8, then you can migrate directly to DB2 9. If you are migrating from DB2 Version 7 or earlier, you will need to migrate to DB2 Version 8 first, and then migrate to DB2 9.

> **NOTE** The methodologies to migrate to DB2 9 or DB2 9.5 are exactly the same. We will discuss migration to DB2 9 to mean both DB2 9 and DB2 9.5 in the following migration discussion.

3.11.2 Migration Steps for a DB2 Server on Windows

In DB2 9, you have the option to migrate an existing DB2 Version 8 installation or to install a new copy of DB2 9, test it, and migrate it manually later. If you migrate your existing Version 8 installation, your DB2 instances and DB2 Administration Server (DAS) are migrated automatically for you. If you install a new copy, you can migrate the instances later by running the **db2imigr** command, and you can manually migrate the DAS by running the **dasmigr** command after the migration.

To migrate to DB2 9 from DB2 Version 8:

- Log in as a Local Administrator or user id with elevated installation privileges.
- Launch the DB2 Setup Wizard to begin installation of DB2 9 code. You will see the options *Work with Existing* and *Install New* on the Install a Product panel as shown in Figure 3.25. You can choose either the *Work with Existing* or *install new* option. If you

choose the *Work with Existing* option, DB2 will migrate your existing DB2 Version 8 instances and the DB2 Administration Server (DAS) automatically for you. If you choose to install a new DB2 9.5 copy, then you must run the db2imigr command to migrate the instances, and the **dasmigr** command to migrate the DAS manually.

- Migrate the databases, if any. Use the **migrate database** command to migrate your databases:

```
db2 migrate database database_alias user username using password
```

where

database_alias is the name or the alias of the database you want to migrate.
username and ***password*** refer to a user with SYSADM authority.

> **NOTE** You may want to test DB2 9.5 before migrating an existing DB2 Version 8 copy. You can first install DB2 9.5 on the server that already has DB2 Version 8 installed. Then create a DB2 9.5 instance, and test your applications and environment. When you are satisfied with you testing, you can migrate your instances using the **db2imigr** and **dasimgr** commands mentioned above.

3.11.3 Migration Steps for a DB2 Server on Linux and UNIX

To migrate to DB2 9:

1. Log on as root.
2. Run the db2setup command to install DB2 9. Select *Install New* on the Install a Product panel to install a new copy of DB2 9. (There is no migrate option for Linux and UNIX as there is for Windows.)
3. Migrate all instances from the same installation path that you indicated during the installation in step 2. Make sure all instances are stopped.

   ```
   db2imigr –u fencedID Instname
   ```

   where

   -u fencedID is the user under which the fenced user-defined functions (UDFs) and stored procedures will run.

   Instname is the login name of the instance owner.
4. Migrate the databases, if any. Use the **migrate database** command to migrate your databases:

   ```
   db2 migrate database database_alias user username using password
   ```

   where

database_alias is the name or the alias of the database you want to migrate.

username and ***password*** refer to a user with SYSADM authority.

3.12 Case Study

Your company has chosen DB2 9.5 Enterprise Server Edition on a Windows machine as your data server. Currently you have DB2 9.5 Personal Edition installed on that machine, because you were learning DB2 on your own time. To install DB2 9.5 Enterprise Server Edition, you do not need to uninstall the DB2 Personal Edition; you can either install a new copy or migrate your existing DB2 9.5 Personal Edition to DB2 9.5 Enterprise Server Edition. You decide to migrate because you want to migrate one of your databases for further testing purposes. When you run the DB2 9.5 Enterprise Server Edition **db2setup** command, the installation starts, but you receive the warning message shown in Figure 3.34.

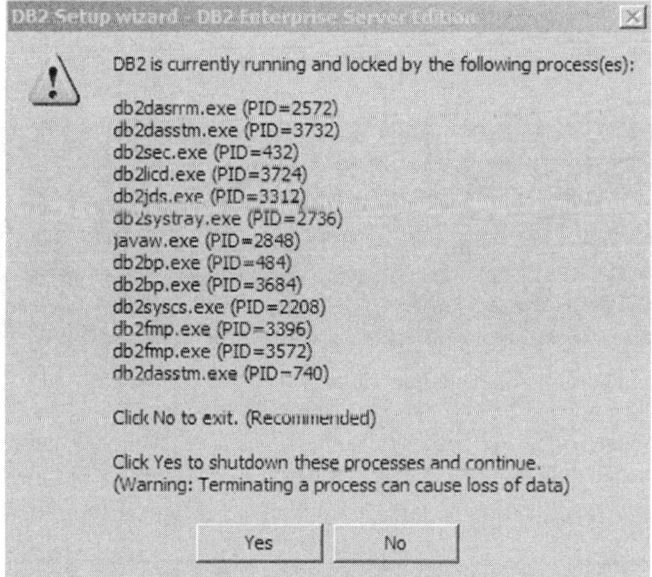

Figure 3.34 Shutting down processes on Windows

You click *Yes* because you were using DB2 PE for training purposes. After this, the installation successfully completes.

Next you issue the command **db2licm -l** to confirm you installed the right product and to review the license status. Figure 3.35 shows the output of the command.

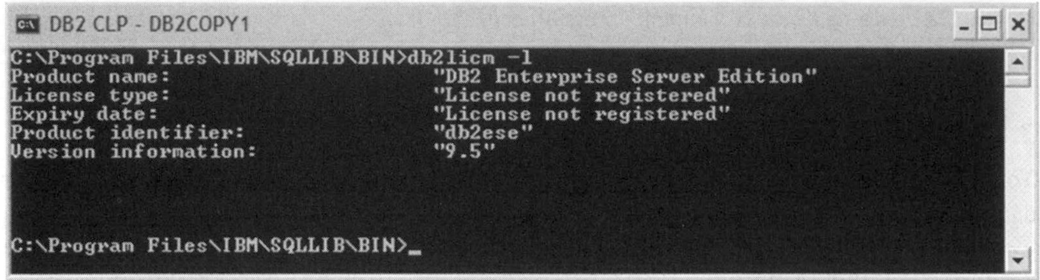

Figure 3.35 Output from the db2licm command

The response confirms that you have DB2 Enterprise Server Edition installed, but now you realize it is not yet *registered*. You tell this to your manager, who calls the 1-800-IBM-SERV number to buy a permanent license.

Next, you issue the **`db2level`** command to ensure you are at the latest Fix Pack. Figure 3.36 shows the command's output.

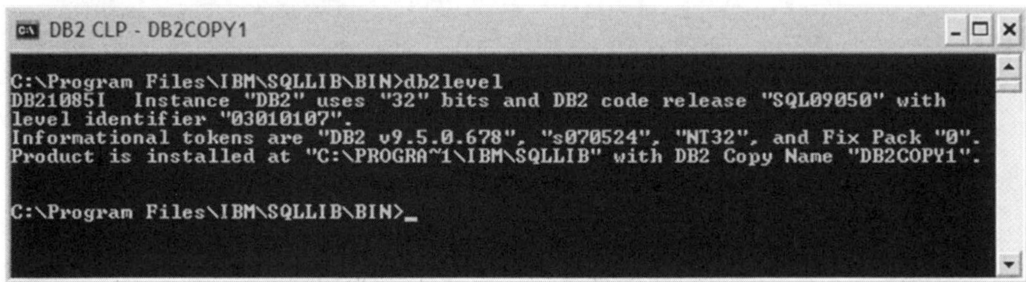

Figure 3.36 Output from the db2licm command

You notice that you are still at Fix Pack 0 (also known as base level or General Availability [GA] level). Since you know that Fix Pack 1 has just been released, you go to the IBM support Web site and download Fix Pack 1. Figure 3.37 shows the DB2 technical support Web site.

> **NOTE** At the time this book was written, DB2 9.5 was still in open beta; therefore, Fix Pack 1 was not available. We use this Fix Pack number hypothetically to illustrate how to work with Fix Packs.

> **NOTE** Web site content changes constantly. The DB2 Technical Support Web site may change in the future or may not look the same as shown in Figure 3.37.

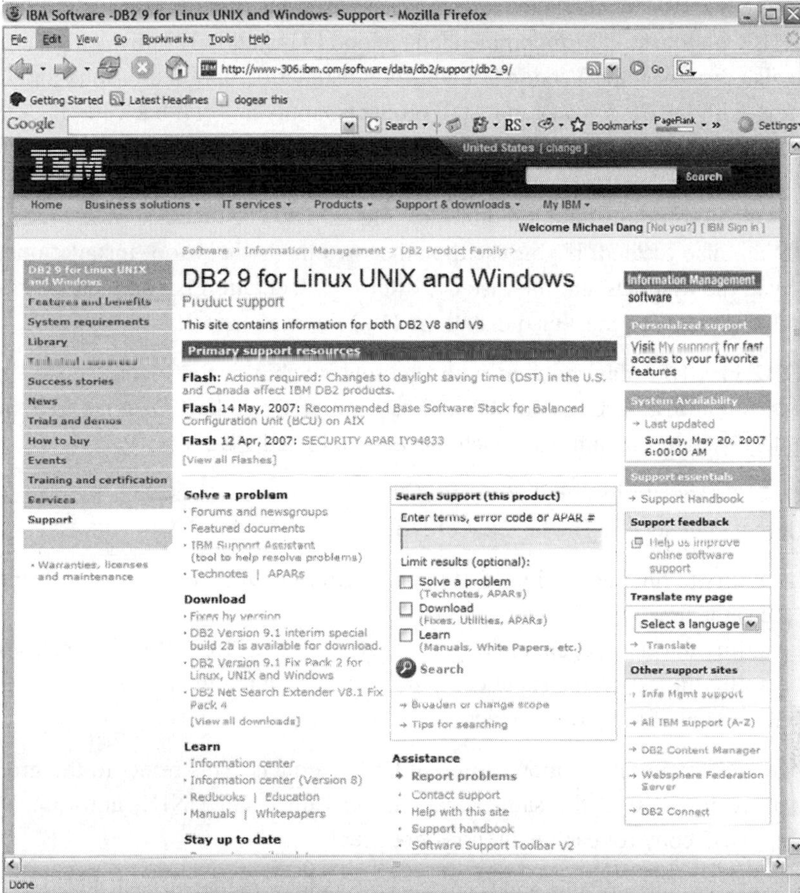

Figure 3.37 The DB2 technical support Web site

After applying Fix Pack 1, you again issue the **db2level** command to confirm it now shows the right Fix Pack level.

Now your company is ready to start working with DB2!

3.13 Summary

In this chapter we discussed four DB2 installation methods:

- Using the DB2 Setup Wizard
- Using a response file
- Using the **db2_install** script
- Using manual installation of DB2 payload files

The first two methods are available on all supported platforms; the last two are only available on Linux and UNIX platforms. The recommended method to install DB2 is by using the DB2 Setup Wizard. We also discussed the Version 9.5 non-root installation option on Linux and UNIX platforms. Starting with DB2 9.5, you can install products, apply and roll back Fix Packs, configure instances, add features, or uninstall products as a non-root user. If you use the DB2 Setup Wizard or the response file methods, you have the choice to create a DB2 instance and the DAS except during the non-root installation on Linux and UNIX. The instance owner user ID and the DAS user ID are also created. If you use the other two methods in root installations, you must manually create the user IDs and the instance after the installation is completed. If you use the manual install method, you must also install the DB2 license manually.

To install DB2 in a DPF environment with multiple machines, the recommended installation method is the Silent install. Copy the DB2 install image from the CD-ROM to a shared disk; then run the DB2 setup program from each machine to install DB2 locally.

A DB2 copy is a separate installation copy of the DB2 9 code. Each DB2 copy can be at the same or different code levels. The benefits of DB2 copies include

- The ability to run applications that require different DB2 versions on the same machine at the same time.
- The ability to run independent copies of DB2 products for different functions.
- The ability to test on the same computer before moving the production database to the latter version of the DB2 product.

A DB2 copy can contain one or more different DB2 products. This refers to the group of DB2 products that are installed at the same location. On Linux and UNIX, non-root installations allow only one DB2 copy for each valid non-root user.

A DB2 Fix Pack contains updates and fixes for problems or defects found during IBM testing, and customer reports. These fixes are also known as Authorized Program Analysis Reports or APARs for short. Fix Packs are cumulative and it is recommended that you keep your DB2 environment running at the latest Fix Pack level to ensure a low-incident operation.

3.14 Review Questions

1. What DB2 installation methods are available on Windows?
2. With a non-root installation, can the user select an installation directory?
3. What is the name of the default instance created by the DB2 Setup Wizard during installation on Linux and UNIX?
4. What is a DB2 Fix Pack also known as?
5. On Linux and UNIX, where are installation logs generated by default? Can you redirect them to a different location?
6. On Windows, where are installation logs generated by default? Can you redirect them to a different location?

7. Two user groups are optionally created on Windows during a DB2 install. What are they?
8. What command needs to be run after you install a DB2 Fix Pack in a root installation on Linux or UNIX?
9. What user rights are granted to an instance owner during installation on Windows?
10. What authority must a user have to install DB2 on Windows?
11. Which of the following is a valid method for installing DB2 on Windows?
    A. The **db2_install** script
    B. The DB2 Setup Wizard
    C. The **db2setup.exe** program
    D. Using the operating system's Add or Remove program utility under the Control Panel
12. Which of the following allows you to install DB2 unattended?
    A. The **db2_install** script
    B. The DB2 Setup Wizard
    C. A response file
    D. Smitty on AIX
13. Which of the following is the TCP/IP port the DB2 Setup Wizard uses to configure the default DB2 instance during installation (assuming TCP/IP is enabled on the system)?
    A. 6000
    B. 20000
    C. 50000
    D. 5000
14. What authority is required for a user to run the db2rfe command in a non-root installation on Linux and UNIX?
    A. Instance owner authority
    B. DAS user authority
    C. Local Administrator authority
    D. Root authority
15. Which of the following user IDs is used by the DB2 GUI tools to perform administration tasks against the local server database instances and databases?
    A. The DAS user ID
    B. The instance owner user ID
    C. The fenced user ID
    D. The DB2 user ID
16. Which of the following is *not* a valid method of creating a response file on Windows?
    A. Using the DB2 Setup Wizard to save the setup and configuration data
    B. Using the **db2_install** script to save the setup and configuration data
    C. Using the response file generator
    D. Modifying one of the sample response files that are provided

17. During installation, which of the following methods prompts you to enter the product keyword (e.g., DB2.ESE, DB2.WSE) for the product you want to install?
    A. The DB2 Setup Wizard
    B. A response file install
    C. The **db2_install** script
    D. Smitty on AIX
18. Which of the following commands should be used to install DB2 on Linux and UNIX using a response file?
    A. **db2setup –r response_file**
    B. **setup /U response_file**
    C. **install –r response_file**
    D. **response_install /U response_file**
19. Which of the following *cannot* be used to install a DB2 license?
    A. The **db2licm** command
    B. The DB2 License Center
    C. The DB2 Setup Wizard
    D. The **db2_install** script
20. Which command is used to provide information about DB2 database systems and features installed on your Linux and UNIX systems?
    A. The **db2licm** command
    B. The **db2cc** command
    C. The **db2ls** command
    D. The **db2level** command

CHAPTER 4

Using the DB2 Tools

How do you work with DB2? How do you issue SQL and/or XQuery statements and enter DB2 commands? Are there graphical tools that can make your administration tasks easier? This chapter provides the answers to all of these questions. DB2 provides a wide range of tools, both graphical and command driven, to help you work with DB2.

In this chapter you will learn about:

- Database command line tools
- Web-based tools
- Database administration tools
- The DB2 information center
- Monitoring tools
- Set up tools
- Application development tools

4.1 DB2 Tools: The Big Picture

Figure 4.1 shows most of the DB2 tools available from the **IBM DB2** menu on the Windows platform and the sequence of items to click to start them. These same tools (except the Command Window and a few others) are available on the Linux and UNIX platforms.

The tools that you see in Figure 4.1 are of two types: command driven and non-command driven. In the next section you will learn about command-driven tools, and in Section 4.4, General Administration Tools, you will be presented with the non-command-driven tools, which are available only using a graphical interface. In most cases you can perform the same DB2 commands, SQL statements, and XQuery statements using either type of tools.

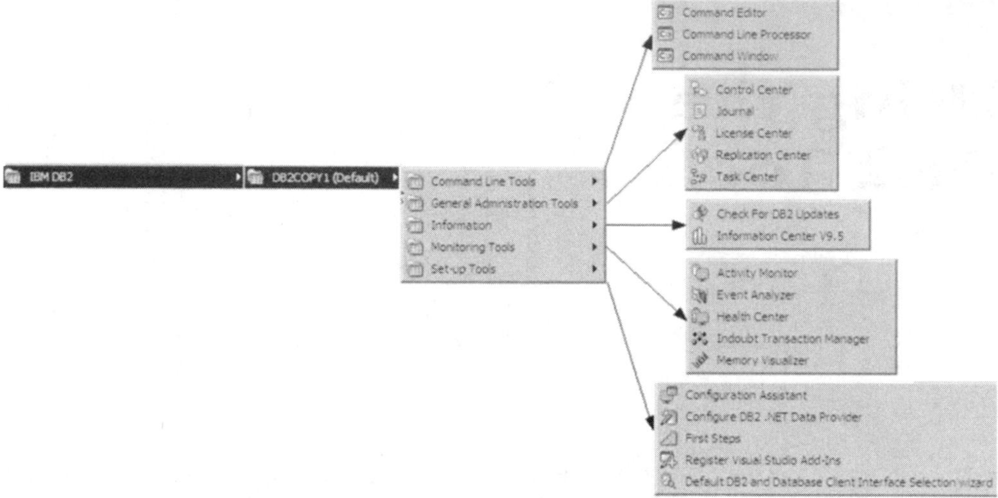

Figure 4.1 The IBM DB2 menu

> **NOTE** Some of the tools described in this section are deprecated in version 9.5, that is, they are still part of the product, but will not be further enhanced. This is done in favor of a new strategy with respect to tools, which is to provide them decoupled from the DB2 code, as separate downloadable Web-based tools. The tools will not only work with DB2, but also with other IBM Data servers; therefore, their name starts with "Data Server" rather than "DB2" as in the case of the Data Server Administration Console (DSAC) Web-based tool. DSAC is described in more detail in Section 4.4, General Administration Tools.

4.2 The Command-Line Tools

All DB2 operations are invoked by DB2 commands, SQL statements, or XQuery statements. For example, to back up a database, you use the **BACKUP DATABASE** command. To create a table, you use the **CREATE TABLE** SQL statement. To parse an XML document you use the FLWOR expression. All of these commands, SQL statements, and XQuery statements can be entered using the command-line tools.

The command-line tools consist of the Command Line Processor (CLP), the Command Window (Windows platform only), and the Command Editor. Since they are command driven, you must have some knowledge of DB2 commands and SQL statements to use them.

> **NOTE** In this chapter we use **DB2 commands** to refer to both types of commands: DB2 system commands and DB2 CLP commands. When a section is only applicable to a given type of command, it will be explicitly indicated. Refer to Section 2.1, SQL Statements, XQuery Statements, and DB2 Commands, for an explanation about the differences between these two types of commands.

4.2.1 The Command Line Processor and the Command Window

The DB2 CLP and the DB2 Command Window are text-based tools used to interact with the DB2 engine. Figure 4.2 shows the relationship between the CLP and the Command Window. Compare each line in the Windows machine versus the Linux/UNIX machine. The equivalent line in each machine has been aligned in the figure.

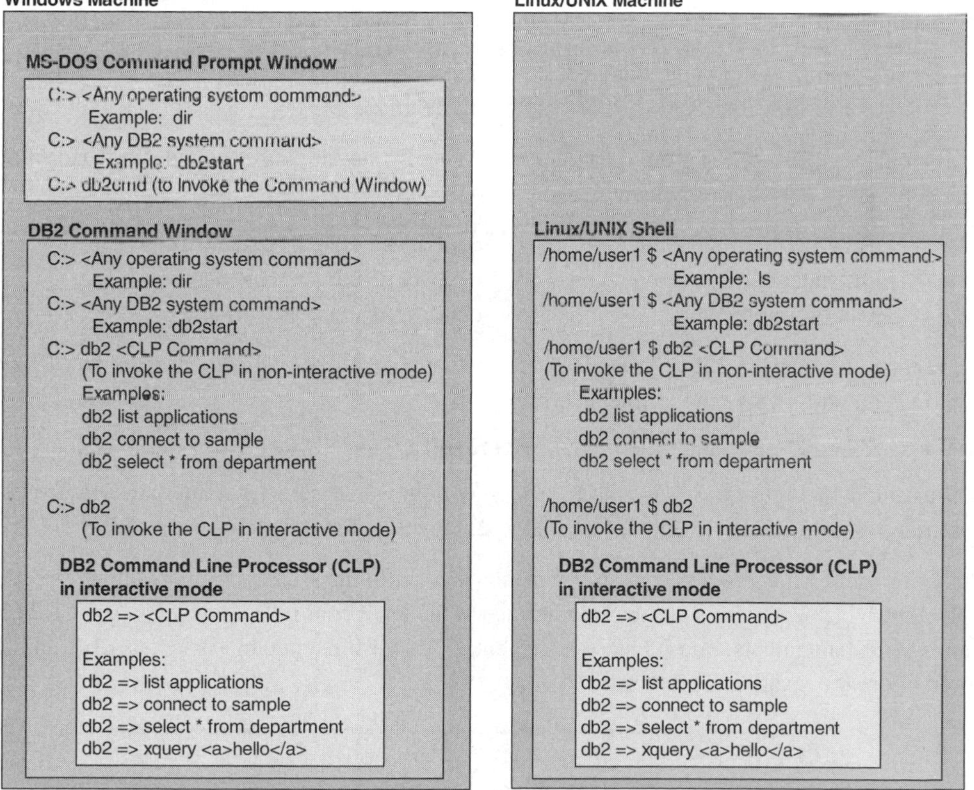

Figure 4.2 The Command Line Processor versus the Command Window

The **Command Window** is only available on Windows; this is due to some architecture differences in Windows versus Linux and UNIX. If you are familiar with the Linux and UNIX platforms, you can think of the Command Window on Windows as the Linux/UNIX shell. Figure 4.2 illustrates this: The commands and statements inside the DB2 Command Window box on the left-hand side of the figure are equivalent to the ones inside the Linux/UNIX shell box on the right-hand side of the figure.

To start the Command Window, click on **Start > Programs > IBM DB2 > DB2COPY1 (Default) > Command Line Tools > Command Window** (see Figure 4.1). Alternatively, to invoke the Command Window from a MSDOS window, issue the command **db2cmd.** This command spawns another window which displays *DB2 CLP* in the title bar. Note that the Command Window looks like any MS-DOS window except for this title bar.

From an MS-DOS window, you can perform operating system commands and DB2 system commands but not DB2 CLP commands, SQL statements, or Xquery statements. However, you can perform all of these from a Command Window.

For example, as shown in Figure 4.2, from the MS-DOS window you can execute the following:

- Operating system commands: **dir**
- DB2 system commands: **db2start**

You can also perform these from the Command Window, and in addition you can perform DB2 CLP commands and SQL statements:

- DB2 CLP command: **db2 list applications**
- SQL statements: **db2 SELECT * FROM department**
- XQuery statements: **db2 "xquery <a>hello</a>"**

If you try to execute a CLP command, SQL statement, or XQuery statement from an MS-DOS window, you will receive the following error:

```
DB21061E Command line environment not initialized
```

as illustrated in Figure 4.3. The figure also shows how the same statement works from the Command Window after it is invoked with the **db2cmd** command.

The **Command Line Processor** is an application written in the C language containing embedded SQL. It provides you with a text-based interface to the DB2 engine that lets you issue CLP commands, SQL statements, and XQuery statements. The CLP executable is called **db2** and it is stored under the ...sqllib/bin directory.

> **NOTE** We recommend that you learn how to use the Command Line Processor, as it is the common tool available with all DB2 versions and clients.

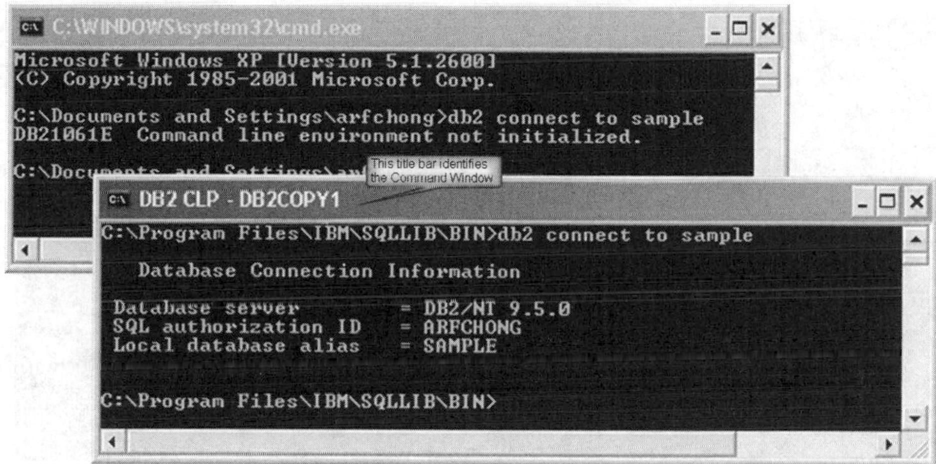

Figure 4.3 Invoking the Command Window from an MS-DOS command prompt

4.2.1.1 Methods to Work with the CLP

There are three ways to issue a DB2 command or SQL statement with the CLP: interactive mode, non-interactive mode, and non-interactive mode using a file as input. These methods are discussed in the following sections.

Method 1: Interactive Mode

You start the CLP in interactive mode by clicking on **Start** > **Programs** > **IBM DB2** > **DB2COPY1 (Default)** > **Command Line Tools** > **Command Line Processor** (see Figure 4.1). Alternatively, from the Command Window or Linux/UNIX shell, you start the CLP in interactive mode by entering **db2** and pressing Enter as shown in Figure 4.4.

After you invoke the CLP in interactive mode, a few messages will appear on the screen, and then your command prompt will change to **db2 =>.** This prompt indicates that you are in interactive mode and that you can type any DB2 CLP command, SQL statement, or XQuery statement.

Table 4.1 lists some common CLP interactive mode commands. The underlined letter in the command shows the shortcut that you can use to invoke the command.

Figure 4.5 shows a few examples of the commands in Table 4.1 in action.

Method 2: Non-Interactive Mode

To work with the CLP in non-interactive mode is equivalent to working with the DB2 Command Window (on Windows) or the Linux/UNIX shell. If you start the CLP in interactive mode, entering the **quit** command takes you to the CLP in non-interactive mode. In this mode you need to prefix the CLP command or SQL statement with the **db2** executable. For example:

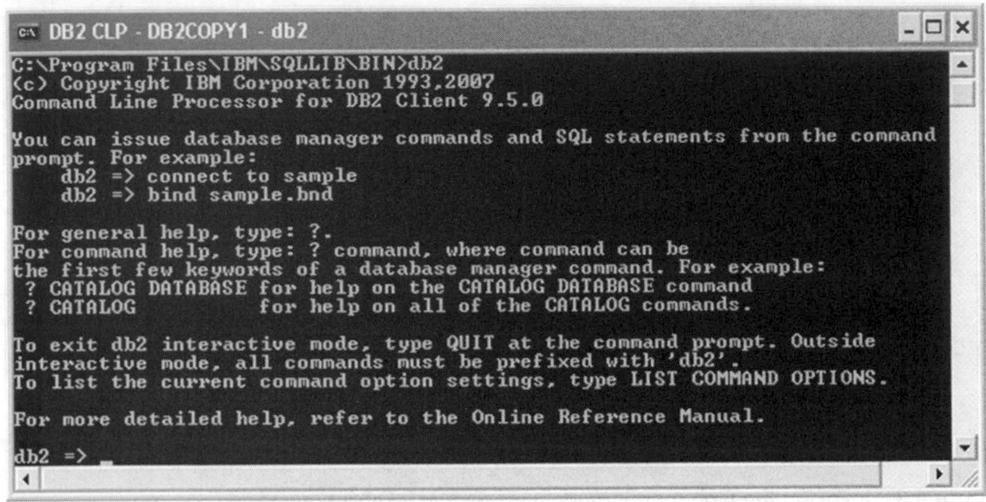

Figure 4.4 The Command Line Processor in interactive mode

Table 4.1 Useful CLP Commands for Working with the CLP in Interactive Mode

Command	Explanation	Example
history	Lists the last 20 commands entered and prefixes each with a number. The maximum number of commands kept in memory can be customized with the DB2 registry variable DB2_CLP_HISTSIZE (see Chapter 5 for information about DB2 registry variables).	**History**
runcmd <*n*>	Reexecutes command number *n* from the list given by the **history** command. If *n* is not specified (or *n* = -1), the previous command is invoked.	To reexecute the third command in the history list: **r 3**
edit <*n*>	Edits the command number *n* using an editor defined by the DB2 registry variable DB2_CLP_EDITOR. If not set, this uses the vi editor on Linux/UNIX and Notepad on Windows.	To edit the fifth command in the history list: **e 5**
Exclamation mark (!)	This is the escape character that lets you issue operating system commands from within the CLP interactive mode.	**!dir**

```
db2 connect to sample
db2 list applications all
db2 select * from employee
db2 "xquery <name>Raul</name>"
```

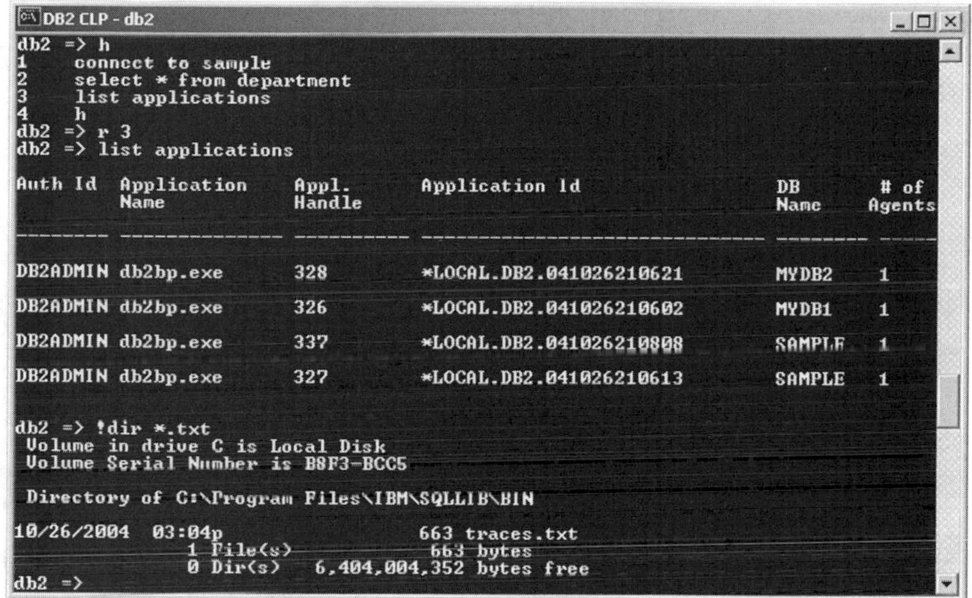
DB2 CLP - db2
db2 => h
1 connect to sample
2 select * from department
3 list applications
4 h
db2 => r 3
db2 => list applications
Auth Id Application Name Appl. Handle Application Id DB Name # of Agents
DB2ADMIN db2bp.exe 328 *LOCAL.DB2.041026210621 MYDB2 1
DB2ADMIN db2bp.exe 326 *LOCAL.DB2.041026210602 MYDB1 1
DB2ADMIN db2bp.exe 337 *LOCAL.DB2.041026210808 SAMPLE 1
DB2ADMIN db2bp.exe 327 *LOCAL.DB2.041026210613 SAMPLE 1
db2 => !dir *.txt
Volume in drive C is Local Disk
Volume Serial Number is B8F3-BCC5
Directory of C:\Program Files\IBM\SQLLIB\BIN
10/26/2004 03:04p 663 traces.txt
1 File(s) 663 bytes
0 Dir(s) 6,404,004,352 bytes free
db2 =>

Figure 4.5 Examples of CLP commands in interactive mode

Using this method you can execute operating system commands in addition to DB2 commands, SQL statements, and XQuery statements from the same window or session.

> **NOTE** References to the Command Window and the CLP on Windows platforms are sometimes used interchangeably in DB2 books to indicate the use of a command-line interface as opposed to a GUI tool.

In practice, many DB2 users prefer to work in this environment because they can use some shortcut key strokes, such as pressing the up arrow key to repeat the last commands on Windows, or to take advantage of operating system mechanisms like piping the output of the CLP to the **more** command on Linux and UNIX to display the output in portions.

Every time you issue the **db2** executable, a "CLP session" is created where a front-end process is invoked. This takes the rest of the statement as input and then closes the process. For example, when you issue

```
db2 list db directory
```

db2 invokes a CLP front-end process that takes **list db directory** as input. Once the CLP digests this command, it implicitly issues the **quit** command to end the CLP front-end process. The front-end and back-end processes are discussed in more detail later in this chapter.

Figure 4.6 shows the CLP in non-interactive mode.

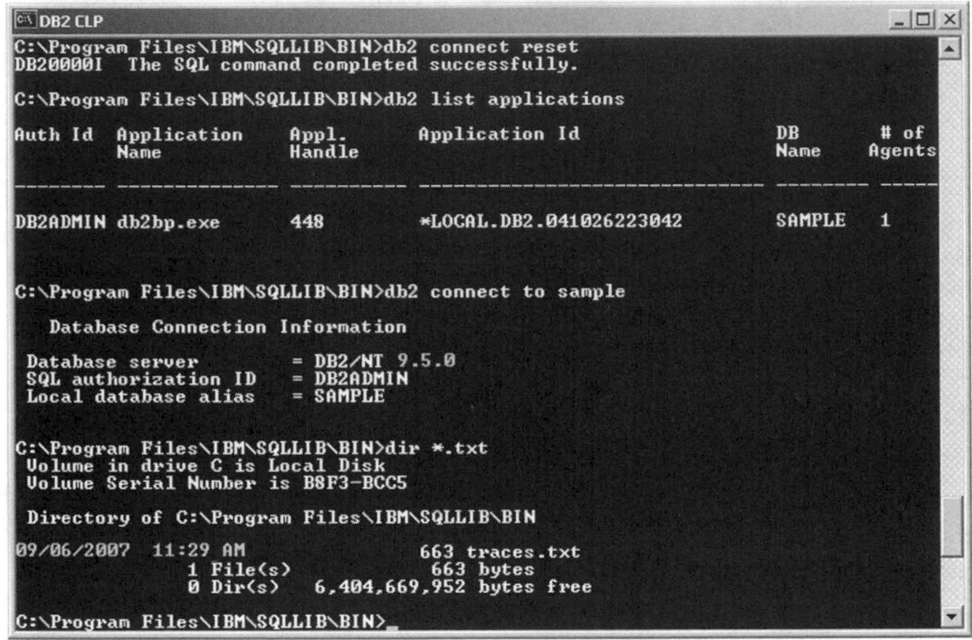

Figure 4.6 The Command Line Processor in non-interactive mode

When invoking the CLP in non-interactive mode, double quotes (") enclosing the CLP command, SQL statement, or XQuery statement may be required if these contain special characters that the operating system may interpret as wildcard characters. This is especially important on Linux and UNIX platforms. If double quotes are not used, the error message that DB2 reports will vary depending on where the wildcard character is used in the statement. For example, if you issue this statement:

```
db2 select * from employee
```

you *may* receive the following error message, since the asterisk (*) is a wildcard character:

```
SQL0104N An unexpected token "*" was found following "select"
```

Use double quotes to avoid parsing errors:

```
db2 "select * from employee"
```

A more deceiving example occurs when you use the greater than (>) character. For example, the statement:

```
db2 select lastname from employee where salary > 10000
```

will be first parsed by the operating system, which will interpret **> 10000** as the redirection of the output to the file *10000*. After executing the above statement, your current directory will have a new file with the name *10000* containing a DB2 syntax error message because only **select lastname from employee where salary** was passed to DB2. Again, to resolve this problem, make sure to enclose the statement in double quotes:

```
db2 "select lastname from employee where salary > 10000"
```

This is particularly important as well when working with XQuery since XML documents use tags enclosed in angle brackets (<, >) which the operating system will interpret completely differently.

Method 3: Non-interactive Mode Using a File as Input

The CLP can use a file containing one or more CLP commands or SQL statements and process them one after the other. This is ideal to develop DB2 database scripts. For example, Figure 4.7 shows the contents of the file *myInput.txt*, which we will use as input to the CLP.

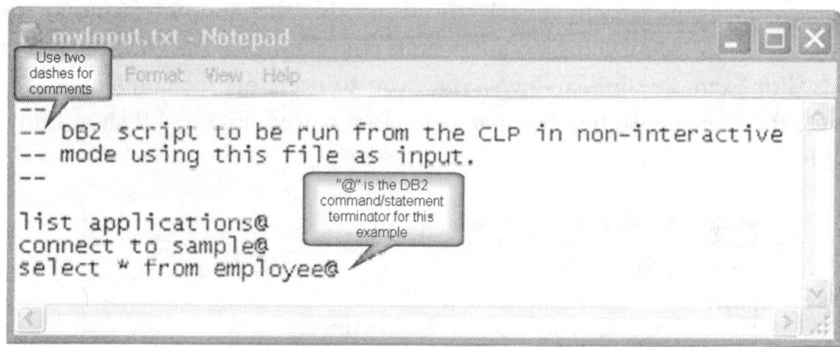

Figure 4.7 Input file to be used by the CLP

To execute this DB2 script file, the **-f** command option (for *file*) followed by the filename is required to indicate to the CLP that this file contains the input. (CLP command options are described in detail in the next section.) If the input file contains a statement terminator character, the **-t** command option (for *terminator*) is required to indicate a terminator character is present. By default, the statement terminator is a semicolon (**;**). If you want to use a different terminator, the ***-dcharacter*** option (for *delimiter*) indicates which delimiter character is being used as the terminator. Use the **-v** option (for *verbose*) to echo the command you are executing. Figure 4.8 provides an example of invoking the CLP using these command options.

> **NOTE** The input file must be a text file. Be aware that invisible characters may cause the DB2 CLP to fail processing the file. If using the Notepad application on Windows, for example, saving the text file with Unicode encoding rather than ANSI encoding will cause this error:
>
> ```
> DB21007E End of file reached while reading the command.
> ```

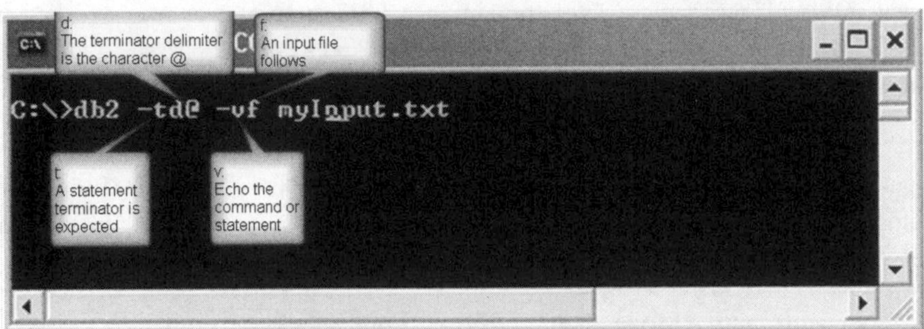

Figure 4.8 Invoking the CLP in non-interactive mode using a file as input

If you prefix each of the CLP commands with **db2** (the CLP executable) in a file and remove the terminator characters, you are effectively converting this file into an operating system script rather than a DB2 script. Depending on the operating system, you may have to make additional modifications. For example, on Windows, you need to use **rem** for comments. You may also need to change the filename so that the *.bat* extension is used. Figure 4.9 shows this for the file *myOS_Input.bat*.

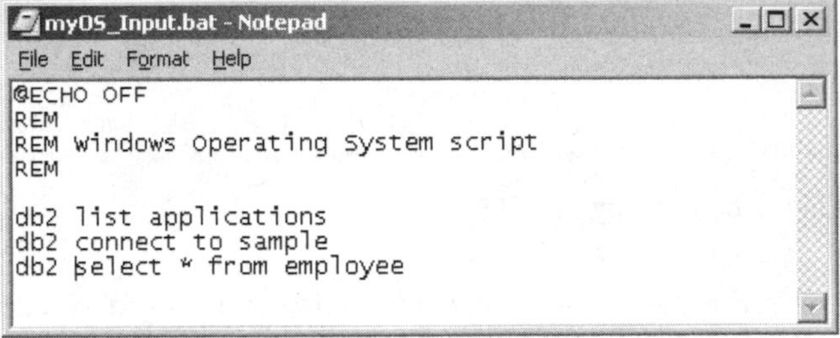

Figure 4.9 Invoking DB2 CLP commands and SQL statements in a Windows script file

On Linux and UNIX platforms, use the pound sign (#) for comments. You may also need to change the permissions of the file so that it is executable. Typically you can use this command to change the file permissions:

```
chmod +x myOS_Input.txt
```

Figure 4.10 shows the same script for a Linux or UNIX platform.

> **NOTE** DB2 scripts do not accept parameters, but operating system scripts do. In other words, if you need to invoke your scripts with parameters, you need to use operating system scripts.

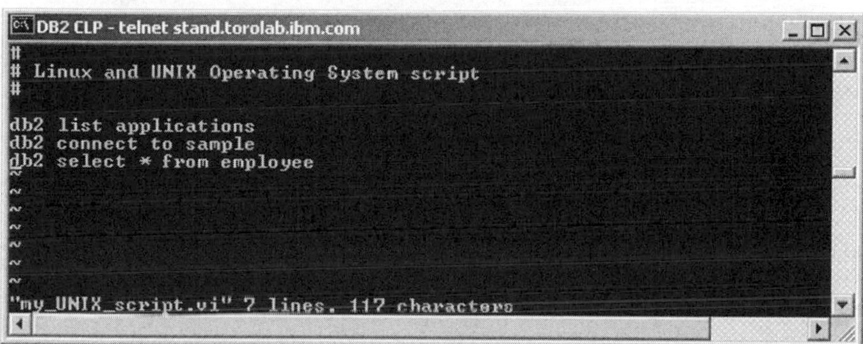

Figure 4.10 Invoking DB2 CLP commands and SQL statements in a Linux/UNIX script file

4.2.1.2 CLP Command Options

The CLP is just another program designed to interact with DB2. Like many other programs, the CLP has been designed to accept several parameter options. The CLP command **`list command options`** displays the available CLP command option parameters (see Figure 4.11).

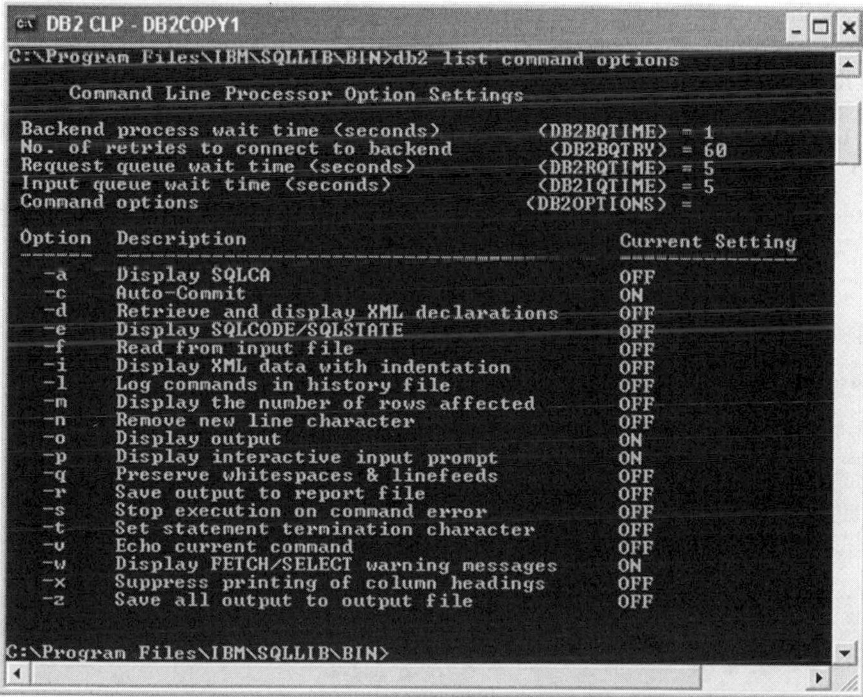

Figure 4.11 CLP command options

To turn on an option, use a dash (-) in the command line. To turn off an option, use a plus symbol (+). Some options are on (or off) by default. For example, to enable autocommit, invoke the CLP as follows:

```
db2 -c insert into employee (firstnme) values ('Raul')
```

After you execute this command, a **COMMIT** statement is automatically issued because autocommit is enabled. (As you can see in Figure 4.11, the Auto-Commit option was already on by default, so including **-c** in the above example is not necessary.)

To disable autocommit, invoke the CLP as follows:

```
db2 +c insert into employee (firstnme) values ('Raul')
```

Note that specifying a command option in the **db2** command applies only to that session of the CLP. Issuing the **db2** command without an option will use the default command option values, or the ones contained in the DB2OPTIONS registry variable, which we discuss later in this section.

You can also change a command option when working with the CLP in interactive mode using the following command:

```
update command options using option value option value...
```

Figure 4.12 shows an example where the **v** option (verbose) is used. This option causes the command or statement to be repeated or echoed when executed as discussed earlier. In Figure 4.12, note that the **SELECT * FROM department** statement is echoed.

If you would like the changes to your CLP options effective across all your CLP sessions, you can set the DB2OPTIONS registry variable with the desired options. In the command:

```
db2set db2options="-v -z myfile.log"
```

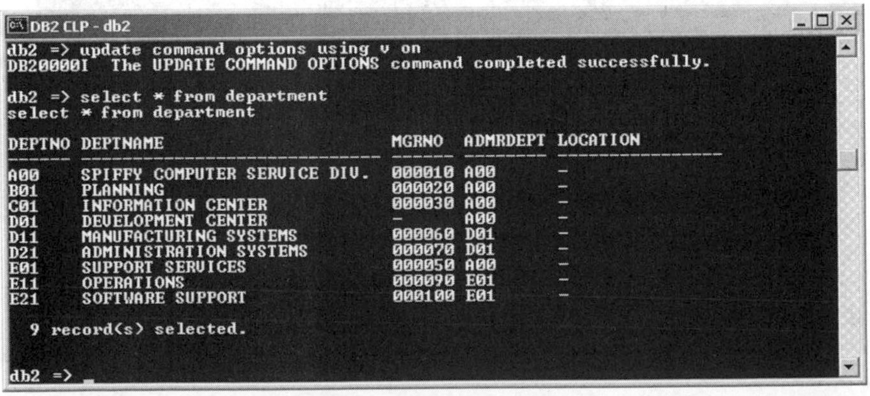

```
DB2 CLP - db2
db2 => update command options using v on
DB20000I  The UPDATE COMMAND OPTIONS command completed successfully.

db2 => select * from department
select * from department

DEPTNO DEPTNAME                             MGRNO  ADMRDEPT LOCATION
------ ------------------------------------ ------ -------- ----------------
A00    SPIFFY COMPUTER SERVICE DIV.         000010 A00      -
B01    PLANNING                             000020 A00      -
C01    INFORMATION CENTER                   000030 A00      -
D01    DEVELOPMENT CENTER                   -      A00      -
D11    MANUFACTURING SYSTEMS                000060 D01      -
D21    ADMINISTRATION SYSTEMS               000070 D01      -
E01    SUPPORT SERVICES                     000050 A00      -
E11    OPERATIONS                           000090 E01      -
E21    SOFTWARE SUPPORT                     000100 E01      -

  9 record(s) selected.


db2 =>
```

Figure 4.12 The CLP in interactive mode

the DB2OPTIONS registry variable is set so that any command executed will be echoed (**-v** option), and the output will be spooled in the file *myfile.log* (**-z myfile.log** option). The changes take effect immediately for the current session and for any other new CLP sessions that you start.

To reset the values to the default, issue this command:

```
db2set db2options=
```

DB2 registry variables are explained in detail in Chapter 5, Understanding the DB2 Environment, DB2 Instances, and Databases.

4.2.1.3 Obtaining Help Information from the CLP

One of the most useful CLP commands is the help command represented by a question mark (**?**). This command provides help on SQL error codes (SQLCODE), DB2 messages, and CLP command syntax. For example:

```
db2 ? SQL0104N
db2 ? DB21004E
db2 ? list applications
```

In addition, using the help command by itself displays the entire list of CLP commands, as shown in Figure 4.13.

NOTE The help (**?**) command can display CLP command syntax, but not SQL statement syntax. Refer to the *DB2 SQL Reference* manual for SQL statement syntax.

Figure 4.14 shows other examples of the help (**?**) command.

4.2.1.4 Line Continuation

There are two ways to use line continuation from the CLP: with the backslash character and with the delimiter terminator character.

Method 1: Using the Backslash (\) Character

You can use the backslash (****) character in either interactive or non-interactive mode. Figure 4.15 first shows an example of using the interactive mode, followed by an example of using the non-interactive mode.

Notice that after entering **** and pressing Enter, the prompt changes to:

```
db2 (cont.) =>
```

Method 2: Using a Delimiter Terminator Character with the CLP in Interactive Mode

Using this method, the CLP is invoked in interactive mode using the terminator delimiter option. For example:

```
db2 -td!
```

After entering this command and pressing Enter, the CLP is invoked in interactive mode. You can wrap commands onto multiple lines until you type the terminator character, which is the exclamation mark (**!**) in the example shown in Figure 4.16.

Use this method when you have statements that include carriage returns. If you copy and paste one of these statements into the CLP, the carriage returns will cause the statement to continue in another line, which is acceptable, because the CLP processes the command after the terminator character is entered.

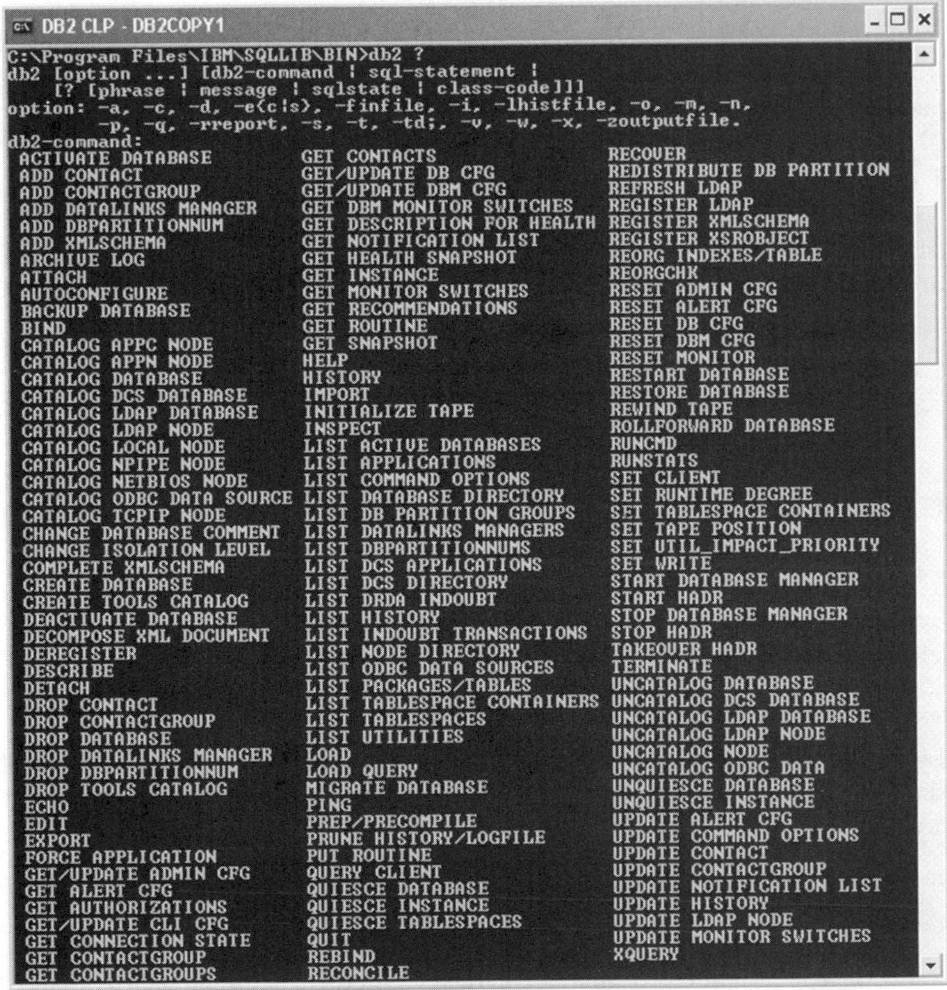

Figure 4.13 Output of the command db2 ?

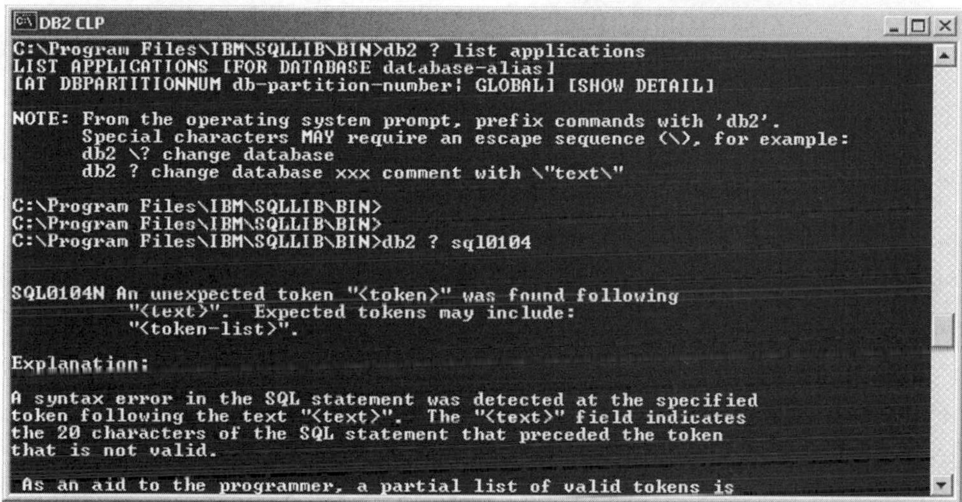

Figure 4.14 The CLP help (?) command

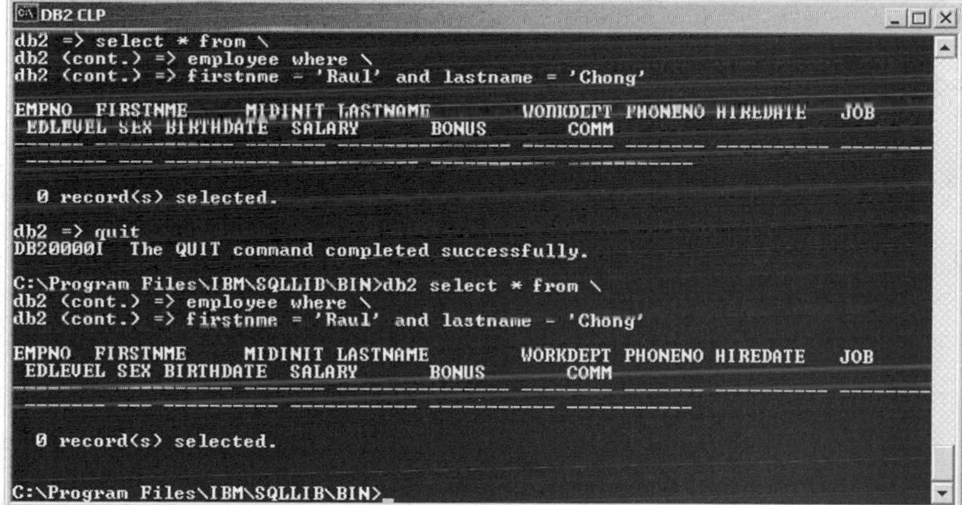

Figure 4.15 Line continuation in the CLP using the backslash continuation character

The following statement has one carriage return character after **`staff`** and one after **`Edwards;`** therefore, use method 2 to start the DB2 CLP in interactive mode:

```
select * from staff
where name = 'Edwards'
and job = 'Sales'
```

After you copy and paste the statement into the CLP, enter the terminator character and press Enter to execute it.

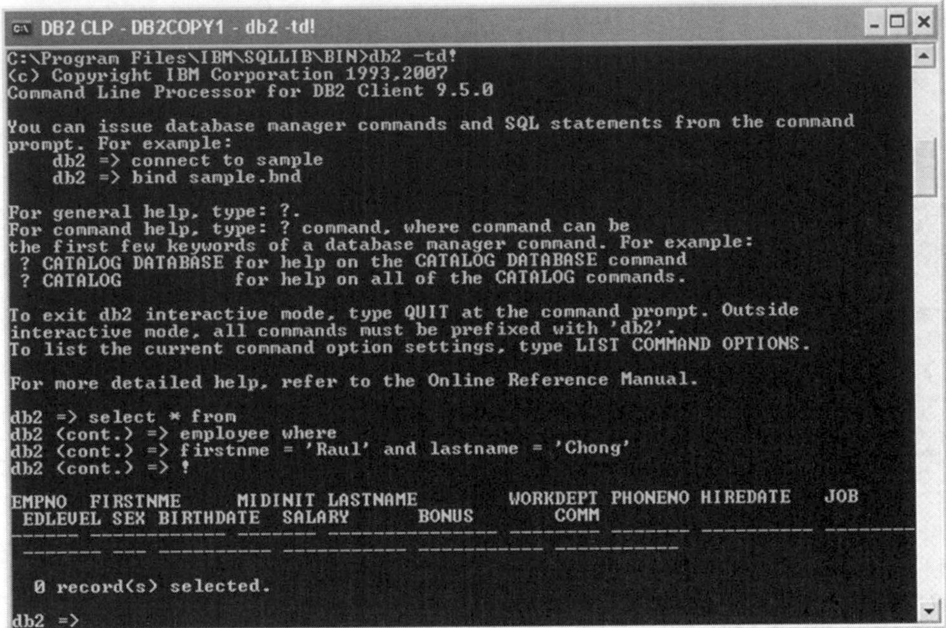

DB2 CLP - DB2COPY1 - db2 -td!
C:\Program Files\IBM\SQLLIB\BIN>db2 -td!
(c) Copyright IBM Corporation 1993,2007
Command Line Processor for DB2 Client 9.5.0
You can issue database manager commands and SQL statements from the command
prompt. For example:
db2 => connect to sample
db2 => bind sample.bnd
For general help, type: ?.
For command help, type: ? command, where command can be
the first few keywords of a database manager command. For example:
? CATALOG DATABASE for help on the CATALOG DATABASE command
? CATALOG for help on all of the CATALOG commands.
To exit db2 interactive mode, type QUIT at the command prompt. Outside
interactive mode, all commands must be prefixed with 'db2'.
To list the current command option settings, type LIST COMMAND OPTIONS.
For more detailed help, refer to the Online Reference Manual.
db2 => select * from
db2 (cont.) => employee where
db2 (cont.) => firstnme = 'Raul' and lastname = 'Chong'
db2 (cont.) => !
EMPNO FIRSTNME MIDINIT LASTNAME WORKDEPT PHONENO HIREDATE JOB
EDLEVEL SEX BIRTHDATE SALARY BONUS COMM
0 record(s) selected.
db2 =>

Figure 4.16 Line continuation in the CLP using a delimiter termination character in interactive mode

4.2.1.5 The CLP Front-End and Back-End Processes

The CLP has both front-end and a back-end processes. The front-end allows you to perform actions without connecting to a database. For example, issuing the command:

```
db2 list db directory
```

does not require a connection to a database. Depending on the operation, the instance need not be started either.

The back-end process is needed when you perform actions against a database. The back-end process is created when you connect to the database in a CLP session and can be identified by the application name *db2bp*. Figure 4.17 shows the output of the **list applications** command, which shows this thread indicating a connection to the *sample* database.

To remove the connection to a database, issue the **connect reset** statement, the **terminate** command, or the **disconnect** statement. **Connect reset** and **terminate** will work even if the process is in the middle of a unit of work. **Disconnect** only works when there is no active unit of work. Closing a window or session without previously issuing a **terminate** command will close the CLP application and front-end process and remove the connection to the database, but does not guarantee that the back-end process will be terminated.

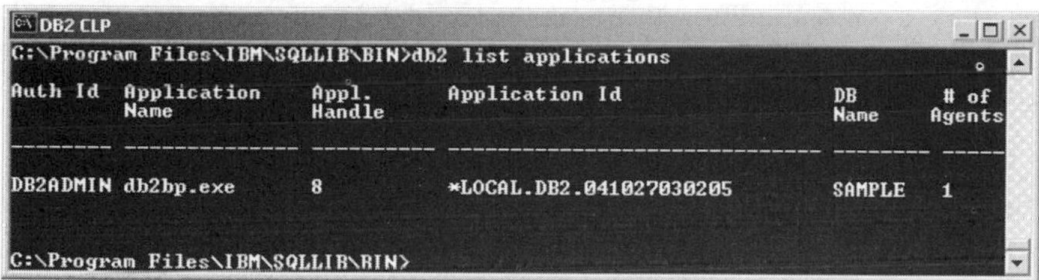
```
C:\Program Files\IBM\SQLLIB\BIN>db2 list applications

Auth Id  Application    Appl.      Application Id                 DB       # of
         Name           Handle                                    Name     Agents
-------- -------------- ---------- ------------------------------ -------- -----
DB2ADMIN db2bp.exe      8          *LOCAL.DB2.041027030205        SAMPLE   1

C:\Program Files\IBM\SQLLIB\BIN>
```

Figure 4.17 The CLP back-end process

> **NOTE** The **terminate** command is the only one that guarantees the back-end process is indeed terminated. Even if the **list applications** command does not display the *db2bp* back-end process running, use the **terminate** command to be certain.

It is important to make sure that the back-end process is terminated because in some circumstances, a change to a parameter, environment variable, or DB2 registry variable will not take effect until this is performed. For example, in a multi-partition environment, the DB2NODE environment variable is used to indicate which partition is the coordinator. After changing the value of this variable, you must issue a **terminate** command for it to take effect.

> **NOTE** We recommend issuing a **terminate** command before a **db2stop** command. This prevents the back-end process from maintaining an attachment to an instance that is no longer active.

4.2.2 The Command Editor

The **Command Editor** is the graphical user interface (GUI) version of the Command Line Processor. The Command Editor offers several other functions in addition to those provided by the CLP and the Command Window.

- The ability to execute multiple DB2 commands and SQL statements interactively and simultaneously. With the CLP, only one command at a time can be executed interactively. If you want to execute multiple commands, you have to save them in a text file and execute the file with the **-f** option as explained in Section 4.2.1.1, Methods to Work with the CLP.
- The ability to save all the commands you typed in the Command Editor window to a file or as a task to be executed from the Task center.
- The ability to display a Visual Explain output of the access path chosen by the DB2 optimizer for an SQL statement. The Visual Explain tool is discussed in the next section.
- The ability to display results in well-formatted tables.

You can start the Command Editor either from the IBM DB2 menu or from the Control Center. (We will talk about the Control Center in Section 4.4, General Administration Tools.) Alternatively, the command **db2ce** starts it from a command-line prompt.

Figure 4.18 shows the start screen of the Command Editor. The Target field is empty until you click on the *Add* button, which displays the Specify Target window. Select a Target type from the pull-down menu, and then select the database you want to work with in the Available targets pull-down menu.

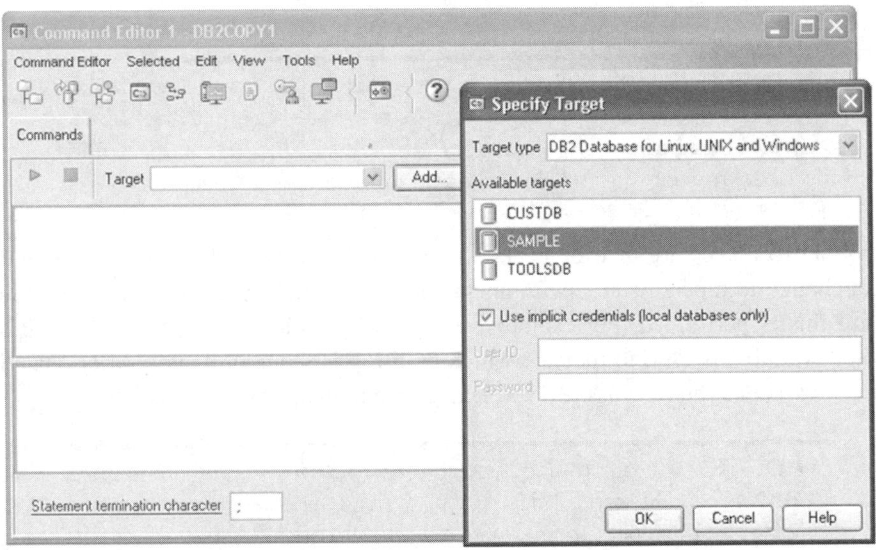

Figure 4.18 The Command Editor lets you choose the database you want to work with.

The Command Editor makes an implicit connection to the database you have chosen. You can then start entering your commands from the command input window (see Figure 4.19).

Figure 4.19 shows the three tabs associated with views in the Command Editor. The tab selected in Figure 4.19 is for the Commands view. This view displays all the commands you have entered. If you want to execute several commands or statements at once, make sure to delimit them with the character specified in the Statement terminator character field (at the bottom of the window). If you entered several commands or statements in the Command Input Window, but would like to execute only a particular one, highlight it. Then you have the following options:

- To execute the command and produce the results, click on the *Execute* button
- To execute the command, produce the results, and the access plan, click on the *Execute and Access Plan* button
- To produce the access plan but not execute the command, click on the *Access Plan* button

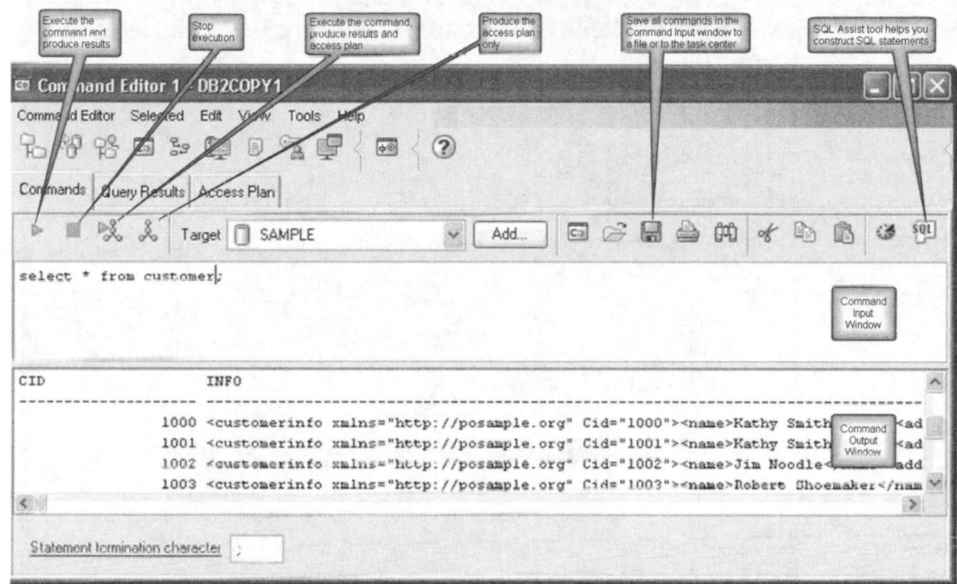

Figure 4.19 The Commands view in the Command Editor

If you choose to execute the command, the results can be displayed in the Command Output Window as shown in Figure 4.19. This is probably the most convenient way of displaying the output, especially when working with XML documents, as you will be able to view at once all the XML documents for all the rows selected. To configure the display of the output this way, make sure to change the display results option under tool settings. From the Command Editor choose **Tools > Tools Settings > Command Editor.** Then uncheck the box **Display results for a single query on the Query Results page.** If you do not change this configuration, you will receive your output in the Query Results view, as shown in Figure 4.20. To view a given XML document, click the button with the three dots.

For non-XML columns, you can directly perform updates by clicking on the corresponding value and making the desired change in the Query Results view. To add or delete an entire row, click the *Add Row* or *Delete Row* button respectively. None of these changes are permanent unless you click on the *Commit* button. If you want to cancel your changes, click on the *Roll Back* button.

If you choose either of the other two options that produce the access plan, a tool called **Visual Explain** is invoked. The next section explains this tool in more detail.

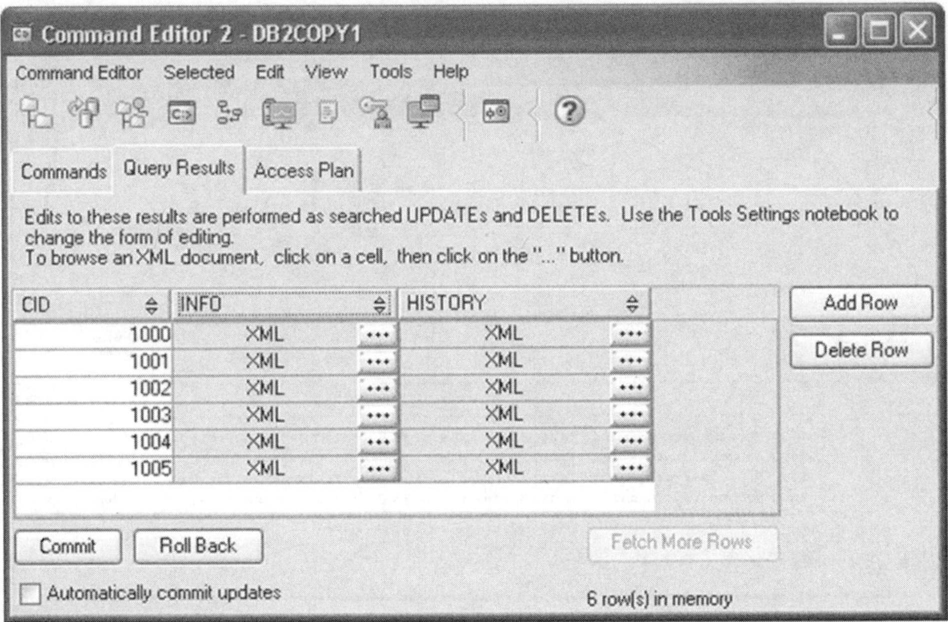

Figure 4.20

4.2.2.1 Visual Explain

DB2 provides an SQL and XQuery facility that stores in "explain" tables detailed information about how DB2 will access the data to satisfy a query request. For example, the information in these explain tables may show that DB2 will scan the table sequentially, or it may show that the data will be accessed through the indexes associated to the table. The method to access the data that DB2 chooses is called the **access plan,** and the particular component of DB2 that makes this decision is called the **DB2 optimizer,** which can be considered the "brain" of DB2. To analyze the access plan, you can use text-based tools like the **`db2exfmt`** and the **`db2expln`** command-line tools; however, it is often useful to display this information in a graph. Use **Visual Explain** to graphically display an access plan for a query.

You can invoke Visual Explain from the Command Editor. Simply enter an SQL or XQuery statement in the Command Editor's Command Input Window, and then press either the *Execute and Access Plan* button or the *Access Plan* button. Figure 4.21 shows the Visual Explain output of the query **`select * from sales.`** In this particular example, the ARFCHONG.SALES table is accessed using a table scan (TBSCAN) with a cost of 7.65 timerons. The smaller "Overview" window is useful when you want to navigate through a large explain. Clicking on a particular section of the overview window will take you to a corresponding section in the larger window. Visual Explain can also be invoked from the Control Center; see Chapter 17, Database Performance Considerations, for more details.

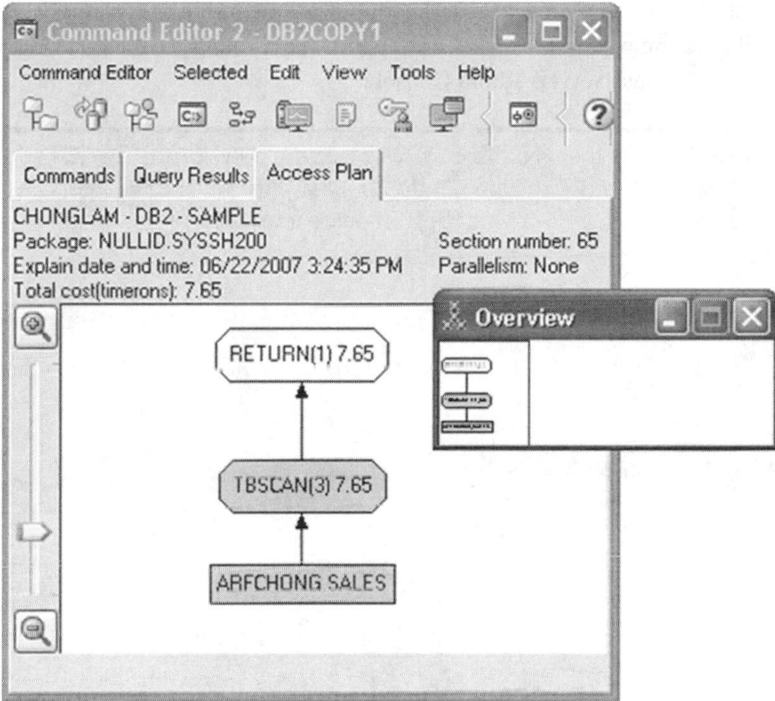

Figure 4.21 The Access Plan view in the Command Editor

9.5

4.3 Web-Based Tools

Web-based tools are not part of the IBM Menu shown in Figure 4.1; however we feel it's important to mention these tools here. The main Web-based tool is the Data Server Administration Console (DSAC).

4.3.1 The Data Server Administration Console

The Data Server Administration Console (DSAC) is a Web-based tool created using numerous open standards, and Web 2.0 technologies such as AJAX. It is a free product for most of its features and downloadable from the Internet. At the time this book was written, there were plans to bundle it with DB2. The DSAC has a smaller disk and memory footprint than previous DB2 tools. You can perform about eighty percent of your administrative tasks using the DSAC. You can use it to manage one DB2 data server, or hundreds of IBM data servers from different platforms such as DB2 for Linux, UNIX and Windows, DB2 for z/OS and IDS. It is fast, simple but powerful, and is task-based. The DSAC has the ability to provide real time and exception-based monitoring, and you can drill down to determine a specific problem. Upgrades to the DSAC are independent of the DB2 server or clients, and this tool does not need the DAS (DB2 Administration server) running, unlike the previous DB2 tools.

The console includes "for-free" and "for-fee" admininstration tooling. The "for-fee" features are grayed out until a license is purchased, and it is applied. Everything from the DSAC is scriptable. Figure 4.22 shows the Data Server Admin Console.

> **NOTE** At the time this book was written, plans for the DSAC had not been finalized. The name of the tool may change, and the interface shown in Figure 4.22 may not be 100 percent accurate.

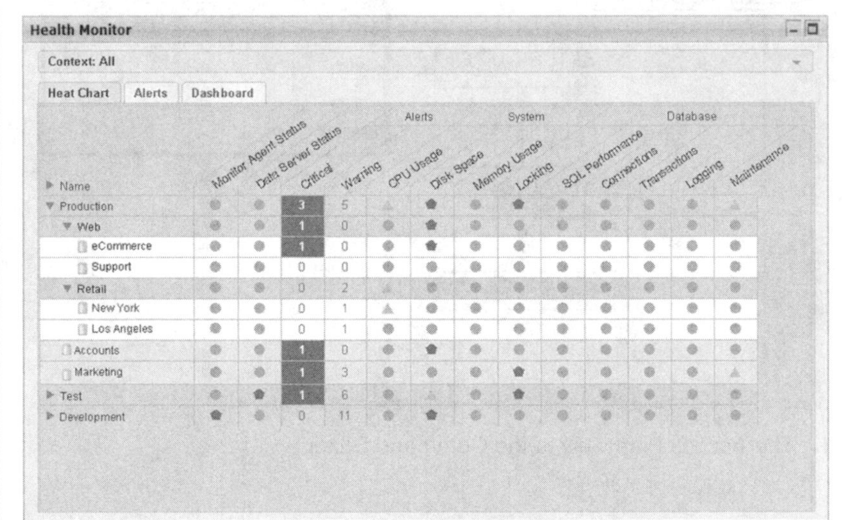

Figure 4.22 The Data Server Admin Console

4.4 General Administration Tools

The tools available under **General Administration Tools** in the DB2 menu are GUI-based. If you are unfamiliar with DB2 commands or SQL statements, the tools in this section allow you to perform all kinds of database administration tasks without having to enter one single DB2 command!

The General Administration Tools consist of the Control Center, the Journal, the License Center, the Replication Center, and the Task Center.

4.4.1 The Control Center

The **Control Center** is one of the most important DB2 GUI administration tools. It provides the following functions:

- A complete picture of all your instances and databases on local and remote systems, including host systems (OS/390 and z/OS platforms). This helps you visualize how your instances and databases are structured.
- Management of your federated database systems (federation was briefly discussed in Chapter 2, DB2 at a Glance: The Big Picture).
- Most database operations, which you would otherwise have to perform using DB2 commands.
- A launchpad for all other GUI tools.
- Many wizards and advisors, which can make your database administration tasks a lot easier.

You can start the Control Center in three different views, as shown in Figure 4.23.

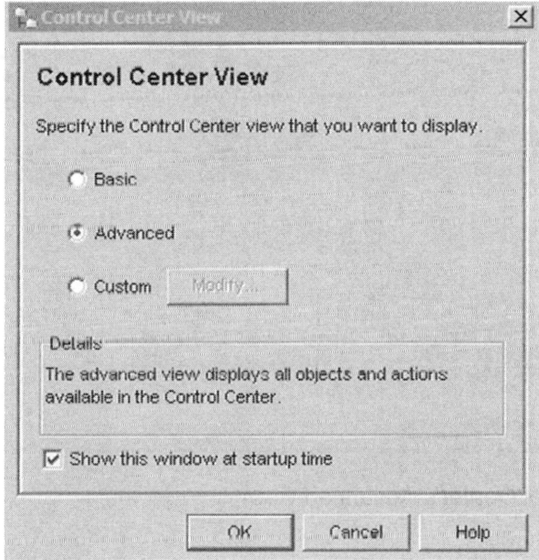

Figure 4.23 The Control Center views

The **Basic** view only shows databases residing locally on the server; it doesn't display instances. The **Advanced** view shows everything: all instances and databases on both the local system and remote systems (if connections have been configured). The **Custom** view allows you to tailor the Object Tree and the object actions to your specific needs.

Figure 4.24 shows the Control Center Advanced view. The **Object Tree** displays the tree structure on your local and remote systems, and the **Contents** pane provides more detail about the specific item selected. The **Object Details** pane displays details and actions that can be performed for the selected object.

For example, in Figure 4.24 the Tables folder in the Object Tree is selected, so the Contents pane displays the list of tables. Since the CUSTOMER table is selected, the Object Details pane shows the table structure as well as other actions like the Create New Table action.

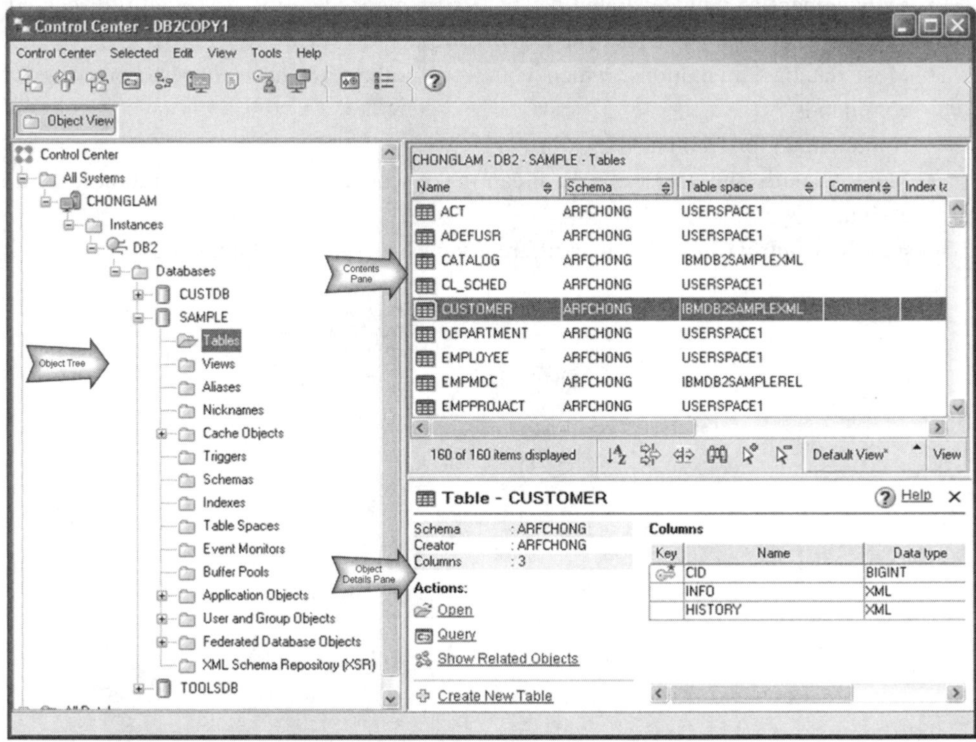

Figure 4.24 The Control Center's Advanced view

You can perform many tasks from the Control Center by right-clicking an object to display its list of operations. Figure 4.25 shows the list of available operations for the database named *SAMPLE.*

As shown in Figure 4.25, **Drop, Connect, Backup,** and **Restore** are among the many available database operations you can perform in the Control Center.

You can also start most of the GUI tools shown in the IBM DB2 menu from the Control Center. Figure 4.26 displays the Control Center toolbar contents. To start the GUI tool, click its toolbar icon.

The Control Center offers several wizards and advisors. They can assist you in many tasks such as backing up a database, creating a table, and setting up high-availability disaster recovery databases. These wizards and advisors are launched by selecting **Tools > Wizards** in the Control Center.

Figure 4.27 shows the list of available wizards and advisors.

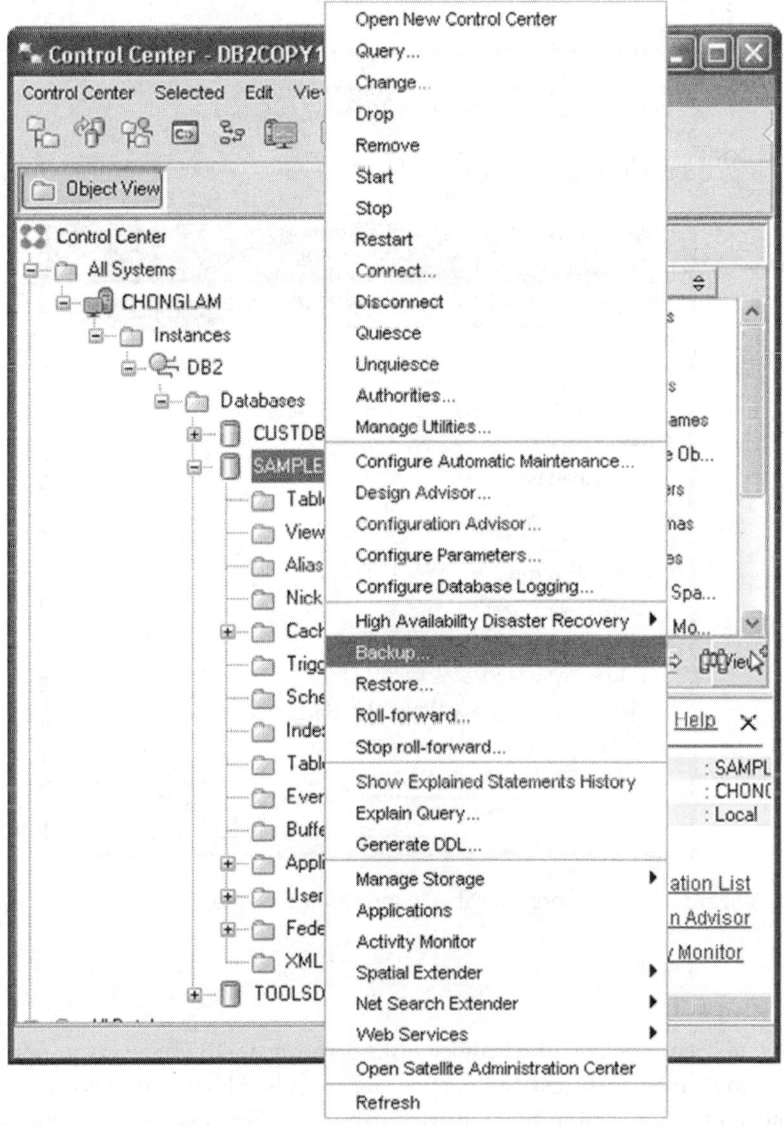

Figure 4.25 Database operations in the Control Center

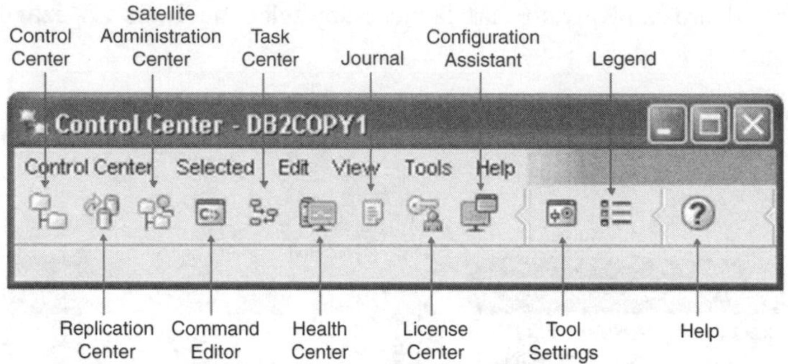

Figure 4.26 The Control Center's toolbar

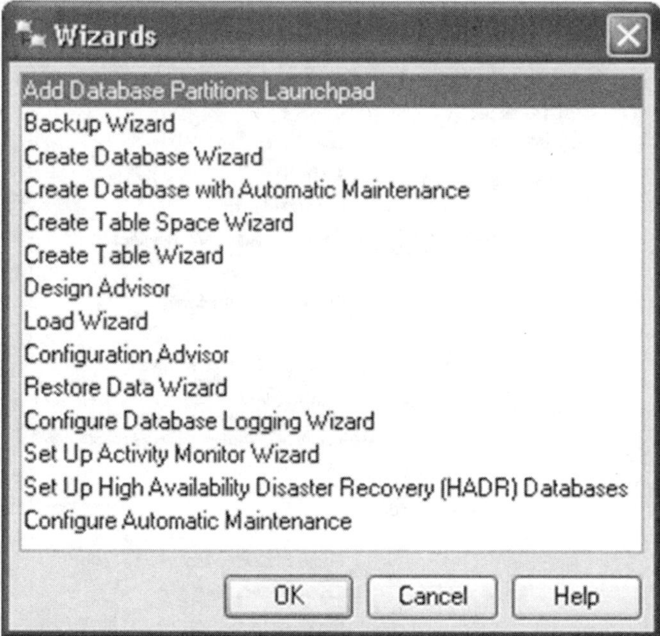

Figure 4.27 Wizards and advisors available in the Control Center

4.4.2 The Journal

The **Journal** tool keeps track of all scheduled tasks performed, DB2 recovery information, DB2 administration tools messages, and Notification log records. Should you need to investigate a problem, you can use this tool to find out what happened. Figure 4.28 shows the Notification Log tab in the Journal.

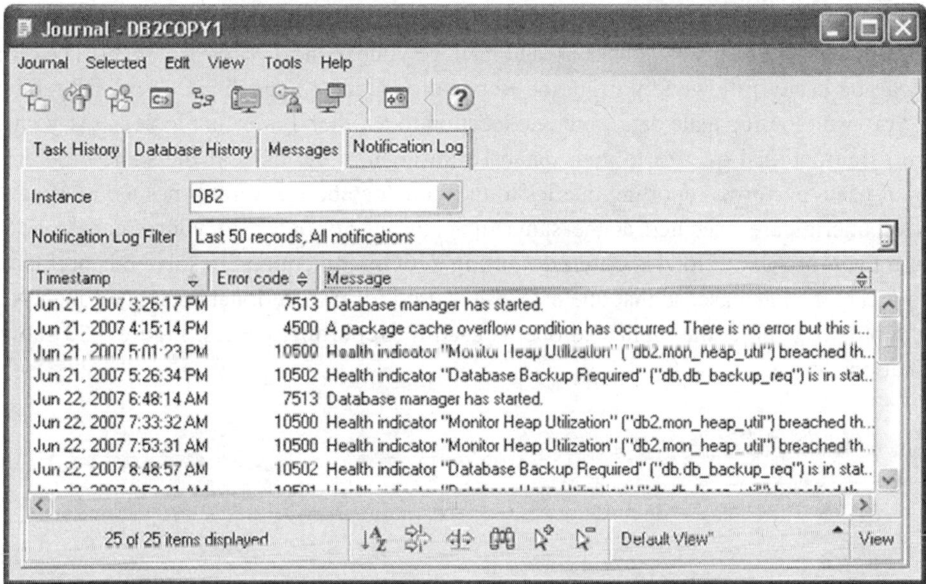

Figure 4.28 The Journal

4.4.3 License Center

You use the **License Center** to install a new license and to display license information for installed products (the **db2licm** command provides equivalent information). You launch the License Center from the Control Center toolbar. Figure 4.29 shows the License Center.

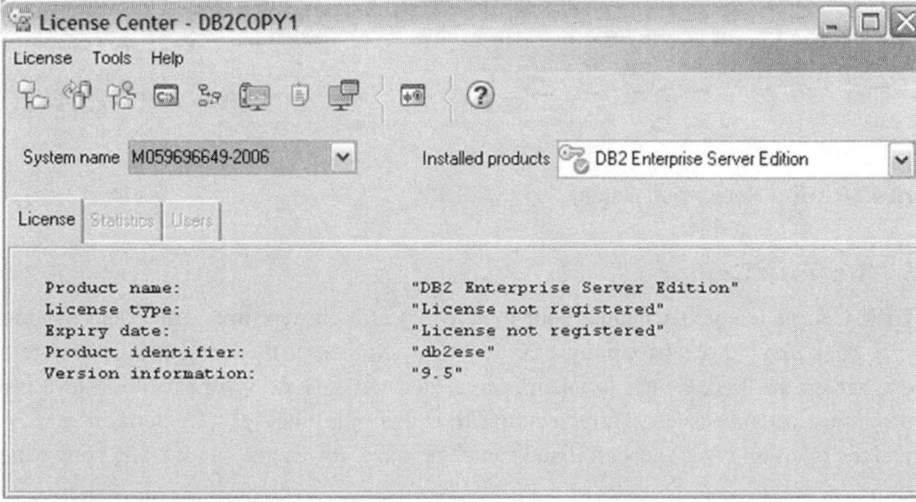

Figure 4.29 The License Center

4.4.4 The Replication Center

The **Replication Center** lets you set up and manage your replication environment. The required steps can be easily followed by using the Replication Center Launchpad. Use DB2 replication when you want to propagate data from one location to another. For example, let's say your users perform transactional queries to your database throughout the day. At the same time, another group of users performs reporting queries to the same database several times a day. When both types of queries are executed at the same time, the performance of your database degrades because the type of workload is different causing a lot of contention. To solve this problem, you can replicate the database, so that one database is used for transactional queries through the day, and the other database, the replicated one, is used for reporting queries. Figure 4.30 shows the Replication Center.

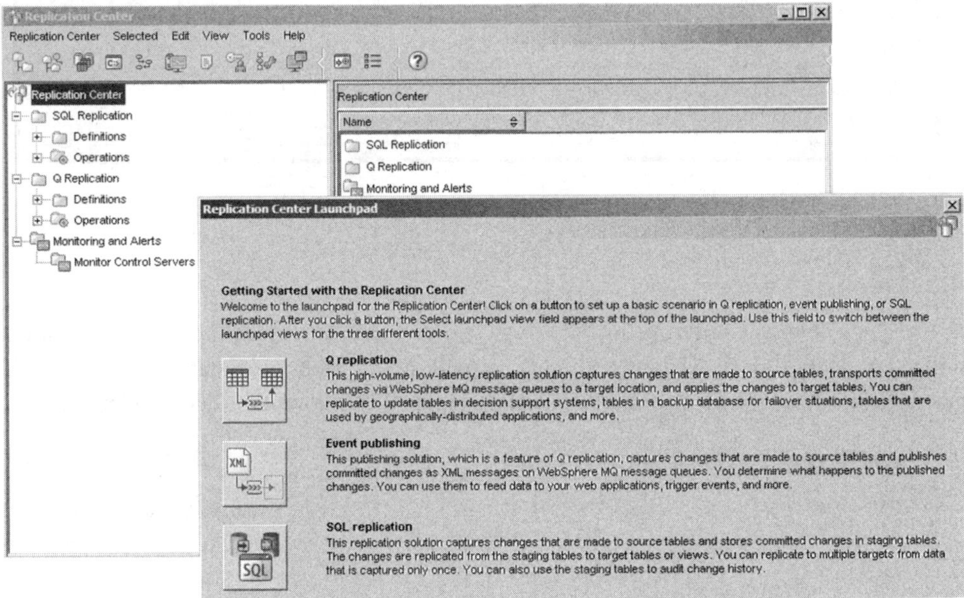

Figure 4.30 The Replication Center

4.4.5 The Task Center

The **Task Center** lets you schedule your jobs to run at a chosen time. You could use the Task Center to back up your database daily at 3:00 A.M. when there is no activity on your system. You can also set up the Task Center to take different actions on successful execution of a task and another action on an unsuccessful execution. For example, the Task Center can send you an e-mail if the operation was successful and can page you if it was not. Figure 4.31 shows the Task Center.

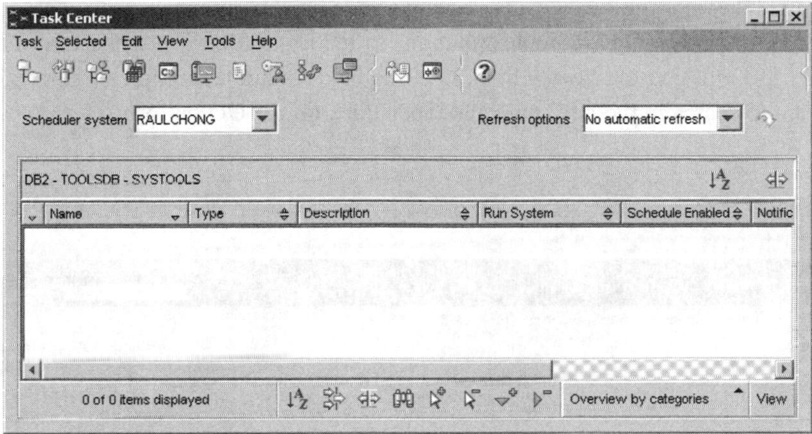

Figure 4.31 The Task Center

> **NOTE** The Tools Catalog database must exist for the Journal and the Task Center to work correctly. You can create this database during the installation process or create it manually using the **CREATE TOOLS CATALOG** command. From the Control Center, you can also choose **Tools > Tools settings >** Scheduler Settings tab, and press on the **Create new** button.

4.5 Information Tools

The **Information** menu (see Figure 4.1) provides access to all DB2 documentation.

4.5.1 Information Center

The **Information Center** gives you access to all DB2 documentation. It comes with a fast search engine allowing you to search on any given topic. The DB2 Information Center can be accessed in three different ways.

- Dynamically through the Internet (at http://publib.boulder.ibm.com/infocenter/db2luw/v9r5/index.jsp).
- Locally on the database server after installing the DB2 Information Center from a separate CD.
- Through a designated server on your company's intranet. The DB2 Information Center must be installed on that server.
- Figure 4.32 shows the Information Center accessed through the Internet. On the left panel there is a list of topics from which you can choose. Each of these topics can be

drilled down to subtopics, and selecting a specific subtopic makes the contents panel on the right side display more information. At the top left corner of the Information Center, you will find the *Search* field. Use this field to input any topic or keyword that you want to search in the DB2 manuals. Then click on the *GO* button.

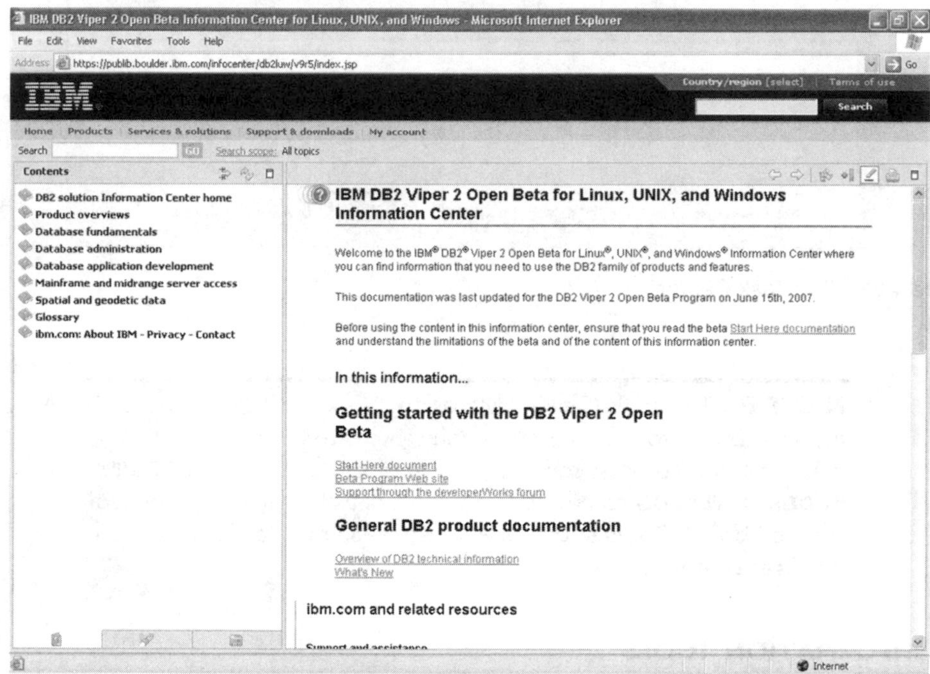

Figure 4.32 The DB2 Information Center

4.5.2 Checking for DB2 Updates

The Information Center Web site (shown in Figure 4.32) is periodically updated with new and current documentation; however, if you have installed the Information Center locally, make sure to check for updates regularly. Use the **Check For DB2 Updates** option in the DB2 menu (see Figure 4.1) to launch the InstallShield Update Service, which is shown in Figure 4.33.

From this site you can download the refreshed DB2 Information Center image and install it on your server. You can also obtain information about updates to the DB2 code and news about DB2 in general.

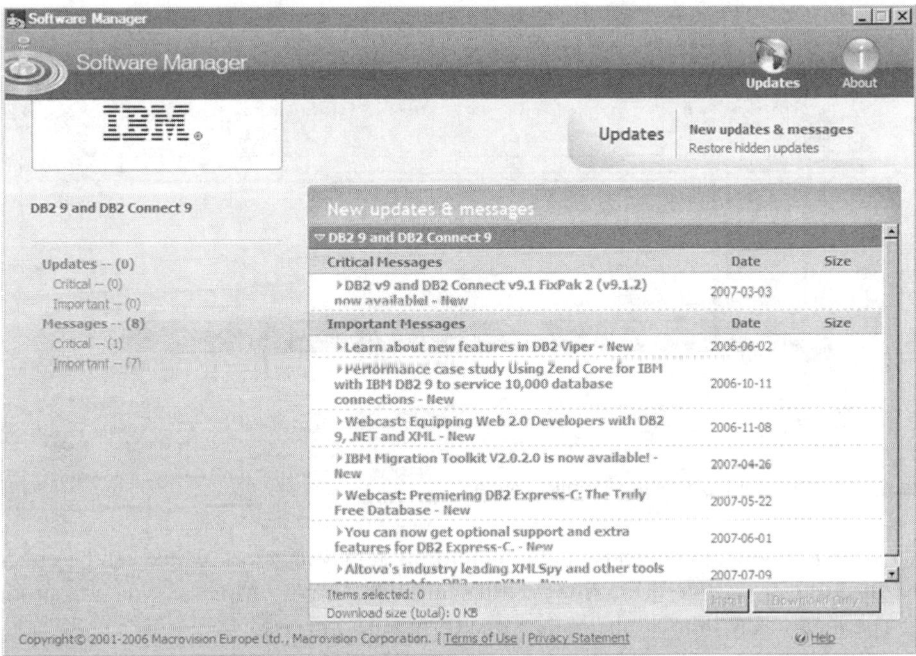

Figure 4.33 Checking for DB2 updates

4.6 Monitoring Tools

As a database administrator, it is important to have a good understanding of your database environment. Some of the things you need to know are the kinds of activities that are happening on the system, the database workload, and memory usage. The **Monitoring tools** watch the database based on the criteria you provide and generate reports.

The graphical Monitoring tools consist of the Activity Monitor, Event Analyzer, Health Center, Indoubt Transaction manager, and the Memory Visualizer.

4.6.1 The Activity Monitor

The **Activity Monitor** helps you monitor the performance of your application and database by tracking monitor data. Among other things, it can help you monitor application concurrency, resource consumption, SQL statement usage, and lock-waiting situations.

You can start the Activity Monitor either from the DB2 menu or using the db2am command. When you start the Activity Monitor, the Set Up Activity Monitor Wizard appears. This wizard prompts you to select from a set of predefined monitoring tasks, as shown in Figure 4.34.

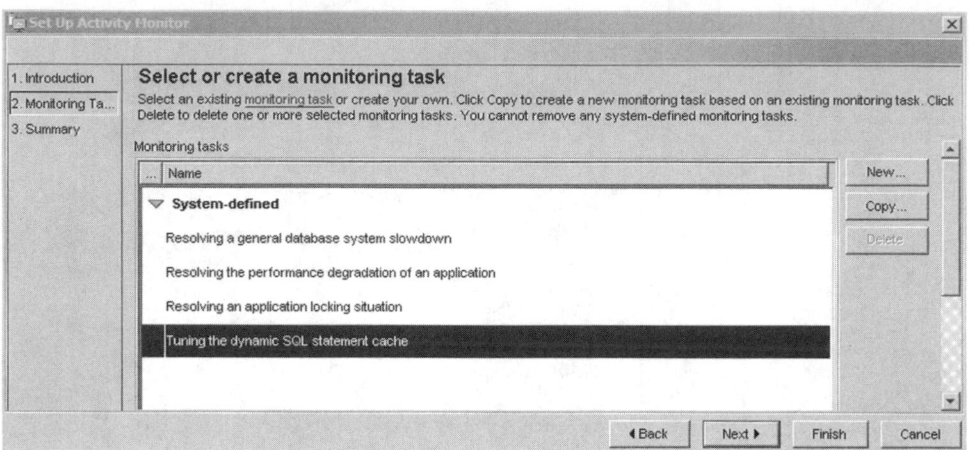

Figure 4.34 The Set Up Activity Monitor Wizard

The data that is monitored depends on the monitoring task you select, which can be either predefined by DB2 or user defined. After setting up your Activity Monitor, you can produce a report. The report shows the results of the selected monitoring task.

Figure 4.35 shows a sample report produced by the Activity Monitor, based on the selected monitoring task *Tuning the dynamic SQL statement cache*. In Figure 4.35, each executed dynamic SQL statement is listed in the left-most column. The other columns display the system resources that have been consumed. Click on the *Details and Recommendations* tab to get more information on the selected report.

To use the Activity Monitor, you must set the following database manager configuration (DBM CFG) parameters to ON: DFT_MON_BUFPOOL, DFT_MON_LOCK, DFT_MON_SORT, DFT_ MON_ STMT, DFT_MON_ TIMESTAMP, AND DFT_MON_UOW.

4.6.2 Event Analyzer

You use Event Monitors for troubleshooting performance problems. After creating an Event Monitor with the **CREATE EVENT MONITOR** statement, the output file produced (normally with an .EVT extension) can be analyzed with the **Event Analyzer.** You can also create Event Monitors in the Control Center by right-clicking on the *Event Monitors* folder for a selected database and choosing **Create.** They can later be analyzed with the Event Analyzer, as shown in Figure 4.36.

In Figure 4.36, the Event Monitor *myeventmonitor1* was created to detect deadlock events. The Event Analyzer is showing one time period for which this type of information was collected. Event Monitors are discussed in more detail in Chapter 17, Database Performance Considerations.

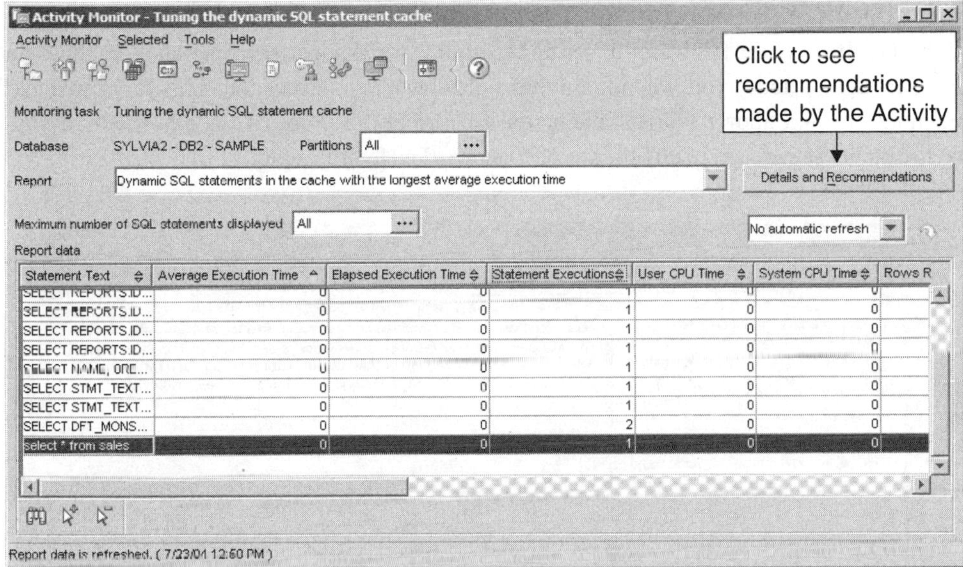

Figure 4.35 An Activity Monitor report

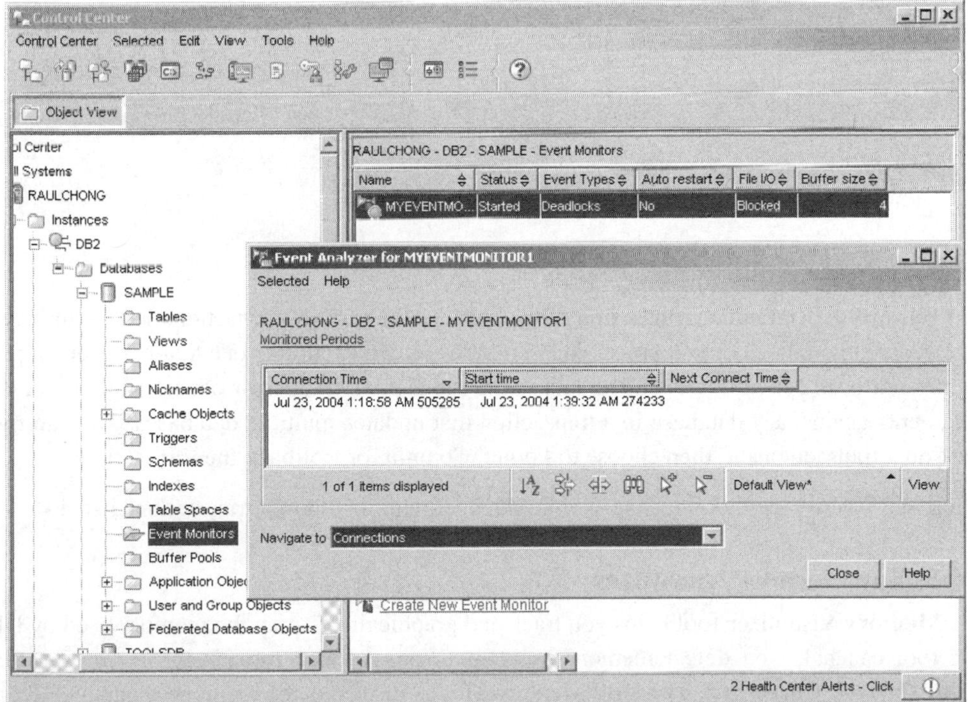

Figure 4.36 The Event Analyzer

4.6.3 Health Center

Use the **Health Center** GUI tool to set up thresholds for key performance and database health indicators, and to notify you when these thresholds have been exceeded. This tool provides recommendations and allows you to take action to correct the problem. In other words, you can have the database manage itself! Figure 4.37 shows the Health Center.

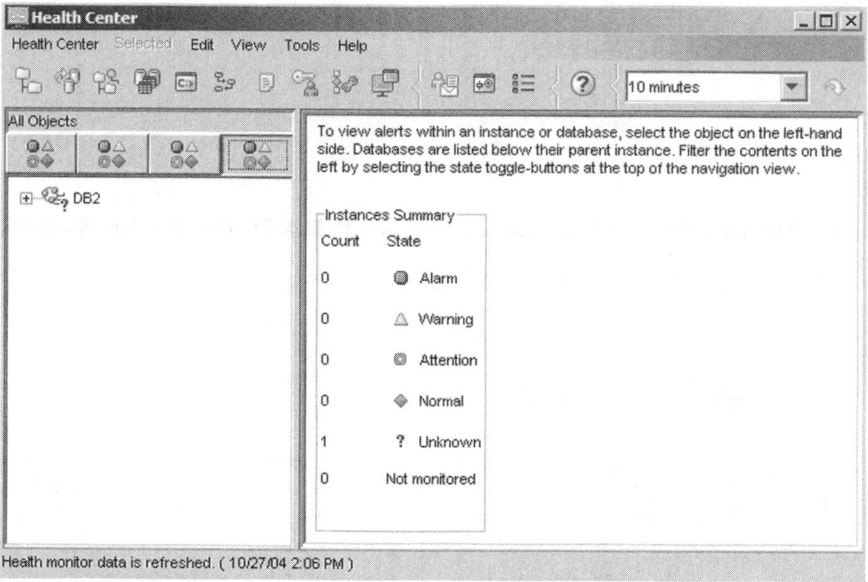

Figure 4.37 The Health Center

4.6.4 Indoubt Transaction Manager

You can use the **Indoubt Transaction Manager** to help resolve transactions left in an indoubt state during two-phase commit processing. An **indoubt transaction** is one that has been prepared but has not been committed or rolled back. This can happen if an error occurs while processing statements against any database in a transaction that updates multiple databases. You can right-click on a transaction and then choose to Forget, Commit, or Rollback the transaction.

Figure 4.38 shows the Indoubt Transaction Manager with no indoubt transactions listed.

4.6.5 The Memory Visualizer

The **Memory Visualizer** tool helps you track and graphically display the memory used by DB2. The tool can help you detect memory problems. You can also modify the memory settings within the tool. Chapter 16, The DB2 Memory Model, discusses the memory usage by DB2 and

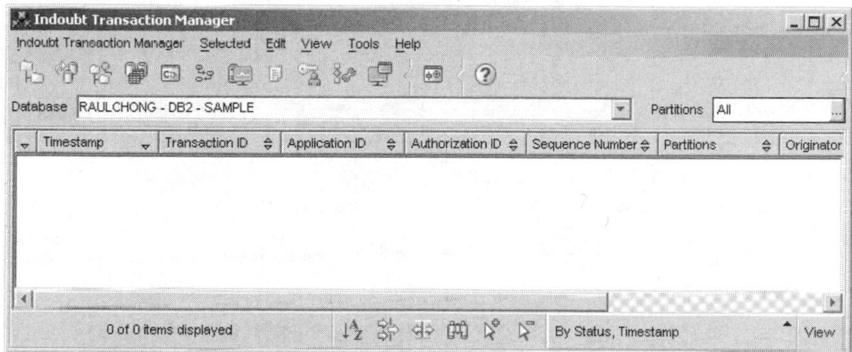

Figure 4.38 The Indoubt Transaction Manager

the **db2mtrk** memory tracker tool, which is a text-based tool equivalent to the Memory Visualizer.

V9.5 With the introduction of the Simplified Memory Configuration Solution in DB2 9.5, the Memory Visualizer user interface shows the new and updated configuration parameters: APPL_MEMORY and INSTANCE_MEMORY. More details on those two configuration parameters are discussed in Chapter 16, The DB2 Memory Model. Moreover, values for the deprecated configuration parameters APPGROUP_MEM_SZ, APP_CTL_HEAP_SZ, and QUERY_HEAP_SZ no longer display for Version 9.5 databases, but are still available in earlier versions of the databases.

Figure 4.39 shows the Memory Visualizer. In the figure, the buffer pools and Lock Manager Heap are being plotted in the graph at the bottom of the window every five seconds. In both cases, the graph shows a straight line, indicating the memory usage for these two are not increasing.

4.7 Setup Tools

The **Setup Tools** get you started with DB2. Using these tools, you can create the *sample* database, which can be used to explore DB2 features. They also help you configure connections to remote databases. The Setup Tools consist of the Configuration Assistant, Configure DB2 .NET Data Provider, First Steps, Register Visual Studio Add-Ins, and Default DB2 and Database Client Interface Selection Wizard.

4.7.1 The Configuration Assistant

The Configuration Assistant helps you:

- Set up connections to databases residing on remote servers using the Add Database Wizard.
- Configure connection properties for local databases.

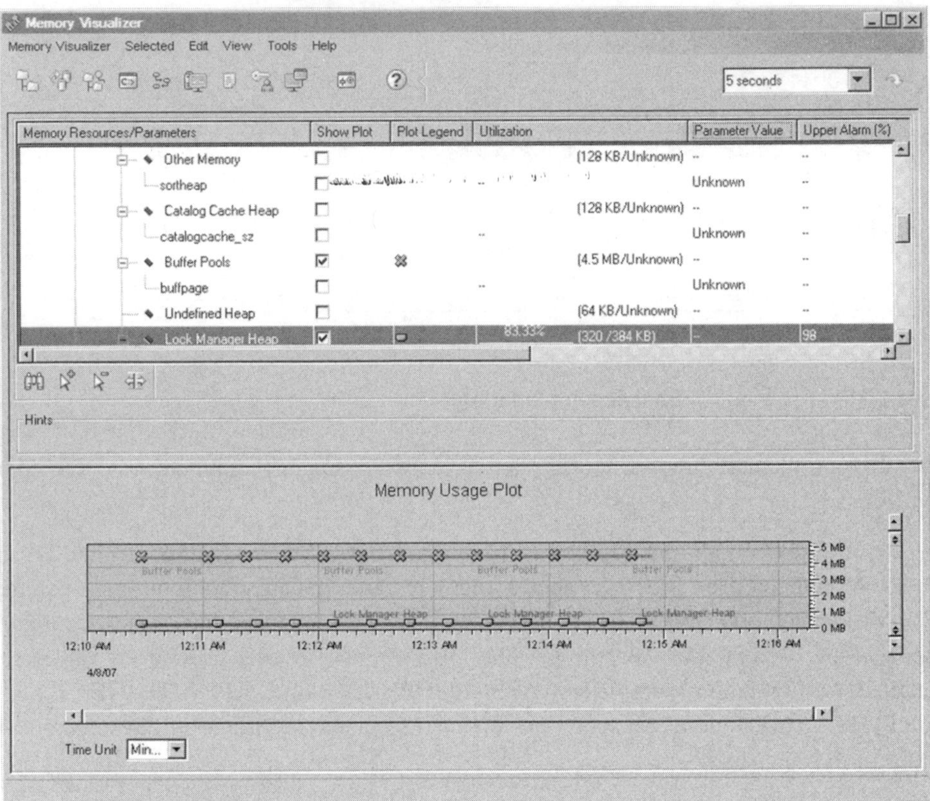

Figure 4.39 The Memory Visualizer

Figure 4.40 shows the Configuration Assistant and the Add Database Wizard. Chapter 6, Configuring Client and Server Connectivity, explains how to use the Configuration Assistant in detail.

4.7.2 Configure DB2 .NET Data Provider

As its name implies, this tools helps you configure the DB2 .NET Data provider, also known as the IBM Data Server Provider for .NET. There are 32-bit and 64-bit versions of the IBM Data Server Provider for .NET, each supporting the 32-bit and 64-bit versions of the .NET Framework version 2.0 CLR respectively. During the installation of the DB2 client or server software, this tool can help you determine which one of these two IBM Data Server Provider for .NET editions will be installed. The tool runs behind the scenes; you will not see a GUI interface coming up when you select it.

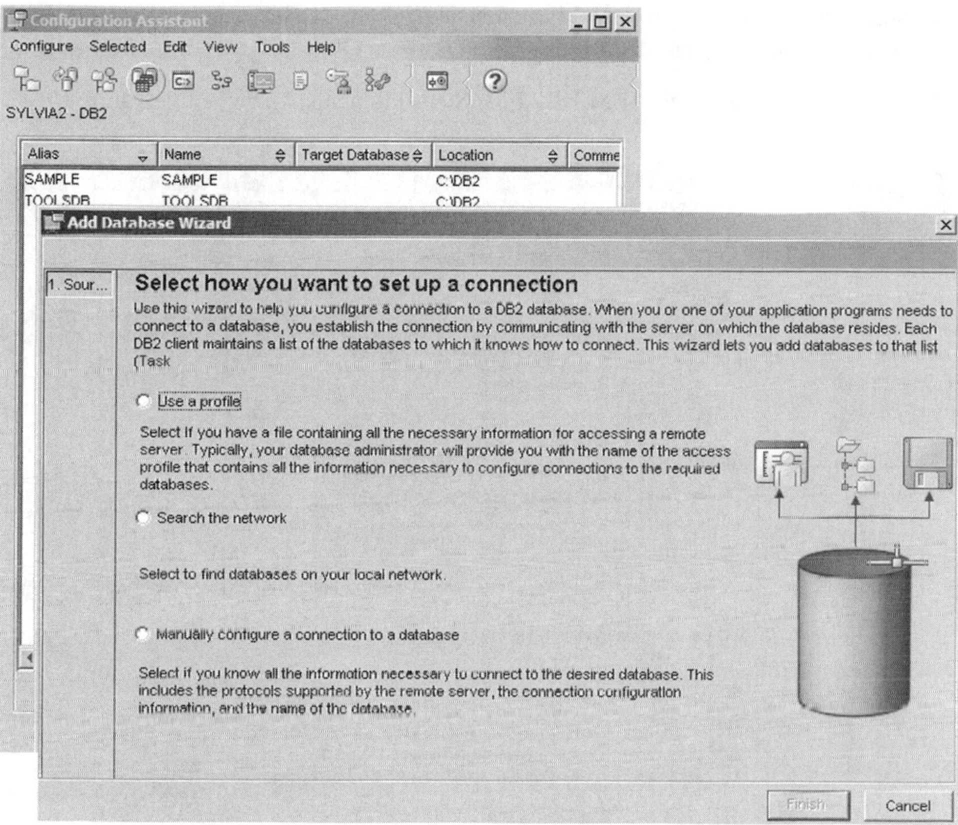

Figure 4.40 The Configuration Assistant

4.7.3 First Steps

The IBM DB2 **First Steps** tool is a good starting point for new DB2 users who want to get familiar with the product. Figure 4.41 shows the operations you can perform using this tool.

The *Database Creation* tab allows you to create a database called *sample* on your local system. The *sample* database is provided with the DB2 product for testing and learning purposes. It comes with a set of predefined tables. You can work with this database just like any other database. The equivalent DB2 command to create this *sample* database is **`db2sampl`**.

From the *Database Creation* tab you can also click on the *Create Your Own Database* button, which walks you through several steps to create your new database, which is configured for optimal performance. You can specify the name of the database and the location where it is going to be created. The equivalent DB2 command to create a new database is **`create database`** and is discussed in Chapter 8, The DB2 Storage Model. After the database is created, you can create tables using the Control Center or SQL statements. The SQL statements to create database objects are described in Chapter 7, Working with Database Objects.

We leave the other options in the IBM DB2 First Steps Launchpad for you to explore.

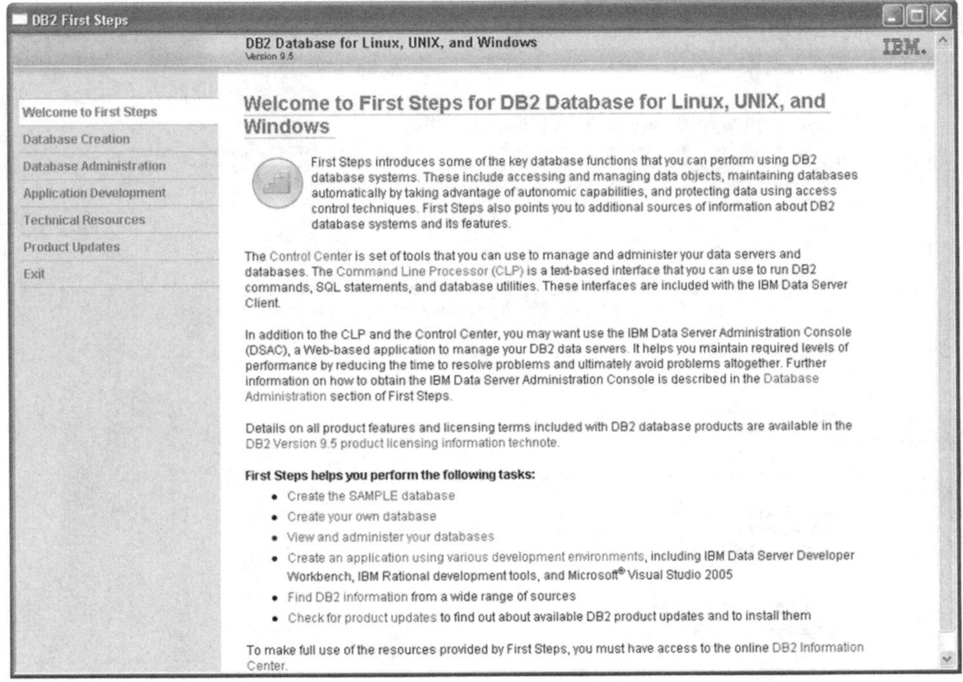

Figure 4.41 The First Steps Launchpad

4.7.4 Register Visual Studio Add-Ins

When you select the **Register Visual Studio Add-Ins** menu item (the second to last item in the **IBM DB2** menu shown in Figure 4.1), it adds a plug-in into Microsoft Visual Studio so that DB2 tools can be invoked from Visual Basic, Visual C++, and Visual InterDev. The add-in inserts the DB2 menu entries into each of these Microsoft development tool's **View, Tools,** and **Help** menus.

V9.5

4.7.5 Default DB2 and Database Client Interface Selection Wizard

This tool only applies to Windows platforms. The Default DB2 and Database Client Interface Selection wizard allows you to select the default DB2 install copy on your computer when there is one or more DB2 copies on your computer. Applications will use this default DB2 install copy by default. This tool can also be used to set the default IBM database client interface (ODBC/CLI driver and .NET provider) copy. You can also launch this wizard by running the

db2swtch.exe command located in the sqllib\bin directory of your DB2 install copy. Figure 4.42 shows the Default DB2 and Database Client Interface Selection Wizard.

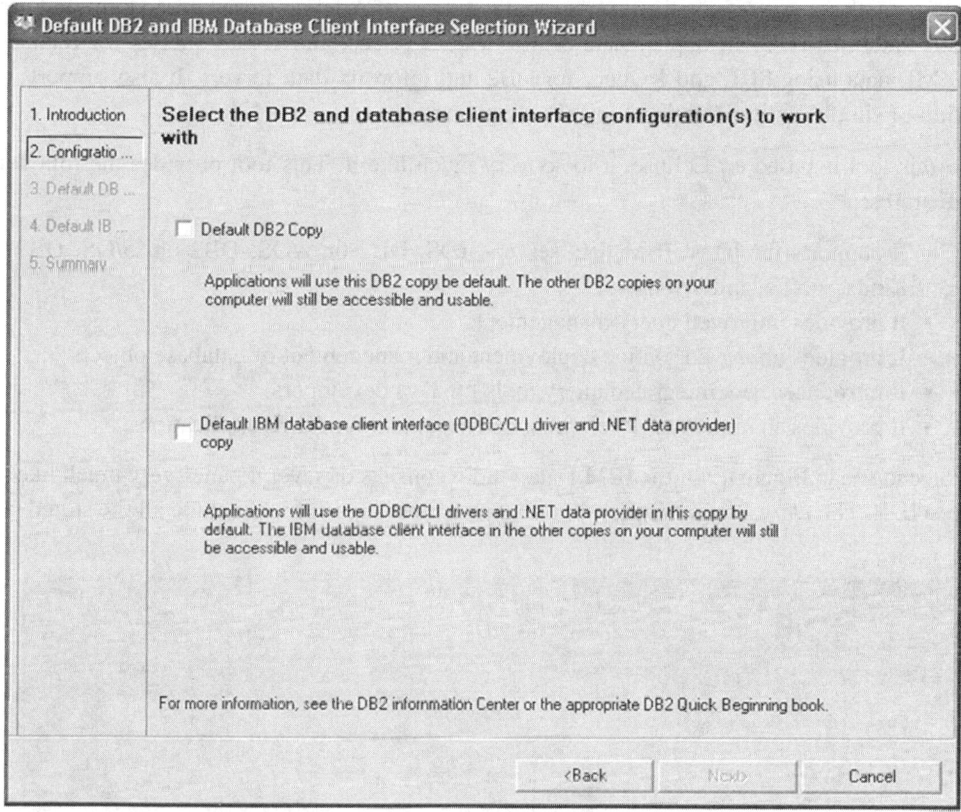

Figure 4.42 The Default DB2 and Database Client Interface Selection Wizard

4.8 Other Tools

Thus far we have covered all the tools illustrated in the IBM DB2 menu (Figure 4.1). There are other tools that are worth discussing here; some of them are available through the Control Center or the Command Editor but not from the IBM DB2 menu. Others are available as a separate download.

V9.5 4.8.1 The IBM Data Studio

The IBM Data Studio is a comprehensive suite of integrated Eclipse tools for the database designer and development DBA. This tool replaces the DB2 Developer Workbench introduced in DB2 9. Prior to DB2 9, there was also another tool called the Development Center. The IBM

Data Studio comes as a separately downloadable image, and can be obtained from the DB2 Express-C Web site (www.ibm.com/db2/express).

This tool can help you reduce the time to create, deploy, and debug stored procedures and user-defined functions (UDFs), deploy data-centric Web services, and create queries for relational and XML data using SQL and XQuery for DB2 and Informix data servers. It also supports the creation of simple Entity-Relationship (ER) diagrams.

Since this tool is based on Eclipse, it looks very much like it. This tool provides the following new features:

- It supports the latest IBM data servers: IDS, DB2 on z/OS, DB2 on i5/OS, DB2 on Linux, UNIX, and Windows
- It provides improved query management.
- It provides improved routine deployment and management of database objects.
- It introduces new integrated query tools for Java developers.
- It provides an improved development environment for XML applications.

As you can see in Figure 4.43, the IBM Data Studio consists of several panes very much like the Eclipse IDE. The *Data Project Explorer* contains your projects, which include all the stored pro-

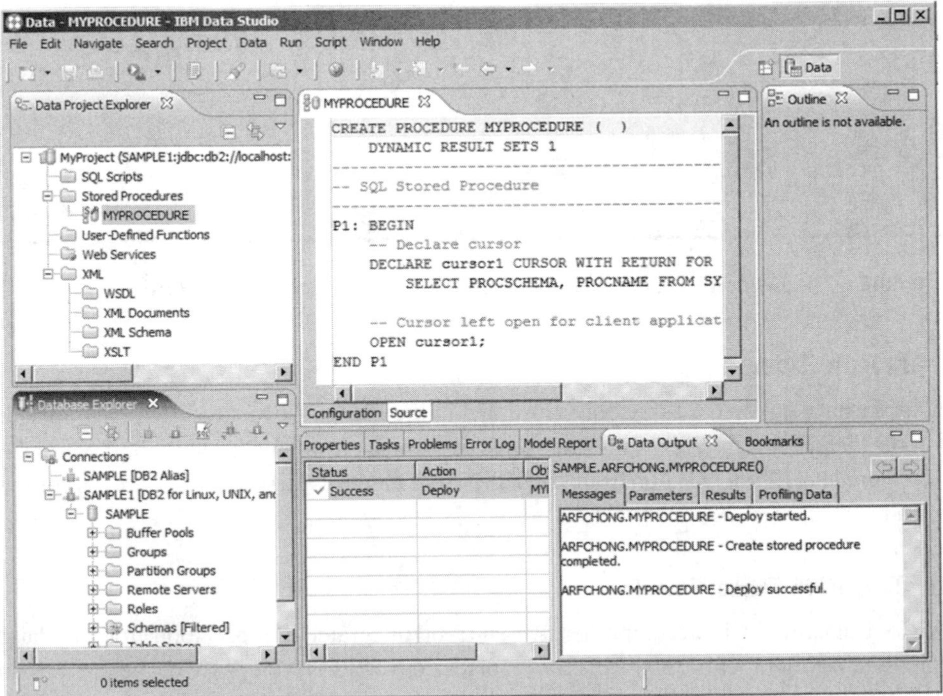

Figure 4.43 The IBM Data Studio

cedures, UDFs, and XML queries stored locally in your machine. The *Database Explorer* displays information about your database connections. At the bottom-right corner, you can see the messages and results after deploying and/or executing your procedures or functions. At the top-right corner, you can work with the code of your procedures and UDFs.

We will discuss more about stored procedures and UDFs in Chapter 7, Working with Database Objects.

4.8.2 SQL Assist

If you are not proficient in SQL, the **SQL Assist** tool can help you build SQL statements step by step. You can launch SQL Assist from the Command Editor by clicking on the SQL Assist icon (refer to Figure 4.19). The built statement will be pasted into the Command Editor where it can be run.

Figure 4.44 shows SQL Assist after being launched from the Command Editor. In the figure, a SELECT statement was chosen. When the FROM clause was selected, a list of schemas and tables was displayed from which you could choose the tables you wanted to work with. At the bottom of the figure, you see the SQL that is generated as you select different choices in SQL Assist.

4.8.3 Satellite Administration Center

The **Satellite Administration Center** is a tool that provides centralized administrative support for satellites. A **satellite** is a DB2 server that is a member of a group of similar DB2 servers, each running the same application and with similar configurations. You launch the Satellite Administration Center from the DB2 Control Center toolbar.

The Satellite Administration Center stores its information in the **satellite control database** (SATCTLDB). This database records, among other things, which satellites are in the environment, the group each satellite belongs to, and which version of the end-user application a satellite is running. This database is on a DB2 server known as the **Satellite Control Server.** To set up and maintain its database configuration, each satellite connects to the satellite control database to download the batches that correspond to its version of the end-user application. The satellite executes these batches locally, and then reports the results back to the satellite control database. This process of downloading batches, executing them, and then reporting the results of the batch execution is known as **synchronization.** A satellite synchronizes to maintain its consistency with the other satellites that belong to its group and are running the same version of the end-user application. For more information about how to install and administer a satellite environment, refer to the Resources section at the end of this book.

4.8.4 The db2pd Tool

The db2pd tool is a command line monitor and troubleshooting tool that collects quick and immediate statistics for DB2 instances and databases. This tool does not degrade the DB2

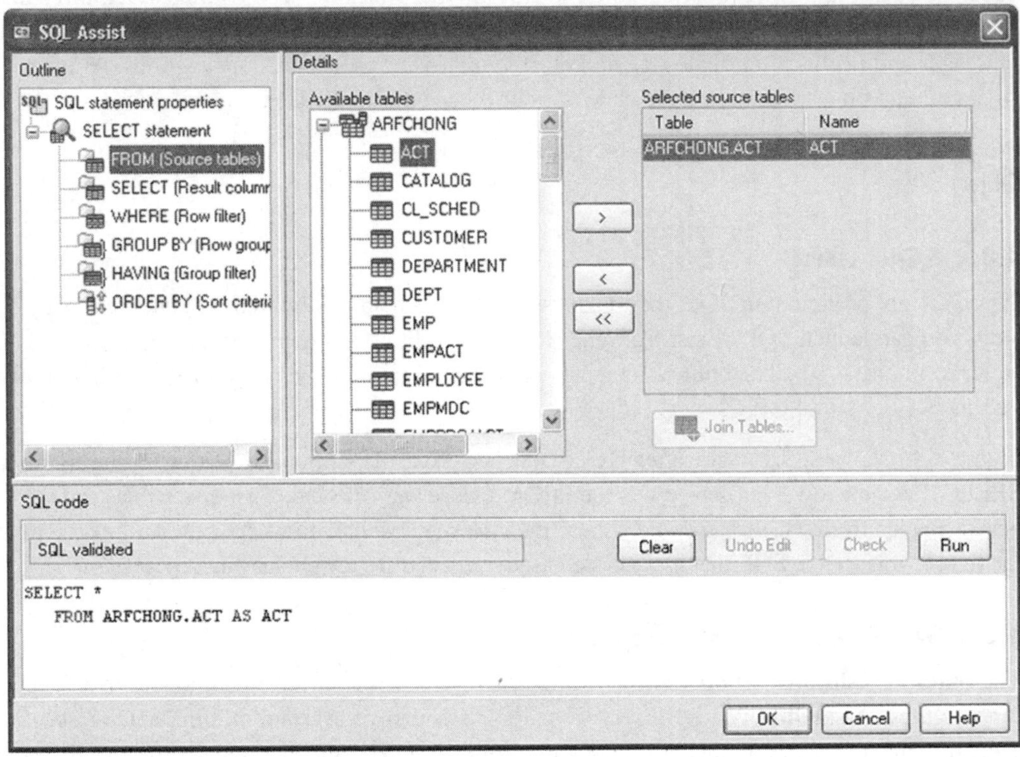

Figure 4.44 SQL Assist

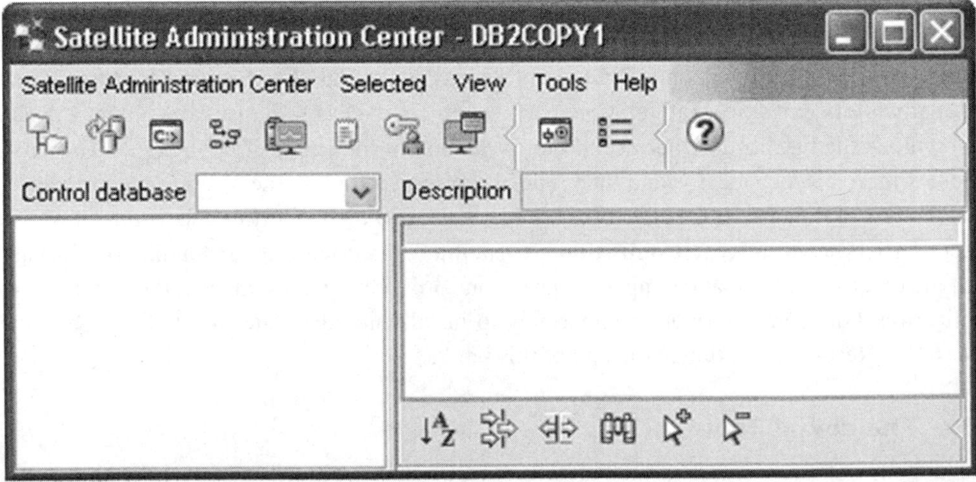

Figure 4.45 The Satellite Administration Center

engine performance because it acquires the information directly from memory, rather than gathering data on the fly. Use this tool for troubleshooting, problem determination, database monitoring, performance tuning, and as an aid in application development design.

The db2pd tool provides many options to display information about database transactions, table spaces, table statistics, dynamic SQL, database configurations, and many other database details; for example

- To display the operating system information, issue

  db2pd –osinfo
- To display all instance-related information, issue

  db2pd –inst
- To display all database-related information to the *sample* database, issue

  db2pd –db sample

Use the **db2pd –help** command to display all the available options. This tool is not available through the graphical interface.

We discuss more about the db2pd tool in Chapter 15, The DB2 Process Model, and Chapter 18, Diagnosing Problems.

4.9 Tool Settings

All of the graphical tools that you can invoke through the Control Center, including the Control Center itself, have a menu for setting up the general tool characteristics. If you select **Tools > Tools Settings** from any of these tools, the window shown in Figure 4.46 is displayed. Note that each tool invokes the same Tools Settings window.

In Figure 4.46, the *Command Editor* tab is selected. You can see that under this tab the Command Editor can be set to automatically commit SQL statements (autocommit is enabled by default). When autocommit is disabled, you must issue the **COMMIT** statement explicitly to commit SQL statements. There are many other settings that you can change under the other tabs, and we encourage you to explore them yourself.

4.10 Case Study

You recently installed DB2 Express-C on your Windows laptop. During the installation, the *DB2* instance was created. Now you want to start using DB2 by creating a database. Since you are new to DB2, you decide to use the DB2 First Steps tool (see Figure 4.41).

You click on *Database creation > Create Sample Database* from the First Steps Launchpad and the screen shown in Figure 4.47 is displayed.

Next you choose the option *XML and SQL objects and data,* which will create a Unicode database, and click OK. Wait for a few minutes for the *sample* database to be created. Alternatively,

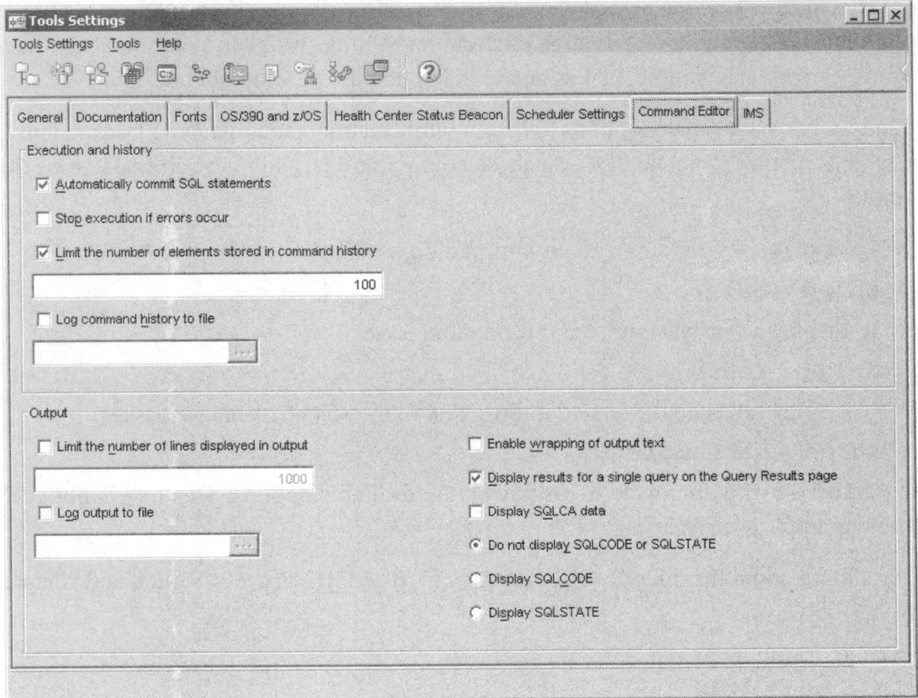

Figure 4.46 The Tools Settings window

you can create the *sample* database from an MS-DOS prompt on Windows or a Linux/UNIX shell using this command:

```
db2sampl -sql -xml
```

> **NOTE** Starting with DB2 9 fixpack 2, the SAMPLE database is automatically created as part of the DB2 installation.

After the database is created, you launch the Control Center by choosing **Start > Programs > IBM DB2 > DB2COPY1 > General Administration Tools > Control Center.**

From the Control Center, choose the *Advanced* view and then expand the *Object Tree* to display the *sample* database and all its database objects (see Figure 4.24).

The *sample* database already has a set of tables defined in it. However, you decide to create a table of your own. To do so, you right-click on the *Tables* folder in the *Object Tree* and choose *Create.* This launches the Create Table Wizard, which will guide you through the process of creating a table. You are presented with the following pages:

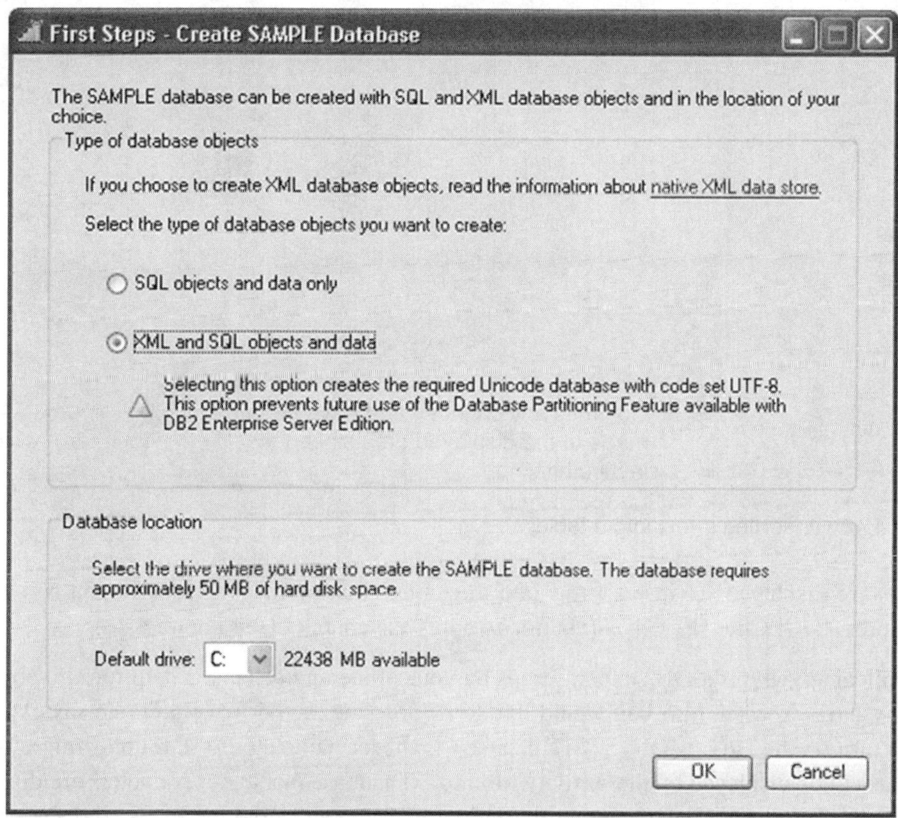

Figure 4.47 First Steps—Create SAMPLE database window

- Identify the schema and name for the new table: In the *Table schema* field, enter the user ID you logged in with. We will discuss the significance of schemas in Chapter 7, Working with Database Objects; for now it is sufficient to enter your user ID. In the *Table name* field, enter the name of the table you want to create, for example, *Table1*.
- Change column definitions for the new table: Click *Add* to add columns one at a time. In the *Column name* field, enter the name of the first column for *Table1*, for example, *Col1*. Choose the data type from the pull-down menu, for example, *INTEGER*. You could create more columns by repeating this step, but one column is sufficient for now.

There are other windows in which you can define the properties of other database objects. However, completing the above two windows is enough to create the table. Click on the *Finish* button to create the table.

Table1 is displayed under the *Tables* folder once it is created (all tables are displayed in the Contents pane of the Control Center—see Figure 4.24). To display the contents of the table, right-click on the table name and choose *Open*. Since nothing has been inserted into *Table1*, no

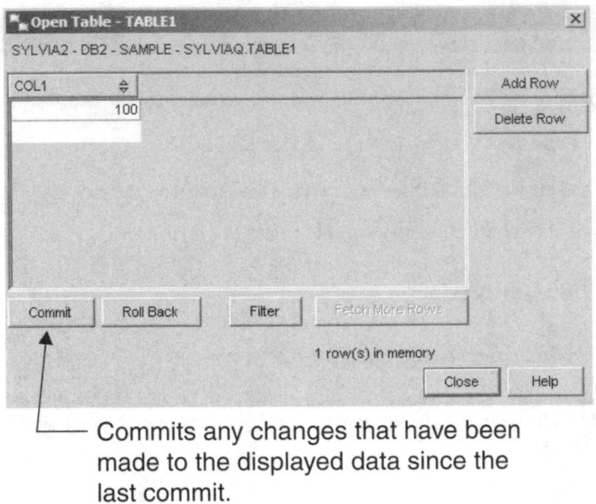

Figure 4.48 Inserting a row into a table

contents are displayed. To insert a row into the table, click on the *Add Row* button and enter a value under *Col1*. Click the *Commit* button to apply the changes (see Figure 4.48).

Your colleague, who is a DB2 expert, drops by your office and offers his help for any problems you may have. You tell him you would like to explore the Activity Monitor. He says you first need to turn on the DFT_MON_STMT database manager parameter to start collecting information that will be displayed by the Activity Monitor. (Database manager parameters are discussed in detail in Chapter 5, Understanding the DB2 Environment, DB2 Instances, and Databases.) He quickly turns this on for you.

Next, you start the Activity Monitor and choose the *sample* database from the *Introduction* page. You see the four predefined functions of the Activity Monitor (see Figure 4.34). You decide to monitor dynamic SQL statements performed on this database. Therefore, you highlight the *Tuning the dynamic SQL statement cache* option and click *Next.*

Figure 4.49 lists the SQL statement items that the Activity Monitor checks. Click *Finish* to complete the Activity Monitor definition and the window shown in Figure 4.50 appears.

To obtain the Activity Monitor report, select one of the four options listed. The Activity Monitor starts monitoring all dynamic SQL statements being executed on the database. If there are users connected to the database, all the dynamic SQL statements they submit will be monitored. Figure 4.51 shows an Activity Monitor report on *Dynamic SQL statements in the cache with the largest number of rows read.*

If there are no other users connected to the system, you can generate some SQL statements yourself. The simplest way to do this from the Control Center is to right-click on a table name and

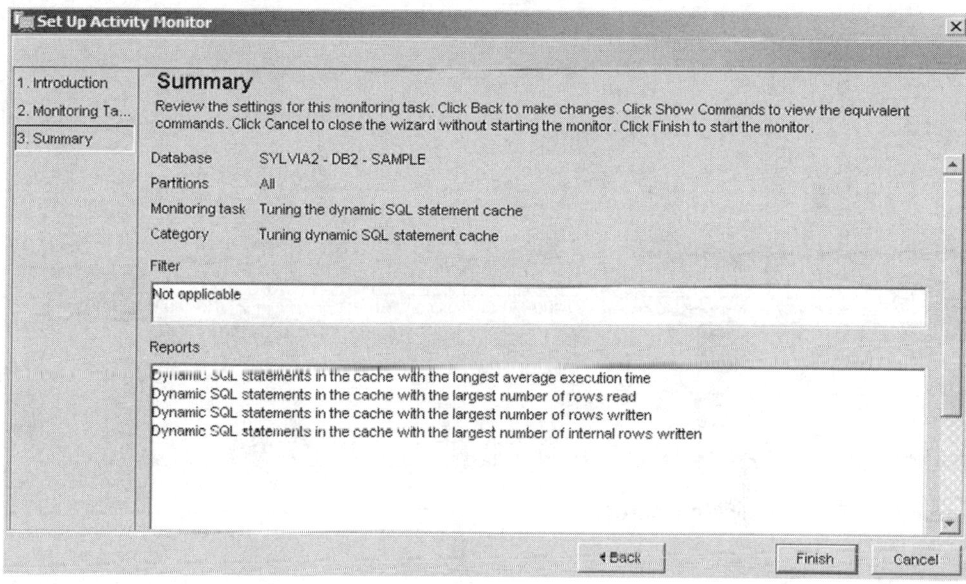

Figure 4.49 Activity Monitor summary page

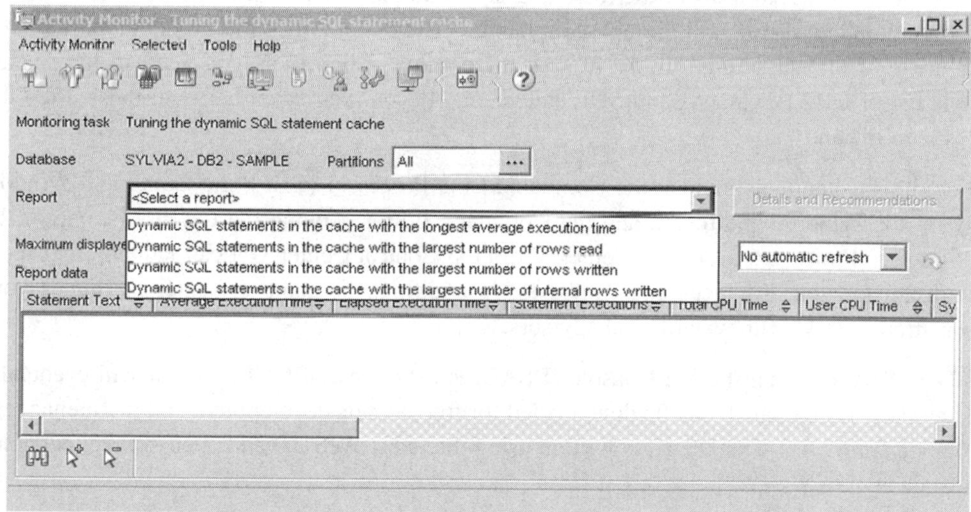

Figure 4.50 Obtaining an Activity Monitor report

choose *Open* to display its contents. This is equivalent to the following SQL statement:

```
SELECT * FROM table_name
```

Though you have not finished exploring all the DB2 tools, this exercise has made you realize how easy to use and powerful they are!

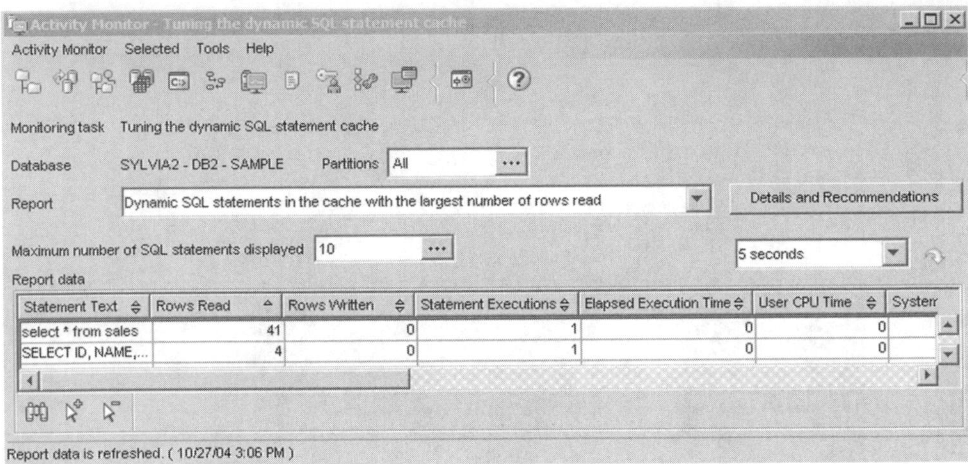

Figure 4.51 The Activity Monitor report

4.11 Summary

This chapter introduced most of the tools that are available in DB2. They come in two categories: the command-driven and the non-command-driven tools. All of the non-command-driven tools are also known as GUI Tools. To use the command line tools you need to have some knowledge of DB2 commands and SQL statements. If you aren't familiar with these, the GUI tools come in handy.

The command-line tools include the Command Line Processor (CLP), the Command Window (only on the Windows platform), and the Command Editor. Among the GUI tools, one of the most powerful ones is the Control Center. From the Control Center you can launch other tools and administer your instances and databases. In addition, the Control Center facilitates your administration tasks with wizards and advisors.

The Data Server Administration Console (DSAC) is a Web-based GUI tool that will eventually replace many DB2 tools. It can be downloaded for free, and its development and maintenance is decoupled from DB2. The DSAC is written using the latest Web 2.0 and open-source technologies, such as AJAX.

The IBM Data Studio provides you with an integrated data management environment that helps you develop and manage database applications throughout the data management lifecycle. It helps you build, test, debug, and deploy stored procedures, user-defined functions (UDFs), SQL and XML queries, and work with Web services.

The monitoring tools generate reports and keep track of your databases according to criteria you provide. These reports are handy for investigating performance problems and setting benchmarks for your database.

4.12 Review Questions

1. Which of the DB2 tools can be used to schedule SQL scripts in DB2?
2. The DB2 Command Window is only available on Windows. What is the equivalent tool on the Linux/UNIX platforms?
3. Which registry variable needs to be changed to set **autocommit** to off permanently for the CLP?
4. When is it handy to start the CLP in interactive mode with a different terminator character as in **db2 -td!**?
5. Which command is necessary to guarantee the CLP back-end process is terminated?
6. How can Visual Explain be invoked?
7. Which tool can be used to develop SQL user-defined functions?
8. Can the DSAC be used to administer DB2 for i5/OS databases?
9. It's 9:00 A.M. and you would like to investigate a problem that happened at 3:00 A.M. Where do you look for more information?
10. How can you obtain the most current information about a given DB2 topic?
11. Which two of the following tools can be used to execute SQL statements against a DB2 database?
    A. Command Window
    B. Command Editor
    C. Command Line Processor
    D. Command Processor
    E. db2cc
12. Which of the following is the default termination character for files processed by the DB2 CLP?
    A. :
    B. ;
    C. |
    D. $
13. If you have the following CLP input file named samp.sql, how many commits will occur during the processing of the db2 –tvf samp.sql command?

```
connect to sample;
select * from org;
select * from dept;
connect reset;
```

A. 0
B. 1
C. 2
D. 3
E. 4

14. The Health Center will alert you when:
    A. A row is deleted from a table
    B. You run the load tool
    C. You exceed a defined threshold on performance characteristics
    D. An SQL statement fails because of incorrect syntax
15. Which of the following tools will give you information about the memory used by DB2 and your DB2 applications?
    A. db2memlist
    B. Memory Visualizer
    C. db2mv
    D. Memory Center
    E. db2mtrk
16. If you have the following CLP input file named samp.sql, how many commits will occur during the processing of the db2 +c –tvf samp.sql command?

```
connect to sample;
select * from org;
select * from dept;
```

    A. 0
    B. 1
    C. 2
    D. 3
    E. 4
17. If you have the following CLP input file named samp.sql, which of the commands below will run this file successfully?

```
connect to sample@
select * from org@
select * from dept@
connect reset@
```

    A. db2 –t@f samp.sql
    B. db2 -td@ -f samp.sql
    C. db2 -t@ -f samp.sql
    D. db2 -td@f samp.sql
18. If your application receives the SQL code -911, which of the following commands can be used to get its description?
    A. db2 ? -911
    B. db2 ? 911N
    C. db2 ? SQL-911
    D. db2 ? SQL911N

19. Which of the following commands cannot be run from the CLP in interactive mode?

A. History

B. Edit

C. Runcmd

D. Repeat

20. Which two of the following can be performed from the CLP in interactive mode?

A. db2 ? SQL911N

B. db2stop

C. list applications

D. select * from staff

CHAPTER 5

Understanding the DB2 Environment, DB2 Instances, and Databases

You need to understand the DB2 environment and the concepts of DB2 instances and databases to work effectively with DB2. DB2 instances and the DB2 environment control many factors that influence DB2's behavior by using configurable parameters at different levels and locations.

In this chapter you will learn about the following:

- The big picture of the DB2 Environment, DB2 instances, and databases
- The environment variables
- The DB2 registry variables
- How to manage and configure a DB2 instance
- How to manage and configure the Database Administration Server
- How to manage and configure databases
- Instance and database design considerations

5.1 The DB2 Environment, DB2 Instances, and Databases: The Big Picture

Figure 5.1 illustrates the different levels in which you can configure your DB2 environment.

You can use

- Environment variables at the operating system level
- The DB2 profile registry variables at the operating system and instance levels
- The Database Manager (DBM) Configuration file at the instance level
- The Database (DB) Configuration file at the database level

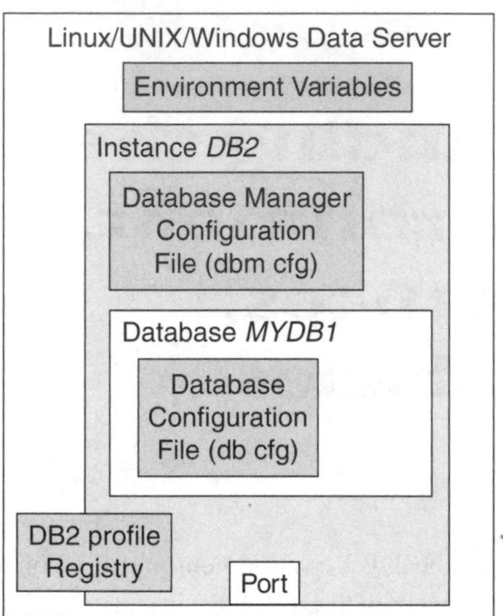

Figure 5.1 The big picture of the DB2 environment, instances, and databases

In the following sections you will learn in detail how to work with all of these variables.

> **NOTE** DB2 provides several levels of configuration that allow users to control the DB2 environment with more flexibility. If you are not an experienced DB2 user, the **Configuration Advisor** graphical tool can set parameter values based on your answers to simple questions about your system. Chapter 17, Database Performance Considerations, discusses this tool in more detail.

5.2 The DB2 Environment

The DB2 environment consists of environment variables and DB2 profile registry variables. These manage, monitor, and control the behavior of a DB2 system.

5.2.1 Environment Variables

Environment variables are set at the operating system level. Most environment variables applicable to DB2 are set automatically during the DB2 installation. For example, the PATH environment variable is updated to point to the DB2 executable code directory.

The two most important environment variables applicable to DB2 are

- DB2INSTANCE, which determines the active instance in your machine
- DB2NODE, which determines the active database partition in a multipartitioned environment.

To review the contents of an environment variable like DB2INSTANCE, you can do the following:

On Windows:

```
echo %DB2INSTANCE%
```

or

```
set DB2INSTANCE
```

On Linux and UNIX:

```
export | grep DB2INSTANCE
```

or

```
set | grep DB2INSTANCE
```

To change the value of an environment variable *temporarily*, use the **set** operating system command on Windows or **export** on Linux and UNIX as shown in the following examples.

On Windows:

```
set DB2INSTANCE=myinst
```

On Linux and UNIX it would depend on the shell that is used.

- For the Korn shell:

  ```
  DB2INSTANCE=myinst
  export DB2INSTANCE
  ```

- For the Bourne shell:

  ```
  export DB2INSTANCE=myinst
  ```

- For the C shell:

  ```
  setenv DB2INSTANCE myinst
  ```

This setting will be lost after you close the window or end the session.

> **NOTE** A common mistake when using the **set** (Windows) or **export** (Linux and UNIX) commands is to leave spaces before and/or after the equal sign (=). No spaces must be used!

To create a new or modify an existing environment variable *permanently*, you can do the following:

- On Windows platforms, use the Control Panel. Figure 5.2 shows an example of using the Control Panel under Windows XP Professional and viewing the environment variable DB2INSTANCE. In the figure, *System* was selected followed by the *Advanced* tab, and then the *Environment Variables* button.

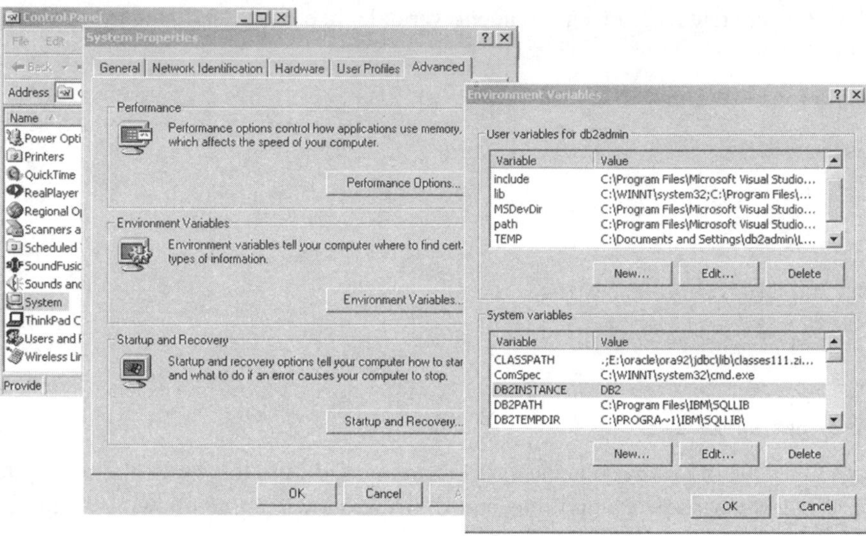

Figure 5.2 Setting an environment variable permanently in Windows

- On Linux and UNIX platforms you can permanently change an environment variable by adding the **export** command in the .login or .profile startup scripts. However, rather than making this change directly, you can edit the script that comes with DB2 to set up the default DB2 environment. Then invoke this script from .login or .profile. DB2 provides the **db2profile** (for the Bourne and Korn shells) script and **db2cshrc** (for the C shell) script, which contain all the required commands to set up this default DB2 environment. These script files are located under the *INSTHOME*/ sqllib directory, where *INSTHOME* represents the instance owner's home directory.

Figure 5.3 shows the **db2profile** script. Note that the DB2INSTANCE environment variable is set in the script file.

```
#############################################################################
# Licensed Materials - Property of IBM
#
# (C) COPYRIGHT International Business Machines Corp. 2007
#
# All Rights Reserved.
#
# US Government Users Restricted Rights - Use, duplication or
# disclosure restricted by GSA ADP Schedule Contract with IBM Corp.
#
#############################################################################
#
# NAME:     db2profile
#
# FUNCTION: This script sets up a default database environment for
#           Bourne shell or Korn shell users.
#
```

Figure 5.3 The db2profile script file for a Linux and UNIX machine

```
# USAGE:     . db2profile
#            This script can either be invoked directly as above or
#            it can be added to the user's .profile file so that the
#            database environment is established during login.
#
#            #### DO NOT EDIT THIS FILE ####
#
#############################################################################
DB2DIR=/opt/IBM/db2/V9.5
# Remember the current DB2INSTANCE environment variable
CUR_INSTNAME=${DB2INSTANCE:=""}
#-----------------------------------------------------------------------
# DB2INSTANCE [Default null, values: Any valid instance name]
# Specifies the instance that is active by default.
#-----------------------------------------------------------------------
DB2INSTANCE=db2inst2
export DB2INSTANCE
INSTHOME=/home/db2inst2
# Function to add or remove certain path to or from the specified
# environment variable.
AddRemoveString()
{
    if [ $# -ne 3 ]; then
       return 0
    fi
    var=$1         #The enviornment variable to be processed
    addrm_str=$2   #The new path to be used
    action=$3      #Action: a -> add, r -> remove
    if [ "X${action?}" != "Xa" -a "X${action?}" != "Xr" ]; then
        return 0  # return without doing anything
    fi
    awkval='$1 != "'${addrm_str?}'"{print $0}'
    newval=`eval /usr/bin/echo \\${$var:-""} | /usr/bin/awk '{for (i=1; i<= NF; ++i)
\
          if( $i != VAR ) print $i":"}' FS=":" VAR=${addrm_str?}`
    newval=`/usr/bin/echo ${newval?} | /usr/bin/sed 's/\: /\:/g'`
    if [ "X${action?}" = "Xa" ]; then
        newval=${newval?}"${addrm_str?}"
    else
        newval=`/usr/bin/echo ${newval?} | /usr/bin/sed 's/:$//'`
    fi
    eval $var=\"${newval?}\"
    unset var addrm_str awkval newval
}

#----------------------------------------------------------------------------
# If DB2 instance environment is being switched from one instances to another,
# the entries for old DB2 instance in the original instance enviornment
# are cleaned up.
#----------------------------------------------------------------------------
if [ -n "${CUR_INSTNAME?}" ]; then
     CUR_INSTHOME=`${INSTHOME?}/sqllib/bin/db2usrinf -d ${CUR_INSTNAME?}`
     path_list="bin adm misc"
     class_list="java/db2java.zip java/db2jcc.jar java/sqlj.zip function \
       java/db2jcc_license_cisuz.jar java/db2jcc_license_cu.jar \
               java/runtime.zip"
```

Figure 5.3 The db2profile script file for a Linux and UNIX machine *(Continued)*

```
    for tmp_entry in ${path_list?}; do
       AddRemoveString PATH ${CUR_INSTHOME?}/sqllib/${tmp_entry?} r
    done
    for tmp_entry in ${class_list?}; do
       AddRemoveString CLASSPATH ${CUR_INSTHOME?}/sqllib/${tmp_entry?} r
    done

    for path_name in LD_LIBRARY_PATH LIBPATH SHLIB_PATH LD_LIBRARY_PATH_32 \
       LD_LIBRARY_PATH_64; do
       for tmp_path in lib lib32 lib64; do
          AddRemoveString ${path_name?} ${CUR_INSTHOME?}/sqllib/${tmp_path?} r
       done
    done

    for path_name in PATH CLASSPATH LD_LIBRARY_PATH LIBPATH SHLIB_PATH \
       LD_LIBRARY_PATH_32 LD_LIBRARY_PATH_64; do
       eval path_value=\$$path_name
       if [ "X${path_value}" = "X" ]; then
          unset ${path_name?}
       else
          export ${path_name?}
       fi
    done
    unset CUR_INSTNAME path_list class_list tmp_entry path_name path_value
fi

#-----------------------------------------------------------------------------
# In DB2 instance environment, the DAS environment needs to be cleaned up.
#-----------------------------------------------------------------------------
DASWORKDIR=${DASWORKDIR:=""}
if [ "X${DASWORKDIR}" != "X" ]; then
  AddRemoveString PATH ${DASWORKDIR?}/bin r
  AddRemoveString PATH ${DASWORKDIR?}/adm r
  for path_name in LIBPATH SHLIB_PATH LD_LIBRARY_PATH; do
      for tmp_path in lib function; do
          AddRemoveString ${path_name?} ${DASWORKDIR?}/${tmp_path?} r
      done
  done
  for path_name in PATH LIBPATH SHLIB_PATH LD_LIBRARY_PATH; do
       if [ "X${path_name}" = "X" ]; then
          unset ${path_name?}
       else
          export ${path_name?}
       fi
  done
fi
#-----------------------------------------------------------------------------

for tmp_path in bin adm misc; do
   AddRemoveString PATH ${INSTHOME?}/sqllib/${tmp_path?} a
done
export PATH
unset tmp_path

#-------------------------------------------------------------------------
# UDB Extender initialization
#-------------------------------------------------------------------------
```

Figure 5.3 The db2profile script file for a Linux and UNIX machine *(Continued)*

```
if [ -f ${INSTHOME}/dmb/dmbprofile ]; then
    . ${INSTHOME}/dmb/dmbprofile
fi

#-----------------------------------------------------------------------
# The following variables are used for JDBC support
#-----------------------------------------------------------------------
CLASSPATH=${CLASSPATH:-""}

if [ -f ${INSTHOME?}/sqllib/java/db2java.zip ]; then
    AddRemoveString CLASSPATH ${INSTHOME?}/sqllib/java/db2java.zip a
fi
if [ -f ${INSTHOME?}/sqllib/java/db2jcc.jar ]; then
    AddRemoveString CLASSPATH ${INSTHOME?}/sqllib/java/db2jcc.jar a
fi
if [ -f ${INSTHOME?}/sqllib/java/sqlj.zip ]; then
    AddRemoveString CLASSPATH ${INSTHOME?}/sqllib/java/sqlj.zip a
fi
if [ -d ${INSTHOME?}/sqllib/function ]; then
    AddRemoveString CLASSPATH ${INSTHOME?}/sqllib/function a
fi

if [ -f ${INSTHOME?}/sqllib/java/db2jcc_license_cisuz.jar ]; then
    AddRemoveString CLASSPATH ${INSTHOME?}/sqllib/java/db2jcc_license_cisuz.jar a
fi

if [ -f ${INSTHOME?}/sqllib/java/db2jcc_license_cu.jar ]; then
    AddRemoveString CLASSPATH ${INSTHOME?}/sqllib/java/db2jcc_license_cu.jar a
fi

AddRemoveString CLASSPATH . a
export CLASSPATH

LIBPATH=${LIBPATH:-"/usr/lib:/lib"}
AddRemoveString LIBPATH ${INSTHOME?}/sqllib/lib64 a
export LIBPATH

#-----------------------------------------------------------------------
# Any user changes to the environment goes into userprofile.  Modifications
# to db2profile may be overwritten in fixpaks.
#-----------------------------------------------------------------------
if [ -f ${INSTHOME?}/sqllib/userprofile ]; then
    . ${INSTHOME?}/sqllib/userprofile
fi
```

Figure 5.3 The db2profile script file for a Linux and UNIX machine *(Continued)*

For the DB2 instance owner, a line to invoke the **db2profile/db2cshrc** script file is automatically added to the .login or .profile file during the instance creation. If you are a DB2 user who is not the instance owner, add the following line to your .login or .profile startup scripts:

.INSTHOME/sqllib/db2profile (for Bourne and Korn shells)

or

source INSTHOME/sqllib/db2cshrc (for C shell)

Executing the above commands will guarantee that your database environment is configured to use DB2.

5.2.2 DB2 Profile Registries

Most DB2-related information is stored in a centralized repository called the **DB2 profile registry.** Depending on the operating system platform where DB2 is installed, variables stored in the DB2 profile registries may be different. The DB2 profile registry variables are commonly referred to as **DB2 registry variables.**

> **NOTE** The word "Registry" always causes confusion when working with DB2 on the Windows platform. The DB2 profile registry variables have no relationship to the Windows registry variables.

The DB2 profile registry consists of the following registries:

- The DB2 Instance-Level Profile Registry: Variables set at this level apply only to a specific instance.
- The DB2 Global-Level Profile Registry: Variables set at this level apply globally to all instances.
- The DB2 Instance Node-Level Profile Registry: Variables at this level apply to a specific partition in a multipartitioned DB2 environment.
- The DB2 Instance Profile Registry: This contains a list of all instances in the system. The command `db2ilist`, which lists all instances in a system, uses this registry as input.

> **NOTE** All variables in the DB2 registries *except* those in the DB2 Instance Profile Registry are the same. The difference is the level at which you set the variable. For example, you can set the DB2COMM registry variable at the instance-level, global-level, or node-level profile registries.

The DB2 registries are stored as binary or text files in different locations depending on the operating system. To modify these registries, do not edit these files directly; instead, use the **db2set** command. Figure 5.4 shows the **db2set** command with the **-all** option, which lists all of the currently set DB2 profile registry variables.

Notice that each registry variable is preceeded with a letter in square brackets. This indicates in which level the variable is set.

- **[i]** indicates the variable has been set at the DB2 Instance-Level Profile Registry using the **-i** option (which is the default). For example, in Figure 5.4 *[i] DB2COMM=ssl* was set using the following command in instance *myinst*:

  ```
  db2set DB2COMM=ssl -i myinst
  ```

Figure 5.4 The db2set -all command

- **[g]** indicates the variable has been set at the DB2 Global-Level Profile Registry using the **-g** option. This setting applies to all instances defined on the DB2 server. For example, in Figure 5.4, *[g] DB2COMM=netbios* was set using this command:

```
db2set DB2COMM=netbios -g
```

- **[e]** indicates a DB2 registry variable has been set as an environment variable using the **set** command (Windows) or **export** command (Linux and UNIX). For example, in Figure 5.4 *[e] DB2COMM=tcpip* was set using this command:

```
set DB2COMM=tcpip
```

Although most DB2 registry variables can be set as environment variables, we recommend setting them as DB2 registry variables using the `db2set` command. Changes to DB2 registry variables do not require a server reboot, while changes to environment variables may require a reboot.

To set a registry variable at the DB2 instance node-level profile registry level, use a command with this syntax:

```
db2set registry_variable=value -i instance_name partition_number
```

> **NOTE** Similar to the **set** operating system command, do not leave spaces before and/or after the equal sign (=) when using the **db2set** command.

> **NOTE** The **db2set** command will not validate the values assigned to the DB2 registry variables. For example in Figure 5.4, DB2COMM was set to the value of netbios. With DB2 9, the netbios and SNA protocols are no longer supported, which means that assigning this value to DB2COMM is ignored.

In Figure 5.4,the DB2COMM registry variable was set three times with different values each at the [e], [i], and [g] levels. When a registry variable is defined at different levels, DB2 will choose the value using the following search order:

1. Environment variable set using the **set/export** operating system commands.
2. DB2 Instance Node-Level Profile Registry
3. DB2 Instance-Level Profile Registry
4. DB2 Global-Level Profile Registry

Based on this search order, for the example in Figure 5.4, the value *tcpip* for the DB2COMM registry variable is the one that takes precedence as it has been set temporarily at the environment level.

Table 5.1 summarizes other options commonly used with the **db2set** command.

Table 5.1 Common db2set Command Options

Command	Explanation
db2set -all	Lists all the currently set DB2 registry variables
db2set –lr	Lists all the DB2 registry variables that can be set
db2set –h	Displays help information about the **db2set** command
db2set *DB2_registry_variable=*	Deletes a variable from the DB2 registry. Note that a blank space follows the equal sign (=).

Some registry variables require that you stop and start the instance (**db2stop/db2start**) for the change to take effect. Refer to the *DB2 Administration Guide: Performance* for a list of variables that have this requirement.

5.3 The DB2 Instance

From a user's perspective, a **DB2 instance** provides an independent environment where database objects can be created and applications can run. Several instances can be created on one server, and each instance can have a multiple number of databases, as illustrated in Figure 5.5.

Because of these independent environments, one instance cannot "see" the contents of another instance; therefore, objects of the same name can exist in two or more instances. In Figure 5.5, the database called *MYDB1* is associated with instance *Development*, and another database also called *MYDB1* is associated with instance *Test*. Instances allow users to have different environments for production, test, and developmental purposes. In addition, independent environments let you perform instance and database operations without affecting other instances. For example, if you stop and start the instance *Test*, the other two instances are not affected.

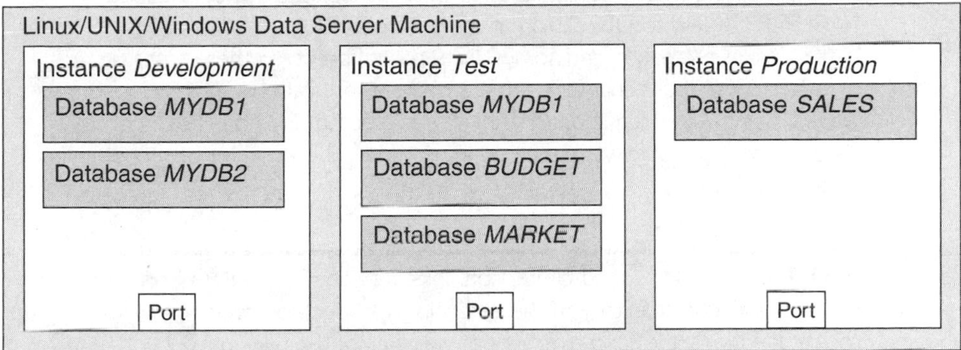

Figure 5.5 A DB2 instance from a user's perspective

From an architectural perspective, an instance serves as a layer between the DB2 binary code and the user database objects. It is important to understand that this is just an association of the DB2 code to the database objects. There is a common misconception among new DB2 users that dropping an instance also drops the databases associated with that instance; this is not necessarily true. When an instance is dropped, the association to the user databases is broken, but it can later be reestablished, as discussed in Chapter 2, DB2 at a Glance: The Big Picture.

Figure 5.6 shows an example of two instances in a Linux and UNIX environment. Databases *MarketDB* and *SalesDB* are associated with instance *#1*. Databases *TestDB* and *ProdDB* are associated with instance *#2*. Each instance has its own configuration files. In this example, both instances are pointing to the same DB2 binary code for DB2 9.5 using **soft links.** On Linux and UNIX, a soft link behaves like an alias to another file. Soft links are also referred to as **symbolic links** or **logical links.**

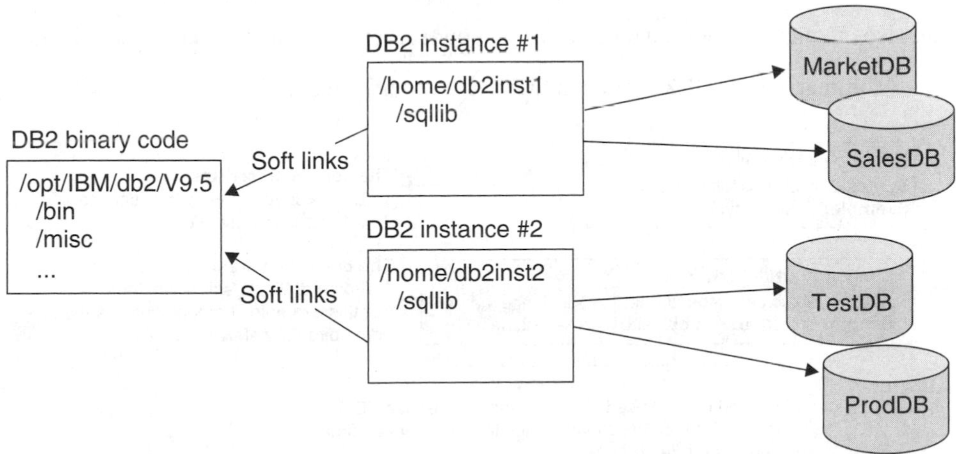

Figure 5.6 The DB2 instance in Linux and UNIX from an architectural prespective

> **NOTE** New to DB2 9.5 are non-root installations in Linux and UNIX. Instance creation and administration is different for these types of installations. In this chapter we focus on root installations, however we will point out, when appropriate, what is different for non-root installations. This topic was discussed in more detail in Chapter 3, Installing DB2.

> **NOTE** On Linux and UNIX, soft links are used as pointers from the instance *sqllib* directory to the DB2 binary code. However, in non-root installations, the *sqllib* directory contains all of the DB2 product files and instance files with no soft links. On Windows, there is a shared install path and all instances access the same libraries and executables.

> **NOTE** In Figure 5.6 the path /opt/IBM/db2/V9.5 is applicable to UNIX only. For Linux, the path is /opt/ibm/db2/V9.5. We will use the UNIX path in most examples.

5.3.1 Creating DB2 Instances

When you install DB2 on the Windows platform, an instance called *DB2* is created by default. On Linux and UNIX you can choose to create the default instance during the installation, change the instance owner's name, or not create an instance so that you can create one later. If you choose to create the default instance on these platforms, this instance is called *db2inst1*. DB2 will create an operating system user with the same name as the instance. This user is known as the **instance owner.**

You can also create new, additional instances on your server using the **db2icrt** command.

Figure 5.7 summarizes the **db2icrt** command and provides examples.

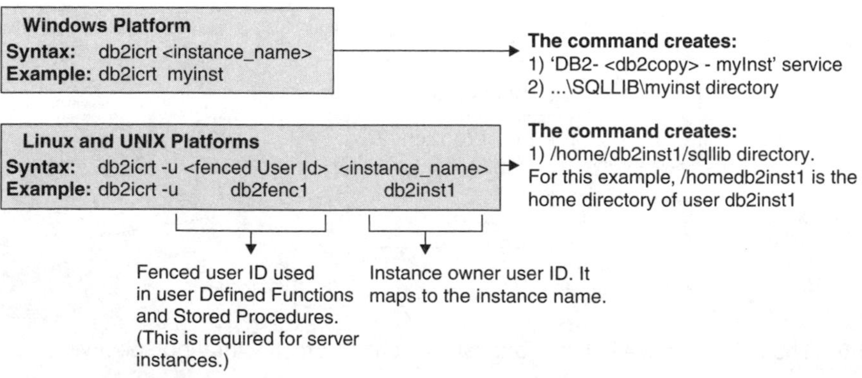

Figure 5.7 The db2icrt command

V9.5

> **NOTE** In non-root installations on Linux and UNIX, the db2icrt command is not supported, as you cannot create other instances. You can only work with the instance created at installation time.

On Windows the **db2icrt** command can be run by a user with Local Administrator authority. The command creates a subdirectory under the SQLLIB directory with the name of the instance just created. In addition, a Windows service *DB2 – db2copy_name – instance_ name* will be created. The first qualifier in DB2-related Windows services is always *DB2*.

V9

> **NOTE** Prior to DB2 9 you could only install one copy of DB2 on a machine running Windows. Starting with DB2 9, several independent copies can be installed at different fix pack levels. To differentiate the Windows services created for each copy, the DB2 copy name-an arbitrary name given to a particular copy of the DB2 code-is incorporated in the service name as show here:
>
> DB2 - db2copy_name - instance_ name.
>
> This is described in more detail in Chapter 3, Installing DB2

On Linux and UNIX you must have root authority or else you need to have the system administrator run the **db2icrt** command for you. You can either use the fully qualified path name to the program or change into the directory to run this command as shown below:

- Run the command **/opt/IBM/db2/V9.5/instance/db2icrt**

  or
- Change into the directory /opt/IBM/db2/V9.5/instance and then invoke the **db2icrt** command.

In addition, on Linux and UNIX, the instance name must match an existing operating system user ID, which becomes the instance owner. This operating system user must exist prior to executing the **db2icrt** command. The **db2icrt** command will create the subdirectory *sqllib* under the home directory of this user.

DB2 on Linux and UNIX also requires a fenced user to run stored procedures and user-defined functions (UDFs) as fenced resources, that is, in a separate address space other than the one used by the DB2 engine. This ensures that problems with these objects do not affect your database or instance. If you have thoroughly tested your stored procedures and UDFs and are confident they will run with no problems, you can use the same ID for the fenced user and the instance owner.

> **NOTE** The terms *instance* and a *DB2 instance* are used interchangeably. On Windows, the default name of the DB2 instance is *DB2*. This sometimes confuses new DB2 users.

NOTE Prior to version 9, the db2icrt command used the -w 64 option to create a 64-bit instance on AIX 5L, HP-UX and Solaris operating systems. This is no longer required starting with DB2 9. With DB2 9 the instance bit size is now determined by the operating system where the product installation is performed.

5.3.2 Creating Client Instances

In general, when we talk about instances in this book we are referring to server instances: fully functional instances created at the DB2 server where your database resides. There are other types of instances that can be created. One of them, the **client instance,** is a scaled-down version of a server instance. A client instance cannot be started or stopped, and databases cannot be created on this type of instance.

You create a DB2 client instance using the **-s** option. For example

```
db2icrt -s CLIENT myclinst
```

creates the client instance *myclinst.* On Linux and UNIX, the operating system user *myclinst* must exist before executing this command. On Windows, an instance does not map to a user ID, so this would not be a requirement.

On a Windows client, the entire machine is considered the DB2 client regardless of the user. On a Linux and UNIX machine the DB2 client is associated with an operating system user.

You need to have a client instance if you have two physically separate Linux and UNIX machines, one containing the DB2 client code (assume it is an application server machine) and the other one containing the DB2 server code (the DB2 server machine). On the client machine a client instance must be created that will associate it to a given operating system user. Logging on as this user lets you perform the commands required to set up connectivity to the DB2 server machine.

If the client and server reside on the same machine containing the DB2 server code, there would be no need to create a client instance, because the operating system user used as the client can "source" the instance owner profile in sqllib/db2profile as described in Section 5.2.1, Environment Variables.

5.3.3 Creating DB2 Instances in a Multipartitioned Environment

In a multipartitioned environment, an instance is only created once: on the machine where the disks to be shared by the other partitions reside. The instance owner's home directory is then exported to all the servers participating in the multipartitioned environment (see Chapter 2, DB2 at a Glance: The Big Picture).

NOTE You can only create a multipartitioned database if you have DB2 Enterprise installed and you have purchased the database partitioning feature (DPF) pack. The DPF is a paper-only license that you need to acquire; you do not need to install any additional products to use this feature.

5.3.4 Dropping an Instance

You can drop an instance if you no longer need it. Before you drop an instance, make sure that it is stopped. Aditionally, on Linux and UNIX ensure that all memory and inter-process communications (IPCs) owned by the instance have been released; this can be done by issuing the **ipclean** command as the instance owner. You can then run the **db2idrop** command to drop the DB2 instance. For example, to drop the instance *myinst*, use the command:

```
db2idrop myinst
```

5.3.5 Listing the Instances in Your System

You can list all instances on your server using the **db2ilist** command. On Windows you can run this command from any Command Window. On Linux and UNIX you may need to change the directory to the path where this command resides, which is under the directory where DB2 was installed (/opt/IBM/db2/V9.5) before running this command.

Alternatively, you can list your instances using the DB2 Control Center. Figure 5.8 shows the steps that are needed.

1. Right-click on the Instances folder.
2. Choose Add Instance.
3. Click on the *Discover* button.

Clicking on *Discover* displays a list of all available instances. You can then select the desired instance(s) to add to the Control Center.

NOTE You cannot create an instance from the Control Center. You can only add an existing instance to the Control Center so it can be displayed and managed more easily with this tool.

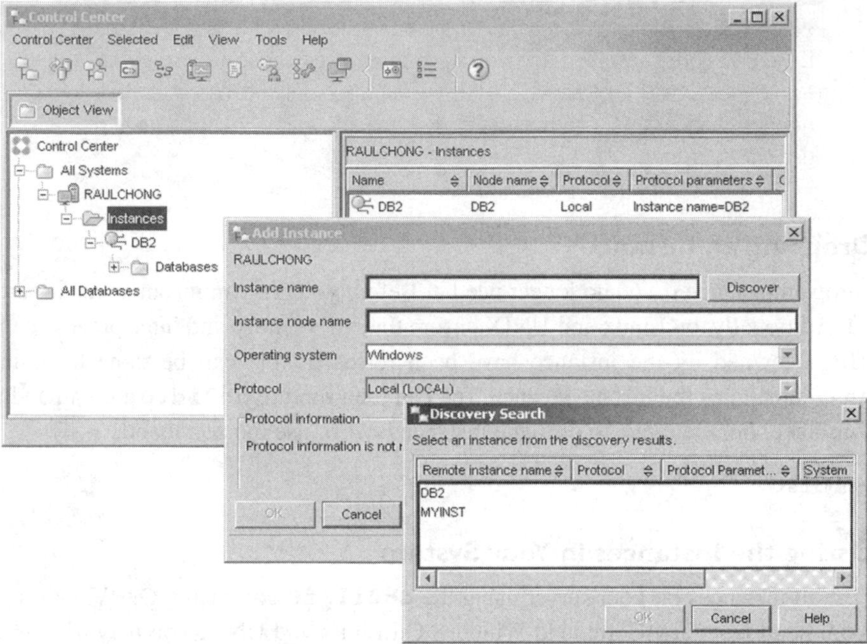

Figure 5.8 Adding instances to the Control Center

5.3.6 The DB2INSTANCE Environment Variable

Use the DB2INSTANCE environment variable to indicate which instance will be affected by your commands, that is, which instance is the active one for your commands. It is particularly important to have this variable set correctly when you have multiple instances in the same DB2 server. For example, if you have two instances, *myinst1* and *myinst2*, and DB2INSTANCE is set to *myinst2*, any command you execute will be directed to the *myinst2* instance. On Linux and UNIX you can switch to another instance by logging on or switching to the corresponding instance owner user ID.

Because DB2INSTANCE is an operating system environment variable, you set this value like any other environment variable for your operating system, as discussed in Section 5.2.1, Environment Variables. Figure 5.9 illustrates setting the DB2INSTANCE environment variable temporarily in the Windows platform using the **set** operating system command. It also illustrates the methods used to determine its current value such as using the command **get instance** (which works on any platform), using the **echo** operating system command, or the **set** operating system command.

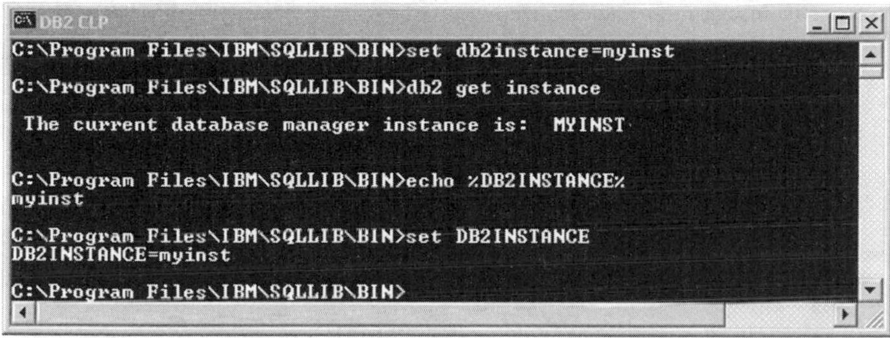

Figure 5.9 Working with the DB2INSTANCE variable

5.3.7 Starting a DB2 Instance

An instance must be started before you can work with it. You can choose to start the instance manually or automatically every time you reboot your machine. To start an instance manually, use the **db2start** command. On Windows, since DB2 instances are created as services, you can also start an instance manually using the **NET START** command. To start an instance automatically on Windows, look for the service corresponding to the DB2 instance by opening the Control Panel, choosing the *Administration Tools* folder, and then double-clicking on *Services*. A Services window similar to the one displayed in Figure 5.10 will appear.

Several DB2 services are listed in Figure 5.10. All of the DB2 services can be easily identified as they are prefixed with *DB2* and include the DB2 installation copy name. For example, the service *DB2 – DB2COPY1 – MYINST* represents the instance *MYINST* using the DB2 installation copy *DB2COPY1*. The service *DB2 – DB2COPY1 – DB2* highlighted in the figure represents the instance named *DB2* using installation copy *DB2COPY1*. As you can see from the figure, this service is set up to be manually started, so you would need to execute a **db2start** command every time the system is restarted for the DB2 instance to be able to work with your databases.

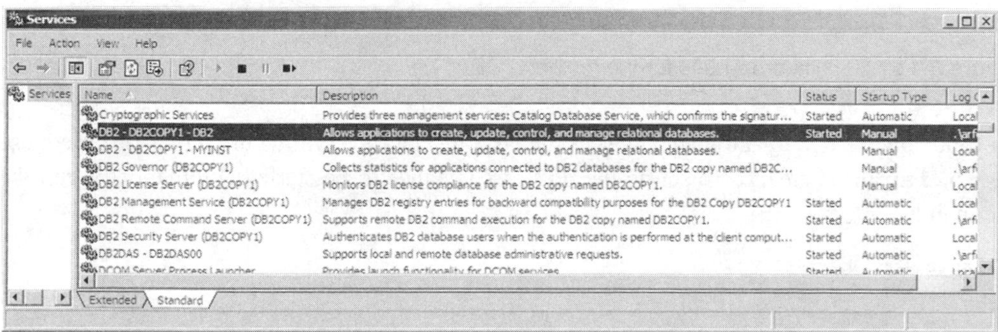

Figure 5.10 Windows services for DB2

You can set up the instance to be automatically started by right-clicking on the *DB2 – DB2COPY1 – DB2* service and choosing **Properties** from the drop-down menu. Once the Properties panel appears, you can change the *Startup type* from *Manual* to *Automatic* (see Figure 5.11).

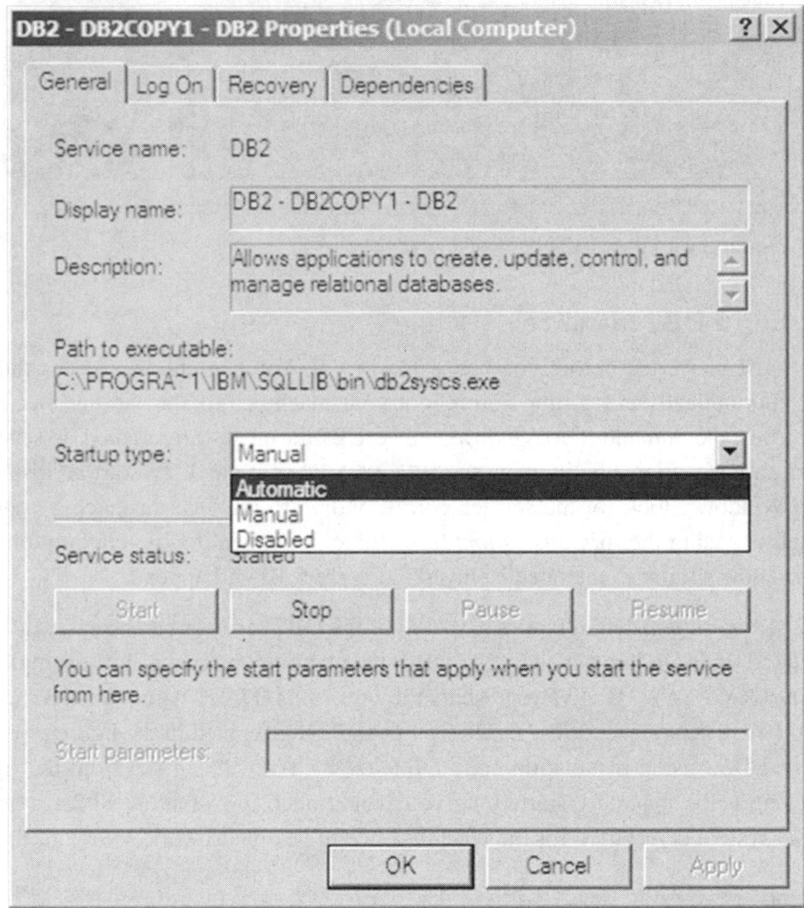

Figure 5.11 Service properties for the instance DB2

On Linux and UNIX, to automatically start the DB2 instance every time the server is started, use the **`db2iauto`** command. To set up the *db2inst1* instance to be started automatically, run the command:

```
db2iauto –on db2inst1
```

> **NOTE** If you are setting up your system for High Availability failover, you *should not* set up the instance to be started automatically.

NOTE The DB2INSTANCE variable indicates which instance is your active instance, that is, the one to which your commands would apply. This is different from instances that are *started*. Many instances can be started at the same time, but only one is your active instance.

V9.5

NOTE On Linux and UNIX, the automatic starting of non-root DB2 instances at system reboot is not supported.

In a multipartitioned environment you only need to run the `db2start` command once, and it will start all of the partitions defined in the db2nodes.cfg file. Notice in the output of the `db2start` command below that there is one message returned for each partition, and each message has the partition number associated with it in the third column. Since the instances are started in parallel, they are not likely to complete in the order specified in the db2nodes.cfg file.

```
db2inst1@aries db2inst1]$ db2start

06-14-2007 4:32:16  1  0  SQL1063N  DB2START processing was successful.
06-14-2007 4:32:16  0  0  SQL1063N  DB2START processing was successful.
06-14-2007 4:32:16  2  0  SQL1063N  DB2START processing was successful.
06-14-2007 4:32:16  3  0  SQL1063N  DB2START processing was successful.
SQL1063N  DB2START processing was successful.
```

There may be times when a database administrator needs to be the only user attached to an instance to perform maintenance tasks. In these situations, use the **`db2start`** option **`admin mode user userId`** so only one user has full control of the instance. You can also do this from the Control Center by rightclicking on the desired instance in the Object Tree and choosing *Start Admin.*

5.3.8 Stopping a DB2 Instance

You can use the **`db2stop`** command to stop a DB2 instance that is currently running. On Windows, verify that the DB2INSTANCE environment variable is correctly set before issuing this command, as discussed in Section 5.2.1, Environment Variables. On Linux and UNIX ensure you are logged on as the instance owner of the instance you want to stop.

On Windows, since the DB2 instances are created as services, you can also stop the instances using the **`NET STOP`** command or stop the service from the Control Panel. To stop an instance from the Control Panel on Windows, rightclick on the service and select *Stop* from the dropdown menu. Once the service is stopped the *Status* column will be blank, as the highlighted line shows in Figure 5.12.

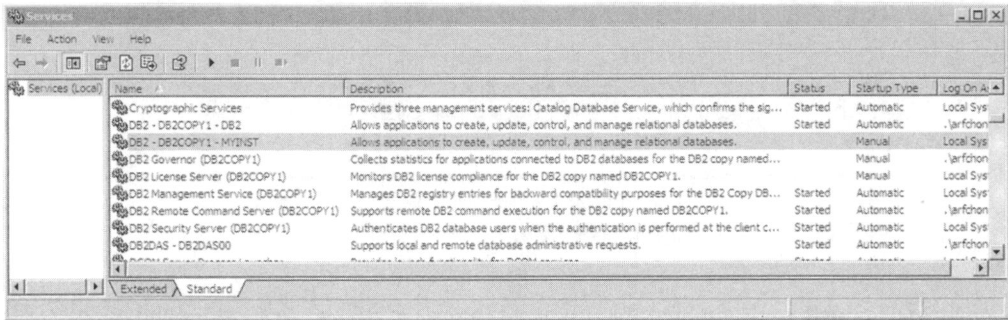

Figure 5.12 A stopped instance

You will not be able to stop the instance if there is a database that is active in the instance or if there are databases with one or more connections. You must first deactivate the database and/or reset the connections. In many cases you will have a large number of DB2 client machines running applications that connect to the database server, and you will not be able to go to each machine to close the application to terminate the connection. In this case you can use the `force` option with the `db2stop` command to force off all active connections and/or activations to stop the instance:

```
db2stop force
```

> **NOTE** A **db2stop force** command has the same effect as issuing the **force applications all** command followed by the db2stop command. However, **db2stop force** prevents new connections from happening while the instance is being stopped. The **force applications** command is discussed in detail in Chapter 12, Understanding Concurrency and Locking.

In a multipartitioned environment you only need to run the **db2stop** command once, and it will stop all of the partitions defined in the db2nodes.cfg file.

> **NOTE** In many DB2 customer environments, the process of issuing a **db2stop** followed by a **db2start** command is called one or more of the following:
>
> - Recycling the instance
> - Bringing the instance down and up
> - Bouncing the instance
> - Stopping and (re)starting the instance
> - Issuing a DB2 stop and start

5.3.9 Attaching to an Instance

To perform instance-level maintenance tasks, you first need to attach to the instance with the **attach** command. Some instance-level operations are

- Listing applications connected to your databases
- Forcing off applications
- Monitoring a database
- Updating the Database Manager Configuration parameters

Users often confuse attaching to an instance and connecting to a database. When in doubt as to which one to use, determine whether the operation is to affect the instance or a particular database. For example, the **list applications** command lists all the applications connected to all the databases in your active instance. This is not an operation that you would perform at the database level, since you want to list all connections to all databases, so an attachment is what is required in this case. (Chapter 6, Configuring Client and Server Connectivity, discusses setting up database connections in detail. In that chapter we describe the **node directory,** which is used to encapsulate connectivity information, such as the hostname of a remote DB2 database server and the port number of the instance.)

> **NOTE** Attachments are only applicable at the instance level; connections are only applicable at the database level.

When you attach to an instance, it can be a local instance or a remote instance. Each instance will have a corresponding entry in the node directory. A local instance resides on the same machine where you issue the **attach** command, while a remote instance resides on some other machine. Other than the active instance specified in the DB2INSTANCE variable, DB2 will look for connectivity information in the node directory for any other instance.

The syntax to attach to the active instance is

```
attach to instance_name_as_indicated_in_DB2INSTANCE
```

For example

```
attach to DB2
```

To attach to a local or remote instance that is not your active instance, use

```
attach to node_name [user userId] [using password]
```

For example

```
attach to mynode user peter using myudbpsw
```

where **mynode** is an entry in the node directory.

Attaching to the active instance (as specified in DB2INSTANCE) is normally done implicitly. However, there are special occasions where you do need to explicitly attach to the active instance, as you will see in following sections.

To detach from the current attached instance, issue the **detach** command:

```
attach to mynode

detach
```

5.3.10 Configuring an Instance

You can set DB2 configuration parameters at the instance level (also known as the database manager level) and at the database level. At the instance level, variables are stored in the Database Manager (DBM) Configuration file. Changes to these variables affect *all* databases associated with this instance. At the database level, variables are stored in the Database Configuration file. Changes to these variables only affect that specific database. In this section we discuss the DBM Configuration file in detail.

When you install DB2 and create an instance, the instance is assigned a default DBM configuration. You can view this configuration by running the **get dbm cfg** command. Figure 5.13 shows the output of this command on a Windows machine.

```
C:\Program Files\IBM\SQLLIB\BIN>db2 get dbm cfg

          Database Manager Configuration

     Node type = Enterprise Server Edition with local and remote clients

 Database manager configuration release level            = 0x0c00

 Maximum total of files open               (MAXTOTFILOP) = 16000
 CPU speed (millisec/instruction)             (CPUSPEED) = 6.140475e-007
 Communications bandwidth (MB/sec)      (COMM_BANDWIDTH) = 1.000000e+002

 Max number of concurrently active databases     (NUMDB) = 8
 Federated Database System Support           (FEDERATED) = NO
 Transaction processor monitor name        (TP_MON_NAME) =

 Default charge-back account           (DFT_ACCOUNT_STR) =

 Java Development Kit installation path       (JDK_PATH) =

 Diagnostic error capture level              (DIAGLEVEL) = 3
 Notify Level                              (NOTIFYLEVEL) = 3
 Diagnostic data directory path               (DIAGPATH) =

 Default database monitor switches
   Buffer pool                         (DFT_MON_BUFPOOL) = OFF
   Lock                                   (DFT_MON_LOCK) = OFF
   Sort                                   (DFT_MON_SORT) = OFF
   Statement                              (DFT_MON_STMT) = OFF
   Table                                 (DFT_MON_TABLE) = OFF
```

Figure 5.13 Contents of the DBM Configuration file

```
   Timestamp                               (DFT_MON_TIMESTAMP) = ON
   Unit of work                                  (DFT_MON_UOW) = OFF
 Monitor health of instance and databases   (HEALTH_MON) = ON

 SYSADM group name                          (SYSADM_GROUP) =
 SYSCTRL group name                        (SYSCTRL_GROUP) =
 SYSMAINT group name                      (SYSMAINT_GROUP) =
 SYSMON group name                          (SYSMON_GROUP) =

 Client Userid-Password Plugin            (CLNT_PW_PLUGIN) =
 Client Kerberos Plugin                  (CLNT_KRB_PLUGIN) = IBMkrb5
 Group Plugin                               (GROUP_PLUGIN) =
 GSS Plugin for Local Authorization      (LOCAL_GSSPLUGIN) =
 Server Plugin Mode                      (SRV_PLUGIN_MODE) = UNFENCED
 Server List of GSS Plugins        (SRVCON_GSSPLUGIN_LIST) =
 Server Userid-Password Plugin          (SRVCON_PW_PLUGIN) =
 Server Connection Authentication            (SRVCON_AUTH) = NOT_SPECIFIED
 Cluster manager                             (CLUSTER_MGR) =

 Database manager authentication          (AUTHENTICATION) = SERVER
 Cataloging allowed without authority     (CATALOG_NOAUTH) = NO
 Trust all clients                        (TRUST_ALLCLNTS) = YES
 Trusted client authentication            (TRUST_CLNTAUTH) = CLIENT
 Bypass federated authentication              (FED_NOAUTH) = NO

 Default database path                         (DFTDBPATH) = C:

 Database monitor heap size (4KB)            (MON_HEAP_SZ) = AUTOMATIC
 Java Virtual Machine heap size (4KB)       (JAVA_HEAP_SZ) = 2048
 Audit buffer size (4KB)                    (AUDIT_BUF_SZ) = 0
 Size of instance shared memory (4KB)  (INSTANCE_MEMORY) = AUTOMATIC
 Backup buffer default size (4KB)              (BACKBUFSZ) = 1024
 Restore buffer default size (4KB)             (RESTBUFSZ) = 1024

 Agent stack size                         (AGENT_STACK_SZ) = 16
 Minimum committed private memory (4KB)     (MIN_PRIV_MEM) = 32
 Private memory threshold (4KB)          (PRIV_MEM_THRESH) = 20000

 Sort heap threshold (4KB)                    (SHEAPTHRES) = 0

 Directory cache support                       (DIR_CACHE) = YES

 Application support layer heap size (4KB)    (ASLHEAPSZ) = 15
 Max requester I/O block size (bytes)           (RQRIOBLK) = 32767
 Query heap size (4KB)                     (QUERY_HEAP_SZ) = 1000

 Workload impact by throttled utilities(UTIL_IMPACT_LIM) = 10

 Priority of agents                             (AGENTPRI) = SYSTEM
 Agent pool size                          (NUM_POOLAGENTS) = AUTOMATIC
 Initial number of agents in pool         (NUM_INITAGENTS) = 0
 Max number of coordinating agents       (MAX_COORDAGENTS) = AUTOMATIC
 Max number of client connections        (MAX_CONNECTIONS) = AUTOMATIC
```

Figure 5.13 Contents of the DBM Configuration file *(Continued)*

```
 Keep fenced process                           (KEEPFENCED) = YES
 Number of pooled fenced processes            (FENCED_POOL) = AUTOMATIC
 Initial number of fenced processes        (NUM_INITFENCED) = 0

 Index re-creation time and redo index build  (INDEXREC) = RESTART

 Transaction manager database name          (TM_DATABASE) = 1ST_CONN
 Transaction resync interval (sec)      (RESYNC_INTERVAL) = 180

 SPM name                                      (SPM_NAME) = RAULCHON
 SPM log size                           (SPM_LOG_FILE_SZ) = 256
 SPM resync agent limit                  (SPM_MAX_RESYNC) = 20
 SPM log path                              (SPM_LOG_PATH) =

 NetBIOS Workstation name                         (NNAME) =

 TCP/IP Service name                           (SVCENAME) = db2c_DB2
 Discovery mode                                (DISCOVER) = SEARCH
 Discover server instance                 (DISCOVER_INST) = ENABLE

 Maximum query degree of parallelism   (MAX_QUERYDEGREE) = ANY
 Enable intra-partition parallelism     (INTRA_PARALLEL) = NO

 Maximum Asynchronous TQs per query    (FEDERATED_ASYNC) = 0

 No. of int. communication buffers(4KB)(FCM_NUM_BUFFERS) = AUTOMATIC
 No. of int. communication channels   (FCM_NUM_CHANNELS) = AUTOMATIC
 Node connection elapse time (sec)         (CONN_ELAPSE) = 10
 Max number of node connection retries (MAX_CONNRETRIES) = 5
 Max time difference between nodes (min) (MAX_TIME_DIFF) = 60

 db2start/db2stop timeout (min)        (START_STOP_TIME) = 10

C:\Program Files\IBM\SQLLIB\BIN>
```

Figure 5.13 Contents of the DBM Configuration file *(Continued)*

Note that the *Node type* entry field at the top of the output identifies the type of instance. For example, in Figure 5.13 this field has the value *Enterprise Server Edition with local and remote clients*. This means it is a server instance. For a client instance the value of this field would be *Client*.

In this book you will learn some of the more important parameters for the DBM Configuration file. For a full treatment of all DBM Configuration parameters, refer to the *DB2 Administration Guide: Performance*.

To update one or more parameters in the DBM Configuration file, issue the command:

```
update dbm cfg
       using parameter_name value parameter_name value ...
```

For example, to update the INTRA_PARALLEL DBM Configuration parameter, issue the following command:

```
update dbm cfg using INTRA_PARALLEL YES
```

Issuing the **get dbm cfg** command after the **update dbm cfg** command shows the newly updated values. However, this does not mean that the change will take effect right away. Several parameters in the DBM Configuration file require a **db2stop** followed by a **db2start** for the new values to be used. For other parameters, the update is dynamic, so a **db2stop/db2start** is not required as the new value takes effect immediately. These parameters are called **configurable online parameters.** If you are updating a configuration parameter of a DB2 client instance, the new value takes effect the next time you restart the client application or if the client application is the CLP, after you issue the **terminate** command.

> **NOTE** Configurable online parameters of the DBM Configuration file can be updated dynamically only if you first explicitly attach to the instance. This also applies to local instances. If you have not performed an attach, the parameter won't be changed until you perform a **db2stop/db2start.**

The Control Center provides the list of DBM Configuration parameters and indicates which ones are configurable online. Refer to Section 5.3.11, Working with an Instance from the Control Center, for details.

To get the current, effective setting for each configuration parameter and the value of the parameter the next time the instance is stopped and restarted, use the **show detail** option of the **get dbm cfg** command. This option requires an instance attachment. If you run this command after changing the INTRA_PARALLEL configuration parameter as above, you will see that the current value is NO, but the next effective or delayed value is YES. The related output from the **get dbm cfg show detail** command would look like the following:

```
C:\Program Files\SQLLIB\BIN>db2 get dbm cfg show detail

Description                                Parameter         Current Value    Delayed Value
-----------------------------------------------------------------------------------------------
...
Enable intra-partition parallelism      (INTRA_PARALLEL) = NO                  YES
```

The **show detail** option is also helpful for determining the actual value of parameters listed as AUTOMATIC. For example, when you issue the **get dbm cfg** command while attached to an instance, you may see output as follows for the INSTANCE_MEMORY parameter:

```
C:\Program Files\SQLLIB\BIN>db2 get dbm cfg
...
Size of instance shared memory (4KB)   (INSTANCE_MEMORY) = AUTOMATIC
```

If you use the **show detail** option, the actual value is displayed:

```
C:\Program Files\SQLLIB\BIN>db2 get dbm cfg show detail
Description                                Parameter       Current Value    Delayed Value
-------------------------------------------------------------------------------------------
...
Size of instance shared memory(4KB)(INSTANCE_MEMORY) = AUTOMATIC(8405) AUTOMATIC(8405)
```

To reset all the DBM Configuration parameters to their default value, use the command **reset dbm cfg.**

5.3.11 Working with an Instance from the Control Center

The instance operations described in the previous sections can also be performed from the Control Center. Figure 5.14 shows the Control Center with the instance *MYINST* selected.

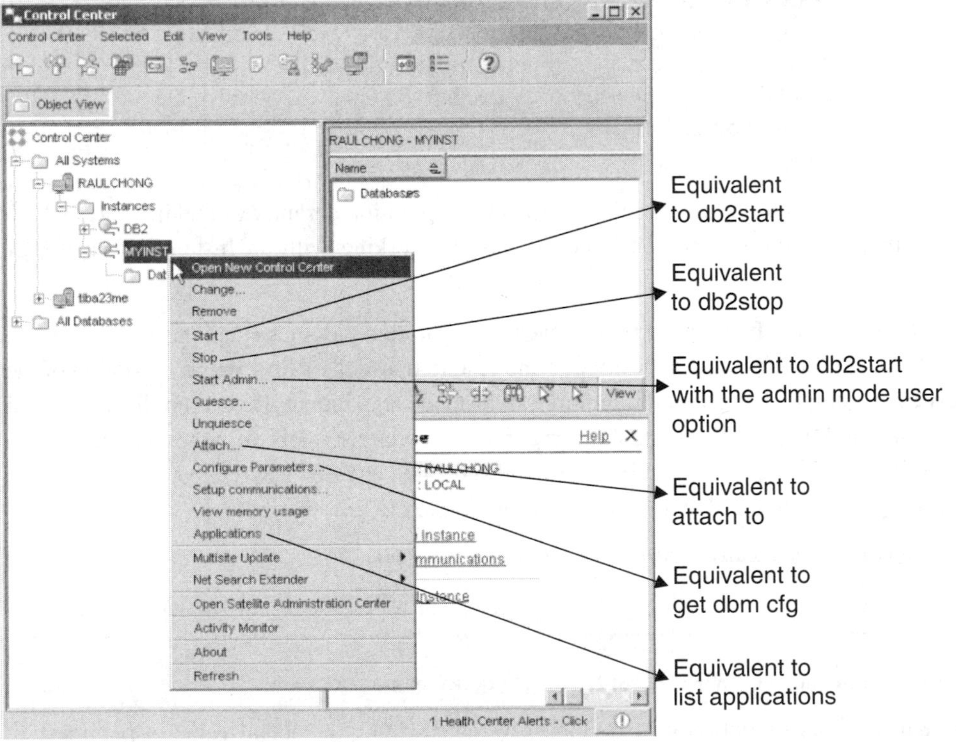

Figure 5.14 Performing instance operations from the Control Center

When you rightclick on the instance, a menu with several options is displayed. Figure 5.14 highlights some of the menu items that map to the instance operations we have already described.

Figure 5.15 shows the DBM Configuration window that appears after selecting **Configure Parameters** from the menu shown in Figure 5.14. In Figure 5.15, the column *Pending Value Effective* indicates when the pending value for the parameter will take effect; for example, immediately or after the instance is restarted. The column *Dynamic* indicates whether the parameter is configurable online or not. The rest of the columns are self-explanatory.

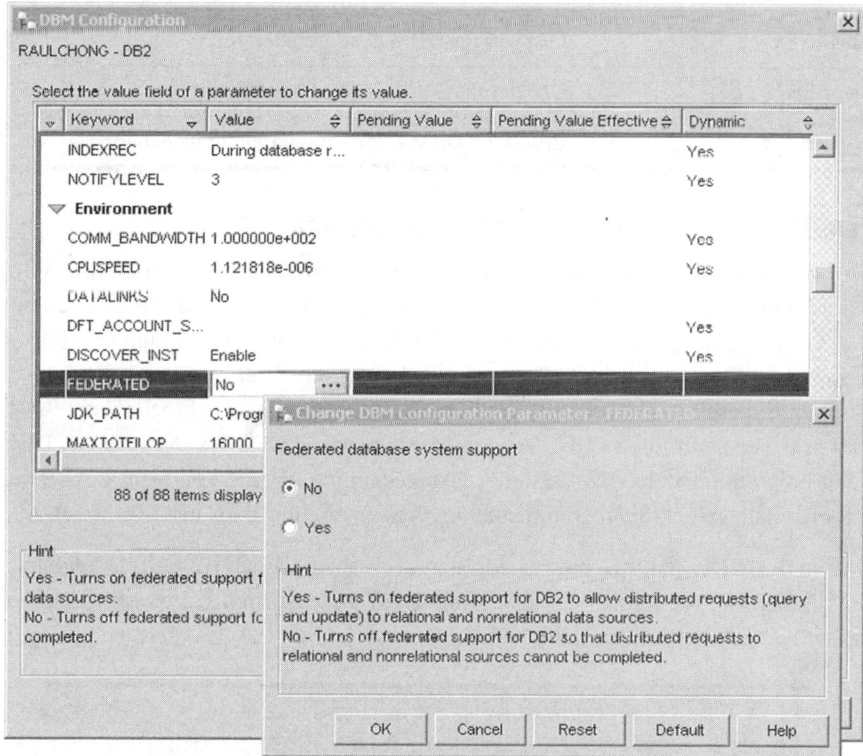

Figure 5.15 Configuring an instance from the Control Center

Figure 5.15 also illustrates how you can update a Database Manager Configuration parameter from the Control Center. For example, after selecting the parameter *FEDERATED* and clicking on the three dots button (...), a pop-up window displays that lists the possible values this parameter can accept. Choose the desired option and click *OK*.

5.3.12 The DB2 Commands at the Instance Level

Table 5.2 summarizes the most common DB2 commands used at the instance level.

Table 5.2 DB2 Instance-Level Commands

Command	Explanation
`db2start`	Starts an instance.
`db2stop`	Stops an instance.
`db2icrt`	Creates a new instance.
`db2idrop`	Drops an instance.
`db2ilist`	Lists all available instances in your system.
`get dbm cfg`	Displays the DBM Configuration file.
`update dbm cfg`	Updates the DBM Configuration file.
`reset dbm cfg`	Resets the DBM Configuration file to its default values.

5.4 The Database Administration Server

The **Database Administration Server** (DAS) is a background process that allows for remote graphical administration of your databases. For example, if you install the DB2 client on your Windows XP laptop and want to connect to a database in Japan using graphical tools, the database in Japan has to have the DAS created and running. There can only be one DAS per machine, even if there are several DB2 installation copies. A DB2 9.x DAS, where 9.x stands for versions 9 or 9.5 can administer DB2 Version 8 instances and DB2 9.x instances. A DB2 Version 8 DAS can only administer DB2 Version 8 instances; therefore, if you have DB2 9.x and DB2 Version 8 on a data server, the recommendation is to ensure the DAS used is the DB2 9.x DAS.

On Linux and UNIX, a DAS user needs to be created. The DB2 profile registry variable DB2ADMINSERVER contains the value of the DAS user. Normally, it is set to *DB2DAS00* on Windows and *dasusr1* on Linux and UNIX.

NOTE DB2 Administration Server and Database Administration Server are used interchangeably to refer to the DAS process.

V9.5

NOTE DB2 9.5 introduces the IBM Data Server Administration Console (DSAC), a graphical tool that can do most of your adminstrative operations. DSAC is the new generation of tools for IBM data servers. It does not need a DAS. Learn more about this tool in Chapter 4, Using the DB2 tools.

5.4.1 The DAS Commands

Table 5.3 summarizes the most common commands for the DAS.

Table 5.3 DAS Commands

Command	Explanation
`db2admin start`	Starts the DAS.
`db2admin stop`	Stops the DAS.
`dascrt`	Creates the DAS in Linux and UNIX.
`dasdrop`	Drops the DAS in Linux and UNIX.
`db2admin create`	Creates the DAS in Windows.
`db2admin drop`	Drops the DAS in Windows.
`get admin cfg`	Displays the DAS admin configuration file.
`update admin cfg`	Updates the DAS admin configuration file.
`reset admin cfg`	Resets the DAS admin configuration file to its default values.

5.5 Configuring a Database

Database configuration and instance configuration are fairly similar. We will use the same format to describe database configuration as we used to discuss instance configuration earlier in this chapter. Database concepts are discussed in more detail in Chapter 7, Working with Database Objects.

A database is set up with a default configuration when you create it. You can view this configuration by running the **get db cfg for *database_name*** command. Figure 5.16 shows the output of this command on a Windows machine.

```
C:\Program Files\IBM\SQLLIB\BIN>db2 get db cfg for sample
```

> **NOTE** If you are connected to a database, issuing the command get **db cfg** displays the contents of database configuration file; you don't need to specify the database name as part of the command.

In this book you will learn some of the more important database configuration parameters. For a full treatment of all database configuration parameters, refer to the *DB2 Administration Guide: Performance*.

To update one or more parameters in the database configuration file, issue the command:

```
update db cfg for database_name
      using parameter_name value  parameter_name value...
```

```
Database Configuration for Database sample

Database configuration release level                    = 0x0c00
Database release level                                  = 0x0c00

Database territory                                      = US
Database code page                                      = 1208
Database code set                                       = UTF-8
Database country/region code                            = 1
Database collating sequence                             = IDENTITY
Alternate collating sequence              (ALT_COLLATE) =
Database page size                                      = 8192

Dynamic SQL Query management          (DYN_QUERY_MGMT) = DISABLE

Discovery support for this database       (DISCOVER_DB) = ENABLE

Restrict access                                         = NO
Default query optimization class         (DFT_QUERYOPT) = 5
Degree of parallelism                      (DFT_DEGREE) = 1
Continue upon arithmetic exceptions   (DFT_SQLMATHWARN) = NO
Default refresh age                   (DFT_REFRESH_AGE) = 0
Default maintained table types for opt (DFT_MTTB_TYPES) = SYSTEM
Number of frequent values retained     (NUM_FREQVALUES) = 10
Number of quantiles retained            (NUM_QUANTILES) = 20

Decimal floating point rounding mode  (DECFLT_ROUNDING) = ROUND_HALF_EVEN

Backup pending                                          = NO

Database is consistent                                  = YES
Rollforward pending                                     = NO
Restore pending                                         = NO

Multi-page file allocation enabled                      = YES

Log retain for recovery status                          = NO
User exit for logging status                            = NO

Self tuning memory                    (SELF_TUNING_MEM) = OFF
Size of database shared memory (4KB)  (DATABASE_MEMORY) = AUTOMATIC
Database memory threshold               (DB_MEM_THRESH) = 10
Max storage for lock list (4KB)              (LOCKLIST) = 50
Percent. of lock lists per application       (MAXLOCKS) = 22
Package cache size (4KB)                   (PCKCACHESZ) = (MAXAPPLS*8)
Sort heap thres for shared sorts (4KB) (SHEAPTHRES_SHR) = 5000
Sort list heap (4KB)                         (SORTHEAP) = 256

Database heap (4KB)                            (DBHEAP) = AUTOMATIC
Catalog cache size (4KB)              (CATALOGCACHE_SZ) = (MAXAPPLS*4)
Log buffer size (4KB)                        (LOGBUFSZ) = 8
Utilities heap size (4KB)                (UTIL_HEAP_SZ) = 5000
Buffer pool size (pages)                     (BUFFPAGE) = 250
SQL statement heap (4KB)                     (STMTHEAP) = AUTOMATIC
```

Figure 5.16 The contents of the database configuration file

```
 Default application heap (4KB)              (APPLHEAPSZ) = AUTOMATIC
 Application Memory Size (4KB)              (APPL_MEMORY) = AUTOMATIC
 Statistics heap size (4KB)                (STAT_HEAP_SZ) = AUTOMATIC

 Interval for checking deadlock (ms)          (DLCHKTIME) = 10000
 Lock timeout (sec)                         (LOCKTIMEOUT) = -1

 Changed pages threshold                 (CHNGPGS_THRESH) = 60
 Number of asynchronous page cleaners   (NUM_IOCLEANERS) = AUTOMATIC
 Number of I/O servers                   (NUM_IOSERVERS) = AUTOMATIC
 Index sort flag                              (INDEXSORT) = YES
 Sequential detect flag                       (SEQDETECT) = YES
 Default prefetch size (pages)          (DFT_PREFETCH_SZ) = AUTOMATIC

 Track modified pages                          (TRACKMOD) = OFF

 Default number of containers                             = 1
 Default tablespace extentsize (pages)    (DFT_EXTENT_SZ) = 32

 Max number of active applications             (MAXAPPLS) = AUTOMATIC
 Average number of active applications        (AVG_APPLS) = AUTOMATIC
 Max DB files open per application             (MAXFILOP) = 32768

 Log file size (4KB)                          (LOGFILSIZ) = 1000
 Number of primary log files                 (LOGPRIMARY) = 3
 Number of secondary log files                (LOGSECOND) = 2
 Changed path to log files                   (NEWLOGPATH) =
 Path to log files                                        = C:\DB2\NODE0000\SQL00
001\SQLOGDIR\
 Overflow log path                      (OVERFLOWLOGPATH) =
 Mirror log path                          (MIRRORLOGPATH) =
 First active log file                                    =
 Block log on disk full                 (BLK_LOG_DSK_FUL) = NO
 Percent max primary log space by transaction  (MAX_LOG) = 0
 Num. of active log files for 1 active UOW(NUM_LOG_SPAN) = 0

 Group commit count                           (MINCOMMIT) = 1
 Percent log file reclaimed before soft chckpt (SOFTMAX) = 100
 Log retain for recovery enabled              (LOGRETAIN) = OFF
 User exit for logging enabled                 (USEREXIT) = OFF

 HADR database role                                       = STANDARD
 HADR local host name                   (HADR_LOCAL_HOST) =
 HADR local service name                 (HADR_LOCAL_SVC) =
 HADR remote host name                 (HADR_REMOTE_HOST) =
 HADR remote service name               (HADR_REMOTE_SVC) =
 HADR instance name of remote server  (HADR_REMOTE_INST) =
 HADR timeout value                        (HADR_TIMEOUT) = 120
 HADR log write synchronization mode     (HADR_SYNCMODE) = NEARSYNC
 HADR peer window duration (seconds)  (HADR_PEER_WINDOW) = 0

First log archive method                 (LOGARCHMETH1) = OFF
Options for logarchmeth1                  (LOGARCHOPT1) =
Second log archive method                (LOGARCHMETH2) = OFF
Options for logarchmeth2                  (LOGARCHOPT2) =
```

Figure 5.16 The contents of the database configuration file *(Continued)*

```
Failover log archive path                    (FAILARCHPATH) =
Number of log archive retries on error      (NUMARCHRETRY) = 5
Log archive retry Delay (secs)            (ARCHRETRYDELAY) = 20
Vendor options                                  (VENDOROPT) =

Auto restart enabled                          (AUTORESTART) = ON
Index re-creation time and redo index build  (INDEXREC) = SYSTEM (RESTART)
Log pages during index build              (LOGINDEXBUILD) = OFF
Default number of loadrec sessions      (DFT_LOADREC_SES) = 1
Number of database backups to retain     (NUM_DB_BACKUPS) = 12
Recovery history retention (days)       (REC_HIS_RETENTN) = 366
Auto deletion of recovery objects     (AUTO_DEL_REC_OBJ) = OFF

TSM management class                      (TSM_MGMTCLASS) =
TSM node name                              (TSM_NODENAME) =
TSM owner                                     (TSM_OWNER) =
TSM password                               (TSM_PASSWORD) =

Automatic maintenance                          (AUTO_MAINT) = ON
  Automatic database backup              (AUTO_DB_BACKUP) = OFF
  Automatic table maintenance            (AUTO_TBL_MAINT) = ON
    Automatic runstats                    (AUTO_RUNSTATS) = ON
      Automatic statement statistics    (AUTO_STMT_STATS) = OFF
    Automatic statistics profiling      (AUTO_STATS_PROF) = OFF
      Automatic profile updates           (AUTO_PROF_UPD) = OFF
    Automatic reorganization                 (AUTO_REORG) = OFF

Enable XML Character operations          (ENABLE_XMLCHAR) = YES
WLM Collection Interval (minutes)      (WLM_COLLECT_INT) = 0
```

Figure 5.16 The contents of the database configuration file *(Continued)*

For example, to update the CHNGPGS_THRESH database configuration parameter in the *sample* database to a value of 20, issue the command:

```
update db cfg for sample using CHNGPGS_THRESH 20
```

Issuing the **get db cfg for *database_name*** command after the **update db cfg** command shows the newly updated values. However, this does not mean the change will take effect right away. Several parameters in the database configuration file require all connections to be removed before the changes take effect on the first new connection to the database. In most production environments, this is the same as an outage as it is not possible to disconnect all users. For other parameters, the update is dynamic, and the new value takes effect immediately after executing the command; these are called **configurable online parameters.**

> **NOTE** Configurable online parameters of the database configuration file can be updated dynamically only if you first connect to the database. If a database connection has not been performed, the parameter will not be changed immediately, but after all connections are removed.

The Control Center provides the list of database configuration parameters and indicates which ones are configurable online. Refer to Section 5.5.1, Configuring a Database from the Control Center, for details.

To get the current, effective setting for each configuration parameter along with the value of the parameter on the first new connection to the database after all connections are removed, use the **show detail** option of the **get db cfg** command. This option requires a database connection. If you run this command after changing the CHNGPGS_THRESH configuration parameter as above, you will see that the current value is 60, but the next effective or delayed value is 20. The related output from the **get db cfg show detail** command would look like the following:

```
C:\Program Files\SQLLIB\BIN>db2 get db cfg for sample show detail

Description                          Parameter        Current Value   Delayed Value
----------------------------------------------------------------------------------
...
Changed pages threshold            (CHNGPGS_THRESH) =      60                  20
```

The **show detail** option is also helpful in determining the actual value of parameters listed as AUTOMATIC. For example, when you issue the **get db cfg** command while connected to a database, you may see output like the following for the MAXAPPLS parameter:

```
C:\Program Files\SQLLIB\BIN>db2 get db cfg
...
Max number of active applications          (MAXAPPLS) =    AUTOMATIC
```

If you use the **show detail** option, the actual value is displayed:

```
C:\Program Files\SQLLIB\BIN>db2 get db cfg show detail

Description                          Parameter        Current Value   Delayed Value
----------------------------------------------------------------------------------
...
Max number of active applications  (MAXAPPLS) =   AUTOMATIC(40)   AUTOMATIC(40)
```

To reset all the database configuration parameters to their default values, use the command **reset db cfg for *database_name*.**

5.5.1 Configuring a Database from the Control Center

You can also configure a database from the Control Center. Figure 5.17 shows the Control Center with the database *SAMPLE* selected. When you right click on the database a menu with several options appears.

Although the Control Center's database menu has *Start* and *Stop* options, as shown in Figure 5.17, these are used to start and stop the instance where the selected database resides. There are no explicit commands to stop and start a database. To "stop" a database, simply ensure that all connections to the database are removed. You can do this with the **force applications** command or by disconnecting each application. The first connection to a database "starts" the database. The commands **activate database** and **deactivate database** are also related to these concepts, although they are mainly used for performance reasons.

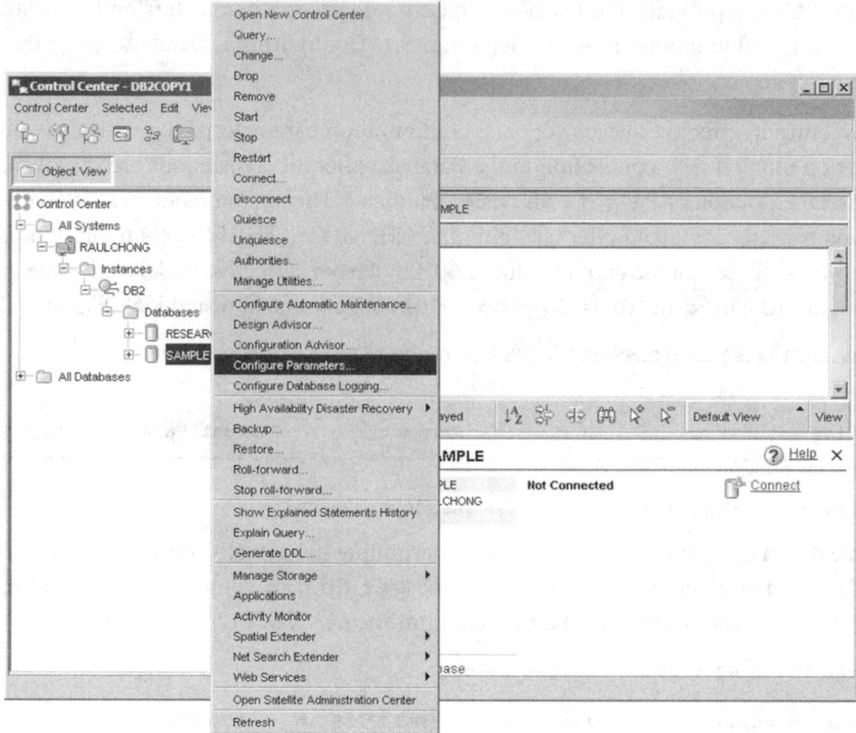

Figure 5.17 Using the Control Center to configure a database

The **activate database** command activates a database by allocating all the necessary database memory and services or processes required. The first connection to the database normally performs these operations; therefore, by using the **activate database** command before connecting, the first connection no longer has to pay the price of this extra overhead. The **deactivate database** command does the opposite; it stops all services or processes needed by the database and releases the memory. A database can be considered "started" when it is activated and "stopped" when it is deactivated.

> **NOTE** The **Restart** command option in Figure 5.17 maps to the **restart database** command, which you can use for recovery purposes when a database is left in an inconsistent state after a crash recovery. Don't use this command if you only want the new value of a database configuration parameter that is not dynamic to take effect. Instead, use the **force applications** command or ensure all applications disconnect from the database.

Figure 5.18 shows the Database Configuration window that appears after selecting **Configure Parameters** from the menu shown in Figure 5.17.

In Figure 5.18 the column *Pending Value Effective* indicates when the pending value for the parameter will take effect, for example, immediately or after the database is "stopped" and "started". The column *Dynamic* indicates whether the parameter is configurable online. The rest of the columns are self-explanatory.

Figure 5.18 also illustrates how you can update a database configuration parameter from the Control Center. After selecting the parameter *DLCHKTIME* and clicking on the three dots button (...), a pop-up window appears displaying the values that this parameter can accept.

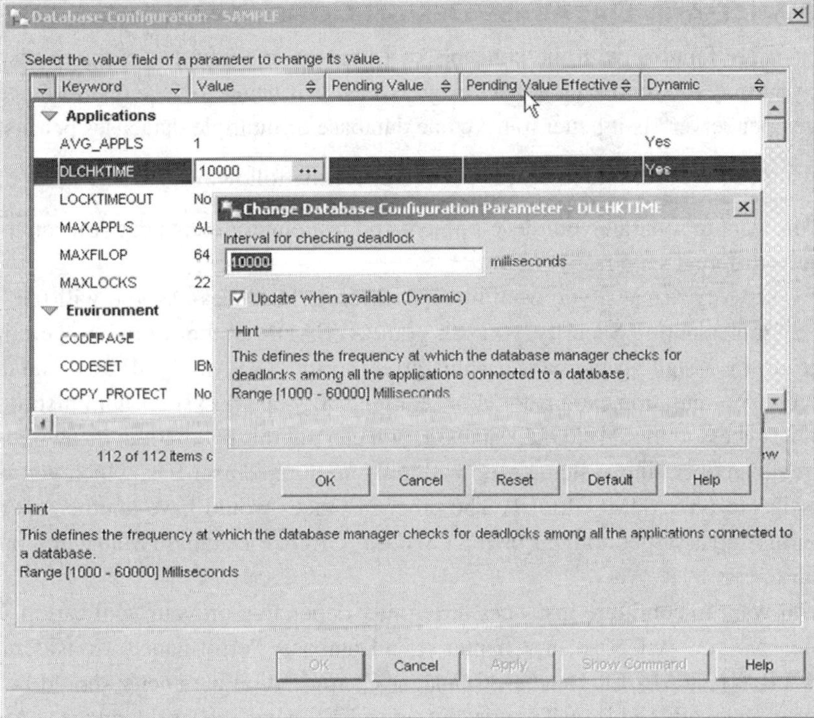

Figure 5.18 Configuring database parameters from the Control Center

5.5.2 The DB2 Commands at the Database Level

Table 5.4 summarizes the most common commands used to configure a database. For more information about database concepts, refer to Chapter 7, Working with Database Objects.

> **NOTE** If a DB2 registry variable, Database Manager Configuration parameter, or database configuration parameter accepts only Boolean values, the values YES and ON and the values NO and OFF respectively are equivalent.

Table 5.4 The DB2 Database-Level Commands

Command	Explanation
`get db cfg`	Displays the database configuration file.
`update db cfg`	Updates the database configuration file.
`reset db cfg`	Resets the database configuration file to its default values.

5.6 Instance and Database Design Considerations

Now that you are familiar with the concepts of instances and how to configure instances and databases, you may be wondering about design issues. Is it better to have one instance or multiple instances per server? Is it better to have one database or multiple databases per instance?

You may want to have multiple instances per server for the following reasons.

- You want to separate your development and test environments but you cannot afford to have different servers.
- For security reasons, you want to have different instances. As you will see in Chapter 11, Implementing Security, you can grant SYSADM authority to an operating system group by assigning the name of this group to the SYSADM_GROUP Database Manager Configuration parameter. For example, if not all system administrators should have access to the *PAYROLL* database, you can put this database in its own instance and create an operating system group with only authorized user IDs, which you would then assign to SYSADM_GROUP. The other instances would have another operating system group assigned to their own SYSADM_GROUP Database Manager Configuration parameter.
- You want to configure instances differently depending on your application. For example, as you will see in Chapter 17, Database Performance Considerations, the INTRA_PARALLEL Database Manager Configuration parameter should be set to NO when the workload is OLTP type, but set to YES when the workload is OLAP (or DSS) type. Because this is an instance-level parameter, all the databases inside the instance will use the same setting. Creating databases that will be used for either OLTP or OLAP in different instances will allow you to set INTRA_PARALLEL correctly for each case.

If the above does not apply to you, in a production environment, we recommend having one instance per server and one database per instance; this will guarantee that all resources are allocated to that one database and instance.

If you do decide to create multiple instances on a server, remember that an instance consumes some resources when started. Chapter 16, The DB2 Memory Model, discusses the memory allocated for instances. In general, an instance does not consume a great amount of resources;

however, the databases inside the instances may consume a lot of memory depending, for example, on the size of their buffer pools. Keep in mind that when you have many instances, each with many databases, the memory used by all the databases and instances when they are active should be less than the physical memory of the machine; otherwise paging or swapping will occur, which will affect the performance of the entire system. With 64-bit instances, these memory limitations are reduced.

> **NOTE** OLTP stands for online transaction processing. The OLTP type of workload implies short transactions performing simple SELECT, INSERT, UPDATE, and DELETE operations affecting a small number of rows. In reality, there are few databases used only for pure OLTP workloads. Most databases are used for a mixed workload.
>
> OLAP stands for online analytical processing and DSS for decision support systems. OLAP and DSS have similar types of workload, and they imply complex SELECT statements, normally using several JOIN operations.

5.7 Case Study

You have just returned from a DB2 training class and would like to practice what you have learned by changing some DB2 registry variables and configuration parameters. The system you are working with has one instance called *DB2* and two databases, *mydb* and *testdb*.

1. First, you save the contents of your configuration files by simply redirecting the output to files. This is just as a precaution in case you need to go back to your current configuration.

```
db2set -all > db2set.bk
db2 get dbm cfg > dbmcfg.bk
db2 get db cfg for mydb > dbcfg_mydb.bk
db2 get db cfg for testdb > dbcfg_testdb.bk
set > environmentVariables.bk
```

   If you do need to go back to your current configuration, review the contents of these files and enter the appropriate commands to set your environment variables correctly (set/export), DBM Configuration file (update dbm cfg), database configuration file (update db cfg), and DB2 registry variables (db2set).
2. Then, you want to verify which instances have been created and which one is the current active one:

```
db2ilist
db2 get instance
```

   The first command lists all instances in your server; in this case, there is only one instance, *DB2*. The second command shows you that the *DB2* instance is the current active instance.

3. Next, since you like to reuse CLP commands that you have typed before, you decide to increase the number of CLP commands that are kept as "history." You don't quite remember which DB2 registry variable has to be modified, so you issue the command:
   ```
   db2set -lr
   ```
   This lists all the DB2 registry variables you can set. You review the list and recognize the registry variable you need: DB2_CLP_HISTSIZE (discussed in Chapter 4, Using the DB2 Tools). You issue the command:
   ```
   db2set DB2_CLP_HISTSIZE=50
   ```
   This command sets the DB2_CLP_HISTSIZE registry variable only for the active instance because the -i option is the default.
4. You decide to make this change globally, so you issue:
   ```
   db2set DB2_CLP_HISTSIZE=50   -g
   ```
   You make sure that there are no spaces before and after the equal (=) sign to avoid getting an error.
5. You confirm that the registry variable is set by issuing the command:
   ```
   db2set -all
   ```
   You notice the same variable is set twice: once at the instance level (denoted by [i]), the other at the global level (denoted by [g]). You change your mind and decide to set this registry variable only for the current instance, not globally. You unset the registry variable as follows:
   ```
   db2set DB2_CLP_HISTSIZE=   -g
   ```
   As indicated in Table 5.1, to unset the value of a DB2 registry variable, leave a blank after the equal sign.
6. Next, you have to bring the instance down and then up by issuing the commands **db2stop** and **db2start** to ensure that the new registry variable value takes effect. Since you are planning to make other changes that may require an instance restart, you decide to wait until you finish all your changes.
   After issuing the **get dbm cfg** command, you decide to make a small change to the SHEAPTHRESH parameter from 20000 to 20005. You will reverse the change afterwards, as you are only testing what you have learned about instance commands for now. You issue the command:
   ```
   db2 update dbm cfg using SHEAPTHRES 20005
   ```
   You want to see the current and delayed values for this parameter, so you issue the command:
   ```
   db2 get dbm cfg show detail
   ```
7. Next, you want to make changes to your database configuration. You check your system with the **list applications** command. You know there are two databases in the instance, *mydb* and *testdb*. The output of the command shows that there are no connections to *mydb*, but *testdb* has 10 users connected to it. Also, other users are working heavily on the test machine, which is running other software. Since you don't want to

interfere with their work, you don't want to connect to the *mydb* database as this would allocate memory for the different database resources. Nonetheless, you do realize that making changes to a Database Configuration parameter does not require you to be connected to the database. After all, the database configuration is a binary file, so you are simply updating this file, and the database does not need to be active. You issue this command to increase the sort heap:

```
db2 update db cfg for mydb using SORTHEAP 1024
```

Since you are not connected to the database, you must specify the database name as part of the command. Given that the database is down, you don't really care whether the parameter SORTHEAP is configurable online or not. The next time there is a connection to the database, the new value will take effect. You do want to make sure the value has indeed been set to 1024, so you issue the command:

```
db2 get db cfg for mydb
```

8. Your boss is calling you, so you need to finish this exercise immediately. You write a note reminding yourself to revert the changes you didn't really want back to the way they were and then issue the **db2stop** and **db2start** commands once the other users in your system finish with their tests.

5.8 Summary

This chapter discussed the DB2 environment and its environment variables and DB2 profile registry. It explained how to list the contents of environment variables and how to modify them either temporarily or permanently.

It also described how to manipulate the DB2 profile registry variables with the **db2set** command. The different levels of the DB2 profile registry were explained, as well as the priority that DB2 takes into consideration when the same variable is set at different levels.

There was a detailed explanation of instances, and it showed how an instance can be created, dropped, started, stopped, and configured. For non-root Linux/UNIX installations, some of the instance administration was different, and this was pointed out. It also described the Database Administration Server (DAS), which is a background process that needs to be running at the database server to allow remote DB2 clients to graphically administer a database server. The chapter also discussed the similarity between configuring instance and database configuration parameters.

After reading this chapter you should have a solid background on how to work and manage instances as well as how to configure a database.

5.9 Review Questions

1. Which environment variable determines the current active instance on your database server?

2. How can you set up your DB2 environment in Linux or UNIX?
3. Which command can you use to remove the DB2COMM registry variable from the DB2 Global-Level Profile Registry?
4. Which command can you use to list all the instances in your server?
5. What authority is required to create a DB2 instance on Linux or UNIX?
6. What authority is required to create a DB2 instance on Windows?
7. What command can be used to remove an unneeded instance from your server?
8. Does the **db2start** command need to be executed once per each database partition?
9. What can you do to gain exclusive access to an instance?
10. What is the difference between an attachment and a connection?
11. Which of the following commands will list all of the available registry variables in DB2?
    A. db2set -a
    B. db2set -all
    C. db2set -lr
    D. db2set -ltr
12. Which two of the following are not database configuration parameters?
    A. SHEAPTHRES
    B. SHEAPTHRES_SHR
    C. BUFFPAGE
    D. MAX_QUERYDEGREE
    E. MAXLOCKS
13. You have three databases: one for development, one for test, and one for production. To ensure that an error in an application in the development database will not affect the other databases, how would you configure these databases?
    A. Combine them into one database using different schemas
    B. Create all the databases in the same instance
    C. Put each database on a different drive/file system on the server
    D. Create each database in a different instance
14. Which of the following commands will show the current and delayed values for the Database Manager Configuration parameters?
    A. get dbm cfg
    B. get dbm cfg show detail
    C. get dbm cfg show all
    D. get complete dbm cfg
15. Which of the following commands updates the DAS configuration?
    A. das update cfg
    B. db2 update dbm cfg for das
    C. db2admin update cfg
    D. db2 update admin cfg

16. Which of the following commands changes the DAS configuration back to the default values?
    A. das reset cfg
    B. db2 reset dbm cfg for das
    C. db2admin reset cfg
    D. db2 reset admin cfg
17. Which of the following commands stops the DB2 instance even if there are active connections to databases in the instance?
    A. db2 force applications all
    B. db2 stop all applications
    C. db2stop force
    D. db2stop applications all
18. Which of the following commands/statements requires an attachment to a remote instance?
    A. db2 list applications
    B. db2 list db directory
    C. db2 select * from employee
    D. db2 create database mydb
19. Which of the following commands can be used to review the contents of the Database Configuration file for the database to which you are currently connected?
    A. db2 list database configuration
    B. db2 list db cfg
    C. db2 get dbm cfg
    D. db2 get db cfg
20. Which two of the following commands do not set the value of the INTRA_PARALLEL parameter to YES?
    A. db2 update database manager configuration using INTRA_PARALLEL YES
    B. db2 update dbm cfg using INTRA_PARALLEL 1
    C. db2 update dbm cfg using INTRA_PARALLEL ON
    D. db2 update database configuration using INTRA_PARALLEL YES

CHAPTER 6

Configuring Client and Server Connectivity

This chapter describes different methods you can use to configure a DB2 client to connect to a DB2 server. The DB2 client can reside on the same machine as the DB2 server or it can be miles away on a different machine. In addition, a DB2 server can work as a DB2 client in some situations.

In this chapter you will learn about:

- The big picture of client server connectivity
- The DB2 directories used for connectivity
- How to configure database connections manually using DB2 commands
- How to configure database connections using the Configuration Assistant
- How to diagnose DB2 connectivity problems

6.1 Client and Server Connectivity: The Big Picture

Figure 6.1 illustrates a simplified view of what is required to connect from a DB2 client to a DB2 data server.

To connect to a **remote database** (a database that resides on a machine/server/LPAR/partition other than the client machine), follow this three-step process.

1. At the server, allow it to accept client connections by turning on the listener processes.

   In Figure 6.1, the information required from the database server is on the right side below the server machine. For example, if you are using the TCP/IP protocol, you need to set the DB2COMM registry variable to *tcpip* to start the DB2 TCP/IP listeners.

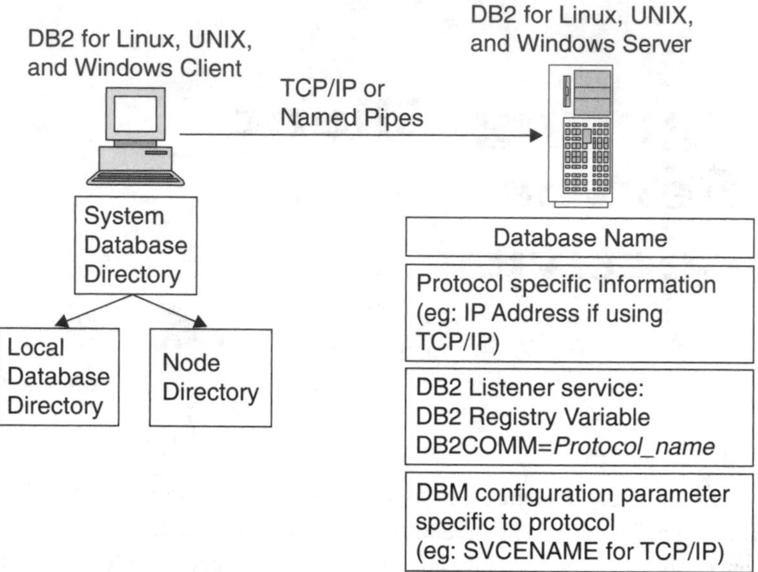

Figure 6.1 The big picture of client and server connectivity

2. Specify the port name or number that a given instance is listening to using the SVCENAME Database Manager Configuration parameter. This is the information you need to give to the client machine in step 3. You will need to stop and restart the instance for the update to take effect.
3. On the client, make sure to enter the connection information (specified in the second step) as well as the server name or IP address correctly into the system and node directories using the **`catalog`** command.

   In Figure 6.1, on the left side below the DB2 client you can see the system database and node directories where you need to store the information obtained in step 1.

For a **local database** (a database that resides in the same instance, on the same machine you are connecting from), the **`create database`** command stores the required information in the system and local database directories automatically for you.

In the next sections you will also learn about the **Database Connection Services** (DCS) directory, which is required to connect to a DB2 server on the z/OS, OS/390, and i5/OS platforms.

We first show you how to enter the information in the DB2 database and node directories using DB2 commands. Once you are familiar with the commands, we show you how to configure client-server connectivity using the Configuration Assistant (CA), which populates these directories behind the scenes.

NOTE The Configuration Assistant and the Configuration Advisor (introduced in Chapter 4, Using the DB2 Tools) are different tools. The Configuration Assistant is mainly used to set up client-server connectivity, while the Configuration Advisor is used exclusively to configure database manager and database configuration parameters.

6.2 The DB2 Database Directories

This section describes the DB2 directories and how they are related. Consider the following statement used to connect to the database with the name or alias *sample*:

```
CONNECT TO sample
```

Given only the database name or alias, how does DB2 know how to find the database *sample*? If *sample* resides on a remote server, how does the client know how to connect to that server?

All database and server information is stored in the DB2 directories. Table 6.1 lists these directories and the corresponding commands to view, insert, and delete their contents. More detailed information about the directories and commands is presented in the next sections.

Table 6.1 The Commands to View, Insert, and Delete the Contents of the DB2 Directories

Directory Name	Command to View Contents	Command to Insert Contents	Command to Delete Contents
System database	**list db directory** or **list database directory**	**catalog db** (for remote and local databases) or **create database** (for local databases only)	**uncatalog db** (for remote and local databases) or **drop database** (for local databases only)
Local database	**list db directory on *path/drive*** or **list database directory on path/drive**	**create database** (for local databases only)	**drop database** (for local databases only)
Node	**list node directory**	**catalog TCPIP node**	**uncatalog node**
DCS	**list dcs directory**	**catalog DCS database**	**uncatalog DCS database**

Note that you cannot update an entry you entered with the **`catalog`** command. You have to delete the entry with the **`uncatalog`** command first, and then insert the correct or updated entry using the **`catalog`** command.

6.2.1 The DB2 Database Directories: An Analogy Using a Book

To understand how the DB2 directories work let's use an analogy. Above the dotted line in Figure 6.2 is the table of contents for a book called *The World*. This table of contents shows that the book is divided into several parts. If you jump to any of these parts, you will see a subset of the table of contents. The Resources section presents information about other books; with that information you can find a given book in a library or bookstore or on the Internet, and once you find the book, the process repeats itself where you first review the table of contents for that book and then look at its different parts.

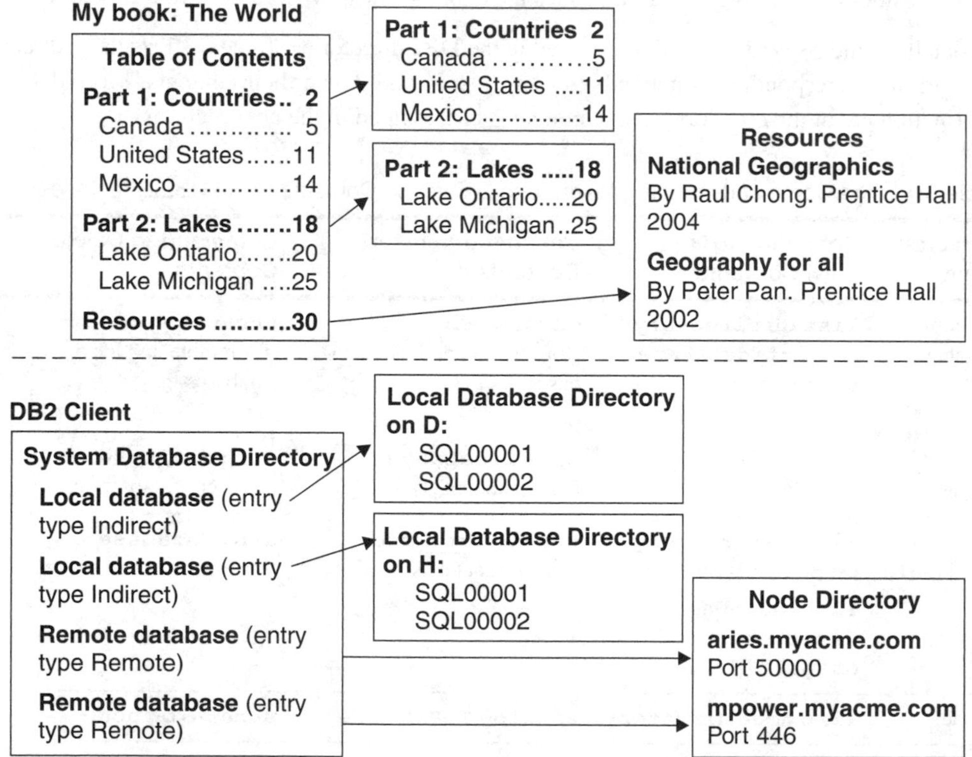

Figure 6.2 The DB2 directories: A book analogy

Similarly, with DB2 directories (shown below the dotted line), whenever you issue a **`CONNECT TO <database>`** statement, DB2 looks for the information in the **system database directory,** which is equivalent to the table of contents: it shows all the databases available for you to connect (or attach) to from this machine. When an entry in this directory has the type *indirect*, it means the database is local (it resides in the current DB2 instance). To look for more information about this local database, you can view the **local database directory,** which is equivalent to the subset of the table of contents. When an entry in the system database directory is **remote,** it means that the database resides in a different instance than the current one, and this instance can be on a different server or the same server. Thus, you need to review the **node directory** for information about how to access this remote server or instance. This is similar to the Resources (or bibliography) section of a book, where information points to a different book with more information about a given topic.

The **Database Connection Services** (DCS) **directory** (not shown in Figure 6.2) contains extra information required when you connect to a host database server like DB2 for OS/390, z/OS and i5/OS.

> **NOTE** In this chapter host database servers like DB2 for OS/390 and z/OS and DB2 for i5/OS will only be used as database servers and not as clients.

6.2.2 The System Database Directory

As mentioned earlier, the system database directory is like a table of contents: it shows you all the databases you can connect to from your system. The system database directory is stored in a binary file with name *SQLDBDIR* and is in the following location:

DB2_install_directory\instance_name\sqldbdir on Windows systems

DB2_instance_home/sqllib/sqldbdir on Linux and UNIX systems

You should not modify this file manually. To display the contents of the system database directory, use the **`list db directory`** command, as shown in Figure 6.3.

The system database directory shown in Figure 6.3 indicates that you can connect to three different databases from this system: *MYHOSTDB*, *MYRMTDB(the alias for the database named RMTDB)*, and *MYLOCDB*. Let's examine each of these database entries in detail starting from the bottom (Database 3 entry) to the top (Database 1 entry).

The relevant fields in Database 3 entry are as follows:

- Database alias = *MYLOCDB*. This indicates the alias you need to use in the **`CONNECT`** statement. It must be a unique name within the system database directory.
- Database name = *MYLOCDB*. This is the actual database name. For this particular entry it is the same as the alias name.
- Directory entry type = *Indirect*. An entry type of *Indirect* means that the database is local; that is, it resides in the same instance where you are currently working.

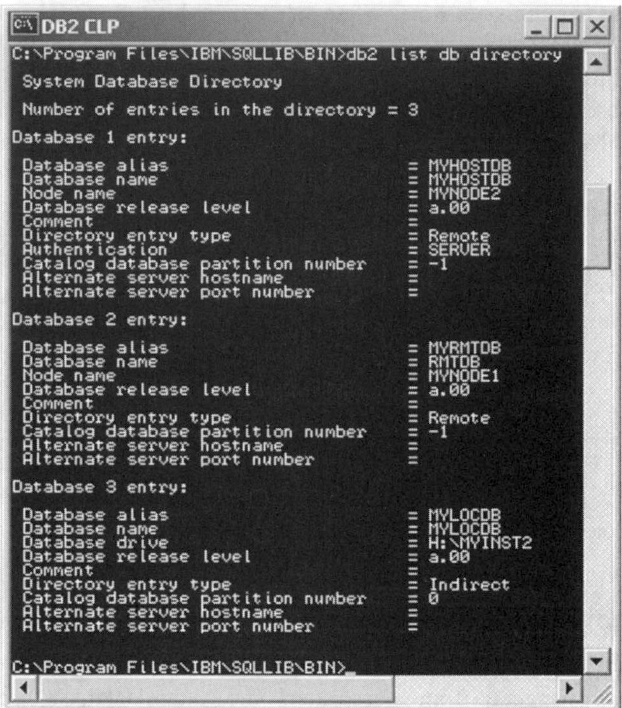
```
C:\Program Files\IBM\SQLLIB\BIN>db2 list db directory

 System Database Directory

 Number of entries in the directory = 3

Database 1 entry:

 Database alias                       = MYHOSTDB
 Database name                        = MYHOSTDB
 Node name                            = MYNODE2
 Database release level               = a.00
 Comment                              =
 Directory entry type                 = Remote
 Authentication                       = SERVER
 Catalog database partition number    = -1
 Alternate server hostname            =
 Alternate server port number         =

Database 2 entry:

 Database alias                       = MYRMTDB
 Database name                        = RMTDB
 Node name                            = MYNODE1
 Database release level               = a.00
 Comment                              =
 Directory entry type                 = Remote
 Catalog database partition number    = -1
 Alternate server hostname            =
 Alternate server port number         =

Database 3 entry:

 Database alias                       = MYLOCDB
 Database name                        = MYLOCDB
 Database drive                       = H:\MYINST2
 Database release level               = a.00
 Comment                              =
 Directory entry type                 = Indirect
 Catalog database partition number    = 0
 Alternate server hostname            =
 Alternate server port number         =

C:\Program Files\IBM\SQLLIB\BIN>_
```

Figure 6.3 A sample DB2 system database directory

- Database Drive = *H:\MYINST2*. From the previous field you know this database is local. This field tells where on the server this database is stored. Note that the example in Figure 6.3 is for a Windows system. For a Linux or UNIX system the field would be *Local database directory* instead of *Database Drive*.

The relevant fields in Database 2 entry that have not been described yet are

- Directory entry type = *Remote*. An entry type of *Remote* means that the database resides on a different instance or server than the one on which you are currently working.
- Node name = *MYNODE1*. From the previous field you know this database is remote. The node name field tells the name of the entry in the node directory where you can find the information about the server and instance that hosts the database.

The relevant field in the Database 1 entry that has not been described earlier is

- Authentication = *SERVER*. This entry indicates that security is handled at the server where the instance is running. Other options are discussed in Chapter 11, Implementing Security.

6.2.3 The Local Database Directory

The local database directory is also stored in a file called *SQLDBDIR*. However, this file is different from the *SQLDBDIR* file for the system database directory in that it resides on every *drive* (in Windows) or *path* (in Linux or UNIX) that contains, or at some time contained, a database. It contains information only for databases on that drive/path, and it is a subset of the system database directory. Use the **`list db directory on`** ***`drive/path`*** command to display the local database directory, as shown in Figure 6.4.

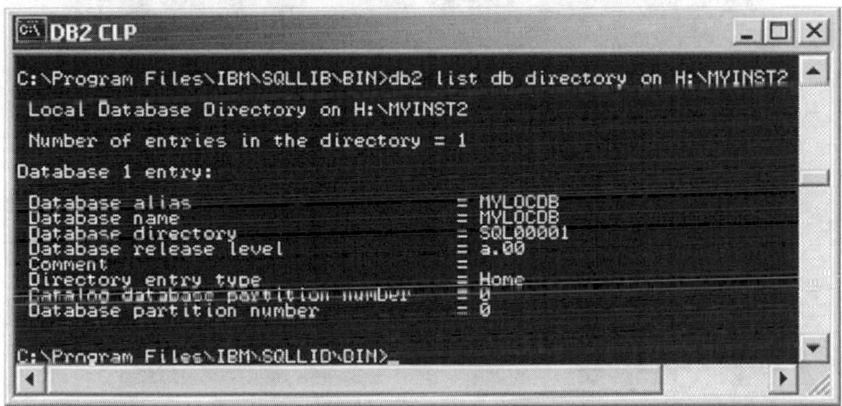

Figure 6.4 A sample DB2 local database directory

Figure 6.4 shows *MYLOCDB* is the only database stored in *H:\MYINST2*. Note that *MYLOCDB* also appeared in the system database directory in Figure 6.3, since the local database directory is a subset of the system database directory. On Windows, the **`create database`** command can only specify a drive, not a path, where a database will be created; therefore, the command **`list db directory on H:`** should return the same output as **`list db directory on H:\MYINST2.`** On Linux and UNIX, a path can be specified with the **`create database`** command; therefore, when using the **`list db directory`** command, specify the full path. Chapter 8, The DB2 Storage Model, explains the **`create database`** command in detail.

The relevant information in the entry of Figure 6.4 is as follows:

- Database directory = *SQL00001*. This is the subdirectory where the database is physically stored in your server.

6.2.4 The Node Directory

The node directory stores information about how to communicate to a remote instance where a given database resides. It is stored in a file called *SQLNODIR* and is in:

DB2_install_directory\instance_name\SQLNODIR on Windows systems

DB2_instance_home/sqllib/sqlnodir on Linux and UNIX systems

One important field in the node directory is the communication protocol used to communicate with the server, as several other fields are displayed depending on this entry. For example, if the node directory contains a TCP/IP entry, then other fields provided are the IP address (or host name) of the server and the service name (or port number) of the instance where the database resides. Figure 6.5 shows an example of the contents of the node directory.

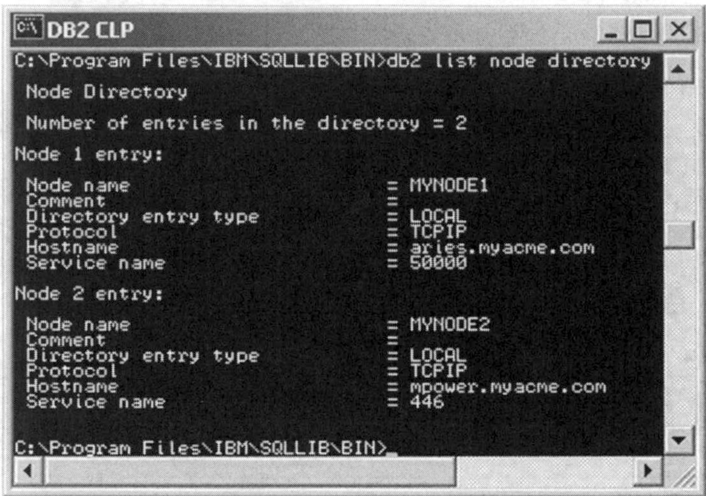

Figure 6.5 A sample DB2 node directory

There are two entries in Figure 6.5. We explain the first one in detail below; the second entry has a similar explanation, and thus will not be described.

Node 1 entry has these relevant fields:

- Node name = *MYNODE1*. This is the name of this node entry. It was chosen arbitrarily.
- Protocol = *TCPIP*. This is the communication protocol that is used to communicate with the remote system.
- Host name = *aries.myacme.com*. This is the host name of the remote database server. Alternatively, the IP address can be provided.
- Service Name = *50000*. This is the TCP/IP port number used by the instance in the remote server to listen for connections.

> **NOTE** Since the node directory contains the information required to connect to an instance, it is not only used by the **CONNECT** statement but also by the **attach** command as described in Chapter 5, Understanding the DB2 Environment, DB2 Instances, and Databases.

6.2.5 The Database Connection Services Directory

The DCS directory is required only when connecting to a host server like DB2 for OS/390, z/OS, and i5/OS. This directory is available only when the DB2 Connect software is installed. Figure 6.6 shows the contents of a sample DCS directory.

Figure 6.6 A sample DCS directory

In Figure 6.6 the relevant fields are as follows:

- Local database name = *MYHOSTDB*. This name must match the corresponding entry in the system database directory.
- Target database name = *HOSTPROD*. Depending on the host, this entry corresponds to the following:

  For DB2 for OS/390 and z/OS: The location name of the DB2 subsystem

  For DB2 for i5/OS: The local RDB name

6.2.6 The Relationship between the DB2 Directories

Now that you have a good understanding of the DB2 directories, let's see how all of them are related by using a few figures.

6.2.6.1 A Local Connection

Figure 6.7 illustrates the process of connecting to a DB2 database. When a user issues the statement:

```
CONNECT TO mylocdb USER raul USING mypsw
```

> **NOTE** You can also issue the CONNECT statement without specifying "USING mypsw". DB2 will prompt you for the password. That way, the password won't be shown in clear text.

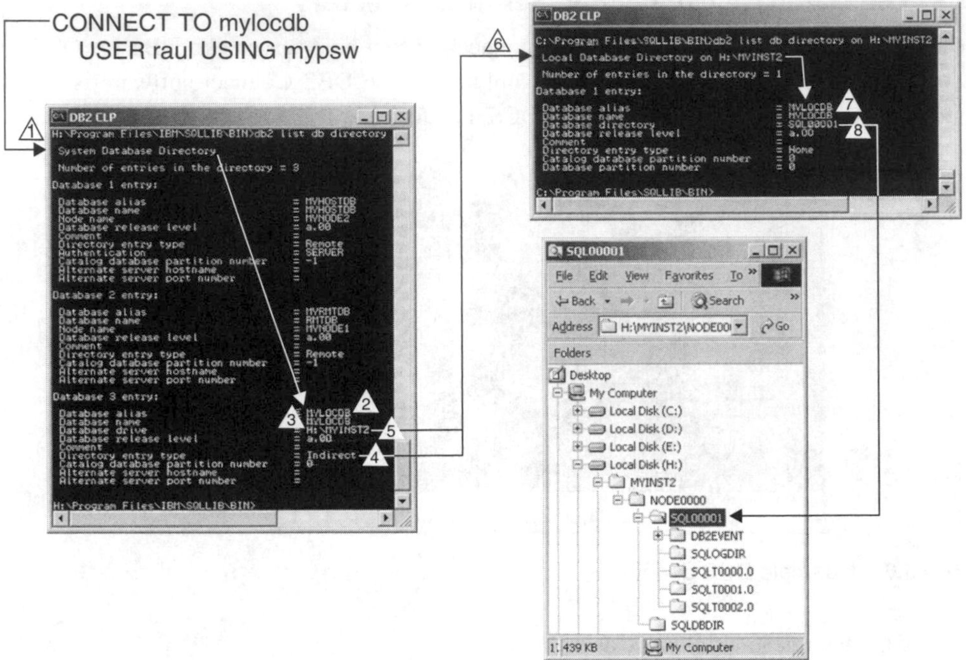

Figure 6.7 The local database connection process

DB2 follows these steps:

1. Looks for the system database directory.
2. Inside the system database directory, looks for the entry with a database alias of *MYLOCDB.*
3. Determines the database name that corresponds to the database alias (in Figure 6.7 the database alias and name are the same).
4. Determines if the database is local or remote by reviewing the *Directory entry type* field. In Figure 6.7, the entry type is *Indirect*, so the database is local.
5. Since the database is local, DB2 reviews the *Database drive* field, which indicates the location of the local database directory. In Figure 6.7, it is *H:\MYINST2*.
6. Looks for the local database directory.
7. Inside the local database directory, DB2 looks for the entry with a database alias that matches the database name of *MYLOCDB*.
8. Determines the physical location where the database resides by looking at the field *Database Directory.* In Figure 6.7, it is *SQL00001.*

6.2.6.2 A Remote Connection to a DB2 Database on another Server

Figure 6.8 illustrates the process of connecting to a remote DB2 database. When a user issues the statement

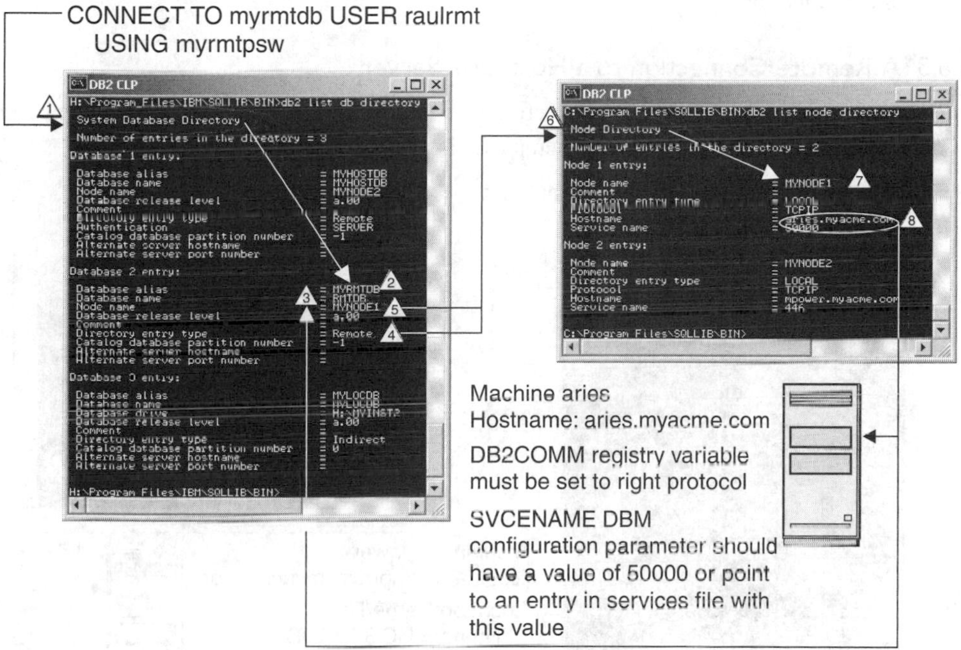

CONNECT TO myrmtdb USER raulrmt USING myrmtpsw
Machine aries
Hostname: aries.myacme.com
DB2COMM registry variable must be set to right protocol
SVCENAME DBM configuration parameter should have a value of 50000 or point to an entry in services file with this value

Figure 6.8 The remote database connection process

```
CONNECT TO myrmtdb USER raulrmt USING myrmtpsw
```

DB2 follows these steps:

1. Looks for the system database directory.
2. Inside the system database directory, looks for the entry with a database alias of *MYRMTDB*.
3. Determines the database name that corresponds to the database alias. In Figure 6.8 the database name is *RMTDB*. This information will later be used in step 8.
4. Determines if the database is local or remote by reviewing the *Directory entry type* field. In Figure 6.8, the entry type is *Remote*, so the database is remote.
5. Since the database is remote, DB2 reviews the *Node name* field, which indicates the entry name to look for in the node directory. In the figure, the node name is *MYNODE1*.
6. Looks for the node directory.
7. Inside the node directory, looks for the entry with a node name of *MYNODE1*.

8. Determines the physical location of the server or instance where the database resides. In this example, the TCP/IP protocol is used, so DB2 looks for the fields *Hostname* and *Service Name*. In Figure 6.8, their values are *aries.myacme.com* and *50000* respectively. With this information and the database name obtained in step 3, DB2 initiates the connection.

6.2.6.3 A Remote Connection to a Host DB2 Server

Figure 6.9 illustrates the process of connecting to a remote DB2 host server, which can be DB2 for z/OS, OS/390, or DB2 for i5/OS. When a user issues the statement:

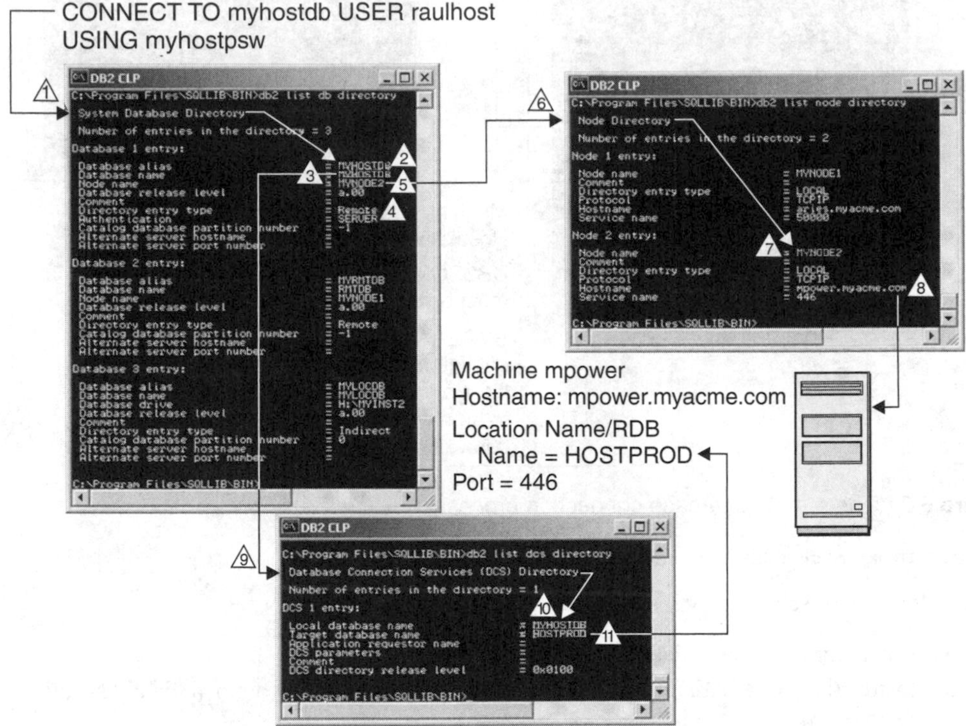

Figure 6.9 The remote host DB2 database connection process

```
CONNECT TO myhostdb USER raulhost USING myhostpsw
```

DB2 follows these steps:

1. Looks for the system database directory.
2. Inside the system database directory, looks for the entry with a database alias of *MYHOSTDB*.

3. Determines the database name that corresponds to the database alias. (In Figure 6.9 the database name and alias are the same.) This information will later be used in step 9.
4. Determines if the database is local or remote by reviewing the *Directory entry type* field. In Figure 6.9, the entry type is *Remote*, so the database is remote.
5. Since the database is remote, DB2 reviews the *Node name* field, which indicates the entry name to look for in the node directory. In the figure, the node name is *MYNODE2*.
6. Looks for the node directory.
7. Inside the node directory, DB2 looks for the entry with a node name of *MYNODE2*.
8. Determines the physical location where the database resides. In this example, the TCP/IP protocol is used therefore DB2 looks for the fields *Hostname* and *Service Name*. In Figure 6.9, their values are *mpower.myacme.com* and *446* respectively.
9. DB2 detects that this is a host database server and thus, with the database name obtained in step 3, it accesses the DCS directory.
10. Inside the DCS directory, DB2 looks for the entry with a local database name of *MYHOSTDB*.
11. Determines the target database name that corresponds to *MYHOSTDB*. In this example it is *HOSTPROD*. With this information and the connectivity information obtained in step 8, DB2 initiates the connection.

6.3 Supported Connectivity Scenarios

In this section, we discuss the following four connectivity scenarios in detail.

- Scenario 1: Local connection from a DB2 client to a DB2 server
- Scenario 2: Remote connection from a DB2 client to a DB2 server
- Scenario 3: Remote connection from a DB2 client to a DB2 host server
- Scenario 4: Remote connection from a DB2 client to a DB2 host server through a DB2 Connect gateway

A DB2 host server can be DB2 for z/OS and VM/VSE, OS/390, or i5/OS.

You can configure a database connection by either:

- Cataloging the DB2 directories using DB2 commands manually
- Using the Configuration Assistant (CA) GUI tool

The Configuration Assistant is explained in Section 6.4, Configuring Database Connections Using the Configuration Assistant.

It is useful to understand how to manually administer the DB2 directories using DB2 commands, so these scenarios focus on using the commands. Once you know how to do this, it will be a breeze to perform the configuration with the Configuration Assistant.

NOTE As discussed in Chapter 1, the clients in DB2 have been renamed to use "IBM Data Server" rather than "DB2" as part of the name. For example, the DB2 Runtime Client has been renamed to IBM Data Server Runtime Client. In this chapter, when we use the term "DB2 Client" to refer to a client using any of the DB2 9 clients such as the IBM Data Server Runtime Client or the IBM Data Server Client

6.3.1 Scenario 1: Local Connection from a DB2 Client to a DB2 Server

Figure 6.10 illustrates a local connection.

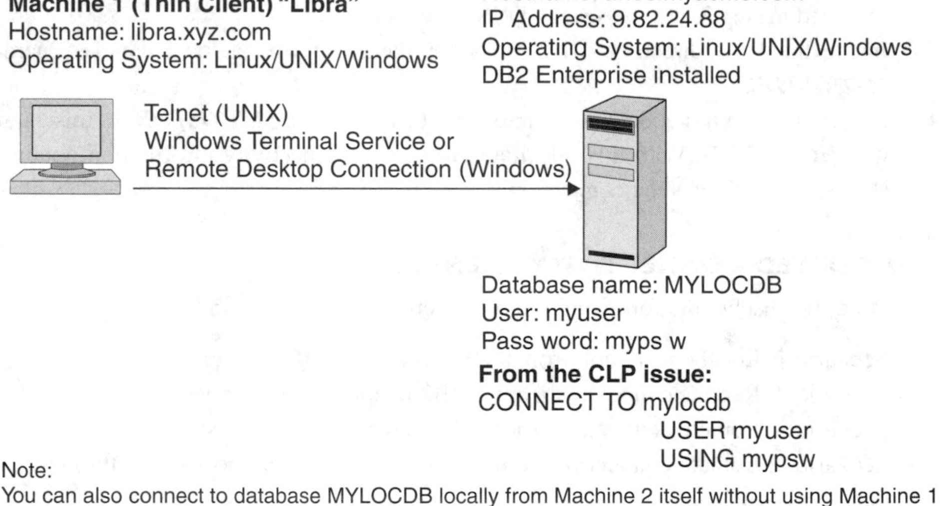

Figure 6.10 The process of connecting locally from a DB2 client to a DB2 Server

Figure 6.10 shows two servers, Machine 1 and Machine 2. Machine 1 is used to connect to Machine 2 using operating system commands or utilities like the Windows Terminal Service or Remote Desktop Connection (on Windows) or telnet (on Linux or UNIX). Once you establish this connection, any command you issue from the keyboard at Machine 1 is equivalent to issuing the command locally at Machine 2. Under this setup, when the **`connect to`** ***`database`*** statement is issued from the keyboard at either Machine 1 or Machine 2, the connection is considered local.

In this configuration, the server must have one of the following installed:

- DB2 Personal
- DB2 Express-C
- DB2 Express
- DB2 Workgroup
- DB2 Enterprise

When you create a database with the **create database** command (or in the Control Center), an entry is automatically created in the system database directory and the local database directory.

You normally do not need to issue **catalog** commands for a local database. However, it is possible for a local database to get "lost" in the system database directory. For example, this can happen if someone issues the **uncatalog database** command to remove the database from the system database directory, or when the system database directory is reset when reinstalling DB2. In these cases, as long as the database was not dropped (either by the **drop database** command or using the Control Center), the database still physically exists on the system, and the entry in the system database directory is simply missing. To get the database back into the system database directory, use this command:

```
catalog db database_name [as database_alias] [on drive/path]
```

where

drive (Windows)/**path** (UNIX) is the location where the database files are physically stored.

Once the database is cataloged, you can connect to it and use it just like before.

> **NOTE** If you drop an instance, the databases that belong to that instance are not dropped, because the databases reside on different directories from that of the instance. To recover these databases, all you need to do is to create a new instance with the same name as the one dropped and catalog the databases back using the **catalog db** command.

6.3.2 Scenario 2: Remote Connection from a DB2 Client to a DB2 Server

In most cases you do not have the authority to log on to the database server to perform a local database connection. Database servers are typically set up so that connections are performed through DB2 clients. In this scenario, DB2 client code is installed on a different machine from the database server machine. The **connect** statement is issued from the DB2 client machine. Figure 6.11 shows a connection from the machine *Libra* to a remote DB2 instance that resides on the server *Aries*.

In this configuration, the machine Libra is considered a client to database server Aries. The client must have one of the following installed:

- DB2 Client
- DB2 Personal
- DB2 Express-C
- DB2 Express
- DB2 Workgroup
- DB2 Enterprise

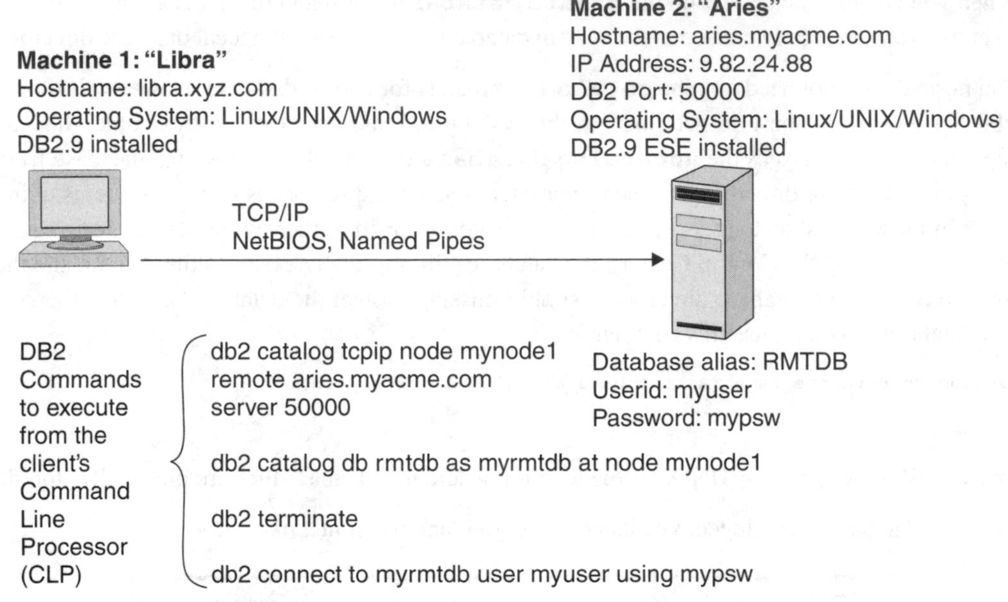
Machine 2: "Aries"
Hostname: aries.myacme.com
IP Address: 9.82.24.88
DB2 Port: 50000
Operating System: Linux/UNIX/Windows
DB2.9 ESE installed
Machine 1: "Libra"
Hostname: libra.xyz.com
Operating System: Linux/UNIX/Windows
DB2.9 installed
TCP/IP
NetBIOS, Named Pipes
DB2 Commands to execute from the client's Command Line Processor (CLP)
db2 catalog tcpip node mynode1 remote aries.myacme.com server 50000
Database alias: RMTDB
Userid: myuser
Password: mypsw
db2 catalog db rmtdb as myrmtdb at node mynode1
db2 terminate
db2 connect to myrmtdb user myuser using mypsw
Note: NetBIOS and Named Pipes are supported protocols if and only if client and server machines are using Windows.

Figure 6.11 The process of connecting remotely from a DB2 client to a DB2 server

The server must have one of the following installed:

- DB2 Express-C
- DB2 Express
- DB2 Workgroup
- DB2 Enterprise

The supported communication protocols are

- TCPIP
- Named Pipes (only if both the client and server are Windows)

To configure the connection shown in Figure 6.11, you need to

- Enable the database server to accept client connections.
- Catalog the node directory and the system database directory on the client.

The following sections describe these steps.

6.3.2.1 Enabling the Database Server to Accept Client Connections

Clients connect to the database server across the network using TCP/IP, or Named Pipes (Windows only). The server must have a process that is running to receive these connect requests. We call this process a **listener** because it "listens" to any request that comes in from the network and tells the database manager to serve it.

V9

> **NOTE** The NetBIOS protocol is no longer supported in DB2 9. NetBIOS is not a valid keyword for the DB2COMM registry variable, and cataloged nodes and databases using this protocol will not work under DB2 9.

6.3.2.1.1 TCP/IP connection

You need to perform the following steps on the database server to set up the listener if you are using the TCP/IP communication protocol.

1. Update the services file to reserve a TCP/IP port for the DB2 instance.
   On Linux and UNIX, the services file is located in /etc/services.
   On Windows, the services file is located in
   C:\Windows\System32\drivers\etc\services for 32-bit processors, and
   C:\Windows\System64\drivers\etc\services for 64-bit processors.
   The entry in the services file must look like this:

   ```
   service_name      port_number      /tcp
   ```

   where
   `service_name` is an arbitrary name to associate with the port number.
   `port_number` is the TCP/IP port number you are going to reserve for this DB2 instance.

   The port number must not already exist in the services file, and it must have a value of 1024 or higher for DB2 on LUW.

2. Update the SVCENAME parameter in the Database Manager Configuration file.

   Log on as the local administrator (Windows) or the instance owner (Linux or UNIX) and issue the following command from the Command Line Processor:

   ```
   update dbm cfg using svcename port_number/service_name
   ```

   You need to specify either a port number or the service name you defined in step 1.

3. Enable TCP/IP support for the instance. Issue the following command:
   `db2set DB2COMM=TCPIP`

4. Stop and restart the instance to make the changes you made in the previous steps effective. Issue **`db2stop`** and **`db2start.`**

NOTE If you are working with the default instance created and configured by the DB2 Setup Wizard, the services file, SVCENAME, and the DB2COMM parameters are already correctly configured for you.

NOTE For discussion on Named Pipes connectivity and set up, please refer to the *Quick Beginnings for DB2 Clients* manual.

6.3.2.2 Cataloging the Node Directory and Database Directory on the Client

After enabling the server to accept client connections, you need to tell the client how to connect to the server. You do this by cataloging the node directory and the system database directory at the client.

6.3.2.2.1 TCP/IP Connection

DB2 9 has built-in support for Internet Protocol Version 6 (IPv6). IPv6 is a new version of the Internet Protocol, designed as a successor to IP version 4 (IPv4), which is what is widely in use. You can now connect to servers using either IPv4 or IPv6.

Use the information in Table 6.2 for completing the procedure in this section.

1. Catalog a TCP/IP node on the client:

```
catalog tcpip/tcpip4/tcpip6 node nodename
remote hostname/IPv4_address/IPv6_address
server service_name/port_number_of_server
```

Table 6.2 TCP/IP Connectivity Worksheet

Parameter	Description	Sample Values
Host name	The host name of the remote server. Use the "tcpip" keyword if you want to specify the hostname instead of the IP address. You can specify the hostname regardless if the server is using an IPv4 or IPv6 address.	aries.myacme.com
IPv4 address	This is the standard 32bit IP address of the remote server specified in decimal format. You should not specify an IPv6 address with the "tcpip4" keyword. The catalog command will not fail, but your subsequent connections will.	9.82.24.88

Table 6.2 TCP/IP Connectivity Worksheet *(Continued)*

Parameter	Description	Sample Values
IPv6 address	This is the new 128bit IP address of the remote server specified in hexadecimal format. You should not specify the IPv4 address with the "tcpip6" keyword. The catalog command will not fail, but your subsequent connections will.	1080:21DA:9C5A:2F3B:02AA:00FF:FE28:417A
Service name	The name that maps to the TCP/IP port number. The service name and port number are used interchangeably.	db2inst1
Port number	The TCP/IP port number where the instance is listening for incoming connections on the server. The service name and port number are used interchangeably.	50000
Node name	An arbitrary name used to identify the remote server. It must be unique in the client's node directory.	Mynode1
Database name	The database on the server. It is the database to which you want to connect.	RMTDB
Database alias (optional)	An alias for the database name. If specified, all connections must use this alias. If not specified, the database alias will be the same as the database name.	MYRMTDB

2. Catalog an entry in the database directory on the client:
   ```
   catalog db database_name [as database_alias] at node nodename
   ```
3. Issue a **`terminate`** command to flush the directory cache:
   ```
   terminate
   ```

Table 6.3 demonstrates how to use these commands based on the examples shown in Figure 6.11 and Figure 6.12. Figure 6.11 and Figure 6.12 show the three node directory entries and three system database directory entries respectively for remote connection to their respective databases. The information in this table applies to all Linux, UNIX, and Windows platforms.

After completing the **`catalog`** commands in Table 6.3, the client's database directory and node directory will look like Figure 6.12 and Figure 6.13 respectively.

6.3.3 Scenario 3: Remote Connection from a DB2 Client to a DB2 Host Server

Figure 6.14 illustrates the configuration used for this scenario. The machine *aries* is considered a client to the database server *mpower*.

The client must have one of the following installed:

- DB2 Connect Personal Edition
- DB2 Connect Enterprise Edition

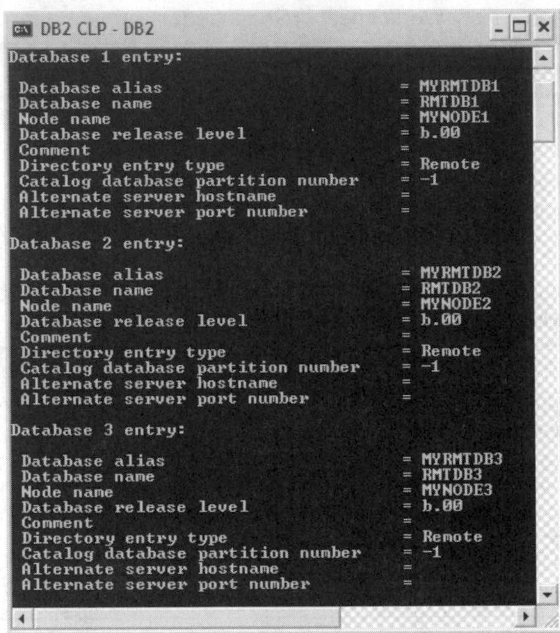
```
DB2 CLP - DB2
Database 1 entry:

 Database alias                       = MYRMTDB1
 Database name                        = RMTDB1
 Node name                            = MYNODE1
 Database release level               = b.00
 Comment                              =
 Directory entry type                 = Remote
 Catalog database partition number    = -1
 Alternate server hostname            =
 Alternate server port number         =

Database 2 entry:

 Database alias                       = MYRMTDB2
 Database name                        = RMTDB2
 Node name                            = MYNODE2
 Database release level               = b.00
 Comment                              =
 Directory entry type                 = Remote
 Catalog database partition number    = -1
 Alternate server hostname            =
 Alternate server port number         =

Database 3 entry:

 Database alias                       = MYRMTDB3
 Database name                        = RMTDB3
 Node name                            = MYNODE3
 Database release level               = b.00
 Comment                              =
 Directory entry type                 = Remote
 Catalog database partition number    = -1
 Alternate server hostname            =
 Alternate server port number         =
```

Figure 6.12 Sample client system database directory for remote connections to DB2 databases

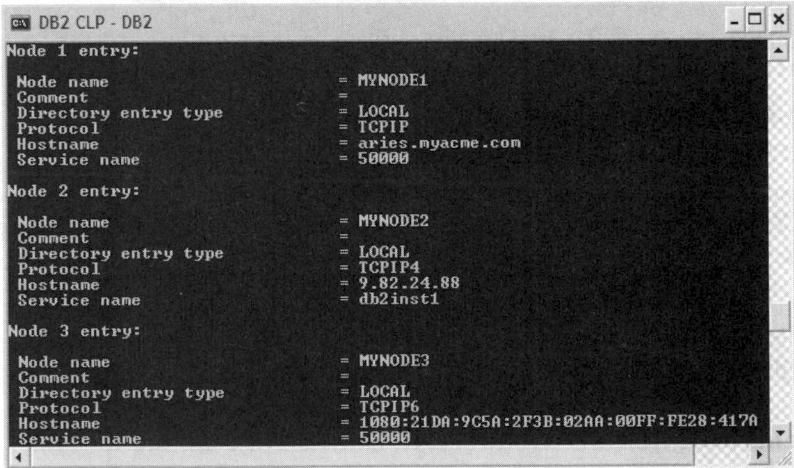
```
DB2 CLP - DB2
Node 1 entry:

 Node name                  = MYNODE1
 Comment                    =
 Directory entry type       = LOCAL
 Protocol                   = TCPIP
 Hostname                   = aries.myacme.com
 Service name               = 50000

Node 2 entry:

 Node name                  = MYNODE2
 Comment                    =
 Directory entry type       = LOCAL
 Protocol                   = TCPIP4
 Hostname                   = 9.82.24.88
 Service name               = db2inst1

Node 3 entry:

 Node name                  = MYNODE3
 Comment                    =
 Directory entry type       = LOCAL
 Protocol                   = TCPIP6
 Hostname                   = 1080:21DA:9C5A:2F3B:02AA:00FF:FE28:417A
 Service name               = 50000
```

Figure 6.13 Sample client system node directory for remote connections to DB2 databases

Machine 1: "aries"
Hostname: aries.myacme.com
IP Address: 9.99.24.88
DB2 Port: 50000
Operating System: Linux/UNIX/Windows
DB2.9 Connect installed
Machine 2: "mpower"
Hostname: mpower.youracme.com
IP Address:158.228.20.3
DB2 Port: 446
Operating System: z/OS, OS/390, or iSeries
DB2 for z/OS and OS/390 or DB2 for iSeries installed
TCP/IP or APPC
DB2 commands to execute from the DB2 Connect Command Line Processor (CLP)
db2 catalog tcpip node mynode2
remote mpower.youracme.com
server 446
db2 catalog db myhostdb
at node mynode2
db2 catalog dcs db myhostdb as hostprod
db2 terminate
db2 connect to myhostdb user myhostid using myhostpsw
Location Name (OS/390
or z/OS) or RDB name (iSeries):
HOSTPROD
userid: myhostid
password: myhostpsw

Figure 6.14 The process of connecting remotely from a DB2 client to a DB2 host server

Table 6.3 Example of Configuring a Remote Connection to a DB2 Server Using TCP/IP

Information You Need to Obtain from Server Machine 2 (*Aries*) to Perform the Commands on Client Machine 1	Command to Run on Client Machine 1 (*Libra*)
Hostname1 = aries.myacme.com IP address = 9.82.24.87 Service name/port # in services file = db2inst 50000	**db2 catalog tcpip node mynode1 remote aries.myacme.com server 50000**
Hostname2 = aries2.myacme.com IP address = 9.82.24.88 Service name/port # in services file = db2inst1 50010	**db2 catalog tcpip4 node mynode2 remote 9.82.24.88 server db2inst1**
Hostname3 = aries.myacme.com IP address (IPv6) = 1080:21DA:9C5A:2F3B:02AA:00FF:FE28:417A Service name/port # in services file = db2inst2 50020	**db2 catalog tcpip6 node mynode3 remote 1080:21DA:9C5A:2F3B:02AA:00FF:FE28:417A server 50020**

(continues)

Table 6.3 Example of Configuring a Remote Connection to a DB2 Server Using TCP/IP *(Continued)*

Information You Need to Obtain from Server Machine 2 (*Aries*) to Perform the Commands on Client Machine 1	Command to Run on Client Machine 1 (*Libra*)
Database alias on Machine 2 = RMTDB Note: The database must exist in the system database directory of Machine 2. If the database alias and the database name are different, then the database alias should be used. Note: *MYRMTDBx* is an alias to the database *RMTDBx*, where *x* is either 1, 2, or 3.Specifying the alias is optional, but if specified, the alias is what you should use in the connect command. Otherwise, use the database name.	**db2 catalog db rmtdb1 as myrmtdb1 at node mynode1** **db2 catalog db rmtdb2 as myrmtdb2 at node mynode2** **db2 catalog db rmtdb3 as myrmtdb3 at node mynode3**
No information needed.	**db2 terminate** Note: This command is needed to make the previous catalog commands effective.
A valid user ID and password that has **CONNECT** privileges to databases RMTDB1, RMTDB2 and RMTDB3. This user ID will be used from Machine 1 to connect to RMTDB.	**db2 connect to myrmtdb1 user userid using password** **db2 connect to myrmtdb2 user userid using password** **db2 connect to myrmtdb3 user userid using password**

The only communication protocol supported is TCP/IP.

> **NOTE** The SNA communication protocol including APPC, APPN and CPI-C is no longer supported in DB2 9.

Setting up a remote connection to a host DB2 database follows the same principle as setting up a connection to a DB2 for Linux, UNIX, and Windows database. You need to configure both the client and the server.

- Enable the database server to accept client connections.
- Catalog the node directory, system database directory, and DCS directory on the client.

6.3.3.1 Enabling the Database Server to Accept Client Connections

We will not go through the host database server configuration in this book. However, at a minimum, for DB2 for z/OS and OS/390, make sure that the distributed data facility (DDF) is running on the mainframe. DDF is the facility in DB2 for z/OS and OS/390 that allows for remote communication support. You can verify this by issuing the **-display ddf** command from the mainframe. To start DDF, issue the **-start ddf** command.

For DB2 for i5/OS, make sure the distributed data management (DDM) is started. DDM is the facility in DB2 for i5/OS that allows for remote communication support. To start DDM from the i5/OS server or to verify that DDM is already started issue

```
STRTTCPSVR SERVER(*DDM)
```

The TCPIP port 446 is usually the default value for DB2 for z/OS.

6.3.3.2 Cataloging the Node Directory, Database Directory, and DCS Directory on the Client

After you have enabled the server to accept client connections, you need to tell the client how to connect to the server. You do this by cataloging the node directory, system database directory, and DCS directory on the client.

6.3.3.2.1 TCP/IP Connection

Use the information in Table 6.4 for completing the procedure in this section.

Table 6.4 TCP/IP Connectivity Worksheet for DB2 Client to DB2 Host Connection

Parameter	Description	Sample Values
Host name or IP address	The host name or IP address of the remote server.	mpower.youracme.com 158.228.10.3
Port number	The TCP/IP port number on which DB2 is listening for incoming connections on the server.	446
Node name	This is an arbitrary name and is used to identify the remote server. It must be unique in the client's node directory.	mynode2
Target database name	The database on the host server. For DB2 for z/OS and OS/ 390 servers, this is the *Location name*. For DB2 for i5/OS servers, this is the *RDB name*.	hostprod
Database name	An arbitrary name you would like to associate with the target database name.	myhostdb
Database alias (optional)	You can optionally specify a database alias for the database name. If specified, all connections must use this alias name; if not specified, the database alias will be the same as the database name.	myhostdb

1. Catalog a TCP/IP node on the client.

```
Catalog tcpip/tcpip4/tcpip6 node nodename
  remote hostname/Ipv4_address/Ipv6_address
    server service_name/port_number_of_server
```

2. Catalog a database directory on the client.

```
catalog db database_name [as database_alias] at node nodename
```

3. Catalog a DCS database directory on the client by issuing the following command from the client's command window:

```
catalog dcs db database_name as target_database_name
```

   The ***database_name*** field must match the ***database_name*** in the **catalog db** command in step 2.

4. Issue the **terminate** command to refresh the cache.

```
terminate
```

Table 6.5 demonstrates how to use these commands based on the example shown in Figure 6.15.

After completing the three catalog commands in Table 6.5, the client machine's system database directory and node directory will look as shown in Figure 6.15.

Table 6.5 Example of Configuring a Remote Connection to DB2 for z/OS and OS/390 or DB2 for i5/OS Database

Information You Need to Obtain from Host Server Machine 2 *(mpower)* to Perform the Commands on Client Machine 1 (*aries*)	Command to Run on Client Machine 1 (*aries*)
Host name of Machine 2 = mpower.youracme.com The TCP/IP port DB2 uses = 446	**db2 catalog tcpip node mynode2 remote mpower.youracme.com server 446**
No information needed.	**db2 catalog db *myhostdb* at node *mynode2*** Note: ***myhostdb*** is an arbitrary database name, but it must match the entry for the DCS directory below.
hostprod = The *Location name* if the server is DB2 for z/OS and OS/390 or *RDB name* if the server is DB2 for i5/OS.	**db2 catalog dcs db myhostdb as hostprod**
No information needed.	**db2 terminate** Note: This command is needed to make the previous **catalog** commands effective.
A valid user ID and password that has connect privilege to the host database.	**db2 connect to myhostdb user *userid* using *password***

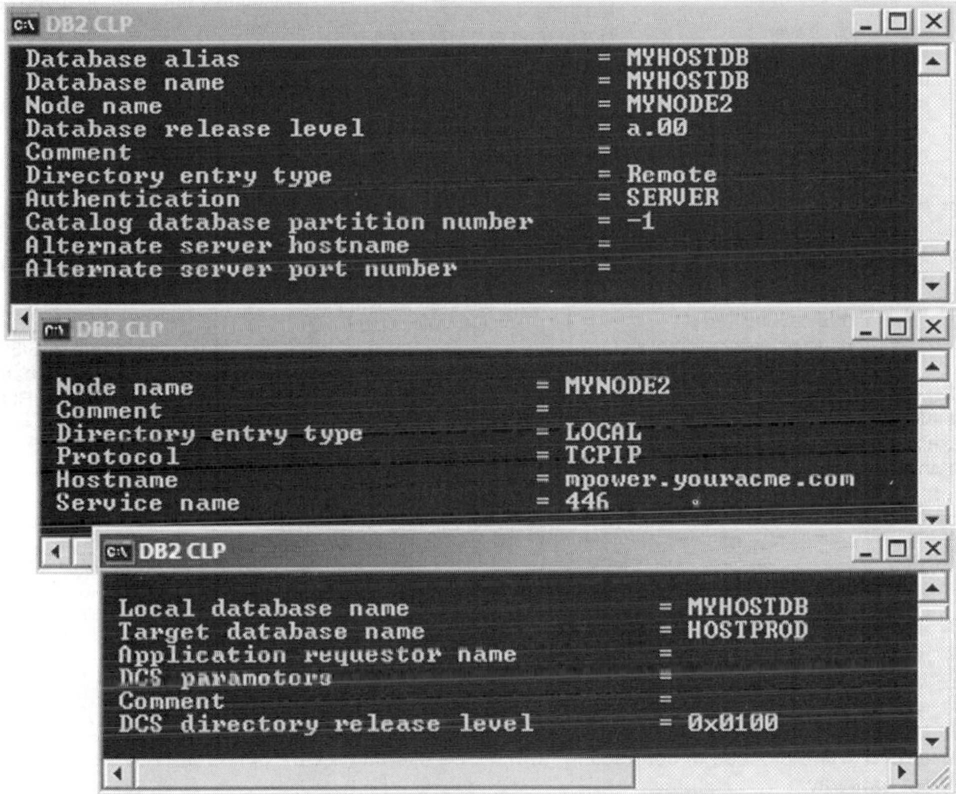
```
Database alias                          = MYHOSTDB
Database name                           = MYHOSTDB
Node name                               = MYNODE2
Database release level                  = a.00
Comment                                 =
Directory entry type                    = Remote
Authentication                          = SERVER
Catalog database partition number       = -1
Alternate server hostname               =
Alternate server port number            =

Node name                        = MYNODE2
Comment                          =
Directory entry type             = LOCAL
Protocol                         = TCPIP
Hostname                         = mpower.youracme.com
Service name                     = 446

Local database name              = MYHOSTDB
Target database name             = HOSTPROD
Application requestor name       =
DCS parameters                   =
Comment                          =
DCS directory release level      = 0x0100
```

Figure 6.15 Sample client's system database directory, node directory, and DCS directory for remote connection to a DB2 host database

6.3.4 Scenario 4: Remote Connection from a DB2 Client to a DB2 Host Server via a DB2 Connect Gateway

Imagine you have 1,000 clients who need to connect to a host database. If you set up the connections using DB2 Connect Personal Edition, you will need to purchase and install DB2 Connect Personal Edition on each of the 1,000 clients. This would be very costly. Wouldn't it be nice if you could only install DB2 Connect once on one machine, and use it as a gateway to service all connections from clients to the host database? Of course! For that scenario you need to use the DB2 Connect Enterprise Edition. Figure 6.16 illustrates this scenario.

In this configuration, Machine 1 is the client, Machine 2 is referred to as the DB2 Connect gateway, and Machine 3 is the host database server.

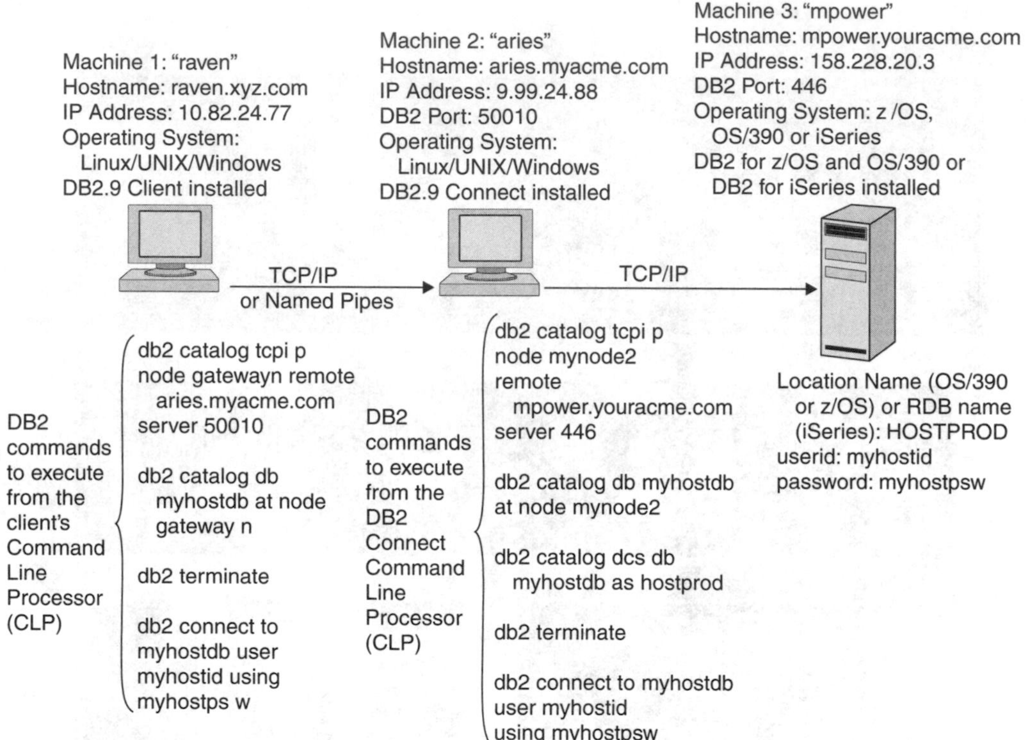
Machine 1: "raven"
Hostname: raven.xyz.com
IP Address: 10.82.24.77
Operating System: Linux/UNIX/Windows
DB2.9 Client installed
Machine 2: "aries"
Hostname: aries.myacme.com
IP Address: 9.99.24.88
DB2 Port: 50010
Operating System: Linux/UNIX/Windows
DB2.9 Connect installed
Machine 3: "mpower"
Hostname: mpower.youracme.com
IP Address: 158.228.20.3
DB2 Port: 446
Operating System: z /OS, OS/390 or iSeries
DB2 for z/OS and OS/390 or DB2 for iSeries installed
TCP/IP
or Named Pipes
TCP/IP
DB2 commands to execute from the client's Command Line Processor (CLP)
db2 catalog tcpi p node gatewayn remote aries.myacme.com server 50010
db2 catalog db myhostdb at node gateway n
db2 terminate
db2 connect to myhostdb user myhostid using myhostps w
DB2 commands to execute from the DB2 Connect Command Line Processor (CLP)
db2 catalog tcpi p node mynode2 remote mpower.youracme.com server 446
db2 catalog db myhostdb at node mynode2
db2 catalog dcs db myhostdb as hostprod
db2 terminate
db2 connect to myhostdb user myhostid using myhostpsw
Location Name (OS/390 or z/OS) or RDB name (iSeries): HOSTPROD
userid: myhostid
password: myhostpsw

Figure 6.16 The process of connecting from a DB2 client to a DB2 server via a DB2 Connect gateway

The DB2 Connect gateway is the only machine that needs to have DB2 Connect Enterprise Edition installed. Its task is to serve as a middleman between the clients and the host database server, since the clients do not have the ability to connect directly to the server. The gateway machine can serve hundreds of clients.

When configuring this type of connection, you can break the three-tier connection into two parts.

- Part one is the gateway-to-host server connection. This is identical to what we discussed in Scenario 3. Follow the same steps as in Section 6.3.3, Scenario 3: Remote Connection from a DB2 Client to a DB2 Host Server, to configure the gateway. Make sure you can connect from the gateway to the host database before proceeding to the next step.
- Part two is the client-to-gateway connection. From the client's perspective, the gateway machine is the database server. (The client does not know anything about the host server mpower.) Thus, when cofiguring this part of the connection, treat the gateway as the server, and follow the same steps described in Section 6.3.2, Scenario 2: Remote Connection from a DB2 Client to a DB2 Server.

6.3.5 Binding Utilities

After a client establishes a connection to a database server, it should be able to access the data in the database. However, if you issue the **import/export** commands or try to run a CLI/ODBC application, you will get SQL0805N "Package not found" error. This is because the client has not bound these utilities to the database server.

Utilities are database programs with embedded SQL; their packages must reside on the database server. Packages are version and Fix Pack level specific; therefore, a package created at the DB2 9, Fix Pack 1 level cannot be used by a client running at DB2 9, Fix Pack 2. If this client needs to use these utilities, it must create packages at its own DB2 level. (Refer to Chapter 7, Working with Database Objects, for a more detailed explanation of packages.)

To create all of these packages at once, run the following commands from an IBM Data Server Client's CLP window:

```
connect to database_alias user userid using password
bind @db2ubind.lst blocking all grant public
bind @db2cli.lst   blocking all grant public
```

If the database server is a host database, you must run one of the following commands on the DB2 Connect machine.

- If the host is DB2 for z/OS or OS/390:

```
bind @ddcsmvs.lst blocking all grant public
```

- If the host is DB2 for i5/OS:

```
bind @ddcs400.lst blocking all grant public
```

You need to use the symbol **@** when you specify a file that contains a list of bind files (with the .lst file extension), rather than a bind file (with the .bnd file extension) itself. The .lst files are in the *install_directory*\bnd directory on Windows and in the *instance_home*/sqllib/bnd directory on Linux or UNIX. Both contain a list of bind files the **bind** command will run against. A package is created for each of these bind files.

> **NOTE** The IBM Data Server Runtime Client does not include the required bind files, so you cannot run the **bind** command from a Runtime Client.

You must bind the utilities for each database you want to access. Binding only needs to be done once by a client. Once a package is successfully bound to the database, all DB2 clients of the same DB2 version and Fix Pack level can use it. If you have different versions and Fix Packs of clients, you must bind the utilities for each client version and Fix Pack level.

> **NOTE** You must have BINDADD authority to create a new package in a database or BIND privilege if the package already exists.

DB2 9.5 introduced automatic binding of the utilities which is performed as part of the process of applying a Fix Pack. Also for Linux and UNIX, the db2iupdt and dasupdt command are automatically bound as part of the Fix Pack upgrade.

6.4 Configuring Database Connections Using the Configuration Assistant

If you don't feel comfortable using DB2 commands, you can use the **Configuration Assistant** (**CA**), a graphical tool to configure connections on a client machine (or a server machine). The CA catalogs the DB2 directories for you.

The CA's **Add Database Wizard** offers three methods to configure a database connection from a client machine.

- **Search the network:** With this method, you do not need to know any communication-specific information about the database server, such as the TCP/IP port and database name. The CA will find that out for you using DB2's Discovery ability and will update the DB2 directories.
- **Use a profile:** A **profile** contains all the information necessary to create a connection between a client and a server. Using the information from a given profile, the CA will update the DB2 directories of the client to allow connections to the chosen database.
- **Manually configure a connection to a database:** You must know the specific connection information of the server, such as host name, port number, and database name. The CA will update the DB2 directories based on the information you provide.

The following sections discuss each of these methods in more detail.

> **NOTE** You can only use the Configuration Assistant to configure connections *from* a client *to* a server. You still need to enable the server to accept client connections *manually* before you start using the CA to configure the client.

6.4.1 Configuring a Connection Using DB2 Discovery in the Configuration Assistant

You can perform Discovery in one of two ways.

- The **search discovery** method searches the network for any DB2 servers accessible by clients. You do not need to know the name of the server. The CA returns a list of valid servers and their database information. Use this method only in a small network where there are not many hubs, otherwise the search process may take a long time to complete.

- The **known discovery** method requires you to provide the server name you want to access, and the CA returns the instance and database information for that server.

Table 6.6 shows the parameters that control DB2 Discovery at the server and the files where they are located.

Table 6.6 The Parameters That Control Discovery at the Server

Configuration File	Parameter Name	Possible Values	Explanation
DAS configuration file	DISCOVER	SEARCH	The default value. Both search and known discovery can be used.
		KNOWN	Only known discovery can be used.
		DISABLE	Discovery method can't be used for instances.
DBM configuration file	DISCOVER _INST	ENABLE	The default value. The instance can be discovered.
		DISABLE	The instance can't be discovered.
Database configuration file	DISCOVER_DB	ENABLE	The default value. The database can be discovered.
		DISABLE	The database can't be discovered.

Table 6.7 shows the parameter that controls DB2 Discovery at the client.

Table 6.7 The Parameter That Controls Discovery at the Client

Configuration File	Parameter Name	Possible Values	Explanation
DBM configuration file	DISCOVER	SEARCH	The default value. The client can issue search and known discovery requests
		KNOWN	The client can only issue known discovery requests.
		DISABLE	Discovery is disabled at the client.

By default, all the instances and databases on a server are visible to all clients using the CA. If you have security concerns, you can control the level of visibility by modifying the values of these parameters. For example, if you set DISCOVER_ INST=DISABLE at the instance level, then the instance and all its databases will not be visible by clients who try to discover them using the CA.

Figure 6.17 shows an example of a database server with two instances and different values for the parameters affecting DB2 discovery.

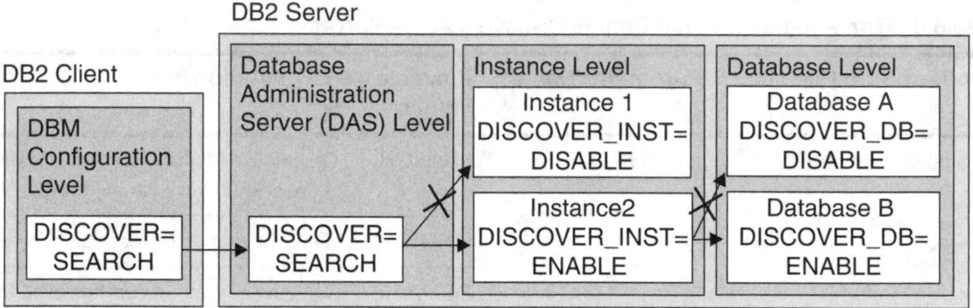

Figure 6.17 Discovery hierarchy

In Figure 6.17, the client can use the CA to see the database server because DISCOVER is set to SEARCH in the server's DAS. The client can see instance 2 but not instance 1. In instance 2, the client can see database B but not A.

> **NOTE** The DAS on each DB2 server you want to locate using Discovery must be configured and running.

The procedure to add a database connection using the discovery method in the CA is

1. Open the CA from the **IBM DB2** menu or enter **db2ca** from a command line. Figure 6.18 shows the CA interface.
2. The databases that are already cataloged on the client are displayed in the CA window. To add more connections, click **Selected** and choose **Add Database Using Wizard.** You will see the Add Database Wizard, shown in Figure 6.19.
3. Choose *Search the network* to use the DB2 Discovery methods. This displays the window shown in Figure 6.20. The systems the client currently knows about are displayed in the *Known systems* folder. *SYLVIA2* is the only known system to this client. If the database server you want to connect to is already in the Known systems folder, expand the tree to look for it. If the database server is not listed, you need to add it to the list.

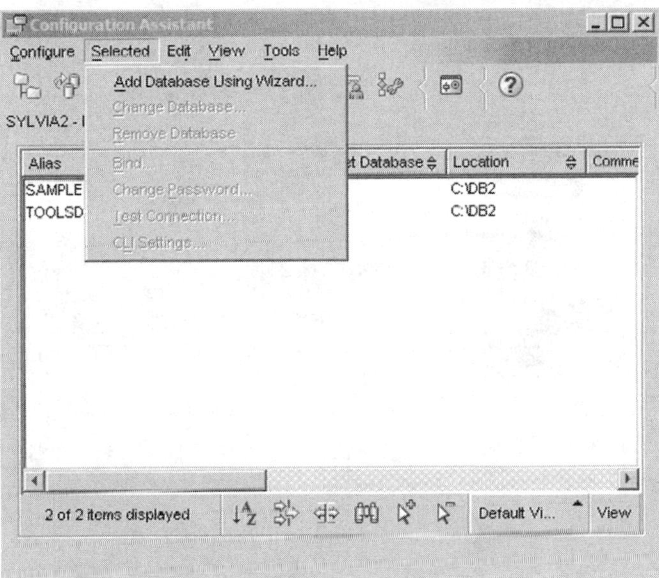

Figure 6.18 The Configuration Assistant (CA)

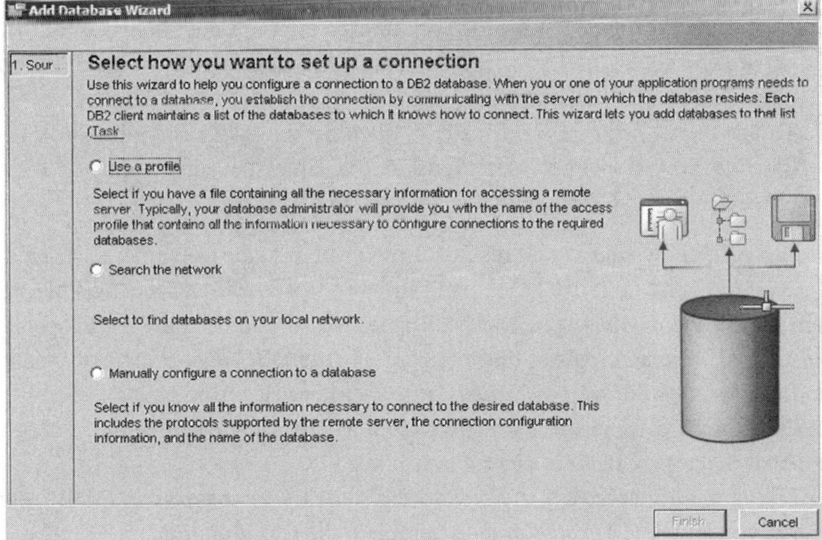

Figure 6.19 Add Database Wizard—Configuration methods

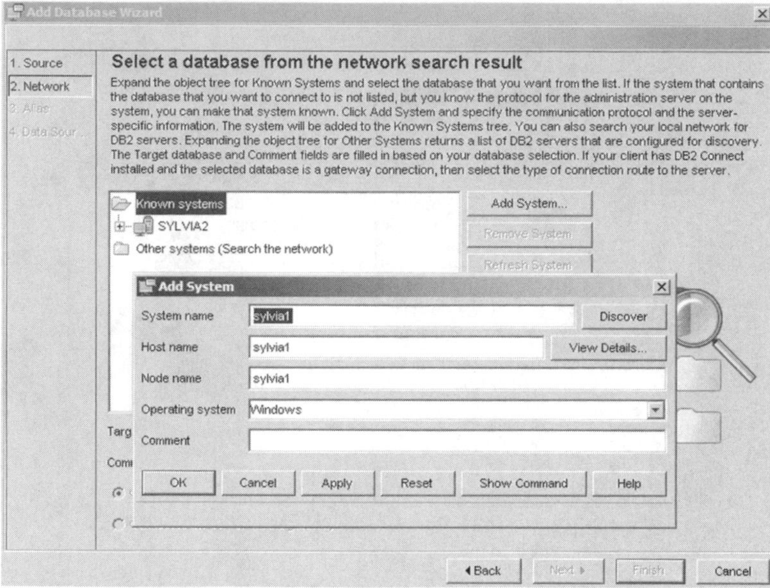

Figure 6.20 Add Database Wizard—Adding a system using the known discovery method

4. You have two choices to add the new system.
   - To use the *search discovery* method, double click on the *Other systems (Search the network)* folder. The CA will then search for and display all database servers that have Discovery enabled on the system.
   - To use the *known discovery* method, click on the *Add System* button. This displays the *Add System* window (see Figure 6.20). Enter the information as required. The Node Name and Comment fields are optional.
5. Figure 6.21 shows the search result for the system name you entered. In this example, the system name is *SYLVIA1*. Expand the tree to see all databases visible on this system. Select the database you want to connect to. If you do not want to specify an alias for the database and register this database as an ODBC data source, you can finish the configuration by clicking the *Finish* button. Otherwise, click *Next*.
6. In Figure 6.22 you can specify a database alias. This is the name you will use during all connect requests. Click *Finish* or *Next*.
7. In Figure 6.23, you have the choice to register this database as an ODBC data source. When you click the *Finish* button to complete the configuration, an Add Database Confirmation window displays. You can click *Close* to return to the CA main window or *Test Connection* to verify the connection to the database.

Figure 6.24 shows the window displayed if you choose to test the connection. The user ID must be valid on the database server.

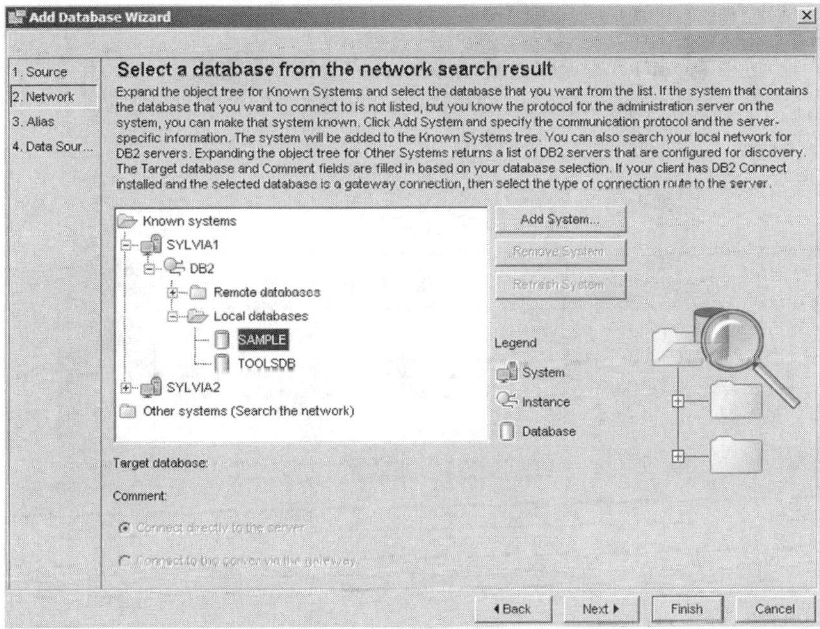

Figure 6.21 Add Database Wizard—Network search result

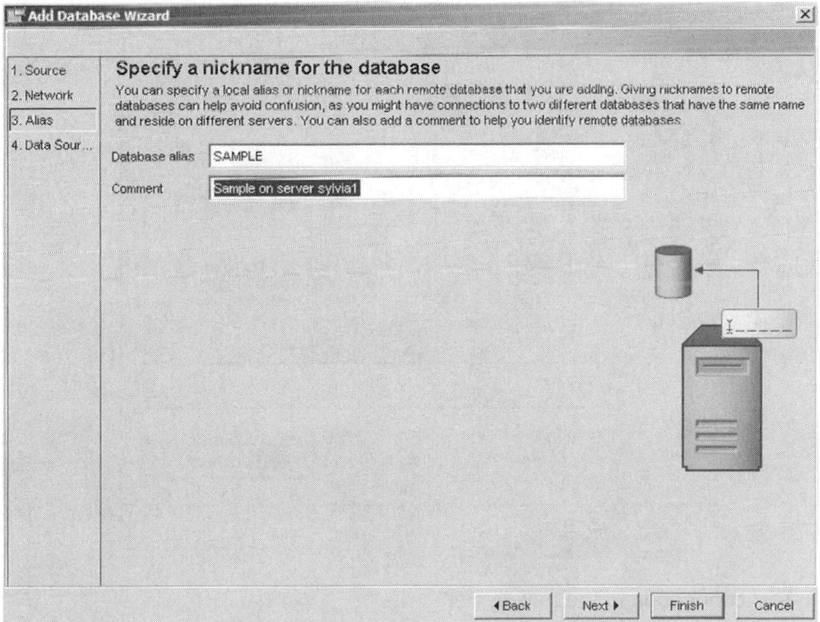

Figure 6.22 Add Database Wizard—Specify a database alias

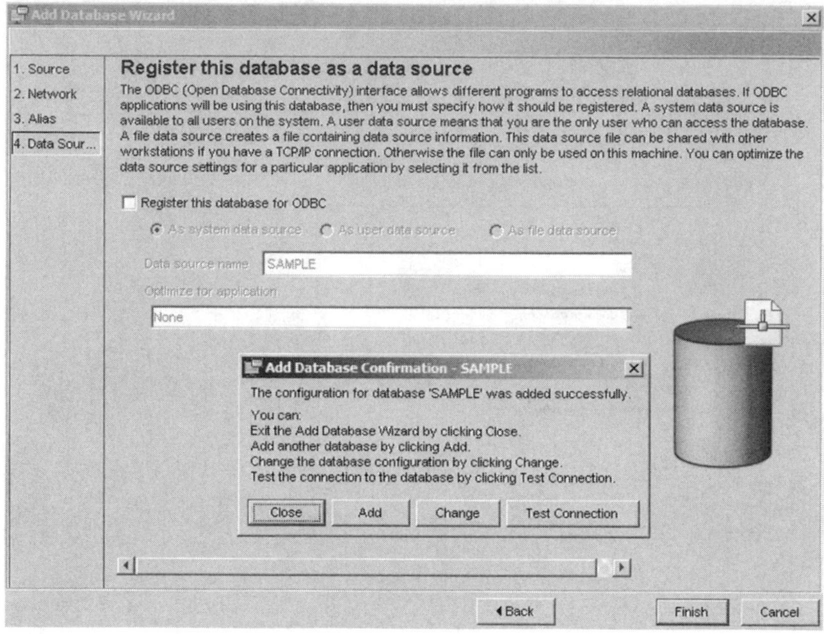

Figure 6.23 Register database as an ODBC data source

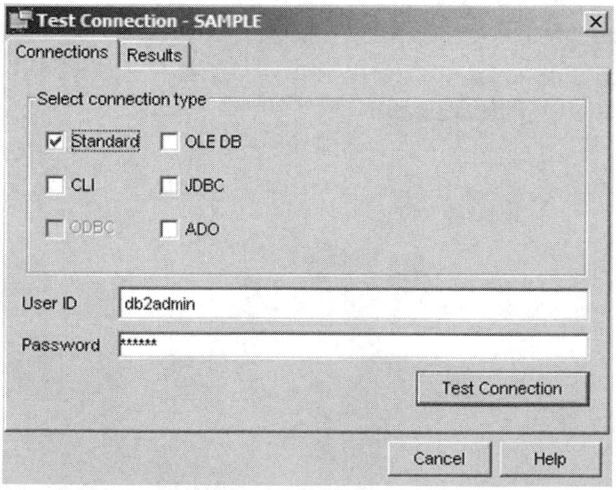

Test Connection - SAMPLE
Connections
Results
Select connection type
Standard
OLE DB
CLI
JDBC
ODBC
ADO
User ID
db2admin
Password
******
Test Connection
Cancel
Help

Figure 6.24 Test connection to the new system

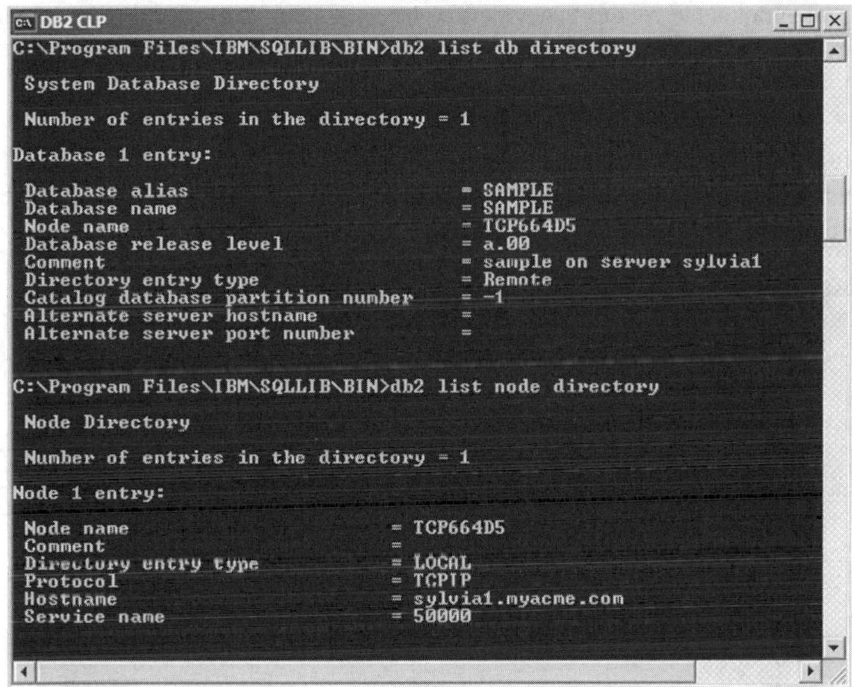
```
C:\Program Files\IBM\SQLLIB\BIN>db2 list db directory

 System Database Directory

 Number of entries in the directory = 1

Database 1 entry:

 Database alias                       = SAMPLE
 Database name                        = SAMPLE
 Node name                            = TCP664D5
 Database release level               = a.00
 Comment                              = sample on server sylvia1
 Directory entry type                 = Remote
 Catalog database partition number    = -1
 Alternate server hostname            =
 Alternate server port number         =

C:\Program Files\IBM\SQLLIB\BIN>db2 list node directory

 Node Directory

 Number of entries in the directory = 1

Node 1 entry:

 Node name                      = TCP664D5
 Comment                        =
 Directory entry type           = LOCAL
 Protocol                       = TCPIP
 Hostname                       = sylvia1.myacme.com
 Service name                   = 50000
```

Figure 6.25 Updated node directory and database directory

The CA automatically updates the node directory and database directory, as shown in Figure 6.25. Note that the node name is an arbitrary name chosen by the CA.

6.4.2 Configuring a Connection Using Access Profiles in the Configuration Assistant

An **access profile** is a file that contains all the information necessary to create a connection between a client and a server. This process automatically catalogs the DB2 directories on the client. Use access profiles if you have many clients that need to be configured to connect to the same DB2 servers.

You can obtain an access profile either from a configured client or from the server itself.

- If you have a client that has been configured to connect to DB2 servers, use this client's CA to export its configuration to an access profile file. You can then transfer this file to other clients and configure them using this information.
- You can use the server's CA to export an access profile that contains information about all the instances that have DISCOVER_INST=ENABLE in the Database Manager Configuration file and all databases that have DISCOVER_DB=ENABLE in the database

configuration file. You can then transfer this access profile to clients and configure them using the information in this file.

6.4.2.1 Using the Configuration Assistant to Export an Access Profile

1. In the Configuration Assistant, choose **Configure > Export Profile.** (You can also do this by using the **db2cfexp** command.) Figure 6.26 shows the three Export Profile options.

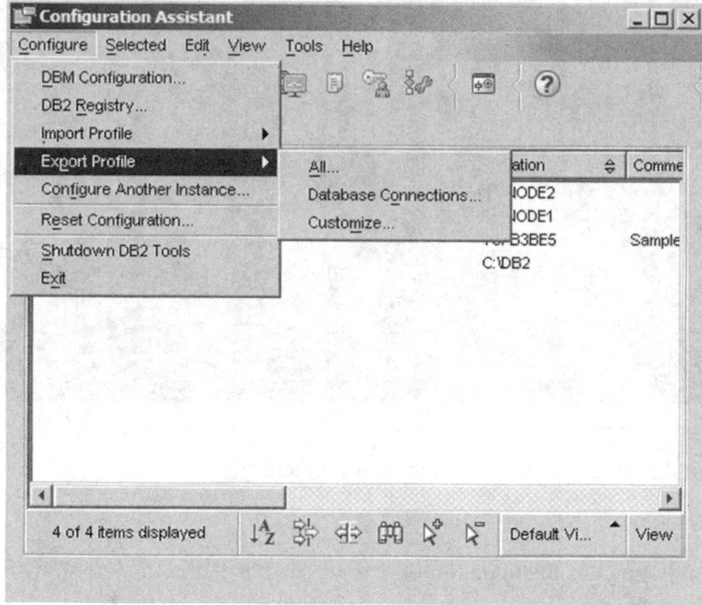

Figure 6.26 Exporting an access profile using the CA

- **All** creates a profile that contains all of the databases cataloged on the system. In addition, the profile includes specific information about the system, such as the DB2 registry variables and Database Manager Configuration.
- **Database Connections** creates a profile that contains only the database catalog information.
- **Customize** lets you select specific databases that are cataloged on the system.

2. In this example, let's select **Customize.** This displays the *Customize Export Profile* window (see Figure 6.27).
3. **From the** *Available database aliases* list, choose the database(s) for which you would like to export the connection information. Then click the > button to transfer it to the *Selected database aliases* list.
4. Enter a filename for the access profile.

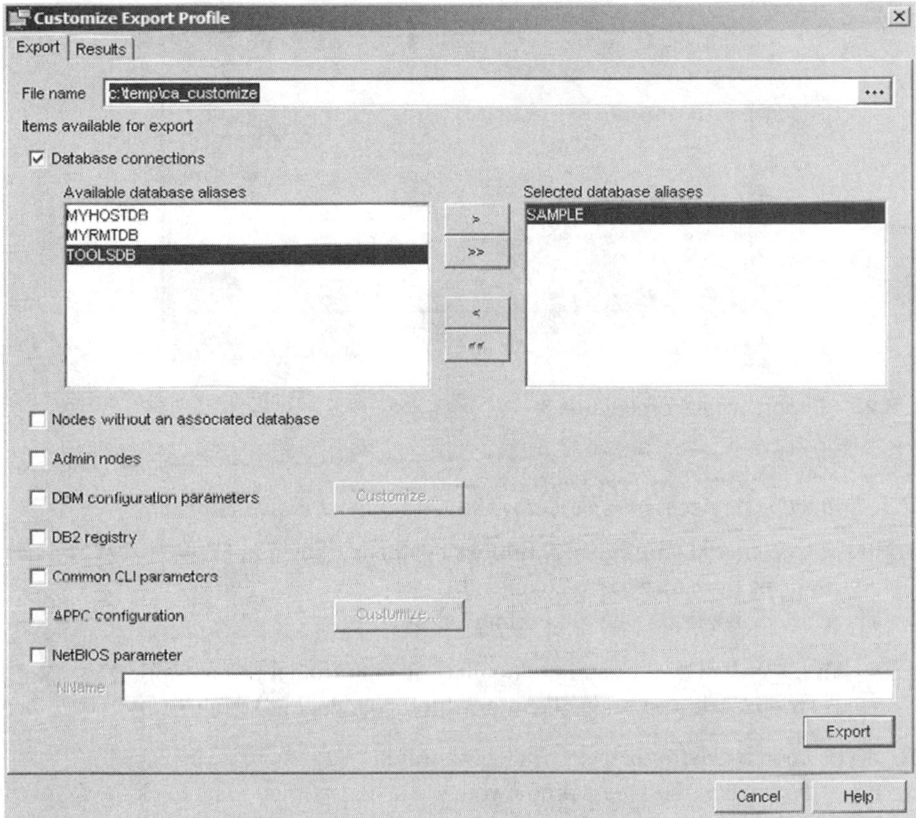

Figure 6.27 The Customize Export Profile window

5. If you want to export specific information about the system, such as DBM Configuration parameters or the DB2 registry, you can do so by checking the boxes beside each option.
6. **Click the** *Export* button. Figure 6.28 shows the export result. If the operation is successful, an access profile file is created in the specified directory.

6.4.2.2 Using the Configuration Assistant to Import an Access Profile

After you have obtained an access profile from either a client or a server, you can use this profile to configure other clients. You transfer the file over to the client you want to configure and start the CA on the client.

There are two ways to import an access profile using the Configuration Assistant.

- Use the CA's Import function
- Use the CA's Add Database Wizard

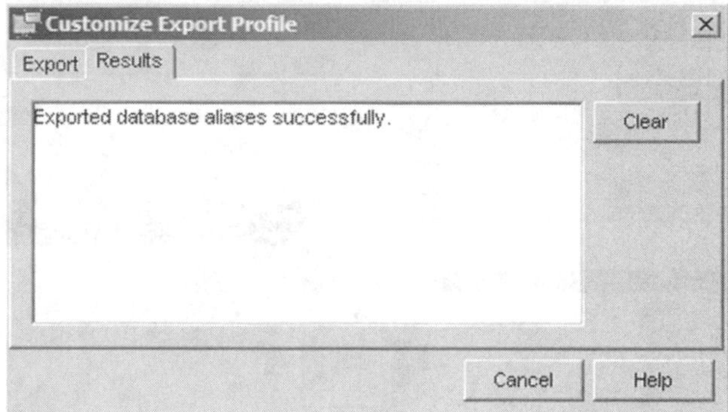

Figure 6.28 Export access profile result

6.4.2.2.1 Importing an Access Profile Using the CA's Import Profile Function

1. In the CA, choose **Configure > Import Profile** as shown in Figure 6.29 (You can also do this using the **`db2cfimp`** command.)
   There are two options when importing a profile.
   - **All** imports all of the configuration information from a given profile.
   - **Customize** lets you select the information you would like to import.
2. If you choose **Customize,** the window shown in Figure 6.30 is displayed.
3. Enter the name of the access profile you would like to import and click the *Load* button. This loads the information in the profile into the *Items available for import* section of the window. You can choose the database(s) you want from the *Available database aliases* list and transfer it to the *Selected database aliases* list.
4. If the profile contains information such as DBM configuration parameters, the DB2 registry, or CLI parameters, the corresponding checkboxes will be available. You can click each checkbox to import that information as well. In Figure 6.30, the checkboxes are grayed out because the associated information is not contained in the access profile.
5. Click the *Import* button and the window shown in Figure 6.31 appears.

If the import is successful, you now have the ability to connect to the database(s) you have chosen. The client's node directory and system database directory have been updated to include this new database.

6.4.2.2.2 Importing an Access Profile Using the CA's Add Database Wizard

You can also import the information in an access profile using the Configuration Assistant's Add Database Wizard. However, when using this method you can only add one database at a time. If you want to add multiple databases, using the Import function discussed in the previous section is a better choice.

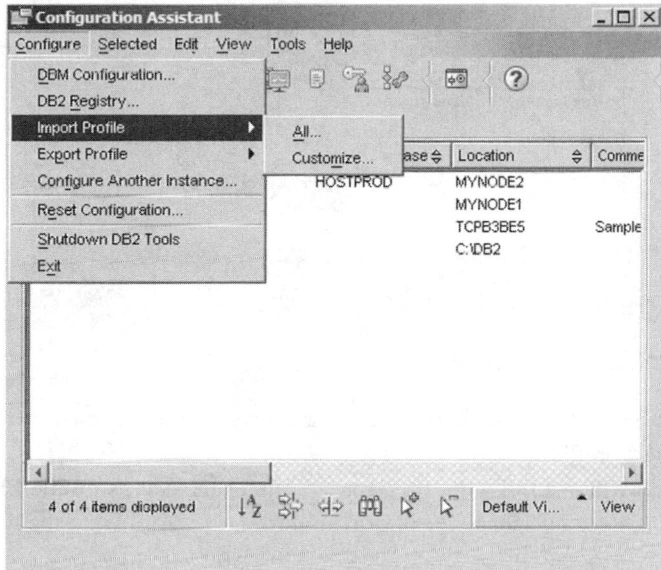

Figure 6.29 Importing the access profile using the CA

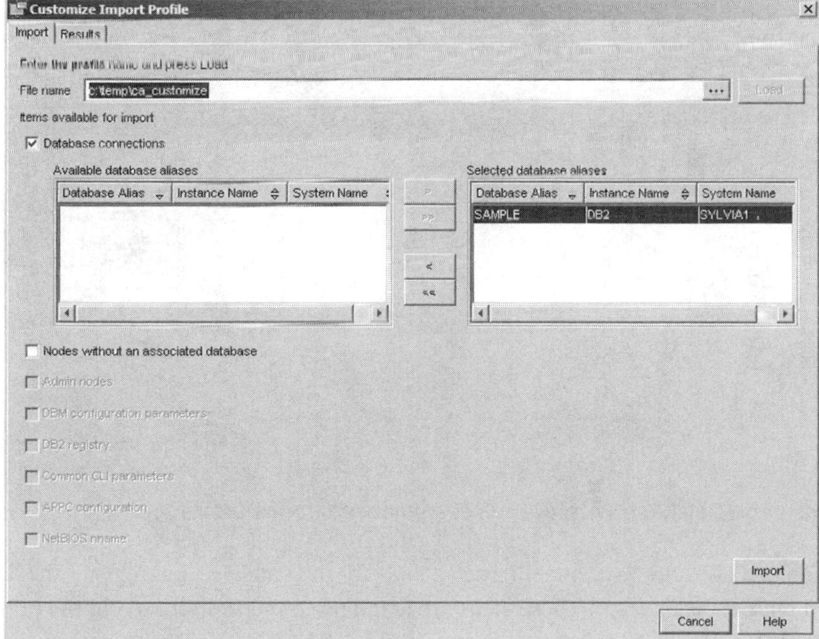

Figure 6.30 The Customize Import Profile window

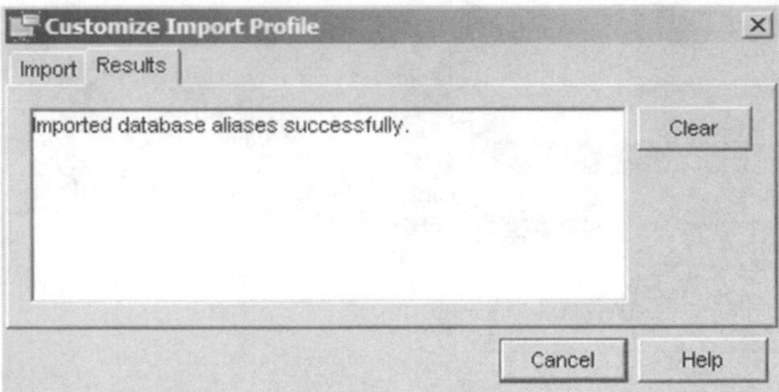

Figure 6.31 Import access profile result

1. From the Select how you want to set up a connection window (shown in Figure 6.19), select Use a profile.
2. The window shown in Figure 6.32 appears. Enter the access profile filename and click the *Load* button. This loads the information from the profile into the window.

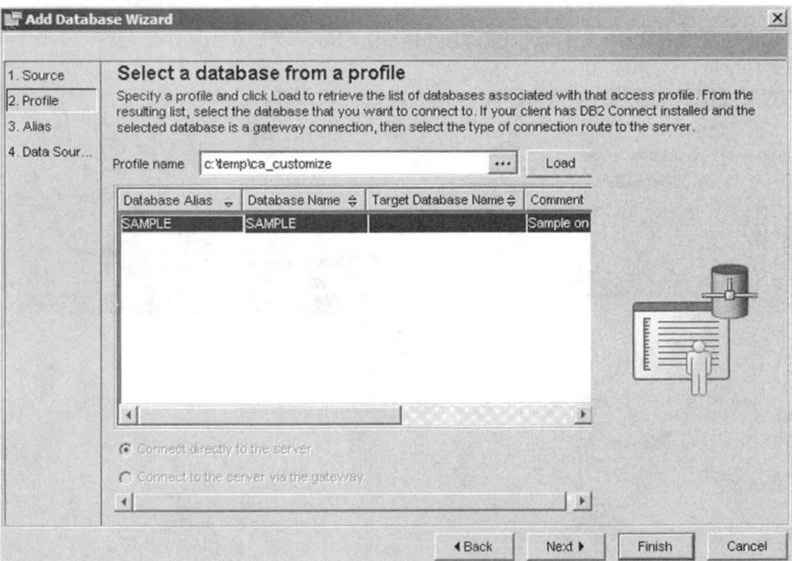

Figure 6.32 Add Database Wizard—Select a database from a profile

3. You can click on *Next* to configure an alias for the database and register the database as an ODBC data source. These steps are identical to those discussed in the previous section. Proceed through the wizard or click *Finish* to complete the import process.

6.4.3 Configuring a Connection Manually Using the Configuration Assistant

You can also manually configure a connection in the Configuration Assistant. Using this method, you must know the specific server connection information, such as host name, port number, and database name. The CA will update the DB2 directories based on the information you provide.

1. In the CA, choose **Selected > Add Database Using Wizard.** Choose *Manually configure a connection to a database* (see Figure 6.18) and click *Next*. The window shown in Figure 6.33 appears.
2. Select the protocol you will use to connect to the database. Also, if the database resides on a host system, check the corresponding box. Click *Next*.
3. Enter the host name or TCP/IP address of the server and the service name or port number that the DB2 instance is using on the server, as shown in Figure 6.34. Click *Next*.

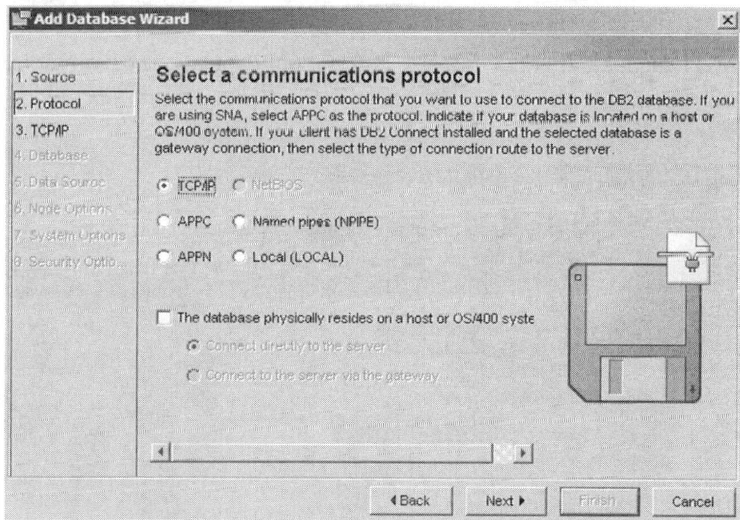

Figure 6.33 Add Database Wizard—Select a communications protocol

4. Enter the database name, as shown in Figure 6.35. The database name in this entry corresponds to the database alias on the server. If you want, complete the optional *Database alias* and *Comment* fields. The alias is what you will use in the **CONNECT** statement. Click *Next*.
5. Once you have completed the screen shown in Figure 6.36, you can choose to either continue through the next screens or you can click *Finish*. If you continue to any of the subsequent screens, you can click *Finish* at any time.

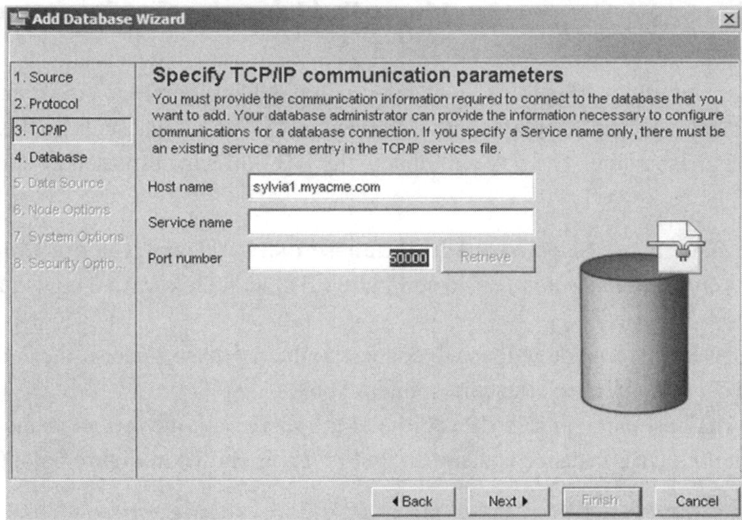

Figure 6.34 Add Database Wizard—Specify TCP/IP communications parameters

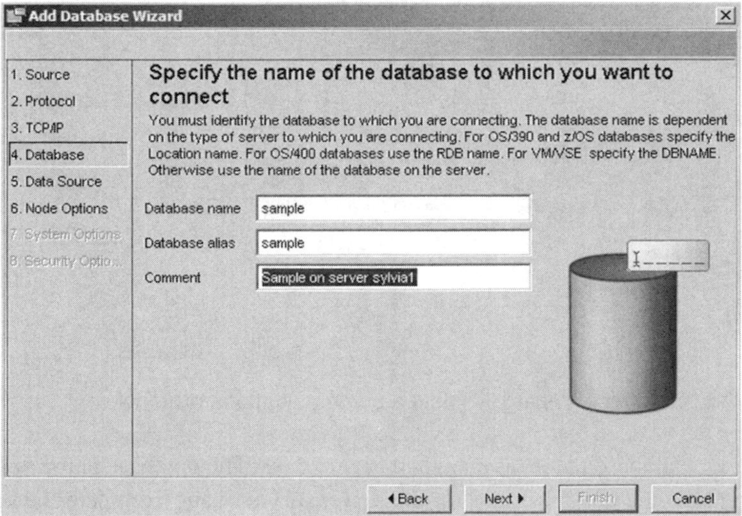

Figure 6.35 Add Database Wizard—Specify database name

6. In the screen shown in Figure 6.37, specify the operating system and instance name on the database server. Since this information affects the behavior of the Control Center, it is important that you fill them in. Click *Next*.

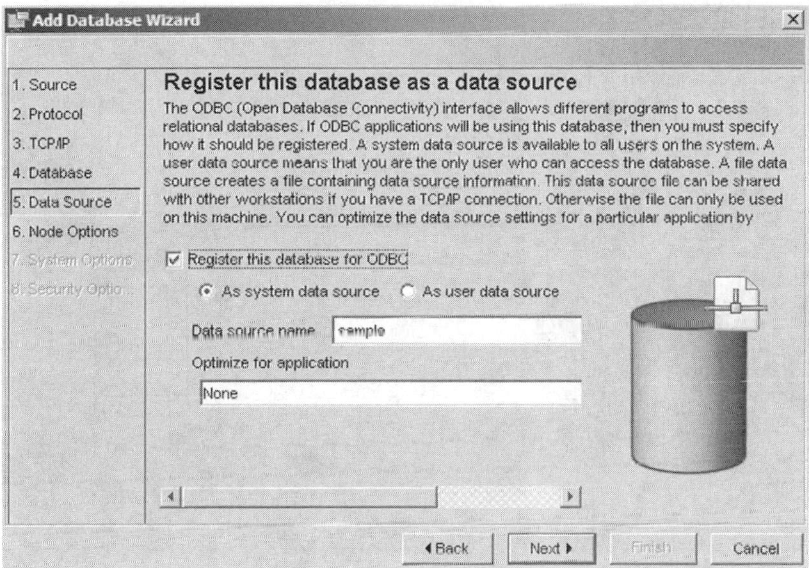

Figure 6.36 Add Database Wizard—Register this database as an ODBC data source

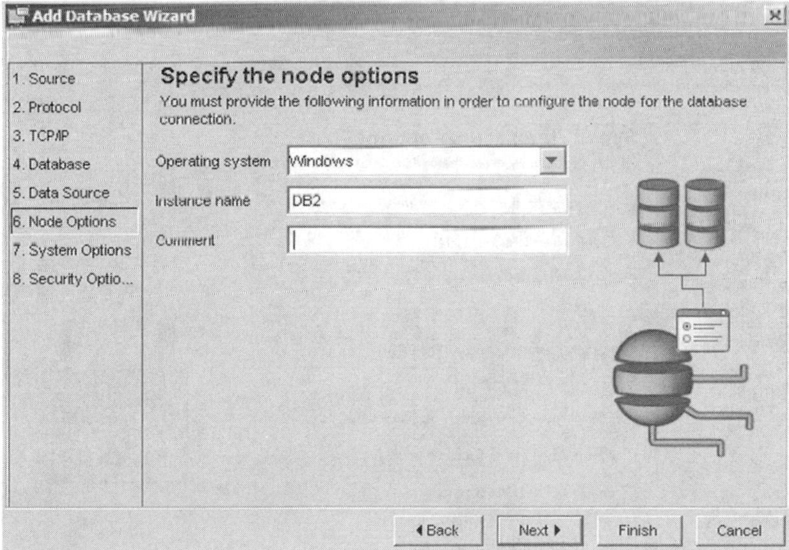

Figure 6.37 Add Database Wizard—Specify the node options

7. In Figure 6.38, enter the system name and host name. The system name is the name you want to use for the database server. If you click on the *View Details* button, the CA will retrieve the TCP/IP name and address information for the server. Click *Next*.

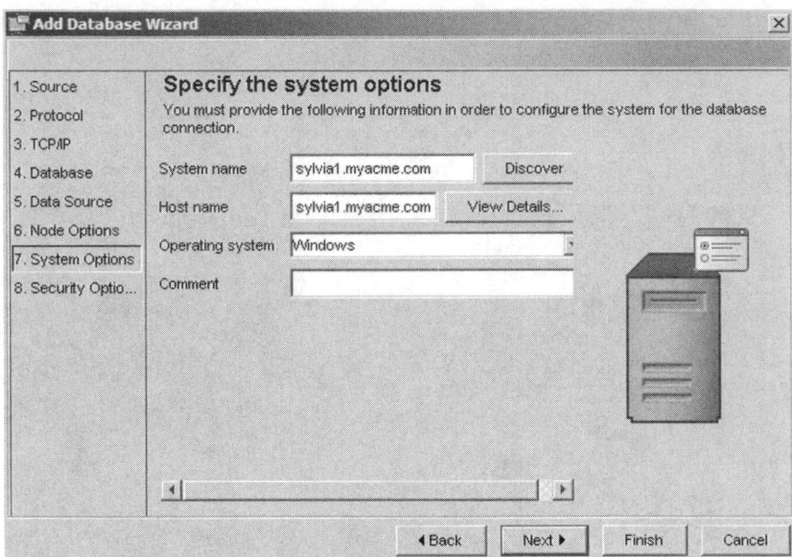

Figure 6.38 Add Database Wizard—Specify the system options

8. In Figure 6.39, choose a security option for this connection and then click *Finish*. The CA will automatically update DB2 directories.

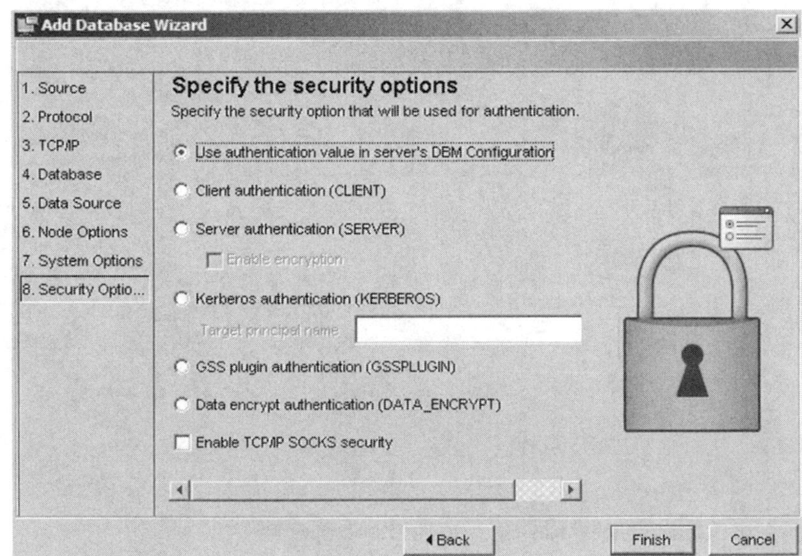

Figure 6.39 Add Database Wizard—Specify the security options

6.4.4 Automatic Client Reroute Feature

What is the typical scenario for your connected client applications when there is an outage at the data server? Can your application logic handle a "SQL30081N A Communication error has been detected" error message when the application encounters a data server communication problem? Does your application simply return an application error to your user, or does it try to re-establish the connection? Even if it does, if the data server is still down, the attempt will be in vain. This is where the automatic client reroute feature comes to the rescue. Automatic client reroute will redirect database client application connections from a primary database server to an alternate database server if the primary database server fails, or if there is a loss of communication between the client application and the primary server.

To enable the automatic client reroute feature, issue the **UPDATE ALTERNATE SERVER** command on the primary database.

Here is the syntax of the command:

```
UPDATE ALTERNATE SERVER FOR DATABASE database-alias
USING HOSTNAME alternate-server-hostname PORT port-number
```

To enable the client reroute feature on the TEST1 database on server1, so that all existing and new client connections will be rerouted to server2 following a takeover, issue the following command on server1:

```
UPDATE ALTERNATE SERVER FOR DATABASE test1 USING HOSTNAME server2.torolab.ibm.com PORT
50000
```

> **NOTE** Port 50000 is the SVCENAME port for the database instance.

The alternate server information is stored in server1's database directory. If you issue a **LIST DB DIRECTORY** command, you will see that the alternate server information (both the hostname and the port number) has been added:

```
Database alias                        = TEST1
Database name                         = TEST1
Local database directory              = C:
Database release level                = b.00
Comment                               =
Directory entry type                  = Indirect
Catalog database partition number     = 0
Alternate server hostname             = server2
Alternate server port number          = 50000
```

When a remote client application connects to this database, the alternate server information is retrieved and gets stored in the database directory of the client as well. Using this information, the client knows which server to connect to in case the primary server, server1, becomes unavailable.

Because the client does not get this alternate server information until it makes a connection to the primary server, the **UPDATE ALTERNATE SERVER** command must be issued before a takeover operation, and you must make sure that the client has at least made one successful connection to it prior to the takeover.

> **NOTE** Refer to Chapter 14, Developing Database Backup and Recovery Solutions, for discussion on how to use automatic client reroute with HADR.

6.4.5 Application Connection Timeout Support

You can now set a connection timeout value for DB2 database connections. A connection timeout value is a limit to the amount of time that an application should wait for a connection. Setting a connection timeout value is useful in case the database server is inaccessible. In this situation, it can take a long time for connection requests to fail and return.

For .NET, CLI, ODBC, and OLE DB applications, you can use the ConnectTimeout configuration keyword to enable connection timeout. For other types of application interfaces, such as the command line processor (CLP), you can set the DB2TCP_CLIENT_CONTIMEOUT registry variable.

For example, update the db2cli.ini file so that all CLI /ODBC applications connecting to database MYDB22 timeout after 10 seconds if a connection cannot be established:

```
; This is a comment line.
[MYDB22]
AutoCommit=0
ConnectTimeout =10
```

Similarly, through the CLP, you can configure all connections to any database to timeout after 10 seconds using the following command:

```
db2set DB2TCP_CLIENT_CONTIMEOUT=10
```

> **NOTE** You can configure the connect timeout support in conjuction with the automatic client reroute feature. In this case, after the connect timeouts on the primary server, client reroute will take over and reestablish the connection on a secondary server.

6.5 Diagnosing DB2 Connectivity Problems

Sometimes database connections fail. In this section, we look at some techniques to diagnose connectivity problems. Figure 6.40 illustrates what happens when you issue a **CONNECT TO *database*** statement. It also shows how the system database, node, and DCS directories are used during the process. For example, when the **CONNECT TO SAMPLE** statement is issued, DB2 first looks for the database *alias* SAMPLE in the system database directory. This is the alias used for the database with the name MYSAMPLE. If the alias is not found, you get an SQL1013N error. If it is found, DB2 checks whether this is a local or remote database. If it is a local database, DB2 initiates a connection to the database MYSAMPLE. If it is a remote database, DB2 checks the node directory to retrieve information about the remote server and then initiates a connection to the server.

The flowchart in Figure 6.40 shows what is involved to establish a database connection. Follow this chart to diagnose connection problems more easily.

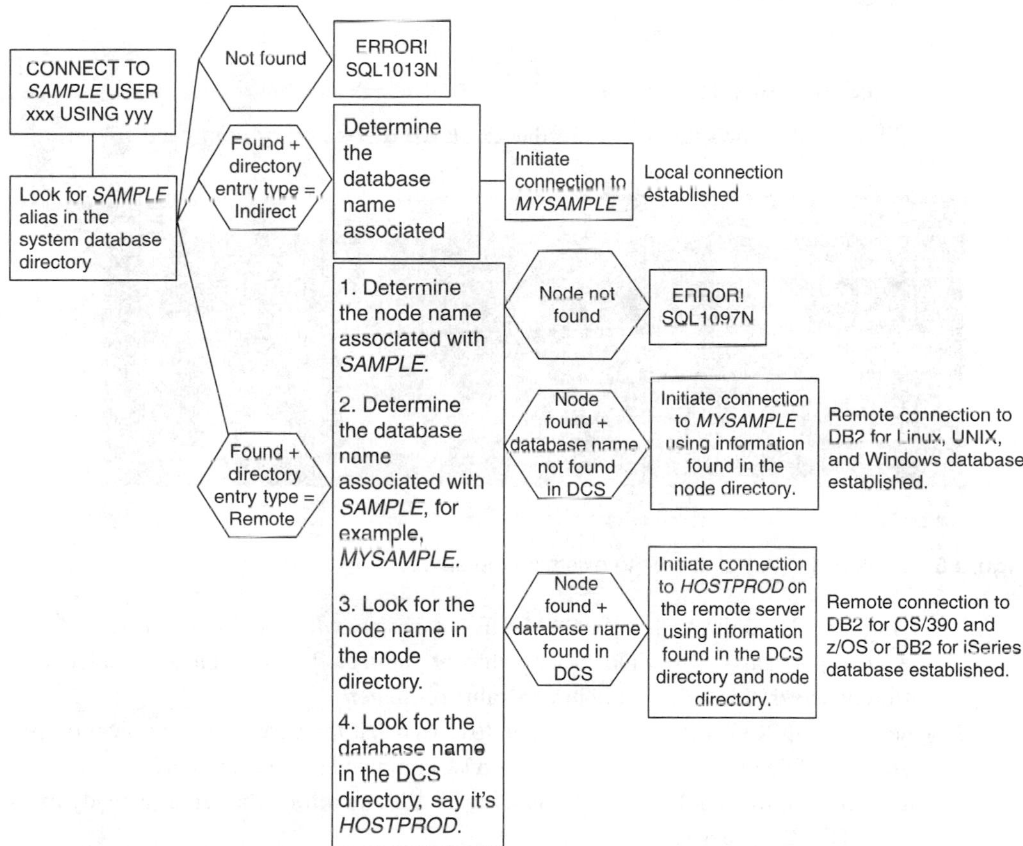

Figure 6.40 Database connection flowchart

6.5.1 Diagnosing Client-Server TCP/IP Connection Problems

SQL30081N Communication error and *SQL1013N Database not found* are the most common connection errors. If either of these errors occurs, you should verify the server and client configurations.

- On the server, verify that the DB2 instance is properly set up to accept client connections.
- On the client, verify that the node directory, database directory, and in the case of a host connection, the DCS directory, are set up correctly.

6.5.1.1 Verifying the Server Configuration

At the database server, follow this procedure to verify its configuration.

1. Verify that the database exists by issuing one of the following commands at the server:

   ```
   list db directory
   ```

   or

   ```
   list db directory show detail
   ```

   Figure 6.41 shows the output for the **`list db directory`** command.

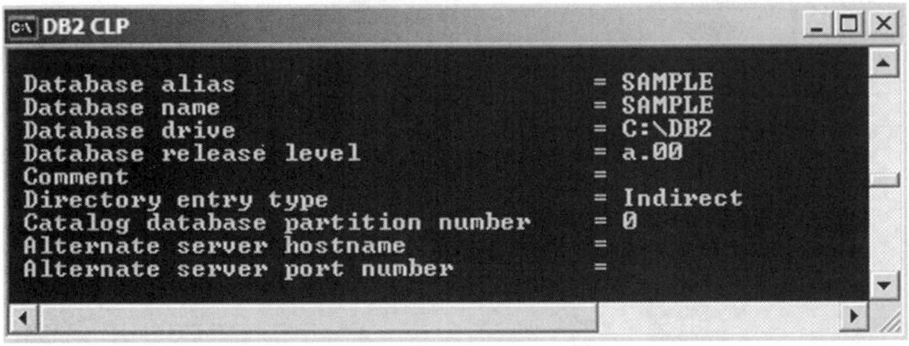

```
DB2 CLP

Database alias                         = SAMPLE
Database name                          = SAMPLE
Database drive                         = C:\DB2
Database release level                 = a.00
Comment                                =
Directory entry type                   = Indirect
Catalog database partition number      = 0
Alternate server hostname              =
Alternate server port number           =
```

Figure 6.41 Verifying that a database exists on the server

   Figure 6.41 confirms that the SAMPLE database resides locally on the server since the *Directory entry type* field has a value of *Indirect*. If the database resided on a different server, this field would have a value of *Remote*.

2. Check the DB2COMM registry variable to verify that the correct communication protocol is specified by using the **`db2set –all`** command (see Figure 6.42).
   Figure 6.42 shows that DB2COMM is set to TCPIP; therefore, the server is ready to listen for TCP/IP requests.
3. Verify that the appropriate configuration parameters are set in the Database Manager Configuration file. Issue the **`get dbm cfg`** command and examine the following.

   - **SVCENAME** must be set to a port number or service name.

   In Figure 6.43, you can see that the SVCENAME is set to a service name, db2c_DB2.

If SVCENAME is set to a service name instead of a port number, confirm that the value listed there is mapped to a unique port number in the operating system's services file. For example:

```
db2c_DB2    50000/tcp    # Connection port for DB2 instance db2inst1
```

If this line does not exist in the services file, use a text editor to add it.

After you have made sure that you can connect locally on the server and that the server is set up correctly to accept client connections, verify the client configuration.

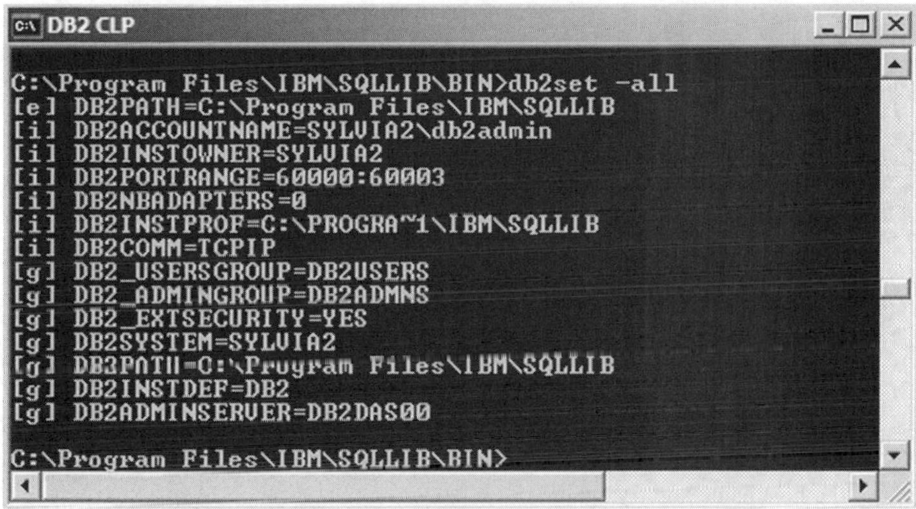

Figure 6.42 Checking the DB2COMM registry variable on the server

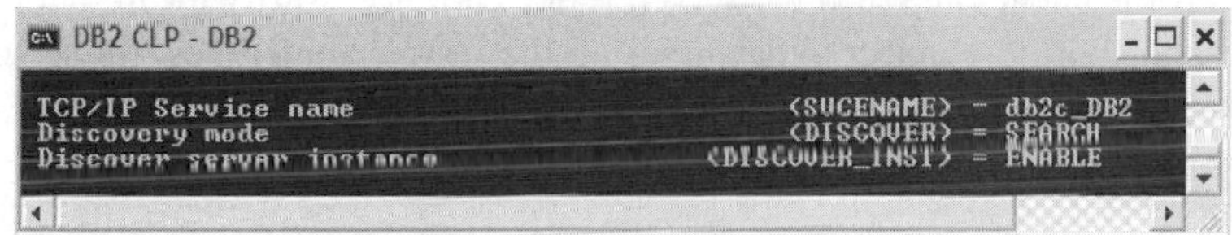

Figure 6.43 Verifying that SVCENAME is correctly set on the server

6.5.1.2 Verifying the Client Configuration

At the client, follow these steps to verify its configuration.

1. Verify that the server connectivity information has been correctly entered in the node directory by using the **`list node directory`** command.

   The service name in the client's node directory is a port number that matches the port number referenced by the SVCENAME on the server. For example, the SVCENAME on the server is set to *db2c_DB2*, as shown in Figure 6.43 and as we saw, this mapped to port 50000 in the server's services file. Therefore, the client needs to specify port 50000 in the node directory, as shown in Figure 6.44.

   Alternatively, the client can specify a service name instead of the port number in the node directory. However, this service name needs to be defined in the client's services file, not the server's services file. For example, the node directory can have the service name *db2conn*. If this is the case, then in the client's services file, you must set *db2conn* to 50000:

   ```
   db2conn     50000/tcp
   ```

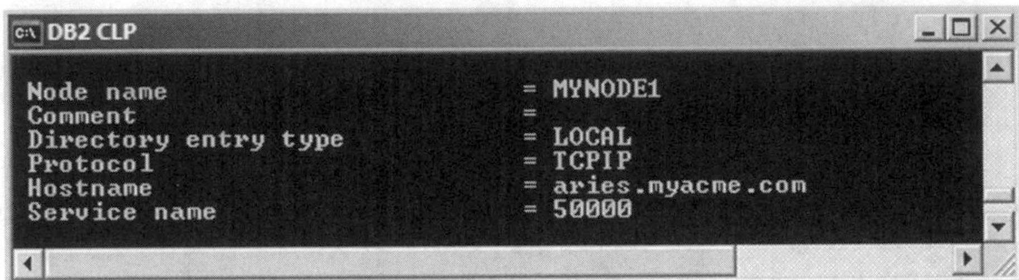

Figure 6.44 Checking the node directory on a client

2. Verify that you can ping the host name exactly as it appears in the node directory. If you cannot, that means there is a problem connecting to the server. Try to ping the IP address of the server. If that works, then recatalog the node using the IP address instead of the host name and try again.

   To recatalog the node directory, you need to first uncatalog the existing node:

   ```
   uncatalog node nodename
   ```

3. Even if the client can reach the server, it does not necessarily mean that the client can access the port to connect to databases on the server. Sometimes, for security reasons, the server port is not open to client connections, or the port is not enabled at all. To test if a port is accessible, you can telnet to the port as follows:

   ```
   telnet hostname or ip address 50000
   ```

   If DB2 is listening on that port on the server, you will see the Telnet window open, but it will hang, since DB2 is not configured to respond to the **`telnet`** command. This means that you have indeed reached that port on the server.
   If you get an immediate error, this means that either:

   - The server is not listening on this port. Refer to Section 6.5.1.1, Verifying the Server Configuration, to resolve this.
   - The port is behind a firewall and is not reachable by clients. Contact your network administrator for assistance.

4. Confirm that the correct database values appear in the database directory using the **`list db directory`** command. The database *name* in the client's database directory must match the database *alias* in the server's database directory (see Figure 6.45).

If the database resides on a host server, verify the DCS directory. Using the **`list dcs directory`** command, ensure that the database name in the database directory matches the database name in the DCS directory (see Figure 6.46). The target database name in the DCS directory must be the Location name if the host server is DB2 for z/OS and OS/390, or the RDB name if the host server is DB2 for i5/OS.

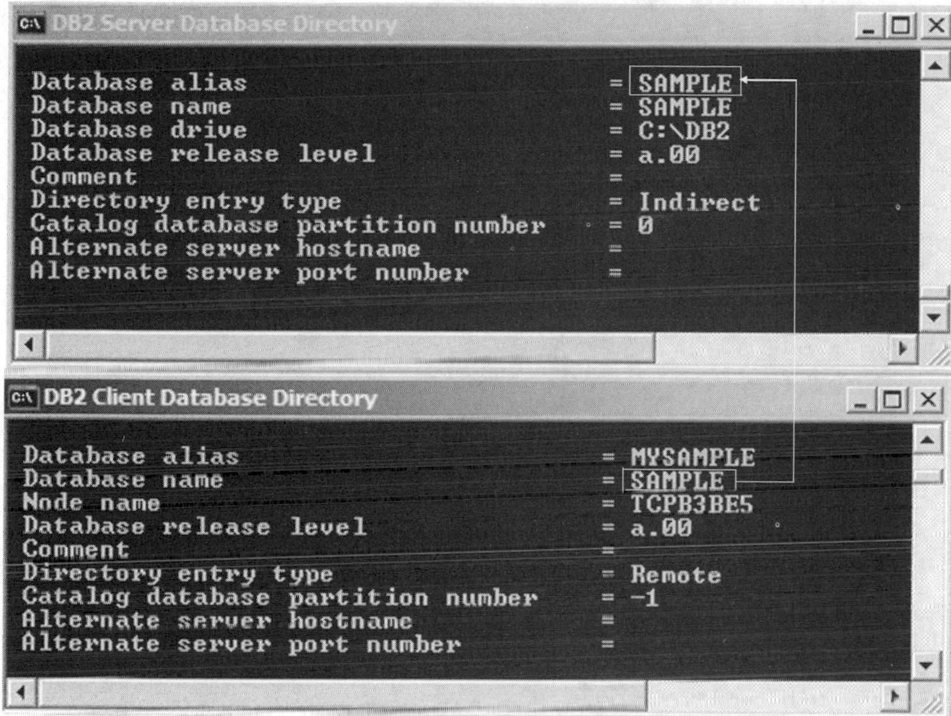

Figure 6.45 Verifying that the database name in the client database directory matches the database alias on the server

Figure 6.47 displays a flowchart for diagnosing client-server connectivity problems. It summarizes what we have discussed so far. The client is a DB2 client; the server can be either a DB2 server or a DB2 Connect gateway.

Figure 6.48 displays a flowchart for diagnosing client-host connectivity problems.

In Figure 6.48, the client has at least DB2 Connect Personal Edition installed (review Scenario 3).

For a three-tier configuration where a DB2 Connect gateway works as the middle tier, the diagnosing path splits into two parts. First, you need to make sure the connection is working from the Connect gateway to the host database. For this, use the flowchart in Figure 6.48. Second, for the client-gateway connection, use the flowchart in Figure 6.47.

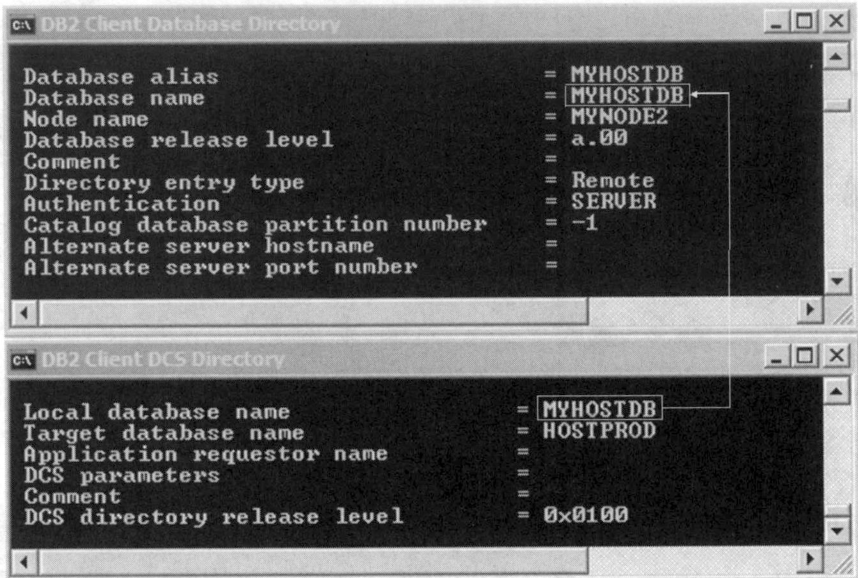

Figure 6.46 Verifying that the database name in the database directory matches the database name in the DCS directory

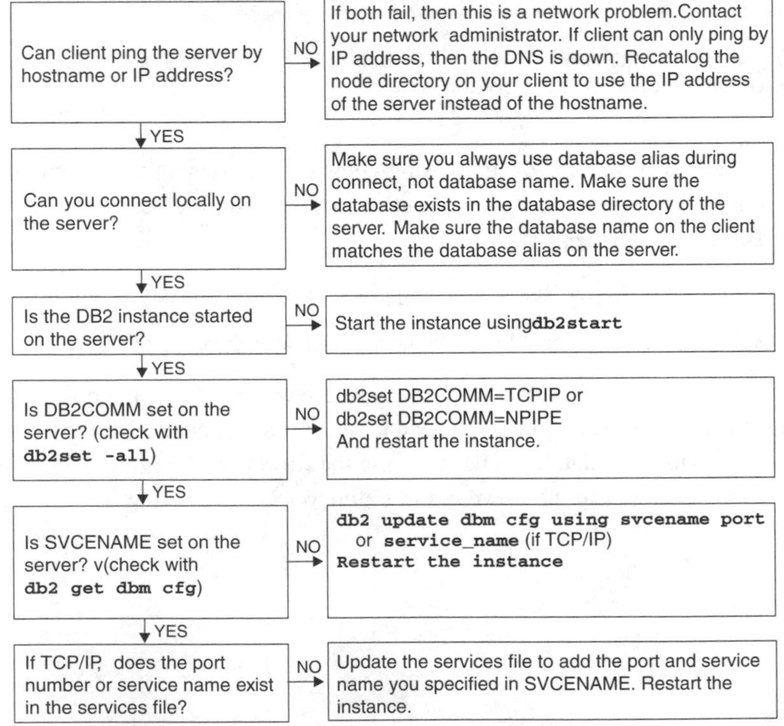

Figure 6.47 Diagnostic flowchart for client-server connectivity problems

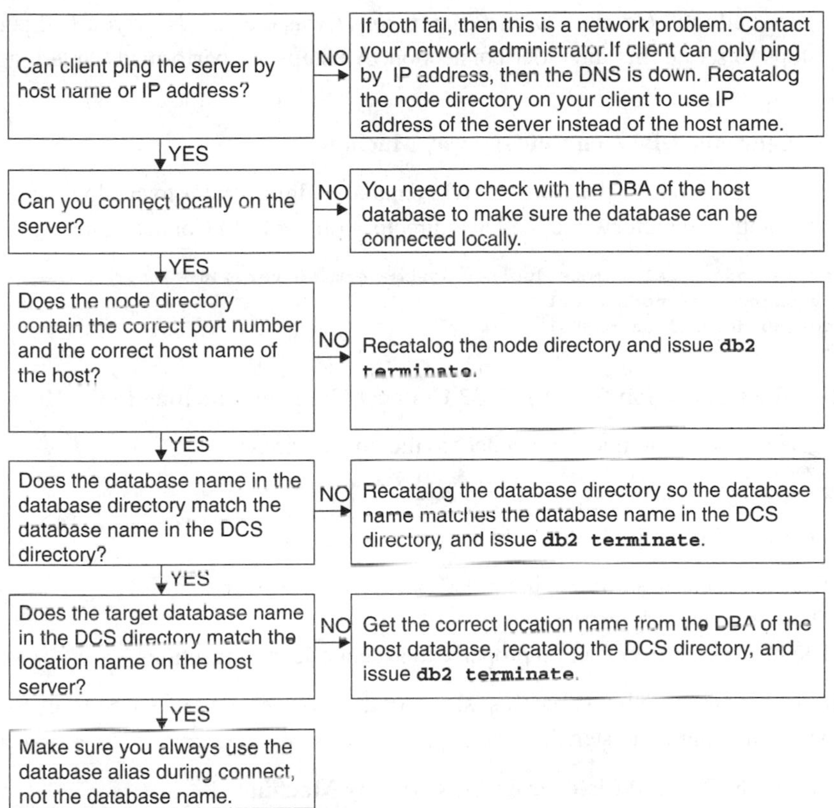

Figure 6.48 Diagnostic path for client-host connectivity problems

6.6 Case Study

You have just installed DB2 Connect Enterprise Edition on an AIX machine. You will use this machine as a DB2 Connect gateway for DB2 clients connecting to your company's DB2 for z/ OS server.

You are given the following information by the database administrator (DBA) of the host database:

```
Hostname      = jupiter.myacme.com
Port Number   = 446
Location Name = OS390L1
User ID       = user1
Password      = userpwd
```

For security reasons, the DB2 for z/OS location name is not to be exposed to the DB2 clients. The clients will refer to the host database using the name DB2PROD.

When you installed DB2 Connect, an instance *db2inst1* was created. Now you will perform the following steps to set up this three-tier connection. All steps are performed while logged on as *db2inst1*.

Step 1: Configure the DB2 Connect Gateway Machine

Use the information given by the DB2 for z/OS database administrator to catalog the node directory, system database directory, and the DCS directory on the DB2 Connect gateway:

```
catalog tcpip node node1 remote jupiter.myacme.com server 446
catalog db db2prod at node node1
catalog dcs db db2prod as os39011
terminate
```

Step 2: Test the Connection from the DB2 Connect Gateway Machine to the Host

Use the following DB2 command to connect to the host database:

```
CONNECT TO db2prod USER user1 USING userpwd
```

If the connection fails, the problem could be that:

- The user ID or password is incorrect.
- There is a network problem.
- The host server is not set up properly to accept client connections.

As the problem is likely to be on the host side, contact your host's DBA first to investigate the problem before moving on to step 3.

Step 3: Enable the TCP/IP Listener on the Gateway Machine

To make this gateway machine capable of accepting client connections, you need to enable the TCP/IP listener for the *db2inst1* instance. If you created the *db2inst1* instance using the DB2 Setup Wizard during product installation, you do not need to perform this step because it has already been done for you. However, since you created *db2inst1* manually using the **db2icrt** command, you need to perform the following steps to enable the TCP/IP listener.

1. Manually add the following entry in the etc/services file:
   ```
   db2conn1 50000/tcp #DB2 connection port for db2inst1
   ```
2. Execute the following DB2 commands:
   ```
   update dbm cfg using svcename db2conn1
   db2set DB2COMM=TCPIP
   db2stop
   db2start
   ```

Step 4: Configure a DB2 Client to Connect to the Host via the Gateway

The DB2 client will connect to the host database via the DB2 Connect gateway. On the client, perform the following commands to catalog the client's node directory and database directory to connect to the gateway. The host name of the gateway is *mercury.myacme.com*.

```
catalog tcpip node node1 remote mercury.myacme.com server 50000
catalog db db2prod at node node1
terminate
```

To connect to the host from the client, execute:

```
CONNECT TO db2prod USER user1 USING userpwd
```

If the connection is successful, proceed to the next step to configure other clients.

Step 5: Configure the Rest of the Clients Using a Client Profile

You need to configure 100 more DB2 clients. You could perform step 4 on all 100 clients, or you can export the catalog information on the client you have just configured and use this profile to configure other clients. Of course, the second option is the faster way.

Since the client is an AIX client without X-Windows installed, you cannot export the client profile using the Configuration Assistant. Therefore, you decide to use the **db2cfexp** and **db2cfimp** commands instead.

On the client that has been configured in step 4, export its catalog information into an access profile *accessprofile* under the /tmp directory:

```
db2cfexp /tmp/accessprofile TEMPLATE
```

FTP the *accessprofile* file to the other clients, and on each of them execute:

```
db2cfimp accessprofile
```

6.7 Summary

In this chapter you learned the how to configure connections from a DB2 client to a DB2 server. Four supported connection scenarios were discussed in detail:

- Local connection from a DB2 client to a DB2 server
- Remote connection from a DB2 client to a DB2 server
- Remote connection from a DB2 client to a DB2 host server
- Remote connection from a DB2 client to a DB2 host server via a DB2 Connect gateway

A local connection occurs when a DB2 client and a DB2 server reside on the same server. A connection from a DB2 client to a DB2 server requires that at least the IBM Data Server Runtime Client be installed on the client machine. On the server machine, at least DB2 Express Edition is required. A connection from a DB2 client to a DB2 host server requires that at least the DB2 Connect Personal Edition software be installed on the client machine. The supported host servers are DB2 for z/OS and OS/390 and DB2 for i5/OS.

TCP/IP is the supported communication protocol for all of the above connections. Named Pipes is supported if both the client and the server are on Windows. Starting with DB2 9, the IPv6 communication protocol was supported. This means that DB2 can connect to servers using IPv4 or IPv6 addresses. Commands have been added or enhanced to provide IPv6 support. For example, the existing CATALOG TCPIP NODE command has been supplemented with the additional commands, CATALOG TCPIP4 NODE and CATALOG TCPIP6 NODE, to enable you to request a particular type of connection.

Connectivity information is stored in four main directories: the system database directory, the local database directory, the node directory, and the DCS directory. The system database directory contains the names and aliases of both remote and local databases. The local database directory contains the names and aliases of databases that exist locally on a particular drive (on Windows) or path (on Linux or UNIX). The information about how to reach a remote server is stored in the client's node directory. For a TCP/IP connection, the remote server's host name or IP address and the DB2 port number are stored. To connect to a database residing on a host server, a DCS directory is also required. An entry in the DCS directory contains the actual database name known to the host server.

There are two methods you can use to configure client-server connections.

- Catalog the node directory, database directory, and DCS directory manually
- Use the Configuration Assistant for automatic configuration

If you use the CA, you can use any of the three CA methods.

- Access profiles
- Search the network
- Manual configuration

After configuring the connections, you need to bind database utilities or else the client will not be able to use any of the database utilities such as import or export. Run the **bind** command on the *db2ubind.lst* file to bind database utilities. If the client is going to run CLI/ODBC applications, run the **bind** command on the *db2cli.lst* file as well to create CLI packages on the server.

If the server is DB2 for z/OS or OS/390, use the *ddcsmvs.lst* file in the **bind** command. If the server is DB2 for i5/OS, use the *ddcs400.lst* file.

The binding of utilities must be done for each database you want to access. Once a package is successfully bound to the database, all DB2 clients of the same type and DB2 level can use it. Step-by-step instructions were provided to help diagnose DB2 connectivity problems. Follow the flowcharts provided to pinpoint where the connetivity issue lies.

6.8 Review Questions

1. Which DB2 directory contains information about all the databases you can connect to from a DB2 client machine?
2. Which command is used to review the contents of the local database directory located in drive H: on a Windows machine?
3. If the system database directory contains an entry with a type of *indirect*, what does this say about the entry?

4. If the SVCENAME database manager parameter has a value of db2_cDB2, which port is being used?
5. Which communication protocols are supported when connecting from a DB2 Connect gateway to a DB2 for z/OS server?
6. Why is DB2 Connect Enterprise Edition the recommended DB2 Connect product to use to support 1,000 clients connecting to a DB2 for i5/OS server?
7. Which command can you use to remove an incorrect entry from the DCS directory?
8. Which command can you use to remove an incorrect entry from the node directory?
9. What should you check to verify that the correct communication protocol is specified?
10. In which case would "Search the network" not be an appropriate choice to set up connectivity to your databases?
11. Given the following command

    ```
    catalog tcpip node srv2 remote server2 server db2port
    ```

    which of the following DB2 directories will be updated?

    A. DCS directory
    B. System database directory
    C. Local database directory
    D. Node directory
12. Which of the following products will not make use of the DCS directory?

    A. DB2 Connect Personal
    B. DB2 Connect Enterprise
    C. DB2 Personal
    D. DB2 Enterprise
13. The following entry appears in the services file of a DB2 client machine

    ```
    db2c_DB2    60000
    ```

    whereas the SVCENAME value for the DB2 instance at the server is 50005. Which of the following commands is the correct one to use?

    A. `catalog tcpip node mynode remote aries server 60000`
    B. `catalog tcpip node mynode remote aries server 50005`
    C. `catalog tcpip node mynode remote aries server db2c_DB2`
    D. `catalog tcpip node mynode remote aries server 50000`
14. Which of the following commands inserts an entry in the system database directory?

    A. `catalog system database directory mydb at node mynode`
    B. `insert into system db value (mydb)`
    C. `create database mydb on F:`
    D. `catalog dcs db mydb`
15. Which of the following commands are required to enable a DB2 server for TCPIP connectivity? (Choose all that apply.)

    A. `update dbm cfg using SVCENAME 50000`
    B. `db2set DB2COMM=TCPIP`

C. **connect to sample**
D. **ping myhost**

16. Which of the following is not a supported method from the DB2 Configuration Assistant?
    A. Manually configure a connection to a database
    B. Search the network
    C. Use a Profile
    D. Unknown discovery
17. Which of the following commands is required to prevent the use of the Discover method for a database server from any DB2 client?
    A. **update admin cfg using DISCOVER disable** (at the server machine)
    B. **update dbm cfg using DISCOVER disable** (at the server machine)
    C. **update admin cfg using DISCOVER disable** (at the client machine)
    D. **update dbm cfg using DISCOVER disable** (at the client machine)
18. Which of the following commands is required to prevent the use of the Discover method only for database mydb while connected to that database?
    A. **update admin cfg using DISCOVER disable**
    B. **update dbm cfg using DISCOVER disable**
    C. **update dbm cfg using DISCOVER_INST disable**
    D. **update db cfg using DISCOVER_DB disable**
19. Which of the following commands will properly catalog a remote DB2 instance accepting TCP/IP connections?
    A. **catalog tcpip4 node mynode1 remote 9.23.223.98 server 1032**
    B. **catalog tcpip6 node mynode1 remote 2001:0db8::1428:57ab server 50000**
    C. **catalog tcpip node mynode1 remote 9.23.223.98 server db2inst1**
    D. **catalog tcpip4 node mynode1 remote aries.acme.com server db2inst1**
20. The command **get dbm cfg | grep DISCOVER** returns two lines in your Linux server:

```
Discovery mode                          (DISCOVER) = SEARCH
Discover server instance           (DISCOVER_INST) = ENABLE
```

    Which command prevents this server from using the Discover method against other server machines?
    A. **db2 update dbm cfg using DISCOVER_INST disable**
    B. **db2 update dbm cfg using DISCOVER disable**
    C. **db2 update dbm cfg using DISCOVER known**
    D. **db2 update dbm cfg using DISCOVER_INST known**

CHAPTER 7

Working with Database Objects

In this chapter we discuss the various objects that may exist in your database, such as tables, indexes, views, sequence objects, and stored procedures. We also describe the different data types supported by DB2. This chapter is closely related to Chapters 8, 9, and 10. Chapter 8, The DB2 Storage Model, explains the implementation and manipulation of several of these objects. Chapter 9, Leveraging the Power of SQL, explains how to work with these database objects using the SQL language, and Chapter 10, Mastering the DB2 pureXML Support, discusses how to work with XML documents in DB2.

In this chapter you will learn about:

- The big picture of the DB2 database objects
- The definitions of databases, database partitions, partition groups, buffer pools, and table spaces
- The DB2 data types
- How to work with tables, indexes, views, and schemas
- The definition of application-related objects like packages, triggers, user-defined functions, stored procedures, and sequences

7.1 DB2 Database Objects: The Big Picture

A database is a collection of database objects. You can create a database on one or more database partitions. A database partition, as its name implies, is part of a database. We discuss these concepts in more detail in the next sections; for now, we introduce you to the DB2 database objects. Figure 7.1 illustrates these objects in a database created in a single-partition environment (database partition 0). The database objects are described next.

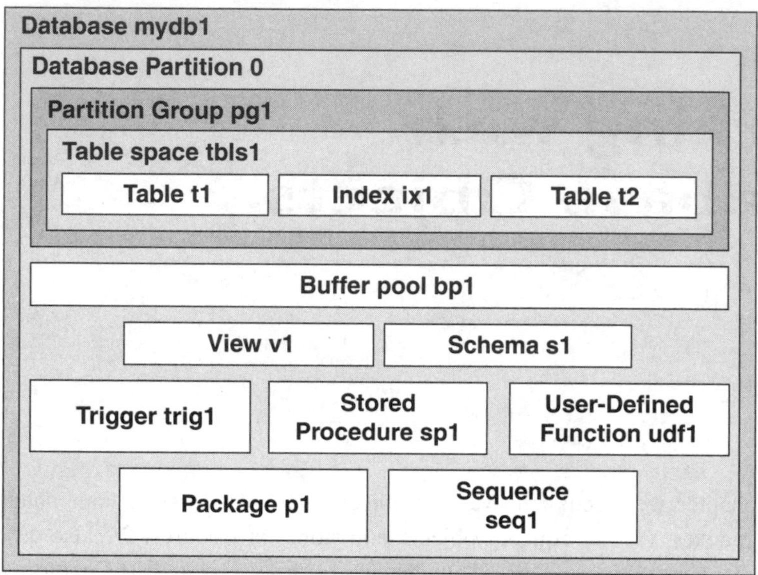

Figure 7.1 An overview of the DB2 database objects

- A **partition group** is a logical database object representing a collection of database partitions. In a single-partition environment, partition groups are not relevant; however, in multi-partition environments, a partition group facilitates the work of a database administrator, as he or she is able to perform database operations on or within several partitions at a time. Partition groups can contain one or more table spaces. In Figure 7.1, partition group *pg1* contains table space *tbls1*.
- **Table spaces** are logical objects that associate tables and indexes to the physical devices where these objects are stored, as well as to the physical memory where the data in these objects is cached when it is being accessed. Tables and indexes must be created inside a table space as illustrated in Figure 7.1, where tables *t1* and *t2* and index *ix1* are all created inside table space *tbls1*.
- **Tables** consist of rows and columns, like spreadsheets. Data can be inserted, deleted, and updated within a table. Figure 7.1 has two tables, *t1* and *t2*.
- **Indexes** are an ordered set of keys each pointing to a row in a table. They improve application performance when looking for specific rows. Indexes can also be used to guarantee the uniqueness of rows. In Figure 7.1, index *ix1* is associated to table *t1*.
- A **buffer pool** is an area in physical memory that caches the database information most recently used. Without buffer pools, every single piece of data has to be retrieved from disk, which is very slow. Buffer pools are associated to tables and indexes through a table space. In Figure 7.1, table space *tbls1* is associated to buffer pool *bp1*, therefore tables *t1* and *t2* and index *ix1* use buffer pool *bp1*.

- A **view** is an alternate way of representing data that exists in one or more tables. A view can include some or all of the columns from one or more tables. It can also be based on other views. In Figure 7.1, view *v1* is based on table *t1*.
- Every object in the database is created with a two-part name separated by a dot: **`schema_name.object_name`**

  The first part of this two-part name is the schema name. A **schema** is an object that provides a logical grouping of other database objects. A schema can be owned by an individual who can control access to the objects within it. Schemas can be implicitly or explicitly specified when accessing an object.
- A **trigger** is an object that contains application logic that is triggered by specific actions like an update to a table. For example, in Figure 7.1, a trigger can be created so that after table *t1* is updated, table *t2* is also updated with some other information.
- A **stored procedure** is an object used to move application logic into your database. By keeping part of the application logic in the database, there are performance improvements as the amount of network traffic between the application and the database is considerably reduced.
- **User-defined functions** (UDFs) allow database users to extend the SQL language by creating functions that can be used anywhere a DB2 built-in function is used. Similar to stored procedures, application logic can be moved to the database by using UDFs.
- A **package** is an object containing the compiled version of your SQL queries as well as the access path that the DB2 optimizer, the brain of DB2, has chosen to retrieve the data for those queries.
- A **sequence** object allows the generation of unique numbers in sequence. These numbers can be used across the database as a unique identifier for tables or for applications.

To create, modify, or delete database objects, you use the Data Definition Language (DDL) consisting of the following SQL statements:

- **`CREATE`**
- **`DECLARE`**
- **`ALTER`**
- **`DROP`**

The following objects can be created and dropped using the **`CREATE`** and **`DROP`** statements, respectively:

- Tables
- Indexes
- Schemas
- Views
- User-defined functions
- User-defined types

- Buffer pools
- Table spaces
- Stored procedures
- Triggers
- Servers (for federated databases)
- Wrappers (for federated databases)
- Nicknames (for federated databases)
- Sequences

You use the **DECLARE** statement to create temporary tables, and the **ALTER** statement to change one or more attributes or characteristics of an existing database object. You can alter most, but not all, of the database objects created with the **CREATE** statement.

The **CREATE**, **DECLARE**, **ALTER**, and **DROP** statements are used throughout this chapter.

7.2 Databases

A database is a collection of information organized into interrelated objects such as table spaces, partition groups, and tables. Each database is an independent unit containing its own system information, temporary space, transaction logs, and configuration files, as illustrated in Figure 7.2.

Figure 7.2 shows two databases, *MYDB1* and *MYDB2*, inside the instance *DB2* in a single-partition environment (Database Partition 0). The box showing *Database Partition 0* is included for completeness; in a single-partition environment you can ignore this box. Since databases are independent units, object names from different databases can be the same. For example, the name of the table space *MyTablespace1* is used in both databases in the figure.

Figure 7.2 also shows the three table spaces that DB2 creates by default when you create a database: SYSCATSPACE, TEMPSPACE1, and USERSPACE1. These table spaces are described in Section 7.4, Table Spaces.

In this chapter we only discuss database objects. Configuration files are discussed in Chapter 5, Understanding the DB2 Environment, DB2 Instances, and Databases. The local database directory is discussed in Chapter 6, Configuring Client and Server Connectivity. Logs are discussed in Chapter 13, Developing Database Backup and Recovery Solutions.

To create a database, use the **CREATE DATABASE** command (Chapter 8, The DB2 Storage Model, discusses this command in detail). To perform operations against database objects, you first need to connect to the database using the **CONNECT** statement (see Chapter 6, Configuring Client and Server Connectivity).

7.2.1 Database Partitions

You can create a single-partition or a multi-partition database, depending on your needs.

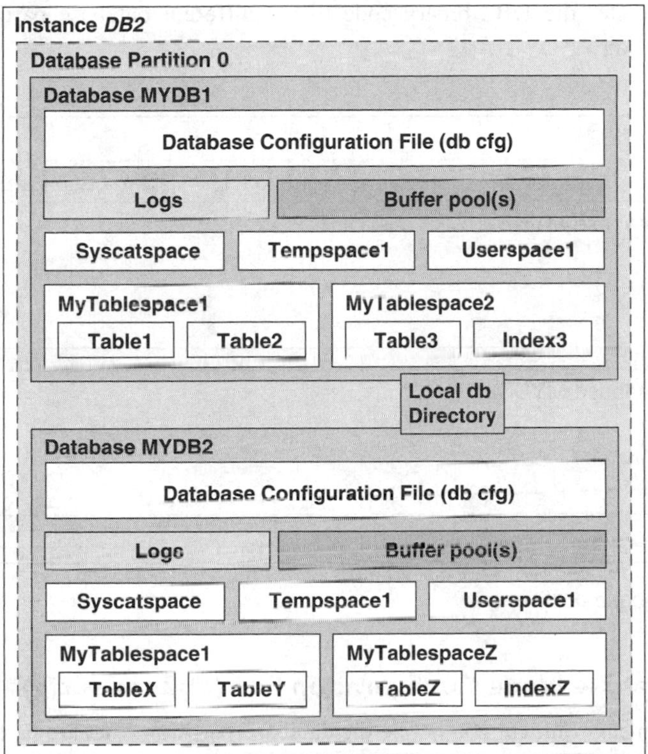

Figure 7.2 A database and its objects

In a multi-partition environment, **a database partition** (or simply **partition**) is an independent part of a database containing its own data, indexes, configuration files, and transaction logs. Database functions are also distributed between all the database partitions. This provides for unlimited scalability.

Multiple database partitions can reside on one physical server; these are sometimes referred to as **logical partitions** sharing the resources of the machine. Database partitions can also reside on different physical servers. The collection of all of these partitions corresponds to one database.

Multi-partition database support uses the database partitioning feature (DPF) of DB2 Enterprise, which comes built-in with the product but requires the purchase of a separate license.

Figure 7.3 shows two databases, *MYDB1* and *MYDB2*, in a multi-partition environment with three database partitions.

As mentioned in Chapter 2, DB2 at a Glance: The Big Picture, an instance associates the DB2 binary code (also called the DB2 copy) to databases. Database partitions, on the other hand, are used to split your database into different parts. Therefore, an instance in a multi-partition environment associates the DB2 binary code to the different database partitions. Figure 7.3 shows this association.

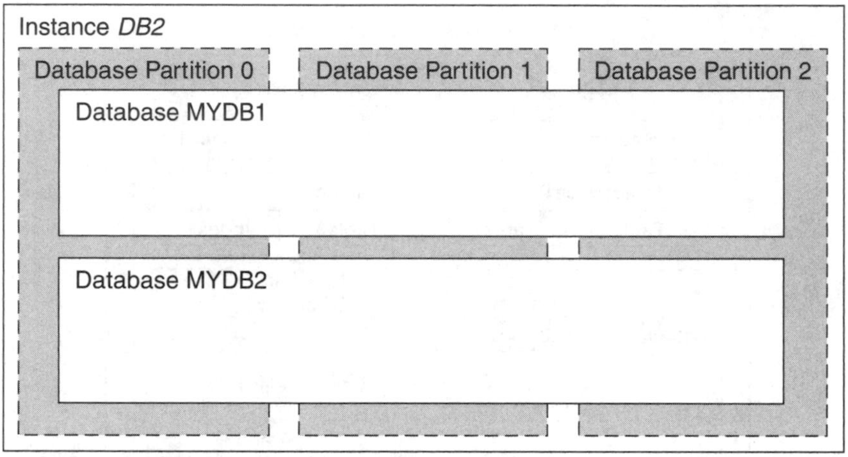

Figure 7.3 Database partitions

7.2.2 The Database Node Configuration File (db2nodes.cfg)

In a multi-partition environment you define the database partitions that are part of your database by entering the appropriate information in the database node configuration file, db2nodes.cfg.

On Linux and UNIX platforms, the db2nodes.cfg file can contain up to five columns, as shown in Table 7.1.

On Windows there is also another column, Computername, which contains the computer name for the machine on which the partition resides. Table 7.2 shows the order of the columns on Windows systems and whether they are required.

When you create an instance in DB2 Enterprise, a default db2nodes.cfg file is created with one row. On Linux and UNIX the default file has three columns and looks like the following:

```
0    myserver    0
```

On Windows the default file has four columns and looks like the following:

```
0    myserver    myserver    0
```

The db2nodes.cfg file is located

- Under the sqllib directory for the instance owner on Linux and UNIX
- Under the SQLLIB*Instance_name* directory on Windows

Table 7.1 Columns of the db2nodes.cfg Configuration File for Linux and UNIX

	Partition Number	Hostname	Logical Port	Netname	Resourcesetname
Is the column required?	Yes.	Yes.	Sometimes.	Sometimes.	Optional.
Description	DB2 uses this column to identify the partition.	The TCP/IP host name of the server where the partition is created.	This column must be used if you want to create more than one partition on the same server. It specifies the logical port for the partition within the server and must be unique within a server.	Supports a host that has more than one active TCP/IP interface, each with its own host name. It is required if you are using a high speed interconnect for inter- partition communication or if the resource-setname column is used.	It specifies the operating system resource that the partition should be started in.

Table 7.2 Columns of the db2nodes.cfg Configuration File for Windows

	Partition Number	Hostname	Computername	Logical Port	Netname	Resourcesetname
Is the column required?	Yes.	Yes.	Yes.	Sometimes.	Sometimes.	Optional.

There is only one db2nodes.cfg file per instance, and all the databases you create under this instance will be partitioned at CREATE DATABASE time based on the contents of this file. To create multiple partitions, edit the db2nodes.cfg file and add an entry for each database partition. For example, assume you have an eight-way SMP server (a server with eight CPUs or cores) running Linux as shown in Figure 7.4.

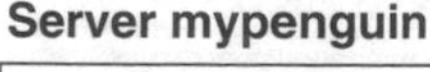

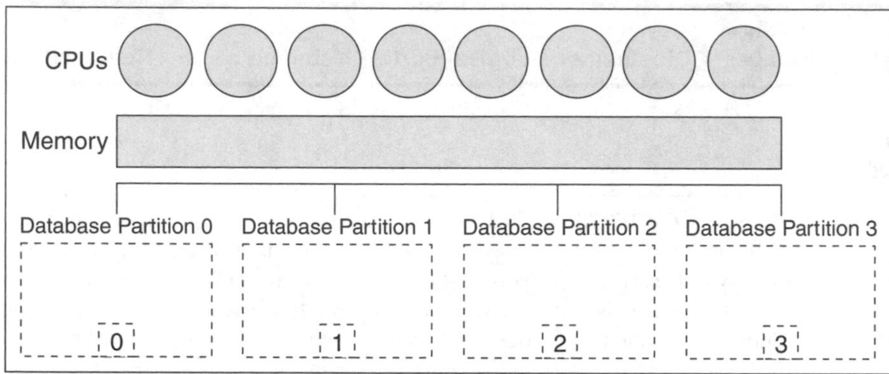

Figure 7.4 An eight-way SMP Linux server with four database partitions

You need to edit the db2nodes.cfg file to make it look like the following:

```
0     mypenguin     0
1     mypenguin     1
2     mypenguin     2
3     mypenguin     3
```

In another scenario, assume you are installing DB2 on a cluster of eight two-way SMP Linux servers, and you want to create one partition on each server as illustrated in Figure 7.5 (not all servers are shown).

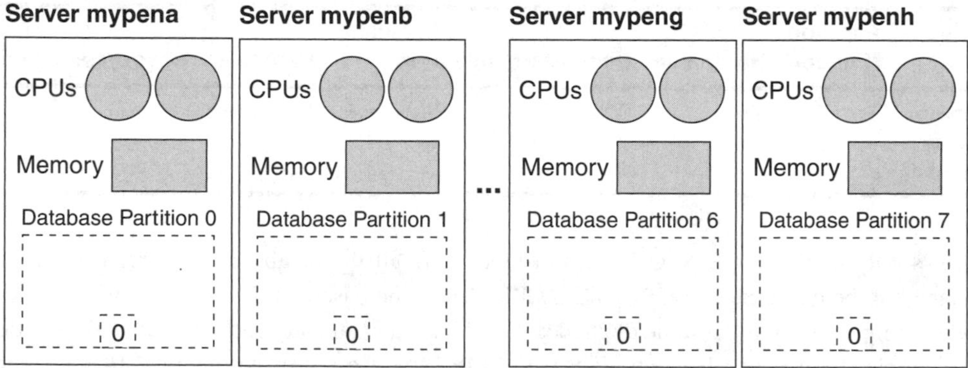

Figure 7.5 A cluster of eight two-way SMP Linux servers with eight partitions in total

You need to edit the db2nodes.cfg file to make it look like the following:

```
0     mypena     0
1     mypenb     0
2     mypenc     0
```

```
3    mypend    0
4    mypene    0
5    mypenf    0
6    mypeng    0
7    mypenh    0
```

In yet another scenario, assume you are installing DB2 on a cluster of four UNIX servers with four CPUs each and you want to create two partitions on each server as shown in Figure 7.6.

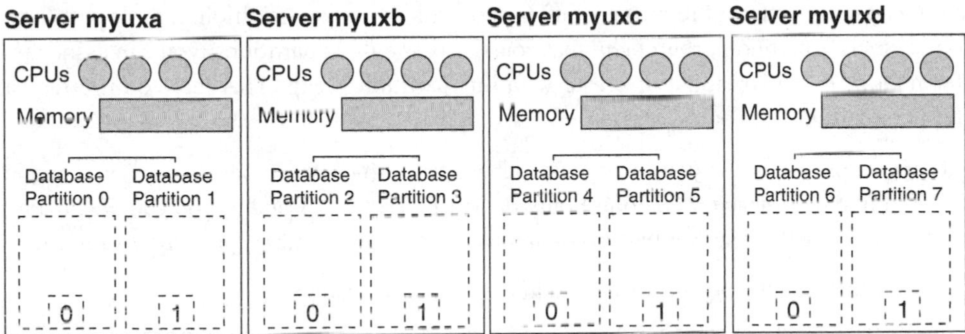

Figure 7.6 A cluster of four four-way SMP UNIX servers with eight database partitions in total

You need to edit the db2nodes.cfg file to make it look like the following:

```
0    myuxa    0
1    myuxa    1
2    myuxb    0
3    myuxb    1
4    myuxc    0
5    myuxc    1
6    myuxd    0
7    myuxd    1
```

On Linux and UNIX you can edit the db2nodes.cfg file with any ASCII editor (for example, vi). On Windows, you should not edit the db2nodes.cfg file directly; instead, use the **db2ncrt** and **db2ndrop** commands to add and remove database partitions, respectively.

You can also use the **db2start** command to add and/or remove a database partition from the DB2 instance and the db2nodes.cfg file as follows.

- Use the **db2start** command with the **add dbpartitionnum** option to add a partition to the database and insert an entry for the partition into the db2nodes.cfg file.
- Use the **db2start** command with the **drop dbpartitionnum** option to remove a partition from the database and delete its entry from the db2nodes.cfg file.

You can also use the **add dbpartitionnum** command to add a partition to the database even if the partition already has an entry in the db2nodes.cfg file. The **drop dbpartitionnum** command will remove the specified partition from the database but will not remove its entry from the instance's db2nodes.cfg file.

7.3 Partition Groups

A database **partition group** is a set of one or more database partitions for the same database. By grouping database partitions, you can perform database operations at the partition group level rather than individually on each partition. This allows for database administration flexibility. For example, let's say you want to create a buffer pool with the same definition in three partitions. If you first create a partition group *pgall* that consists of the three partitions, you can associate the buffer pool *bp1* you are about to create with this partition group. This lets you use the same buffer pool definition on each partition.

Partition groups also allow you to associate table spaces to database partitions. For example, if you would like table space *tbls1* to use only database partitions 1 and 2, you can create a partition group *pg12* with these two partitions, and then associate the table space *tbls1* to *pg12.*

Figure 7.7 illustrates the objects discussed in the preceding examples.

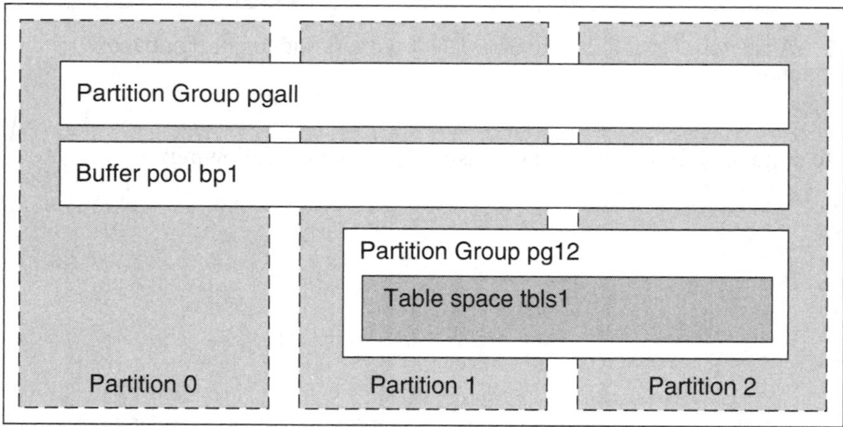

Figure 7.7 Partition groups

In Figure 7.7 the buffer pool definition is repeated across all the partitions. If you create the buffer pool with 20,000 4K pages, each partition will allocate 20,000 4K pages. Note that the 20,000 4K pages are *not* split across all three partitions as the figure may suggest.

To create a partition group, use the **CREATE DATABASE PARTITION GROUP** statement. Refer to Chapter 8, The DB2 Storage Model, for more details.

When you create a database, three partition groups are created by default.

- **IBMCATGROUP** is the partition group where the DB2 catalog table space (SYSCATSPACE) resides. It consists of only one partition, the one where the **CREATE DATABASE** command is issued.
- **IBMTEMPGROUP** is the partition group where the system temporary table space (TEMPSPACE1) resides. It spans all partitions.
- **IBMDEFAULTGROUP** is the partition group where the user table space (USERSPACE1) resides. It spans all partitions.

These default partition groups are discussed in detail in Chapter 8, The DB2 Storage Model.

7.4 Table Spaces

A table space is a logical object in your database. It is used to associate your logical tables and indexes to their physical storage devices (containers or storage paths) and physical memory (buffer pools). All tables and indexes must reside in table spaces. With DB2 9 a table can span table spaces as we discuss in Section 7.8.8, Partitioned Tables.

7.4.1 Table Space Classification

Table spaces can be classified based on how the table space is managed and on what type of data they contain.

Based on how the table space is managed, a table space can be one of the following types.

- **System-managed space (SMS):** This type of table space is managed by the operating system and requires minimal administration.
- **Database-managed space (DMS):** This type of table space is managed by the DB2 database manager, and it requires some administration.
- **Automatic Storage:** This type of table space can be either SMS or DMS, and the space is managed by the DB2 database manager, but it requires minimal administration. The database manager determines which containers are to be assigned to the table space, based upon the storage paths that are associated with the database. Automatic storage table spaces can be SMS if the table space type is temporary or DMS if the table space type is Regular or Large. The table space types are described below.

Based on the type of data it contains, a table space can be one of the following types.

- **Regular:** Use this type of table space to store any kind of data (including indexes) except temporary data. This type is allowed in both, SMS and DMS table spaces. It is the only type allowed for SMS table spaces, and it is also the default type for SMS table spaces when no type is specified.
- **Large:** Use this type of table space to store any kind of data (including indexes) except temporary data. This type is only allowed on DMS table spaces. It is also the default type for DMS table spaces when no type is specified.

- **Temporary:** Use this type of table space to hold temporary data. In turn, temporary table spaces can be further classified as two types.
    - **System:** These table spaces hold temporary data required by DB2 to perform operations such as sorts or joins, which cannot be completed in memory and require space for processing the result set.
    - **User:** These table spaces hold temporary data from tables created with the **DECLARE GLOBAL TEMPORARY TABLE** statement. This type of table is explained in Section 7.8.12, Temporary Tables.

> **NOTE** System temporary table spaces and user temporary table spaces are commonly confused. Remember that system temporary table spaces are used by DB2, while user temporary table spaces are used by users when they declare global temporary tables.

To create a table space, use the **CREATE TABLESPACE** statement. A table space can be created with any of these page sizes: 4K, 8K, 16K, and 32K. A corresponding buffer pool of the same page size must exist prior to issuing this statement. Refer to Chapter 8, The DB2 Storage Model, for details.

7.4.2 Default Table Spaces

When a database is created, the following table spaces are created in the database by default.

- **SYSCATSPACE** contains the DB2 system catalog tables and views. This set of tables and views contains system information about all the objects in the database.
- **TEMPSPACE1** is used for system temporary data when DB2 needs temporary tables to process large sort or join operations.
- **USERSPACE1** is the table space where tables and indexes are initially created by default if a table space name has not been explicitly indicated in the **CREATE TABLE** statement. Section 7.8.2, User Tables, describes in detail the rules followed when a table space is implicitly assigned to a table.

V9

> **NOTE** With DB2 9, SYSCATSPACE is created as a DMS REGULAR table space, and USERSPACE1 is created as a DMS LARGE table space. With DB2 9, DMS table spaces are created as LARGE by default, while in previous versions they were created as REGULAR.

7.5 Buffer Pools

The database **buffer pool** is a piece of memory used by DB2 to temporarily store (cache) both data and index pages when they are read from disk to be scanned or modified. The buffer pool improves the performance of the database because the pages can be accessed much more quickly from memory than from disk.

When you create a database, a default buffer pool, IBMDEFAULTBP, is automatically created. This buffer pool is associated with the default table spaces SYSCATSPACE, TEMPSPACE1, and USERSPACE1, and you cannot drop it.

To create a buffer pool, use the **CREATE BUFFERPOOL** statement. This statement allows you to define, among other things, how large the buffer pool will be and which page size it will use. Refer to Chapter 8, The DB2 Storage Model, for details.

7.6 Schemas

A **schema** is a database object used to logically group other database objects together. Every database object name has two parts:

```
schema_name.object_name
```

This two-part name (also known as the fully qualified name) must be unique within the database. Here are some examples:

```
db2admin.tab1
mary.idx1
sales.tblspace1
```

When you create an object, it is always created within a schema, even if you do not explicitly specify the schema name. When you do not specify the schema name, DB2 uses your **authorization ID** (the ID used to connect to the database) as the object's schema. If you connect to a database as *peter* and in a query specify a table simply as *tab1*, DB2 will interpret this as *peter.tab1*.

> **NOTE** A schema does *not* need to map to a user ID. Any user with the appropriate authorization can create a schema. For example, assuming user *peter* has the correct authorizations, he can create the schema *foo*, where *foo* does not map to any user.

To create the schema *user1*, use the **CREATE SCHEMA** statement as follows:

```
CREATE SCHEMA user1
```

Or, if you are connected to the database as *user1*, when you create the first new object using this connection without explicitly typing the schema name, DB2 will automatically create the schema *user1* and then the object. This assumes you have the appropriate authorization, in this case, the IMPLICIT_SCHEMA privilege. The following statement creates the schema *user1*, followed by the table *table1*.

```
CREATE TABLE table1 (mycol int)
```

You are connected to the database as *user1*; you can also create objects under a different schema. In this case, explicitly indicate the schema name, for example:

```
CREATE TABLE newuser.table1 (mycol int)
```

This statement creates a table called *table1* in the schema *newuser*. If the schema doesn't already exist, it is created. Although running both of these **CREATE TABLE** statements results in two tables in the database called *table1*, they are different tables because one is in the schema *user1*, and the other is in the schema *newuser*.

> **NOTE** Creating schemas implicitly or explicitly requires the user to have the appropriate authorizations or privileges. Refer to Chapter 11, Implementing Security, for more details.

When you access a database object, you can omit the schema name. Let's say you are connected to the database as *user1*, and you issue the following statement:

```
SELECT * FROM table1
```

This statement references table *user1.table1*.

If the table you want to access is *newuser.table1*, you must explicitly include the schema name:

```
SELECT * FROM newuser.table1
```

You cannot alter a schema, but you can drop it (as long as no objects exist within the schema) and recreate it with the new definition. Use the **DROP SCHEMA** statement to drop a schema:

```
DROP SCHEMA newuser RESTRICT
```

You must specify the **RESTRICT** keyword; it is part of the **DROP SCHEMA** syntax and serves as a reminder that you cannot drop a schema unless it is unused.

7.7 Data Types

Before continuing with our discussion of database objects, you need to understand the data types supported by DB2. A **data type** indicates what type of data can be saved in a column or variable and how large it can be. DB2 data types are either:

- Built-in data types
- User-defined types (UDTs)

7.7.1 DB2 Built-in Data Types

DB2 provides several built-in data types, which can be classified into the following categories:

- Numeric
- String

- Datetime
- Extensible Markup Language

Figure 7.8 summarizes the built-in data types supported in DB2.

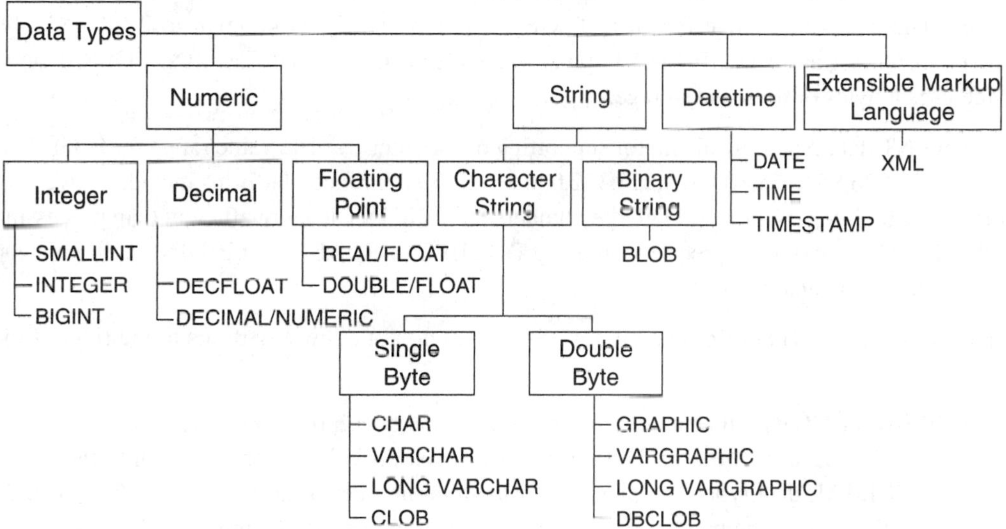

Figure 7.8 The DB2 built-in data types

NOTE With DB2 9, the DATALINK data type and the Data Links Manager are no longer supported. DB2 9 introduces the new data type XML.

NOTE DB2 9.5 introduces the new data type DECFLOAT.

7.7.1.1 Numeric Data Types

The numeric data types include the following:

- Small integer (SMALLINT)
- Integer (INT or INTEGER)
- Big integer (BIGINT)
- DECIMAL/NUMERIC
- REAL/FLOAT
- DOUBLE/FLOAT
- Decimal floating-point (DECFLOAT)

A SMALLINT uses the least amount of storage in the database for each value. The data value range for a SMALLINT is –32768 to 32767. The precision for a SMALLINT is 5 digits to the left of the decimal. Each SMALLINT column value uses 2 bytes of database storage.

An INTEGER uses twice as much storage as a SMALLINT but has a greater range of possible values. The data value range for an INTEGER data type is –2,147,483,648 to 2,147,483,647. The precision for an INTEGER is 10 digits to the left of the decimal. Each INTEGER column value uses 4 bytes of database storage.

The BIGINT data type is available for supporting 64-bit integers. The value range for BIGINT is –9,223,372,036,854,775,808 to 9,223,372,036,854,775,807. Since platforms include native support for 64-bit integers, processing large numbers with BIGINT is more efficient than processing with DECIMAL and more precise than using DOUBLE or REAL. Each BIGINT column value uses 8 bytes of database storage.

The SMALLINT, INTEGER, and BIGINT data types do not allow any digits to the right of the decimal.

A DECIMAL or NUMERIC data type is used for numbers with fractional and whole parts. The DECIMAL data is stored in a packed format. You must provide the precision and scale when using a DECIMAL data type. The precision is the total number of digits (ranging from 1 to 31 digits), and the scale is the number of digits in the fractional part of the number.

> **NOTE** If you do not explicitly specify the precision and scale, DB2 will use a default value of DECIMAL(5,0), that is, a precision of 5 digits and a scale of 0 digits.

A REAL or FLOAT data type is an approximation of a number. The approximation requires 32 bits or 4 bytes of storage. To specify a single-precision number using the REAL data type, you must define its length between 1 and 24 (especially if you use the FLOAT data type, as it can represent both single- and double-precision numbers and is determined by the integer value specified).

A DOUBLE or FLOAT data type is also an approximation of a number. The approximation requires 64 bits or 8 bytes of storage. To specify a double-precision number using the FLOAT data type, you must define its length between 25 and 53.

The DECFLOAT data type, new in DB2 9.5, is useful in business applications that deal with exact decimal values such as financial applications where monetary values are manipulated. It supports the 16-digit and 34-digit decimal floating-point encodings, corresponding to 8 bytes and 16 bytes of storages respectively. While the FLOAT data type provides binary approximations to decimal data, DECFLOAT provides exact decimal values. DECFLOAT provides the accuracy of DECIMAL with some of the performance advantages of FLOAT.

7.7.1.2 String Data Types

You can define string or character columns as either fixed length or variable length. The character string data types include the following:

- Character (CHAR)
- Variable character (VARCHAR)
- Long variable character (LONG VARCHAR)
- Character large object (CLOB)
- GRAPHIC
- VARGRAPHIC
- LONG VARGRAPHIC
- Double-byte character large object (DBCLOB)

A CHAR column is stored as a fixed-length field in the database; if the string you enter is shorter than the defined length of the column, the string will be padded with blanks. This wastes space within the database if you tend to store strings that are a lot shorter than the length of the column. A fixed-length character column can have a maximum length of 254 characters. If no length is specified, DB2 will use the default length of 1 character.

A VARCHAR column stores only the characters entered for the string, and its maximum size closely corresponds to the page size for the table. For example, for a table created in a table space with a 32K page size, the maximum length of a VARCHAR string is 32,672 characters.

A LONG VARCHAR column also stores only the characters entered for the string, but it does not store them in the data object with the other columns. LONG VARCHAR is a special data type stored in a separate long object. The maximum length of a LONG VARCHAR string is 32,700 characters.

NOTE You can use the FOR BIT DATA clause of CHAR, VARCHAR, and LONG VARCHAR data types to indicate the data will be stored as a sequence of bytes (binary data). The clause can be used for non-traditional data like video and audio. Code page conversions do not occur because data is compared bit by bit.

GRAPHIC data types use 2 bytes of storage to represent a single character. There are three types:

- GRAPHIC: fixed length with a maximum of 127 characters
- VARGRAPHIC: varying length with a maximum of 16,336 characters
- LONG VARGRAPHIC: varying length with a maximum of 16,350 characters

> **NOTE** The LONG VARCHAR and LONG VARGRAPHIC data types are deprecated, meaning that they are still supported but are no longer enhanced. These data types are not manipulated in the buffer pool but are accessed directly from disk, a direct input/output (I/O) operation, so using them may impact performance. Instead, use the VARCHAR or VARGRAPHIC data types, respectively, because their maximum lengths are very close to those of the LONG data types, but VARCHAR and VARGRAPHIC provide better performance.

When a VARCHAR data type's maximum size of 32,672 bytes is not enough to hold your data, use large objects. Large objects (LOBs) can store data greater than 32K up to 2GB in size. They are typically used to store information such as an audio file, or a picture. Though XML documents can also be stored as LOBs, with DB2 9 we recommend you to use the XML data type instead in order to take advantage of pureXML technology.

Three kinds of LOB data types are provided with DB2:

- Binary large object (BLOB)
- Single-byte character large object (CLOB)
- Double-byte character large object (DBCLOB)

BLOBs store variable-length data in binary format and are ideal for storing video or audio information in your database. This data type has some restrictions; for example, you cannot sort by this type of column.

CLOBs store large amounts of variable-length single-byte character set (SBCS) or multibyte character set (MBCS) character strings, for example, large amounts of text such as white papers or long documents.

DBCLOBs store large amounts of variable-length double-byte character set (DBCS) character strings, such as large amounts of text in Chinese.

Similar to LONG VARCHAR and LONG VARGRAPHIC data types, LOBs are accessed directly from disk without going through the buffer pool, so using LOBs is slower than using other data types. In addition, because changes to a database are logged in transaction log files, these files might get filled quickly when modifying a LOB column. To prevent this from happening, the **CREATE TABLE** statement has the **NOT LOGGED** option for LOB columns. For LOB columns defined as more than 1GB in size, **NOT LOGGED** is required.

The **CREATE TABLE** statement also has the **COMPACT** option for LOBs to allocate just the necessary disk space. However, if you perform an update to the LOB column that would increase the size of the LOB, DB2 would need to allocate more space at that time, which incurs a performance penalty. Note that this option does not compress the LOBs.

> **NOTE** Do not use LOBs to store data less than 32K in size. Instead, use VARCHAR or VARCHAR FOR BIT DATA, which can hold a maximum of 32,672 bytes. This will help with database performance.

7.7.1.3 Datetime Data Types

Date and time data types are special character data types used to store date and/or time values in specific formats. These data types are stored in an internal format by DB2, and use an external format for the users. DB2 supports three datetime data types: DATE, TIME, and TIMESTAMP.

- The DATE type stores a date value (month, day, and year). Its external format is MM-DD-YYYY or MM/DD/YYYY.
- The TIME type stores a time value (hour, minute, and second). Its external format is HH:MM:SS or HH.MM.SS.
- The TIMESTAMP type combines the DATE and TIME types but also stores the time down to the nanosecond. Its external format is MM-DD-YYYY-HH.MM.SS.NNNNNN.

7.7.1.4 Extensible Markup Language Data Type

The Extensible Markup Language data type, XML, is a data type that is part of the SQL standard with XML extensions (SQL/XML). This new data type allows for storing well-formed XML documents natively (in a parsed-hierarchical manner) internally in a DB2 database. The XML data type can be transformed to a serialized string value using the XMLSERIALIZE function, and a serialized string value can be transformed into an XML value using the XMLPARSE function. These functions are discussed in more detail in Chapter 10, Mastering the DB2 pureXML Support.

7.7.2 User-Defined Types

User-defined types (UDTs) allow database users to create or extend the use of data types to their own needs. UDTs can be classified as DISTINCT, STRUCTURE, or REFERENCE. This section discusses only DISTINCT types. Please refer to the *DB2 SQL Reference* manual for the other kinds of UDTs.

A DISTINCT UDT can enforce business rules and prevent data from being used improperly. UDTs are built on top of existing DB2 built-in data types.

To create a UDT, use the **CREATE DISTINCT TYPE** statement:

```
CREATE DISTINCT TYPE type_name AS built-in_datatype WITH COMPARISONS
```

The **WITH COMPARISONS** clause is required for all data types, except BLOB, CLOB, DBCLOB, LONG VARCHAR, and LONG VARGRAPHIC data types. This clause causes DB2 to create system-generated SQL functions that perform casting between the types; these are known as casting functions.

For example, let's say you create two UDTs, *celsius* and *fahrenheit*:

```
CREATE DISTINCT TYPE  celsius   AS integer WITH COMPARISONS
CREATE DISTINCT TYPE fahrenheit AS integer WITH COMPARISONS
```

The first statement creates a casting function named *celsius*, and the second statement creates a casting function named *fahrenheit*.

Now, let's say you create a table using the newly created UDTs:

```
CREATE TABLE temperature
       (country          varchar(100),
        average_temp_c   celsius,
        average_temp_f   fahrenheit
       )
```

Table *temperature* keeps track of the average temperature of each country in the world in both Celsius and Fahrenheit. If you would like to know which countries have an average temperature higher than 35 degrees Celsius, you can issue this query:

```
SELECT country FROM temperature WHERE average_temp_c > 35
```

Would this query work? At first, you may think it will, but remember that *average_temp_c* has data type *celsius*, while 35 is an INTEGER. Even though *celsius* was created based on the INTEGER built-in data type, this comparison cannot be performed as is. To resolve this problem, use the casting function generated with the creation of the *celsius* UDT as shown below:

```
SELECT country FROM temperature WHERE average_temp_c > celsius(35)
```

UDTs enforce business rules by preventing illegitimate operations. For example, the following query will not work:

```
SELECT country FROM temperature WHERE average_temp_c = average_temp_f
```

Because column *average_temp_c* and *average_temp_f* are of different data types, this query will result in an error. If UDTs had not been created and the INTEGER built-in data type had been used instead for both columns, the query would have worked—but what meaning in real life would that have?

To drop a UDT, use the statement **`DROP DISTINCT TYPE type_name`**. This will also drop the casting functions associated to the UDT.

7.7.3 Choosing the Proper Data Type

It is important to choose the proper data type because this affects performance and disk space. To choose the correct data type, you need to understand how your data will be used and its possible values. Table 7.3 summarizes what you should consider.

Table 7.3 Choosing the Proper Data Types

Question	Data Type
Is your data variable in length, with a maximum length of fewer than 10 characters?	CHAR
Is your data variable in length, with a minimum length of 10 characters?	VARCHAR
Is your data fixed in length?	CHAR
Is your data going to be used in sort operations?	CHAR, VARCHAR, DECIMAL, INTEGER
Is your data going to be used in arithmetic operations?	DECIMAL, REAL, DOUBLE, BIGINT, INTEGER, SMALLINT
Does your data require decimals?	DECIMAL, REAL, DOUBLE, FLOAT
Do you need to store very small amounts of non-traditional data like audio or video?	CHAR FOR BIT DATA, VARCHAR FOR BIT DATA, LONG VARCHAR FOR BIT DATA
Do you need to store non-traditional data like audio or video, or data larger than a character string can store?	CLOB, BLOB, DBCLOB
Does the data contain timestamp information?	TIMESTAMP
Does the data contain time information?	TIME
Does the data contain date information?	DATE
Do you need a data type to enforce your business rules that has a specific meaning (beyond DB2 built-in data types)?	User-defined type
Will you work with XML documents in your database?	XML
Is your data variable in length, with a maximum length of fewer than 10 characters?	CHAR

NOTE For the first two rows of Table 7.3 we chose CHAR versus VARCHAR depending on the length of the data. If the maximum length is fewer than 10 characters, we suggest using a CHAR data type; otherwise, we recommend VARCHAR. Normally for small variable-length columns, a CHAR column provides better performance. We chose the value of 10 characters based on our experience, but it may vary depending on your data.

7.8 Tables

A **table** is an unordered set of records, consisting of rows and columns. Each column has a defined data type, and each row represents an entry in the table. Figure 7.9 shows an example of a table with *n* rows and *m* columns. The *sales_person* column with a VARCHAR data type is the first column in the table, followed by the *region* column with a CHAR data type, and the *year* column with an INTEGER data type. The *info* column is the *m*th column in the table and has an XML data type.

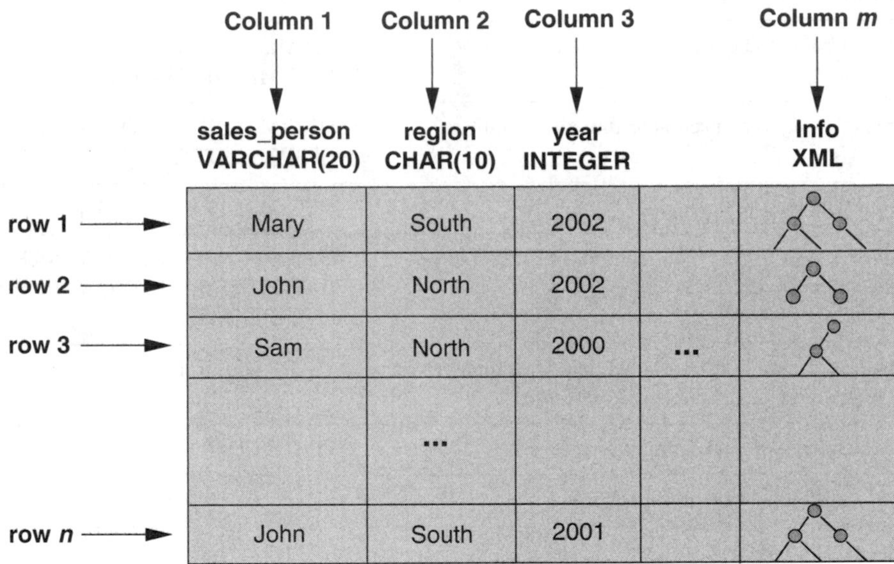

Figure 7.9 An example of a table

7.8.1 Table Classification

Tables in DB2 can be classified as illustrated in Figure 7.10. You will learn more about each of these tables in the next sections.

7.8.2 System Catalog Tables

DB2 automatically creates system catalog tables when a database is created. They always reside in the SYSCATSPACE table space. System catalog tables contain information about all the objects in the database. For example, when you create a table space, its information will be loaded into one or more system catalog tables. When this table space is referenced during a later operation, DB2 checks the corresponding system catalog tables to see whether the table space exists and whether the operation is allowed. Without the system catalog tables, DB2 will not be able to function.

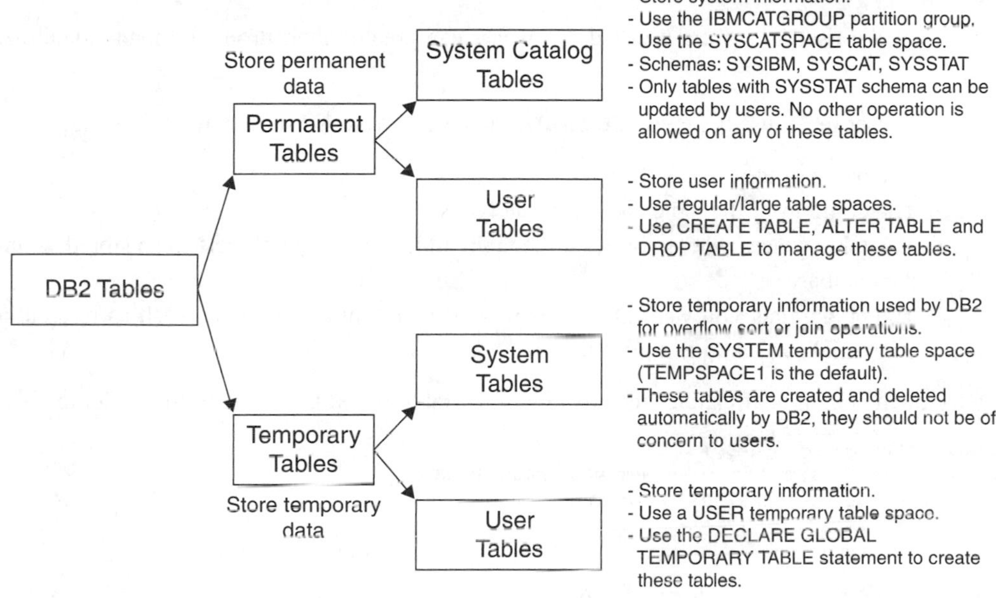

Figure 7.10 Classification of tables in DB2

Some of the information contained in system catalog tables includes the following:

- Definitions of all database objects
- Column data types of the tables and views
- Defined constraints
- Object privileges
- Object dependencies

System catalog tables or views use the SYSIBM, SYSCAT, or SYSSTAT schemas.

- The **SYSIBM schema** is used for the base system catalog tables.
- The **SYSCAT schema** is used for views defined on the system catalog tables. DB2 users should normally query the SYSCAT views rather than the SYSIBM tables for information.
- **The SYSSTAT schema** is used for views containing information about database statistics and is also based on the system catalog tables.

Although you cannot update the tables and views residing under the SYSIBM and SYSCAT schemas, you can update the views under the SYSSTAT schema. Updating these views can sometimes influence the DB2 optimizer to choose a different access path.

Refer to Appendix D, Using the DB2 System Catalog Tables, for details about the system catalog tables.

7.8.3 User Tables

User tables are used to store a user's data. A user can create, alter, drop, and manipulate user tables.

To create a user table, use the **CREATE TABLE** statement. You can specify the following:

- The name of the table
- The columns of the table and their data types
- The table spaces where you want the table, index, and long objects to be stored within the database
- The constraints you want DB2 to build and maintain on the table, such as referential constraints and unique constraints

The following example illustrates the creation of the table *myemployees* with four columns.

```
CREATE TABLE myemployees (
        empID     INT            NOT NULL PRIMARY KEY,
        empname   VARCHAR(30)    NOT NULL,
        info XML,
        history   CLOB)
```

In which table space would the table *myemployees* be created? In cases where a table space is not specified, as in this example, follow the flow chart shown in Figure 7.11 to determine what table space would be used.

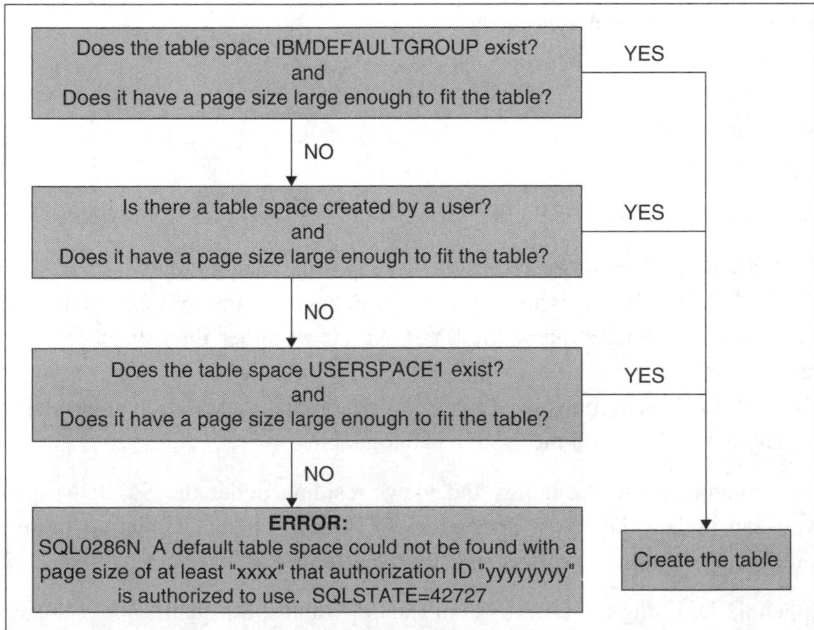

Figure 7.11 Guidelines for determining how the default table space is chosen for a table

This next example uses the same **CREATE TABLE** situation, but it indicates the table spaces to be used for the table data, index, and long objects.

```
CREATE TABLE myemployees (
             empID     INT            NOT NULL PRIMARY KEY,
             empname   VARCHAR(30)    NOT NULL,
             info      XML,
             history   CLOB)
             IN datadms
       INDEX IN indexdms
       LONG  IN largedms
```

Use the **IN** clause to specify the table space where the table data will reside. Use the **INDEX IN** clause to specify where all indexes for the table will reside. Use the **LONG IN** clause to indicate where the XML, LOB, LONG VARCHAR, or LONG VARGRAPHIC objects will reside.

> **NOTE** If different table spaces are used for the table, index, and long data, all of these table spaces must be DMS. In addition, the table space where the long data is to be stored must be defined as a *large* table space.

> **NOTE** In previous versions of DB2, *large* table spaces were known as *long* table spaces. Though the syntax of the **CREATE TABLESPACE** statement uses the **LARGE** clause, the syntax of the **CREATE TABLE** statement still uses **LONG**.

Figure 7.12 shows the command used to create the table *myemployees* and also the corresponding table space commands to create the required table spaces. Note that all of the statements are creating LARGE table spaces, even for the first two statements where LARGE is not explictly provided since this is the default for DMS table spaces.

You can also create a table based on the definition of another table, for example:

```
CREATE TABLE clone LIKE myemployees
```

The table *clone* will have the same definition as the table *myemployees*, however, other objects like constraints, indexes, or triggers associated to the table are not copied. Table data is not copied either.

Another alternative is to create the table structure based on the result of a query, as shown next:

```
CREATE TABLE clone2 AS (SELECT * FROM myemployees) DEFINITION ONLY
```

The **DEFINITION ONLY** clause is required so that only the structure of the table is copied; otherwise, you would be creating a materialized query table (MQT), which is described in Section 7.8.11, Materialized Query Tables and Summary Tables.

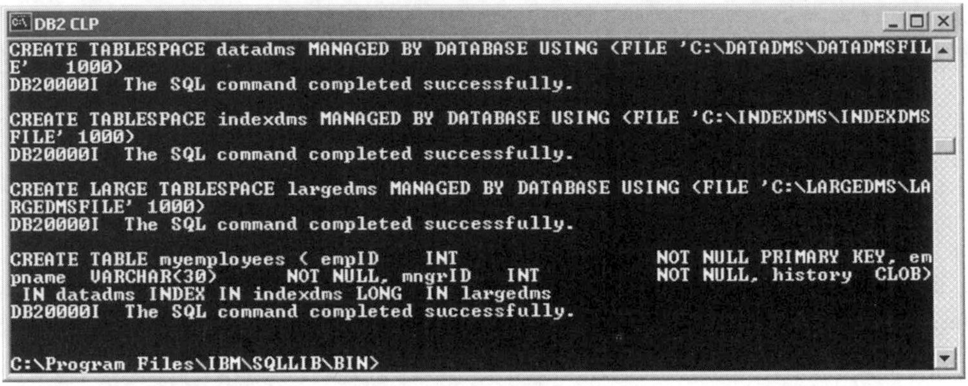

```
DB2 CLP
CREATE TABLESPACE datadms MANAGED BY DATABASE USING (FILE 'C:\DATADMS\DATADMSFIL
E'   1000)
DB20000I  The SQL command completed successfully.

CREATE TABLESPACE indexdms MANAGED BY DATABASE USING (FILE 'C:\INDEXDMS\INDEXDMS
FILE' 1000)
DB20000I  The SQL command completed successfully.

CREATE LARGE TABLESPACE largedms MANAGED BY DATABASE USING (FILE 'C:\LARGEDMS\LA
RGEDMSFILE' 1000)
DB20000I  The SQL command completed successfully.

CREATE TABLE myemployees ( empID    INT                   NOT NULL PRIMARY KEY, em
pname  VARCHAR(30)      NOT NULL, mngrID   INT        NOT NULL, history  CLOB)
 IN datadms INDEX IN indexdms LONG  IN largedms
DB20000I  The SQL command completed successfully.

C:\Program Files\IBM\SQLLIB\BIN>
```

Figure 7.12 Creating a table where table, index, and long data are stored in different DMS table spaces

Once you have created a table, you cannot change the column names or data types; however, you are allowed to increase the length of VARCHAR columns or add new columns to the end of the table. You can do this with the **ALTER TABLE** statement. For example, to add the column *address* to the table *myemployees*, use this statement:

```
ALTER TABLE myemployees ADD COLUMN address CHAR(45)
```

You cannot remove a column from a table using the **ALTER TABLE** statement. If you want to remove a column from a table, you have two choices:

- Use a view to hide the column you want removed. (Views are discussed in Section 7.12, Views.)
- Drop the table and recreate it.

To drop a table and all its contents, use the **DROP TABLE** statement, for example:

```
DROP TABLE myemployees
```

7.8.4 Default Values

In the **CREATE TABLE** statement, you can use the **DEFAULT** clause for a given column to provide a default value for the column. This means that when you use an **INSERT** statement to insert a row that does not provide a value for the column, the default value specified in the **DEFAULT** clause will be used. For example, let's say you create the table *company* with this statement:

```
CREATE TABLE company (
       companyID        INTEGER,
       companyName      VARCHAR(30),
       city             VARCHAR(20) DEFAULT 'TORONTO'
       )
```

Inserting a record with either of the following two statements provides the same result.

```
(1) INSERT INTO company  (companyID, companyName,  city)
                VALUES (   111    ,  'cityOne' , DEFAULT)
(2) INSERT INTO company  (companyID, companyName)
                VALUES (   111,      'cityOne' )
```

The following row would be inserted.

```
COMPANYID       COMPANYNAME                            CITY
----------- ------------------------------ --------------------
        111 cityOne                                    TORONTO
```

In the first **INSERT** statement, the **DEFAULT** keyword is used. In the second **INSERT** statement, the third column (*city*) is not included in the statement. In both cases, this means that the default value as defined in the table is inserted for that column.

What about the table columns that do not have a **DEFAULT** clause? What is inserted when test columns are omitted from the **INSERT** statement? In such scenarios, DB2 will insert a NULL, assuming the column accepts NULL values. If the column does not accept NULL values, you will receive an error. (We describe NULLs in the next section.) For example, the result of this statement:

```
      INSERT INTO company  (city)
                 VALUES ('ATLANTA')
```

```
is:
COMPANYID       COMPANYNAME                            CITY
----------- ------------------------------ --------------------
          -  -                                         ATLANTA
```

The dash (–) represents a NULL value.

The columns of a table can also be defined with the **DEFAULT** keyword just by itself. In such a scenario, DB2 will use default values depending on the data type of the column. Typically, DB2 chooses a zero for numeric data types and a blank for character strings. For example, let's recreate the table *company* as follows:

```
CREATE TABLE company (
       companyID         INTEGER      DEFAULT,
       companyName       VARCHAR(30)  DEFAULT,
       city              VARCHAR(20)  DEFAULT 'TORONTO'
       )
```

Issuing the following statement:

```
      INSERT INTO company  (city)
                 VALUES (DEFAULT)
```

returns:

```
COMPANYID       COMPANYNAME                            CITY
----------- ------------------------------ ------------
          0                                            TORONTO
```

This example shows that because the columns *companyID* and *companyName* are both defined with the **DEFAULT** clause just by itself, DB2 chose a default value of zero for column *companyID*, which is an INTEGER, and a blank for column *companyName*, which is a VARCHAR.

7.8.5 Using NULL Values

NULL values represent an unknown state. For example, let's review the contents of the table *student*, which contains NULL values.

```
NAME                 MARK
-------------------- -----------
Peter                        100
Mary                          60
John                           -
Raul                          80
Tom                            -
```

John and Tom were sick the day of the exam, therefore the teacher put NULL values for their marks. This is different than giving them a mark of zero. If you issue this statement:

```
SELECT avg(mark) as average FROM student
```

The result is:

```
AVERAGE
-----------
         80
```

Note that the average was calculated as follows: (100 + 60 + 80) / 3. The total number of students considered in the calculation was three, not five, because NULL values were not taken into consideration in the calculation.

Your business requirements dictate when NULL values are allowed in your columns. Let's review another example to illustrate when using **NOT NULL** is appropriate. The following statement creates a table that stores a company phone directory.

```
CREATE TABLE telephoneDirectory (
    empID       CHAR(3)        NOT NULL PRIMARY KEY,
    phone_no    VARCHAR(15)    NOT NULL,
    deptname    VARCHAR(20)    NOT NULL DEFAULT 'Marketing',
    position    VARCHAR(30)    DEFAULT 'Clerk'
)
```

In the example, let's assume the business requirements indicate that the column *empID* must uniquely identify a row. Thus, *empID* should be created as NOT NULL so that NULL values are not accepted; otherwise, several rows may have NULLs, which would not make the rows unique.

Next, the column *phone_no* is also defined as NOT NULL per the business requirements. If the purpose of this table is to store telephone numbers, it's understandable that this column does not accept NULLs.

The third column, *deptname*, is defined as NOT NULL with a **DEFAULT** value of Marketing. This means that a NULL value is not accepted, and when the column is omitted in an **INSERT** statement, the default value of Marketing is used. For example, if you issue this statement:

```
INSERT INTO telephoneDirectory (empID, phone_no)
                    VALUES ('111', '905-123-4567')
```

The result is:

```
EMPID PHONE_NO        DEPTNAME             POSITION
----- --------------- -------------------- -----------------------
111   905-123-4567    Marketing            Clerk
```

The fourth column, *position*, allows NULL values and has a default value of Clerk. This case was explained in Section 7.8.3, Default Values. The NOT NULL DEFAULT *value* clause works the same as the DEFAULT *value* clause only that NULL values are not allowed.

7.8.6 Identity Columns

An identity column is a numeric column in a table that automatically generates a unique numeric value in sequence for each row inserted. A unique identifier is often used in applications to identify a specific row. Unlike sequence objects, which we discuss in Section 7.17, Sequences, identity columns are bound to the table they are defined on. There can be only one identity column per table. DB2 can generate the identity column values in two ways.

- Generated always: The values are always generated by DB2. Applications are not allowed to provide an explicit value.
- Generated by default: The values can be explicitly provided by an application; if no value is given, DB2 generates one. In this case, however, DB2 cannot guarantee the uniqueness of the value generated.

To create an identity column, use the **CREATE TABLE** statement with the **GENERATED** clause and make sure it contains the **IDENTITY** keyword because **GENERATED** can also be used to generate other values automatically that are not identity columns. Here is an example.

```
CREATE TABLE product (
       productno   INTEGER GENERATED ALWAYS AS
                          IDENTITY (START WITH 200 INCREMENT BY 1),
       description VARCHAR(50) )
```

The column *productno* is an INTEGER defined as an identity column that is always generated. The value generated will start from 200, and it will be incremented by 1. Let's perform a few **INSERT** statements and see the results obtained.

```
INSERT INTO product VALUES (DEFAULT,'banana');           --->inserts 200,banana
INSERT INTO product (description) VALUES ('apple');      --->inserts 201,apple
INSERT INTO product VALUES (300,'pear');                 --->error SQL0798N
COMMIT;

INSERT INTO product (description) VALUES ('orange');     --->inserts 202,orange
ROLLBACK;
```

```
INSERT INTO product (description) VALUES ('plum');      --->inserts 203,plum
COMMIT;
```

The following query shows the final result.

```
SELECT * FROM product;

PRODUCTNO   DESCRIPTION
----------- ------------
        200 banana
        201 apple
        203 plum
```

The first two **INSERT** statements show that two identity column values were generated: 200 and 201. The third **INSERT** statement returns an error because you cannot explicitly insert a value for an identity column generated as **ALWAYS.** After the third **INSERT** statement, we issue a **COMMIT** to guarantee these rows are stored in the database. The fourth **INSERT** statement causes another identity column value, 202, to be generated; however, we issue a **ROLLBACK** statement right after, so this row is not stored in the database. Note that the final **INSERT** statement, which inserts the product plum, generates a value of 203, not 202 since 202 was generated and assigned to the previous statement. (**COMMIT** and **ROLLBACK** statements are explained in more detail in Chapter 14, Developing Database Backup and Recovery Solutions.)

> **NOTE** An identity column value is generated only once. Once the value has been generated, even if a **ROLLBACK** statement is performed, it will not be generated again.

Now let's review another example, this time creating the same table *product* with the **GENERATED BY DEFAULT** clause.

```
CREATE TABLE product (
       productno    INTEGER GENERATED BY DEFAULT AS
                             IDENTITY (START WITH 200 INCREMENT BY 1),
       description VARCHAR(50) )
```

Next, we insert a few rows.

```
INSERT INTO product VALUES (DEFAULT,'banana');          --->inserts 200,banana
INSERT INTO product (description) VALUES ('apple');     --->inserts 201,apple
INSERT INTO product VALUES (300,'pear');                --->inserts 300,pear
INSERT INTO product VALUES (201,'orange');              --->inserts 201,orange
COMMIT;
INSERT INTO product (description) VALUES ('papaya');    --->inserts 202,papaya
ROLLBACK;
INSERT INTO product (description) VALUES ('plum');      --->inserts 203,plum
COMMIT;
```

The following query shows the final result.

```
SELECT * FROM product

PRODUCTNO   DESCRIPTION
----------- --------------------
        200 banana
        201 apple
        300 pear
        201 orange
        203 plum
```

The first two **INSERT** statements show that two identity column values were generated: 200 and 201. For the third and fourth **INSERT** statements, we explicitly provided the values 300 and 201, respectively, for the identity column. Note that DB2 did not return an error as in the previous example because we defined the identity column as **GENERATED BY DEFAULT.** After the fourth **INSERT** statement, we issue a **COMMIT** to guarantee these rows are stored in the database. The fifth **INSERT** statement causes another identity column value, 202, to be generated; however, we issue a **ROLLBACK** statement right after, so this row is not stored in the database. Note that the final **INSERT** statement, which inserts the product plum, generates a value of 203, not 202.

The following final example illustrates a **GENERATED** value, which is not an identity column. The example uses **GENERATED ALWAYS,** but you can also use **GENERATED BY DEFAULT.**

```
CREATE TABLE income (
 empno      INTEGER,
 salary     INTEGER,
 taxRate    DECIMAL(5,2),
 netSalary DECIMAL(7,2) GENERATED ALWAYS AS (salary * (1 - taxRate))
)
```

If you insert the following row:

```
INSERT INTO income (empno, salary, taxRate) VALUES (111, 50000, 0.3)
```

the result is

```
EMPNO       SALARY      TAXRATE NETSALARY
----------- ----------- ------- ---------
        111       50000    0.30  35000.00
```

DB2 generates the value of the last column *NETSALARY* based on the *SALARY* and *TAXRATE* columns.

7.8.7 Constraints

Constraints allow you to create rules for the data in your tables. You can define four types of constraints on a table.

- **A unique** constraint ensures that no duplicate key values can be entered in the table.
- **A referential** constraint ensures that a value in one table must have a corresponding entry in a related table.
- **A check** constraint ensures that the values you enter into the column are within the rules specified when the table was defined.
- **An informational** constraint allows you to enforce or not enforce a constraint.

These constraints are discussed further in the following sections.

7.8.7.1 Unique Constraints

A unique constraint indicates that the values for a given column must all be unique. A unique constraint is defined in the **CREATE TABLE** or **ALTER TABLE** statements using the **UNIQUE** clause or the **PRIMARY KEY** clause. A primary key, as you will see in the next section, is also a unique constraint.

All the columns that make up a unique constraint must be defined as NOT NULL. For the following example, the column *empID* must be defined as NOT NULL because it is the primary key. The column *deptID* must also be defined as NOT NULL because it is a unique constraint.

```
CREATE TABLE employ (
       empID    INT          NOT NULL PRIMARY KEY,
       name     CHAR(30)     ,
       deptID   INT          NOT NULL UNIQUE
       )
```

Now, let's perform a few **INSERT** statements in sequence.

```
INSERT INTO employ VALUES (111, 'Peter', 999)--> inserts 111, Peter, 999
INSERT INTO employ VALUES (111, 'Peter', 123)--> SQL0803N error, duplicate primary key 111
INSERT INTO employ VALUES (789, 'Peter', 999)--> SQL0803N error, duplicate unique key 999
```

This example illustrates that an error (SQL0803N) occurs if the value you attempt to insert for a unique or primary key column is not unique (it already exists in the table).

Unique constraints are implemented using unique indexes. When a **CREATE TABLE** statement has the **UNIQUE** or **PRIMARY KEY** keywords, DB2 automatically creates a corresponding unique index. The name of this system-generated index starts with "SQL" followed by a timestamp. For the example just shown, two unique indexes were generated with these names:

```
SQL070922135806320
SQL070922135806460
```

Both indexes were created on September 22, 2007, at 1:58 p.m.

Though you would normally not refer to an index name directly in an application, a good index name may be helpful when analyzing an explain output. An explain output, as you will see in Chapter 17, Database Performance Considerations, displays the access path DB2 chooses to access your data for a given query. Therefore, rather than letting DB2 generate system names for your indexes, we recommend using the **ALTER TABLE** statement in the case of primary key columns and the **CONSTRAINT** clause to explicitly give names to the indexes. For example, let's rewrite the **CREATE TABLE** statement used in the previous example as follows:

```
CREATE TABLE employ (
       empID    INT        NOT NULL,
       name     CHAR(30)   ,
       deptID   INT        NOT NULL CONSTRAINT unique_dept_const UNIQUE
       )

ALTER TABLE employ ADD CONSTRAINT employ_pk PRIMARY KEY (empID)
```

In this example, we removed the **PRIMARY KEY** clause of the **CREATE TABLE** statement and added an **ALTER TABLE** statement. The **ALTER TABLE** statement allowed us to put in a name for the constraint (*employ_pk*), which also becomes the name of the corresponding unique index.

Instead of the **ALTER TABLE** statement, you can also use the following two statements with the same result:

```
CREATE UNIQUE INDEX employ_pk ON employ (empID)
ALTER TABLE employ ADD PRIMARY KEY (empID)
```

In this case, the **CREATE UNIQUE** statement explicitly creates the unique index and specifies the desired name for the index. Next, the **ALTER TABLE** statement indicates that the same column used for the unique index is also used as the primary key. After executing the **ALTER TABLE** statement, you will receive this warning message:

```
SQL0598W  Existing index "EMPLOY_PK" is used as the index for the primary key or a
unique key. SQLSTATE=01550
```

This warning is acceptable because this is in fact what is desired.

In the previous **CREATE TABLE** statement, we also added a unique constraint using the clause **CONSTRAINT unique_dept_const UNIQUE**. With this clause, DB2 generates a corresponding unique index with the name *unique_dept_const*.

You can also use the **ALTER TABLE** statement to add a unique constraint, as shown in this example:

```
ALTER TABLE employ ADD CONSTRAINT unique_dept_const UNIQUE (deptID)
```

7.8.7.2 Referential Constraints

Referential constraints are used to support referential integrity. Referential integrity allows your database to manage relationships between tables.

7.8.7.2.1 Using Primary, Unique, and Foreign Keys to Establish Referential Integrity

Referential integrity can be better explained with examples. Assume you have two tables, as illustrated in Figure 7.13.

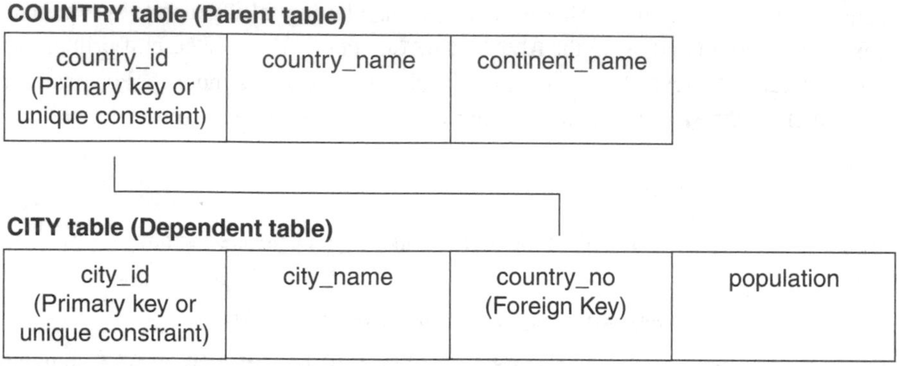

COUNTRY table (Parent table)

country_id (Primary key or unique constraint)	country_name	continent_name

CITY table (Dependent table)

city_id (Primary key or unique constraint)	city_name	country_no (Foreign Key)	population

Figure 7.13 Referential integrity between two tables

The figure shows the tables *country* and *city,* where *country* is the parent table containing information about all the countries in the world, and *city* is the dependent table containing information about a particular city for a given country. Note that the column *country_ID* and the column *country_no* are used to establish a relationship between the two tables.

The *country_ID* column is a primary key column. A primary key consists of one or more columns; it is a special case of a unique constraint. While there can be many unique constraints in a table, there can be only one primary key. A primary key is used to establish a referential integrity relationship with another table.

The *country_no* column, known as the foreign key column, will reference the primary key column of the parent table. Because of this relationship, the *country_no* column cannot have a value that does not exist in the *country_ID* column. The data type for this column must be compatible with the primary key column of the parent table. For the example illustrated in Figure 7.13, if the parent key column is defined as type INTEGER, the foreign key column can be defined as type DECIMAL because it is a numeric data type for which conversion is allowed; however, it cannot be defined as type CHAR. Other than this restriction, the foreign key can be treated like any other column. It can use the **NOT NULL, UNIQUE,** and even **PRIMARY KEY** clauses.

To establish the referential integrity relationship between the two tables, let's look at the corresponding **CREATE TABLE** statements for both tables.

```
CREATE TABLE country (
       country_ID      INT            NOT NULL PRIMARY KEY,
       country_Name    VARCHAR(30)    NOT NULL,
       continent_Name  CHAR(15)
       )

CREATE TABLE city (
       city_ID         INT            NOT NULL PRIMARY KEY,
       city_name       VARCHAR(30)    NOT NULL,
       country_no      INT            REFERENCES country,
       population      INT
       )
```

Note that the **CREATE TABLE** statement for the *city* table includes the **REFERENCES** clause and that it does not need to specify any column of the parent table *country*. DB2 will automatically look for the primary key column of the parent table to establish the relationship.

What if there is no primary key column for the parent table but a unique constraint instead? What if the parent table contains more than one unique constraint? In such cases, use the **REFERENCES** clause followed by the correct column name(s). For example, let's say we actually created the *country* table in Figure 7.13 with no primary key but two unique constraints, as follows.

```
CREATE TABLE country (
       country_ID        INT              NOT NULL UNIQUE,
       country_Name      VARCHAR(30)      NOT NULL,
       continent_Name    CHAR(15)         NOT NULL UNIQUE
       )
```

To establish referential integrity using the column *country_ID*, this column must be specified in the **CREATE TABLE** statement for the *city* table, as shown below.

```
CREATE TABLE city (
       city_ID           INT              NOT NULL PRIMARY KEY,
       city_name         VARCHAR(30)      NOT NULL,
       country_no        INT              REFERENCES country(country_ID),
       population        INT
       )
```

> **NOTE** A unique constraint on a column that has been defined as NOT NULL can also be referenced by a foreign key clause because a primary key is basically the same as a unique constraint.

You can also use the **ALTER TABLE** statement to add a foreign key, for example:

```
ALTER TABLE city
      ADD FOREIGN KEY (country_no) REFERENCES country (country_ID)
```

This statement would add to the table *city* the foreign key using column *country_no*, which would reference column *country_ID* in table *country*.

> **NOTE** Using primary keys, unique keys, and foreign keys is one method to implement referential integrity. Another method is to use triggers. By using triggers, you can code your own logic that may differ from the rules described in this section. Triggers are discussed in Section 7.14.
>
> You cannot establish referential integrity between a relational column and an element in an XML document. If some sort of relationship like this is required, you may think about using Triggers to implement such relationship.

7.8.7.2.2 Referential Integrity Implications on SQL Operations

The enforcement of referential integrity has implications on **INSERT, UPDATE,** and **DELETE** operations, which must follow certain rules. To explain these rules, let's look at the following example using Figure 7.14.

COUNTRY table (Parent table)

country_ID (Primary key or unique constraint)	country_name	continent_name
1	Canada	North America

CITY table (Dependent table)

city_id (Primary key or unique constraint)	city_name	country_no (Foreign Key)	population
11	Toronto	1	8,000,000
22	Montreal	1	6,000,000
33	Calgary	1	5,000,000

DISTRICT table (Dependent table)

district_id (Primary key or unique constraint)	district_name	city_no (Foreign Key)	registrations
111	North York	11	300
222	Markham	11	900

Figure 7.14 An example to illustrate SQL operations under referential integrity

We used the first two tables, *country* and *city*, in previous examples. In this particular example, we have inserted a few records in each of these tables. A new table, *district*, which is dependent on table *city*, is also illustrated. Here is the **CREATE TABLE** statement for the table *district*.

```
CREATE TABLE district (
      district_ID      INT             NOT NULL PRIMARY KEY,
      district_name    VARCHAR(30)     NOT NULL,
      city_no          INT             REFERENCES city,
      registrations    INT
      )
```

The following cases are examined.

Inserting to a Parent Table

What would happen if the following record were inserted in table *country*?

```
INSERT INTO country  VALUES (2,'Spain',4)
```

Because *country* is the parent table at the top of Figure 7.14, any value can be inserted into this table without a need to worry about the dependent tables.

Inserting to a Dependent Table

What would happen if the following record were inserted in table *city*?

```
INSERT INTO city      VALUES (44,'Vancouver',3,4000000)
```

Table *city* is dependent on table *country* based on column *country_no* (the third column in the *city* table). This **INSERT** statement is trying to insert a record with a value of 3 for the *country_no* column. From Figure 7.14 you can see this value is not present in table *country*; therefore, this record cannot be inserted and an error would be returned.

Deleting a Row from the Parent Table

What would happen if the following record were deleted from table *country*?

```
DELETE FROM country WHERE country_name = 'Canada'
```

This **DELETE** statement would fail with an error SQL0532N because there are related dependent rows. This is the default behavior, also called the **NO ACTION** delete rule.

You can specify **DELETE** rules in the **CREATE TABLE** statement of the dependent table. In addition to **NO ACTION,** you can use the following rules.

- **RESTRICT:** The behavior is exactly the same as the **NO ACTION** rule. The difference is when this constraint is enforced. For more details, refer to the *DB2 SQL Reference* manual.
- **CASCADE:** All the dependent rows will be deleted when the parent table row is deleted.
- **SET NULL:** All the dependent rows will have the value of the foreign key column set to NULL, if NULLs are allowed; otherwise, an error is returned. All the other columns remain unchanged.

For example, let's say we actually created the table *city* as follows.

```
CREATE TABLE city (
       city_ID        INT           NOT NULL PRIMARY KEY,
       city_name      VARCHAR(30)   NOT NULL,
       country_no     INT           REFERENCES country(country_ID)
                                    ON DELETE CASCADE,
       population     INT
       )
```

Note that we added the clause **ON DELETE CASCADE** to the foreign key column *country_no*.

If we execute the following statement again, will it work this time?

```
DELETE FROM country WHERE country_name = 'Canada'
```

The answer is no. Though we defined the **CASCADE** rule correctly in the *city* table, we did not define it in the *district* table. All dependent tables need to be defined using **CASCADE** if you want all the dependent rows to be deleted. In this example, if we had defined the *district* table correctly, all the rows of all the tables would have been deleted.

Deleting a Row from a Dependent Table

You can delete a row from a dependent table with no implications unless the dependent table is the parent table of another table.

Updating a Row from the Parent Table

You cannot update the primary key of the parent table. To ensure you don't duplicate an existing value, DB2 does not allow this operation.

Updating a Row from a Dependent Table

You can update the foreign key of a dependent table only if the new value already exists in the parent table and the foreign key is defined as **NOT NULL.** This is the default behavior, which corresponds to the **NO ACTION** update rule.

For example, issuing this statement:

```
UPDATE city SET country_no = 7 WHERE city_name = 'Montreal'
```

would return error SQL0530N, which indicates the value of 7 does not exist in the parent table.

The other **UPDATE** rule possible is **RESTRICT,** which behaves similarly to the **NO ACTION** rule. The difference is when the rule enforcement takes place. For details about this rule, please review the *DB2 SQL Reference* manual.

You can specify **UPDATE** rules on the **CREATE TABLE** statement of a dependent table. For example, we could have created the *city* table as follows (on top of the **DELETE** rules of the previous example).

```
CREATE TABLE city (
       city_ID         INT             NOT NULL PRIMARY KEY,
       city_name       VARCHAR(30)     NOT NULL,
       country_no      INT             REFERENCES country(country_ID)
                                       ON DELETE CASCADE
                                       ON UPDATE RESTRICT,
       population      INT
)
```

7.8.7.3 Check Constraints

Check constraints are used to enforce data integrity at the table level. Once the check constraint is defined, every **INSERT** or **UPDATE** operation must satisfy the constraint; otherwise, you will receive an error. For example, let's create the table *student*.

```
CREATE TABLE student (
       student_ID      INT            NOT NULL PRIMARY KEY,
       name            VARCHAR(30)    NOT NULL,
       sex             CHAR(1)        NOT NULL
       CONSTRAINT sex_check_const CHECK (sex in ('M', 'F'))
       )
```

This table has the check constraint *sex_check_const* defined which verifies that the column *sex* has the values of M or F. Now let's attempt the following statement.

```
INSERT INTO student VALUES (1, 'Tom', 'Z')
```

We will receive an error SQL0545N because the value Z does not satisfy the check constraint.

You can also add a check constraint with the **ALTER TABLE** statement, as shown here.

```
ALTER TABLE student
      ADD CONSTRAINT sex_check_const CHECK (sex in ('M', 'F'))
```

If you are adding a check constraint with the **ALTER TABLE** statement to a table that already has data, DB2 will check the entire table to make sure the existing data satisfies the check constraint. If it doesn't, the **ALTER TABLE** statement will fail with error SQL0544N.

If you do not want DB2 to check the table when a check constraint is added, you can use the **SET INTEGRITY** statement. This statement turns off check constraint and referential constraint checking. For example, let's say we create the *student* table without a check constraint and insert some rows that will later be invalid for the check constraint.

```
CREATE TABLE student (
       student_ID      INT            NOT NULL PRIMARY KEY,
       name            VARCHAR(30)    NOT NULL,
       sex             CHAR(1)        NOT NULL
       )
INSERT INTO student VALUES (1, 'Tom',  'Z')
INSERT INTO student VALUES (2, 'Mary', 'A')
```

Now we attempt to add the following check constraint.

```
ALTER TABLE student
      ADD CONSTRAINT sex_check_const CHECK (sex in ('M', 'F'))
```

You receive error SQL0544N, as indicated earlier. Thus, use the **SET INTEGRITY** command to turn off constraint checking so that you can add the constraint.

```
SET INTEGRITY FOR student OFF
```

At this point, the *student* table is put in CHECK PENDING state, a state that allows only a few operations on the table, like **ALTER TABLE.** Other operations such as **SELECT, INSERT, UPDATE,** and **DELETE** are disallowed.

After turning off constraint checking, you can repeat the **ALTER TABLE** statement, which this time should be successful. Use the **SET INTEGRITY** statement again to turn constraint checking on as follows:

```
SET INTEGRITY FOR student CHECK IMMEDIATE UNCHECKED
```

The **IMMEDIATE UNCHECKED** option turns on check constraints again but does not check the existing table data. Alternatively, you can also issue:

```
SET INTEGRITY FOR student IMMEDIATE CHECKED
```

In this case, the **IMMEDIATE CHECKED** option turns on check constraints again and also checks the existing table data. If a violation is encountered, the table will remain in CHECK PENDING state. The **SET INTEGRITY** statement has an option to move the violating records to an exception table.

```
SET INTEGRITY FOR student IMMEDIATE CHECKED
    FOR EXCEPTION IN student USE my_exception_table
```

The name of the exception table in this example is *my_exception_table*. This table must exist with at least the same columns as the original source table, in this case, the *student* table. After this **SET INTEGRITY** statement is executed, the violating rows would be moved to the exception table, and the CHECK PENDING status would be removed. For more details about the **SET INTEGRITY** statement, refer to the *DB2 SQL Reference* manual.

7.8.7.4 Informational Constraints

Prior to Version 8.1, DB2 always enforced constraints once you defined them. Though you can turn constraint checking off with the **SET INTEGRITY** statement, this is mainly used to perform table alterations to add new constraints to existing tables, as you saw in the previous section. Using the **SET INTEGRITY** statement puts your table in CHECK PENDING status, which prevents you from performing many operations on your table.

What if your application already performs constraint checking, and thus there is no need for DB2 to check the data again? For example, large applications such as SAP, PeopleSoft, and Siebel are written to check the constraints before they insert the data into DB2. In this case, defining the constraint in DB2 would cause extra overhead if DB2 is also enforcing the rule and revalidating the constraint. However, if you do not define these constraints, the DB2 optimizer cannot use them to its advantage in choosing the most optimal access plans. (Chapter 17, Database Performance Considerations, explains the DB2 optimizer in more detail.)

Informational constraints allow you to specify whether or not DB2 should enforce the constraint and whether or not it can be used by the optimizer to choose the best access plan for the application statements.

The default operation when you create a constraint is that it is always enforced and can be used by the optimizer. You can change this default behavior by using informational constraints, which are implemented by using the following clauses of the **CREATE TABLE** statement.

- **ENFORCED:** This is the default option. Use this clause if you want DB2 to check the constraints for every operation on the table.
- **NOT ENFORCED:** Use this clause if you do not want DB2 to check the constraints for every operation on the table.
- **ENABLE QUERY OPTIMIZATION:** Use this clause so that the DB2 optimizer can use the knowledge of the constraint when building the plan for accessing the table or referenced tables.
- **DISABLE QUERY OPTIMIZATION:** Use this clause if you want the DB2 optimizer to ignore the constraints defined on your table.

The following example illustrates how informational constraints work.

```
CREATE TABLE student (
       student_ID       INT              NOT NULL PRIMARY KEY,
       name             VARCHAR(30)      NOT NULL,
       sex              CHAR(1)          NOT NULL
       CONSTRAINT sex_check_const CHECK (sex in ('M', 'F'))
       NOT ENFORCED
       ENABLE QUERY OPTIMIZATION
       )
```

Note that the constraint for table *student* will not be enforced, but the constraint is used for query optimization. Now let's perform the following statements.

```
(1)  INSERT INTO student VALUES (5, 'John', 'T')
(2)  SELECT * FROM student WHERE sex = 'T'
```

The first statement executes successfully—a T can be inserted for the *sex* column because the constraint *sex_check_const* is not enforced.

The second statement returns zero records because query optimization is enabled. Therefore, the optimizer does not scan the table but checks the constraints defined for the *sex* column in the DB2 catalog tables and assumes it has only values of M or F, quickly returning a result of zero records. Of course, this result is incorrect. If you want to obtain the correct result, disable query optimization. You can do this with the **ALTER TABLE** statement:

```
ALTER TABLE student
      ALTER CHECK sex_check_const DISABLE QUERY OPTIMIZATION
```

If you perform the second statement again, this time you should get one record.

```
   SELECT * FROM student WHERE sex = 'T'
 STUDENT_ID NAME                              SEX
----------- ------------------------------ ---
          5 John                              T
```

> **NOTE** After issuing the **ALTER TABLE** statement to enable or disable query optimization, make sure to issue a **terminate** command if working from the CLP so the change will take effect.

> **NOTE** Use informational constraints only if you are certain the data to be inserted or updated has been correctly checked by your application. Normally you want to use the options **NOT ENFORCED** and **ENABLE QUERY OPTIMIZATION** together because you want DB2 to reduce overhead by not performing constraint checking, but having the DB2 optimizer take into account the constraint definition.

7.8.8 Not Logged Initially Tables

The **NOT LOGGED INITIALLY** clause of the **CREATE TABLE** statement allows you to create a table that will not be logged when an **INSERT, UPDATE, DELETE, CREATE INDEX, ALTER TABLE,** or **DROP INDEX** operation is performed in the same unit of work in which the **CREATE TABLE** statement was issued. For example, let's say you execute the following statements in a script.

```
CREATE TABLE products (
       productID     INT,
       product_Name VARCHAR(30)
       )
       NOT LOGGED INITIALLY;

INSERT INTO products VALUES (1,'door');
INSERT INTO products VALUES (2,'window');
...
INSERT INTO products VALUES (999999,'telephone');

COMMIT;

INSERT INTO products VALUES (1000000,'television');
UPDATE products SET product_name = 'radio' where productID = 3456;

ALTER TABLE products ACTIVATE NOT LOGGED INITIALLY

INSERT INTO products VALUES (1000001,'desk');
INSERT INTO products VALUES (1000002,'table');
...
INSERT INTO products VALUES (1999999,'chair');

COMMIT;
```

Any operation from the **CREATE TABLE** statement until the first **COMMIT** is not logged. Once the **COMMIT** is issued, any subsequent operation is logged. For this example, the **INSERT** and **UPDATE** statements after the first **COMMIT** are logged.

After creating the table as **NOT LOGGED INITIALLY,** if you would like to turn off logging temporarily again, you can use the **ALTER TABLE** statement with the **ACTIVATE NOT LOGGED INITIALLY** clause, as shown in the example. Any operations between the **ALTER TABLE** and the second **COMMIT** are not logged.

> **NOTE** You can use the statement **ALTER TABLE table_name ACTIVATE NOT LOGGED INITIALLY** only for tables that were originally created with the **NOT LOGGED INITALLY** clause.

You can also use the **WITH EMPTY TABLE** clause as part of the **ALTER TABLE table_name ACTIVATE NOT LOGGED INITIALLY** statement to remove all the data of the table. This method is faster than using a **DELETE FROM *table_name*** statement. For example, to remove all the rows of the table *products*, issue

```
ALTER TABLE products ACTIVATE NOT LOGGED INITIALLY WITH EMPTY TABLE
```

V9

7.8.9 Partitioned Tables

With partitioned tables you can now create a table that can span multiple table spaces. In addition, queries can be directed automatically only to the partitions where the data resides. For example, if you partition a table based on the month, and a user runs a query that is calculating the total sales for March, the query need only access the data for March, not the data for any other month.

There are two forms of the create table syntax that can be used to create a partitioned table, the short form and the long form. For example, the two statements below will create a table with the same table partitioning scheme.

```
CREATE TABLE t1(c1 INT)
      IN tbsp1, tbsp2, tbsp3, tbsp4
      PARTITION BY RANGE(c1)
            (STARTING FROM (1) ENDING (200) EVERY (50))

CREATE TABLE t1(c1 INT)
      PARTITION BY RANGE(t1)
            (STARTING FROM (1) ENDING(50)  IN tbsp1,
                               ENDING(100) IN tbsp2,
                               ENDING(150) IN tbsp3,
                               ENDING(200) IN tbsp4)
```

In both cases above, the first table partition (numbers from 1 to 50) will be placed in table space tbsp1, the second table partition in tbsp2, the third table partition in tbsp3, and the fourth table partition in tbsp4 as shown in Figure 7.15 below.

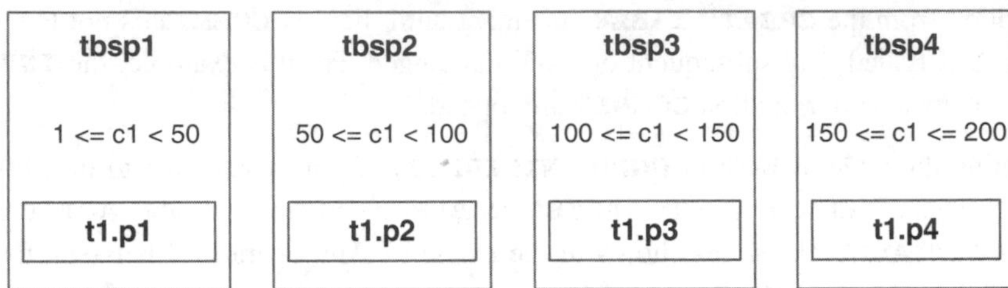

Figure 7.15 An example to illustrate partitioned tables

For a table that will have date ranges, you can either specify explicit start and stop values for the ranges, or you can leave it open ended using the special registers MINVALUES and MAXVALUES.

The table defined as:

```
CREATE TABLE sales(sdate DATE, customer INT)
     PARTITION BY RANGE(sdate)
        (STARTING '1/1/2006'  ENDING '3/31/2006',
         STARTING '4/1/2006'  ENDING '6/30/2006',
         STARTING '7/1/2006'  ENDING '9/30/2006',
         STARTING '10/1/2006' ENDING '12/31/2006')
```

would look like the following:

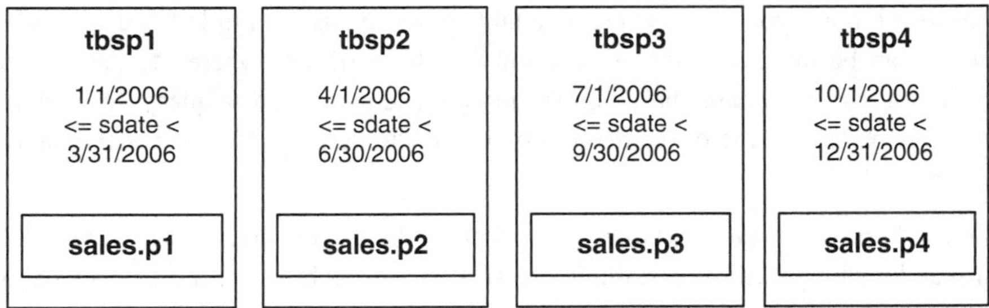

Figure 7.16 Table partitioned by date every three months

If you attempt to enter a row with a date in 2005, you will get the following error.

```
DB21034E  The command was processed as an SQL statement because it was not a valid Com-
mand Line Processor command.  During SQL processing it returned:
SQL0327N  The row cannot be inserted into table "DSNOW.SALES2" because it is outside
the bounds of the defined data partition ranges.  SQLSTATE=22525
```

However, you can also define the table so that the first range will accept all dates up to March 31, 2006 as follows:

```
CREATE TABLE sales(sdate DATE, customer INT)
     PARTITION BY RANGE(sdate)
        (STARTING MINVALUE     ENDING '3/31/2006',
         STARTING '4/1/2006'   ENDING '6/30/2006',
         STARTING '7/1/2006'   ENDING '9/30/2006',
         STARTING '10/1/2006'  ENDING '12/31/2006')
```

By default the range boundaries are inclusive, so to avoid leaving holes in the table, you can create the ranges using the EXCLUSIVE option for the ending boundary as follows:

```
CREATE TABLE sales4(sdate DATE, customer INT)
       IN tbsp1, tbsp2, tbsp3, tbsp4
       PARTITION BY RANGE(sdate)
           (STARTING MINVALUE        ENDING '3/31/2006' EXCLUSIVE,
            STARTING '3/31/2006'     ENDING '6/30/2006' EXCLUSIVE,
            STARTING '6/30/2006'     ENDING '9/30/2006' EXCLUSIVE,
            STARTING '9/30/2006'     ENDING '12/31/2006')
```

This table will look the same as Figure 7.16 above.

As you add new data to the table, you can create a new stand-alone table, load data into the table, and then attach the table to the range partitioned table as follows.

```
CREATE TABLE sales1Q07(sdate DATE, customer INT) in tbsp5

load from sales.del of del replace into sales1Q07

ALTER TABLE sales4 ATTACH PARTITION
      STARTING ('1/1/2007')
      ENDING ('3/31/2007')  FROM sales1Q07

set integrity for table sales off
```

Now the table will look like the following:

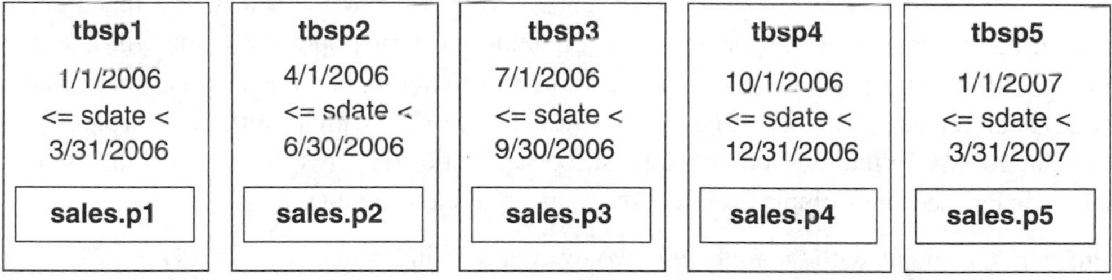

Figure 7.17 Partitioned table after attaching a partition

7.8.9.1 Detaching Partitions

You can remove the old table partitions using the DETACH command, however you need to know the name of the table partition to do this. You can either look up the table partition name using the Control Center, or the **DESCRIBE DATA PARTITIONS SHOW DETAIL** command, or name the table partitions when you are creating the table as follows:

```
CREATE TABLE carsales(sale_date DATE, VIN char(30))
       PARTITION BY RANGE(sale_date)
           (part q106 STARTING MINVALUE         ENDING '3/31/2006' EXCLUSIVE,
            part q206 STARTING '3/31/2006'      ENDING '6/30/2006' EXCLUSIVE,
            part q306 STARTING '6/30/2006'      ENDING '9/30/2006' EXCLUSIVE,
            part q406 STARTING '9/30/2006'      ENDING '12/31/2006')
```

You can then detach the table partition for the first quarter of 2006 into the table q106 as follows:

```
alter table carsales detach partition q106 into q106
```

V9 7.8.10 Row Compression

In DB2 9 you can now choose to compress the data in your tables. This provides a number of advantages such as:

- Decreased disk storage costs since the data and corresponding logs are compressed on disk
- Decreased I/O bandwidth consumption since there is less data being sent across the I/O channels
- Increased memory efficiency since the data is compressed in the buffer pools

However, these advantages come at some cost. Because the data in the buffer pool is compressed, it must be uncompressed before any rows are returned to the users or applications accessing the database.

DB2 utilizes a dictionary based compression. The dictionary is built by scanning the data (or a representative sample of the data), and then any further data added to the table, or updated within the table will also examine the dictionary to determine if data within that row can be compressed.

Compression works by replacing repeating strings within a row of data with a much smaller symbol. For example, if you have a table that includes customer addresses, you will likely find repeated information since there is a number of people living in the same city. For these customers DB2 can replace common strings like "Dallas, TX, 23456" with a short 12 bit symbol. Since DB2 can do this for the most common, most repeated cities (or any other series of bytes) in the table, you can see how compression will result in significant savings.

Consider an example with the following two rows of data in a table:

```
Fred  Smith  500  1000  Plano  Texas  24355
John  Smith  500  2000  Plano  Texas  24355
Sam   Smith  600  8000  Plano  Texas  24355
```

We can see that there are a number of repeating strings in these rows. But, DB2 not only looks for repeating strings in columns, it can also look for these repeating strings across columns, or within a column. So let's take the example above and examine the compression dictionary that DB2 would build for these rows.

We see that the name **Smith** is repeated in all 3 rows, so that would be the first entry in the dictionary. The department 500 is also repeated (but only in two rows, as is the address Plano, Texas, 24355. But look closer, if we look at the fourth column, we see that both rows, end in 000, so really the string 000 Plano Texas 24355 is repeated, and we can replace this entire string with a symbol. So for this data, the dictionary would contain 3 values as shown below.

01	Smith
02	500
03	000 Plano Texas 24355

Now, DB2 can store the first two rows on disk as follows:

```
Fred 01 02 1 03
John 01 02 2 03
```

Figure 7.18 summarizes the process of working with row compression. You first need to enable row compression using the COMPRESS clause of the CREATE TABLE or the ALTER TABLE statements. Next, a compression dictionary needs to be built with the REORG or INSPECT utilities. With DB2 9.5, the dictionary can be automatically created as well. Finally, you can verify the compression characteristics by running a DB2 snapshot, querying the SYSCAT.TABLES view, or running the function ADMIN_GET_TAB_COMPRESS_INFO. Each of the rectangles in the figure is described in more detail in the next sections.

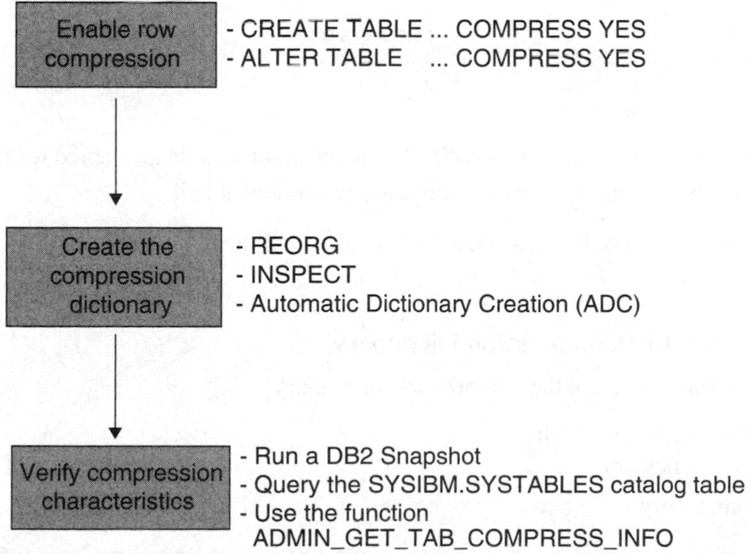

Figure 7.18 Working with row compression

7.8.10.1 Enabling Row Compression

Compression is enabled at the table level either when the table is created or by altering an existing table using the CREATE or ALTER TABLE statements. The syntax of these statements is shown below.

```
CREATE TABLE <table name> --->
         |---COMPRESS NO---|
----+-----------------+---->
         |---COMPRESS YES--|

ALTER TABLE <table name> --->
  --+--------------------+---->
         |---COMPRESS--+-YES--+--|
                       |--NO--|
```

For example, if user **ARFCHONG** wants to create the table **MYEMP** as a compressed table, he can issue this command:

```
create table myemp (
    EMP_ID integer not null,
    EMP_LAST_NAME varchar(20) not null,
    EMP_FIRST_NAME varchar(20) not null
)COMPRESS YES;
```

To verify that compression is enabled for a table, you can issue this statement:

```
SELECT name, compression
  FROM sysibm.systables
 WHERE creator = 'ARFCHONG' and name = 'MYEMP'
```

The output would look like this:

```
NAME                                  COMPRESSION
------------------------------------- -----------
MYEMP                                 R
  1 record(s) selected.
```

A value of 'R' in the column COMPRESSION, means that the table is enabled for row compression. A value of 'N', means that row compression was not enabled.

Enabling row compression does not mean that the data will be compressed right away. A dictionary must first be built as described in the next section.

7.8.10.2 Creating the Compression Dictionary

There are three ways to create the compression dictionary:

- Using the REORG utility
- Using the INSPECT tool
- Automatically

The REORG utility and the INSPECT tool are explained in more detail in Chapter 13, Maintaining Data, and Chapter 14, Developing Database Backup and Recovery Solutions, respectively.

Automatically creating the compression dictionary is described in more detail in Section 7.8.9.4 Automatic Dictionary Creation.

When REORG or INSPECT are used to create the compression dictionary, DB2 will examine all of the data in the table at the time these utilities are run. If the table has not already been loaded, you can build the dictionary by loading a representative sample of the data first and running REORG with the RESETDICTIONARY clause. Later you can load the remaining data once the dictionary has been built. You can also build the dictionary using the INSPECT tool, and then reorg the table using the new dictionary.

When the dictionary is created for a table, and the table has compression turned on, all inserts, updates, loads, and imports will honor the dictionary.

The REORG utility provides the RESETDICTIONARY and KEEPDICTIONARY clauses to determine whether a dictionary is rebuilt or kept after running this REORG.

Table 7.4 shows the outcome if the REORG is run using the RESETDICTIONARY option.

Table 7.5 shows the outcome if the REORG is run using the KEEPDICTIONARY option.

Table 7.4 Using REORG with the RESETDICTIONARY clause

Table COMPRESSION Attribute	Dictionary Exists	Result Outcome
YES	YES	Build new dictionary; rows compressed
YES	NO	Build new dictionary; rows compressed
NO	YES	Remove dictionary; all rows uncompressed
NO	NO	No effect

Table 7.5 Using REORG with the KEEPDICTIONARY clause

Table COMPRESSION Attribute	Dictionary Exists	Result Outcome
YES	YES	Preserve dictionary; rows compressed
YES	NO	Build dictionary; rows compressed
NO	YES	Preserve dictionary; all rows uncompressed
NO	NO	No effect

For example, continuing with the table **myemp** created in the previous section, let's assume you loaded the data from a delimited ASCII file **myemp.del** using these commands from the CLP:

```
LOAD from myemp.del of del replace into myemp;
SET INTEGRITY for myemp immediate checked;
REORG table myemp;
```

The LOAD, SET INTEGRITY and REORG commands are explained in more detailed in Chapter 13, Maintaining Data. The REORG command issued above will build the dictionary as this is the default behavior.

7.8.10.3 Verifying Compression Characteristics

There are three ways you can verify the effectiveness of row compression:

- Obtain a DB2 snapshot while the table is being REORGed
- Query the SYSIBM.SYSTABLES table
- Use the function ADMIN_GET_TAB_COMPRESS_INFO

For the first method, while the table is being REORGed, you can determine if it is rebuilding or keeping the dictionary, and also monitor the number of rows that have been compressed by getting a snapshot for the table. From the CLP, you can run this command:

```
get snapshot for all > output.txt
```

This assumes the appropriate monitor switches have been turned on. Chapter 17, Database Performance Considerations provides more information about snapshots. For the above example, the output of the snapshot will be redirected to the file **output.txt.** In that file, search for a section like the one shown below.

```
Reorg Type            =
        Reclustering
        Table Reorg
        Replace Compression Dictionary
        Allow Read Access
        Recluster Via Table Scan
        Rebuild Data Dictionary
        Reorg Data Only
Reorg Index           =  1
Reorg Tablespace      =  2
Start Time            =  08/16/2006 11:16:16.530771
Reorg Phase           =  2 - Build
Max Phase             =  4
Phase Start Time      =  08/16/2006 11:16:16.556749
Status                =  Started
Current Counter       =  0
Max Counter           =  0
Completion            =  0
Rows Compressed       =  980
Rows Rejected         =  0
Rows Time             =
```

In the output above, note that for this example, the dictionary is being rebuilt, and the number of rows compressed is 980.

For the second method, you can query the catalog table SYSIBM.SYSTABLES, however, ensure that you update the catalog information using the RUNSTATS command which is also explained in more detailed in Chapter 13, Maintaining Data. Continuing with the example used in previous sections, you would do

```
RUNSTATS on table arfchong.myemp

SELECT AVGROWSIZE                 A,
       PCTROWSCOMPRESSED          B,
       AVGROWCOMPRESSIONRATIO C,
       AVGCOMPRESSEDROWSIZE       D,
       PCTPAGESSAVED              E
FROM syscat.tables
WHERE tabname = 'MYEMP' and tabschema = 'ARFCHONG'
```

The output would be

```
A      B              C              D      E
------ -------------- -------------- ------ ------
    68  +1.00000E+002  +2.13341E+000     68     52

  1 record(s) selected.
```

Note the column PCTPAGESAVED with alias 'E' has a value of 52. This means that with row compression, this table can save 52% in pages used.

V9.5 For the third method, you can verify and retrieve the compression characteristics via the administrative table function ADMIN_GET_TAB_COMPRESS_INFO which was introduced with DB2 9.5. The syntax of this function is shown below.

```
>>-ADMIN_GET_TAB_COMPRESS_INFO—(--tabschema--,--tabname--,--exemode--)-><
```

exemode in the above syntax refers to the execution mode, which can be one of these two values:

- 'REPORT'—Reports compression information as of last generation. This is the default value.
- 'ESTIMATE'—Generates new compression information based on the current table.

For example, let's continue using the ARCHONG.MYEMP table which was compressed earlier. Let's say that the table data has evolved over an extended period of time, and thus you want to determine whether a new compression dictionary should be built in order to establish a more acceptable compression ratio. To do this, you need to compare the compression statistics based on the current table data to those when the dictionary was initially built. This can be achieved with these two statements.

```
SELECT PAGES_SAVED_PERCENT, BYTES_SAVED_PERCENT FROM
TABLE(SYSPROC.ADMIN_GET_TAB_COMPRESS_INFO('ARFCHONG', 'MYEMP', 'REPORT')) AS T

SELECT PCT_PAGES_SAVED, PCT_BYTES_SAVED FROM
TABLE(SYSPROC.ADMIN_GET_TAB_COMPRESS_INFO('ARFCHONG', 'MYEMP', 'ESTIMATE')) AS T
```

7.8.10.4 Automatic Dictionary Creation

In DB2 9.5, in order to alleviate the administrative aspects of managing data row compression, compression dictionaries are automatically created as part of table population operations, such as INSERT, IMPORT, and LOAD INSERT. When large amounts of data are added to a table such that a threshold is passed, (the default threshold is 1MB), automatic creation of the compression dictionary is triggered. This is known as Automatic Dictionary Creation (ADC).

In order for ADC to be applicable, compression has to be enabled for the table, and no compression dictionary should exist. For INSERT processing (SQL INSERT or IMPORT INSERT), the triggering of ADC is based on a default table size policy. For LOAD INSERT, ADC is triggered based on the amount of data processed by the LOAD utility. With the introduction of ADC, you no longer need to know whether a compression dictionary already exists or whether one needs to be created. Once a sufficient amount of data is available, ADC is set in motion to create a compression dictionary and insert it into the table. Subsequent data moved into the table will be compressed using the compression dictionary. In addition, the LOAD REPLACE utility now allows explicit compression dictionary management. You can keep the existing compression dictionary if one exists via the KEEPDICTIONARY option, or you can now create a new compression dictionary even if one already exists via the RESETDICTIONARY option.

7.8.11 Table Compression

You can compress tables to a certain extent by using the **VALUE COMPRESSION** clause of the **CREATE TABLE** statement. This clause tells DB2 that it can use a different internal format for the table rows so that they occupy less space. In a sense, this clause turns on compression for the table; however, you need to specify another clause, **COMPRESS SYSTEM DEFAULT,** for each column that you want to compress. Only the columns whose values are normally NULL or the system default value of 0 can be compressed. Also, the data type must not be DATE, TIME, or TIMESTAMP. If the data type is a varying-length string, this clause is ignored. Here's an example:

```
CREATE TABLE company (
       company_ID     INTEGER    NOT NULL PRIMARY KEY,
       name           CHAR(10),
       address        VARCHAR(30)         COMPRESS SYSTEM DEFAULT,
       no_employees   INTEGER    NOT NULL COMPRESS SYSTEM DEFAULT
      )
         VALUE COMPRESSION
```

The column *address* would be ignored since it's a VARCHAR column, and the column *no_employees* would be compressed. Table compression saves space especially for tables used in data warehousing applications where many rows contain NULLs or the system default value of 0. However, **UPDATE** operations may be impacted when changing to a different value than the default of 0 because the compressed value would first have to be expanded and then updated.

For an existing table containing data, you can enable table compression using the **ALTER TABLE** statement, as shown in this example.

```
ALTER TABLE city ACTIVATE VALUE COMPRESSION

ALTER TABLE city
      ALTER COLUMN population COMPRESS SYSTEM DEFAULT
```

In this example, we enable compression by using the first statement, and then we specify which column to compress by using the second statement. In addition, if the table *city* were populated, the **REORG** utility would have to be executed on the table for the compression to take effect on the existing rows. Chapter 13, Maintaining Data, discusses the **REORG** utility in more detail.

7.8.12 Materialized Query Tables and Summary Tables

Materialized query tables (MQTs) allow users to create tables with data based on the results of a query. The DB2 optimizer can later use these tables to determine whether a query can best be served by accessing an MQT instead of the base tables. Here is an example of an MQT:

```
CREATE SUMMARY TABLE my_summary
          AS  (SELECT  city_name, population
                 FROM country A, city B
                WHERE  A.country_id = B.country_no)
          DATA INITIALLY DEFERRED
          REFRESH DEFERRED
```

The **SUMMARY** keyword is optional. The **DATA INITIALLY DEFERRED** clause indicates that DB2 will not immediately populate the *my_summary* MQT table after creation, but will populate it following the **REFRESH TABLE** statement:

```
REFRESH TABLE my_summary
```

The **REFRESH DEFERRED** clause in the **CREATE SUMMARY TABLE** statement indicates that the data in the table is refreshed only when you explicitly issue a **REFRESH TABLE** statement. Alternatively, you can create the MQT with the **REFRESH IMMEDIATE** clause, which means DB2 immediately refreshes the data when the base tables are changed.

DB2 checks the registry variable *CURRENT REFRESH AGE* to determine whether or not the MQT contains up-to-date information. This registry can have a value from 0 up to 99999999999999 (9,999 years, 99 months, 99 days, 99 hours, 99 minutes, and 99 seconds), which indicates the maximum duration the DB2 optimizer can wait since the last **REFRESH TABLE** statement was issued on an MQT to consider MQT tables in its calculations. For example, if an MQT were refreshed today, and the *CURRENT REFRESH AGE* has a value of 5 days, then the DB2 optimizer can consider the MQT in its calculations for the next 5 days. If the value of this register is 0, only the tables created with the **REFRESH IMMEDIATE** clause can be used for optimization.

7.8.13 Temporary Tables

Temporary tables can be classified as system or user tables. DB2 manages system temporary tables in the system temporary table space. DB2 creates and drops these tables automatically. Since users don't have control over system temporary tables, we don't discuss them any further in this section.

You create user temporary tables inside a user temporary table space. For example, the following statement creates a user temporary table space called *usrtmp4k*.

```
CREATE USER TEMPORARY TABLESPACE usrtmp4k
       MANAGED BY SYSTEM USING ('C:\usrtmp')
```

User temporary tables, referred to as temporary tables from here on, store temporary data, that is, data that will be destroyed after a session or when a connection ends. Temporary tables are typically used in situations where you need to compute a large result set from an operation, and you need to store the result set temporarily to continue with further processing.

Though transaction logging is allowed with temporary tables, most users don't need to log temporary data. In fact, not having transaction logging for this type of table improves performance.

Temporary tables exist only for one connection; therefore, there are no concurrency or locking issues.

To create a temporary table, use the **DECLARE** statement. Here's an example.

```
DECLARE GLOBAL TEMPORARY TABLE temp_table1 (col1 int, col2 int)
  ON COMMIT PRESERVE ROWS
  NOT LOGGED
  IN  usrtmp4k
```

Table *temp_table1* is created in *usrtmp4k*, the user temporary table space we created earlier.

DB2 uses the schema *session* for all temporary tables regardless of the user ID connected to the database. After you create a temporary table, you can access it just like any regular table. The following statement inserts a row into table *temp_table1*.

```
INSERT INTO session.temp_table1 (1,2)
```

The following statement selects all the rows in table *temp_table1*:

```
SELECT * FROM session.temp_table1
```

You can drop and alter temporary tables, but you cannot create views or triggers against them. Indexes are allowed.

> **NOTE** When working with temporary tables, make sure to explicitly specify the schema *session*. If you work with objects without specifying the schema, DB2 defaults to the authorization ID or connection ID.

7.9 Indexes

Indexes are database objects that are built based on one or more columns of a table. They are used for two main reasons:

- To improve query performance. Indexes can be used to access the data faster using direct access to rows based on the index key values.
- To guarantee uniqueness when they are defined as unique indexes.

7.9.1 Working with Indexes

To create an index, use the **CREATE INDEX** statement. This statement requires at a minimum:

- The name of the index
- The name of the associated table
- The columns that make up the index (also known as index keys)

In addition, you can specify the following:

- Whether the index is unique (enforce uniqueness for the key values) or non-unique (allow duplicates)
- Which order DB2 should use to build and maintain the key values: ascending (**ASC,** the default) or descending (**DESC**) order
- Whether to create **INCLUDE** columns that are not part of the index key but are columns often retrieved by your queries

For example, let's consider the following statement.

```
CREATE UNIQUE INDEX company_ix
       ON company (company_ID ASC, name DESC)
       INCLUDE (no_employees)
```

This statement creates a unique index *company_ix*. This index is associated to the table *company* based on the columns *company_ID* in ascending order and *name* in descending order.

V9 Bi-directional scans are allowed by default in indexes, primary keys and unique keys, which means that an index can be traversed in both directions. Prior to V9, the clause **ALLOW REVERSE SCANS** had to be explicitly stated to allow for this to be in effect.

In addition, an **INCLUDE** column *no_employees* was added to the index definition. This column does not belong to the index key, that is, the index will not be built and maintained taking this column into consideration. Instead, an **INCLUDE** column is useful for performance reasons. Assuming the users of table *company* often retrieve the *no_employees* column, without the **INCLUDE** column, DB2 would first have to access the index page and then the data page. Rather than performing two access operations, why not add the desired column in the index?

Now let's consider another example that shows how an index looks. The following statement was used to create a table containing the sales records of a company.

> **NOTE** **INCLUDE** columns in an index can improve performance at the cost of having a larger index. The effect of adding an **INCLUDE** column versus including the column as part of the index key is the same; however, the maintenance cost of updating **INCLUDE** columns is less than that of updating key columns.

```
CREATE TABLE sales (
       sales_person     VARCHAR(30)  NOT NULL,
       region           CHAR(5)      NOT NULL,
       number_of_sales  INT          NOT NULL,
       year             INT
       )
```

Figure 7.19 illustrates the contents of this table.

sales_person	region	number_of_ sales	year
Mary	South	10	2007
John	North	9	2005
Sam	North	8	2005
Mary	East	12	2006
John	West	13	2006
Sam	South	12	2006
Mary	West	15	2007
Sam	South	15	2007
Mary	East	12	2007
John	West	12	2005
Sam	North	14	2006
John	South	21	2007

Figure 7.19 The sales table

Let's define an index on the *sales_person* column of the *sales* table using the following **CREATE INDEX** statement.

```
CREATE INDEX index1 ON sales (sales_person)
```

When DB2 builds the index *index1*, it creates pointers to the data pages of each record in the table. Each record is identified by a record ID (RID). An index on the *sales_person* column is shown in Figure 7.20.

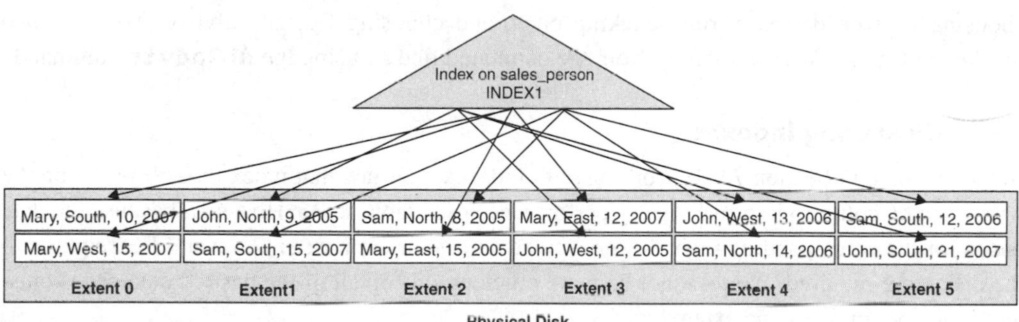

Figure 7.20 An index defined on the sales_person column

Rows are stored on physical disks, and disks are divided into extents. An extent contains a fixed number of pages. We will talk about pages and extents in detail in Chapter 8, The DB2 Storage Model. For now, we will treat extents as portions of the disk.

Let's say you issue the following query:

```
SELECT * FROM sales WHERE sales_person = 'Sam'
```

For this query, DB2 would use index *index1,* and as you can see from Figure 7.16, it would follow the pointers to extents 1, 2, 4, and 5; all of these extents have a data page with a record where the salesperson is Sam. An index gives you a direct access to the records you are looking for. Without an index, DB2 may scan all the data pages in all the extents for the table. This operation is known as a **table scan**, and for very large tables, it can be a very expensive operation.

Once an index has been created, it cannot be modified. To add or remove a key column from the index, you must drop and recreate the index. To drop an index, use the **DROP INDEX** statement. For example:

```
DROP INDEX index1
```

> **NOTE** An index automatically created by the database manager when a primary key or unique constraint was defined cannot be dropped with the **DROP INDEX** statement. To drop these indexes, use the **ALTER TABLE** statement with the **DROP PRIMARY KEY or DROP UNIQUE *constraint_name*** clauses, respectively.

Indexes can improve query performance considerably; however, the more indexes you define on a table, the more the cost incurred when updating the table because the indexes will also need to be updated. The larger you define the size of an index (based on the number of key columns and their columns sizes), the more the cost to update the index. Choose your indexes wisely.

The Index Advisor, part of the Design Advisor tool, can recommend indexes for you based on a specific query or a set of queries. You can launch the Design Advisor from the Control Center by choosing a given database, right-clicking on it, and choosing Design Advisor. You can also invoke the Design Advisor directly from the command line by using the **db2advis** command.

7.9.2 Clustering Indexes

In the example in Section 7.9.1, Working with Indexes, you saw that index *index1* (based on the *sales_person* column) improved query performance over table scans. However, because the data pages for the corresponding records were spread across different extents, several I/O requests to the disk were required. Would it not be more efficient to keep all of the desired data pages clustered together on the same extent?

You can achieve this by using a clustering index. A clustering index is created so that the index pages physically map to the data pages. That is, all the records that have the same index key are physically close together. Figure 7.21 illustrates how *index1* works when created as a clustering index using the **CLUSTER** clause as follows.

```
CREATE INDEX index1 ON sales (sales_person) CLUSTER
```

In the figure, when you issue this query:

```
SELECT * FROM sales WHERE sales_person = 'Sam'
```

DB2 would still use index *index1* but it requires less I/O access to the disk because the desired data pages are clustered together on extents 4 and 5.

> **NOTE** There can be only one clustering index per table.

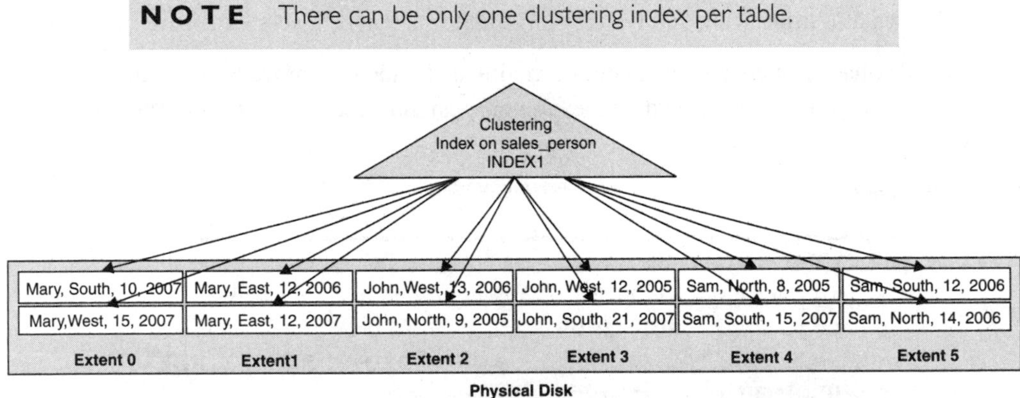

Figure 7.21 A clustering index on the sales_person column

> **NOTE** Indexes can be created on XML document elements, attributes or values. Chapter 10, Mastering the DB2 pureXML Support, discusses this in more detail.

7.10 Multidimensional Clustering Tables and Block Indexes

Multidimensional clustering (MDC), as its name implies, allows for clustering of the physical data pages in multiple dimensions. For example, using the *sales* table illustrated previously in Figure 7.19, you can cluster the data based on two dimensions: *sales_person* and *year* columns. This method of clustering has several benefits over clustering indexes.

- With MDC, the data pages are physically clustered by several dimensions simultaneously. With clustering indexes, only one cluster index is allowed per table; the other indexes in the table are unclustered.
- MDC guarantees clustering over time even though frequent **INSERT** operations are performed. Thus, less maintenance and overhead is required. With clustering indexes, this is not the case. As data pages are filled up, a clustered **INSERT** operation may encounter the situation where the row to insert does not fit into the right page to maintain the clustering of the data. In such cases, the row may end up on a page that is not close to the other related rows. Clustering indexes require an administrator to perform periodic table reorganizations to recluster the table and set up pages with additional free space to accommodate future clustered **INSERT** requests.
- MDC uses **block indexes,** indexes that point to an entire block of pages. These are smaller indexes than regular and clustering indexes, which point to a single record.

> **NOTE** MDC is primarily intended for data warehousing environments; however, it can also work in online transaction processing (OLTP) environments.

7.10.1 MDC Tables

Let's redefine our *sales* table as an MDC table, using dimensions *sales_person* and *year*.

```
CREATE TABLE sales (
       sales_person      VARCHAR(30)  NOT NULL,
       region            CHAR(5)      NOT NULL,
       number_of_sales   INT          NOT NULL,
       year              INT
       )
ORGANIZE BY DIMENSIONS (sales_person, year)
```

DB2 places records that have the same *sales_person* and *year* values in physical locations that are close together as they are inserted into the table. These locations are called blocks. A block can be treated as an extent. The size of an extent can be defined in the **CREATE TABLESPACE** statement. The minimum size for a block is two pages, like extents.

Figure 7.22 illustrates the contents of the *sales* table using the new MDC definition. For simplicity, in this example a block can hold only two records.

The figure shows this MDC table is physically organized such that records having the same *year* and *sales_person* values are grouped together into separate blocks. For example, all records in block 0 have *sales_person* = John and *year* = 2005. All records in block 4 have *sales_person* = Mary and *year* = 2007.

When a block is filled, DB2 will allocate a new block or reuse an old block for the new records inserted. In Figure 7.22, block 4 was filled, and thus block 5 had to be created.

Blocks that have the same dimension values are grouped into cells. Each cell represents a unique combination of the dimension values. If there are X different values for *sales_person*, and Y different values for *year*, there are X*Y number of cells. In Figure 7.22, you see the table *sales* has three values for dimension *sales_person*, namely, John, Mary, and Sam. It also has three values for dimension *year*, namely, 2005, 2006, and 2007. Therefore, nine cells are illustrated, one for each combination.

A cell contains only the necessary blocks to store the records that have the dimension values of that cell. If there are no records (as in the case of cell 4 in Figure 7.22), no blocks will be allocated.

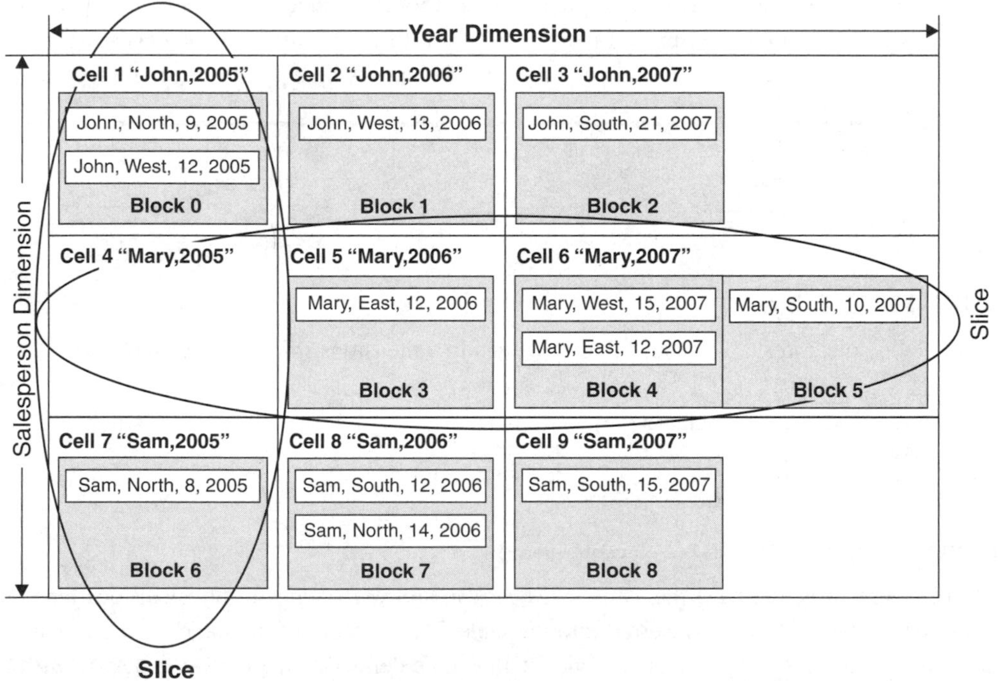

Figure 7.22 The sales table defined as an MDC table

In Figure 7.22, we also illustrate the concept of a slice. A slice consists of all the cells that belong to a specific value of a dimension. Figure 7.22 highlights two out of six slices, one for dimension *year* with a value of 2005 and the other for dimension *sales_person* with a value of Mary.

7.10.2 Block Indexes

Block indexes are pointers to a block, not a single record. A block index points to the beginning of each block, which has a unique block ID (BID). MDC tables use only block indexes. Figure 7.23 shows a comparison between a regular index and a block index.

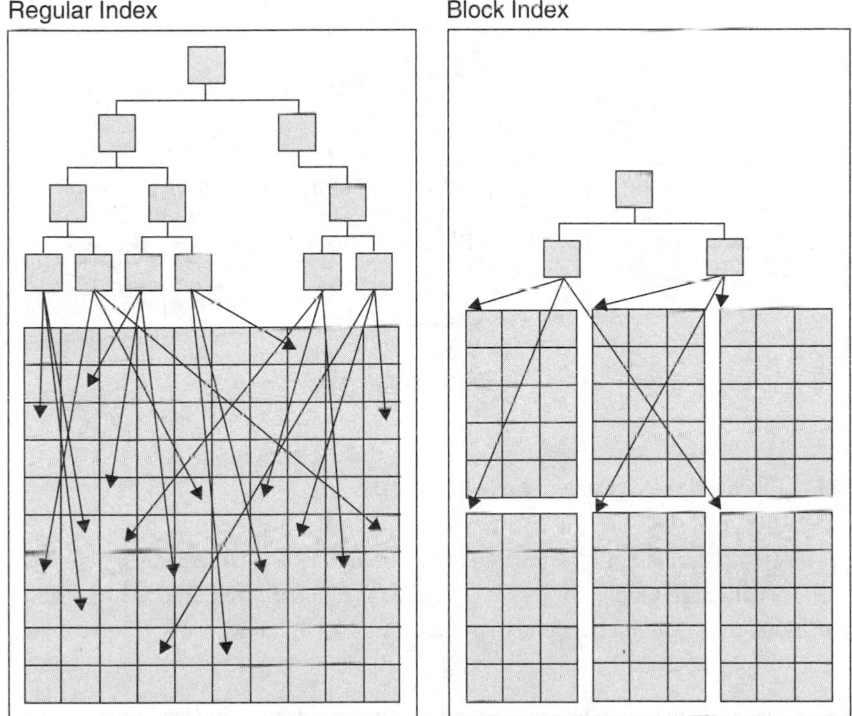

Figure 7.23 A regular (RID) index versus a block index

A block index has the following advantages over a regular index.

- Block indexes are significantly smaller than regular indexes because they point to a block rather than a record. The reduced size makes index scans much faster.
- Less maintenance overhead is associated with block indexes. They only need to be updated when adding the first record to a block and removing the last record from a block.
- Prefetching is done in blocks, thus the amount of I/O is reduced.

An MDC table defined with even a single dimension can benefit from block indexes and can be a viable alternative to a regular table using a clustering index.

When an MDC table is created, a dimension block index is created for each specified dimension. For our *sales* table, two dimension block indexes are created, one for the *sales_person* dimension and one for the *year* dimension, as illustrated in Figure 7.24.

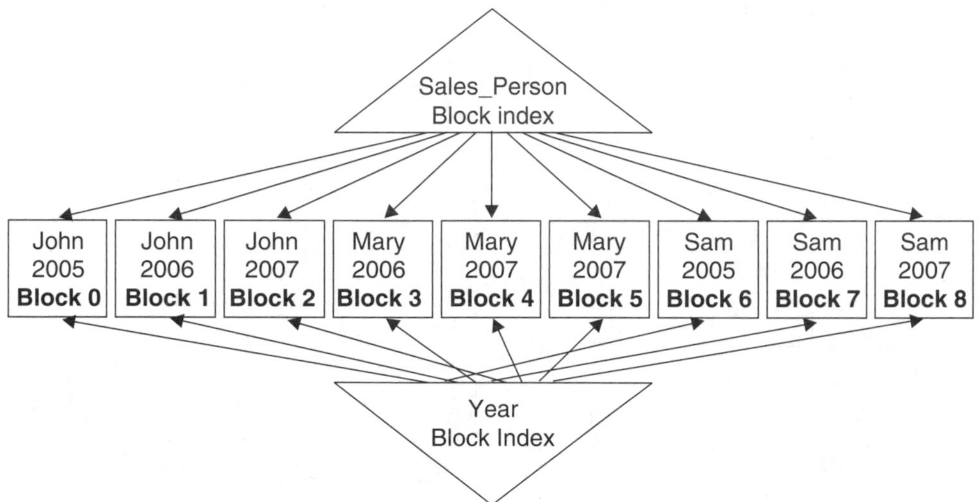

Figure 7.24 Block indexes for sales_person and year

A query requesting records that have *sales_person* = John can use the *sales_person* block index to quickly access all three blocks (blocks 0, 1, and 2) that satisfy this criteria. Another query can use the *year* block index to independently access all blocks that have *year* = 2007 (blocks 2, 4, 5, and 8).

In addition to the dimension block indexes, a **composite block index** is also created during MDC table creation. A composite block index contains all columns across all dimensions and is used to maintain the clustering of data over **INSERT** and **UPDATE** activity. If a single dimension block index already contains all the dimension key columns, a composite block index is not created.

7.10.3 The Block Map

A block map is an array containing an entry for each block of an MDC table. The entry indicates whether or not a block is in use. Each block has a unique identifier (BID) and also an **IN_USE** status bit. When a **DELETE** operation removes the last record in a block, DB2 frees the block by changing its **IN_USE** status bit and removing its BID from all block indexes. When new records are inserted and they can no longer fit into existing blocks, DB2 first scans for free blocks, looking for ones without the **IN_USE** bit set. If a free block is found, DB2 reuses it, updates its **IN_USE** bit, and adds its BID to block indexes.

Reusing free blocks greatly reduces fragmentation and in turn minimizes the need to reorganize the MDC table even though pages within the blocks may be fragmented.

7.10.4 Choosing Dimensions for MDC Tables

Choosing the right dimensions for an MDC table is crucial for obtaining the maximum advantages MDC can provide. You should consider the following.

- Choose columns with the lowest cardinality.

  One of the advantages of using block indexes is that they point to a block rather than a record; therefore, there are fewer pointers to traverse. If each block contains only one record, the block index essentially becomes a regular index. You should try to minimize the number of blocks by increasing the number of records they can contain. You can achieve this by choosing columns with the lowest cardinality, that is, the lowest number of distinct values. For example, a column like *region*, with possible values of North, South, East, and West, is a good choice. A column like *employee_id*, which uniquely identifies each employee of a company that has 100,000 employees, is definitely a bad choice.
- Choose the correct block size (extent size).

  MDC tables allocate space in blocks. The entire block is allocated even if only one record is inserted. For example, if your block can hold 100 pages, and on average only 10 records are inserted per block (assuming only one record can fit in a page), then 90% of the space is wasted. Thus, make sure you choose the correct block size.
- Choose the right number of dimensions.

  The higher the number of dimensions, the more possible combinations you can have, and therefore the higher the number of possible cells. If there are many cells, each cell will likely contain only a few records, and if that is the case, the block size needs to be set to a small number.

> **NOTE** The Design Advisor tool can make recommendations on what dimensions to choose for a given table.

7.11 Combining DPF, Table Partitioning, and MDC

For ultimate flexibility, and maximum performance, you can combine DPF, table partitioning and MDC. DPF will parallelize everything across all data partitions, while table partitioning and MDC will drastically reduce the I/O required to scan the data and build the result set.

The following statement illustrates how to combine the three types of partitioning.

```
CREATE TABLE carsales
 (custID INT, sales date, make char(30), model char(30), color char(30))
      DISTRIBUTE BY HASH (custID)
```

```
PARTITION BY RANGE (sales)
   STARTING FROM ('01/01/2006')
   ENDING ('12/31/2006')  EVERY 1 months)
ORGANIZE BY DIMENSIONS (make, model, color)
```

In the example above, consider a query looking only for a specific make, model and color of car, sold in a specific month, for example all red, Ford, Mustangs sold in February, 2006. In this case the query will run automatically, and in parallel, across all database partitions, but within each database partition only needs to access the data in the February table partition, and then only needs to access the data block(s) containing red, Ford, Mustangs. No data blocks for other makes, models, or colors of cars need be read.

Figure 7.25 below shows how these partitioning schemes work together to optimize data access.

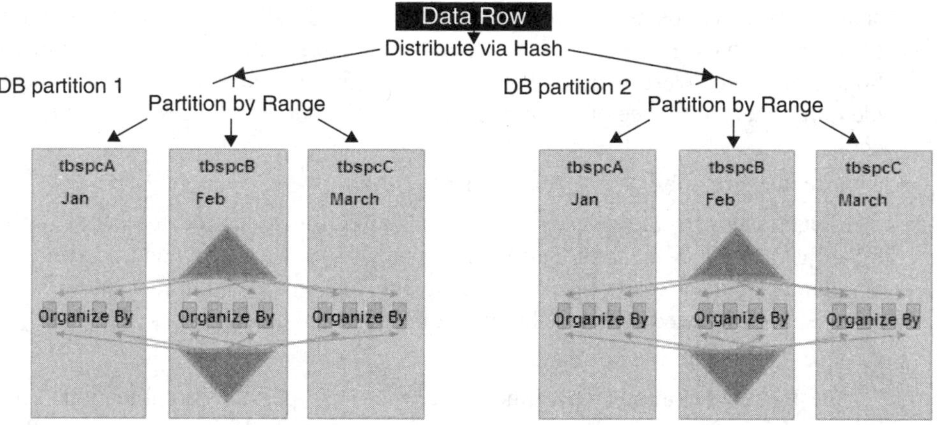

Figure 7.25 Combining DPF, table partitioning, and MDC

7.12 Views

A view is a virtual table derived from one or more tables or other views. It is virtual because it does not contain any data, but a definition of a table based on the result of a **SELECT** statement. Figure 7.26 illustrates view *view1* derived from table *table1*.

A view does not need to contain all the columns of the base table. Its columns do not need to have the same names as the base table, either. This is illustrated in Figure 7.26, where the view consists of only two columns, and the first column of the view has a different name than the corresponding column in the base table. This is particularly useful for hiding confidential information from users.

You can create a view using the **CREATE VIEW** statement. For example, to create the view *view1* shown in Figure 7.26, issue this statement.

View1

ID	Name
001	John
002	Mary
003	Sam
004	Julie

Table1

Employee_ID	Name	Salary	Deptno
001	John	60000	101
002	Mary	60000	101
003	Sam	65000	111
004	Julie	70000	112

Figure 7.26 A view derived from a table

```
CREATE VIEW view1 (id, name)
    AS SELECT employee_id, name FROM table1
```

To display the contents of *view1*, use the following statement.

```
SELECT * FROM view1
```

You can also create views based on multiple tables. Figure 7.27 shows a view created from two tables.

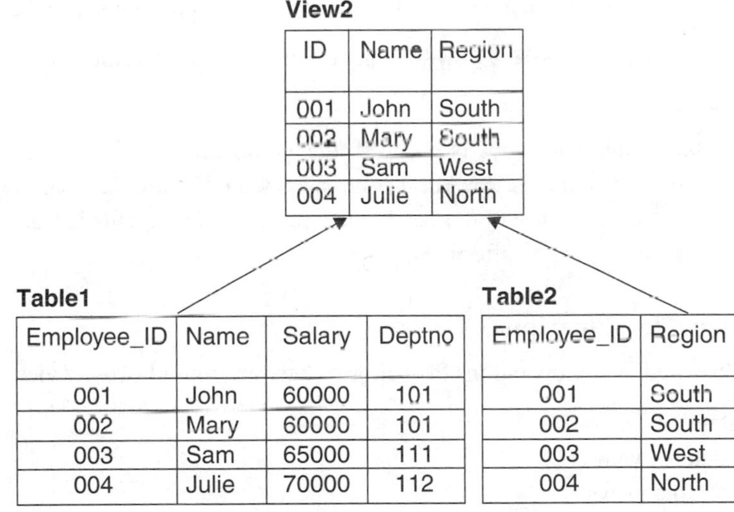

View2

ID	Name	Region
001	John	South
002	Mary	South
003	Sam	West
004	Julie	North

Table1

Employee_ID	Name	Salary	Deptno
001	John	60000	101
002	Mary	60000	101
003	Sam	65000	111
004	Julie	70000	112

Table2

Employee_ID	Region
001	South
002	South
003	West
004	North

Figure 7.27 A view derived from two tables

Here is the corresponding **CREATE VIEW** statement for Figure 7.27.

```
CREATE VIEW view2 (id, name, region)
AS SELECT table1.employee_id, table1.name, table2.region
    FROM table1,table2
   WHERE table1.employee_id = table2.employee_id
```

With this statement we have combined the information of *table1* and *table2* into *view2*, while limiting access to the salary information.

When you create a view, its definition is stored in the system catalog table SYSCAT.VIEWS. This table contains information about each view such as its name, schema, whether or not it is read-only, and the SQL statement used to create the view. For example, in Figure 7.28 we show part of the information for views *view1* and *view2* in SYSCAT.VIEWS.

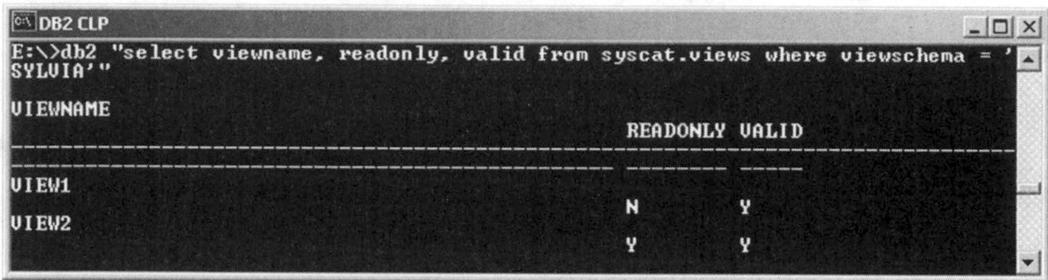

Figure 7.28 View definitions stored in the SYSCAT.VIEWS table

When a view is referenced in a query, DB2 reads and executes the view definition from the SYSCAT.VIEWS table, pulls the data from the base table, and presents it to the users.

To remove a view, use the **DROP VIEW** statement. For example, to remove the view *view1* use

```
DROP VIEW view1
```

If any of the base tables or views is dropped, the views that are dependent on them will be marked invalid and the value in the VALID column shown in Figure 7.28 will be set to X instead of Y. When this happens, you will not be able to use these views. This is true even if you have recreated the base table or view afterward.

7.12.1 View Classification

Views are classified by the operations they allow. There are four classes of views:

- Deleteable views
- Updatable views
- Insertable views
- Read-only views

In the SYSCAT.VIEWS catalog table, when the value of the column READ-ONLY is Y, this indicates that the view is read-only; otherwise, it is either a deleteable, updatable, or insertable view. Figure 7.29 shows *view2* is a read-only view, but *view1* is not.

Figure 7.29 illustrates the relationship between the different types of views. The views are discussed further in the next sections.

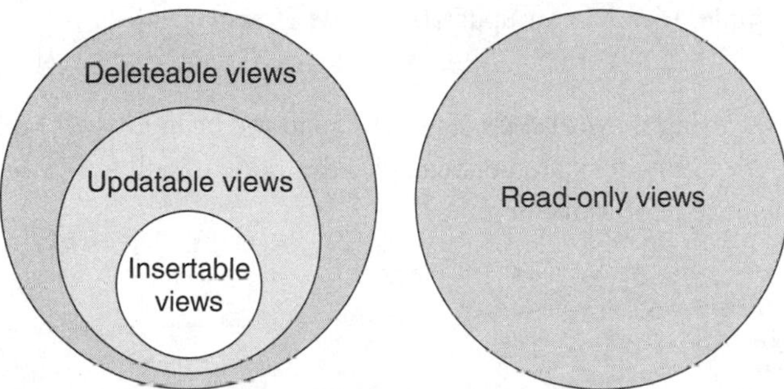

Figure 7.29 View classifications and relationships

7.12.1.1 Deleteable Views

A **deleteable view** allows you to execute the **DELETE** statement against it. All of the following must be true.

- Each **FROM** clause of the outer fullselect identifies only one base table (with no **OUTER** clause), a deleteable view (with no **OUTER** clause), a deleteable nested table expression, or a deleteable common table expression (cannot identify a NICKNAME used with federated support).
- The outer fullselect does not include a **VALUES** clause.
- The outer fullselect does not include a **GROUP BY** clause or a **HAVING** clause.
- The outer fullselect does not include column functions in the **SELECT** list.
- The outer fullselect does not include **SET** operations (**UNION, EXCEPT,** or **INTERSECT**), with the exception of **UNION ALL.**
- The base tables in the operands of a **UNION ALL** must not be the same table, and each operand must be deleteable.
- The select list of the outer fullselect does not include **DISTINCT.**

For further detail, refer to the *DB2 SQL Reference* manual. In our previous example, *view1* is a deleteable view. However, *view2* is not because it does not follow the first rule. In *view2*'s definition, the **SELECT** statement contains two base tables in the **FROM** clause.

7.12.1.2 Updatable Views

An updatable view is a special case of a deleteable view. A view is updatable when at least one of its columns is updatable. All of the following must be true.

- The view is deleteable.
- The column resolves to a column of a base table (not using a dereference operation), and the **READ ONLY** option is not specified.
- All the corresponding columns of the operands of a **UNION ALL** have exactly matching data types (including length or precision and scale) and matching default values if the fullselect of the view includes a **UNION ALL.**

In our previous example, *view1* is an updatable view. However, *view2* is not because it is not deleteable.

You can update *view1* using the **UPDATE** statement, and the changes will be applied to its base table. For example, the following statement changes the value of column *employee_id* to 100 for records with the *name* value of Mary in *table1*.

```
UPDATE view1 SET id='100' WHERE name = 'Mary';
```

7.12.1.3 Insertable Views

An insertable view allows you to execute the **INSERT** statement against it. A view is insertable when all of its columns are updatable. For example, *view1* fits this rule. The following statement will insert a row into *table1*, which is the base table of *view1*.

```
INSERT INTO view1 VALUES ('200', 'Ben');
```

Figure 7.30 displays the contents of *table1* after executing the **INSERT** statement on *view1*. Note that the *salary* and *deptno* columns for Ben contain NULL values because these two columns are not contained in *view1*.

```
DB2 CLP
E:\>db2 select * from table1

EMPLOYEE_ID NAME                                      SALARY
----------- ----------------------------------------- ------
100         Mary                                       60000
003         Sam                                        65000
004         Julie                                      70000
005         Steve                                          -
006         Clair                                          -
200         Ben                                            -

  6 record(s) selected.
```

Figure 7.30 Contents of table1 after inserting a row into view1

If *table1* were defined such that NULL values were not allowed in one of the *salary* or *deptno* columns, the **INSERT** statement would fail, and *view1* would not be an insertable view.

7.12.1.4 Read-Only Views

A read-only view is not deleteable. In Figure 7.27, shown earlier, *view2* is a read-only view. Its read-only property is also stored in the SYSCAT.VIEWS table, which is shown in Figure 7.28.

> **NOTE** Even if a view is read-only, **INSERT, UPDATE,** and **DELETE** operations are still possible by using an **INSTEAD OF** trigger. For more information, see Section 7.14, Triggers.

7.12.2 Using the WITH CHECK OPTION

You can define a view to selectively display a subset of rows of its base table by using the **WHERE** clause in the **CREATE VIEW** statement. To ensure that all the **INSERT** and **UPDATE** operations conform to the criteria specified in the **WHERE** clause of the view, you can use the **WITH CHECK OPTION** clause. For example, let's create the view *view3* derived from table *table1* (see Figure 7.22) as follows.

```
CREATE VIEW view3 (id, name,deptno)
       AS SELECT employee_id, name, deptno
            FROM table1
           WHERE deptno = 101
       WITH CHECK OPTION
```

If you issue a **SELECT * FROM view3** statement, you will obtain the following result.

```
ID  NAME                 DEPTNO
--- -------------------- -----------
001 John                         101
002 Mary                         101
```

Only two rows are retrieved because these are the only rows that satisfy the **WHERE** clause. What happens if you issue the following statement?

```
INSERT INTO view3 VALUES ('007','Shawn',201)
```

This statement fails because 201 does not conform to the criteria of the **WHERE** clause used in the **CREATE VIEW** definition, which is enforced because of **WITH CHECK OPTION.** If *view3* had not been defined with this clause, the **INSERT** statement would have succeeded.

7.12.3 Nested Views

Nested views are ones based on other views, for example:

```
CREATE VIEW view4
       AS SELECT * FROM view3
```

In this example, *view4* has been created based on *view3*, which was used in earlier examples. The **WITH CHECK OPTION** clause specified in *view3* is still in effect for *view4*; therefore, the following **INSERT** statement fails for the same reason it fails when inserting into *view3*.

```
INSERT INTO view4 VALUES ('007','Shawn',201)
```

When a view is defined with the **WITH CHECK OPTION** clause, the search condition is propagated through all the views that depend on it.

7.13 Packages

A **package** is a database object consisting of executable SQL, including the access path the DB2 optimizer will take to perform the SQL operation.

To explain how a package works, let's review Figure 7.31, which illustrates the preparation of a C application program with embedded SQL.

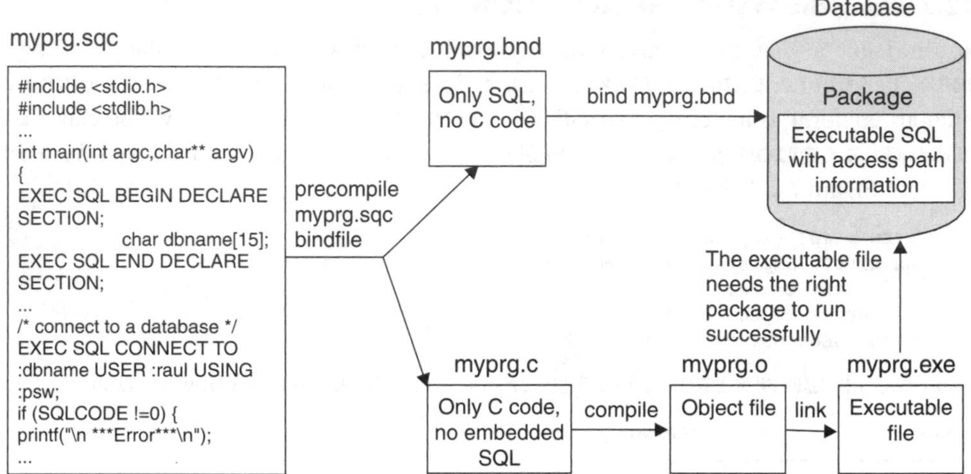

Figure 7.31 How a package is obtained

In the figure, the C program myprg.sqc contains embedded SQL. Issuing the **precompile** command (also known as the **prep** command) with the **bindfile** option generates two files, the myprg.bnd bind file containing only SQL information and the myprg.c file containing only C code.

The bind file will be compiled using the **bind** command to obtain a package that is stored in the database. To issue the **bind** command, a connection to the database must exist.

The myprg.c file will be compiled and linked like any regular C program. The resulting executable file myprg.exe has to be in sync with the package stored in the database to successfully execute.

7.14 Triggers

A trigger is a database object associated to a table or a view that contains some application logic, which is executed automatically upon an **INSERT, UPDATE,** or **DELETE** operation on the table or view. For example, you can use a trigger:

- To validate the input in an **INSERT** statement
- To compare the new value of a row being updated to an old value
- To insert logging information to another table for audit trail purposes when a row is deleted

Triggers can be classified as **BEFORE, AFTER,** or **INSTEAD OF** triggers.

BEFORE triggers are activated before any table data is affected by the triggering SQL statement. For example, if you are inserting a row into a table, the **BEFORE** trigger is activated first, before the **INSERT** is completed.

AFTER triggers are activated after the triggering SQL statement has successfully completed. For example, if a **DELETE** operation on table *A* completed successfully, an **AFTER** trigger could be invoked to perform an **INSERT** on table *B*.

INSTEAD OF triggers are used to perform **INSERT, UPDATE,** or **DELETE** operations on views where these operations are otherwise not allowed. Though read-only views cannot be modified, the underlying tables can; thus, by using an **INSTEAD OF** trigger, you can make sure that logic is triggered when the view is affected, but the action is performed on the tables themselves.

To create a trigger, use the **CREATE TRIGGER** statement as demonstrated here.

```
CREATE TRIGGER default_time
       NO CASCADE BEFORE INSERT ON schedule
       REFERENCING NEW AS n
       FOR EACH ROW
       MODE DB2SQL
       WHEN (n.start_time IS NULL)
             SET n.start_time = '12:00'
```

This example shows a **BEFORE** trigger that is activated when an **INSERT** statement is performed on table *schedule*. If the row being inserted has a value of NULL for column *start_time*, the code will assign a value of 12:00 and then continue with the **INSERT** operation. The **REFERENCING NEW** clause simply indicates a way to identify the new value of a column.

Here is another example, this time for an **AFTER** trigger.

```
CREATE TRIGGER audit_qty
       AFTER UPDATE OF quantity ON inventory
       REFERENCING OLD AS o NEW AS n
       FOR EACH ROW
       MODE DB2SQL
       INSERT INTO sold
          VALUES (n.product_ID, n.daysold, o.quantity - n.quantity)
```

This **AFTER** trigger can be used in the following scenario. Let's say you administer a convenience store. You would like to know how many items of each product are sold per day; therefore, you perform a count every night and update your database with the new count. With the help of this **AFTER** trigger, you can easily query the *sold* table, which is automatically updated when you update the column *quantity* of table *inventory*. The number of items sold for the day is obtained by substracting the old quantity value minus the new quantity value.

Next we show an example of an **INSTEAD OF** trigger.

```
CREATE TRIGGER update_view2
       INSTEAD OF UPDATE
       ON view2
       REFERENCING OLD AS o NEW AS n
       FOR EACH ROW
       MODE DB2SQL
       BEGIN ATOMIC
          UPDATE table2
```

```
    SET region = n.region
    WHERE region = o.region;
END
```

This example demonstrates how a read-only view can still be updated by using **INSTEAD OF** triggers. In the example, the trigger updates the *region* column of table *table2* when the view *view2* (a read-only view) is updated.

7.15 Stored Procedures

Stored procedures are programs whose executable binaries reside at the database server. They serve as subroutines to calling applications, and they normally wrap multiple SQL statements with flow logic. Figure 7.32 depicts a situation in which stored procedures are useful.

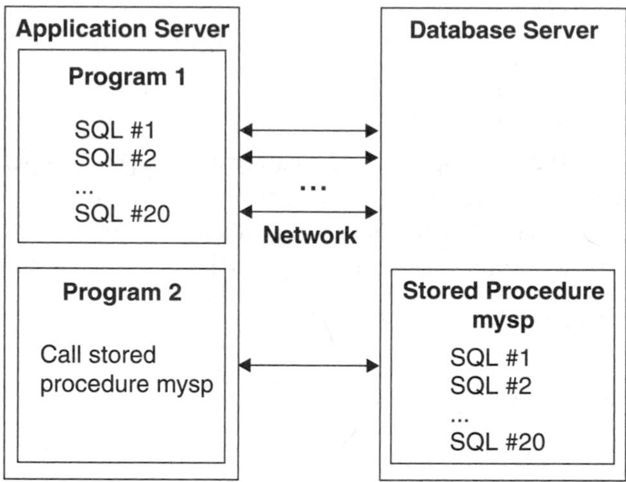

Figure 7.32 Reducing network traffic by using stored procedures

In the figure, *Program 1* and stored procedure *mysp* execute the same set of SQL statements. *Program 1*, however, does not perform as well as *Program 2* because of the extra overhead of sending each SQL statement through the network and waiting for its return. On the other hand, *Program 2* only needs to call the stored procedure *mysp* once and then wait for its return. Because *mysp* performs all the SQL statements within the database server, there is minimal network overhead.

Besides improving response time for applications running on a different server than the database server, stored procedures also provide a central location to store database application logic. This allows for a single place to maintain your code.

You can write stored procedures in several languages, such as C, Java, and SQL PL. SQL PL procedures are the most popular ones because they are easy to learn, provide very good performance, and are very compatible across the DB2 platforms, including DB2 for z/OS and DB2 for i5/OS.

To create a stored procedure in the database, use the **CREATE PROCEDURE** statement. Stored procedures that do not use the SQL PL language are known as external procedures. For this type of procedure, the **CREATE PROCEDURE** statement simply registers the procedure to DB2. The executable code is normally kept under the sqllib\function\routine subdirectory.

In the case of SQL PL stored procedures, the source code is included with the **CREATE PROCEDURE** statement. Moreover, executing the **CREATE PROCEDURE** statement will compile the code, bind the SQL statements, and create the necessary packages.

The following is an example of an SQL PL stored procedure created in the database *sample* (which is provided with DB2).

```
CREATE PROCEDURE CSMMGR.NEW_SALARY (IN  p_empno    CHAR(6),
                                    OUT p_empName VARCHAR(30) )
       LANGUAGE SQL
---------------------------------------------------------------------
-- SQL Stored Procedure used to update the salary of an employee
---------------------------------------------------------------------
P1: BEGIN
  DECLARE v_firstName VARCHAR(12);
  DECLARE v_lastName  VARCHAR(15);

  UPDATE employee SET salary = salary * 1.05
         WHERE empno = p_empno;

  SELECT lastname, firstnme INTO v_lastName, v_firstName
    FROM employee WHERE empno = p_empno;

  SET p_empName = v_lastName || ', ' || v_firstName;
END P1
```

> **NOTE** We recommend using the IBM Data Studio tool to develop, debug, and test your SQL PL stored procedures. From the tool you can also drop and alter procedures.

> **NOTE** We recommend the book *DB2 SQL PL: Essential Guide for DB2 UDB on Linux, UNIX, Windows, i5/OS, and z/OS* by Zamil Janmohamed, Clara Liu, Drew Bradstock, Raul Chong, Michael Gao, Fraser McArthur, and Paul Yip for a detailed explanation of the SQL PL language.

To change the properties of your stored procedures, you can use the **ALTER PROCEDURE** statement. To drop a stored procedure, use the **DROP PROCEDURE** statement.

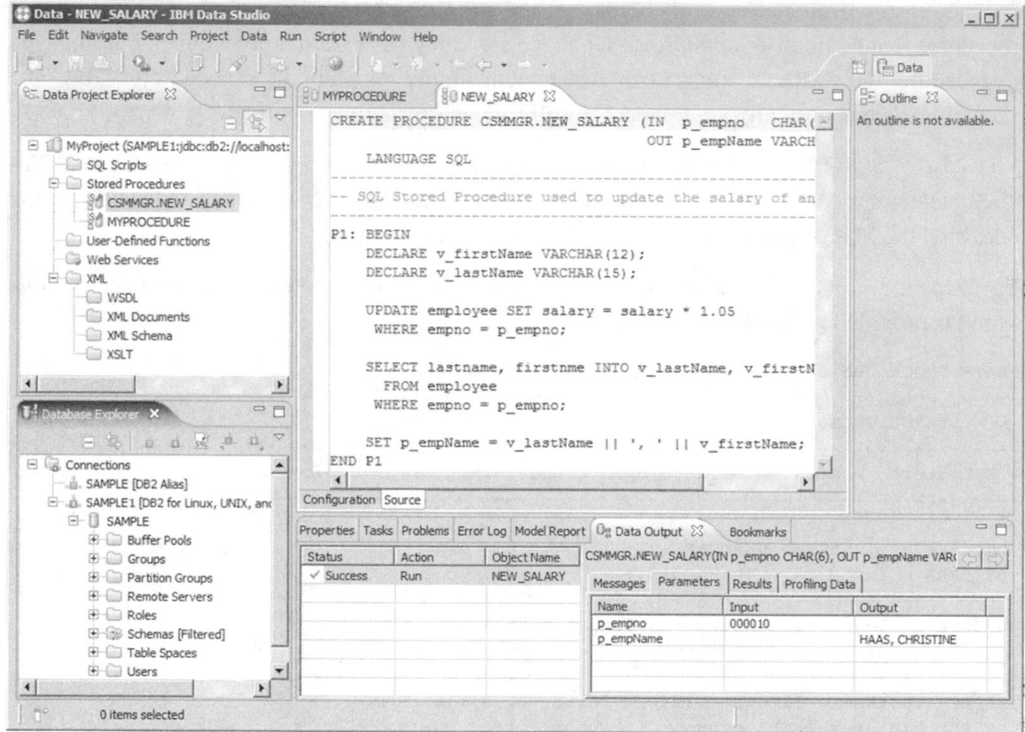

Figure 7.33 Using the IBM Data Server Developer Workbench to develop, test, and run the CSMMGR.NEW_SALARY stored procedure

Stored procedures are also classified as fenced or unfenced. A **fenced stored procedure** runs in a different address space than the DB2 engine. This guarantees that a failure from the procedure will not corrupt the DB2 engine itself. In Linux and UNIX, a fenced user needs to be created to work with fenced stored procedures. Refer to Chapter 5, Understanding the DB2 Environment, DB2 Instances, and Databases, for details.

An **unfenced stored procedure** runs in the same address space as the DB2 engine. In terms of performance, unfenced stored procedures run faster than fenced ones; however, there is a risk that unfenced procedures may corrupt DB2 information, so you should make sure to test these procedures thoroughly.

7.16 User-Defined Functions

DB2 provides built-in functions that allow you to manipulate your data within an SQL statement. For example, the **`year`** function can retrieve the year of a timestamp column, as shown here.

```
db2 select year(current timestamp) from sysibm.sysdummy1

1
-----------
       2005
```

In addition to built-in functions, DB2 allows you to create your own functions. These user-**defined functions** (UDFs) allow you to simplify database application development by moving some of the logic to the database. A UDF takes zero to many input parameters and returns a value, a row or a table. To create a UDF, use the **CREATE FUNCTION** statement.

UDFs can be classified as follows.

- **Sourced functions:** These functions are created on top of DB2 built-in functions. Here's an example.

```
CREATE FUNCTION trim (p_var1 VARCHAR(50))
      RETURNS VARCHAR(50)
      RETURN RTRIM(LTRIM(p_var1))
```

In this example, **RTRIM** is a DB2 built-in function that removes all the blanks at the end of a string. **LTRIM** is a DB2 built-in function that removes all the blanks at the beginning of a string. The UDF **trim** is created to remove blanks at the beginning and the end of a string by using these two built-in functions. To test the function, you can use the **VALUES** statement as follows:

```
VALUES (trim('       hello    ')
which returns:
1
--------------------------------------------------
hello
```

- **SQL functions:** These functions are written in SQL PL language. They can return a scalar value, a single row, or a table of data. The following code shows an example of an SQL UDF returning a scalar value: the rounded salary of an employee.

```
CREATE FUNCTION csmmgr.salary_round(p_empno CHAR(6))
    RETURNS INTEGER
    LANGUAGE SQL
F1: BEGIN ATOMIC
    DECLARE v_salary INTEGER;
    SET v_salary = (SELECT ceiling(salary) FROM employee
                    WHERE empno = p_empno);
    RETURN v_salary;
END
```

This function takes an employee number as input and returns the salary rounded to the highest integer value. SQL functions can be developed by using the IBM Data Studio, as illustrated in Figure 7.34.

- **External functions:** These functions are defined in the database with references to object code libraries that are written in C, Java, or OLE. Consider this example.

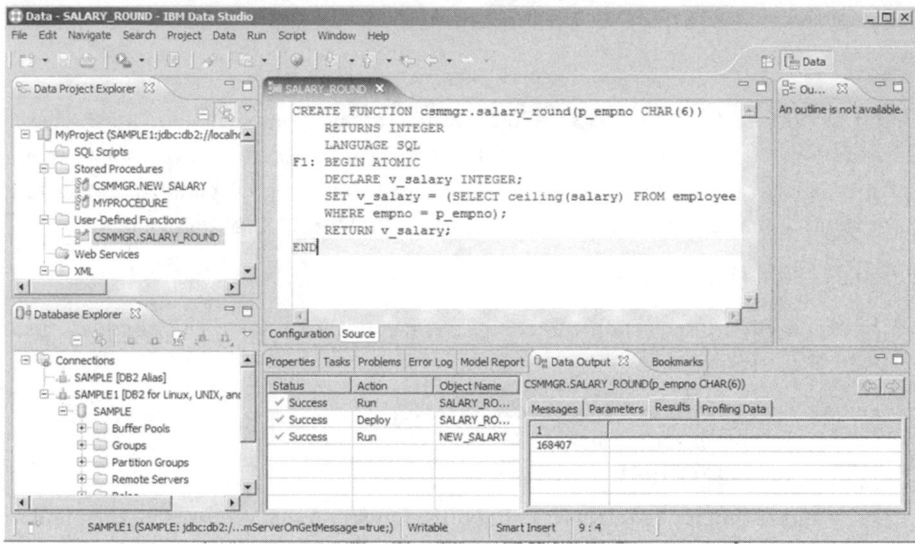

Figure 7.34 Using the IBM Data Studio tool to develop, test, and run the ***csmmgr.salary_round*** user-defined function

```
CREATE FUNCTION csmmgr.db2killapp(INT)
        RETURNS INT
        EXTERNAL NAME 'db2killapplib!db2killapp'
        LANGUAGE C
        PARAMETER STYLE SQL
        NOT FENCED
        RETURNS NULL ON NULL INPUT
        NOT DETERMINISTIC
        NO SQL
        NO EXTERNAL ACTION
```

This statement registers the UDF **csmmgr.db2killapp** to DB2. It is an external function written in C. The C executable code is stored in the *db2killapplib* library, which is stored under the sqllib\function subdirectory.

7.17 Sequences

A **sequence** is a database object that allows automatic generation of values. Unlike identity columns, this object does not depend on any table—the same sequence object can be used across the database.

To create a sequence, use the **CREATE SEQUENCE** statement as demonstrated here.

```
CREATE SEQUENCE myseq AS INTEGER
       START WITH 1 INCREMENT BY 1
       NO MAXVALUE
       NO CYCLE
       CACHE 5
```

This statement creates the sequence *myseq*, which is of type INTEGER. The sequence starts with a value of 1 and then increases by 1 each time it's invoked for the next value.

The **NO MAXVALUE** clause indicates there is no explicit maximum value in which the sequence will stop; therefore, it will be bound by the limit of the data type, in this case, INTEGER.

The **NO CYCLE** clause indicates the sequence will not start over from the beginning once the limit is reached.

CACHE 5 indicates five sequence numbers will be cached in memory, and the sixth number in the sequence would be stored in a catalog table. Sequence numbers are cached in memory for performance reasons; otherwise, DB2 needs to access the catalog tables constantly to retrieve the next value in line. What would happen if your computer crashed and the following numbers were in the cache: 5, 6, 7, 8, and 9? These numbers would be lost, and the next time DB2 needed to retrieve a number, it would obtain the number from the catalog tables. In this example, 10 is the next number to be generated. If you are using the sequence number to generate unique identifiers, which must be in sequence with no gaps allowed, this would not work for you. The solution would be to use the **NO CACHE** clause to guarantee sequentially generated numbers with no gaps, but you will pay a performance cost.

For the sequence value, you can use any exact numeric data type with a scale of zero, including SMALLINT, INTEGER, BIGINT, and DECIMAL. In addition, any user-defined distinct type based on these data types can hold sequence values.

> **NOTE** The options supported for sequence objects are the same as the ones for identity columns.

Table 7.6 shows other statements you can use with sequences.

Table 7.6 Other Statements Used with Sequences

Statement	Explanation
ALTER SEQUENCE	Alters the characteristics of a sequence, like the increment value
DROP SEQUENCE	Drops the sequence
NEXTVAL FOR ***sequence_name*** or **NEXT VALUE FOR** ***sequence_name***	Retrieves the next value generated in the sequence
PREVVAL FOR ***sequence_name*** or **PREVIOUS VALUE FOR** ***sequence_name***	Retrieves the previous value generated in the sequence

7.18 Case Study

1)

You have been given the task of creating several DB2 database objects for a proof-of-concept exercise on a single-partition environment. You start by creating the database *testdb* on your Windows server's E: drive as follows:

```
CREATE DATABASE testdb ON E:
```

This command takes a few minutes to complete as it creates several default database objects, including the default table spaces (SYSCATSPACE, TEMPSPACE1, and USERSPACE1) and the default buffer pool (IBMDEFAULTBP). Because this is just a test database, you decide to use the USERSPACE1 default table space for your user tables and the default buffer pool.

After the database is created, before you can create any object, you need to connect to the database; thus you perform this operation:

```
CONNECT TO testdb
```

Given that this is a single-partition environment, you don't bother about creating partition groups. Therefore, you start with the creation of your tables. The requirements for this proof-of-concept exercise indicate that you need to create a table for the departments in your organization. Every department must have a department ID, which must be unique within the organization. Every department must also have a name and a manager ID. Because all three of these columns are required, you need to define them as NOT NULL. To ensure that the department ID is unique, you have two options: create a unique index or define the column as the primary key for the table. You decide to create a primary key because you want to define relationships between the department ID in this table and other tables later.

Therefore, you create the table as follows.

```
CREATE TABLE dept (
       deptID     INT        NOT NULL PRIMARY KEY,
       deptname   CHAR(30)   NOT NULL,
       mngrID     INT        NOT NULL)
```

You also could have created the table in two steps as follows.

```
CREATE TABLE dept (
       deptID     INT        NOT NULL,
       deptname   CHAR(30)   NOT NULL,
       mngrID     INT        NOT NULL)

ALTER TABLE dept ADD PRIMARY KEY (deptID)
```

Next, because your applications tend to scan the table looking for department names on a regular basis, you create an index on the *deptname* column in the *dept* table as follows.

```
CREATE INDEX deptnmx ON dept (deptname)
```

Next, you create the table of employees for your organization. Every employee has an employee ID, first and last names, and a salary. In addition, every employee belongs to a department. You issue the following statement to create the *emp* table.

```
CREATE TABLE emp (
       empID    INT              NOT NULL PRIMARY KEY,
       fname    CHAR(30)         NOT NULL,
       lname    CHAR(30)         NOT NULL,
       deptID   INT              NOT NULL,
       salary   DECIMAL (12,2)
       )
```

Because your applications scan the table looking for employees' names on a regular basis, you also create an index on the first and last name columns in the table as follows.

```
CREATE INDEX empnmx ON emp (lname, fname)
```

The employee and department tables are related: the department table is the parent table, and the employee table is the dependent table; therefore, any department ID in the employee table must exist in the department table. To establish this relationship, you create a referential constraint as follows.

```
ALTER TABLE emp ADD FOREIGN KEY (deptID) REFERENCES dept
```

Alternatively, you could have set up the same referential constraint by using a unique constraint in the dept table instead of the primary key as follows.

```
CREATE TABLE dept (
       deptID     INT        NOT NULL,
       deptname   CHAR(30)   NOT NULL,
       mngrID     INT        NOT NULL
       )
ALTER TABLE dept ADD CONSTRAINT deptun UNIQUE (deptID)
ALTER TABLE emp  ADD FOREIGN KEY (deptID) REFERENCES dept (deptID)
```

This is important because you may want to have more than one referential constraint for the same base table, and this allows you to reference different keys in the parent table.

There is also a requirement to enforce a rule that no employee can have a salary greater than $100,000.00; therefore, you create a check constraint as follows.

```
ALTER TABLE emp
      ADD CONSTRAINT salary CHECK (salary <= 100000.00)
```

After the alter table successfully completes, you test the **CHECK** constraint with the following statement.

```
INSERT INTO emp VALUES (123, 'Sam ', 'Johnson ', 345, 100005)
```

This **INSERT** statement fails as expected with this message.

```
SQL0545N  The requested operation is not allowed because a row does not satisfy the
check constraint "MYSCHEMA.EMP.SALARY". SQLSTATE=23513
```

You know your applications already perform the salary check constraint before the data is entered into DB2, so you wonder if you can remove this constraint in DB2. However, when you ask your manager, he says the problem with that approach is that DB2 would not know that those rules exist and may therefore need to do extra checks that could cause inefficient access. To overcome this, you create informational constraints so that the DB2 optimizer knows about the rules when building the optimal access plan, but DB2 does not enforce the rules when the data is being manipulated. Therefore, you change the constraint you created earlier.

First you drop the constraint.

```
ALTER TABLE emp DROP CONSTRAINT salary
```

Then you recreate it again as follow:

```
ALTER TABLE emp ADD CONSTRAINT salary
      CHECK (salary < 100000.00)
      NOT ENFORCED ENABLE QUERY OPTIMIZATION
```

You save all of these commands in a script file. Next, because several developers in your company will use this *testdb* database to test different things, you decide to create the objects again, but this time using a different schema. Because you have SYSADM authority, you can issue the following commands.

```
CREATE SCHEMA developer1
SET CURRENT SCHEMA developer1
```

You then execute the script file, which creates all the objects again, but in a different schema.

And that's it for your proof-of-concept exercise!

2)

In this second case study assume that you are building a new table that will be quite large, and will likely contain a lot of repeated values. Start off by connecting to the sample database. Create a copy of the staff table as follows:

```
create table stf like staff
```

Enable compression for the table:

```
alter table stf compress yes
```

Next load a representative sample of the data into the table:

```
insert into stf select * from staff
```

Build the compression dictionary:

```
reorg table mytable resetdictionary
```

Load the table with "all" of the data by running the folllwing statement ten times:

```
insert into stf select * from staff
```

Create a table to store the car sales for the year 2006, and partition the table by month:

```
CREATE TABLE carsales(sale_date DATE,
                      make  char(30),
                      model char(30),
                      color char(30))
PARTITION BY RANGE(sale_date)
  ( STARTING '1/1/2006'
    ENDING '12/31/2006'
           EVERY 1 MONTH )
```

Create a table and add a new partition for January 2007:

```
CREATE TABLE jansales (sale_date DATE,
                       make  char(30),
                       model char(30),
                       color char(30))

ALTER TABLE carsales attach partition
      starting ('2007-01-01')
      ending ('2007-03-31')  FROM jansales
```

And that's it! This second case study showed you how to work with row compression and table partitioning.

7.19 Summary

This chapter discussed the concept of databases, database partitions, and the DB2 database objects. It explained how to work with various DB2 database objects such as partition groups, table spaces, buffer pools, tables, views, indexes, schemas, stored procedures, and so on. Some of these objects are further explained in Chapter 8, The DB2 Storage Model.

The chapter also discussed the DB2 data types (DB2 built-in and user-defined types), which are used as ways to define the columns of a table or as parameters to stored procedures and functions.

Table objects were discussed in detail because there are many topics associated with tables, such as constraints, referential integrity, the use of NULLs, identity columns, table compression, and row compression.

This chapter also described indexes and the different clauses of the **CREATE INDEX** statement such as **INCLUDE.** More complex subjects such as range partitioning, or multidimensional clustering (MDC) tables, were also discussed. MDC tables allow for greater flexibility to cluster your data by several dimensions.

Views and their classification (deleteable, updatable, insertable, and read-only) were also explored.

The chapter also introduced application-related objects such as packages, triggers, stored procedures, user-defined functions, and sequences. Although this is not a DB2 application development book, this chapter provided you with the foundation to understand these objects.

Referring to the figures presented in the chapter should help you remember all the concepts introduced.

7.20 Review Questions

1. Consider the following instructions/commands/statements:

```
Login to your Linux server as user JDOE
su db2inst1 (switch user to db2inst1)
CONNECT TO sample USER foo USING bar
SELECT * FROM t1
```

   Which table will you select data from?

   A. JDOE.t1
   B. db2inst1.t1
   C. foo.t1
   D. bar.t1

2. Which of the following is not created when you create a database?

   A. IBMDEFAULTBP
   B. IBMDEFAULTSPACE
   C. IBMDEFAULTGROUP
   D. SYSCATSPACE
   E. IBMTEMPGROUP

3. Which of the following objects will ensure rows are assigned a unique value across multiple tables?

   A. Identity column
   B. Unique index
   C. Sequence
   D. Row ID

4. Which of the following commands will delete all rows from the table *t1* without logging?

   A. Truncate table
   B. Delete * from t1 no log
   C. Alter table t1 activate not logged initially with truncate
   D. Alter table t1 activate not logged initially with empty table

5. To ensure that a column can contain only the values T or F, which option should you choose?

   A. Create a unique index on the column.
   B. Create a check constraint on the column.
   C. Specify the column as NOT NULL.
   D. Create a view on the table.

6. When deleting a row from a table that has a primary key defined, which of the following options on a foreign key clause will delete all rows with the same value in the foreign key table?
   A. Restrict
   B. Cascade
   C. Drop
   D. Set NULL
7. Which two of the following can be referenced by a foreign key constraint?
   A. Unique index
   B. Unique constraint
   C. Check constraint
   D. Primary key
   E. Identity column
8. Given the table created as follows:

```
CREATE TABLE product (
       productno   INTEGER GENERATED ALWAYS AS
                           IDENTITY (START WITH 0 INCREMENT BY 5),
       description VARCHAR(50) )
```

   And these statements:

```
INSERT INTO product VALUES (DEFAULT,'banana')
INSERT INTO product (description) VALUES ('apple')
INSERT INTO product VALUES (300,'pear');
```

   How many rows will be in the table?
   A. 0
   B. 1
   C. 2
   D. 3
9. Consider the following statement.

```
CREATE TABLE wqwq (c1 DECIMAL)
```

   What will the precision and scale be for column *c1*?
   A. Precision = 15, scale = 0
   B. Precision = 15, scale =15
   C. Precision = 5, scale = 0
   D. Precision = 5, scale = 10
10. Which of the following is not a supported type of trigger?
   A. **INBETWEEN**
   B. **AFTER**
   C. **INSTEAD OF**
   D. **BEFORE**

11. Which of the following does not belong to a database?
    A. Schema
    B. Logs
    C. Registry variables
    D. System catalogs
12. Consider the following statement.

    ```
    CREATE TABLE foo (c1 INT NOT NULL PRIMARY KEY, c2 INT)
    ```

    How many database objects are created?
    A. 1
    B. 2
    C. 3
    D. 4
13. Consider the following db2nodes.cfg file.

    ```
    0 mysrv1 0
    1 mysrv1 1
    2 mysrv2 0
    3 mysrv2 1
    ```

    How many servers are the partitions running on?
    A. 1
    B. 2
    C. 3
    D. 4
14. Which of the following options can be used to partition data across multiple servers?
    A. Organize by
    B. Partition by
    C. Spread by
    D. Distribute by
15. To create the table space *ts1* successfully in the database *sample*, place the following steps in the correct order.

    ```
    1. CREATE TABLESPACE ts1 PAGESIZE 16K BUFFERPOOL bp1
    2. CONNECT TO sample
    3. CREATE BUFFERPOOL bp1 SIZE 100000 PAGESIZE 16K
    ```

    A. 1, 2, 3
    B. 3, 2, 1
    C. 2, 1, 3
    D. 2, 3, 1
16. Which of the following objects' definitions can be altered by using the **ALTER** statement?
    A. Table
    B. View
    C. Index
    D. Schema

17. A package contains which of the following? (Choose all that apply.)
 A. Executable SQL statements
 B. The access path that the DB2 optimizer chooses to retrieve the data
 C. A collection of stored procedures and functions
 D. A list of bind files

18. Tables with the same name can be created within the same database by creating them in which of the following?
 A. Different partitions
 B. Different partition groups
 C. Different table spaces
 D. Different schemas

19. Which of the following can be used to obtain the next value of the sequence *seq1*? (Choose all that apply.)
 A. seq1.nextValue
 B. NEXTVAL FOR seq1
 C. NEXT VALUE FOR seq1
 D. seq1.next

20. Which of the following statements is true?
 A. A user temporary table space is created with the create temporary table statement.
 B. The creation of a user temporary table space will fail if no system temporary table space is available.
 C. A user temporary table is created in TEMPSPACE1.
 D. A user temporary table space is needed so that declared global temporary tables can be declared.

21. Which of the following commands or statements will enable compression for a table?
 A. REORG
 B. RUNSTATS
 C. INSPECT
 D. CREATE
 E. ALTER

22. Which of the following commands will remove an existing range from a table and create a new table with the data from that range?
 A. DETACH
 B. ALTER
 C. CREATE
 D. REORG

CHAPTER 8

The DB2 Storage Model

This chapter describes how DB2 stores its objects on disk and introduces the concepts of storage paths, table spaces, containers, pages, and extents. It discusses how you can create and modify these objects on your data server and database so that your system will perform as optimally as possible and so that you do not run out of space when working with the database.

In this chapter you will learn about:

- DB2's storage model
- Database creation and structure
- Storage paths
- Partition groups
- Table spaces
- Containers
- Extents
- Pages
- Buffer pools

8.1 THE DB2 STORAGE MODEL: THE BIG PICTURE

This section provides an overview of the DB2 storage model. In Figure 8.1 you can see the interaction between the different database objects as they relate to the DB2 storage model. This figure presents a combination of physical and logical views of the primary database objects.

Figure 8.1 illustrates a user retrieving some data from the table *t2*. From this user's perspective, the information he needs is stored in a table, and how and where it is stored on disk is irrelevant. When this user issues the SQL statement

```
SELECT ProdId FROM t2 WHERE ProdName = 'Plum'
```

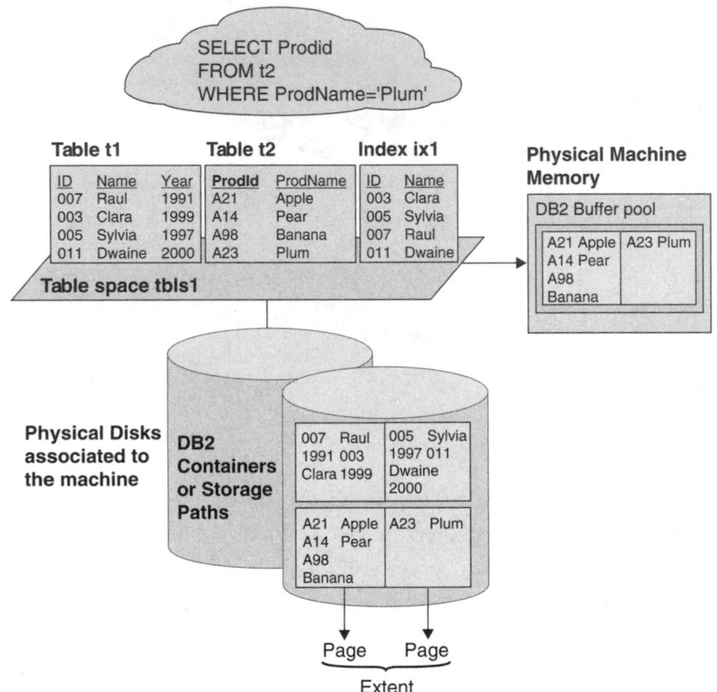

Figure 8.1 View of the DB2 database objects

the column from the specified rows in the table is retrieved by DB2 and returned to the user. Behind the scenes, DB2 may need to read a number of pages of data from one or more physical disks or from memory to provide this information to the user.

DB2 stores table and index data on **pages,** which are the smallest unit of storage in a DB2 database. Figure 8.1 shows four pages for the table *t2*, and each page contains one or more rows from the tables *t1* and *t2* and one or more key values for the index *ix1* on table *t1*.

When DB2 processes SQL statements, it must scan the data and/or index pages. DB2 only scans these pages in the buffer pools. If the page is already in a buffer pool due to the processing of other SQL statements, DB2 can process the request immediately. If the page is not in the buffer pool, DB2 must read it from disk and place it in the buffer pool, as shown on the right side of Figure 8.1.

Rather than reading one page at a time, DB2 can group pages together into **extents** and read multiple pages with each I/O request. In Figure 8.1 you can see that pages are grouped together in extents of two pages. You can also see that the tables and indexes are stored in table spaces. Table spaces are a logical layer between your logical tables and your physical resources such as memory and disks. **Containers** are the physical storage for the table spaces.

To optimize performance, DB2 lets you specify the table spaces in which you want your tables and indexes stored. You can also associate buffer pools with specific table spaces so that you can optimize the placement of tables and indexes within memory.

8.2 Databases: Logical and Physical Storage of Your Data

This section discusses how DB2 logically and physically creates databases.

8.2.1 Creating a Database

As mentioned in Chapter 2, DB2 at a Glance: The Big Picture, you use the **CREATE DATABASE** command to create a database. The basic syntax of the command is

```
CREATE DATABASE database name ON drive(s)/path(s)
```

The database name:

- Can be a maximum of eight characters long
- Cannot contain all numbers
- Cannot start with a number
- Cannot contain spaces
- Must be unique within the same DB2 instance

V9 In DB2 9, there is a new storage option called Automatic Storage. With automatic storage, you can have DB2 automatically manage the space in your table spaces. Automatic storage requires you to specify one or more **storage paths** when you create the database. A storage path is just a piece of storage, whether that be a drive, a path, or file system; you tell DB2 to use it to store the database. When you create table spaces later on for logically separating your database objects such as tables or indexes, the table spaces will automatically be striped across all of the storage paths assigned to the database. The storage path can be a drive, or a path on a file system. AUTOMATIC STORAGE is an option on the CREATE DATABASE command that allows you to specify whether the database will or will not use automatic storage. If this is set to YES, or AUTOMATIC STORAGE is not specified, then automatic storage would be turned on. If this is set to NO, automatic storage would not be enabled for the database.

If automatic storage is disabled when the database is created, DB2 creates the database on the drive or path specified by the DFTDBPATH Database Manager Configuration parameter. On Windows this will be a drive, and on Linux and UNIX this will be the path to a file system. By default, the DFTDBPATH configuration parameter specifies the drive where DB2 is installed on Windows. On Linux and UNIX it is the instance owner's home directory.

When you do specify the drives or the paths for the database or the database storage paths, keep the following in mind.

- They cannot be a LAN drive, an NFS mounted file system, or a General Parallel File System (GPFS).
- The file systems or drives cannot be a read-only device.
- The instance owner must have write permission on the drives or file systems.

There must be sufficient space available on the drives or file systems to hold at least the system catalogs. In addition, in the **CREATE DATABASE** command you can optionally specify:

- The database partition number for the catalog table space (for multipartition environments).
- The definition of the temporary and default user table spaces if you do not want to use the default locations..
- The code set and territory allow you to specify the character set that you want DB2 to use to store your data and return result sets.
- The collating sequence lets you specify how DB2 should sort data when you create indexes or use the **SORT** or **ORDER BY** clauses in SELECT statements.
- Whether you want to automatically configure the instance for the specified workload.

When a database is created using the default syntax of the **CREATE DATABASE** command, several objects are created.

- The partition group IBMCATGROUP, which contains
  - The table space SYSCATSPACE (catalog table space), which contains the DB2 catalog tables and views
- The partition group IBMTEMPGROUP, which contains
  - The table space TEMPSPACE1 (system temporary table space)
- The partition group IBMDEFAULTGROUP, which contains
  - The table space USERSPACE1 (user table space)
- The buffer pool IBMDEFAULTBP
- A database configuration file

Figure 8.2 below shows these default objects that are created when you create a database.

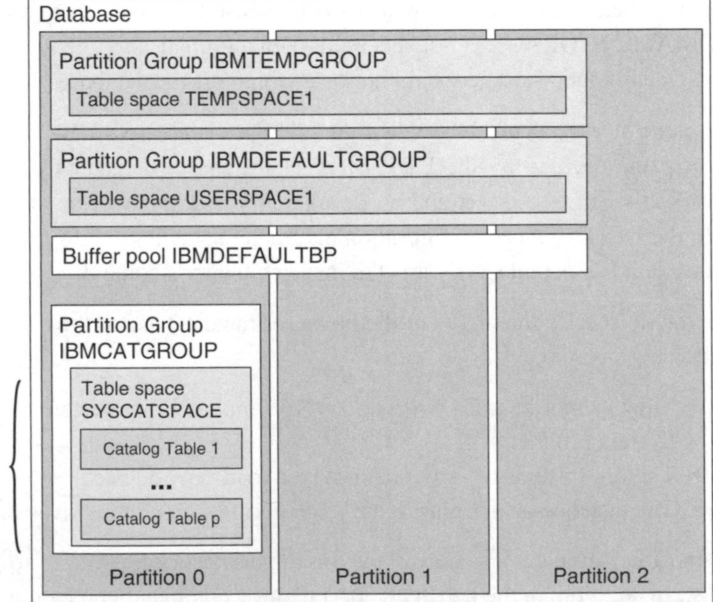

Figure 8.2 A database with default database objects created

When you create a database you can specify different locations and table space types for the temporary and user table spaces.

```
CREATE DATABASE sales ON /data1, /data2, /data3
    TEMPORARY TABLESPACE MANAGED BY SYSTEM USING ('/temp')
```

The example above lets the catalog and user table spaces default to the database storage paths (/data1, /data2, and /data3). You are also specifying to use an SMS table space for the temporary table space, and this temporary table space will use the file system /temp.

You can also create the user table space as a DMS table space as shown below:

```
create database sales on /data1, /data2, /data3
    temporary tablespace managed by system using ('/temp')
    user tablespace managed by database using (file '/userspc/cont1' 40M)
```

SMS and DMS table spaces are discussed in detail in Section 8.4, Table Spaces.

The **CREATE DATABASE** command in a multipartition environment automatically takes the contents of the database partition configuration file (db2nodes.cfg) into consideration. The partition where you issue the **CREATE DATABASE** command becomes the catalog partition for the database, and the system catalog tables for this database will be created on that partition. If you do not explicitly connect to a database partition or server, the database will be created with the system catalogs on the first partition in the db2nodes.cfg file.

8.2.2 Database Creation Examples

In this section we provide two examples of how to create a database. The first example is for a single-partition environment, and the second example is for a multipartition environment.

8.2.2.1 Creating a Database in a Single-Partition Environment

Let's say you are working on a single partition DB2 environment running on a Windows server and the DB2 instance name you created is *myinst*. If you issue the command:

```
CREATE DATABASE sales ON D:
```

several directories will be created on the D: drive as shown in Figure 8.3.

Continuing with the example, you can create two additional databases, *test* and *prod,* using the following commands:

```
CREATE DATABASE test ON D:
CREATE DATABASE prod ON D:
```

Figure 8.4 shows the additional directories these commands create.

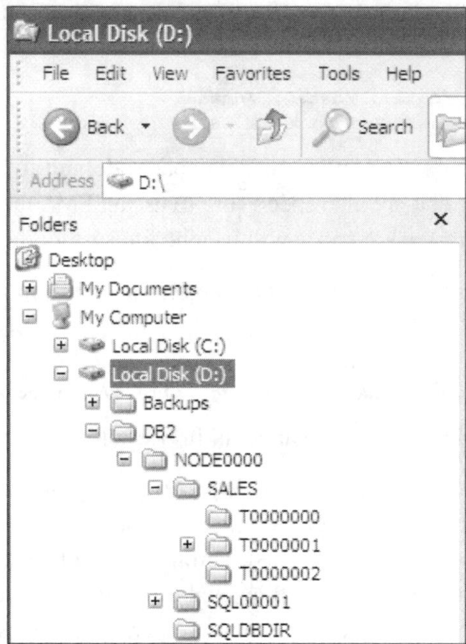

Figure 8.3 Directories created when a database is created

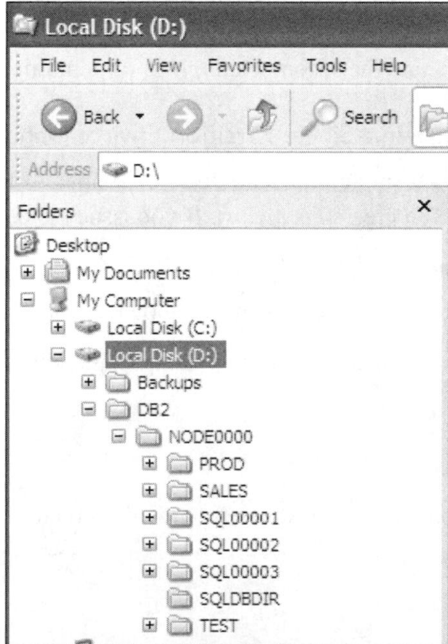

Figure 8.4 Directories created for the databases sales, test, and prod

Table 8.1 below shows the database name and the directories that DB2 created when the database was created.

Table 8.1 Directory Names for Databases

Database Name	Directory Names
Sales	SQL00001 and SALES
Test	SQL00002 and TEST
Prod	SQL00003 and PROD

Using the **`LIST DB DIRECTORY ON drive/path`** lets you map the SQL*xxxxx* directory to the actual database name, where *xxxxx* in SQL*xxxxx* represents digits. In this case if you issue the command:

```
LIST DB DIRECTORY ON D:
```

you would get the output shown in Figure 8.5.

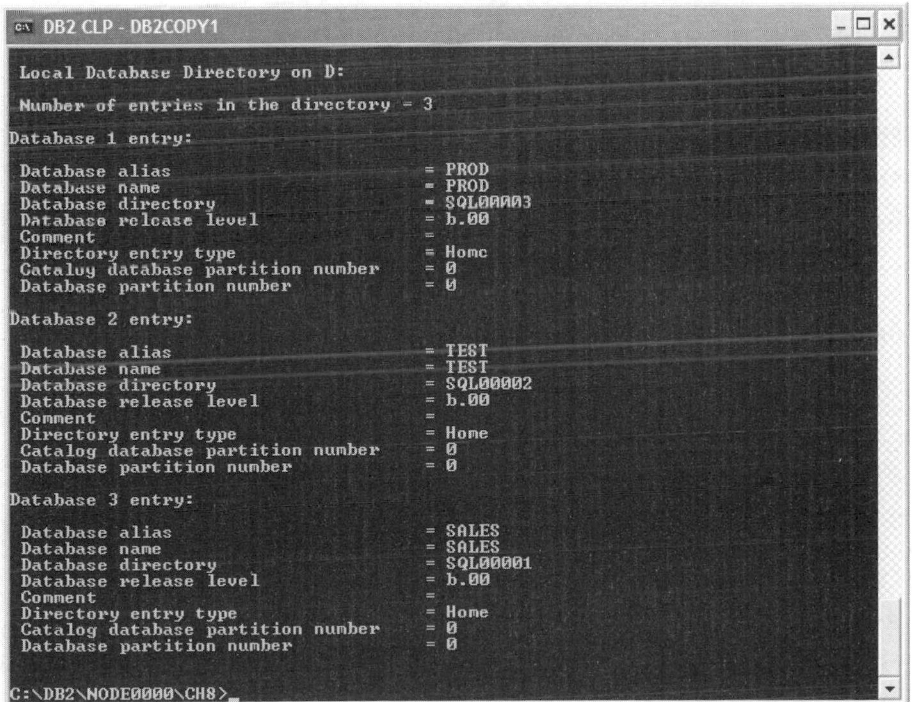

Figure 8.5 Output from the command list db directory on D:

If you drop one of these databases, its SQL*xxxxx* directory and the directory with the database's name will be deleted. If you create a new database at a later time, the SQLxxxxx directory name will be reused. For example, if you drop the database *test*, the directories SQL00002 and TEST will be deleted. If you then create a new database called *QA*, the directory SQL00002 will be recreated (along with the QA directory used for the QA database).

8.2.2.2 Creating a Database in a Multipartition Environment

Let's say you are working on a DB2 multipartition environment running on a single SMP Linux server with the following db2nodes.cfg file:

```
0    mylinx1    0
1    mylinx1    1
2    mylinx1    2
```

If you log in as the instance owner *db2inst1* on this server and create a database with this command:

```
create database sales on /data
```

the directory structure shown in Figure 8.6 will be created.

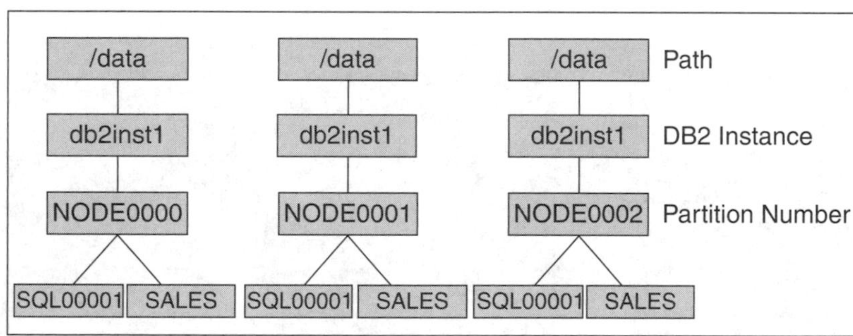

Figure 8.6 Directory structure for a three-partition database

As Figure 8.6 illustrates, there are three NODE*xxxx* directories, one for each database partition. The NODE*xxxx* directory is named based on the database instance's expanded four-digit partition number designated in the first column in the db2nodes.cfg file. Since the partition numbers used in the db2nodes.cfg file are 0, 1, and 2, these directories are NODE0000, NODE0001, and NODE0002.

8.2.3 Listing Databases

When you create a database with the **CREATE DATABASE** command, entries in the system database directory and local database directory are automatically entered. To list the system database directory contents, issue the command:

```
list db directory
```

To list the local database directory contents, issue the command:

```
list db directory on drive/path
```

Chapter 6, Configuring Client and Server Connectivity, discusses the system and local database directories in detail.

8.2.4 Dropping Databases

If you no longer need the data in a database, you can drop the database from the system using the **DROP DATABASE** command. This command removes the database from the local and system database directories and deletes all table spaces, tables, logs, and directory structure supporting the database. After dropping a database, the space is immediately available for reuse.

For example, if you run the command

```
DROP DATABASE sales
```

the entries in the system and local database directories for this database are removed, and the database's SQL*xxxxx* and SALES directories are also removed. The local database directory (SQLDBDIR) is *not* removed when you drop a database, because there may be other databases in the same path or on the same drive.

> **NOTE** The only supported way to remove a database is to use the DROP DATABASE command. Manually deleting the SQL*xxxxx* directory for the database is not supported, because it leaves the database entries in both the local and system database directories.

8.2.5 The Sample Database

DB2 contains a program to create a sample database that can be used for testing, or for learning purposes when you first start working with DB2. To create this database the instance must be started, and then you can run the command **db2sampl.** This creates a new database called *sample*, and the database will contain some tables with a few rows of data in each.

Use the command's **-k** option if you would like the *sample* database to be created with primary keys. In addition, you can specify the path if you would like this database to be created in a different location. For example, the command

```
db2sampl /data -k
```

creates the *sample* database in the */data* path, and the tables in the database have primary keys associated with them.

You can also create a sample database with XML data using the command:

```
db2sampl /data -xml
```

8.3 Database Partition Groups

In a multipartition environment, a database partition is an independent subset of a database that contains its own data, indexes, configuration files, and transaction logs. A partition group is a logical grouping of one or more database partitions that lets you control the placement of table spaces and buffer pools within the database partitions.

8.3.1 Database Partition Group Classifications

Partition groups are classified based on the number of database partitions they contain.

- Single-partition partition groups contain only one database partition.
- Multipartition partition groups contain more than one database partition.

Figure 8.7 shows four database partition groups.

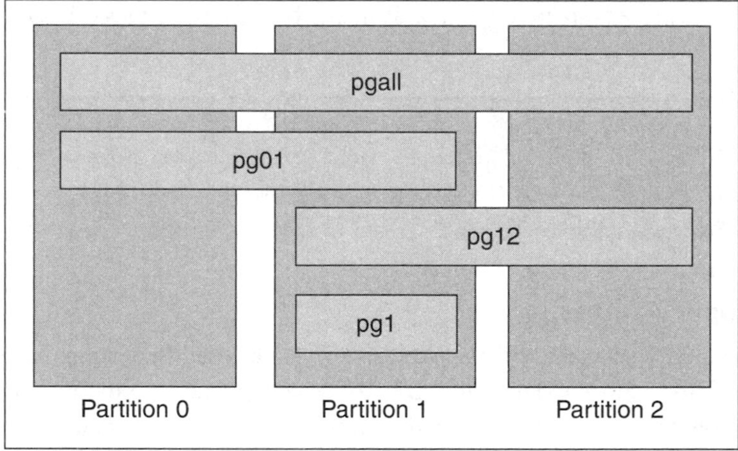

Figure 8.7 Database partition Groups

- *pgall* is a multipartition partition group that spreads across all the database partitions.
- *pg01* is a multipartition partition group that spreads across partitions 0 and 1.
- *pg12* is a multipartition partition group that spreads across partitions 1 and 2.
- *pg1* is a single-partition partition group that resides on database partition 1.

> **NOTE** Database partitions can belong to more than one partition group. For example, in Figure 8.7 database partition 1 is part of all four partition groups.

8.3.2 Default Partition Groups

When you create a database, DB2 automatically creates three partition groups within that database. Table 8.2 describes these partition groups.

Table 8.2 Default Partition Groups

Partition Group Name	Description
IBMDEFAULTGROUP	By default, this partition group contains all database partitions that you have defined in the db2nodes.cfg file. This is the default partition group for any tables that you create. You can alter this partition group to either add or remove database partitions. This partition group cannot be dropped.
IBMTEMPGROUP	This partition group spans all database partitions that you have defined in the db2nodes.cfg file. This partition group is where all temporary tables created during database processing are placed. This partition group cannot be dropped.
IBMCATGROUP	This partition group only exists on the database's catalog partition. The catalog partition is the partition where you executed the CREATE DATABASE command. This is the partition where the system catalog tables are created. This partition group cannot be altered to either add or remove database partitions. This partition group cannot be dropped.

> **NOTE** If you create a user temporary table space, you must create it in the IBMDEFAULTGROUP or any other partition group that you have created. DB2 does not allow you to create a user temporary table in the IBMTEMPGROUP. (User temporary table spaces are used for declared global temporary tables, which are described in Chapter 7, Working with Database Objects.)

8.3.3 Creating Database Partition Groups

You create a database partition group with the statement **`CREATE DATABASE PARTITION GROUP`**. The statement also records the partition group definition in the database system catalog tables.

The following commands show how to create the partition groups you see in Figure 8.8. For this example assume that the db2nodes.cfg file contains the following entries for the database partitions numbered 0, 1, and 2:

```
0      mylinx1     0
1      mylinx1     1
2      mylinx1     2
```

Starting with *pgall*, there are two ways to create this partition group using the **CREATE DATABASE PARTITION GROUP** statement:

```
create database partition group pgall on dbpartitionnums (0,1,2)
```

or

```
create database partition group pgall on all dbpartitionnums
```

You would create the other partition groups in Figure 8.8 as follows:

```
create database partition group pg01 on dbpartitionnums (0,1)
create database partition group pg12 on dbpartitionnums (1,2)
create database partition group pg1  on dbpartitionnums (1)
```

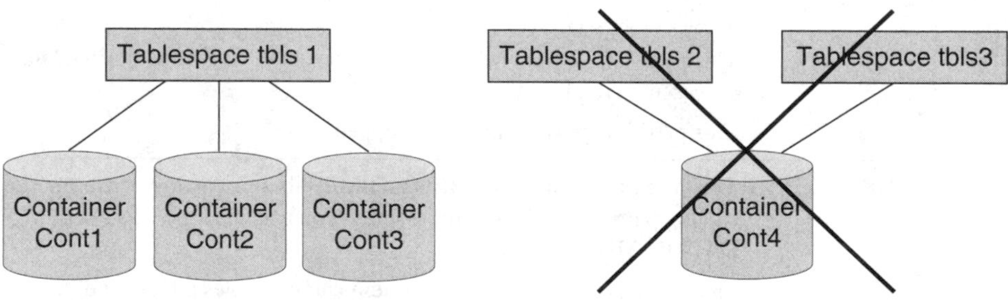

Figure 8.8 One table space can contain multiple containers, but a container can be associated to only one table space

8.3.4 Modifying a Database Partition Group

You can modify a partition group with the **ALTER DATABASE PARTITION GROUP** statement. This statement changes the definition of an existing partition group by adding or removing partitions. If you want to add a new partition to the partition group, that partition must already be defined in the db2nodes.cfg file.

Continuing with the example from the previous section, you can add a new database partition to the instance by editing the db2nodes.cfg file and adding a fourth line:

```
0      mylinx1          0
1      mylinx1          1
2      mylinx1          2
3      mylinx1          3
```

If you now want to alter the partition group *pgall* to add partition number 3, issue this statement:

```
alter database partition group pgall add dbpartitionnum (3)
```

Notice that partition number 1 in this example is one part of all partitions groups. To reduce some of the load on that partition you can remove it from partition group *pgall*, as follows:

```
alter database partition group pgall drop dbpartitionnum (1)
```

8.3.5 Listing Database Partition Groups

You can list all partition groups in your database with the **LIST DATABASE PARTITION GROUP** statement. This lists all the partition groups that are defined in the database, regardless of which database partition you are currently connected to. The following is the output of this statement for the example we have been discussing.

```
DATABASE PARTITION GROUP
---------------------------------------------
IBMCATGROUP
IBMDEFAULTGROUP
PGALL
PG01
PG1
PG12
```

To see which partitions are included in each partition group, use the **SHOW DETAIL** option with the **LIST DATABASE PARTITION GROUP** statement. This option provides additional information, including:

- PMAP_ID: The partitioning map associated with the partition group
- DATABASE PARTITION NUMBER: The database partition number as defined in the db2nodes.cfg file
- IN_USE: The status of the database partition

The output of this command contains three columns, and one row for each database partition that is part of the partition group, with the exception of the IBMTEMPGROUP.

```
DATABASE PARTITION  DATABASE PARTITION       IN_USE
GROUP               NUMBER

------------------  -------------------      -------
IBMCATGROUP         0                        Y
IBMDEFAULTGROUP     0                        Y
IBMDEFAULTGROUP     1                        Y
IBMDEFAULTGROUP     2                        Y
IBMDEFAULTGROUP     3                        Y
PGALL               0                        Y
PGALL               1                        Y
PGALL               2                        Y
PGALL               3                        Y
PG01                2                        Y
PG01                3                        Y
PG12                2                        Y
PG12                3                        Y
PG1                 2                        Y
```

> **NOTE** This information is also available in the system catalog view SYSCAT.NODEGROUPDEF.

8.3.6 Dropping a Database Partition Group

While a partition group does not consume any system resources, if a partition group is not being used, you can drop it using the **DROP DATABASE PARTITION GROUP** statement. If you wanted to drop the partition group *pg12* from our example, use the statement:

```
DROP DATABASE PARTITION GROUP pg12
```

8.4 Table Spaces

As discussed in Chapter 7, Working with Database Objects, a table space is a logical, not physical, database object. You cannot point to anything on disk or your server and say "This is my table space." In DB2, all tables and indexes must be created in table spaces. Therefore, it is important to understand how to create and change table spaces.

A table space is a collection of one or more underlying physical storage devices known as **containers.** This allows you complete control over the placement of the containers on the disks, devices, and file systems available on your server.

There are two types of table spaces depending on how the physical space is allocated: system managed space (SMS) and database managed space (DMS). SMS table spaces store data in operating system files, and space for tables is allocated on-demand. In DMS table spaces, the database manager controls the storage space. You provide a list of devices or files and their size to belong to a table space when the DMS table space is defined, and DB2 then allocates the defined amount of space.

Before we can continue discussing table spaces, it is important to explain how a table space's containers work and how data is striped across the containers in a table space, based on extents.

8.4.1 Containers

When you create a table space that is not using automatic storage, you define the container(s) for the table space to define the physical storage of the table space. How you define the container depends on the type of table space that you are creating. For SMS table spaces, a container can only be a directory. For DMS table spaces, a container can either be a file or a logical device or drive name.

When you create the table space, you have to define at least one container. A table space can have a number of containers associated with it, but once it has been defined, a container can belong to one and only one table space. Figure 8.8 illustrates this.

8.4.2 Storage Paths

If you create the database using automatic storage, then you will have specified at least one storage path for the database. You can create table spaces and they will automatically use the database's storage paths. If you created the database without automatic storage, or migrated the database from a previous version of DB2 that did not support automatic storage you can add table spaces which use automatic storage.

When you create tables and indexes in the table space, they will be striped across the storage paths, in the same manner as with containers. The major differences between storage paths and containers are:

- You do not specify the table space or storage type for storage paths.
- Storage paths can be used by multiple table spaces, or even databases.

8.4.3 Pages

DB2 stores table and index data on a **page**, which is the smallest unit of storage in a DB2 database. DB2 creates and manages the pages in the table space automatically, but you can control the page size for your table spaces. If you do not explicitly specify the page size when you create the table space, DB2 will use the default size of 4K. DB2 supports four different page sizes: 4K, 8K, 16K, and 32K.

It is important to note that a row within a table cannot span pages (i.e., the entire row must fit on a single page). The page size for the table must be large enough to hold all of the columns in the table. For example, if a table is created as follows:

```
CREATE TABLE mytable (lastname   CHAR(100),
                      firstname  CHAR(100),
                      address    CHAR(4000)
                     )
```

the total space required to store a row is the sum of the column sizes, and this exceeds the size of a 4K page. Therefore, this table must be created in a table space with a page size is of at least 8K.

Tables are described in detail in Chapter 7, Working with Database Objects.

> **NOTE** Once you have created a table space with a given page size, you cannot alter the page size. The only option is to drop and recreate the table space using a different page size.

8.4.4 Extents

An **extent** is a collection of consecutive pages in a table space. For performance reasons, DB2 reads and writes extents of pages rather than single pages to optimize I/O. An extent can only contain pages for one object. For example, DB2 will not allow one page within an extent to belong to table A and another one to index A or table B.

If you are familiar with RAID (redundant array of inexpensive disks) or striped file systems, you understand the concept of **striping—**where data is written to the various underlying disks in pieces. DB2 does the same basic operation within its table spaces. When you create a table space with more than one container, DB2 writes the data to the containers in a round-robin fashion. DB2 fills an extent in one container, then fills an extent in the next container, and so on until it has written an extent in all of the containers in the table space. DB2 will then fill the second extent in each of the containers, and so on.

For example, if you create a table space with four containers or four storage paths, and create a table in that table space, as you add data to the table, the data will be striped across the table space containers as follows: The first extent of pages for the table is placed in the first container or storage path (i.e., Container 0 or storage path A). Next, extent number one is written to Container 1 or storage path B, extent number two is written to Container 2 or storage path C, and extent number three is written to Container 3 or storage path D. At this point there is one extent in each of the four containers or storage paths, so DB2 will start striping the data back at the first container or storage path. Therefore, extent number four will be written to Container 0 or storage path A, extent number five will be written to Container 1 or storage path B, and so on as more data is added to the table. Figure 8.9 illustrates this.

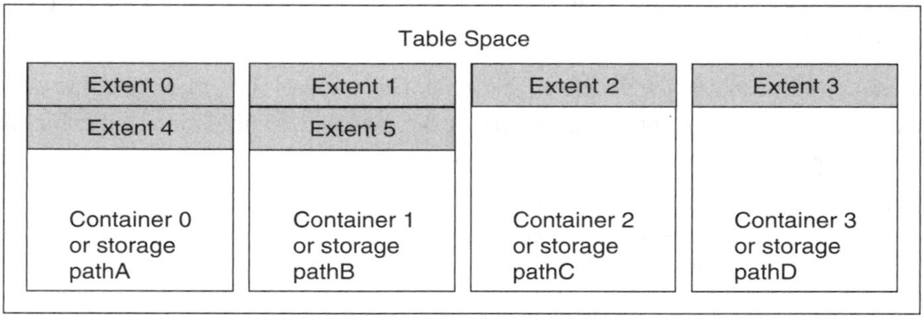

Figure 8.9 Table spaces, containers, storage paths, and extents

> **NOTE** The first extent (Extent 0) for each object can start in any of the defined containers. Not all objects start in the first Container 0 or storage path.

You can control the extent size when you create a table space with the **EXTENTSIZE** clause of the **CREATE TABLESPACE** statement. If you do not explicitly specify the extent size when you create the table space, DB2 uses the default extent size based on the database configuration parameter DFT_EXTENT_SZ.

> **NOTE** Once you have created a table space with a given extent size, you cannot alter the extent size. The only option is to drop and recreate the table space to use a different extent size.

8.4.5 Creating Table Spaces

You create a table space with the **CREATE TABLESPACE** statement. When you create a table space, you can define the following:

The type of data that the table space will store; includes one of these keywords:

- REGULAR
- LARGE
- SYSTEM TEMPORARY
- USER TEMPORARY

To indicate the type of table space based on how it is managed, you can use these keywords:

- AUTOMATIC STORAGE
- SYSTEM (for SMS table spaces)
- DATABASE (for DMS table spaces)

Although each of these options for specifying the table space storage type are mutually exclusive, if your table space is MANAGED BY AUTOMATIC STORAGE, DB2 will determine what type of storage to use under the covers.

- To indicate the page size to use for all tables and indexes in the table space use
  - PAGESIZE *integer* (4K is the default)
- To indicate the extent size for the table space use
  - EXTENTSIZE *number of pages* (the default is determined by the database configuration file parameter DFT_EXTENT_SZ)
- To indicate the name of the buffer pool associated to this table space use
  - BUFFERPOOL *buffer pool name*. This buffer pool must exist before you create the table and must have the same page size as you specify for the table space. By default, the table space will be associated with the IBMDEFAULTBP buffer pool. You can change this when you create the table space since the page size of the table space must match the page size of the associated buffer pool. If you are using a multipartitioned database, you also need to tell DB2 in which partition group to create the table space.

In addition, you can optionally specify the following table space characteristics:

- The I/O characteristics of the table spaces and its containers:
  - The overhead, which is the same as the seek time for the disks. The default is 12.67 milliseconds. If you have one kind of disk, then you can usually find this value on the disks or from the manufacturer. If you have a mixture of disks in the table space, you need to calculate the average overhead, seek time, and latency for the disks.

- The transfer rate for the disks specifies the amount of time (in milliseconds) required for the I/O subsystem to read one page from disk into memory. As with the overhead, if you are using a mixture of disk types, calculate an average value for this parameter.
  - The prefetch size for the table space, which indicates the number of pages fetched ahead of time to improve performance. DB2 uses the database configuration file parameter DFT_PREFTECH_SZ if you do not specify this value.
- The database partition group where the table space will be created

  Allow dropped table recovery. If you accidentally drop a table and this option is enabled, you can specify the RECOVER TABLE ON option when you are rolling forward so that the table will not be deleted and you can recover the table's data. This option can only be specified for a REGULAR table space.

LARGE table spaces use a larger RID size. This drastically increases the number of rows that can be on each page, since each RID points to a row. It also increases the maximum number of pages that can be in a table space, so you are no longer stuck with a maximum size of 64 GB f or table spaces (assuming a 4K page size).

8.4.6 Automatic Storage

When you create a database with automatic storage, the table spaces do not need to use the MANAGED BY clause. You can use the MANAGED BY clause, and explicitly define the table space container(s), or you can skip the MANAGED BY clause and the table space will use AUTOMATIC STORAGE. If you create a database without automatic storage, when you create a table space, you must specify the container(s) using either the MANAGED BY SYSTEM or MANAGED BY DATABASE clauses.

Automatic storage table spaces use space in the storage paths defined for the database or table space, and can grow automatically as the table space is getting close to being full. DB2 will choose whether to use SMS or DMS for the underlying storage for the table space depending on its data type (i.e. temp or regular).

When you create a table space using automatic storage, you define its initial size, maximum size, and growth increment. As the table space begins to fill up, DB2 will automatically grow the table space by the specified increment.

You can add storage paths to a table space defined to use automatic storage, and these "new" storage paths will be used for new data that is added.

8.4.6.1 Creating Automatic Storage Table Spaces

You then need to use the **CREATE TABLESPACE** statement, which will then use the database's storage paths for the table space by default. For example, the following statement creates a table space named *auto1* :

```
CREATE TABLESPACE auto1 managed by automatic storage
```

To create a table space using automatic storage that will start at 100MB, and grow up to a maximum of 750MB, in increments of 50MB, use the following statement:

```
CREATE TABLESPACE auto1 managed by automatic storage
    initialsize 100MB
    increasesize 50MB
    maxsize 750MB
```

8.4.7 SMS Table Spaces

System-managed space (SMS) table spaces use the file system manager to manage the tables and indexes stored within the table space. The only type of container allowed for an SMS table space is a directory, which you specify in the **CREATE TABLESPACE** statement. When you create tables and indexes, DB2 creates a file for every object within the table space inside the directory containers.

Since you cannot add containers to an SMS table space using the **ALTER TABLESPACE** statement, it is very important for you to create the table space on a file system with enough space.

> **NOTE** Although you cannot normally add containers to an SMS table space directly, you can increase the size of the existing file system containers using operating system commands. You can add a container to an SMS table space on a partition where there are no existing containers for the table space using the SYSTEM CONTAINER clause. You can also add a container indirectly, by backing up the database and performing a redirected restore.

8.4.7.1 Creating SMS Table Spaces

You need to use the **CREATE TABLESPACE** statement with the **MANAGED BY SYSTEM** clause to create an SMS table space. You also specify the path for the containers for the table space. For example, the following statement creates an SMS table space *space1* using one directory container *'c:\space1'*:

```
CREATE TABLESPACE space1
   MANAGED BY SYSTEM USING ('c:\space1')
```

Note that the path is included with the **USING** keyword. You can specify this as an absolute or a relative path. The above example uses an absolute path (it completely specifies the location of the directory). This is the same example, but using a relative path:

```
CREATE TABLESPACE space1
   MANAGED BY SYSTEM USING ('space1')
```

A relative path is relative to the database directory (i.e., the SQL*xxxxx* directory) where the database is created. The command above creates the following directory, assuming the active instance is *DB2*, and there is only one database created on the C: drive on Windows:

```
C:\DB2\NODE0000\SQL00001\SPACE1
```

For the instance *db2inst1* with only one database created on /mydata file system on Linux or UNIX, the above command creates the directory:

```
/mydata/db2inst1/NODE0000/SQL00001/space1
```

> **NOTE** If the directory you specify does not exist, DB2 will create it. If the directory does exist, it cannot contain any files or subdirectories

You can create more than one container for the table space as follows:

```
create tablespace space1
managed by system using
('c:\space1',  'd:\space1')
```

or

```
create tablespace space1
managed by system using
('/data1/space1', '/data1/space2')
```

> **NOTE** In the preceding examples you created the containers on the same drive and file system. In practice you should not do this, as this is not an optimal configuration and could cause I/O contention.

If you create a table in an SMS table space, DB2 creates a file for each object, and stores the information for the object in that file. Whenever you create a table it is assigned an object ID. Each of the files that are created for an object associated with the same table will be assigned the same object ID by DB2 if the table is in an SMS table space. This object ID is then used in the filename for the objects in an SMS table space.

If you look inside an SMS table space directory container, you will see several files named SQL*xxxxx*.DAT, SQL*xxxxx*.INX, SQL*xxxxx*.LB, SQL*xxxxx*.LBA, and SQL*xxxxx*.LF. If the table space has more than one container, DB2 creates the same files in all of the table space's containers.

8.4.8 DMS Table Spaces

DB2 manages the storage and retrieval of database objects from within the table space with **database-managed space** (**DMS**) table spaces. When you create a DMS table space, the only types of containers that can be specified are files, logical drives, or logical devices (raw devices). With DMS table spaces, when you create tables and indexes, DB2 places the pages for these objects in the table space and keeps track of where things are located.

8.4.8.1 Creating DMS Table Spaces

To create a DMS table space, specify **MANAGED BY DATABASE** with the **CREATE TABLESPACE** statement. You then specify the path for the containers as follows:

```
CREATE TABLESPACE tablespace_name
    MANAGED BY DATABASE USING
        (FILE 'file_name' size)
```

or

```
CREATE TABLESPACE tablespace_name
    MANAGED BY DATABASE USING
        (DEVICE 'device_name' size)
```

> **NOTE** If the file already exists, DB2 checks to make sure it is not used as a container for another tablespace. If it is not already used, DB2 will use the file. If you are using a logical drive or raw logical device, you must first create the drive or device using operating system commands.

8.4.8.1.1 Using Device Containers

If you are building a table space on Linux or UNIX and want to use a raw device, you must first create a logical volume using the tools provided by your operating system. If you are using Windows, create a disk partition that can be used as the container, but you need to remember *not* to format the partition to create a file system.

It is important to note the size of these volumes or partitions, so that when you are creating the table space and assigning the containers to the devices you do not waste space. Since the volume/partition cannot be used for any other purpose, you might as well size the container to use the whole device/partition.

> **NOTE** You can extend or resize the container later to use up the free space if you do leave some space on the logical volumes/disk partitions.

When you create the table space, you can specify the size of the containers in either:

- Number of pages based on the page size for the table space (the default)
- Actual size in KB, MB, or GB

The following are two examples of creating DMS table spaces with device containers.

```
CREATE TABLESPACE ts1 MANAGED BY DATABASE USING
    (DEVICE '/dev/rmydisk1' 20000)

CREATE TABLESPACE ts2 MANAGED BY DATABASE USING
    (DEVICE '\\.\G:' 200MB)
```

8.4.8.1.2 Using File Containers

As with SMS containers, when you specify the name for a file container, you can use either a relative filename or the absolute filename. When you issue the **CREATE TABLESPACE** statement you specify the container name(s) and size(s). If the file exists, DB2 checks to see if the file is the right size and if it is used for any other purpose. If it is the right size and not used for another purpose, DB2 will use the file. If it is not the right size but is not used for any other purpose, DB2 will either expand or shrink the file to make it the right size. If the file does not exist, DB2 will create it with the size that you specfied.

In the same manner as with device containers, you can specify the size of the containers in either:

- Number of pages based on the page size for the table space (the default)
- Actual size in KB, MB, or GB

The following are two examples of creating DMS table spaces with file containers.

```
CREATE TABLESPACE ts1 MANAGED BY DATABASE USING
      (file '/myfile1' 2GB)

CREATE TABLESPACE ts2 MANAGED BY DATABASE USING
      (file 'C:\dbfiles\ts2' 20000)
```

8.4.9 Table Space Considerations in a Multipartition Environment

When you create table spaces in a multipartition database, the table space may be defined on more than one database partition. As discussed earlier, the partition group that you specify for the table space determines on which partitions the table space will be created.

If you are using a cluster of Linux servers with one database partition on each server, and each server has its own set of physical disks, this process is a lot less confusing. However, given the popularity of SAN storage and Network Attached Storage (NAS), and the growing use of large UNIX-based SMP servers, there are many times when the database partitions will be sharing the same underlying disks. In this case it is very important that you take the time to determine a naming convention for your table spaces and containers.

You can specify the container name on each database partition using the ON DBPARTITION-NUM parameter:

```
CREATE TABLESPACE ts2 MANAGED BY DATABASE
      USING (FILE '/dbfiles/ts2c1p0' 2GB) ON DBPARTITIONNUM (0)
      USING (FILE '/dbfiles/ts2c1p1' 2GB) ON DBPARTITIONNUM (1)
      USING (FILE '/dbfiles/ts2c1p2' 2GB) ON DBPARTITIONNUM (2)
      USING (FILE '/dbfiles/ts2c1p3' 2GB) ON DBPARTITIONNUM (3)
```

DB2 also lets you use an expression to automatically add the partition number into the container name so the container names will be unique across the database. This partition expression can be used anywhere within the name of the container and must be preceded by a space. The expression is **$N** and can be used as follows:

```
CREATE TABLESPACE ts2 MANAGED BY DATABASE
      USING (FILE '/dbfiles/ts2c1p $N' 2GB)
```

For the same four-partition database as above, it would create the containers:

/dbfiles/ts2c1p0 on partition 0
/dbfiles/ts2c1p1 on partition 1
/dbfiles/ts2c1p2 on partition 2
/dbfiles/ts2c1p3 on partition 3

You can also use this expression if the table space has more than one container:

```
CREATE TABLESPACE ts2 MANAGED BY DATABASE
      USING (FILE '/dbfiles/ts2c1p $N' 2GB,
      FILE '/dbfiles/ts2c2p $N' 2GB)
```

For the same four-partition database as above, it would create the containers:

/dbfiles/ts2c1p0 on partition 0
/dbfiles/ts2c2p0 on partition 0
/dbfiles/ts2c1p1 on partition 1
/dbfiles/ts2c2p1 on partition 1
/dbfiles/ts2c1p2 on partition 2
/dbfiles/ts2c2p2 on partition 2
/dbfiles/ts2c1p3 on partition 3
/dbfiles/ts2c2p3 on partition 3

8.4.10 Listing Table Spaces

You can get a list of the table spaces in your database using the **LIST TABLESPACES** command. This command lists every table space in the database to which you are currently connected, as well as the following information:

- The table space ID (the internal ID that DB2 uses for the table space)
- The table space name
- The table space storage type (DMS or SMS)
- The table space contents (Regular (any data), Large, or Temporary)
- The state of the table space

Figure 8.10 shows an example of the output of the **LIST TABLESPACES** command.

You can get more information about table spaces by specifying the **SHOW DETAIL** option. This provides the following additional information about the table spaces:

- The total number of pages
- The number of usable pages
- The number of used pages
- The number of free pages
- The table space high-water mark (in pages)
- The page size (in bytes)

- The extent size (in bytes)
- The prefetch size (in pages)
- The number of containers in the table space

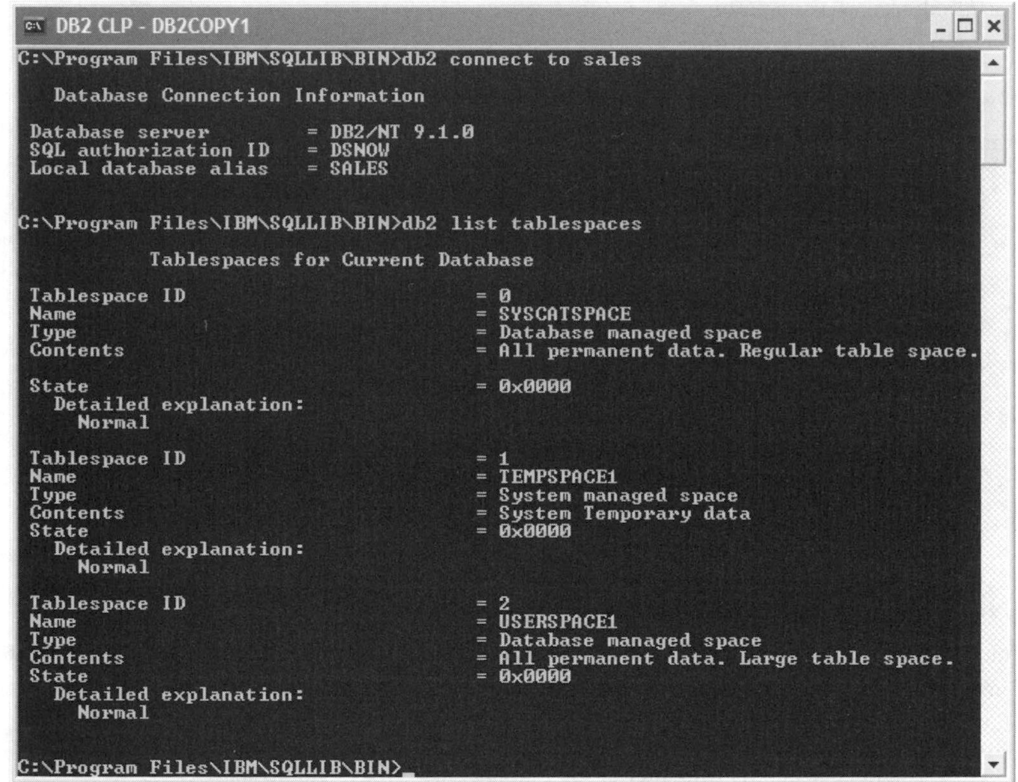

```
DB2 CLP - DB2COPY1
C:\Program Files\IBM\SQLLIB\BIN>db2 connect to sales

   Database Connection Information

 Database server        = DB2/NT 9.1.0
 SQL authorization ID   = DSNOW
 Local database alias   = SALES


C:\Program Files\IBM\SQLLIB\BIN>db2 list tablespaces

           Tablespaces for Current Database

 Tablespace ID                        = 0
 Name                                 = SYSCATSPACE
 Type                                 = Database managed space
 Contents                             = All permanent data. Regular table space.

 State                                = 0x0000
   Detailed explanation:
     Normal

 Tablespace ID                        = 1
 Name                                 = TEMPSPACE1
 Type                                 = System managed space
 Contents                             = System Temporary data
 State                                = 0x0000
   Detailed explanation:
     Normal

 Tablespace ID                        = 2
 Name                                 = USERSPACE1
 Type                                 = Database managed space
 Contents                             = All permanent data. Large table space.
 State                                = 0x0000
   Detailed explanation:
     Normal


C:\Program Files\IBM\SQLLIB\BIN>_
```

Figure 8.10 Output from the command LIST TABLESPACE

Figure 8.11 shows an example of the output of the **LIST TABLESPACES SHOW DETAIL** command.

You can use this extra information to examine how full your table spaces are, so you can take action if the table space is getting close to being full.

For SMS table spaces, the information does *not* indicate how full the table space is since DB2 is not aware of the size of the file system. The Health Monitor, which is part of DB2, does examine the file system size when it looks at the percentage of free space for the table space, so you can use this to make sure your table space is not filling the file system.

You can also get information about the table spaces in a database using the **GET SNAPSHOT FOR TABLESPACES** command. This command provides the following information:

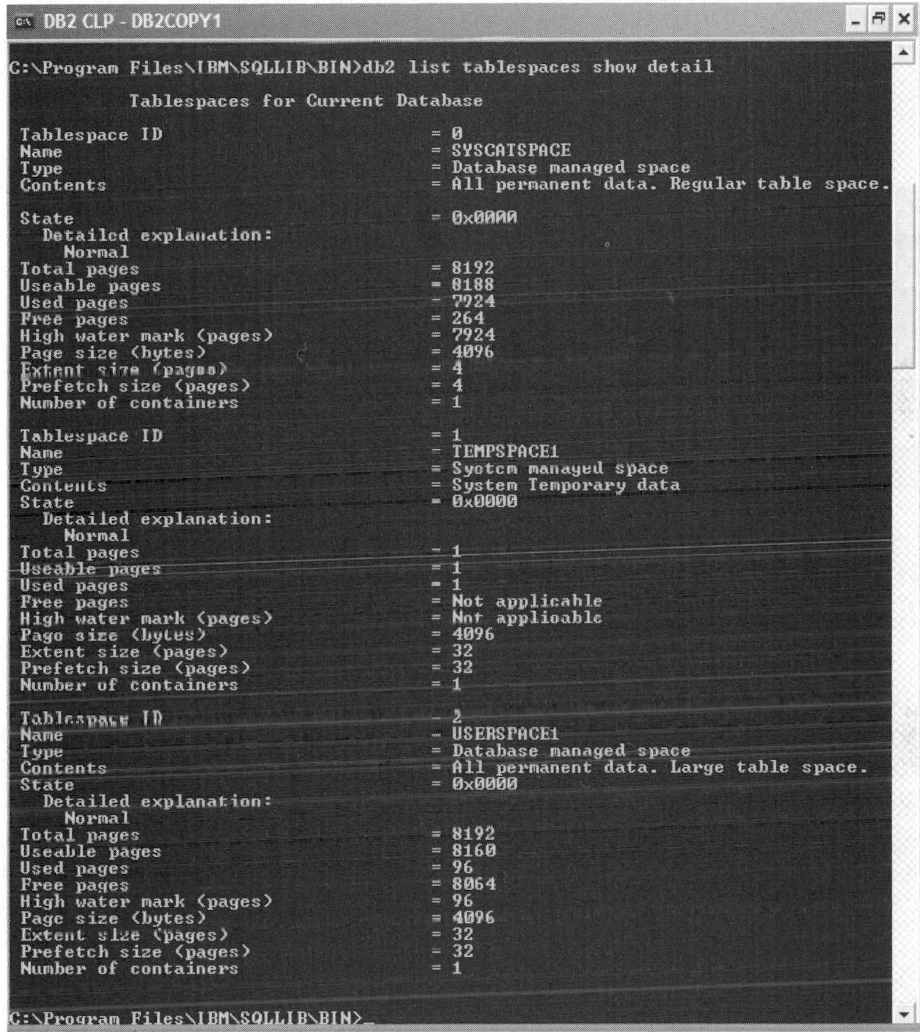

```
C:\Program Files\IBM\SQLLIB\BIN>db2 list tablespaces show detail

           Tablespaces for Current Database

 Tablespace ID                        = 0
 Name                                 = SYSCATSPACE
 Type                                 = Database managed space
 Contents                             = All permanent data. Regular table space.

 State                                = 0x0000
   Detailed explanation:
     Normal
 Total pages                          = 8192
 Useable pages                        = 8188
 Used pages                           = 7924
 Free pages                           = 264
 High water mark (pages)              = 7924
 Page size (bytes)                    = 4096
 Extent size (pages)                  = 4
 Prefetch size (pages)                = 4
 Number of containers                 = 1

 Tablespace ID                        = 1
 Name                                 = TEMPSPACE1
 Type                                 = System managed space
 Contents                             = System Temporary data
 State                                = 0x0000
   Detailed explanation:
     Normal
 Total pages                          = 1
 Useable pages                        = 1
 Used pages                           = 1
 Free pages                           = Not applicable
 High water mark (pages)              = Not applicable
 Page size (bytes)                    = 4096
 Extent size (pages)                  = 32
 Prefetch size (pages)                = 32
 Number of containers                 = 1

 Tablespace ID                        = 2
 Name                                 = USERSPACE1
 Type                                 = Database managed space
 Contents                             = All permanent data. Large table space.
 State                                = 0x0000
   Detailed explanation:
     Normal
 Total pages                          = 8192
 Useable pages                        = 8160
 Used pages                           = 96
 Free pages                           = 8064
 High water mark (pages)              = 96
 Page size (bytes)                    = 4096
 Extent size (pages)                  = 32
 Prefetch size (pages)                = 32
 Number of containers                 = 1

C:\Program Files\IBM\SQLLIB\BIN>_
```

Figure 8.11 Output from the LIST TABLESPACES SHOW DETAIL command

- The table space ID (the internal ID that DB2 uses for the table space)
- The table space storage type (DMS or SMS)
- The table space contents (Regular (any data), Large, or Temporary)
- The page size for the table space
- The extent size for the table space
- The prefetch size for the table space
- The current buffer pool used by the table space
- The buffer pool used at the next database startup
- The table space state
- The size (in pages)

- The number of usable pages
- The number of used pages
- The number of pending free pages
- The number of free pages
- The table space high-water mark
- An indicator of whether rebalancing is occurring (rebalancing is discussed in Section 8.4.11.2, Shrinking a DMS Table Space)
- The minimum point in time for roll forward recovery
- The number of table space quiescers
- The number of containers
- Container information such as
  - The container name
  - The container ID
  - The container type
  - The total pages in the container
  - The number of usable pages in the container
  - The stripe set number
  - An indicator of whether the container is accessible
- The table space map for DMS table spaces

Table 8.3 summarizes the differences between SMS and DMS table spaces. As you can see, both table space types stripe the extents in a round-robin fashion across the containers. SMS tables spaces grow and shrink as data is added or deleted, while DMS table spaces are preallocated when the table space is created. Both types of table spaces provide very good performance. If you use automatic storage, DB2 will automatically choose the optimal underlying table space for the type of data that will be stored in the table space. For example, for a temporary table space, it will choose SMS, but for a regular table space it will choose DMS.

Table 8.3 Comparing SMS and DMS Characteristics

Characteristic	SMS	DMS
Striping	Yes.	Yes.
Object management	Operating system using unique filenames.	DB2.
Space allocation	Grows/shrinks on demand.	Preallocated.
Ease of administration	Easy.	Average.
Performance	Very Good.	Best. Can achieve up to 5 to 10 percent advantage with raw containers. Index, LOBs, and data for a single table can be spread across table spaces.

8.4.11 Altering a Table Space

You can change the size and other characteristics—such as the prefetch size, overhead, and transfer rate—of all types of table spaces in your databases using the **ALTER TABLESPACE** statement. You can also change buffer pool assigments and bring an offline table space back online. The storage characteristics can only be modified for automatic storage and DMS table spaces.

To change the I/O characteristics for your table spaces, you must first connect to the database, then use the **ALTER TABLESPACE** statement with the parameter you want to change. For example:

```
ALTER TABLESPACE   ts2    PREFETCHSIZE 128
ALTER TABLESPACE   ts1    OVERHEAD      10
ALTER TABLESPACE   mytspc TRANSFERRATE 100
```

8.4.11.1 Enlarging a DMS Table Space

You can change the amount of space available for your automatic storage or DMS table spaces by adding either storage paths or containers to the table space. For DMS table spaces you can also increase the size of the current containers in the table space.

> **NOTE** You cannot add or remove containers from SMS table spaces. However, you can add a container to an SMS table space on a partition where there are no existing containers for the table space using the **SYSTEM CONTAINER** clause.

To add a new container to an existing table space, use the **ADD** clause of the **ALTER TABLESPACE** statement. If you do not explicitly tell DB2 at which offset within the table space (aka stripe set) to add the container, DB2 will choose the stripe set based on the size of the existing containers and the new container(s). When you run the **ALTER TABLESPACE** command, DB2 may need to asynchronously rebalance the data in the table space so that it is balanced across the containers evenly. If you do not want DB2 to rebalance the data, which can affect the performance of your system, you can specify the **BEGIN NEW STRIPE SET** clause; this essentially adds the container to the bottom of the table space for use as new data is added.

Let's look at some examples of adding containers to table spaces using the following table space:

```
CREATE TABLESPACE myts MANAGED BY DATABASE USING
    (FILE 'cont0' 50,
    FILE 'cont1' 50,
    FILE 'cont2' 30)
```

The following commands can be used to add containers to the table space:

```
ALTER TABLESPACE myts ADD (FILE 'cont3' 60)
ALTER TABLESPACE myts ADD (FILE 'cont3a' 60, FILE 'cont3b' 40)
ALTER TABLESPACE myts ADD (FILE 'cont3' 60) BEGIN NEW STRIPE SET
```

To make the containers in an existing table space bigger, you can either extend them or resize them. The **EXTEND** option increases the container by the size specified, while the **RESIZE** option changes the size of the container to the new size specified. You can also use the **RESIZE** option to increase or reduce the size of a container.

Let's continue using the same table space as given earlier to illustrate these options. To recap, the table space was created as follows:

```
CREATE TABLESPACE myts MANAGED BY DATABASE USING
    (FILE 'cont0' 50,
    FILE 'cont1' 50,
    FILE 'cont2' 30)
    EXTENTSIZE 10
```

To increase the size of the third container (that is, *cont2*) to 50 pages like the other containers, you can use either of the following commands:

```
ALTER TABLESPACE myts
    EXTEND (FILE 'cont2' 20)
```

or

```
ALTER TABLESPACE myts
    RESIZE (FILE 'cont2' 50)
```

To increase the size of all the containers to 100 pages, you can use one of the following commands:

```
ALTER TABLESPACE myts
    EXTEND (FILE 'cont0' 50,  FILE 'cont1' 50,  FILE 'cont2' 70)
```

or

```
ALTER TABLESPACE myts
    RESIZE  (FILE 'cont0' 100,
      FILE 'cont1' 100,
      FILE 'cont2' 100)
```

or

```
ALTER TABLESPACE myts
    RESIZE (all containers 100)
```

To increase the size of all of the containers by 100 pages, you can use the command:

```
ALTER TABLESPACE myts
    EXTEND  (all containers 100)
```

8.4.11.2 Shrinking a DMS Table Space

If you find that you have a lot of free space in some of your table spaces, you may be able to free up that space for use by other table spaces or for other file systems on your server. You can reduce the amount of space available for your DMS table spaces by dropping or removing containers from the table space or by reducing the size of the current containers in the table space.

DB2 will not let you remove a container or shrink the existing container(s) if the result would not leave enough space in the table space to hold all of the existing data stored in the table space. Also, DB2 will not **REORG** the data and indexes in the table space to remove free space from within the pages.

8.4.11.2.1 The Table Space High-Water Mark

You also cannot reduce the number of table space containers or shrink the existing containers so that the table space would be smaller than its high water mark. The **high-water mark** is the first page after the highest page number that has been allocated within the table space. This is not always going to be the same as the number of used pages, because you may have inserted some data, established the table space high-water mark, and then deleted some data. The table space will then show these pages where the data was deleted are available for use, but the high-water mark will not be moved down. Figure 8.12 illustrates the concept of the table space high-water mark. In the figure, consider the following:

- The table space has 1,000 usable pages and its extent size is 100. Therefore, there will be ten extents in the tablespace.
- By default, Extents 0, 1, and 2 will be used for the table space overhead.
- If you create a table named *org*, Extent 3 will be allocated for its object map, and Extent 4 will be allocated for its table object.

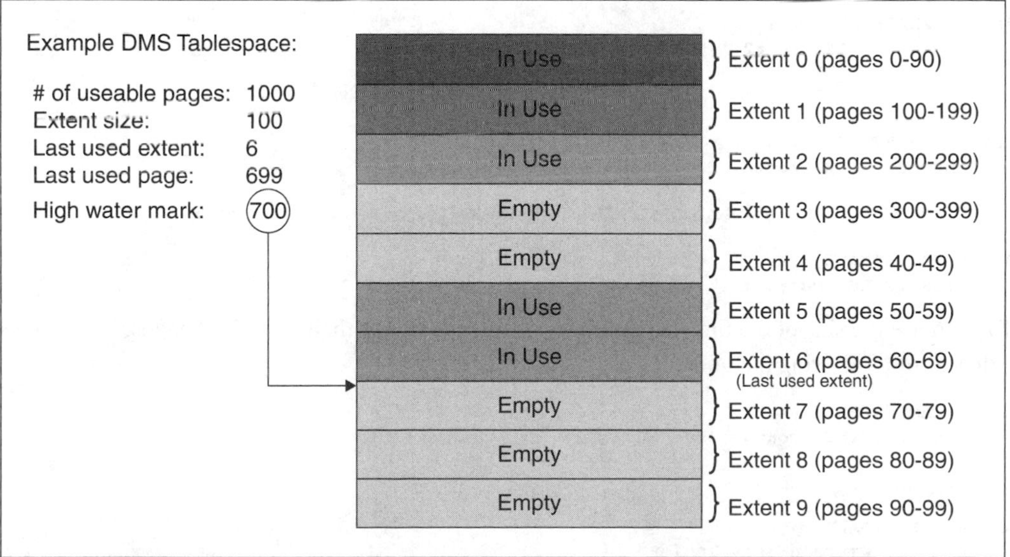

Figure 8.12 The table space high-water mark

- If you create a table named *dept*, Extent 5 will be allocated for its object map, and Extent 6 will be allocated for its table object.
- If you drop the table *org*, Extents 3 and 4 will be freed up for reuse by other data and/or objects. There will be five extents in use, which means that the total number of pages used by the tables would be 400.
- The highest allocated page number in this tablespace is 699, which means that the high-water mark is 700 (699 + 1).

DB2 will not allow you to drop a container or reduce the size of the containers if you are attempting to remove more extents from the table space than are above the table space high-water mark. In this example, there are three extents above the high water mark, so you can reduce the table space by a maximum of three extents.

Let's step through some other examples. For these, assume that the high-water mark is not an issue and that there is enough free space available in the table space to allow the operation to complete successfully.

Assume that you have a table space created with the following command:

```
CREATE TABLESPACE myts MANAGED BY DATABASE USING
    (FILE 'cont0' 250,
    FILE 'cont1' 300,
    FILE 'cont2' 200)
    EXTENTSIZE 10
```

To decrease the size of the third container (*cont2*) to be only 150 pages, you can use either of the following commands:

```
ALTER TABLESPACE myts
    RESIZE (FILE 'cont2' 150)
```

or

```
ALTER TABLESPACE myts
    REDUCE (FILE 'cont2' 50)
```

To remove the third container (*cont2*) from the table space, you can use the command:

```
ALTER TABLESPACE myts
    DROP (FILE 'cont2')
```

To decrease the size of the first and second containers to make them both 200 pages, you can use either of the following methods:

```
ALTER TABLESPACE myts
    RESIZE (FILE 'cont0' 200)
```

plus

```
ALTER TABLESPACE myts
    RESIZE (FILE 'cont1' 200)
```

or

```
ALTER TABLESPACE myts
    RESIZE (FILE 'cont0' 200, file 'cont1' 200)
```

It is better to call the **ALTER TABLESPACE** statement once and specify both of the containers that you want to change rather than doing this in two steps. If you do this in two steps like in the first example, DB2 needs to complete a rebalance of the data after the first **ALTER TABLESPACE** command, and another one after the second **ALTER TABLESPACE** command. If you do this with one **ALTER TABLESPACE** command, DB2 only needs to rebalance the data once, saving time and causing less impact on the system.

When you alter a table space to either add or remove space, the table space may need to be rebalanced. The table space snapshot includes information about any table space rebalancing that may be occurring. If a rebalance is occurring, the rebalancer mode field will be either forward (starting from page zero and working down through the table space), or reverse (starting at the end of the table space and working up through the table space). The snapshot will also show when the rebalance was started and how many extents in the table space still need to be moved as part of the rebalance process. The following is part of the table space snapshot that shows this information.

```
High water mark (pages)                    = 21771
Rebalancer Mode                            = Reverse
    Start Time                             = 01-16-2004 11:02:33.000000
    Restart Time                           = 01-16-2004 11:02:33.000000
    Number of extents processed            = 1102
    Number of extents remaining            = 484
    Last extent moved                      = 1160
```

8.4.11.3 Dropping a Table Space

While an SMS table space will not consume any space unless there are objects (i.e., tables and indexes) in the table space, a DMS table space will continue to hold all of its allocated space. If you create a table space and find that you did not create any objects in the table space, it is good practice to drop the table space.

Dropping a table space can also be a very fast and efficient method for dropping tables. If you drop a table space and there are tables in the table space, then DB2 will drop the tables as well, as long as there are no objects for the tables in other table spaces (i.e., the data object for the table is in one table space while the index object is in another table space). When you drop a table space this way, DB2 does not log all of the row and page deletions as it does for a drop table operation; therefore, this can be a much more efficient method to drop a table, especially if you have only that table defined in the table space.

To drop a table space you use the **DROP TABLESPACE** statement:

```
DROP TABLESPACE myts
```

This removes all entries for the table space from the system catalogs as well as its entries in the table spaces file, and it drops all objects defined wholly within the table space.

8.5 Buffer Pools

The database buffer pools are the area where all of the work in a database really happens. All regular data and index keys are read, scanned, updated, inserted, and deleted within the database buffer pools.

The database buffer pool area is a piece of real memory that is used by DB2 to temporarily store (cache) the regular data and index pages when they are read from disk to be scanned or modified. The buffer pool area improves the performance of the database, since the pages can be accessed much more quickly from memory than from disk.

When you connect to a database, the database buffer pools (along with the lock list, database heap, and so on) are allocated in memory. When you (and anyone else using the database) disconnect all applications from the database, this memory is freed back to the operating system.

If your applications frequently connect to and disconnect from the database, you should consider activating the database (using the **ACTIVATE DATABASE** command) so that the buffer pools and all database-related memory remain allocated. This eliminates the overhead of allocating all of this memory each time an application connects to the database. When you then want to "close" the database, use the **DEACTIVATE DATABASE** command.

8.5.1 Creating Buffer Pools

When you create a database, DB2 creates a default buffer pool named IBMDEFAULTBP. On Linux and Windows the default buffer pool is 250 pages or 1MB, while on UNIX the default buffer pool is 1,000 pages or 4MB. You cannot drop the default buffer pool, but you can change its size using the **ALTER BUFFERPOOL** statement.

You can also create additional buffer pools if your data and workloads can benefit from isolating the different database objects into their own separate work areas. You can use the **CREATE BUFFERPOOL** statement to create a new buffer pool and can specify the following information with this statement:

- The name of the buffer pool. This name cannot already be used within the database and cannot begin with the characters SYS or IBM.
- Whether to create the buffer pool immediately or wait until the database is stopped and restarted.
- If you tell DB2 to create the buffer pool immediately but there is not enough memory available, DB2 will instead create it deferred.
- The default option is immediate.
- The database partition group on which to create the buffer pool. If you do not specify a database partition group, the buffer pool will be created on all partitions.

- The page size used for the buffer pool. The default page size is 4K or 4096 bytes.
- The size of the buffer pool, specified in the number of pages.
- In a partitioned database, this will be the default size for all database partitions where the buffer pool exists.
- The **EXCEPT ON DBPARTITIONNUMS** clause allows the buffer pool to have different sizes on the different database partitions.
- The number of pages to be created in the block-based area of the buffer pool. This area cannot be more than 98 percent of the total buffer pool size. Specifying a value of 0 will disable block I/O for the buffer pool.
- The number of pages within a given block in the block-based area of the buffer pool. The block size must be between 2 and 256 pages; the default value is 32 pages.

> **NOTE** The page size and buffer pool name cannot be altered once it has been defined for a buffer pool.

Enabling block-based I/O by setting NUMBLOCKPAGES to a value greater than zero can help performance for applications that perform a lot of sequential prefetching.

> **NOTE** NUMBLOCKPAGES does not need to be set to allow prefetching to occur.

To examine buffer pools in more detail, let's look at a few examples. Consider a database that is used for an online Web-based ordering application. Performance is fine most of the time, but once a week management runs some reports that cause the system to slow down. In examining the reports you notice that there are large, multiple joins that create a large temporary table. To isolate the creation of the temporary table from overwhelming the buffer pool, you can create a 10,000-page buffer pool dedicated to the temporary table space as follows:

```
CREATE BUFFERPOOL tempbp SIZE 10000
```

You then need to tell the table space to use the buffer pool:

```
ALTER TABLESPACE tempspace1 BUFFERPOOL tempbp
```

As mentioned earlier, the default page size for a database is 4K. If you want to create a table that is more than 4005 bytes, you need to create a table space with a larger page size. But before you can create this table space, you need to create a buffer pool with the same page size. For this example, assume that a 16K page size is best for this table.

```
CREATE BUFFERPOOL bp16k SIZE 100000 PAGESIZE 16K
```

You can then create the table space as follows:

```
CREATE TABLESPACE tspc16k PAGESIZE 16K BUFFERPOOL bp16k
```

If you know that this table will be scanned a lot and that it would benefit from sequential prefetch, you could set aside a portion of the buffer pool for block-based I/O as follows:

```
CREATE BUFFERPOOL bp16k
    SIZE 100000
    PAGESIZE 16K
    NUMBLOCKPAGES 24000
    BLOCKSIZE 256
```

If you specify a block size that is larger than 98 percent of the buffer pool size, you will get the following error.

```
SQL20150N The number of block pages for a buffer pool is too large for the size of the
buffer pool. SQLSTATE=54052
```

> **NOTE** If you are using block-based I/O, you should ensure that the block size you set is based on the table space's extent size.

If you are creating a buffer pool in a multipartition database, and the table space you are creating the buffer pool for is in a database partition group that is not defined on all database partitions, you can specify in which partition group the buffer pool will be created:

```
CREATE BUFFERPOOL bp16k
    SIZE 100000
    PAGESIZE 16K
    NUMBLOCKPAGES 24000
    BLOCKSIZE 256
    DATABASEPARTITIONGROUP pg16k
```

If you are creating a buffer pool in a multipartition database and you want the buffer pool to be sized larger on some database partitions, you can specify these partitions and their sizes as follows:

```
CREATE BUFFERPOOL bp16k
    SIZE 100000
    PAGESIZE 16K
    NUMBLOCKPAGES 24000
    BLOCKSIZE 256
    EXCEPT ON DBPARTITIONNUMS 1,2,3 SIZE 200000
```

In this case you can also use the commands:

```
CREATE BUFFERPOOL bp16k
    SIZE 100000
    PAGESIZE 16K
    NUMBLOCKPAGES 24000
    BLOCKSIZE 256
    EXCEPT ON DBPARTITIONNUMS 1 TO 3 SIZE 200000
```

or

```
CREATE BUFFERPOOL bp16k
    SIZE 100000
    PAGESIZE 16K
```

```
    NUMBLOCKPAGES 24000
    BLOCKSIZE 256
    EXCEPT ON DBPARTITIONNUM 1 SIZE 200000
    EXCEPT ON DBPARTITIONNUM 2 SIZE 200000
    EXCEPT ON DBPARTITIONNUM 3 SIZE 200000
```

8.5.2 Altering Buffer Pools

You can change some of the attributes of a buffer pool using the **ALTER BUFFERPOOL** statement. DB2 allows you to change the following:

- Size
- Database partition group
- Block-based area
- Block size
- Enabling or disabling extended storage

Given a buffer pool created with the statement:

```
CREATE BUFFERPOOL bp16k
    SIZE 100000
    PAGESIZE 16K
    NUMBLOCKPAGES 24000
    BLOCKSIZE 256
    DATABASEPARTITIONGROUP PG16K
```

to make the buffer pool twice as large, you would use the statement:

```
ALTER BUFFERPOOL bp16k
    SIZE 200000
```

Notice that since you did not want to change the block-based area size or the block size, you did not specify these options in the **ALTER BUFFERPOOL** statement.

To make the size of the block-based area 32,000 pages instead of 24,000 pages, you would use the statement:

```
ALTER BUFFERPOOL bp16k
    NUMBLOCKPAGES 32000
```

To allocate this buffer pool also on the partitions in the database partition group *pg1234*, use the statement:

```
ALTER BUFFERPOOL bp16k
    DATABASEPARTITIONGROUP pg1234
```

8.5.3 Dropping Buffer Pools

You will not be able to drop any buffer pools that are associated with a table space. Before you can drop the buffer pool you will need to associate the table space with a different buffer pool using the **ALTER TABLESPACE** statement.

Once there are no longer any table spaces associated with the buffer pool, you can drop the buffer pool using the **DROP BUFFERPOOL** statement. This will release the memory back to the operating system for use by other DB2-related buffers and heaps, or for other application memory requests.

To drop the buffer pool BP16K, use the statement:

```
DROP BUFFERPOOL bp16k
```

8.6 Case Study

Let's start by creating a database named mydb on your Windows server using automatic storage.

Your server was configured with four physical hard drives that are to be dedicated to your database, so you want to create a new database that will use these drives. Once you have formatted the four drives using the operating system tools and given them the labels G, H, I, and J drives, you are ready to create the table space.

The storage paths for the database will be the C: and D: drives as follows:

```
CREATE DATABASE mydb ON G:, H:, I:, J: AUTOMATIC STORAGE YES
```

First you need to connect to the database:

```
CONNECT TO mydb
```

You can then create the table space:

```
CREATE TABLESPACE myts MANAGED BY AUTOMATIC STORAGE
```

To optimize access to data in this table space you can add a new buffer pool, and then assign the *myts* table space to use the buffer pool:

```
CREATE BUFFERPOOL mytsbp SIZE 50000
ALTER TABLESPACE myts BUFFERPOOL mytsbp
```

You have a table with a large number of columns that will not fit the default 4K page, so you will need to create a new table space with a larger page size. However, before you can create the table space you must first create a buffer pool with the page size you intend to use for the table space:

```
CREATE BUFFERPOOL my16kbp SIZE 50000 PAGESIZE 16K
CREATE TABLESPACE myts16k
    PAGESIZE 16k
    MANAGED BY DATABASE USING
    (FILE 'g:\ts16k' 50000,
    FILE 'h:\ts16k' 50000,
    FILE 'i:\ts16k' 50000,
    FILE 'j:\ts16k' 50000)
    BUFFERPOOL my16kbp
```

To create the table you need to specify the 16K page size table space:

```
CREATE TABLE foo
    (c1 VARCHAR(2500),
     c2 VARCHAR(2500)
    ) IN myts16K
```

You execute the command:

```
CREATE TABLE foo2
    (c1 VARCHAR(250),
     c2 VARCHAR(250)
    )
```

and DB2 puts the table in the first user-created table space, *myts*. You can verify this by querying the SYSCAT.TABLES catalog view:

```
SELECT tabname, tbspace FROM syscat.tables
    WHERE tabname='FOO2'
```

You want to create another table and store any indexes defined on the table in a different table space, so you must specify the data and index table spaces when you create the table. You first need to create the index table space.

```
CREATE TABLESPACE INXts16k
    PAGESIZE 16K
    MANAGED BY DATABASE USING
    (FILE 'g:\INX16k' 500,
    FILE 'h:\INX16k' 500,
    FILE 'i:\INX16k' 500,
    FILE 'j:\INX16k' 500)
    BUFFERPOOL my16kbp
```

You can then create the table and specify that the data will be stored in the table space *myts16k*, and the index in the table space will be *INXts16k*.

```
CREATE TABLE staff
    (empid INT,
    fname VARCHAR(30),
    lname VARCHAR(30),
    deptid INT
    )
    IN myts16K
    INDEX IN INXts16K
```

When you now create any indexes on the staff table, they will be placed in the *INXts16K* table space.

```
CREATE INDEX staffx ON staff (empid)
```

As you can see above, the index table space only has 2,000 pages of space defined. Since you anticipate having a large number of rows in this table, you enlarge the table space:

```
ALTER TABLESPACE INXts16k EXTEND (ALL CONTAINERS 40000)
```

Your users want to create some tables for storing personal information. This information is not accessed by your applications, and is accessed infrequently. You decide that this is a perfect place to use automatic storage so you do not have to manage the table space. In order to ensure that the table space does not need attention, you can let it grow automatically up to 500GB if you wish. Since the database was already created using automatic storage, the default in DB2 9, you can simply creare the tabe space as follows:

```
CREATE TABLESPACE scratch
INITIALSIZE 20MB
INCREASESIZE 10MB
MAXSIZE 500GB
```

8.7 Summary

In this chapter you learned about the DB2 storage model, a topic that is closely related to the database objects discussed in Chapter 7, Working with Database Objects. This chapter described databases and the various components that are part of databases. Table spaces and containers define the logical and physical storage of your tables and indexes, while partition groups are used to give you control over where your table spaces will be stored in a multipartition database.

As data is inserted into your tables, pages are also written to the table's data and index objects. When the table space has multiple containers, DB2 will fill these on a round-robin basis among the extents, filling an extent at a time. When you then access your data, it must first be read into the database's buffer pool(s) to be scanned and read. You can assign table spaces to specific buffer pools, and give these buffer pools different sizes to optimize your performance.

8.8 Review Questions

1. What is the largest number of partitions supported by DB2?
2. What is the name of the buffer pool created automatically by DB2 in every database?
3. For the table created as:

   ```
   CREATE TABLE mytable (col1   VARCHAR(100),
                         Col2   int,
                         Col3   VARCHAR(9000)
                        )
   ```

   what is the minimum page size required?
4. What type of object is stored in the DB2 file *SQL00018.DAT*?
5. What command can be used to determine the amount of free space in a table space?
6. Which type of table space is preallocated when it is created?
7. Which type of table space can grow and shrink as tables grow and shrink within it?
8. When can a user-defined table space not be dropped?
9. What is the main reason for creating a block-based area in your buffer pool?
10. Which command can be used to determine if a rebalance is occurring due to the addition or removal of a container in the table space?
11. Which of the following page sizes is not supported by DB2?
    A. 2K
    B. 4K
    C. 8K
    D. 16K
    E. 32K

12. If a database has 12 table spaces all using an 8K page size, what is the minimum number of buffer pools that must exist in the database?
    A. 1
    B. 2
    C. 8
    D. 12
13. Given the following db2nodes.cfg file:

```
0 mysrv1 0
1 mysrv1 1
2 mysrv2 0
3 mysrv2 1
```

    what is the largest table that can exist in a database created in this instance?
    A. 64GB
    B. 256GB
    C. 1TB
    D. 2TB
14. Given the following db2nodes.cfg file for the instance *inst1*:

```
0 mysrv1 0
1 mysrv1 1
2 mysrv2 0
3 mysrv2 1
```

    and the command **`create database foo on /data,`** which directories will be created under the /data directory?
    A. NODE0002 and NODE0003
    B. NODE0000 and NODE0001
    C. DB2
    D. inst1
15. Given the following db2nodes.cfg file for the instance *inst1*:

```
0 mysrv1 0
1 mysrv1 1
2 mysrv2 0
3 mysrv2 1
```

    and the command **`create database foo on /data,`** which directories will be created under the /data/inst1 directory on server *mysrv2*?
    A. NODE0002 and NODE0003
    B. NODE0000 and NODE0001
    C. NODE0002
    D. NODE0000, NODE0001, NODE0002, and NODE0003

16. Given a newly created nonpartitioned instance on Windows named *DB2* and the command **`create database foo on C:`**, how many directories will be created under the subdirectory C:\DB2\NODE0000\SQL00001?

A. 1
B. 2
C. 3
D. 4
E. 5

17. Given the following sequence of events:

1. Create database *sample* on C:.
2. Create database *sales* on C:.
3. Create database *test* on C:.
4. **`drop db sales`**
5. **`create db my_sales`**

which subdirectory will the database *my_sales* be located in?

A. SQL00001
B. SQL00002
C. SQL00003
D. SQL00004

18. Given the following db2nodes.cfg file for the instance *inst1*:

```
0 mysrv1 0
1 mysrv1 1
2 mysrv2 0
3 mysrv2 1
```

and the following sequence of commands:

```
telnet myserv2
create database foo on /data
```

which of the following is the catalog partition for the database *foo*?

A. Partition 0
B. Partition 1
C. Partition 2
D. Partition 3

19. To create the table space *TS1* successfully in the database *sample*, place the following steps in the correct order:

1. `CREATE TABLESPACE ts1 PAGESIZE 16K BUFFERPOOL bp1`
2. `CONNECT TO sample`
3. `CREATE BUFFERPOOL bp1 SIZE 100000 PAGESIZE 16K`

A. 1, 2, 3
B. 3, 2, 1
C. 2, 1, 3
D. 2, 3, 1

20. Given a database with six partitions, which of the following statements will create a buffer pool with a size of 100MB on partitions 1, 2, 3, 4, and 5, and a size of 150MB on partition 0?

A.
```
CREATE BUFFERPOOL BP1
SIZE 100MB on all DBPARTITIONNUMS
except DBPARTITIONNUM 0 size 150MB
```

B.
```
CREATE BUFFERPOOL BP1
SIZE 100MB on DBPARTITIONNUMS 1,2,3,4,5
150MB on DBPARTITIONNUM 0
```

C.
```
CREATE BUFFERPOOL BP1
SIZE 150MB
except on DBPARTITIONNUMS 1,2,3,4,5 size 100MB
```

D.
```
CREATE BUFFERPOOL BP1
SIZE 100MB on DBPARTITIONNUMS 1,2,3,4,5
SIZE 150MB on DBPARTITIONNUM 0
```

CHAPTER 9

Leveraging the Power of SQL

Structured Query Language (SQL) lets users access and manipulate data in relational database management systems. Now that you have learned about the fundamentals of DB2, this chapter shows you how to leverage the power of SQL to work with relational data that is stored in DB2 databases. The examples provided in this chapter use the sample database. In Chapter 10, Mastering the DB2 pureXML Support, we discuss SQL/XML functions. SQL/XML is an extension of the SQL language that includes support for accessing XML data. You can now issue SQL queries that can access both, relational and XML data. Chapter 8, The DB2 Storage Model, describes the sample database in more detail.

In this chapter you will learn about:

- The **SELECT** SQL statement to query data
- The **INSERT, UPDATE,** and **DELETE** SQL statements to modify data
- Recursive SQL statements
- How to query data that just got inserted, updated, or deleted in the same SQL statement
- The **MERGE** SQL statement to combine insert, update, and/or delete operations in one statement

> **NOTE** If you are following the examples in this chapter using the Command Line Processor (CLP), the Command Window, or the Command Editor, these tools have autocommit enabled by default, so the changes you make will be stored permanently to the table. Refer to Chapter 4, Using the DB2 Tools, for more information.

9.1 Querying DB2 Data

You use the **SELECT** statement to query tables or views from a database. At a minimum, the statement contains a **SELECT** clause and a **FROM** clause. The following are two examples of **SELECT** statements. This first example uses the wildcard symbol (*) to indicate that all columns from the *employee* table are selected:

```
SELECT * FROM employee;
```

In this example, the column names *empno, firstname*, and *lastname* are specified in the **SELECT** statement:

```
SELECT empno, firstnme, lastname FROM employee;
```

9.1.1 Derived Columns

When data is retrieved from a table using the **SELECT** clause, you can derive or calculate new columns based on other columns. The DESCRIBE command is a handy command to display table definitions, which for this section, can help you determine how to derive other columns based on existing ones. Let's find out what columns are defined in the *employee* table.

```
DESCRIBE TABLE employee
```

Figure 9.1 illustrates how to derive the column *totalpay* by adding the *salary* and *comm* columns.

```
SELECT empno, firstnme, lastname, (salary + comm) AS totalpay
  FROM employee

EMPNO  FIRSTNME     LASTNAME        TOTALPAY
------ ------------ --------------- ------------
000010 CHRISTINE    HAAS               156970.00
000020 MICHAEL      THOMPSON            97550.00
000030 SALLY        KWAN               101310.00
000050 JOHN         GEYER               83389.00
000060 IRVING       STERN               74830.00
. . .
```

Figure 9.1 Example of a derived column

Note that *totalpay* is the name for the derived column specified in the SELECT statement. If it is not specified, DB2 will use the column number as the column name. In the example below, *(salary + comm)* is the fourth column in the SELECT list, hence a number 4 is used as the column name.

```
SELECT empno, firstnme, lastname, (salary + comm) FROM employee
```

9.1.2 The SELECT Statement with COUNT Aggregate Function

The **COUNT** option lets you get a row count of the result set. For example, the SQL statement in Figure 9.2 returns the number of rows in the *sales* table whose *region* column has the value *Quebec*. In this case, there are 12 records that match this criteria.

```
SELECT COUNT(*)
  FROM sales
 WHERE region = 'Quebec'

1
-----------
         12
  1 record(s) selected.
```

Figure 9.2 Example of a SELECT statement with COUNT aggregate function

9.1.3 The SELECT Statement with DISTINCT Clause

To eliminate duplicate rows in a result set among the columns specified in the **SELECT** statement, use the **DISTINCT** clause. The SQL statement in Figure 9.3 selects the distinct, or unique values of the *region* column of the *sales* table.

```
SELECT DISTINCT region FROM sales

REGION
---------------
Manitoba
Ontario-North
Ontario-South
Quebec
  4 record(s) selected.
```

Figure 9.3 Example of a SELECT statement with DISTINCT clause

You can also use the **DISTINCT** clause in the **SELECT** statement with **COUNT** function. For example, the SQL statement in Figure 9.4 returns the number of distinct or unique values in the region column of the *sales* table.

The output shows that there are four distinct values for the region column in the *sales* table. This value is the same as we saw with the **SELECT DISTINCT region FROM sales** result obtained in Figure 9.3.

```
SELECT COUNT (DISTINCT region) FROM sales

1
-----------
          4

  1 record(s) selected.
```

Figure 9.4 Example of a SELECT statement with COUNT function and DISTINCT clause

9.1.4 DB2 Special Registers

DB2 **special registers** are memory values/registers that allow DB2 to provide information to an application about its environment. These registers can be referenced in SQL statements. The most commonly used special registers are listed in Table 9.1. For a complete list of DB2 special registers, refer to the *DB2 SQL Reference Guide*.

Table 9.1 DB2 Special Registers

DB2 Special Registers	Descriptions
CURRENT DATE or CURRENT_DATE	A date based on the time-of-day clock at the database server. If this register is referenced more than once in a single statement, the value returned will be the same for all references.
CURRENT ISOLATION	Identifies the isolation level for any dynamic SQL statements issued within the current session. This special register can be modified using the **SET CURRENT ISOLATION** statement.
CURRENT LOCK TIMEOUT	Specifies the number of seconds that an application will wait to obtain a lock. This special register can be modified using the **SET CURRENT LOCK TIMEOUT** statement.
CURRENT PACKAGE PATH	Identifies the path to be used when resolving references to packages. This special register can be modified using the **SET CURRENT PACKAGE PATH** statement.
CURRENT PATH or CURRENT_PATH	Identifies the SQL path used to resolve procedure, functions, and data type references for dynamically prepared SQL statements. The value of this special register is a list of one or more schema names. This special register can be modified using the **SET PATH** statement.
CURRENT SCHEMA or CURRENT_SCHEMA	Identifies the schema name used to qualify unqualified database objects in dynamic SQL statements. The default value is the authorization ID of the current user. This special register can be modified using the SET CURRENT SCHEMA statement.
CURRENT TIME or CURRENT_TIME	A time based on the time-of-day clock at the database server. If this register is referenced more than once in a single statement, the value returned will be the same for all references.

Table 9.1 DB2 Special Registers *(Continued)*

DB2 Special Registers	Descriptions
CURRENT TIMESTAMP or CURRENT_TIMESTAMP	A timestamp based on the time-of-day clock at the database server. If this register is referenced more than once in a single statement, the value returned will be the same for all references.
CURRENT USER or CURRENT_USER	Specifies the authorization ID to be used for statement authorization.
SESSION_USER	Specifies the authorization ID to be used for the current session. This is the same as the USER special register.
SYSTEM_USER	Specifies the authorization ID of the user who connected to the database.
USER	Specifies the runtime authorization ID used to connect to the database.

To display the value of a special register, use the following statement:

```
VALUES special_register
```

For example, to display the value of the CURRENT TIMESTAMP special register, issue:

```
VALUES CURRENT TIMESTAMP
```

SQL also supports expressions using DB2 special registers. Figure 9.5 uses the CURRENT DATE register to derive the *retiredate* column.

```
SELECT empno, firstnme, lastname
     , (salary + comm) AS totalpay
     , CURRENT DATE AS retiredate
  FROM employee

EMPNO  FIRSTNME     LASTNAME        TOTALPAY     RETIREDATE
------ ------------ --------------- ------------ ----------
000010 CHRISTINE    HAAS               156970.00 10/12/2006
000020 MICHAEL      THOMPSON            97550.00 10/12/2006
000030 SALLY        KWAN               101310.00 10/12/2006
000050 JOHN         GEYER               83389.00 10/12/2006
000060 IRVING       STERN               74830.00 10/12/2006
. . .
```

Figure 9.5 Example of using DB2 special registers in a SELECT statement

As indicated in Table 9.1, some of the special registers are updatable. For example, to change the value of the CURRENT ISOLATION special register to RR (Repeatable Read), issue:

```
SET CURRENT ISOLATION RR
```

9.1.5 Scalar and Column Functions

Invoking a function against the column values can be very useful to derive new column values. Consider the following example where you want to obtain the name of the day for each employee's hire date. You can use the **DAYNAME** built-in function supplied by DB2 as shown in Figure 9.6.

```
SELECT empno, firstnme, lastname
     , (salary + comm) AS totalpay
     , DAYNAME(hiredate) AS dayname
  FROM employee

EMPNO  FIRSTNME     LASTNAME        TOTALPAY     DAYNAME
------ ------------ --------------- ------------ ------------
000010 CHRISTINE    HAAS               156970.00 Sunday
000020 MICHAEL      THOMPSON            97550.00 Friday
000030 SALLY        KWAN               101310.00 Tuesday
000050 JOHN         GEYER               83389.00 Friday
000060 IRVING       STERN               74830.00 Sunday
. . .
```

Figure 9.6 Example of a scalar function

The function **DAYNAME** used in Figure 9.6 is called a scalar function. A scalar function takes input values and returns a single value. Another type of function, called a column function, operates on the values of an entire column. The example in Figure 9.7 shows how to calculate the average value of the *salary* column in the employee table.

```
SELECT DECIMAL( AVG(salary), 9, 2 ) AS avgsalary
  FROM employee

AVGSALARY
-----------
   58155.35
  1 record(s) selected.
```

Figure 9.7 Example of a column function

The AVG column function, which is a built-in function, calculates the average of a specified column. In this example, it calculates the average of all the salary values in the employee table. Notice that the DECIMAL function is also used; this casts the average result to a decimal representation with a precision of 9, and scale of 2. Casting is discussed in the next section.

9.1.6 The CAST Expression

There are many occasions when a value with a given data type needs to be converted to a different data type. For example, when manipulating data using the **DATE** and **TIMESTAMP** data types, **TIMESTAMP** might need to be cast to **DATE.** Figure 9.8 illustrates such an example.

```
SELECT CURRENT TIMESTAMP, CAST(CURRENT TIMESTAMP AS DATE)
  FROM SYSIBM.SYSDUMMY1

1                          2
-------------------------- ----------
2006-10-12-12.42.16.828000 10/12/2006

  1 record(s) selected.
```

Figure 9.8 Example of a CAST expression

9.1.7 The WHERE clause

For better performance, you should always write your SQL statements so that only the required data is returned. One way to achieve this is to limit the number of columns to be retrieved by explicitly specifying the column names in the **SELECT** statement (as illustrated in previous examples). The other way is to limit the number of rows to be retrieved using the **WHERE** clause. Figure 9.9 illustrates an example of a **SELECT** statement that returns employees who are managers with a salary greater than $1,000.00.

```
SELECT empno, firstnme, lastname
  FROM employee
 WHERE salary > 1000
   AND job = 'MANAGER'

EMPNO  FIRSTNME     LASTNAME
------ ------------ ---------------
000020 MICHAEL      THOMPSON
000030 SALLY        KWAN
000050 JOHN         GEYER
000060 IRVING       STERN
000070 EVA          PULASKI
000090 EILEEN       HENDERSON
000100 THEODORE     SPENSER
  7 record(s) selected.
```

Figure 9.9 Example of a WHERE clause

9.1.8 Using FETCH FIRST *n* ROWS ONLY

Sometimes the result set returned contains hundreds, or thousands of rows and you may only need the first few rows from the result set. Use the **FETCH FIRST *n* ROWS ONLY** clause of the **SELECT** statement to accomplish this. For example, to only return the first three rows from the example illustrated in Figure 9.9, use the statement shown in Figure 9.10. Note that the actual result of the query does not change, but you instructed DB2 to return only the first *n* rows of the result set.

```
SELECT empno, firstnme, lastname
  FROM employee
 WHERE workdept > 1000
   AND job = 'MANAGER'
 FETCH FIRST 3 ROWS ONLY

EMPNO  FIRSTNME     LASTNAME
------ ------------ ---------------
000020 MICHAEL      THOMPSON
000030 SALLY        KWAN
000050 JOHN         GEYER
  3 record(s) selected.
```

Figure 9.10 Example of FETCH FIRST *n* ROWS ONLY

9.1.9 The LIKE Predicate

The **LIKE** predicate lets you search for patterns in character string columns. In SQL, the percent sign (%) is a wildcard character that represents zero or more characters. It can be used any place in the search string, and as many times as you need it.

The other wildcard character used with the **LIKE** predicate is the underline character (_). This character represents one and only one character. In Figure 9.11, it matches items in *workdept* that have strings exactly three characters long, with the first two characters of D2.

For example, the SQL statement in Figure 9.11 returns all the rows in the employee table where the *lastname* column starts with the letter M or the *workdept* column contains 3 characters starting with "D2".

```
SELECT empno, firstnme, lastname, workdept FROM employee
WHERE lastname LIKE 'M%' OR workdept LIKE 'D2_'

EMPNO  FIRSTNME     LASTNAME        WORKDEPT
------ ------------ --------------- --------
000070 EVA          PULASKI         D21
000230 JAMES        JEFFERSON       D21
000240 SALVATORE    MARINO          D21
000250 DANIEL       SMITH           D21
000260 SYBIL        JOHNSON         D21
000270 MARIA        PEREZ           D21
000320 RAMLAL       MEHTA           E21
200240 ROBERT       MONTEVERDE      D21
  8 record(s) selected.
```

Figure 9.11 Example of a LIKE predicate

9.1.10 The BETWEEN Predicate

The **BETWEEN** predicate lets you search for all the rows whose value falls between the values indicated. For example, the SQL statement in Figure 9.12 returns all the rows from the employee table whose salary is between $40,000 and $50,000.

```
SELECT firstnme, lastname, salary FROM employee
WHERE salary BETWEEN 40000 AND 50000

FIRSTNME     LASTNAME        SALARY
------------ --------------- -----------
SEAN         O'CONNELL          49250.00
MASATOSHI    YOSHIMURA          44680.00
JENNIFER     LUTZ               49840.00
JAMES        JEFFERSON          42180.00
SALVATORE    MARINO             48760.00
DANIEL       SMITH              49180.00
SYBIL        JOHNSON            47250.00
WING         LEE                45370.00
JASON        GOUNOT             43840.00
DIAN         HEMMINGER          46500.00
EILEEN       SCHWARTZ           46250.00
  11 record(s) selected.
```

Figure 9.12 Example of a BETWEEN predicate

9.1.11 The IN Predicate

The **IN** predicate lets you search rows based on a set of values. The SQL statement in Figure 9.13 returns all the rows from the *sales* table where the value in the *sales_date* column is either *03/29/1996* or *04/01/2006*.

9.1.12 The ORDER BY Clause

SQL does not return the results retrieved in a particular order; the order of a result may be different each time a **SELECT** statement is executed. To sort the result set, use the **ORDER BY** clause as shown in Figure 9.14.

You must specify the column names in the **ORDER BY** clause; column numbers are not allowed. Refer to Section 9.1.1, Derived Columns, for example of column numbers.

Notice that *lastname* is sorted in ascending order in the example above. You can explicitly specify the keyword ASC or omit it because it is the default behavior. To sort the result set in descending order, simply use the DESC keyword instead.

```
SELECT * FROM sales
WHERE sales_date IN ('03/29/1996', '04/01/2006')

SALES_DATE SALES_PERSON    REGION          SALES
---------- --------------- --------------- -----------
03/29/1996 LEE             Ontario-North             2
04/01/2006 LUCCHESSI       Ontario-South             3
04/01/2006 LUCCHESSI       Manitoba                  1
04/01/2006 LEE             Ontario-South             8
04/01/2006 LEE             Ontario-North             -
04/01/2006 LEE             Quebec                    8
04/01/2006 LEE             Manitoba                  9
04/01/2006 GOUNOT          Ontario-South             3
04/01/2006 GOUNOT          Ontario-North             1
04/01/2006 GOUNOT          Quebec                    3
04/01/2006 GOUNOT          Manitoba                  7

  11 record(s) selected.
```

Figure 9.13 Example of an IN predicate

```
SELECT empno, firstnme, lastname
  FROM employee
 WHERE job='MANAGER'
 ORDER BY lastname ASC

EMPNO  FIRSTNME     LASTNAME
------ ------------ ---------------
000050 JOHN         GEYER
000090 EILEEN       HENDERSON
000030 SALLY        KWAN
000070 EVA          PULASKI
000100 THEODORE     SPENSER
000060 IRVING       STERN
000020 MICHAEL      THOMPSON

  7 record(s) selected.
```

Figure 9.14 Example of an ORDER BY clause

9.1.13 The GROUP BY...HAVING Clause

When you need to group multiple rows into a single row based on one or more columns, the **GROUP BY** clause comes in handy. Let's use an example to explain the usage of this clause. Figure 9.15 sums up the salary of all the employees. The GROUP BY clause groups the results by *workdept* which returns the total salary of the employees for each department.

The **HAVING** clause then specifies which of the combined rows are to be retrieved. In the statement in Figure 9.15, only department names starting with *E* are retrieved.

```
SELECT workdept, SUM(salary) AS total_salary
  FROM employee
 GROUP BY workdept
HAVING workdept LIKE 'E%'
WORKDEPT TOTAL_SALARY
-------- ---------------------------------
E01                               80175.00
E11                              317140.00
E21                              282520.00

  3 record(s) selected.
```

Figure 9.15 Example of GROUP BY and HAVING clauses

9.1.14 Joins

Sometimes information that you want to retrieve does not reside in a single table. You can join the rows in two or more tables in a **SELECT** statement by listing the tables in the FROM clause. Consider the example in Figure 9.16.

```
SELECT empno, firstnme, lastname, deptname, mgrno
  FROM employee, department
 WHERE workdept = deptno
   AND admrdept = 'A00'

EMPNO  FIRSTNME     LASTNAME        DEPTNAME                      MGRNO
------ ------------ --------------- ----------------------------- -----
000010 CHRISTINE    HAAS            SPIFFY COMPUTER SERVICE DIV.  000010
000020 MICHAEL      THOMPSON        PLANNING                      000020
000030 SALLY        KWAN            INFORMATION CENTER            000030
000050 JOHN         GEYER           SUPPORT SERVICES              000050
000110 VINCENZO     LUCCHESSI       SPIFFY COMPUTER SERVICE DIV.  000010
000120 SEAN         O'CONNELL       SPIFFY COMPUTER SERVICE DIV.  000010
000130 DELORES      QUINTANA        INFORMATION CENTER            000030
000140 HEATHER      NICHOLLS        INFORMATION CENTER            000030
200010 DIAN         HEMMINGER       SPIFFY COMPUTER SERVICE DIV.  000010
200120 GREG         ORLANDO         SPIFFY COMPUTER SERVICE DIV.  000010
200140 KIM          NATZ            INFORMATION CENTER            000030

   11 record(s) selected.
```

Figure 9.16 Example of an INNER join

The example in Figure 9.16 retrieves a list of employees, their department names, and manager's employee numbers whose administrative department (*admrdept*) is *A00*. Since the *employee* table only stores the department number of the employees and not the department names, you need to join the *employee* table with the *department* table. Note that the two tables are joined in the **FROM** clause. Only records with matching department numbers (*workdept* = *deptno*) are retrieved.

This type of join is called an **inner join**; it results in matched rows that are present in both joined tables. The **INNER JOIN** keywords can be omitted as demonstrated in Figure 9.16. However, if you choose to explicitly use the **INNER JOIN** syntax, the **SELECT** statement in Figure 9.16 can be rewritten as the following SQL statement.

```
SELECT empno, firstnme, lastname, deptname, mgrno
  FROM employee INNER JOIN department
    ON workdept = deptno
 WHERE admrdept='A00'
```

Note that the **INNER JOIN** clause is used in the **FROM** clause. The **ON** keyword specifies the join predicates and categorizes rows as either joined or not-joined. This is different from the **WHERE** clause, which is used to filter rows.

There are three other types of joins: **LEFT OUTER JOIN, RIGHT OUTER JOIN,** and **FULL OUTER JOIN.** Outer joins are useful when you want to include rows that are present in the left table, right table, or both tables, in addition to the rows returned from the implied inner join. A table specified on the left side of the **OUTER JOIN** operator is considered the left table, and the table specified on the right side of the **OUTER JOIN** operator is considered the right table.

A left outer join includes rows from the left table that were missing from the inner join. A right outer join includes rows from the right table that were missing from the inner join. A full outer join includes rows from both the left and right tables that were missing from the inner join. Figures 9.17, 9.18, 9.19 demonstrate information to be retrieved and an example of each join.

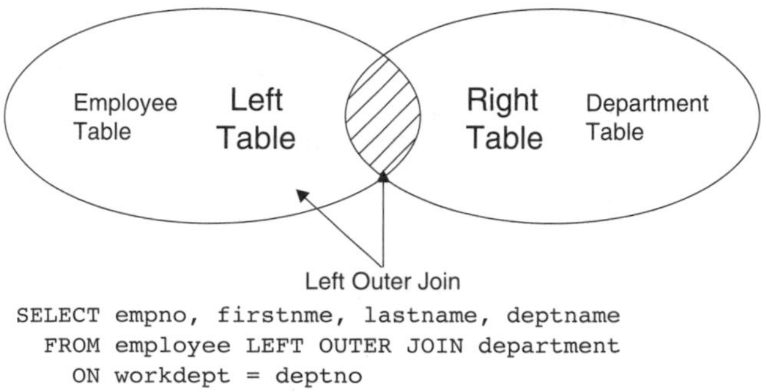


```
SELECT empno, firstnme, lastname, deptname
  FROM employee LEFT OUTER JOIN department
    ON workdept = deptno
```

Figure 9.17 Example of a LEFT OUTER join

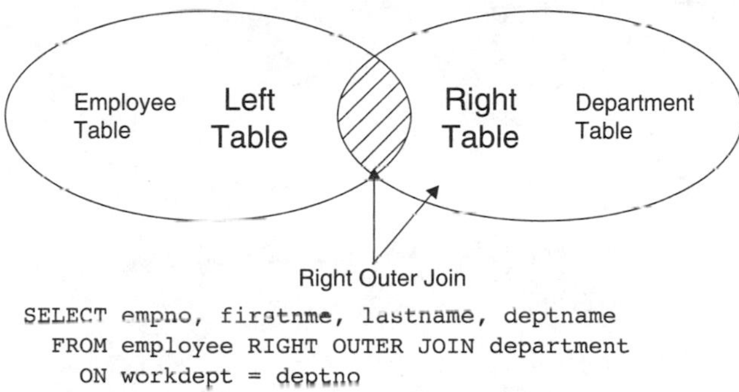


```
SELECT empno, firstnme, lastname, deptname
  FROM employee RIGHT OUTER JOIN department
    ON workdept = deptno
```

Figure 9.18 Example of a RIGHT OUTER join

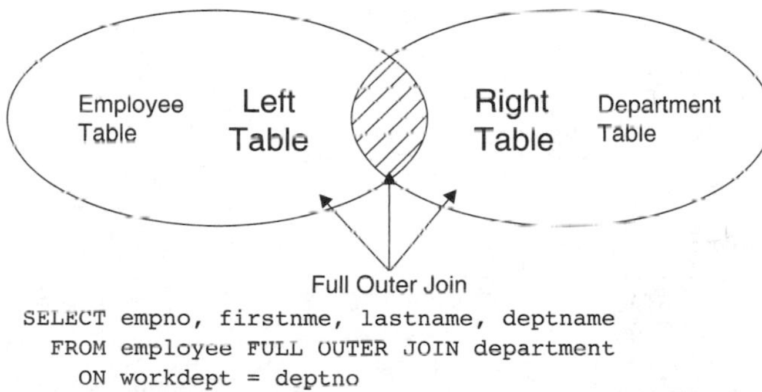


```
SELECT empno, firstnme, lastname, deptname
  FROM employee FULL OUTER JOIN department
    ON workdept = deptno
```

Figure 9.19 Example of a FULL OUTER join

9.1.15 Working with NULLs

A NULL in DB2 represents an unknown value. The following is an example of how to return all rows where the value of *midinit* is NULL.

```
SELECT empno FROM employee WHERE midinit IS NULL
```

When working with NULL values, the **COALESCE** function comes in very handy: It checks whether the input is NULL and replaces it with the specified value if it is NULL. Refer to Figure 9.20 for an example that returns 0 if the value in the *comm* column is NULL.

9.1.16 The CASE Expression

When you want to perform different operations based on the evaluation of a column or value, you can use the **CASE** expression in an SQL statement to simplify your code. The example in Figure 9.21 introduces this expression.

```
SELECT id, name, COALESCE(comm, 0) AS comm
  FROM staff
 FETCH FIRST 6 ROWS ONLY

ID     NAME      COMM
------ --------- ---------------
    10 Sanders              0.00
    20 Pernal             612.45
    30 Marenghi             0.00
    40 O'Brien            846.55
    50 Hanes                0.00
    60 Quigley            650.25

  6 record(s) selected.
```

Figure 9.20 Example of the COALESCE function

```
SELECT firstnme, lastname,
  CASE
    WHEN salary <= 40000 THEN 'Need a raise'
    WHEN salary > 40000 AND salary <= 50000 THEN 'Fair pay'
    ELSE 'Overpaid'
  END AS comment
FROM employee

FIRSTNME     LASTNAME        COMMENT
------------ --------------- ------------
MAUDE        SETRIGHT        Need a raise
RAMLAL       MEHTA           Need a raise
WING         LEE             Fair pay
JASON        GOUNOT          Fair pay
DIAN         HEMMINGER       Fair pay
GREG         ORLANDO         Need a raise
KIM          NATZ            Overpaid
KIYOSHI      YAMAMOTO        Overpaid
. . .
```

Figure 9.21 Example of a CASE expression

In Figure 9.21, the values of the *salary* column are evaluated. If the value is less than or equals to $40,000, the string *Need a raise* is returned. If the value is between $40,000 and $50,000, *Fair pay* is returned. For all other values, *Overpaid* is returned.

9.1.17 Adding a Row Number to the Result Set

Recall that the **FETCH FIRST *n* ROWS ONLY** clause lets you return only the first *n* rows. What if you want to return row 30 and above? The **ROWNUMBER** and **OVER** functions solve this problem. Figure 9.22 shows a column derived with sequential row numbers generated by **ROWNUMBER() OVER()**.

```
SELECT ROWNUMBER() OVER() AS rowid, firstnme, lastname FROM employee

ROWID                FIRSTNME     LASTNAME
-------------------- ------------ ---------------
                   1 CHRISTINE    HAAS
                   2 MICHAEL      THOMPSON
                   3 SALLY        KWAN
                   4 JOHN         GEYER
                   5 IRVING       STERN
                   6 EVA          PULASKI
                   7 EILEEN       HENDERSON
                   8 THEODORE     SPENSER
                   9 VINCENZO     LUCCHESSI
                  10 SEAN         O'CONNELL
                  11 DELORES      QUINTANA
                  12 HEATHER      NICHOLLS
                  13 BRUCE        ADAMSON
                  14 ELIZABETH    PIANKA
                  15 MASATOSHI    YOSHIMURA
                  16 MARILYN      SCOUTTEN
                  17 JAMES        WALKER
                  18 DAVID        BROWN
                  19 WILLIAM      JONES
                  20 JENNIFER     LUTZ
                  21 JAMES        JEFFERSON
                  22 SALVATORE    MARINO
                  23 DANIEL       SMITH
                  24 SYBIL        JOHNSON
                  25 MARIA        PEREZ
                  26 ETHEL        SCHNEIDER
                  27 JOHN         PARKER
                  28 PHILIP       SMITH
                  29 MAUDE        SETRIGHT
                  30 RAMLAL       MEHTA
                  31 WING         LEE
                  32 JASON        GOUNOT
                  33 DIAN         HEMMINGER
                  34 GREG         ORLANDO
                  35 KIM          NATZ
                  36 KIYOSHI      YAMAMOTO
                  37 REBA         JOHN
                  38 ROBERT       MONTEVERDE
                  39 EILEEN       SCHWARTZ
                  40 MICHELLE     SPRINGER
                  41 HELENA       WONG
                  42 ROY          ALONZO
  42 record(s) selected.
```

Figure 9.22 Example 1: Using ROWNUMBER() OVER()

To return rows higher than 30, use the **ROWNUMBER()OVER()** expression to the **FROM** clause. Figure 9.23 shows this trick.

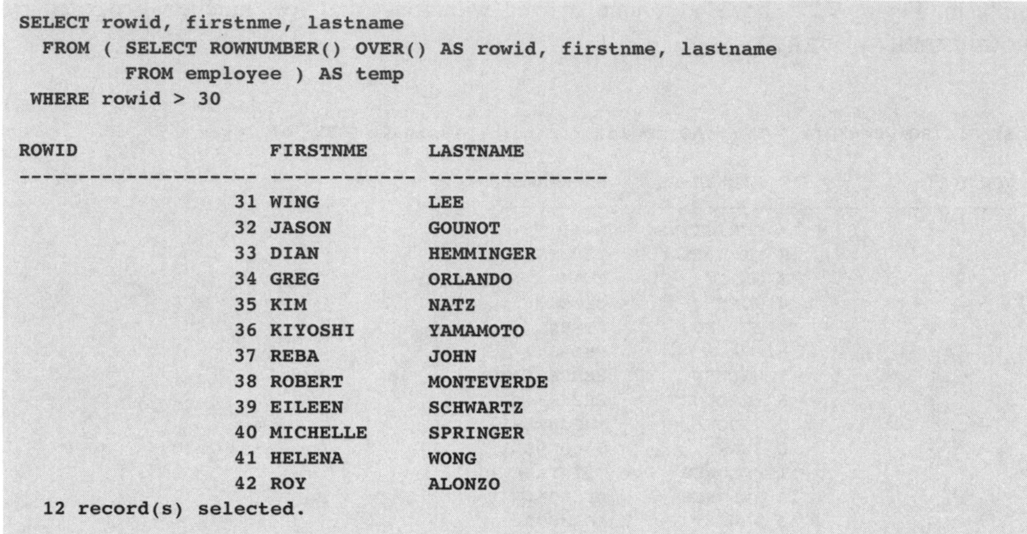

```
SELECT rowid, firstnme, lastname
  FROM ( SELECT ROWNUMBER() OVER() AS rowid, firstnme, lastname
         FROM employee ) AS temp
 WHERE rowid > 30

ROWID                FIRSTNME     LASTNAME
-------------------- ------------ ---------------
                  31 WING         LEE
                  32 JASON        GOUNOT
                  33 DIAN         HEMMINGER
                  34 GREG         ORLANDO
                  35 KIM          NATZ
                  36 KIYOSHI      YAMAMOTO
                  37 REBA         JOHN
                  38 ROBERT       MONTEVERDE
                  39 EILEEN       SCHWARTZ
                  40 MICHELLE     SPRINGER
                  41 HELENA       WONG
                  42 ROY          ALONZO
  12 record(s) selected.
```

Figure 9.23 Example 2: Using ROWNUMBER() OVER()

You can also sort the result set before numbering the rows, as shown in Figure 9.24.

```
SELECT rowid, firstnme, lastname
FROM ( SELECT ROWNUMBER() OVER( ORDER BY salary, comm ) AS rowid,
             firstnme, lastname
         FROM employee) AS temp
WHERE rowid > 30
ROWID                FIRSTNME     LASTNAME
-------------------- ------------ ---------------
                  31 HEATHER      NICHOLLS
                  32 KIM          NATZ
                  33 REBA         JOHN
                  34 IRVING       STERN
                  35 DELORES      QUINTANA
                  36 JOHN         GEYER
                  37 THEODORE     SPENSER
                  38 EILEEN       HENDERSON
                  39 MICHAEL      THOMPSON
                  40 EVA          PULASKI
                  41 SALLY        KWAN
                  42 CHRISTINE    HAAS
  12 record(s) selected.
```

Figure 9.24 Example 3: Using ROWNUMBER() OVER()

9.2 Modifying Table Data

You modify table data using the **INSERT, UPDATE, DELETE,** and **MERGE** statements. Most of the clauses and functions described in the previous section also work with these statements. We will use some examples to explain their basic usages.

Note MERGE statements are discussed in Section 9.4 The MERGE Statement.

You can specify all the column values in the **INSERT** statement like this:

```
INSERT INTO employee
VALUES ( '000998', 'SMITH', 'A', 'JOHN',  NULL, NULL, NULL, NULL, 18,
        'M', NULL, NULL, NULL, NULL )
```

Alternatively, you can explicitly specify the column list for which values will be provided in the **INSERT** statement:

```
INSERT INTO employee (empno, firstnme, midinit, lastname, edlevel)
VALUES ( '000999', 'SMITH', 'A', 'JOHN', 18 );
```

For columns that are not named in the INSERT statement, NULL or default value if defined will be inserted for a nullable column. On the other hand if a NOT NULL column has a default value defined, that value will be inserted. Otherwise, the INSERT will fail with *SQL0407 Assignment of a NULL value to a NOT NULL column is not allowed.*

You can also insert multiple rows in one **INSERT** statement as shown below:

```
INSERT INTO employee (empno, firstnme, midinit, lastname, edlevel)
VALUES ( '000999', 'SMITH', 'A', 'JOHN', 18 )
     , ( '000998', 'LOPEZ', 'M', 'JEN' , 18 )
     , ( '000997', 'FRASER', 'B', 'MARC', 28 );
```

A multi-row insert can also be achieved with values obtained from a **SELECT** statement:

```
INSERT INTO employee_temp ( SELECT * FROM employee );
```

It is fairly straightforward to update one or more rows in a table by simply assigning the new values in the **SET** clause of an UPDATE statement:

```
UPDATE employee SET salary = salary * 1.5, comm = 0
 WHERE empno='000999';
```

The next **UPDATE** statement updates the *employee* table and sets the *hiredate* with value of the DB2 special register **CURRENT DATE.** It also sets the *workdept* to the department number selected from the *department* table.

```
UPDATE employee
   SET (hiredate, workdept) = (SELECT CURRENT DATE, deptno
                                 FROM department
                                WHERE deptname='PLANNING')
WHERE empno='000999';
```

The **DELETE** statement is used to delete rows from a table. To remove all rows from the *employee* table, use the following statement:

```
DELETE FROM employee;
```

To remove only certain rows, use the **WHERE** clause to filter the rows:

```
DELETE FROM employee WHERE workdept IS NULL;
```

To remove rows with a row number greater than 100, use the **ROWNUMBER()OVER()** functions like this:

```
DELETE FROM
 (SELECT ROWNUMBER() OVER(ORDER BY empno) AS rowid
   FROM employee)
WHERE rowid > 100
```

9.3 Selecting from UPDATE, DELETE, or INSERT

While the **INSERT, UPDATE,** and **DELETE** statements change data in the specified tables, they only return a message indicating whether or not the statement completed successfully and an indicator of the number of rows being affected. If the statement completed successfully, you need to issue a separate SQL statement to find out what changed. In the next example, to determine which rows are to be deleted, you first issue a **SELECT** statement to capture the rows you will be deleting with a subsequent **DELETE** statement. Both statements have the same **WHERE** condition to filter the same rows.

```
SELECT empno, firstnme, lastname FROM employee WHERE workdept = 'A00';
DELETE FROM employee WHERE workdept = 'A00';
```

Rather than issuing two separate statements, they can be optimized to use just one SQL statement like this:

```
SELECT empno, firstnme, lastname
  FROM OLD TABLE (DELETE FROM employee WHERE workdept = 'A00');
```

Whenever a table is inserted, updated, or deleted, DB2 maintains one or more internal temporal tables known as transition tables. You specify the transition tables with the **NEW TABLE** and **OLD TABLE** clauses. Depending on the SQL operation, different transition tables are available. Refer to Table 9.2 for a summary of their availability.

Table 9.2 Availability of Transition Tables Depending on the SQL Statement Issued

SQL Statement	NEW TABLE	OLD TABLE
INSERT	Yes	No
UPDATE	Yes	Yes
DELETE	No	Yes

To demonstrate a **SELECT** from **UPDATE** query, consider the following example in which you want to increase the salary of all the employees in department A00. If you use the **OLD TABLE** clause, you can perform the update and return the old salaries as they were before the update. This is good for building an audit table to track the changes to important tables.

```
SELECT salary
   FROM OLD TABLE (UPDATE employee
                      SET salary = salary * 1.1
                    WHERE workdept = 'A00')
```

Similarly, if you want to retrieve the new salary, you can use the **NEW TABLE** clause instead:

```
SELECT salary
  FROM NEW TABLE (UPDATE employee
                     SET salary = salary * 1.1
                   WHERE workdept IS NULL )
```

SELECT from **INSERT** works just like the preceding example:

```
SELECT salary
   FROM NEW TABLE (INSERT INTO employee
                     (empno, firstnme, midinit, lastname, edleve, salaryl)
                   VALUES ( '000999', 'SMITH', 'A', 'JOHN', 18, 45000 ))
```

You cannot retrieve the new and old salary values using both the **NEW TABLE** and **OLD TABLE** clauses. To do this, use the **INCLUDE** clause.

```
SELECT salary as new_salary, old_salary
  FROM NEW TABLE ( UPDATE employee INCLUDE (old_salary DECIMAL(9,2))
                      SET salary     = salary * 1.10,
                          old_salary = salary
                    WHERE workdept = 'A00')
```

The **INCLUDE** clause in the nested **UPDATE** statement creates a new column that can be selected using the outer **SELECT** statement. You can see that the *old_salary* gets the old salary value while the table column *salary* is increased by 10 percent.

Finally, let's look at the **FINAL TABLE** clause. When executing an **INSERT, UPDATE,** or **DELETE** statement, there may still be **AFTER** triggers or referential constraints that result in further modification of data in the table. Using **FINAL TABLE** can prevent these types of changes.

For instance, assume that an **AFTER** trigger is defined to delete all rows from the *employee* table when an employee's salary is updated. If **FINAL TABLE** is used, the **UPDATE** statement will fail. This protects you from any unforeseen side-effects not visible to the application.

For example, an error is received if the following SQL statement is issued:

```
SELECT salary
  FROM FINAL TABLE ( UPDATE employee
                        SET salary = salary * 1.1
                      WHERE workdept = 'A00')
SQL0989N  AFTER trigger "AUDIT_TRIG" attempted to modify a row in table
"EMPLOYEE" that was modified by an SQL data change statement within a FROM clause.
SQLSTATE=560C3
```

NOTE Trigger is a type of application database object that defines a set of actions to be performed in response to an insert, update, or delete operation on a specified table. Triggers are discussed in Chapter 7, Working with Database Objects.

9.4 The MERGE Statement

The **MERGE** statement combines an **INSERT** statement with an **UPDATE** or **DELETE** statement. For example, if a row in table *T1* also exists in table *T2*, the existing row in *T2* should be updated. If a row in *T1* does not exist in *T2*, it should be inserted into *T2*. A new and efficient way to code this logic can be implemented with one statement: the **MERGE** statement. Figure 9.25 shows this **MERGE** statement.

```
MERGE INTO T2 as target
    USING (SELECT ... FROM T1) AS source
       ON target.id=source.id
    WHEN NOT MATCHED THEN
        INSERT INTO T2 ...
    WHEN MATCHED THEN
        UPDATE T2 SET ...
```

Figure 9.25 Example of a MERGE statement

Figure 9.26 illustrates the syntax of the **MERGE** statement. The **MERGE** statement has a lot of details; see the *DB2 SQL Reference* manual for more examples and additional information.

```
>>-MERGE INTO--+-table-name-------+---------------------------->
               +-view-name--------+
               '-(--fullselect--)-'

>--+-----------------------+--USING--table-reference----------->
   '-| correlation-clause |-'

>--ON--search-condition---------------------------------------->

   .-----------------------------------------------------------.
   V                                                           |
>----WHEN--| matching-condition |--THEN--+-| modification-operation |+>
                                         '-signal-statement---------'

   .-ELSE IGNORE-.
>--+-------------+---------------------------------------------><
```

Figure 9.26 Syntax of the MERGE statement

> **NOTE** Refer to Chapter 1, Introduction to DB2, for a description of the DB2 syntax diagram conventions.

9.5 Recursive SQL

Recursive SQL is a powerful way to query hierarchies of data. Organizational structures, bills-of-material, product classifications, and document hierarchies are all examples of hierarchical data. Let's use an example to demonstrate how a recursive SQL statement is written.

Assume that there is a table called *children* with definition and date as shown in Figure 9.27.

```
CREATE TABLE children ( person_id INTEGER
                      , name      VARCHAR(50)
                      , age       INTEGER
                      , gender    CHAR(1)
                      , parent_id INTEGER )
PERSON_ID   NAME      AGE         GENDER PARENT_ID
----------- -------- ----------- ------ -----------
          1 Apple             10 F              10
          2 Zoe               11 F               3
          3 John              30 M              13
          4 Mary              25 F              24
          5 Peter             14 M               4
          6 Jenny             13 F               4
         24 Robert            60 M              30

  7 record(s) selected.
```

Figure 9.27 Sample data in the children table

To retrieve the ancestors of *Jenny*, you would use the recursive query shown in Figure 9.28.

```
WITH temptab (person_id, name, parent_id) AS          (1)
     (SELECT person_id, name, parent_id               (2)
        FROM children
       WHERE name = 'Jenny'

      UNION ALL                                       (3)

      SELECT c.person_id, c.name, c.parent_id         (4)
        FROM children c, temptab super
       WHERE c.person_id = super.parent_id            (5)

) SELECT * FROM temptab
```

Figure 9.28 A recursive SQL example

A **common table expression (CTE)** temporarily stores data as the query execution progresses. It can be referenced in other places within the query. Each use of a specific CTE within a complex query shares the same temporary view. Figure 9.29 illustrates the syntax of a common table expression.

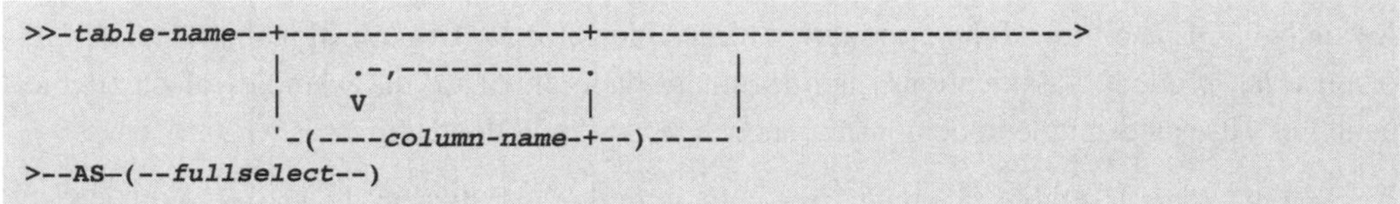

```
>>-table-name--+-----------------+----------------------------->
               |     .-,----------.      |
               |     V            |      |
               '-(----column-name-+--)-----'
>--AS-(--fullselect--)
```

Figure 9.29 Syntax of a common table expression

Back to the example in Figure 9.28, the CTE is called *temptab* and it is created with the **WITH** clause on line (1). The definition of the CTE is specified at lines (2), (3), and (4) inside the parentheses.

Line (2) obtains the initial result set which contains the record with the name 'Jenny'. Then, the recursion takes place by joining each row in *temptab* with its parents (4). The result of one execution of this recursion is added to *temptab* via **UNION ALL** at line (3).

The final query (5) extracts the *person_id*, *name*, and *parent_id* out of the *temptab* CTE.

The recursive SQL will return Jenny's parents and their parents, similar to Figure 9.30.

```
PERSON_ID   NAME                          PARENT_ID
----------- ----------------------------- -----------
SQL0347W  The recursive common table expression "DB2ADMIN.TEMPTAB" may contain an
infinite loop.  SQLSTATE=01605

          6 Jenny                         4
          4 Mary                          24
         24 Robert                        30

  3 record(s) selected with 1 warning messages printed.
```

Figure 9.30 Result of a recursive SQL

Notice that a warning message is also returned indicating that the CTE may contain an infinite loop. To avoid an infinite loop, you can specify the maximum number of recursive levels in the query, as shown in Figure 9.31.

```
WITH temptab (person_id, name, parent_id, level) AS
     (SELECT person_id, name, parent_id, 1
        FROM children
       WHERE name = 'Jenny'

      UNION ALL

      SELECT c.person_id, c.name, c.parent_id, super.level + 1
        FROM children c, temptab super
       WHERE c.person_id = super.parent_id
         AND level < 5

) SELECT * FROM temptab
```

Figure 9.31 A recursive SQL example with a maximum number of recursive levels

9.6 The UNION, INTERSECT, and EXCEPT Operators

UNION, INTERSECT, and **EXCEPT** are operators that can be used to obtain the union, intersection, and difference between *fullselect*, *subselect*, or *values-clause*. Figure 9.32 shows the syntax diagram of the **UNION**, **INTERSECT,** and **EXCEPT** operators.

```
>>-+-subselect---------+--------------------------------------->
   +-(fullselect)------+
   '-| values-clause |-'

   .-------------------------------------------.
   V                                           |
>----+-----------------------------------------+-+------------->
     '-+-UNION---------+--+-subselect---------+-'
       +-UNION ALL-----+  +-(fullselect)------+
       +-EXCEPT--------+  '-| values-clause |-'
       +-EXCEPT ALL----+
       +-INTERSECT-----+
       '-INTERSECT ALL-'

>--+-----------------+--+--------------------+----------------><
   '-order-by-clause-'  '-fetch-first-clause-'
```

Figure 9.32 Syntax diagram of the UNION, INTERSECT, and EXCEPT operators

9.6.1 The UNION and UNION ALL Operators

A **UNION** operation combines two sets of columns and removes duplicate rows. Specifying **UNION ALL** gives the same result as the **UNION** operation, but it also includes the duplicate rows. Consider the two tables, R1 and R2, in Figure 9.33.

```
R1                  R2
------------        -----------
Apple               Apple
Apple               Apple
Apple               Banana
Banana              Banana
Banana              Banana
Cranberry           Cranberry
Cranberry           Mango
Cranberry
Orange
```

Figure 9.33 R1 and R2 tables

Figure 9.34 shows the results of the **UNION** and **UNION ALL** operations on the two tables illustrated in Figure 9.33. As you can see, the **UNION** operator removes duplicates.

```
SELECT R1 FROM R1 AS R1_UNION_R2
 UNION SELECT R2 AS R1_UNION_R2 FROM R2
 ORDER BY R1_UNION_R2

R1_UNION_R2
------------------
Apple
Banana
Cranberry
Mango
Orange

SELECT R1 AS R1_UNION_ALL_R2 FROM R1
 UNION ALL
SELECT R2 AS R1_UNION_ALL_R2 FROM R2
 ORDER BY R1_UNION_ALL_R2

R1_UNION_ALL_R2
------------------------
Apple
Apple
Apple
Apple
Apple
Banana
Banana
Banana
Banana
Banana
Cranberry
Cranberry
Cranberry
Cranberry
Mango
Orange
```

Figure 9.34 Examples of UNION and UNION ALL

9.6.2 The INTERSECT and INTERSECT ALL Operators

An **INTERSECT** operation retrieves the matching set of distinct values from two columns; **INTERSECT ALL** returns the set of matching rows. The examples in Figure 9.35 use tables R1 and R2 from Figure 9.33.

```
SELECT R1 AS R1_INTERSECT_R2 FROM R1
INTERSECT SELECT R2 AS R1_INTERSECT_R2 FROM R2
 ORDER BY R1_INTERSECT_R2

R1_INTERSECT_R2
------------------
Apple
Banana
Cranberry

SELECT R1 AS R1_INTERSECT_ALL_R2 FROM R1
INTERSECT ALL
SELECT R2 AS R1_INTERSECT_ALL_R2 FROM R2
 ORDER BY R1_INTERSECT_ALL_R2

R1_INTERSECT_ALL_R2
------------------------
Apple
Apple
Banana
Banana
Cranberry
```

Figure 9.35 Examples of INTERSECT and INTERSECT ALL

9.6.3 The EXCEPT and EXCEPT ALL Operators

An **EXCEPT** operation retrieves the set of distinct values that exist in the first table but not in the second table. **EXCEPT ALL** returns the set of rows that exist only in the first table. The examples in Figure 9.36 use tables R1 and R2 from Figure 9.33.

9.7 Case Study

Let's review some of the SQL statements you have learned in this chapter. This section gives scenarios and then shows the commands and resulting output.

1. Return a result of *deptno*, *admrdept*, and a derived *comment* column from the *department* table where *deptname* contains the string *CENTER*. Order the result with the first column of the result set.

```
SELECT deptno
     , admrdept
     , 'it is a center' AS comment
  FROM department
```

```
SELECT R1 AS R1_EXCEPT_R2 FROM R1
EXCEPT
SELECT R2 AS R1_EXCEPT_R2 FROM R2
ORDER BY R1_EXCEPT_R2

R1_EXCEPT_R2
------------------
Mango

SELECT R1 AS R1_EXCEPT_ALL_R2 FROM R1
EXCEPT ALL
SELECT R2 AS R1_EXCEPT_ALL_R2 FROM R2
ORDER BY R1_EXCEPT_ALL_R2

R1_EXCEPT_ALL_R2
------------------------
Apple
Cranberry
Cranberry
Mango
```

Figure 9.36 Examples of EXCEPT and EXCEPT ALL

```
 WHERE deptname
  LIKE '%CENTER%'
 ORDER BY 1

DEPTNO ADMRDEPT COMMENT
------ -------- --------------
C01    A00      it is a center
D01    A00      it is a center

  2 record(s) selected.
```

2. Return the *name* and *id* of staffs whose year of service is NOT NULL. Order the result by *years* and *id*. Fetch only the first five rows of the result.

```
SELECT years
     , name
     , id
  FROM staff
 WHERE years IS NOT NULL
ORDER BY years DESC, id DESC
FETCH FIRST 5 ROWS ONLY

YEARS  NAME      ID
------ --------- ------
    13 Graham       310
    12 Jones        260
```

```
    10 Quill          290
    10 Lu             210
    10 Hanes           50

  5 record(s) selected.
```

3. Return a list of employees who do not work as a **SALESREP** in the **OPERATIONS** department.

```
SELECT a.empno, a.lastname, b.deptno AS dept
  FROM employee a, department b
 WHERE a.workdept = b.deptno
   AND a.job      <> 'SALESREP'
   AND b.deptname = 'OPERATIONS'

EMPNO  LASTNAME        DEPT
------ --------------- ----
000090 HENDERSON       E11
000280 SCHNEIDER       E11
000290 PARKER          E11
000300 SMITH           E11
000310 SETRIGHT        E11

  5 record(s) selected.
```

4. Insert multiple rows into the *emp_act* table.

```
INSERT INTO emp_act VALUES
     ('200000' ,'ABC' ,10 ,NULL ,'2006-10-22',CURRENT DATE)
    ,('200000' ,'DEF' ,10 ,1.4  ,NULL        ,DATE (CURRENT TIMESTAMP))
    ,('200000' ,'IJK' ,10 ,1.4  ,'2006-10-22', DEFAULT)

DB20000I  The SQL command completed successfully.
```

5. Insert the result of a query into the *emp_act* table.

```
INSERT INTO emp_act
    SELECT LTRIM(CHAR(id + 600000))
         , SUBSTR(UCASE(name),1,6)
         , 180
         , 100
         , CURRENT DATE
         , CURRENT DATE + 100 DAYS
      FROM staff

DB20000I  The SQL command completed successfully.
```

6. Update multiple rows in the *emp_act* table using a result of a query.

```
UPDATE emp_act
   SET ( emstdate
       , projno ) = ( SELECT CURRENT DATE + 2 DAYS
                           , MIN(CHAR(id))
```

```
                                 FROM staff
                                WHERE id <> 33 )
  WHERE empno LIKE '600%'

DB20000I  The SQL command completed successfully.
```

7. Delete records from the emp_act table where emstdate is greater than 01/01/2007.

```
DELETE FROM emp_act WHERE emstdate > '01/01/2007'
DB20000I  The SQL command completed successfully.
```

8. Query records just inserted.

```
SELECT * FROM NEW TABLE (
    INSERT INTO emp_act VALUES
         ('200000' ,'ABC' ,10 ,NULL ,'2006-10-22',CURRENT DATE)
        ,('200000' ,'DEF' ,10 ,1.4  ,NULL, DATE (CURRENT TIMESTAMP))
        ,('200000' ,'IJK' ,10 ,1.4  ,'2006-10-22', DEFAULT)
      )

EMPNO  PROJNO ACTNO  EMPTIME EMSTDATE   EMENDATE
------ ------ ------ ------- ---------- ----------
200000 abc        10       - 10/22/2006 04/23/2007
200000 DEF        10    1.40 -          04/23/2007
200000 IJK        10    1.40 10/22/2006 -

  3 record(s) selected.
```

9. Query records just deleted.

```
SELECT * FROM OLD TABLE (
    DELETE FROM emp_act WHERE emstdate > '01/01/2003' )

EMPNO  PROJNO ACTNO  EMPTIME EMSTDATE   EMENDATE
------ ------ ------ ------- ---------- ----------
200000 abc        10       - 10/22/2006 04/23/2007
200000 abc        10       - 10/22/2006 04/23/2007
20000  IJK        10    1.40 10/22/2006 -

  3 record(s) selected.
```

10. Query records just inserted in the order they were inserted.

```
SELECT empno
     , projno
     , actno
     , row#
  FROM FINAL TABLE
       ( INSERT INTO emp_act (empno, projno, actno)
```

```
                INCLUDE ( row# SMALLINT )
                 VALUES ('300000', 'XXX', 999, 1)
                      , ('300000', 'YYY', 999, 2) )
  ORDER BY row#

 EMPNO  PROJNO ACTNO  ROW#
 ------ ------ ------ ------
 300000 XXX       999      1
 300000 YYY       999      2

 record(s) selected.
```

9.8 Summary

This chapter shows the power of SQL statements to manipulate relational data stored in a DB2 database, using statements that include a **SELECT, INSERT, UPDATE,** and a **DELETE.** In the SQL statements, you can use DB2 special registers to obtain information about the environment such as the current date and current user connected to the database.

Besides the basic SQL statements to manipulate data, you can also use column and scalar functions, cast expressions, **WHERE** clauses, **ORDER BY** clauses, **GROUP BY** clauses, **FETCH FIRST *n* ROWS ONLY** options, and many other features to customize the result that you want to obtain.

It is very common that data requested is from more than one table. Inner and outer joins are used to combine data from two or more tables in a **SELECT** statement.

SQL enhancement returns selective data from data being deleted, updated, or inserted in a single SQL statement, which provides a simplified and optimized way to write SQLs. For example, rather than issuing two separate statements to query data you are going to delete and then perform the delete, DB2 lets you combine the two operations in a single statement. It definitely simplifies the application code as well as improves performance in most cases.

The **MERGE** statement was first introduced in DB2 Version 8. It combines an **INSERT** with an **UPDATE** or **DELETE** statement.

9.9 Review Questions

1. Given the following *employee* table:

```
 empno     firstnme      lastname        salary
 ---------------------------------------------
 000010    Peter         Smith         38752.00
 000020    Christine     Haas          52234.00
 000030    John          Geyer         38250.00
 000040    Irving        Poon          40175.00
 000050    Eva           Pulaski       36170.00
```

How many rows are returned from the following SQL statement?

```
SELECT empno
  FROM employee
 WHERE lastname LIKE 'P%'
   AND salary > 38500
```

A. 1
B. 2
C. 3
D. 4
E. 5

2. Given the following table *t1*:

```
     id    job      bonus
----------------------------
     1     Mgr       -
     2     Sales     10
     3     Mgr       -
     4     DBA       15
```

Which of the following SQL statements will retrieve the rows that have unknown values in the *bonus* column?

A. SELECT * FROM t1 WHERE bonus = NULL
B. SELECT * FROM t1 WHERE bonus = ''
C. SELECT * FROM t1 WHERE bonus = '' OR bonus = 'NULL'
D. SELECT * FROM t1 WHERE bonus IS NULL
E. SELECT * FROM t1 WHERE bonus = '' OR bonus = ""

3. Given the following table *t1* in a DB2 9 database:

```
     id    job      bonus
----------------------------
     1     Mgr       -
     2     Sales     10
     3     Mgr       -
     4     DBA       15
```

Which of the following describes the result if this statement is executed?

```
SELECT id, job FROM OLD TABLE (DELETE FROM t1 WHERE bonus IS NULL)
```

A. The statement will fail because a SELECT statement cannot contain a DELETE statement.
B. The statement will succeed if no row is found for the DELETE statement.
C. The statement will succeed and return the number of rows deleted with the DELETE statement.
D. The statement will succeed and return the number of rows left in *t1* after the DELETE statement is executed.

4. Given the following tables:

```
Student_classA
      NAME           AGE
---------------------
      Mary            30
      Peter           35
      John            45
      Lilian          38
      Raymond         26
      Lilian          24
      Peter           38
      Peter           40
Student_classB
      NAME           AGE
---------------------
      Paul            26
      Peter           35
      Peter           29
      Christ          32
      Raymond         26
      Lilian          24
```

If the following SQL statement is executed, how many rows will be returned?

```
SELECT name FROM student_classA
INTERSECT
SELECT name FROM student_classB
```

A. 1
B. 2
C. 3
D. 4
E. 5

5. If you are working on a UNIX system and you want to select all rows from the org table, which of the following commands must be used?

A. db2 select * from org
B. db2 select(*) from org
C. db2 "select * from org"
D. db2 "select(*) from org"

6. Which of the following statements will return only 30 rows from the employee table?
   A. SELECT FIRST 30 ROWS FROM employee
   B. SELECT * FROM employee READ FIRST 30 ROWS ONLY
   C. SELECT * FROM employee OPTIMIZE FOR 30 ROWS
   D. SELECT * FROM employee FETCH FIRST 30 ROWS ONLY
7. Which of the following is a valid wildcard character in a LIKE clause of a SELECT statement?
   A. %
   B. _
   C. *
   D. @
8. Given the following **CREATE TABLE** statement:

```
CREATE TABLE employee
( id    INTEGER NOT NULL
, name VARCHAR(50)
, dept VARCHAR(10) NOT NULL DEFAULT 'A00'
, PRIMARY KEY (id) )
```

   Which two of the following statements will execute successfully?
   A. INSERT INTO employee VALUES (NULL, NULL, 'A00')
   B. INSERT INTO employee (name, dept) VALUES ('Peter', DEFAULT)
   C. INSERT INTO employee (id, name) VALUES (1234, 'Peter')
   D. INSERT INTO employee (id) VALUES (1234)
9. Given the following table:

```
CREATE TABLE employee
( id    INTEGER NOT NULL
, name VARCHAR(50)
, dept VARCHAR(10) NOT NULL DEFAULT 'A00'
, PRIMARY KEY (id) )
```

   If the following **SELECT** statement is executed, which of the following describes the order of the rows in the result returned?

```
SELECT id FROM employee
```

   A. The rows are not sorted in any particular order.
   B. The rows are sorted by id in ascending order.
   C. The rows are sorted by id in descending order.
   D. The rows are ordered based on the sequence of when the data were inserted into the table.
10. Given the following table, *newborn*:

```
baby_name       birth_date        doctor_name
--------------------------------------------------
JEREMY          05/22/2005        REICHER
KATHY           03/03/2005        WONG
```

```
CHLOE          01/23/2005      RICCI
WESLEY         10/24/2004      ATKINSON
FIONA          12/25/2004      JOHNSON
```

Which of the statements returns the list of baby names and their doctors who were born five days ago?

A. **SELECT baby_name, doctor_name**

```
FROM newborn
WHERE birth_date = DAYADD(TODAY, 5)
```

B. **SELECT baby_name, doctor_name**

```
FROM newborn
WHERE birth_date = CURRENT DATE - 5 DAYS
```

C. **SELECT baby_name, doctor_name**

```
FROM newborn
WHERE birth_date < TODAY - 5 DAYS
```

D. **SELECT baby_name, doctor_name**

```
FROM newborn
WHERE birth_date = DAYADD(CURRENT DATE, 5)
```

11. Given a table created using the statement:

```
CREATE TABLE foo (c1 INT, c2 INT, c3 INT)
```

To retrieve only the columns c1 and c3 from the table, which of the following statements should be used?

A. SELECT * FROM foo
B. SELECT c1,c3 FROM foo
C. SELECT 1,3 FROM foo
D. SELECT columns 1 and 3 FROM foo

12. To insert the current date into the column named dt in the table foo, which of the following statements should be used?

A. INSERT INTO foo (dt) VALUES date
B. INSERT INTO foo (dt) VALUES current date
C. INSERT INTO foo (dt) VALUES (date)
D. INSERT INTO foo (dt) VALUES (currentdate)

13. Which of the following statements deletes all the rows from the table?

A. DELETE FROM foo
B. DELETE * FROM foo
C. DELETE (SELECT * FROM foo)
D. DELETE ALL FROM foo

14. Given the following tables:

```
Table T                    Table S

col 1     col2             col 1     col2
-------   ------           -------   ------
2         Raul             2         Susan
4         Mary             5         Clara
8         Tom              6         Jenny
9         Glenn            9         Luisa
```

How many rows will the following MERGE statement return?

```
MERGE INTO t USING s
      ON   t.col1 = s.col1
      WHEN MATCHED THEN
       UPDATE SET t.col2 = s.col2
      WHEN NOT MATCHED THEN
           INSERT VALUES (s.col1, s.col2)
```

A. 0
B. 2
C. 4
D. 6
E. 8

15. Given the same tables as in question 14, how many rows will the following statement return?

```
SELECT * FROM t INNER JOIN s ON s.col1 = t.col1
```

A. 0
B. 1
C. 2
D. 3
E. 4

16. Given the same tables as in question 14, how many rows will the following statement return?

```
SELECT * FROM t FULL OUTER JOIN s ON s.col1 = t.col1
```

A. 0
B. 2
C. 4
D. 6
E. 8

17. Given the same tables as in question 14, how many rows will the following statement return?

```
SELECT * FROM t LEFT OUTER JOIN s ON s.col1 = t.col1
```

A. 0
B. 2
C. 4
D. 6
E. 8

18. Given the same tables as in question 14, how many rows will the following statement return?

```
SELECT * FROM t RIGHT OUTER JOIN s ON s.col1 = t.col1
```

A. 0
B. 2
C. 4
D. 6
E. 8

19. Assuming the table *employee* has 32 records, how many rows will the following statement return?

```
SELECT empno, salary
   FROM FINAL TABLE (INSERT INTO employee
                  (empno, firstnme, midinit, lastname, edlevel)
                   VALUES ('000999', 'SMITH', 'A', 'JOHN', 18 ),
                          ('001000', 'JOHNSON', 'A', 'TOM', 22 )
                  )
```

A. 0
B. 2
C. 32
D. 34
E. 36

20. Assuming the table *employee* has 10 records, how many records will there be in total after executing the following statement?

```
SELECT salary
   FROM NEW TABLE (INSERT INTO employee
                        (empno, firstnme, midinit, lastname, edlevel)
                        VALUES ('000999 ', 'SMITH ', 'A ', 'JOHN ', 18 ),
                               ('001000 ', 'JOHNSON ', 'A ', 'TOM ', 22 ) )
```

A. 0
B. 2
C. 4
D. 10
E. 12

CHAPTER 10

Mastering the DB2 pureXML Support

XML stands for e**X**tensible **M**arkup **L**anguage. Why is it increasingly popular? How does it impact the business world? Why do you want to exchange information in XML format? Why are we talking about XML with databases? This chapter provides the answers to all of these questions. We first provide some basic introduction to XML, then we look at the different XML capabilities offered by DB2.

In this chapter you will learn about:

- The fundamentals of XML
- Well-formed and validated XML documents
- XML namespaces and XML schema
- XPath expressions
- The pureXML support in DB2
- XQuery and SQL/XML languages
- XML schema support and validation in DB2
- Indexes over XML data
- XML performance considerations

NOTE pureXML support was introduced with DB2 9; therefore this entire chapter is new. We will not use the DB2 9 icon [V9] throughout the chapter starting from this point. However, we will use the DB2 9.5 icon [V9.5] for the new features added with that release of DB2.

10.1 XML: The Big Picture

This section provides an overview of XML from a business perspective. It helps us understand why XML is so important today. Many of the ideas in this section were also discussed in Chapter 1, Introduction to DB2.

Figure 10.1 is split into two sections divided by the box containing the text "eXtensible Markup Language (XML)." Above this box, we see different concepts or technologies that are keys in today's business world. Below this box you see concepts that are more specific to how XML works.

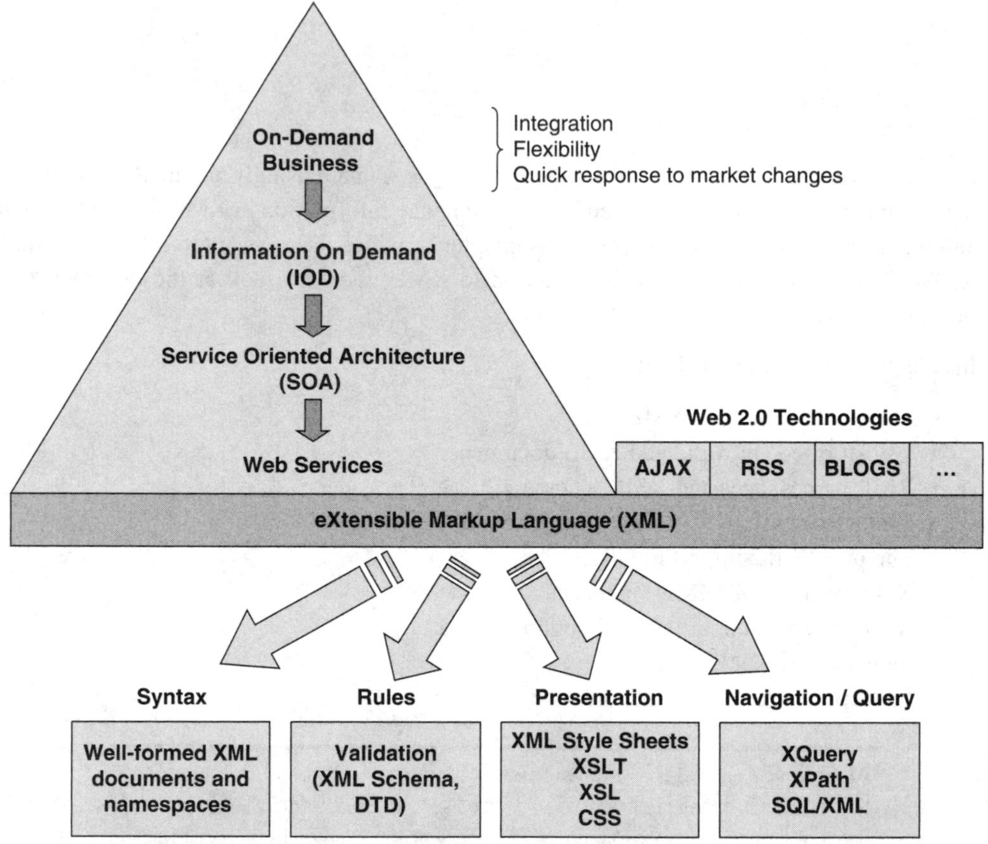

Figure 10.1 High-level overview of the XML

Why is XML so important today? This question can be answered by reviewing the top part of Figure 10.1. There are two main reasons.

1. XML is the foundation of Information on Demand.

   As illustrated by the triangle on the left of the figure, all the concepts inside the triangle, which were discussed earlier in Chapter 1, Introduction to DB2, depend on one another, and at the base is XML. This means that without XML, these concepts would be hard to implement; therefore XML is the foundation of Information on Demand, which is the foundation of an on-demand business.

2. **XML is the foundation of Web 2.0 technologies.**

   XML is the enabling technology of many Web 2.0 technologies such as Web services, AJAX, Atom, RSS, and blogs. This is highlighted in Figure 10.1, which shows XML at the base of all of these technologies. These tools and technologies were also described in Chapter 1, Introduction to DB2.

   XML is the ideal enabling technology because it is a language that describes itself and is very flexible: It can be easily extended; it can be transformed to other formats; is independent of the platform or vendor; and is easy to share. XML is a hierarchical data model ideal to store semi-structured information. For simplicity, at this stage of this chapter, you can think of an XML document simply as a text document with tags; however, as you will see later, XML is a lot more than that. For example, <name>Raul</name> is an XML document.

Below the "eXtensible Markup Language (XML)" box in Figure 10.1 the concepts and standards that make up an XML document are highlighted.

With respect to syntax, an XML document is a well-formed XML document when it follows the right syntax as defined by the World Wide Web Consortium (W3C) XML standard. XML namespaces, though optional, can help avoid name collisions in an XML document by providing prefixes to XML elements.

Ensuring that an XML document follows certain rules, data types, or a predefined structure is known as validation. Validation can be performed through Document Type Definitions (DTD) or XML Schema Definitions (XSD).

With respect to presentation, given an XML document, you can easily transform it to a format that the media knows how to present. For example, use XSLT (eXtensible Stylesheet Language Transformation) to transform XML documents into HTML documents so that data can be accurately displayed on a Web browser. Simply apply a different XML stylesheet to the same XML document, and you can present the content data on a browser in a different look and feel.

In terms of navigation, when you want to search for a specific content in an XML document you can use different languages such as XQuery, XPath, and SQL/XML.

> **NOTE** In this chapter we provide a brief introduction to XML covering only the concepts needed to understand the basics. For a complete description of XML please review any of the many books on the subject.

10.1.1 What Is XML?

XML is a language designed to describe data; its focus is on describing *what the data is*. To further understand what XML is, let's compare it to HTML (Hyper Text Markup Language) given that HTML is known by most people nowadays. HTML is a language designed to describe how to display data; its focus is on presentation, *how the data looks*. Additionally, HTML provides a fixed set of predefined tags while XML allows you to define your own tags to describe your data. This is one of the reasons for the "X" in XML: you can extend the language based on your needs. XML is not a replacement of HTML, instead it complements HTML. You can think of XML as a superset of HTML. XML is a hierarchical data model and is comprised of nodes such as elements and attributes. XML elements are containers of information and can also contain other elements. Figure 10.2 shows an example of an XML document.

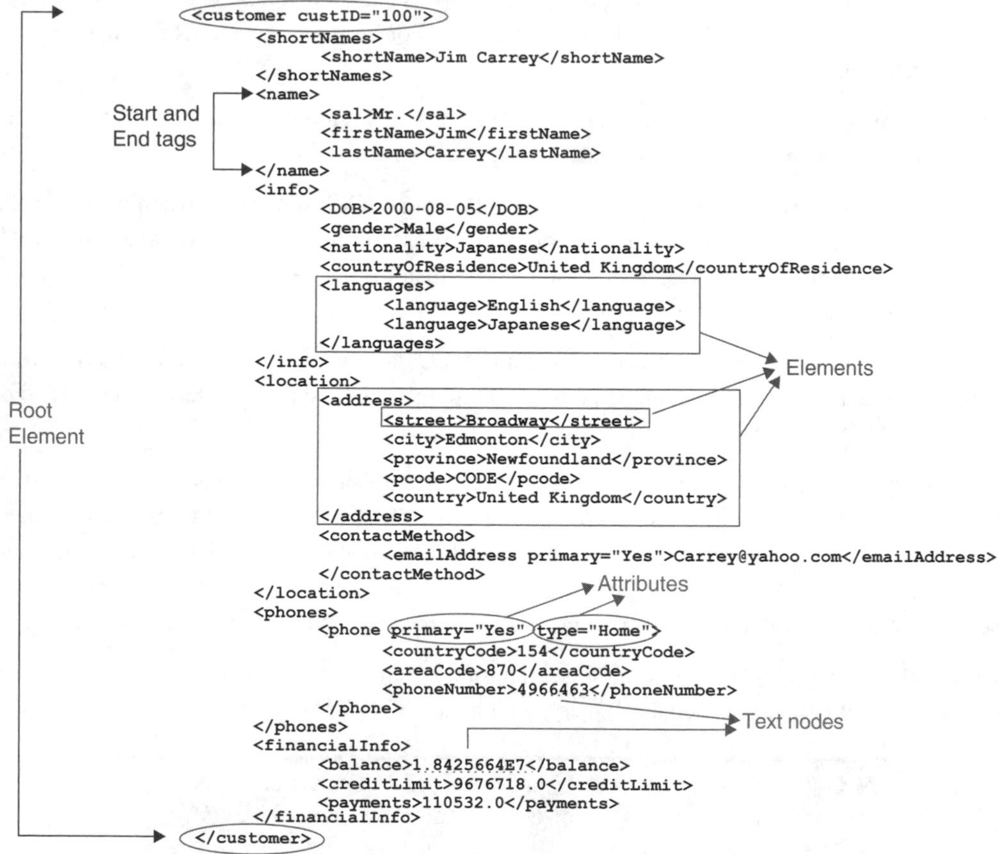

```
<customer custID="100">
    <shortNames>
        <shortName>Jim Carrey</shortName>
    </shortNames>
    <name>
        <sal>Mr.</sal>
        <firstName>Jim</firstName>
        <lastName>Carrey</lastName>
    </name>
    <info>
        <DOB>2000-08-05</DOB>
        <gender>Male</gender>
        <nationality>Japanese</nationality>
        <countryOfResidence>United Kingdom</countryOfResidence>
        <languages>
            <language>English</language>
            <language>Japanese</language>
        </languages>
    </info>
    <location>
        <address>
            <street>Broadway</street>
            <city>Edmonton</city>
            <province>Newfoundland</province>
            <pcode>CODE</pcode>
            <country>United Kingdom</country>
        </address>
        <contactMethod>
            <emailAddress primary="Yes">Carrey@yahoo.com</emailAddress>
        </contactMethod>
    </location>
    <phones>
        <phone primary="Yes" type="Home">
            <countryCode>154</countryCode>
            <areaCode>870</areaCode>
            <phoneNumber>4966463</phoneNumber>
        </phone>
    </phones>
    <financialInfo>
        <balance>1.8425664E7</balance>
        <creditLimit>9676718.0</creditLimit>
        <payments>110532.0</payments>
    </financialInfo>
</customer>
```


Figure 10.2 An XML document and its components

Table 10.1 describes the items in Figure 10.2.

Table 10.1 XML Document Components

XML Document Component	Description	Example from Figure 10.2
Element	An element is a logical unit of information in an XML document and is used to describe a piece of information. It is comprised of two tags, an opening tag, for example **<street>**, and a closing tag, for example **</street>.** Note that the closing tag has an extra "/". An element can occur once or multiple times in a row.	`<street>` `Broadway` `</street>`
Root element (or root node)	The root element must contain all other elements.	`<customer>` `< ...>` `< ...>` `</customer>`
Attribute	These are pieces of information that can appear within an element's opening tag. An element can have multiple attributes but each attribute can occur only once per element. Unlike elements, attributes cannot contain other nodes.	`<phone primary = "Yes"` `type = "Home">` `</phone>`
Text nodes	This is the information provided within the tags of an element.	`<language>` `English` `</language>`

10.1.2 Well-Formed Versus Valid XML Documents

Well-formed XML documents and valid XML documents are two different concepts often confused.

A **well-formed** XML document is a document that follows these basic rules.

1. It must have one and only one root element.
2. Each element begins with a start tag and ends with an end tag.
3. An element can contain other elements, attributes, or text nodes.
4. Attribute values must be enclosed in double quotes. Text nodes, on the other hand, should not.

Table 10.2 shows examples of XML documents that are well-formed and *not* well-formed.

As mentioned in Table 10.2, XML document tag names are case sensitive; for example **<name>** is different from **<Name>.**

For the complete set of rules and definitions of a well-formed XML document, refer to the W3C recommendation at http://www.w3.org/TR/REC-xml.

Table 10.2 Examples of Well-Formed and Not Well-Formed XML Documents

XML Document	Why It's Not Well Formed	Well-Formed Version
<author> **<name>Raul** **</author>**	Missing ending tag for **<name>**.	**<author>** **<name>Raul</name>** **</author>**
<author></author> **<name>Raul</name>**	There is no root element.	**<author>** **<name>Raul</name>** **</author>**
<author> **<name>Raul</author>** **</name>**	Starting and ending tags not matching.	**<author>** **<name>Raul</name>** **</author>**
<author id = 1> **<name>Raul</name>** **</author>**	Attribute **id** is not enclosed in double quotes.	**<author id = “1”>** **<name>Raul</name>** **</author>**
<author id = “1”> **<name>“Raul”</name>** **</author>**	The information content **Raul** should not be enclosed in quotes.	**<author id = “1”>** **<name>Raul</name>** **</author>**
<author> **<name>Raul</NAME>** **</author>**	Starting and ending tags not matching for element **name**. Tag names are case sensitive.	**<author>** **<name>Raul</name>** **</author>**

A **valid** XML document is

1. A well-formed XML document.
2. A document compliant with the rules defined in an XML schema document or a Document Type Definition (DTD) document.

Validation is the process of checking whether a given XML document is valid with respect to a particular XML schema or DTD. An XML schema defines the structure, content, and data types of XML documents.

> **NOTE** DTD, though still used, is the "older" method to perform validation. In this book we focus on the "newer" method of using XML schemas.

You can choose to validate or not to validate an XML document. Validation can be performed at various levels of your infrastructure, for example, in the application server and/or your DB2 database. Validation can help you ensure that the data complies with predefined rules and is in a format that the application expects. Validation may not be required if the XML data is produced by a trusted source.

Before taking a closer look at XML schemas and validation, let's first introduce the concept of a namespace in the next section.

10.1.3 Namespaces in XML

There may be situations where your application interacts with XML documents provided from different independent sources where element names are the same. For example, one such source may be using the tag "address" to represent the address of a customer, while another source may be using the same tag "address" to represent the address of a financial institution such as a bank. This name collision can cause confusion and may result in application errors. Namespaces in XML are used to prevent this problem. You can declare a default namespace which would be used for all XML elements in the XML document, or you can declare a namespace with a prefix to be used on specific XML elements. Figure 10.3 shows an XML document with XML namespaces using prefixes.

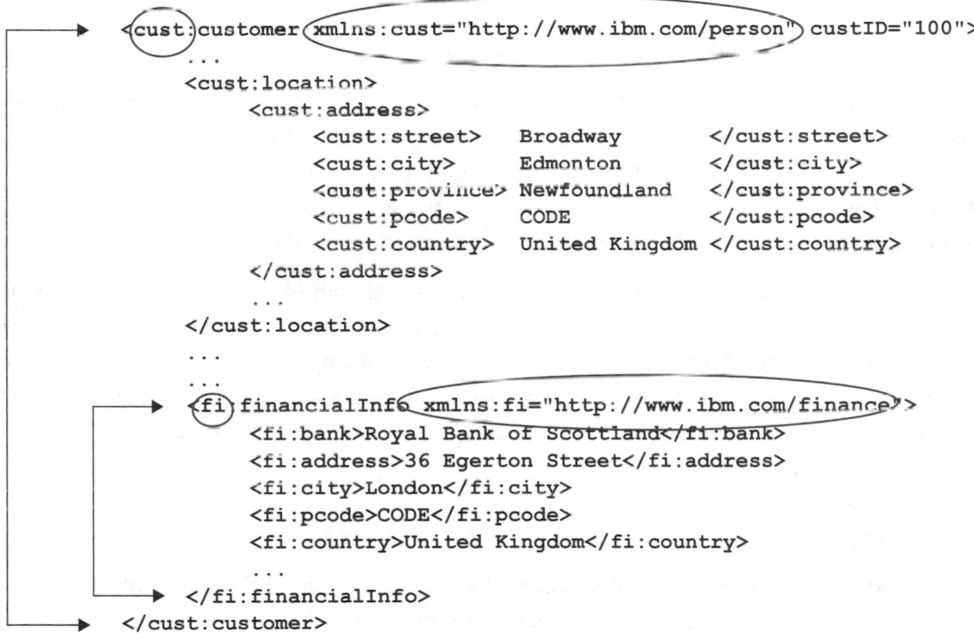

Figure 10.3 XML namespace declarations for nested XML elements

In Figure 10.3 the ellipses on the first line highlight an XML namespace definition. Let's analyze this line in more detail:

```
<cust:customer xmlns:cust="http://www.ibm.com/person" custID="100">
```

xmlns:cust="http://www.ibm.com/person" means that we want to define a namespace using the prefix *cust* to represent the Universal Resource Identifier (URI) "http://www.ibm.com/person".

A URI, which typically looks like a Uniform Resource Locator (URL), is a unique identifier. For example, http://www.ibm.com/db2v9 and http://abc.def.ghi/uri are URIs. Note that a URI does not have to point to a real Web page; it is just an identifier.

The prefix *cust* can be used in the same line that it is defined

```
<cust:customer .....>
```

Note as well that multiple namespaces can be defined in the root element or any element of the document. Once the prefix and namespace have been declared, all elements using the prefix can be easily distinguished from other elements. For example, in Figure 10.3 we see

```
<cust:address>      ... </cust:address>
...
```

and

```
<fi:address>36 Egerton Street</fi:address>
```

Because the element address is used with prefixes, we can distinguish that **<cust:address>** is the element whose namespace uses the prefix **cust,** while **<fi:address>** is the element whose namespace uses the prefix **fi.** As long as both prefixes are associated to different URIs they can provide this distinction. If both prefixes (**cust** and **fi**) were assigned to the same URI then **<fi:address>** and <**cust:address>** are considered identical elements.

An XML namespace applies to the current element and all sub-elements and attributes that it contains. For example in Figure 10.3, the elements **customer, location, address, street, city, province, pcode** and **country,** belong to the **cust** namespace. Note that this namespace is overridden by the namespace with prefix **fi** defined later on in the document. The scope of the namespace with prefix **fi** is just within the **financialInfo** element, its sub-elements and attributes.

10.1.4 XML Schema

As mentioned earlier, an XML schema defines the structure of an XML document. We will use the example below to demonstrate what makes up an XML schema. Let's take a look at the XML document (*address.xml*) in Figure 10.4.

The XML schema file (*address.xsd*) that defines the elements of *address.xml* is illustrated in Figure 10.5. In the figure we have included the numbers (1), (2), (3), and so on to different sections in the document to make it easier to explain the different blocks in the XML schema document.

```
<location>
    <address>
        <street>78 Harrison Garden Blvd</street>
        <city>Toronto</city>
        <province>Ontario</province>
        <pcode>L5N 6G3</pcode>
        <country>Canada</country>
    </address>
    <contactMethod>
         <emailAddress primary="Yes">Carrey@yahoo.com</emailAddress>
    </contactMethod>
</location>
```

Figure 10.4 XML document address.xml

```
(1)-- <xsd:schema xmlns:xsd="http://www.w3.org/2001/XMLSchema">

(2)--  <xsd:element name="location">
         <xsd:complexType>
           <xsd:sequence>
             <xsd:element ref="address"/>
             <xsd:element ref="contactMethod"/>
           </xsd:sequence>
         </xsd:complexType>
     </xsd:element>

(3)--  <xsd:element name="address">
         <xsd:complexType>
           <xsd:sequence>
             <xsd:element ref="street"/>
             <xsd:element ref="city"/>
             <xsd:element ref="province"/>
             <xsd:element ref="pcode"/>
             <xsd:element ref="country"/>
           </xsd:sequence>
         </xsd:complexType>
       </xsd:element>

 (4)-- <xsd:element name="contactMethod">
         <xsd:complexType>
           <xsd:sequence>
             <xsd:element ref="emailAddress"/>
           </xsd:sequence>
         </xsd:complexType>
       </xsd:element>

 (5)-- <xsd:element name="emailAddress">
         <xsd:complexType>
           <xsd:attribute name="primary" type="xsd:string"/>
```

Figure 10.5 XML schema file address.xsd

```
        </xsd:complexType>
      </xsd:element>
  (6)-- <xsd:element name="street"   type="xsd:string"/>
      <xsd:element name="city"     type="xsd:string"/>
      <xsd:element name="province" type="xsd:string"/>
      <xsd:element name="pcode"    type="xsd:string"/>
      <xsd:element name="country"  type="xsd:string"/>

    </xsd:schema>
```

Figure 10.5 XML schema file address.xsd *(Continued)*

> **NOTE** In Figure 10.5 we use a XML schema with a specific style that uses unnamed complex types and "ref" to refer to other elements. A different and equally popular style is to define **named** complex types to reference a certain element by its type rather than by using "ref". In DB2 there is no preference for one style over the other.

First of all, an XML schema is itself an XML document. In block (1) note the definition of the namespace:

```
<xsd:schema xmlns:xsd="http://www.w3.org/2001/XMLSchema">
…
</xsd:schema>
```

Its root element is called **schema,** and this must be used to identify this XML document as an XML schema document.

Its namespace uses the prefix **xsd** and it's defined with the URI **http://www.w3.org/2001/XMLSchema.**

In block (2), we have

```
<xsd:element name="location">
   <xsd:complexType>
     <xsd:sequence>
       <xsd:element ref="address"/>
       <xsd:element ref="contactMethod"/>
     </xsd:sequence>
   </xsd:complexType>
</xsd:element>
```

This block defines the element **location** as an element of complex type because it contains other elements. The other elements it contains are **address** and **contactMethod.**

Similarly to the explanation for block (2), in block (3) we have the definition for element **address,** which is of complex type because it contains other elements such as **street, city, province, pcode,** and **country.**

In block (4) we have the definition for element **contactMethod,** which is of complex type because it contains another element, namely **emailAddress.**

Block (5) indicates that **emailAddress** is also of complex type because it contains the attribute **primary.** In this block we also see that **primary** is defined as a string, a simple type.

In Block (6) we see that the other elements: **street, city, province, pcode,** and **country** are all simple types of string.

An element defined with the simple type can contain only built-in data types included in the XML Schema definition (for example, xsd:string, xsd:date, xsd:integer, etc.) or user-defined data types. Notice also that there is an attribute defined in the **emailAddress** element (block (5)). An attribute definition is very similar to an element.

You can provide a default or a fixed value to a simple element or attribute. For example, we use the **default** keyword to set a default value of "BR" for the **country** element when no other value is specified.

```
<xsd:element name="country" type="xsd:string" default="BR"/>
```

To specify a fixed value for the **primary** attribute when no other value is accepted, the keyword **fixed** is used as shown here.

```
<xsd:attribute name="primary" type="xsd:string" fixed="yes"/>
```

It is often very useful to restrict certain values or patterns to elements or attributes. There are many possible constraints you can put on the data types. The following example shows you how to define a pattern if the content of the **pcode** element must contain six digits where each digit must be between 0 and 7.

```
<xsd:element name="country">
  <xsd:simpleType>
    <xsd:restriction base="xs:string">
            <xsd:pattern value="[0-7][0-7][0-7][0-7][0-7][0-7]"/>
    </xsd:restriction>
  </xsd:simpleType>
</xsd:element>
```

Note that [0-7] is repeated six times to indicate that element **pcode** can at most have six digits.

In this other example, assume you want the content of the **country** element to be only one of the acceptable values listed. Notice that the **country** element uses the **countryType** type which has a string-base data type and a list of acceptable values. These values are specified in the **enumeration** elements.

```
<xsd:element name="country" type="countryType"/>

<xsd:simpleType name="countryType">>
    <xsd:restriction base="xs:string">
        <xsd:enumeration value="Brazil"/>
```

```
        <xsd:enumeration value="Canada"/>
        <xsd:enumeration value="China"/>
        <xsd:enumeration value="India"/>
        <xsd:enumeration value="Russia"/>
        <xsd:enumeration value="United States"/>
    </xsd:restriction>
</xsd:simpleType>
```

10.1.5 Working with XML Documents

SQL is a language used to query relational data as we saw in Chapter 9, Leveraging the Power of SQL. It works with rows and columns of a table. With SQL you can retrieve entire XML documents stored in columns defined with the XML data type; however, if you want to retrieve only parts of an XML document you need either XQuery or SQL with XML extensions, also known as SQL/XML.

10.1.5.1 XML Parsers: DOM Versus SAX

In general, application developers need to parse XML documents after retrieving them from a database in order to process them. Though this book is not focusing on application development, this section may help Database Administrators (DBAs) understand the work developers must do to process XML documents.

There are two methods to parse an XML document as shown in Figure 10.6, Document Object Model (DOM) and Simple API for XML (SAX).

Using the DOM parser, the input XML document in serialized format is read and converted into a parsed-hierarchical format, which has a tree structure. This is performed at runtime when the entire tree is loaded into memory at once, and traversed using specialized methods. Since the entire tree has to be built first and loaded into memory, this method is resource intensive. Even though it may not be that good for performance, it is easier to use than a SAX parser.

Using the SAX parser, the input XML document is parsed into a stream of events which are processed by your application. This method is faster and uses less memory; however, it is harder to use since your application needs to perform most of the work. In particular, navigating upwards or backwards in the document tree is easy with DOM but more difficult with SAX where you are responsible for buffering the relevant events that you may want to revisit.

XML parsers only work with well-formed XML documents. Syntax errors will be returned if any of the well-formed rules are violated.

NOTE With DB2 9.5 we support JDBC 4.0 where a simple API call is enough to retrieve XML from DB2 in DOM or SAX format. In other words, this parsing is done for you, simplifying the Java application development work.

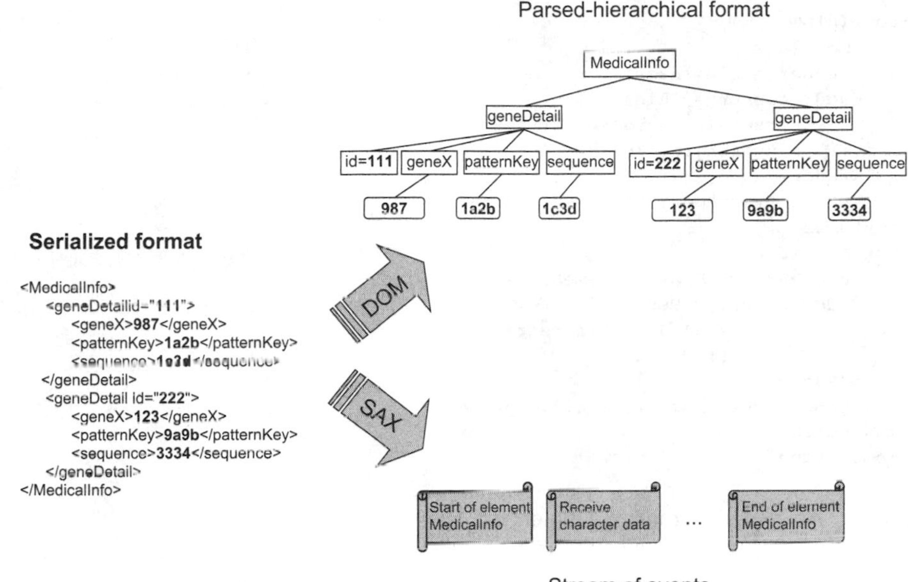

Figure 10.6 DOM versus SAX parsers

As we will see in Section 10.2, pureXML in DB2, DB2 uses SAX parsing when an XML document is first inserted into the database to build its internal tree format from the stream of events.

10.1.5.2 XQuery and XPath

XQuery is a W3C standard and is the language for searching and extracting XML data. XQuery includes the FLWOR expression which allows for great flexibility when querying XML documents. The FLWOR expression is discussed in more detail in Section 10.3.1.3 XQuery with FLWOR Expressions.

XQuery also includes XPath, which is a language that uses path expressions to navigate XML documents. You can think of XPath as navigating a tree built by a parser such as DOM. Although XPath navigation over a tree is the most intuitive way to think about it, XPath navigation can just as well be accomplished over a stream of SAX events, or over a binary XML format.

Navigating a tree is something you probably have already done without noticing it. How do you change directories in Windows, Linux or UNIX using the command line? You use the **`change directory (cd)`** operating system command. Using **`cd`** you specify the directory paths by using slashes. Similarly, with XPath you traverse a tree by defining path expressions, that is, you specify element and attribute names separated by slashes. Each slash denotes a *step* in the path.

The best way to learn more about XPath is by using an example. Assume you have the XML document illustrated in Figure 10.7.

```
<customerInfo>
   <customer id ="1">
        <name>Xie Jin</name>
        <addr country="China">
            <street>12 Guang Rd</street>
            <city>Beijing</city>
        </addr>
        <phone type="work">8891-987</phone>
   </customer>
   <customer id ="2">
        <name>Stuart Fraser</name>
        <addr country="Peru">
            <street>334 Junin</street>
            <city>Lima</city>
        </addr>
        <phone type="home">987-6121</phone>
   </customer>
</customerInfo>
```

Figure 10.7 An XML document customerInfo.xml

The corresponding tree representation of this *customerInfo.xml* XML document is shown in Figure 10.8.

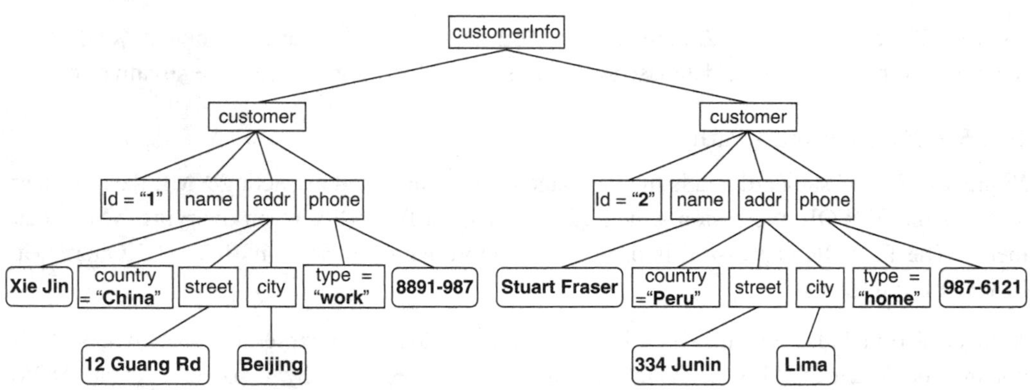

Figure 10.8 Tree representation of customerInfo.xml

Each XML document has a single root element which is sitting at the top of the tree in Figure 10.8. Under the root element, you can have element, attribute, text, namespace, comment, and process-instruction nodes. Process-instruction nodes are not present in the example above. They are used to provide instructions for processing the XML to generate the output. The most popular use of XML processing instructions includes XSL (Extensible Stylesheet Language) or CSS (Cascading Style Sheets) to format the XML document. Detailed explanation of these stylesheets is outside of the scope of this book; however, you can get an idea of how they work with this example of a process-instruction node where the type and filename of the stylesheet is provided.

```
<?xml-stylesheet type="text/css" href="licenserpt.css"?>
```

10.1.5.2.1 XPath Expressions

XPath takes advantage of expressions to more easily locate elements and attributes. Table 10.3 provides some useful XPath expressions.

Table 10.3 Some Common XPath Expressions

/	Selects from the root node.
//	Selects nodes in the document from the current node that match the select.
text()	Specifies the text node under an element.
@	Specifies an attribute.
*	Matches any element node.
@*	Matches any attribute node.

Table 10.4 illustrates the output of different XPath expressions using as input the *customer-info.xml* file illustrated in Figure 10.8.

Table 10.4 Examples of XPath Expressions

XPath Expressions	Result Description	Result
/customerInfo	Selects the root element *customerInfo*.	The entire XML document as shown in Figure 10.7
/customerInfo/*/phone/text()	Selects the text node under the *phone* element of *customerInfo*.	**8891-987** **987-6121**
/customerInfo//addr/@country	Selects the *country* attribute under the *addr* element of *customerInfo*.	**China** **Peru**
//phone	Selects all *phone* elements in the document.	**<phone type="work">** **8891-987** **</phone>** **<phone type="home">** **987-6121** **</phone>**

(continues)

Table 10.4 Examples of XPath Expressions *(Continued)*

XPath Expressions	Result Description	Result
//phone/text()	Selects text node of all *phone* elements in the document.	`8891-987` `987-6121`
//@type	Selects all *type* attributes in the document.	`work` `home`

/customerInfo/customer/addr/*	Selects all *elements* under the *addr* element.	`<street>`
		`12 Guang Rd`
		`</street>`
		`<city>`
		`Beijing`
		`</city>`
		`<street>`
		`334 Junin`
		`</street>`
		`<city>`
		`Lima`
		`</city>`

/customerInfo/customer/phone[@*]	Selects all *phone* elements under *customerInfo,* which have any attribute.	`<phone type="work">`
		`8891-987`
		`</phone>`
		`<phone type="home">`
		`987-6121`
		`</phone>`

You can also use predicates in XPath to find a specific node or a node that contains a specific value. Predicates are always surrounded by square brackets. Table 10.5 provides some examples using Figure 10.8 as the input XML document.

Table 10.5 Examples of XPath Expressions with Predicates

XPath Expressions	Result Description	Result

`/customerInfo/`
`customer[1]/`
`phone/text()`
	Selects the **phone** element text node under the first **customer** of **customerInfo.**	`8891-987`

`/customerInfo/`
`customer`
`[last()]/name`
	Selects the **name** of the last **customer** element in the document.	`<name>`
		`Stuart Fraser`
		`</name>`

Table 10.5 Examples of XPath Expressions with Predicates *(Continued)*

XPath Expressions	Result Description	Result
//addr[@country='Peru']	Selects all **addr** elements with **country** attribute = 'Peru' in the document.	**<addr country="Peru"> <street> 334 Junin </street> <city> Lima </city> </addr>**
//addr[city='Beijing']	Selects all **addr** elements in the document that has a **city** element with a value of 'Beijing'.	**<addr country="China"> <street> 12 Guang Rd </street> <city> Beijing </city> </addr>**
/customerInfo/*/phone[@type]	Selects all **phone** elements under **customerInfo** which has an attribute named type.	**<phone type="work"> 8891-987 </phone> <phone type="home"> 987-6121 </phone>**
/customerInfo//phone[@type='home']	Selects all **phone** elements under **customerInfo** which has an attribute named type with a value of 'home'.	**<phone type="home"> 987-6121 </phone>**

10.1.5.3 SQL/XML

SQL/XML is an extension of the SQL language. It provides support for using XML in the context of a relational database system. As part of the SQL 2006 ANSI/ISO standard, SQL/XML defines a mechanism for using SQL and XML together. This standard includes the following:

- The XML data type which treats XML data in the database as XML and not as character data. This data type was discussed in Chapter 7, Working with Database Objects.

- XML publishing functions to publish the existing SQL data converted into XML documents.
- Conversion functions to convert the XML data type to CHAR, VARCHAR, or CLOB data type and back.
- Functions to use XQuery and XPath in SQL statements.

Table 10.6 lists the SQL/XML functions supported in DB2. We discuss some of these functions in subsequent sections.

Table 10.6 SQL/XML Functions Supported in DB2

Function Name	Description
XMLVALIDATE	Validates XML value against an XML schema and type-annotates the XML value.
XMLEXISTS	Determines if an XQuery returns a result (i.e. a sequence of one or more items).
XMLQUERY	Executes an XQuery and returns the result sequence.
XMLTABLE	Executes an XQuery and returns the result sequence as a relational table (if possible).
XMLCAST	Casts to or from an XML type.
XMLELEMENT	Creates an XML element.
XMLATTRIBUTES	Used within XMLELEMENT to create attributes.
XMLFOREST	Produces a forest of XML elements from a list of SQL values.
XMLCONCAT	Concatenates a list of XML values.
XMLNAMESPACES	Provides XML namespace declarations in an XML element.
XMLAGG	Groups a set of XML rows.
XMLCOMMENT	Generates an XQuery comment node.
XMLPI	Generates an XQuery processing instruction node.
XMLTEXT	Generates an XQuery text node.
XMLDOCUMENT	Generates an XQuery document node.
XMLSERIALIZE	Converts an XML value into character/BLOB data.
XMLPARSE	Parses character/BLOB data, produces XML value.

10.1.6 XML versus the Relational Model

The relational model to store data is the most prevalent in the industry today. Most applications work well with relational databases. Why are we focusing so much on XML then? What are the specific advantages of working with XML (based on the hierarchical model) versus the relational model?

There are several reasons why you would like to work with XML documents instead of using the relational model.

1. If you will be storing semi-structured type of information, for example the DNA of people, then XML documents are more appropriate. Figure 10.9 provides an example where the same information is stored in a relational table, and on XML.

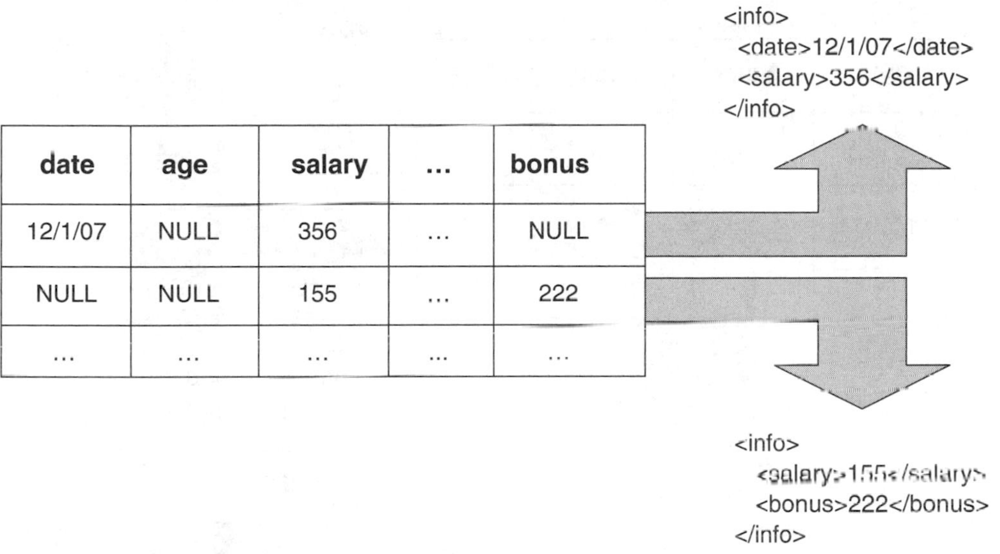

date	age	salary	...	bonus
12/1/07	NULL	356	...	NULL
NULL	NULL	155	...	222
...	...	...	...	...

Figure 10.9 Storing data in a relational table and XML

In Figure 10.9, using the relational table requires the use of many NULLs; therefore, it is inefficient, and applications may require code to deal with complex mappings. Using XML to represent each row is better as it avoids placing data into multiple columns, it uses only two elements versus 1000 columns, and it can be transformed and extended. Moreover, storing data this way also simplifies mapping.

2. If the schema or structure of your database changes constantly, using XML is a better choice. Normally with relational databases a database architect spends a good amount of time in the design of the database using Entity-Relationship (ER) diagrams, and creating logical and physical designs. It is important to have a good design, because the relational model is more appropriate for fixed schemas, or schemas that will not often change. For example, if you are developing an application builder, it may be better to use XML, because in an application builder you will be expecting users to add, delete, or modify fields. The application may have to drop and recreate tables for this purpose if a relational database is used; however, with XML there is no need for this. In XML you can simply add or remove an XML element when a field is added or removed to the structure respectively. Figure 10.10 shows an example illustrating this case.

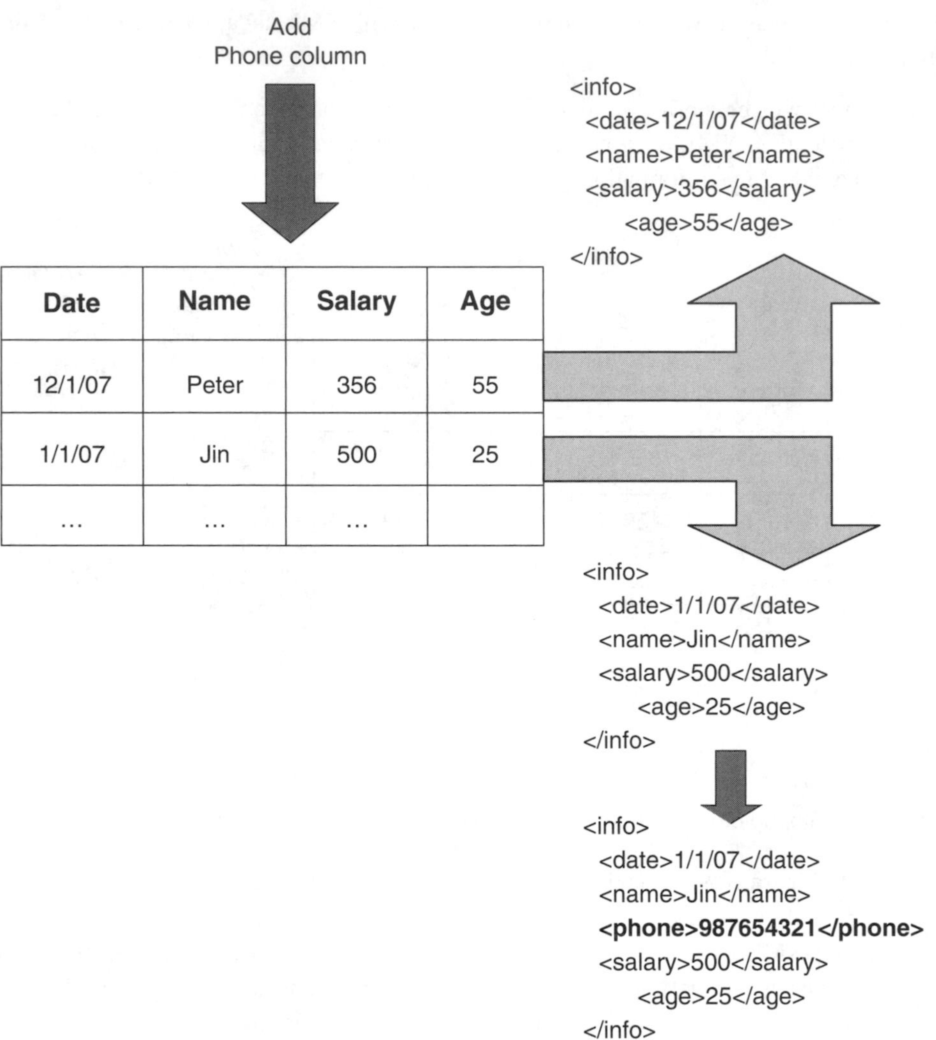

Figure 10.10 Making changes to the schema

In Figure 10.10 let's assume you would like to add the **Phone** column between the **Name** and **Salary** columns. Behind the scenes the data server may have to unload the existing data, drop the table, recreate it with the right columns including the **Phone** column, and load the data back. Compare this process to how easy this change would be done in XML. In XML if a document needs to store the phone information, the **phone** element can be added to the particular XML document. In Figure 10.10, **Peter** does not have a telephone number, but **Jin** does; therefore the figure shows the phone element for **Jin.**

3. Your data may be too complex to be easily modeled in a relational schema.
4. Your schema may be fixed but within that schema you have a lot of variability and different options.

5. For data exchange: You receive XML data, need to process it, and send it out also as XML. If you used a relational database, the XML data would first need to be converted to relational data for processing, and then back to XML to send these data out. This incurs extra cost and complexity.

Table 10.7 lists the differences between the two models.

Table 10.7 Relational Versus Hierarchical (XML) Model

Relational	Hierarchical (XML)
Relational data is flat	XML data is nested.
Relational model is set oriented. Sets are unordered.	XML retrieves sequences (the order matters).
Relational data is structured.	XML data is semi-structured.
Relational data has a strong schema, unlikely to change often.	XML data has a flexible schema, appropriate for constant changes.
Use NULL for an unknown state.	NULLs don't exist. Don't add any XML element.
Based on the ANSI/ISO industry standards.	Based on the W3C industry standards.

10.1.7 XML and Databases

The previous sections described why XML is important, and also the fact that XML and relational data are different. You may be wondering then, what does XML have to do with databases? There are two main reasons.

1. Databases are great to manage large amounts of information.

   XML documents can be stored in files, XML repositories, or databases. IBM and many other companies believe databases provide the best solution. Databases are a mature technology that is best to store large amounts of data. They provide a secure environment, and can quickly and efficiently search for specific information. Databases also allow for persistency, recoverability, and so on. All the advantages of using a database to store data apply also to XML documents. After all, XML documents are data just like any other forms of data.

   What about XML repositories? Why would they not be good to store XML documents? XML repositories are software developed specifically to store XML documents. There are not that many of these repositories in the market today, and they were developed at the time databases did not provide good support to store XML documents in an efficient manner. Software companies developing XML repositories are actually reinventing the wheel: They are developing software to provide the same features a database already has! Their technology is not as robust as using database technology, while database technology has matured over the years.

2. Storing XML data in databases allows for integration of relational and XML data in a single query.

   By storing relational and XML documents together, you can integrate new XML data with existing relational data, and combine SQL with XPath or XQuery into one query. Moreover, relational data can be published as XML, and vice versa. Through integration, databases can better support Web applications, SOA, and Web services. For example let's take a look at the table in Figure 10.11.

PATIENTS table

NAME	SEX	AGE	COFFEE	SMOKE	DNA
Elizabeth	F	65	35	15	geneX = 987
Raul	M	47	10	0	geneX = 987
...					
Tina	F	58	4	10	geneX = 123

Figure 10.11 Integrating relational with XML data

In Figure 10.11 the table **PATIENTS** stores relational data such as the **NAME, SEX, AGE,** the years the person has been drinking coffee (column **COFFEE**), and the years the person has been smoking (column **SMOKE**). In addition, the last column of the table is storing the **DNA** of each patient as an XML document. Because XML is based on the hierarchical model, we are representing XML documents in the figure as trees which are hierarchical in nature. Now let's say you work at a medical research facility, and your goal is to determine relationships between different factors (such as age, years smoking, etc.) and specific genes, say "gene X with a value of 987." By storing relational and XML data in the same table you could run SQL/XML queries that would allow you to perform different interesting tests. For example, you could run a query to answer the following question:

"Show me the names of all the women who are older than 55 years old, who have been drinking coffee for more than 15 years, and who have been smoking for more than 10 years, where geneX has a value of 987." The query would look like this in DB2:

```
(1) ---    SELECT name from PATIENTS
(2) ---    WHERE xmlexists('$p/Patient/MedicalDetail[geneX="987"]'
(3) ---                      passing PATIENTS.DNA as "p")
(4) ---              and sex = 'F'
(5) ---              and age > 55
(6) ---              and coffee > 15
(7) ---              and smoke > 10
```

In the query, lines (1), (4), (5), (6) and (7) are using SQL as explained in Chapter 9, Leveraging the Power of SQL. In line (2) we are calling the **XMLEXISTS** function, which is part of the SQL 2006 standard (SQL with XML extensions) and will be described in more detail in a later section. **$p** in line (2) indicates that **p** is a variable; this variable is defined in line (3) which indicates that variable **p** holds the column **PATIENTS.DNA,** in other words, variable **p** holds the XML document. Once we know what the variable **p** is holding, it should be easy to understand that in **$p/Patient/MedicalDetail[geneX="987"]** we are using XPath to navigate the tree until we test for the value of geneX to be equal to "987."

Running this type of query can lead to discovering relationships between factors such as drinking coffee or smoking and given genes that may be related to some diseases. In other words, this type of analysis could potentially lead to the discovery of cures for certain diseases. This is just a fictitious example, but we hope it helps you understand why it is beneficial to integrate both types of data. We discuss more queries like this in later sections of this chapter.

10.1.7.1 Methods to Store and Work with XML Documents in Databases

There are three methods to store XML documents in databases:

- Using a CLOB or varchar column
- Using the "shredding" (also known as decomposition) method
- Using pureXML.

10.1.7.1.1 Using a CLOB or VARCHAR Column

XML documents can be stored intact as plain unparsed text. This process is quite simple, but ignores the internal structure of the XML documents. The underlying storage can be a CLOB column or a VARCHAR column within a database. Outside of databases, you can use files within the file system. Processing XML documents stored this way is not flexible and not good for performance. Figure 10.12 illustrates this method.

10.1.7.1.2 Using the Shredding Method to Store XML Documents

Figure 10.13 illustrates how XML documents are stored using the shredding method. This method shreds or decomposes the XML document into small pieces, where each piece is stored in a column of a relational table. This forces the hierarchical XML data model into the flat relational model. Extra join columns are required to keep the relationship between the tables. This

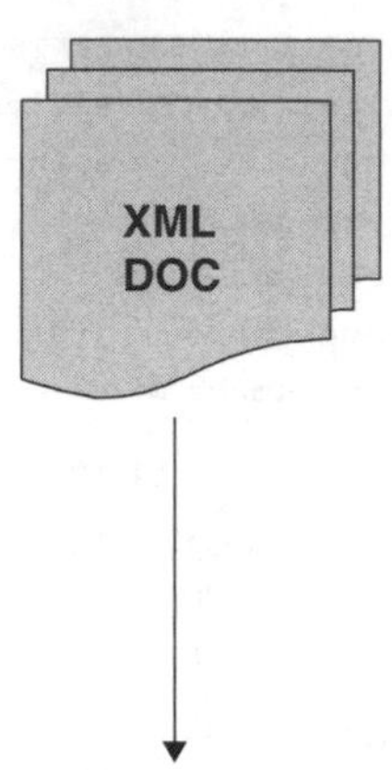

name varchar(30)	**dna** CLOB/varchar
Jin	**XML DOC**
Raul	**XML DOC**
...	...

Figure 10.12 Using a CLOB or VARCHAR column to store XML documents

method is not flexible when it comes to changing an XML document because propagating this change may require the creation of more tables and/or fields, and several columns may need to be populated with NULL values. In addition, this method is not good for performance because if you would like to compose the original XML document back to the way it was, you would have to perform a multi-way SQL JOIN operation which is expensive. Some XML documents that are shredded may require many tables; therefore, the performance for this type of document would be very bad with too many JOIN operations.

Shredding XML documents implies that if you issue an XQuery or XPath statement, this statement has to first be mapped to SQL so that the relational engine can process it.

10.1.7.1.3 Using pureXML

pureXML implies that XML is stored in a parsed hierarchical format at INSERT time. This is good for performance at query time, because there is no need to build this tree for processing as

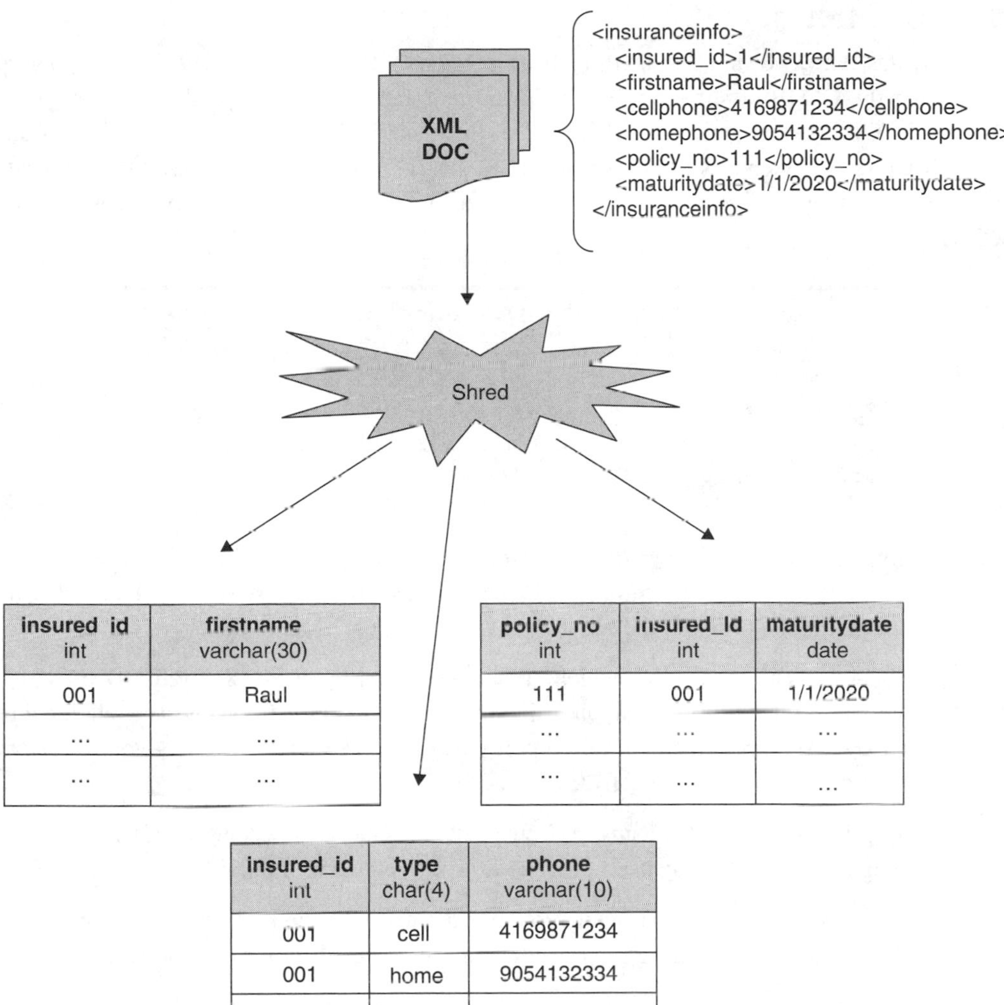

insured_id int	firstname varchar(30)
001	Raul
...	...
...	...

policy_no int	insured_id int	maturitydate date
111	001	1/1/2020
...	...	...
...	...	...

insured_id int	type char(4)	phone varchar(10)
001	cell	4169871234
001	home	9054132334
...	...	...

Figure 10.13 Using the shredding method to store XML documents

it was built in advance. It also means that the engine that processes this XML document, can handle hierarchical structures and does not need to do any mapping to SQL, but can directly process the XML; remember that XML documents are based on the hierarchical model. In other words, the storage format is the same as the processing format, there is no mapping required. We explain pureXML in DB2 in the next section.

10.2 PUREXML IN DB2

DB2 provides pureXML support starting from version 9. Prior to version 9, DB2 supported XML using the CLOB or shredding methods and required the XML extender software. IBM calls DB2's XML technology **"pureXML"** rather than "native XML." The reason for using this term is because other vendors use the term "native XML" just because they have an XML data type; however, they still store XML documents using the CLOB method or the shredding method.

> **NOTE** The XML extender as well as the "shredding" technique is still supported with DB2 9.5; however, this is not the recommended way to store XML documents. The code to implement the shredding technique was also further enhanced and improved in DB2 9. We briefly discuss this method in Section 10.10 Annotated XML Schema Decomposition.

XML is fully integrated in all layers of DB2, from XML storage, XML indexing, XML querying, APIs for client applications, utilities, and application support, to XML performance. Figure 10.14 illustrates this and provides the big picture of DB2's pureXML technology.

In Figure 10.14 a client application, which can be written in ODBC/CLI, .NET, JDBC/SQLJ, PHP, COBOL, embedded SQL, and so on, using the corresponding API can access relational or XML data. These APIs were modified to support pureXML. There are two ways you can query XML and relational data together in DB2:

- Using SQL/XML (either using SQL by itself or XQuery embedded in SQL)
- Using XQuery (either by itself or using SQL embedded in XQuery)

XML documents are stored in tables using columns defined with the XML data type, and internally stored as a parsed hierarchical tree as shown in Figure 10.14 for the column **`dna`**.

To allow for efficient XML data processing, XML indexes are supported. DB2 also provides support for XML Schema so that XML documents can be validated during inserts and updates. Validation of an XML document is optional.

Utilities such as IMPORT, EXPORT, RUNSTATS, BACKUP, RESTORE are all XML enabled with DB2 9. Graphical tools are also extended to work with XML.

In the next sections we discuss pureXML in more detail.

10.2.1 pureXML Storage in DB2

pureXML storage means that XML documents are internally stored in hierarchical format, as parsed trees. This is possible starting with DB2 9 by first creating a UNICODE database, followed

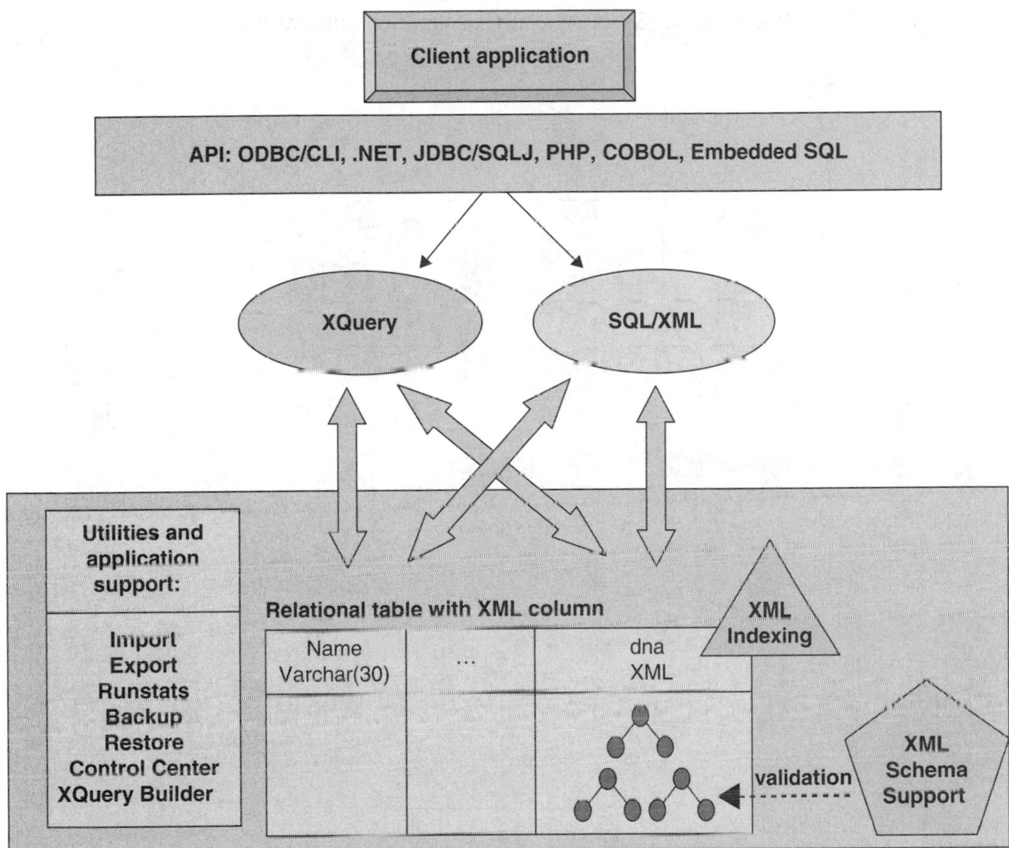

Figure 10.14 pureXML in DB2 9: The big picture

by creating a table using columns with the XML data type. The XML data type was introduced with the SQL/XML standard, and is new in DB2 9. Figure 10.15 provides an overview of the pureXML storage in DB2.

As you can see in Figure 10.15, the table **PATIENTS** has several columns, but specifically it illustrates a relational column called **NAME,** and an XML column called **DNA.** Relational column values are inserted and stored as usual. XML documents are inserted using either the INSERT SQL statement, the IMPORT utility or the LOAD utility, and this will be discussed in a later section. The XML document itself is not stored within the row, but rather a descriptor pointing to it, also illustrated in Figure 10.15. When the XML document is inserted into the database, DB2 parses the XML document and stores it internally as a parsed tree using the XQuery Data Model (XDM). This tree is persistent. DB2 uses an IBM version of the Xerces parser (a popular parser which is a DOM and SAX parser). Figure 10.16 illustrates this process.

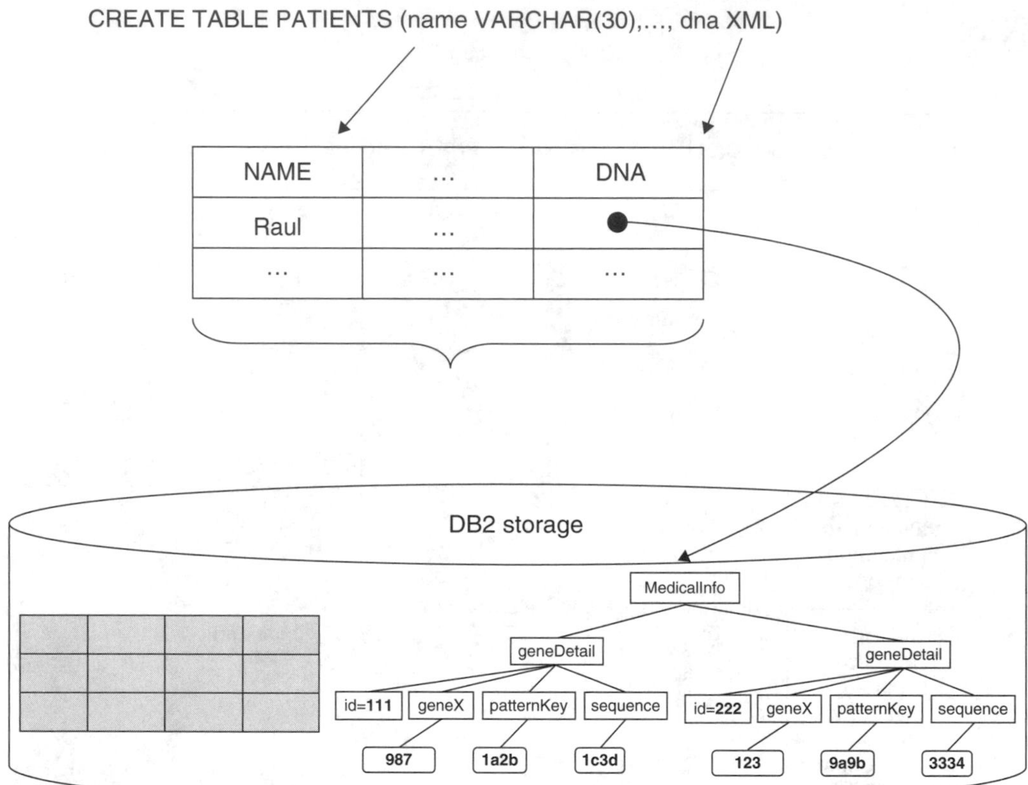

Figure 10.15 pureXML storage in DB2

Moreover, in order to save space and improve performance of queries using XPath expressions, DB2 will convert the tag element names and other information of the XML document into integer values. This is illustrated in Figure 10.17.

At the top of Figure 10.17 we illustrate the XML document in parsed-hierarchical format. We also show a "Path table", which is created per database. The path table provides the list of all distinct paths to all nodes and attributes in the XML document. At the bottom of the figure we illustrate the same tree in internal format where the element and attributes names have been replaced by integers. The mapping information between the integers and the tag names is stored in the catalog table SYSIBM.SYSXMLSTRINGS, which basically behaves as a dictionary. Using this dictionary, the SYSIBM.SYSXMLPATHS catalog table stores the unique paths using the integer values rather than the string values. Note that certain tag names and paths typically occur many times in your XML data but require only a single entry in the string table and path table, respectively.

Serialized format

```
<MedicalInfo>
    <geneDetail id="111">
        <geneX>987</geneX>
        <patternKey>1a2b</patternKey>
        <sequence>1c3d</sequence>
    </geneDetail>
    <geneDetail id="222">
        <geneX>123</geneX>
        <patternKey>9a9b</patternKey>
        <sequence>3334</sequence>
    </geneDetail>
</MedicalInfo>
```

Parsed-hierarchical format

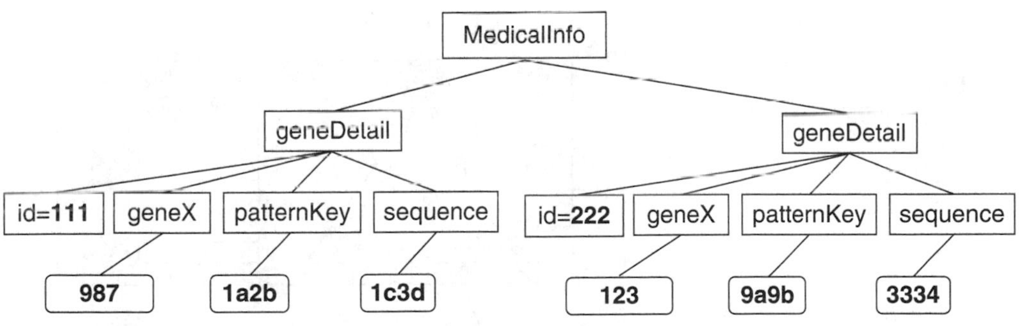

Figure 10.16 XML documents stored as parsed-hierarchical trees in DB2

In terms of storage at the page level, DB2 creates several internal objects when data is stored in tables. A DAT object holds the data of the table, an INX object includes the indexes, and with DB2 9, a new object called the XML Data (XDA) object holds the XML data pages. Figure 10.18 illustrates these objects and their relationship.

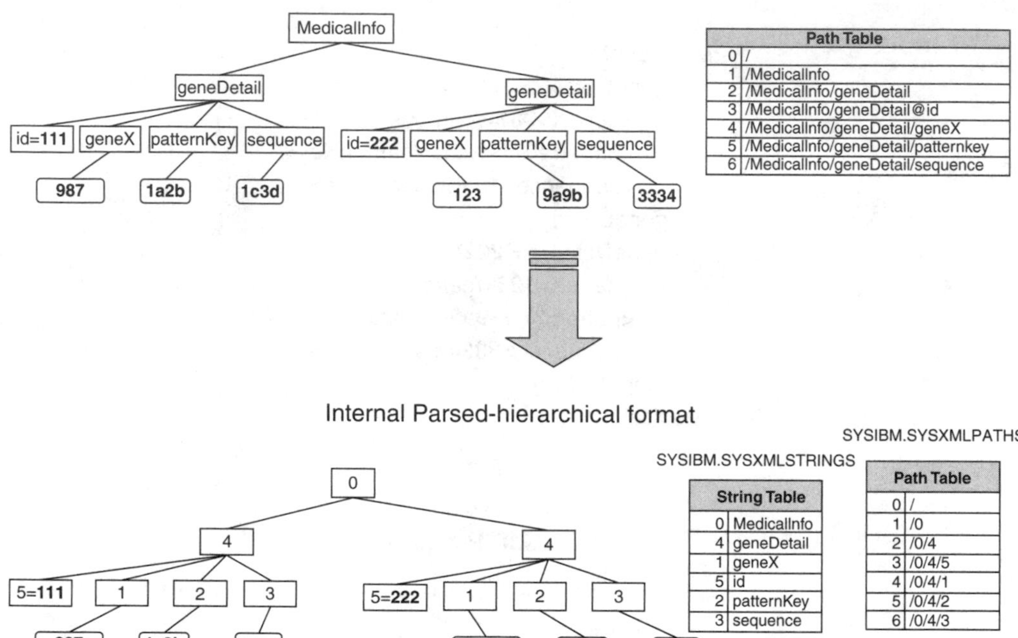

Figure 10.17 Internal storage of an XML document

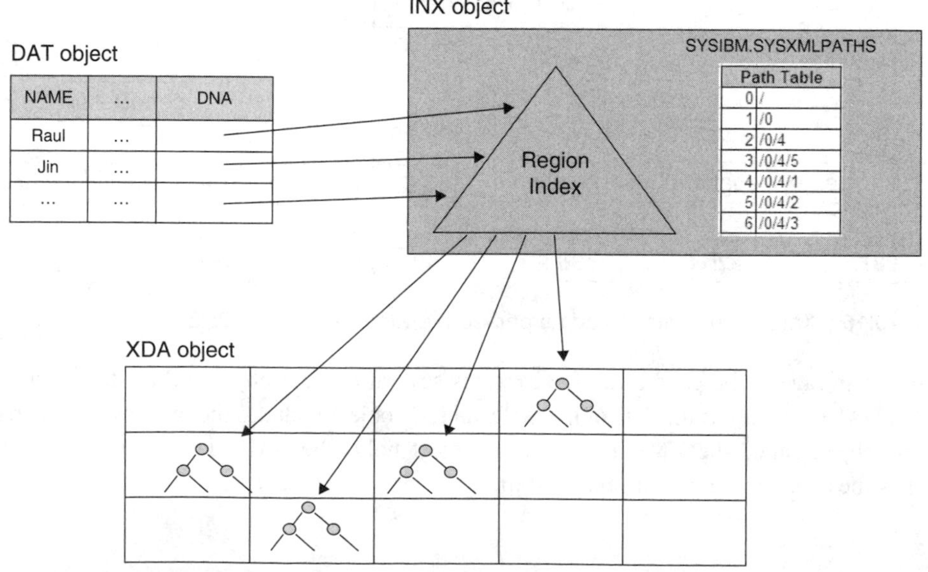

Figure 10.18 Internal objects created in an SMS table space and their relationship

In the figure, the DAT object includes the table data, and for the XML column (DNA in this example), it includes pointers to the region index, which points to the corresponding XML data in the XDA object. A region is a set of nodes of an XML document stored within a page. When an XML document doesn't fit on one page, it is split into regions, and the region index captures how this XML document is divided up internally. The fewer regions per document, the less index region entries are required and the better the performance is. Region indexes are described in more detail in Section 10.8.1, System Indexes. Figure 10.19 illustrates three regions created for one XML document and stored in different pages.

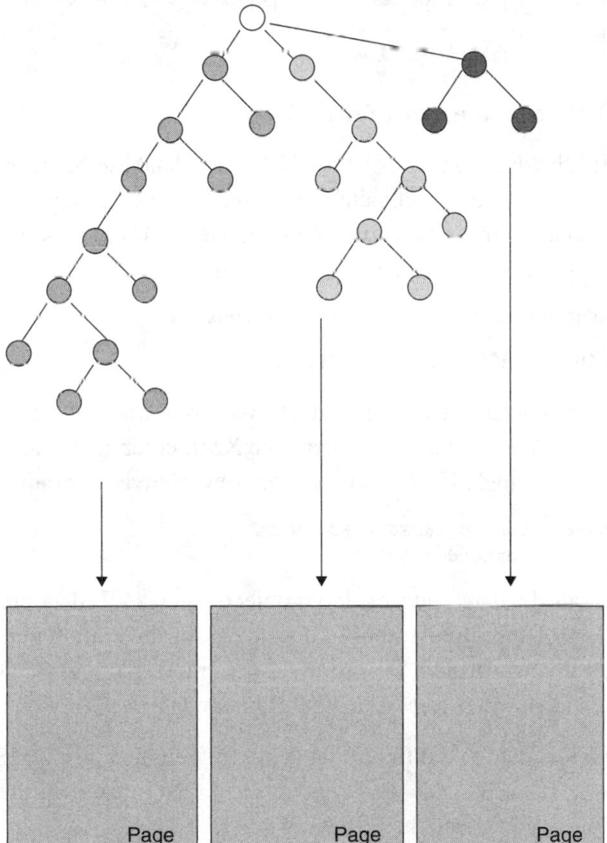

Figure 10.19 Regions

The maximum size of an XML document allowed in DB2 is 2GB. This means that if you have a table with two XML columns and two rows, each of the four XML documents in the table can be of at most 2GB each.

From a user's perspective, all you need to do to use pureXML storage is the following:

1. Create a UNICODE database (Only for DB2 9)
2. Create a table with an XML data type column

> **NOTE** In DB2 9.5, the requirement of creating a database as UNICODE to support pureXML is removed.

> **NOTE** pureXML support is only provided in single partition databases at this time.

1. Create a UNICODE database (Only for DB2 9)

To support pureXML, the database must be a UNICODE database because all the data will be stored in UTF-8 regardless of the document encoding, locale or codepage of the database. To create a UNICODE database from the command line, use the UTF-8 code set and a compatible territory code. We use the US territory code in this example.

```
CREATE DATABASE XMLDB USING CODESET UTF-8 TERRITORY US
```

2. Create a table with an XML data type column

The XML data type introduced in DB2 9 enables you to define table columns to store well-formed XML documents. You can have more than one XML column in a table. Each non-nullable XML column contains one single XML document per row. Here is an example:

```
CREATE TABLE customer ( custid INTEGER NOT NULL
                      , custorder XML )
```

In SMS table spaces, all the data, indexes, large objects, and XML data are stored in the same table space. In Figure 10.18 we used an SMS table space for illustration purposes; however, this is not recommended for performance. We discuss this in more detail in Section 10.11.1, Choosing Correctly Where and How to Store Your XML Documents.

If you want to store XML data in a different table space, you must use DMS table spaces. Also for performance, use a LARGE table space using the LONG clause in the CREATE TABLE statement. For example if you create the following table:

```
CREATE TABLE customer ( custid INTEGER NOT NULL
                      , custorder XML )
          IN DATATSPACE
    INDEX IN IDXTSPACE
    LONG  IN LARGETSPACE
```

All the XML documents are stored in the LARGETSPACE table space indexes including XML indexes, if they exist, will go to the IDXTSPACE table space; all other regular data goes to the DATATSPACE table space.

10.2.2 Base-Table Inlining and Compression of XML Data

V9.5

With DB2 9.5, XML documents that are small enough can be inlined in the base table instead of being stored in the separate XDA area. For example, in a database or table space with 16KB pages you could define the following table, which allows XML documents that can be stored within 10240 bytes or less, to reside in the DAT object.

```
CREATE TABLE customer ( custid INTEGER NOT NULL
                      , custorder XML inline length 10240)
```

Only documents that require more than the specified inline length will still be stored in the XDA object and require regions index entries. Applications that mostly process large numbers of small documents can benefit from inlining in terms of performance. Also, the row compression feature introduced in DB2 9 also applies to inlined documents and can greatly reduce the XML storage consumption on disk. This in turn reduces the XML I/O activity, which again benefits performance.

Note that inlining of XML documents reduces the number of rows per page in the DAT object. Queries which only access relational columns will therefore have to read a larger number of pages and may suffer in performance. Hence, inlining and choosing an inline length can be subject to performance trade-offs.

10.2.3 The pureXML Engine

Now that you understand how XML data is internally stored in DB2, you should realize that this internal storage requires its own engine interface to access it. The relational engine by itself can not parse an XML document. Figure 10.20 illustrates how the DB2 engine works.

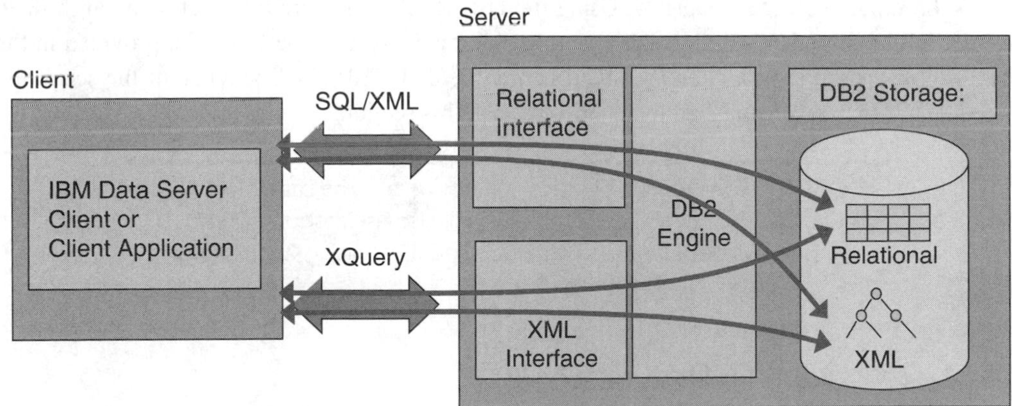

Figure 10.20 pureXML engine interfaces

In Figure 10.20, a client issues SQL, SQL/XML or XQuery statements and these statements will be processed by the appropriate interface depending on whether you are trying to access relational data or XML data, or both.

When working on XML data you can perform queries in two ways, using XQuery or using SQL/XML. For inserts, use the SQL INSERT statement, the IMPORT utility or the LOAD utility. For update and delete operations, use an SQL UPDATE and an SQL DELETE respectively.

In the next sections we discuss these operations and other features of pureXML, such as its support for indexes and XML schema validation, in more detail.

10.3 Querying XML Data

To query XML data you can use XQuery or SQL/XML. If you are working with XQuery, there are two important functions to identify the XML data that is input to the query:

```
db2-fn:sqlquery
db2-fn:xmlcolumn
```

Earlier in Table 10.6 we listed different SQL/XML functions. In this section we describe some of the most important SQL/XML functions such as:

```
XMLTABLE
XMLQUERY
```

and some important predicates such as:

```
XMLEXISTS
```

In the next sections you can learn and practice using these functions. If you would like to follow along, ensure you have created the SAMPLE database as described in the case study of Chapter 4, Using the DB2 Tools, Section 4.10. As we will be building more complex queries based on previous examples, we recommend you to store the queries in a text file, and run them as a script using the DB2 Command Window (Or Linux/UNIX shell) in non-interactive mode using this file as the input. Refer to Chapter 4, Using the DB2 Tools, for more information about how to use the DB2 Command Window and scripting. Alternatively, edit the script file provided in the Web site of this book (www.ibmpressbooks.com/title/0131580183). The name of the script file is *myxquery.db2* and contains all the queries used in this section.

> **NOTE** For the sake of space and clarity, in some cases we will show only snippets of the output. We will also use a dotted line to separate rows because most XML documents are long, and this way they can be identified more easily.

10.3.1 Querying XML Data with XQuery

To use XQuery as the primary language to query XML data in DB2, all queries must begin with the keyword **xquery**, otherwise DB2 will assume you are working with SQL. Two XQuery functions are supported to retrieve data.

```
db2-fn:xmlcolumn('xml-column-name')
db2-fn:sqlquery('fullselect-sql-statement')
```

10.3.1.1 The db2-fn:xmlcolumn Function

The **db2-fn:xmlcolumn** function takes an XML column name as its input argument. The column name uses this syntax: **SQL-schema-name.table-name.xml-column-name**

The **SQL-schema-name** is optional; whereas the table (or view or alias) and XML column names are mandatory. Note that the input argument is case sensitive. It must match the schema, table, and column names defined in DB2, which are usually in uppercase by default. Here is the first example of an XQuery statement.

Example #1:

```
xquery db2-fn:xmlcolumn('CUSTOMER.INFO')
```

This XQuery statement retrieves all the XML documents stored in the XML column **INFO** of the **CUSTOMER** table. The following would be the output of the above XQuery statement.

```
INFO
--------------------------------------------------------------------

<customerinfo xmlns="http://posample.org" Cid="1000"><name>Kathy
Smith</name><addr country="Canada"><street>5 Rosewood</street>
<city>Toronto</city><prov-state>Ontario</prov-state>
<pcode-zip>M6W 1E6</pcode-zip></addr><phone type="work">416-555-1358
</phone></customerinfo>
--------------------------------------------------------------------

<customerinfo xmlns="http://posample.org" Cid="1001"><name>Kathy
Smith</name><addr country="Canada"><street>25 EastCreek</street>
<city>Markham</city><prov-state>Ontario</prov-state>
<pcode-zip>N9C 3T6</pcode-zip></addr><phone type="work">905-555-7258
</phone></customerinfo>
--------------------------------------------------------------------

...
--------------------------------------------------------------------

<customerinfo xmlns="http://posample.org" Cid="1005"><name>Larry
Menard</name><addr country="Canada"><street>223 NatureValley Road
</street><city>Toronto</city><prov-state>Ontario</prov-state>
<pcode-zip>M4C 5K8</pcode-zip></addr><phone type="work">905-555-9146
</phone><phone type="home">416-555-6121</phone><assistant><name>Goose Defender
</name><phone type="home">416-555-1943</phone></assistant>
</customerinfo>


  6 record(s) selected.
```

Given that this query is retrieving the entire XML document and not just parts of it, an equivalent SQL statement would be:

```
SELECT info FROM customer
```

SQL would not work, however, when you need only parts of the XML document. In that case use XQuery or SQL/XML.

Each row in the result table of an XQuery is an XML value obtained from the evaluation of the expression. In this example, each row is an XML document with all its elements and attributes.

Example #2:

Example #1 showed you how to use XQuery to retrieve the entire XML document using the **db2-fn:xmlcolumn** function. In example #2, you can retrieve specific elements of the XML document using XPath, as you can see below:

```
xquery db2-fn:xmlcolumn('CUSTOMER.INFO')/customerinfo/phone
```

Note that the above query is very similar to Example #1, however, we are appending the XPath expression **/customerinfo/phone** to just retrieve the phone elements. Running the above query will actually return zero records because, as you see in Figure 10.18, each document has the namespace **xmlns="http://posample.org"** declared; therefore, this should be included in the query as shown in Example #3.

Example #3:

```
xquery
declare default element namespace "http://posample.org";
db2-fn:xmlcolumn('CUSTOMER.INFO')/customerinfo/phone
```

In the second line of the above query, we declare a default element namespace so that it is used for both the *customerinfo* and *phone* elements in the XQuery. Alternatively, you can declare a namespace with a prefix as shown in Example #4.

Example #4:

```
xquery
declare namespace ns="http://posample.org";
db2-fn:xmlcolumn('CUSTOMER.INFO')/ns:customerinfo/ns:phone
```

We first declare the namespace with an arbitrary string prefix of *ns*, and then we prefix each element name used in the query with this string. You should now get the expected result as shown below – all the *phone* elements just under the *customerinfo* element from all documents in the column INFO.

```
1
<phonexmlns="http://posample.org"type="work">416-555-1358</phone>
<phonexmlns="http://posample.org"type="work">905-555-7258</phone>
<phonexmlns="http://posample.org"type="work">905-555-7258</phone>
 ...
<phonexmlns="http://posample.org"type="work">905-555-9146</phone>
<phonexmlns="http://posample.org"type="home">416-555-6121</phone>

  11 record(s) selected.
```

Let's now illustrate other examples using some of the XPath statements explained in earlier sections.

NOTE If you are following along with the examples above using the DB2 Command Editor, at the bottom-left corner of this tool the Statement termination character is set to a semicolon (;) by default. Given that the namespace definition in the above examples must end with a semicolon, this would cause a conflict, because DB2 will think it's the end of the entire statement. To solve this problem in the DB2 Command Editor, simply change the statement termination character for any other character than the semicolon.

Example #5:

Select the text node under the *phone* elements of *customerinfo*.

```
xquery
declare default element namespace "http://posample.org";
db2-fn:xmlcolumn('CUSTOMER.INFO')/customerinfo/phone/text()
```

The result would be:

```
1
416-555-1358
905-555-7258
905-555-7258
...
416-555-3376
905-555-9146
416-555-6121

  11 record(s) selected.
```

Example #6:

Select all *phone* elements anywhere in the document.

```
xquery
declare default element namespace "http://posample.org";
db2-fn:xmlcolumn('CUSTOMER.INFO')//phone
```

The result would be:

```
1
<phonexmlns="http://posample.org"type="work">416-555-1358</phone>
<phonexmlns="http://posample.org"type="work">905-555-7258</phone>
<phonexmlns="http://posample.org"type="work">905-555-7258</phone>
 ...
<phonexmlns="http://posample.org"type="work">905-555-9146</phone>
<phonexmlns="http://posample.org"type="home">416-555-6121</phone>
<phonexmlns="http://posample.org"type="home">416-555-1943</phone>

  13 record(s) selected.
```

Example #7:

Select all elements under the *customerinfo* element that have any attribute.

```
xquery
declare default element namespace "http://posample.org";
db2-fn:xmlcolumn('CUSTOMER.INFO')/customerinfo/phone[@*]
```

The result would be:

```
1
<phonexmlns="http://posample.org"type="work">416-555-1358</phone>
<phonexmlns="http://posample.org"type="work">905-555-7258</phone>
<phonexmlns="http://posample.org"type="work">905-555-7258</phone>
<phonexmlns="http://posample.org"type="work">905-555-7258</phone>
<phonexmlns="http://posample.org"type="home">416-555-2937</phone>
<phonexmlns="http://posample.org"type="cell">905-555-8743</phone>
<phonexmlns="http://posample.org"type="cottage">613-555-3278</phone>
<phonexmlns="http://posample.org"type="work">905-555-4789</phone>
<phonexmlns="http://posample.org"type="home">416-555-3376</phone>
<phonexmlns="http://posample.org"type="work">905-555-9146</phone>
<phonexmlns="http://posample.org"type="home">416-555-6121</phone>

11record(s)selected.
```

10.3.1.2 The db2-fn:sqlquery Function

The **db2-fn:sqlquery** function allows you to embed SQL statements in XQuery. The argument of the function must be a full SELECT SQL statement which returns a single-column result set, where this column must be of type XML. Here is an example.

Example #1:

```
xquery
db2-fn:sqlquery('select info from customer')
```

The result is equivalent to the result of

```
xquery db2-fn:xmlcolumn('CUSTOMER.INFO')
```

which returns a result set of six documents stored in the **INFO** XML column. Use XPath expressions to get to information you are interested in as shown in Example #2.

> **NOTE** While XQuery is case sensitive, SQL is not; this means that if a statement combines the use of XQuery with SQL, you only need to be careful about the case in the XQuery part. Thus in the db2-fn:sqlquery function, since the argument of this function is a SQL statement, this SQL statement can be in any case. Refer to Appendix B, Use of Uppercase Versus Lowercase in DB2 for more details.

Example #2:

The following XQuery returns all the phone elements that have a type attribute with a value of "home" under the *customerinfo* element.

```
xquery
declare default element namespace "http://posample.org";
```

```
db2-fn:sqlquery('select info from customer')
    /customerinfo/phone[@type='home']
```

The result would be:

```
1
<phonexmlns="http://posample.org"type="home">416-555-2937</phone>
<phonexmlns="http://posample.org"type="home">416-555-3376</phone>
<phonexmlns="http://posample.org"type="home">416-555-6121</phone>

  3 record(s) selected.
```

Note that in this example the use of the db2-fn:sqlquery function is not really needed because we are retrieving all the rows for the XML column INFO, and after that we use XPath. This very well could have been done using only XQuery. Typically the db2-fn:sqlquery is used to narrow down the set of input XML documents based on relational predicates, or to construct input XML documents from relational values. The next examples illustrate this.

Example #3:

This example illustrates that you can perform table joins and filtering within the **db2-fn:sqlquery** function before passing the result for XPath evaluation. For example, this query joins the CUSTOMER and PURCHASEORDER tables and returns names of the items ordered by customer with ID 1002.

```
xquery
declare default element namespace "http://posample.org";
db2-fn:sqlquery('select porder
                   from customer a, purchaseorder b
                  where a.cid = b.custid
                    and a.cid = 1002')
    /PurchaseOrder/item/name
```

The result would be:

```
1
<namexmlns="http://posample.org">SnowShovel,Basic22inch</name>
 ...
<namexmlns="http://posample.org">SnowShovel,Deluxe24inch</name>
<namexmlns="http://posample.org">IceScraper,Windshield4inch</name>

  6 record(s) selected.
```

Example #4:

This is another example of table joins within the **db2-fn:sqlquery** function including filtering of some rows based on some predicates. Notice how the single quotation marks are used to enclose the 'Shipped' condition and double quotation marks are used to enclose the SQL statement.

```
xquery
declare default element namespace "http://posample.org";
db2-fn:sqlquery("select porder
```

```
                  from customer a, purchaseorder b
                 where a.cid = b.custid
                   and a.cid = 1002
                   and b.status = 'Shipped'")
    /PurchaseOrder/item/name
```

The result would be:

```
1
----------------------------------------------------------------------
<namexmlns="http://posample.org">SnowShovel,Basic22inch</name>
<namexmlns="http://posample.org">SnowShovel,Basic22inch</name>
<namexmlns="http://posample.org">SnowShovel,Deluxe24inch</name>
<namexmlns="http://posample.org">IceScraper,Windshield4inch</name>

  4 record(s) selected.
```

10.3.1.3 XQuery with FLWOR Expressions

The FLWOR expression stands for **F**or, **L**et, **W**here, **O**rder, **R**eturn. This expression is useful to manipulate XML documents and return another XML document, an HTML document, or a combination of both. It is also useful for computing joins between XML documents, and sorting the results. Table 10.8 describes the FLWOR expression in more detail. Note that the FLWOR expression is part of XQuery which is case sensitive, therefore all the clauses in FLWOR should be in lower case as shown in Table 10.8.

Table 10.8 The FLWOR Expression

FLWOR Clause	Description	Clause Required?
for	Iterates over the result of the expression and binds variable to each item returned.	Optional
let	Binds a variable to the result of the expression. This expression is different from the one in the FOR clause.	Optional
where	Eliminates items of the iteration.	Optional
order	Reorders items of the iteration.	Optional
return	Constructs results of the query.	Mandatory

The FLWOR expression iterates over sequences and bind variables to intermediate results. Figure 10.21 illustrates the syntax diagram of the FLWOR expression.

Let's take a look at some examples using the FLWOR expression.

Example #1:

This example queries the INFO XML column in the CUSTOMER table. It obtains a list of phone numbers for each customer who lives in Canada. We have added the numbers (1), (2), (3), and so on to explain what each line does.

```
   .--------------------.
   V                    |
>>---+-| for clause |-+-+--+------------------+---------------->
     '-| let clause |-'    '-where--Expression-'

>--+----------------------------------------+---------------->
   |            .-,------------------------. |
   |            V              .-ascending--. | |
   '-order by----Expression--+------------+-+-'
                               '-descending-'

>--return--Expression------------------------------------------><

for clause

      .-,------------------------------------------------------.
      V                                                         |
|--for----$VariableName--+----------------------------+--in--Expression-+--|
                         '-at--$PositionalVariableName-'

let clause

      .-,----------------------------.
      V                              |
|--let----$VariableName--:=--Expression-+----------------------|
```

Figure 10.21 Syntax diagram of the FLWOR expression

```
(1)-- xquery
(2)-- declare default element namespace 'http://posample.org';
(3)--   for $i in db2-fn:xmlcolumn("CUSTOMER.INFO")
(4)--   let $cname :=$i/customerinfo/name
(5)-- where $i/customerinfo/addr/@country="Canada"
(6)-- order by $cname
(7)-- return
(8)--     <CustPhone>
(9)--        {$cname, $i/customerinfo/phone}
(10)--    </CustPhone>
```

So let's explain the above query line by line:

(1) As mentioned earlier, you must start any XQuery statement with the **xquery** command; otherwise DB2 will assume you are issuing SQL statements.

(2) This line declares the namespaces to avoid name collisions.

(3) This line starts the FLWOR expression with the for clause. Using this clause we are iterating over the the result sequence produced by the function **db2-fn:xmlcolumn("CUSTOMER.INFO").** The variable "$i" is bound to one item in that sequence at a time. In this query, each item is a document from the column INFO. Recall that any string prefixed with a dollar (**$**) sign indicates a variable.

(4) The let clause is used to assign to the variable $cname the subdocument represented by the XPath expression **$i/customerinfo/name.** In other words, the variable $cname now contains the sequence of all the name elements (including the tags) from the document currently assigned to $i.
(5) The where clause is used for filtering; in this case we are filtering based on the attribute **country** so that it matches the string "Canada"
(6) The order by clause is used for sorting
(7) The return clause indicates the output of this FLWOR expression follows
(8), (9), (10) provide the structure of the XML documents that this FLWOR expression will return. Note that the comma in **{$cname, $i/customerinfo/phone}** will not appear in the output.

The result of this query is shown below.

```
1
<CustPhone xmlns="http://posample.org"><name>Jim Noodle</name>
<phone type="work">905-555-7258</phone></CustPhone>
--------------------------------------------------------------------
<CustPhone xmlns="http://posample.org"><name>Kathy Smith</name>
<phonetype="work">416-555-1358</phone></CustPhone>

--------------------------------------------------------------------
 …
--------------------------------------------------------------------
<CustPhone xmlns="http://posample.org"><name>Robert Shoemaker</name>
<phone type="work">905-555-7258</phone>
<phone type="home">416-555-2937</phone>
<phone type="cell">905-555-8743</phone>
<phonetype="cottage">613-555-3278</phone></CustPhone>

  6 record(s) selected.
```

10.3.1.4 Join Operations with XQuery

This section describes how to join two or more XML documents together. The queries in this section may look complex; however, once you have the basic understanding of each clause and XPath expression, the statements can be easy to understand, and you can build on this knowledge to perform advanced processing such as groupings, aggregations, and nested FLWOR expressions. Let's take a look at this first example.

Example #1:

You can join two XML documents by nesting FLWOR expressions. This syntax may be the easiest to understand. The example below retrieves a list of the details of all unshipped products.

```
(1)-- xquery
(2)-- declare default element namespace 'http://posample.org';
(3)-- for $i in db2-fn:sqlquery
(4)--     ("select porder
(5)--         from purchaseorder
```

```
(6)--          where status='Unshipped'")
(7)--      for $j in db2-fn:sqlquery
(8)--           ("select description from product")
(9)--  where $i/PurchaseOrder/item/partid = $j/product/@pid
(10)-- return
(11)--      <UnshippedProd ponum="{$i/PurchaseOrder/@PoNum}">
(12)--          <proddesc>
(13)--              { $j/product/description/details }
(14)--          </proddesc>
(15)--     </UnshippedProd>
```

The explanation of most of the lines is the same as in previous examples. A few things to highlight are:

In line (6), the WHERE clause is for the SQL statement, not for the FLWOR expression.

In line (9), the WHERE clause is for the FLWOR expression.

Lines (3) to (6) are used to bind variable $i (this is also known as variable assignment).

Lines (7) to (8) are used to bind variable $j.

In line (9) is where the JOIN takes place.

Note that the FOR clause is nested. The first FOR clause iterates over the PORDER XML document and the other one iterates over the DESCRIPTION XML document. The WHERE clause in FLWOR is used here to specify the join predicate, namely the *partid* element and the *pid* attribute in the PORDER and DESCRIPTION documents respectively.

Here is the output:

```
1
<UnshippedProd xmlns="http://posample.org" ponum="5000"><proddesc>
<details>Basic Snow Shovel, 22 inches wide, straight handle with D-Grip</details></
proddesc></UnshippedProd>

----------------------------------------------------------------------
<UnshippedProd xmlns="http://posample.org" ponum="5000"><proddesc>
<details>Super Deluxe Snow Shovel, 26 inches wide, ergonomic battery heated curved
handlewithupgradedD-Grip</details></proddesc></UnshippedProd>

  2 record(s) selected.
```

Example #2:

```
(1)-- xquery
(2)-- declare default element namespace 'http://posample.org';
(3)--     for $i in db2-fn:sqlquery("select porder
(4)--                                    from purchaseorder
(5)--                                   where status='Unshipped'")
(6)--     let $partno := $i/PurchaseOrder/item/partid
(7)--     return
(8)--     <UnshippedProd ponum="{$i/PurchaseOrder/@PoNum}">
```

```
(9)--          <proddesc>
(10)--            { db2-fn:xmlcolumn('PRODUCT.DESCRIPTION')
(11)--              /product[@pid=$partno]/description/details}
(12)--          </proddesc>
(13)--      </UnshippedProd>
```

Lines (1), (2) and (7) were explained in previous examples.

Lines (3) to (5) are used to assign to variable $i the XML documents stored in column **porder** where the status is "Unshipped."

Line (6) is used to assign to the variable **partno** the **partid** element for all XML documents stored in variable $i.

Lines (8) to (13) describe the structure of the XML documents to return. Note especially in line (10) we are obtaining the "details" element from XML documents stored in the column **DESCRIPTION** of another table, table **PRODUCT.** And in line (11) the JOIN condition is defined as **[@pid=$partno].**

In summary, the for clause returns a list of purchase orders that has not been shipped. The variable **$partno** is bound to the **$partid** found in these purchase orders. The XML document in the PRODUCT table is then joined with the PORDER XML documents by evaluating the expression **product[@pid=$partno].** Therefore, the result of this XQuery returns the product description of each unshipped product. Here is the output.

```
1
<UnshippedProd xmlns="http://posample.org" ponum="5000">
<proddesc><details>Basic Snow Shovel, 22 inches wide, straight handle
with D-Grip</details><details>Super Deluxe Snow Shovel, 26 inches wide, ergonomic
battery heated curved handle with upgraded D-Grip</details>
</proddesc></UnshippedProd>

  1 record(s) selected.
```

10.3.2 Querying XML Data with SQL/XML

In the previous section, you were introduced to XQuery using it as the primary language to query XML data. In this section, we use SQL as the primary language embedded with XQuery. For this purpose, we need to work with the following functions:

- XMLQUERY
- XMLTABLE
- XMLSERIALIZE

and the following predicate:

- XMLEXISTS

10.3.2.1 XMLQUERY

XMLQUERY is an SQL scalar function that returns the result of an XQuery expression as an XML sequence. Example #1 gives us the first taste about using this function.

Example #1:

```
(1)-- SELECT XMLQUERY (
(2)--          'declare default element namespace "http://posample.org";
(3)--          $d/customerinfo/phone' passing INFO as "d" )
(4)--  FROM CUSTOMER
```

Lines (1) and (4) are simply using SQL, and invoking the XMLQUERY function.

Line (2) is declaring the namespace as we have done in previous examples.

Line (3) is the key line to understand. It first specifies the XPath expression **$d/customer-info/phone.** Any string prefixed with the dollar sign ($) represents a variable, this means that "d" is a variable. The variable value is assigned using the line **passing INFO as "d".** This means that we are assigning to variable "d" the column INFO, which is the one containing the XML documents. In other words, the variable d has the XML document of a given row (and you will be iterating for all the rows in the table using SELECT). Now that you know that variable "d" contains the XML document, you then use XPath to navigate through that document when you use **$d/customerinfo/phone.** The XMLQUERY function returns the result using the XML data type.

V9.5 The functions XMLQUERY, XMLTABLE and the predicate XMLEXISTS often use the clause **passing <XML column name> as "<variable name>"** to bind the variable with the XML documents from the XML column for further processing. For example, in the previous query, **passing INFO as "d"** was used. With DB2 9.5 this can be done implicitly, where by default, DB2 will create a variable with the same name as the XML column. The above query could be rewritten as follows:

```
(1)-- SELECT XMLQUERY (
(2)--          'declare default element namespace "http://posample.org";
(3)--          $INFO/customerinfo/phone' )
(4)--  FROM CUSTOMER
```

> **NOTE** As indicated earlier, SQL is not case sensitive, but XQuery is. SQL columns are normally stored in uppercase in the Catalog, therefore when XQuery refers to them, uppercase must be used. For implicit variable binding, the variable must use uppercase to match the column name.

Since there are six rows in the CUSTOMER table, six rows are returned by this query. Each row contains a sequence of the *phone* elements found in each XML document. You therefore see the first record in the output below only has one *phone* element and the last record has two *phone* elements.

```
1

<phone xmlns="http://posample.org" type="work">416-555-1358</phone>
---------------------------------------------------------------------
<phone xmlns="http://posample.org" type="work">905-555-7258</phone>
---------------------------------------------------------------------
<phone xmlns="http://posample.org" type="work">905-555-7258</phone>
---------------------------------------------------------------------
<phone xmlns="http://posample.org" type="work">905-555-7258</phone>
<phone xmlns="http://posample.org" type="home">416-555-2937</phone>
<phone xmlns="http://posample.org" type="cell">905-555-8743</phone>
<phone xmlns="http://posample.org" type="cottage">613-555-3278</phone>
---------------------------------------------------------------------
<phone xmlns="http://posample.org" type="work">905-555-4789</phone>
<phone xmlns="http://posample.org" type="home">416-555-3376</phone>
---------------------------------------------------------------------
<phone xmlns="http://posample.org" type="work">905-555-9146</phone>
<phonexmlns="http://posample.org"type="home">416-555-6121</phone>

  6 record(s) selected.
```

Example #2:

The XMLQUERY function always returns results of type XML. If you need to compare XML values with non-XML values in a query, you must explicitly cast the XML type to a compatible data type. In the example below, the query joins the PURCHASEORDER and CUSTOMER tables together. It uses the customer ID as the join predicate. CUSTID in the PURCHASEORDER table is a BIGINT value, whereas result of **$d/customerinfo/@Cid** returned by XMLQUERY is an XML value. We need to first cast the XML value to BIGINT using XMLCAST before the comparison can succeed. In order to sort by the XML values returned from the XMLQUERY results, you must also cast them to values that SQL can order on. For example:

```
select cid
     , poid
     , xmlquery (
          'declare default element namespace "http://posample.org";
           $d//name' passing porder as "d")
from purchaseorder p, customer c
where p.custid = XMLCAST ( XMLQUERY ('declare default element namespace
                                              "http://posample.org";
                     $d/customerinfo/@Cid' passing info as "d") AS BIGINT)
```

This join between an XML and relational value is here expressed at the SQL level. An index on custid could be used to speed up the processing. Note that the XMLCAST operation would fail if the XMLQUERY would return a sequence of more than one item. The same join can also be expressed at the XML level, using XMLEXISTS.

Example #3 and Example #4 describe a scenario using XMLQUERY and XMLEXISTS where oversimplifying an SQL/XML query may result in bad query performance. We will discuss the XMLEXISTS predicate in more detail in the next section; for now it is enough to know that it is a predicate that can be used in the WHERE clause to filter rows.

Example #3:

```
SELECT XMLQUERY (
           'declare default element namespace "http://posample.org";
            $d/customerinfo[name="Larry Menard"]/phone'
                passing INFO as "d" )
  FROM CUSTOMER
1
------------------------------------------------------------------------
<phone xmlns="http://posample.org" type="work">905-555-9146</phone>
<phone xmlns="http://posample.org" type="home">416-555-6121</phone>

  6 record(s) selected.
```

Example #4:

```
SELECT XMLQUERY (
           'declare default element namespace "http://posample.org";
            $d/customerinfo/phone' passing INFO as "d" )
  FROM CUSTOMER
 WHERE XMLEXISTS ('declare default element namespace
                  "http://posample.org";
                  $d/customerinfo[name="Larry Menard"]'
                  passing INFO as "d" )
1
------------------------------------------------------------------------
<phone xmlns="http://posample.org" type="work">905-555-9146</phone>
<phone xmlns="http://posample.org" type="home">416-555-6121</phone>

  1 record(s) selected.
```

The output of example #3 indicates there are 6 records; however, it seems to show only 1 (consisting of two XML phone elements). The condition **`[name="Larry Menard"]`** has only one matching row in the *customer* table. Because there is a *phone* element specified after the condition, DB2 is evaluating every row for the condition and for each row, it retrieves the associated *phone* element. Since there is no name match for the first five rows, values for the *phone* element are an empty sequence. While when working with relational data you would get a NULL value represented by a dash ("-"), when working with XML data you just get nothing. Despite the fact that this query is not returning exactly what you were expecting, the index as well cannot be used.

On the other hand, the results for example #4 indicate there is only 1 record returned, which is the expected behavior, and also it will use an index. You should always use the WHERE clause in an SQL/XML query to filter out unwanted rows.

10.3.2.2 XMLEXISTS

Use the XMLEXISTS predicate to filter the rows to select. Let's take a look at a simple example.

Example #1:

```
SELECT cid
  FROM customer
 WHERE xmlexists('declare default element namespace "http://posample.org";
                 $c/customerinfo/addr[pcode-zip="M6W 1E6"]'
                  passing CUSTOMER.INFO as "c")
```

In the example, the **`cid`** column is selected for those customers who have a zip code of **`"M6W 1E6"`** but the zip code is not a column, but an element in the XML document.

The output of this query is:

```
CID
--------------------
                1000

  1 record(s) selected.
```

Example #2:

In this example we use both the XMLQUERY and the XMLEXISTS functions. Filtering rows to be returned can be done using the WHERE clause just like what you would do in the SQL language. For example, the query below returns *phone* elements for customers with CID less than 1003 and where the *city* element equals to "Markham." The second WHERE condition makes use of the XMLEXISTS predicate. It restricts the rows returned to only those that contain an XML document matching the result of the given XQuery expression.

```
SELECT CID, XMLQUERY (
     'declare default element namespace "http://posample.org";
     $d/customerinfo/phone' passing INFO as "d" )
  FROM CUSTOMER
 WHERE CID < 1003
   AND XMLEXISTS (
           'declare default element namespace "http://posample.org";
           $d//addr[city="Markham"]' passing INFO as "d" )
```

The result is shown below.

```
CID                  2
-------------------- -------------------------------------------------
                1001 <phone xmlns="http://posample.org"
type="work">905-555-7258</phone>
--------------------------------------------------------------------------
                1002 <phone xmlns="http://posample.org"
type="work">905-555-7258</phone>

  3 record(s) selected.
```

The XMLEXISTS function will return one of the following for each row that is evaluated in the WHERE clause:

- FALSE if the embedded XQuery returns an empty sequence
- TRUE if the embedded XQuery returns a non empty sequence

Now, let's analyze the behavior of the following two queries in Example #3 and #4:

Example #3:

```
SELECT XMLQUERY ('$d/apartment' passing DETAIL as "d" )
  FROM apartment
 WHERE XMLEXISTS ('$d/apartment[suite="Paradise"]'
                  passing DETAIL as "d");
```

Example #4:

```
SELECT XMLQUERY ('$d/apartment' passing DETAIL as "d" )
  FROM apartment
 WHERE XMLEXISTS ('$d/apartment/suite="Paradise"'
                  passing DETAIL as "d");
```

and let's assume that the index idx1 had been previously created as follows:

```
CREATE INDEX idx1 on apartment(detail)
    GENERATE KEY USING XMLPATTERN '/apartment/suite'
    AS SQL VARCHAR(30);
```

We discuss more about XML indexes in Section 10.8. Comparing the query in Example #3 versus the one in Example #4, the only difference is in the following line:

Query in Example #3:

```
WHERE XMLEXISTS ('$d/apartment[suite="Paradise"]'
```

Query in Example #4:

```
WHERE XMLEXISTS ('$d/apartment/suite="Paradise"'
```

The output is exactly the same, however, the query in Example #3 uses index idx1, while the query in Example #4 does not, hence the performance of the query in Example #3 is a lot faster than the one in Example #4. Why was the index not used in Example #4?

Let's explain the behavior of XMLEXISTS with Figures 10.22 and 10.23. Figure 10.22 represents the evaluations performed by the query in Example #3. The inner box represents the evaluation of the clause:

`$d/apartment[suite="Paradise"]`, which returns a sequence with suite = "Paradise" when the condition is satisfied, or an empty sequence if it's not. This value is then passed to the other box for XMLEXISTS, which will evaluate to a Boolean False when an empty sequence is provided, and this is passed to the SELECT statement (the outermost box), which would not select any rows.

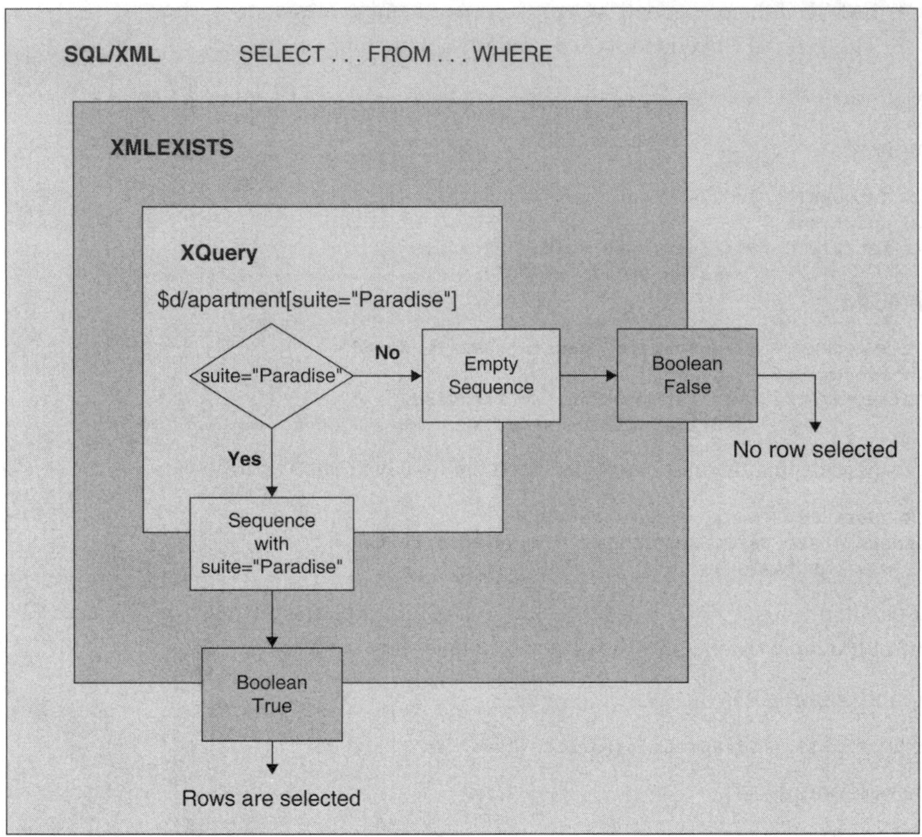

Figure 10.22 SQL/XML with XMLEXISTS consideration

On the other hand, in Figure 10.23, the inner box represents the evaluation of the clause

`$d/apartment/suite="Paradise"`, which returns a Boolean true when the condition is satisfied, or a Boolean false when it's not. This value is then passed to the other box for XMLEXISTS, which will evaluate to a Boolean True when either a False or True are provided, and this is passed to the SELECT statement (the outer most box), which would select any rows. In other words, in this case rows will always be selected even though the condition inside the XQuery does not match. Since all rows are selected regardless, the DB2 optimizer is not going to use the index.

10.3.2.3 XMLTABLE

Another SQL/XML function available for querying XML data is the table function XMLTABLE. Because it is a table function, it allows you to execute an XQuery expression and return values as a table instead of an XML sequence. Another interesting characteristic of this function

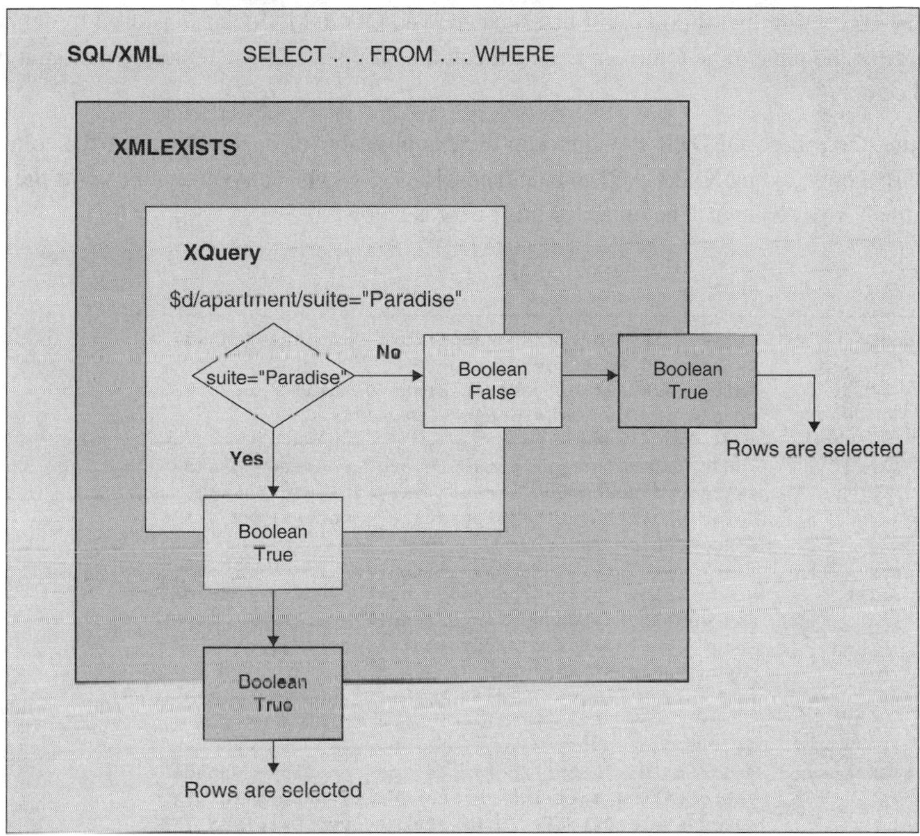

Figure 10.23 SQL/XML with XMLEXISTS consideration

is that you can specify columns of any SQL data type including the XML data type. Therefore, you can 'make' a table with columns in regular SQL and XML data types. For example, the query in Example #1 returns a table with a column of type CHAR(50) and another column of type XML.

Example #1

```
SELECT T.*
  FROM XMLTABLE (
      XMLNAMESPACES (DEFAULT 'http://posample.org')
      , 'db2-fn:xmlcolumn("CUSTOMER.INFO")'
         COLUMNS "NAME"  CHAR(50) PATH '/customerinfo/name'
               , "ADDR"  XML      PATH '/customerinfo/addr' ) AS T
ORDER BY T.NAME
```

A default namespace is declared using the XMLNAMESPACES function. Every XQuery expression in the XMLTABLE function call will use this default namespace binding. The

XQuery expression that follows will be executed. The COLUMNS clause is used to define the structure of the table to be returned. For each column, you specify an XQuery expression in the PATH clause.

Note that there is an ORDER BY clause in the example above. Because the NAME column is implicitly converted by XMLCAST to data type CHAR(50), you can conveniently sort the result using the NAME column. The output of this query is below.

```
NAME              ADDR
----------------- ----------------------------------------------------
Jim Noodle        <addr xmlns="http://posample.org" country="Canada">
                  <street>25 EastCreek</street>
                  <city>Markham</city><prov-state>Ontario</prov-state>
                  <pcode-zip>N9C 3T6</pcode-zip></addr>
----------------------------------------------------------------------
Kathy Smith       <addr xmlns="http://posample.org" country="Canada">
                  <street>5 Rosewood</street><city>Toronto</city>
                  <prov-state>Ontario</prov-state><pcode-zip>M6W 1E6
                  </pcode-zip></addr>
----------------------------------------------------------------------
Kathy Smith       <addr xmlns="http://posample.org" country="Canada">
                  <street>25 EastCreek</street><city>Markham</city>
                  <prov-state>Ontario</prov-state><pcode-zip>N9C 3T6
                  </pcode-zip></addr>
----------------------------------------------------------------------
...
----------------------------------------------------------------------
Robert Shoemaker  <addr xmlns="http://posample.org" country="Canada">
                  <street>1596 Baseline</street><city>Aurora</city>
                  <prov-state>Ontario</prov-state><pcode-zip>N8X 7F8
                  </pcode-zip></addr>

  6 record(s) selected.
```

Let's look at a similar example but with a different XQuery expression to show various ways of writing the query.

Example #2

```
SELECT T.*
  FROM CUSTOMER c
     , XMLTABLE (
          XMLNAMESPACES (DEFAULT 'http://posample.org')
        , '$d/customerinfo/addr' PASSING c.INFO as "d"
           COLUMNS "NAME"  CHAR(50) PATH '../name'
                 , "CID"   BIGINT   PATH '../@Cid'
                 , "PHONE" CHAR(15) PATH '../phone'
                 , "ADDR"  XML      PATH '.' )
AS T
ORDER BY T.NAME
```

In this example, we didn't use the **db2-fn:xmlcolumn** function. Instead, we join the CUSTOMER table with the XMLTABLE resulting table. You should be familiar with the

XQuery expression **'$d/customerinfo/addr' PASSING c.INFO as "d"** by now. It evaluates the expression and obtains all the *addr* elements from the INFO XML column and binds them to the variable *$d*. Four columns are defined; three using an SQL data type and one using an XML data type. The SQL/XML statement actually fails after few rows are processed. If you refer to the XML documents in the SAMPLE database, you see that there are four phone numbers assigned to customer Robert Shoemaker. If the XQuery expression in the PATH clause returns more than one item, in this case four phone elements for one customer, the data type of that column must be in XML type. Therefore, for the query to work, you must change the line

```
, "PHONE" CHAR(15) PATH '../phone'
```

to

```
, "PHONE" XML       PATH '../phone'
```

Alternatively you could rewrite the query to produce one row per phone number, in which case the other values such as cid and name would be repeated for each phone.

Note that if the XQuery expression in the PATH clause returns an empty sequence, a NULL value is returned for that column. Here is the result of the query.

```
NAME                                              CID
PHONE
ADDR
-------------------------------------------------- --------------------
Jim Noodle                                                        1002
<phonexmlns="http://posample.org"type="work">905-555-7258</phone>
<addr xmlns="http://posample.org" country="Canada"><street>25 EastCreek
</street><city>Markham</city><prov-state>Ontario</prov-state><pcode-zip>N9C 3T6
</pcode-zip></addr>
-----------------------------------------------------------------------
Kathy Smith                                                       1000
<phonexmlns="http://posample.org"type="work">416-555-1358</phone>
<addr xmlns="http://posample.org" country="Canada"><street>5 Rosewood
</street><city>Toronto</city><prov-state>Ontario</prov-state><pcode-zip>M6W 1E6
</pcode-zip></addr>
-----------------------------------------------------------------------
Kathy Smith                                                       1001
<phonexmlns="http://posample.org"type="work">905-555-7258</phone>
<addr xmlns="http://posample.org" country="Canada"><street>25 EastCreek
</street><city>Markham</city><prov-state>Ontario</prov-state><pcode-zip>N9C 3T6
</pcode-zip></addr>
-----------------------------------------------------------------------
 ...
-----------------------------------------------------------------------
Robert Shoemaker                                                  1003
<phone xmlns="http://posample.org" type="work">905-555-7258</phone>
<phone xmlns="http://posample.org" type="home">416-555-2937</phone>
<phone xmlns="http://posample.org" type="cell">905-555-8743</phone>
<phonexmlns="http://posample.org"type="cottage">613-555-3278</phone>
<addr xmlns="http://posample.org" country="Canada"><street>1596 Baseline
</street><city>Aurora</city><prov-state>Ontario</prov-state><pcode-zip>N8X 7F8
</pcode-zip></addr>

  6 record(s) selected.
```

10.3.2.4 XML Serialization

At this point, you have probably tried few or all of the examples illustrated above using the DB2 CLP. You are now ready to write your own application and apply the knowledge of XQuery and SQL/XML you just learned. While you are writing the queries and testing the results from a client application, you realize that the programming language you use does not support the XML data type. All the XML data returned are implicitly converted to Binary Large Objects (BLOBs). Why is that? What can you do to control this conversion? The answer is XML serialization.

XML serialization is the process of converting XML data from its hierarchical format to a serialized string format. Think of it as a process to flatten a tree with branches and nodes to a piece of paper so that the client application can work with and process the data. If the client supports XML data, the DB2 data server sends the returned XML data to the client and lets the client serialize the data implicitly. However, if the client does not support XML data, the DB2 data server will implicitly serialize the XML data before sending it to the client. Implicit XML serialization simplifies the application code, is more efficient to send data to clients as XML data, and allows the clients to handle the XML data properly.

While we recommend implicit XML serialization as much as possible, there are cases you may consider using explicit XML serialization. The first consideration was brought up earlier in this section. By default, the DB2 data server converts XML data to BLOB if the client doesn't support the XML data type. If you want the retrieved data to be of some other data type, you then want to perform an explicit XML serialization. By the way, converting XML data type to BLOB is the best choice of data type because it results in fewer encoding issues. Encoding is covered later in this section.

Another situation is when the XML documents are very large. Unlike large objects, there are no locators for XML data. If XML data is converted to CLOB or BLOB, LOB locators can be used to refer to a LOB value to improve performance. Each LOB locator is a 4-byte value, which is very tiny compared to the actual size of the XML document.

Figure 10.24 shows the syntax of the XMLSERIALIZE scalar function you use to explicitly serialize XML documents.

```
                       .-CONTENT-.
>>-XMLSERIALIZE--(--+---------+---------------------------------->

>--XML-expression--AS--| data-type |----------------------------->

    .-------------------------------------.
    V .-VERSION--'1.0'---------------. (1) |
>----+-------------------------------+-----+--)------------------><
       | .-EXCLUDING XMLDECLARATION-. |
       '-+-INCLUDING XMLDECLARATION-+-'

data-type
```

Figure 10.24 The XMLSERIALIZE function syntax

```
                    .-(1)-----------.
|--+-+-CHARACTER-+--+---------------+-------------------------+--|
   | '-CHAR------'  '-(--integer--)-'                         |
   +-+-VARCHAR----------------+--(--integer--)----------------+
   | '-+-CHARACTER-+--VARYING-'                               |
   |   '-CHAR------'                                          |
   |                                  .-(1M)----------------. |
   +-+-CLOB----------------------+--+---------------------+-+
   | '-+-CHARACTER-+--LARGE OBJECT-'  '-(--integer--+---+--)-' |
   |   '-CHAR------'                               +-K-+      |
   |                                               +-M-|      |
   |                                               '-G-'      |
   |                            .-(1M)----------------.       |
   '-+-BLOB-----------------+--+---------------------+--------'
     '-BINARY--LARGE OBJECT-'  '-(--integer--+---+--)-'
                                             +-K-+
                                             +-M-+
                                             '-G-'
```

Figure 10.24 The XMLSERIALIZE function syntax *(Continued)*

We can easily serialize an example used above. For example, the following statement used earlier with explicit XML serialization will look like this.

```
SELECT XMLSERIALIZE (
  XMLQUERY ('declare default element namespace "http://posample.org";
           $d/customerinfo/phone' passing INFO as "d" )
  AS BLOB (500k))
FROM CUSTOMER
```

There is an optional clause to specify whether an XML declaration is included in the result. If the INCLUDING XMLDECLARATION option is used, the following string is included in the result.

```
<?xml version="1.0" encoding="UTF-8"?>
```

After the XML data is serialized, the result is encoded with UTF-8 regardless of the usage of the INCLUDING XMLDECLARATION option. If the serialized output is in character data type, the character string sent from the data server to the client will be converted to the code page of the client. Assume the client code page is not UTF-8 and the INCLUDING XMLDECLARATION option is used (which has **encoding="UTF-8"** in the result), there may be a possibility of running into data loss or truncation problems during code page conversion. To avoid code page conversion, you may want to consider using BLOB as the serialized data type or use host variables in the application code.

10.4 SQL/XML Publishing Functions

Publishing functions allow you to publish relational data from tables as an XML document. In other words, publishing functions allow you to do the opposite of the XMLTABLE function previously discussed. SQL/XML publishing functions support was available in versions prior to

DB2 9. There are about ten SQL/XML publishing functions that can be used together to construct XML documents. We illustrate some of these functions in the example below.

Example #1:

```
SELECT XMLCONCAT(
    XMLPI( NAME "xml-stylesheet"
          , 'type="text/css" href="licenserpt.css"' )
  , XMLELEMENT( NAME "license-compliance-checks"
              , XMLAGG ( XMLELEMENT
                         ( NAME "feature"
                         , XMLATTRIBUTES (featureid AS "id")
                         , XMLELEMENT( NAME "name", feature )
                         , XMLELEMENT( NAME "function", function )
                         , XMLELEMENT( NAME "evaluation", evaluation )
                         , XMLELEMENT( NAME "detail", detail )
                         ) ORDER BY feature, function
                       ) ) )
  FROM licensetab
```

This SQL statement queries the LICENSETAB table and obtains the details about the features available in the current DB2 server. It returns these values as part of a single XML document using the XMLCONCAT function. The XMLPI function specifies the processing instruction, which in this case is an XML stylesheet and associated information. XML elements and attributes are specified in the XMLELEMENT and XMLATTRIBUTES functions. As soon as you have the stylesheet *licenserpt.css* specified in the XML document, you can use any browser to display the content in a Web-based report. The output is shown below.

```
<?xml-stylesheet type="text/css" href="licenserpt.css"?>
<license-compliance-checks>
    <feature id="801">
        <name>High Availability Feature</name>
        <function>High Availability Disaster Recovery</function>
        <evaluation>HADR_DB_ROLE = STANDARD</evaluation>
        <detail>HADR is NOT being used</detail>
    </feature>
    <feature id="802">
        <name>Performance Optimization Feature</name>
        <function>Intraquery parallelism</function>
        <evaluation>INTRA_PARALLEL = NO</evaluation>
        <detail>Intraquery parallelism is DISABLED</detail>
    </feature>
    <feature>
        <name>Performance Optimization Feature</name>
        <function>Materialized Query Tables</function>
        <evaluation>MQT =&gt; DB2INST1.ADEFUSR</evaluation>
        <detail/>
    </feature>
    <feature>
        <name>Performance Optimization Feature</name>
        <function>Materialized Query Tables</function>
        <evaluation>MQT =&gt; DB2INST1.TESTMQT</evaluation>
        <detail/>
    </feature>
</license-compliance-checks>
```

For further information about the SQL/XML publishing functions, please refer to the DB2 manuals.

V9.5

10.5 Transforming XML Documents Using XSLT Functions

XSLT transformation is the standard method used to transform XML data into other formats such as plain text, HTML or other forms of XML. In DB2 you can use the XSLTRANSFORM function for this purpose where the XML document is taken from the database. XSLTRANSFORM uses stylesheets to convert XML into other data formats. You can convert part or all of an XML document and select or rearrange the data using XPath and the built-in functions of XSLT. XSLTRANSFORM function can accept XSLT parameters at run time.

To illustrate the use of the XSLTRANSFORM function, consider this table:

```
CREATE TABLE myXMLtable (myXMLdoc xml, myXSLdoc CLOB(1M))
```

For this particular example, the XSLT stylesheet is stored in the column myXSLdoc, however it is not a requirement to store it in the table. To invoke the XSLTRANSFORM function issue:

```
SELECT XSLTRANSFORM (myXMLdoc USING myXSLdoc AS CLOB(1M))
  FROM myXMLtable
```

The type of the myXMLdoc parameter can be XML, CLOB, BLOB, and varchar. The XSLTRANSFORM function is also supported in partitioned databases (DPF).

10.6 Inserting XML Data into a DB2 Database

There are three ways to move XML data into a table.

1. Using the SQL INSERT statement
2. Using the IMPORT utility
3. Using the LOAD utility (in DB2 9.5)

The IMPORT and LOAD utilities are covered in Chapter 13, Maintaining Data; therefore we will defer the explanation about how to use this method to that chapter. In this chapter we concentrate on how to insert XML data with the INSERT statement.

There are two basic requirements when inserting XML data into an XML column.

1. The XML document must be well-formed.
2. The XML data to be inserted must be in XML hierarchical format. This can be done by implicit or explicit XML parsing as discussed earlier.

Below is a simple example about how to INSERT an XML document into a table. XML parsing is done implicitly. From a user's perspective, you basically treat the XML document as a string.

Example 1:

```
CREATE TABLE clients(id integer, name varchar(25), addr XML)
```

```
INSERT INTO clients VALUES (88, 'Jin Chong', 'Perfect',
   '<address>888 Nighthawk Trail, Mississauga, ON, 98210</address>')
```

In Section 10.6.1, XML Parsing, we provide other examples for INSERT where explicitly parsing is done using XMLPARSE.

Example 2:

Here is another example of inserting XML data using the XMLTABLE function. For this example you first need to create the table SHIPADDRESS in the SAMPLE database as follows:

```
CONNECT TO SAMPLE

CREATE TABLE SHIPADDRESS (name char(50), address xml)

INSERT INTO shipaddress
    SELECT T.*
      FROM XMLTABLE (
          XMLNAMESPACES (DEFAULT 'http://posample.org')
          , 'db2-fn:xmlcolumn("CUSTOMER.INFO")'
             COLUMNS "NAME"  CHAR(50) PATH '/customerinfo/name'
                    , "ADDR"  XML       PATH 'document{/customerinfo/addr}'
) AS T
```

The INSERT statement is inserting all the rows and columns from table T. Table T is built from the XMLTABLE function, which defines the table columns using elements from the XML documents stored in the INFO column of the CUSTOMER table.

You can optionally have DB2 validate the XML document during insertion. This process makes sure XML documents to be stored in the database are valid against a registered XML schema. XML validation and XML schema support in DB2 is discussed in detail in Section 10.9 XML Schema Support and Validation in DB2.

10.6.1 XML Parsing

XML parsing is the process opposite to XML serialization. It converts XML data from its serialized string format to hierarchical format. XML parsing can be performed implicitly by DB2 or explicitly. Implicit XML parsing occurs when you assign a host variable, parameter marker, or SQL expression with a string data type to an XML column in an INSERT, UPDATE, DELETE, or MERGE statement. This was explained in earlier sections. Explicit XML parsing occurs when you use the XMLPARSE function.

The XMLPARSE function parses the XML data and returns it in XML data type. The syntax of this function is quite simple as shown in Figure 10.25.

```
                                                .-STRIP WHITESPACE----.
>>-XMLPARSE--(--DOCUMENT--string-expression--+---------------------+--)-><
                                                '-PRESERVE WHITESPACE-'
```

Figure 10.25 The XMLPARSE function syntax

Here is an example of the XMLPARSE function. For illustration purposes and clarity, we are not showing the entire XML document.

```
INSERT INTO customer (cid, info, history) VALUES (
     , 1
     , XMLPARSE( DOCUMENT '<?xml version="1.0" encoding="UTF-8"?>. . .
                 <customerinfo> . . .
                 <street>5 Rosewood</street> <city>Toronto</city> . . .
                 </customerinfo>'
                 PRESERVE WHITESPACE)
     , NULL)
```

The behavior of options STRIP WHITESPACE and PRESERVE WHITESPACE are self explanatory. They are used to control preservation of whitespace characters that appear between elements. This whitespace is known as the boundary whitespace. In the above example, the space between `</street>` and `<city>` is the boundary whitespace.

You can also strip or perverse boundary whitespace during implicit XML parsing with the DB2 registry variable CURRENT IMPLICIT XMLPARSE OPTION. It accepts values STRIP WHITESPACE or PRESERVE WHITESPACE. Default is STRIP WHITESPACE.

XMLPARSE is supported only in Unicode databases. The XML document string will be converted to the database server code page. However this code page may be different from the one specified in the XML declaration `<?xml version="1.0" encoding="UTF-8"?>`. Data loss or truncation may occur during the code page conversion. Similar to the XML serialization encoding consideration, use host variables to store the character string input and then apply it to the XMLPARSE function if possible. Otherwise, a BLOB data type should be specified as the argument to avoid code page conversion.

Another example of the XMLPARSE function with parameter markers and a cast of the XML data to BLOB is demonstrated below.

```
INSERT INTO customer (cid, info, history) VALUES (
     , ?
     , XMLPARSE( DOCUMENT CAST (? AS BLOB) PRESERVE WHITESPACE )
     , ? )
```

10.7 Updating and Deleting XML Data

The XQuery language has been a W3C candidate recommendation for a few years now. The XQuery Update Facility for updating XML data, however, is not yet standardized. In DB2 9, updating XML data was supported using the SQL UPDATE statement. A stored procedure was also available for this purpose but provided as a separate download from the IBM developerWorks Web site. Refer to the Resources section for details on this Web site. Using the SQL UPDATE statement, entire new XML document had to be specified, even if you wanted to only change part of the document, such as one element or text node. Using the stored procedure, you could specify which part of the document you wanted to change; however, behind the scenes, the entire XML document was updated on disk.

V9.5 With DB2 9.5 we can now perform sub-document updates (with the transform expression), which is a lot more efficient. This allows you to replace, insert, delete or rename nodes in an XML document. You can also change the value of a node without replacing the node itself, typically to change an element or attribute value, which is a very common type of update.

To perform an update operation you need to use the TRANSFORM expression. Since the TRANSFORM expression is part of the XQuery language, you can use it anywhere you normally use XQuery, for example in a FLWOR expression or in the XMLQUERY function in an SQL/XML statement. The most typical use is in an SQL UPDATE statement to modify an XML document in an XML column.

Figure 10.26 shows the syntax of the TRANSFORM expression extracted from the DB2 manuals.

```
>>-transform--| copy clause |--| modify clause |--| return clause |-><

copy clause

       .-,---------------------------------------.
       V                                         |
|--copy----$VariableName--:=--CopySourceExpression-+------------|

modify clause

|--modify--ModifyExpression-------------------------------------|

return clause

|--return--ReturnExpression-------------------------------------|
```

Figure 10.26 The syntax of the TRANSFORM expression

The **copy** clause is used to assign to a variable the XML documents you want to process.

In the **modify** clause, you can invoke an **insert, delete, rename, or replace** expression. These expressions allow you to perform updates to your XML document. For example, if you want to add new nodes to the document, you would use the **insert** expression, to delete nodes from an XML document, use the **delete** expression, to rename an element or attribute in the XML document, use the **rename** expression, and to replace an existing node with a new node or sequence of nodes, use the **replace** expression. The **replace value of** expression can only be used to change the value of an element or attribute.

The **return** clause returns the result of the transform expression.

Let us show you two examples below, one with SQL as the primary language, and the other one with XQuery as the primary language to illustrate UPDATE operations. As a prerequisite, you need to create the following table:

```
CREATE TABLE customers(
  id           integer primary key not null,
  name         varchar(50),
  age          integer,
  contactinfo xml)
```

Example #1:

```
(1)-- UPDATE customers
(2)-- SET contactinfo = xmlquery( 'declare default element namespace
(3)--                                  "http://posample.org";
(4)--      transform
(5)--      copy $newinfo := $c
(6)--           modify do insert <email2>my2email.gm.com</email2>
(7)--                           as last into $newinfo/customerinfo
(8)--      return $newinfo' passing contactinfo as "c")
(9)-- WHERE id = 100
```

In Example #1, lines (1), (2), and (9) are part of the SQL UPDATE syntax. In Line (2) the XMLQUERY function is invoked, which calls the transform expression in line (4). The transform expression block goes from line (4) to line (8), and it is used to insert a new node into the XML document containing the **email2** element.

Note that updating the elements in an XML document through a view is not supported.

Example #2:

```
(1)-- xquery
(2)-- declare default element namespace "http://posample.org";
(3)-- transform
(4)-- copy $person := db2-fn:sqlquery(
(5)--    "select contactinfo from customers where id=100")/Address
(6)-- modify(
(7)--    do replace value of $person/Address/city with 'Toronto',
(8)--    do insert <email2>my2email@gm.com</email2> as last into $person )
(9)-- return $person
```

In Example #2, lines (1) and (2) have been explained in earlier examples.

Line (3) invokes the transform expression. In the transform expression, you specify:

- A copy of the XML document using the **copy** expression as shown in Line(4). In this example, the copy of the XML document is bound to variable **person**, and not all the XML documents in the table are selected, only the ones filtered by the **db2-fn:sqlquery** function.

- What you plan to modify using the **modify** expression as shown in line (6). Within **modify**, a replace of a text node value is provided, as well as information about an insert of a new node.

Deleting entire XML documents from tables is as simple as when using the SELECT statement in SQL/XML. Use the SQL DELETE statement and specific any necessary WHERE predicates such as in the example below.

Example #3:

```
DELETE FROM customer
 WHERE XMLEXISTS (
          'declare default element namespace "http://posample.org";
          $d//addr[city="Markham"]' passing info as "d" )
```

In this example we delete all the rows which have XML documents containing the **city** element with a value of "Markham."

If you would like to delete only part of an XML document, you are, in effect, updating the XML document. Updates of an XML document were discussed earlier in this section. For this case you would have to use the transform expression, and invoke the modify clause with the delete expression.

> **NOTE** Because XML support is fully integrated in DB2, the MERGE statement also works with XML data.

10.8 XML Indexes

Accessing XML documents using pureXML would not be efficient without the appropriate XML indexes created. In pureXML, there are two types of indexes:

- System indexes
- User-created indexes

10.8.1 System Indexes

As the name implies, system indexes are created and used by DB2. There are two types.

- XML Region Index

  This type of index is created by DB2 when the first XML column is created or added to the table. This is a single index for all the XML columns within the table. The XML region index captures how an XML document is divided up internally into regions, which was discussed in Section 10.2.1, pureXML Storage in DB2.

- XML Path Index
  This type of index is created by DB2 for each XML column created or added to the table. The XML path index records all unique paths which exist within XML documents stored within an XML column. A subset of these paths is stored in the global catalog path table SYSIBM.SYSXMLPATHS. These indexes are used to improve the performance during queries.

When an XML document is inserted into the table, DB2 starts building these internal system indexes. Figure 10.27 illustrates these indexes.

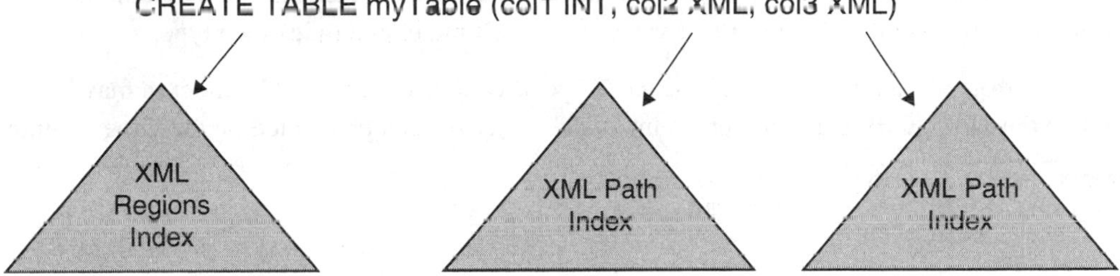

Figure 10.27 XML system indexes

10.8.2 User-Created Indexes

Like the regular indexes over relational data, user-created indexes are created to improve query performance. These indexes are defined on an XML column, and are implemented just like relational indexes using B-Trees. XML indexing is more granular than just indexing the entire XML document; nodes within the documents can be indexed. These qualifying nodes are evaluated based on the XML pattern expression in the CREATE INDEX statement.

For example the following statement creates an XML index *custidx* on the INFO column.

```
CREATE INDEX custidx ON customer(info)
    GENERATE KEY USING XMLPATTERN '/customerinfo/@Cid'
    AS SQL DOUBLE
```

The *info* column is an XML column in the *customer* table. The nodes qualified by the path expression specified in the XMLPATTERN clause are indexed. In this case, index keys are created on the *Cid* attribute nodes. This clause is called the XML index specification. The XMLPATTERN allows for an XPath expression without predicates. On the other hand, the following XPath expression would not be allowed in the index specification because it has a predicate:

```
/customerinfo/phone[@type='home']
```

In addition, you need to indicate the data type of the indexed values. Four SQL data types are allowed:

VARCHAR,
DATE,

TIMESTAMP, and
DOUBLE.

Since the *Cid* XML attribute in this example is numeric, the SQL data type of DOUBLE is used. Note that if you inserted an XML document where *@Cid* is not numeric, the index would not prevent the insertion but would not contain an index entry for that document. This is perfectly safe because the index would only be used to evaluate numeric predicates, so the absence of non-numeric values from the index would never lead to incomplete query results.

V9.5 In DB2 9.5 you can add the clause **reject invalid values** to the CREATE INDEX statement to prevent this situation. The clause **ignore invalid values** is the default, and as it name states, it will allow for inserts of values that don't match the index data type.

Although you can only have one XML index specification, multiple XML indexes may be created on the same XML column. For example, these indexes can be created on the same column:

```
CREATE INDEX custidx1 ON customer(info)
    GENERATE KEY USING XMLPATTERN '/customerinfo/@Cid'
    AS SQL DOUBLE

CREATE INDEX custidx2 ON customer(info)
    GENERATE KEY USING XMLPATTERN '/customerinfo/@Cid'
    AS SQL VARCHAR(10)
```

Notice that the indexes are basically the same except that index keys in *custidx1* are using the DOUBLE data type and index keys in *custidx2* are using the VARCHAR(10) data type. This is perfectly reasonable if you have XQuery predicates that match *Cid* as a character string and as a number. You can also choose between VARCHAR(n), where n represents a number, and VARCHAR HASHED for character strings. VARCHAR(n) allows you to specify the maximum length of the character; values that are longer than this length will not be indexed. VARCHAR HASHED on the other hand, has no length limit for the character string. The system will generate an 8-byte hash code over the entire string. VARCHAR HASHED however, will only be used for equality look-ups and not range scans, while VARCHAR(n) works for both.

XML namespace and default namespace declarations are optional in the index specification for element and attribute names in the XML pattern. Here are two examples where the namespace has been included in the **CREATE INDEX** statement.

```
CREATE INDEX custidx1 ON customer(info)
    GENERATE KEY USING XMLPATTERN
        'declare default element namespace "http://posample.org";
        /customerinfo/addr/city/text()'
    AS SQL VARCHAR(50)

CREATE INDEX custidx1 ON customer(info)
    GENERATE KEY USING XMLPATTERN
        'declare namespace n="http://posample.org";
        /n:customerinfo/n:addr/n:city/text()'
    AS SQL VARCHAR(50)
```

To index elements in any namespace, you can use wildcards for the namespace prefixes and avoid the namespace declaration.

```
CREATE INDEX custidx1 ON customer(info)
    GENERATE KEY USING XMLPATTERN
        '/*:customerinfo/*:addr/*:city/text()'
    AS SQL VARCHAR(50)
```

You can also create unique XML indexes. Unique indexes for relational data enforce uniqueness across all rows in a table, and unique XML indexes essentially do the same. A unique XML index enforces uniqueness across all documents and within each document in the XML column. However, this uniqueness applies specifically to the data type of the index and the XML path to the node. For example, consider the table and XML unique index defined below.

```
CREATE TABLE apartment
    ( apartid   INT
    , apartname VARCHAR(20)
    , detail    XML);

CREATE UNIQUE INDEX apartindex ON apartment(detail)
    GENERATE KEY USING XMLPATTERN '/apartment/suite/@id' AS SQL DOUBLE;
```

The above statements create the table **apartment** with the **detail** column defined as an XML column. The index **apartindex** is created on the pattern **'/apartment/suite/@id'** using the SQL data type of DOUBLE. Note that the pattern in the XMLPATTERN clause is not verified until an index key is inserted or evaluated. If you were to put **'/blah/abc/123/@id'** in the XML index specification, the CREATE UNIQUE INDEX statement will still be successful. However, the index will never be used because there will typically not be any node satisfying that path. Let's now insert a row to the *apartment* table.

```
INSERT INTO apartment
    VALUES ( 1
           , 'Haven'
           , XMLPARSE (DOCUMENT '<apartment name="Haven">
             <suite id="1001" sqfeet="835">Paradise<ammenities>
             <rooms>2</rooms><den>0</den><laundry>Yes</laundry>
             </ammenities><maintenance payment="monthly">300
             </maintenance></suite></apartment>'))
```

The row is inserted successfully, and the appropriate index entry is created. As a test, if you issue the same INSERT statement again, you will receive an SQL0803N error indicating the insert failed because of duplicate values, id="1001" for an index key in the *apartment* table. This shows us that a unique index enforces uniqueness within a single XML column across all documents whose nodes are qualified by the XML pattern.

The above example only demonstrates the unique constraint applies to the XML path to the node and the value of the node. The data type of the index is also a key to how the unique constraint is defined. For example, if the INSERT statement were to insert **suite id="10A"** to the *apartment* instead as shown below,

```
INSERT INTO apartment
    VALUES ( 1
           , 'Haven'
           , XMLPARSE (DOCUMENT '<apartment name="Haven">
             <suite id="10A" sqfeet="835">Paradise<ammenities>
             <rooms>2</rooms><den>0</den><laundry>Yes</laundry>
             </ammenities><maintenance payment="monthly">300
             </maintenance></suite></apartment>'))
```

multiple executions of such INSERT statement will be successful even though the unique index **apartindex** we defined earlier exists. This is because the value "10A" cannot be cast to the DOUBLE data type; hence no index entry is inserted. Therefore, the constraint bound by the unique index does not apply. If you want the data type of the index to be a hard constraint, use the "reject invalid values" clause in the index definition.

10.8.3 Conditions for XML Index Eligibility

Now that you know how to create XML indexes, perhaps you are wondering when an XML index can be used for a query predicate. There are three necessary conditions for XML index eligibility.

- The query predicate must match the XML index data type.
- The XMLPATTERN specified in the index is equally or less restrictive than the query predicate, that is, the XML index must contain everything that the predicate is asking for.
- The text node and **text()** function must be used consistently in the query predicate and the index definitions.

In the discussion of the XML unique index above, it was brought to your attention that the data type of the index and the actual value of relevant node in the XML document matters. They must match. This concept also applies to whether the XML index can be used for an XML query. We will use the same table and XML index definition illustrated earlier, which we are copying again below for clarity.

```
CREATE UNIQUE INDEX apartindex ON apartment(detail)
    GENERATE KEY USING XMLPATTERN '/apartment/suite/@id' AS SQL DOUBLE
```

Consider the following query and the associated explain plan in Figure 10.28.

```
SELECT XMLQUERY ('$d/apartment' passing DETAIL as "d")
  FROM apartment
 WHERE XMLEXISTS ('$d/apartment/suite[@id=1001]' passing DETAIL as "d")
```

> **NOTE** Visual explain and other execution path monitoring tools are discussed in Chapter 17, Database Performance Considerations.

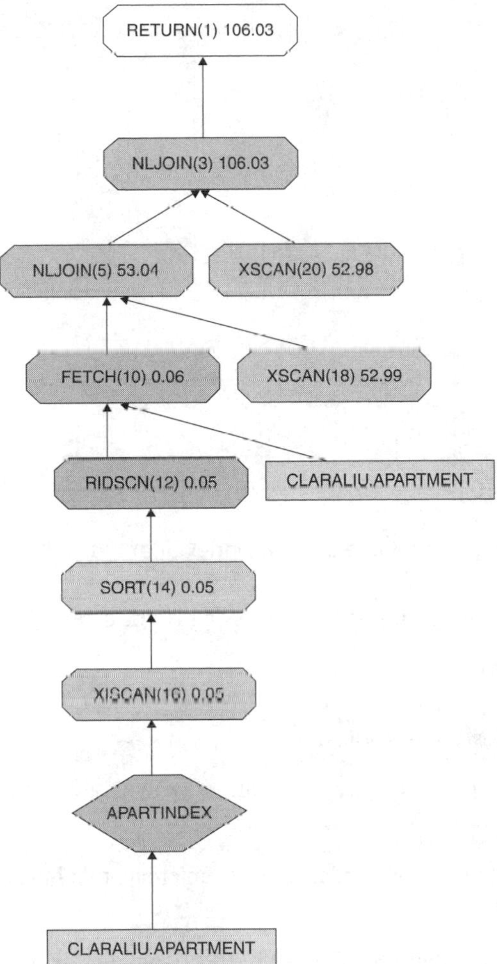

Figure 10.28 XQuery that uses an XML index

You can see in the explain plan from Figure 10.28 that the *apartindex* is used because **`suite[@id=1001]`** in the predicate matches the index data type, DOUBLE. On the other hand, if **`suite[@id="1001"]`** is used, *apartindex* cannot be used because **`"1001"`** is a string. For example, in the XQuery statement below we use **`suite[@id="1001"]`** instead of **`suite[@id=1001]`** as the query predicate. The visual explain illustrated in Figure 10.29 shows that the entire *apartment* table is scanned.

```
SELECT XMLQUERY ('$d/apartment' passing DETAIL as "d" )
  FROM apartment
 WHERE XMLEXISTS ('$d/apartment/suite[@id="1001"]' passing DETAIL
                   as "d")
```

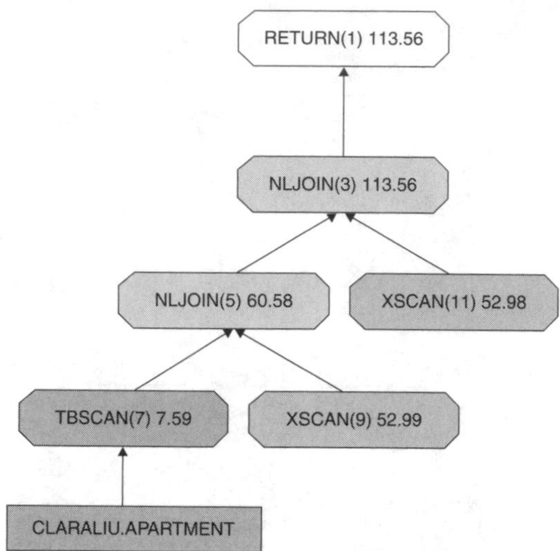

Figure 10.29 XQuery that cannot use the XML index apartindex

There are three operators designed just for processing XML data:

1. XSCAN for XML scan and navigation,
2. XISCAN for XML index access, and
3. XANDOR for XML index joins.

These new XML-specific join and query evaluation methods evaluate multiple predicates concurrently with minimal index I/O.

If you want both queries to use XML indexes, you can create two indexes; one in DOUBLE type and another one in VARCHAR type.

The second condition states that the XMLPATTERN specified in the index is equally or less restrictive than the query predicate. For example, you have an index defined as shown below.

```
CREATE INDEX idx1 on apartment(detail)
    GENERATE KEY USING XMLPATTERN '/apartment/suite'
    AS SQL VARCHAR(30);
```

The following XQuery can be used and as shown in the visual explain of Figure 10.30, the index is indeed used given that the index definition is as equally restrictive as the query predicate.

```
SELECT XMLQUERY ('$d/apartment' passing DETAIL as "d" )
  FROM apartment
 WHERE XMLEXISTS ('$d/apartment[suite="Paradise"]'
                  passing DETAIL as "d");
```

However, with the same index ***idx1*** defined earlier, the following queries will not use the index.

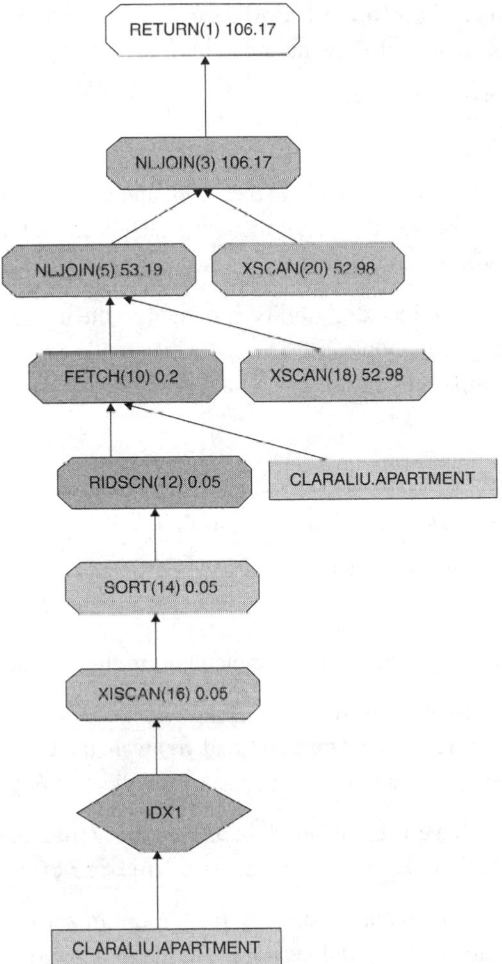

Figure 10.30 Visual Explain of an XQuery statement using an index that is as restrictive as the query predicate

```
SELECT XMLQUERY ('$d/apartment' passing DETAIL as "d" )
  FROM apartment
 WHERE XMLEXISTS ('$d//suite="Paradise"'
                  passing DETAIL as "d");

SELECT XMLQUERY ('$d/apartment' passing DETAIL as "d" )
  FROM apartment
 WHERE XMLEXISTS ('$d/apartment/*="Paradise"'
                  passing DETAIL as "d");
```

The index specification is more restrictive than the query predicates; hence the index cannot be used. Both queries have the same visual explain plan illustrated in Figure 10.31.

To satisfy both predicates **'$d/apartment/suite="Paradise"** and **$d//suite="Paradise"**, you can create the following index instead.

```
CREATE INDEX idx2 on apartment(detail)
    GENERATE KEY USING XMLPATTERN '//suite'
    AS SQL VARCHAR(30);
```

Of course you can also use **'//text()'** as the XML index specification to index all the text contents in the document. However, this is not recommended because this means you are indexing almost everything. This will be too expensive for insert, update, and delete operations.

The third and last condition for index eligibility is related to the usage of the **text()** function. The text node and **text()** function must be used consistently in the query predicate and the index definitions. For example, if you use this XPath statement

```
'/apartment/suite'
```

it will return something like

```
<suite id="1001" sqfeet="835">Paradise . . . </suite> .
```

On the other hand, if you issue this other XPath statement

```
'/apartment/suite/text()',
```

the result will return the text content of the *suite* element, in this example, 1001.

You should take this into consideration when specifying the XMLPATTERN in the index definition. If you have a predicate **'/apartment/suite'** and you want the DB2 optimizer to use an index, XMLPATTERN for such index should be the same as the predicate **'/apartment/suite'**.

On the other hand, if you have a predicate **'/apartment/suite/text()'**, you should define the index with XMLPATTERN **'/apartment/suite/text()'**.

In conclusion, the three conditions are necessary for the optimizer to consider an XML index; however, even if all conditions satisfy, it does not mean the index will be chosen. As you will see in Chapter 17, Database Performance Considerations, the DB2 optimizer is cost-based. This means it has to evaluate the overall cost with the size, statistics of the table and so on. Having eligible indexes defined in the database is only one of the many factors.

10.9 XML Schema Support and Validation in DB2

An XML schema defines the building blocks of an XML document. DB2's support for XML schema involves several components as illustrated in Figure 10.32.

Figure 10.32 shows at the center the XML Schema Repository (XSR) containing several XML Schemas. These XML schemas have been registered in the XSR using CLP commands, stored procedures, or applications as shown on the left side of the figure. When an XML document is inserted into an XML column, you can optionally validate it against an XML schema previously

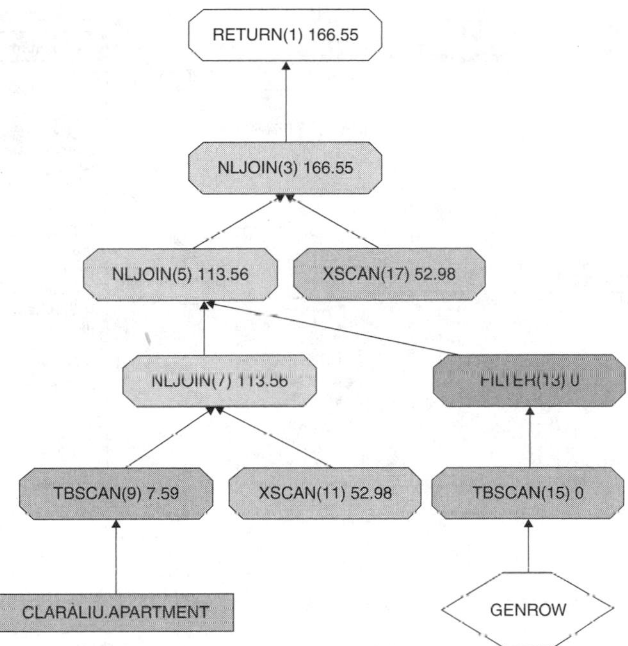

Figure 10.31 XQuery that cannot use the idx1 index

stored in the XSR. You can optionally validate per row inserted using the XMLVALIDATE function, or per column using a BEFORE trigger.

10.9.1 XML Schema Repository

The XML Schema Repository (XSR) is a repository that stores copies of registered XML schemas, external entities and DTDs in DB2. XML schemas, external entities and DTDs are known as XSR objects. At the same time, each XML schema can contain one or more XML schema documents (xsd).

When an XML document contains a reference to a Uniform Resource Identifier (URI) that points to an associated XML schema or DTD, this URI is required to validate the XML document.

10.9.1.1 Registering XSR Objects

XSR objects must be registered through the CLP, stored procedures, or Java applications. To register an XML schema follow these steps:

1. Register the primary XML schema document.

   For example, let's register the xsd stored in **c:/temp/customer.xsd** to the XMLschema named **store.custschema,** where **store** is the qualifier and **custschema** is the XML schema name. The xsd also includes the URI **'http://**

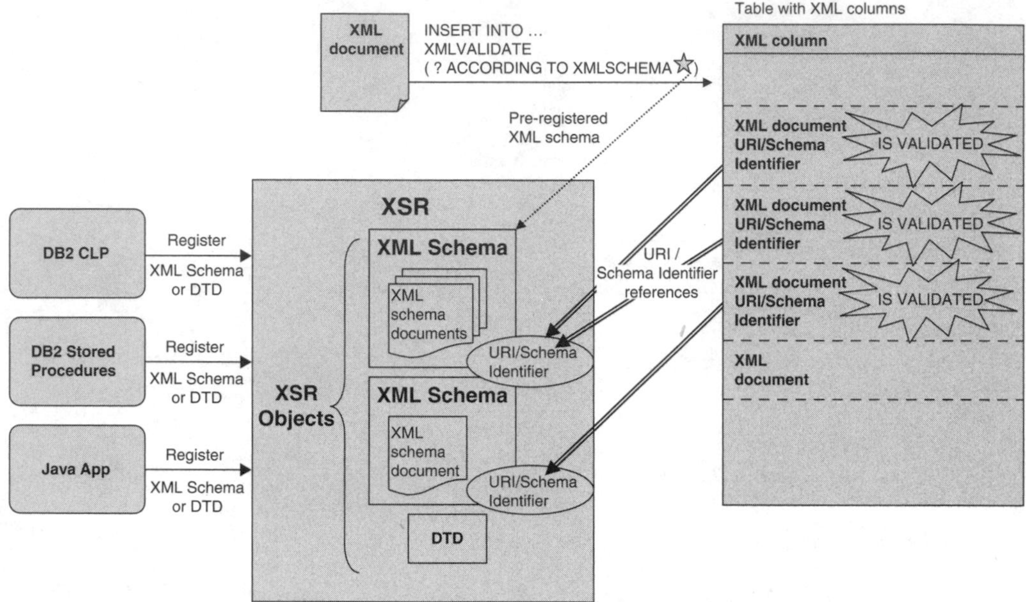

Figure 10.32 Overview of XML schema support and validation in DB2

posample.org/CUSTOMER' which can be referenced in the XML documents stored in XML columns.

From the CLP you would issue this command:

```
REGISTER XMLSCHEMA 'http://posample.org/CUSTOMER'
FROM 'file://c:/temp/customer.xsd'
AS store.custschema
```

Using a stored procedure you can issue the following CALL statement, assuming the host variable **:content_host_var** contains the content of the xsd:

```
CALL SYSPROC.XSR_REGISTER
( 'store', 'custschema'
, 'http://posample.org/CUSTOMER'
, :content_host_var, NULL);
```

2. Optionally, you may add other xsd in the XML schema. The following command will add the xsd **c:/temp/address.xsd** to the XML schema **store.custschema** with URI **'http://posample.org/ADDRESS'.**

   From the CLP, issue:

```
ADD XMLSCHEMA DOCUMENT TO store.custschema
ADD 'http://posample.org/ADDRESS'
FROM 'file://c:/temp/address.xsd'
```

   Using a stored procedure, use:

```
CALL SYSPROC.XSR_ADDSCHEMADOC
```

```
( 'store', 'custschema'
, 'http://posample.org/ADDRESS'
, :content_host_var, NULL);
```

3. Finally, you complete the registration process by the COMPLETE XMLSCHEMA command.

   From the CLP issue:

```
COMPLETE XMLSCHEMA store.custschema
```

   Using a stored procedure, issue:

```
CALL SYSPROC.XSR_COMPLETE ('store', 'custschema', NULL, 0);
```

   From a Java application you can invoke the same stored procedures to perform this registration. If your XML schema consists of only one schema document, then the REGISTER and COMPLETE can be combined in a single command.

10.9.1.2 Obtaining Information about Registered XML Schemas

Information about the XML schema registered in the XSR can be found in the system catalog views. Table 10.9 provides a brief description of each view.

Table 10.9 System Catalog Views Specific to XSR Objects

System Catalog Views	Description
SYSCAT.XSROBJECTS	Details of each XSR object such as the object name, its SQL schema, target namespace, and schema location.
SYSCAT.XSROBJECTCOMPONENTS	Details of the XSR object components.
SYSCAT.XSROBJECTDEP	Information about objects that are depended on the XSR object.
SYSCAT.XSROBJECTHIERARCHIES	Details of the hierarchical relationship between the XSR object and its component.
SYSCAT.XSROBJECTAUTH	User or group that has USAGE privileges on the XSR object.

10.9.2 XML Validation

Once an XML schema is registered in the XSR, you can start using it to validate XML documents. Validation is optional, it is not a requirement enforced by DB2; however, just like any other constraint placed in the database, XML validation ensures the accuracy of the XML document structure so that applications working with these XML documents perform less error checking or verification. XML validation may increase CPU time for insert operations and may reduce throughput. You may consider avoiding schema validation if it is not really necessary or if the application is already checking the structure of the XML documents.

10.9.2.1 Performing Validation

Validation can be performed in three ways.

1. Using the XMLVALIDATE function

   You can invoke the XMLVALIDATE function whenever you are inserting or updating XML documents. This means that validation is performed per row inserted or updated since the SQL INSERT or SQL UPDATE statements are used. For example, below is an INSERT statement that validates the whole XML document according to the registered XML schema **store.custschema** defined earlier. The relevant lines in the statement below are highlighted in bold.

```
INSERT INTO customer (cid, info, history) VALUES (
     , 1
     , XMLVALIDATE (
        XMLPARSE( DOCUMENT '<?xml version="1.0" encoding="UTF-8"?>. . .
                  <customerinfo> . . .
                  <street>5 Rosewood</street> <city>Toronto</city> . . .
                  </customerinfo>'
                  PRESERVE WHITESPACE )
        ACCORDING TO XMLSCHEMA ID store.custschema )
     , NULL)
```

   If you use a parameter marker to pass the document to the insert statement, then the XMLPARSE function inside XMLVALIDATE is not needed, that is.:

```
INSERT INTO customer (cid, info, history) VALUES (
, 1
, XMLVALIDATE (? ACCORDING TO XMLSCHEMA ID store.custschema )
, NULL)
```

   You can also validate just an element within the XML document as shown in the example below where the XML document is validated according to **store.custschema** only for the **street** element which has a namespace of **'http://posample.org/'**.

```
INSERT INTO customer (cid, info, history) VALUES (
, 1
, XMLVALIDATE (
  XMLPARSE( DOCUMENT '<?xml version="1.0" encoding="UTF-8"?>. . .
             <customerinfo> . . .
            <street>5 Rosewood</street> <city>Toronto</city> . . .
            </customerinfo>'
            PRESERVE WHITESPACE )
  ACCORDING TO XMLSCHEMA ID store.custschema
  NAMESPACE 'http://posample.org/'
  ELEMENT "street"  )
, NULL)
```

V9.5

2. Using a trigger with the XMLVALIDATE function

   You can create a BEFORE trigger to call the XMLVALIDATE function, which would allow the validation check to be performed automatically for you. Note that the "when" condition in the following trigger is optional. It is used only to validate documents, which were not validated in the insert statement. Without the "when" condition you force (re)validation of *all* incoming documents against a specific schema.

```
CREATE TRIGGER myValid NO CASCADE BEFORE INSERT ON myTable
REFERENCING NEW AS n
FOR EACH ROW
MODE DB2SQL
BEGIN ATOMIC
WHEN (n.myCol2 is not validated)
  set (n.myCol2) = xmlvalidate(n.myCol2 ACCORDING TO XMLSCHEMA URI 'http://
my-namespace');
END
```

3. Using a CHECK constraint

   The IS VALIDATED predicate can enforce that an XML document has been validated when used as a CHECK constraint when you create or alter a table. This is illustrated in the next two statements below.

```
CREATE TABLE car
( car_id INTEGER NOT NULL
, car_detail XML
, car_option_pkg XML
, CONSTRAINT ck_validcar CHECK ( car_detail IS VALIDATED );

ALTER TABLE car ADD CONSTRAINT ck_validoption
    CHECK ( car_option_pkg IS VALIDATED );
```

   In the above two examples we have highlighted in bold the lines of interest. These lines show that a CHECK constraint is set up to verify an XML column has been validated.

V9.5 In DB2 9.5, the IS VALIDATED predicate is extended to specify the given XML SCHEMA to perform the validation against. For example, we could rewrite one of the above examples as follows:

```
ALTER TABLE car
  ADD CONSTRAINT ck validoption
  CHECK ( car_option_pkg IS VALIDATED
          ACCORDING TO XMLSCHEMA ID JOHN.MYSCHEMA);
```

You can also specify a list of schema identifiers in the check constraint:

```
ALTER TABLE T2
  ADD CONSTRAINT CK_VALIDATED
  CHECK (XMLCOL IS VALIDATED
         ACCORDING TO XMLSCHEMA ID IN (RICK.MYSCHEMA, RICK.SCHEMA2,
                                       RICK.SCHEMA3)
      )
```

10.9.2.2 The IS VALIDATED Predicate

The predicate "IS VALIDATED" can be used to check whether an XML document has been validated with the XMLVALIDATE function. For example, you can use this predicate as follows:

```
SELECT cid FROM customer
   WHERE info IS VALIDATED;
```

The above SELECT statement will retrieve the column **cid** from the **CUSTOMER** table for any rows where the XML document in the **INFO** column has been validated.

10.9.2.3 Determining the Schema of a Previously Validated Document

When a document is validated and stored, DB2 remembers the XSR object ID of the schema against which each document was validated. The information is available to applications to aid them with schema versioning and evolution. The function XSROBJECTID can be applied to any XML document, or part of a document, to obtain the ID of the schema that was used for validation. This ID can then be used to look up the SQL identifier of the schema, or the full schema document, in the XSR. The function can also be used to find all documents for a given schema. This however requires examining every document. Hence, if this is a frequent operation you may want to keep the schema ID or name in an additional relational column with an index on it. For example

```
select xsrobjectid(myXMLcol)
from myTable
where …..

select myXMLcol
from myTable
where xsrobjectid(myXMLcol) =   <…>
```

V9.5

10.9.3 Compatible XML Schema Evolution

When working with XML documents, your XML schema may evolve. This evolution is often compatible, that is, you may add optional elements or attributes, increase the size of string types, or increase the number of allowed occurrences of repeating elements; and this may not affect the overall structure of your schema. Compatible XML schema evolution will have no or minimal impact on your applications, as opposed to non-compatible XML schema evolution.

DB2 9.5 introduces the UPDATE XMLSCHEMA command to update your XML schemas. The syntax of this command is shown in Figure 10.33.

```
>>-UPDATE XMLSCHEMA--xmlschema1--WITH--xmlschema2--------------->

>--+-----------------+----------------------------------------><
   '-DROP NEW SCHEMA-'
```

Figure 10.33 Syntax diagram of the UPDATE XMLSCHEMA command

To use this command, your old and new schema must have been registered beforehand. The command will compare both schemas for compatibility, and if the schemas are not compatible, an error message will be returned. If the schemas are compatible, the old schema will be replaced by the new one. The existing XML documents will look like they were validated by the new XML schema. But the existing XML documents are not touched, inspected, or modified in any way. The schema update is an inexpensive catalog operation only.

For example to update the XMLSCHEMA raul.oldschema with raul.newschema, issue this command:

```
UPDATE XMLSCHEMA RAUL.OLDSCHEMA
WITH RAUL.NEWSCHEMA
DROP NEW SCHEMA
```

The last line in the example is optional and indicates that the new XML schema should be dropped after it is used to update the original XML schema.

The same functionality to update XML Schemas is provided through the stored procedure XSR_UPDATE.

10.10 Annotated XML Schema Decomposition

Earlier in this chapter we described the different methods to store XML documents in a database. Besides pureXML, one other method was called "Shredding" (also known as "decomposition"), where you store content from an XML document in relational columns, and another method called "CLOB/varchar" where you store XML documents using a CLOB or varchar column. The support of these last two methods was possible in previous versions using the DB2 XML Extender.

Although pureXML is often the best choice for managing XML in DB2, there can be good and valid reasons for shredding. For example, if XML is only the transport & exchange format of the data, if the XML format is no longer relevant once it reaches the database, if the XML structure is very regular in nature and therefore easy to map to a relational schema, if the XML structure is stable and unlikely to change over time, and if SQL applications need to consume the data (such as BI reporting tools or business application packages), the shredding XML to relational format can still be a good choice.

Therefore, DB2 9 also provides better support for the decomposition method. It provides richer functionality and significantly better performance than shredding with the XML Extender.

Starting with DB2 9, decomposition annotations are specified in XML schemas. These annotations specify the details of the decomposition such as the name of the target table, how the elements and attributes are mapped to the target table, and what XML data is to be mapped. An XML schema captured in the XSR can also be annotated and used for XML document decomposition.

Here is a snippet of a sample XML schema with decomposition annotations.

```
<xs:element name="publications">
  <xs:complexType>
    <xs:sequence>
      <xs:element name="textbook" maxOccurs="unbounded"
        db2-xdb:rowSet="TEXTBOOKS" db2-xdb:column="DETAILS">
```

```
        <xs:complexType>
          <xs:sequence>
            <xs:element name="isbn" type="xs:string">
            <xs:element name="author" type="xs:string" maxOccurs="unbounded">
            <xs:element name="publicationDate" type="xs:gYear">
            <xs:element name="university" type="xs:string" maxOccurs="unbounded">
          <xs:sequence>
         <xs:attribute name="title" type="xs:string" use="required"
           db2-xdb:rowSet="TEXTBOOKS" db2-xdb:column="TITLE">
        <xs:complexType>
      <xs:element>
    <xs:sequence>
  <xs:complexType>
<xs:element>
```

The above XML schema snippet looks like any regular XML schema document except that it has annotations prefixed with **db2-xdb** that belong to namespace **http://www.ibm.com/xmlns/prod/db2/xdb1.**

From the above example, this line

```
<xs:element name="textbook" maxOccurs="unbounded"
db2-xdb:rowSet="TEXTBOOKS" db2-xdb:column="DETAILS">
```

indicates the mapping between the *textbook* element and the *details* column.
A summary of the decomposition annotations is provided in Table 10.10. Please refer to the Information Center for a complete explanation with examples.

Table 10.10 Summary of the Decomposition Annotations

Category	Action	XML Decomposition Annotation
Specifying the SQL schema.	Specify the default SQL schema for all tables that do not specify their SQL schema.	**db2-xdb:default-SQLSchema**
	Specify an SQL schema different from the default for a specific table.	**db2-xdb:table (<db2-xdb:SQLSchema> child element)**
Mapping XML elements or attributes to target tables.	Map a single element or attribute to single column and table pair.	**db2-xdb:rowSet** with **db2-xdb:column** as attribute annotations or **db2-xdb:rowSetMapping**
	Map a single element or attribute to one or more distinct column and table pairs.	**db2-xdb:rowSetMapping**
	Map multiple elements or attributes to single column and table pair.	**db2-xdb:table**

Table 10.10 Summary of the Decomposition Annotations *(Continued)*

Specify the XML data to be decomposed.	Specify the type of content to be inserted for an element of complex type (text, string, or markup).	**db2-xdb: contentHandling**
	Specify any content transformation to be applied before insertion.	**db2-xdb:normalization** **db2-xdb:expression** **db2-xdb:truncate**
	Filter the data to be decomposed based on the item's content or the context in which it appears.	**db2-xdb:condition** **db2-xdb:locationPath**

Once the annotated schema document is ready, it must be registered in the XSR. To do so, simply append ENABLE DECOMPOSITION to the REGISTER XMLSCHEMA command as shown in this example:

```
REGISTER XMLSCHEMA 'http://posample.org/CUSTOMER'
    FROM 'file://c:/temp/customer.xsd'
      AS store.custschema
  ENABLE DECOMPOSITION
```

With the ALTER XSROBJECT command, you can enable or disable an XML schema easily as shown below:

```
ALTER XSROBJECT store.custschema DISABLE DECOMPOSITION
```

Upon successful registration of the annotated schema, issue the DECOMPOSE XML DOCUMENT command to start the decomposition process. For example, the following command validates and decomposes the *address.xml* XML document according to the registered XML schema *store.custschema*.

```
DECOMPOSE XML DOCUMENT address.xml
    XMLSCHEMA store.custschema
    VALIDATE
```

In addition to these CLP commands, similar stored procedures are available, which allow you to invoke the decomposition through an API or from other stored procedures.

Migration from XML Extender shredding is easy and desirable to benefit from the higher performance of the new decomposition with DB2 9. In the XML Extender, data access definitions (DADs) were used to define the mapping from XML to relational tables. A tool is available to convert a DAD to an annotated schema for shredding in DB2 9. See www-128.ibm.com/developerworks/db2/library/techarticle/dm-0604pradhan/ for details.

10.11 XML Performance Considerations

Chapter 17, Database Performance Considerations covers performance topics about DB2 in general. We decided to keep XML-related topics as closely together as possible; therefore, this topic about XML performance is in this chapter, and not in Chapter 17. However, some concepts like "the DB2 optimizer" or "visual explain" are further discussed in Chapter 17, so you may want to read that chapter before reading this section.

XML performance and optimization is based on three main criteria:

1. Choosing correctly where and how to store your XML documents
2. Creating appropriate indexes and using SQL/XML and XQuery statements efficiently
3. Ensuring that statistics on XML columns are collected accurately

10.11.1 Choosing Correctly Where and How to Store Your XML Documents

If the table space that stores the XML document has a small page size (such as 4KB) and XML documents are anything but small, a single document may span multiple or many pages. To minimize the number of pages being accessed when working with the XML document, you want to choose a larger page size for the XML data. However, the relational part of the table and indexes may need a smaller page size. To accomplish best performance for both relational and XML data, it is recommended to use DMS table spaces. You can place the XML data and indexes in separate table spaces. Then, you can tune the table spaces separately with different page sizes and other table space characteristics. But, multiple page sizes, table spaces and buffer pools also increase the complexity and administration overhead of your database. Hence, you should use multiple page sizes only if you really know that you get a significant performance gain in return. A medium page size such as 8k or 16k may provide adequate performance for both the XML and relational data of your application.

Additionally, choose your document granularity such that it matches the predominant level of access and ideally also the granularity of your logical business objects. For example, in an order processing application where each order is an independent logical object and typically processed separately from other orders, it make sense to use one XML document per order rather than larger documents which, say, contain all orders for a full week. Smaller documents tend to provide better performance than larger ones.

10.11.2 Creating Appropriate Indexes and Using SQL/XML and XQuery Statements Efficiently

Creating indexes over XML data appropriately, and using SQL/XML and XQuery statements efficiently are two topics that are highly related to each other. A useful guideline is to define indexes "as precisely" as possible, to ensure lean indexes and minimal index maintenance overhead. For example, an index on **`/customer/name`** can be better than an index on **`//name`** if there are “name” elements at various paths in the document but only the customer name actually needs to be indexed. Also, indexes on `//*` on `//text()` can have a significant adverse effect on insert, update, or delete performance. This is because you want your queries to be as precise as possible so that DB2 does not fetch unnecessary data. This will also help for index eligibility. If you recall, the index definition must be equally or less restrictive than the query predicates to be considered. In Section 10.8.2, User-Created Indexes, we described in more detail XML index eligibility.

10.11.3 Ensure That Statistics on XML Columns Are Collected Accurately

The DB2 optimizer is the “brain” of DB2. It determines the best access path to access your data the fastest. The DB2 optimizer needs Catalog statistics to be up to date in order to calculate the best access plan; therefore, the RUNSTATS utility should be run often. Chapter 13, Maintaining Data, explains this utility in more detail. This utility has been enhanced to support pureXML, which means that statistics are also collected over XML data, and its indexes.

10.12 pureXML Restrictions

This section provides an overview of some key restrictions of the pureXML. For further detail, refer to the documentation. Most restrictions are related to XML columns use.

1. XML columns are restricted as follows:
   - can be part of an index only if the index is an index over XML data
   - can be referenced in CHECK constraints only in conjunction with a VALIDATED predicate
   - can be referenced in the triggered-action of a BEFORE TRIGGER only to invoke the XMLVALIDATE function from a SET statement, to SET values to NULL, or to leave values of type XML unchanged
   - cannot be included as columns of keys, including primary, foreign, and unique keys, dimension keys of multi-dimensional clustering (MDC) tables, sequence keys of range-clustered tables, distribution keys, and data partitioning keys.
   - cannot have a default value specified by the WITH DEFAULT clause; if the column is nullable, the default for the column is NULL
   - cannot be used in a range-clustered table (RCT)
   - cannot be used in a multi-dimensional clustering (MDC) table
   - cannot be used in a table with a distribution key
   - cannot be used in a table partitioned by range
   - cannot be used in a CCSID UNICODE table in a non-Unicode database
   - cannot be included in typed tables and typed views
   - cannot be referenced in generated columns
   - cannot be specified in the select-list of scrollable cursors
   - cause data blocking to be disabled when retrieving XML data

2. pureXML is not supported with the database partitioning feature. In DB2 9.5, pureXML is supported in the catalog node of a partitioned database.
3. Federation of XML data in XML columns is only allowed between IBM Data servers.
4. SQL replication is not supported; only Q-Replication is supported.

10.13 Case Study

Prerequisite:

This case study requires XML documents and files that are provided in the Web site for this book. Look for the section "About the Web site" in this book for more details. We will assume you have copied those files to the directory C:\UnderstandingDB2 as shown in Figure 10.34.

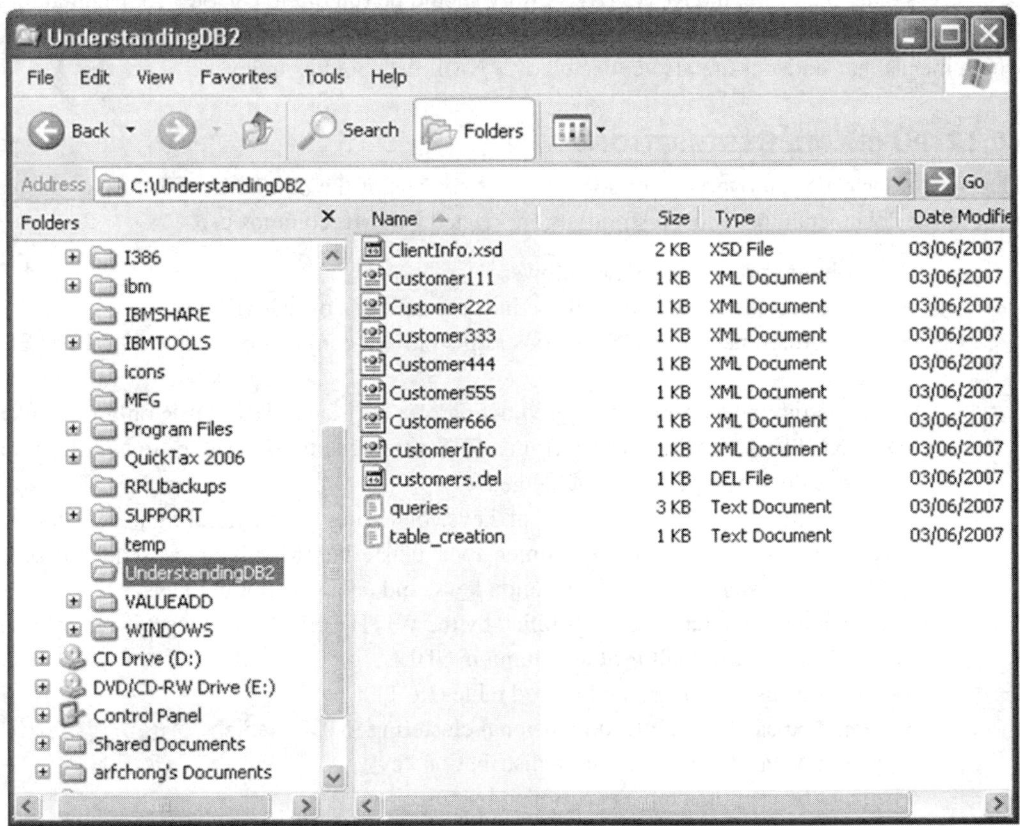

Figure 10.34 Input files required for this case study

Your manager has asked you to prepare a report about the customers of your company. Some of the information from these customers is stored in XML documents stored in files; some other information is stored in a delimited ASCII file. Since you know DB2 well, and know about pureXML technology, you decide to store all of this information together in a DB2 table. In the directory C:\UnderstandingDB2, you have all the input XML document files, conveniently named **Customer111.xml**, **Customer222.xml**, and so on. In addition, you have created the file **customers.del** which includes the delimited ASCII file you had before, and a pointer to the XML files. This delimited ascii file will be used by the IMPORT utility (which will be explained in Chapter 13, Maintaining Data).

Next, you create a script file and input this information:

1. You create a UNICODE database in order to have pureXML support.

```
CREATE DATABASE custdb using codeset UTF-8 territory US;
```

2. Then you connect to the new database, and create the customers table as shown here.

```
CONNECT TO custdb;

CREATE TABLE customers(
 id          integer primary key not null,
 name        varchar(50),
 age         integer,
 contactinfo xml);
```

3. Next, you realize one of the customer's information was not in the delimited ASCII file, and it didn't have an XML document either. You decide to input this information manually using an INSERT statement as shown here.

```
INSERT into customers values (100, 'Allan Murali', 33,
  '<addr>123 Lincoln Ave., Ottawa, ON, 00112</addr>');
```

4. Finally, you load the rest of the records using the IMPORT utility (more on this in Chapter 13, Maintaining Data).

```
IMPORT FROM "C:\UnderstandingDB2\customers.del" of del
  xml from "C:\UnderstandingDB2"
  INSERT INTO CUSTOMERS (ID, NAME, AGE, CONTACTINFO);
```

5. Once your script file is complete with the above statements, you save it with the name **table_creation.txt,** and you run it from the DB2 Command Window (in Windows) or the Linux/UNIX shell as follows:

```
db2 –tvf table_creation.txt
```

6. After running successfully the script file, you will have a database with the table CUSTOMERS, which contains relational and an XML column. Open the Control Center, locate the CUSTOMERS table, open it, and you should find the information illustrated in Figure 10.35 The window showing the XML document tree corresponds to the second row.

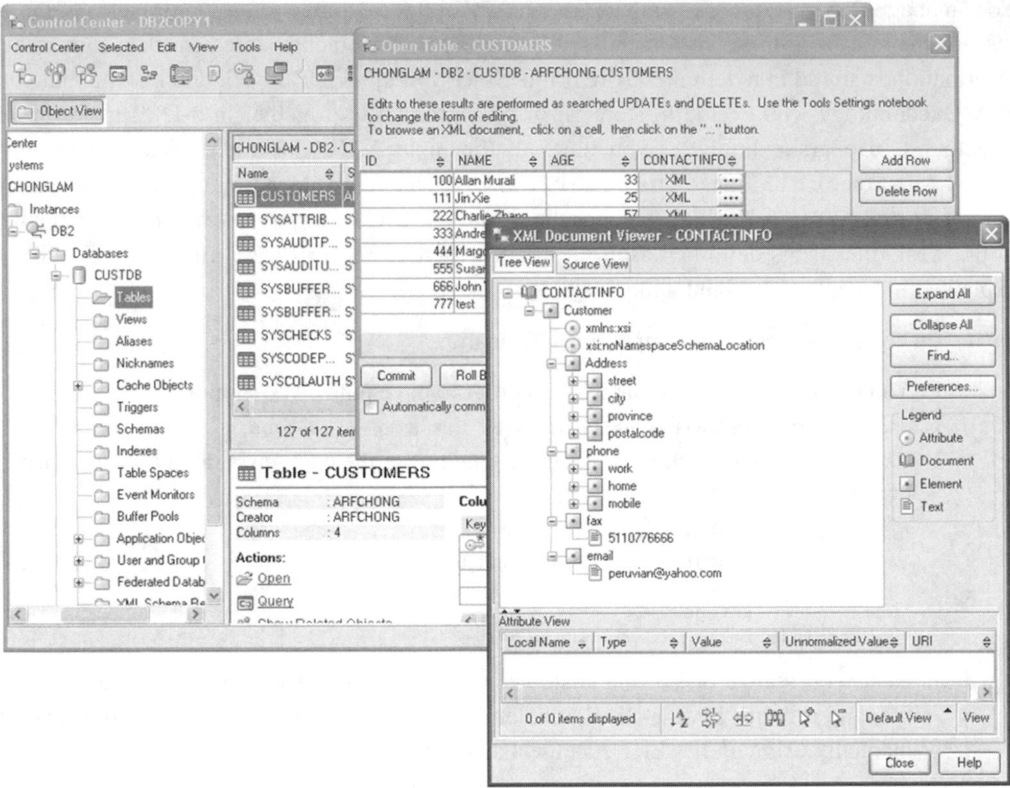

Figure 10.35 The CUSTOMERS table from the Control Center

7. You would like to add several queries to your application, but you want to test them first from the Command Editor; therefore, you open the Command Editor, ensure you are connected to the CUSTDB database, and start testing XQuery statements.

8. First you want to find out the name of the customers who live in a city with postal code "98273". If you look at the XML document tree from the Control Center, you determine the XPath expression that is required, and issue this SQL/XML query:

```
SELECT name FROM customers
WHERE xmlexists('$c/Customer/Address[postalcode="98273"]'
passing CUSTOMERS.CONTACTINFO as "c")
The correct answer to this query should be "Jin Xie"
```

9. Next, you would like to retrieve all the e-mails of customers who are 25 years of age. You would like to offer a special promotion to this type of customer. To obtain this information, you run this query:

```
SELECT xmlquery('$c/Customer/email/text()'
                passing contactInfo as "c")
```

```
 FROM customers
WHERE age = 25
```

The correct answer to this query should be:

```
1
---------------------------------------------------------------------
peruvian@yahoo.com
1 record(s) selected.
```

10. You would like to run XQuery statements rather than SQL/XML to obtain the fax information of all customers.

```
xquery
for $y in db2-fn:xmlcolumn('CUSTOMERS.CONTACTINFO')
                            /Customer/fax/text()
return $y
The correct answer to this query should be:
1--------------------------------------------------------------------
5110776666
5585555555

 2 record(s) selected.
```

11. You are happy with the results so far. Then you realize one of the records for the customer with ID of 100 has incorrect information. Therefore you run the following SQL UPDATE statement:

```
update customers set contactInfo=(
xmlparse(document'<Customer>
<Address>
   <street>5401 New Address ave.</street>
   <city>New City</city>
   <province>NC</province>
   <postalcode>98765</postalcode>
</Address>
<phone>
   <work>3331233000</work>
   <home>3121111111</home>
   <mobile>3082222222</mobile>
</phone>
   <fax>3081236666</fax>
<email>newemail@newplace.com</email>
</Customer>'))
where id = 100
```

After the UPDATE operation, you verify through the Control Center that the new values have been correctly updated. With these excellent results, you start writing your application, which would invoke the queries tested, and that would generate a report for your manager.

10.14 Summary

In this chapter, you were introduced to the fundamentals of XML such as the concepts of a well-formed versus a valid XML document, XML namespaces, XML schema, and the languages to query XML data, namely XQuery, XPath, and SQL/XML.

With version 9 DB2 provides seamless integration of XML with relational data. Hierarchical XML data is stored in XML columns for which data storage is highly optimized. DB2 stores XML data in the original hierarchical format of the XML documents. This pureXML storage model improves performance of queries that use SQL/XML or XQuery expressions.

XQuery with FLWOR expressions also allow you to construct well-formed XML documents and to restructure the XML data. FLWOR stands for FOR, LET, WHERE, ORDER BY, and RETURN. The expression allows for iterating through documents, binding a variable to the result of the expression, eliminating and reordering items of the iteration, and finally constructing results of the query.

The SQL language has been extended to work with XML data; this is known as SQL/XML. Examples of new SQL/XML functions are XMLQUERY, XMLTABLE, XMLEXISTS, and XMLCAST. You can also construct XML documents from relational data using publishing functions such as XMLCONCAT, XMLELEMENT, XMLAGG, XMLATTRIBUTES, and so on.

When working with XML data, you should be aware of XML serialization and parsing because the programming language you are using may not support XML data type. Several codepage considerations were also mentioned in this chapter.

XML schema support in DB2 is the key to XML document validation. The XML schema repository stores copies of registered XML schemas in DB2. XML schema registration can be as simple as issuing the REGISTER XMLSCHEMA and COMPLETE XMLSCHEMA commands. XML schema captured in the XML repository can also be used for XML document decomposition. You simply need to specify decomposition annotations in the XML schemas.

10.15 Review Questions

1. What are some key characteristics of pureXML?
2. Why is query performance better with pureXML than with other methods such as shredding or CLOB?
3. What's the difference between a well-formed XML document, and a validated XML document?
4. What is annotated XML Schema decomposition?
5. Can you validate different XML documents in the same column using different XML schemas?
6. Which are the three conditions for XML index eligibility?
7. I would like to get the best performance for my application. Should I store the data as XML or as relational?

8. Can XML documents be stored and managed when using the Database Partitioning Feature?
9. Is row compression applicable to XML data?
10. Is anybody in the industry using pureXML at all?
11. Which of the following is not an SQL/XML function:
    A. XMLPI
    B. XMLNODE
    C. XMLELEMENT
    D. XMLPARSE
12. Given the following XML document:

```
<dept bldg="101">
    <employee id="901">
        <name>John Doe</name>
        <phone>408 555 1212</phone>
        <office>344</office>
    </employee>
    <employee id="902">
        <name>Peter Pan</name>
        <phone>408 555 9918</phone>
        <office>216</office>
    </employee>
</dept>
```

    What is the output of the following XPath expression:

```
//employee[office="344" or office="216"]/@id
```

    A. 901
       902
    B. 901, 902
    C. <id>901</id>, <id>902</id>
    D. 902
13. Using the same XML document as in question #2, what would be the output of the following XPath expression?

```
/dept/employee[2]/@id
```

    A. 901
    B. 902
    C. @901
    D. @902
14. Using the same XML document as in question #2, what would be the output of the following XQuery statement?

```
xquery
for $d in db2-fn:xmlcolumn("DEPT.DEPTDOC")/dept
let $emp := $d//employee/name
where $d/@bldg > 95
order by $d/@bldg
```

```
return
   <EmpList>
   {$d/@bldg, $emp}
   </EmpList>
```

A.

```
<EmpList>
  101, John Doe
  101, Peter Pan
</EmpList>
```

B.

```
<EmpList>
  101,<name>John Doe</name>
  101,<name>Peter Pan</name>
</EmpList>
```

C.

```
<EmpList>
  101<name>John Doe</name>
        <name>Peter Pan</name>
</EmpList>
```

D.

```
<EmpList>
  101<name>John Doe</name>
  101<name>Peter Pan</name>
</EmpList>
```

15. Which of the following statements return the same output

(I) xquery db2-fn:xmlcolumn('CUSTOMER.INFO')
(II) select info from customer
(III) xquery db2-fn:xmlcolumn("CUSTOMER.INFO")
(IV) XqUeRy db2-fn:xmlcolumn('CUSTOMER.INFO')

A. (I), (II), (IV)
B. (I), (II), (III)
C. (I), (III)
D. (I), (II)

16. Which of the following strings can be used with XMLPARSE?

A. <name>Peter</name>
B. <?xml-stylesheet type="text/css" href="licenserpt.css"?>
C. <?xml version="1.0" encoding="UTF-8"?>
D. Peter

17. Which function can be used to embed SQL in an XQuery expression?

A. XMLEXISTS
B. db2-fn:xmlcolumn
C. db2-fn:sqlquery
D. XMLQUERY

18. Which of the following operators is not used for XML data?

A. XSCAN

B. XISCAN

C. XANDOR

D. XMLJOIN

19. Given the following index:

```
CREATE INDEX myindex on patients(dna)
    GENERATE KEY USING XMLPATTERN '/geneX/pattern'
    AS SQL VARCHAR(30);
```

Which of the following statements does not meet index eligibility:

A.

```
SELECT XMLQUERY ('$d/geneX' passing DNA as "d" )
  FROM patients
 WHERE XMLEXISTS ('$d/geneX[pattern="ABC"]'
                  passing DNA as "d");
```

B.

```
select xmlquery ('$d/genex' passing DNA as "d" )
  from patients
 where xmlexists ('$d/genex[pattern="ABC"]'
                  passing DNA as "d");
```

C.

```
SELECT XMLQUERY ('$d/geneX' passing DNA as "d" )
  FROM patients
 WHERE XMLEXISTS ('$d//geneX[pattern="ABC"]'
                  passing DNA as "d");
```

D. None of the above

20. Which of the following has all the methods to validate an XML document in DB2?

I) An AFTER trigger

II) A BEFORE trigger

III) A CHECK constraint

IV) The XMLVALIDATE function on an INSERT statement

A. II, III, IV

B. II, IV

C. I, II, III, IV

D. II, III

CHAPTER 11

Implementing Security

All tasks and concepts presented in the previous chapters assumed you had the administrative rights, or privileges, to set up client and server connectivity, execute SQL statements, create database objects, and so on. In the real world, administrative rights are typically given only to selected individuals. In addition, the ability for users to access data (i.e., privileges) must be controlled in order to comply with business and regulatory requirements. DB2 uses a number of components to support various security schemes. This chapter discusses each of the security components and provides examples to illustrate different implementation scenarios.

In this chapter you will learn about:

- The big picture of the DB2 security model
- Different authentication methods that DB2 supports
- Authentication methods using customized loadable libraries
- Label-Based Access Control (LBAC)
- LBAC security policies, security label components, security labels, and exemptions
- How to enable data encryption
- Database operations you can perform with the various administrative authorities
- Controlling access to database objects
- Obtaining the authorities and privileges information from the metadata
- Considerations for Windows domain users

11.1 DB2 Security Model: The Big Picture

The DB2 security model consists of four major components: authentication, administrative authorization, database object security (also known as database object privileges), and row and column level security via Label-Based Access Control (LBAC). Figure 11.1 illustrates these components.

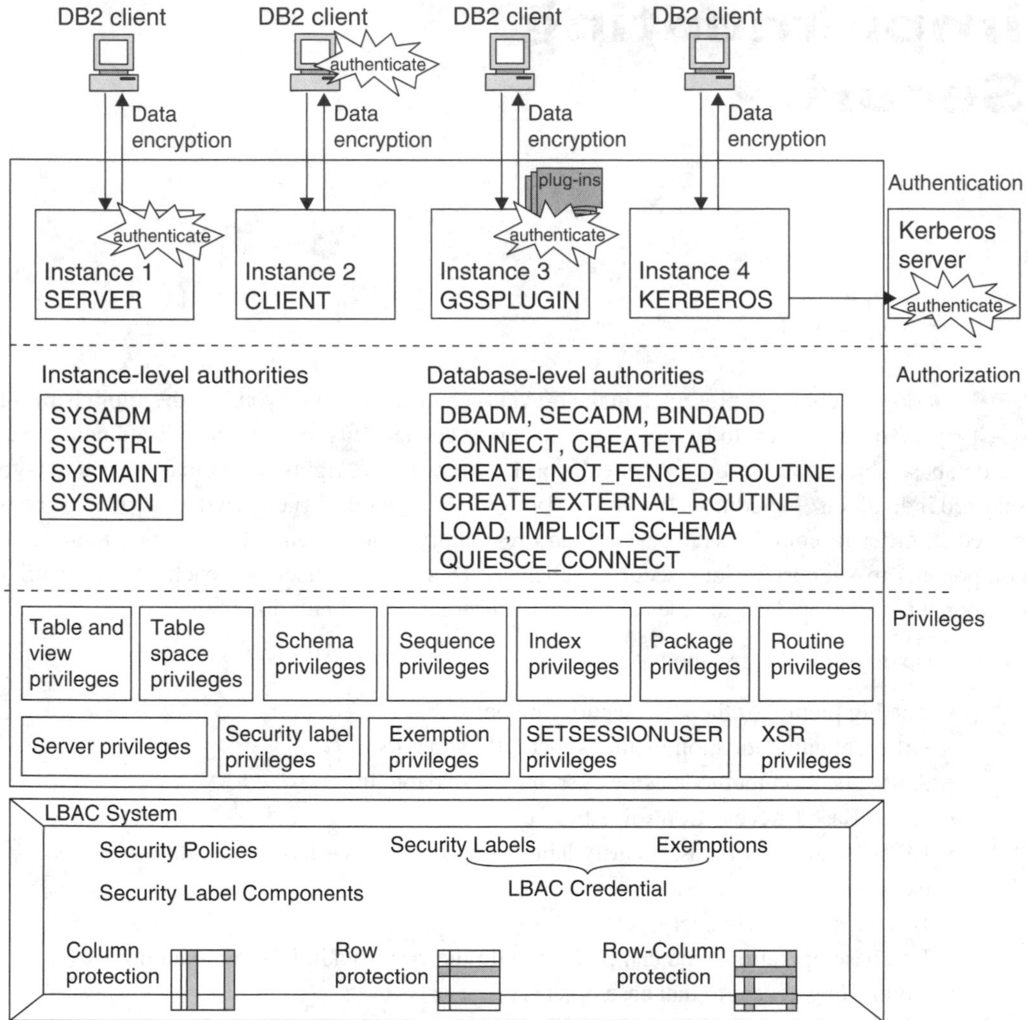

Figure 11.1 The big picture of the DB2 security model

A combination of external security services and internal DB2 privilege mechanisms handle DB2 security. As shown in Figure 11.1, a user goes through the authentication process before he is allowed to connect to the database. Once the user ID and password have been verified (either on the server or the client), an internal DB2 process takes over and makes sure that the user is authorized to (i.e. has the privileges to) perform the requested operations and/or see the requested data. This is represented by the Authorization and Privileges components in Figure 11.1.

11.2 AUTHENTICATION

Authentication is the process of validating the supplied user ID and password with a security facility. This authentication occurs when you try to connect to a database or attach to an instance. The security facility is external to DB2; user IDs and passwords are not stored in a DB2 server. Authentication can occur at any of the following:

- At a DB2 server using Operating system authentication (Figure 11.1, Instance 1)
- At a DB2 client using Operating system authentication (Figure 11.1, Instance 2)
- Using a customized loadable library via Generic Security Service (GSS) (Figure 11.1, Instance 3)
- Using a Kerberos security service (Figure 11.1, Instance 4)

The authentication process also determines which operating system groups the user belongs to while not using GSS or Kerboros. Group membership lookup is essential because it lets users inherit certain authorities or privileges through the groups they belong to.

The following sections describe how to configure the authentication type at the DB2 server and at the client respectively. The combination of the client and server authentication configurations determines where and how the authentication will take place (the authentication method).

11.2.1 Configuring the Authentication Type at a DB2 Server

To configure the authentication type at a DB2 server, you use the Database Manager (DBM) Configuration parameter AUTHENTICATION. If you are not already familiar with DBM Configuration parameters, refer to Chapter 5, Understanding the DB2 Environment, DB2 Instances, and Databases. For completeness, we are including the command here to display the current DBM parameter settings:

```
get dbm cfg
```

From the output, locate the following line where the authentication type is specified:

```
Database manager authentication          (AUTHENTICATION) = SERVER
```

SERVER is the default authentication type of an instance. Figure 11.2 shows this authentication type.

To change the value to the KERBEROS authentication type, for example, use this DB2 command:

```
update dbm cfg using authentication KERBEROS
```

Alternatively, you can use the Control Center to make this change. Chapter 4, Using the DB2 Tools, describes the Control Center in detail.

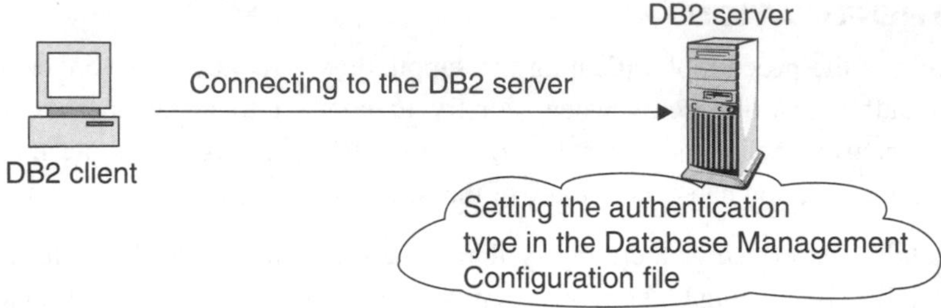

Figure 11.2 Configuring the authentication type at a DB2 server

Table 11.1 summarizes the values the AUTHENTICATION parameter accepts.

Table 11.1 Description of the Authentication Types

Authentication Type	Description
SERVER	Authenticates users at the DB2 server. This is the default value.
SERVER_ENCRYPT	Authenticates users at the DB2 server. When the user ID and password are sent to the server, they are both encrypted.
DATA_ENCRYPT	Authenticates users at the DB2 server, userID, password and user data are all encrypted.
DATA_ENCRYPT_CMP	Authenticates users at the DB2 server, userID, password and user data are all encrypted if both the DB2 server and client support data encryption. SERVER_ENCRYPT will be used instead if the client does not support data encryption.
KERBEROS	Authenticates users at a Kerberos server.
KRB_SERVER_ENCRYPT	Authenticates users at a Kerberos server if both the DB2 server and client support Kerberos security service. SERVER_ENCRYPT will be used instead if the client does not support Kerberos security service.
GSSPLUGIN	Authenticates users using an external GSS Application Programming Interface (GSSAPI)-based security mechanism.
GSS_SERVER_ENCRYPT	Authenticates users using an external GSSAPI-based security mechanism if both the DB2 server and client support GSS. Use SERVER_ENCRYPT instead if the client does not support GSS.
CLIENT	Authenticates users at the DB2 client depending on the settings of two other configuration parameters: TRUST_CLNTAUTH and TRUST_ALLCLNTS.

The output of the **get dbm cfg** command includes another authentication-related parameter, called server connection authentication (SRVCON_AUTH):

```
Server Connection Authentication          (SRVCON_AUTH) = NOT_SPECIFIED
```

This parameter sets the authentication type at the DB2 server for incoming database connections. Note that only database connections evaluate the value of this parameter. Explicit instance attachment and operations that require implicit instance attachment still use AUTHENTICATION to resolve the authentication type.

By default, SRVCON_AUTH has a value of NOT_SPECIFIED. In this case, the value of AUTHENTICATION is used instead.

11.2.2 Configuring the Authentication Type at a DB2 Client

When a client is configured to connect to a database, you need to catalog the node and the database. The **catalog database** command has an option called AUTHENTICATION that allows you to indicate the authentication type to be used when connecting to the specified database from a DB2 client as shown in Figure 11.3.

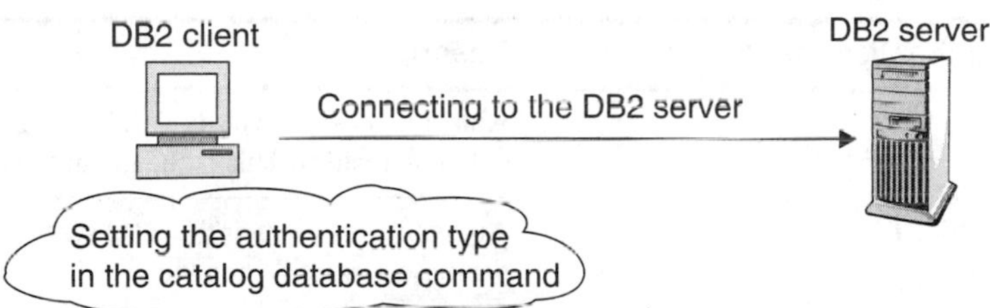

Figure 11.3 Configuring the authentication type at a DB2 client

Figure 11.4 illustrates the syntax of the **catalog database** command. To execute this command, you need to have either SYSADM or SYSCTRL authority or the database manager configuration parameter CATALOG_NOAUTH is set to ON. Setting CATALOG_NOAUTH to ON means database cataloging is allowed without authority. Adminstrative authorities are discussed in Section 11.4, CATALOG_NOAUTH .

If authentication type is not specified in the **catalog database** command, SERVER_ENCRYPT is used. This authentication type must be supported by the server to ensure that the correct authentication type is used; otherwise an error is returned.

To change this setting, explicitly specify the AUTHENTICATION keyword along with one of the supported values shown in Table 11.2. The following is an example of using GSSPLUGIN authentication.

```
catalog db sample at node dbsrv authentication gssplugin
```

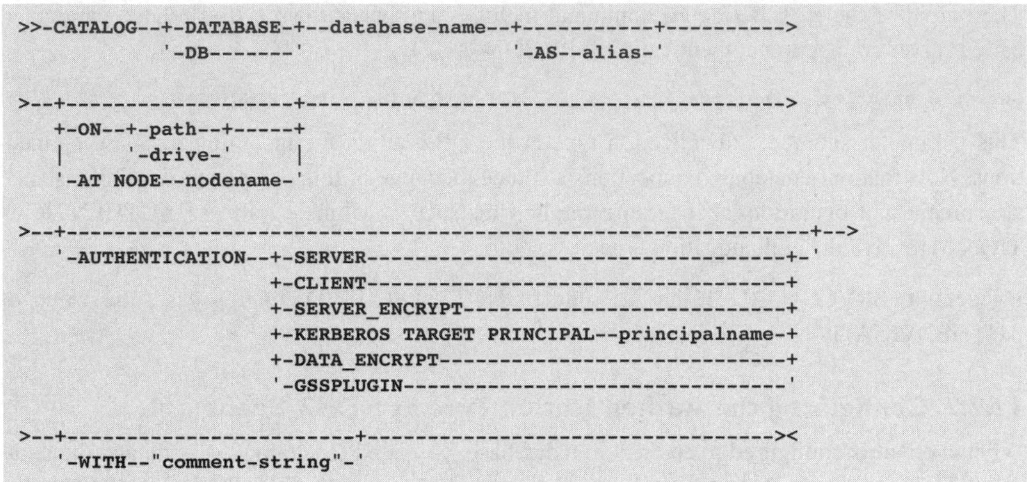

```
>>-CATALOG--+-DATABASE-+--database-name--+-----------+--------->
            '-DB-------'                 '-AS--alias-'

>--+-----------------+----------------------------------------->
   +-ON--+-path--+-----+
   |     '-drive-'     |
   '-AT NODE--nodename-'

>--+--------------------------------------------------------+-->
   '-AUTHENTICATION--+-SERVER-------------------------------+-'
                     +-CLIENT-------------------------------+
                     +-SERVER_ENCRYPT-----------------------+
                     +-KERBEROS TARGET PRINCIPAL--principalname-+
                     +-DATA_ENCRYPT-------------------------+
                     '-GSSPLUGIN----------------------------'

>--+---------------------+---------------------------------><
   '-WITH--"comment-string"-'
```

Figure 11.4 Syntax of the CATALOG DATABASE command

Table 11.2 Authentication Types Supported at DB2 Clients

Supported Authentication Values	Description
SERVER	Authenticates users at the DB2 server where the database resides. This is the default value.
SERVER_ENCRYPT	Authenticates users at the DB2 server where the database resides. When the user ID and password are sent to the server, they are both encrypted.
KERBEROS	Authenticates users at a Kerberos server.
TARGET PRINCIPAL *principalname*	Fully qualify the Kerberos principal name for the target server. For UNIX and Linux systems, use a name like: • name/instance@REALM • For Windows 2000, *principalname* is the logon account of the DB2 server service, which may look like one of the following: • userid@DOMAIN • userid@xxx.xxx.xxx.com • domain\userid
DATA_ENCRYPT	Authenticates users at the DB2 server. In addition, data encryption must be used for the connections.

Table 11.2 Authentication Types Supported at DB2 Clients *(Continued)*

Supported Authentication Values	Description
GSSPLUGIN	Authenticates users with an external GSSAPI-based security mechanism.
CLIENT	Authenticates users at the DB2 client depending on the settings of two other configuration parameters: TRUST_CLNTAUTH and TRUST_ALLCLNTS

11.2.3 Authenticating Users at/on the DB2 Server

As mentioned earlier, authenticating a user and the associated password at the DB2 server is the default behavior. The DBM configuration parameter at the server and the authentication option in the database directory entry are both set to SERVER. DB2 does not maintain any user and password information. This implies that the user ID and password pair must be defined in the security facility built in the operating system of the server. Figure 11.5 demonstrates a few scenarios of server authentication.

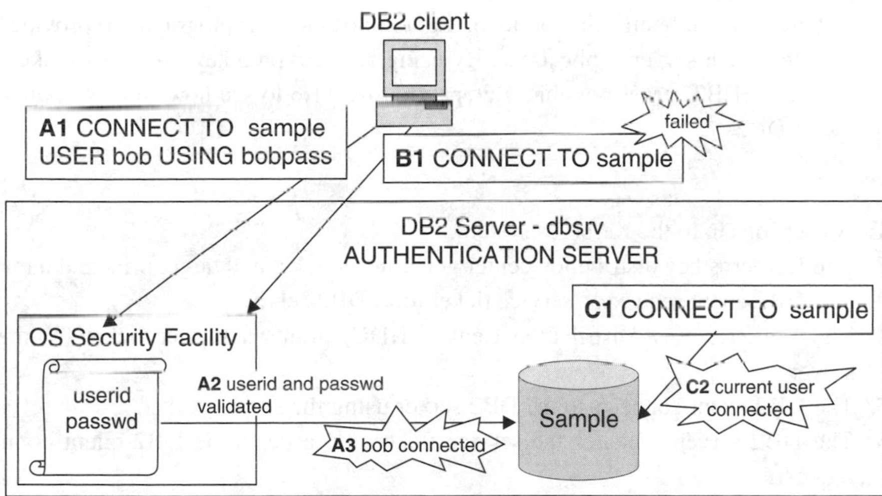

Figure 11.5 Example of SERVER authentication

> **NOTE** As long as the database server authentication type is set to SERVER, authentication will always take place at the server.

In Scenario A, A1 issues a **CONNECT** statement to connect to the SAMPLE database that is remotely located in the *dbsrv* DB2 server. The user ID *bob* and the password *bobpass* are also provided. These pieces of information are validated by the DB2 server security facility at A2. Once validated, *bob* is connected to SAMPLE in A3 provided that he has the appropriate CONNECT privilege (privileges are discussed later in this chapter).

Scenario B uses the same environment except that no user ID and password are provided in the **CONNECT** statement. When a remote database connection is requested, it is mandatory to supply a user ID and password. Therefore, the **CONNECT** statement specified in B1 fails.

Scenarios A and B are both remote requests. It is also very common to make local database connections from the DB2 server itself. Scenario C demonstrates such a request. Since you must have already logged into the server console with a valid user ID and password, it is not necessary to supply a user ID and password in the **CONNECT** statement at C1. If you choose to connect to the database with a different user ID, then you need to issue the **CONNECT** statement with the user ID and password you want as shown in A1.

The SERVER_ENCRYPT authentication type behaves exactly the same as SERVER authentication except that both the user ID and password are encrypted.

11.2.4 Authenticating Users Using the Kerberos Security Service

Kerberos is a network authentication protocol that employs key cryptography to provide strong authentication for client/server applications. By using an encrypted key, Kerberos makes single sign-on to a remote DB2 server possible. Refer to Figure 11.6 to see how Kerberos authentication works with DB2.

In Figure 11.6:

1. A user logs in to the Kerberos system.
2. The Kerberos key distribution center generates a ticket and target principal name.
3. The DB2 client requests a service ticket for a DB2 server.
4. The Kerberos Key Distribution Center (KDC) grants a service ticket for the DB2 server.
5. The DB2 client connects to the DB2 server using the service ticket.
6. The DB2 server validates the service ticket and accepts the DB2 client connection request.

The AUTHENTICATION type KERBEROS allows Kerberos-enabled clients to be authenticated at the Kerberos server. Although Kerberos is gaining popularity, there will be clients that do not have Kerberos support enabled. To accommodate these clients and at the same time ensure all clients are able to connect securely, you can set the authentication type at the DB2 server as KRB_SERVER_ENCRYPT. This option allows all Kerberos-enabled clients to be authenticated with Kerberos security service, while other clients use SERVER_ENCRYPT authentication instead.

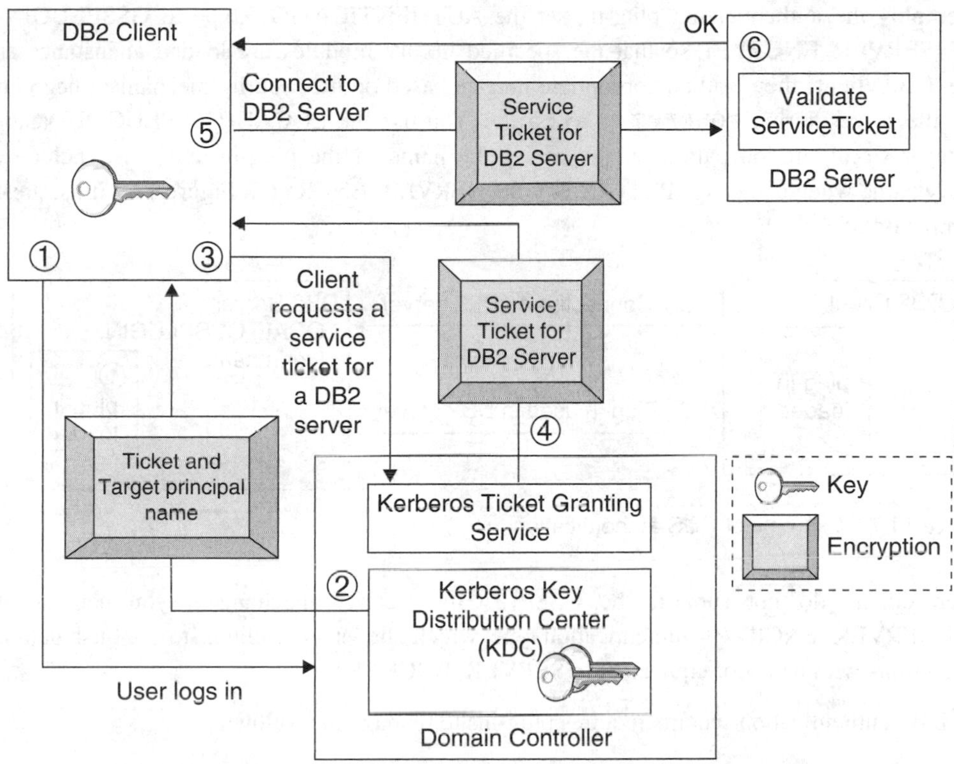

Figure 11.6 Example of Kerberos authentication

Table 11.3 summarizes the resolved authentication types based on different client and server authentication settings related to Kerberos.

Table 11.3 Summary of Kerberos-Related Client/Server Authentication Types

Client Specification	Server Specification	Client/Server Resolution
KERBEROS	KRB_SERVER_ENCRYPT	KERBEROS
Any other setting	KRB_SERVER_ENCRYPT	SERVER_ENCRYPT

11.2.5 Authenticating Users with Generic Security Service Plug-ins

You can write authentication mechanisms to implement your own security model. These authentication modules follow the Generic Security Service (GSS) Application Programming Interface (GSSAPI) standard as documented in the Internet's Requests for Comments (RFC) (see www.rfc-editor.org/rfc.html).

To employ the authentication plug-in, set the AUTHENTICATION type to GSSPLUGIN or GSS_SERVER_ENCRYPT so that the specified library modules are loaded at instance start time. DB2 clients then load an appropriate plug-in based on the security mechanism negotiated with the server during **`CONNECT`** or **`attach.`** You use the LOCAL_GSSPLUGIN Database Manager Configuration parameter to specify the name of the plug-in and must include the library name when using GSSPLUGIN or GSS_SERVER_ENCRYPT. Figure 11.7 illustrates an example of GSS.

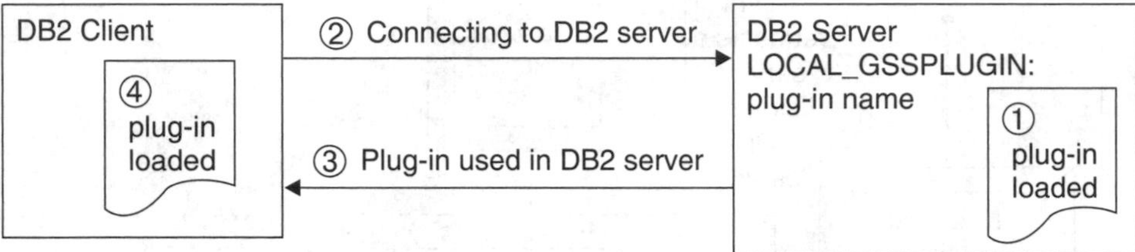

Figure 11.7 Example of GSS authentication

When clients do not support the GSSPLUGIN security mechanism, you can use the GSS_SERVER_ENCRYPT authentication type, which allows those clients to establish database connections with behavior equivalent to SERVER_ENCRYPT.

The DB2 authentication scheme requires plug-ins to manage the following:

- Group membership
- Authentication at the client
- Authentication at the server

If you do not specify the loadable libraries, DB2-supplied plug-Ins are used instead. A few Database Manager Configuration parameters are used to support authentication plug-ins, and they are listed in Table 11.4.

Table 11.4 Database Manager Parameters for Authentication Plug-Ins

Database Manager Parameter	Description
GROUP_PLUGIN	The name of the group management plug-in library.
CLNT_PW_PLUGIN	The name of the client-side password authentication plug-in. The functions in the named plug-in will also be used for local instance-level actions if the AUTHENTICATION parameter is set to SERVER, CLIENT, SERVER_ENCRYPT, DATAENC, or DATAENC_COMP.

Table 11.4 Database Manager Parameters for Authentication Plug-Ins *(Continued)*

Database Manager Parameter	Description
CLNT_KRB_PLUGIN	The name of the client-side Kerberos plug-in. This plug-in will also be used for local instance-level actions, that is, when the AUTHENTICATION parameter is set to KERBEROS or KRB_SERVER_ENCRYPT.
SRVCON_PW_PLUGIN	The name of the server-side password authentication module.
SRVCON_GSSPLUGIN_LIST	The list of names of all GSSAPI plug-ins separated by commas. The number of plug-ins supported by the server is unlimited; however, the maximum length of the list of plug-in names is 256 characters, and each plug-in name must be fewer than 32 characters. This list should be stated with the most preferred plug-in first.
SRV_PLUGIN_MODE	Indicates if the plug-in is to be run in fenced or unfenced mode. (**Fenced** means that the plug-ins run in a different address space from the DB2 system controller process and **unfenced** means executing the plug-ins in the same address space.) It is recommended to run user-defined modules in fenced mode to protect the system controller. Since this is an instance-level parameter, it applies to all plug-ins within the same instance. The default value is FENCED.

DB2 provides sample plug-ins so you can develop your own plug-ins more easily. You must place the library files in the designated directory where DB2 looks for:

- Client-side user authentication plug-ins in the directory
  $DB2PATH/security32/plugin/client (for Linux/UNIX 32-bit)
  $DB2PATH/security64/plugin/client (for Linux/UNIX 64-bit)
  $DB2PATH\security\plugin\instance-name\client (for Windows)
- Server-side user authentication plug-ins in the directory
  $DB2PATH/security32/plugin/server (for Linux/UNIX 32-bit)
  $DB2PATH/security64/plugin/server (for Linux/UNIX 64-bit)
  $DB2PATH\security\plugin\instance-name\server (for Windows)
- Group plug-ins in the directory
  $DB2PATH/security32/plugin/group (for Linux/UNIX 32-bit)
  $DB2PATH/security64/plugin/group (for Linux/UNIX 64-bit)
  $DB2PATH\security\plugin\instance-name\group (for Windows)

You specify the name of the plug-in as a Database Manager Configuration parameter. Use the full name of the library file, but do not include the file extension or the path. For example, to configure the group plug-in, issue:

```
update dbm cfg using group_plugin mygrplib
```

11.2.6 Authenticating Users at/on the DB2 Client(s)

When you want to allow DB2 clients to perform their own authentication, set the server authentication type to CLIENT. This setting does not mean that client authentication applies to every client; qualified clients are determined by two other DBM Configuration parameters—TRUST_ALLCLNTS and TRUST_CLNTAUTH.

TRUST_ALLCLNTS (as you can tell from the name) specifies whether DB2 is going to trust all clients. DB2 categorizes clients into these types:

- **Untrusted** clients do not have a reliable security facility.
- **Trusted** clients have reliable security facilities like Windows Server, AIX, z/OS, and Linux.
- **Distributed Relational Database Architecture** (DRDA) clients are on host legacy systems with reliable security facilities, including DB2 for z/OS, DB2 for i5/OS, and DB2 for VM and VSE.

> **NOTE** Even though all DB2 clients use the DRDA database communication protocol to communicate with DB2 servers, only clients running on mainframe legacy systems are considered as DRDA clients for historical and backward compatibility reasons.

TRUST_ALLCLNTS accepts any of the values summarized in Table 11.5.

Table 11.5 Values Allowed for TRUST_ALLCLNTS

TRUST_ALLCLNTS value	Description
YES	Trusts all clients. This is the default setting. Authentication will take place at the client. See the exception mentioned in the TRUST_CLNTAUTH discussion.
NO	Trust only clients with reliable security facilities (i.e., trusted clients). Untrusted clients must provide user ID and password for authentication to take place at the server.
DRDAONLY	Trusts only clients that are running on iSeries, zSeries, VM, and VSE platforms. All other clients must provide user IDs and passwords.

You can specify a more granular security scheme with TRUST_ALLCLNTS. For example, you can let trusted clients perform authentication on their own and, at the same time, force untrusted clients to be authenticated at the server.

Consider a scenario in which you log into a Windows machine as *localuser* and connect to the remote database without specifying a user ID and password. *localuser* will be the connected authorization ID at the database. What if you want to connect to the database with a different user ID, for example, *poweruser*, who has the authority to perform a database backup? To allow such behavior, use TRUST_CLNTAUTH to specify where authentication will take place if a user ID and password are supplied in a **CONNECT** statement or **attach** command. Table 11.6 presents the values for TRUST_CLNTAUTH.

Table 11.6 Values Allowed for TRUST_CLNTAUTH

TRUST_CLNTAUTH Value	Description
CLIENT	Authentication is performed at the client; user ID and password are not required.
SERVER	Authentication is done at the server only if the user ID and password are supplied.

DB2 evaluates TRUST_ALLCLNTS and TRUST_CLNTAUTH only if you set AUTHENTICATION to CLIENT on the DB2 server. Figures 11.8, 11.9, 11.10, and 11.11 illustrate how to use these parameters.

In Figure 11.8, TRUST_ALLCLNTS is set to YES, so all clients are considered trusted and can perform their own authentication.

In Figure 11.9, TRUST_ALLCLNTS is set to NO, so only trusted clients perform their own authentication. Authentication for untrusted clients is done at the server.

In Figure 11.10, TRUST_CLNAUTH is set to SERVER. When user ID and password are specified in the **CONNECT** statement, authentication is performed at the server.

In Figure 11.11, TRUST_CLNTAUTH is set to SERVER and both clients provide user ID and password in the **CONNECT** statement. Hence, authentication is performed at the server for both clients.

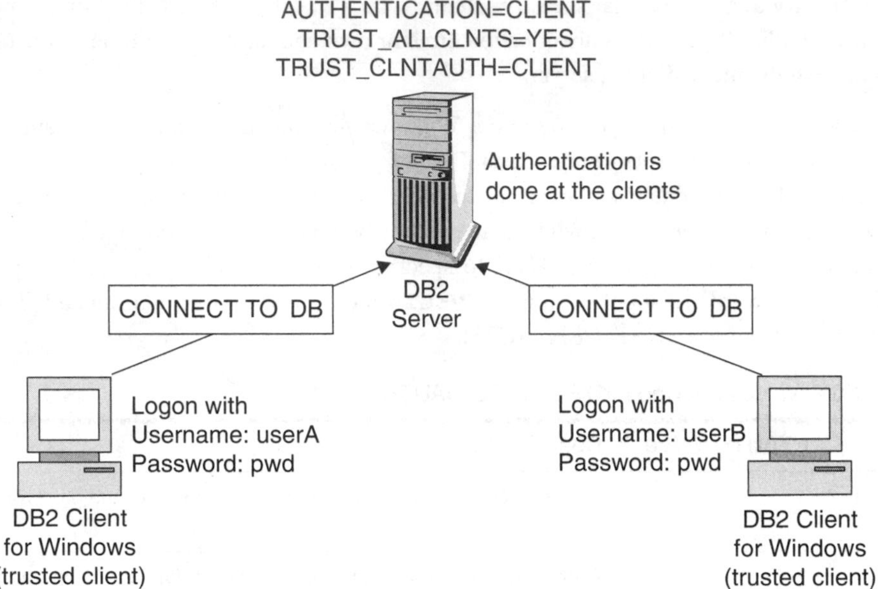

Figure 11.8 Example 1: TRUST_ALLCLNTS and TRUST_CLNTAUTH

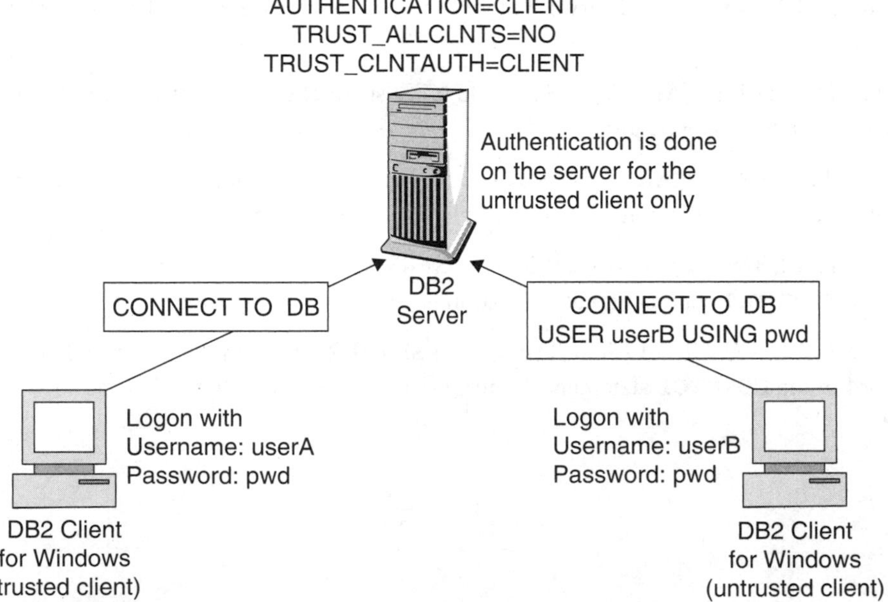

Figure 11.9 Example 2: TRUST_ALLCLNTS and TRUST_CLNTAUTH

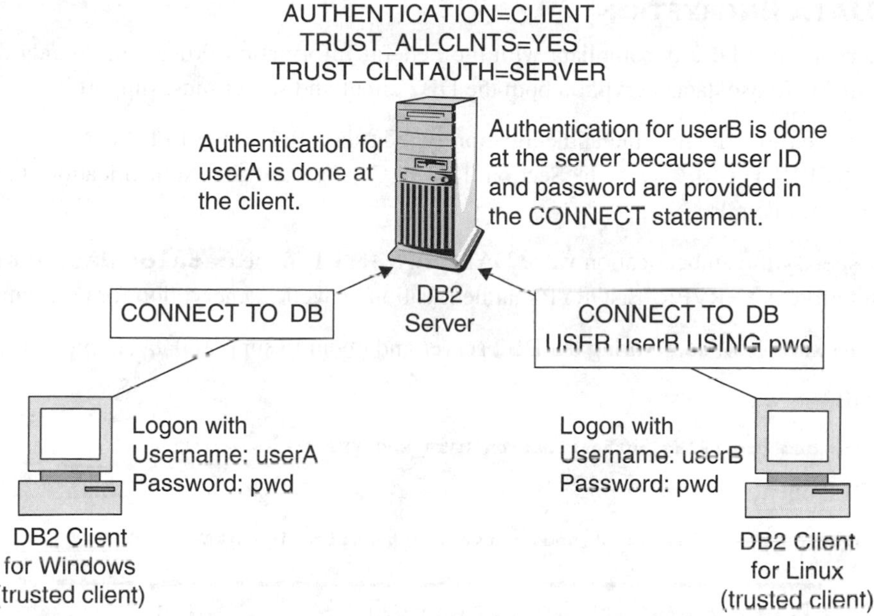

Figure 11.10 Example 3: TRUST_ALLCLNTS and TRUST_CLNTAUTH

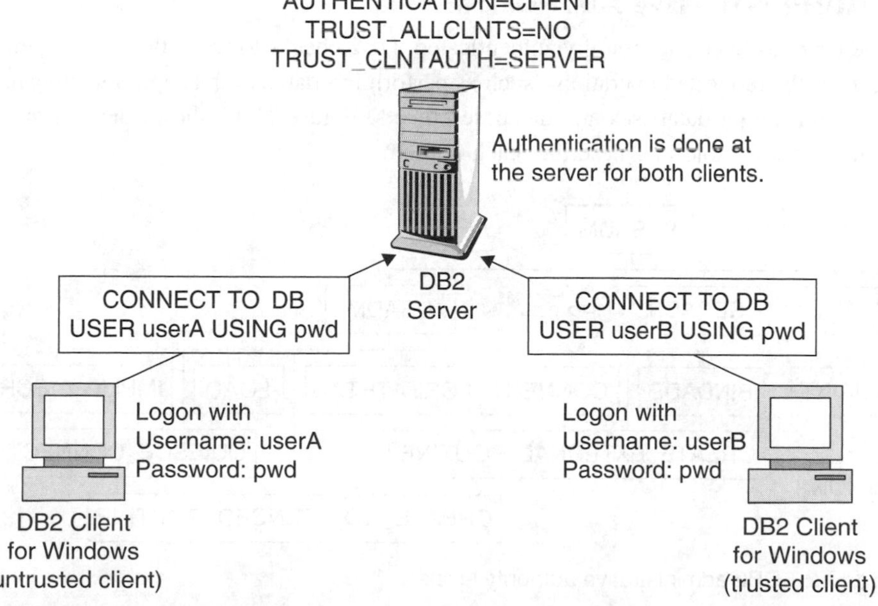

Figure 11.11 Example 4: TRUST_ALLCLNTS and TRUST_CLNTAUTH

11.3 Data Encryption

Data encryption in DB2 is compliant with the Federal Information Processing Standard 140-2 (FIPS 140-2). To use data encryption both the DB2 client and server must support it.

First, you need to configure the authentication type at the DB2 server to DATA_ENCRYPT or DATA_ENCRYPT_CMP. Refer to Section 11.2.1, Configuring the Authentication Type at a DB2 Server for details.

Second, specify the authentication value DATA_ENCRYPT in the **catalog database** command. It enforces SERVER_ENCRYPT authentication as well as encryption for user data.

Here is an example of configuring the DB2 server and client to support data encryption.

On the DB2 server:

```
db2 update dbm cfg using authentication DATA_ENCRYPT
```

On the DB2 client:

```
db2 catalog database bankdb at node server1 authentication DATA_ENCRYPT
```

> **NOTE** Authentication type DATA_ENCRYPT_CMP is not valid in the **catalog database** command. If DATA_ENCRYPT is used in the command, make sure the DB2 server supports data encryption.

11.4 Administrative Authorities

Once the user has been successfully authenticated, DB2 checks to see if the user has the proper authority for the requested operations, such as performing database manager maintenance operations and managing databases and database objects. Figure 11.12 shows the authorities supported in DB2 and Table 11.7 describes each of them.

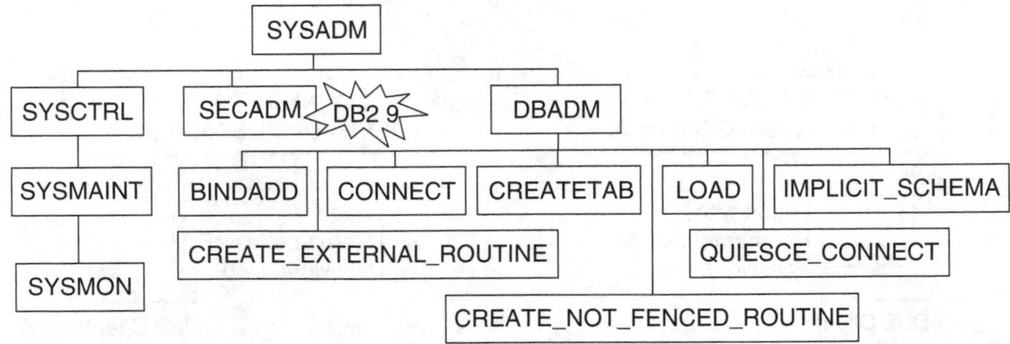

Figure 11.12 DB2 administrative authority levels

Table 11.7 Descriptions of DB2 Administrative Authority Levels

DB2 Administrative Authority	Description
SYSADM	These users have the highest authority level and full privileges for managing the instance. They also have access to all data in the underlying databases.
SYSCTRL	These users have certain privileges in managing the instance, its databases, and database objects. They can create new databases, but do not have access to the data. For example, they cannot issue statements such as **DELETE FROM employee** or **SELECT * FROM employee.**
SYSMAINT	Similar to SYSCTRL, SYSMAINT users have certain privileges in managing the instance, its databases, and database objects. However, they cannot create new databases and do not have access to the data. For example, these users cannot issue statements such as **DELETE FROM employee** or **SELECT * FROM employee.**
SYSMON	These users can turn snapshot monitor switches on, collect snapshot data, and access other database system monitor data. No other task can be performed unless the required authority or privileges are granted to the same user by other means.
SECADM	SECADM is a database-level authority. This authority can only be granted to a user by a user with SYSADM authority. Only the user who is granted SECADM (not even SYSADM) can create, drop, grant, and revoke securityobjects such as security labels, security label components, security policies, trusted contexts and roles. SECADM can also transfer ownership on objects from one user to another.
DBADM	Database-level authority that allows users to perform administrative tasks on the specified database. Note that they also have full data access to the database.
LOAD	These users can only run the load utility against the specified database. Before the user can load data into a table, he or she must also have the privilege to INSERT and/or DELETE on the target table. (Database object privileges are discussed in more detail in the next section.)
CONNECT	Grants users access the database. Without the CONNECT authority, a user cannot connect to the database even though he or she is successfully authenticated by the security facility.
BINDADD	Allows users to create new packages in the database.
CREATETAB	Allows users to create new tables in the database.

(continues)

Table 11.7 Descriptions of DB2 Administrative Authority Levels *(Continued)*

DB2 Administrative Authority	Description
CREATE_NOT_FENCED_ROUTINE	Allows users to create nonfenced routines such as user-defined functions and stored procedures. When a nonfenced routine is invoked, it executes in the database manager's process rather than in its own address space.
IMPLICIT_SCHEMA	Allows users to create a schema implicitly via database object creation. For example, if *bob* wants to create a table *jeff.sales* and the schema *jeff* does not already exist, *bob* needs to hold the IMPLICIT_SCHEMA authority for this database.
QUIESCE_CONNECT	Allows users to access the database while it is quiesced. When a database is quiesced, only users with SYSADM, DBADM, and QUIESCE_CONNECT authorities can connect to the database and perform administrative tasks.
CREATE_EXTERNAL_ROUTINE	Allows users to create routines written in external languages such as C, Java, and OLE.

To give you a better idea of what the system, SECADM, and DBADM authorities can and cannot do, Table 11.8 summarizes some common functions and the authorities required to perform them. For functions that are not listed here, refer to the DB2 manuals. The manuals clearly list the authorities and privileges needed to execute commands and SQL statements.

Table 11.8 Summary of DB2 Administrative Authorities

Function	SYSADM	SYSCTRL	SYSMAINT	SYSMON	SECADM	DBADM
Update Database Manager Configuration parameters	YES	NO	NO	NO	NO	NO
Grant/revoke DBADM authority	YES	NO	NO	NO	NO	NO
Establish/change SYSCTRL authority	YES	NO	NO	NO	NO	NO
Establish/change SYSMAINT authority	YES	NO	NO	NO	NO	NO
Force users off the database	YES	YES	NO	NO	NO	NO
Create/drop databases	YES	YES	NO	NO	NO	NO
Restore to new database	YES	YES	NO	NO	NO	NO

Table 11.8 Summary of DB2 Administrative Authorities *(Continued)*

Function	SYSADM	SYSCTRL	SYSMAINT	SYSMON	SECADM	DBADM
Update database configuration parameters	YES	YES	YES	NO	NO	NO
Back up databases/table spaces	YES	YES	YES	NO	NO	NO
Restore to existing database	YES	YES	YES	NO	NO	NO
Perform roll forward recovery	YES	YES	YES	NO	NO	NO
Start/stop instances	YES	YES	YES	NO	NO	NO
Restore table spaces	YES	YES	YES	NO	NO	NO
Run traces	YES	YES	YES	NO	NO	NO
Obtain monitor snapshots	YES	YES	YES	YES	NO	NO
Query table space states	YES	YES	YES	NO	NO	YES
Prune log history files	YES	YES	YES	NO	NO	YES
Quiesce table spaces	YES	YES	YES	NO	NO	YES
Quiesce databases	YES	NO	NO	NO	NO	YES
Quiesce instances	YES	YES	NO	NO	NO	NO
Load tables	YES	NO	NO	NO	NO	YES
Set/unset check pending status	YES	NO	NO	NO	NO	YES
Create/drop event monitors	YES	NO	NO	NO	YES	YES
Create/drop security label components	NO	NO	NO	NO	YES	NO
Create/drop security policies	NO	NO	NO	NO	YES	NO
Create/drop security labels	NO	NO	NO	NO	YES	NO
Create/drop roles	NO	NO	NO	NO	YES	NO

(continues)

Table 11.8 Summary of DB2 Administrative Authorities *(Continued)*

Function	SYSADM	SYSCTRL	SYSMAINT	SYSMON	SECADM	DBADM
Create/drop trusted contexts	NO	NO	NO	NO	YES	NO
Grant/revoke security lables	NO	NO	NO	NO	YES	NO
Grant/revoke LBAC rule exemptions	NO	NO	NO	NO	YES	NO
Grant/revoke setsession-user privileges	NO	NO	NO	NO	YES	NO
Grant/revoke roles	NO	NO	NO	NO	YES	NO
Execute TRANSFER OWNERSHIP statement	NO	NO	NO	NO	YES	NO

11.4.1 Managing Administrative Authorities

Now that you understand the roles of different authorities in DB2, it's time to show you how to "give" a user or a group of users an authority. The verb *give* is used because a user receives the system and database authorities through different commands and statements.

Recall that SYSADM, SYSCTRL, SYSMAINT, and SYSMON are system authorities for an instance. You set these with the Database Manager Configuration parameters by assigning a user group defined in the operating system or security facility to the associated parameters. The following are the entries for the configuration parameters:

```
SYSADM group name        (SYSADM_GROUP) =
SYSCTRL group name       (SYSCTRL_GROUP) =
SYSMAINT group name      (SYSMAINT_GROUP) =
SYSMON group name        (SYSMON_GROUP) =
```

On Windows, the parameters are set to NULL, which indicates that the members of the Windows **Administrators** group have all of these system authorities. On Linux and UNIX systems, the primary group of the instance owner is the default value for all the SYS*_GROUP.

To set any of the system groups, you use the **update dbm** command. For example, if *admgrp* and *maintgrp* are valid groups, the following command configures the SYSADM_GROUP and SYSMAINT_GROUP:

```
update dbm cfg using sysadm_group admgrp sysmaint_group maintgrp
```

This command does not validate the existence of the group. It is your responsibility to enter a valid group name. To reset them to the default value of NULL, specify:

```
update dbm cfg using sysadm_group NULL
```

> **NOTE** In resetting DBM and DB configuration parameters to the default value, you must use NULL in uppercase. DB2 treats the lowercase *null* as an input value.

Since the SYS*_GROUP parameters are not configurable online, you need to stop and restart the instance for the changes to take effect.

You grant and revoke database authorities with the **GRANT** and **REVOKE** statements to a user, a role, or group of users. Figures 11.13 and 11.14 show the syntax of these statements, and Figure 11.15 illustrates how to use them.

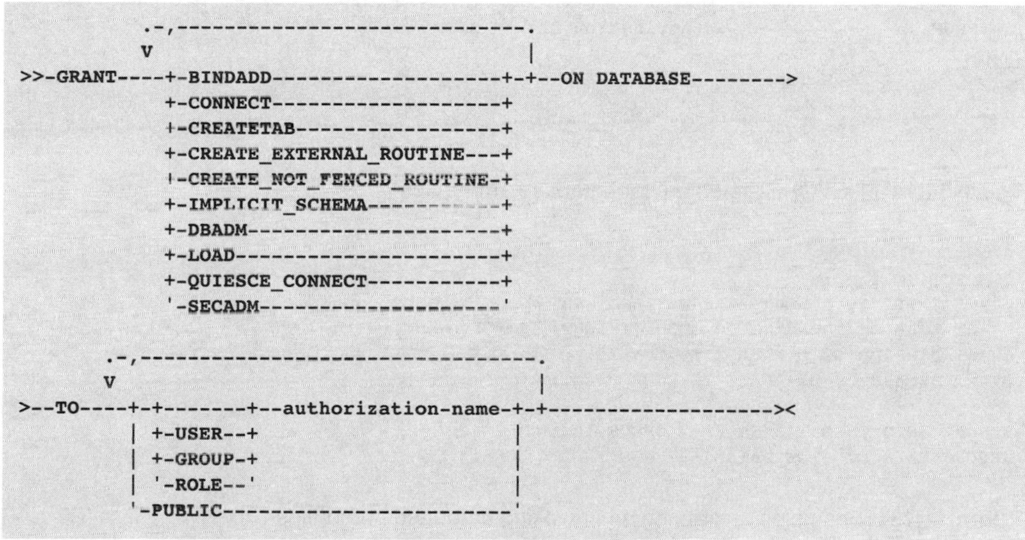

```
            .-,-----------------------------.
            V                               |
>>-GRANT----+-BINDADD-------------------+-+--ON DATABASE-------->
            +-CONNECT-------------------+
            +-CREATETAB-----------------+
            +-CREATE_EXTERNAL_ROUTINE---+
            +-CREATE_NOT_FENCED_ROUTINE-+
            +-IMPLICIT_SCHEMA-----------+
            +-DBADM---------------------+
            +-LOAD----------------------+
            +-QUIESCE_CONNECT-----------+
            '-SECADM--------------------'

        .-,---------------------------------.
        V                                   |
>--TO----+-+-------+--authorization-name-+-+--------------------><
         | +-USER--+                     |
         | +-GROUP-+                     |
         | '-ROLE--'                     |
         '-PUBLIC------------------------'
```

Figure 11.13 GRANT statement for database authorities

V9.5 You must first connect to the target database before you specify the authority or authorities you want to grant or revoke to/from a user, group, or role. A role is a new database object introduced in DB2 9.5 to simplify management of authorization. Roles are the equivalent of in-database groups, as described in Chapter 7, Working with Database Objects. The keywords USER, GROUP, and ROLE are optional for both **GRANT** and **REVOKE** statements. However, if you have a user ID, group name or role name defined with the same name, you must specify **USER, GROUP,** or **ROLE** explicitly; otherwise you will receive an error message.

Notice that the last example of Figure 11.15 uses the keyword PUBLIC. PUBLIC is not the name of a group defined in the operating system or in the external security facility; it is a special group to which everyone belongs. PUBLIC by default receives a few database authorities and/or database object privileges depending on the type of operations performed. Refer to the next section for more information about implicit privileges.

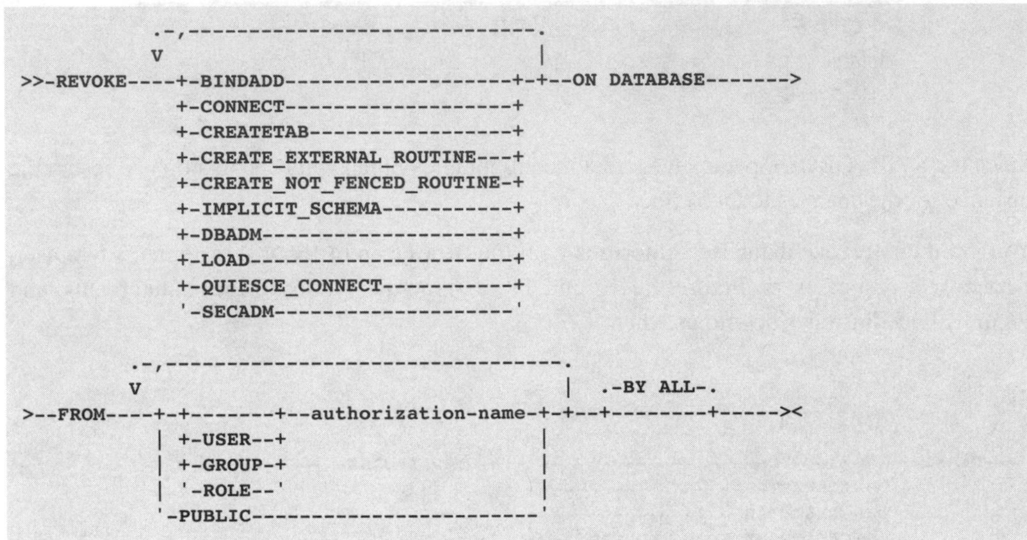

```
             .-,---------------------------.
             V                             |
>>-REVOKE----+-BINDADD-------------------+-+--ON DATABASE------->
             +-CONNECT-------------------+
             +-CREATETAB-----------------+
             +-CREATE_EXTERNAL_ROUTINE---+
             +-CREATE_NOT_FENCED_ROUTINE-+
             +-IMPLICIT_SCHEMA-----------+
             +-DBADM---------------------+
             +-LOAD----------------------+
             +-QUIESCE_CONNECT-----------+
             '-SECADM--------------------'

           .-,--------------------------------.
           V                                  |   .-BY ALL-.
>--FROM----+-+-------+--authorization-name-+-+--+--------+----><
           | +-USER--+                     |
           | +-GROUP-+                     |
           | '-ROLE--'                     |
           '-PUBLIC------------------------'
```

Figure 11.14 REVOKE statement for database authorities

```
CONNECT TO sample;
GRANT IMPLICIT_SCHEMA, CREATETAB ON DATABASE TO USER john;
GRANT LOAD ON DATABASE TO GROUP loadgrp, USER john;
GRANT BINDADD ON DATABASE TO PUBLIC;
GRANT SECADM ON DATABASE TO USER peter;

REVOKE LOAD ON DATABASE FROM GROUP loadgrp;
REVOKE CREATETAB ON DATABASE FROM PUBLIC;
```

Figure 11.15 Examples of granting and revoking database authorities

SECADM was a new database authority introduced in DB2 9. It must be granted to a user explicitly. Any attempt to grant SECADM to a group, a role, or to PUBLIC will result in an error. Notice in Table 11.8, operations that can be performed by SECADM cannot be performed by another user, not even SYSADM.

The **REVOKE** statement uses the BY ALL option as its default. This means that this command revokes each named authority (as well as privileges—that will be discussed later in this chapter) from all named users and/or groups who were explicitly granted those authorities (and privileges). However, there is no cascade effect to also revoke authorities (and privileges) that were implicitly granted. Stay tuned for the implicit privileges discussion in the following section.

> **NOTE** Connect privileges are granted to PUBLIC by default, and should be revoked after the creation of the database and explicit connect priviledges granted.

11.5 DATABASE OBJECT PRIVILEGES

Controlling access to database objects is as important as authenticating users and managing administrative authorities. Privileges give users the right to access each individual database object in a specific way. Privileges can be granted explicitly and implicitly. The following sections list all the supported privileges for each database object and discuss implicit privileges.

If you are not familiar with any database objects discussed in the following sections, see Chapter 7, Working with Database Objects.

11.5.1 Schema Privileges

There are three schema privileges.

- CREATEIN allows users to create objects within the schema.
- ALTERIN allows users to alter objects within the schema.
- DROPIN allows users to drop objects within the schema.

For example, you can specify the **GRANT** and **REVOKE** statements against a given schema, as shown in the syntax diagrams in Figures 11.16 and 11.17.

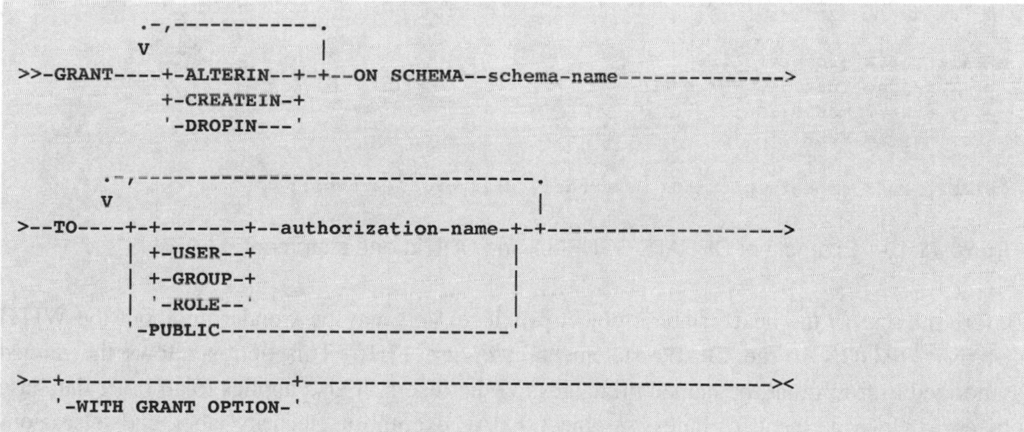

```
            .-,-----------.
            V             |
>>-GRANT----+-ALTERIN--+-+--ON SCHEMA--schema-name-------------->
              +-CREATEIN-+
              '-DROPIN---'

        .-,--------------------------------.
        V                                  |
>--TO----+-+-------+--authorization-name-+-+-------------------->
         | +-USER--+                     |
         | +-GROUP-+                     |
         | '-ROLE--'                     |
         '-PUBLIC------------------------'

>--+-------------------+---------------------------------------><
   '-WITH GRANT OPTION-'
```

Figure 11.16 GRANT syntax diagram for schema privileges

Previously we introduced the IMPLICIT_SCHEMA database authority, which allows the grantee to create a schema via the creation of database objects. You can also create a new schema explicitly using the **CREATE SCHEMA** statement, for example:

```
CONNECT TO sample USER dbowner;
CREATE SCHEMA dev AUTHORIZATION devuser;
```

The **CREATE SCHEMA** statement requires that user *dbowner* has the SYSADM or DBADM authorities on database *SAMPLE*. This creates a schema called *dev* where *devuser* is the schema owner.

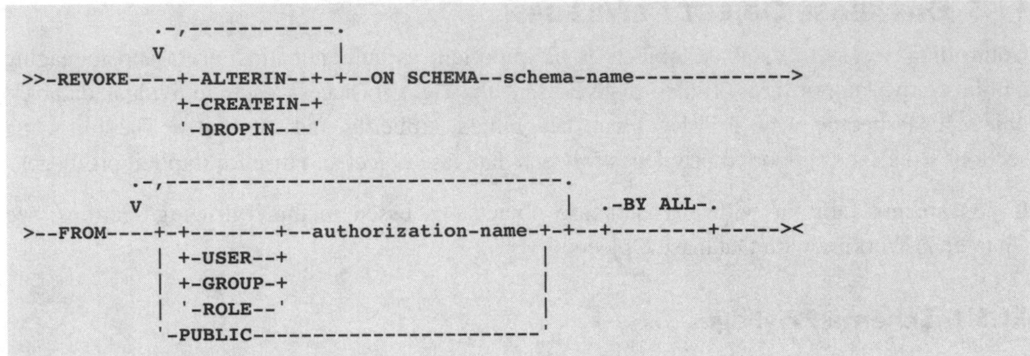

```
            .-,------------.
            V              |
>>-REVOKE----+-ALTERIN--+-+--ON SCHEMA--schema-name------------->
             +-CREATEIN-+
             '-DROPIN---'

          .-,--------------------------------.
          V                                  |  .-BY ALL-.
>--FROM----+-+-------+--authorization-name-+-+--+--------+----><
           | +-USER--+                     |
           | +-GROUP-+                     |
           | '-ROLE--'                     |
           '-PUBLIC------------------------'
```

Figure 11.17 REVOKE syntax diagram for schema privileges

You can also create a schema and database objects within that schema in one SQL statement. Figure 11.18 demonstrates a straightforward example. You simply fully qualify the object name with the schema. For example, in Figure 11.18, the table *dairyprod* and index *prodindx* are created in the schema of *grocery*. Schema *grocery* will be automatically created if it does not already exist.

```
CREATE TABLE grocery.dairyprod
    ( prodno SMALLINT NOT NULL
    , desc VARCHAR(100)
    , qty INTEGER );

CREATE INDEX grocery.prodindx ON grocery.dairyprod (prodno);
```

Figure 11.18 Example of CREATE SCHEMA and DDL in one statement

Before moving to the next database object privilege, you may be wondering about the WITH GRANT OPTION in the **GRANT** statement in Figure 11.16. This option allows the named authorized user to grant the named privileges to other users. It also applies to all other database object privileges (except for index, xsrobject, LBAC exemption, security label, and setsession-user privileges).

11.5.2 Table Space Privileges

Tables and table spaces are logical objects, as discussed in Chapter 7, Working with Database Objects. Tables are logically stored in table spaces, and table spaces are associated to physical storage devices. You need some USE privileges to be able to define tables in a table space. Figures 11.19 and 11.20 show the **GRANT** and **REVOKE** syntax diagrams with the USE privilege available for a specific table space. When a table space is created, its USE privilege is granted to PUBLIC by default. If you want to restrict usage of the table space, you should revoke the USE privilege from PUBLIC and grant it to selected users or groups individually.

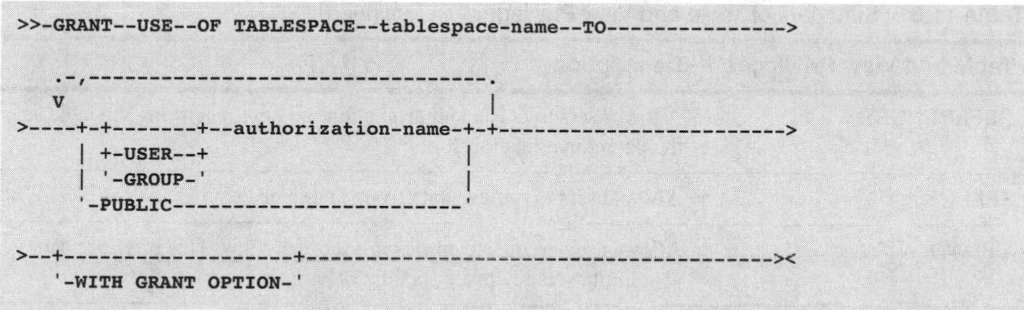

```
>>-GRANT--USE--OF TABLESPACE--tablespace-name--TO--------------->

   .-,--------------------------------.
   V                                  |
>----+-+-------+--authorization-name-+-+------------------------>
     | +-USER--+                      |
     | '-GROUP-'                      |
     '-PUBLIC-------------------------'

>--+-------------------+---------------------------------------><
   '-WITH GRANT OPTION-'
```

Figure 11.19 GRANT syntax diagram for package privileges

```
>>-REVOKE USE OF TABLESPACE--tablespace-name--FROM-------------->

   .-,--------------------------------.
   V                                  |  .-BY ALL-.
>----+-+-------+--authorization-name-+-+--+--------+-----------><
     | +-USER--+                      |
     | | +-GROUP-+                    |
     | '-ROLE--'                      |
     '-PUBLIC-------------------------'
```

Figure 11.20 REVOKE syntax diagram for table space privileges

The following examples show how to grant and revoke the table space privileges.

```
GRANT USE OF TABLESPACE userspace1 TO USER db2admin;
REVOKE USE OF TABLESPACE userspace1 FROM PUBLIC;
```

11.5.3 Table and View Privileges

There are quite a number of privileges you can control for tables and views. Table 11.9 describes these privileges.

Table 11.9 Summary of Table and View Privileges

Table and View Privileges	Descriptions
CONTROL	Provides users with all privileges for a table or view as well as the ability to grant those privileges (except CONTROL) to others.
ALTER	Allows users to alter a table or view.
DELETE	Allows users to delete records from a table or view.
INDEX	Allows users to create an index on a table. This privilege does not apply to views.
INSERT	Allows users to insert an entry into a table or view.

(continues)

Table 11.9 Summary of Table and View Privileges *(Continued)*

Table and View Privileges	Descriptions
REFERENCES	Allows users to create and drop a foreign key, specifying the table as the parent in a relationship.
SELECT	Allows users to retrieve data from a table or view.
UPDATE	Allows users to update entries in a table or view. This privilege can also limit users to update specific columns only.
ALL PRIVILEGES	Grants all the above privileges except CONTROL on a table or view.

Figures 11.21 and 11.22 show the **GRANT** and **REVOKE** syntax diagrams for table and view privileges respectively.

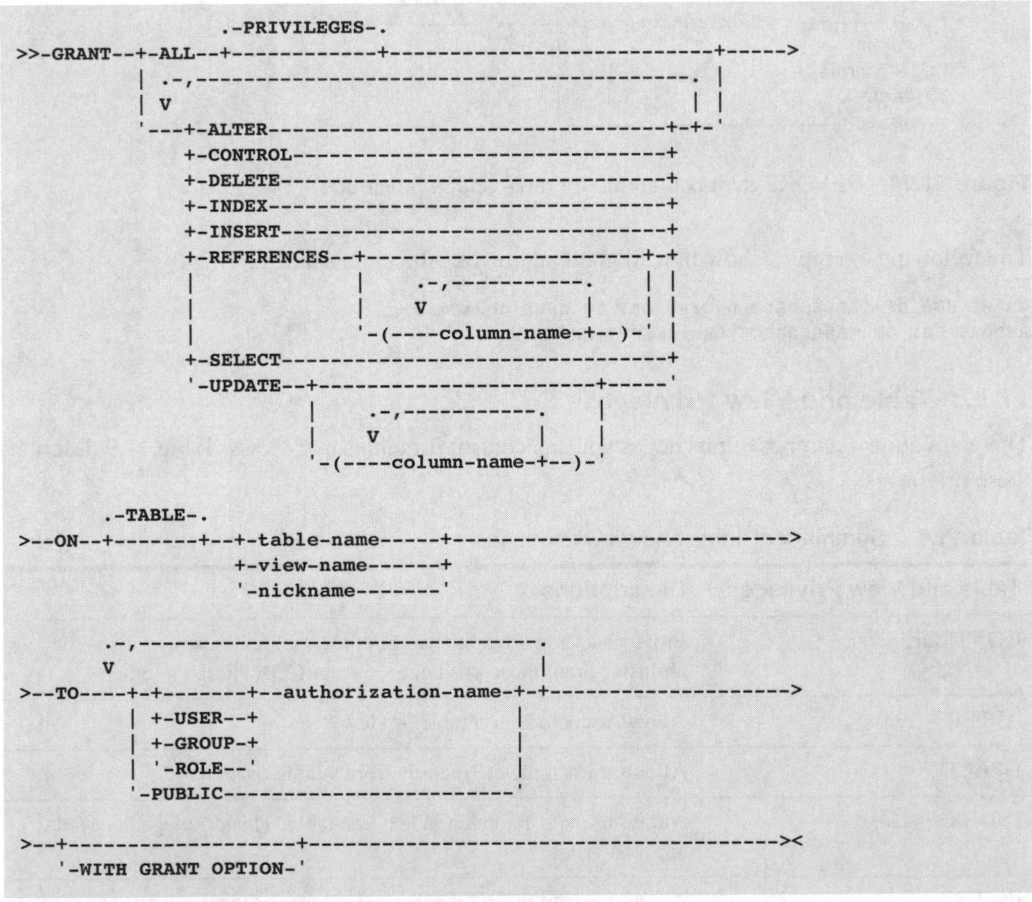

```
                   .-PRIVILEGES-.
>>-GRANT--+-ALL--+------------+--------------------------+----->
          | .-,----------------------------------------. |
          | V                                          | |
          '---+-ALTER-------------------------------+-+-'
              +-CONTROL-----------------------------+
              +-DELETE------------------------------+
              +-INDEX-------------------------------+
              +-INSERT------------------------------+
              +-REFERENCES--+---------------------+-+
              |             |      .-,----------.  | |
              |             |      V            |  | |
              |             '-(----column-name-+--)-' |
              +-SELECT------------------------------+
              '-UPDATE--+-----------------------+-----'
                        |     .-,----------.    |
                        |     V            |    |
                        '-(----column-name-+--)-'

        .-TABLE-.
>--ON--+-------+--+-table-name-----+---------------------------->
                  +-view-name------+
                  '-nickname-------'

        .-,--------------------------------.
        V                                  |
>--TO----+-+-------+--authorization-name-+-+-------------------->
         | +-USER--+                     |
         | +-GROUP-+                     |
         | '-ROLE--'                     |
         '-PUBLIC------------------------'

>--+-------------------+---------------------------------------><
   '-WITH GRANT OPTION-'
```

Figure 11.21 GRANT syntax diagram for table and view privileges

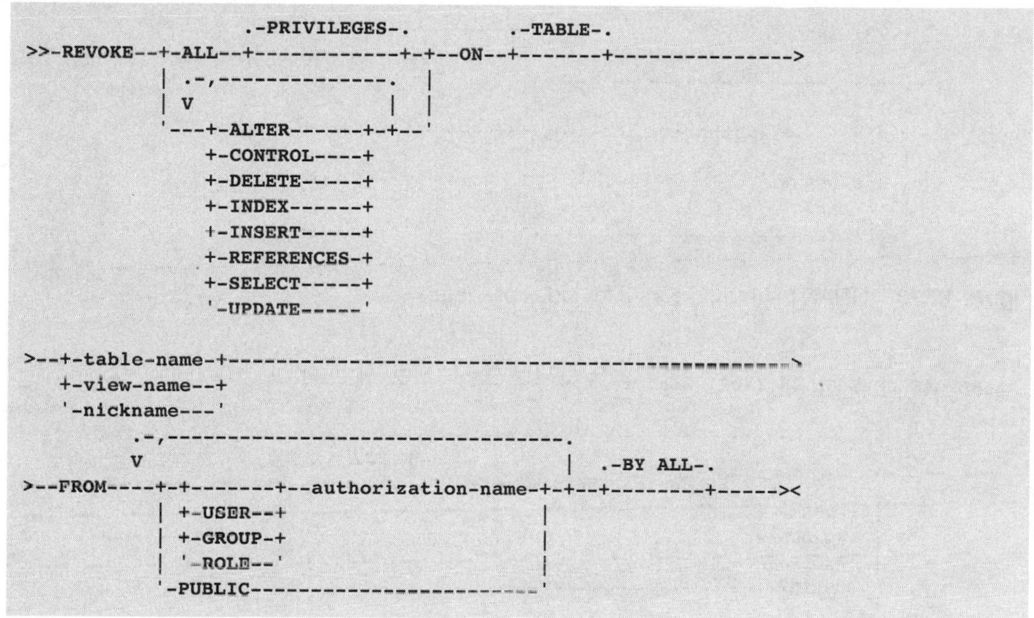

```
                  .-PRIVILEGES-.        .-TABLE-.
>>-REVOKE--+-ALL--+------------+-+--ON--+-------+--------------->
           | .-,--------------.  |
           | V                |  |
           '---+-ALTER------+-+--'
               +-CONTROL----+
               +-DELETE-----+
               +-INDEX------+
               +-INSERT-----+
               +-REFERENCES-+
               +-SELECT-----+
               '-UPDATE-----'

>--+-table-name-+----------------------------------------------->
   +-view-name--+
   '-nickname---'

         .-,--------------------------------.
         V                                  |  .-BY ALL-.
>--FROM----+-+-------+--authorization-name-+-+--+--------+-----><
           | +-USER--+                     |
           | +-GROUP-+                     |
           | '-ROLE--'                     |
           '-PUBLIC------------------------'
```

Figure 11.22 REVOKE syntax diagram for table and view privileges

The following examples show how to grant and revoke some table and view privileges.

```
GRANT ALL PRIVILEGES ON TABLE employee TO USER db2admin WITH GRANT OPTION;
GRANT UPDATE ON TABLE employee (salary, comm) TO GROUP db2users;
REVOKE CONTROL ON TABLE employee FROM PUBLIC;
```

The **GRANT** and **REVOKE** statements discussed above also apply to **nicknames** (database objects that represent remote tables and views residing in different databases). The remote databases can be databases in the DB2 family or non-DB2 databases. This feature is known as **federated database support** and was briefly discussed in Chapter 2, DB2 at a Glance: The Big Picture.

11.5.4 Index Privileges

Privileges for managing indexes is fairly straightforward: you can only drop an index after it is created. To change an index key, for example, you need to drop the index and recreate it. The CONTROL privilege allows the grantee to drop the index. Figures 11.23 and 11.24 list **GRANT** and **REVOKE** statements with index privileges.

The following examples show how to grant and revoke index privileges.

```
GRANT CONTROL ON INDEX empind TO USER db2admin;
REVOKE CONTROL ON INDEX empind FROM db2admin;
```

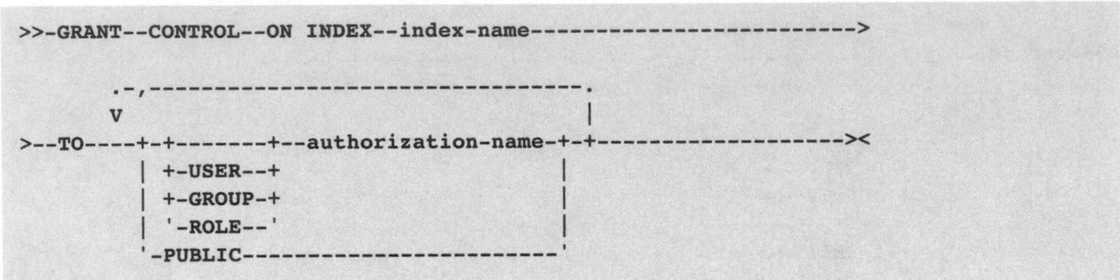

```
>>-GRANT--CONTROL--ON INDEX--index-name------------------------->

         .-,--------------------------------.
         V                                  |
>--TO----+-+-------+--authorization-name-+-+-------------------><
         | +-USER--+                     |
         | +-GROUP-+                     |
         | '-ROLE--'                     |
         '-PUBLIC-----------------------'
```

Figure 11.23 GRANT syntax diagram for index privileges

```
>>-REVOKE CONTROL ON INDEX--index-name------------------------->

           .-,--------------------------------.
           V                                  |  .-BY ALL-.
>--FROM----+-+-------+--authorization-name-+-+--+--------+-----><
           | +-USER--+                     |
           | +-GROUP-+                     |
           | '-ROLE--'                     |
           '-PUBLIC-----------------------'
```

Figure 11.24 REVOKE syntax diagram for index privileges

11.5.5 Package Privileges

A **package** is a database object that contains the data access plan of how static SQL statements will be executed. A package needs to be bound to a database before its associated program can execute it. The following are the privileges you use to manage packages.

- BIND allows users to rebind an existing package.
- EXECUTE allows users to execute a package.
- CONTROL provides users the ability to rebind, drop, or execute a package as well as the ability to grant the above privileges to other users and/or groups.

Figures 11.25 and 11.26 show the **GRANT** and **REVOKE** statements for package privileges respectively.

The following examples show how to grant and revoke package privileges:

```
GRANT EXECUTE, BIND ON PACKAGE emppack1 TO GROUP db2grp WITH GRANT OPTION;
REVOKE BIND ON PACKAGE emppack1 FROM USER db2dev;
```

11.5.6 Routine Privileges

To be able to use a routine, a user must be granted with its associated EXECUTE privilege. As illustrated in Figures 11.27, and 11.28, EXECUTE is the only routine privilege, but it applies to all types of routines: functions, methods, and stored procedures.

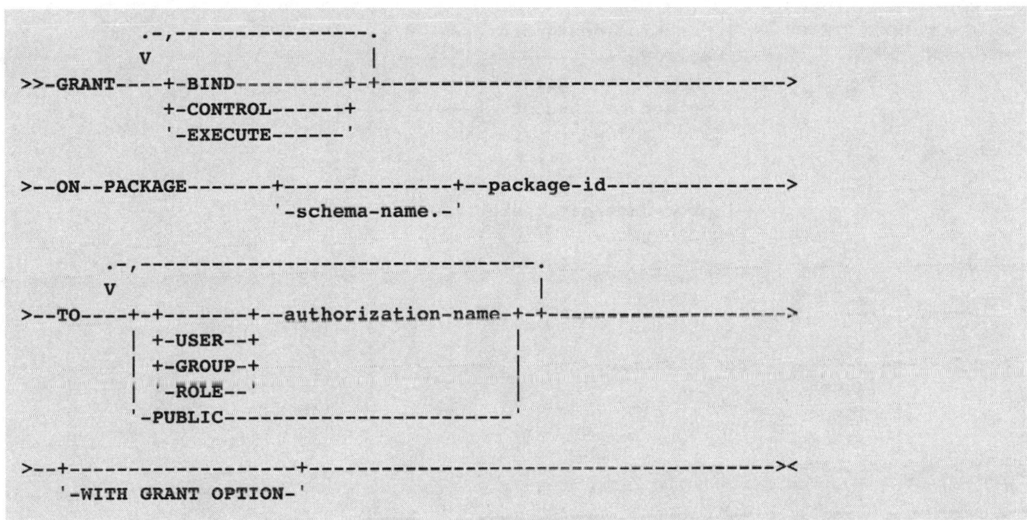

```
           .-,---------------.
           V                 |
>>-GRANT----+-BIND---------+-+---------------------------------->
            +-CONTROL------+
            '-EXECUTE------'

>--ON--PACKAGE-------+--------------+--package-id--------------->
                     '-schema-name.-'

       .-,--------------------------------.
       V                                  |
>--TO----+-+-------+--authorization-name-+-+-------------------->
         | +-USER--+                     |
         | +-GROUP-+                     |
         | '-ROLE--'                     |
         '-PUBLIC------------------------'

>--+-------------------+---------------------------------------><
   '-WITH GRANT OPTION-'
```

Figure 11.25 GRANT syntax diagram for package privileges

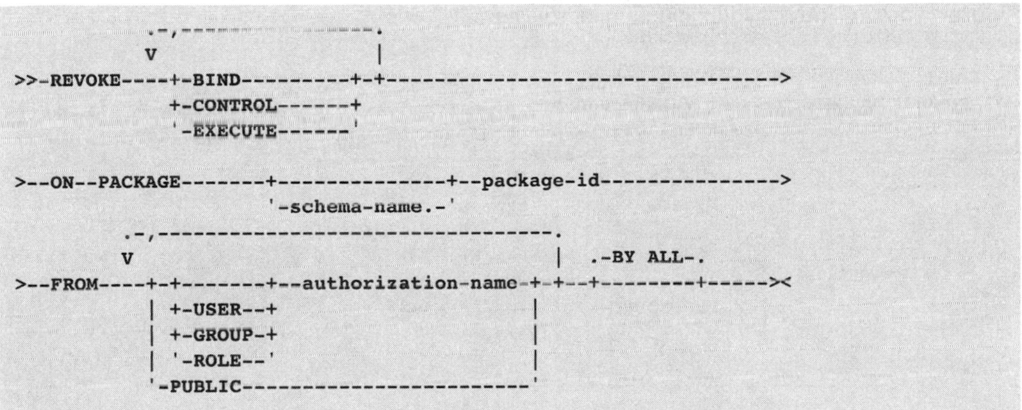

```
            .-,---------------.
            V                 |
>>-REVOKE----+-BIND---------+-+--------------------------------->
             +-CONTROL------+
             '-EXECUTE------'

>--ON--PACKAGE-------+--------------+--package-id--------------->
                     '-schema-name.-'
        .-,--------------------------------.
        V                                  |  .-BY ALL-.
>--FROM----+-+-------+--authorization-name-+-+--+--------+-----><
           | +-USER--+                     |
           | +-GROUP-+                     |
           | '-ROLE--'                     |
           '-PUBLIC------------------------'
```

Figure 11.26 REVOKE syntax diagram for package privileges

The following examples show how to grant and revoke routine privileges:

```
GRANT EXECUTE ON PROCEDURE salary_increase TO USER db2admin WITH GRANT OPTION;
REVOKE EXECUTE ON PROCEDURE salary_increase FROM USER db2admin;
```

11.5.7 Sequence Privileges

A **sequence object** generates unique, sequential numeric values. By default, the group PUBLIC can use any sequence object unless they are controlled by the USAGE privilege, as shown in Figure 11.29. You can restrict usage of certain sequence objects by revoking USAGE from PUBLIC.

```
>>-GRANT EXECUTE ON--+-| function-designator |----------+------->
                     +-FUNCTION--+---------+--*---------+
                     |           '-schema.-'            |
                     +-| method-designator |------------+
                     +-METHOD * FOR--+-type-name------+-+
                     |               '-+---------+--*-' |
                     |                 '-schema.-'      |
                     +-| procedure-designator |---------+
                     '-PROCEDURE--+---------+--*--------'
                                  '-schema.-'

      .-,--------------------------------.
      V                                  |
>--TO----+-+-------+--authorization-name-+-+-------------------->
         | +-USER--+                       |
         | +-GROUP-+                       |
         | '-ROLE--'                       |
         '-PUBLIC-------------------------'

>--+-------------------+---------------------------------------><
   '-WITH GRANT OPTION-'
```

Figure 11.27 GRANT syntax diagram for routine privileges

```
>>-REVOKE EXECUTE ON--+-| function-designator |----------+------>
                      +-FUNCTION--+---------+--*---------+
                      |           '-schema.-'            |
                      +-| method-designator |------------+
                      +-METHOD * FOR--+-type-name------+-+
                      |               '-+---------+--*-' |
                      |                 '-schema.-'      |
                      +-| procedure-designator |---------+
                      '-PROCEDURE--+---------+--*--------'
                                   '-schema.-'

        .-,--------------------------------.
        V                                  |
>--FROM----+-+-------+--authorization-name-+-+------------------>
           | +-USER--+                       |
           | +-GROUP-+                       |
           | '-ROLE--'                       |
           '-PUBLIC-------------------------'

   .-BY ALL-.
>--+--------+--RESTRICT----------------------------------------><
```

Figure 11.28 REVOKE syntax diagram for routine privileges

There may also be cases where you want to change the sequence object definition, such as the minimum, maximum, and incremental values. You probably want to limit the ability to alter a sequence object to only a few users. Use the ALTER privilege (shown in Figures 11.29 and

11.30) to do that. RESTRICT is the default behavior that prevents the sequence from being dropped if dependencies exist.

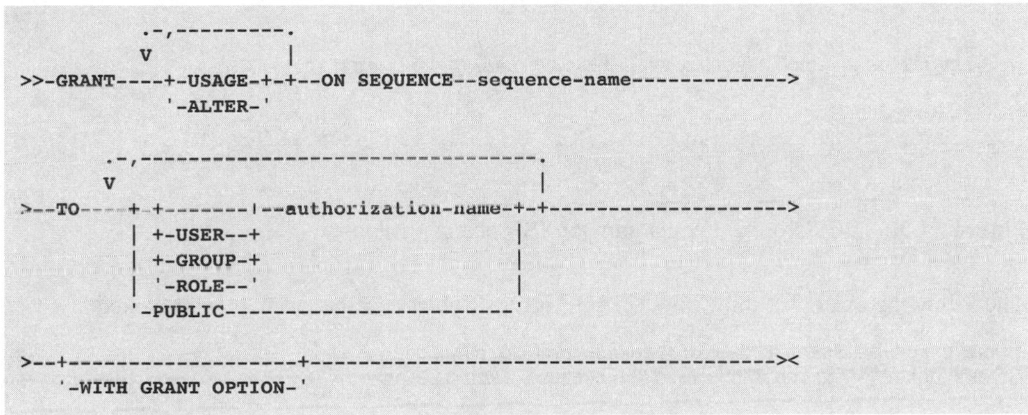

Figure 11.29 GRANT syntax diagram for sequence privileges

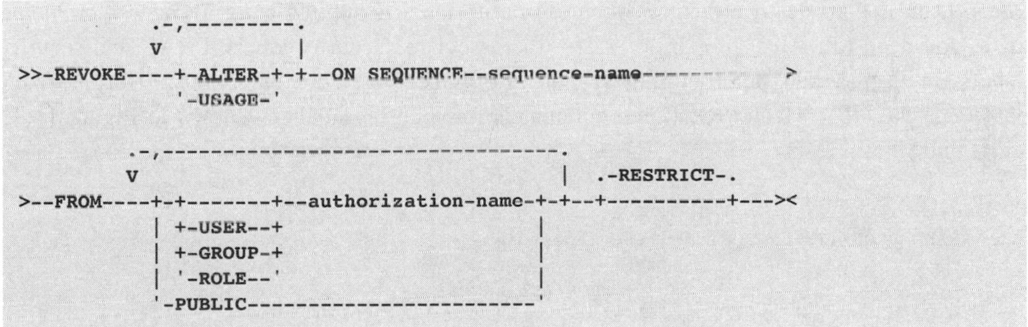

Figure 11.30 REVOKE syntax diagram for sequence privileges

The following examples show how to grant and revoke sequence privileges.

```
GRANT USAGE, ALTER ON SEQUENCE empseq TO USER d2admin WITH GRANT OPTION;
REVOKE ALTER ON SEQUENCE empseq FROM db2admin RESTRICT;
```

11.5.8 XSR Object Privileges

XSR objects are registered XML schemas or DTDs in the XML schema repository. Before they can be used for XML validation or annotated XML schema decomposition, you must have the USAGE privilege on the XSR object. Please refer to Chapter 10 Mastering the DB2 Native XML Support for more details on XML. Figures 11.31 and 11.32 present the syntax diagrams of GRANT and REVOKE for this privilege.

```
>>-GRANT USAGE ON--XSROBJECT--xsrobject-name--TO--PUBLIC-------><
```

Figure 11.31 GRANT syntax diagram for XSR object privileges

```
>>-REVOKE USAGE ON--XSROBJECT--xsrobject-name--FROM--PUBLIC----->

   .-BY ALL-.
>--+--------+--------------------------------------------------><
```

Figure 11.32 REVOKE syntax diagram for XSR object privileges

The following examples show how USAGE on XSR object can be granted and revoked.

```
GRANT USAGE ON XSROBJECT store.custschema TO PUBLIC
REVOKE USAGE ON XSROBJECT store.custschema FROM PUBLIC
```

11.5.9 Security Label Privileges

Security labels are database objects used in a LBAC system to define a certain set of security rules. Data is considered protected when a security label is applied to it. To access protected data, you need to receive proper access for the associated security labels. LBAC and security labels are discussed in more detail in Section 11.6, Label-Based Access Control. Here, we will introduce the GRANT and REVOKE commands for security labels as shown in Figure 11.33 and Figure 11.34 respectively.

```
>>-GRANT SECURITY LABEL--security-label-name-------------------->

                                 .-FOR ALL ACCESS---.
>--TO USER--authorization-name--+------------------+-----------><
                                 +-FOR READ ACCESS--+
                                 '-FOR WRITE ACCESS-'
```

Figure 11.33 GRANT syntax diagram for security label privileges

```
>>-REVOKE SECURITY LABEL--security-label-name--FROM USER--authorization-name-><
```

Figure 11.34 REVOKE syntax diagram for security label privileges

Note that you can grant all, read only, or write only access to any user with a security label. This is a very important step to limit access to protected data from every user. The statements themselves are quite straightforward. The security label must already be defined in the database catalogs and it must be qualified with a security policy.

```
GRANT SECURITY LABEL SALES_POLICY.EAST_COAST TO USER bobby
GRANT SECURITY LABEL SALES_POLICY.ASIA TO USER wong FOR READ ACCESS
GRANT SECURITY LABEL SALES_POLICY.ASIA TO USER betty FOR WRITE ACCESS
REVOKE SECURITY LABEL SALES_POLICY.ASIA FROM user wong
```

11.5.10 LBAC Rule Exemption Privileges

LBAC rule exemption behaves exactly like the name implies. The user will have an exemption on the access rule for the LBAC security policy identified in the statement. The indicated rule will not be enforced for that user.

Figure 11.35 shows that you can be exempted from any of the six or all LBAC rules. Only a user with SECADM authority can execute this GRANT statement. You can also revoke an exemption to a LBAC access rule via the REVOKE statement shown in Figure 11.36.

```
>>-GRANT EXEMPTION ON RULE------------------------------------->

>--+-DB2LBACREADARRAY-----------------+--FOR--policy-name------->
   +-DB2LBACREADSET-------------------+
   +-DB2LBACREADTREE------------------+
   +-DB2LBACWRITEARRAY--+-WRITEDOWN-+-+
   |                    '-WRITEUP---' |
   +-DB2LBACWRITESET------------------+
   +-DB2LBACWRITETREE-----------------+
   '-ALL------------------------------'

>--TO USER--authorization-name---------------------------------><
```

Figure 11.35 GRANT syntax diagram for exemption privileges

```
>>-REVOKE EXEMPTION ON RULE------------------------------------>

>--+-DB2LBACREADARRAY-----------------+--FOR--policy-name------->
   +-DB2LBACREADSET-------------------+
   +-DB2LBACREADTREE------------------+
   +-DB2LBACWRITEARRAY--+-WRITEDOWN-+-+
   |                    '-WRITEUP---' |
   +-DB2LBACWRITESET------------------+
   +-DB2LBACWRITETREE-----------------+
   '-ALL------------------------------'

>--FROM USER--authorization-name-------------------------------><
```

Figure 11.36 REVOKE syntax diagram for exemption privileges

```
GRANT EXEMPTION ON RULE DB2LBACWRITETREE FOR SALES_POLICY TO USER mary
REVOKE EXEMPTION ON RULE ALL FOR SALES_POLICY FROM USER bobby
```

The first example grants an exemption for write access for the SALES_POLICY to *mary*. The next example revokes the exemptions on all of the predefined rules for SALES_POLICY from *bobby*.

11.5.11 SET SESSION AUTHORIZATION Statement and SETSESSIONUSER Privilege

DB2 special registers USER, CURRENT USER, SYSTEM_USER, SESSION_USER were intrdouced in Section 9.1.4, DB2 Special Registers. Inside an application program or on the CLP, you can change the value of the SESSION_USER special register with the SET SESSION AUTHORIZATION statement. The syntax diagram of the statement is shown in Figure 11.37.

```
                                .-=-.
>>-SET--+-SESSION AUTHORIZATION-+--+---+------------------------>
        '-SESSION_USER----------'

>--+-authorization-name-+--+----------------------+------------><
   +-USER---------------+  '-ALLOW ADMINISTRATION-'
   +-CURRENT_USER-------+
   +-SYSTEM_USER--------+
   +-host-variable------+
   '-string-constant----'
```

Figure 11.37 Syntax diagram of the SET SESSION AUTHORIZATION statement

You can explicitly specify an authorization name in the statement like the following. It sets the SESSION_USER special register to *bobby*.

```
SET SESSION AUTHORIZATION = bobby
```

Alternatively, you can use the value stored in another special register. The example below sets SESSION_USER to the SYSTEM_USER special register.

```
SET SESSION_USER = SYSTEM_USER
```

The ALLOW ADMINISTRATION means that certain administration operations can be specified prior to this statement within the same unit of work. The administration operations include:

- Data definition language (DDL)
- GRANT and REVOKE statements
- LOCK TABLE statement
- COMMIT and ROLLBACK statements
- Special registers SET statements

To invoke the SET SESSION AUTHORIZATION or the equivalent SET SESSION_USER statement, you need the SETSESSIONUSER privilege on an authorization ID. Figure 11.38 and 11.39 introduce the GRANT and REVOKE commands for the SETSESSIONUSER privilege on an authorization ID.

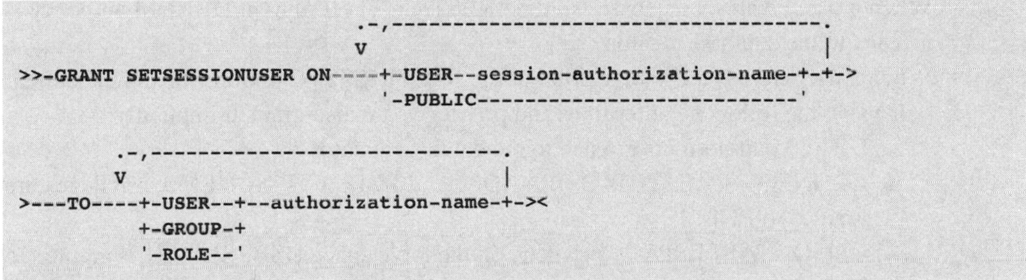

Figure 11.38 GRANT syntax diagram of the SETSESSIONUSER privilege

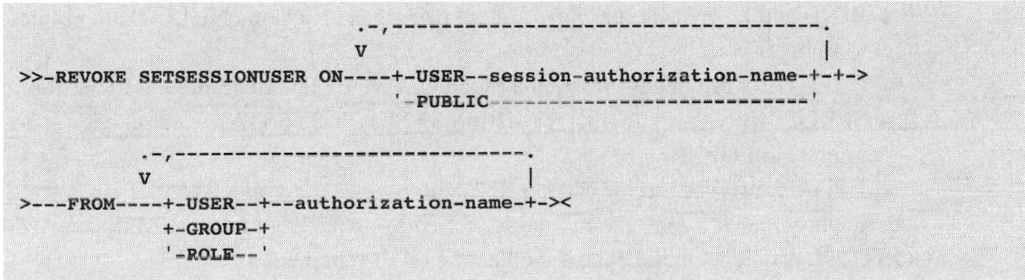

Figure 11.39 REVOKE syntax diagram of the SETSESSIONUSER privilege

The following examples show how to GRANT and REVOKE the SETSESSIONUSER privilege.

```
GRANT SETSESSIONUSER ON USER kevin, USER bobby, GROUP dbadmin TO GROUP devadmin
REVOKE SETSESSIONUSER ON USER bobby FROM GROUP devadmin.
```

The first example allows users in group *devadmin* to set the session authorization ID as users *kevin*, *bobby*, and group *dbadmin*.

The second example revokes *devadmin's* ability to set session authorization ID as *bobby*.

11.5.12 Implicit Privileges

As discussed previously, DB2 privileges usually are granted explicitly with **GRANT** statements. In some cases users may also obtain privileges implicitly or indirectly by performing certain operations. You should pay attention to these privileges and determine whether they are valid per the security policies in your company.

- A user who is granted DBADM authority is also implicitly granted BINDADD, CONNECT, CREATETAB, CREATE_EXTERNAL_ROUTINE, CREATE_ NOT_FENCED_ROUTINE, IMPLICIT_SCHEMA, QUIESCE_CONNECT, LOAD privileges.

- When a user creates a database with the RESTRICTIVE option, DBADM authority is granted to the database creator.
- When a user creates a database without the RESTRICTIVE option (this is the default behavior), the following authorities and privileges are also granted implicitly:
  - DBADM authority is granted to the database creator.
  - CONNECT, CREATETAB, BINADD, and IMPLICIT_SCHEMA privileges are granted to PUBLIC.
  - USE OF TABLESPACE privilege on the table space USERSPACE1 is granted to PUBLIC.
  - EXECUTE with GRANT privileges on all procedures in schema SQLJ and on all functions and procedures in schema SYSPROC are granted to PUBLIC.
  - BIND and EXECUTE privileges on all packages in schema NULLID are granted to PUBLIC.
  - CREATEIN privileges on schema SQLJ and NULLID are granted to PUBLIC.
  - SELECT privileges to the SYSIBM, SYSCAT, SYSSTAT catalog views are granted to PUBLIC.
  - UPDATE privilege to the SYSSTAT catalog views are granted to PUBLIC.
- A user who creates a table, view, index, schema, or package automatically receives CONTROL privilege on the database object he or she creates.

If a program is coded with static SQL statements, packages that contain data access plans are generated and bound to the database at compile time. When a user executes the package, explicit privileges for database objects referenced in the statements are not required. The user only needs EXECUTE privilege on the package to execute the statements. However, this does not mean that the user has direct access to the underlying database objects.

Consider the example illustrated in Figure 11.40. A package *dev.pkg1* containing **`UPDATE`**, **`SELECT`**, and **`INSERT`** statements is bound to the database. A user who only has EXECUTE privilege on *dev.pkg1* can only manipulate table *t1* through the package. He cannot issue **`SELECT`**, **`UPDATE`**, and **`INSERT`** statements directly to *t1*.

As mentioned earlier in this chapter, when a privilege is revoked, there is no cascade effect to also revoke the implicit privileges. For example, if user *bob* is granted DBADM authority, he also implicitly receives the privileges BINDADD, CONNECT, CREATETAB, CREATE_NOT_FENCED, and IMPLICIT_SCHEMA. Assuming, for some reason, DBADM is revoked from *bob* with this statement:

```
REVOKE dbadm FROM USER bob
```

bob no longer has DBADM authority, but he still has BINDADD, CONNECT, CREATETAB, CREATE_NOT_FENCED, and IMPLICIT_SCHEMA authorities. Each of them must be explicitly revoked if you want to remove all authorities from *bob*.

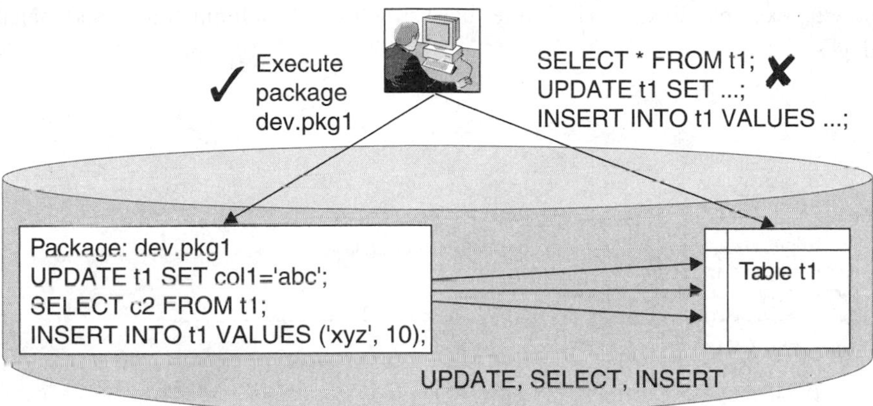

Figure 11.40 Example of controlling database object access via packages

V9.5 11.5.13 Roles and Privileges

In the last decade Role-Based Access Control (RBAC) has emerged as an access control model, which has been quickly adopted by a large number of software products, and in particular by Relational Database Management Systems (RDBMS). The central notion of RBAC is that users do not have discretionary access to enterprise objects. Instead, access permissions are associated with roles, and users are made members of appropriate roles. RBAC greatly simplifies management of authorization while providing an opportunity for system administrators to control access to enterprise objects at a level of abstraction that is close to the structure of their enterprise.

With the implementation of roles in DB2 9.5, the assignment and update of privileges are much simplified. Once the privileges are assigned or updated at the role level, you no longer need to perform the same operations to each user granted that role. Moreover, the privileges that you as a user gained through membership in one or more roles are considered for authorization when you create views, triggers, materialized query tables (MQTs), static SQL and SQL routines. Prior to version 9.5, this has been a major problem for DB2 as groups are managed by the operating system and DB2 has no way of knowing when membership in these groups changes so that it can invalidate the database objects (e.g., packages) created by users who relied on their group privileges to succeed.

After creating a role, the security administrator (who holds SECADM authority) can grant or revoke a role to or from a user, group, or another role (shown in Figures 11.41 and 11.42). In addition, the security administrator can delegate the management of membership in a role to an authorization ID by granting the authorization ID membership in the role with the **WITH ADMIN OPTION.**

The following example illustrates how roles have simplified the administration and management of privileges:

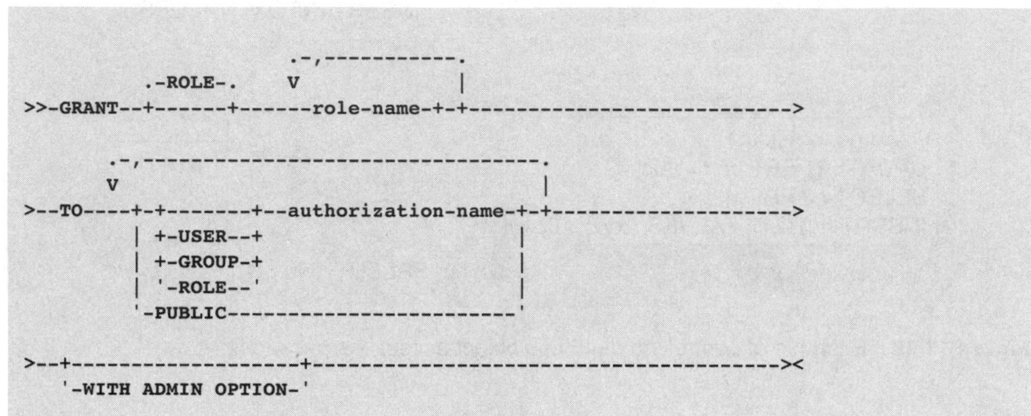

```
                              .-,-----------.
          .-ROLE-.     V             |
>>-GRANT--+------+------role-name-+-+--------------------------->

        .-,--------------------------------.
        V                                  |
>--TO----+-+-------+--authorization-name-+-+-------------------->
         | +-USER--+                     |
         | +-GROUP-+                     |
         | '-ROLE--'                     |
         '-PUBLIC------------------------'

>--+-------------------+---------------------------------------><
   '-WITH ADMIN OPTION-'
```

Figure 11.41 GRANT ROLE syntax diagram

```
                                                  .-,---------.
                                   .-ROLE-.  V            |
>>-REVOKE--+-------------------+--+------+----role-name-+-------->
           '-ADMIN OPTION FOR-'
         .-,--------------------------------.
         V                                  |  .-BY ALL-.
>--FROM----+-+-------+--authorization-name-+-+--+--------+------><
           | +-USER--+                     |
           | +-GROUP-+                     |
           | '-ROLE--'                     |
           '-PUBLIC------------------------'
```

Figure 11.42 REVOKE ROLE syntax diagram

Usage Scenario

Alice is a teller at the bank, and has the privilege to SELECT from tables, CUSTOMER, CHECKING, and SAVINGS. One day Alice changes her job and the database administrator has to revoke her privilege on those tables. The bank later hires two new tellers, Lisa and Tom. The database administrator again has to grant SELECT privilege on the tables to the new tellers.

Without database roles:

```
CONNECT TO sample;
GRANT SELECT ON TABLE customer TO USER alice;
GRANT SELECT ON TABLE checking TO USER alice;
GRANT SELECT ON TABLE savings TO USER alice;
REVOKE SELECT ON TABLE customer FROM USER alice;
REVOKE SELECT ON TABLE checking FROM USER alice;
REVOKE SELECT ON TABLE savings FROM USER alice;
GRANT SELECT ON TABLE customer TO USER lisa;
GRANT SELECT ON TABLE checking to USER lisa;
GRANT SELECT ON TABLE savings to USER lisa;
GRANT SELECT ON TABLE customer TO USER tom;
GRANT SELECT ON TABLE checking to USER tom;
GRANT SELECT ON TABLE savings to USER tom;
```

With database roles:

```
CONNECT TO sample;
CREATE ROLE teller;
GRANT SELECT ON TABLE customer TO ROLE teller;
GRANT SELECT ON TABLE checking TO ROLE teller;
GRANT SELECT ON TABLE customer TO ROLE teller;
GRANT ROLE teller TO USER alice;
REVOKE ROLE teller FROM USER alice;
GRANT ROLE teller TO USER lisa;
GRANT ROLE teller TO USER tom;
```

There are more examples in DB2 Information Center, which demonstrates the advantages of using database roles.

11.5.14 TRANSFER OWNERSHIP Statement

When a database object is created, the authorization ID that was used to create the object was registered as the owner of that database object by default in the system catalogs. For example in the SYSCAT.TABLES catalog view, the OWNER column captures the authorization ID under which the table, view, or alias was created. If this authorization ID is no longer applicable (e.g. the person has left the team or company), the TRANSFER OWNERSHIP SQL statement is very handy to change the ownership of a database object to another authorization ID. The OWNER column for that database object is replaced by the new owner in the associated system catalog tables or views.

This SQL statement can only be executed by the original owner of the object or a user with the SECADM authority. Syntax diagram of the TRANSFER OWNERSHIP statement can be found in Figure 11.43.

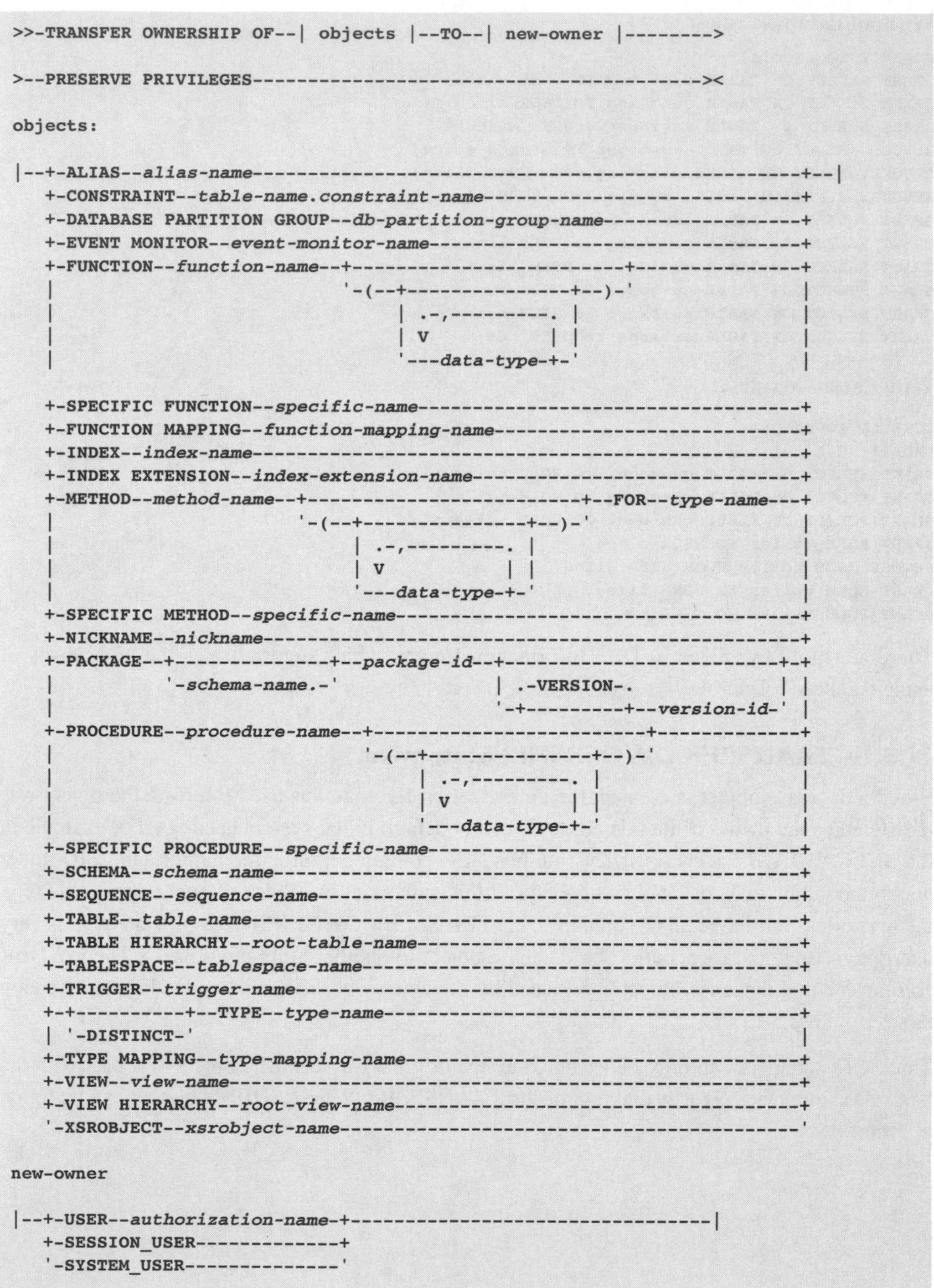

```
>>-TRANSFER OWNERSHIP OF--| objects |--TO--| new-owner |-------->

>--PRESERVE PRIVILEGES-----------------------------------------><

objects:

|--+-ALIAS--alias-name--------------------------------------------------+--|
   +-CONSTRAINT--table-name.constraint-name-----------------------------+
   +-DATABASE PARTITION GROUP--db-partition-group-name------------------+
   +-EVENT MONITOR--event-monitor-name----------------------------------+
   +-FUNCTION--function-name--+-------------------------+---------------+
   |                          '-(--+---------------+--)-'               |
   |                               | .-,---------. |                    |
   |                               | V           | |                    |
   |                               '---data-type-+-'                    |
   +-SPECIFIC FUNCTION--specific-name-----------------------------------+
   +-FUNCTION MAPPING--function-mapping-name----------------------------+
   +-INDEX--index-name--------------------------------------------------+
   +-INDEX EXTENSION--index-extension-name------------------------------+
   +-METHOD--method-name--+-------------------------+--FOR--type-name---+
   |                      '-(--+---------------+--)-'                   |
   |                           | .-,---------. |                        |
   |                           | V           | |                        |
   |                           '---data-type-+-'                        |
   +-SPECIFIC METHOD--specific-name-------------------------------------+
   +-NICKNAME--nickname-------------------------------------------------+
   +-PACKAGE--+--------------+--package-id--+-------------------------+-+
   |          '-schema-name.-'              | .-VERSION-.             | |
   |                                        '-+---------+--version-id-' |
   +-PROCEDURE--procedure-name--+-------------------------+-------------+
   |                            '-(--+---------------+--)-'             |
   |                                 | .-,---------. |                  |
   |                                 | V           | |                  |
   |                                 '---data-type-+-'                  |
   +-SPECIFIC PROCEDURE--specific-name----------------------------------+
   +-SCHEMA--schema-name------------------------------------------------+
   +-SEQUENCE--sequence-name--------------------------------------------+
   +-TABLE--table-name--------------------------------------------------+
   +-TABLE HIERARCHY--root-table-name-----------------------------------+
   +-TABLESPACE--tablespace-name----------------------------------------+
   +-TRIGGER--trigger-name----------------------------------------------+
   +-+----------+--TYPE--type-name--------------------------------------+
   | '-DISTINCT-'                                                       |
   +-TYPE MAPPING--type-mapping-name------------------------------------+
   +-VIEW--view-name----------------------------------------------------+
   +-VIEW HIERARCHY--root-view-name-------------------------------------+
   '-XSROBJECT--xsrobject-name------------------------------------------'

new-owner

|--+-USER--authorization-name-+---------------------------------|
   +-SESSION_USER-------------+
   '-SYSTEM_USER--------------'
```

Figure 11.43 Syntax diagram of the TRANSFER OWNERSHIP statement

As seen in Figure 11.43, this SQL statement works with many database objects. The new owner must be a user. Here are a couple of examples.

```
TRANSFER OWNERSHIP OF TABLE acct.employee TO USER roger PRESERVE PRIVILEGES
```

The above example will change the OWNER value from *acct* to *roger* for table *acct.employee* in the SYSCAT.TABLES view. The PRESERVE PRIVILEGES is a mandatory clause which keeps all existing privileges presently held by the current owner of the object, even after the transfer. If you want to remove access on any specific database objects from this current owner, you need to execute the respective REVOKE statements accordingly.

Assume the following view *acct.payroll* has SELECT and INSERT dependencies on an underlying table *acct.employee*.

```
TRANSFER OWNERSHIP OF VIEW acct.payroll TO USER ed PRESERVE PRIVILEGES
```

If the database object you are trying to transfer has dependent objects as it does in this case, then the new owner must have the same privileges on the dependent object. In our example above, the new owner *ed* must also have SELECT and INSERT privileges on *acct.employee*.

V9 11.6 Label-Based Access Control (LBAC)

Label-based access control (LBAC) gives you complete control over who can access the data in your tables and views. LBAC lets you decide the precise privileges users have on the columns and rows in the tables. It is much like combining predicates, views and privileges into one very powerful, easy to administer package.

The power of LBAC is that you do not need to define and manage hundreds of views in order to define the fine grained access that more and more companies require due to the increased awareness of data security in today's environment.

All LBAC settings or configuration are performed by the *security administrator*, who is the user that has been granted SECADM authority by the system administrator for the instance. The security settings or configurations then define the security policy. This policy describes the criteria used to decide what data each user can see in the table or view.

Only one policy can be defined per table, but each table can have its own security policy. The security policy is made up of at least one (but usually more) security label. Users who want to access data in the table or view need to have the appropriate security label granted to them. When there's a match, access is permitted; without a match, access is denied. There are three types of security labels:

- Row security labels. A security label associated with a data row or record in a database table.
- Column security labels. A security label associated with a column in a database table.
- User security labels. A security label granted to a database user.

A security label is composed of security label components, and there are three types of components that you can use to build your security labels:

- **Sets.** A set is a collection of elements where the order in which those elements appear is not important. All elements are deemed equal. In this case, as shown in Figure 11.44, the set indicates whether or not a specific drug is available for sale in a state. In this example, the X indicates a drug cannot be sold in that state.

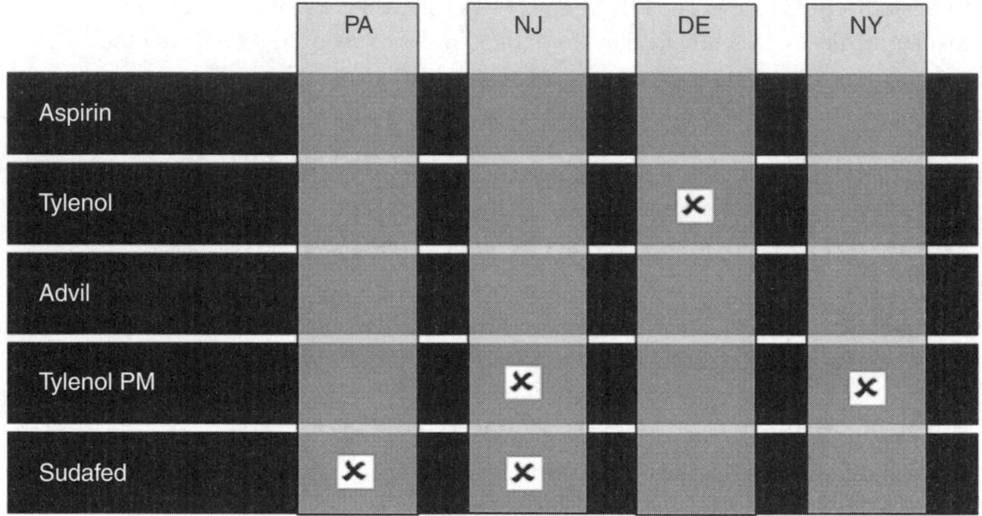

PA
NJ
DE
NY
Aspirin
Tylenol
Advil
Tylenol PM
Sudafed

Figure 11.44 Security Set

- **Arrays.** An array is an ordered set that can be used to represent a simple hierarchy. In an array, the order in which the elements appear is important. For example, the first element ranks higher than the second element and the second higher than the third. In Figure 11.45, we would see Confidential first, then Private, then Public since the first element is ranked higher. We also see that the scope of data that can be accessed decreases as the ranking decreases. In this example, each ranking can see the data in its level, as well as all data below that level.
- **Trees.** A tree represents a more complex hierarchy that can have multiple nodes and branches. For example, trees can be used to represent organizational charts. You use a security policy to define the security label components that make up a particular security label. In Figure 11.46, the General can see all data, and has the highest security classification. As you go down through the ranks, each lower level has a lower classification level, and can see less data. At the bottom is the enlisted person, who can see almost nothing.

If you try to read protected rows in a table that your LBAC credentials do not allow you to read, DB2 acts as if those rows do not exist. Those rows will not be returned to you if you select them,

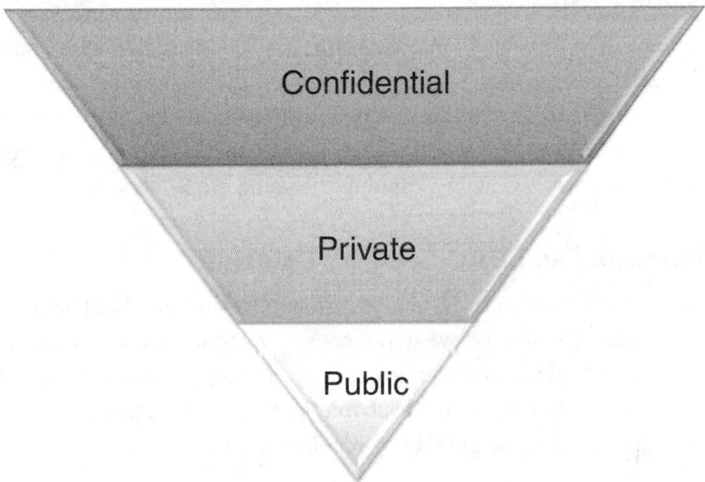

Figure 11.45 Security Array

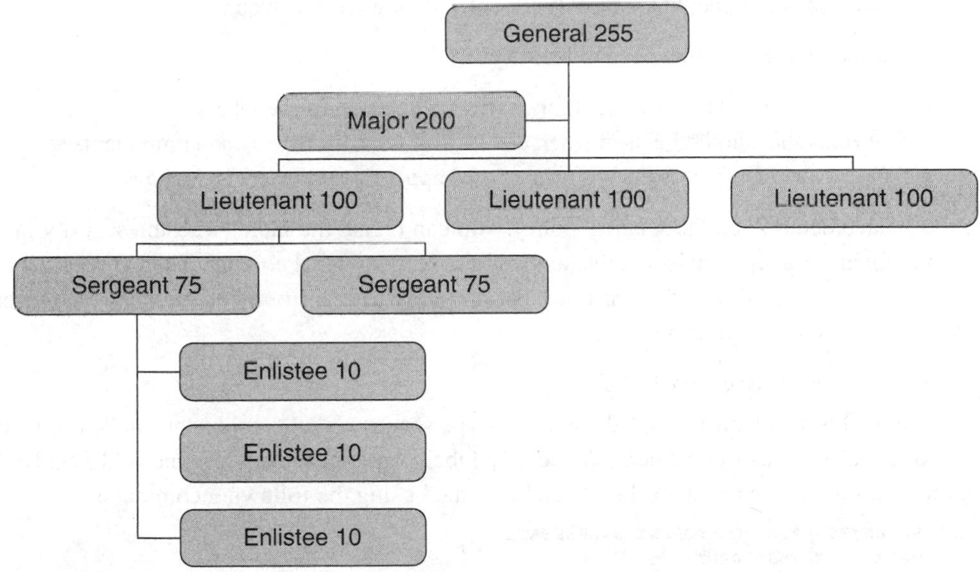

Figure 11.46 Security Tree

and you cannot delete or update the rows. Even aggregate functions ignore rows that your LBAC credentials do not allow you to read. The COUNT(*) function, for example, will return a count only of the rows that you have read access to. It is as if they do not exist at all.

11.6.1 Views and LBAC

You can define a view on a protected table the same way you can define one on a non-protected table. When the view is accessed the LBAC protection on the underlying table is enforced on top of any row or column restrictions enforced by the view. Since the LBAC credentials that are used to determine what rows to return are based on the authorization ID, two users accessing the same view might see different rows even when running the same query.

11.6.2 Implementing an LBAC Security Solution

The following sections provide an overview of how you would go about setting up LBAC protection on a specific table. In this case we will discuss how to implement security on your corporate **sales** table. The sales table is used to track every item sold by your sales force, and you want to be sure that people are not claiming other people's sales, or poaching sales oportunities, since there are large bonuses at stake, for the sales force, and their managers.

In this case you want your:

- VP of Sales to be able to see all identified opportunities, as well as completed sales
- State Sales Executives to see only the prospective and completed sales in their state
- Individual sales people to see only the sales they were involved in

To build the security policy, you need to identify:

- The security labels, and what components will be part of the labels
- The rules that should be used when comparing security labels and components
- Any optional behaviors that you want to be applied when users access data

Once you have determined the security policy, you can create the table (with the security label column defined) or alter an existng table and add the security label column. Then you attach the security policy to the table and grant users the appropriate security labels to allow or prevent them from accessing the protected data.

Step 1a: Defining the Security Label

From your analysis, you have decided that a tree-type security label component can be used with each individual state as the element. A security label component with a name SALESSTATE with the states as shown in Figure 11.44 can be created using the following command:

```
CREATE SECURITY LABEL COMPONENT SALESSTATE
       TREE ('STATES' ROOT,
             'PA' UNDER 'STATES',
             'NJ' UNDER 'STATES ',
             'NY' UNDER 'STATES ',
             'DE' UNDER 'STATES ' )
```

Step 1b: Defining the Security Policy

After the security label component has been created, you then need to create the security policy. A security policy with a name SALESPOLICY that uses SALESSTATE can be created as follows:

```
CREATE SECURITY POLICY SALESPOLICY
     COMPONENTS SALESSTATE
     WITH DB2LBACRULES
     RESTRICT NOT AUTHORIZED WRITE SECURITY LABEL
```

Step 1c: Defining the Security Labels

Since each state's sales executive need only see the sales and opportunities in their state, you should define a security label for each state, each state's sales executive, and the VP of sales. The security labels will be based on the overall SALESPOLICY created previously. The security labels should be created as follows:

```
CREATE SECURITY LABEL SALESPOLICY.PA
     COMPONENT SALESSTATE 'PA'

CREATE SECURITY LABEL SALESPOLICY.NJ
     COMPONENT SALESSTATE 'NJ'

CREATE SECURITY LABEL SALESPOLICY.NY
     COMPONENT SALESSTATE 'NY'

CREATE SECURITY LABEL SALESPOLICY.DE
     COMPONENT SALESSTATE 'DE'

CREATE SECURITY LABEL SALESPOLICY.STATES
     COMPONENT SALESSTATE 'STATES'
```

Step 2: Creating and Protecting the SALES Table

```
CREATE TABLE SALES (SALES_DATE DATE,
    SALES_PERSON VARCHAR (15),
    STATE CHAR (2),
    SALES INTEGER,
    MARGIN INTEGER,
    STATETAG DB2SECURITYLABEL)
    SECURITY POLICY SALESPOLICY
```

In the example above, the state of the sale, and the security tag are the same. but since we normally do not query the security tag separately, we still need to store the state.

Step 3: Loading Data

The following data will be loaded into the table for this example:

SALES_DATE	SALES_PERSON	STATE	SALES	MARGIN	STATETAG
04/21/2007	SUMMER	PA	9000	50	PA
03/31/2007	FROST	DE	1000	40	DE
05/29/2007	SNOW	NY	3000	40	NY
04/20/2007	GREEN	NJ	2000	40	NJ

Step 4: Granting Security Labels to the Users

> **NOTE** SECADM authority is required to execute commands for granting labels to users.

After the SALES table has been created and protected no users can access the table until security labels have been granted. To allow each state's sales executive access to his state's data, grant each of them the security label that corresponds to his state. If you only want them to read the data, you can grant only read authority, but since they also might want to change the data, this example will grant read and write access.

```
GRANT SECURITY LABEL SALESPOLICY.PA
    TO USER Dwaine FOR ALL ACCESS

GRANT SECURITY LABEL SALESPOLICY.NY
    TO USER Chris FOR ALL ACCESS

GRANT SECURITY LABEL SALESPOLICY.NJ
    TO USER Larry FOR ALL ACCESS

GRANT SECURITY LABEL SALESPOLICY.DE
    TO USER Phil FOR ALL ACCESS

GRANT SECURITY LABEL SALESPOLICY.STATES
    TO USER Alyssa FOR ALL ACCESS
```

11.6.3 LBAC In Action

This next section will examine how users access the table, and what data they will see.

Example 1

If Alyssa, the VP of Sales attempts to insert some data into the SALES table, it will be successful since she has read and write permission on all states.

```
INSERT into SALES VALUES (
    '06/02/2007',
    'LUCAS',
    'NY',
    1400,
    20,
    SECLABEL_BY_NAME('SALESPOLICY', 'NY'));
```

If Larry tries to insert a sale for Phil, the insert will fail since Larry works in NJ, not in DE.

```
INSERT into  SALES VALUES (
     '06/02/2007',
     'SMITH',
     'DE,
     1500,
     12,
     SECLABEL_BY_NAME ('SALESPOLICY', 'DE'))
```

Example 2

If Larry tries to read the sales information for NY so that he can "scoop" some sales, he will not get any data.

```
SELECT sales_date, sales_person, state, sales, margin
      from  SALES where state='NY'
```

In this case no data row is returned since the row in the table for this state is protected by security label SALESPOLICY.NY, and the security label that Larry holds is not authoized to read that row.

Example 3

Larry tries to read all of the sales data from the SALES table by issuing the command:

```
SELECT sales_date, sales_person, region, sales, margin
    from  SALES;
```

In this case, only the rows with the sales policy NJ in the STATETAG are returned.

11.6.4 Column Level Security

You can use LBAC to protect columns in the same manner as shown for protecting rows.

Referential Integrity Constraints and LBAC

While LBAC can work on tables with referential constraints defined on them, you need to consider the following.

- LBAC read access rules are NOT applied for internally generated scans of child tables. This is to avoid having orphan children.
- LBAC read access rules are NOT applied for internally generated scans of parent tables.
- LBAC write rules are applied when a CASCADE operation is performed on child tables.

LBAC provides a mechanism for protecting rows and/or columns in your tables, and ensuring that only the people with permission can see or alter the data in the tables.

11.7 Authority and Privilege Metadata

Up to this point we have introduced different authorities and privileges. Now we will show you where all this security information is stored and how to easily retrieve it.

Just like most of the information about a database, authorities and privileges metadata is stored in the catalog tables and views listed in Table 11.10. For a complete list of all DB2 catalog tables and descriptions, refer to Appendix D, Using the DB2 System Catalog Tables, or the *DB2 SQL Reference* manual.

Table 11.10 System Catalog Views Containing Authority and Privilege Metadata

Catalog View	Description
SYSCAT.COLAUTH	Stores column privileges for each grantee. Column privileges are granted through table and view privileges. The two privilege types are Update and Reference.
SYSCAT.DBAUTH	Stores database authorities for each grantee.
SYSCAT.INDEXAUTH	Stores index privileges for each grantee.
SYSCAT.PACKAGEAUTH	Stores package privileges for each grantee.
SYSCAT.PASSTHRUAUTH	Stores information about authorizations to query data sources in pass-through sessions. Pass-through sessions (not discussed in this book) are used in federated database environments.
SYSCAT.ROLEAUTH	Stores database roles granted to users, groups, roles or PUBLIC.
SYSCAT.ROUTINEAUTH	Stores routine privileges for each grantee.
SYSCAT.SCHEMAAUTH	Stores schema privileges for each grantee.
SYSCAT.SEQUENCEAUTH	Stores sequence privileges for each grantee.
SYSCAT.TABAUTH	Stores table privileges for each grantee.
SYSCAT.TBSPACEAUTH	Stores table space privileges for each grantee.
SYSCAT.XSROBJECTAUTH	Stores XSR object USAGE privileges for each grantee.
SYSCAT.SECURITYLABELS	Stores information of security labels.
SYSCAT.SECURITYLABEL-ACCESS	Stores database authorization IDs and types of access to security labels defined in the database.
SYSCAT.SECURITYLABEL-COMPONENTS	Stores information of security label components.
SYSCAT.SECURITYLABEL-COMPONENTELEMENTS	Stores element value for each security label component.

Table 11.10 System Catalog Views Containing Authority and Privilege Metadata *(Continued)*

Catalog View	Description
SYSCAT.SECURITYPOLICY	Stores information of security policies.
SYSCAT.SECURITYPOLICY-COMPONENTRULES	Stores read and write access rules for each security label component of its associated security policy.
SYSCAT.SECURITYPOLICY-EXEMPTIONS	Stores information of security policy exemptions.

While querying the catalog views can give you everything (and sometimes more than) you want to know, the following are a few commands and tools you will find handy.

From the DB2 CLP, you can obtain the authorities of users connected to the database in the current session with this command:

```
get authorizations
```

The command extracts and formats information stored in SYSCAT.DBAUTH. It lists the database authorities for the users. In addition to showing the authorities directly granted to the current user, it also shows implicit authorities inherited. Figure 11.47 shows the output of this command.

You can also retrieve the same result from the DB2 Control Center. Right-click on the database you want to know about and then select **Authorities** (see Figure 11.48). This displays the Database Authorities window (see Figure 11.49), where you can manage database-level authorities for existing and new users and groups.

> **NOTE** Recall that user IDs and user groups are defined outside of DB2 (e.g., the operating system of the DB2 server). The user IDs and user groups shown in the Control Center refer to existing users and groups at the external security facility level. To add an existing user to the Control Center, use the *Add User* button.

To manage privileges for each individual database object, right click on the target object from the Control Center and select **Privileges** (see Figure 11.50).

Using the window shown in Figure 11.51, you can manage the privileges associated to the object. For example, you can grant or revoke particular privileges of a table for a particular user or for all users.

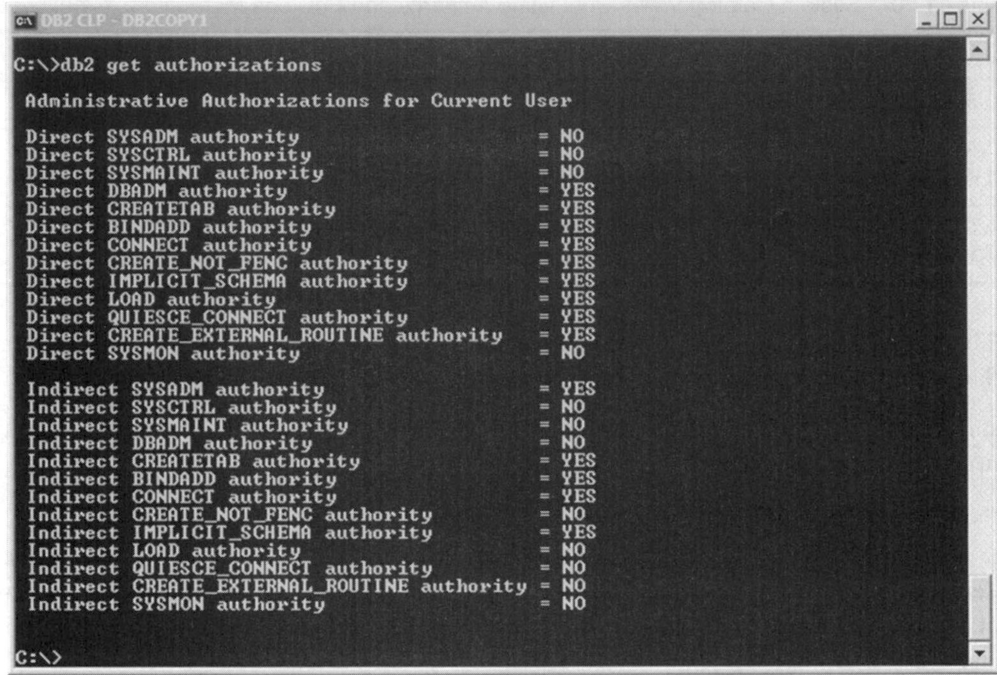

Figure 11.47 Output of the get authorizations command

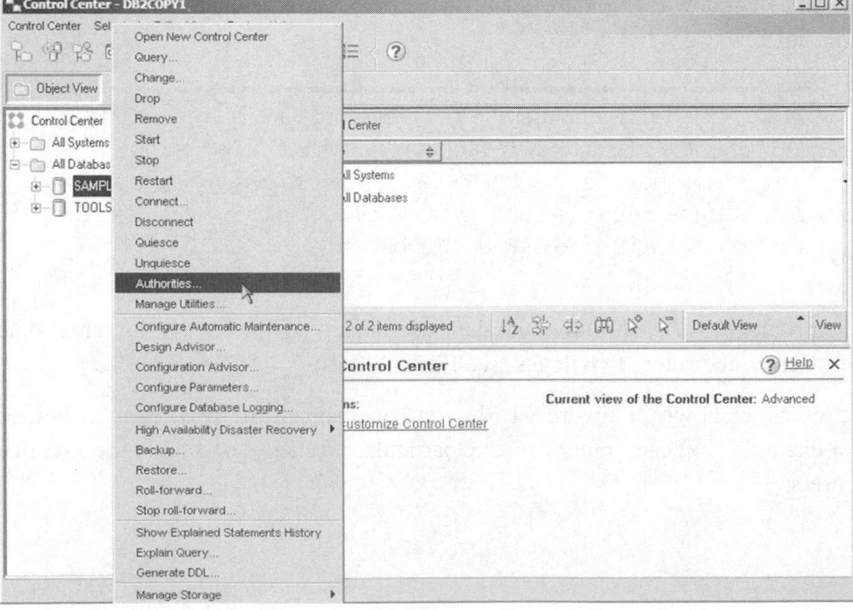

Figure 11.48 Obtaining database authorities from the Control Center

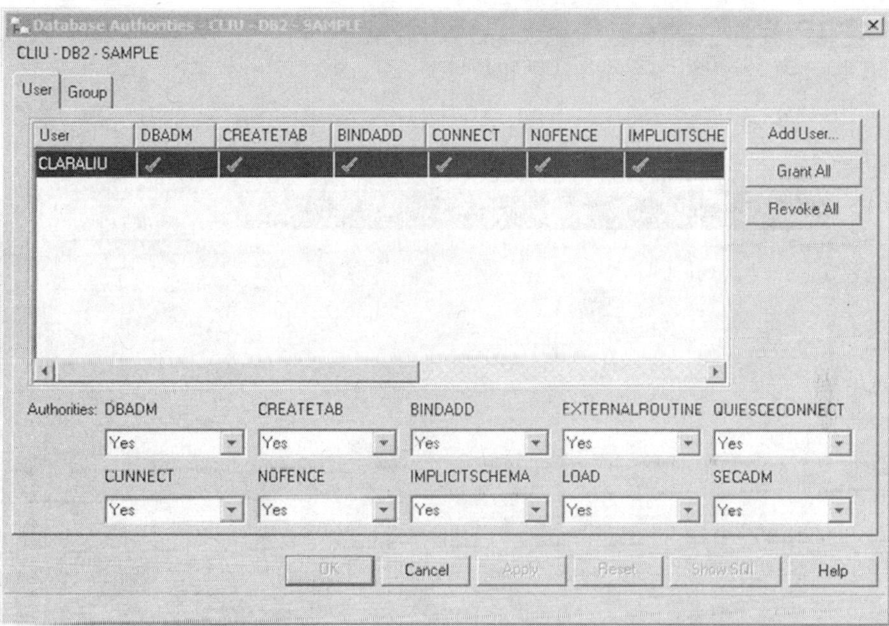

Figure 11.49 Managing database authorities from the Control Center

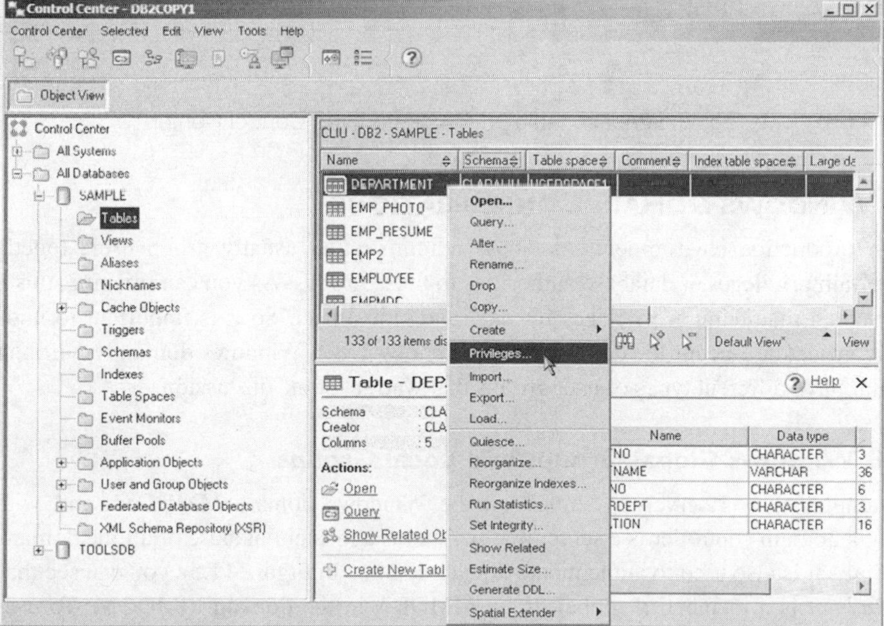

Figure 11.50 Managing database object privileges from the Control Center

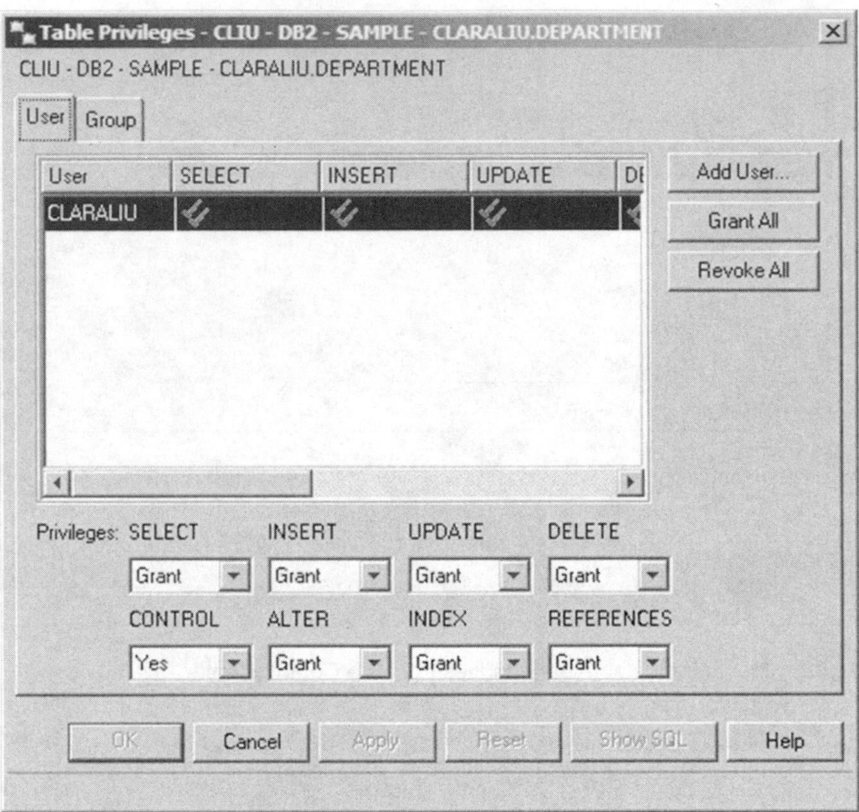

Figure 11.51 Managing database table privileges from the Control Center

11.8 Windows Domain Considerations

In most production environments, database administrators usually group users together and grant certain privileges or database authorities to those groups. As you can imagine, this is more efficient than maintaining privileges for each individual user. So it is important to understand how the groups are being looked up for the users by DB2. Windows domain environments in particular have different types of user groups that warrant some discussion.

11.8.1 Windows Global Groups and Local Groups

For example, a DB2 server is defined on the Windows domain MMDOM, and within the domain, a domain controller is a server that maintains a master database of all the domain users' credentials. It is also used to authenticate domain logons. In Figure 11.52 you can see that a user ID *db2admin* is a member of global group MMDBA in the domain MMDOM. To use global groups, you must include them inside a local group on the DB2 server. When DB2 enumerates all the groups that a person is a member of, it also lists the local groups the user is a member of indirectly. Permission to access the database and/or object must be granted to this local group.

Figure 11.53 shows a second scenario, where the same user ID, *db2admin*, is also defined locally at the DB2 server and is a member of a local group called DB2DBA.

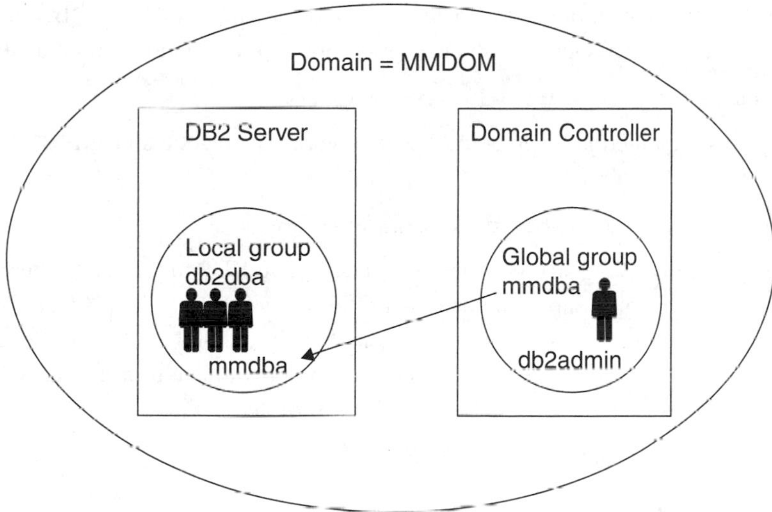

Figure 11.52 Support of global groups in DB2

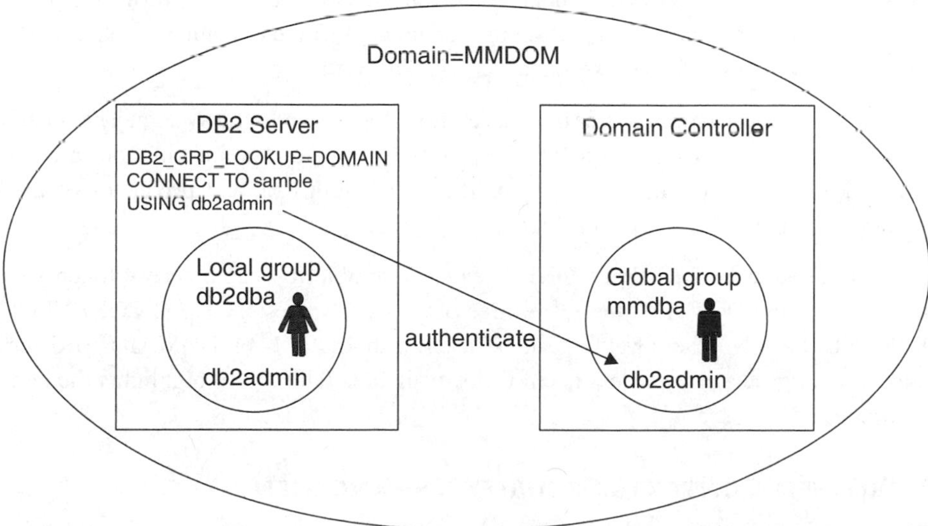

Figure 11.53 Support of LOCAL or DOMAIN group lookup

A user connects to the database as *db2admin* and tries to drop a table. Which group do you want DB2 to enumerate for *db2admin*? It is important for DB2 to enumerate the right group because local group DB2DBA might only hold SELECT privileges on the table, whereas the global group MMDBA has SYSADM authority.

The first option is to include the Windows domain with the user ID during authentication, such as in the **CONNECT** statement or the **attach** command. The fully qualified DB2 authentication ID can be as long as 30 characters. This makes group lookup on Windows more deterministic.

```
CONNECT TO sample USER mmdba/db2admin USING password
```

Note that the fully qualified authentication ID also works in **GRANT** and **REVOKE** statements. For example:

```
GRANT SELECT ON TABLE employee TO USER mmdba/db2admin
```

Alternatively, use the DB2 registry variable DB2_GRP_LOOKUP to tell DB2 where to validate user accounts and perform group member lookup. Set the variable to LOCAL to force DB2 to always enumerate groups and validate user accounts locally on the DB2 server. Set the variable to DOMAIN to force DB2 to always enumerate groups and validate user accounts on the Windows domain to which the user account belongs. For example:

```
db2set DB2_GRP_LOOKUP = DOMAIN
```

11.8.2 Access Tokens

If a user wants to log onto his or her laptop as a domain user in a disconnected environment, Windows supports this via cached credentials. When a credential is cached, information kept from the last logon is referenced if the machine cannot contact the domain controller. DB2 supports this behavior by using an access token.

An access token is created after a user has successfully logged on to the system. The token is an object that describes the security context of a process or thread. The information in an access token includes the identity, all of the groups the user belongs to, and privileges of the user account associated with the process or thread.

You can also use the DB2_GRP_LOOKUP registry variable to enable access token support. Besides LOCAL and DOMAIN, there are three other valid values: TOKEN, TOKENLOCAL, and TOKENDOMAIN. These values can be used with LOCAL or DOMAIN to determine where to look up groups if an access token is not available. Table 11.11 highlights the behavior of these values.

V9.5 11.9 Trusted Contexts Security Enhancement

The three-tiered application model has gained great popularity in recent years with the emergence of web-based technologies and the Java 2 Enterprise Edition (J2EE) platform. Examples of such applications include IBM WebSphere Application Server, and BEA WebLogic. In a

Table 11.11 DB2_GRP_LOOKUP Registry Variable Settings

DB2_GRP_LOOKUP Setting	Description
TOKEN	Enables access token support to look up all groups that the user belongs to at the location where the user account is defined.
LOCAL, TOKENLOCAL	Enables access token support to look up local groups or to fallback to use LOCAL group lookup if an access token is not available.
DOMAIN, TOKENDOMAIN	Enables access token support to look up domain groups or to fall-back to DOMAIN group lookup if an access token is not available.

three-tiered application model, the middle tier is responsible for authenticating the users running the client applications and for managing the interactions with the database server. While the three-tiered application model has many benefits, having all interactions with the database server occur under the middle tier's authorization ID raises some security concerns as follows:

- Loss of end user identity within the database server
- Diminished user accountability
- Overgranting of privileges to the middle tier's authorization ID

The trusted contexts feature introduced in DB2 9.5 can very well address these security challenges. A trusted context is a database object that defines a trust relationship for a connection between the database and an external entity such as an application server. By using trusted contexts, the actual user's identity and database privileges will be used for database requests performed by the middle tier on behalf of that user.

A typical scenario of using trusted contexts is:

1. The security administrator (who holds SECADM authority) creates a trusted context database object to define a trust relationship between the database and the mid-tier. The trust relationship is based upon attributes, such as system authorization ID, IP address, and data stream encryption.
2. The application developer uses proper APIs to initiate an explicit trusted connection or to switch the user on the current explicit trusted connection. Such application will allow the middle-tier to establish an explicit trusted connection to the database, which gives the middle-tier the ability to switch the current user ID on the connection to a different user ID, with or without authentication.

There are more examples in the DB2 Information Center, which illustrates how to use and develop your applications using trusted contexts in a three-tier application model.

11.10 Case Study

Assume that you have just created a database (SAMPLE) in a DB2 instance (DB2) for application testing. Before the testers can access the database, you need to make sure they have all the necessary privileges and authorities to perform requested database operations.

First of all, you want to enforce that all client authentications are validated at the server. To retrieve the current authentication setting, issue the following command:

```
get dbm cfg
```

The result indicates that user IDs and passwords will be authenticated at the DB2 server:

```
Database manager authentication          (AUTHENTICATION) = SERVER
```

Recently, a company-wide alert announced that encryption should be used wherever possible to prevent eavesdropping. To do this, you can update the database manager authentication to SERVER_ENCRYPT so that both user IDs and passwords are encrypted.

You decide to update the authentication type using the **update dbm cfg** command:

```
update dbm cfg using authentication server_encrypt
```

You then stop and restart the DB2 instance.

Besides encrypting user IDs and passwords, data requested from and returned to the database can also be encrypted. You configure this at each DB2 client using the following command:

```
catalog db sample at node dbsrv authentication sql_authentication_dataenc_cmp
```

Besides configuring the DB2 clients and server to perform secured authentication and data encryption, data access must be restricted to authorized users only. As you can see from the result of the **get dbm cfg** command, the system groups all default to NULL (i.e., users who have system administrative or root privileges).

To make sure only the assigned users can perform DB2 administrative tasks, you set the system groups to the appropriate groups:

```
update dbm cfg using sysadm grpadmin sysctrl grpctrl
     sysmaint grpmaint sysmon grpmon
```

Cynthia, who is a member of the *grpadmin* group, connects to the SAMPLE database and issues the following statements:

```
CREATE TABLE topsecret_table
     ( empno         CHAR(6)
     , name          VARCHAR(50)
     , perf_grade    CHAR(1)
     , salary_inc_pct INTEGER);

INSERT INTO topsecret_table
     VALUES ('000010', 'Bill', 'F', 0)
          , ('000020', 'John', 'A', 80)
          , ('000030', 'Kathy','C', 20);
```

The *topsecret_table* was successfully created and populated because *Cynthia* is a member of the SYSADM group who can perform any operation on the instance and its associated databases.

Bill found out that he will be getting an *F* grade in his performance review and will not get any salary increase. Being a member of the *grpmaint* group, he thinks he has the authority to update the records in the *topsecret_table* table. Therefore, he connects to the SAMPLE database and issues the following statement:

```
UPDATE topsecret_table
   SET perf_grade = 'A', salary_inc_pct = 100
 WHERE empno = '000010'
```

The update was not successful. The following error was received:

```
SQL0551N  "DB2USER" does not have the privilege to perform operation "UPDATE" on
object "DB2ADMIN.EMPLOYEE".  SQLSTATE=42501
```

This works as expected because users who have just the SYSCTRL, SYSMAINT, or SYSMON authority do not have the ability to retrieve or modify data. They only have the authority to perform system maintenance or monitor tasks.

By default, four privileges are granted to PUBLIC when a database is created. You should lock down the database by revoking privileges that are implicitly granted:

```
REVOKE CONNECT, CREATETAB, BINADD, IMPLICIT_SCHEMA
    ON DATABASE FROM PUBLIC
```

Then, grant privileges to users which they only need.

```
GRANT SELECT, UPDATE, DELETE, INDEX ON TABLE employee TO USER john
```

11.11 Summary

This chapter introduced the DB2 security model. To connect to a DB2 database, user and password authentication is performed outside of DB2 using the security facility provided by the operating system of the DB2 server, by Kerberos, or through customized security plug-ins. Security plug-ins are loadable library modules that implement security mechanisms to be used for user authentication.

Setting the authentication type at the DB2 server and client determines where authentication will take place. At the DB2 server, authentication type is defined in the Database Manager Configuration file. DB2 clients specify an authentication type for each database it connects to when the database is being cataloged.

Once a user is successfully authenticated, the user must have appropriate database authorities and/or privileges before he or she can perform database tasks and operations. Database authorities are required for a user to perform database administration tasks such as database creation or database backup.

Database privileges for various types of database objects are granted and revoked through the **GRANT** and **REVOKE** statements. With the implementation of Role-Based Access Control (RBAC) in DB2 9.5, the assignment and update of priviledges are much simplified by granting priviledges to roles instead of individual user IDs.

Label-Based Access Control (LBAC) lets you decide exactly who has read and write data access to individual rows and columns in tables.

There are special considerations for a DB2 server on Windows configured in a Windows domain, for example, for local or global group lookup. DB2 lets you use the registry variable DB2_GRP_ LOOKUP to identify where the user is being enumerated for group resolution.

11.12 Review Questions

1. Where does DB2 store information about the users who can access DB2?
2. Besides performing user ID and password authentication at the DB2 server or DB2 client, what other authentication mechanisms does DB2 support?
3. When does a user need the BINDADD privilege on a database?
4. If *bob* is connected to a database and wants to create a table *foo* in the *ts1* table space, what privileges must he have to run the following statement?
   ```
   CREATE TABLE mary.foo (c1 INT, c2 INT) IN ts1
   ```
5. A user ID *bob* who is a member of group *dba* is defined on the DB2 server. Why would the following fail to give SYSCTRL authority to user *bob*?
   ```
   update dbm cfg using sysctrl bob
   ```
6. In a Windows environment where a DB2 server is defined inside a domain called *domprod*, user ID *db2admin* is only defined in the domain controller as a member of the global group *glbgrp*. If you want to log on to the DB2 server as the domain user *domprod\db2admin* and perform tasks such as creating a new database, what are the three key steps you have to take?
7. You want to authenticate users at the clients. What are the three types of clients that the parameter TRUST_ALLCLNTS evaluates?
8. You have just created a database. Other than the members of the SYSADM group, you want to allow only *bob* to create new tables in the database. What DCL command do you have to issue?
9. *Mary* wrote an embedded SQL program with static SQL statements. A package is created and bound to the database. What privilege does *bob* need to use the package?
10. Given the following Database Manager Configuration parameters on your DB2 instance running on the Linux Server DBL1:
    ```
    Database manager authentication        (AUTHENTICATION) = CLIENT
    Trust all clients                      (TRUST_ALLCLNTS) = NO
    Trusted client authentication          (TRUST_CLNTAUTH) = CLIENT
    ```
    If you are connecting to the database from a Windows ME client, where will authentication take place?

11. If you are connecting to a DB2 database on a UNIX server named DBX1 from a Linux client named DBL1, where will the user ID be authenticated by default?
    A. DBL1
    B. DBX1
12. If you have configured DB2 with the authentication set to SERVER_ENCRYPT, which of the following describes what is encrypted?
    A. Data
    B. Data and user IDs
    C. User IDs and passwords
    D. Data, user IDs, and passwords
13. Given the following Database Manager Configuration parameters on your DB2 instance running on the Linux Server DBL1:

```
Database manager authentication              (AUTHENTICATION) = CLIENT
Trust all clients                            (TRUST_ALLCLNTS) = YES
Trusted client authentication                (TRUST_CLNTAUTH) = CLIENT
```

    If you are connecting to the database from a Windows ME client, where will authentication take place?
    A. The client
    B. The server
14. Which two of the following DB2 authorities can select data from tables?
    SYSADM
    A. SYSCTRL
    B. SYSMAINT
    C. DBADM
    D. SYSMON
15. Which of the following can be encrypted with DB2?
    A. User IDs
    B. Passwords
    C. All data
    D. User IDs, passwords, and data
16. Which of the following groups can create and drop event monitors?
    A. SYSADM
    B. SYSMON
    C. SYSCTRL
    D. SYSMAINT
17. Which of the following authorities cannot take a DB2 trace?
    A. SYSADM
    B. SYSMON
    C. SYSCTRL
    D. SYSMAINT

18. Given the following:

- User1 grants CREATEIN privilege on the schema *foo* to Fred with grant option.
- Joe grants CREATEIN privilege on the schema *foo* to Barney with grant option.
- User1 revokes CREATEIN privilege on the schema *foo* from Fred.
- Barney grants CREATEIN privilege on the schema *foo* to Wilma.
- Wilma grants CREATEIN privilege on the schema *foo* to Betty.

Which of the following still have CREATEIN privilege on the schema *foo*?

A. Barney
B. Barney and Wilma
C. Barney, Wilma, and Betty
D. No one

19. Given the table space *tsp1* that is created with default options, which of the following sets of commands will ensure only the group *grp1* can use the table space?

A. GRANT USE OF TABLESPACE tsp1 TO grp1
B. GRANT USER OF TABLESPACE tsp1 TO grp1 WITH GRANT OPTION
C. REVOKE USE OF TABLESPACE FROM ALL
D. GRANT USE OF TABLESPACE tsp1 TO GRP1
E. REVOKE USE OF TABLESPACE FROM PUBLIC
F. GRANT USE OF TABLESPACE tsp1 TO GRP1

20. If a DBA wants to find out whether user *bob* has CREATETAB privileges, which of the following system catalog tables should the DBA query?

A. SYSCAT.TABAUTH
B. SYSCAT.TABLES
C. SYSCAT.DBAUTH
D. SYSCAT.SCHEMAAUTH

CHAPTER 12

Understanding Concurrency and Locking

You need to establish or define some rules and locking semantics to guarantee data integrity in case more than one user tries to update the same row of data in a multi-user database environment. DB2 uses four isolation levels to support different levels of concurrency. Each isolation level is implemented by slightly different locking behaviors. In this chapter we will look at their differences and some examples of how they can be used in the application. As a database administrator or an application developer you will find it very helpful to know troubleshooting skills to identify locking problems, and this chapter covers DB2 monitoring tools to do this.

In this chapter you will learn about:

- The big picture of the DB2 locking mechanism
- Different concurrency scenarios
- The DB2 isolation levels
- How DB2 isolation levels affect locking
- Troubleshooting tools that come with DB2 to identify locking problems
- Avoiding locking problems

12.1 DB2 Locking and Concurrency: The Big Picture

Figure 12.1 provides an overview of the DB2 locking mechanism using isolation levels. Isolation levels can be configured by various methods. Depending on the isolation level specified, DB2 performs locking differently. The following sections discuss these in more detail.

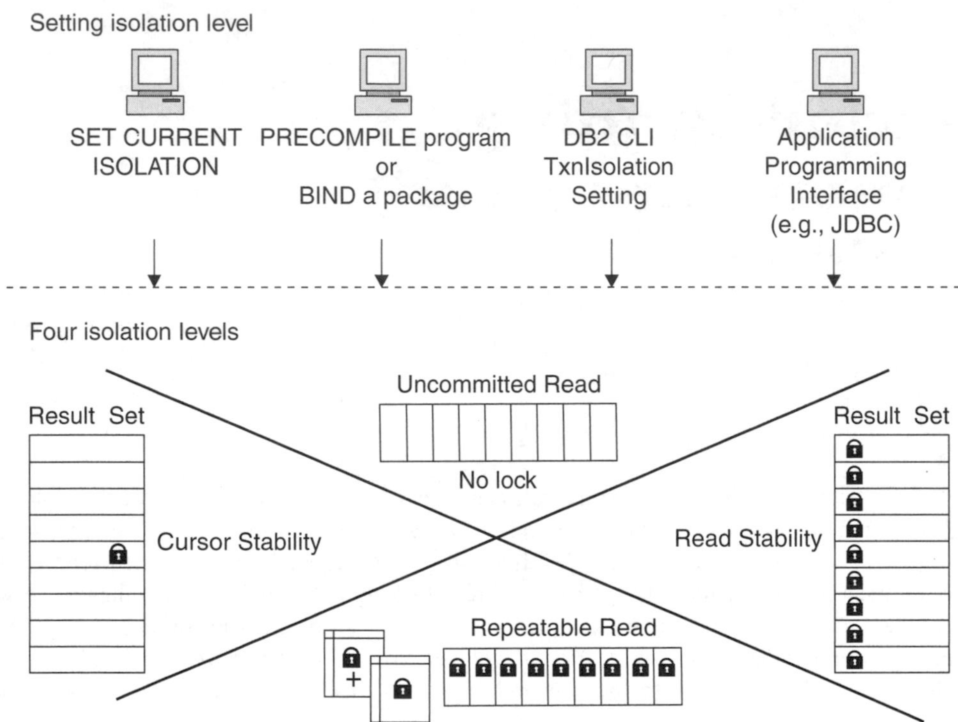

Figure 12.1 Overview of locking and concurrency

12.2 Concurrency and Locking Scenarios

Like many other database systems, DB2 provides support for concurrent data access. While the database is being accessed and manipulated by multiple users, it is important to keep data integrity by using database locking. Before getting into detailed discussions about DB2 locking, you should first understand various concurrent data access scenarios you may encounter and how each DB2 isolation level can prevent these scenarios from occurring or allow these scenarios to occur, if desired.

12.2.1 Lost Updates

Assume there is an airline reservation system with multiple agents answering calls for seat reservations. A table called *reservations* is defined to store flight numbers, seat assignments, and passenger names. Each seat on every flight is represented by a single row of data. Figure 12.2 shows the *reservations* table.

Suppose customer Harry Jones wants to reserve a seat on Flight 512 and calls the reservation center. An agent, Sam, receives the call and finds the only seat available, 4A, for Harry. While Harry is confirming the itinerary with his wife, Sam maintains the available seat on his screen.

Flight	Seat	Passenger_name
512	1C	John Smith
512	1D	Arnold Page
512	23A	Tim Chan
512	13B	Bernard Reid
512	4A	–

Figure 12.2 Sample content of the reservations table

At this time, agent Mary is helping another customer, Billy Bee, to fulfill his request. Mary also finds 4A, the last seat on Flight 512.

Eventually, Harry decides to confirm the seat and Sam assigns seat 4A to Harry. However, Mary does not see Harry's update and she assigns the same seat to Billy. Both seat assignments are successful, but guess who gets the seat? If the list of seats is retrieved again, you will see that the second update overwrites the first one (see Figure 12.3). Hence, Sam loses the seat assignment and Harry will not be able to get on the plane as he expects.

Flight	Seat	Passenger_name
512	1C	John Smith
512	1D	Arnold Page
512	23A	Tim Chan
512	13B	Bernard Reid
512	4A	Billy Bee

Figure 12.3 Sample content of the updated reservations table

This example demonstrates that if there is no mechanism in place to maintain the accuracy of data, it is possible to lose updates without knowing it or until the customers find out for themselves.

By default, DB2 acquires a lock on every record that the agent is updating. This default behavior cannot be changed. With this type of lock, no other agent can update the same row of data. If this reservation system is implemented in DB2, this scenario of lost update will never occur. When Sam is updating the record, all other read operations (except uncommitted read) and all write operations to the same row of data will wait until Sam's transaction is completed. Once Sam has committed the change, Mary will see the new seat assignment in her next data retrieval, so Billy will not be assigned to the seat.

Two terms are introduced here that warrant some discussion. A **transaction** (also known as a **unit of work**) is a sequence of SQL statements that the database manager treats as a whole. Any reading from or writing to the database is performed in a transaction. At the end of a transaction, the application can **COMMIT** or **ROLLBACK** the changes. Once you issue a **COMMIT** operation, changes are written to the database. A **ROLLBACK** operation causes the changes within the transaction to be rolled back. Transactions are discussed in more detail in Chapter 14, Developing Database Backup and Recovery Solutions.

12.2.2 Uncommitted Reads

Using the same flight reservation example, assume Sam is updating a row to assign a seat. Since DB2 locks the row by default, no other agent can read or update the same record. Meanwhile, the manager wants to run a report to determine how many passengers are scheduled to fly on Flight 512. Because of the default locking behavior, the manager's request has to wait until Sam's update is completed. However, if the manager's application is implemented to read uncommitted data, the manager can run the report without waiting for Sam to complete his transaction. This type of read is called an **uncommitted read** or a **dirty read.** However, changes Sam makes are not guaranteed to be written to the database. Therefore, if he decides to roll back the changes, the manager will get a different result when running the report again.

Whether an uncommitted read is desireable or not, it is based on the application design. As you can imagine, applications with the ability to read uncommitted data can respond promptly because there is no need to acquire and wait for locks. However, you must understand that the data retrieved is *not* committed data, which means that the data may not be the same the next time you query it.

12.2.3 Nonrepeatable Reads

Suppose Harry asks Sam to find an aisle seat on Flight 512. Sam issues a query and retrieves a list of available seats on the flight. Figure 12.4 shows such a list where (the NULL value) in the Passenger Name column means the seat is not assigned.

Flight	Seat	Passenger_name
512	5B	–
512	6E	–
512	8C	–
512	13E	–
512	15E	–

Figure 12.4 Available seats on Flight 512

In this aircraft model, only C and D seats are aisle seats. There is only one aisle seat available on this flight, seat 8C. Before Sam reserves seat 8C for Harry, no lock is acquired on this row highlighted in Figure 12.4. At this time, Mary has assigned and committed the same aisle seat to another customer, Billy. When Sam is ready and tries to assign Seat 8C to Harry, the update fails because the seat is no longer available. If the same query is issued, Figure 12.5 shows that seat 8C is no longer available.

Flight	Seat	Passenger_name
512	5B	–
512	6E	–
512	13E	–
512	15E	–

Figure 12.5 Updated available seats on Flight 512

This is an example of a **nonrepeatable read** scenario for which a different result set is returned with the same query within the same transaction. To avoid this situation, all the rows returned from the result set, shown in Figure 12.4, should be locked. This way, no other user can update the rows currently being read until the transaction is completed. However, concurrency will be decreased because of the extra locks being held.

12.2.4 Phantom Reads

A **phantom read** is similar to a nonrepeatable read: while rows currently read are not updatable or removable by another user, new rows *can* be inserted into the tables that fall under the query criteria.

The flight reservation application is designed in a way that all rows in a result set are locked. Due to the demand of this particular flight, the airline decides to upgrade the aircraft to a larger one so that more passengers can be served. Since more seats are added to the flight, the same query used before to obtain available seat will now return extra rows. If the aircraft upgrade is made in the middle of another query transaction, the next execution of the same query will result in extra "phantom" rows. Depending on the situation, reading phantom rows may or may not be desireable with the application. To avoid this behavior, extra locking is required.

12.3 DB2 Isolation Levels

DB2 provides four isolation levels to control locking behavior. From the lowest isolation level to the highest these are

- Uncommitted read
- Cursor stability
- Read stability
- Repeatable read

These isolation levels use different locking strategies, so you can choose the level of data protection depending on the application design.

12.3.1 Uncommitted Reads

Uncommitted read (UR) is the lowest isolation level but provides the highest concurrency to the database applications. When you configure an application to perform uncommitted reads, the application will not acquire any row locks to read data. However, a nonrestrictive table lock is required (see Section 12.5, DB2 Locking, for more information). Since no row locks are acquired, there is no conflict with any read or write operations undergoing on the same data. With this isolation level, uncommitted reads, nonrepeatable reads, and phantom reads can occur.

Figure 12.6 shows an example of two applications accessing the same row. Assume that App A locks row 2 for an update operation. No other application can make changes to row 2 until App A commits or rolls back. The only concurrent operation that can be issued against row 2 is an uncommitted read as illustrated by App B.

No row lock is acquired for read operations for applications configured with the UR isolation level. For any update, insert, or delete operation, an application with UR will still hold locks obtained to perform these operations until the transaction is committed or rolled back. App C in Figure 12.6 illustrates this.

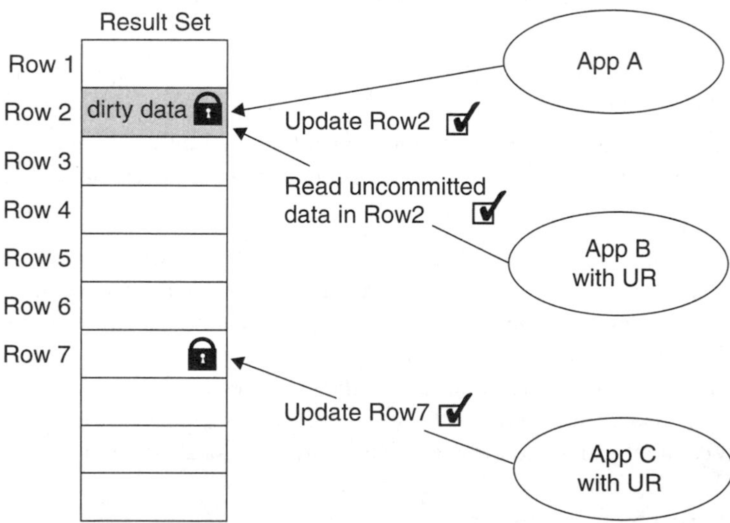

Figure 12.6 Concurrent data access with the uncommitted read isolation level

12.3.2 Cursor Stability

Cursor stability (CS) is the default DB2 isolation level. This isolation level works well with most applications because it uses a degree of locking sufficient to protect data, and at the same time it also provides a high level of concurrency. As the name of this isolation level implies, it uses a mechanism to provide a stable read on the latest row accessed. DB2 will only lock the row currently being read.

A cursor can be viewed as a pointer to one row in a set of rows (also called a **result set**). You need to OPEN the cursor so that it is positioned just before the first row of the result set. To move the cursor to the next row, you execute a FETCH operation. As a best practice, you should CLOSE the cursor when it is no longer required.

When a cursor is opened, no lock is acquired until the application fetches the first row of the result set. In the same unit of work, if the application fetches the second row, DB2 will release the previous row lock and acquire a lock on the second row. In Figure 12.7, App A with a CS isolation level fetches row 2. This application will only lock the row it is reading: row 2. When App D tries to alter that particular row, it has to wait.

In Figure 12.7 App B holds a lock on row 7 for read (fetching). At the same time, App C obtains a share lock and can still read the same row. Therefore, with isolation level CS, concurrent reads are still possible.

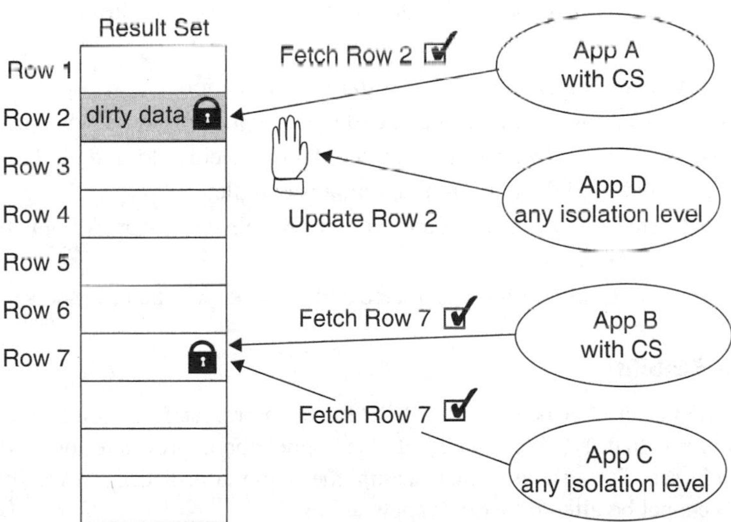

Figure 12.7 Concurrent read with two applications in cursor stability isolation level

Using isolation level CS, nonrepeatable read and phantom read scenarios can still occur; however, the uncommitted read scenario is not possible.

Now you understand that a row lock is released when the application with CS reads the next row. But what happens if the application makes changes to a row while it is being read? Figure 12.8 illustrates this scenario.

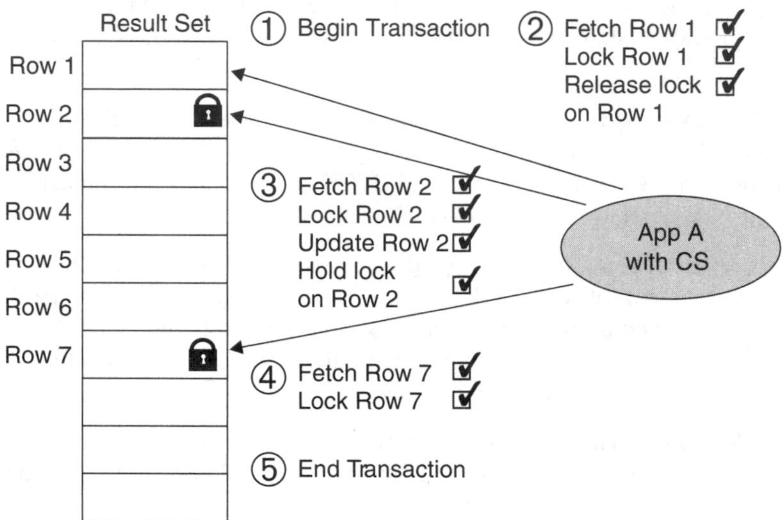

Figure 12.8 Reading and updating data with cursor stability isolation level

(1) App A uses CS isolation level and starts a transaction.
(2) App A locks row 1 for read. App A releases the lock on row 1 when it fetches row 2.
(3) Row 2 is locked. During the read, the App A decides to update the row. The lock will be held until the current transaction is completed (5).
(4) App A fetches row 7 and acquires a lock. At this point App A holds two locks: one for read and one for update.
(5) The current transaction is completed and all locks will be released.

12.3.3 Read Stability

Read stability (RS) is another isolation level DB2 uses to protect data. Unlike CS, RS not only locks the current row that is being fetched; it also applies the appropriate locks to all rows that are in the result set. This ensures that within the same transaction, rows that have been previously read cannot be altered by other applications

Figure 12.9 shows that all the rows in the result set are locked even when the cursor is only processing a particular row. No wait is necessary if more than one application reads the same set of rows concurrently. However, any update operation will have to wait until the reads are completed.

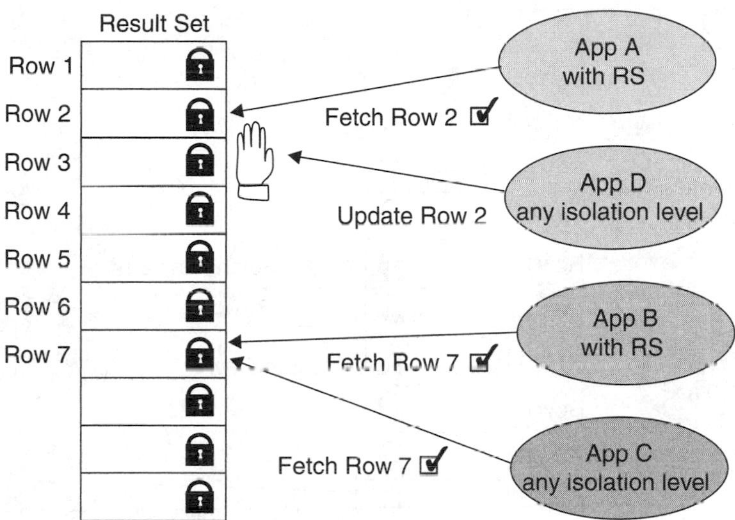

Figure 12.9 The read stability isolation level

RS causes DB2 to perform more locking than the UR or CS isolation levels. With RS, the uncommitted read and nonrepeatable read scenarios cannot occur; however, phantom reads can still happen.

Similar to the other isolation levels, if an application with RS updates a row, a lock will be held until the transaction is completed.

12.3.4 Repeatable Reads

Repeatable (RR) read is the highest and most restrictive isolation level. It also gives you the lowest concurrency. Similar to RS, applications with RR force DB2 to lock all the rows in the result set as well as rows that are accessed to build the result set. A query that involves a two-table join is issued and DB2 decides to perform table scans on both tables to obtain the result. This isolation level locks all the rows in the two tables. If a row is read by the application using RR, no other application can alter it until the transaction is completed. This ensures that your result set is consistent throughout the duration of the unit of work. One consideration is that the additional locking can greatly reduce concurrency.

In Figure 12.10, you can see that behavior for applications A, B, C, and D is the same as RS. However, even if App E tries to update a row in table T1 that is not in the result set, it still has to wait until the lock is released.

With repeatable read isolation level, none of the locking scenarios can occur. Applications with RR can only read committed data and perform repeatable read.

Table 12.1 summarizes the four isolation levels and locking scenarios that may occur.

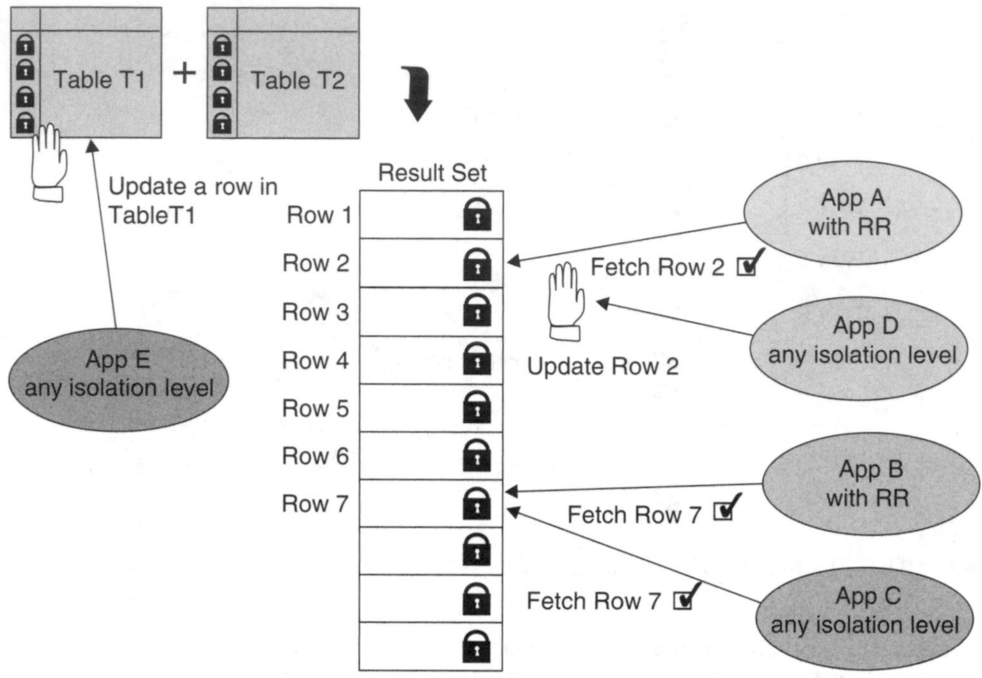

Figure 12.10 The repeatable read isolation level

Table 12.1 Four Isolation Levels and Locking Scenarios

Locking Scenarios	Uncommitted Read	Cursor Stability	Read Stability	Repeatable Read
Lost update	No	No	No	No
Uncommitted read	Yes	No	No	No
Nonrepeatable read	Yes	Yes	No	No
Phantom read	Yes	Yes	Yes	No

12.4 Changing Isolation Levels

The isolation level is not bound to a database. Each application and statements within an application can use a different isolation level so that a different locking mechanism can be applied. Isolation levels can be set at different levels:

- Session level
- Application level
- Statement level

The following sections describe each of these levels.

12.4.1 Using the DB2 Command Window

The current isolation level is stored in a DB2 special register called CURRENT ISOLATION. The special register is a value with two characters (data type of CHAR(2)) of the current isolation level for any dynamic SQL statements issued within the current session.

To obtain the current isolation level value, connect to the database and issue either of these statements:

```
VALUES CURRENT ISOLATION
SELECT CURRENT ISOLATION FROM sysibm.sysdummy1
```

The following are the possible values:

- UR (uncommitted read)
- CS (cursor stability)
- RS (read stability)
- RR (repeatable read)
- Blank (means that the default isolation level is used)

To change the isolation level, use the **SET CURRENT ISOLATION** statement. Figure 12.11 shows the syntax diagram for this statement.

```
       .-CURRENT-.                    .-=-.
>>-SET--+---------+--ISOLATION--+---+--+-UR----+---------------><
                                       +-CS----+
                                       +-RR----+
                                       +-RS----+
                                       '-RESET-'
```

Figure 12.11 Syntax diagram for the SET CURRENT ISOLATION command

Figure 12.12 demonstrates a few examples of how to set and obtain the current isolation level.

It is important to understand that changes to this DB2 register affect only the current session. Subsequent dynamic SQL statements executed in this session will use this isolation level. The change only applies for dynamic SQL statements. For static SQL statements or packages, you can control the isolation level through the DB2 **bind** command discussed in the next section.

12.4.2 Using the DB2 PRECOMPILE and BIND Commands

To execute an SQL statement, it must be compiled into an executable form that DB2 understands. This executable form of the statement is known as the **data access plan.** Data access plans are stored in database objects called **packages.**

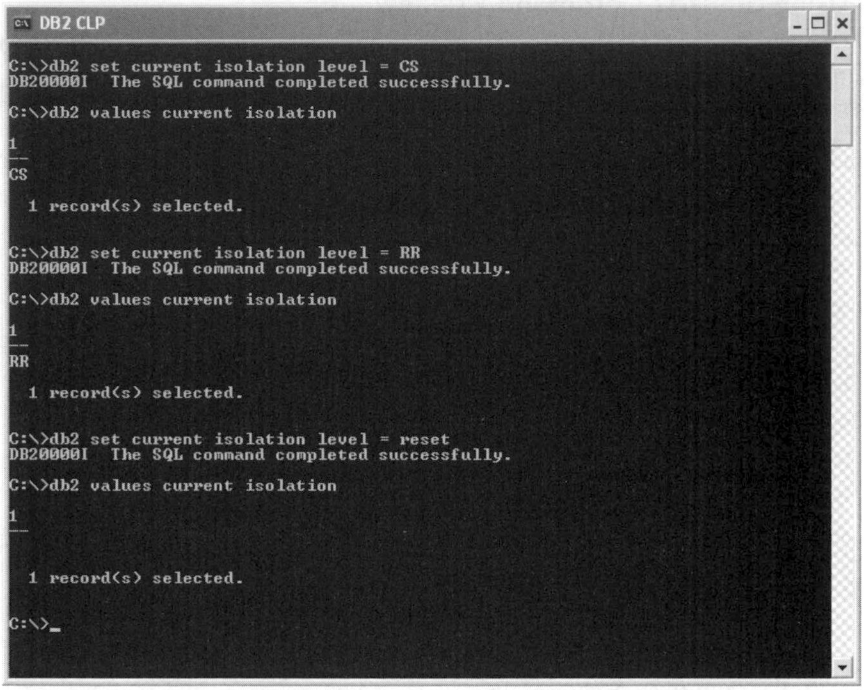

```
DB2 CLP
C:\>db2 set current isolation level = CS
DB20000I  The SQL command completed successfully.

C:\>db2 values current isolation

1
--
CS

  1 record(s) selected.

C:\>db2 set current isolation level = RR
DB20000I  The SQL command completed successfully.

C:\>db2 values current isolation

1
--
RR

  1 record(s) selected.

C:\>db2 set current isolation level = reset
DB20000I  The SQL command completed successfully.

C:\>db2 values current isolation

1
--


  1 record(s) selected.

C:\>_
```

Figure 12.12 Examples of the SET CURRENT ISOLATION LEVEL command

Data access plans for dynamic SQL statements are created at execution time. DB2 uses the most current table and index statistics, configuration parameters, and DB2 register settings (such as CURRENT ISOLATION) to evaluate and generate the most optimal plan.

When an application with static SQL statements is precompiled, the prepared statements are stored in a bind file generated by the DB2 precompiler. To create the database access plan from the bind file, you need to invoke the bind utility. The utility takes the bind file as input, creates a package that contains the data access plan, and binds it to the database.

Both the DB2 **precompile** and **bind** commands let you specify some characteristics of how the package should be executed, like the query optimization level, use of row blocking, and the isolation level. For example, if you want to precompile or bind a package using a nondefault isolation level, use:

```
precompile appfile.sqc isolation RR
```

or

```
bind bindfilename.bnd isolation RR
```

where *appfile.sqc* is an embedded C program containing static SQL, and *bindfilename.bnd* is a bind file containing SQL in internal format that is to be bound into a package.

Once the package is bound, you can use the system catalog tables or DB2 Control Center to find out the isolation level specified.

Using the system catalog tables, you can issue the following query:

```
SELECT pkgschema, pkgname, isolation FROM syscat.packages
```

Using the DB2 Control Center, navigate to the folders **Instance > Database > Application Objects > Packages.** You should see the isolation level column on the right panel, as shown in Figure 12.13. For example, the package highlighted in Figure 12.13 was bound with isolation level CS.

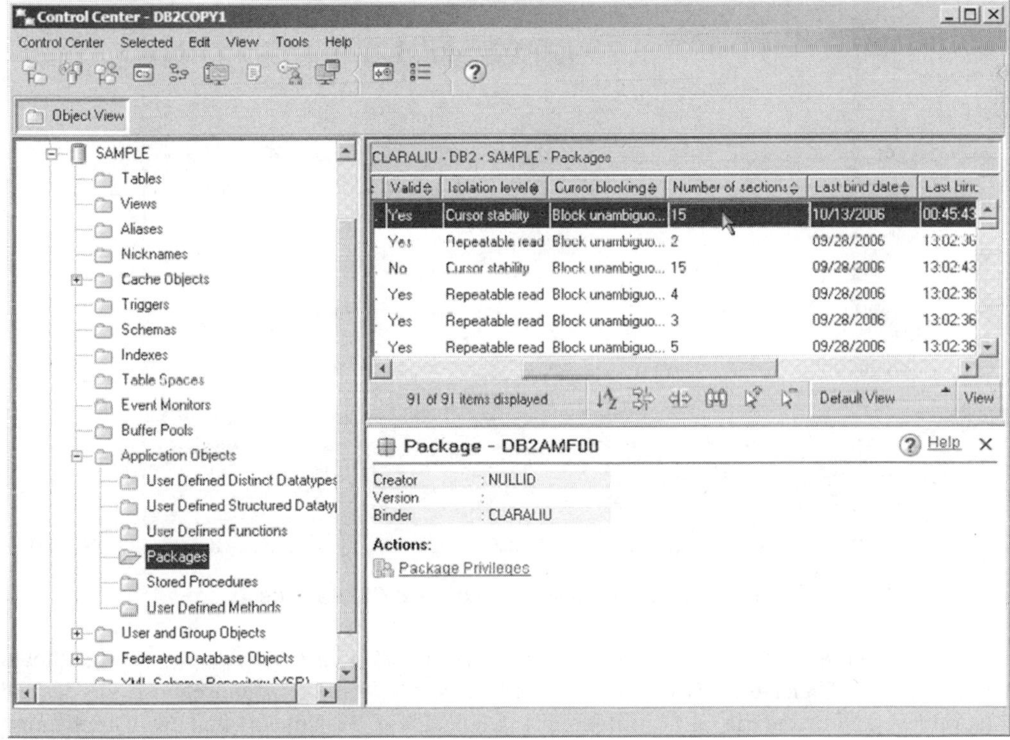

Figure 12.13 Using the Control Center to retrieve the isolation level of packages

12.4.3 Using the DB2 Call Level Interface

The DB2 call level interface (CLI) is the IBM callable SQL interface to DB2 database servers. It is a C/C++ application programming interface (API) for database access. If your application is using the DB2 CLI API, you can also set the isolation level with the CLI setting.

At the DB2 client, launch the Configuration Assistant. Right click on the database you want to set the isolation level for, and select **CLI Settings** (see Figure 12.14).

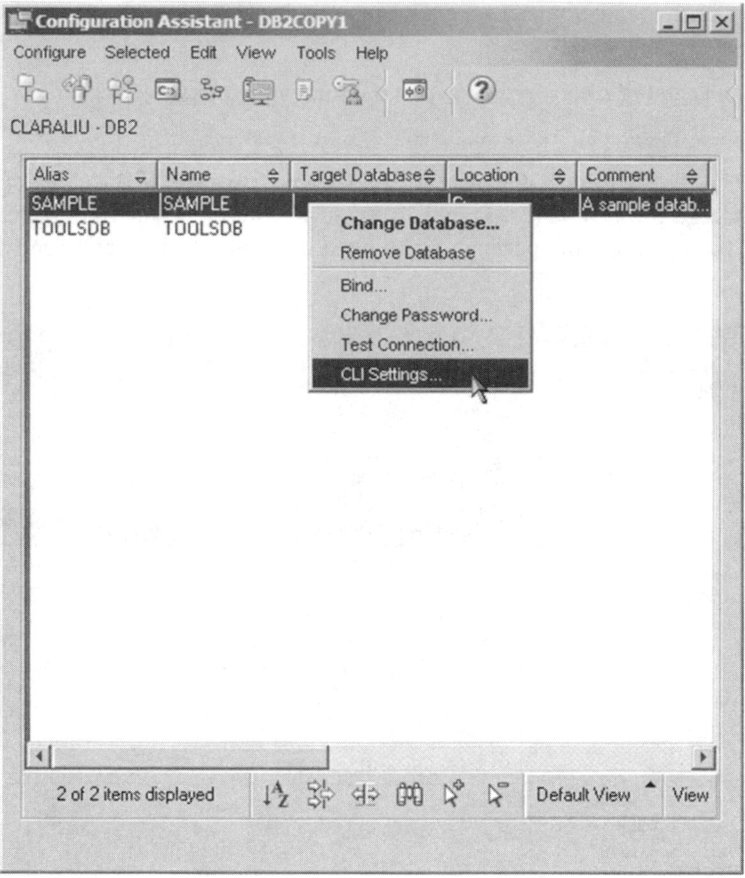

Figure 12.14 Using the Configuration Assistant to access CLI settings

Switch to the *Settings* tab and click *Add*. This displays the *Add CLI Parameter* window as shown in Figure 12.15. Under the list of CLI keywords, select *TxnIsolation* and choose the desired isolation level. Note that the CLI settings apply to a database. This means that every application connecting to the database through this DB2 client will use the isolation level specified.

If the Configuration Assistant is not available at the client, you can also update the DB2 CLI initialization file (db2cli.ini) directly. The file is located at the DB2 install directory. Insert *TxnIsolation* under the database name you want and enter the isolation level you want to use. Each isolation level is identified by a number (see Table 12.2). The following example shows how to set the isolation for the SAMPLE database to repeatable read.

```
[SAMPLE]
DBALIAS=SAMPLE
TXNIsolation=8
```

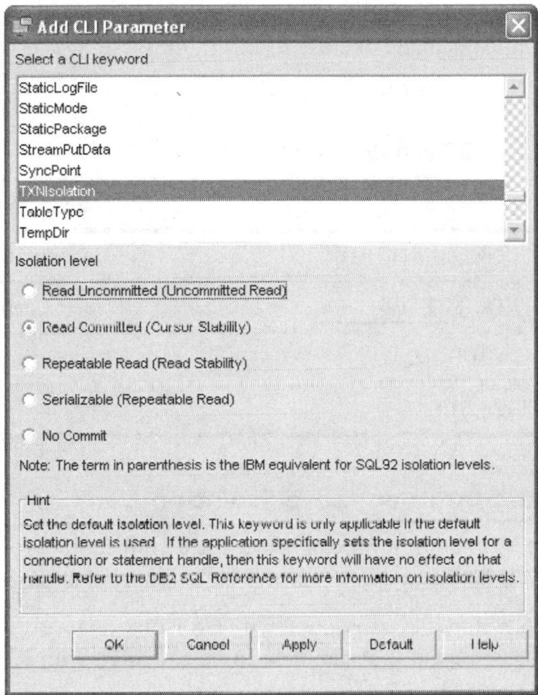

Figure 12.15 Setting the isolation level from the DB2 Configuration Assistant

Table 12.2 DB2 CLI Values for the Isolation Levels

	Uncommitted Read	Cursor Stability	Read Stability	Repeatable Read
TXNIsolation Value	1	2	4	8

12.4.4 Using the Application Programming Interface

In addition to the CLI, DB2 provides various types of programming interfaces that your application can use. The Java Common Client for DB2 is one example. Most APIs such as Java Database Connectivity (JDBC) provide an option to specify the isolation level. A code snippet from a JDBC program is listed in Figure 12.16. For other APIs, check with the associated programming documentations.

```
Class.forName("com.ibm.db2.jcc.DB2Driver");
Connection con=null;
con = DriverManager.getConnection (jdbc:db2:sample,username,password);
con.setTransactionIsolation(TRANSACTION_READ_UNCOMMITTED);
```

Figure 12.16 Snippet of a JDBC program to specify an isolation level

The names of the isolation levels used in APIs are usually different from those used in DB2. JDBC and DB2 isolation level mappings are listed in Table 12.3. For other APIs, refer to the documentation.

Table 12.3 Comparable JDBC and DB2 Isolation Levels

JDBC	DB2
TRANSACTION_READ_UNCOMMITTED	Uncommitted read
TRANSACTION_READ_COMMITTED	Cursor stability
TRANSACTION_REPEATABLE_READ	Read stability
TRANSACTION_SERIALIZABLE	Repeatable read

12.4.5 Working with Statement Level Isolation Level

So far, you have seen that isolation level can be set for a connection. To provide more granular concurrency control, DB2 has the ability to specify isolation level at the statement level.

Suppose an application has started a transaction with CS isolation level. To increase concurrency of a particular statement, you want the statement to be executed with RR isolation level. To do so, use the isolation clause **WITH RR:**

```
UPDATE employee SET salary = 10000 WHERE empno='000010' WITH RR
```

Similarly, you can apply the **WITH** clause to the **INSERT, DELETE,** and **SELECT** statements. The same clause in the **SELECT** statement has an extra option for the RR and RS isolation level. Figure 12.17 shows the syntax diagram of the **SELECT** statement's isolation clause.

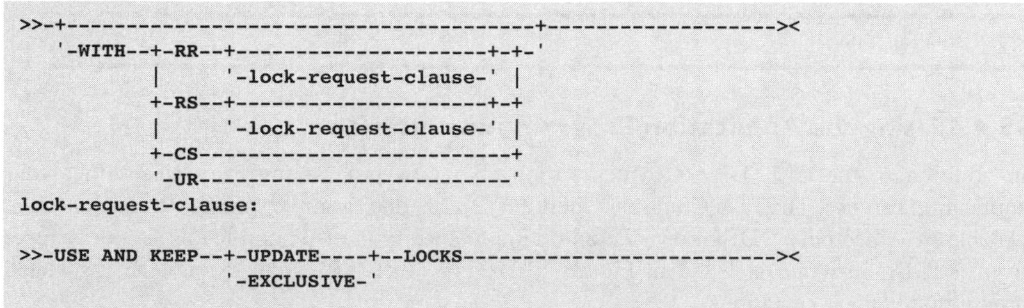

Figure 12.17 Syntax diagram of the SELECT statement's isolation clause

The **lock-request-clause** is optional and specifies the type of lock that DB2 will acquire and hold. The owner of an UPDATE lock can update the row being locked. Concurrent processes can only read the data in the locked object but cannot update it. EXCLUSIVE lock, on the other hand, is a more restrictive type of lock. It does not allow concurrent processes to acquire any lock on the data.

A **SELECT** statement with the isolation clause will look similar to the following:

```
SELECT empno, lastname, firstnme
  FROM employee
 WHERE deptno='A01'
  WITH RR USE AND KEEP EXCLUSIVE LOCKS
```

12.5 DB2 Locking

DB2 uses various levels of locking to provide concurrent data access and at the same time protect the data. Depending on the operations requested, the database manager can acquire locks on table rows, table blocks, tables, table spaces, buffer pools, and databases. Locks are acquired implicitly by DB2 according to the semantics defined by the isolation level.

> **NOTE** Table blocks are groups of records that block-based indexes point to. These block-based indexes are called multi-dimensional clustering (MDC) indexes.

12.5.1 Lock Attributes

During normal data manipulation processing, DB2 uses row-level locking by default. You can override this rule to acquire table-level locking instead. The **ALTER TABLE** statement with the **LOCKSIZE** option forces DB2 to obtain a table level lock whenever the table is accessed. The statement will look like this:

```
ALTER TABLE employee LOCKSIZE TABLE
```

This setting is retained until you execute:

```
ALTER TABLE employee LOCKSIZE ROW
```

The only objects that you can explicitly lock are databases, tables, and table spaces. To explicitly lock a database, use the **CONNECT** statement with the appropriate lock mode. For example:

```
CONNECT TO sample IN EXCLUSIVE MODE
```

This causes an exclusive lock to be applied to the database. It prevents concurrent application from executing any operations at the database. This lock mode is useful when exclusive administrative tasks must be performed. You can also connect to the database in SHARE MODE, which allows other concurrent connections to the database but prevents other users from connecting in exclusive mode.

> **NOTE** When you need to perform exclusive administrative tasks at the instance, rather than the database level, use the **start database manager admin mode** command as explained in Chapter 5, Understanding the DB2 Environment, DB2 Instances, and Databases.

Table spaces for a particular table can be quiesced. **Quiescing** a table space is like locking a table space so that administrative tasks (e.g., a load operation) can be performed. With the different quiesce modes, shown in Figure 12.18, DB2 obtains different types of locks for the table and its associated table space(s). The syntax diagram of the **QUIESCE TABLESPACES FOR TABLE** command is presented in Figure 12.18.

```
>>-QUIESCE TABLESPACES FOR TABLE--+-tablename--------+---------->
                                  '-schema.tablename-'

>--+-SHARE------------+----------------------------------------><
   +-INTENT TO UPDATE-+
   +-EXCLUSIVE--------+
   '-RESET------------'
```

Figure 12.18 Syntax diagram of the quiesce tablespaces for table command

If you have quiesced the table spaces with a restrictive mode, access to tables within those tablespaces is not allowed. For example, this command:

```
QUIESCE TABLESPACES FOR TABLE employee EXCLUSIVE
```

puts strict table space locking on the table space where table *employee* is stored, and on the table *employee*. The state of the table space changes to QUIESCED EXCLUSIVE. No other access to the table spaces is allowed. This means that access to another table that is stored in the same table space is not allowed. You will receive the following error.

```
SQL0290N Table space access is not allowed SQLSTATE=55039
```

To unquiesce the table space, issue the same **QUIESCE TABLESPACES FOR TABLE** command but with the **RESET** option.

You can also lock a table explicitly with the **LOCK TABLE** statement. Similarly, different lock modes are available as shown in Figure 12.19. The **LOCK TABLE** statement locks the specified table until the transaction is completed.

```
>>-LOCK TABLE--+-table-name-+--IN--+-SHARE-----+--MODE---------><
               '-nickname---'      '-EXCLUSIVE-'
```

Figure 12.19 Syntax diagram of the LOCK TABLE statement

Each lockable object can be locked in a different mode; this represents the type of access allowed for the lock owner. Different lock modes also control the type of access permitted for concurrent users of the locked object.

12.5.1.1 Table-Level Lock Modes

Table and row locks are the most common types of locks being used. Figure 12.20 shows the table-level lock modes. The table lock modes IN, IS, IX, and SIX are used to support row-level locking. An application requires an IN lock on the table before it can perform an uncommitted read. The IS, IX, and SIX locks permit row-level locking while preventing more exclusive locks on the table by other applications.

The other table lock modes—S, U, X, and Z—are strict table locking and do not use row level locking. For example, if an application holds an X lock on a table, the lock owner can read or update any data in the table but cannot obtain a row lock. Refer to Table 12.4 for a summary of all table lock modes.

Table Lock Mode	Description	
IN	Intent None	Row locking also used
IS	Intent Share	Row locking also used
IX	Intent eXclusive	Row locking also used
SIX	Share with Intent eXclusive	Row locking also used
S	Share	Strict table locking
U	Update	Strict table locking
X	eXclusive	Strict table locking
Z	Superexclusive	Strict table locking

Figure 12.20 Table Lock Mode Compatibility Chart

12.5.1.2 Row Lock Modes

Row lock modes require support of some kind of table lock. The minimum table locks DB2 must acquire before obtaining a row lock are listed in Figure 12.21. For example, an application can lock a row in Share mode if it also holds an IS lock on the table.

Besides table and row locks, there are other types of objects DB2 locks. Table 12.4 presents a summary of lockable objects and lock modes. *Y* means that the lock mode applies to that type of object; a dash means that it does not apply.

Row Lock Mode	Description	Minimum Table Lock Required
S	**S**hare	IS
U	**U**pdate	IX
X	e**X**clusive	IX
W	**W**eak Exclusive	IX
NS	**N**ext Key **S**hare	IS
NW	**N**ext Key **W**eak exclusive	IX

Figure 12.21 Row Lock Mode Compatibility Chart

Table 12.4 Lock Modes Summary

Lock Mode	Buffer Pool	Table Space	Table Block	Table	Row	Description
IN (**I**ntent **N**one)	–	Y	Y	Y	–	The lock owner can read any data in the object, including uncommitted data, but cannot update any of it. Other concurrent applications can read or update the table.
IS (**I**ntent **S**hare)	–	Y	Y	Y	–	The lock owner can read data in the locked object but cannot update its data. Other applications can read or update the object.
NS (**N**ext Key **S**hare)	–	–	–	–	Y	The lock owner and all concurrent applications can read, but not update, the locked row. This lock is acquired on rows of a table where the isolation level of the application is either RS or CS. NS lock mode is not used for next-key locking. It is used instead of S mode during CS and RS scans to minimize the impact of next-key locking on these scans.
S (**S**hare)	–	–	Y	Y	Y	The lock owner and all concurrent applications can read but not update the locked data.

Table 12.4 Lock Modes Summary *(Continued)*

Lock Mode	Buffer Pool	Table Space	Table Block	Table	Row	Description
IX (**I**ntent e**X**clusive)	–	Y	Y	Y	–	The lock owner and concurrent applications can read and update data. Other concurrent applications can both read and update the table.
SIX (**S**hare with **I**ntent e**X**clusive)	–	–	Y	Y	–	The lock owner can read and update data. Other concurrent applications can read the table.
U (**U**pdate)	–	–	Y	Y	Y	The lock owner can update data. Other units of work can read the data in the locked object but cannot update it.
NW (**N**ext Key **W**eak Exclusive)	–	–	–	–	Y	When a row is inserted into an index, an NW lock is acquired on the next row. The lock owner can read but not update the locked row. This lock mode is similar to an X lock, except that it is also compatible with W and NS locks.
X (e**X**clusive)	Y	–	Y	Y	Y	The lock owner can both read and update data in the locked object. Only uncommitted read applications can access the locked object.
W (**W**eak Exclusive)	–	–	–	–	Y	This lock is acquired on the row when a row is inserted into a table. The lock owner can change the locked row. This lock is used during insertion into a unique index to determine if a duplicate value is found. This lock is similar to an X lock except that it is compatible with the NW lock. Only uncommitted read applications can access the locked row.

(*continues*)

Table 12.4 Lock Modes Summary *(Continued)*

Lock Mode	Buffer Pool	Table Space	Table Block	Table	Row	Description
Z (Super Exclusive)	–	Y	–	Y	–	This lock is acquired on a table in certain conditions, such as when the table is altered or dropped, an index on the table is created or dropped, and for some types of table reorganization. No other concurrent application can read or update the table.

NOTE If you use multidimensional clustering (MDC) tables, you can impose table block locks.

Figures 12.22 and 12.23 (from the DB2 manual *Administration Guide: Performance*) present lock mode compatibility charts for table and row locks respectively. *NO* means the requesting application must wait for the lock to be released and *YES* means the lock can be granted.

Mode of Lock for App A \ Mode of Lock for App B	IN	IS	S	IX	SIX	U	X	Z
IN	YES	YES	YES	YES	YES	YES	YES	NO
IS	YES	YES	YES	YES	YES	YES	NO	NO
IX	YES	YES	NO	YES	NO	NO	NO	NO
S	YES	YES	YES	NO	NO	YES	NO	NO
SIX	YES	YES	NO	NO	NO	NO	NO	NO
U	YES	YES	YES	NO	NO	NO	NO	NO
X	YES	NO	NO	NO	NO	NO	NO	NO
Z	NO	NO	NO	NO	NO	NO	NO	NO

Figure 12.22 Table lock mode compatibility chart

Mode of Lock for App A \ Mode of Lock for App B	S	U	X	W	NS	NW
S	YES	YES	NO	NO	YES	NO
U	YES	NO	NO	NO	YES	NO
X	NO	NO	NO	NO	NO	NO
W	NO	NO	NO	NO	NO	YES
NS	YES	YES	NO	NO	YES	YES
NW	NO	NO	NO	YES	YES	NO

Figure 12.23 Row lock mode compatibility chart

Let's use an example to demonstrate how to use the charts. Assume that application A is holding an IX lock on a table. Looking at the compatibility chart in Figure 12.22, you can see that another application can only lock the same table in IN, IS, or IX mode as highlighted with the circles in the figure.

If application B requests an IS lock at the table level and tries to read some rows in the table, use the row lock chart in Figure 12.23 to determine the compatibility of concurrent data access. As long as application A holds locks that are compatible with the lock mode application B is requesting, both applications can work concurrently with each other. For example, if application A is holding a U lock on a row, application B can only obtain an S or NS lock (refer to compatibility values circled in Figure 12.23). Otherwise, application B must wait for application A to complete its transaction.

12.5.2 Lock Waits

A discussion of DB2 locking mechanisms is not really complete if lock wait and deadlock scenarios are not covered. As the number of concurrent applications increases, the possibility of running into situations with incompatible locks is relatively higher. In the examples used to describe the behavior of the different isolation levels, you saw how an application might have to wait for a lock. This is known as **lock wait.** Deadlocks are discussed in the next section.

It is generally not possible to totally avoid lock wait as concurrency increases. After all, DB2 relies on the locking mechanism to keep data integrity. However, you should minimize lock waits and each wait length as much as possible. They put a hold on processing the statements, hence, they affect performance.

Note that you should minimize lock waits and the duration of each wait. You can use the database configuration parameter called LOCKTIMEOUT to define how long an application is going to wait for a lock. By default, LOCKTIMEOUT is set to -1, which stands for infinite wait. We recommend setting it to a finite number that works well with your application and business requirement.

If an application reaches the LOCKTIMEOUT value, it receives the following message:

```
SQL0911N The current transaction has been rolled back because of a deadlock or
timeout.  Reason code "68".
```

Reason code 68 indicates the transaction is rolled back due to a lock timeout. LOCKTIMEOUT applies to any application connecting to the database. In some cases, you may want to set the timeout duration for a given application rather than providing the same value for all applications. You can directly control how long an individual application will wait for a lock using the **`set current lock timeout`** command. This command overrides the LOCKTIMEOUT parameter and stores the new value in the DB2 special register CURRENT LOCK TIMEOUT. This would be useful, for example, in a system where there is a mixed workload of long-running reports as well as update batch jobs. Figure 12.24 gives the syntax of the command.

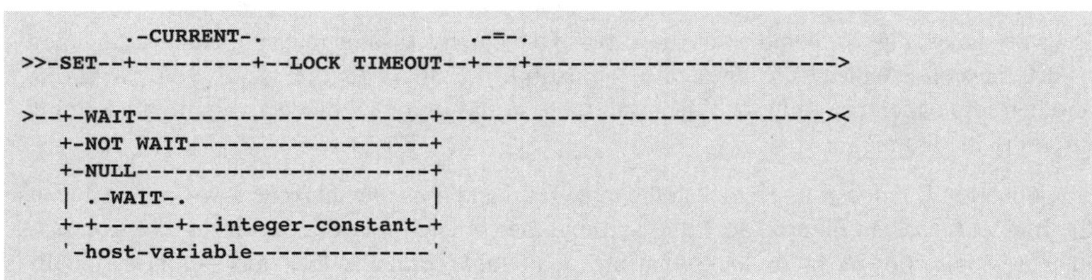

```
        .-CURRENT-.                .-=-.
>>-SET--+---------+--LOCK TIMEOUT--+---+------------------------>

>--+-WAIT-----------------------+------------------------------><
   +-NOT WAIT-------------------+
   +-NULL-----------------------+
   | .-WAIT-.                   |
   +-+------+--integer-constant-+
   '-host-variable--------------'
```

Figure 12.24 Syntax diagram of the set current lock timeout command

You can set the lock timeout period to the following.

- WAIT specifies that the application will wait infinitely for a lock.
- NOT WAIT specifies that the application will not wait for locks that cannot be obtained.
- NULL specifies that the application will use the value of the LOCKTIMEOUT database configuration parameter as the duration to wait for locks.
- WAIT *integer_constant* specifies an integer value of how long the application will wait for a lock. The value -1 will have the same behavior as WAIT (without an integer value). A value of 0 is equivalent to specifying NOT WAIT.

To validate the value of the CURRENT LOCK TIMEOUT special register, you can use the **VALUES** statement:

```
VALUES CURRENT LOCK TIMEOUT
```

12.5.3 Deadlocks

There is another undesirable lock scenario to avoid: deadlock. **Deadlock** is a situation when two applications are waiting for locks that the other is holding. Consider the situation in Figure 12.25.

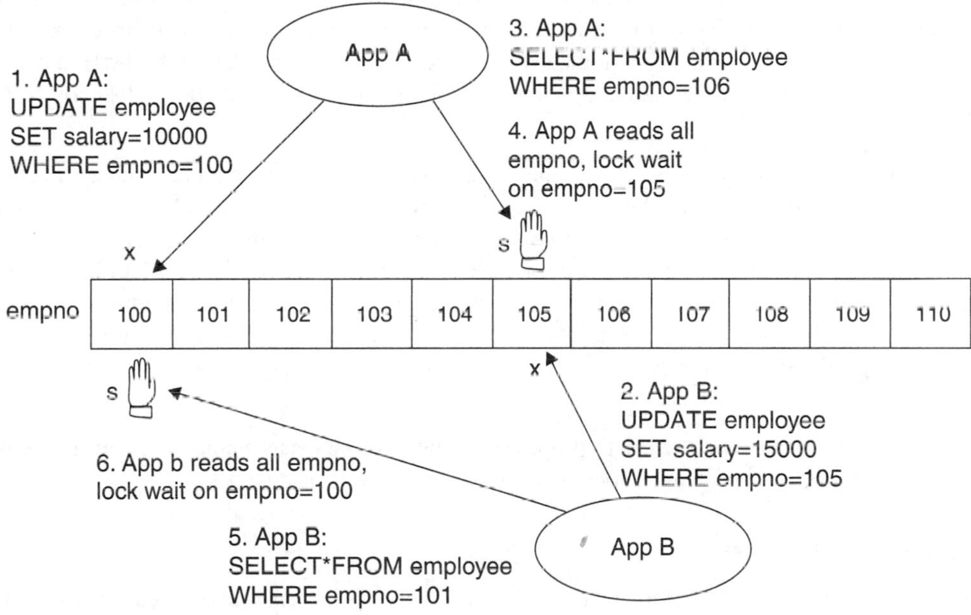

Figure 12.25 Example of a deadlock situation

(1) App A starts a transaction and updates the record where *empno* = 100. The record is locked by App A with an X lock.

(2) App B starts a transaction and updates the record where *empno* = 105. The record is locked by App B with an X lock.

(3 and 4) In the same transaction as (1), App A queries the table and scans for *empno* = 106. Assume that DB2 chooses to use a table scan to read each *empno* and see if it is 106. To perform a read, App A needs an S lock on every row. An S lock cannot be obtained for *empno* = 105 because the row is locked by App B with an incompatible lock, X.

(5 and 6) Similarly, App B is executing the same program to search for *empno* = 101. Assume that it also has to scan all the rows. App B will stop and wait for *empno* = 100 that is being locked by App A.

Apps A and B in this example now encounter a deadlock situation. DB2 has a deadlock detector running around the clock to identify any deadlock. Once one is detected, it will randomly pick a victim and roll back its transaction. By rolling back, all the locks that particular application is holding will be released. This allows the other application that is involved in the deadlock to complete its processing.

The application that got rolled back will receive the message:

```
SQL0911N The current transaction has been rolled back because of a deadlock or
timeout.  Reason code "2".
```

Reason code 2 means that the transaction is rolled back due to a deadlock. The failed user application is then responsible to report the error and retry the transaction if necessary. The deadlock detector is activated periodically as determined by the DLCHKTIME database configuration parameter. The default value for this parameter is 10,000 milliseconds (10 seconds).

To avoid deadlocks or any unnecessary lock waits, you need to understand your application. Design the application and tune the database in a way that the application will only read the data it requires. Figure 12.25 shows an example of two applications manipulating data on different rows. Why would it still encounter a deadlock? The key to this particular problem is that DB2 scans every *empno* value to see if the row qualifies the queries. If only a portion of the values are scanned, the applications may not run into a deadlock. This can be achieved by creating proper indexes and maintaining current database statistics so DB2 can choose a more efficient data access plan.

A deadlock may still occur even with proper indexing and database maintenance. In that case, you can make use of a new feature lock deferral, which is discussed next.

12.5.4 Lock Deferral

You can enable lock deferral for CS or RS isolation level scans with the DB2_EVALUNCOMMITTED registry variable. With lock deferral, DB2 can then evaluate the row before trying to lock it. To enable this feature issue the command:

```
db2set DB2_EVALUNCOMMITTED=ON
```

To disable it issue:

```
db2set DB2_EVALUNCOMMITTED=
```

Figure 12.26 shows that lock deferral no longer requires App A to put an S lock on *empno* = 105. App A can then read the *empno* = 106 row. Similar logic applies to App B.

To also skip all uncommitted deleted and inserted rows, you should also set both the DB2_SKIPDELETED and DB2_SKIPINSERTED registry variables to ON.

```
db2set DB2_SKIPDELETED=ON
db2set DB2_SKIPINSERTED=ON
```

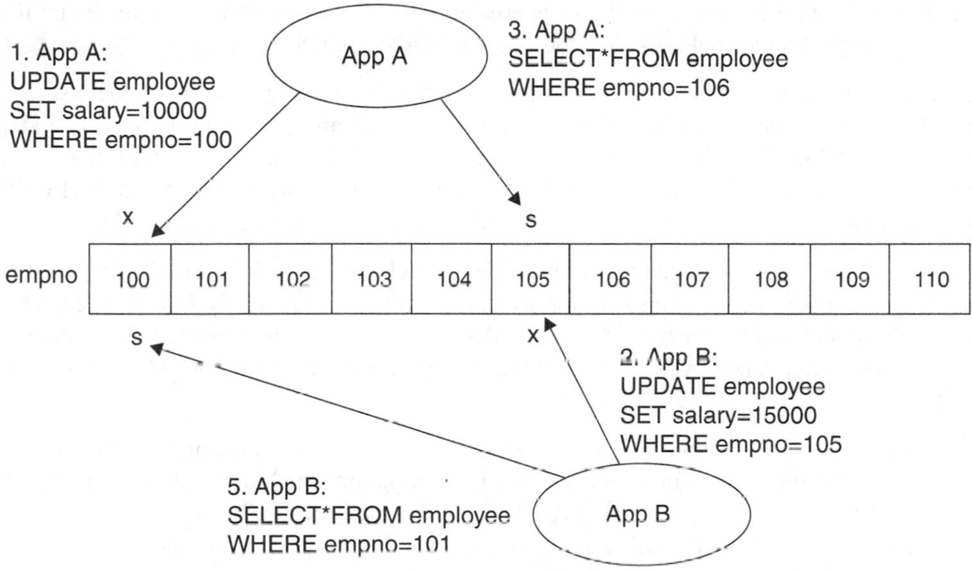

Figure 12.26 Deadlock problem resolved with EVALUNCOMMITTED enabled

12.5.5 Lock Escalation

When DB2 acquires a lock on an object, it allocates memory for each lock from the database shared memory area called the *locklist*. A tunable database configuration parameter by the same name lets you indicate the maximum storage allowed for locks in each database. To resize the locklist, update the LOCKLIST parameter with a new value in units of 4K.

Regardless of the type of lock, each lock uses about 36 bytes of memory on 32-bit DB2 instances and 56 bytes of memory on 64-bit DB2 instances. As the number of locks being held by all applications connected to the database increases, it is possible that the locklist will get full. When this happens, DB2 attempts to free memory by allocating a table lock and releasing the row locks. This internal operation is called **lock escalation.**

Lock escalation degrades performance because it can significantly reduce database concurrency. When you monitor your database, you should ideally see very few to no escalations. It is important to tune the LOCKLIST parameter appropriately so that lock escalations are avoided.

The MAXLOCKS database configuration parameter also has a direct effect on lock escalation. MAXLOCKS defines the percentage of the total locklist permitted to be allocated to a single application. Proper configuration of MAXLOCKS prevents any one application from using up all the memory available in the locklist. When the number of locks an application holds reaches the MAXLOCKS percentage, DB2 escalates the row locks of the particular application to a table lock. The table with the most row locks is escalated first. Lock escalation continues until the percentage of the locklist held is below the value of MAXLOCKS.

The database manager determines which locks to escalate by looking through the locklist for the application and finding the table with the most row locks. If after replacing these with a single table lock, the MAXLOCKS value is no longer exceeded, lock escalation will stop. If not, escalation continues until the percentage of the locklist held is below the value of MAXLOCKS. The MAXLOCKS parameter multiplied by the MAXAPPLS parameter cannot be less than 100.

As the number of row locks being held increases, the chance of locking escalations occurring also increases. Take this into consideration when choosing isolation levels. For example, the RR isolation level locks all the rows in the result set as well as the rows referenced to build the result set. With this isolation level you should choose an appropriate value for your MAXLOCKS and LOCKLIST parameters.

Starting in DB2 9, self tuning memory simplifies the task of memory configuration by automatically setting values for memory configuration parameters. Among these, MAXLOCK and LOCKLIST are set to AUTOMATIC by default, which means that the memory usage is dynamically sized as the workload requirements change. For more information about self tuning memory allocation, refer to Chapter 17, Database Performance Considerations.

12.6 Diagnosing Lock Problems

We have discussed how isolation levels affect the DB2 locking strategy. The various lock modes allow DB2 to provide diversified concurrent scenarios. For many applications the locking mechanism works transparently, but for others, issues such as lock waits, deadlocks, and lock escalations can occur.

DB2 has a comprehensive set of tools that you can use to obtain information about locking. In the following sections we will look at some of the tools that are available and how they can be used to troubleshoot locking problems.

12.6.1 Using the list applications Command

The **`list applications`** command issued with the **`show detail`** clause shows the status of each application. Use this command as the first diagnostic step if you suspect a lock wait condition exists. You can also use the Control Center to get similar information. From the object tree right click on the desired instance name and choose **Applications.** Note, however, that not all the columns from the **`list applications show detail`** command are reported by the Control Center.

Figure 12.27 shows the output of the **`list applications show detail`** command. The output is over 240 bytes wide; to understand locking behavior, focus on the output columns listed in Table 12.5.

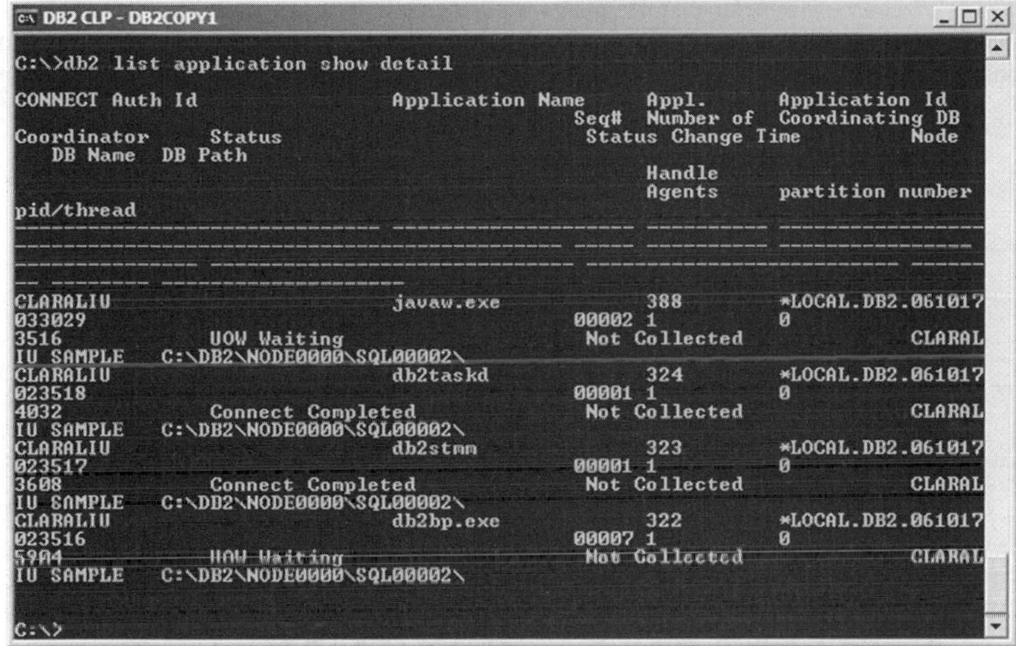

Figure 12.27 Output of the list applications show detail command

Table 12.5 Output Columns of the list applications show detail Command

Output Column	Description
Status	A value of *Lock-wait* means the application is blocked by a lock held by a different application. Don't be confused by a value of *UOW Waiting*, which means that the application (unit of work) is in progress and not blocked by a lock. It is simply not doing any work at the moment.
Status Change Time	This is of particular interest for an application with *Lock-wait* status. The value shows when the lock wait began. Note that the UOW monitor switch must be on for the status change time to be reported.
Appl. Handle	The handle is a unique ID for an active application. Being able to identify the application handle is important when it is holding locks that are causing contention problems. You can use the application handle in the **`FORCE APPLICATION`** command to terminate its current transaction.

12.6.2 Using the force application Command

You can use the **`force application`** command in conjunction with the **`list applications`** command to resolve concurrency problems. A typical scenario occurs when user *Bob* issues a query that does not COMMIT. He then goes for a one-hour coffee break, leaving other users unable to continue their work because Bob's query is holding several locks on the same objects. In this scenario, a DBA can issue a **`list applications`** command to identify that the connection is from Bob by looking at the *Appl. Handle* column, as shown in Figure 12.28.

```
DB2 CLP

C:\>db2 list application

Auth Id  Application    Appl.      Application Id                 DB       # of
         Name           Handle                                    Name     Agents
-------- -------------- ---------- ------------------------------ -------- -----
MARY     db2bp.exe      212        *LOCAL.DB2.041026160829        SAMPLE   1
DB2ADMIN db2bp.exe      209        *LOCAL.DB2.041026160826        SAMPLE   1
BOB      db2bp.exe      208        *LOCAL.DB2.041026160825        SAMPLE   1

C:\>db2 force application (208)
DB20000I  The FORCE APPLICATION command completed successfully.
DB21024I  This command is asynchronous and may not be effective immediately.

C:\>db2 list application

Auth Id  Application    Appl.      Application Id                 DB       # of
         Name           Handle                                    Name     Agents
-------- -------------- ---------- ------------------------------ -------- -----
MARY     db2bp.exe      212        *LOCAL.DB2.041026160829        SAMPLE   1
DB2ADMIN db2bp.exe      209        *LOCAL.DB2.041026160826        SAMPLE   1

C:\>_
```

Figure 12.28 The force application command

Figure 12.28 shows there are three connections to the *SAMPLE* database. Next, the DBA identifies user BOB whose connection has the application handle of 208, and issues the command:

`db2 force application (208)`

The command executes asynchronously, meaning that it will not wait for the connection to be terminated to return. After a few seconds, when he issues the **`list applications`** command again, he sees that Bob's connection has been removed, allowing the other connections to continue their work.

To force several connections in one command use the syntax:

`db2 force application (`*`Appl. Handle, Appl. Handle,`*` ... )`

There may be situations when you need to force all the connections against all the databases in the instance. In such situations use the **`all`** option of the **`force application`** command:

```
db2 force application all
```

> **NOTE** The **force application** command does not prevent other users from connecting to a database.
>
> The **force application** command always preserves database integrity, so only users who are idling or executing interruptible database operations can be terminated.

12.6.3 Using the Snapshot Monitor

You can use the **Snapshot Monitor** to capture information about a database and any connected applications at a specific time. Snapshot monitoring provides the majority of the useful information for dealing with lock issues. Before you can obtain snapshot information in full extent, you must turn on the monitor switches. See Section 17.7, The Snapshot Monitor, for a detailed discussion on setting monitor switches and capturing information. In this section we focus on the relevant commands required to continue with our lock diagnostic discussion.

Turn on all the monitor switches with this command:

```
db2 update monitor switches using bufferpool on lock on sort on
     statement on table on timestamp on uow on
```

To get a database snapshot, issue

```
db2 get snapshot for all on database_name
```

From the output of this command you obtain the following snapshot monitoring components in sequence. Snapshots that are most relevant to locking have an asterisk (*) after them.

- Database snapshot*
- Buffer pool snapshot
- Dynamic SQL snapshot
- Application snapshot*
- Table space snapshot
- Database lock snapshot*
- Table snapshot

The database snapshot part of the result contains a good summary of the locking information for the specified database. Figure 12.29 shows only the pertinent lines to locking from a sample database snapshot output.

If you want to "zoom" into each application and understand the types of locks they are holding, examine the application snapshots. Figure 12.30 shows the most important subset of information for an application in a lock wait situation.

```
 Database Snapshot
. . . .

Locks held currently = 8
Lock waits = 0
Time database waited on locks (ms) = 315704
Lock list memory in use (Bytes) = 1692
Deadlocks detected = 0
Lock escalations = 0
Exclusive lock escalations = 0
Agents currently waiting on locks = 1
Lock Timeouts = 0
```

Figure 12.29 Database snapshot with lock-related information

```
 Application Snapshot

Application handle       = 14                              (1)
Application status       = Lock-wait
Status change time       = 08-15-2007 14:30:36.907312
Snapshot timestamp       = 08-15-2007 14:30:43.414574
Time application waited on locks (ms)    = 6507            (2)
Total time UOW waited on locks (ms)      = 6507
UOW start timestamp      = 08-15-2007 14:30:36.889356
Statement start timestamp        = 08-15-2007 14:30:36.890986
Dynamic SQL statement text:
select * from org                                          (3)

ID of agent holding lock         = 13
Application ID holding lock      = *LOCAL.DB2.011905182946
Lock name        = 0x02000200000000000000000054
Lock attributes          = 0x00000000
Release flags    = 0x00000001
Lock object type         = Table
Lock mode        = Exclusive Lock (X)                      (4)
Lock mode requested      = Intention Share Lock (IS)       (5)
Name of tablespace holding lock          = USERSPACE1
Schema of table holding lock             = WILKINS
Name of table holding lock               = ORG
Lock wait start timestamp                = 08-15-2007 14:30:36.907318
```

Figure 12.30 Application snapshot with lock-related information

In Figure 12.30:

(1) You can see that application handle 14 is in a lock-wait state.

(2) It has been waiting for 6,507 milliseconds for locks.

(3, 5) It is currently executing a SELECT statement and requesting an Intent Share (IS) lock on a table.

(4) However, application handle 13 holds an exclusive (X) lock on the same table.

To further investigate the problem, you can use the **list application** command and see what application handle 13 is doing and check its application snapshot for more information.

Like the application snapshot, the database lock snapshot has a section for each connected application (see Figure 12.31).`

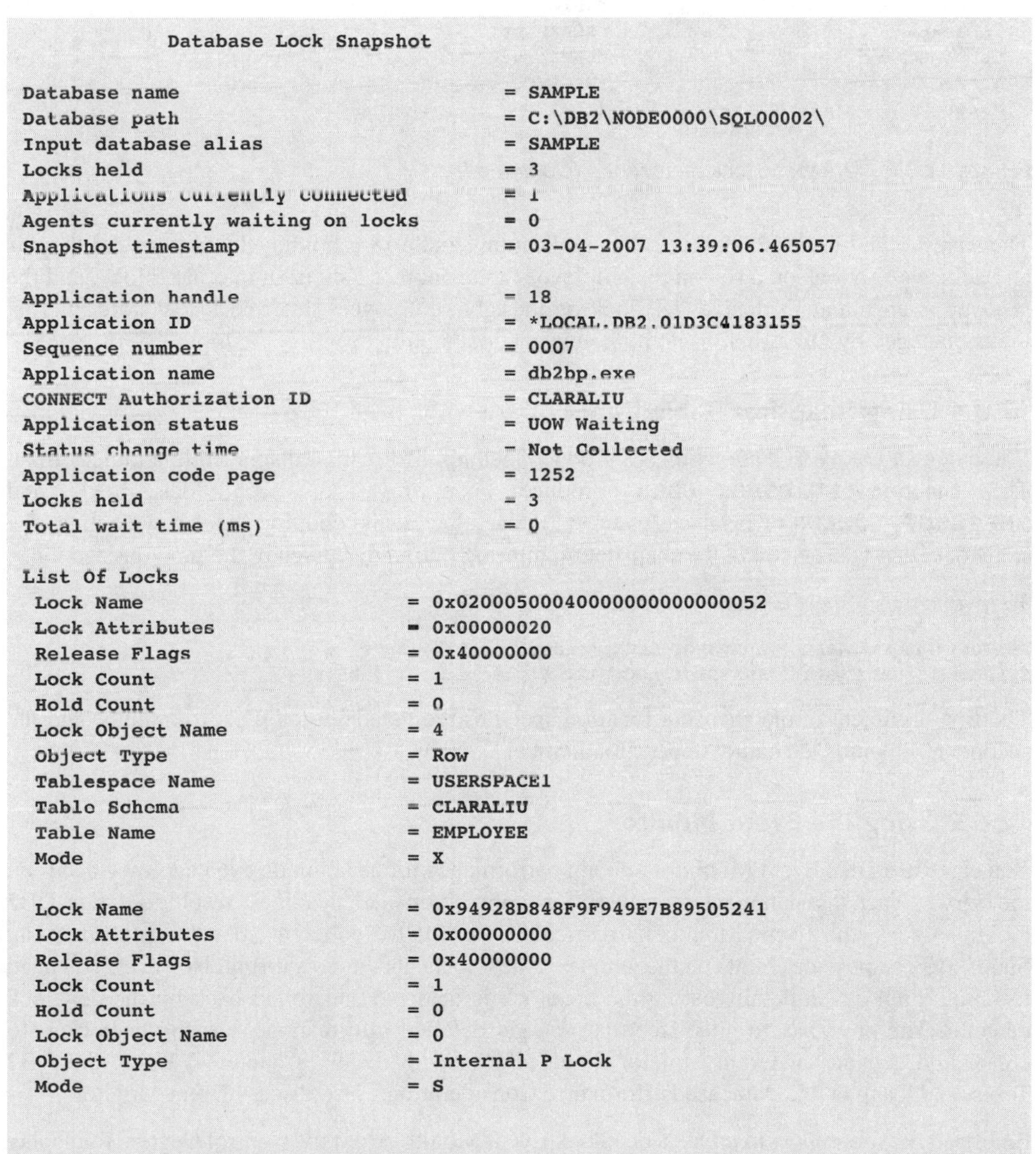

```
            Database Lock Snapshot

Database name                               = SAMPLE
Database path                               = C:\DB2\NODE0000\SQL00002\
Input database alias                        = SAMPLE
Locks held                                  = 3
Applications currently connected            = 1
Agents currently waiting on locks           = 0
Snapshot timestamp                          = 03-04-2007 13:39:06.465057

Application handle                          = 18
Application ID                              = *LOCAL.DB2.01D3C4183155
Sequence number                             = 0007
Application name                            = db2bp.exe
CONNECT Authorization ID                    = CLARALIU
Application status                          = UOW Waiting
Status change time                          = Not Collected
Application code page                       = 1252
Locks held                                  = 3
Total wait time (ms)                        = 0

List Of Locks
 Lock Name                   = 0x02000500040000000000000052
 Lock Attributes             = 0x00000020
 Release Flags               = 0x40000000
 Lock Count                  = 1
 Hold Count                  = 0
 Lock Object Name            = 4
 Object Type                 = Row
 Tablespace Name             = USERSPACE1
 Table Schema                = CLARALIU
 Table Name                  = EMPLOYEE
 Mode                        = X

 Lock Name                   = 0x94928D848F9F949E7B89505241
 Lock Attributes             = 0x00000000
 Release Flags               = 0x40000000
 Lock Count                  = 1
 Hold Count                  = 0
 Lock Object Name            = 0
 Object Type                 = Internal P Lock
 Mode                        = S
```

Figure 12.31 Database lock snapshot

```
Lock Name                        = 0x02000500000000000000000054
Lock Attributes                  = 0x00000000
Release Flags                    = 0x40000000
Lock Count                       = 1
Hold Count                       = 0
Lock Object Name                 = 5
Object Type                      = Table
Tablespace Name                  = USERSPACE1
Table Schema                     = CLARALIU
Table Name                       = EMPLOYEE
Mode                             = IX
```

Figure 12.31 Database lock snapshot *(Continued)*

The snapshot in Figure 12.31 shows that application handle 18 is holding 3 locks. One of them is an exclusive (X) lock on a row in the employee table, another lock is an internal P lock, and the last one is an Intent Exclusive (IX) lock on the table employee. (Internal P locks are internal locks managed by DB2; there is nothing you can do about them.)

12.6.4 Using Snapshot Table Functions

You can also invoke SQL functions to produce locking information displayed in a table format. The function **SNAPSHOT_LOCK** produces one row for each lock held, and **SNAPSHOT_LOCKWAIT** produces one row for each lock wait condition. Each row contains the same data that is provided in the snapshot monitoring output discussed in the previous section.

To invoke these snapshot table functions, use:

```
SELECT * FROM TABLE ( SNAPSHOT_LOCK ('sample', 0) ) AS s
SELECT * FROM TABLE ( SNAPSHOT_LOCKWAIT ('sample', 0) ) AS s
```

The first argument of the snapshot function specifies the database you want to monitor and the second argument is the database partition number.

12.6.5 Using the Event Monitor

You can use a DB2 Event Monitor to obtain performance information on events as they occur on the server, such as statement or transaction completion and deadlock resolution. For DB2 locking issues, the Event Monitor is particularly useful for collecting deadlock information. Snapshots can provide counts on the number of deadlocks that are occurring. However, you need to obtain application details before the deadlock is detected and rolled back by the deadlock detector. The only way to guarantee that you get detailed information on each deadlock is to create and activate an Event Monitor for deadlocks with details. Chapter 4, Using the DB2 Tools, and Chapter 17, Database Performance Considerations, also discuss Event Monitors.

Figure 12.32 shows how to create a deadlock Event Monitor from the Control Center. To display the Create Event Monitor window, right click on the Event Monitors folder under database you want to monitor, and then click on **Create.** In the Create Event Monitor window, specify the name of the Event Monitor. Under *Event Types*, select *Deadlocks* and also check the *With details* option. Then click *OK*. After clicking *OK*, the new Event Monitor is created and started.

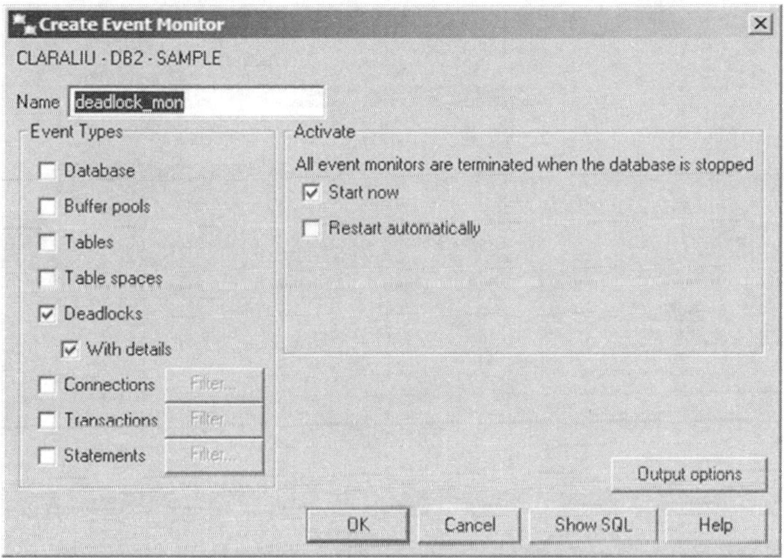

Figure 12.32 Stopping event monitoring and analyzing Event Monitor records

If a deadlock occurs, the DB2 deadlock detector identifies the two applications involved and rolls back one of the transactions. From the Control Center, right click on the Event Monitor you just created and choose *Stop Event Monitoring* (see Figure 12.33). Next, from the Control Center right click again on the Event Monitor you just created and choose *Analyze Event Monitor Records*. This displays the Event Analyzer window, (see Figure 12.34).

From the Event Analyzer window, select the *Deadlocked Connection* as shown in Figure 12.34.

At this point you will see the connections that were involved in the deadlock. You can then drill down to the Data Elements on any connection for more information as shown in Figure 12.35.

In the Data Elements window (see Figure 12.36), you will see the statements that are involved and the locks the application is holding. For example, from Figure 12.36 you can tell that five locks were held on the *employee* table when the statement **SELECT * FROM employee** was executing.

12.6.6 Using the Activity Monitor

Chapter 4, Using the DB2 Tools, introduced the activity monitor. We limit our discussion in this chapter to locking-related topics.

Set up the Activity Monitor by selecting the database you want to monitor as illustrated in Figure 12.37.

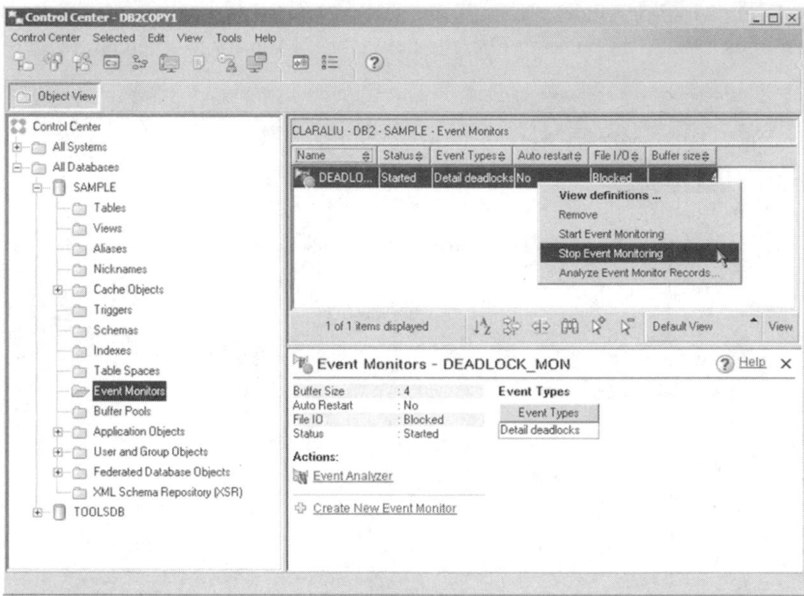

Figure 12.33 Stopping event monitoring and analyzing Event Monitor records

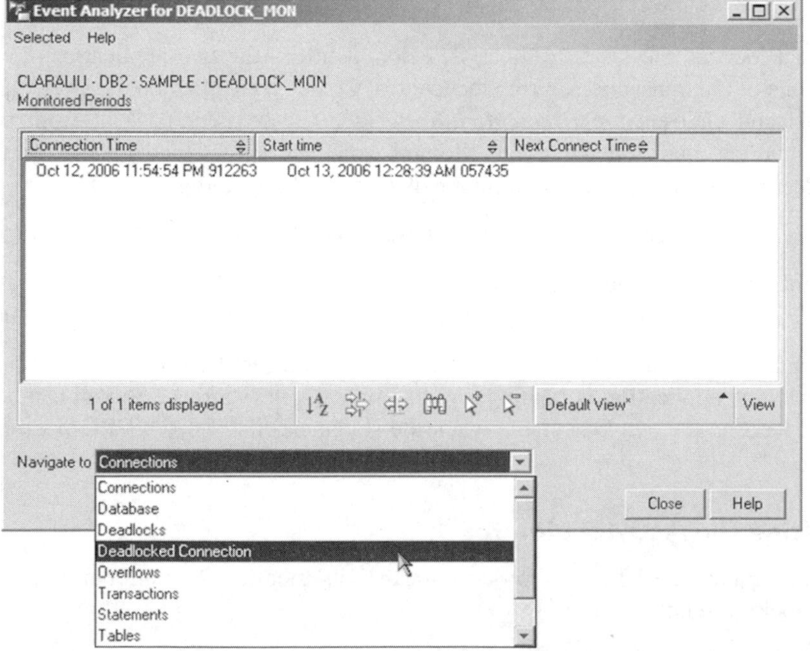

Figure 12.34 Navigating to the deadlocked connection

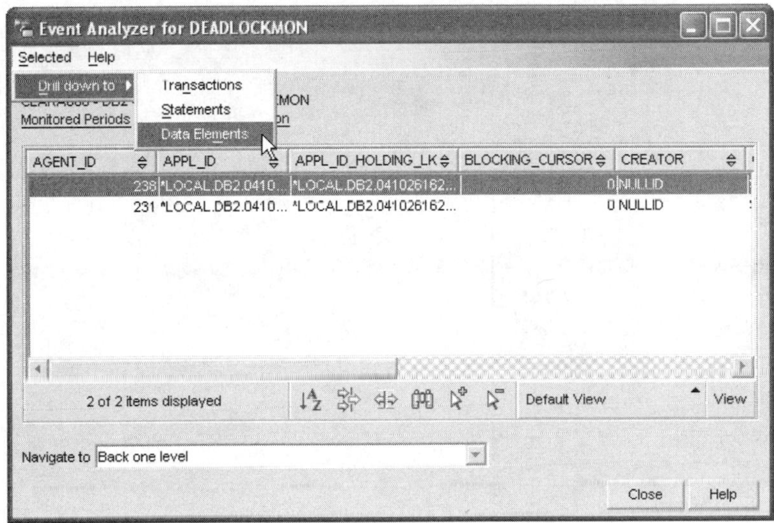

Figure 12.35 Drilling down to the data elements of a particular application

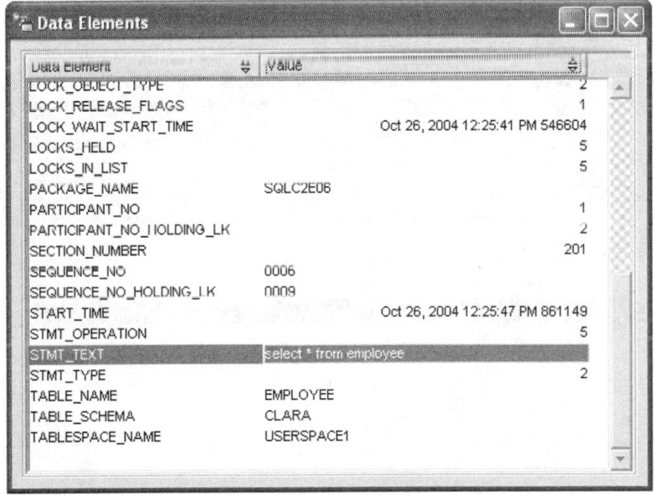

Figure 12.36 Data elements in an application

Select or create a monitoring task. There are a few system-defined monitoring tasks. One of them is used to capture locking information, which is highlighted in Figure 12.38. You can also create a new monitoring task by clicking the *New* button.

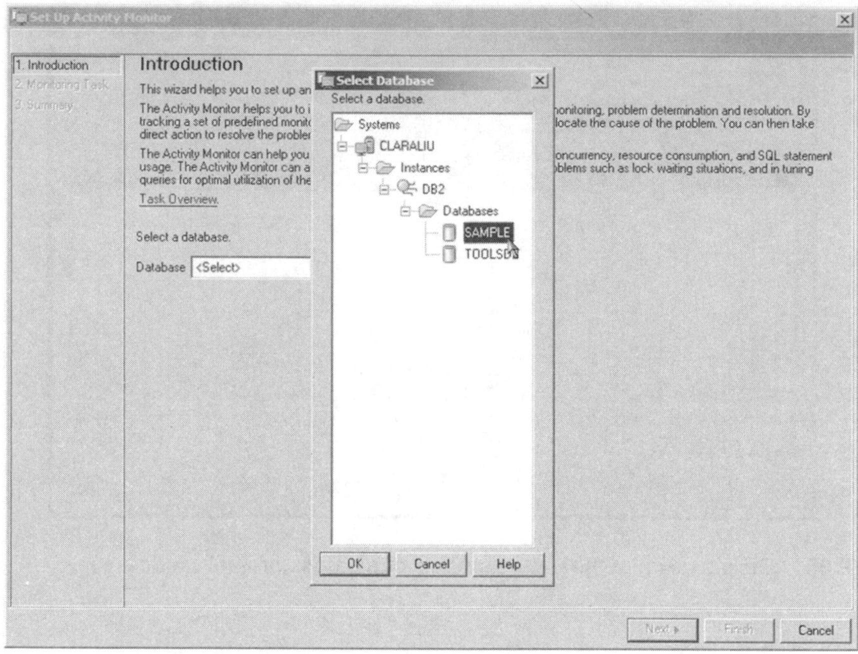

Figure 12.37 Setting up the Activity Monitor

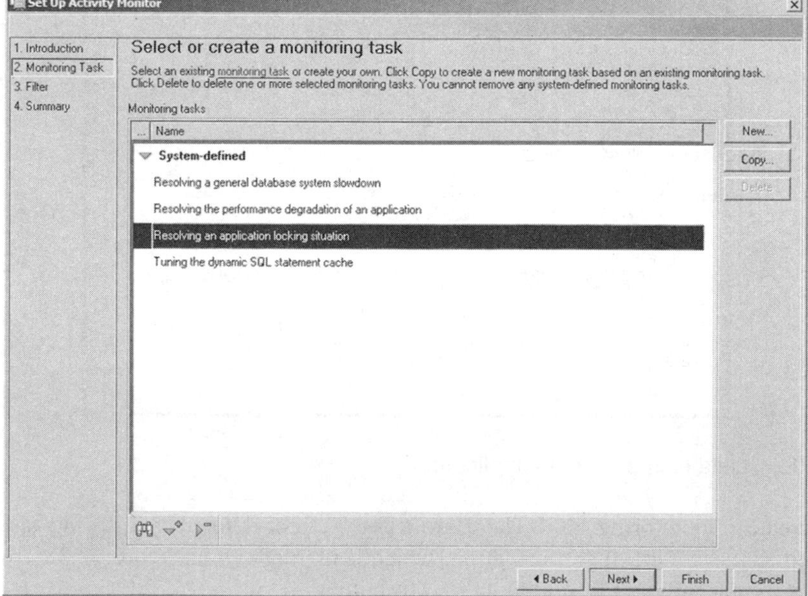

Figure 12.38 Selecting or creating a monitoring task

You can see In Figure 12.39 that you can choose to monitor all or selected applications. Click *Finish* to complete the Activity Monitor setup.

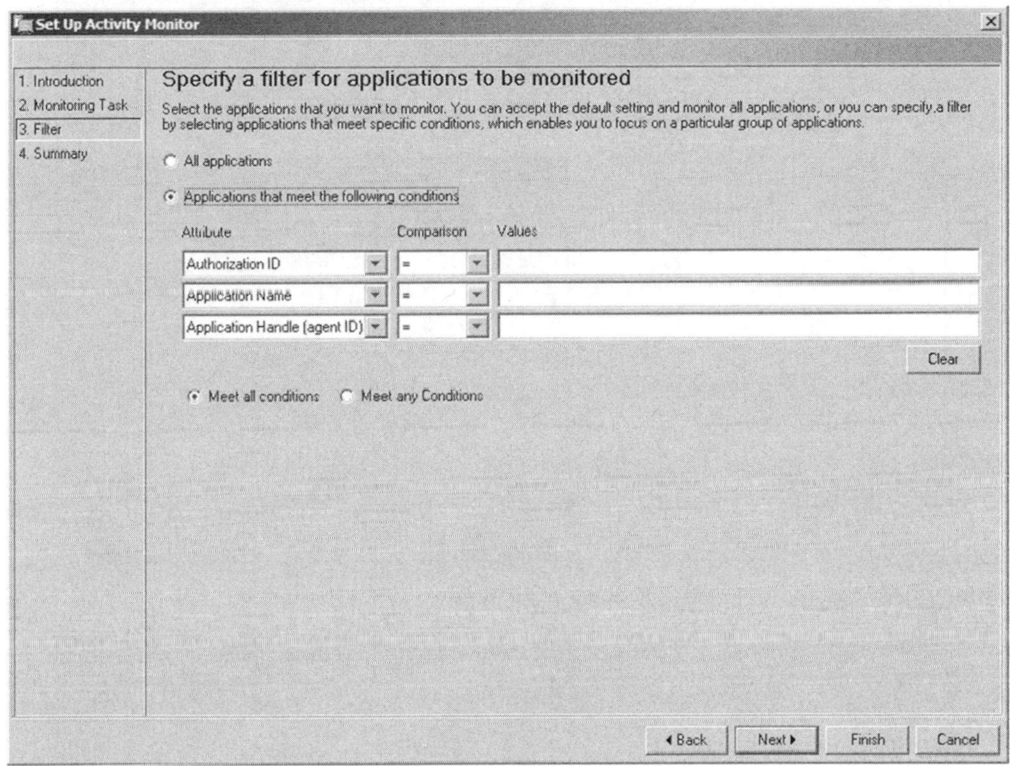

Figure 12.39 Specifying applications to be monitored

As applications are connected to the database, the activity and status of each will be listed under *Report data* (see Figure 12.40).

To zoom into a particular application and examine its associated lock chains, right click on the application handle number and choose **Show Lock Chains** (see Figure 12.41).

You will get a pictorial view of the locks being held by the application in the Lock Chain dialog. Click on the *Legend* button to find out what each icon means (see Figure 12.42).

You can also see the lock details for each node by selecting *Show Lock Details* as shown in Figure 12.43.

You can use the similar information (shown in Figure 12.44) for detailed locking analysis.

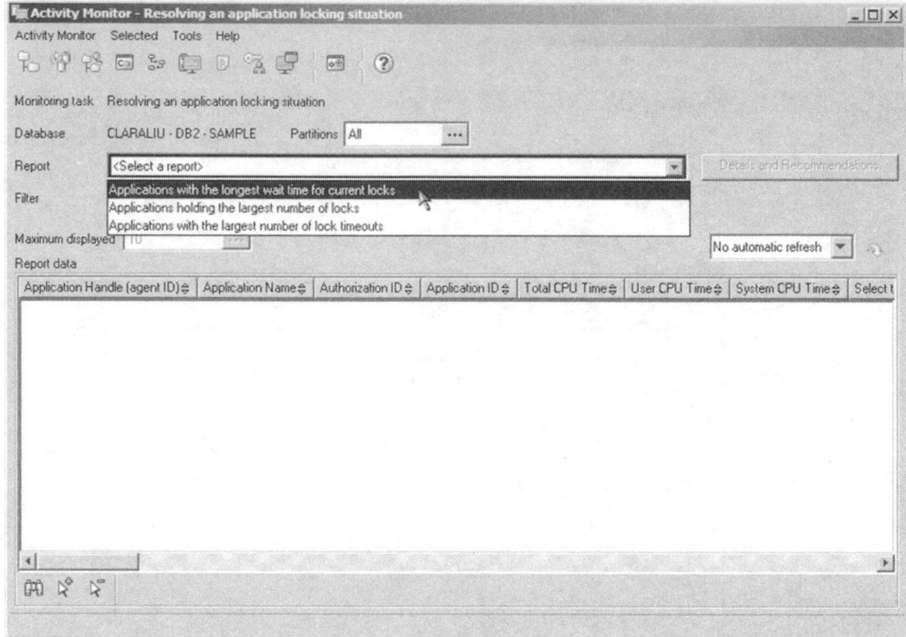

Figure 12.40 Selecting the type of information to be reported

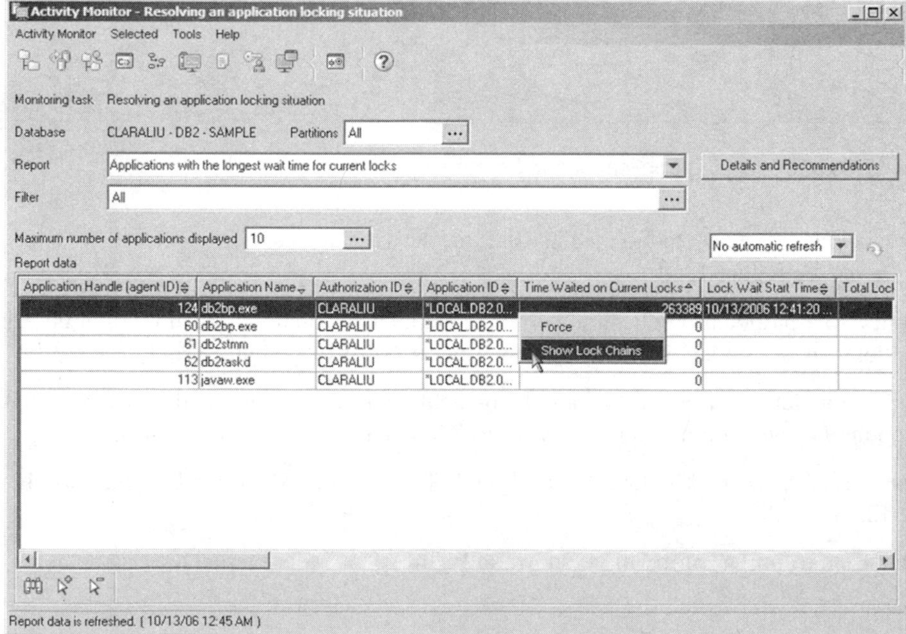

Figure 12.41 Showing an application's lock chains

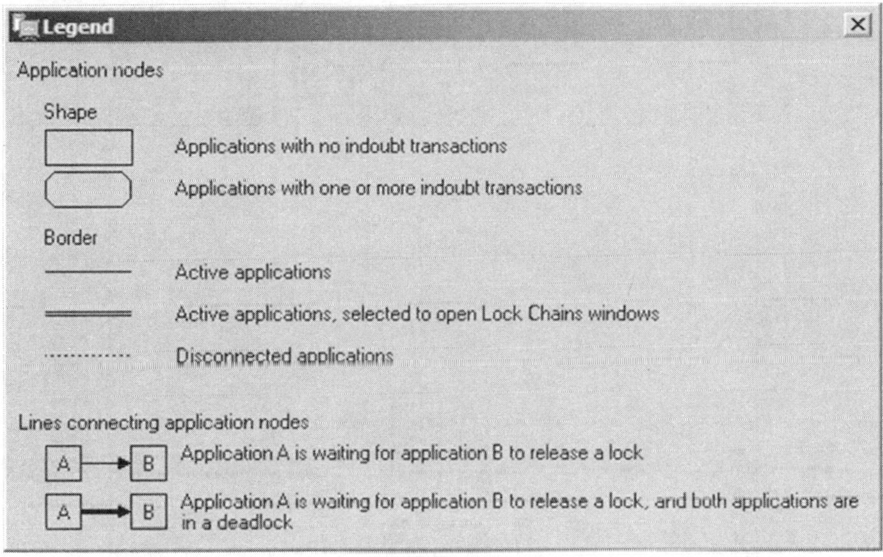

Figure 12.42 Lock details

12.6.7 Using the Health Center

The Health Center is a graphical tool used to analyze and improve the health of DB2. It provides four indicators in the Application Concurrency category: lock escalation rate, lock list utilization, percentage of applications waiting on locks, and deadlock rate. You can set warning and alarm levels for the indicators, enable the indicators, and define an action to be taken when the thresholds are reached, such as taking a snapshot in the Health Center. The Health Center is discussed in more detail in Chapter 4, Using the DB2 Tools.

12.7 Techniques to Avoid Locking

It is good to know how to diagnose locking problems, but it is even better to know how to prevent them. Avoiding locking problems requires a good application design. The following is a list of items you should consider when developing your applications. For a detailed explanation of these and other techniques, refer to the *DB2 UDB Administration Guide*, and *DB2 UDB Application Development Guide.*

- Choose the appropriate isolation level: UR, CS, RS, or RR. As discussed earlier, UR allows for the most concurrency and the least number of locks required, while RR allows for the least concurrency and the most number of locks required. For example, if your application is used for estimation purposes and the exact value of columns is not needed, isolation UR should be used. Choosing the right isolation level guarantees that DB2 takes the right amount of locks that your application requires. In addition, catalog locks are acquired even in uncommitted read applications using dynamic SQL or XQuery statements.

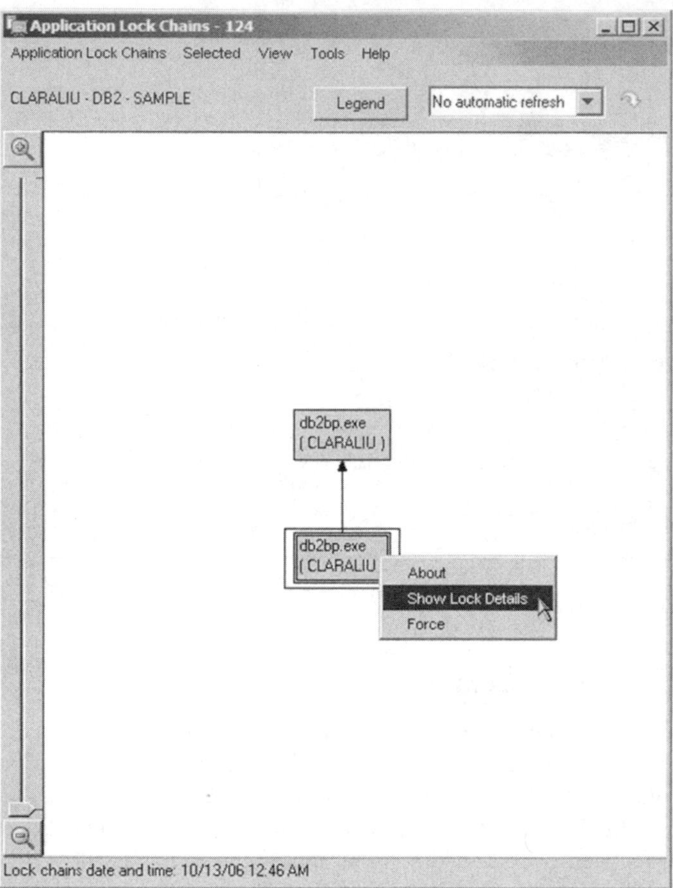

Figure 12.43 Showing an application's lock details

- Issue **COMMIT** statements as frequently as the application logic allows. Issuing a **COMMIT** incurs I/O costs because data is flushed to disk, but it releases locks allowing for more concurrency. Issue **COMMIT** statements even for read-only applications, since S locks are taken (unless using UR Isolation).
- Specify the **FOR FETCH ONLY** clause in the **SELECT** statement. This clause prevents exclusive locks from being taken. The **FOR READ ONLY** clause is equivalent.
- Perform **INSERT, UPDATE,** and **DELETE** statements at the end of a unit of work if possible. These operations require exclusive locks, and they are kept until the end of the UOW (commit/roll back). Putting these statements at the end of a UOW allows for maximum concurrency.

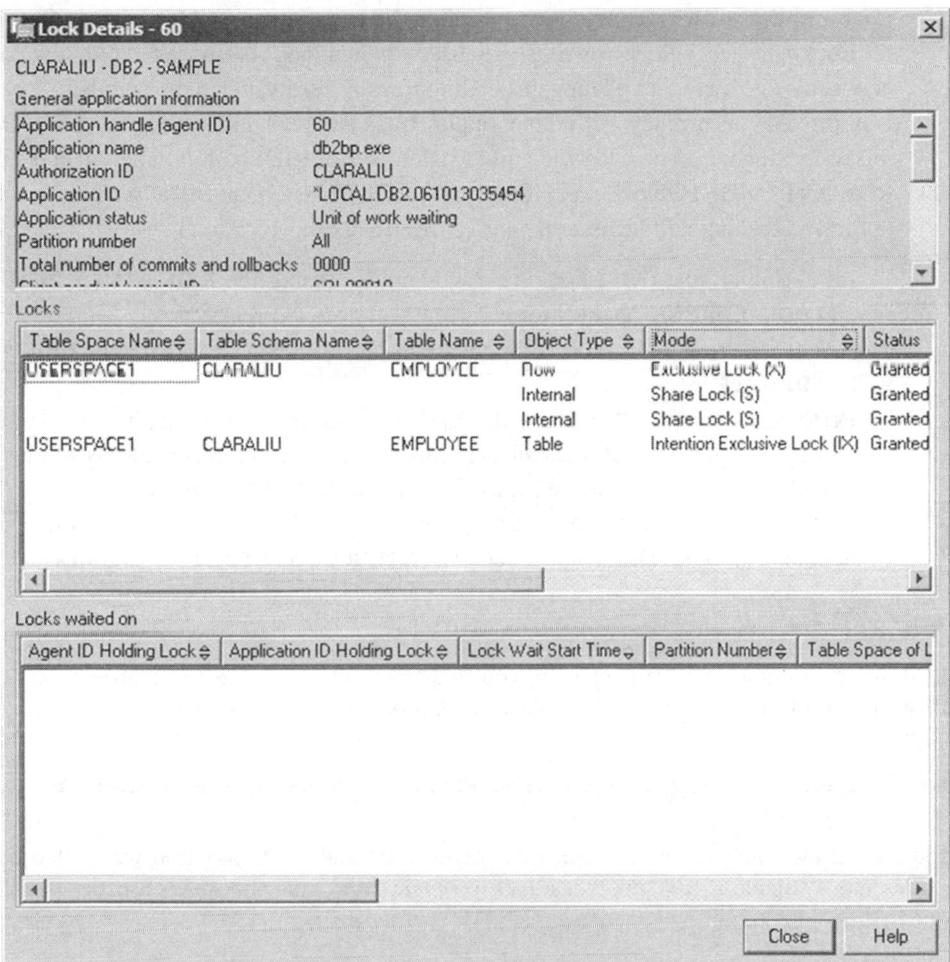

Figure 12.44 Lock details

- Avoid lock escalations impacting concurrency by tuning the **LOCKLIST** and MAX-LOCKS database configuration parameters.
- When declaring cursors, be specific about their use. If the cursor is to be used only for reads, include the **FOR READ ONLY** clause in the declaration; if the cursor is to be used for updates, include the **FOR UPDATE** clause. In addition, you can specify the columns to be updated in the **FOR UPDATE** clause. For example:

```
DECLARE mycur1 CURSOR FOR
    SELECT * FROM employee WHERE salary > 10000
    FOR UPDATE OF firstnme, lastname
```

By explicitly declaring the use of the cursor, DB2 will choose the correct locks.

- Enable optimistic locking in your application. With verison 9.5, DB2 enabled Optimistic Locking, a technique for SQL database applications that do not hold row locks between selecting, and updating or deleting rows. The advantage of optimistic locking is improved concurrency, since other applications can read and write those rows. Optimistic locking uses a new Row Identifier (RID_BIT or RID) built in function and a new ROW CHANGE TOKEN expression with the SQL statements. The typical way that optimistic locking will be used in your application is shown below:
    1. In the initial query, **SELECT** the row identifier (using the **RID_BIT()** function) and **ROW CHANGE TOKEN** for each row you need to process.
    2. Release the row locks so other applications can **SELECT, INSERT, UPDATE,** and **DELETE** from the tabe.
    3. Perform a searched **UPDATE** or **DELETE** on the target rows, using the row identifier and **ROW CHANGE TOKEN** in the search condition, optimistically assuming the unlocked row has not changed since the original **SELECT** statement.
    4. If a row has changed, the **UPDATE** operation will fail and the application logic must handle the failure. For instance, retry the **SELECT** and **UPDATE** operations.

12.8 Case Study

On a Monday morning, a developer calls you and requests assistance to resolve a deadlock problem. You find that two identical applications are being executed concurrently and receive this SQL0911 error:

```
SQL0911N The current transaction has been rolled back because of a deadlock or
timeout.  Reason code "2".
```

Reason code *2* indicates that a deadlock was encountered and the transaction was rolled back. Few tools are available to diagnose deadlock problems and you choose to use the deadlock Event Monitor.

Data from the deadlock Event Monitor shows that:

- Application A updated a row in the *employee* table.
- At the same time, application B updated another row in the *employee* table as well.
- Before both applications commited their updates, they queried the *employee* table again for some additional information.

This caused a deadlock like the one in Figure 12.25. To resolve the locking problem, you enable lock deferral with:

```
db2set DB2_EVALUNCOMMITTED=YES
```

That same day, an application is promoted from the Development environment to the Test environment. The application is a reservation system that is expected to handle requests from at most 200 users concurrently. On the very first run of the application, there are many locking issues, so you are asked to review the application design. Using monitoring information like snapshots (discussed in Chapter 17, Database Performance Considerations), you first note that there is an incredible number of lock escalations. You review the LOCKLIST and MAXLOCKS parameters and decide to increase LOCKLIST by 50 percent. A second run of the application performs a lot better, and the snapshots for this run show there are no longer lock escalation problems, but still there are locking issues.

Next, you review the SQL issued by the application using the snapshots. All the cursors defined in the application are ambiguous; that is, they have not been defined with a **FOR READ ONLY** or **FOR UPDATE** clause, so DB2 may not be choosing the correct locking. You also note that the transactions are very long; in other words, **COMMIT** statements are not issued frequently enough. You voice these concerns to the application developers, who decide to stop the testing while they implement your suggestions.

12.9 Summary

In this chapter you learned about locking scenarios that you may encounter when a database is concurrently manipulated. Some scenarios might be desirable, but some are not. To control the behavior of how DB2 handles concurrent database access, use the different isolation levels.

There are four types of isolation levels: uncommitted read, cursor stability (the default), repeatable read, and read stability. The behavior of DB2 locking and lock attributes are controlled by the isolation level specified for the database. When an application is holding many locks that have exceeded its quota (through the setting of MAXLOCKS), lock escalation may occur. Lock escalation should be minimized as much as possible because it significantly reduces the concurrency of the database.

There are command line tools as well as graphical tools that can help you identify and solve locking problems, and you can implement techniques when developing your applications to avoid locking.

12.10 Review Questions

1. A batch operation is encountering lock escalations. If it is the only application running when the lock escalation occurs, which database configuration parameter can be used to reduce the lock escalations?
2. Sam issues a **SELECT** statement that returns the following result set of three rows:

```
Name        Seat
----------------
Liu         1A
Chong       14F
Snow        3B
```

   Without committing or rolling back the current transaction, he issues the same **SELECT** statement again. The following is returned:

```
Name        Seat
----------------
-           1A
Chong       14F
Qi          3B
```

   Why is that?

3. What database objects can a DB2 user explicitly lock using a DB2 command or statement?
4. If an application holds a U lock on a row, what lock must another application request to access this row concurrently?
5. What does error SQL0911N with reason code *68* mean?
6. What does error SQL0911N with reason code *2* mean?
7. A user complained about poor performance. With the DB2 Snapshot Monitor you obtained the following information:

```
Locks held currently = 855
Lock waits = 1123
Time database waited on locks (ms) = 3157040000
Lock list memory in use (Bytes) = 16920
Deadlocks detected = 0
Lock escalations = 103
Exclusive lock escalations = 0
Agents currently waiting on locks = 38
Lock Timeouts = 2232
```

   How would you troubleshoot the high number of lock escalations?
8. What tools that come with DB2 can assist you in diagnosing lock problems?
9. The following is captured by the Snapshot Monitor. What does it tell you?

```
Application Snapshot

Application handle                    = 14
Application status                    = Lock-wait
Status change time                    = 08-15-2007 14:30:36.907312
Snapshot timestamp                    = 08-15-2007 14:30:43.414574
Time application waited on locks (ms) = 6507
Total time UOW waited on locks (ms)   = 6507
UOW start timestamp                   = 08-15-2007 14:30:36.889356
Statement start timestamp             = 08-15-2007 14:30:36.890986
Dynamic SQL statement text:
select * from org

ID of agent holding lock              = 13
Application ID holding lock           = *LOCAL.DB2.011905182946
Lock name                             = 0x02000200000000000000000054
Lock attributes                       = 0x00000000
Release flags                         = 0x00000001
Lock object type                      = Table
Lock mode                             = Exclusive Lock (X)
Lock mode requested                   = Intention Share Lock (IS)
Name of tablespace holding lock       = USERSPACE1
Schema of table holding lock          = WILKINS
Name of table holding lock            = ORG
Lock wait start timestamp             = 08-15-2007 14:30:36.907318
```

10. Bob was connected to the *sample* database. He turned auto-commit OFF and issued the following statement:

```
UPDATE employee SET salary = salary * 1.5 WHERE empno='000010'
```

A database administrator, Mike, who had just joined the company was monitoring the system. He noticed that Bob had acquired a table lock on the *employee* table. Since Bob did not commit or roll back the transaction, no one can access the table (except for UR applications). Mike asked Bob to commit or roll back the transaction. That released the locks and business went on as usual. Then another user, Mary, issued the following statement:

```
SELECT name, salary FROM employee WHERE empno = '000020'
```

Mary also had auto-commit turned OFF and didn't commit or rollback the transaction. Once again, the *employee* table was locked.

Mike is concerned about these two locking incidents. Could you assist him with what might be the cause?

11. Which of the following is not a DB2 isolation level?
    A. Uncommitted read
    B. Cursor stability
    C. Cursor with hold
    D. Repeatable read
12. On which of the following objects does DB2 not obtain locks?
    A. Row
    B. Page
    C. Table
    D. Table space
13. Which of the following is the default isolation level in DB2?
    A. Uncommitted read
    B. Cursor stability
    C. Read stability
    D. Repeatable read
14. Which of the following isolation levels typically causes the most locks to be obtained?
    A. Uncommitted read
    B. Cursor stability
    C. Read stability
    D. Repeatable read
15. Which of the following isolation levels does not obtain row level locks?
    A. Uncommitted read
    B. Cursor stability
    C. Read stability
    D. Repeatable read
16. Which of the following isolation levels lets you see data that has been updated by other applications before it is committed?
    A. Uncommitted read
    B. Cursor stability

  C. Read stability
  D. Repeatable read

17. Given a transaction that issues the same SQL statement twice. Which of the following isolation levels will allow new rows to be returned in the result set, but will not allow rows to be removed from the result set?
  A. Uncommitted read
  B. Cursor stability
  C. Read stability
  D. Repeatable read
18. If the current session has an isolation level of CS, which of the following will change the isolation level to UR for the current statement?
  A. Select * from foo use UR
  B. Select * from foo with UR
  C. Select * from foo isolation UR
  D. Select * from foo UR
19. Using the **`alter table`** statement, which two of the following can you change the locksize to?
  A. Column
  B. Page
  C. Row
  D. Index
  E. Table
20. To specify that your application should return immediately rather than wait for a lock, which of the following commands must be used?
  A. Set lock timeout = nowait
  B. Set lock timeout = not wait
  C. Set lock timeout = NULL
  D. Set lock nowait

CHAPTER 13

Maintaining Data

Moving data from one database server to another is a very common task in a production environment and in almost every phase of the development cycle. For example, a developer may want to export data from a production database and load it into her tables for testing. In a production environment, a database administrator may want to export a few tables from production to a test database server to investigate a performance problem.

DB2 provides a number of utilities so that you can accomplish these tasks very easily. We will introduce each utility and discuss different options supported.

In this chapter you will learn about:

- The big picture of the DB2 data movement utilities
- Different file formats used to move data
- The EXPORT utility
- The IMPORT utility
- The LOAD utility
- The DB2MOVE utility
- The DB2RELOCATEDB utility
- How to generate the Data Definition Language for a database
- The different data maintenance utilities such as RUNSTATS, REORG, REORGCHK, REBIND

13.1 DB2 Data Movement Utilities: The Big Picture

Figure 13.1 presents the big picture of the DB2 data movement utilities. The utilities provide a way to move data from one database to another. The source and target databases can be the same instance, in different instances on the same server, on different servers on the same platform, or on different platforms entirely. For example, you can move data stored in DB2 on z/OS to a database defined in DB2 on a Linux server. Data movement within DB2 is very efficient and flexible.

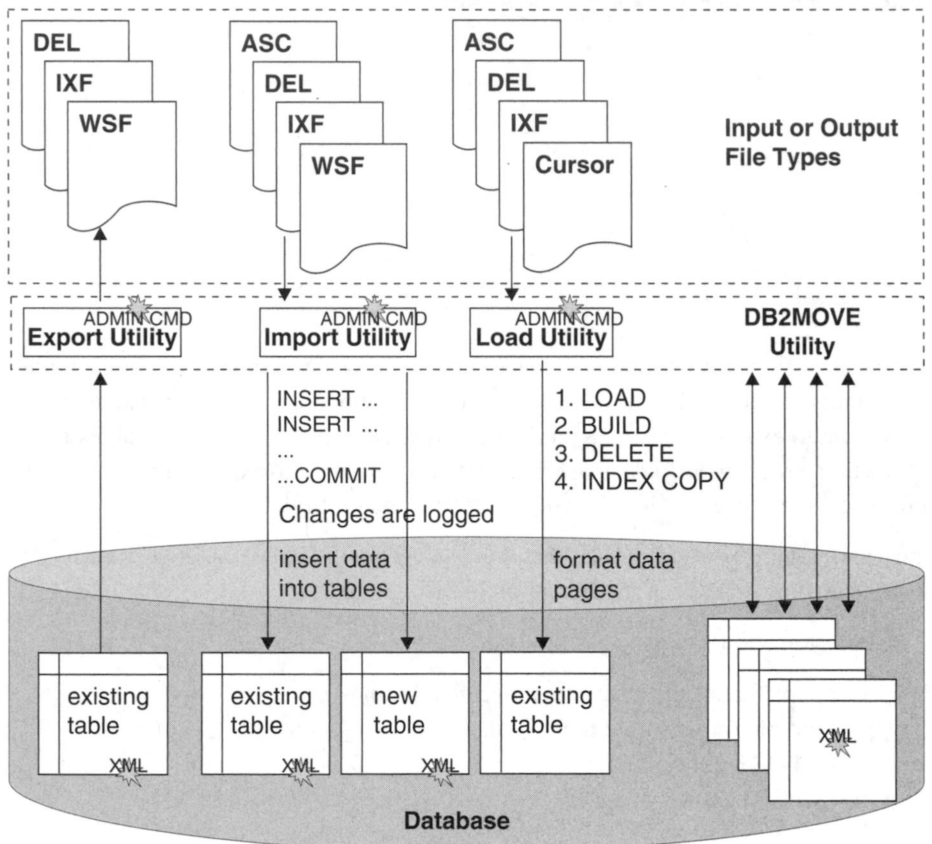

Figure 13.1 DB2 data movement utilities

Figure 13.1 shows that all data movement utilities use a file either for input or output. The file can be of types DEL, IXF, ASC, WSF, and Cursor.

To extract data from a table in a database, you use the export utility. The import and load utilities insert data from the input files into a specified table. **db2move** is a batch version of the data movement utilities; it can export, import, or load multiple tables with just one command. Each utility is discussed in more detail in the sections that follow.

13.2 Data Movement File Formats

Before learning about moving data between DB2 databases and/or other data sources, it is important to first understand the file formats that the data movement utilities use. You can choose from five different file formats:

- Delimited ASCII (DEL)
- Non-delimited ASCII (ASC)
- PC version of Integrated Exchange Format (PC/IXF)
- Worksheet format (WSF)
- Cursor

13.2.1 Delimited ASCII (DEL) Format

As the name implies, this file format contains a stream of ASCII characters that are separated by row and column delimiters. Comma (,) is the default column delimiter and the carriage return is the default row delimiter. For character strings, DB2 uses double quotes (" ") as the string delimiter. For example, a DEL file will look similar to Figure 13.2. Note that all the string data is surrounded by a pair of double quotes and each column value is separated by a comma.

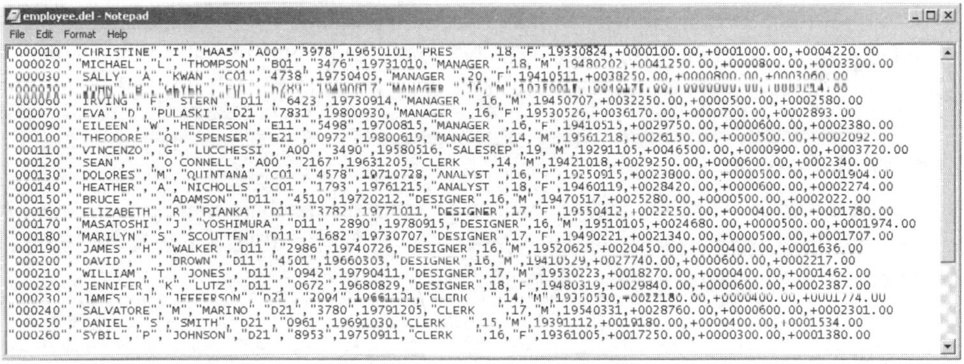

```
employee.del - Notepad
File  Edit  Format  Help
"000010","CHRISTINE","I","HAAS","A00","3978",19650101,"PRES    ",18,"F",19330824,+0000100.00,+0001000.00,+0004220.00
"000020","MICHAEL","L","THOMPSON","B01","3476",19731010,"MANAGER ",18,"M",19480202,+0041250.00,+0000800.00,+0003300.00
"000030","SALLY","A","KWAN","C01","4738",19750405,"MANAGER ",20,"F",19410511,+0038250.00,+0000800.00,+0003060.00
[illegible]
"000060","IRVING","F","STERN","D11","6423",19730914,"MANAGER ",16,"M",19450707,+0032250.00,+0000500.00,+0002580.00
"000070","EVA","D","PULASKI","D21","7831",19800930,"MANAGER ",16,"F",19530526,+0036170.00,+0000700.00,+0002893.00
"000090","EILEEN","W","HENDERSON","E11","5498",19700815,"MANAGER ",16,"F",19410515,+0029750.00,+0000600.00,+0002380.00
"000100","THEODORE","Q","SPENSER","E21","0972",19800619,"MANAGER ",14,"M",19561218,+0026150.00,+0000500.00,+0002092.00
"000110","VINCENZO","G","LUCCHESSI","A00","3490",19580516,"SALESREP",19,"M",19291105,+0046500.00,+0000900.00,+0003720.00
"000120","SEAN"," ","O'CONNELL","A00","2167",19631205,"CLERK   ",14,"M",19421018,+0029250.00,+0000600.00,+0002340.00
"000130","DOLORES","M","QUINTANA","C01","4578",19710728,"ANALYST ",16,"F",19250915,+0023800.00,+0000500.00,+0001904.00
"000140","HEATHER","A","NICHOLLS","C01","1793",19761215,"ANALYST ",18,"F",19460119,+0028420.00,+0000600.00,+0002274.00
"000150","BRUCE"," ","ADAMSON","D11","4510",19720212,"DESIGNER",16,"M",19470517,+0025280.00,+0000500.00,+0002022.00
"000160","ELIZABETH","R","PIANKA","D11","3782",19771011,"DESIGNER",17,"F",19550412,+0022250.00,+0000400.00,+0001780.00
"000170","MASATOSHI","J","YOSHIMURA","D11","2890",19780915,"DESIGNER",16,"M",19510105,+0024680.00,+0000500.00,+0001974.00
"000180","MARILYN","S","SCOUTTEN","D11","1682",19730707,"DESIGNER",17,"F",19490221,+0021340.00,+0000500.00,+0001707.00
"000190","JAMES","H","WALKER","D11","2986",19740726,"DESIGNER",16,"M",19520625,+0020450.00,+0000400.00,+0001636.00
"000200","DAVID"," ","BROWN","D11","4501",19660303,"DESIGNER",16,"M",19410529,+0027740.00,+0000600.00,+0002217.00
"000210","WILLIAM","T","JONES","D11","0942",19790411,"DESIGNER",17,"M",19530223,+0018270.00,+0000400.00,+0001462.00
"000220","JENNIFER","K","LUTZ","D11","0672",19680829,"DESIGNER",18,"F",19480319,+0029840.00,+0000600.00,+0002387.00
"000230","JAMES","J","JEFFERSON","D21","2094",19661121,"CLERK   ",14,"M",19350530,+0022180.00,+0000400.00,+0001774.00
"000240","SALVATORE","M","MARINO","D21","3780",19791205,"CLERK   ",17,"M",19540331,+0028760.00,+0000600.00,+0002301.00
"000250","DANIEL","S","SMITH","D21","0961",19691030,"CLERK   ",15,"M",19391112,+0019180.00,+0000400.00,+0001534.00
"000260","SYBIL","P","JOHNSON","D21","8953",19750911,"CLERK   ",16,"F",19361005,+0017250.00,+0000300.00,+0001380.00
```

Figure 13.2 Sample DEL file

13.2.2 Non-Delimited ASCII (ASC) Format

The ASC file format is also known as **fixed length ASCII file format** because each column length in the file has the same length as defined for the corresponding column definition in the table. For example, variable-length character column definitions in a table are padded with blanks in an ASC file and represented using their maximum length. Figure 13.3 shows the same data as in Figure 13.2 but in ASC format.

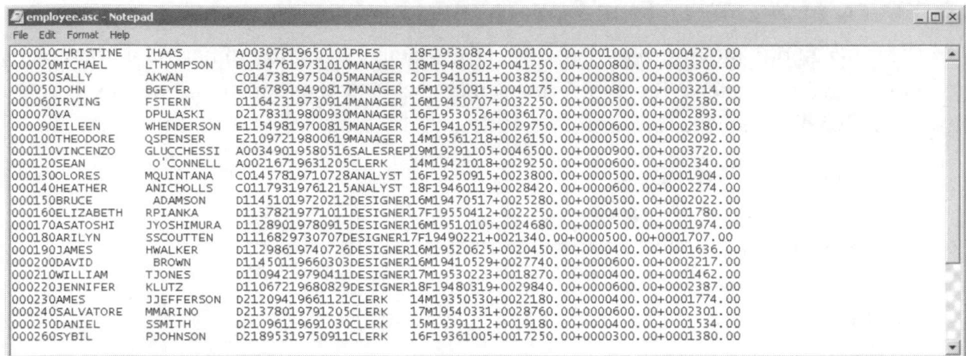
```
employee.asc - Notepad
File Edit Format Help
000010CHRISTINE   IHAAS       A00397819650101PRES     18F19330824+0000100.00+0001000.00+0004220.00
000020MICHAEL     LTHOMPSON   B01347619731010MANAGER 18M19480202+0041250.00+0000800.00+0003300.00
000030SALLY       AKWAN       C01473819750405MANAGER 20F19410511+0038250.00+0000800.00+0003060.00
000050JOHN        BGEYER      E01678919490817MANAGER 16M19250915+0040175.00+0000800.00+0003214.00
000060IRVING      FSTERN      D11642319730914MANAGER 16M19450707+0032250.00+0000500.00+0002580.00
000070VA          DPULASKI    D21783119800930MANAGER 16F19530526+0036170.00+0000700.00+0002893.00
000090EILEEN      WHENDERSON  E11549819700815MANAGER 16F19410515+0029750.00+0000600.00+0002380.00
000100THEODORE    QSPENSER    E21097219800619MANAGER 14M19561218+0026150.00+0000500.00+0002092.00
000110VINCENZO    GLUCCHESSI  A00349019580516SALESREP19M19291105+0046500.00+0000900.00+0003720.00
000120SEAN         O'CONNELL  A00216719631205CLERK   14M19421018+0029250.00+0000600.00+0002340.00
000130OLORES      MQUINTANA   C01457819710728ANALYST 16F19250915+0023800.00+0000500.00+0001904.00
000140HEATHER     ANICHOLLS   C01179319761215ANALYST 18F19460119+0028420.00+0000600.00+0002274.00
000150BRUCE        ADAMSON    D11451019720212DESIGNER16M19470517+0025280.00+0000500.00+0002022.00
000160ELIZABETH   RPIANKA     D11378219771011DESIGNER17F19550412+0022250.00+0000400.00+0001780.00
000170ASATOSHI    JYOSHIMURA  D11289019780915DESIGNER16M19510105+0024680.00+0000500.00+0001974.00
000180ARILYN      SSCOUTTEN   D1116829730707DESIGNER17F19490221+0021340.00+0000500.00+0001707.00
000190JAMES       HWALKER     D11298619740726DESIGNER16M19520625+0020450.00+0000400.00+0001636.00
000200DAVID        BROWN      D11450119660303DESIGNER16M19410529+0027740.00+0000600.00+0002217.00
000210WILLIAM     TJONES      D11094219790411DESIGNER17M19530223+0018270.00+0000400.00+0001462.00
000220JENNIFER    KLUTZ       D11067219680829DESIGNER18F19480319+0029840.00+0000600.00+0002387.00
000230AMES        JJEFFERSON  D21209419661121CLERK   14M19350530+0022180.00+0000400.00+0001774.00
000240SALVATORE   MMARINO     D21378019791205CLERK   17M19540331+0028760.00+0000600.00+0002301.00
000250DANIEL      SSMITH      D21096119691030CLERK   15M19391112+0019180.00+0000400.00+0001534.00
000260SYBIL       PJOHNSON    D21895319750911CLERK   16F19361005+0017250.00+0000300.00+0001380.00
```

Figure 13.3 Sample ASC file

13.2.3 PC Version of IXF (PC/IXF) Format

PC/IXF (or simply IXF) files cannot be edited with a normal text editor. It uses the IXF data interchange architecture, which is a generic relational database exchange format that lets you move data among DB2 databases. PC/IXF can only be used for moving data between DB2 databases because it is an IBM proprietary format. In addition to data, the file also contains the data types and structure of the table. Therefore it can be used to first create the table in the target database and then import data.

13.2.4 WSF Format

WSF files are Lotus 1-2-3 and Symphony worksheets that the database manager supports. Any filenames with these extensions are accepted: WKS, WK1, WRK, WR1, and WJ2. WSF files are mainly used for moving data between DB2 and these worksheets.

13.2.5 Cursor

Alternatively, you can you load data into a table using a cursor. The cursor must be declared with an SQL query first before it can be referenced in the **`load`** command. You can only use the cursor file format with the load utility. Section 13.5.2.2, Loading from a CURSOR, shows how to use this format.

13.3 The DB2 EXPORT Utility

The export utility extracts data from a table into a file. Figure 13.4 shows the syntax diagram of the **`export`** command.

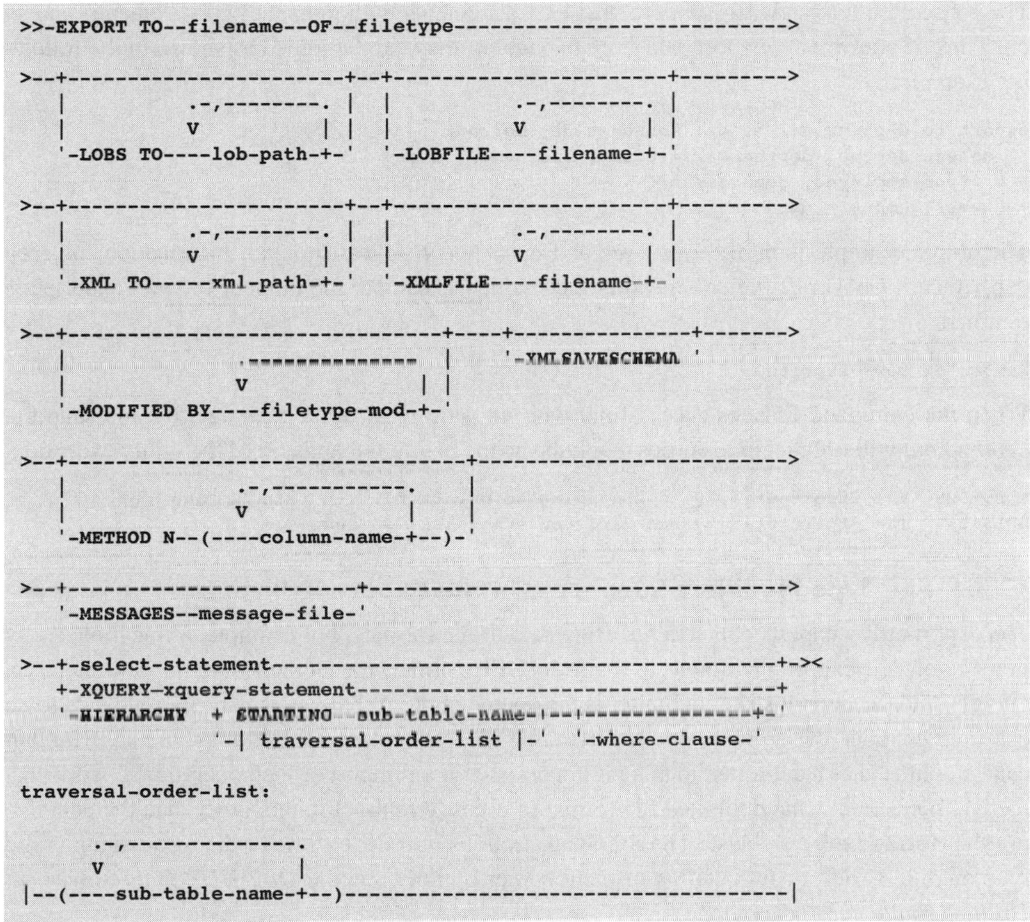

```
>>-EXPORT TO--filename--OF--filetype---------------------------->

>--+-----------------------+--+-----------------------+--------->
   |        .-,--------.   |  |          .-,--------.  |
   |        V          |   |  |          V          |  |
   '-LOBS TO----lob-path-+-'  '-LOBFILE----filename-+-'

>--+-----------------------+--+-----------------------+--------->
   |        .-,--------.   |  |          .-,--------.  |
   |        V          |   |  |          V          |  |
   '-XML TO-----xml-path-+-'  '-XMLFILE----filename-+-'

>--+-------------------------------+----+---------------+------->
   |             .--------------.  |    '-XMLSAVESCHEMA-'
   |             V              |  |
   '-MODIFIED BY----filetype-mod-+-'

>--+-------------------------------+---------------------------->
   |             .-,-----------.   |
   |             V             |   |
   '-METHOD N--(----column-name-+--)-'

>--+-----------------------+------------------------------------>
   '-MESSAGES--message-file-'

>--+-select-statement-----------------------------------------+-><
   +-XQUERY-xquery-statement----------------------------------+
   '-HIERARCHY--+-STARTING--sub-table-name-+--+---------------+-'
                '-| traversal-order-list |-'  '-where-clause-'

traversal-order-list:

      .-,--------------.
      V                |
|--(----sub-table-name-+--)-------------------------------------|
```

Figure 13.4 Syntax diagram of the export command

As you can see, the command supports many different options. Let's start with a simple export command and discuss how to use the options to customize the command. The following example of the **export** command exports all the rows in the *employee* table to the file *empdata.ixf* in IXF format.

```
export to empdata.ixf of ixf select * from employee
```

All the keywords in this command are mandatory, that is, you have to provide the output filename, specify the file format, and the **SELECT** statement that will retrieve the rows to be exported. The exported file can be in a format of DEL, IXF, or WSF.

Using the optional **messages** clause, you can specify a filename where warning and error messages of the export operation are logged. If no message file accompanies the **messages** clause, the messages are written to standard output. Though optional, we highly recommend you use this clause so that all the messages generated by the utility are saved.

The **export** command also supports **SELECT** statements with joins, nested statements, and so on. Thus, if you want to export data from two tables, they can be joined as shown in the following example:

```
export to deptmgr.del of del messages deptmgr.out
   select deptno, deptname, firstnme, lastname, salary
     from employee, department
    where empno = mgrno
```

The above example joins the *employee* and *department* tables to obtain information for each department manager. If the command is successfully executed, the number of rows exported is returned.

```
Number of rows exported: 8
```

When the command finishes successfully with no warning or error message, the message file *deptmgr.out* will only include entries that indicate the beginning and end of the utility execution.

```
SQL3104N  The Export utility is beginning to export data to file "c:\deptmgr.del".
SQL3105N  The Export utility has finished exporting "8" rows.
```

13.3.1 File Type Modifiers Supported in the Export Utility

The export utility exports data to a file using default file formats. For example, as mentioned earlier, if you are exporting a table to a file in DEL format, the default column delimiter is a comma, and the default string delimiter is the double quote. What happens if the table data to be exported contains these delimiters as part of the data? The file exported may contain data that can be confused as a delimiter, making it impossible for an import or load operation to work correctly. To customize the delimited file format to use different delimiters other than the defaults, use the **modified by** clause. The following sections introduce some of the most common file type modifiers. For a complete list of the modifier options, see the *DB2 UDB Data Movement Utilities Guide and Reference*.

13.3.1.1 Changing the Column Delimiter

To use a column delimiter other than the comma, specify the **coldel** file type modifier in the **modified by** clause. The following example specifies to use a semicolon as the column modifier. Note that there is no space between the keyword **coldel** and the semicolon.

```
export to deptmgr.del of del
  modified by coldel;
  messages deptmgr.out
  select deptno, deptname, firstnme, lastname, salary
    from employee, department
   where empno = mgrno
```

13.3.1.2 Changing the Character Delimiter

You can enclose character strings with a different delimiter by using the keyword **chardel.** Continuing with the previous example, the character delimiter used here is a pair of single quotes.

```
export to deptmgr.del of del
  modified by coldel; chardel''
  messages deptmgr.out
  select deptno, deptname, firstnme, lastname, salary
    from employee, department
   where empno = mgrno
```

13.3.1.3 Changing the Date Format

You can also export data in a specific date format you prefer by using the **timestampformat** modifier.

```
export to deptmgr.del of del
  modified by coldel; chardel'' timestampformat="yyyy.mm.dd hh:mm"
  messages deptmgr.out
  select deptno, deptname, firstnme, lastname, salary
    from employee, department
   where empno = mgrno
```

13.3.1.4 Changing the Code Page

In many cases, the code page of the target database server is not the same as the source server. To ensure data is handled correctly in the target server, you should pay attention to the code page of the exported data. By default, data exported is in the same code page as the application for which the **export** command is invoked. With the export utility, you can use the **codepage** modifier to convert character data from the application.

```
export to deptmgr.del of del
  modified by coldel; chardel'' timestampformat="yyyy.mm.dd hh:mm"
              codepage=1208
  messages deptmgr.out
  select deptno, deptname, firstnme, lastname, salary
    from employee, department
   where empno = mgrno
```

Note that this modifier cannot be used with the **lobinsfile** modifier, which is discussed in the next section.

13.3.2 Exporting Large Objects

DB2 supports the following types of large objects: character large objects (CLOBs), binary large objects (BLOBs), and double-byte character large objects (DBCLOBs). LOB values can be as large as 2GB for CLOBs and BLOBs and 1GB for DBCLOBs. Due to these sizes, the export utility by default extracts only the first 32KB of data of the LOB values in the export file. To extract the entire LOB, you must use the **lobs to** or **lobfile** clause or the **lobsinfile** modifier.

The **lobs to** clause specifies the directories in which the LOB files will be stored. If no **lobs to** clause is found, LOB data is written to the current working directory. You can specify more than one path as the LOB file target directories, and there will be at least one file per LOB path.

Providing user-specified filenames to the extracted LOB files will be very helpful if you want to identify them on the file system later. The **lobfile** clause can be used for this purpose. Each LOB file will have a sequence number as the file extension, for example *lobfile.001*, *lobfile.002*, *lobfile.003*, and so on.

> **NOTE** When either the **lobs to** or **lobfile** clause is specified, the **lobsinfile** behavior is implicitly activated. However, it is always a good practice to explicitly specify the **lobsinfile** modifier to avoid confusion with the **lobsinsepfile** modifier, which will be discussed later.

All the LOB values for a particular LOB column are stored in a single file that is separate from the regular export data file. The export data file, however, contains a LOB location specifier (LLS) to link the regular data for the row with the LOB data of this row. Since all LOB values are stored in one file, the LLS string indicates the starting position (offset) where the associated LOB data can be found and the length of the LOB. The format of the LLS is

```
filename.ext.nnn.mmm
```

where

- *filename.ext* is the name of the file that contains the LOB.
- *nnn* is the offset (measured in bytes) of the LOB within the file.
- *mmm* is the length (measured in bytes) of the LOB.

For example, the following **export** command generates three files. One file is the message file, *mgrresume.out*. Another file, *mgrresume.del*, is the data file, which contains all data columns for the rows except the LOB data. The third file, *resume.001*, is the file containing the LOB values for all rows.

```
export to mgrresume.del of del
  lobs to c:\lobs
  lobfile resume
  modified by lobsinfile
  messages mgrresume.out
   select deptno, deptname, firstnme, lastname, resume
     from employee a, emp_resume b
    where a.empno = b.empno
```

Note that the output file *mgrresume.del* contains the LLS instead of the LOB data. Figure 13.5 illustrates the contents of *mgrresume.del*. Notice that in the third column the LLS value is *resume.001.0.1313*, which means that the LOB of this record is stored in file *resume.001*. It begins at an offset of 0 bytes, and then follows by the size of the LOB (1313 bytes). The following LLS entry shows that the LOB data for the next row is also stored in file *resume.001.0.1313,* starting at offset 1313 and with a length of 1817 bytes. The next entry would start at offset 3130 (1313 + 1817). If the indicated size in the LLS is 0, the LOB is considered to have a length of 0. If the length is –1, the LOB is considered to be NULL, and the offset and filename are ignored.

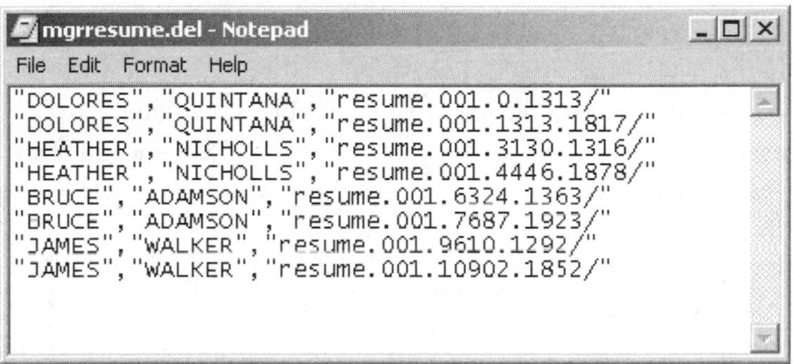

Figure 13.5 A sample export data file with LOB location specifier (LLS)

Starting in DB2 9, you can export each LOB data into separate files instead of concatenating the data into a LOB file. The LOB options described earlier remain the same, except that the **lobsinsepfile** modifier is used instead. Here is an example using the **lobsinsepfile** modifier.

```
export to mgrresume.del of del
  lobs to c:\lobs
  lobfile resume
  modified by lobsinsepfile
  messages mgrresume.out
   select deptno, deptname, firstnme, lastname, resume
     from employee a, emp_resume b
    where a.empno = b.empno
```

With this **export** command, the export utility will write LOB data into files called *resume.ext.lob* such as *resume.001.lob*, *resume.002.lob*, *resume.003.lob*, and so on. They are all located in the LOB path *c:\lobs*.

13.3.3 Exporting XML Data

With the introduction of native XML support in DB2 9, the export utility is extended to also support XML. By default, the export utility exports XML data to a file or files separate from the rest of the exported relational data. For example, the following **export** command is issued on the *product* table, which has one XML column defined.

```
export to prodexport.del of del
    messages msg.out
    select * from product
```

In this example, the export utility will generate two output files. One of them is the *prodexport.del* file, which contains relational data of the table as well as the XML data specifier (XDS). XDS is a string represented as an XML tag named XDS. It has attributes that describe information about the actual XML data in the column. These are the attributes you might see in an XDS string:

- **FIL** specifies the name of the file that contains the XML data.
- **OFF** specifies the byte offset of the XML data in the file named by the **FIL** attribute.
- **LEN** specifies the length in bytes of the XML data in the file named by the **FIL** attribute.
- **SCH** specifies the fully qualified SQL identifier of the XML schema used to validate this XML document.

From Figure 13.6, you can see that the first XML data is stored in *prodexport.del.001.xml* starting at the 0 byte offset, and it has a length of 290 bytes. Similarly, the second XML data is also stored in the same file *prodexport.del.001.xml* starting at the 290 byte offset and is 303 bytes long.

File: prodexport.del

```
"100-100-01",,,,,,"<XDS FIL='prodexport.del.001.xml' OFF='0' LEN='290' />"
"100-101-01",,,,,,"<XDS FIL='prodexport.del.001.xml' OFF='290' LEN='303' />"
"100-103-01",,,,,,"<XDS FIL='prodexport.del.001.xml' OFF='593' LEN='337' />"
"100-201-01",,,,,,"<XDS FIL='prodexport.del.001.xml' OFF='930' LEN='255' />"
```

Figure 13.6 Content of prodexport.del

The other file generated by the export utility in this example is *prodexport.del.001.xml,* which contains the actual XML data. Every XML data exported are concatenated and written to this file. To get a better idea, refer to Figure 13.7.

File: prodexport.del.001.xml

```
<?xml version="1.0" encoding="UTF-8" ?><product xmlns="http://posample.org"
pid="100-100-01"><description><name>Snow Shovel, Basic 22 inch</name><detai
ls>Basic Snow Shovel, 22 inches wide, straight handle with D-Grip</details>
<price>9.99</price><weight>1 kg</weight></description></product><?xml versi
on="1.0" encoding="UTF-8" ?><product xmlns="http://posample.org" pid="100-
101-01"><description><name>Snow Shovel, Deluxe 24 inch</name><details>A Del
uxe Snow Shovel, 24 inches wide, ergonomic curved handle with D-Grip</detai
ls><price>19.99</price><weight>2 kg</weight></description></product><?xml
version="1.0" encoding="UTF-8" ?><product xmlns="http://posample.org" pid="
100-103-01"><description><name>Snow Shovel, Super Deluxe 26 inch</name><det
ails>Super Deluxe Snow Shovel, 26 inches wide, ergonomic battery heated cur
ved handle with upgraded D-Grip</details><price>49.99</price><weight>3 kg</
weight></description></product><?xml version="1.0" encoding="UTF-8" ?><prod
uct xmlns="http://posample.org" pid="100-201-01"><description><name>Ice Scr
aper, Windshield 4 inch</name><details>Basic Ice Scraper 4 inches wide, foa
m handle</details><price>3.99</price></description></product>
```

Figure 13.7 Content of prodexport.del.001.xml

Both *prodexport.del* and *prodexport.del.001.xml* in the above example are stored in the current directory of where the **export** command is executed. Similar to exporting large objects, you can specify the path(s) where the exported XML documents will go and the base filename of the output files. Consider the following example.

```
export to prodexport.del of del
    xml to d:\xmlpath
    xmlfile proddesc
    modified by xmlinsepfiles xmlnodeclaration xmlchar
    xmlsaveschema
    messages msg.out
    select * from product
```

Here, the relational data of the *product* table is exported to the *prodexport.del* file. All XML data is then written to the directory specified in the **XML TO** clause, *d:/xmlpath.* The files with XML data are named *proddesc.ext.xml,* where *ext* is a sequence number, for example, *proddesc.001.xml, proddesc.002.xml, proddesc.003.xml*, and so on. The base filename is defined with the **XMLFILE** option.

A few modifiers are also used in the example. Here is a summary of all the XML related modifiers:

- **XMLINSEPFILES** causes the export utility to write each exported XML document to a separate XML file.
- **XMLNODECLARATION** indicates that the XML data is exported without an XML declaration tag. An XML declaration tag, **<?xml version="1.0" encoding="UTF-8" ?>,** contains attributes of the XML version and encoding information. It is by default written at the beginning of an XML document.
- **XMLCHAR** indicates that the XML data is written in the character codepage. By default, XML data is written out in Unicode. When this modifier is used, the value of the **codepage** file type modifier or the application codepage will be used instead.
- **XMLGRAPHIC** indicates that the exported XML data will be encoded in the UTF-16 codepage regardless of the **codepage** file type modifier or the application codepage. Note that **XMLGRAPHIC** is not used in this example.

The last option introduced here is **XMLSAVESCHEMA.** When an XML document is inserted, it can be validated against an XML schema. The **XMLSAVESCHEMA** option causes the export utility to also save the XML schema information for every exported XML data. A fully qualified SQL identifier of that schema will be stored as an SCH attribute inside the corresponding XML data specifier (XDS). Note that if the exported XML document was not validated against an XML schema or the schema object no longer exists in the database, an SCH attribute will not be included in the corresponding XDS. Figure 13.8 illustrates the sample result of the above **export** command with XML options and modifiers.

File: prodexport.del

```
"100-100-01",,,,,,"<XDS FIL='prodexport.del.001.xml' />"
"100-101-01",,,,,,"<XDS FIL='prodexport.del.002.xml' SCH='DB2INST1.PRODUCT' />"
"100-103-01",,,,,,"<XDS FIL='prodexport.del.003.xml' SCH='DB2INST1.PRODUCT' />"
"100-201-01",,,,,,"<XDS FIL='prodexport.del.004.xml' />"
```

File: proddesc.001.xml

```
<product xmlns="http://posample.org" pid="100-100-01"><description><name>Snow
Shovel, Basic 22 inch</name><details>Basic Snow Shovel, 22 inches wide, straigh
t handle with D-Grip</details><price>9.99</price><weight>1 kg</weight></descrip
tion></product>
```

File: proddesc.002.xml

```
<product xmlns="http://posample.org" pid="100-101-01"><description><name>Snow
Shovel, Deluxe 24 inch</name><details>A Deluxe Snow Shovel, 24 inches wide, erg
onomic curved handle with D-Grip</details><price>19.99</price><weight>2 kg</wei
ght></description></product>
```

File: proddesc.003.xml

```
<product xmlns="http://posample.org" pid="100-103-01"><description><name>Snow
Shovel, Super Deluxe 26 inch</name><details>Super Deluxe Snow Shovel, 26 inches
wide, ergonomic battery heated curved handle with upgraded D-Grip</details><pri
ce>49.99</price><weight>3 kg</weight></description></product>
```

File: proddesc.004.xml

```
<product xmlns="http://posample.org" pid="100-201-01"><description><name>Ice
Scraper, Windshield 4 inch</name><details>Basic Ice Scraper 4 inches wide, foam
handle</details><price>3.99</price></description></product>
```

Figure 13.8 Output of an **export** command

Perhaps you only want to export selected XML elements and attributes but not the entire XML document. Simply apply the SQL/XML or XQuery lanugage you learned in Chapter 10, Mastering the DB2 pureXML Support, to the **export** command. As an example, the following command will export six records of the XML *phone* elements. Each record is stored in separate files. Content of one of the exported record is captured in Figure 13.9.

```
export to custexport.del of del
    xmlfile custphone
    modified by xmlinsepfiles xmlnodeclaration
    select xmlquery ('declare default element namespace "http://posample.org";
                      $d/customerinfo/phone' passing INFO as "d" )
      from customer
```

File: custphone.006.xml

```
<phone xmlns="http://posample.org" type="work">905-555-9146</phone><phone
xmlns="http://posample.org" type="home">416-555-6121</phone>
```

Figure 13.9 Content of custphone.006.xml

13.3.4 Specifying Column Names

The **method n** (column names) option is useful when a column is derived from one or more columns. For example, if you use the following **select** statement in the **export** command:

```
select empno, firstnme, lastname, salary * 1.3
  from employee
 where workdept='A00'
```

the following shows what the output of the **select** statement would be. Notice that the last column in the select list is a derived column that does not have a column name.

```
EMPNO  FIRSTNME     LASTNAME        4
------ ------------ --------------- -------------
000010 CHRISTINE    HAAS                  130.000
000110 VINCENZO     LUCCHESSI           60450.000
000120 SEAN         O'CONNELL           38025.000
```

The import utility (which is discussed in more detail in Section 13.4, The DB2 IMPORT Utility) can be executed with a **create** option that lets you create the target table if it does not already exist before data is imported. The input file must also contain the definition of the table. If you were to import the above result with the **create** option, the newly created table would have the fourth column named *4*. Rather than using a number, you can provide a more descriptive name using the **AS** clause in the **select** statement:

```
export to newsalary.ixf of ixf
  messages newsalary.out
  select empno, firstnme, lastname, salary * 1.3 as new_salary
    from employee
   where workdept='A00'
```

Alternatively, use the **method n** option to explicitly specify all the column names. This option is only supported when the export file format is IXF or WSF.

```
export to newsalary.ixf of ixf
  messages newsalary.out
  method n ('EMPLOYEENO', 'FIRSTNAME', 'LASTNAME', 'NEWSALARY')
  select empno, firstnme, lastname, salary * 1.3
    from employee
   where workdept='A00'
```

With the **method n** clause and the specified columns, the resulting file will contain the new column names:

```
EMPLOYEENO FIRSTNAME    LASTNAME         NEWSALARY
---------- ------------ --------------- -------------
000010     CHRISTINE    HAAS                  130.000
000110     VINCENZO     LUCCHESSI           60450.000
000120     SEAN         O'CONNELL           38025.000
```

13.3.5 Authorities Required to Perform an Export

There is no special authorization requirement to perform an export. Any authenticated user is able to execute the **export** command. However, the user must be able to access the data of the table being exported. Therefore, the user must hold SYSADM, DBADM, CONTROL, or SELECT privileges on each table or view referenced in the **select** statement of the command.

13.3.6 Exporting a Table Using the Control Center

You can also perform an export from the Control Center. In the Control Center, right click on the table you want to export and select the **Export** option as shown in Figure 13.10.

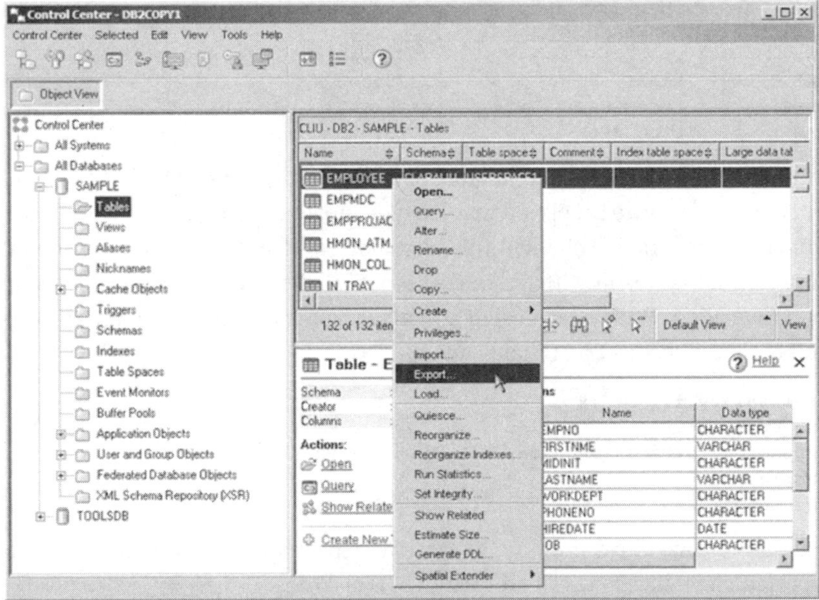

Figure 13.10 Exporting data from the Control Center

This displays the Export Table dialog (see Figure 13.11). You can specify all the options discussed earlier in this chapter in this dialog, such as the output file, message file, file format, and the **select** statement.

To specify the column names, LOB, and XML options, switch to the *Columns* tab (illustrated in Figure 13.12).

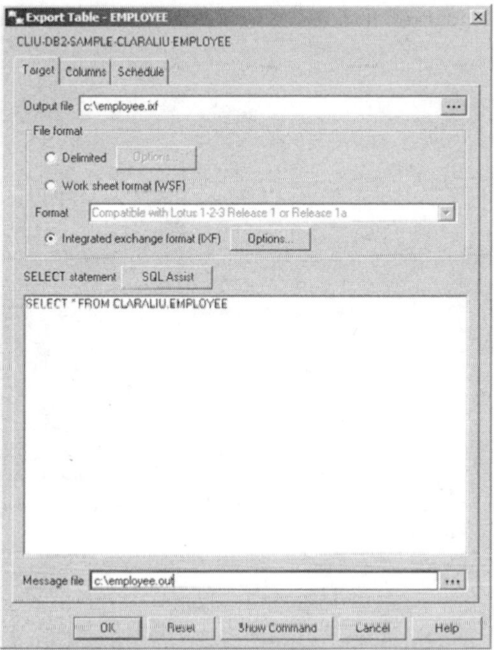

Figure 13.11 The Export Table dialog

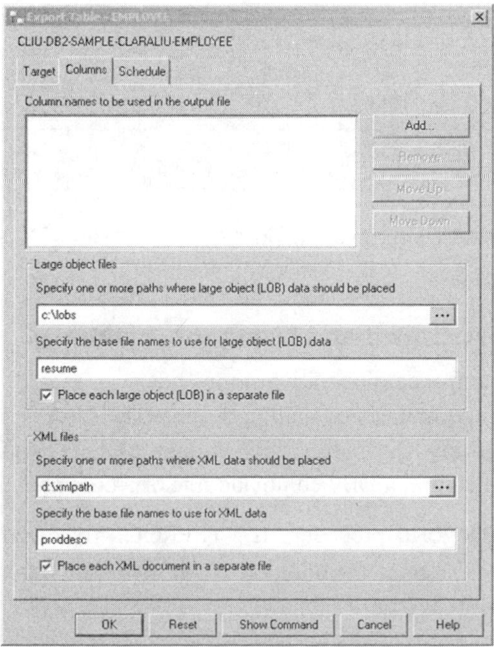

Figure 13.12 Specifying column names, LOB, and XML options for the export operation

The last tab, *Schedule*, lets you run the export now or schedule it to run at some other time (see Figure 13.13).

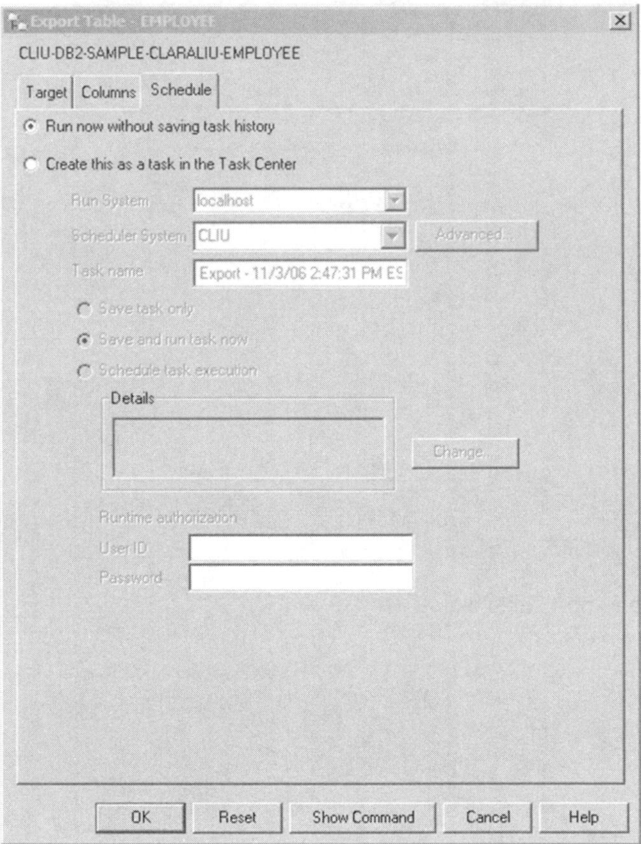

Figure 13.13 Specifying when to run the export

V9 13.3.7 Run an export Command Using the ADMIN_CMD Procedure

Starting in DB2 9, you can run administrative commands such as **`export, import, load, reorg,`** and **`runstats`** commands by calling the **`ADMIN_CMD`** procedure. The advantage of doing this is that you can now administer DB2 through SQL. This procedure can be invoked from any SQL-based application, a DB2 command line or a command script.

The schema of the **`ADMIN_CMD`** procedure is SYSPROC. You need EXECUTE privilege to invoke the procedure. In addition, performing an export operation requires you to have appropriate privileges as discussed in Section 13.5.9.

The syntax and behavior of the **export** command supported in the **ADMIN_CMD** procedure is exactly the same as shown in Figure 13.4 with one exception. Rather than saving the messages for the export operation in a file stored in a server directory, messages are saved on the server in the database. Note that **messages on server** is used in the example below.

```
call sysproc.admin_cmd
    ( 'export to employee.del of del messages on server select * from employee' )
```

The command returns a result set with three columns:

- ROWS_EXPORTED—number of rows exported
- MSG_RETRIEVAL—an SQL statement of how to retreive the message, for example:

  ```
  SELECT SQLCODE
       , MSG
    FROM TABLE(SYSPROC.ADMIN_GET_MSGS('23230_CLARALIU')) AS MSG
  ```

- MSG_REMOVAL—an SQL statement of how the message can be removed, for example:

  ```
  CALL SYSPROC.ADMIN_REMOVE_MSGS('23230_CLARALIU')
  ```

13.4 The DB2 IMPORT Utility

The import utility inserts data from an input file into a table or a view. The utility performs inserts as if it was executing **INSERT** statements. Just like normal insert operations, DB2 validates the data and checks against the table definitions, constraints (such as referential integrity and check constraints), and index definitions. Triggers are also invoked.

The utility supports options and import modes that let you customize its behavior. The syntax diagram of the **import** command is very long; Figure 13.14 shows only a portion of it. Please refer to the *DB2 Command Reference* for the complete syntax diagram.

Although the syntax diagram may seem complex, it is quite easy to understand and follow. Let's start with a simple **import** command and discuss the mandatory options. To a certain degree, the **import** command is structured much like the **export** command: You have to specify the input filename, format of the file, and the target table name, for example:

```
import from employee.ixf of ixf
  messages employee.out
  insert into employee
```

This command takes the file *employee.ixf,* which is in the IXF format, as the input and inserts the data rows from the file into the *employee* table. The import utility supports input files in ASC, DEL, IXF, and WSF formats. We also recommend that you specify the optional clause **messages** to save the error and warning messages and the import status. In Section 13.4.4, Restarting a Failed Import, you will see that the message file can be used to identify where to restart an interrupted import operation.

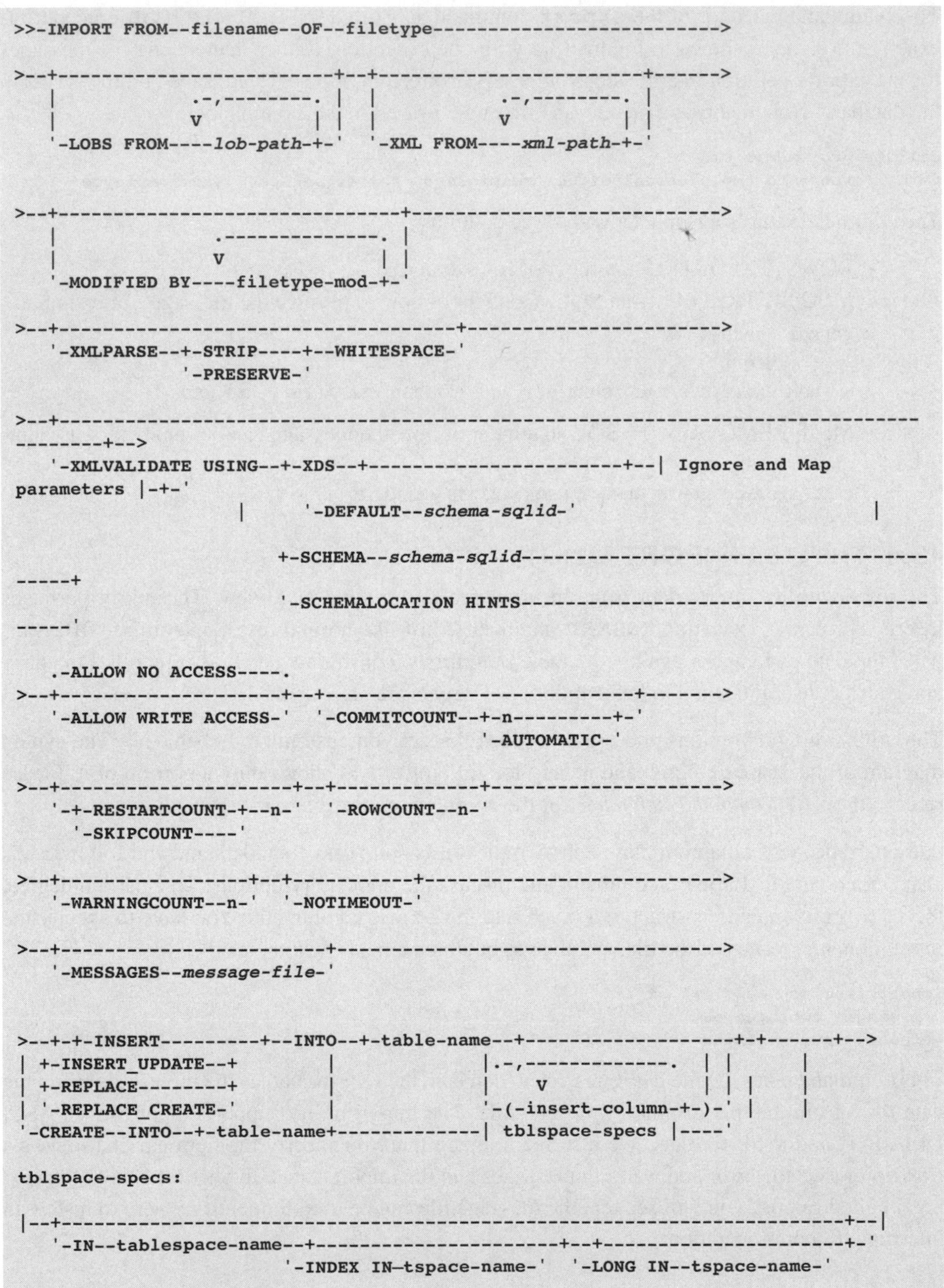

```
>>-IMPORT FROM--filename--OF--filetype------------------------->

>--+-----------------------+--+----------------------+------>
   |            .-,--------. |  |           .-,--------. |
   |            V          | |  |           V          | |
   '-LOBS FROM----lob-path-+-'  '-XML FROM----xml-path-+-'


>--+------------------------------+---------------------------->
   |          .---------------.  |
   |          V               |  |
   '-MODIFIED BY----filetype-mod-+-'

>--+-------------------------------------+--------------------->
   '-XMLPARSE--+-STRIP----+--WHITESPACE-'
               '-PRESERVE-'

>--+-----------------------------------------------------------------------
--------+-->
   '-XMLVALIDATE USING--+-XDS--+----------------------+--| Ignore and Map
parameters |-+-'
                        |       '-DEFAULT--schema-sqlid-'                  |

                        +-SCHEMA--schema-sqlid------------------------------------
-----+
                        '-SCHEMALOCATION HINTS------------------------------------
-----'

   .-ALLOW NO ACCESS----.
>--+--------------------+--+----------------------------+------->
   '-ALLOW WRITE ACCESS-'  '-COMMITCOUNT--+-n---------+-'
                                          '-AUTOMATIC-'

>--+--------------------+--+------------+-------------------->
   '-+-RESTARTCOUNT-+--n-'  '-ROWCOUNT--n-'
     '-SKIPCOUNT----'

>--+-----------------+--+-----------+------------------------->
   '-WARNINGCOUNT--n-'  '-NOTIMEOUT-'

>--+-----------------------+----------------------------------->
   '-MESSAGES--message-file-'


>--+-+-INSERT---------+--INTO--+-table-name--+-------------------+-+------+-->
 | +-INSERT_UPDATE--+         |             |.-,-------------.  | |      |
 | +-REPLACE--------+         |             |  V              | | |      |
 | '-REPLACE_CREATE-'         |             '-(-insert-column-+-)-' |      |
 '-CREATE--INTO--+-table-name+-------------| tblspace-specs |----'

tblspace-specs:

|--+--------------------------------------------------------------------+--|
   '-IN--tablespace-name--+----------------------+--+---------------------+-'
                          '-INDEX IN-tspace-name-'  '-LONG IN--tspace-name-'
```

Figure 13.14 Simplified syntax diagram of the import command

13.4.1 Import Mode

The previous example uses **insert** to indicate that new data is to be appended to the existing *employee* table. Table 13.1 lists the modes supported by the import utility.

Table 13.1 Import Modes

Mode	Description
INSERT	Adds the imported data to the table without changing the existing table data. The target table must already exist.
INSERT_UPDATE	Adds the imported data to the target table or updates existing rows with matching primary keys. The target table must already exist defined with primary keys.
CREATE	Creates the table, index definitions, and row contents. The input file must use the IXF format because this is the only format that stores table and index definitions.
REPLACE	Deletes all existing data from the table and inserts the imported data. The table definition and index definitions are not changed.
REPLACE_CREATE	If the table exists, this option behaves like the **replace** option. If the table does not exist, this option behaves like the **create** option, which creates the table and index definitions and then inserts the row contents. This option requires the input file to be in IXF format.

Figures 13.15, 13.16, and 13.17 demonstrate some of the import modes and other options.

In Figure 13.15, the input data of specific columns are selected from the DEL input file and imported into the *empsalary* table. This table must exist in order to use the **replace** option. The **warningcount** option indicates that the utility will stop after 10 warnings are received. If this option is not specified or is set to zero, the import operation will continue regardless of the number of warnings issued.

```
import from employee.del of del
  messages empsalary.out
  warningcount 10
  replace into empsalary (salary, bonus, comm)
```

Figure 13.15 Example 1: import command

In Figure 13.16, the **import** command deletes all the rows in the table (if table *newemployee* exists) and inserts the row contents. If the *newemployee* table does not exist, the command creates the table with definitions stored in the IXF input file and inserts the row contents. In addition to specifying the columns you want to import as demonstrated in Figure 13.15, you can also limit the number of rows to be imported using the **rowcount** option. In Figure 13.16, the number of rows to import is limited to the first 1000 rows.

```
import from employee.ixf of ixf
  messages employee.out
  rowcount 1000
  replace_create into newemployee
```

Figure 13.16 Example 2: import command

If the **create** option is demonstrated in Figure 13.17, you can also specify which table space the new table is going to be created in. The **in** clause tells DB2 to store the table data in a particular table space, and the **index in** clauses indicates where the index is to be stored.

```
import from employee.ixf of ixf
  messages newemployee.out
  create into newemployee in datats index in indexts
```

Figure 13.17 Example 3: import command

13.4.2 Allow Concurrent Write Access

While the import utility is adding new rows to the table, the table by default is locked exclusively to block any read/write activities from other applications. This is the behavior of the **allow no access** option. Alternatively, you can specify **allow write access** in the command to allow concurrent read/write access to the target table. A less restrictive lock is acquired at the beginning of the import operation. Note that this option is not compatible with the **replace, create,** or **replace_create** import options.

Both the **allow write access** and **allow no access** options require some type of table lock. It is possible that the utility will be placed in lock-wait state and eventually will be terminated due to a lock timeout. You can specify the **notimeout** option so that the utility will not time out while waiting for locks. This option supersedes the LOCKTIMEOUT database configuration parameter.

13.4.3 Regular Commits during an Import

The import utility inserts data into a table through normal insert operations. Therefore, changes made during the import are logged, and they are committed to the database upon successful completion of the import operation. By default, an import, behaves like an atomic compound statement for which more than one insert is grouped into a transaction. If any insert fails, the rest of the inserts will not be committed to the database.

If you were to import a few million rows into a table, you would need to make sure there was enough log space to hold the insertions because they are treated as one transaction. However, sometimes it is not feasible to allocate large log space just for the import. There is an import option available for this reason. You can specify the **commitcount n** option to force a commit after every *n* records are imported. With **commitcount automatic,** the utility will commit automatically at an appropriate time to avoid running out of active log space and avoid lock escalation.

Figure 13.18 shows the messages captured during the following **import** command. Note that a COMMIT is issued every 1,000 rows. The message file also serves as a very good progress indicator, because you can access this file while the utility is running.

```
import from employee.ixf of ixf
  commitcount 1000
  messages newemp.out
  create into newemployee in datats index in indexts
```

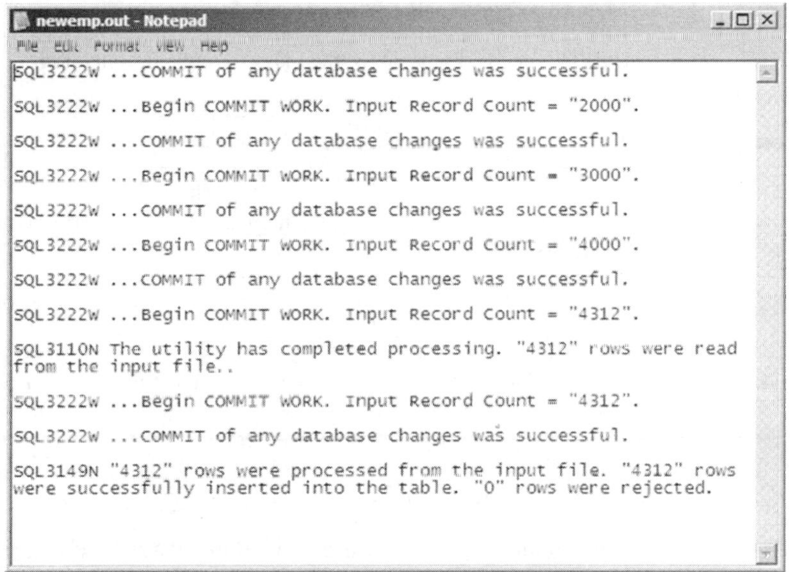

Figure 13.18 Importing with intermediate commits

13.4.4 Restarting a Failed Import

If you have import failures due to invalid input, for example, you can use the message file generated from an **import** command that uses the **commitcount** and **messages** options to identify which record failed. Then you could issue the same **import** command with **restartcount n** or **skipcount n** to start the import from record *n*+1. This is a very handy method to restart a failed import. Here is an example:

```
import from employee.ixf of ixf
  commitcount 1000
  skipcount 550
  messages newemployee.out
  create into newemployee in datats index in indexts
```

13.4.5 File Type Modifiers Supported in the Import Utility

The import utility also has the **modified by** clause to allow customization. Some modifiers supported in the export utility also apply to the import utility. A few of them are outlined here. Refer to the *DB2 Data Movement Utilities Guide and Reference* for a complete listing specific to the import utility. Table 13.2 shows a short list of the type of modifiers supported.

Table 13.2 Modifier Types

Modifier Type	Description
compound=x	x number of statements will be attempted to insert each time.
index-schema=schema	Uses the specified schema for the index during index creation.
striptblanks	Truncates any trailing blank spaces when loading data into a variable-length field.
lobsinfile	Indicates that LOB data is being imported. The utility will check the LOBS FROM clause to get the path of the input LOB files. Import large objects will be discussed later.
xmlchar	Indicates that the XML documents are encoded in the character code page. Import XML data will be discussed later.
xmlgraphic	Indicates that the XML documents are encoded in the specified graphic code page.

13.4.5.1 Handling Target Tables with Generated and Identity Columns

Tables with generated columns or identity columns are defined in a way that column values will be automatically generated when records are inserted into the tables. Since import operations perform inserts in the background, new values will be generated at the target server. Therefore, you need to decide whether values stored in the source input file should be used or if new values should be generated. The import utility supports a few file type modifiers to take care of that.

The file modifier **generatedignore** forces the import utility to ignore data for all generated columns presented in the data file. The utility generates the values of those columns. The file modifier **identityignore** behaves the same way as **generatedignore.**

You can use the **generatemissing** modifier to inform the import utility that the input data file contains no data for the generated columns (not even NULLs), and the import utility will therefore generate a value for each row. This behavior also applies to **identitymissing** modifier.

13.4.6 Importing Large Objects

If you are exporting LOB data in separate files (as described in Section 13.3.2, Exporting Large Objects), you need to tell the import utility the location and name of the files. Consider the following **import** command:

```
import from mgrresume.ixf of ixf
    lobs from c:\lobs1, c:\lobs2, c:\lobs3
    modified by lobsinfile
    commitcount 1000
    messages mgrresume.out
    create into newemployee in datats index in indexts long in lobts
```

This command takes *mgrresume.del* as the input file. With the **lobsinfile** modifier, the utility searches the paths specified in the **lobs from** clause for the LOB location specifier (LLS). Recall that each LOB data has an LLS that represents the location of a LOB in a file stored in the LOB file path.

Notice that an additional clause, **long in lobts,** is added to the **create into** option. It indicates that all LOB data will be created and stored in *lobts* table space. If this clause is omitted, LOB data will be stored in the same table space with the other data. Typically, we recommend that you use DMS table space and keep regular data, LOB data, and indexes in different table spaces.

V9 13.4.7 Importing XML Data

To import XML documents, use the **xml from** option to specify one or more paths where the documents are stored. Otherwise, the **import** utility will look for the XML files in the current directory.

You can choose how the XML documents are parsed; strip whitespace or preserve whitespace. If the **xmlparse** option is not specified, the parsing behavior for XML documents will be determined by the **CURRENT XMLPARSE OPTION** special register. Here is an example of these two options.

```
import from myfile.ixf of ixf
    xml from d:\xmlpath
    xmlparse preserve whitespace
    messages msg.out
    insert into newtable
```

When you insert or update an XML document, you might want to determine whether the structure, content, and data types of the XML document are valid. The import utility also supports XML validation through the use of the **xmlvalidate** option. Table 13.3 lists three possible methods.

Table 13.3 XML Validation Methods with the Import Utility

XML Validation Method	Description
USING XDS	Recall that you can export XML schema information and store it in the SCH attribute of the XML Data Specifier (XDS). The value of the SCH attribute will be used to perform validation. If there is no SCH attribute in the XDS, either the DEFAULT, IGNORE, or MAP will be considered.
USING SCHEMA schema-sqlid	Use the XML schema specified in this clause.
USING SCHEMA LOCA-TION HINTS	Validate the XML documents against the schemas identified by the XML schema location hints in the source XML documents.

```
import from myfile.ixf of ixf
    xml from d:\xmlpath
    xmlparse preserve whitespace
    xmlvalidate using xds
        default S1.SCHEMA_A
        ignore (S1.SCHEMA_X, S1.SCHEMA_Y, S1.SCHEMA_Z)
        map (S1.SCHEMA_A, S1.SCHEMA_B)
    commitcount 500 restartcount 30000
    messages msg.out
    insert into newtable
```

The above **import** command will:

- Insert data from *myfile.ixf* and XML files located in *d:\xmlpath.*
- Whitespace is preserved when the XML document is parsed.
- Each XML document is validated using the schema information identified in the SCH attribute of the XDS. However, if XDS for any particular row doesn't contain a SCH attribute, S1.SCHEMA_A will be used instead. This is specified by the **default** option.
- For SCH attribute specified as S1.SCHEMA_X, or S1.SCHEMA_Y, or S1.SCHEMA_Z, validation will not be performed for the imported XML document. This is specified by the **ignore** option.
- If the SCH attribute is specified as S1.SCHEMA_A, it will then be mapped to S1.SCHEMA_B. Note that although the **DEFAULT** clause specifies S1.SCHEMA_A, any subsequent mapping will not be performed. This is specified by the **map** option.
- The import utility will issue a commit after every 500 rows are imported.
- The import operation is started at record 30,001 because the first 30,000 records are skipped.
- Any errors, warnings, and informational messages are written to the *msg.out* file.
- New data are inserted (or appended) into the *newtable*.

This example only gives you some idea of how the imported XML documents can be validated. There are more examples in the DB2 Information Center, which demonstrates the power of the **xmlvalidate** option.

13.4.8 Select Columns to Import

There are three ways to select particular columns you want to import. **method l** uses the starting and ending position (in bytes) for all columns to be imported. This method only supports ASC files; for example:

```
import from employee.asc of asc
    messages employee.out
    method l (1 5, 6 14, 24 30)
    insert into employee
```

This command imports three selected columns of data into the *employee* table: bytes 1 to 5 from the first column, bytes 6 to 14 from the second column, and bytes 24 to 30 from the third column.

The other two methods specify the names of the columns (**method n**) or the field numbers of the input data (**method p**). **method n** is only valid for IXF files and **method p** can be used with IXF or DEL files. The following shows examples of the **method n** and **method p** clauses in the **import** command.

```
import from employee.ixf of ixf
    messages employee.out
    method n (empno, firstnme, lastname)
    insert into employee (empno, firstnme, lastname)
import from employee.ixf of ixf
    messages employee.out
    method p (1, 2, 4)
    insert into employee (empno, firstnme, lastname)
```

13.4.9 Authorities Required to Perform an Import

Depending on the options you have chosen for the import, specific authorization and privileges are required. Since SYSADM and DBADM hold the highest authority for an instance and a database respectively, both of them can issue **import** commands with all of the options discussed above. For users who do not have SYSADM and DBADM privileges, refer to Table 13.4 for the privileges required to perform each import option. If you are not already familiar with DB2 security, refer to Chapter 11, Implementing Security.

V9

> **NOTE** Starting in DB2 9, special considerations are required when you are importing data into tables that have protected columns and/or rows. The authorization ID must have LBAC credentials that allow write access to all protected columns and/or rows in the table. Refer to Chapter 11, Implementing Security, for LBAC specifics.

Table 13.4 Privileges Required for Different Import Scenarios

Import Scenario	Privileges Required
Import to an existing table with the **insert** option	CONTROL privilege on each participating table or view or INSERT and SELECT privileges on each participating table or view.
Import to an existing table using the **insert_update** option	CONTROL privilege on the table or view or INSERT, SELECT, UPDATE, and DELETE privileges on each participating table or view.
Import to an existing table using the **replace** or **replace_create** option	CONTROL privilege on the table or view or INSERT, SELECT, and DELETE privileges on the table or view.

(continues)

Table 13.4 Privileges Required for Different Import Scenarios *(Continued)*

Import Scenario	Privileges Required
Import to a new table using the **create** or **replace_create** option	CREATETAB authority on the database and USE privilege on the table space and IMPLICIT_SCHEMA authority on the database, if the implicit or explicit schema name of the table does not exist or CREATEIN privilege on the schema, if the schema name of the table refers to an existing schema
Import to a hierarchy table that does not already exist using the **CREATE** option *or* the **REPLACE_CREATE** option. This import scenario requires one of the authorities listed on the right. (Note that this book does not cover hierarchy tables.)	CREATETAB authority on the database and USE privilege on the table space and: IMPLICIT_SCHEMA authority on the database, if the schema name of the table does not exist or CREATEIN privilege on the schema, if the schema of the table exists or CONTROL privilege on every subtable in the hierarchy if the **replace_create** option on the entire hierarchy is used

13.4.10 Importing a Table Using the Control Center

You can invoke the import utility from the Control Center by right clicking on the target table and selecting **Import.** Figure 13.19 shows the Import table dialog:

V9 13.4.11 Run an import Command with the ADMIN_CMD Procedure

The syntax and behavior of an **import** command executed by the **ADMIN_CMD** procedure is the same as described in Section 13.3.7 except for the messages of the import operation.

```
call sysproc.admin_cmd
    ('import from employee.del of del messages on server insert into myemp')
```

A result set of eight columns is returned with the information such as rows read, skipped, inserted, updated, rejected, committed, SQL statements to retrieve and remove messages generated by the IMPORT utility.

13.5 The DB2 Load Utility

The load utility is another tool you can use to insert data into a table. Note that you cannot run the load utility against a view; the target must be a table that already exists. The major difference

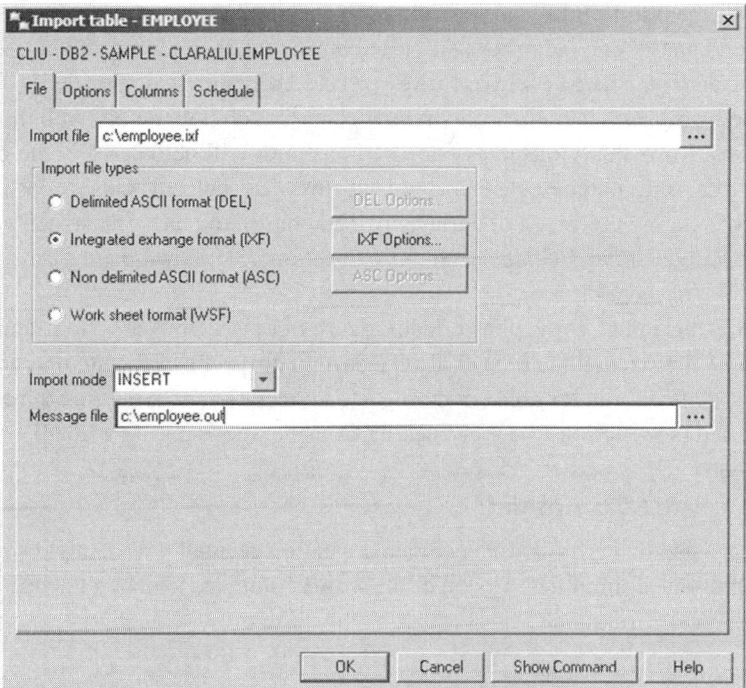

Figure 13.19 Invoking the import utility from the Control Center

between a load and an import is that a load is much faster. Unlike the import utility, data is not written to the database using normal insert operations. Instead, the load utility reads the input data, formats data pages, and writes directly to the database. Database changes are not logged and constraint validations (except unique constraint) are not performed during a load operation.

13.5.1 The Load Process

Basically, a complete load process consists of four phases.

1. During the **load phase,** the load utility scans the input file for any invalid data rows that do not comply with the table definition; for example, if a table column is defined as INTEGER but the input data is stored as "abcd". Invalid data will not be loaded into the table. The rejected rows and warnings will be written to a dump file specified by the **`dumpfile`** modifier. Valid data is then written into the table. At the same time, table statistics (if the **`statistics use profile`** option was specified) and index keys are also collected. If the **`savecount`** option is specified in the **`load`** command, points of consistency are recorded in the message file. Consistency points are established by the load utility. They are very useful when it comes to restarting the load operation. You can restart the load from the last successful consistency point.

2. During the **build phase,** indexes are produced based on the index keys collected during the load phase. The index keys are sorted during the load phase, and index statistics are collected (if the **`statistics use profile`** option was specified).
3. In the load phase, the utility only rejects rows that do not comply with the column definitions. Rows that violated any unique constraint will be deleted in the **delete phase.** Note that only unique constraint violated rows are deleted. Other constraints are not checked during this phase or during any load phase. You have to manually check it after the load operation is complete. Refer to Section 13.5.8, Validating Data against Constraints, for more information.
4. During the **index copy phase,** index data is copied from a system temporary table space to the original table space. This will only occur if a system temporary table space was specified for index creation during a load operation with the **`read access`** option specified (see Section 13.5.2.5, Locking Considerations during a Load).

13.5.2 The LOAD Command

The load utility is so powerful that its command can be executed with many different options. Figure 13.20 presents a simplified version of the **`load`** command syntax diagram.

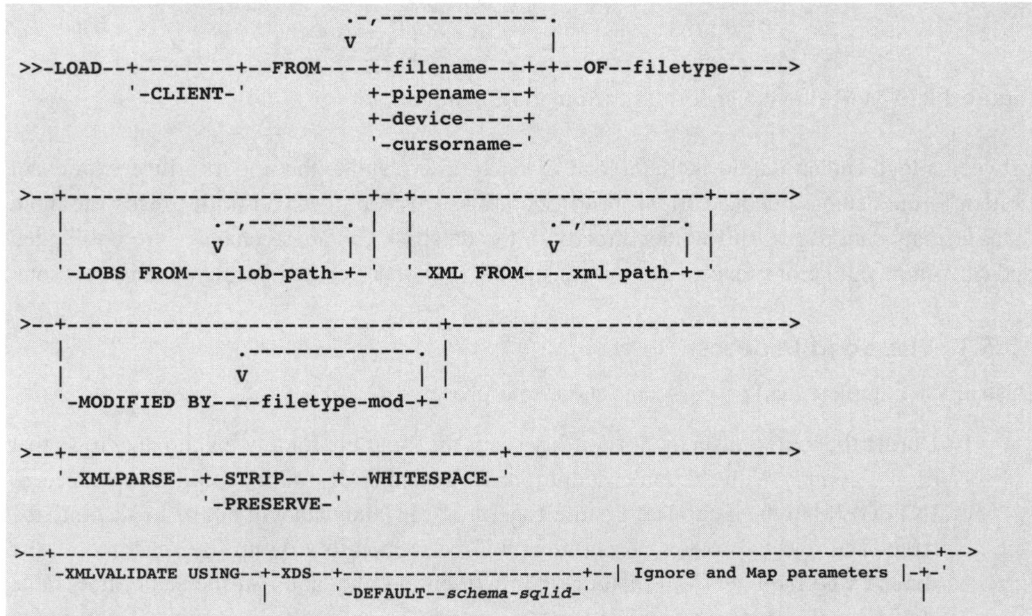

```
                                   .-,--------------.
                                   V                |
>>-LOAD--+--------+--FROM----+-filename---+-+--OF--filetype----->
         '-CLIENT-'           +-pipename---+
                              +-device-----+
                              '-cursorname-'

>--+-------------------------+--+-----------------------+------>
   |          .-,--------.  |  |          .-,--------.  |
   |          V          |  |  |          V          |  |
   '-LOBS FROM----lob-path-+-'  '-XML FROM----xml-path-+-'

>--+-------------------------------+---------------------------->
   |             .--------------.  |
   |             V              |  |
   '-MODIFIED BY----filetype-mod-+-'

>--+-------------------------------------+---------------------->
   '-XMLPARSE--+-STRIP----+--WHITESPACE-'
               '-PRESERVE-'

>--+---------------------------------------------------------------------------------+-->
   '-XMLVALIDATE USING--+-XDS--+-----------------------+--| Ignore and Map parameters |-+-'
                        |      '-DEFAULT--schema-sqlid-'                               |
```

Figure 13.20 Simplified syntax diagram of the load command

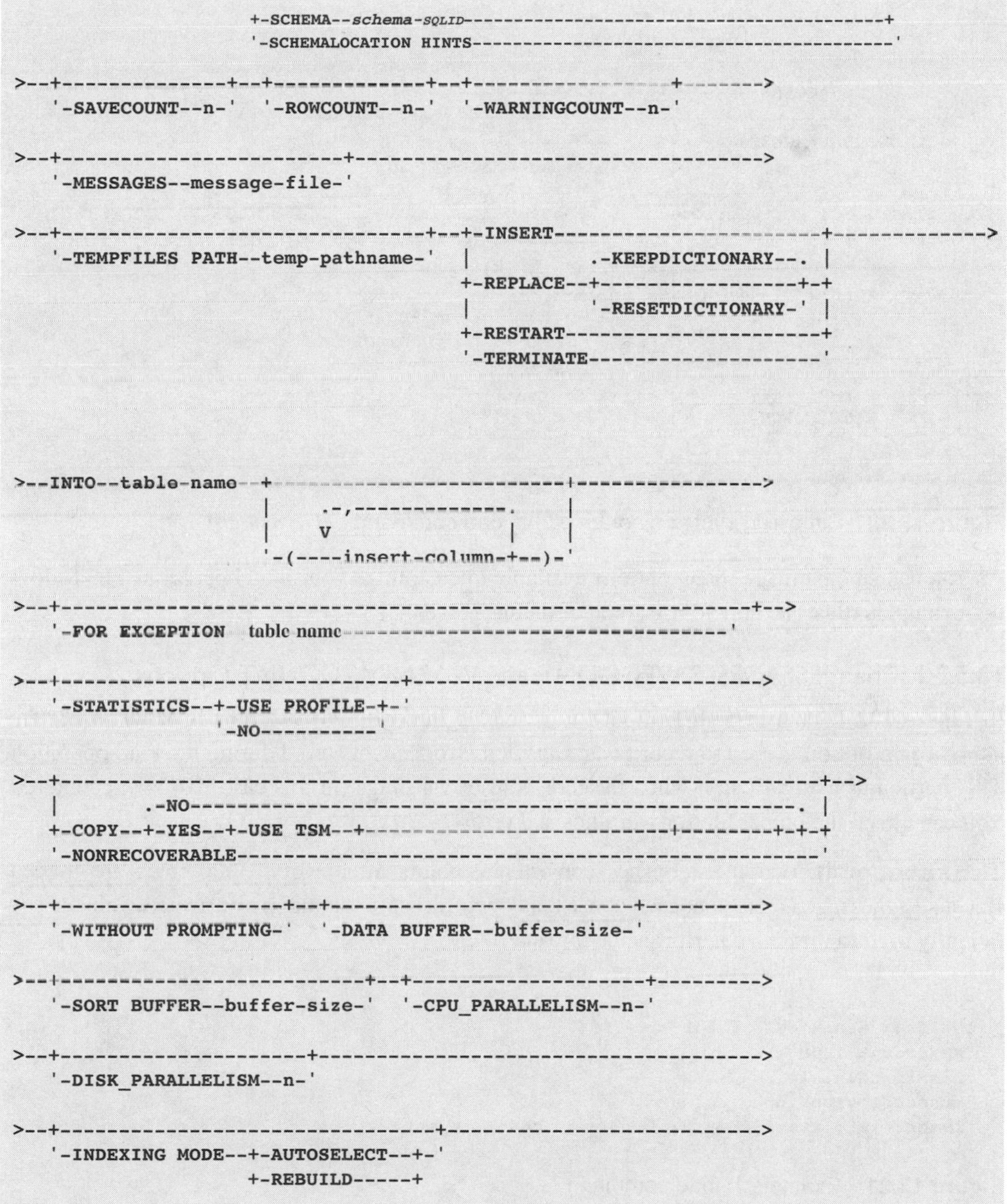

```
                        +-SCHEMA--schema-SQLID-----------------------------------------+
                        '-SCHEMALOCATION HINTS-----------------------------------------'

>--+--------------+--+-------------+--+----------------+-------->
   '-SAVECOUNT--n-'  '-ROWCOUNT--n-'  '-WARNINGCOUNT--n-'

>--+-----------------------+------------------------------------>
   '-MESSAGES--message-file-'

>--+-------------------------------+--+-INSERT-----------------------+------------->
   '-TEMPFILES PATH--temp-pathname-'  |           .-KEEPDICTIONARY--. |
                                      +-REPLACE--+-----------------+-+
                                      |           '-RESETDICTIONARY-' |
                                      +-RESTART----------------------+
                                      '-TERMINATE--------------------'


>--INTO--table-name--+------------------------+---------------->
                     |    .-,-------------.   |
                     |    V               |   |
                     '-(----insert-column-+--)-'

>--+-------------------------------------------------------+-->
   '-FOR EXCEPTION  table name---------------------------------'

>--+---------------------------+------------------------------>
   '-STATISTICS--+-USE PROFILE-+-'
                 '-NO----------'

>--+-------------------------------------------------------------------+-->
   |      .-NO-----------------------------------------------------.  |
   +-COPY--+-YES--+-USE TSM--+--------------------------+--------+-+-+
   '-NONRECOVERABLE----------------------------------------------------'

>--+------------------+--+--------------------------+---------->
   '-WITHOUT PROMPTING-'  '-DATA BUFFER--buffer-size-'

>--+--------------------------+--+-------------------+--------->
   '-SORT BUFFER--buffer-size-'  '-CPU_PARALLELISM--n-'

>--+--------------------+--------------------------------------->
   '-DISK_PARALLELISM--n-'

>--+------------------------------+------------------------->
   '-INDEXING MODE--+-AUTOSELECT--+-'
                    +-REBUILD-----+
```

Figure 13.20 Simplified syntax diagram of the load command *(Continued)*

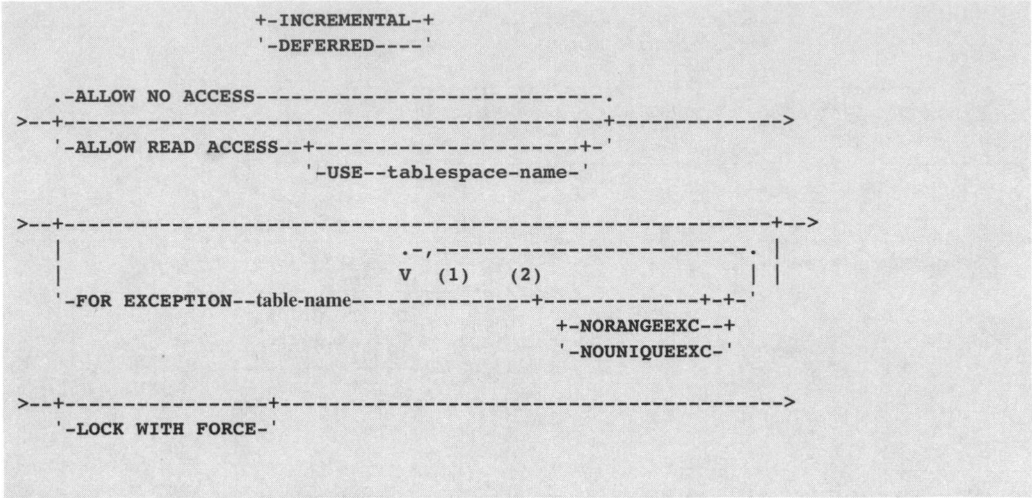

```
                    +-INCREMENTAL-+
                    '-DEFERRED----'

   .-ALLOW NO ACCESS-----------------------------.
>--+---------------------------------------------+------------->
   '-ALLOW READ ACCESS--+----------------------+-'
                        '-USE--tablespace-name-'

>--+----------------------------------------------------------+-->
   |                                   .-,--------------------------. |
   |                                   V  (1)   (2)                 | |
   '-FOR EXCEPTION--table-name---------------+-------------+-+-'
                                             +-NORANGEEXC--+
                                             '-NOUNIQUEEXC-'

>--+----------------+------------------------------------------->
   '-LOCK WITH FORCE-'
```

Figure 13.20 Simplified syntax diagram of the load command *(Continued)*

As you can see, there are many options available to customize your load operation. The following examples illustrate how to use some of them.

13.5.2.1 The MESSAGES, SAVECOUNT, and WARNINGCOUNT Options

In Figure 13.21, data in a DEL input file is loaded into a list of columns in table *stock*. The **messages** option is used to record warnings and errors encountered during the load operation. This particular load will stop when the threshold of warnings (in this case, 10) is encountered. You can check the output file for warnings and errors.

The **savecount** option establishes consistency points after every 1,000 rows are loaded. Because a message is issued at each consistency point, ensure that the **savecount** value is sufficiently high to minimize performance impact.

```
load from stock.del of del
  savecount 1000
  warningcount 10
  messages stock.out
  insert into stock(itemid, itemdesc, cost, inventory)
```

Figure 13.21 Example 1: load command

Consistency points are established during the load phase. You can use them to restart a failed or terminated load operation. By specifying the same **load** command but replacing **insert** with the **restart** option, the load operation will automatically continue from the last consistency point.

To terminate a load, issue the same **load** command but use the **terminate** option in place of **insert;** for example:

```
load from stock.del of del
  savecount 1000
  warningcount 10
  messages stock.out
  terminate
```

13.5.2.2 Loading from a CURSOR

The load utility supports four file formats: IXF, DEL, ASC, and CURSOR (described in Section 13.2, Data Movement File Formats). When using the CURSOR file type as demonstrated in Figure 13.22, the cursor must be already declared but does not need to be opened. The entire result of the query associated with the specified cursor will be processed by the load utility. You must also ensure that the column types of the SQL query are compatible with the corresponding column types in the target table.

```
declare cur1 cursor as select * from oldstock;
load from cur1 of cursor
  messages curstock.out
  insert into stock
```

Figure 13.22 Example 2: load command

13.5.2.3 MODIFIED BY dumpfile and Exception Table

As mentioned earlier, the load process goes through four phases. During the load phase, data that does not comply with the column definition will not be loaded. Rejected records can be saved in a dump file by using the **modified by dumpfile** modifier. If **dumpfile** is not specified, rejected records are not saved. Since the load utility will not stop unless it reaches the warning threshold if one is specified, it is not easy to identify the rejected records. Hence, it is always a good practice to use the modifier and validate the message file after a load is completed. Figure 13.23 shows how to use **modified by dumpfile.**

```
load from stock.ixf of ixf
 modified by dumpfile=stockdump.dmp
 messages stock.out
 replace into stock
 for exception stockexp
```

Figure 13.23 Example 3: load command

Assume that the input file *stock.ixf* contains the data in Table 13.5. '

Table 13.5 Data Stored in the Input File stock.ixf

itemid	itemdesc	inventory
10	~~~	1
20	~~~	–
30	~~~	3
30	~~~	4
40	~~~	X
50	~~~	6
50	~~~	7
80	~~~	8

The target table *stock* is defined with three columns using this **CREATE TABLE** statement:

```
CREATE TABLE stock
        ( itemid     INTEGER NOT NULL
        , itemdesc   VARCHAR(100)
        , inventory INTEGER NOT NULL
        , PRIMARY KEY (itemid) )
```

Notice that the second and fifth records in *stock.ixf* do not comply with the NOT NULL and numeric definitions. If the **load** command shown in Figure 13.23 is executed, a dump file (*stockdump.dmp*) is created to save rows that are not loaded due to incompatible data type and the nullability attribute. Table 13.6 shows that the dump file *stockdump.dmp* contains the rows not loaded.

Table 13.6 Rows Not Loaded but Stored in the Dump File stockdump.dmp

itemid	itemdesc	inventory
20	~~~	–
40	~~~	X

Recall that in the third load phase, the load process deletes rows that violate any unique constraint defined in the target table. You can save the deleted rows in a table called an **exception table** using the **for exception** option. If an exception table is not specified, the rows will be discarded.

You need to create an exception table manually before you can use it. The table should have the same number of columns, column types, and nullability attributes as the target table to be loaded. You can create such a table with this command:

```
CREATE TABLE stockexp LIKE stock
```

Because the **load** utility does not clean up the exception table, it contains invalid rows from previous load operations unless you remove existing rows before invoking the utility. To log when and why rows are rejected, you can add two other optional columns to the end of the exception table. The first column is defined as a TIMESTAMP data type to record when the record was deleted. The second column is defined as CLOB (32K) or larger and tracks the constraint names that the data violates. To add columns to the table, use the **ALTER TABLE** statement:

```
ALTER TABLE stockexp
  ADD COLUMN load_ts TIMESTAMP
  ADD COLUMN load_msg CLOB(32k)
```

Like the *dumpfile* modifier, it is a good practice to also use the exception table, especially if unique violations are possible. The exception table illustrated in Table 13.7 contains rows that violated the unique constraints.

Table 13.7 Exception Table stockexp

itemid	itemdesc	inventory
30	~~~	4
50	~~~	7

Figure 13.24 shows the big picture of the concepts of *dumpfile* and the exception table.

(1) Create the target table *stock*.
(2) Issue the **load** command with **modified by dumpfile, messages,** and **for exception** options.
(3) Rows that do not comply with the table definition (NOT NULL and numeric column) are recorded in the *stockdump.dmp* file.
(4) Rows that violated the unique constraint are deleted from the *stock* table and inserted into the exception table.
(5) Four rows are successfully loaded into the *stock* table.

13.5.2.4 Loading from a Client

In all the examples you have seen so far, the load commands are executed from the database server, and the input files are located on the database server. You may sometimes want to invoke a load operation from a remote client as well as using a file that resides at the client. To do so, specify the **client** keyword in the command as demonstrated in Figure 13.25.

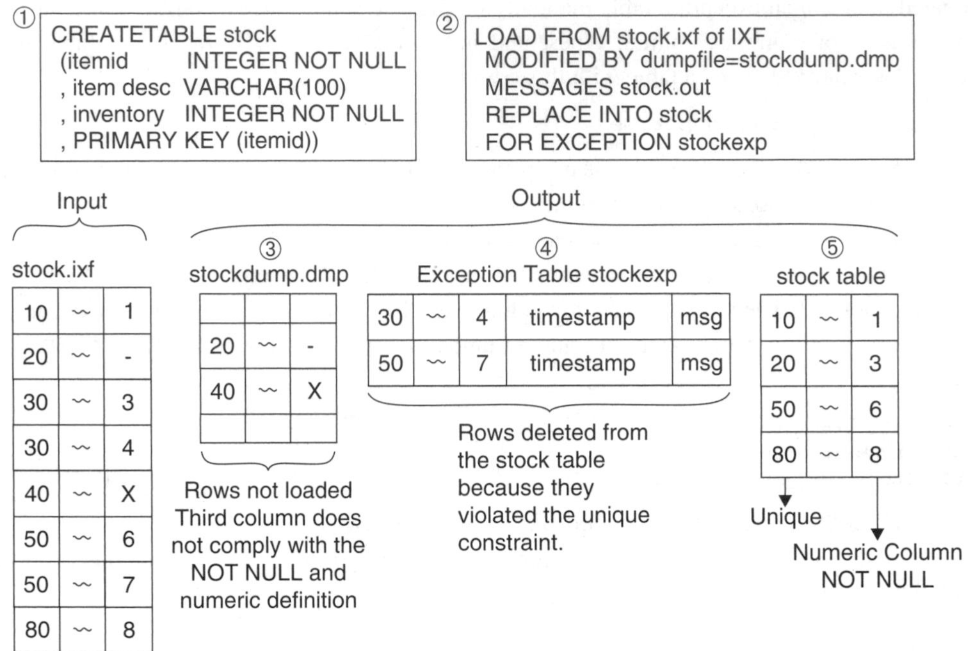

Figure 13.24 Loading data with dumpfile and an exception table

```
load client from stock.ixf of ixf
  modified by dumpfile=stockdump.dmp
  rowcount 5000
  messages stock.out
  tempfiles path c:\loadtemp
  replace into stock
  for exception stockexcept
  lock with force
```

Figure 13.25 Example 4: load command

You cannot load a CURSOR file type from a client. The *dumpfile* and *lobsinfile* modifiers (discussed in the following sections) refer to files on the server even when the command includes the **client** keyword.

> **NOTE** Use the **load client** command when the input file resides on the client from which you are issuing the command. Use the *dumpfile*, *tempfile*, and *lobsinfile* modifiers for files located on the DB2 server.

The **rowcount** option works exactly the same as the one supported by the import utility. You can control the number of rows to be loaded with this option.

During the load process, the utility uses temporary files. By default, it allocates temporary files from the directory where the **load** command was issued. To explicitly specify a path for this purpose, use the **tempfiles** option as shown in Figure 13.25. Notice that the example also uses the **replace** mode, which replaces the old data in the target table with the new data.

13.5.2.5 Locking Considerations during a Load

The utility acquires various locks during the load process. If you choose to give the load operation a higher priority than other concurrent applications, you can specify the **lock with force** option (in Figure 13.25) to immediately terminate other applications that are holding conflicting locks so that the load utility does not have to wait for locks.

By default, no other application can access the target table that is being loaded. The utility locks the target table for exclusive access until the load completes. You can set this default behavior with the **allow no access** option. This is the only valid option for **load replace.**

You can increase concurrency by locking the target table in share mode and allowing read access. In Figure 13.26, the **allow read access** option is enabled, which lets readers access data that existed before the load. New data will not be available until the load has completed.

```
load from stock.ixf of ixf
  modified by dumpfile=stockdump.dmp
  messages stock.out
  replace into stock
  for exception stockexcept
  allow read access
  indexing mode incremental
```

Figure 13.26 Example 5: load command

13.5.2.6 The INDEXING MODE Option

The last option in Figure 13.26, **indexing mode,** indicates whether the load utility is to rebuild indexes or to extend them incrementally. This is done in the build phase. You can use the options in Table 13.8.

Table 13.8 INDEXING MODE Options for the load Command

INDEXING MODE option	Description
REBUILD	Forces all indexes to be rebuilt.
INCREMENTAL	Extends indexes with new data.

(continues)

Table 13.8 INDEXING MODE Options for the load Command *(Continued)*

INDEXING MODE option	Description
AUTOSELECT (default)	The load utility will automatically choose between REBUILD or INCREMENTAL mode.
DEFERRED	Indexes will not be rebuilt but will be marked as needing a refresh. An index will be rebuilt when it is first accessed or when the database is restarted.

13.5.3 File Type Modifiers Supported in the load Utility

The file type modifiers supported in the load utility are as comprehensive as those supported in the export and import utilities. The following section discusses a few of the modifiers. Refer to the *DB2 Data Movement Utilities Guide and Reference* for a complete list of load utility modifiers.

13.5.3.1 Leaving Free Space in Data and Index Pages

When you insert data into a table with the insert, import, or load operations, DB2 tries to fit as much of the data into the data and index pages as possible. Consider pages tightly packed as shown in Figure 13.27.

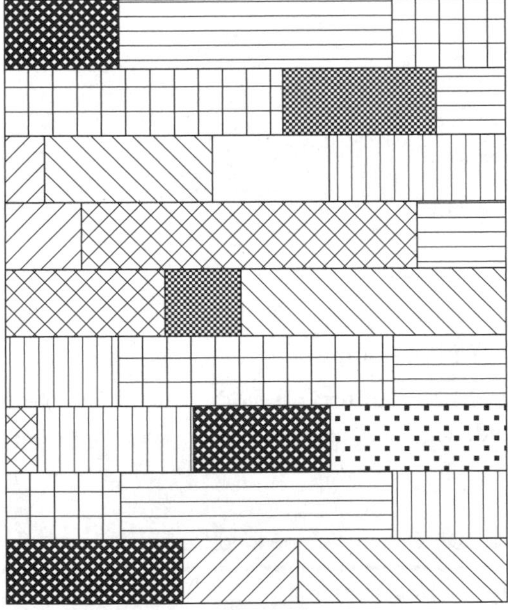

Figure 13.27 A tightly packed data or index page

When a certain record is updated with data larger than the original size, new data might not be able to fit into the original data page. DB2 will then search for the next free page to store the updated record. The updated record is referenced from the original page by a **pointer.** When a request comes in to retrieve the record, DB2 first locates the original data page and then searches for the new data page as referenced by the pointer. This is called **page overflow** (see Figure 13.28). The higher the number of page overflows, the more time DB2 will spend finding the data or index page. Hence, you want to avoid page overflows as much as possible to improve performance.

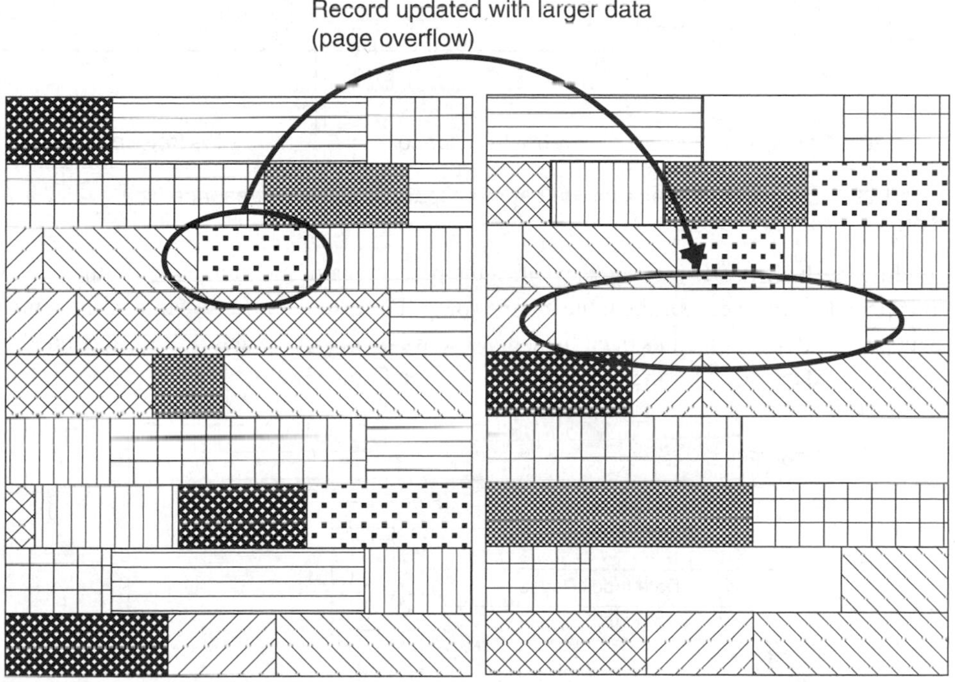

Figure 13.28 Page Overflow

To minimize page overflows, you can customize the table definition so that certain free space is reserved so that the pages are not tightly packed. The **`CREATE TABLE`**, **`ALTER TABLE`**, and **`CREATE INDEX`** statements have options for leaving free space in data and/or index pages. The **`load`** command also has options to override the default set for the target table. You can specify this using the file type modifiers: **`indexfreespace`**, **`pagefreespace`**, and **`totalfreespace`**.

Modifiers **`pagefreespace=x`** and **`indexfreespace=x`** can be used to specify the percentage of each data and/or index page that is to be left as free space. For example, Figure 13.29 illustrates leaving 20 percent of free space on each data and index page.

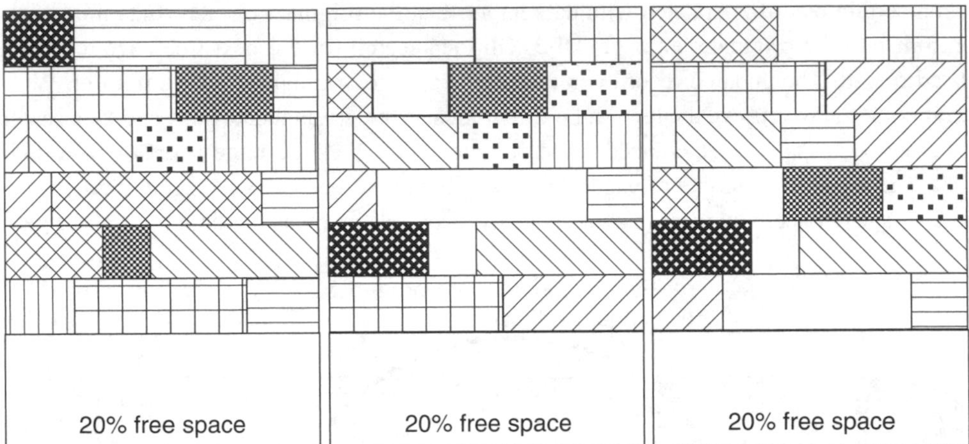

Figure 13.29 Leaving free space for the pagefreespace and indexfreespace file modifiers

The modifier **totalfreespace=x** specifies the percentage of the total pages in the table that is to be appended to the end of the table as free space. For example, if **x** = 20, and the table has 100 data pages after the data has been loaded, 20 additional empty pages will be appended. The total number of data pages for the table will be 120 (see Figure 13.30).

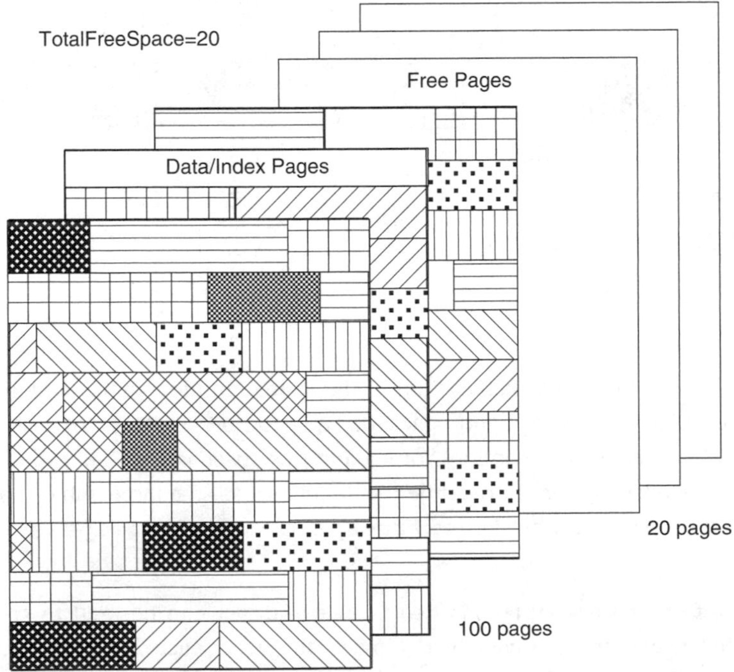

Figure 13.30 Using the totalfreespace file modifier

13.5.4 Loading Large Objects

The load utility uses the same option and modifier as the import utility to specify the path where LOBs are stored. For example, the following command lists the directories where LOBs are stored with the **lobs from** option.

```
load from stock.ixf of ixf
  lobs from c:\lobs1, c:\lobs2, c:\lobs3
  modified by dumpfile=stockdump.dmp lobsinfile
  messages stock.out
  replace into stock
  for exception stockexcept
```

V9.5 13.5.5 Loading XML Data

The **import** utility is a good solution for inserting a small number of XML documents, but in DB2 9.5 the **load** utility can be used to insert large volumes of XML data at very high speeds.

The load utility uses the same options and modifier as the import utility described in Sections 13.4.5 and 13.4.7 to specify the path where the XML documents are stored, decide how the documents are parsed, and validate whether the structure, content, and data types of the XML document are valid.

Here is an example to illustrate different options while loading XML data.

```
load from myfile.del of del
    xml from d:\xmlpath
    xmlparse strip whitespace
    xmlvalidate using schema S1.SCHEMA_A
    savecount 5000
    messages msg.out
    insert into newtable
```

The **load** command above will

- Insert data from the file *myfile.del* and XML files located in the path or directory *d:\xmlpath*.
- Remove embedded whitespace when the XML document is parsed.
- Validate each XML document using the schema with the SQL identifier "S1.SCHEMA_A". The SCH attribute of the XDS in the XML column will be ignored.
- Establish consistency points after every 5,000 rows are loaded.
- Write any errors, warnings, and informational messages to the *msg.out* file.
- Insert (or append) new data into the table named *newtable*.

This example only gives you some idea of how to load XML data. There are more examples in the DB2 Information Center, which demonstrates the strong support of the load utility on populating XML data columns.

13.5.6 Collecting Statistics

During the load phase of the process, the load utility also collects table statistics if you specify **`statistics.`** You can either collect statistics using the statistic profile with **`the statistics use profile`** option, or specify not to collect statistics with the **`statistics no`** option. A **statistic profile** is a set of options that specify which statistics are to be collected, such as table, index, or distribution statistics.

If you choose not to collect statistics during the load, you should always update the statistics at your earliest convenience. When large amounts of new data are inserted into a table, you should update the statistics to reflect the changes so that the optimizer can determine the most optimal access plan.

13.5.7 The COPY YES/NO and NONRECOVERABLE Options

Recall that changes made to the target tables during the load are not logged. This is one of the characteristics of the load utility that improves performance. However, it also takes away the ability to perform roll forward recovery for the load operation. DB2 puts the table space where the target table resides in backup pending state when the load operation begins. After the load completes, you must back up the table space or database. This ensures that the table space can be restored to the point where logging is resumed if you ever need to restore the table space restore. This is the behavior of the load option **`copy no.`** You can also specify **`copy yes`** if archival logging is enabled. With **`copy yes,`** a copy of the loaded data will be saved and the table space will not be in backup pending state upon load completion. However, this negatively impacts the performance of the load. Table space status related to load operation will be discussed later in this chapter.

When you cannot afford to have a window to perform a table space backup after the load is complete but you also need the load to complete as fast as possible, neither **`copy yes`** nor **`copy no`** is a good solution. You may want to consider using the option **`nonrecoverable`** if the target table can be re-created and data can be reloaded.

The **`nonrecoverable`** option specifies that the target table is marked as nonrecoverable until the associated table space is backed up. In case of failure, such as disk or database failure, the table space needs to be restored and rolled back. The roll forward utility marks the data being loaded as *invalid* and skips the subsequent transactions for the target table. After the roll forward operation is completed, the target table is not accessible and it can only be dropped. Note that other tables in the same table space are not affected by this option.

13.5.8 Validating Data against Constraints

The load utility checks for invalid data and unique constraints during the load process. However, other constraints such as referential integrity and check constraints are not validated. DB2 therefore puts target tables defined with these constraints in check pending state. This forces you to manually validate the data before the tables are available for further processing.

The **set integrity** command gives you the ability to do just that. The command can be as simple as the following, which immediately validates data against the constraints for table *stock*.

```
set integrity for stock immediate checked
```

There are many other options; refer to the *DB2 UDB Command Reference* for the complete syntax of the command.

13.5.9 Performance Considerations

You can further speed up the load performance by taking advantage of the extra hardware resources you might have on the machine. Table 13.9 lists options and modifiers you can use.

Table 13.9 Options and Modifiers That Improve Load Performance

Performance-Related Modifiers	Description
DATA BUFFER	Specifies the number of 4KB pages to use as buffered space for transferring data within the load utility.
SORT BUFFER	Specifies the amount of memory used to sort index keys during the load operation.
CPU_PARALLELISM	Specifies the number of processes that the load utility will spawn for parsing, converting, and formatting records during the load operation.
DISK_PARALLELISM	Specifies the number of processes that the load utility will spawn for writing data to the table space containers.
FASTPARSE	Reduces syntax checking on input data. Note that this modifier may not detect invalid data.
ANYORDER	Specifies that preserving source data order is not required.

13.5.10 Authorities Required to Perform a Load

To perform a load, you must have SYSADM, DBADM, or LOAD authority. With the LOAD authority, you also need specific privileges on the target tables depending on the mode used in the **load** command. For example, you need INSERT privileges on the table when the load utility is invoked in INSERT mode. If you use REPLACE mode, you need INSERT and DELETE privileges on the target table.

Note that you also need appropriate access to the exception table if one is specified. In addition, when using the **copy yes** option, you need SYSADM, SYSCTRL, or SYSMAINT authority because a backup is performed during the load operation.

> **NOTE** Starting in DB2 9, special considerations are required when you are loading data into a table that has protected columns and/or rows. The authorization ID must have LBAC credentials that allow write access to all protected columns and/or rows in the table. Refer to Chapter 11, Implementing Security, for LBAC specifics.

13.5.11 Loading a Table Using the Control Center

The Control Center provides a graphical tool to invoke a load operation. Right click on the target table and select **Load** to start the Load Wizard (Figure 13.31). The Load Wizard walks you through the process of loading a table.

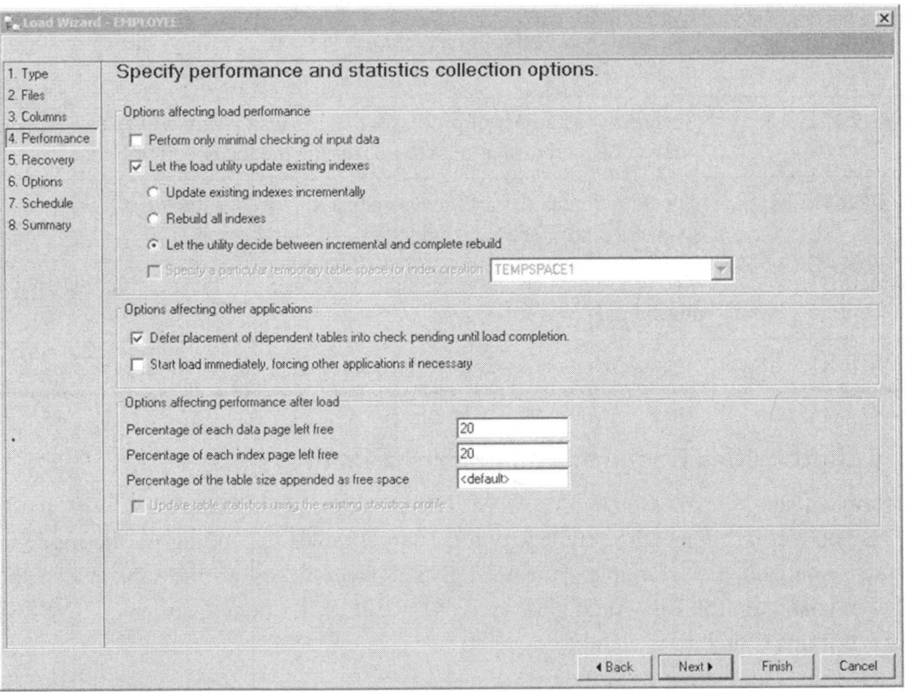

Figure 13.31 Loading a table from the Control Center

13.5.12 Run a load Command with the ADMIN_CMD Procedure

The data must reside on the database server to be loaded with the ADMIN_CMD procedure. Running a load command with the **ADMIN_CMD** procedure does not allow the data that resides on a remote client server to be loaded. This means the CLIENT keyword is not supported. In addition, messages of the load operation are kept on the server in the database. Here is an example.

```
call sysproc.admin_cmd
    ('load from employee.del of del messages on server replace into myemp')
```

A result set is returned with information rows read, skipped, loaded, rejected, deleted, committed, partitioned, SQL statements to retrieve and remove the message.

13.5.13 Monitoring a Load Operation

During the phases of a load, the target table and its associated table spaces are in different states. By checking the state of the table and table space, you can tell which phase the load operation is currently in. Before introducing the tools to obtain this information, let's first discuss the different table and table space states.

13.5.13.1 Table States

Table 13.10 lists the states in which tables can be placed by the database manager. You can control some of these; others are caused by the load utility.

Table 13.10 Table States

Table State	Description
Normal	The table is in normal state.
Set Integrity pending	The table is placed in check pending because it has constraints that have not yet been verified. When the load operation begins, it places tables with constraints (foreign key constraint and check constraint) in this state.
Load in progress	Load is in progress on this table.
Load pending	A load operation has been activated on this table. However, it was aborted before data could be committed. Issue the **load** command with the **terminate, restart,** or **replace** option to bring the table out of this state.
Read access only	The table data is available for read access queries. Load operations using the **allow read access** option placed the table in this state.
Unavailable	The table is unavailable. You can drop or restore it from a backup. Rolling forward through a non-recoverable load operation will place a table in this state.

(continues)

Table 13.10 Table States *(Continued)*

Table State	Description
Not load restartable	When information required for a load restart operation is unreliable, the table will be placed in this state. This prevents a load restart operation from taking place. For example, a table is placed in this state when a roll forward operation is started after a failed load operation that has not been successfully restarted or terminated.
Type-1 indexes	Type-1 indexes are used in DB2 prior to Version 8. Tables currently using type-1 indexes can be converted to type-2 indexes using the REORG utility with CONVERT option. Type-2 indexes provide significant locking enhancements. They are also required to perform some online maintenance tasks, such as REORG.
Unknown	The table state cannot be determined.

13.5.13.2 Table Space States

Table 13.11 lists the states in which table spaces can be placed by the database manager.

Table 13.11 Table Space States

Table State	Description
Normal	The table space is in normal state.
Quiesced: SHARE	The table space has been quiesced in SHARED mode.
Quiesced: UPDATE	The table space has been quiesced in UPDATE mode.
Quiesced: EXCLUSIVE	The table space has been quiesced in EXCLUSIVE mode.
Load pending	A table space is put in this state if a load operation has been active on one of its associated tables but has been aborted before data could be committed.
Delete pending	A table space is put in this state if one of its associated tables is undergoing the delete phase of a load operation but has been aborted or failed.
Backup pending	A table space is put in this state after a Point In Time roll forward operation, or after a load operation with the `no copy` option. You must back up the table space before using it. If it is not backed up, then you cannot update the table space, and only read-only operations are allowed.
Roll forward in progress	A table space is put in this state when a roll forward operation on that table space is in progress. Once the roll forward operation completes successfully, the table space is no longer in roll forward-in-progress state. The table space can also be taken out of this state if the roll forward operation is cancelled.

Table 13.11 Table Space States *(Continued)*

Table State	Description
Roll forward pending	A table space is put in this state after it is restored or following an I/O error. After it is restored, the table space can be rolled forward to the end of the logs or to a Point In Time. Following an I/O error, the table space must be rolled forward to the end of the logs.
Restore pending	A table space is put in this state if a roll forward operation on that table space is cancelled, or if a roll forward operation on that table space encounters an unrecoverable error, in which case the table space must be restored and rolled forward again.
Load in progress	A table space is put in this state if it is associated with a load operation. The load in progress state is removed when the load operation is completed or aborted.
Reorg in progress	An REORG operation is in progress on one of the tables associated to the table space.
Backup in progress	A backup is in progress on the table space.
Storage must be defined	For DB2 database manager internal use only.
Restore in progress	A restore is in progress on the table space.
Offline and not accessible	DB2 failed to access or use one or more containers associated to the table space, so the table space is placed offline. To take the table space out of this state, repair the containers.

13.5.13.3 Load Querying

DB2 has two utilities that you can use to obtain the table state. Figure 13.32 presents the syntax diagram of one of them, the **load query** command.

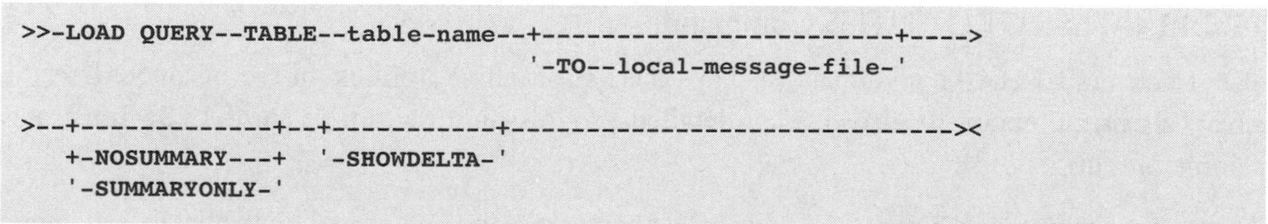

```
>>-LOAD QUERY--TABLE--table-name--+-----------------------+---->
                                  '-TO--local-message-file-'

>--+-------------+--+-----------+------------------------------><
   +-NOSUMMARY---+  '-SHOWDELTA-'
   '-SUMMARYONLY-'
```

Figure 13.32 Syntax diagram of the load query command

You can specify the following command to check the status of the load operation:

```
load query table stock to c:/stockstatus.out
```

The output file *stockstatus.out* might look similar to Figure 13.33.

```
SQL3501W  The table space(s) in which the table resides will not be placed in backup
pending state since forward recovery is disabled for the database.

SQL3109N  The utility is beginning to load data from file "stock.del"

SQL3500W  The utility is beginning the "LOAD" phase at time "03-21-2007
11:31:16.597045".

SQL3519W  Begin Load Consistency Point. Input record count = "0".

SQL3520W  Load Consistency Point was successful.

SQL3519W  Begin Load Consistency Point. Input record count = "104416".

SQL3520W  Load Consistency Point was successful.

SQL3519W  Begin Load Consistency Point. Input record count = "205757".

SQL3520W  Load Consistency Point was successful.

SQL3532I  The Load utility is currently in the "LOAD" phase.

Number of rows read         = 205757
Number of rows skipped      = 0
Number of rows loaded       = 205757
Number of rows rejected     = 0
Number of rows deleted      = 0
Number of rows committed    = 123432
Number of warnings          = 0

Tablestate:
  Load in Progress
```

Figure 13.33 Sample output of a load query command

13.5.13.4 The LIST UTILITIES Command

The **list utilities** command displays the list of active utilities on the instance. Use the **show detail** option to also display detailed progress information. Figure 13.34 illustrates sample output.

The report generated in Figure 13.34 indicates that a load was performed on the database *sample* and includes a brief description of the operation. *Progress Monitoring* tells you the current phase of the load and the number of rows already loaded and to be loaded.

The table space in which the load target table resides will be placed in backup pending state if **COPY NO** (the default) option is specified. The utility places the table space in this state at the beginning of the load operation. The table spaces stays in backup pending mode even when the load is complete until you perform a database or table space level backup.

```
list utilities show detail

ID                                    = 1
Type                                  = LOAD
Database Name                         = SAMPLE
Partition Number                      = 0
Description                           = OFFLINE LOAD Unknown file type AUTOMATIC
                                        INDEXING INSERT COPY NO
Start Time                            = 03/15/2007 00:41:08.767650
Progress Monitoring:
   Phase Number                       = 1
      Description                     = SETUP
      Total Work                      = 0 bytes
      Completed Work                  = 0 bytes
      Start Time                      = 03/15/2007 00:41:08.786501
   Phase Number [Current]             = 2
      Description                     = LOAD
      Total Work                      = 11447 rows
      Completed Work                  = 5481 rows
      Start Time                      = 03/15/2007 00:41:09.436920
```

Figure 13.34 Output of the list utilities command

Figure 13.35 shows how to retrieve the table space status.

```
list tablespaces show detail

Tablespace ID                            = 2
 Name                                    = USERSPACE1
 Type                                    = System managed space
 Contents                                = Any data
  State                                   = 0x0000
   Detailed explanation:
     Backup pending
 Total pages                             = 527
 Useable pages                           = 527
 Used pages                              = 527
 Free pages                              = Not applicable
 High water mark (pages)                 = Not applicable
 Page size (bytes)                       = 4096
 Extent size (pages)                     = 32
 Prefetch size (pages)                   = 16
 Number of containers                    = 1
```

Figure 13.35 Retrieving the table space status

13.6 The DB2MOVE Utility

You can only operate the export, import, and load utilities on one table at a time. To move a large number of tables between DB2 databases, use the **db2move** utility. Supported actions in the command are **export, import, load,** and **copy.** Based on the action you request, the utility calls the DB2 export, import, and load application programming interfaces (APIs) accordingly. Refer to Figure 13.36 for options supported by **db2move.**

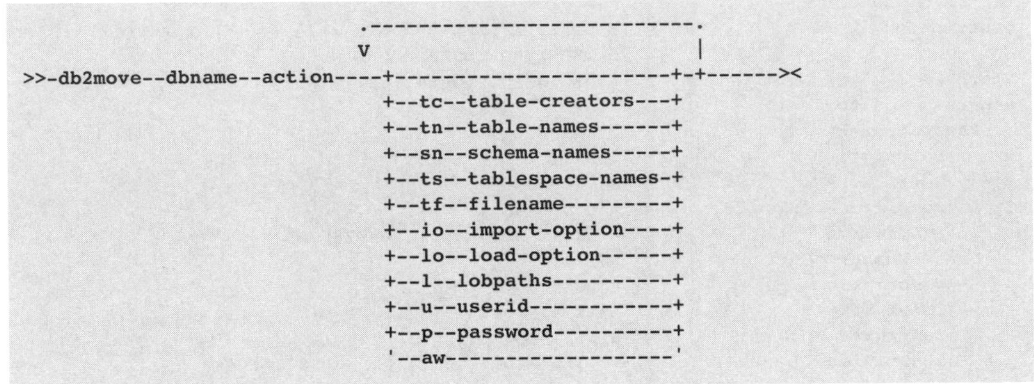

```
                                  .---------------------------.
                                  V                           |
>>-db2move--dbname--action----+-----------------------+-+------><
                              +--tc--table-creators---+
                              +--tn--table-names------+
                              +--sn--schema-names-----+
                              +--ts--tablespace-names-+
                              +--tf--filename---------+
                              +--io--import-option----+
                              +--lo--load-option------+
                              +--l--lobpaths----------+
                              +--u--userid------------+
                              +--p--password----------+
                              '--aw-------------------'
```

Figure 13.36 Syntax diagram of the db2move command

The **db2move** command can also be used without any options. This example exports all tables in the *sample* database:

```
db2move sample export
```

To import tables with schema *dbaadmin* and schemas that start with *dbauser*, you can specify the **–tc** option and provide a list of schema names; the command also accepts the wildcard (*).

```
db2move sample import –tc dbaadmin,dbauser*
```

You can also specify the replace mode and *lobpath*:

```
db2move sample load –lo replace -l c:\lobpath1,c:\lobpath2
```

There is no specific authorization prerequisite to invoke this utility. However, the user ID must have the correct authorization and/or privileges for the associated utility (export, import, and load) to take action.

The behavior of the **export, import,** and **load** actions is exactly the same as described in the previous sections. The only action you probably are not familiar with is **copy.** It duplicates tables in a schema or schemas into a target database. Only tables with exactly the same schema names specified in the **–sn** option will be copied (via export). If multiple schema names are specified, use commas to separate them without blank spaces. For example:

```
db2move sample copy -sn db2inst1,prodschema
    -co target_db acctdb user peter using petepasswd ddl_and_load
```

The above **db2move** command copies supported objects under the schema db2inst1 and prodschema. The **–co target_DB** option that follows makes the command more interesting. It specifies the target database in which the schemas are going to be copied. This option is mandatory when the **copy** action is specified. In addition, the target database must be different from the source database. You may provide the user and password with the **user** and **using** options when connecting to the target database.

By default, supported objects from the source schema will be created and tables will be populated in the target database. This is the behavior of the **ddl_and_load** mode. Two other modes are available: **ddl_only** and **load_only.** As the names imply, **ddl_only** only creates all the supported objects from the source schema and **load_only** loads all specified tables from the source to the target database. Note that tables must already exist in the target database when this option is used.

Sometimes you may want to rename the schema when copying the objects to the target database. The **schema_map** option can be used for this purpose. You simply provide one or more pairs of schema mappings like the following:

```
schema_map ((source_schema1,target_schema1),(source_schema2,target_schema2))
```

Extra attention is recommended when **SCHEMA_MAP** is used. Only the schema of the object itself is renamed; qualified objects inside the object body remain unchanged. For example, in the following view:

```
CREATE VIEW FOO.v1 AS 'SELECT c1 FROM FOO.T1'
```

if the schema is renamed from FOO to BAR, only the schema of the view is changed. The underlying definition of the view is preserved. The above example will be mapped to the following. Note that *BAR.v1* created in the target database might fail if *FOO.T1* is not defined.

```
CREATE VIEW BAR.v1 AS 'SELECT c1 FROM FOO.T1'
```

A similar mapping idea also applies to table spaces. For example, you want the copied tables to be stored in a different table space name from the source database. The **db2move** command is extended to let you specify table space name mappings. Consider the following option:

```
tablespace_map ((TS1,TS2),(TS2,TS3), sys_any)
```

The above table space name mapping indicates that source TS1 is mapped to target TS2, source TS2 is mapped to target TS3. The **sys_any** indicates that the remaining table spaces will use table spaces chosen by the database manager based on the table space selection algorithm. Let's put the pieces together in an example.

```
db2move sample copy -sn db2inst1,prodschema
    -co target_db acctdb user peter using petepasswd load_only
        schema_map ((db2inst1,db2inst2),(prodschema,devschema))
        tablespace_map sys_any
        nonrecoverable
```

This command copies supported objects with the schema names *db2inst1* and *prodschema* from the *sample* database to the *acctdb* database. The authorization id *peter* and the associated password are used to connect to *acctdb*. The target tables already exist in *acctdb* and the tables will be repopulated. All objects under the *db2inst1* and *prodschema* schemas are now under *db2inst2* and *devschema* respectively. Instead of using the table space name defined in the *sample* database, the default table space in *acctdb* will be used instead.

The **NONRECOVERABLE** option allows the user to immediately use the table spaces after the copy is completed. Backups of the table spaces are not required but highly recommended at the earliest time.

13.7 The db2relocatedb Utility

The **db2relocatedb** utility renames a database and relocates a database or part of a database you specify in the configuration file. This tool makes the necessary changes to the DB2 instance and database files.

You can alter the following properties of a database using the **db2relocatedb** utility:

- The database name
- The instance it belongs to
- The database directory
- The database partition number
- The log directory (if it does not reside in the database directory)
- The location of table space containers (if they do not reside in the database directory)

The syntax for the db2relocatedb command is

```
db2relocatedb –f configuration_file_name
```

The format of the configuration file is

```
DB_NAME=oldName,newName
DB_PATH=oldPath,newPath
INSTANCE=oldInst,newInst
NODENUM=nodeNumber
LOG_DIR=oldDirPath,newDirPath
CONT_PATH=oldContPath1,newContPath1
CONT_PATH=oldContPath2,newContPath2
...
```

If the *sample* database belongs to instance db2inst1 and was created under /data, to rename the *sample* database to *sample1*, edit a configuration file as follows and run the **db2relocatedb** command using this file:

```
DB_NAME=SAMPLE,SAMPLE1
DB_PATH=/data
INSTANCE=db2inst1
```

To move the *sample* database from the instance *db2inst1* on path /data to instance *db2inst2* on the same path, do the following:

- Move all the files in /data/db2inst1 to /data/db2inst2
- Edit a configuration file as follows and run **db2relocatedb** using this file:

```
DB_NAME=SAMPLE
DB_PATH=/data
INSTANCE=db2inst1, dn2inst2
```

If the *sample* database belongs to instance *db2inst1*, was created under /data, and has a SMS table space container /home/db2inst1/ts1 that must be moved to /home/db2inst1/ts/ts1, do the following:

- Copy all the files in /home/db2inst1/ts1 to /home/db2inst1/ts/ts1.
- Edit a configuration file and run **db2relocatedb** using this file:

```
DB_NAME=SAMPLE
DB_PATH=/data
INSTANCE=db2inst1
CONT_PATH=/home/db2inst1/ts1,/home/db2inst1/ts/ts1
```

Refer to the file *Command_and_SQL_Examples.pdf* included with the CD-ROM accompanying this book for more examples on how to use **db2relocatedb.**

13.8 Generating Data Definition Language

So far this chapter has introduced tools and utilities that you can use to extract data and table definitions using export. In cases when you just want to extract the definition of a table, the **db2look** command comes in very handy.

db2look extracts the Data Definition Language (DDL) of database objects. Besides that, the tool can also generate the following:

- UPDATE statistics statements
- Authorization statements such as GRANT statements (also known as the Data Control Language (DCL)
- **update** commands for the following Database Manager Configuration parameters:
  - cpuspeed
  - intra_parallel
  - comm_bandwidth
  - nodetype
  - federated
  - fed_noauth
- **update** commands for the following database configuration parameters:
  - locklist
  - dft_degree
  - maxlocks
  - avg_appls
  - stmtheap
  - dft_queryopt

- The **db2set** command for the following DB2 registry variables:
    - DB2_PRED_FACTORIZE
    - DB2_CORRELATED_PREDICATES
    - DB2_LIKE_VARCHAR
    - DB2_SORT_AFTER_TQ
    - DB2_ORDERED_NLJN
    - DB2_NEW_CORR_SQ_FF
    - DB2_PART_INNER_JOIN
    - DB2_INTERESTING_KEYS

The syntax diagram for the **db2look** command in Figure 13.37 shows all the supported options.

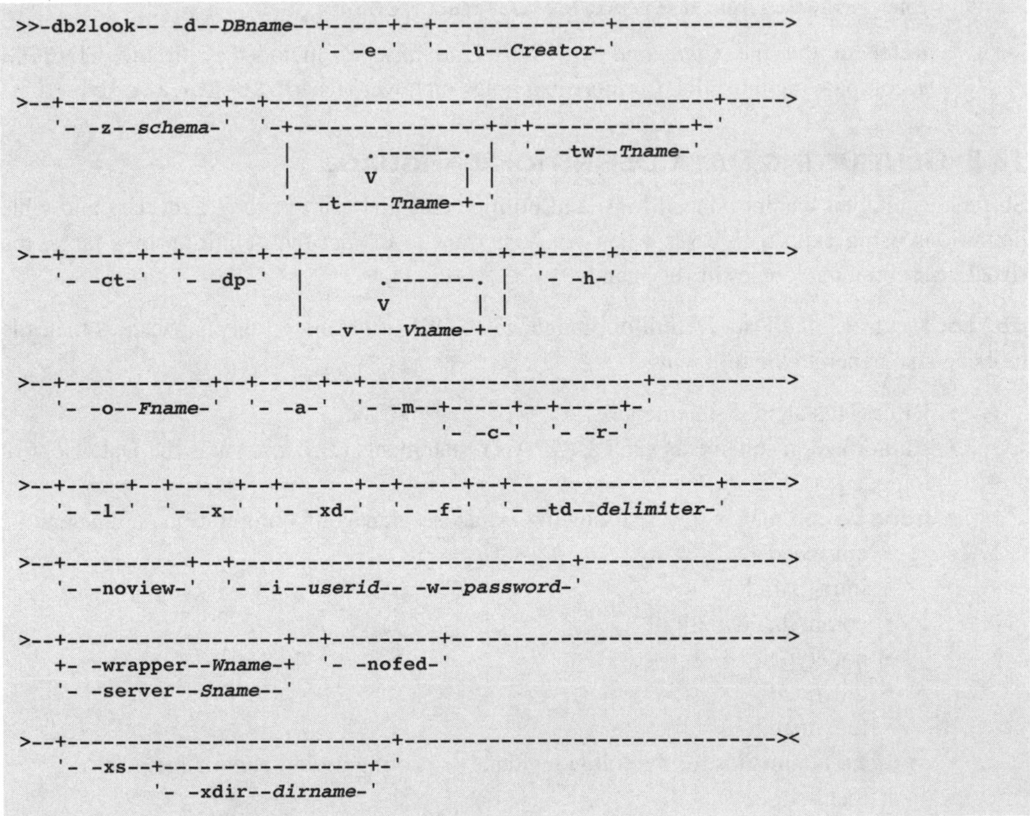

```
>>-db2look-- -d--DBname--+-----+--+--------------+-------------->
                         '- -e-'  '- -u--Creator-'

>--+-------------+--+-----------------------------------+----->
   '- -z--schema-'  '-+----------------+--+-------------+-'
                      |    .--------.  |  '- -tw--Tname-'
                      |    V        |  |
                      '- -t----Tname-+-'

>--+------+--+------+--+----------------+--+-----+-------------->
   '- -ct-'  '- -dp-'  |    .--------.  |  '- -h-'
                       |    V        |  |
                       '- -v----Vname-+-'

>--+------------+--+-----+--+----------------------+----------->
   '- -o--Fname-'  '- -a-'  '- -m--+-----+--+-----+-'
                                   '- -c-'  '- -r-'

>--+-----+--+-----+--+------+--+-----+--+-----------------+----->
   '- -l-'  '- -x-'  '- -xd-'  '- -f-'  '- -td--delimiter-'

>--+----------+--+---------------------------+----------------->
   '- -noview-'  '- -i--userid-- -w--password-'

>--+------------------+--+---------+---------------------------->
   +- -wrapper--Wname-+  '- -nofed-'
   '- -server--Sname--'

>--+-------------------------+-------------------------------><
   '- -xs--+-----------------+-'
           '- -xdir--dirname-'
```

Figure 13.37 Syntax diagram of the db2look command

Refer to the *DB2 Command Reference Manual* for more information about each option. The following examples demonstrate how the command can be used.

- In the *sample* database, the command generates the DDL of objects created by *db2admin* under the schema *prod*. It also generates authorization statements. The output file *db2look.sql* captures this result.
  ```
  db2look –d sample –u db2admin –z prod –e –x –o db2look.sql
  ```
- In the *sample* database, the command extracts the DDL from the *staff*, *department*, and *employee* tables, and generates UPDATE statements used to replicate statistics of the tables and the associated **runstats** commands.
  ```
  db2look –d sample –t staff department employee –m -r
  ```
- In the *sample* database, the command generates the DDL for all the database objects including the authorization statements, and stores the result in *db2look.sql*.
  ```
  db2look –d sample –xd –o db2look.sql
  ```
- In the *sample* database, the command extracts the DDL from the *customer* and *porder* tables. It also exports all files necessary for XML schemas registration. The XSR objects are stored in *c:\xsddir*.
  ```
  db2look –d sample –t customer porder –xs –xdir c:\xsddir
  ```

13.9 DB2 Maintenance Utilities

Performing maintenance activities on your databases is essential to ensure that they are optimized for performance and recoverability. In this section, we introduce a few utilities that you should use regularly to ensure the database is healthy and optimized.

13.9.1 The RUNSTATS Utility

DB2 utilizes a sophisticated cost-based optimizer to determine how data is being accessed. Its decisions are heavily influenced by statistical information about the size of the database tables and indexes. Therefore, it is important to keep the database statistics up to date so that an efficient data access plan can be chosen. The RUNSTATS utility updates statistics about the physical characteristics of a table and the associated indexes. Characteristics include the number of records (cardinality), the number of pages, the average record length, and so on.

The **runstats** command supports many different options; a small fraction of the syntax diagram is shown in Figure 13.38. Refer to the *DB2 Command Reference* for details on each option.

```
>>-RUNSTATS--ON TABLE--table name--+-USE PROFILE------------+--->
                                   '-| Statistics Options |-'

>--+-----------------------------------+----------------------><
   '-UTIL_IMPACT_PRIORITY--+----------+-'
                           '-priority-'
```

Figure 13.38 Partial syntax diagram of the runstats command

The following examples illustrate how to use this command.

- This command collects statistics on the table *db2user.employee* while letting readers and writers access the table while the statistics are being calculated.

```
runstats on table db2user.employee allow write access
```

- This command collects statistics on the table *db2user.employee*, as well as on the columns *empid* and *empname* with distribution statistics. While the command is running, the table is only available for read-only requests.

```
runstats on table db2user.employee with distribution
    on columns ( empid, empname ) allow read access
```

- The following command collects statistics on the table *db2user.employee* and detailed statistics on all its indexes.

```
runstats on table db2user.employee and detailed indexes all
```

- This command collects statistics on the table *db2user.employee* with distribution statistics on only 30 percent of the rows.

```
runstats on table db2user.employee with distribution
    tablesmple bernoulli(30)
```

You can be very specific when it comes to collecting statistics on the database objects. Different combinations of **runstats** options can be used to collect table statistics, index statistics, distribution statistics, sampling information, and so on. To simplify statistics collection, you can save the options you specified when you issue the **runstats** command in a statistics profile. If you want to collect the same statistics repeatedly on a table and do not want to retype the command options, you simply specify the **use profile** option.

```
runstats on table db2user.employee use profile
```

This command collects statistics on *db2user.employee* using the options saved in the statistics profile for that table. So, how do you set a statistics profile? It is as easy as using the **set profile only** option.

```
runstats on table db2user.employee
    with distribution on columns (empid, empname)
    set profile only
```

Notice that the option will only set the profile; the **runstats** command will not run. If you need to modify a previously registered statistics profile, use the **update profile only** option. Similarly, this option will only update the profile without running the **runstats** command. If you want to update the profile as well as update the statistics, use the **update profile** option instead.

```
runstats on table db2user.employee
    with distribution default
    num_freqvalues 50 num_quantiles 50
    update profile
```

In order to maintain efficient database operation, statistics should be collected regularly. You should find regular windows of reduced database activity so that database statistics can be collected without affecting the database performance. In some environments, this may not be possible.

Starting in DB2 9, automatic statistics collection allows DB2 to automatically run the **runstats** utility in the background to ensure the most current database statistics are available. The automatic statistics collection feature is enabled by default for any new database created in DB2 9. You can disable it by explicitly setting the AUTO_RUNSTATS database configuration parameter to OFF. In order to minimize the performance impact of automatic statistics collection, throttling of the **runstats** utility can be used to limit the amount of resources consumed by the utility. When the database activity is low, the utility runs more aggressively. On the other hand, when the database activity increases, the resources allocated to executing **runstats** are reduced. Here is how to specify the level of throttling.

```
runstats on table db2user.employee
    with distribution default
    num_freqvalues 50 num_quantiles 50
    util_impact_priority 30
```

The acceptable priority value ranges from 1 to 100. The highest priority (meaning unthrottled) is represented by the value 100 and the value 1 represents the lowest priority. Default priority level is 50.

> **NOTE** The ADMIN_CMD procedure also supports execution of the **runstats** command.

13.9.2 The REORG and REORGCHK Utilities

As data is inserted, deleted, and updated in the database, the data might not be physically placed in a sequential order, which means that DB2 must perform additional read operations to access data. This usually requires more disk I/O operations, and we all know such operations are costly. To minimize I/O operations, you should consider physically reorganizing the table to the index so that related data are located close to each other.

> **NOTE** Refer to Section 13.5.3.1, Leaving Free Space in Data and Index Pages, for a discussion of page overflows, leaving free space in data, and index pages.

An index is said to have a **high cluster ratio** when the data with equal or near key values is physically stored close together. The higher the cluster ratio, the better rows are ordered in index key sequence. Figure 13.39 shows the difference between indexes with high and low cluster ratio.

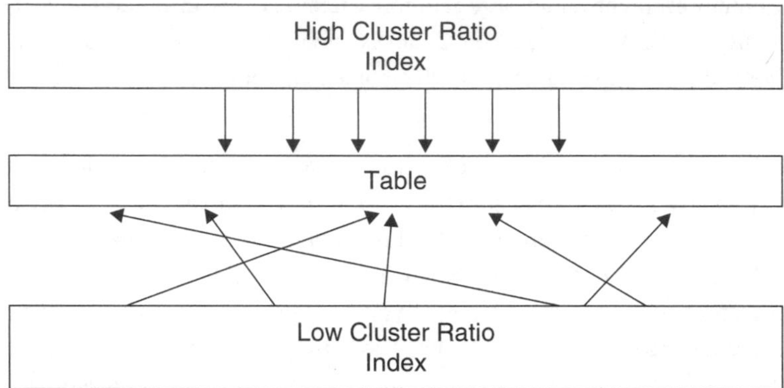

Figure 13.39 Indexes with high and low cluster ratio

An index's cluster ratio is part of the database statistics. You will learn in Chapter 17, Database Performance Considerations, that keeping database statistics is very important when it comes to performance. REORGCHK is a data maintenance utility that has an option to retrieve current database statistics or update the database statistics. It generates a report on the statistics with indicators identifying tables and indexes that should be reorganized (or defragmented). Using the statistics formulae, **reorgchk** marks the tables or indexes with asterisks (*) if there is a need to REORG. Figure 13.40 shows the syntax diagram of the **reorgchk** command.

```
              .-UPDATE STATISTICS--.
>>-REORGCHK--+--------------------+----------------------------->
              '-CURRENT STATISTICS-'

   .-ON TABLE USER-----------------.
>--+-------------------------------+---------------------------><
   '-ON--+-SCHEMA--schema-name---+-'
         |         .-USER-------. |
         '-TABLE--+-SYSTEM-----+-'
                  +-ALL--------+
                  '-table-name-'
```

Figure 13.40 Syntax diagram of the reorgchk command

For example, the following command generates a report of the current statistics on all tables that are owned by the runtime authorization ID:

```
reorgchk current statistics on table user
```

This command updates the statistics and generates a report on all the tables created under the schema *smith*:

```
reorgchk update statistics on schema smith
```

Figure 13.41 shows a sample output of a **reorgchk** command. You can see that the report contains table and index statistics. Every table and index defined in the database is listed. If statistics are not collected for the table or index, a dash (–) is displayed.

```
Table statistics:

F1: 100 * OVERFLOW / CARD < 5
F2: 100 * (Effective Space Utilization of Data Pages) > 68
F3: 100 * (Required Pages / Total Pages) > 80

SCHEMA    NAME                        CARD     OV     NP     FP    TSIZE  F1  F2  F3 REORG
------------------------------------------------------------------------------------------
SYSIBM    SYSATTRIBUTES                  -      -      -      -        -   -   -   - ---
SYSIBM    SYSBUFFERPOOLNODES             -      -      -      -        -   -   -   - ---
SYSIBM    SYSBUFFERPOOLS                 1      0      1      1       52   0   - 100 ---
SYSIBM    SYSCHECKS                      -      -      -      -        -   -   -   - ---
SYSIBM    SYSCODEPROPERTIES              -      -      -      -        -   -   -   - ---
SYSIBM    SYSCOLAUTH                     -      -      -      -        -   -   -   - ---

Index statistics:

F4: CLUSTERRATIO or normalized CLUSTERFACTOR > 80
F5: 100*(KEYS*(ISIZE+9)+(CARD-KEYS)*5) / ((NLEAF-NUM_EMPTY_LEAFS)*INDEXPAGESIZE) > 50
F6: (100-PCTFREE)*((INDEXPAGESIZE-96)/(ISIZE+12))**(NLEVELS-2)*(INDEXPAGESIZE-96)/
(KEYS*(ISIZE+9)+(CARD-KEYS)*5) < 100
F7: 100 * (NUMRIDS DELETED / (NUMRIDS DELETED + CARD)) < 20
F8: 100 * (NUM EMPTY LEAFS / NLEAF) < 20

SCHEMA   NAME                     CARD  LEAF ELEAF LVLS ISIZE NDEL KEYS  F4 F5 F6 F7 F8 REORG
---------------------------------------------------------------------------------------------
Table: SYSIBM.SYSATTRIBUTES
SYSIBM   IBM83                       -     -     -    -     -    -    -   -  -  -  -  - -----
SYSIBM   IBM84                       -     -     -    -     -    -    -   -  -  -  -  - -----
SYSIBM   IBM85                       -     -     -    -     -    -    -   -  -  -  -  - -----
Table: SYSIBM.SYSBUFFERPOOLNODES
SYSIBM   IBM69                       -     -     -    -     -    -    -   -  -  -  -  - -----
Table: SYSIBM.SYSBUFFERPOOLS
SYSIBM   IBM67                       1     1     0    1    22    0    1 100  -  -  0  0 -----
SYSIBM   IBM68                       1     1     0    1    10    0    1 100  -  -  0  0 -----
Table: SYSIBM.SYSCHECKS
SYSIBM   IBM37                       -     -     -    -     -    -    -   -  -  -  -  - -----
```

Figure 13.41 Sample output of the **reorgchk** command

To reorganize tables or indexes, use the REORG utility. It reorganizes data for a table and/or index. Although data is physically rearranged, DB2 provides the option of performing this online or offline. By default, offline REORG lets other users read the table. You can restrict table access by specifying the **allow no access** option. Online REORG (also called **inplace REORG**) does not support read or write access to the table. Since data pages are rearranged, concurrent applications have to wait for REORG to complete with the current pages. You can easily stop, pause, or resume the process with the appropriate options. Figure 13.42 illustrates the syntax diagram of the **reorg** command.

The following command reorganizes table *db2user.employee* and its index *db2user.idxemp*. The operation lets others perform writes to the same table.

```
reorg table db2user.employee index db2user.idxemp inplace allow write access
```

To pause a REORG operation, issue the command with the same options but specify the **pause** option:

```
reorg table db2user.employee index db2user.idxemp inplace pause
```

```
>>-REORG------------------------------------------------------->

>--+-TABLE--table-name--| Table Clause |-----------------+------>
   '-+-INDEXES ALL FOR TABLE--table-name--| Index Clause |-'
     '-INDEX--index-name--+-----------------------+-'
                          '-FOR TABLE--table-name-'


>--+-------------------------------+--------------------------><
   '-| Database Partition Clause |-'

Table Clause:

|--+-------------------+------------------------------------------>
   '-INDEX--index-name-'
     .-ALLOW READ ACCESS-.
>--+-+-------------------+--+---------------+--+------------+--+-------------+-+--|
   | '-ALLOW NO ACCESS---'  '-USE--tbspace-'  '-INDEXSCAN-'  '-LONGLOBDATA-' |
   |           .-ALLOW WRITE ACCESS-.                          .-START--.    |
   '-INPLACE--+-+--------------------+--+------------------+--+--------+-+---'
              | '-ALLOW READ ACCESS--'  '-NOTRUNCATE TABLE-'  '-RESUME-' |
              '-+-STOP--+-------------------------------------------------'
                '-PAUSE-'
Index Clause:

   .-ALLOW READ ACCESS--.
|--+--------------------+--+-------------------------+---------|
   +-ALLOW NO ACCESS----+  |                  .-ALL---. |
   '-ALLOW WRITE ACCESS-'  +-CLEANUP ONLY--+-------+-+
                           |                  '-PAGES-' |
                           '-CONVERT-----------------'
```

Figure 13.42 Syntax diagram of the reorg command

You can also reorganize an index. If the **cleanup** clause is used as shown in one of the examples below, a cleanup will be done instead of a reorganization.

```
reorg index db2user.idxemp for table db2user.employee allow write access
reorg index db2user.idxemp for table db2user.employee cleanup only
```

> **NOTE** The REORG utility rearranges the data physically but does not update the database statistics. Therefore, it is important to always execute a RUNSTATS upon completion of a REORG.

V9 One of the most prominent features introduced in DB2 9 is the ability to perform row compression. DB2 shrinks row sizes by building and utilizing a compression dictionary, which is used as an alphabet to compress rows of data in tables. The data dictionary used to compress and expand the rows in the table is built when a table marked with the COMPRESS attribute is being reorganized. V9.5 Moreover, in DB2 9.5, in order to minimize the administrative effort, compression dictionaries can be automatically created as part of the table data population operations, such as

INSERT, IMPORT, and LOAD INSERT, when certain conditions are met. Refer to Chapter 7, Working with Database Objects, which introduces this new feature in more detail.

Two options in the REORG TABLE command affect the behaviour of whether a compression dictionary will be created; namely KEEPDICTIONARY and RESETDICTIONARY. When compression is enabled for a particular table, KEEPDICTIONARY basically preserves the dictionary if it exists and the REORG utility uses it to compress the table data. A dictionary will be built if one does not already exist.

On the other hand, the RESETDICTIONARY option causes the REORG utility to build a new dictionary regardless of its existence. In addition, the RESETDICTIONARY option will drop the dictionary if the table is no longer enabled with compression. Refer to the Table 13.12 for a summary of the KEEPDICTIONARY and RESETDICTIONARY options behavior.

NOTE The ADMIN_CMD procedure also supports execution of the **reorg** command.

Table 13.12 Summary of the Behavior of the KEEPDICTIONARY and RESETDICTIONARY REORG Option

REORG OPTION	COMPRESS Attribute Set on the Table?	Dictionary Exists?	Behavior
KEEPDICTIONARY	Y	Y	Preserve dictionary; rows compressed
KEEPDICTIONARY	Y	N	Build dictionary; rows compressed
KEEPDICTIONARY	N	Y	Preserve dictionary; all rows uncompressed
KEEPDICTIONARY	N	N	No dictionary; all rows uncompressed
RESETDICTIONARY	Y	Y	Build new dictionary; rows compressed
RESETDICTIONARY	Y	N	Build new dictionary; rows compressed
RESETDICTIONARY	N	Y	Remove dictionary; all rows uncompressed
RESETDICTIONARY	N	N	No dictionary; all rows uncompressed

13.9.3 The REBIND Utility and the FLUSH PACKAGE CACHE Command

Before a database application program or any SQL statement can be executed, DB2 precompiles it and produces a package. A **package** is a database object that contains compiled SQL statements used in the application source file. DB2 uses the packages to access data referenced in the SQL statements. How does the DB2 optimizer choose the data access plan for these packages? It relies on database statistics at the time the packages are created.

For static SQL statements, packages are created and bound to the database at compile time. If statistics are updated to reflect the physical database characteristics, existing packages should also be updated. The REBIND utility lets you re-create a package so that the current database statistics can be used. The command is very simple:

```
rebind package package_name
```

When you execute dynamic SQL statements, they are not known until the application is run. They are precompiled at runtime and stored in the package cache. If statistics are updated, you can flush the cache so that dynamic SQL statements are compiled again to pick up the updated statistics. Use the following command:

```
flush package cache dynamic
```

13.9.4 Database Maintenance Process

You have just learned about a few database maintenance utilities: RUNSTATS, REORG, REORGCHK, REBIND, and FLUSH PACKAGE. Figure 13.43 summarizes the maintenance process that you should perform regularly against your database.

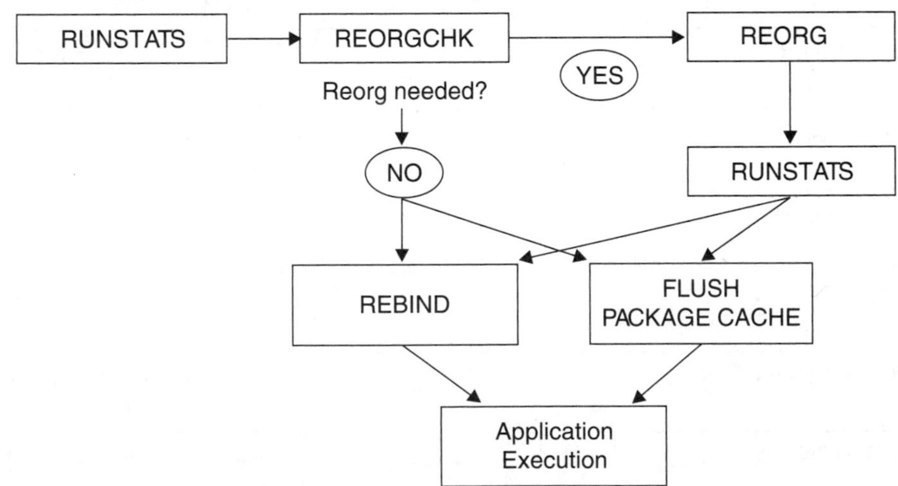

Figure 13.43 Database maintenance process

13.9.5 Automatic Database Maintenance

Maintaining a database can be quite time consuming to plan and execute, as you can see in Figure 13.43. DB2 includes several automatic features, including the automatic maintenance capability. They are enabled by default when you create a new database in DB2 9. The automatic database maintenance capability is adopted by most of the utilities, namely, database backups, update statistics, update statistics with statistics profiles, and data reorganization.

The Configure Automatic Maintenance Wizard is all you need to enable and configure automatic maintenance. Launch the wizard from the Control Center (refer to Figure 13.44) or the Health Center.

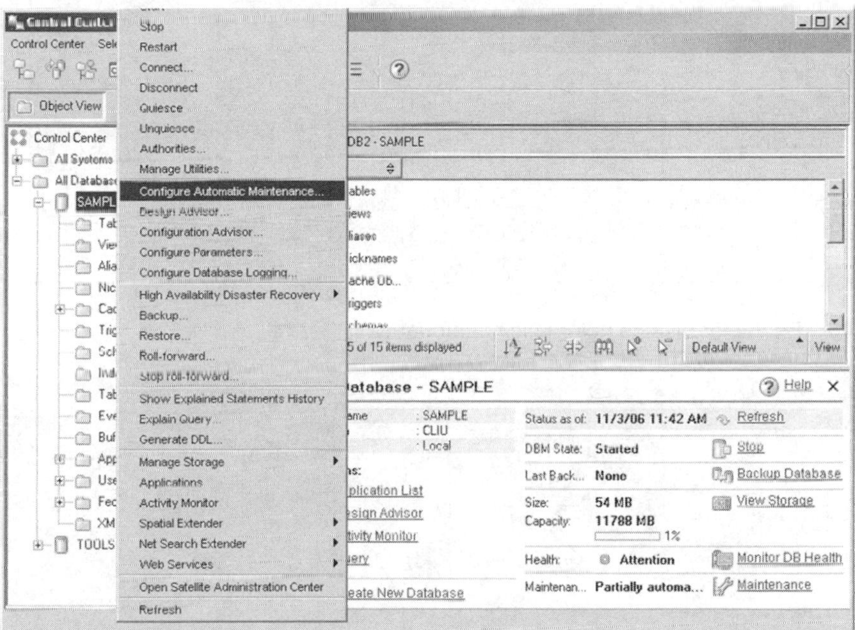

Figure 13.44 Lauch the Configure Automatic Maintenance wizard from the DB2 Control Center

The wizard allows you to

- Define the maintenance windows for the maintenance activities to be automatically executed. Choose periods that have low or no activity.
- Choose people to be notified if automatic maintenance fails.
- Choose maintenance activities for DB2 to handle automatically.
- Specify the evaluation criteria DB2 uses to determine if maintenance is required.

Refer to the Figures 13.45 through 13.50, which demonstrate each configuration step.

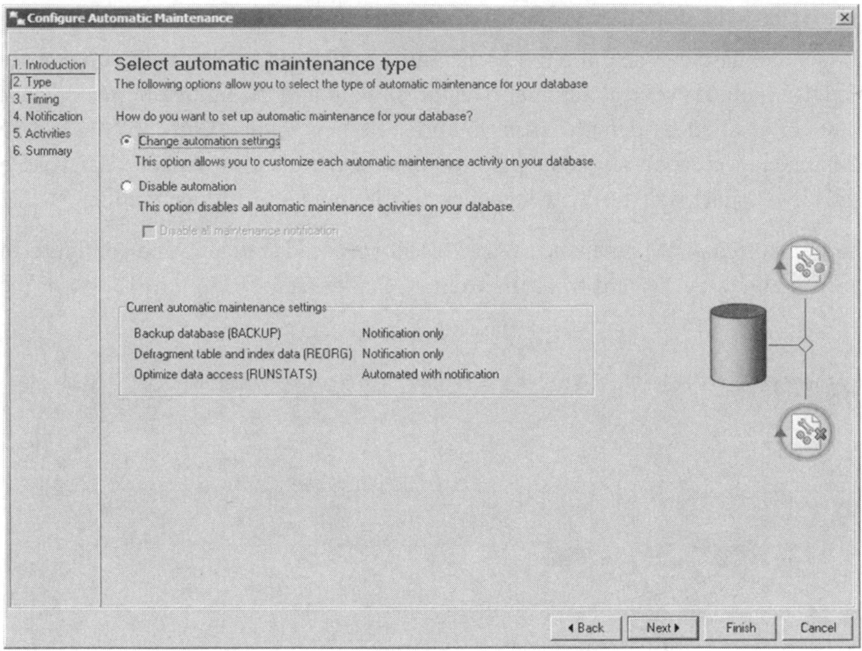

Figure 13.45 Enable or disable automatic maintenance

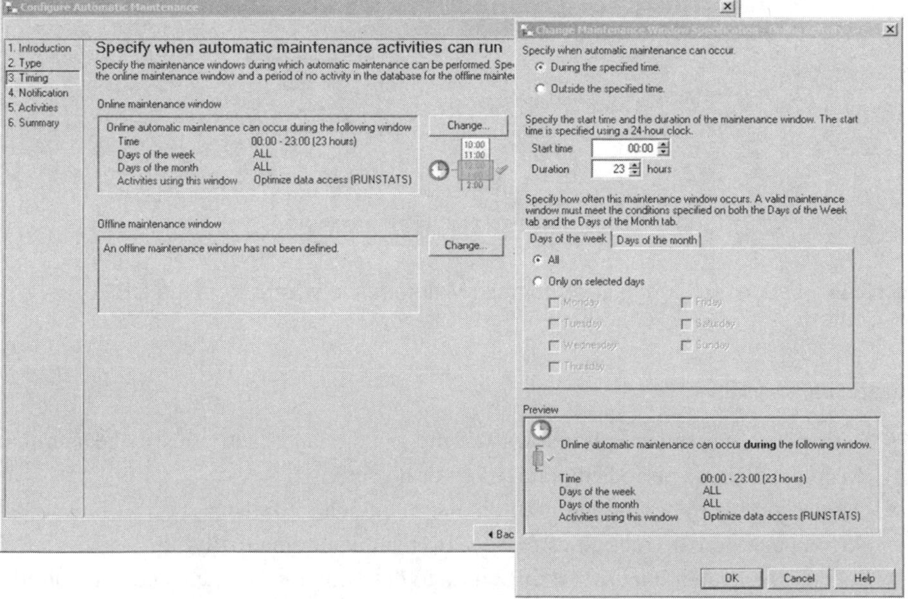

Figure 13.46 Specify database maintenance window

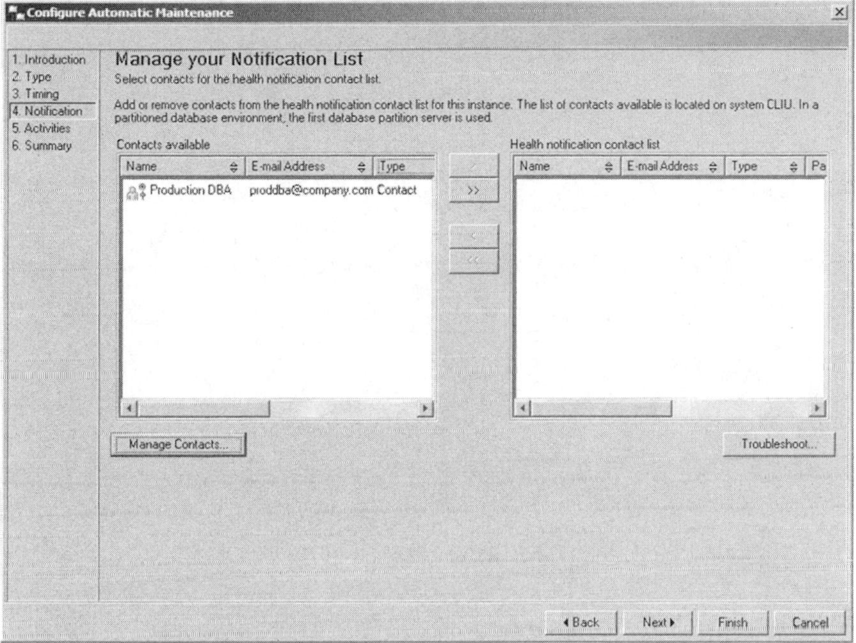

Figure 13.47 Manage the notification list

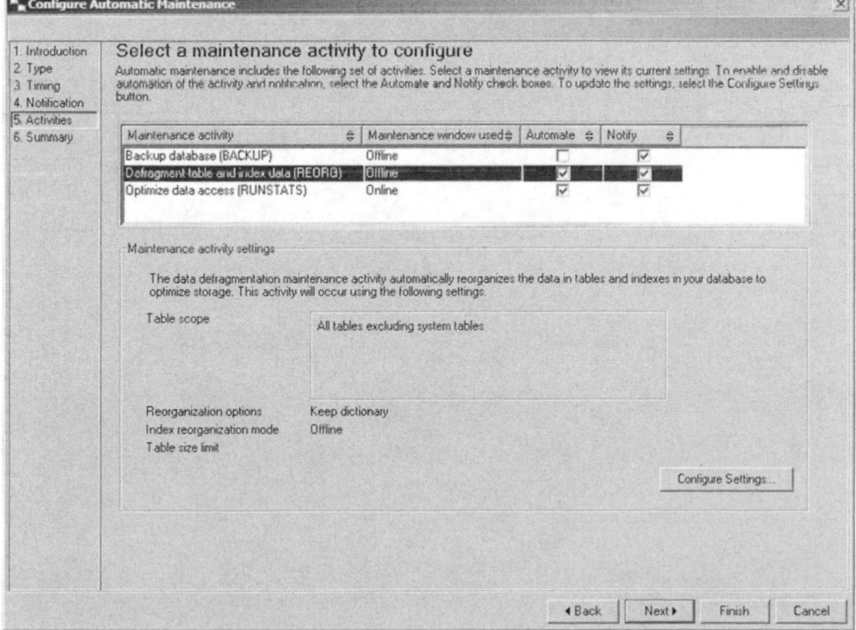

Figure 13.48 Configure the maintenance activities

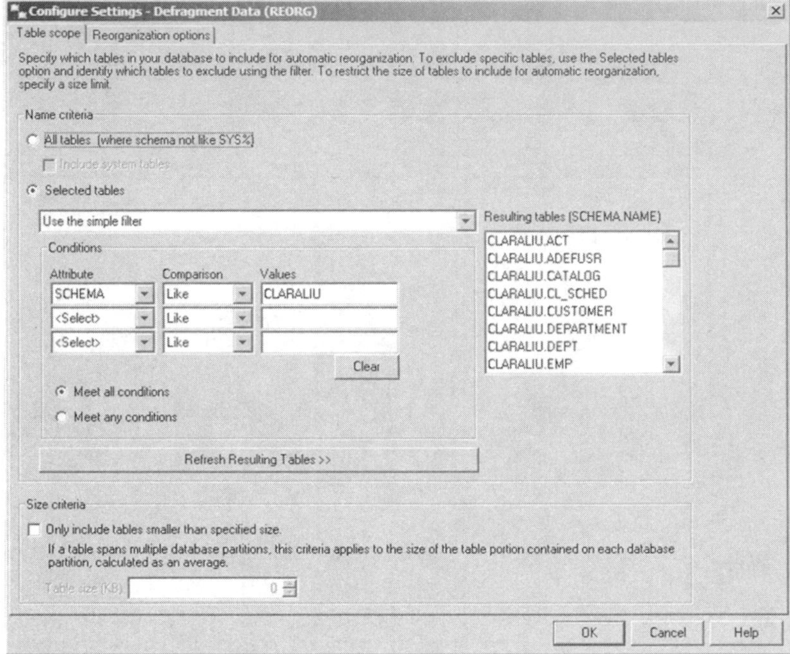

Figure 13.49 Configure settings for each maintenance activity

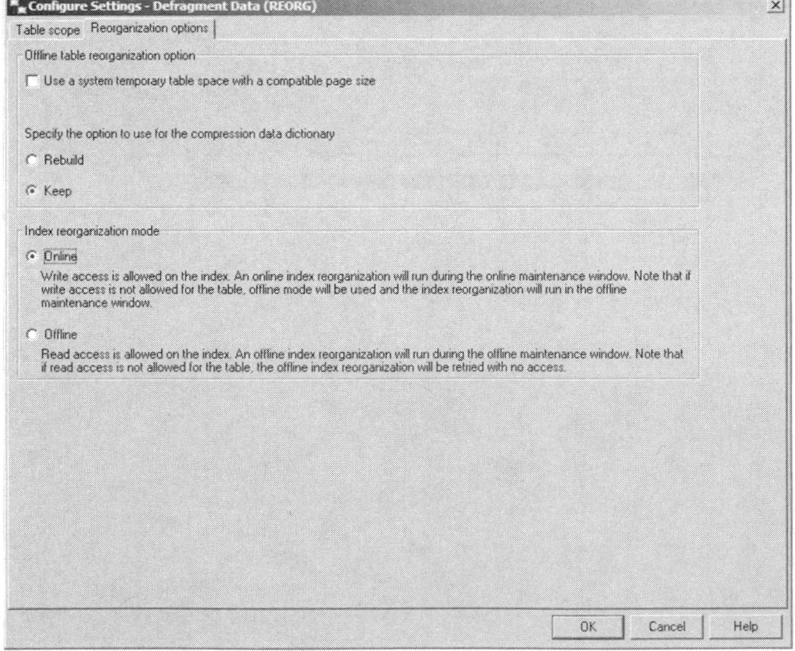

Figure 13.50 More configuration options

If you prefer enabling automatic maintenance using the command-line interface, you can update the following database configuration parameters and control the behavior by turning them ON or OFF.

- Automatic maintenance (auto_maint)
  - Automatic database backup (auto_db_backup)
  - Automatic table maintenance (auto_tbl_maint)
    - Automatic runstats (auto_runstats)
    - Automatic statistics profiling (auto_stats_prof)
    - Automatic profile updates (auto_prof_upd)
    - Automatic reorganization (auto_reorg)

13.10 Case Study

Assume your company wants to deploy a new accounting application very soon, but the finance department director has demanded more thorough testing. The only test machine available for testing has DB2 for Windows installed. However, you need to obtain data from a DB2 for AIX database server. Since the source and target platforms are different and not every table and views are required for testing, you choose to use data movement utilities to move data to the Windows server.

First, you connect to the source server and then export the required tables with this command:

```
export to newsalary.ixf of ixf
  xml to xmlpath
  xmlfile acctdesc
  modified by xmlinsepfiles xmlchar
  messages newsalary.out
  select empno, firstnme, lastname, salary * 1.3 as new_salary
    from employee
   where workdept='A00'
```

You find out that the accounting application needs all of the 100 tables under the schema *acct*. To save the time and effort of typing the **export** command for each of the 100 tables, you choose to use the **db2move** command.

```
db2move proddb export -sn acct
```

Because the output files are in IXF format, you can create the tables and import data directly to the target database using the import utility.

```
import from newsalary.ixf of ixf
  xml from xmlpath
  xmlparse preserve whitespace
  messages newsalary.out
  create into newsalary in datats index in indexts
```

Note that a new table called *newsalary* is created in the *datats* table space and that its indexes are stored in the *indexts* table space.

After the first few successful completions of the import operation, you realize that you cannot finish all the imports within the estimated time. The import utility performs insert statements behind the scenes, and thus activates constraint checking, logging, and triggers. The load utility, on the other hand, goes behind the DB2 engine and loads the data directly to the pages. You can choose to perform logging as well as performing only primary and unique key checks. Thus, for the sake of performance, you decide to change the plan and use the load utility instead.

To capture all rows that violated unique constraints of the target table, you create an exception table with this statement:

```
CREATE TABLE salaryexp
( empno CHAR(6), firstnme VARCHAR(12), lastname VARCHAR(15)
, new_salary DECIMAL(9,2), load_ts TIMESTAMP, load_msg CLOB(2K))
```

Since you are not that familiar with the syntax of the **load** command, you decide to use the Control Center to invoke the load utility. Each graphical tool has a *Show Command* button. You click on this button because you want to store the **load** command generated in a script so you can use it in the future. You obtain the following command, which you can issue later:

```
load from newsalary.ixf of ixf
  modified by dumpfile=salarydump.dmp
  rowcount 5000
  messages salary.out
  tempfiles path c:\loadtemp
  create into salary
  for exception salaryexp
```

After the load is completed successfully, the table is not accessible (by default) due to table space backup pending. Therefore, you need to perform a table space or database backup (see Section 14.4, Performing Database and Table Space Backups).

If the table has any constraints defined, such as referential integrity and check constraint, you need to validate the data integrity with the following command:

```
set integrity for newsalary immediate checked
```

The target tables should be ready and accessible for testing.

As the testing is progressing, you realize that the performance of the report generator reduces after each monthly inventory update. You first reorganize the tables and update the statistics of the tables with the following commands:

```
reorg table inventory_parts indexes all keepdictionary

runstats on table inventory_parts
    with distribution default
    num_freqvalues 50 num_quantiles 50
    util_impact_priority 30
```

Because the table *inventory_parts* is enabled for row compression, the KEEPDICTIONARY option is specified to preserve the dictionary. Rather than performing the maintenance tasks manually, you have decided to turn on automatic maintenance. You simply specify the maintenance window and the maintenance tasks you would like to enable, all through the Control Center > Configure Automatic Maintenance.

13.11 Summary

In this chapter you were introduced to the different data movement utilities that come with DB2. The utilities support the following file formats: DEL, ASC, IXF, WSF, and CURSOR.

The export utility extracts data from a table or view into a file. The **export** command can be very simple. At a minimum, you should specify the output filename (where exported data is stored), its file format, the message file name, and a **SELECT** statement.

The import utility, on the other hand, inserts data into a specified table or view from a file. You can choose to import to an existing or new table (or view). By default, DB2 only issues one COMMIT at the very end of the import operation. In case of failure during the import, all the changes will be rolled back, and you will need to restart the import from the beginning. Alternatively, you can use options such as **commitcount, restartcount,** and **skipcount** to enable the ability of restarting an import.

The load utility is another method to insert data into a specified table or view and is much faster. The utility formats the data pages while bypassing DB2 buffering and logging. The utility is composed of four phases: load, build, delete, and index copy. You can check the load message file or the status of the table or use the **load query** command to monitor the load operation.

The **db2move** utility can be used to move more than one table using just one command. The utility lets you specify the action: export, import, or load. This utility comes in very handy when many tables need to be moved.

The RUNSTATS, REORG, and REORGCHK utilities are very important data maintenance utilities that should be performed regularly to ensure that the most optimal data access plans are used. You should also review the automatic database maintenance capabilities DB2 provides. It will save you a lot of time in planning and scheduling maintenance activities.

13.12 Review Questions

1. Which data movement utility supports the CURSOR input file type?
2. What other privileges are needed to load a table if the person already has LOAD authority?
3. Bob creates the *stock* table:

```
CREATE TABLE stock ( id         INTEGER NOT NULL
                   , name       VARCHAR(10)
                   , bandlevel INTEGER NOT NULL
                   , PRIMARY KEY (id) )
```

   He then loads the table with this **load** command:

```
load from stock.del of del
    modified by dumpfile=stockdump.dmp
    messages stock.out
    replace into stock
    for exception stockexp
```

The input file *stock.del* looks like this:

```
10, "AAA", 30
20, "BBB", -
30, "CCC", 3
30, "DDD", 4
40, "EEE", x
```

After the **load** command is executed, which rows will be stored in the *stockdmp.dmp* file?

4. With the same target table definition, **load** command, and input file as in question 3, which rows will be stored in the *stockexp* exception table?
5. A table is created with the following statement:

```
CREATE TABLE employee
    ( id    SMALLINT NOT NULL
    , name VARCHAR(10)
    , job  CHAR(5) CHECK (job IN ('Sales', 'Mgr', 'Clerk') )
    , PRIMARY KEY (id))
```

If this **load** command is issued, what state would the *employee* table be in?

```
load from emp2.del of del insert into emp2
```

6. A table is created with the following statement:

```
CREATE TABLE employee
    ( id    SMALLINT NOT NULL
    , name VARCHAR(10)
    , job  CHAR(5) CHECK (job IN ('Sales', 'Mgr', 'Clerk') )
    , PRIMARY KEY (id))
```

If this **import** command is issued, what state would the *employee* table be in?

```
import from emp2.del of del insert into emp2
```

7. What will this command do?

```
db2look –d department –a –e –m –x –f –o db2look.sql
```

8. Bob just completed a load operation to insert 300,000 rows of data into various tables. He performed a **RUNSTATS** to update the database statistics so that the DB2 optimizer knows about the new data. However, when the user logs in and runs the application, the performance is not acceptable. The application is mainly coded in static SQL and SQL stored procedures. What can Bob do to improve performance?
9. Bob tries to execute the following command:

```
import from largeinputfile.ixf of ixf
    messages import.out
   create into newtable in datats index in indexts
```

However, he receives log full errors. What can he do to solve this problem?

10. What is the prerequisite for a table to be imported with the **insert_update** option?

11. Which of the following tools will read data from an ASCII file and add them to a table?
    A. insert
    B. merge
    C. load
    D. export
    E. import
12. Which of the following tools will read data from an ASCII file and add them to a view?
    A. insert
    B. merge
    C. load
    D. export
    E. import
13. Which of the following formats is not supported by the import utility?
    A. IXF
    B. DEL
    C. ASC
    D. XLS
14. You want to import the following rows of data in the file *foo.txt* into the table *foo*:

    ```
    "Hello"|"World"
    "Goodbye"|"Cruel World"
    ```

    Which of the following commands must you run?
    A. Import from foo.txt of txt insert into foo
    B. Import from foo.txt of del insert into foo
    C. Import from foo.txt of pipedel insert into foo
    D. Import from foo.txt of del modified by coldell insert into foo
15. Which of the following utility creates a compression dictionary for a table that is enabled for row compression?
    A. Export
    B. Import
    C. Load
    D. Reorg
    E. Runstats
16. Which of the following tools, commands, or statements can be used to rename a database?
    A. Rename database
    B. db2relocatedb
    C. db2move
    D. db2renamedb

17. Which of the following tools can capture statistics on the data it adds to the table?
    A. Export
    B. Import
    C. Load
18. Which of the following are true?
    A. The load utility locks the whole table space for the table being loaded.
    B. The load utility locks the whole table being loaded.
    C. The load utility by default locks only the existing data in the table until the load completes.
    D. The load utility allows read access to all data that existed in the table before the load was run.
19. Which of the following command(s) can populate XML data into a targe table?
    A. Load
    B. Import
    C. Load and Import
20. Given a table is defined with PCTFREE = –1, which of the following tools will not leave free space in a table for subsequent inserts?
    A. Load
    B. Import
    C. Reorg

CHAPTER 14

Developing Database Backup and Recovery Solutions

A power failure may hit your database system while it is busy processing. A user may accidentally drop a very important table that you really need. What can you do to ensure that the data in the database remains consistent even when processing has been interrupted by a power failure? How can you recover a table that has been accidentally dropped? DB2's backup and recovery methods are designed to help you in these situations.

In this chapter you will learn about:

- The concept of transaction logging and the various logging strategies
- How to perform a database backup
- How to perform a database restore
- How to perform a roll forward operation
- How log shipping works
- How split mirroring works and how to use a split mirror to provide high availability
- How HADR works and how to setup an HADR pair
- The fault monitor

14.1 Database Recovery Concepts: The Big Picture

The most basic concept of recovery is ensuring that you can restore committed information, that is, information you explicitly saved using the COMMIT statement. This can be performed in different ways that may utilize backups (saved images of your entire database), and logs (saved operations performed against your database). Figure 14.1 shows the big picture of database recovery concept.

At t1, a database backup operation is performed. This operation creates a database backup image. After the backup operation, the database continues to process transactions. These transactions change the data in the database. All changes are logged in files called log files.

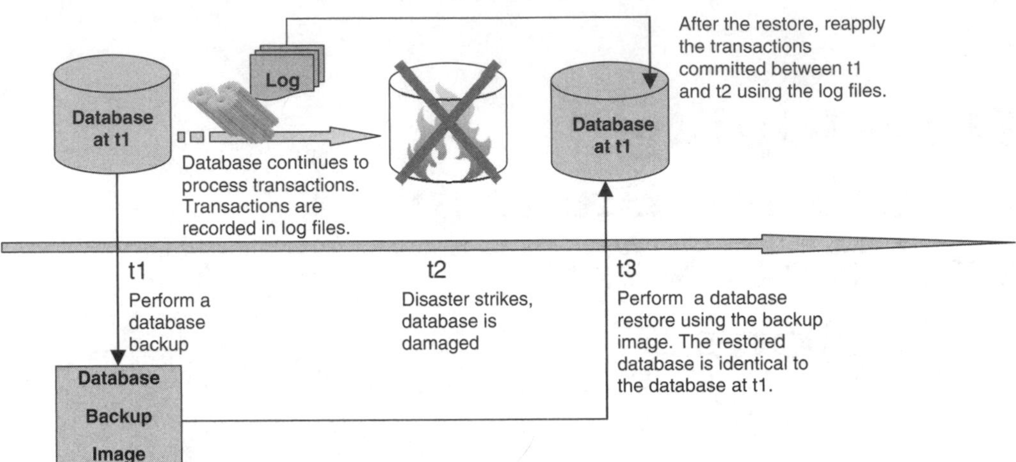

Figure 14.1 Basic concept of database recovery

At t2, a problem that damages the database occurs. To make the database accessible again, you can restore the database using the backup image taken at t1. The restored database will be identical to the database at time t1. But what about the transactions that occurred between t1 and t2? Because all transactions have been logged in the database log files, you might be able to replay the transactions by applying the log files on top of the restored database. If you replay the transactions to a point in time just before the disaster had struck, then you will be able to recovery all committed data. This chapter will build on this basic scenario.

14.1.1 Recovery Scenarios

To prevent the loss of your data, you need to have a recovery strategy, ensure that it works, and consistently practice and follow it. The following are some recovery scenarios you should consider.

- System outage: A power failure, hardware failure, or software failure can cause your database to be in an inconsistent state.
- Transaction failure: Users may inadvertently corrupt your database by modifying it with incorrect data or deleting useful data.
- Media failure: If your disk drive becomes unusable, you may lose all or part of your data.
- Disaster: The facility where your database server is located may be damaged by fire, flooding, power loss, or other catastrophe.

14.1.2 Recovery Strategies

To plan your recovery strategy, ask yourself:

- Can the data be loaded from another source?
- How much data can we afford to lose?

- How much time can we afford to be down?
- What storage resources are available for storing backups and log files?
- Can we have a server available to take over in the event of a failure?

14.1.3 Unit of Work (Transaction)

A **unit of work** (UOW), also known as a **transaction,** consists of one or more SQL statements that end with a **COMMIT** or **ROLLBACK** statement. All of the statements inside this UOW are treated as a complete entity, which ensures data and transactional consistency. A typical example used to explain this concept is that of a customer trying to transfer $100 from his or her savings account to their checking account. The UOW in this case would include all of the following to ensure consistency:

```
UPDATE SAVINGS account set balance = balance – 100 dollars
UPDATE Checking account set balance = balance + 100 dollars
COMMIT
```

If these statements are not treated as a unit and a hardware failure occurs after the first update and before the second update, then this person loses $100! Since the statements are treated as a complete entity, this will never happen because DB2 knows that the unit of work did not complete if a **COMMIT** was not issued. When the system is restarted after the failure, DB2 will automatically **ROLLBACK** all of the statements in the transaction, meaning it will bring the database back to the state prior to the beginning of the transaction.

> **NOTE** An analogy for understanding the **COMMIT** statement is to compare it to the *Save* button in word processing software. When you click this button, you expect your text document to be saved. Changes made after you save the document are lost if your server crashes, but what was saved will remain on disk. Similarly, when you issue a **COMMIT** statement, changes made to the database are guaranteed. If your server crashes, anything that was committed can be recovered, and anything that was not will be lost.

14.1.4 Types of Recovery

There are three types of recovery in DB2:

- Crash recovery
- Version recovery
- Roll forward recovery

Each of these types of recovery is discussed in detail in the next sections.

14.1.4.1 Crash Recovery

Crash recovery protects a database from being left in an inconsistent state following an abnormal termination. An example of an abnormal termination is a power failure. Using the banking example above, if a power failure occurred after the update statements, but prior to the **COMMIT** statement, the next time DB2 is restarted and the database accessed, DB2 will **ROLLBACK** the **UPDATE** statements. Note that statements are rolled back in the reverse order that they were performed originally. This ensures that the data is consistent, and that the person still has the $100 in his or her savings account.

By default, DB2 automatically initiates crash recovery when a database is accessed for the first time following an abnormal termination. You can disable the automatic crash recovery by setting the database configuration parameter AUTORESTART to OFF. If you do that, you will need to perform crash recovery manually using the **RESTART DATABASE** command if the database terminates abnormally. If you do not restart the database manually in the event of a system crash, you will receive the following error when you try to connect to the database:

```
SQL1015N The database must be restarted because the previous session did not conclude
normally.
```

Generally, leave AUTORESTART set to ON unless you have a specific reason to change it.

14.1.4.2 Version Recovery

Version recovery allows you to restore a snapshot of the database taken at a point in time using the **BACKUP DATABASE** command.

The restored database will be in the same state it was in when the **BACKUP** command completed. If further activity was performed against the database after this backup was taken, those updates are lost. For example, assume you back up a database and then create two tables, *table1* and *table2*. If you restore the database using the backup image, your restored database will not contain these two tables.

Referring to Figure 14.1, at time t3, version recovery will recover all data in the database at t1. Any transactions that occurred after t1 will be lost.

14.1.4.3 Roll Forward Recovery

Roll forward recovery extends version recovery by using full database and table space backups in conjunction with the database log files. A backup must be restored first as a baseline, and then the logs are reapplied to this backup image. Therefore, all committed changes you made *after* you backed up the database can be applied to the restored database. Using the previous example with roll forward recovery you have a number of choices to restore your database:

- You can restore the database using only the backup image. This is identical to version recovery. In this case, the restored database will not contain *table1* and *table2*.
- You can restore the database using the backup image, and then roll forward the logs to the point after *table1* was created. In this case, the restored database will contain *table1* but not *table2*.
- You can restore the database using the backup image, and then roll forward the logs to the point after *table2* was created. In this case, the restored database will contain *table1* and *table2, but no transactions after that point in time.*

- You can restore the database using the backup image, and then roll forward the logs all the way to the end of the logs. In this case, the restored database will contain both *table1* and *table2, and all committed transactions that occurred on the database.*

By default, crash recovery and version recovery are enabled. You will learn how to enable roll forward recovery in Section 14.2.4, Logging Methods.

Refering to Figure 14.1, roll forward recovery begins after time t3 where version recovery has restored the database image from t1. Any transactions that were committed will be applied to the database and any transactions not committed will be rolled back. The database will be at a consistent state the same as it was just before the disaster occurred.

14.2 DB2 Transaction Logs

DB2 uses transaction logs to record all changes to your database so that they can be rolled back if you issue the ROLLBACK command, reapplied or rolled back in the event that you need to restore a database backup, or during crash recovery.

> **NOTE** An analogy for understanding the use of transaction logs is to compare it to the *autosave* feature that many word processing software programs have. When this autosave feature kicks in, the word processing software is saving information for you. Similarly, with DB2, operations such as updates, deletes, and so on, are saved in log files whether they have been committed or not. If they were commited, they will certainly be saved.

14.2.1 Understanding the DB2 Transaction Logs

The ability to perform both crash recovery and roll forward recovery is provided by the database transaction logs. **Transaction logs** keep track of changes made to database objects and their data. During the recovery process, DB2 examines these logs and decides which changes to redo or undo.

Logs can be stored in files or on raw devices, although the latter is deprecated functionality. In this chapter, we use files in our examples for simplicity. To ensure data integrity and for performance reasons, DB2 uses a "write-ahead logging" mechanism to write to the logs before writing (externalizing) the database changes to disk, and before returning control to the application. To illustrate this process, assume a user issues the following statements:

```
UPDATE t1 SET year = 2000 WHERE ID = '007'
UPDATE t1 SET year = 2001 WHERE ID = '011'
COMMIT
UPDATE t1 SET year = 2004 WHERE ID = '003'
```

Table *t1* and its index *ix1* are shown in the logical view of Figure 14.2.

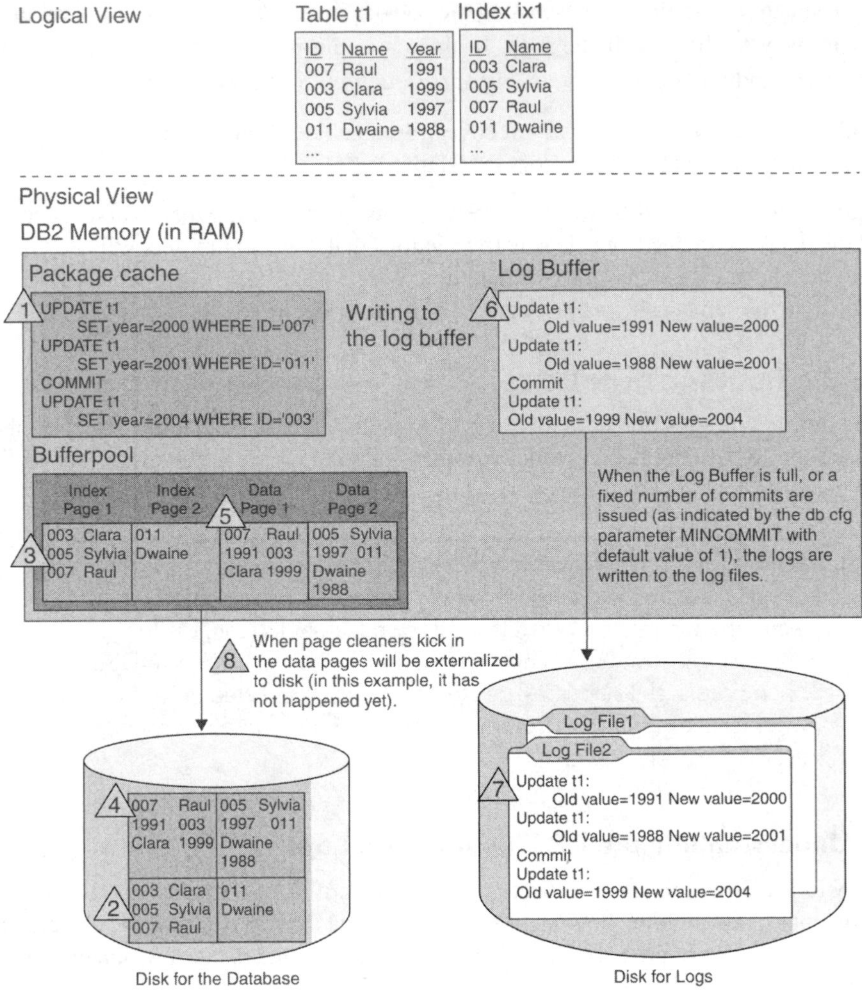

Figure 14.2 Concept of transaction logging

As each statement is executed, the following takes place (the figure uses the first UPDATE statement for illustration purposes).

- The DB2 optimizer parses the query and determines that using index *ix1* is the fastest way to retrieve the desired data. An index page access followed by a data page access is required.
- The statement and access plan information is stored in the package cache (1).
- The extent containing the desired index page (2) is brought from disk to the buffer pool (3) if the page is not already in the buffer pool. The index points to a record in the data

page, and thus the extent containing the pertinent data page (4) is also brought from disk to the buffer pool (5) if it is not already in the buffer pool.

- The **UPDATE** operation takes place in the buffer pool.
- The **UPDATE** operation is recorded in the log buffer. The old and new values are kept in case the operation needs to be rolled back or undone (6).

DB2 constantly checks to see if the log buffer is full, if MINCOMMIT commits have been performed, or if one second has lapsed. If any of these factors have occurred, the information in the log buffers is written to the log file on disk (7).

> **NOTE** The MINCOMMIT database configuration parameter indicates the minimum number of **COMMIT** statements required before writing from the log buffer to the log files on disk.

As you may have determined, log files will contain committed and uncommitted changes. When crash recovery happens, DB2 will undo any statements that were not committed, and will redo any statements that were committed, so that the database is left transactionally consistent.

Note too that the rows that were changed in the buffer pool and that were recorded in the log files may not have been saved to the database disks. The changed rows will eventually be written to disk when "page cleaner" processes are run to "clean" the modified (or dirty) pages from the buffer pool (8). This is not done immediately after the statement is executed or when the transaction commits for performance reasons. DB2 is already storing the information in the log files on disk to ensure data integrity, and the change is reflected in the buffer pool, so there is no need to perform an I/O right away to store the changed pages to disk.

When data is committed and also saved to disk, the data is considered to be **externalized.**

> **NOTE** We discuss the DB2 optimizer and page cleaners in detail in Chapter 17, Database Performance Considerations.

14.2.2 Primary and Secondary Log Files

The *Disk for Logs* in Figure 14.2 is known as the **active log directory** or **log space.** Its location is specified in the database configuration parameter *Path to log files*.

The size of the log space is controlled by three database configuration parameters. Table 14.1 discusses what these parameters are.

For example, let's say you have the following values in your database configuration:

```
Log file size (4KB)             (LOGFILSIZ)  = 1000
Number of primary log files     (LOGPRIMARY) = 3
Number of secondary log files   (LOGSECOND)  = 2
Path to log files                            = C:\mylogs\
```

Table 14.1 Log Parameters

Log Parameters	Description/Usage
LOGPRIMARY	Indicates the number of primary log files that are allocated in the active log directory. Primary log files are allocated during the first database connect or during database activation by the **ACTIVATE DATABASE** command.
LOGSECOND	Controls the maximum number of secondary log files that can be allocated in the active log directory. Secondary log files are allocated dynamically one at a time as needed, when there are no more primary logs available for transaction processing.
LOGFILSIZ	Specifies the size of the log files (in number of 4KB pages).

Since each file is 4MB (1000 × 4KB), and there are a total of 5 log files (3 primary logs and 2 secondary logs), the log space is 20MB.

> **NOTE** The maximum number of log files (logprimary + logsecond) cannot exceed 256 files. If infinite logging is set (see Section 14.2.4.3), then LOGPRIMARY cannot exceed 256 files.

When the first connection is made to a database, or the database is activated, the primary log files are created and allocated on disk. In the example configuration above, as soon as the first connection to the database is established, three primary log files of 1000 4KB-pages each are allocated or initialized. If you examine the C:\mylogs directory, you will see these three files:

```
2007-05-10 08:06p 4,104,192 S0000000.LOG
2007-05-10 08:06p 4,104,192 S0000001.LOG
2007-05-10 08:06p 4,104,192 S0000002.LOG
3 File(s) 12,312,576 bytes
```

Now, let's say you decide to perform the following transaction, which inserts a million records into a table:

```
INSERT INTO TABLE1 VALUES(1);
INSERT INTO TABLE1 VALUES(2);
...
INSERT INTO TABLE1 VALUES(1000000);
COMMIT;
```

DB2 will fill up the first log file, continue with the second log file, and then the third log file. After it fills up the third log file, there are no more primary logs available (remember that LOGPRIMARY is set to 3, so a maximum of three primary logs can exist at any time). At this point DB2 will dynamically allocate a secondary log file. Once the first secondary log file is filled up, DB2 will attempt to allocate another secondary log file. Because this was the first secondary log file, this will succeed. When this log file is filled, DB2 will attempt to allocate another secondary log file. However, because this example has LOGSECOND set to 2 and there are already two secondary log files allocated, DB2 cannot allocate another secondary log file. If LOGSECOND was set to a number more than 2, this process of allocating secondary log files will continue until the maximum number of secondary log files is reached.

At the point when the maximum number of secondary log files is reached, if DB2 needs more log space to complete the transaction, a **log full** condition occurs. This means there is not enough room left in the logs to record and complete the transaction. The transaction encountering this log full condition will be rolled back. (Section 14.2.4, Logging Methods, discusses how DB2 tries to reuse the old logs first, if possible, before creating a new one. DB2 uses an algorithm that reduces the chances of encountering a log full condition.)

Log full is an undesirable condition. Not only is all of the work performed up to this point within the transaction lost, but the rollback will also take some time. For this reason, it is important to ensure that you allocate enough log space to accommodate your workload, and particularly your longest or largest transactions.

Generally, you do not want to allocate a huge number of PRIMARY logs, because they are allocated or initialized when the database is activated. If you specify a large number, DB2 can spend some time creating/initializing these files, causing the first connection to the database to take a long time. If your transaction workload is generally small throughout the day, all that log space will be wasted. You may want to specify enough LOGSECOND log files to handle a spike in your workload (e.g., a heavier workload with long transactions at the end of a month) and have just enough primary logs to cover the normal workloads.

Another undesirable condition is a **log disk full** condition. Unlike a log full condition, where DB2 runs out of logging space because the maximum number of primary and secondary log files have been reached, a log disk full condition occurs when the drive or file system that hosts the active log directory is physically full, meaning no more log files can be created, even though the maximum numbers of primary and secondary log files may not have been reached. This condition could be caused by the file system being too small or the active log directory becoming filled by too many inactive (archive) log files. (You will learn what inactive logs are in the next section.)

By default, a transaction that receives a log disk full error will fail and will be rolled back, just as in the case of a log full condition. However, you can change this behavior by setting the database configuration parameter BLK_LOG_DSK_FUL to YES. Setting this parameter to YES causes applications to block (or wait) instead of rolling back when DB2 encounters a disk full error when writing to the log files. While the applications are waiting (or blocked), DB2 attempts to create the log file every five minutes until it succeeds. After each attempt, DB2 writes a message to the administration notification log. The way to confirm that your application is blocked because of a log disk full condition is to monitor the administration notification log.

> **NOTE** The administration notification log is discussed in Chapter 18, Diagnosing Problems.

Until the log file is successfully created, any user application that attempts to update table data will not be processed. Read-only queries may not be directly affected; however, if a query needs to access data that is locked by an update request or a data page that is fixed in the buffer pool by the updating application, read-only queries will also appear to hang.

Once you have determined that DB2 is waiting because the log disk is full, you can resolve the situation by deleting inactive log files, moving inactive log files to another file system, or by increasing the size of the file system so that a new log file can be created.

14.2.3 Log File States

The state of a log is determined by whether the transactions that are recorded in it have been committed and whether or not they have been externalized to disk. There are three log file states: active, online archive, and offline archive.

14.2.3.1 Active Logs

A log is considered **active** if any of the following applies:

- It contains transactions that have not yet been committed or rolled back.
- It contains transactions that have been committed but whose changes have not yet been written to the database disk (externalized).
- It contains transactions that have been rolled back but whose changes have been written to the database disk (externalized).

In Figure 14.2 log file 2 is an active log because it contains a transaction that has not yet been committed (the last **UPDATE** statement). Log file 2 also contains a transaction that has been committed but has not been externalized to disk (the first two **UPDATE** statements).

Imagine that at this point a power failure occurs and everything in the buffer pool is lost. The only place where you can find a record of these transactions is in the database log files. When the database is restarted, it will go through crash recovery.

DB2 first looks at what is known in the log control file to determine the oldest of the following:

- The oldest committed transaction that has not been externalized
- The oldest uncommitted transaction that has been externalized

After determining the recovery starting point, it then determines what log contains this particular transaction.

DB2 will then redo or undo all transactions from that point forward, until it reaches the end of the logs.

Figure 14.2 indicates that no page cleaning has occurred, so the committed and uncommitted transactions are still in the buffer pool and not externalized. DB2 then finds the oldest transaction needing recovery, and identifies that it starts in log file 1. DB2 will first open log file 1 and read its contents. DB2 will redo the transactions that have a **COMMIT**, and undo the transactions that do not. Figure 14.2 shows DB2 will redo all of the updates in log file 1 and the first two **UPDATE** statements in log file 2. Since the last update was not committed, it will not be replayed. All of the active log files, by definition, are required for crash recovery. If you lose the active logs, crash recovery cannot complete, and the database will be inaccessible.

Active logs typically reside in the active log path. If you have enabled infinite logging, active log files may need to be retrieved from the archive site. (Infinite logging is covered in Section 14.2.4, Logging Methods.)

14.2.3.2 Online Archive Logs

Online archive logs are files that contain only committed, externalized transactions. In other words, they are logs that are no longer active, and therefore no longer needed for crash recovery.

Online archive logs still reside in the active log directory. This is why they are called "online." The term *online archive logs* may sound complicated, but all it means is that inactive logs reside in the active log directory.

Although these logs are no longer needed for crash recovery, they are retained for roll forward recovery. You will see why in Section 14.2.4, Logging Methods.

14.2.3.3 Offline Archive Logs

File systems and disk drives have limited space. If all of the online archive logs are kept in the active log directory, this directory will soon be filled up, causing a log disk full condition. Therefore, the online archive logs should be moved out of the active log directory as soon as possible. You can do this manually, or DB2 can invoke a program or procedure to do this for you. Once this has been done, these logs become **offline archive logs.**

Like the online archive logs, offline archive logs are also retained for roll forward recovery.

14.2.4 Logging Methods

DB2 supports three logging methods: circular logging, archival logging, and infinite active logging.

14.2.4.1 Circular Logging

Circular logging is the default logging mode for DB2. As the name suggests, in this method the logs are reused in a circular mode. For example, if you have three primary logs, DB2 uses them in this order: Log #1, Log #2, Log #3, Log #1, Log #2....

Note that in the above sequence Log #1 and Log #2 are reused. When a log file is reused, its previous contents are completely overwritten. Therefore, a log can be reused if and only if the transactions it contains have already been committed or rolled back and externalized to the database disk. In other words, the log must not be an active log. This ensures DB2 will have the necessary logs for crash recovery if needed. Figure 14.3 shows how circular logging works.

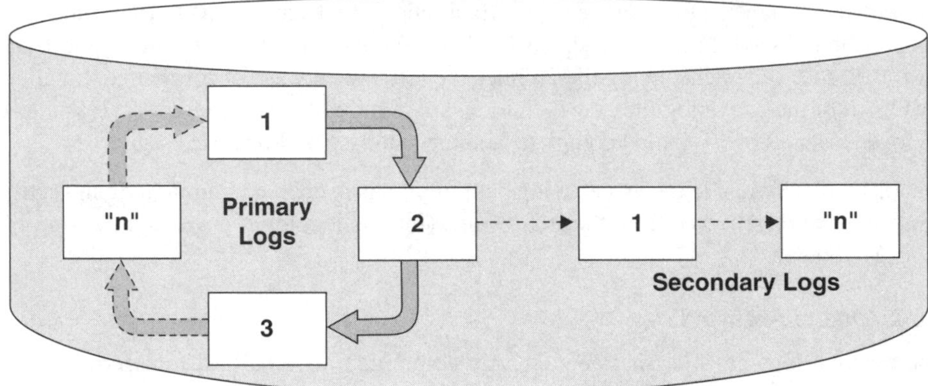

Figure 14.3 Circular logging

Although the ability to recover from a crash is assured, you cannot reapply the transactions that were in these logs, because they have been overwritten. Therefore, circular logging only supports crash recovery and version recovery, not roll forward recovery.

14.2.4.2 Archival Logging

Archival logging keeps the log files even after they contain committed and externalized data. To enable archival logging, you can change the value of the LOGARCHMETH1 database configuration parameter. We will discuss the possible values for the LOGARCHMETH1 parameter later in this section.

With archival logging, roll forward recovery is supported. The contents of inactive logs are saved rather than overwritten; therefore, they can be reapplied during roll forward recovery. Depending on the value set in LOGARCHMETH1, you can have the log files copied or saved to various locations. When the log is needed during roll forward recovery, DB2 retrieves it from that location and restores it into the active log directory.

With archival logging, if you have three primary logs in a database, DB2 will allocate them in this order: Use Log #1, use Log #2, use Log #3, archive Log #1 (when no longer active), create and use Log #4, archive Log #2, create and use Log #5.... Notice that the log number increases as new logs are required. Figure 14.4 shows how archival logging works.

How DB2 archives and retrieves a log file depends on the value set in the LOGARCHMETH1 database parameter. The possible values are OFF, LOGRETAIN, USEREXIT, TSM, and VENDOR and are discussed in detail in Table 14.2.

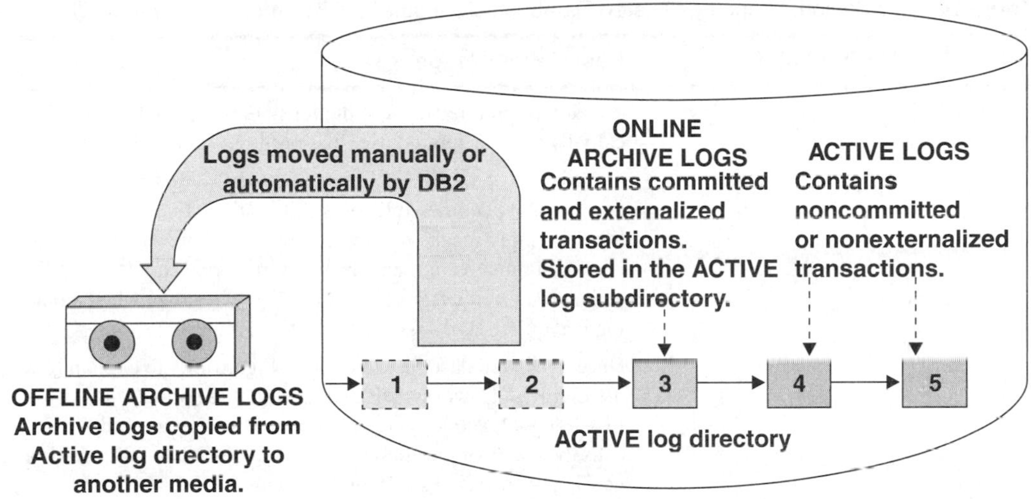

Figure 14.4 Archival logging

Table 14.2 Additional Logging-Related Database Configuration Parameters

LOGARCHMETH1 Values	Description/Usage
OFF	Archival logging is disabled and circular logging is used.
LOGRETAIN	The log files will be retained in the active log directory. Let's use the example in Figure 14.4 to demonstrate how LOGRETAIN works. DB2 starts with three primary logs: log #1, log #2, and log #3. When DB2 fills up all these three logs, it checks if log #1 has become inactive. If it has, DB2 renames log #1 to log #4. The set of primary logs then becomes log #2, log #3, and log #4. If log #1 is still active, DB2 creates log #4 as secondary log. When a new log is needed, DB2 checks if log #2 has become inactive. If it has, DB2 renames log #1 as log #5. If not, it creates log #5 as a secondary log. The process is repeated until LOGSECOND is reached, at which point the log full condition occurs. Note with LOGRETAIN, inactive log files are never overwritten. In Figure 14.4, even though log #1 and log #2 have already become inactive, they still remain in the active log directory. (At this point, they are online archive logs.) You have to manually move them to a different location or the active log directory will soon be filled up by these logs. However, you should never delete these logs without making a copy of them somewhere, because they may be needed for roll forward recovery. After logs #1 and #2 have been moved to another location, they become offline archive logs

(continues)

Table 14.2 Additional Logging-Related Database Configuration Parameters *(Continued)*

LOGARCHMETH1 Values	Description/Usage
USEREXIT	The archive and retrieval of the logs are performed automatically by a user-supplied user exit program called **db2uext2.** The user exit program archives a log file to a different location as soon as it becomes full, even if it is still active. Archiving a log file simply means making a copy of it somewhere; the log itself still remains in the active log directory. If the log is still active, DB2 will not reuse it. If the log is inactive, when a new log is required, DB2 will rename it and reuse it. Once again, let's use the example in Figure 14.4 to explain how the USEREXIT works. DB2 starts with three primary logs: log#1, log #2, and log #3. As soon as these logs are full, DB2 calls the user exit program to archive them. When DB2 needs a new log, it checks to see if log #1 is active. If log #1 is still active, DB2 creates secondary log #4. If log #1 is inactive, DB2 renames log #1 to log #4 and reuses it (instead of creating a new log #4). This helps to eliminate the overhead of creating a new file. There is no loss of data in reusing a log that has been archived, because its copy can always be retrieved when needed. When logs are needed during recovery, DB2 calls the user exit program to retrieve the necessary logs. Because everything is handled by the user exit program, you should not manipulate the log files manually. Doing so may potentially interfere with the user exit program. There is no need to use user exit programs anymore, but user exit support is still available for backwards compatibility.
DISK:directory	With this setting, archival logging uses a similar algorithm as in USEREXIT. The only difference is instead of calling the user exit program, DB2 will automatically archive the logs from the active log directory to the specified *directory.* During recovery, DB2 will automatically retrieve these logs back to the active log directory.
TSM:[management class name]	With this setting archival logging uses a similar algorithm as in USEREXIT. The only difference is that the logs will be archived on the local Tivoli Storage Manger (TSM) server. The management class name parameter is optional. If not specified, the default management class is used.
VENDOR:*library*	With this setting, archival logging uses a similar algorithm as in USEREXIT. The only difference is that logs are archived using the specified vendor library.

You can optionally configure the LOGARCHMETH2 parameter. This parameter specifies the secondary archive log method, and can be set using the same values as for LOGARCHMETH1. If set, logs will be archived to both this destination and the destination specified by the LOGARCHMETH1 parameter.

In addition to LOGARCHMETH1 and LOGARCHMETH2, Table 14.3 lists a number of other logging-related database parameters.

Table 14.3 Additional Logging-Related Database Configuration Parameters

DB CFG Parameters	Description
FAILARCHPATH	Failover archive path. Specifies a third target to archive log files if the primary and secondary archival paths fail. The medium must be disk. It is a temporary storage area for the log files until the primary path(s) becomes available again, at which time the log files will be moved from this directory to the primary archive path(s). By moving the log files to this temporary location, log directory full situations might be avoided.
NUMARCHRETRY	Specifies the number of retries attempted on primary target(s) before archiving to FAILARCHPATH. The default is 5.
ARCHRETRYDELAY	Specifies the number of seconds between retry attempts. The default is 20 seconds.
LOGARCHOPT1 and LOGARCHOPT2	Specifies a string that is passed on to the TSM server or vendor APIs. For TSM, this field is used to allow the database to retrieve logs that were generated on a different TSM node or by a different TSM user. The string must be provided in the following format: **"-fromnode=*nodename* -fromowner=*ownername*"** where ***nodename*** is the name of the TSM node that originally archived the log files, and ***ownername*** is the name of the TSM user who originally archived the log files. Each log archive options field corresponds to one of the log archive methods: LOGARCHOPT1 is used with LOGARCHMETH1, and LOGARCHOPT2 is used with LOGARCHMETH2.

14.2.4.3 Infinite Active Logging

Infinite active logging is built on top of archival logging. With circular logging and archival logging, log space can potentially be filled with active logs if you have very long running transactions. If you have long-running transactions you can use infinite active logging so that you do not run out of log, or log disk, space.

To enable infinite active logging:

- Archive logging must be enabled with one of the automatic archival methods; that is, LOGARCHMETH1 must be set to one of USEREXIT, DISK, TSM, or VENDOR.
- Set the LOGSECOND database configuration parameter to –1.

When archival logging is enabled, a log is marked for archival as soon as it becomes full. However, DB2 leaves the log in the log directory until it becomes inactive for performance reasons, and then renames the file for reuse. With infinite logging, DB2 still archives the log as soon as it is full, but it does not wait for it to become inactive before it renames the file for reuse. This guarantees that the active log directory will never fill up, because any logs can be reused once they are filled and archived. Note that the use of infinite active logging can prolong crash recovery times as active logs may need to be retrieved from the archive site.

14.2.4.4 Log Mirroring

Even with all the protection provided by DB2 logging, there is still a concern of someone accidentally deleting an active log file, or a disk crash that causes data corruption in your database. Mirroring the log files helps protect your database from these potential disasters. Log mirroring allows you to specify a secondary path for the database to manage copies of the active logs. DB2 will attempt to write the log buffer to the log files in both places. When one log path is damaged for whatever reason, DB2 can continue to read and write to the other log path, keeping the database up and running.

To enable log mirroring, set the MIRRORLOGPATH database configuration parameter to a valid drive, path, or device.

Make sure you place your secondary log path on a physically separate disk or disk array (preferably one that is also on a different disk controller and in a different cabinet). This way, the disk drive, or disk controller will not be a single point of failure. When log mirroring is first enabled, it will not become active and used until the next database restart. When there is a failure to either the active log path or the mirror log path, the database will mark the failing path as "bad," write a message to the administration notification log, and write subsequent log records to the remaining "good" log path only. The next time DB2 will attempt to write to the "bad" path is when the current log file is full or truncated and it starts writing to the next log file. If the failure has been fixed at that time, then DB2 will continue to write to both log paths. If the failure has not been fixed, then DB2 will not attempt to use the path again until the next log file is required. DB2 will continue to perform this verification check on the "bad" path each time it starts a new log file until the failure is fixed, and DB2 can write to both log paths again. DB2 will not synchronize the logs in the two log paths, but will keep track of access errors that occured, so that the correct path is used when log files are archived. If one log path has already been marked bad, and a failure occurs while the writing to the good path, the database will stop.

14.2.5 Handling the DB2 Transaction Logs

DB2 logs are crucial for roll forward recovery. A missing or corrupted log file will cause roll forward recovery and crash recovery to fail, and can potentially render the database inaccessible. We recommend that you do not manipulate any logs manually.

If it becomes necessary to work with the log files for some reason, exercise extreme care. Never remove log files based solely on their timestamps. Understanding how log files are timestamped may save you from losing active logs and creating a potential disaster.

When the primary log files are created at database activation, they are *all* given a timestamp based on the activation time. These timestamps do not change until DB2 writes transaction updates to the logs, one log file at a time. These logs are kept in the active log directory, even though they may be empty. For example, if LOGPRIMARY is set to 20, then 20 log files will be created with timestamp A. Suppose transactions begin and write to logs 1 through 10 at timestamps greater than A. At this point in time, you still have 20 logs in the active log directory. Logs 1 through 10 will have timestamps greater than A. Logs 11 through 20 will have timestamps at exactly A. Assume that these logs (logs 1 to 10) span multiple days of work. In this scenario, you may think that logs 11 to 20 are older logs, because of their older timestamps, and can be removed. In fact, these logs are still active logs. If you remove them, and DB2 requires those logs (e.g., the next log required would be log 11), the database will crash and be marked as corrupted. The only way to recover is to restore from a recent backup. Therefore, we highly recommend that you let DB2 handle the logs automatically.

To determine which log files are active and which ones are not, look at the value of the *First active log file* parameter in the database configuration. All the logs prior to the value are inactive; all the log files starting at the value are active—therefore, you should not touch them.

For example, if the first active log file is S0000005.LOG, then logs 0, 1, 2, 3, and 4 are inactive. All the logs starting at log 5 are active.

14.3 Recovery Terminology

Depending on the type of backups that you take, there are different methods that you can use to recover your database in the event of an error. In addition, the configuration you choose for your database will determine whether you can use the database logs to reapply transactions that might otherwise be lost if you need to restore your database from a backup.

14.3.1 Logging Methods versus Recovery Methods

Circular logging supports only crash and version recovery. Archival logging supports all types of recovery: crash, version, and roll forward.

14.3.2 Recoverable versus Nonrecoverable Databases

Recoverable databases can be recovered using crash or roll forward recovery, and as discussed before, archival logging is required to support roll forward recovery. Nonrecoverable databases do not support roll forward recovery and use only circular logging. Table 14.4 shows which logging and recovery methods work together.

Table 14.4 Summary of Logging and Recovery Methods

Logging Method	Supports Crash Recovery	Supports Version Recovery	Supports Roll Forward Recovery	Recoverable Database
Circular Logging (LOGARCHMETH1 = OFF)	Yes	Yes	No	No
Archival Logging (LOGARCHMETH1 = LOGRETAIN, USEREXIT, DISK, TSM, or VENDOR)	Yes	Yes	Yes	Yes

14.4 Performing Database and Table Space Backups

There are two different granularities that you can choose for your backups, and you have two different options for how the backup can be performed. You can choose to back up the entire database or one or more table spaces from within the database. You can also choose whether you want the backup to be taken online or offline. The next section will discuss what an online or offline backup is. These options can be combined to give you a very flexible recovery mechanism for your databases.

14.4.1 Online Access versus Offline Access

In the following sections we use the terms "online" and "offline" quite often. An **online** *backup* allows other applications or processes to connect to the database, as well as read and modify data while the operation is running. An **offline** *backup* does *not* allow other applications or processes to access the database and its objects while the operation is being performed.

14.4.2 Database Backup

A **database backup** is a complete copy of your database objects. In addition to the data, a backup copy contains information about the table spaces, containers, the system catalog, database configuration file, the log control file, and the recovery history file. Note that a backup does *not* contain the Database Manager Configuration file or the values of registry variables.

You must have SYSADM, SYSCTRL, or SYSMAINT authority to perform a backup.

Figure 14.5 shows the syntax diagram of the **BACKUP DATABASE** command:

To perform an offline backup of the sample database and store the backup copy in the directory d:\mybackups, use the following command on Windows.

```
>>--BACKUP--+-DATABASE-+--database-alias------------------------->
            '-DB-------'

 >--+-------------------------------------+-------------------->
    '-USER--username--+-----------------+-'
                      '-USING--password-'

>--+-----------------------------------------------------------------+-->
   |                         .-,-----------------------------.|      |
   |                         V                                |      |
   '-ON-++-DBPARTITIONNUM--+-(-db-partn-num1-+----------------+-+-)---------+-'
       |'-DBPARTITIONNUMS-'                  '-TO-db-partn-num2-'    |
       '-ALL DBPARTITIONNUMS--+-----------------------------------------------+-'
       |                             .-,-----------------------------.|     |
   |           V          |  |
   '-EXCEPT-+-DBPARTITIONNUM--+--(--db-partn-num1--+-----------------+-+---)-'
            '-DBPARTITIONNUMS-'                   '-TO-db-partn-num2-'

 >--+------------------------------------+--+-------+-------->
    |           .-,--------------.        |  '-ONLINE-'
    |           V                |        |
    '-TABLESPACE--(----tablespace-name-+--)-'

 >--+--------------------+------------------------------->
    '-INCREMENTAL--+-------+-'
                   '-DELTA-'

 >--+----------------------------------------------------------------------
----------+-->
    +-USE--+-TSM--+--+-----------------------------+--+----------------------
--+------+
    |      '-XBSA-'  '-OPTIONS--+-"options-string"-+-'  '-OPEN--num-sessions--
SESSIONS-'   |
    |      '  '             '-@--file-name-----'                              |
    |    +-SNAPSHOT--+-------------------+-+------------------------+------
--------|
   |         LIBRARY -'library-name'  '-OPTIONS--+-"options-string"-+-'
|
   |                                              '-@--file-name-----'
|
    +-TO----+-dir-+-+---------------------------------------------------------
---------+
    |       '-dev-'
    >--+-------------------------+--+------------------+------>
    '-WITH--num-buffers--BUFFERS-'  '-BUFFER--buffer-size-'

 >--+-------------+------------------------------------->
    '-PARALLELISM--n-'

 >--+-------------------------------------------------------+-->
    '-COMPRESS--+------------------------+--+------------------+-'
                '-COMPRLIB--name--+---------+-'  '-COMPROPTS--string-'
                                  '-EXCLUDE-'
                                                  .-EXCLUDE LOGS-.
>--+---------------------------------+--+-------------+----->
   '-UTIL_IMPACT_PRIORITY--+----------+-'  '-INCLUDE LOGS-'
                           '-priority-'
 >--+------------------+---------------------------------><
    '-WITHOUT PROMPTING-'
```

Figure 14.5 Syntax diagram of the Backup Database command

```
BACKUP DATABASE sample
TO d:\mybackups
```

The d:\mybackups directory must be created before the backup can be performed. To perform an offline backup of the sample database and store the backup copy in two separate directories, use the following command for Linux/UNIX shown in Figure 14.6:

```
BACKUP DATABASE sample                    (1)
TO /db2backup/dir1, /db2backup/dir2       (2)
WITH 4 BUFFERS                            (3)
BUFFER 4096                               (4)
PARALLELISM 2                             (5)
```

Figure 14.6 Backup Database command example

where:

(1) Indicates the name (or alias) of the database to back up.
(2) Specifies the location(s) where you want to store the backup file. DB2 will write to both locations in parallel.
(3) Indicates how many buffers from memory can be used during the backup operation. Using more than one buffer can improve performance.
(4) Indicates the size of each buffer in 4KB pages.
(5) Specifies how many media reader and writer threads are used to take the backup.

If not specified, DB2 automatically chooses optimal values for the number of buffers, the buffer size, and the parallelism settings. The values are based on the amount of utility heap available, the number of processors available, and the database configuration. The objective is to minimize the time it takes to complete the backup operation.

Notice there is no keyword for **OFFLINE** in the syntax, as this is the default mode.

If you have a 24×7 database, shutting down the database is not an option. To perform backups to ensure the database's recoverability, you can perform online backups instead. You must specify the keyword **ONLINE** in the **BACKUP DATABASE** command as shown below:

```
BACCKUP DATABASE sample
ONLINE
TO /dev/rdir1, /dev/rdir2
```

Because there are users accessing the database while it is being backed up, it is likely that some of the changes made by these users will not be stored in data and index pages in the backup image. A transaction may be in the middle of processing when the backup was taken. This means the backup image likely contains a database that is in an inconsistent state.

If this online backup is used to restore a database, as soon as the restore operation finishes, DB2 places the database in roll forward pending state. A roll forward operation must be performed to bring the database back to a consistent state before you can use it. To do this you must roll forward to at least the time when the backup completed.

If you have set LOGARCHMETH1 to USEREXIT, DISK, TSM, or VENDOR, DB2 automatically retrieves the logs into the active log directory. Otherwise, if LOGRETAIN was set, you must retrieve the log files manually before rolling forward the database. To perform the roll forward, all logs that were active at the time of the backup must be in, or copied into, the active log directory when needed.

> **NOTE** Archival logging must be enabled to perform online backups.

To backup the logs as part of the backup copy, use the **INCLUDE LOGS** option of the **BACKUP DATABASE** command. When you specify this, the logs will be backed up along with the database during an online backup operation. This ensures that if the archived logs are not available, the backup will still be recovered to a minimum Point In Time (PIT) using the logs that are included in the backup image. If you want to restore to a later PIT, additional log files may be required.

For example, to take an online backup of the SAMPLE database along with the logs, using the destination directory /dev/rdir1, issue the command shown below.

```
BACKUP DATABASE sample
ONLINE
TO /dev/rdir1 INCLUDE LOGS
```

> **NOTE** The INCLUDE LOGS option is not available to partitioned (DPF) environments until DB2 9.5. Please read the next section for more information.

14.4.2.1 Database Backup on DPF Environments

Prior to DB2 9.5, whenever you needed to back up your database on a partitioned environment, you were required to run multiple backup commands. Due to the way that the connection logic worked, you were required to back up the DB2 catalog partition first, and then back up all the other data partitions. (For more details on Database Partitioning Feature, please refer to Chapter 2, DB2 at a Glance, The Big Picture.) The following example contains the typical commands you would issue to back up all catalog and data nodes for the database *test* in a partitioned environment:

```
db2_all "<<+0<   db2 backup db test"
db2_all "<<-0<|| db2 backup db test"
```

The first command backed up the catalog partition (partition 0). The second command backed up all the data partitions. The disadvantage of this was that each partition would finish the backups asyncronously, and therefore each backup file would receive a different timestamp; for example:

```
$ db2_all "db2 backup db test"
Backup successful. The timestamp for this backup image is : 20070501143307
linuxbox: db2 backup db test completed ok
Backup successful. The timestamp for this backup image is : 20070501143310
linuxbox: db2 backup db test completed ok
```

The different backup timestamps on each partition posed a minor challenge when it came time to restore the database. You will learn more about the restore process later in this chapter. The important idea to understand here is that you need to make sure that all data is consistent across the different partitions, and therefore you need to determine a minimum point in time where this is true. Although that is not difficult to do, it does require some work and intervention from the DBA.

Starting in DB2 9.5, you can now back up a database in a partitioned environment in one simple step. This is refered to as a Single System View (SSV). When you run the **BACKUP DATABASE** command from the catalog node of a partitioned database, you can use a new clause to specify which partitions to include in the backup. The specified partitions will be backed up simultaneously, and the backup timestamp associated with all specified partitions will be the same. You can include the log files required to restore and recover the database up to the minimum recovery time with the backup image of each partition; for example:

```
db2 backup db test on all dbpartitionnums
db2 backup db test on dbpartitionnums (0, 3)
db2 backup db test on all dbpartitionnums except dbpartitionnums (1,2)
```

The first command will back up all the database partitions for database *test*. The second command will only back up the catalog partition (0) and partition (3). The third command will back up all partitions for *test* exception partitions (1) and (2). The following example shows that all backup files (3 data partitions and 1 catalog partition) will have the same timestamp when the backup completes:

```
$ db2 backup db test on all dbpartitionnums to /backups
Part  Result
----  ------------------------------
0000  DB20000I  The BACKUP DATABASE command completed successfully.
0001  DB20000I  The BACKUP DATABASE command completed successfully.
0002  DB20000I  The BACKUP DATABASE command completed successfully.
0003  DB20000I  The BACKUP DATABASE command completed successfully.
Backup successful. The timestamp for this backup image is : 20070502030405
```

You can now use the **INCLUDE LOGS** option in an online **BACKUP DATABASE** command for a partitioned database as shown below:

```
db2 backup db test on all dbpartitionnums online INCLUDE LOGS
```

14.4.3 Table Space Backup

In a database where only some of your table spaces change considerably, you may opt not to back up the entire database but only specific table spaces. To perform a table space backup, you can use the following syntax:

```
BACKUP DATABASE sample
TABLESPACE (syscatspace, userspace1, userspace2)
ONLINE
TO /db2tbsp/backup1, /db2tbsp/backup2
```

The keyword TABLESPACE indicates this is a table space backup, not a full database backup. You can also see from the example that you can include as many table spaces as desired in the backup. Temporary table spaces cannot be backed up using a table space level backup.

You should back up related table spaces together. For example, if using DMS table spaces where one table space is used for the table data, another one for the indexes, and another one for LOBs, you should back up all of these table spaces at the same time so that you have consistent information. This is also true for table spaces containing tables defined with referential constraints between them.

14.4.4 Incremental Backups

As database sizes continue to grow, the time and resources required to back up and recover these databases also grows substantially. Full database and table space backups are not always the best approach when dealing with large databases, because the storage requirements for multiple copies of such databases are enormous.

To address this issue, DB2 provides incremental backups. An **incremental backup** is a backup image that contains only pages that have been updated since the previous backup was taken. In addition to updated data and index pages, each incremental backup image also contains all of the initial database metadata (such as database configuration, table space definitions, database history, and so on) that is normally stored in full backup images.

There are two kinds of incremental backups.

- In incremental **cumulative** backups, DB2 backs up all of the data that has changed since the last full database backup.
- In **delta** backups, DB2 backs up only the data that has changed since the last successful full, cumulative, or delta backup.

Figure 14.7 illustrates these concepts.

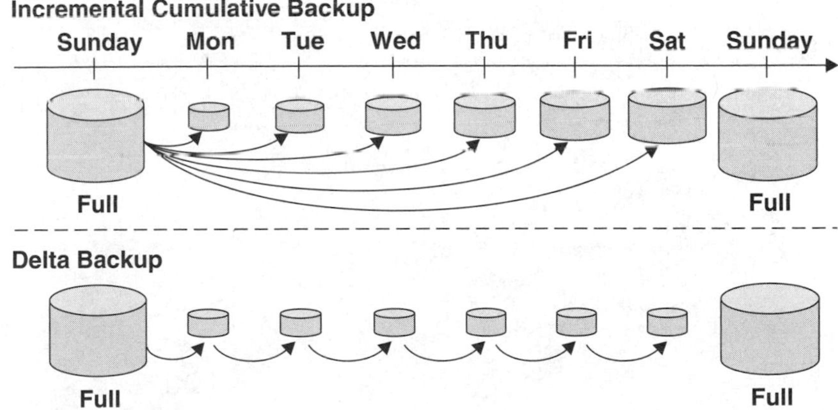

Figure 14.7 Incremental and delta backups

For incremental backups, if there was a crash after the incremental backup on Friday, you would restore the first Sunday's full backup, followed by the incremental backup taken on Friday.

For delta backups, if there was a crash after the delta backup on Friday, you would restore the first Sunday's full backup, followed by each of the delta backups taken on Monday through Friday inclusive.

To enable incremental and delta backups, the TRACKMOD database configuration parameter must be set to YES. This allows DB2 to track database modifications so that the backup utility can detect which database pages must be included in the backup image. After setting this parameter to YES, you must take a full database backup to have a baseline against which incremental backups can be taken.

To perform a cumulative incremental backup on the SAMPLE database to directory /dev/rdir1, issue:

```
BACKUP DB sample
INCREMENTAL TO /dev/rdir1
```

To perform a delta backup on the SAMPLE database to the directory /dev/rdir1, issue:

```
BACKUP DB sample
INCREMENTAL DELTA TO /dev/rdir1
```

14.4.5 Backing Up a Database with the Control Center

You can use the Backup Wizard to perform backups. From the Control Center, expand your database folder, right-click on the database name you wish to back up and select **Backup.** The database Backup Wizard appears. Figure 14.8 shows that you can choose to perform either a database-level backup or a table space-level backup. From here, the Backup Wizard will guide you through the options.

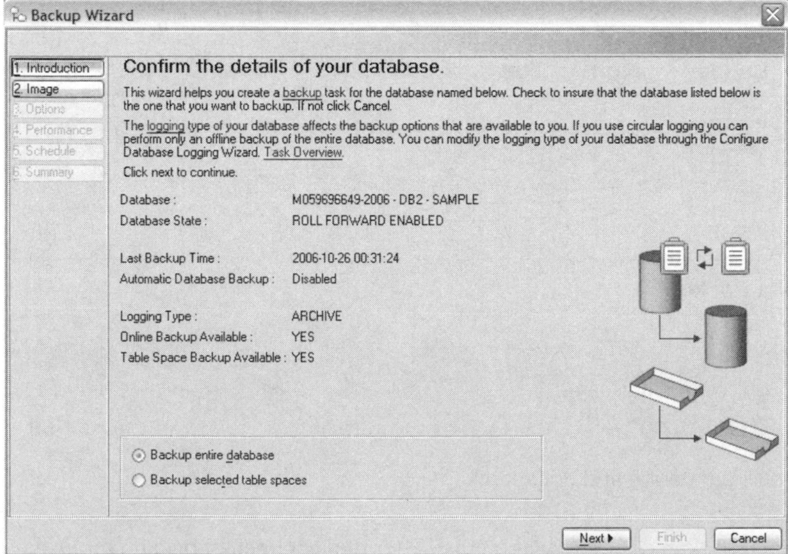

Figure 14.8 Incremental and delta backups

14.4.6 The Backup Files

The backup images are stored as files. The name of the backup file contains the following parts:

- Database alias
- Type of backup (0=Full database, 3=Table space, 4=Copy from LOAD)
- Instance name
- Database partition (always NODE0000 for a single-partition database)
- Catalog partition number (always CATN0000 for a single-partition database)
- Timestamp of the backup
- The image sequence number

V9 The naming convention applies to all platforms. In Figure 14.9, you can see the full filename of each backup image.

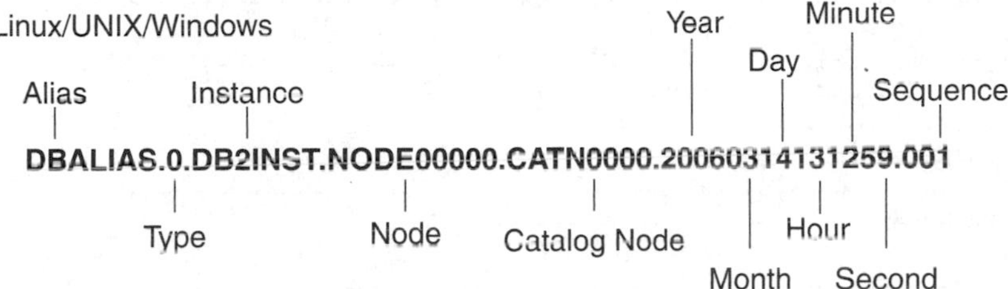

Figure 14.9 Backup file name hierarchy

For example, the command (on a Windows server):

```
BACKUP DATABASE sample to D:\tmp
```

produces the backup image shown in Figure 14.10.

```
DB2 CLP - DB2
11/09/2006  04:16 PM    <DIR>          .
11/09/2006  04:16 PM    <DIR>          ..
11/09/2006  04:16 PM        81,453,056 SAMPLE.0.DB2.NODE0000.CATN0000.2006110916
1623.001
               1 File(s)     81,453,056 bytes
               2 Dir(s)  33,761,030,144 bytes free
```

Figure 14.10 Backup file on Windows

The backup image can be found in the directory specified in the **BACKUP DATABASE** command, or the directory where the command is issued from.

> **NOTE** Do not change the name of the backup file. You will not be able to restore your database if you do.

14.5 Database and Table Space Recovery Using the RESTORE DATABASE Command

You can restore a backup image using the **RESTORE DATABASE** command. You can choose to recover everything in the image, or just an individual table space, or multiple table spaces.

14.5.1 Database Recovery

You can restore a database backup image and create a new database or you can restore over top of an existing database. You need SYSADM, SYSCTRL, or SYSMAINT authority to restore into an existing database, and SYSADM or SYSCTRL authority restore to a new database.

Figure 14.11 shows the syntax diagram of the **RESTORE DATABASE** command.

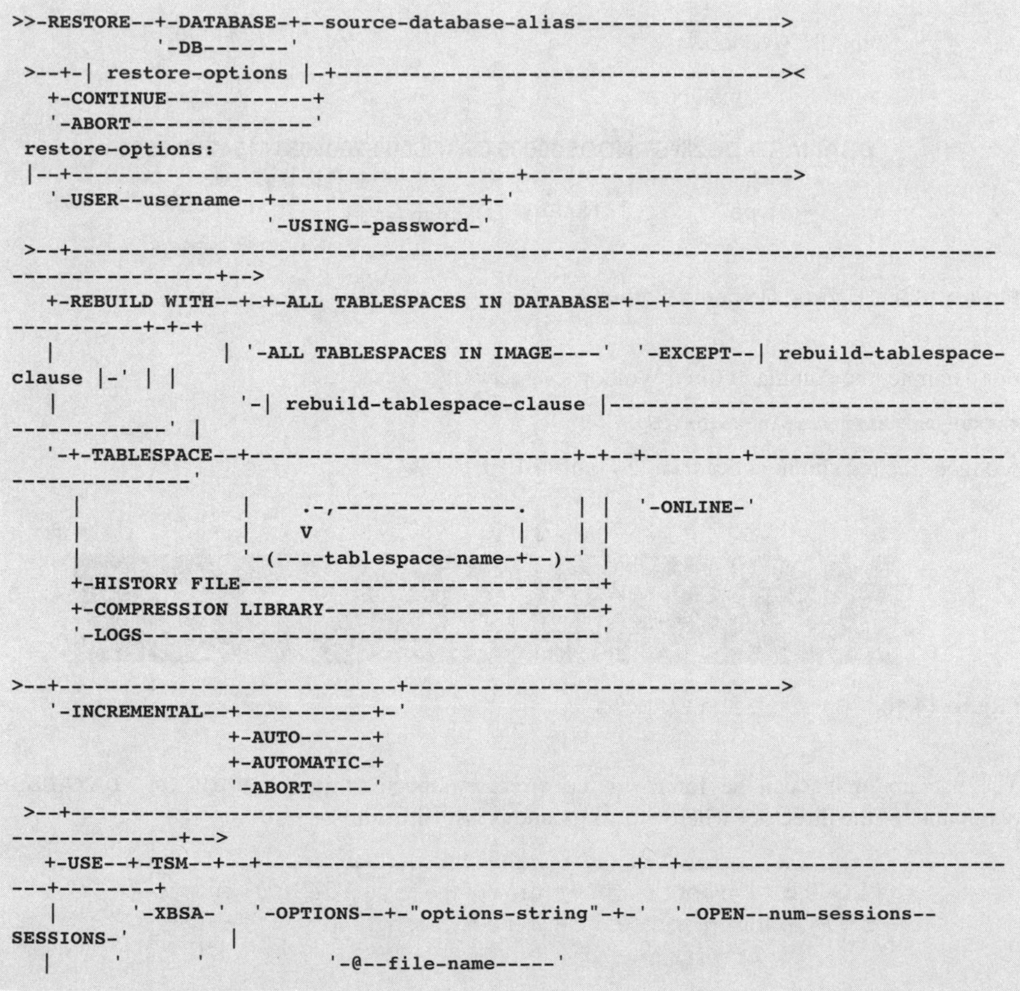

```
>>-RESTORE--+-DATABASE-+--source-database-alias----------------->
            '-DB-------'
 >--+-| restore-options |-+------------------------------------><
   +-CONTINUE------------+
   '-ABORT---------------'
 restore-options:
 |--+-------------------------------------+--------------------->
   '-USER--username--+-----------------+-'
                     '-USING--password-'
 >--+-------------------------------------------------------------
-----------------+-->
   +-REBUILD WITH--+-+-ALL TABLESPACES IN DATABASE-+--+-------------------------
-----------+-+-+
   |               | '-ALL TABLESPACES IN IMAGE----'  '-EXCEPT--| rebuild-tablespace-
clause |-' | |
   |                '-| rebuild-tablespace-clause |-------------------------------
-------------' |
   '-+-TABLESPACE--+---------------------------+-+--+-------+--------------------
---------------'
     |             |    .-,---------------.    | |  '-ONLINE-'
     |             |    V                 |    | |
     |             '-(----tablespace-name-+--)-' |
     +-HISTORY FILE------------------------------+
     +-COMPRESSION LIBRARY-----------------------+
     '-LOGS--------------------------------------'

>--+-------------------------+----------------------------->
   '-INCREMENTAL--+-----------+-'
                  +-AUTO------+
                  +-AUTOMATIC-+
                  '-ABORT-----'
 >--+-------------------------------------------------------------
--------------+-->
   +-USE--+-TSM--+--+-----------------------------+--+--------------------------
---+--------+
   |       '-XBSA-'  '-OPTIONS--+-"options-string"-+-'  '-OPEN--num-sessions--
SESSIONS-'         |
   |       '       '             '-@--file-name-----'
```

Figure 14.11 Syntax diagram of the Restore Database command

```
|
  |   '-SNAPSHOT--+---------------------+-+------------------------+'
|
   |             -LIBRARY- 'library-name'  '-OPTIONS--+-"options-string"-'
|
   |                                                   '-@--file-name---'
|
   +-FROM----+-directory-+-+-------------------------------------------------
-----------+
   |         '-device----'
|
>--+-------------------+------------------------------------>
   '-TAKEN AT--date-time-'
 >--+-----------------------------------------------+---------->
   + TO  target-directory-------------------------+
   +-DBPATH ON--target-directory-------------------+
   '-ON--path-list--+-----------------------------+-'
                    '-DBPATH ON--target-directory-'
 >--+----------------------------+--+---------------------+---->
   '-INTO--target-database-alias-'  '-LOGTARGET--directory-'
 >--+---------------------+--+-----------------------+---->
   '-NEWLOGPATH--directory-'  '-WITH--num-buffers--BUFFERS-'
 >--+------------------+--+------------------+------------->
   '-BUFFER--buffer-size-'  '-DLREPORT--filename-'
 >--+---------------------+--+---------------+------------->
   '-REPLACE HISTORY FILE-'  '-REPLACE EXISTING-'
 >--+------------------------------------+----------------->
   '-REDIRECT--+------------------------+-'
               '-GENERATE SCRIPT--script-'
 >--+--------------+--+-------------+---------------------->
   '-PARALLELISM--n-'  '-COMPRLIB--name-'
 >--+-----------------+--+----------------------+---------->
   '-COMPROPTS--string-'  '-WITHOUT ROLLING FORWARD-'
 >--+-----------------+------------------------------------|
   '-WITHOUT PROMPTING-'
 rebuild-tablespace-clause:
                     .-,--------------.
                    V                 |
|--TABLESPACE--(----tablespace-name-+--)------------------------|
```

Figure 14.11 Syntax diagram of the Restore Database command *(Continued)*

To perform a restore of the sample database, you can use the syntax shown in Figure 14.12.

```
RESTORE DATABASE sample    (1)
FROM C:\DBBACKUP           (2)
TAKEN AT 20070428131259    (3)
WITHOUT ROLLING FORWARD    (4)
WITHOUT PROMPTING          (5)
```

Figure 14.12 Restore Database command example

where:

(1) Indicates the name of the database image to restore.

(2) Specifies the location where the input backup image is located.

(3) If there is more than one backup image in the directory, this option identifies the specific backup based on the timestamp, which is part of the backup filename.

(4) If a database has archival logging enabled, a restore operation puts the database in roll forward pending state, regardless of whether the backup was online or offline. If restoring from an offline backup, you can choose not to roll forward. This option tells DB2 not to place the database in roll forward pending state. When restoring from an online backup, the "without rolling forward" option cannot be used, as you must roll forward to at least the time that the backup completed.

(5) Specifies that the restore is to be performed unattended. Action that normally requires user intervention will return an error message. When using a removable media device, such as tape or diskette, you will be prompted when the end of the device is reached, even if this option is specified.

Note that there is no keyword **OFFLINE** in the RESTORE DATABASE syntax, as this is the default mode. In fact, for the **RESTORE** utility, this is the only mode allowed if you are restoring a whole database.

In Section 14.4.2, Database Backup, we mentioned that the **INCLUDE LOGS** option allows you to back up the logs needed for roll forward recovery. If you specified this option, when restoring the database, you need to provide a location to restore the log files with the **LOGTARGET** option. You can also choose to only restore the log files without restoring the backup image.

For example, on Windows, to restore the SAMPLE database from a backup image residing in the C:\DBBACKUP directory and restore the log files to the directory C:\DB2\NODE0000\SQL00001\SQLOGDIR, issue the following command:

```
RESTORE DATABASE sample
FROM C:\DBBACKUP
LOGTARGET C:\DB2\NODE0000\SQL00001\SQLOGDIR
```

To restore just the logs to the same directory, issue:

```
RESTORE DATABASE sample
LOGS FROM C:\DBBACKUP
LOGTARGET C:\DB2\NODE0000\SQL00001\SQLOGDIR
```

14.5.2 Table Space Recovery

You can restore table spaces either from a full database backup or from a table space backup.

Figure 14.13 shows an example of a table space restore:

```
RESTORE DATABASE sample                          (1)
TABLESPACE ( mytblspace1 )                       (2)
ONLINE                                           (3)
FROM /db2tbsp/backup1, /db2tbsp/backup2          (4)
```

Figure 14.13 Restore database command with tablespace option

where:

(1) Indicates the name of the database image to restore.

(2) Indicates that this is a table space restore, and specifies the name of the table space(s) to restore from the backup image.

(3) Indicates this is an online restore. Note that for user table spaces, both online and offline restores are allowed.

(4) Specifies the location where the backup file is located.

14.5.3 Table Space Recovery Considerations

After a table space is restored, it is *always* placed in roll forward pending state. To make the table space accessible, the table space must be rolled forward to its minimum PIT. This minimum PIT ensures that the table space is consistent with the system catalogs.

For example:

1. Say at time t1 you took a full database backup that included table space *mytbls1*.
2. At time t2 you created table *myTable* in the table space *mytbls1*. This set the minimum PIT for recovery of the table space mytbs1 to time t2.
3. At time t3 you decided to restore only table space mytbls1 from the database backup taken at t1.
4. After the restore is complete, table space mytbls1 will be placed in roll forward pending state. If you were allowed to roll forward to a point prior to the minimum PIT, table space mytbls1 will not contain the table myTable, but the system catalog would say that the table exists in that mytbls1. To avoid inconsistencies like this, DB2 forces you to roll forward at least to the minimum PIT when you restore a table space.

A minimum PIT for a table space is updated when DDL statements are run against the table space or against tables in the table space. To determine the minimum PIT of recovery for a table space you can do either of the following:

- Execute the **LIST TABLESPACES SHOW DETAIL** command
- Obtain a table space snapshot: **GET SNAPSHOT FOR TABLESPACE ON dbname.**

In offline mode, the system catalog table space (SYSCATSPACE) must be rolled forward to the end of logs to ensure that the database is consistent. We discuss more about the **ROLLFORWARD** command in the next section.

14.5.4 Restoring a Database with the Control Center

You can use the Restore Data Wizard to restore a database or a table space. In the Control Center, expand the database folder, right-click on the database you want to restore, and select **Restore.** The Restore Data Wizard is launched.

Figure 14.14 shows that you have the options to restore to an existing database, a new database, or only the history file. The Restore Data Wizard guides you through the restore command options. (We will discuss the history file in Section 14.7, Recovering a Dropped Table.)

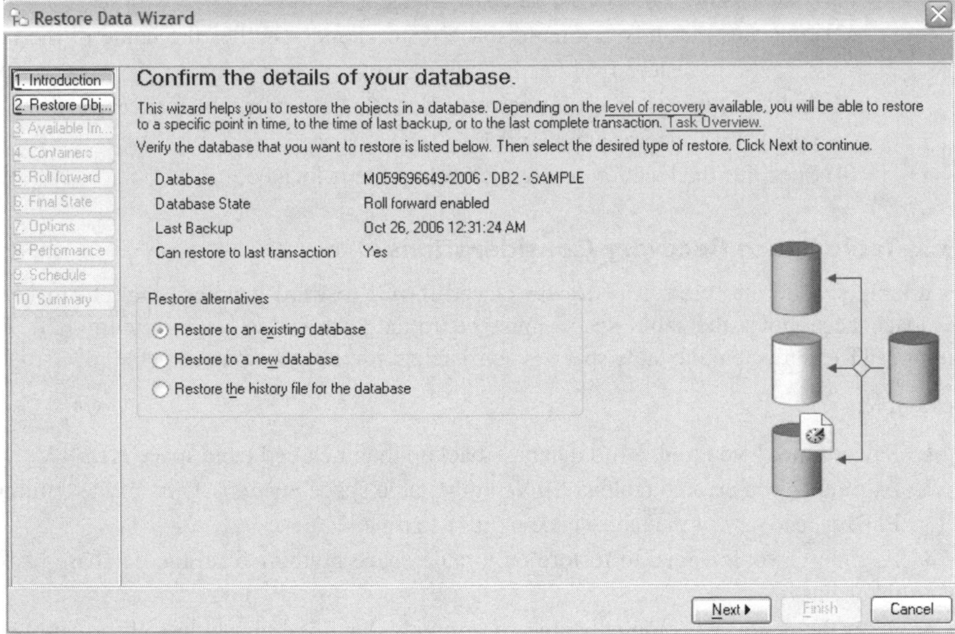

Figure 14.14 The Restore Data Wizard

14.5.5 Redirected Restore

We mentioned earlier that a backup file includes information about the table spaces and containers. For example, let's say one of the table spaces, TS2, has a DMS file container */database/ts2/cont1*. This information is stored in the backup image. When you restore this backup image to a different server (or even to the same server using a different database name), DB2 will try to create the exact same container. If the directory does not exist, DB2 will try to create it. But most likely this will fail because the instance owner does not have the proper authority.

In this case, a regular restore will not work. However, a **redirected restore** solves this problem. During a redirected restore, you can specify new paths for the table space containers, and data will be restored to the new containers.

To change the container definitions during a redirected restore, you first need to obtain the current container definitions in the source database. Use the **LIST TABLESPACES** command to list all the table spaces including their table space IDs, and then use the **LIST TABLESPACE CONTAINERS FOR tablespace ID** command to obtain the container definition for each table space. Once you have this information, you can proceed with the redirected restore operation.

14.5.5.1 Classic Redirected Restore

A redirected restore is performed in three steps:

1. Start the restore operation, but pause it so that you can change the table space definitions. To do this, include the **REDIRECT** keyword as part of the **RESTORE** command. The following shows an example of the command and output:

```
RESTORE DATABASE DB2CERT FROM C:\DBBACKUP
INTO NEWDB REDIRECT
SQL1277N Restore has detected that one or more table space containers are
inaccessible, or has set their state to 'storage must be defined'.
DB20000I The RESTORE DATABASE command completed successfully.
```

2. Specify the container definition for any table space you want to change.

```
SET TABLESPACE CONTAINERS FOR 0 USING (FILE "d:\newdb\cat0.dat" 5000)
SET TABLESPACE CONTAINERS FOR 1 USING (FILE "d:\newdb\cat1.dat" 5000)
...
SET TABLESPACE CONTAINERS FOR n USING (PATH "d:\newdb2")
```

   In this example, **n** represents an ID of one of the table spaces in the backup. When using redirected restore, you cannot change the type of the table space from DMS to SMS or vice versa. The types must stay the same.

3. Restore the data itself into the new containers by including the keyword **CONTINUE** in the RESTORE command:

```
RESTORE DATABASE DB2CERT CONTINUE
```

You can also use redirected restore to add containers to SMS table spaces. As discussed in Chapter 7, Working with Database Objects, SMS table spaces cannot be altered to add a container. Redirected restore provides a workaround to this limitation by redefining the containers.

14.5.5.2 Redirected Restore Using an Automatically Generated Script

V9

Rather than performing the above steps manually, the restore utility allows you to generate a redirected restore script by issuing the **RESTORE** command with the **REDIRECT** and the **GENERATE SCRIPT** options. When the **GENERATE SCRIPT** option is used, the restore utility extracts container information from the backup image, and generates a CLP script that includes all of the detailed container information. You can then modify any of the paths or container sizes in the script, and run the CLP script to re-create the database with the new set of containers.

For example, to perform a redirected restore of the DB2TEST database using a script, follow these steps:

1. Use the restore utility to generate a redirected restore script.

   ```
   RESTORE DATABASE DB2TEST FROM C:\DBBACKUP INTO NEWDB REDIRECT GENERATE SCRIPT
   NEWDB.CLP WITHOUT ROLLING FORWARD
   ```

   This creates a redirected restore script called NEWDB.CLP. You can edit this script to fit your environment and then run it in the DB2 command window. An excerpt of the newdb.clp script is shown in Figure 14.15.

```
-- ***************************************************************************
-- ** automatically created redirect restore script
-- ***************************************************************************
UPDATE COMMAND OPTIONS USING S ON Z ON NEWDB_NODE0000.out V ON;
SET CLIENT ATTACH_DBPARTITIONNUM 0;
SET CLIENT CONNECT_DBPARTITIONNUM 0;
-- ***************************************************************************
-- ** automatically created redirect restore script
-- ***************************************************************************
RESTORE DATABASE DB2TEST
-- USER username
-- USING 'password'
FROM 'C:\dbbackup' TAKEN AT 20060516120102
-- ON 'D:'
-- DBPATH ON 'target-directory'
INTO NEWDB
-- NEWLOGPATH 'D:\DB2\NODE0000\SQL00001\SQLOGDIR\'
-- WITH num-buff BUFFERS
-- BUFFER buffer-size
-- REPLACE HISTORY FILE
-- REPLACE EXISTING REDIRECT
-- PARALLELISM n WITHOUT ROLLING FORWARD
-- WITHOUT PROMPTING
;
-- ***************************************************************************
-- ** table space definition
-- ***************************************************************************
-- ***************************************************************************
-- ** Tablespace name = SYSCATSPACE
-- ** Tablespace ID = 0
-- ** Tablespace Type = Database managed space
-- ** Tablespace Content Type = All permanent data. Regular table
space.
-- ** Tablespace Page size (bytes) = 4096
-- ** Tablespace Extent size (pages) = 4
-- ** Using automatic storage = Yes
-- ** Auto-resize enabled = Yes
```

Figure 14.15 Sample redirected restore script excerpt

```
-- ** Total number of pages = 16384
-- ** Number of usable pages = 16380
-- ** High water mark (pages) = 8872
-- ***************************************************************************
-- ***************************************************************************
-- ** Tablespace name = TEMPSPACE1
-- ** Tablespace ID = 1
-- ** Tablespace Type = System managed space
-- ** Tablespace Content Type = System Temporary data
-- ** Tablespace Page size (bytes) = 4096
-- ** Tablespace Extent size (pages) = 32
-- ** Using automatic storage = Yes
-- ** Total number of pages = 1
-- ***************************************************************************
-- ***************************************************************************
-- ** Tablespace name = USERSPACE1
-- ** Tablespace ID = 2
-- ** Tablespace Type = Database managed space
-- ** Tablespace Content Type = All permanent data. Large table
space.
-- ** Tablespace Page size (bytes) = 4096
-- ** Tablespace Extent size (pages) = 32
-- ** Using automatic storage = Yes
-- ** Auto-resize enabled = Yes
-- ** Total number of pages = 8192
-- ** Number of usable pages = 8160
-- ** High water mark (pages) = 1888
-- ***************************************************************************
-- ***************************************************************************
-- ** Tablespace name = TBS1
-- ** Tablespace ID = 5
```

Figure 14.15 Sample redirected restore script excerpt *(Continued)*

The "**--**" indicates a comment. The **SET TABLESPACE CONTAINER** command is only created for table spaces that are not set up to use automatic storage. For table spaces that are using automatic storage, their containers are handled by DB2 automatically, so there is no need to reset them.

2. Open the redirected restore script in a text editor to make any modifications that are required. You can modify the restore options, as well as container layout and paths.

3. Run the modified redirected restore script as follows:

   db2 –tvf NEWDB.CLP

   The output of the script will be written into a file called *dbname_nodenumber.out*. In our example above, the filename will be db2test_000.out.

14.6 Database and Table Space Roll Forward

If you have to restore your database or a table space in one of your databases, you will lose any changes made since the backup was taken unless you have archival logging enabled and use the **ROLLFORWARD** command to replay the logs for your database.

14.6.1 Database Roll Forward

If a backup operation is performed online, there may be users connected to the database in the middle of a transaction. Thus, an online backup contains the backup image of a database that is potentially in an inconsistent state. After restoring an online backup image, the database is immediately placed in roll forward pending state. You must run the **ROLLFORWARD DATABASE** command to bring the database back to a normal state.

If you performed an offline backup but your database is configured to use archival logging, then the database is also placed in a roll forward pending state following a restore. In this case, you do not need to use the **ROLLFORWARD** command because an offline backup implies that the database is already in a consistent state. To avoid this, use the **WITHOUT ROLLING FORWARD** option in the **RESTORE DATABASE** command. You need SYSADM, SYSCTRL, or SYSMAINT authority to execute the **ROLLFORWARD** command.

During the roll forward process, the transactions in the log files are applied. You can apply all the changes in the log files, that is, roll forward to the end of logs, or you can roll forward to a PIT. This means DB2 will traverse the logs and redo or undo all database operations recorded in the logs up to the specified PIT. However, you must roll forward the database to at least the minimum recovery time. This is the earliest point in time to which a database must be rolled forward to ensure database consistency. If you attempt to roll forward but fail to do so, you will receive the following error message:

```
SQL1275N The stoptime passed to roll-forward must be greater than or equal to
"timestamp", because database "dbname" on node(s) "0" contains information later than
the specified time.
```

The **timestamp** given in the error message is the minimum PIT to which you must roll forward the database.

Starting in DB2 9.5, the minimum recovery time is automatically determined for you if you specify the new END OF BACKUP option in the **ROLLFORWARD DATABASE** command.

During roll forward processing, DB2 does the following:

1. Looks for one log file at a time in the active log directory.
2. If found, reapplies transactions from the log file.
3. If the log file is not found in the active log directory, DB2 searches for the logs in the OVERFLOWLOGPATH, if specified in the **ROLLFORWARD DATABASE** command.
4. If the log file is not found in the overflow log path use the method specified in the LOGARCHMETH1 database configuration parameter to retrieve the log file from the archive path.

5. If DB2 does not find the log file in the active log directory, and you did not specify the **OVERFLOWLOGPATH**, then the logs have to be retrieved from their archive location. The method used is determined by the LOGARCHMETH1 parameter. If it is set to LOGRETAIN, then you have to retrieve the logs manually. If it is set to USEREXIT, then the user exit program **db2uext2** is called to retrieve the log file. If it is set to DISK, TSM, or VENDOR, then DB2 automatically retrieves the log file from the respective archive locations.

Once the log is found in the active log directory or from the **OVERFLOWLOGPATH** option, DB2 reapplies the transactions it contains and then goes to retrieve the next file it needs.

Figure 14.16 shows the simplified syntax diagram of the **ROLLFORWARD DATABASE** command.

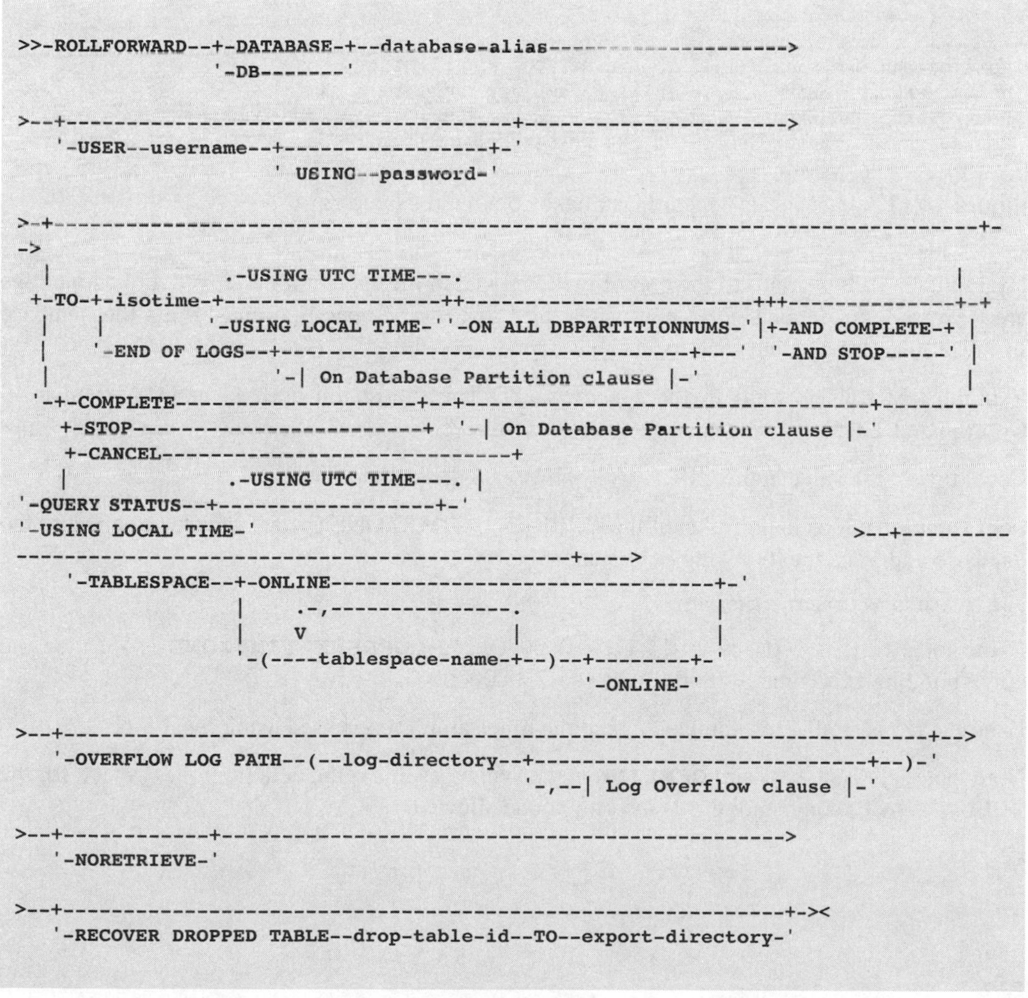

```
>>-ROLLFORWARD--+-DATABASE-+--database-alias-------------------->
                '-DB-------'

>--+-------------------------------------+---------------------->
   '-USER--username--+-----------------+-'
                     ' USING--password-'

>-+-------------------------------------------------------------------------+-
->
  |                 .-USING UTC TIME---.                                    |
  +-TO-+-isotime-+------------------++---------------------+++-------------+-+
  |    |         '-USING LOCAL TIME-''-ON ALL DBPARTITIONNUMS-'|+-AND COMPLETE-+ |
  |    '-END OF LOGS--+----------------------------------+---'  '-AND STOP-----' |
  |                   '-| On Database Partition clause |-'                     |
  '-+-COMPLETE--------------------+--+----------------------------------+--------'
    +-STOP------------------------+  '-| On Database Partition clause |-'
    +-CANCEL----------------------------+
    |              .-USING UTC TIME---. |
    '-QUERY STATUS--+------------------+-'
                    '-USING LOCAL TIME-'                              >--+---------
---------------------------------------------+---->
     '-TABLESPACE--+-ONLINE--------------------------------+-'
                   |     .-,---------------.              |
                   |     V                 |              |
                   '-(----tablespace-name-+--)--+--------+-'
                                                '-ONLINE-'

>--+-----------------------------------------------------------------+-->
   '-OVERFLOW LOG PATH--(--log-directory--+--------------------------+--)-'
                                          '-,--| Log Overflow clause |-'

>--+-------------+---------------------------------------------->
   '-NORETRIEVE-'

>--+-------------------------------------------------------+-><
   '-RECOVER DROPPED TABLE--drop-table-id--TO--export-directory-'
```

Figure 14.16 Syntax diagram of the Rollforward Database command

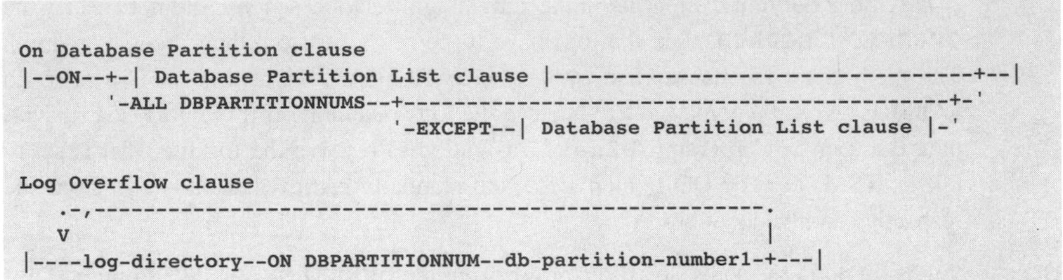

```
On Database Partition clause
|--ON--+-| Database Partition List clause |------------------------------+--|
       '-ALL DBPARTITIONNUMS--+------------------------------------------+-'
                              '-EXCEPT--| Database Partition List clause |-'

Log Overflow clause
   .-,-----------------------------------------------------------.
   V                                                             |
|----log-directory--ON DBPARTITIONNUM--db-partition-number1-+---|
```

Figure 14.16 Syntax diagram of the Rollforward Database command *(Continued)*

To perform a roll forward of the *sample* database you can use any of the following statements as shown in Figure 14.17.

```
ROLLFORWARD DATABASE sample TO END OF LOGS AND COMPLETE                    (1)
ROLLFORWARD DATABASE sample TO timestamp AND COMPLETE                      (2)
ROLLFORWARD DATABASE sample TO timestamp USING LOCAL TIME AND COMPLETE     (3)
ROLLFORWARD DATABASE sample TO END OF BACKUP AND STOP                      (4)
```

Figure 14.17 Multiple Rollforward Database command examples

Example (1) rolls forward to the end of the logs, which means that all archived and active logs are traversed. At the end, DB2 completes the roll forward operation and brings the database from roll forward pending state to a usable state.

Example (2) rolls forward to the specified PIT. The timestamp used is in UTC (Universal Coordinated Time), which can be calculated as follows:

Local time—the value in the CURRENT_TIMEZONE special register

For example, to look at the value of the CURRENT_TIMEZONE special register, connect to the database and issue the following SQL statement:

```
db2 "VALUES (CURRENT_TIMEZONE)"
```

If the local time is 2006-09-29-14.42.38.000000, and **CURRENT_TIMEZONE** is -5, then the corresponding UTC time is 2006-09-29-19.42.38.000000.

Example (3) is similar to example (2), but the timestamp is expressed using local time.

Note that there is no keyword **OFFLINE** in the syntax, as this is the default mode. In fact, for the **ROLLFORWARD** command, this is the only mode allowed.

Example (4) instructs DB2 to determine the minimum PIT that database *sample* is allowed to roll forward to, and then will roll forward to that PIT and bring the database from roll forward pending state to a usable state.

14.6.2 Table Space Roll Forward

You can perform table space roll forwards either online or offline, except for the system catalog table space (SYSCATSPACE), which can only be rolled forward offline. The following is an example of a table space **ROLLFORWARD**:

```
ROLLFORWARD DATABASE sample
TO END OF LOGS AND COMPLETE
TABLESPACE ( userspace1 ) ONLINE
```

The options in this example have already been explained in Section 14.6.1, Database Roll Forward. The only difference is the addition of the **TABLESPACE** option, which specifies the table space to be rolled forward.

14.6.3 Table Space Roll Forward Considerations

If the registry variable DB2_COLLECT_TS_REC_INFO is enabled, only the log files required to recover the table space are processed. The **ROLLFORWARD** command will skip over log files that are not required, which may speed recovery time.

You can use the **QUERY STATUS** option of the **ROLLFORWARD** command to list the log files that DB2 has already processed, the next archive log file required, and the timestamp of the last committed transaction since roll forward processing began; for example:

```
ROLLFORWARD DATABASE sample QUERY STATUS USING LOCAL TIME
```

After a table space PIT roll forward operation completes, the table space is placed into backup pending state. A backup of the table space or database must be taken because all updates made to it between the PIT that the table space was recovered to and the current time have been lost.

14.6.4 Roll Forward a Database Using the Control Center

You can use the Rollforward Wizard to perform a roll forward. In the Control Center, expand the database folder, right-click on the target database, and select **Rollforward** from the menu. The database must be in roll forward pending state to invoke the Rollforward Wizard. Figure 14.18 shows that you can choose to roll forward to the end of logs or to a PIT. The Rollforward Wizard guides you through the roll forward command options.

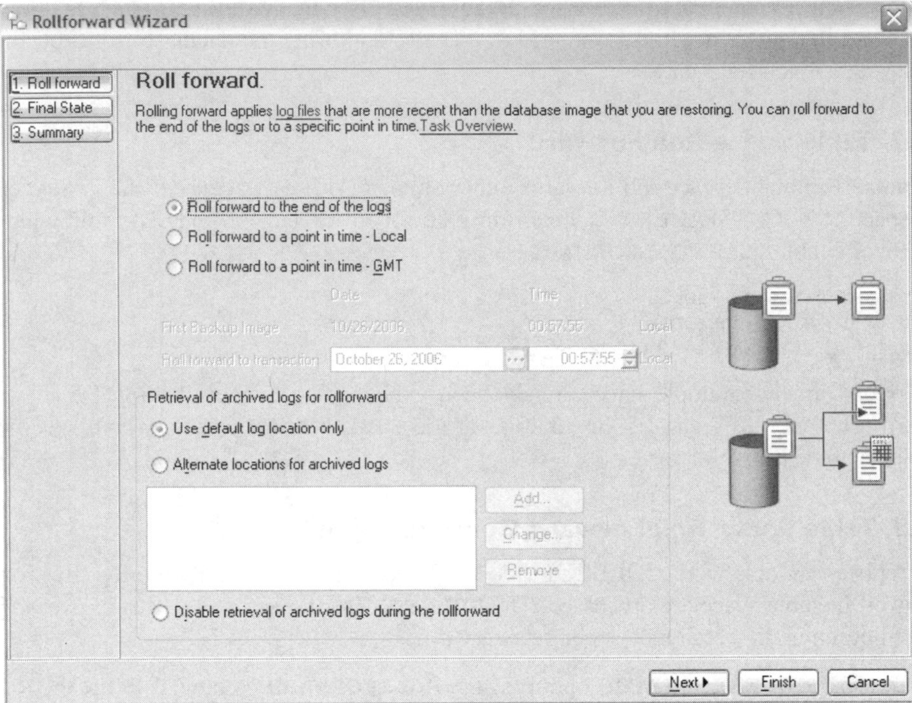

Figure 14.18 The Rollforward Wizard

14.7 Recovering a Dropped Table

You may accidentally drop a table that has data you still need. To recover such a table, you could perform a database (not a table space) restore operation, followed by a database roll forward operation to a PIT before the table was dropped. However, all of the changes you made after the table was dropped are lost. This process may be time consuming if the database is large and the backup is old, and your database will be unavailable during recovery.

DB2 offers a dropped table recovery feature that makes recovering a dropped table much easier. This feature lets you recover your dropped table data using table space-level restore and roll forward operations. This is faster than database-level recovery, and your database remains available to users.

For a dropped table to be recoverable, the table space in which the table resides must have the **DROPPED TABLE RECOVERY** option turned on. By default, dropped table recovery is enabled for newly created data table spaces. To toggle this feature, use the **ALTER TABLESPACE** statement. To determine if a table space is enabled for dropped table recovery, you can query the **DROP_RECOVERY** column in the SYSCAT.TABLESPACES catalog table.

```
SELECT TBSPACE, DROP_RECOVERY FROM SYSCAT.TABLESPACES
```

> **NOTE** The **DROPPED TABLE RECOVERY** option is limited to regular table spaces only, and does not apply to temporary table spaces and table spaces containing LOBs, LONG VARCHARs, or XML data.

To recover a dropped table, perform the following steps.

1. Identify the dropped table by invoking the **LIST HISTORY** command with the **DROPPED TABLE** option. This command displays the dropped table ID in the Backup ID column and shows the DDL statement to recreate the table.

   ```
   LIST HISTORY DROPPED TABLE ALL FOR dbname
   ```

2. Restore a database-level or table space-level backup image taken before the table was dropped.

   ```
   RESTORE DB dbname TABLESPACE (tablespace_name) ONLINE
   ```

3. Create an export directory to which files containing the table data are to be written. In a partitioned database environment, this directory must either be accessible to all database partitions or exist on each partition.
4. Roll forward to a PIT after the table was dropped using the **RECOVER DROPPED TABLE** option on the **ROLLFORWARD DATABASE** command. Alternatively, roll forward to the end of the logs, so that updates to other tables in the table space or database are not lost.

   ```
   ROLLFORWARD DB dbname
   TO END OF LOGS TABLESPACE ONLINE
   RECOVER DROPPED TABLE dropped_table_id
   TO export_directory
   ```

   If successful, subdirectories under this export directory are created automatically for each database partition. These subdirectories are named NODE*nnnn*, where *nnnn* represents the database partition number. Data files containing the dropped table data as it existed on each database partition are exported to a lower subdirectory called *data*; for example:

   ```
   \export_directory\NODE0000\data
   ```

   The *data* file is a delimited file.

5. Re-create the table using the **CREATE TABLE** statement from the recovery history file, obtained in step 1.
6. Import the table data that was exported during the roll forward operation into the table.

   ```
   IMPORT FROM data OF DEL INSERT INTO table
   ```

> **NOTE** The DB2 Recovery Expert is a multi-platform tool that you can use to easily recover a dropped table and its dependent objects, including indexes, authorizations, DDL, and data. See the Resources section for more information about this tool.

14.8 The Recovery History File

DB2 keeps tracks of all the backup, restore, load, and roll forward operations performed on a database in a file called db2rhist.asc, also known as the **recovery history file.** There is a recovery history file for each database, and it is stored in the directory where the database resides. The file is automatically updated when any of the following events occurs:

- A database or table space is backed up
- A database or table space is restored
- A database or table space is rolled forward
- A database is automatically rebuilt and more than one image is restored
- A table space is created
- A table space is altered
- A table space is quiesced
- A table space is renamed
- A table space is dropped
- A table is loaded
- A table is dropped
- A table is reorganized
- A database is recovered

To see the entries in the recovery history file, use the **LIST HISTORY** command. For example, to list all the backup operations performed on the SAMPLE database, issue

```
LIST HISTORY BACKUP ALL FOR sample
```

Figure 14.19 shows the output of the List History Backup command:

For each backup operation performed, an entry like the one shown in Figure 14.19 is entered in the history file. The following list summaries the information that is recorded:

- The time of the operation: 20060929122918001
- The command used: DB2 BACKUP SAMPLE OFFLINE
- The table spaces that were backed up: SYSCATSPACE, USERSPACE1, and SYSTOOLSPACE
- The location of the backup image: d:\temp\SAMPLE.0\DB2\NODE0000\CATN0000\20060929

If an error occurred during the operation, the error will be recorded as well.

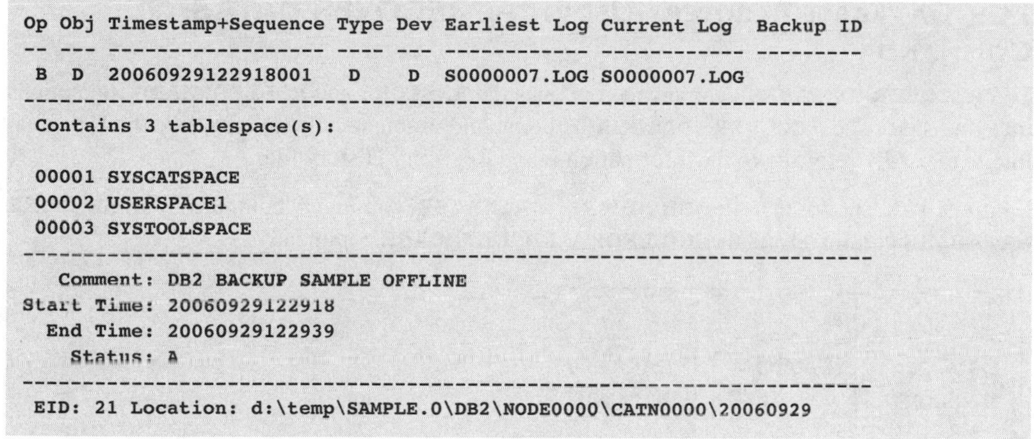

```
Op Obj Timestamp+Sequence Type Dev Earliest Log Current Log  Backup ID
-- --- ------------------ ---- --- ------------ ------------ ---------
 B  D  20060929122918001    D   D  S0000007.LOG S0000007.LOG
----------------------------------------------------------------------
 Contains 3 tablespace(s):

 00001 SYSCATSPACE
 00002 USERSPACE1
 00003 SYSTOOLSPACE
-------------------------------------------------------------------------
   Comment: DB2 BACKUP SAMPLE OFFLINE
Start Time: 20060929122918
  End Time: 20060929122939
    Status: A
-------------------------------------------------------------------------
 EID: 21 Location: d:\temp\SAMPLE.0\DB2\NODE0000\CATN0000\20060929
```

Figure 14.19 Sample List History Backup output

With the recovery history file, you can easily track all your backup operations, restore operations, and more.

V9.5 Although you have always been able to manually prune and update the status of recovery history file entries, it is highly recommended that you configure DB2 to automatically do this for you to avoid manual errors.

To configure DB2 to automatically delete unneeded backup images:

1. Set the AUTO_DEL_REC_OBJ database configuration parameter to ON.
2. Set the num_db_backups database configuration parameter to the number of backups to keep (default is 12).
3. Set the rec_his_retentn database configuration parameter to the number of days of recovery history information to keep (default is 366).

The num_db_backups database configuration parameter defines the number of database backup images to retain for a database.

The rec_his_retentn database configuration parameter defines the number of days that historical information on backups will be retained.

For example, if you take weekly backups on the sample database, and would like DB2 to keep at least a month's worth of backups, and prune everything older than 45 days, you can run the following commands:

```
db2 update db cfg for sample using auto_del_rec_obj on;
db2 update db cfg for sample using num_db_backups 4;
db2 update db cfg for sample using rec_his_retentn 45;
```

14.9 Database Recovery Using the RECOVER DATABASE Command

The **RECOVER DATABASE** command combines the **RESTORE** and **ROLLFORWARD** operations into one step. The **RECOVER DATABASE** command automatically determines which backup image to use by referring to the information in the Recovery History file.

Figure 14.20 shows that the **RECOVER DATABASE** command combines the **RESTORE DATABASE** command and the **ROLLFORWARD DATABASE** command.

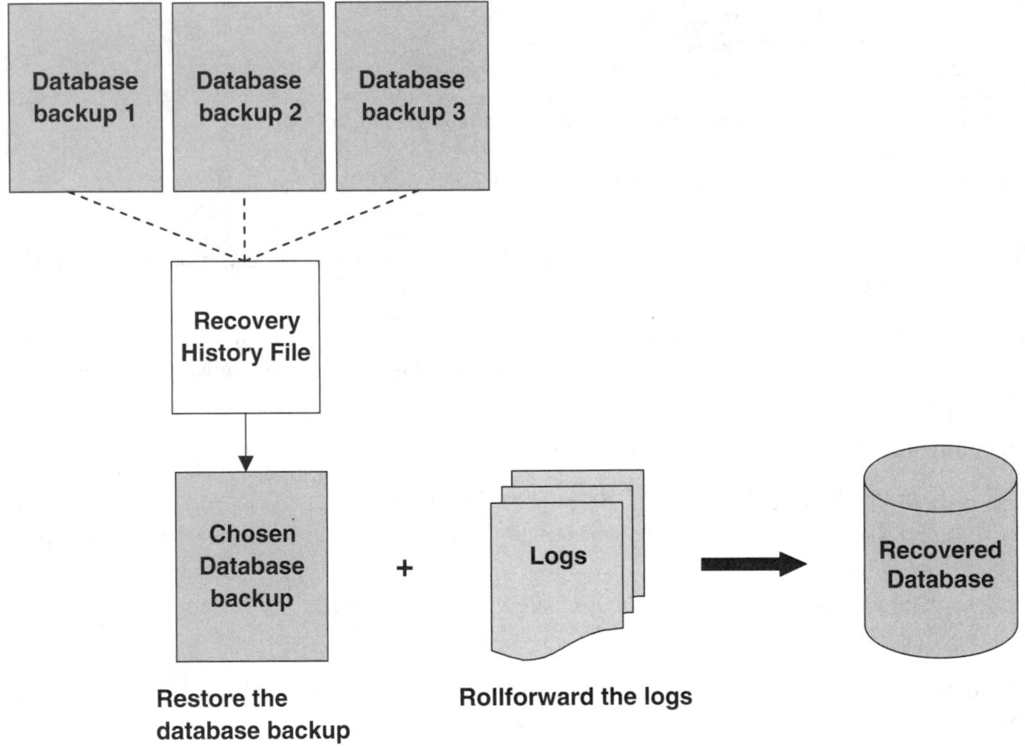

Figure 14.20 How the Recover Database command works

Figure 14.21 shows the syntax diagram of the **RECOVER DATABASE** command.

Let's look at some examples:

- To recover the SAMPLE database from the most recently available backup image and roll forward to end of logs, use

  ```
  RECOVER DB sample
  ```

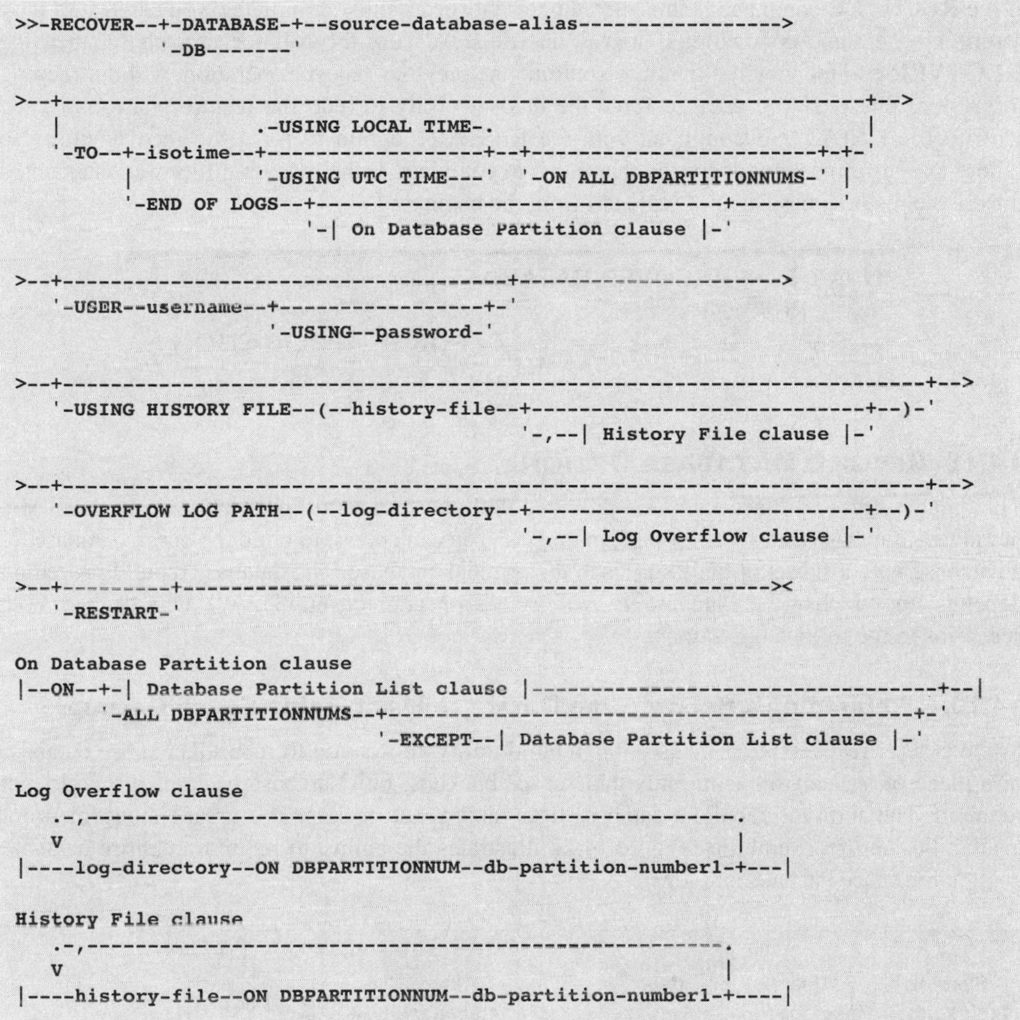

```
>>-RECOVER--+-DATABASE-+--source-database-alias----------------->
            '-DB-------'

>--+-----------------------------------------------------------+-->
   |                   .-USING LOCAL TIME-.                     |
   '-TO--+-isotime--+------------------+--+----------------------+-+-'
         |          '-USING UTC TIME---'  '-ON ALL DBPARTITIONNUMS-' |
         '-END OF LOGS--+----------------------------------+---------'
                        '-| On Database Partition clause |-'

>--+-------------------------------------+---------------------->
   '-USER--username--+-----------------+-'
                     '-USING--password-'

>--+-------------------------------------------------------------+-->
   '-USING HISTORY FILE--(--history-file--+-------------------------+--)-'
                                          '-,--| History File clause |-'

>--+-------------------------------------------------------------+-->
   '-OVERFLOW LOG PATH--(--log-directory--+-------------------------+--)-'
                                          '-,--| Log Overflow clause |-'

>--+---------+-----------------------------------------------><
   '-RESTART-'

On Database Partition clause
|--ON--+-| Database Partition List clause |----------------------------+--|
       '-ALL DBPARTITIONNUMS--+--------------------------------------------+-'
                              '-EXCEPT--| Database Partition List clause |-'

Log Overflow clause
   .-,------------------------------------------------------.
   V                                                        |
|----log-directory--ON DBPARTITIONNUM--db-partition-number1-+---|

History File clause
   .-,-----------------------------------------------------.
   V                                                       |
|----history-file--ON DBPARTITIONNUM--db-partition-number1-+----|
```

Figure 14.21 Syntax diagram of the Recover Database command

- To recover the SAMPLE database to the PIT 2006-09-21-14.50.00 (note that the PIT is specified in local time, not UTC time), issue
  RECOVER DB sample TO 2006-09-21-14.50.00
- To recover the SAMPLE database to a PIT that is no longer contained in the current history file, you need to provide a history file from this time period

```
RECOVER DB sample
    TO 2003-12-31-04:00:00
    USING HISTORY FILE (/home/user/old1999files/db2rhist.asc)
```

V9 If the **RECOVER** command is interrupted before it successfully completes, you can restart it by rerunning the same command. If it was interrupted during the roll forward phase, then the **RECOVER** command will attempt to continue the previous recover operation, without redoing the restore phase. If you want to force the recover utility to redo the restore phase, issue the RECOVER DATABASE command with the RESTART option to force the recover utility to ignore any prior recovery operation that failed to complete. If the recover utility was interrupted during the restore phase, then it will start from the beginning.

> **NOTE** A **RECOVER DATABASE** will not complete if DB2 is unable to retrieve log files, or it was interrupted by the user, for example, if a Ctrl-C was pressed or if a **FORCE APPLICATION** command was issued.

V9 14.10 Rebuild Database Option

The database rebuild functionality is provided with the restore utility. It allows you to build a brand new database using a set of backup images. You can choose to build the entire database, or a database with a subset of table spaces in the original database. The database rebuild procedure depends on whether the database is recoverable or nonrecoverable. We will discuss both scenarios in the following sections.

14.10.1 Rebuilding a Recoverable Database Using Table Space Backups

In the case of recoverable databases, the rebuild utility allows you to rebuild an entire database or a piece of a database, using only table space backups. Full database backups are no longer required. The ability to rebuild a database from table space backups is a great enhancement for availability and recoverability. Figure 14.22 illustrates the ability to rebuild an entire database using table space backups and logs.

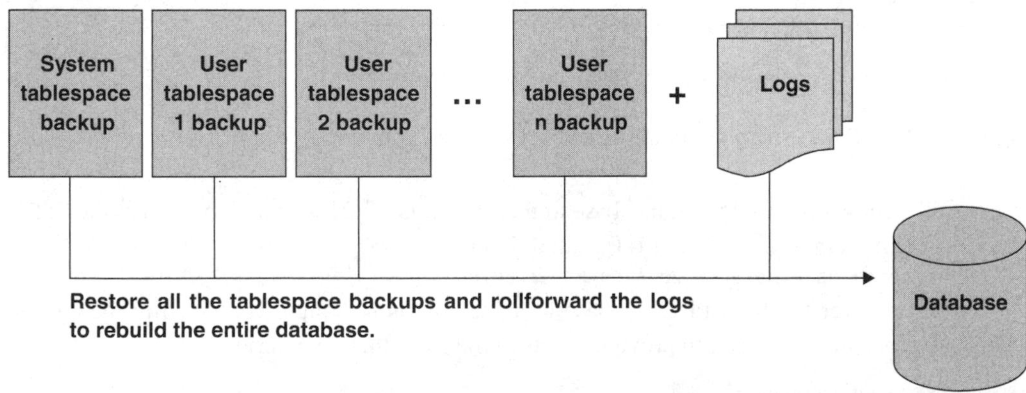

Figure 14.22 Rebuilding the entire database using table space backups and logs

Let's say you have a recoverable database called TEST. One night, there was a power failure. The disk where the database was stored was damaged. The database is not accessible anymore, and you want to recover the database.

The database has the following table spaces:

- SYSCATSPACE (system catalogs)
- TEMPSPACE1 (system temporary table space)
- USERSPACE1 (user data table space)
- USERSPACE2 (user data table space)
- USERSPACE3 (user data table space)

The following are available to you:

- All of the database log files. Because the logs are stored on a separate archive device, they were unharmed.
- You do NOT have any database level backups but you do have table space backups as shown in Table 14.5.

Table 14.5 Backup Image Information

Backup Image	Backup Image Description
TEST.3.DB2.NODE0000.CATN0000.200 70605135047.001	Backup of SYSCATSPACE and USERSPACE1
TEST.3.DB2.NODE0000.CATN0000.200 70606135136.001	Backup of USERSPACE2 and USERSPACE3
TEST.3.DB2.NODE0000.CATN0000.200 70608135208.001	Backup of USERSPACE3

If you were to use the restore and roll forward methods discussed in the previous sections, in order to recover the database to the most recent point in time, you would need to restore a database backup and then roll forward the database to end of logs. Unfortunately, in this case, this is not possible because a full database backup is not available—there are only table space backups available. If you attempted a typical restore command on any of the table space backups, you would receive the following error:

```
db2 restore db test taken at 20070608135208
SQL2560N The target database is not identical to the source database for a restore
from a table space level backup.
```

With the database rebuild functionality, you now can rebuild the TEST database with only table space backups and logs. To rebuild a database, specify the **REBUILD** option in the **RESTORE DATABASE** command.

The following steps will rebuild the TEST database to the most recent point in time.

1. Issue a **RESTORE DATABASE** command with the **REBUILD** option:

```
db2 restore db test rebuild with all tablespaces in database taken at
20070608135208
```

The first step in a rebuild process is to identify the rebuild target image. The rebuild target image should be the most recent backup image that you want to use in your rebuild operation. It is known as the target image because it defines the structure of the database to be rebuilt, including the table spaces that can be restored, the database configuration, and the log sequence. It can be any type of backup (full, table space, incremental, online or offline). In this example, the most recent backup image is TEST.3.DB2.NODE0000.CATN0000.20070608135208.001; therefore we use it as the target image of the rebuild operation.

After this command is executed successfully, the structure of the TEST database is restored. You can retrieve information from the restored database such as the database configuration and its history. If you issue a **LIST HISTORY** command (**`db2 list history all for test`**), the output shown in Figure 14.23 is returned.

```
Op Obj Timestamp+Sequence Type Dev Earliest Log Current Log Backup ID
-- --- ------------------ ---- --- ------------ ------------ --------------
R D 20070619121107001      F                                20070608135208
---------------------------------------------------------------------------
Contains 1 tablespace(s):
00001 USERSPACE3
---------------------------------------------------------------------------
Comment:    RESTORE TEST WITH RF
Start Time: 20070619121107
End Time:   20070719121108
Status:     A
---------------------------------------------------------------------------
EID: 7 Location:
Op Obj Timestamp+Sequence Type Dev Earliest Log Current Log Backup ID
-- --- ------------------ ---- --- ------------ ------------ --------------
R P 20070619121108001      F                                20070605135047
---------------------------------------------------------------------------
Contains 2 tablespace(s):
00001 USERSPACE1
00002 SYSCATSPACE
---------------------------------------------------------------------------
Comment: RESTORE TEST WITH RF
Start Time: 20070619121108
End Time:   20070619121113
Status:     A
---------------------------------------------------------------------------
```

Figure 14.23 Sample List History output

```
EID: 8 Location:
Op Obj Timestamp+Sequence Type Dev Earliest Log Current Log Backup ID
-- --- ------------------ ---- --- ------------ ------------ --------------
R P 20070619121113001      F                                20070606135136
----------------------------------------------------------------------------
Contains 1 tablespace(s):
00001 USERSPACE2
----------------------------------------------------------------------------
Comment: RESTORE TEST WITH RF
Start Time: 20070619121113
End Time:   20070619121114
Status:     A
----------------------------------------------------------------------------
EID: 9 Location:
Op Obj Timestamp+Sequence Type Dev Earliest Log Current Log Backup ID
-- --- ------------------ ---- --- ------------ ------------ --------------
R D 20070619121107         R       S0000001.LOG S0000003.LOG 20070618135208
----------------------------------------------------------------------------
Contains 4 tablespace(s):
00001 USERSPACE3
00002 USERSPACE2
00003 USERSPACE1
00004 SYSCATSPACE
----------------------------------------------------------------------------
Comment: REBUILD TEST WITH RF
Start Time: 20070619121107
End Time:   20070619121115
Status:     A
----------------------------------------------------------------------------
EID: 10 Location:
```

Figure 14.23 Sample List History output *(Continued)*

There are 4 entries in the **LIST HISTORY** command output shown in Figure 14.23. They are all related to the rebuild operation.

The first entry, EID: 7, indicates a restore operation on the backup image 20070608135208, and the table space restored was USERSPACE3. (Recall that this backup image only contains USERSPACE3.) However, all table spaces were specified using the **ALL TABLESPACES** option, so the rest of the table spaces are also restored. This is reflected in the rest of the **LIST HISTORY** output.

Using the information in the backup history file, the restore utility finds the backup images of all the table spaces to be restored and restores them. After the restore, the table spaces are placed in roll-forward pending state. From the **LIST HISTORY** output, you can see that each table space is flagged with 'WITH RF', which indicates a roll forward is required following the restore.

For the restore to work, all backup images must exist in the locations as indicated in the history file. Otherwise, an error is returned stating the restore utility cannot find a required image.

2. Issue a **ROLLFORWARD DATABASE** command with the **TO END OF LOGS** option:

```
db2 rollforward db test to end of logs
```

After all table spaces have been restored, they are put in a roll forward pending state. You need to roll forward the database to bring the database back to a normal state.

To roll forward a database during a rebuild operation, all log files for the time frame between the earliest and most recent backup images used must be available for the roll forward utility to use. If you want to roll forward to a point in time more recent than the last backup, all the log files created after that backup must also be available.

In our example, all logs are still in the log path specified by the LOGPATH database configuration parameter and the roll forward utility will find them there. This is why the location of the logs files was not specified in the **ROLLFORWARD DATABASE** command.

3. Issue a **ROLLFORWARD DATABASE** command with the **STOP** option:

```
db2 rollforward db test stop
```

At this point, you should be able to connect to the TEST database, and all table spaces should be in a NORMAL state.

14.10.2 Rebuilding a Recoverable Database Using Only a Subset of the Table Space Backups

As demonstrated in the previous section, the database rebuild functionality allows you to rebuild an entire database using only table space backups and the database logs. What makes this utility even more interesting is that you do not need to have all table space backups available to rebuild a database. Figure 14.24 shows that we can build a database with only a subset of the table spaces as well.

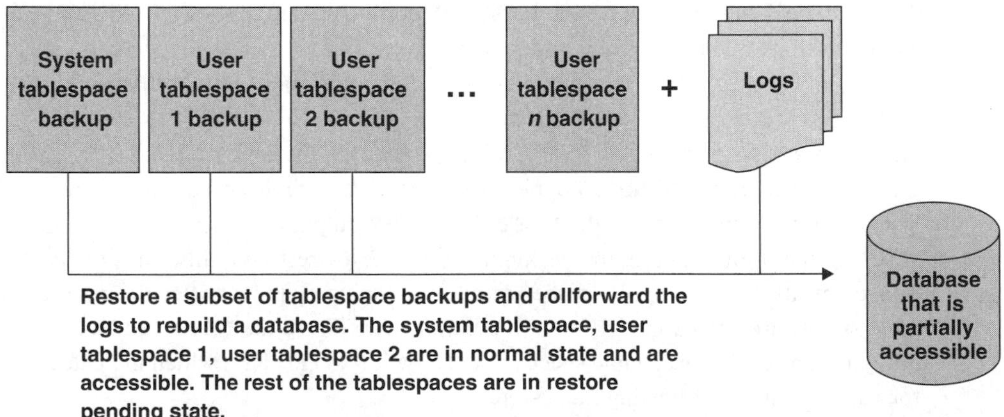
System tablespace backup
User tablespace 1 backup
User tablespace 2 backup
...
User tablespace n backup
+
Logs
Database that is partially accessible
Restore a subset of tablespace backups and rollforward the logs to rebuild a database. The system tablespace, user tablespace 1, user tablespace 2 are in normal state and are accessible. The rest of the tablespaces are in restore pending state.

Figure 14.24 Rebuilding a partially accessible database using only a subset of table space backups and logs

Let's reuse the last example. Suppose that the data in USERSPACE1 and USERSPACE2 is really important to our users, and that two table spaces must be restored as soon as possible following the power failure. USERSPACE3 is not as important and it is large. If we restore all the table spaces, it will take a long time. It would be nice to rebuild a usable database with only USERSPACE1 and USERSPACE2 in it, so users can access the database right away. When there is time later, USERSPACE3 can be restored. The following steps show how this can be done using the database rebuild utility.

1. Issue a **RESTORE DATABASE** command with the **REBUILD** option, specifying only a subset of the table spaces that you want restored:

```
db2 restore db test rebuild with tablespace
(SYSCATSPACE,USERSPACE1,USERSPACE2) taken at 20060916135136
```

   Although you only wanted to restore USERSPACE1 and USERSPACE2, you must restore SYSCATSPACE as well, because this table space holds all the system catalog information. Without it, DB2 would not know anything about the structure of this database.

   Note the target image that must be specified in the above command is the image that contains USERSPACE2 and USERSPACE3. This is the most recent backup that contains the table spaces to be restored. Although, image *20060917135208* is the latest backup of the three, we cannot use it because it does not contain USERSPACE1, USERSPACE2, or SYSCATSPACE.

   The following command has the same effect:

```
db2 restore db test rebuild with all tablespaces in database except tablespace
(USERSPACE3) taken at 20060916135136
```

2. Issue a **ROLLFORWARD DATABASE** command with the **TO END OF LOGS** option:

```
db2 rollforward db test to end of logs
```

3. Issue a **ROLLFORWARD DATABASE** command with the **STOP** option:

```
db2 rollforward db test stop
```

   You may choose to roll forward to a point in time (PIT) instead of end of logs. The PIT you choose must be greater than the timestamp of the backup image you used in the restore.

   At this point, the TEST database is in a normal state and all of the table spaces that were restored are in NORMAL state. USERSPACE3 is in RESTORE PENDING state since it was not restored.

   You can restore USERSPACE3 at a later time, using a normal table space restore (i.e. without the **REBUILD** option).

4. Issue a **RESTORE DATABASE** command and specify the table space to be restored:

```
db2 restore db test tablespace (USERSPACE3) taken at 20060917135208
```

5. Issue a **ROLLFORWARD DATABASE** command with the **TO END OF LOGS** option and specify the table space to be rolled forward:

```
db2 rollforward db test to end of logs tablespace (USERSPACE3)
```

6. Issue a **ROLLFORWARD DATABASE** command with the **STOP** option:

```
db2 rollforward db test stop
```

Now all four table spaces of the TEST database should be in NORMAL states.

The ability to bring only a subset of table spaces online is useful in a production environment recovery situation like the above. It is also useful in a test environment, where you only need to restore a subset of table spaces for interested parties.

14.10.3 Rebuilding a Recoverable Database Using Online Backup Images That Contain Log Files

When rebuilding a recoverable database, you can either use database backups or table space backups. The backups can also be either online or offline.

If you have an online backup image that contains log files, and you wish to use these logs to rollfoward the database, you can retrieve the logs from the image using the **LOGTARGET** option of the **RESTORE DATABASE** command.

Let's reuse the TEST database from the previous example. Suppose that the backup image, *TEST.3.DB2.NODE0000.CATN0000.20060917135208.001* was an online backup image that included logs. To recover the entire database using the table space backups and the logs that are stored in the backup image, issue the following commands:

1. Issue a **RESTORE DATABASE** command with the **LOGTARGET** option. During the restore, the logs are extracted to the location specified by **LOGTARGET.**

```
db2 restore db test rebuild with all tablespaces in database taken at
20060917135208 logtarget /logs
```

2. Issue a **ROLLFORWARD DATABASE** command with the **TO END OF LOGS** option and specify the location of the logs:

```
db2 rollforward db test to end of logs overflow log path (/logs)
```

   Note the **OVERFLOW LOG PATH** option is used to specify the log location.

3. Issue a **ROLLFORWARD DATABASE** command with the **STOP** option:

```
db2 rollforward db test stop
```

14.10.4 Rebuilding a Recoverable Database Using Incremental Backup Images

Incremental backup images can also be used to rebuild a database. When an incremental image is involved in the rebuild process, by default, the restore utility tries to use automatic incremental restore for all incremental images. This means that if you do not use the **INCREMENTAL AUTOMATIC** option of the **RESTORE DATABASE** command, but the target image is an incremental backup image, the restore utility will issue the rebuild operation using automatic incremental restore. If the target image is not an incremental image, but another required image is an incremental image, then the restore utility will also make sure those incremental images are restored using automatic incremental restore. The restore utility will behave in the same way whether you specify the **INCREMENTAL AUTOMATIC** option or not.

If you specify the **INCREMENTAL** option without the **AUTOMATIC** option, you will need to perform the entire rebuild process manually. The restore utility will just restore the initial metadata from the target image, as it would in a regular manual incremental restore. You will then need to complete the restore of the target image using the required incremental restore chain. Then you will need to restore the remaining images to rebuild the database. This process can be quite cumbersome.

It is recommended that you use automatic incremental restore to rebuild your database. Only in the event of a restore failure, should you attempt to rebuild a database using manual methods.

14.10.5 Rebuilding a Recoverable Database Using the Redirect Option

Since the rebuild functionality is part of the restore utility, you can rebuild a database using the redirect method, as in redirected restore. The following rebuilds the entire TEST database to the most recent point in time using the **REDIRECT** option:

1. Issue a **RESTORE DATABASE** command with the **REBUILD** and the **REDIRECT** option:

```
db2 restore db test rebuild with all tablespaces in database taken at
20060917135208 redirect
```

2. Issue a **SET TABLESPACE CONTAINERS** command for each table space whose containers you want to redefine. For example:

```
db2 set tablespace containers for 3 using (file '/newuserspace2' 10000)
db2 set tablespace containers for 4 using (file '/newuserspace3' 15000)
```

3. Issue a **RESTORE DATABASE** command with the **CONTINUE** option:

```
db2 restore db test continue
```

4. Issue a **ROLLFORWARD DATABASE** command with the **TO END OF LOGS** option. (This assumes all logs are accessible in the logpath directory; otherwise, use the **OVERFLOW LOG PATH** option to specify the alternate log path.)

```
db2 rollforward db test to end of logs
```

5. Issue a **ROLLFORWARD DATABASE** command with the **STOP** option:

```
db2 rollforward db test stop
```

At this point the database can accept connections and all table spaces should be in a NORMAL state.

14.10.6 Rebuilding a Nonrecoverable Database

All rebuild methods we have discussed so far work for nonrecoverable databases as well. The main differences are:

- If a database is nonrecoverable, you can only use a database backup image as the target image in the rebuild operation, since table space backups are not available to nonrecoverable databases.
- When the restore completes you can connect to the database right away; no roll forward operation is required. However, any table spaces not restored are put in DROP PENDING state, and they cannot be recovered.

Let's look at an example.

Suppose you have a nonrecoverable database MYDB. MYDB has 3 table spaces: SYSCATSPACE, USERSP1, and USERSP2. A full database backup was taken at *20060921130000*.

You rebuild the database using only SYSCATSPACE and USERSP1:

```
db2 restore db mydb rebuild with tablespace (SYSCATSPACE, USERSP1) taken at
20060921130000
```

Following the restore, the database is able to accept connections. If you issue the **LIST TABLESPACES** command you will see that the SYSCATSPACE and USERSP1 are in a NORMAL state, while USERSP2 is in a DROP PENDING state. You can now work with the two table spaces that are in NORMAL state.

If you want to take a database backup, you must first drop USERSP2 using the **DROP TABLESPACE** command; otherwise, the backup will fail.

14.10.7 Database Rebuild Restrictions

The ability to rebuild a database makes the restore utility more robust. However, there are a few restrictions:

- You must rebuild the SYSCATSPACE table space.
- You cannot perform a rebuild operation using the Control Center. You must either issue commands using the Command Line Processor (CLP) or use the corresponding application programming interfaces (APIs).

- The **REBUILD** option cannot be used against a pre-DB2 9 backup image unless the image is that of a full offline database backup. If the target image is an offline database backup, then only the table spaces in this image can be used for the rebuild. The database will need to be migrated after the rebuild operation successfully completes. Attempts to rebuild using any other type of pre-DB2 9 target image will result in an error.
- The **REBUILD** option cannot be issued against a target image from a different operating system than the one being restored on unless the target image is a full database backup, and the operating systems images are compatible. If the target image is a full database backup, then only the table spaces in this image can be used for the rebuild.

14.11 Backup Recovery through Online Split Mirroring and Suspended I/O Support

Although the online backup method provides the ability to take a database backup without having to bring down the database, for a large database, this process and the process of restoring from the backup, could be time consuming.

DB2's split mirroring and suspended I/O support solve this problem. With split mirroring, you can take a disk mirror image of the current database using your operating system's utility and put this mirror image into a new database. This process has the following advantages over the traditional DB2 backup method:

- It eliminates backup operation overhead from the primary server.
- It is a faster way to set up a new database using the mirror image. No DB2 restore operation is necessary.

14.11.1 Split Mirroring Key Concepts

Splitting a mirror means creating an "instantaneous" copy of the source database by copying the directories or file systems of the database to a hard disk. When required, this disk copy (a.k.a flash copy) can be used to clone a new, but identical database, or used as a backup copy to restore the original database.

The method you choose to split the mirror is not within the control of DB2. You could take a file system copy of the database directory if you wish. However, we strongly recommend that you use intelligent storage devices, such as the IBM Enterprise Storage Server (ESS), known as "Shark," and the EMC Symmetrix 3330. Using the FlashCopy technology, the ESS can establish near instantaneous copies of the data entirely within itself. The instant split feature of EMC TimeFinder software on Symmetrix is also capable of splitting the mirror in a similar manner.

> **NOTE** DB2 9.5 has introduced an automatic way of acquiring split mirrors or flash copies. Check out Section 14.11.7, Integrated Flash Copy, for a sneak peak on how it works.

A split mirror of a database must include the entire contents of the database directory, all the table space containers, and the local database directory. The active log directory may or may not need to be included, depending on how you want to use this split mirror image. This will be discussed later.

When splitting a mirror, it is important to ensure that there are no page writes occurring on the database. DB2's **suspended I/O** support allows you to perform split mirror operations without having to shut down the database. The idea is to put the database into write suspend mode before splitting the mirror, and after the split, resume normal I/O activities.

While the database is in write suspended mode, all its table spaces are placed in SUSPEND_WRITE state. All read operations continue to function normally. However, some transactions may have to wait if they require disk I/O. These transactions will proceed normally once the write operations on the database are resumed.

14.11.2 The db2inidb Tool

You cannot use the **RESTORE DATABASE** command to restore your split mirror or flash copy of your databases. To initialize the disk copy into a usable DB2 database, you need to use the **db2inidb** command.

The db2inidb command has the syntax shown in Figure 14.25.

```
>>-db2inidb--database_alias--AS--+-SNAPSHOT-+------------------>
                                 +-STANDBY--+
                                 '-MIRROR---'
>--+----------------------------+-----------------------------><
   '-RELOCATE USING--configFile-'
```

Figure 14.25 Syntax diagram of the DB2INIDB command

You can initialize a mirror in three different ways:

- **Snapshot** uses the split mirror to clone a database.
- **Standby** uses the split mirror to create a standby database.
- **Mirror** uses the split mirror as a backup image of the primary database.

Both the Snapshot option and the Standby option create a new, but identical database to the source database, using the mirror image. Therefore, the split mirror database cannot exist on the same system as the source database, because it has the same structure as the source database. If the split mirror database must exist on the same system as the source database, specify the RELOCATE USING *configuration-file* option when issuing the **db2inidb** command. This restriction does not apply to the Mirror option (you will see why in Section 14.11.5, Creating a Backup Image of the Primary Database Using the db2inidb Mirror Option).

The format of the relocate configuration file (text file) is shown in Figure 14.26. Use the configuration file to relocate the database directory structures.

```
DB_NAME=oldName,newName
DB_PATH=oldPath,newPath
INSTANCE=oldInst,newInst
NODENUM=nodeNumber
LOG_DIR=oldDirPath,newDirPath
CONT_PATH=oldContPath1,newContPath1
CONT_PATH=oldContPath2,newContPath2
  ...
STORAGE_PATH=oldStoragePath1,newStoragePath1
STORAGE_PATH=oldStoragePath2,newStoragePath2
```

Figure 14.26 Relocate configuration file

We will now look at each of the options in detail.

14.11.3 Cloning a Database Using the db2inidb Snapshot Option

This option creates a near instantaneous copy of the source database at the time when I/O was suspended. Hence, the name "snapshot." During the initialization process, the split mirror database goes through a crash recovery. After the crash recovery is completed, the database is ready for use right away. Any outstanding uncommitted work at the time of the split mirror is rolled back.

Follow the steps outlined in Table 14.6 to create a **clone** database using the **db2inidb snapshot** option.

Table 14.6 Create a Clone Database Using db2inidb Snapshot Option

	What to Do	How to Do It
Step 1	Suspend I/O on the source database.	**CONNECT TO source-database-alias** **SET WRITE SUSPEND FOR DATABASE**
Step 2	Split the mirror.	To split the mirror, you can choose to use the file system copy method, or use any vendor products mentioned earlier. If you choose to use a vendor product, make sure you consult the documentation applicable to your device on how to create a split mirror. Regardless of the variations on the split mirror process, all of the following must be split mirrored at the same time: The entire contents of the database directories All the table space containers The local database directory. The active log directory, if it does not reside in the database directory

(continues)

Table 14.6 Create a Clone Database Using db2inidb Snapshot Option *(Continued)*

	What to Do	How to Do It
Step 3	Resume I/O on the source database	Once the split copy completes, you can resume I/O activities on the source database by issuing the following command on the source database. You must use the same connection session from step 1 when issuing this command. **`SET WRITE RESUME FOR DATABASE`**
Step 4	Make the split mirror accessible	On the target machine, create the same DB2 instance as it is on the source machine. Copy the split mirror obtained from step 2 to exactly the same paths as they are on the source machine. If the split mirror copy is on a network drive, you must first mount the network drive to the target machine. Run the following command to catalog the database on the target machine: **`CATALOG DATABASE database-name AS database-alias ON path`** where *database-alias* must match the database alias of the source database. *path* must match the database path of the source database. (Use the **`LIST DB DIRECTORY`** command to display the database path, or check the DB_STORAGE_PATH field in the SYSIBMADM.DBPATHS view, as shown in Figure 14.14.)
Step 5	Initialize the split mirror database to be a clone database	Start the instance on the target machine using the **`db2start`** command. Initialize the split mirror database using the snapshot option: **`DB2INIDB database-alias AS SNAPSHOT`**

The **`db2inidb`** command initiates crash recovery, which rolls back all uncommitted transactions at the time of the split mirror, thereby making the database consistent. It is essential to have all of the log files from the source that were active at the time of the split. The active log directory must not contain any log file that is not a part of the split mirror. After the completion of the crash recovery, the database is available for operation.

Figure 14.27 summarizes the split mirror process using the snapshot option.

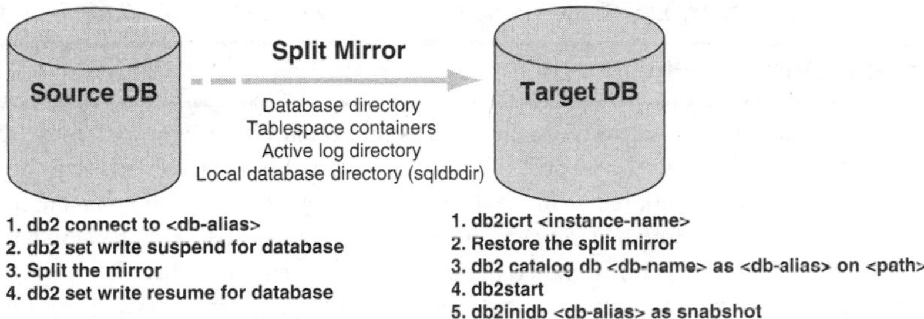
Split Mirror
Source DB
Target DB
Database directory
Tablespace containers
Active log directory
Local database directory (sqldbdir)
1. db2 connect to <db-alias>
2. db2 set write suspend for database
3. Split the mirror
4. db2 set write resume for database
1. db2icrt <instance-name>
2. Restore the split mirror
3. db2 catalog db <db-name> as <db-alias> on <path>
4. db2start
5. db2inidb <db-alias> as snabshot

Figure 14.27 Split mirror using the snapshot option

14.11.4 Creating a Standby Database Using the db2inidb Standby Option

The db2inidb standby option creates a standby database for the **source** database. We also refer to the source database as the primary database here.

When a split mirror is initialized as a standby database, it is placed in *roll forward pending* state. You can then continually apply the inactive log files from the primary database as they become available, keeping the standby database current with the primary database. The log shipping method we discussed earlier is used here to make the logs available to the standby database. If a failure occurs on the primary database, you can use the standby database to take over the primary database role.

Follow the steps outlined in Table 14.7 to create a **standby** database using the **`db2inidb standby`** option.

Table 14.7 Create a Standby Database Using db2inidb Standby Option

	What to Do	How to Do It
Step 1	Suspend I/O on the source database	**`CONNECT TO source-database-alias`** **`SET WRITE SUSPEND FOR DATABASE`**
Step 2	Split the mirror	Use the appropriate method to split mirror the primary database. The split mirror must contain the following: The entire contents of the database directory All the table space containers The local database directory You do *not* need to split the active log directory in this scenario. We will talk about how logs are handled later.
Step 3	Resume I/O on the source database	**`SET WRITE RESUME FOR DATABASE`**

(continues)

Table 14.7 Create a Standby Database Using db2inidb Standby Option *(Continued)*

	What to Do	How to Do It
Step 4	Make the split mirror accessible	Follow the same steps as in the snapshot scenario to make the split mirror accessible. If the active log directory of the primary database does not reside in the database directory, then you must manually create this on the target server. (Remember, this is because the active log directory is not included in the split mirror in this scenario.)
Step 5	Initialize the split mirror database as a standby database	The following command initializes the database and puts it in a roll forward pending state, so logs from the primary database can be applied: `DB2INIDB database-alias AS STANDBY`
Step 6	Apply primary archived logs to standby database	Continuously apply the logs that have been archived by the primary database to the standby database using the **ROLLFORWARD DATABASE** command. In order to keep the standby database as current as possible, new inactive log files (logs that have been archived) from the primary database should be continually applied on the standby database as they become available. This is done by issuing the **ROLLFORWARD DATABASE** command on the standby database without using the **STOP** or **COMPLETE** option. In order to make the logs files accessible to the standby database; you can use the log shipping method discussed in Section 14.11.1. Continuously apply the archived logs to the standby database using the **ROLLFORWARD DATABASE** command: `ROLLFORWARD DB database-alias TO END OF LOGS`
Step 7	Bring the standby database online	In case of a failure on the primary database, you want the standby database to take over the primary database role by switching the database online. To switch the standby database online, perform the following: Make the active log path accessible to the standby database. In step 6, we have only retrieved and applied the archived logs produced by the primary database to the standby database. The active logs have not been applied yet. When you are ready to bring the standby database online, you must also retrieve the active logs from the primary database and apply them on the standby. This retrieval process can be done manually, i.e., copy the active logs from the primary database to the *logpath* directory of the standby server. Roll forward the database to end of logs and stop with the following command: `ROLLFORWARD DB database-alias TO END OF LOGS AND STOP` After the roll forward process is completed, the database is ready for use.

Figure 14.28 summarizes the split mirror process using the standby options:

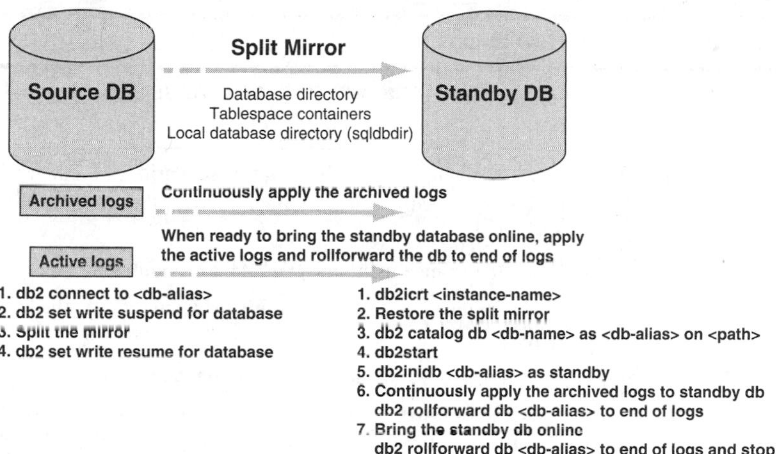
Source DB
Split Mirror
Database directory
Tablespace containers
Local database directory (sqldbdir)
Standby DB
Archived logs
Continuously apply the archived logs
When ready to bring the standby database online, apply the active logs and rollforward the db to end of logs
Active logs
1. db2 connect to <db-alias>
2. db2 set write suspend for database
3. Split the mirror
4. db2 set write resume for database
1. db2icrt <instance-name>
2. Restore the split mirror
3. db2 catalog db <db-name> as <db-alias> on <path>
4. db2start
5. db2inidb <db-alias> as standby
6. Continuously apply the archived logs to standby db
db2 rollforward db <db-alias> to end of logs
7. Bring the standby db online
db2 rollforward db <db-alias> to end of logs and stop

Figure 14.28 Split mirror using the standby option

14.11.5 Creating a Backup Image of the Primary Database Using the db2inidb Mirror Option

The **`mirror`** option of the **`db2inidb`** command is used to create a quick mirror file backup of the source database. The split mirror can be used to restore the source database if needed. This procedure can be used instead of performing the backup and restore database operations on the source database.

Follow the steps outlined in Table 14.8 to create a backup image of the source database using the **`db2inidb mirror`** option.

Table 14.8 Create a Backup Image of the Source Database Using db2inidb Snapshot Option

	What to Do	How to Do It
Step 1	Suspend I/O on the source database	**`CONNECT TO source-database-alias`** **`SET WRITE SUSPEND FOR DATABASE`**
Step 2	Split the mirror	Use the appropriate method to split mirror the primary database. The split mirror must contain the following: The entire contents of the database directory All the table space containers The local database directory You do *not* need to split the active log directory in this scenario.

(continues)

Table 14.8 Create a Backup Image of the Source Database Using db2inidb Snapshot Option *(Continued)*

	What to Do	How to Do It
Step 3	Resume I/O on the source database	**SET WRITE RESUME FOR DATABASE**
Step 4	Restore the source database using the split mirror image	There is no "target" database in this scenario. The intent of the mirror option is to use the mirror copy to recover the source database when needed. Stop the instance using the **db2stop** command. Copy the data files of the split mirror database over the original database. Start the instance using the **db2start** command. Issue the following command to initialize the split mirror database. This replaces the source database with the split mirror image and places it into a roll forward pending state, so logs can be reapplied: **DB2INIDB database-alias AS MIRROR** Roll forward the database to end of logs. After the roll forward process is completed, the database is ready for use: **ROLLFORWARD DB database-alias TO END OF LOGS AND COMPLETE**

Figure 14.29 summarizes a split mirror procedure using the mirror option.

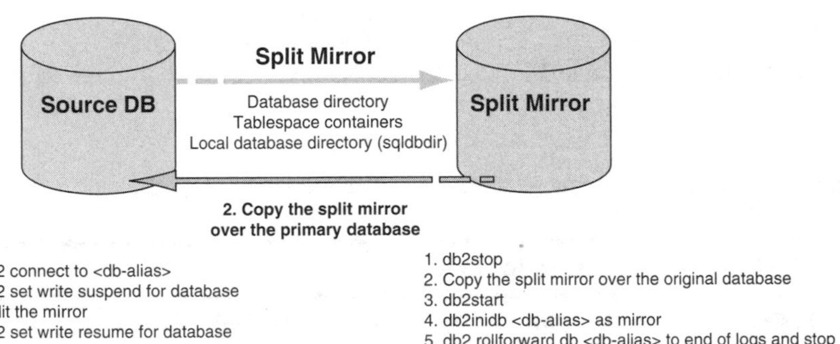

Figure 14.29 Split mirror using the mirror option

14.11.6 Split Mirroring in Partitioned Environments

In a partitioned database environment, you must suspend the I/O on each partition during the split mirror process. The I/O must be resumed on each partition afterwards. The same applies to the **db2inidb** tool, which must be run on each partition to initialize the database on that partition.

Because each partition is treated independently, the partitions can be suspended independently of one another. That means you do not need to issue a **db2_all** to suspend I/O on all of the partitions. If each partition is to be suspended independently, the catalog partition must be suspended last. This is because an attempt to suspend I/O on any of the non-catalog nodes requires a connection to the catalog partition for authorization. If the catalog partition is suspended, then the connection attempt may hang.

The **db2inidb** tool does not require any connections to the database. Therefore, you can run the tool independently on each split mirror, or you can use **db2_all** to run it on all partitions simultaneously. The only requirement is for the database manager to be started.

Let's look at an example. To suspend writes on a database with 3 partitions, 0, 1, 2, with partition 0 being the catalog partition, issue the following commands:

```
export DB2NODE=1
db2 terminate
db2 connect to database-alias
db2 set write suspend for database
"make mirror or copy"
db2 set write resume for database

export DB2NODE=2
db2 terminate
db2 connect to database-alias
db2 set write suspend for database
"make mirror or copy
db2 set write resume for database

export DB2NODE=0
db2 terminate
db2 connect to database-alias
db2 set write suspend for database
"make mirror or copy"
db2 set write resume for database
```

To run db2inidb on all partitions simultaneously, issue

```
db2_all "db2inidb database-alias as standby/snapshot/mirror"
```

V9.5

14.11.7 Integrated Flash Copy

We saw in the last section how useful split mirroring or flash copying can be, but the entire process can be tedious and complicated. Starting in DB2 9.5, there is fully intergrated flash copy functionality in the **BACKUP DATABASE** and **RESTORE DATABASE** commands.

All you need to do is edit a configuration file called dbname.fcs (eg. testdb.fcs) to indicate the type of storage device you are using. DB2 will use an integrated library and automatically go out and identify all required source LUN(s) (Logical Unit Number) and chose the available target LUN(s). The profile is normally located in the $DB2DIR/acs directory; for example:

```
$DB2DIR/acs/testdb.fcs
```

This directory must reside in an NFS directory, so that the profile(s) can be accessed from the production and backup systems.

We discussed the **BACKUP DATABASE** command earlier in the chapter, and showed the syntax in Figure 14.5. You will notice that there is an option to use snapshot. That new option is used to initiate the integrated flash copy. This type of backup is also called a snapshot backup due to the use of the snapshot option. To back up the TESTDB database as a flash copy, simply enter the following command:

```
db2 backup db testdb use snapshot
```

To restore the above image, simply enter the following command:

```
db2 restore db testdb use snapshot
```

At time of this writing, the only anticipated storage devices that are fully supported with the integrated flash copy functionality are IBM ESS, DS6000, DS8000, IBM N-Series, and Network Appliance Netfiler support. IBM is working with other vendors to provide integrated support in future releases. For the time being, published interface specifications are available to allow other storage vendors to integrate with DB2.

> **NOTE** At the time of writing, the beta image used to test our examples did not include the Integrated Flash Copy capability; therefore, we have not been able to test it. Although we are not able to provide more details at this time, you can see how useful this integration can be. We leave further exploration of this functionality to the reader.

14.12 Maintaining High Availability with DB2

Business continuity is vital to business success. In today's interconnected world, virtually every aspect of your business' operations is vulnerable to disruption. High Availability (HA) has become a key business and IT requirement. High availability is the term that is used to describe systems that are operational for a desirably long length of time.

An HA system usually consists of a primary database and a secondary or standby database. We will use standby databases instead of secondary databases for the rest of this chapter. The database that is currently running is referred to as the primary database. All transactions go through this database. The standby database is usually a mirror of the primary database, but not always. If the primary database fails, the standby database takes over the existing transactions, and becomes the new primary database.

14.12.1 Log Shipping

Log shipping is a method where transaction logs are automatically copied from a primary database server to a standby database server.

The standby database is always initialized by restoring a backup image of the primary database. The primary database continues to process transactions after the standby database has been initialized. In order to keep the standby database in sync with the primary database, the standby database must have the ability to continuously apply the logs produced by the primary database. If a takeover operation is required, the standby database can do so quickly, without having to apply the all the logs from the beginning.

The **ROLLFORWARD DATABASE** command is used to apply log files produced by the primary database on the standby database. In fact, the command must be invoked continually on the standby database, so that logs are applied whenever they become available. This process can be scripted and scheduled to run periodically. Using log shipping, you can make the log files produced by the primary database available to the secondary database and continuously apply them.

14.12.1.1 Setting Up Log Shipping

The key to setting up log shipping is to configure the primary database such that it archives logs to a location that is accessible by the standby database, in other words, a shared drive, tape device, or disk array. Figure 14.30 shows an overview of log shipping.

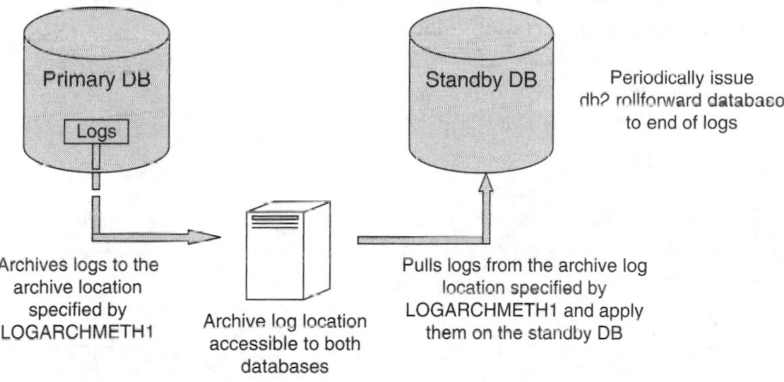

Figure 14.30 Overview of log shipping

You can set the log archival location on the primary database by setting the LOGARCHMETH1 database parameter. The location must be accessible from the standby server, such as a mounted network drive or shared drive.

On the standby database, set the LOGARCHMETH1 parameter to the same value as that on the primary database. When a **ROLLFORWARD DATABASE** command is issued on the standby database, DB2 pulls the logs from this archival location and applies them to the standby database. Figure 14.30 shows that the archive logs of the primary database are written to some kind of shared drive or server to which the standby database also has access.

To ensure redundancy, you can also configure the LOGARCHMETH2 parameter on the primary database. When LOGARCHMETH2 is set, logs are archived to both locations set by LOGARCHMETH1 and LOGARCHMETH2.

Note that for log shipping to work, both systems must be running the same version of DB2, and on the same operating system. Another option to set up log shipping is to use a user exit program on the standby database to continuously retrieve the archived log files from the primary database server or log archive device.

14.12.2 Overview of DB2 High Availability Disaster Recovery (HADR)

DB2 **High Availability Disaster Recovery (HADR)** is a database replication feature that provides a high availability and disaster recovery solution. HADR is currently available for single-partitioned databases only.

An HADR setup includes two databases, the primary and the standby. For recovery purposes, these databases should be created on different machines or servers. The primary machine is where the source database is stored (see Figure 14.31). The standby server stores a database that is cloned from the source database. It can be initialized using database restore, or by split mirroring. When HADR is started, log records are received and replayed on the secondary database. Through continuous log replay, the secondary database keeps an up-to-date replica of the primary database and acts as a standby database.

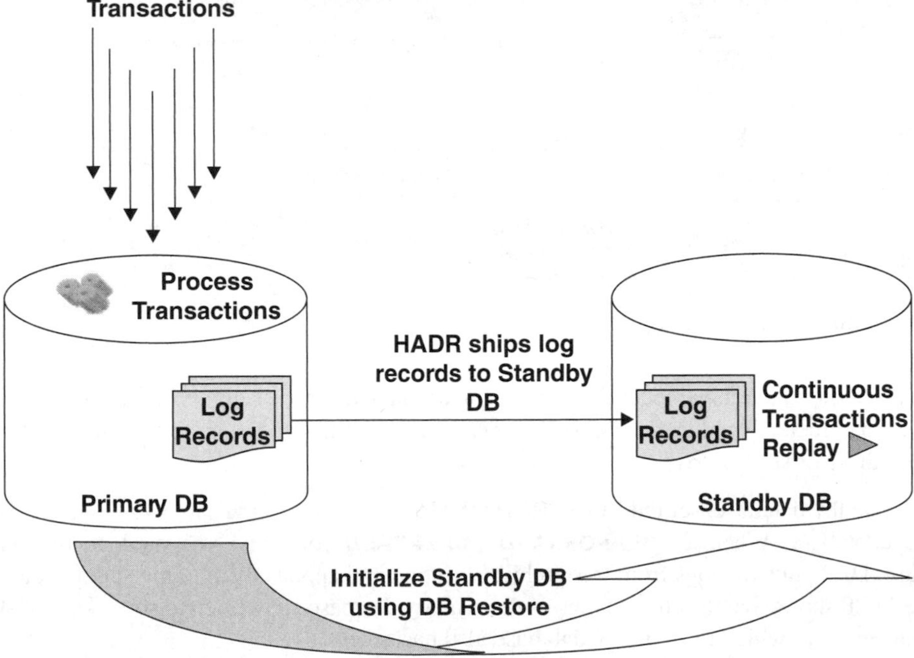

Figure 14.31 Overview of HADR

When a failure occurs on the primary, the standby database can take over the transactional workload and become the new primary database (see Figure 14.32). If the failed machine becomes available again, it can be resynchronized and catch up with the new primary database. The old primary database then becomes the new standby database (see Figure 14.33).

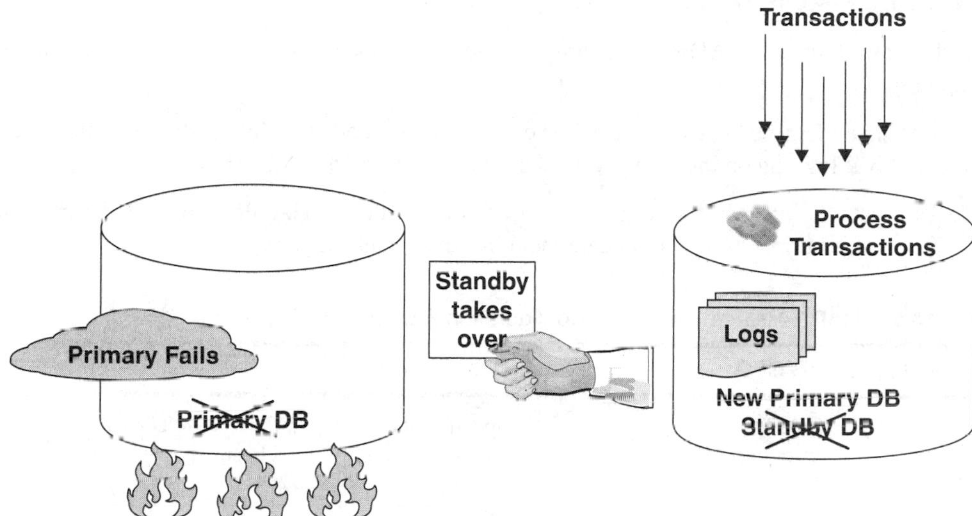

Figure 14.32 Standby database taking over primary role

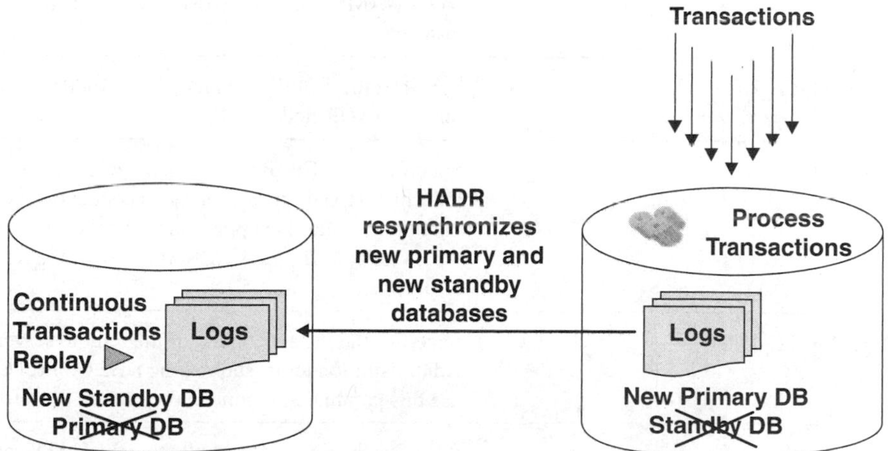

Figure 14.33 New Standby database resynchronizes and catches up with the new primary DB

> **NOTE** HADR is currently not supported with Database Partitioned Feature (DPF).

14.12.2.1 HADR Setup

In order to set up an HADR environment, you must update some database configuration parameters.

After you have identified the HADR pair (i.e., the primary and standby databases), you need to enable archival logging on the primary database (see Section 14.2.4.2, Archival Logging).

Table 14.9 lists the database configuration parameters related to HADR, and their descriptions. We will see an example of how to update them in subsequent sections.

Table 14.9 HADR-Related Database Configuration Parameters

HADR-Related DB CFG	Description
HADR_LOCAL_HOST	Specifies the local host for HADR TCP/IP communication. Either a host name or an IP address can be used.
HADR_LOCAL_SVC	Specifies the TCP/IP service name or port number for which the HADR process accepts connections on the local host. This port cannot be the same as the SVCENAME or SVCENAME +1 of the HADR instance.
HADR_REMOTE_HOST	Specifies the TCP/IP host name or IP address of the remote HADR node.
HADR_REMOTE_SVC	Specifies the TCP/IP service name or port number for which HADR process accepts connections on the remote node. This port cannot be the same as the SVCENAME or SVCENAME +1 of the remote instance.
HADR_REMOTE_INST	Specifies the instance name of the remote server. Administration tools, such as the DB2 Control Center, use this parameter to contact the remote server.
HADR_TIMEOUT	Specifies the time (in seconds) that the HADR process waits before considering a communication attempt to have failed. The default value is 120 seconds.

Table 14.9 HADR-Related Database Configuration Parameters *(Continued)*

HADR-Related DB CFG	Description
HADR_SYNCMODE	Specifies the synchronization mode. It determines how primary log writes are synchronized with the standby when the systems are in peer state. Valid values are: SYNC, NEARSYNC, ASYNC. The default value is NEARSYNC (Peer state will be discussed later in this section.)
HADR_DB_ROLE	Specifies the current role of a database. Valid values are STANDARD, PRIMARY, and STANDBY. STANDARD means the database is not HADR-enabled.

14.12.2.2 HADR Database States

When the standby database is first started, it enters the local catch-up state. Log files (if any) found in the local log path will be read and replayed on the standby database. Figure 14.34 shows the valid HADR database states.

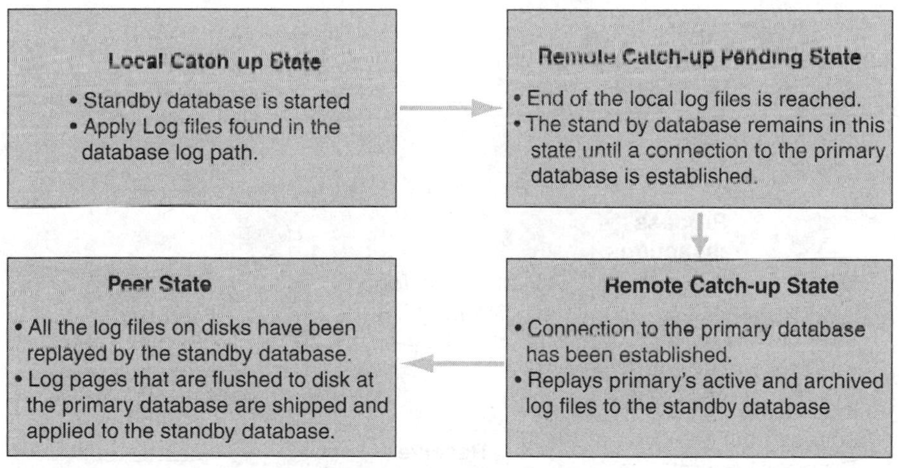

Figure 14.34 HADR database states

When the end of local log file is reached, the standby database enters the remote catch-up state. It replays log pages from the primary's archived logs as well as the active logs until the standby database is caught up to the last active log. Note that if the primary database was not active while HADR was being setup, this process is not required.

When all of the log files on the primary system have been replayed, the primary and standby databases enter the **peer state.**

In the peer state, log pages are shipped and applied to the standby database whenever the primary database flushes log pages to disk. You can specify one of the three synchronization modes to protect from potential loss of data. Details of the synchronization modes are discussed in the next section.

14.12.2.3 HADR Synchronization Modes

Recall that when a HADR pair is in the peer state, log pages that are flushed to the log file on disk at the primary database are shipped to and applied on the standby database. To indicate how log page shipping and writing is managed between the primary and standby databases, a synchronization mode is specified. There are three synchronization modes: **SYNC** (Synchronous), **NEARSYNC** (Near Synchronous), and **ASYNC** (Asynchronous).

SYNC

In synchronous mode (see Figure 14.35), log writes are considered successful only when:

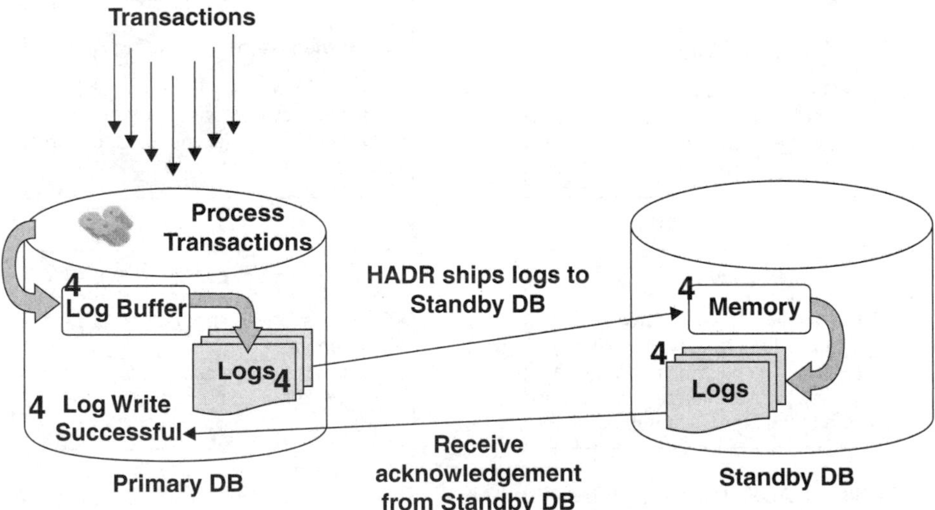

Figure 14.35 Synchronization mode—SYNC

- Log pages are written to log files on the primary database
- The primary database has received acknowledgement from the standby database that log pages are successfully written to log files on the standby database

NEARSYNC

Log records in the primary and standby database are almost (or near) synchronous (see Figure 14.36) because log writes are considered successful only when:

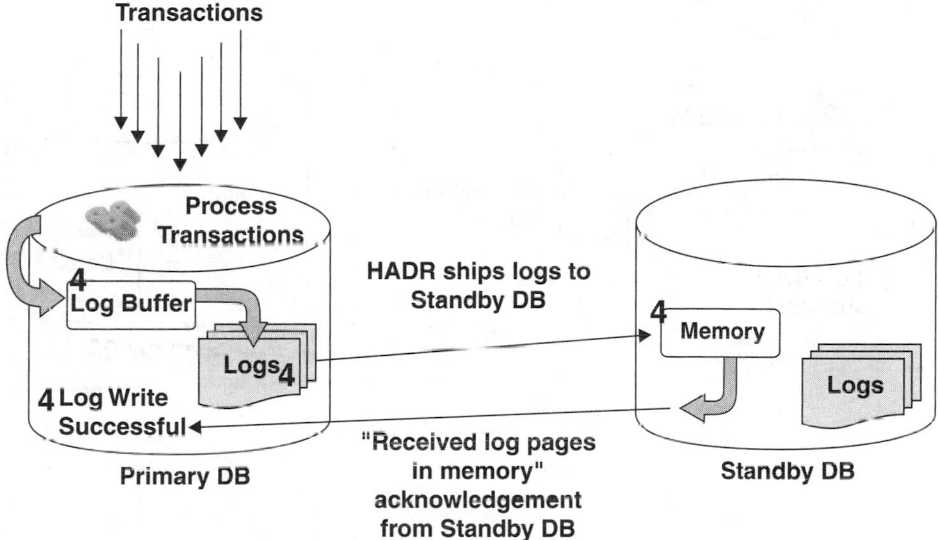

Figure 14.36 Synchronization mode—NEARASYNC

- Log records have been written to the log files on the primary database
- The primary database has received acknowledgement from the standby database that the log records have been received and copied into memory on the standby server

ASYNC

In this mode, the primary database does not wait for acknowledgement from the standby database (see Figure 14.37). Log writes are considered successful when:

- Log records have been written to the log files on the primary database
- Log records have been sent to the standby database; no acknowledgement is expected

14.12.2.4 HADR Commands Overview

HADR is managed by three simple commands:

- START HADR
- STOP HADR
- TAKEOVER HADR

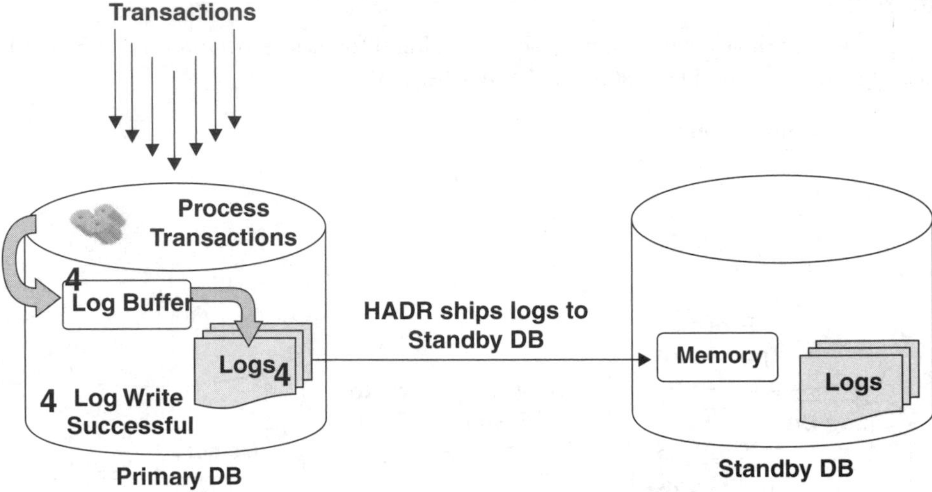

Figure 14.37 Synchronization mode—ASYNC

Figure 14.38 shows their respective syntax diagrams.

```
START HADR ON DATABASE database-alias
[USER userid] [USING password]
AS PRIMARY | STANDBY [BY FORCE]

STOP HADR ON DATABASE database-alias
[USER userid] [USING password]

TAKEOVER HADR ON DATABASE database-alias
[USER userid] [USING password]
[BY FORCE]
```

Figure 14.38 Syntax diagram of the Start HADR command

Issuing the **START HADR** command with either the **AS PRIMARY** or **AS STANDBY** option sets the database role to the one specified if the database is not already in that role. This command also activates the database, if it is not already activated.

The **STOP HADR** command changes an HADR database (either primary or standby) into a standard database. Any database configuration parameters related to HADR remain unchanged so that the database can easily be reactivated as an HADR database.

The **TAKEOVER HADR** command, which you can issue on the standby database only, changes the standby database to a primary database. When you do not specify the **BY FORCE** option, the primary and standby databases switch roles. When you specify the **BY FORCE** option, the standby database unilaterally (without changing the primary to standby) switches to become the primary database. In this case, the standby database attempts to stop transaction processing on the old primary database. However, there is no guarantee that transaction processing will stop. Use the **BY FORCE** option to takeover with extreme caution. Ensure that the current primary has definitely failed, or shut it down, prior to issuing the **TAKEOVER HADR** command with the **BY FORCE** option. Failure to do so may result in both the old primary and new primary databases becoming active. Existing applications may continue to process transactions on the old primary, while new applications may access the new primary. This phenomenon is sometimes known as the "split brain" syndrome. This is obviously undesirable.

14.12.2.5 Setting Up and Initializing HADR

Now that you have learned the concept of HADR, let's look at an example showing how to set up a HADR environment.

In this example, we are going to set up a HADR environment for a database called TEST1 will be set up. TEST1 resides on database server server1 under instance DB2INST1. The service port number, or SVCENAME, of DB2INST1 is 50000.

The other database server, server2, will be used as the standby server. TEST1 currently does not exist on the standby server. Table 14.10 summaries this information.

Table 14.10 Summary of HADR Environment

Server Name	Instance Name	SVCENAME or Port Number	Database Name
server1	DB2INST1	50000	TEST1
server2	DB2INST1	50000	—

To initialize HADR for the first time, you need to perform the five steps shown in Figure 14.39.

1. Identify the primary and the standby servers. Determine the host name, host IP address, and the service name or port number for each of the HADR databases.

   In this example, the primary server is *server1* and the standby server is *server2*.

   You need to make sure that these two servers can communicate with each other through TCP/IP. If hostname resolution does not work, try using the server's TCP/IP address.

2. Create the standby database by cloning the primary database.

   There are two options to clone the primary database.

   One option is to take a backup of the primary database, and restore it on the standby server. This option uses the standard backup and restore method.

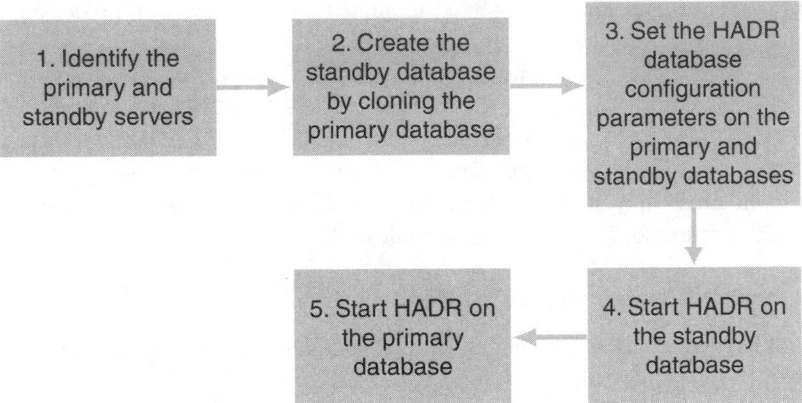

Figure 14.39 Steps to initialize a HADR environment

The other option to clone the primary database is by split mirroring. Make a split mirror of the primary database and initialize it on the standby server. When initializing the mirror, the standby option must be used with the db2inidb command; the mirror and the snapshot options will not work.

In this example, the backup/restore method is used.

First, take a backup of the primary database, TEST1, on server1:

```
BACKUP DB test1
```

Next, move the backup image to the standby server and restore it.

Note that strict symmetry of table space and container configuration is required on the standby database. The name, path, and size of the containers must match the primary database. The names of the databases must be the same. If any of the configurations do not match, HADR may fail to replicate the data to the standby database. Therefore, before restoring the database, make sure the standby server has the same architectural set up as the primary server.

We must restore the backup image to the same location as it is on the primary server. The following output is taken from a **LIST DB DIRECTORY** command on the primary server:

```
Database alias                         = TEST1
 Database name                          = TEST1
 Local database directory               = C:
 Database release level                 = b.00
 Comment                                =
 Directory entry type                   = Indirect
 Catalog database partition number      = 0
 Alternate server hostname              =
 Alternate server port number           =
```

Note that the database resides on the C: drive on the primary server. When restoring the backup image on the standby server, it must be restored on the C: drive as well. On the standby server, issue the following command to restore the TEST1 database:

```
RESTORE DB test1 TO C:
```

After the restore is completed, the database is put in roll forward pending state. This is because the backup was taken from a database that is enabled for archival logging. DO NOT issue the **ROLLFORWARD DATABASE** command to bring the database out of the roll forward pending state. The database must remain in this state in order to start HADR as a standby database properly.

3. Set the following HADR configuration parameters on both the primary and standby databases.

- HADR_LOCAL_HOST
- HADR_LOCAL_SVC
- HADR_REMOTE_HOST
- HADR_REMOTE_SVC
- HADR_REMOTE_INST
- HADR_SYNCMODE
- LOGINDEXBUILD

It is recommended to set the database configuration parameter **LOGINDEXBUILD** to ON in a HADR environment. Otherwise, any index creation, re-creation, or reorganization on the current or future primary database server may not be recoverable on the current or future standby database server using HADR. Those indexes that cannot be recovered will be marked as invalid and will be rebuilt implicitly either at the end of the HADR takeover process or after the HADR takeover process when the underlying tables are accessed.

On each server, an unused TCP/IP port is needed for HADR use. There are no strict rules for choosing a port number for HADR, as long as it is not being used by another application, and it is not equal to SVCENAME or SVCENAME+1.

For example, on the primary server, port 70000 is used for HADR. Update the Windows\System32\drivers\etc\services file to add the following line:

```
Hadr_port            70000/tcp
```

On the standby server, port 80000 is for HADR. Add the following line to the services file on the standby server:

```
Hadr_port            80000/tcp
```

The default value for **HADR_SYNCMODE,** NEARSYNC, will be used.

Now that all the information needed to configure the HADR parameters is available, issue the following commands to configure the parameters on the standby server:

```
UPDATE DB CFG FOR test1 USING HADR_LOCAL_HOST server2.torolab.ibm.com
UPDATE DB CFG FOR test1 USING HADR_LOCAL_SVC 80000
UPDATE DB CFG FOR test1 USING HADR_REMOTE_HOST server1.torolab.ibm.com
UPDATE DB CFG FOR test1 USING HADR_REMOTE_SVC 70000
UPDATE DB CFG FOR test1 USING HADR_REMOTE_INST db2inst1
UPDATE DB CFG FOR test1 USING LOGINDEXBUILD on
```

On the primary database server, configure the same set of parameters as shown below:

```
UPDATE DB CFG FOR test1 USING HADR_LOCAL_HOST server1.torolab.ibm.com
UPDATE DB CFG FOR test1 USING HADR_LOCAL_SVC 70000
UPDATE DB CFG FOR test1 USING HADR_REMOTE_HOST server2.torolab.ibm.com
UPDATE DB CFG FOR test1 USING HADR_REMOTE_SVC 80000
UPDATE DB CFG FOR test1 USING HADR_REMOTE_INST db2inst1
UPDATE DB CFG FOR test1 USING LOGINDEXBUILD on
```

4. Start HADR on the standby database using the **START HADR** command:

```
START HADR ON DB test1 AS STANDBY
```

It is recommended that you start the standby database before starting the primary database. If you start the primary database first, the startup procedure will fail if the standby database is not started within the time period specified by the **HADR_TIMEOUT** database configuration parameter.

5. Start HADR on the primary database:

```
START HADR ON DB test1 AS PRIMARY
```

HADR is now started on the primary and standby databases.

When the primary server is first started, it waits for the standby server to contact it. If the standby server does not make contact with the primary after a specific period of time, HADR will not start. This timeout period is configurable using the HADR_TIMEOUT configuration parameter (see Table 14.9). This behavior is designed to avoid two systems accidentally starting up as the primary at the same time.

During the HADR startup process, the databases go through the following states: local catch-up, remote catch-up pending, remote catch-up and peer. Logs are shipped automatically from the primary server to the standby server, and then replayed on the standby server. This is to ensure that the standby database is up to date with the primary database.

It is highly recommended that the database configuration parameters and database manager configuration parameters be identical on the systems where the primary and standby databases reside. Otherwise, the standby database will not perform the same way as the primary database.

14.12.2.6 Performing a Takeover—Switching Database Roles

In the case where the primary server becomes unavailable, you can perform a HADR takeover operation and let the standby database take over the primary database role, ensuring minimal interruption to users that are connected. You can perform a HADR takeover in one of the following ways:

- Switch the database roles between the primary and standby, that is, standby becomes primary, primary becomes standby
- Failover from primary to standby

We look at the first database role switching option in this section, and the failover option in the next section.

The database role switching option causes any applications currently connected to the HADR primary database to be forced off. This action is designed to work in coordination with DB2's automatic client reroute feature. With automatic client reroute enabled, existing connections are forced off during the takeover, and reestablished to the new primary server after the takeover. New client connections to the old primary database will be automatically rerouted to the new primary database. (Automatic client reroute is covered in more detail in Section 14.12.2.9.)

To switch database roles, issue the **TAKEOVER HADR** command on the standby database. Note that the command can only be issued on the standby database and only when it is in peer state. You can get the HADR status of a database using the **GET SNAPSHOT** command; for example

```
GET SNAPSHOT FOR DATABASE ON test1
```

The following command initiates a HADR database switching role operation from the standby database TEST1:

```
TAKEOVER HADR ON DB test1
```

14.12.2.7 Performing a Takeover—Failover

The failover option itself does not switch database roles. During a failover operation, the standby database takes over the primary database role without having the primary database switching to standby.

This option should only be used when the primary database becomes unavailable, and you want the current standby database to become the new primary database. If the primary database is still active and you execute a HADR failover, you will potentially lose data, or result in having two primary databases. This is sometimes referred to as the "split brain" syndrome.

Before issuing the **TAKEOVER** command, make sure the failed primary database is completely disabled. When a database encounters internal errors, normal shutdown commands might not completely shut it down. You might need to use operating system commands to remove resources such as processes, shared memory, or network connections. If the primary database is not completely disabled, the standby database will still send a message to the primary database asking it to shutdown. However, the standby database will not wait for the confirmation to come back from the primary database that it has successfully shut down. The standby database will immediately switch to the role of primary database.

To perform a HADR failover, issue the **TAKEOVER** command with the **BY FORCE** option on the standby database. Note that the command can only be issued on the standby database and only when it is in peer state or remote catch-up pending state.

The following command initiates a HADR failover operation on database TEST1

```
TAKEOVER HADR ON DB test1 BY FORCE
```

14.12.2.8 Summary of the Takeover Behavior with Respect to Database States

Tables 14.11 and 14.12 summarize the behavior of the **TAKEOVER HADR** command when issued on the standby database, with respect to the HADR state.

Table 14.11 Without BY FORCE Option

Standby Database State	Takeover Behavior
Peer	The primary and standby databases switch roles.
Local catch-up or remote catch-up	ERROR
Remote catch-up pending	ERROR

Table 14.12 With BY FORCE Option

Standby Database State	Takeover Behavior
Peer	The standby notifies the primary to shut itself (the primary) down. The standby stops receiving logs from the primary, finishes replaying the logs it has already received, and then becomes a primary. The standby does *not* wait for any acknowledgement from the primary to confirm that it has received the takeover notification or that it has shut down.
Local catch-up OR remote catch-up	ERROR
Remote catch-up pending	Standby database becomes a primary database.

14.12.2.9 The Automatic Client Reroute Feature and HADR

Up until now, you have seen how to set up a HADR environment and how to perform a takeover using both the database role switching option, and the failover option. The HADR feature can make a database highly available. If the primary database goes down, the standby database will take over and becomes the new primary.

However, this does not mean that client applications are automatically aware of this takeover, and are smart enough to connect to the new primary server instead of the old primary server following a takeover. In fact, with HADR enabled, clients do not automatically connect to the new primary database following a takeover. They still try to connect to the old primary, and fail because the primary server has either become the standby server (database role switching), or has been completely disabled (failover).

The DB2 automatic client reroute feature can be used to make applications highly available. When a HADR environment is enabled with the automatic client reroute feature, after a takeover, all current and new client connections are automatically rerouted to the new primary server, so that the applications can continue their work with minimal interruption.

> **NOTE** DB2 automatic client reroute is not only a feature of HADR. It can be used for situations where there is a loss of communication between the client application and DB2 data server outside of a HADR environment. Refer to Chapter 6 for information on how to configure a remote client connection.

14.12.2.10 Stopping HADR

Use the **STOP HADR** command to stop HADR operations on the primary or standby database. You can choose to stop HADR on one or both of the databases. If you are performing maintenance on the standby system, you only need to stop HADR on the standby database. If you want to stop using HADR completely, you can stop HADR on both databases.

If you want to stop the specified database but you still want it to maintain its role as either an HADR primary or standby database, do not issue the **STOP HADR** command. If you issue the **STOP HADR** command, the database will become a standard database and may require reinitialization in order to resume operations as an HADR database. Instead, issue the **DEACTIVATE DATABASE** command.

For example, to stop HADR on the TEST1 database, issue the following command:

```
STOP HADR ON DB test1
```

14.12.2.11 The HADR Wizard

You can setup and configure HADR using the HADR wizard, which is available from the Control Center.

The wizard guides you through the tasks required to set up the HADR environment, such as stopping and starting HADR, and switching database roles. To launch the wizard, go to the Control Center and right-click on the target database and select High Availability Disaster Recovery (see Figure 14.40). You can choose to set up or manage HADR.

If you choose to setup HADR, a step-by-step wizard is launched, as shown in Figure 14.41.

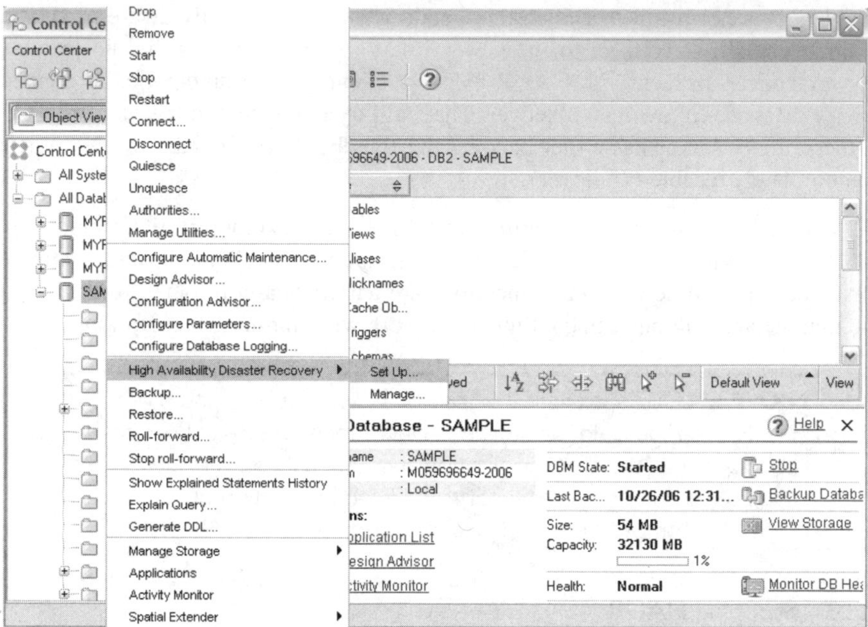

Figure 14.40 Launching the HADR wizard from the Control Center

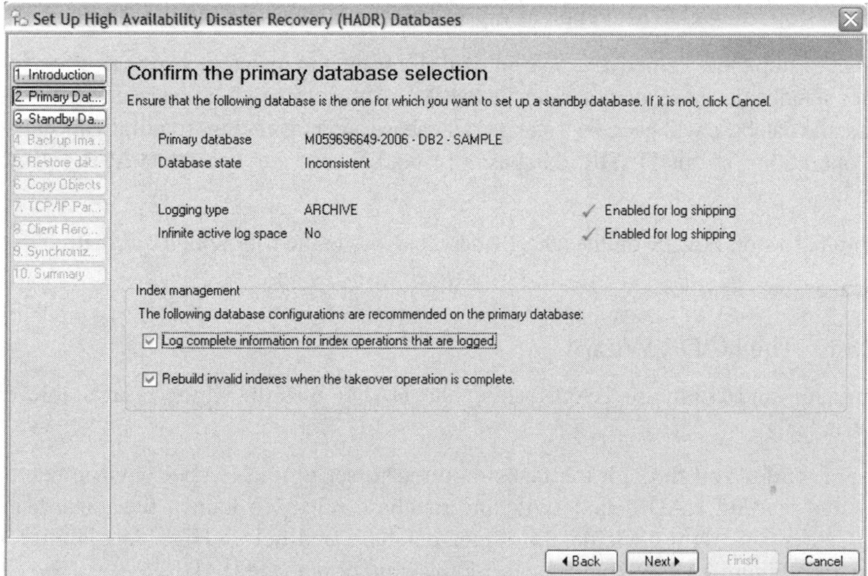

Figure 14.41 Setting up the HADR environment

> **NOTE** If you use the Control Center to set up a HADR environment, the automatic client reroute feature is automatically enabled.

14.13 The Fault Monitor

It is 3 A.M., and your system administrator is tired. In his wisdom, he wanted to kill an application process that was hanging. Instead, he mistyped the process ID by one digit, inadvertently killing the db2sysc process. You will learn in Chapter 15, The DB2 Process Model, that the db2sysc process is the main DB2 system controller. The instance is shut down, but the system administrator is not familiar with DB2 and does not know how to start it up again. He is not even aware of the problem, until an hour later, when you are paged because DB2 is down. Wouldn't it be nice if DB2 was smart enough to notice that the db2sysc process was terminated, and somehow restart it? The answer is, it is, and it can.

14.13.1 The Fault Monitor Facility (Linux and UNIX Only)

DB2 uses a **Fault Monitor Facility** to increase the availability of DB2 instances and databases. The fault monitor is solely responsible for keeping the instance it is monitoring up and running. If the **db2stop** command is issued, the fault monitor ignores it. If the DB2 instance it is monitoring terminates unexpectedly in any other way (like the case of killing the db2sysc process), the fault monitor will attempt to restart the instance automatically.

> **NOTE** If you are using any form of high availability clustering product such as HACMP or MSCS, you must turn the fault monitor facility off. Instance startup and shutdown will be controlled by the clustering product.

14.13.2 Fault Monitor Registry File

The Fault Monitor Facility will create a fault monitor registry file for every instance on a physical machine when the fault monitor daemon is started. The values in this file specify the behavior of the fault monitor. The file can be found in the *~/sqllib/* directory and is named *fm.<machine_name>.reg*. This file should be configured or altered using the **db2fm** command.

The Fault Monitor Coordinator (FMC) is the process of the Fault Monitor Facility that is started at system startup. The init daemon starts the FMC and will restart it if it terminates abnormally. The FMC starts one fault monitor for each DB2 instance. Each fault monitor runs as a daemon process and has the same user privileges as the DB2 instance. Once a fault monitor is started, it is monitored to make sure that it does not exit prematurely. If a fault monitor fails, it is restarted by the FMC. Each fault monitor is, in turn, responsible for monitoring one DB2 instance. If the DB2 instance fails, the fault monitor will restart it.

Figure 14.42 shows you the default fault monitor registry entries.

```
FM_ON = no
FM_ACTIVE = yes
START_TIMEOUT = 600
STOP_TIMEOUT = 600
STATUS_TIMEOUT = 20
STATUS_INTERVAL = 20
RESTART_RETRIES = 3
ACTION_RETRIES = 3
NOTIFY_ADDRESS = <instance_name>@<machine_name>
```

Figure 14.42 Default Fault Monitor Registry Entries.

The registry file can be altered using the **db2fm** command. The syntax for the DB2 fault monitor command is shown in Figure 14.43.

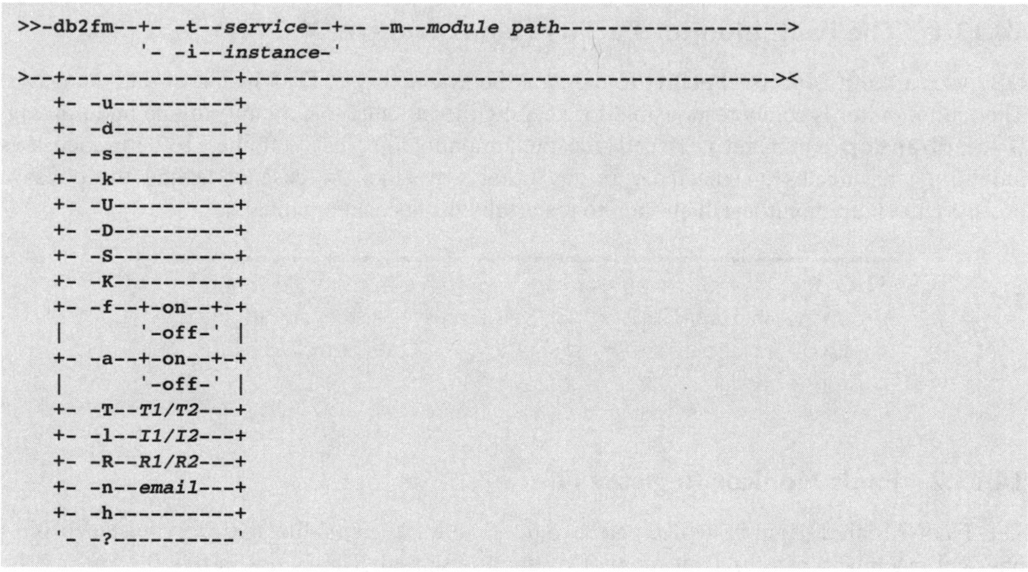

```
>>-db2fm--+- -t--service--+-- -m--module path------------------->
          '- -i--instance-'
>--+--------------+------------------------------------------><
   +- -u----------+
   +- -d----------+
   +- -s----------+
   +- -k----------+
   +- -U----------+
   +- -D----------+
   +- -S----------+
   +- -K----------+
   +- -f--+-on--+-+
   |      '-off-' |
   +- -a--+-on--+-+
   |      '-off-' |
   +- -T--T1/T2---+
   +- -l--I1/I2---+
   +- -R--R1/R2---+
   +- -n--email---+
   +- -h----------+
   '- -?----------'
```

Figure 14.43 Syntax Diagram of db2fm command

Now that you know how DB2 fault monitoring works, let's take a look at an example.

14.13.3 Setting Up the DB2 Fault Monitor

We mentioned that the **init daemon** is responsible for starting the DB2 FMC when the server is started. It is also responsible for *respawning* the FMC whenever it goes down. DB2 automatically writes the following line in the /etc/inittab when you install DB2.

```
fmc:2:respawn:/usr/opt/db2_09_01/bin/db2fmcd #DB2 Fault Monitor Coordinator
```

To check if the FMC is currently running on your system, you can query its status with the **DB2 Fault Monitor Controller Utility (FMCU).** The **FMCU** must be run as root because it accesses the system's inittab file. To query the status, issue the following **db2fmcu** command as root:

```
db2fmcu
```

If the FMC status is down, the result will show

```
FMC: down
```

Run the following command as root to start up the FMC daemon:

```
db2fmcu -u -p /opt/IBM/db2/V9.1/bin/db2fmcd (UNIX)
```

or

```
db2fmcu -u -p /opt/ibm/db2/V9.1/bin/db2fmcd (Linux)
```

If successful, the result will show

```
FMC: up: PID = 18602
```

> **NOTE** You can prevent the FMC from running by typing the following command as root: **db2fmcu -d.**

Once the FMC is active, you can start the fault monitor daemon for each instance. For each DB2 instance for which you want to start the fault monitor, type the following commands:

```
db2iauto -on db2instname
db2fm -i db2instname -f on
db2fm -i db2instname -U
```

where **db2instname** is the name of the DB2 instance for which you want to start the fault monitor. The first command sets the DB2AUTOSTART registry variable to ON. This enables the FMC to automatically start the instance when the server is started. The second command creates the fault monitor registry file and updates the FM_ON parameter to YES in the file. The third command starts the **db2fmd** fault monitor daemon. If your instance is brought offline, the FMC daemon will notice it, and bring it back online. If for some reason the FMC daemon is killed, the init daemon will respawn the FMC daemon.

> **NOTE** The fault monitor will only become inactive if the db2stop command is issued. If a DB2 instance is shut down in any other way, the fault monitor will start it up again.

14.14 Case Study

You have just been assigned a new task: to clone the production database PROD1 on a Windows server to another Windows test server. These are the criteria:

- The cloned database name is TEST1.
- The containers for TEST1 must be redefined. They must reside on the D: drive of the test server.
- TEST1 must contain the most recent data in PROD1.

1. First, take a backup of the database PROD1. Because PROD1 is a 24×7 production database, it is not possible to perform an offline backup. Therefore, you decide to perform an online backup:

```
db2 backup db prod1 online to d:\temp
```

The backup image is created as:

```
D:\temp\PROD1.0\DB2\NODE0000\CATN0000\20040414\170803.001
```

2. Obtain the table space container information on PROD1. This information is needed to define table space containers for the test database.

A. First, list all table spaces in PROD1, as shown in Figure 14.44.

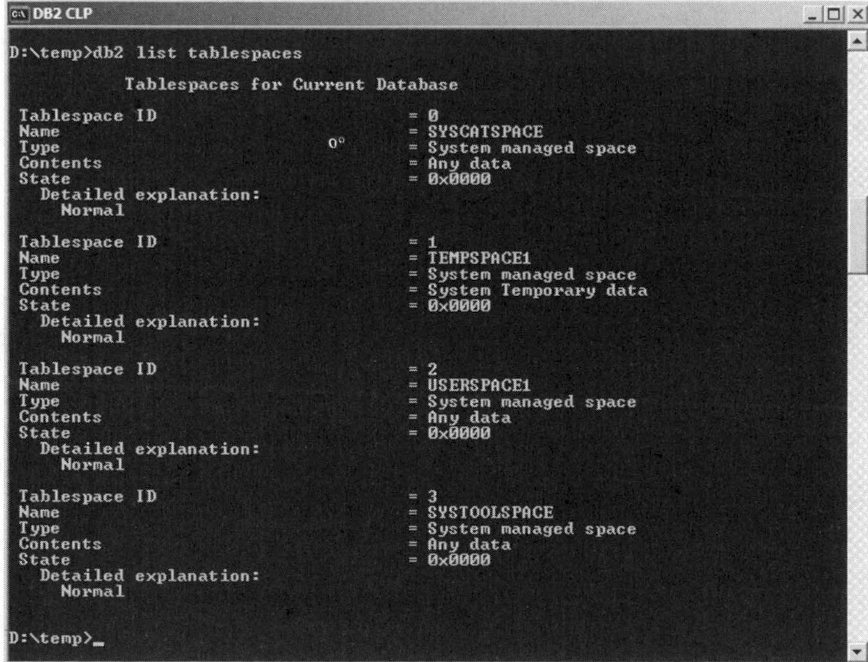

Figure 14.44 Getting table space infermation from PRODI

B. Then, list the containers for each table space, as shown in Figure 14.45.

Since all three table spaces are SMS table spaces, all the containers are directories.

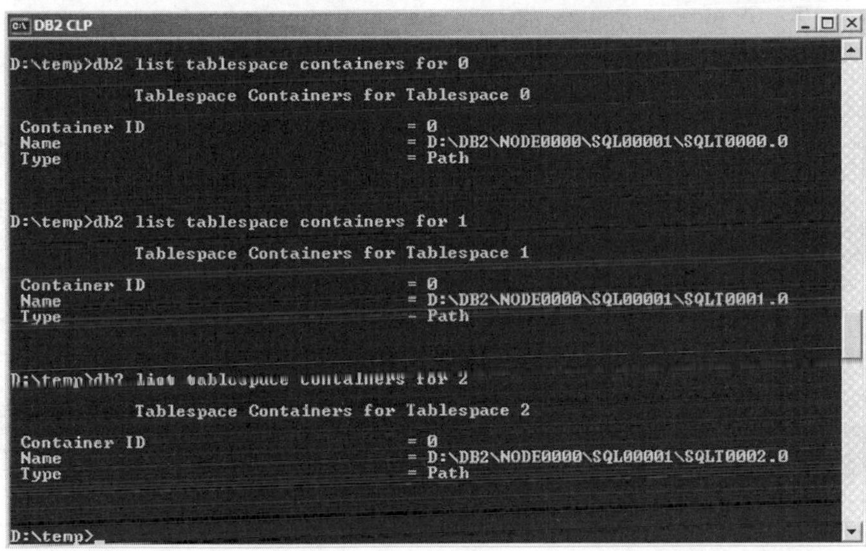

Figure 14.45 Getting container information from PROD1

3. Transfer the backup image over to the test server. FTP the backup image, including the folders and directories starting at D:\temp, over to the test server.
4. Perform a database redirected restore and define the table space containers for database TEST1, as shown in Figure 14.46.

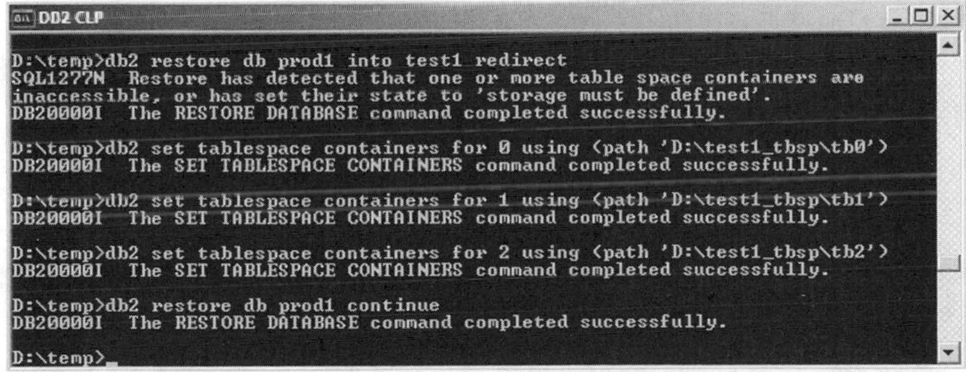

Figure 14.46 Performing redirected restore of PROD1 into TEST1

5. Perform a roll forward on the newly restored database TEST.
   A. At this point, you cannot connect to TEST1 yet. A connect attempt will receive the error SQL1117N, signifying a ROLL FORWARD PENDING state.

B. To roll forward, you need to find out which logs are needed. Run the **ROLLFORWARD DATABASE** command with the **QUERY STATUS** option (see Figure 14.47).

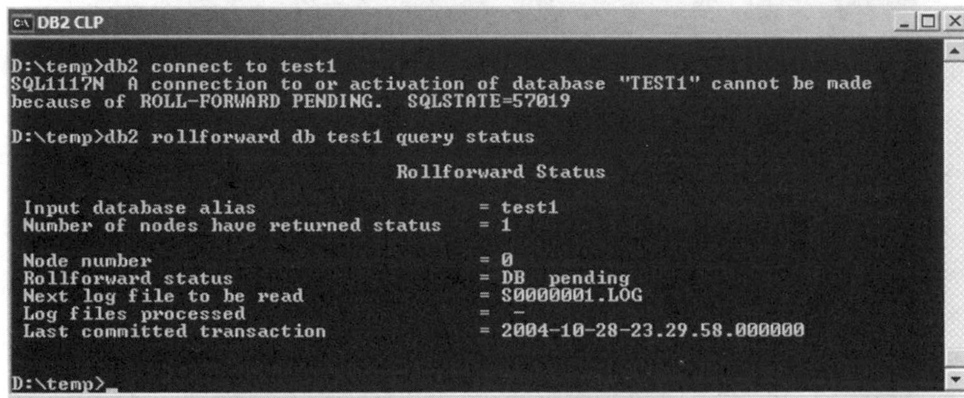

DB2 CLP
D:\temp>db2 connect to test1
SQL1117N A connection to or activation of database "TEST1" cannot be made because of ROLL-FORWARD PENDING. SQLSTATE=57019
D:\temp>db2 rollforward db test1 query status
Rollforward Status
Input database alias = test1
Number of nodes have returned status = 1
Node number = 0
Rollforward status = DB pending
Next log file to be read = S0000001.LOG
Log files processed = -
Last committed transaction = 2004-10-28-23.29.58.000000
D:\temp>

Figure 14.47 Finding out which logs are needed to perform roll forward

Figure 14.47 shows the next log file to be read is S0000000.LOG. This means that you have to transfer all the logs in the active log directory of PROD1, starting at S0000000.LOG, to the active log directory of TEST1.

C. To find out where the active log directory is for PROD1, issue the **GET DB CFG FOR prod1** command. The active log directory is indicated as **Path to log files.**

```
Path to log files D:\DB2\NODE0000\SQL00003\SQLOGDIR\
```

D. The logs in this directory are: S0000000.LOG, S0000001.LOG, S0000002.LOG, and S0000003.LOG. Transfer all of these logs to the test server and into the active log directory of TEST1, which is on D:\DB2\NODE0000\SQL00001\ SQLOGDIR\. (If you list this directory, you will see that it is currently empty.)

E. Perform a roll forward operation on TEST1, as shown in Figure 14.48.

6. Connect to TEST1 and verify that it contains the correct data.

```
DB2 CLP
D:\temp>db2 rollforward db test1 to end of logs and complete

                                 Rollforward Status

 Input database alias                   = test1
 Number of nodes have returned status   = 1

 Node number                            = 0
 Rollforward status                     = not pending
 Next log file to be read               =
 Log files processed                    = S0000001.LOG - S0000004.LOG
 Last committed transaction             = 2004-10-29-00.01.52.000000

DB20000I  The ROLLFORWARD command completed successfully.
```

Figure 14.48 Performing the roll forward operation on TEST1

14.15 Summary

In this chapter you have learned about units of work, (UOW), logging methods, and different backup and recovery strategies.

A unit of work (UOW) is composed of one or more statements and completed by a **COMMIT** or **ROLLBACK** statement. If a UOW is interrupted in the middle of processing, all statements executed up to that point will be rolled back. This ensures data integrity.

When a database is activated, DB2 allocates a number of primary logs, based on the setting of the LOGPRIMARY database configuration parameter. When the primary log space fills up, DB2 allocates secondary logs, one at a time. When the maximum number of secondary logs is reached, specified by the LOGSECOND database parameter, DB2 encounters a log full condition. At this point, uncommitted transactions are rolled back.

There are three types of database recovery: crash, version, and roll forward recovery. Crash recovery and version recovery are the defaults. To enable roll forward recovery, you need enable archival logging.

There are three logging methods available in DB2: circular, archival, and infinite active logging. Circular logging is the default logging method. However, it does not support roll forward recovery. Archival logging is enabled by setting the LOGARCHMETH1 database configuration parameter. Both archival logging and infinite active logging support roll forward recovery. Log mirroring is valuable in maintaining a redundant active log path.

The **RECOVER DATABASE** command combines both the **RESTORE** and **ROLLFORWARD** commands into one easy step. The **RECOVER DATABASE** command can continue where it left off if it is interrupted. Alternatively, it is possible to start the recover process from the beginning by specifying the **RESTART** option.

DB2 monitors instances using the Fault Monitor facility to improve database availability. If there is a fault that brings down an instance, the fault monitor can sense the disruption, and bring the instance back up automatically.

Log shipping is used to build a standby database on another server, in case the primary database fails. A backup of the primary database is taken and restored onto the standby database. The **ROLLFORWARD DATABASE** command should be continuously executed on the standby server to keep the standby server synchronized with the primary. To activate standby database if the primary fails, issue the **ROLLFORWARD DATABASE** command with the **STOP** option. This will enable connectivity to the standby database.

HADR setup requires a primary and secondary server. Log pages that are flushed to the log file on disk at the primary database are constantly shipped and applied to the secondary database. When a failure occurs on the primary database, a takeover operation is initiated on the secondary database, which then becomes the new primary. Since the secondary database is already online, failover can be accomplished very quickly, resulting in minimal downtime. There are 3 HADR synchronization modes (SYNC, NEARSYNC, and ASYNC), which can be selected depending on availability and performance requirements. The DB2 automatic client reroute feature can be enabled with HADR to allow your applications to reconnect to the secondary database if a failure has occurred on the primary.

Write suspend (suspended I/O) support offers a much faster way to perform database backups. This is achieved by taking an instantaneous disk copy of the primary database while it is in a write-suspend mode. During this time, all write operations on the database are suspended; however, other database functions still function normally. After the split mirror is completed, the database is returned to its normal state. No restore operation is needed to restore the split mirror. Instead, you use the **db2inidb** command to initialize the split mirror database. There are three ways you can initialize the split mirror: as a clone database, a standby database, or a backup image of the primary database.

Review Questions

1. Besides crash recovery, what are the other two types of database recovery?
2. What option allows you to back up the logs along with the database?
3. When are secondary logs created and destroyed?
4. What condition triggers the logs to be flushed from the log buffer to log files?
5. TRUE or FALSE: The automatic reroute feature can only be used with HADR?
6. What is the danger with the TAKEOVER BY FORCE scenario?
7. What should you do when you find out that an index is corrupted?
8. How do you determine the minimum recovery time for a table space?
9. Which of the following requires manual archival and retrieval of log files?
   A. USEREXIT
   B. DISK
   C. LOGRETAIN
   D. VENDOR
10. A Unit of Work consists of one or more statements, and is terminated by which of the following?
    A. COMMIT
    B. TERMINATE
    C. RESET
    D. ROLL BACK
11. Which of the following is the default logging method used by DB2?
    A. Infinite logging
    B. Circular logging
    C. Archival logging
    D. Round-robin logging

12. Which of the following database configuration parameters specifies the redundant active log path?
    A. FAILARCHPATH
    B. LOGARCHOPT1
    C. MIRRORLOGPATH
    D. LOGARCHMETH1
13. Given a mirror image of a source database, what must you do to restore the database image to a new server?
    A. RESTORE DATABASE image on the new server
    B. ROLLFORWARD logs to end of file
    C. Unmirror the source database image onto the new server using the same method you used to split the mirror
    D. Use the DB2INIDB tool with mirror option
14. Given that you must restore a database from backup, which of the following objects must be available in order to recover the transactions performed after a backup was taken?
    A. Table space backups
    B. Buffer pools
    C. Logs
    D. Database snapshot output
15. Given the following database configuration information:

```
Number of primary log files (LOGPRIMARY) = 5
Number of secondary log files (LOGSECOND) = 5
Path to log files = C:\logsforDB1\
```

    which of the following correctly lists the contents of the C:\logsforDB1 directory immediately after issuing the activate database command for the database, if log retain is *not* enabled?

    A. Directory of C:\LOGSFORDB1\

```
2004-03-10 06:06p 1,032,192 S0000000.LOG
2004-03-10 06:06p 1,032,192 S0000001.LOG
2004-03-10 06:06p 1,032,192 S0000002.LOG
2004-03-10 06:06p 1,032,192 S0000003.LOG
2004-03-10 06:06p 1,032,192 S0000004.LOG
```

    B. Directory of C:\MYLOGS\

```
2004-03-10 06:06p 1,032,192 S0000001.LOG
2004-03-10 06:06p 1,032,192 S0000002.LOG
2004-03-10 06:06p 1,032,192 S0000003.LOG
2004-03-10 06:06p 1,032,192 S0000004.LOG
2004-03-10 06:06p 1,032,192 S0000005.LOG
```

C. Directory of C:\LOGSFORDB1\

```
2004-03-10 06:06p 1,032,192 S0000000.LOG
2004-03-10 06:06p 1,032,192 S0000001.LOG
2004-03-10 06:06p 1,032,192 S0000002.LOG
2004-03-10 06:06p 1,032,192 S0000003.LOG
2004-03-10 06:06p 1,032,192 S0000004.LOG
2004-03-10 06:06p 1,032,192 S0000005.LOG
2004-03-10 06:06p 1,032,192 S0000006.LOG
2004-03-10 06:06p 1,032,192 S0000007.LOG
2004-03-10 06:06p 1,032,192 S0000008.LOG
2004-03-10 06:06p 1,032,192 S0000009.LOG
```

D. Directory of C:\MYLOGS\

```
2004-03-10 06:06p 1,032,192 S0000001.LOG
2004-03-10 06:06p 1,032,192 S0000002.LOG
2004-03-10 06:06p 1,032,192 S0000003.LOG
2004-03-10 06:06p 1,032,192 S0000004.LOG
2004-03-10 06:06p 1,032,192 S0000005.LOG
2004-03-10 06:06p 1,032,192 S0000006.LOG
2004-03-10 06:06p 1,032,192 S0000007.LOG
2004-03-10 06:06p 1,032,192 S0000008.LOG
2004-03-10 06:06p 1,032,192 S0000009.LOG
2004-03-10 06:06p 1,032,192 S0000010.LOG
```

16. Which of the following activates infinite active log space?

A. **Logsecond = 0**

B. **Logprimary = 0**

C. **Logsecond =-1**

D. **Logprimary = -1**

17. Which of the following configuration parameters enables on backups?

A. Logsecond = 0

B. Logarchmeth1 = off

C. Logarchmeth1 = logretain

D. Mirror log path = userexit

18. Which of the following is not allowed during a redirected restore?

A. Change from DMS file to DMS raw containers

B. Change from DMS file to SMS containers

C. Change the number of containers in an SMS table space

D. Change the number of containers in a DMS table space

19. Given a DB2 client in the Central time zone, and a DB2 server in the Eastern time zone, when the command **`ROLLFORWARD DATABASE sample TO timestamp USING LOCAL TIME`** is issued on the client, which time is used?

A. The time on the client

B. The time on the server

C. The UTC time

D. The GMT time

20. Which of the following is not a valid option for the **db2inidb** command?
   A. Standby
   B. Mirror
   C. Snapshot
   D. Backup

CHAPTER 15

The DB2 Process Model

Have you ever wondered what happens "behind the scenes" when your application connects to the data server? What handles the request? What actually does the work and returns you the results? When you check your system, you may see many threads spawned under the main DB2 system engine process. What are these threads, and what are they used for? Understanding the different DB2 threads and how DB2 works will help you determine the nature of a problem more easily.

In this chapter you will learn about:

- The DB2 process model
- The threaded engine infrastructure
- The various types of DB2 agents
- Monitoring and tuning the usage of DB2 agents

15.1 The DB2 Process Model: The Big Picture

Figure 15.1 shows the DB2 engine process model. This illustrates what happens behind the scenes when a client application connects to a DB2 database.

As shown in Figure 15.1, a client application connects to the DB2 data server using one of the supported communication protocols.

- Local client applications connect to the data server using the Inter-Process Communication (IPC) protocol such as shared memory and semaphores.
- Remote client applications connect to the data server using the TCP/IP, or Named Pipes communication protocol.

> **NOTE** Named Pipes are only supported on Windows platforms.

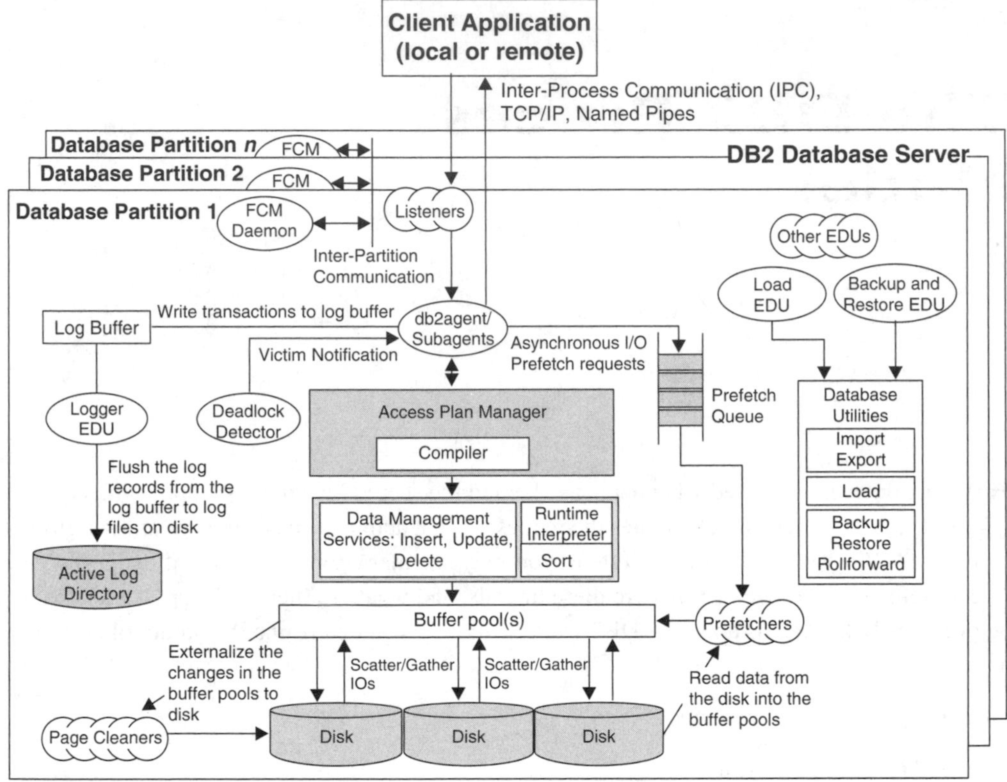

Figure 15.1 The DB2 process model

When a client application connects to the database, the connection request is first accepted by an agent known as the **listener.** There are different listeners for different communication protocols:

- *db2ipccm* for local client connections
- *db2tcpcm* for remote TCP/IP connections
- *db2tcpdm* for TCP/IP discovery tool requests

The Configuration Assistant (CA) on the DB2 client makes discovery requests when it is searching the network for remote DB2 servers and their databases. The remote connection listeners are enabled when the DB2COMM registry variable and the appropriate Database Manager Configuration parameters are set (see Chapter 6, Configuring Client and Server Connectivity).

The *db2ipccm* listener is enabled by default; therefore no additional steps are required.

After the listener accepts a client-application connection, it will assign a **coordinator agent,** *db2agent,* to work on behalf of that application. This agent will communicate with the application and handle all its requests. If the database server instance is multi-partitioned, or if

INTRA_PARALLEL is set to YES, the coordinator agent will distribute the work to a number of subagents, and its role changes to coordinating these subagents.

> **NOTE** Both the subagents and coordinator agents work on behalf of the application. They both can be referred to as **worker agents** for the application.

If the access plan provided by the **Access Plan Manager** indicates that prefetching is needed, then the worker agents send the prefetch requests to a **prefetch queue.** (**Prefetching** means that one or more pages are retrieved from disk into the buffer pool in the expectation that they will be required by an application. Prefetching helps improve performance by reducing the I/O wait time.)

The prefetch request queue is monitored by agents called **prefetchers,** which take the requests from the queue and service each request by retrieving the required data from disk into the buffer pools.

The amount of data to retrieve for each prefetch request is determined by the prefetch size of the specific table space where the data is stored. (You can optionally specify this value in the **CREATE TABLESPACE** and the **ALTER TABLESPACE** statements, using the PREFETCHSIZE parameter.) If the prefetch size is not specified for a table space, then DB2 uses the value for the DFT_PREFETCH_SZ configuration parameter as the default. The default value is AUTOMATIC. Any parameter set to AUTOMATIC indicates that DB2 will calculate the value. In this case, DB2 will calculate an appropriate prefetch size for a table space based on the extent size, the number of containers, and the number of physical spindles per container. This frees you from having to determine the appropriate value for the table space prefetch size. The number of prefetchers is determined by the NUM_IOSERVERS database configuration parameter, which has a default value of AUTOMATIC.

Once the required data is in the buffer pools, the worker agents then perform the updates requested by the application. These updates stay in the buffer pools until a later time, when the **page cleaners** kick in and start writing the changes from the buffer pool to disk in batches. Page cleaners are backup processes that are independent of the application agents. They look for pages from the buffer pool that are no longer needed and write the pages back to disk. The number of page cleaners is determined by the NUM_IOCLEANERS database configuration parameter, which has a default value of AUTOMATIC. (See Chapter 17, Database Performance Considerations, for information about how the number of page cleaners and prefetchers impacts performance.)

All transactions made by the application are logged into DB2 transaction logs by the **logger** agent. Logging ensures data recoverability (see the discussion on data recovery in Chapter 14, Developing Database Backup and Recovery Solutions).

There are other database agents that exist in a DB2 engine, such as the **load agent** shown in Figure 15.1.

In a DPF environment, the same set of agents exists in each database partition. The **Fast Communications Manager** (FCM) agents are responsible for interpartition communications.

15.2 Threaded Engine Infrastructure

Prior to DB2 9.5, DB2 on Linux and UNIX used the process based model in which each agent ran in its own process, while DB2 on Windows used a multi-threaded model. In Version 9.5, DB2 introduces the threaded engine infrastructure on Linux and UNIX to provide a consistent threading architecture across all DB2 server platforms. Such design change not only requires less system resources, but also simplifies DB2 implementation and administration. The most two significant advantages introduced by the threaded engine infrastructure are the Simplified Memory configuration and the Automatic Agent configuration, which are discussed across the rest of this chapter, and Chapter 16, The DB2 Memory Model.

15.2.1 The DB2 Processes

In the new threaded engine model, all **Engine Dispatchable Units** (EDUs) are implemented as **threads** inside the main engine process. So the number of DB2 processes has decreased significantly.

Table 15.1 lists and describes the DB2 processes available in Version 9.5.

Table 15.1 The DB2 Processes

Process Name	Description	Platform
db2acd	The autonomic computing daemon. Used to perform client-side automatic tasks, such as health monitor, automatic maintenance utilities, and the new admin scheduler. This process was formerly called db2hmon. It runs multiple threads that establish connections to the database engine to perform this work. **Note:** The health-monitor process runs as a DB2 fenced mode process, and it appears as db2fmp on Windows.	Linux and UNIX only
db2ckpwd	Checks user IDs and passwords on the DB2 server. Since DB2 relies on operating system-level authentication, this thread verifies the user ID and password when a user or application connects to a database on the server. This authentication will occur when authentication is set to SERVER or when a connection is made from a nonsecure operating system.	Linux and UNIX only
db2fmcd	The fault monitor coordinator daemon. One per physical machine.	UNIX only

Table 15.1 The DB2 Processes *(Continued)*

Process Name	Description	Platform
db2fmd	The fault monitor daemon that is started for every instance of DB2 that is monitored by the fault monitor. It is monitored by the coordinator daemon (*db2fmcd*), so if you kill the *db2fmd* process, *db2fmcd* will bring it back up.	UNIX only
db2fmp	Fenced processes that run user code on the server outside the firewall for both stored procedures and user-defined functions. The db2fmp is always a separate process, but may be multithreaded depending on the types of routines it executes. **Note:** This process replaces both the db2udf and db2dari processes that were used in previous versions of DB2.	All
db2sysc	The main DB2 system controller or engine. In DB2 9.5, there is only one multithreaded main engine process for the entire partition. All Engine Dispatchable Units (EDUs) are threads inside this process. Without this process, the database server cannot function. On Windows the process name is db2syscs.	All
db2vend	The fenced vendor process introduced in DB2 9.5. In a threaded engine, DB2 cannot afford to have vendor code changing its signal masks, launching new threads, corrupting agents' stacks. So all vendor code runs in this process outside of the engine.	Linux and UNIX only
db2wdog	The DB2 watchdog. The watchdog is the parent of the main engine process, db2sysc. It is responsible for the following internal tasks: • Clean up IPC resources if the db2sysc process abnormally terminates. • Spawn db2fmp processes as well as the health-monitor process. Upon the abnormal termination of those processes, clean up db2fmp system resources and restart the health monitor if needed. • Set the agent absolute scheduling priority. Note that setting absolute agent priority is not supported for nonroot install.	Linux and UNIX only

> **NOTE** The Global Daemon Spawner (db2gds) process on Linux and UNIX platforms no longer exists in the threaded engine.

On AIX, Linux, and HP-UX, use the **`ps –fu instancename`** command to display the DB2 processes owned by the instance. Alternatively, you can use the **`db2_local_ps`** command, which displays the DB2 processes for an instance under each database partition. Note that the *db2wdog* process is owned by root, not the instance owner. Its sole purpose is to watch for the system controller.

On Solaris, the default **/usr/bin/ps** command only shows *db2sysc* for all processes (e.g., db2wdog and db2acd). To display the DB2 processes with their actual names, use the **db2ptree** command.

Figure 15.2 shows the list of DB2 processes after an instance is started by **db2start.** The instance name is *db2inst1*, and it has two database partitions.

```
     UID    PID   PPID  C    STIME    TTY  TIME CMD
    root 491738      1  0 13:25:25      -  0:02 /opt/IBM/db2/V9.5/bin/db2fmcd
    root 778382      1  0 14:32:16      -  0:02 db2wdog 0
    root 340050      1  0 14:32:19      -  0:00 db2wdog 1
    root 467004 594148  0 14:32:18      -  0:00 db2ckpwd 0
    root 532498 594148  0 14:32:18      -  0:00 db2ckpwd 0
    root 569548 594148  0 14:32:18      -  0:00 db2ckpwd 0
    root 692452 684248  0 14:32:19      -  0:00 db2ckpwd 1
    root 700592 684248  0 14:32:19      -  0:00 db2ckpwd 1
    root 741556 684248  0 14:32:19      -  0:00 db2ckpwd 1
db2inst1 794864 778382  0 14:32:20      -  0:00 db2acd 0
db2inst1 282730 778382  0 14:32:18      -  0:00 db2sysc 0
db2inst1 184562 340050  0 14:32:19      -  0:00 db2sysc 1
db2inst1 475244 340050  0 14:32:19      -  0:02 db2acd 1
```

Figure 15.2 DB2 processes after an instance is started

15.3 The DB2 Engine Dispatchable Units

Each oval shown in Figure 15.3 represents a DB2 thread. The DB2 engine is where these threads live; hence these threads are called DB2 Engine Dispatchable Units or **EDUs.** Therefore, a coordinator agent, a page cleaner, and a subagent are all EDUs.

In the new threaded engine model, the EDUs are implemented as threads across Linux, UNIX, and Windows platforms. All EDUs are peers, and have access to each other's memory and handles (e.g., file handles, sockets) because they all run inside a single process.

Figure 15.3 shows the hierarchy for some main DB2 EDUs and a firewall between the client applications and the DB2 engine because the client applications run in a different address space from the DB2 engine. This way, if applications behave in an inappropriate manner, they will not overwrite DB2's internal buffers or files within the DB2 engine.

The *db2fmp* process is the fenced-mode process; it is responsible for executing fenced-stored procedures and user-defined functions outside the firewall. If stored procedures and functions are defined as unfenced, then they will run within the same address space as the DB2 engine. By doing so, the performance of stored procedures and functions can be improved. However, there is an added potential risk to the DB2 engine: These stored procedures and functions can potentially

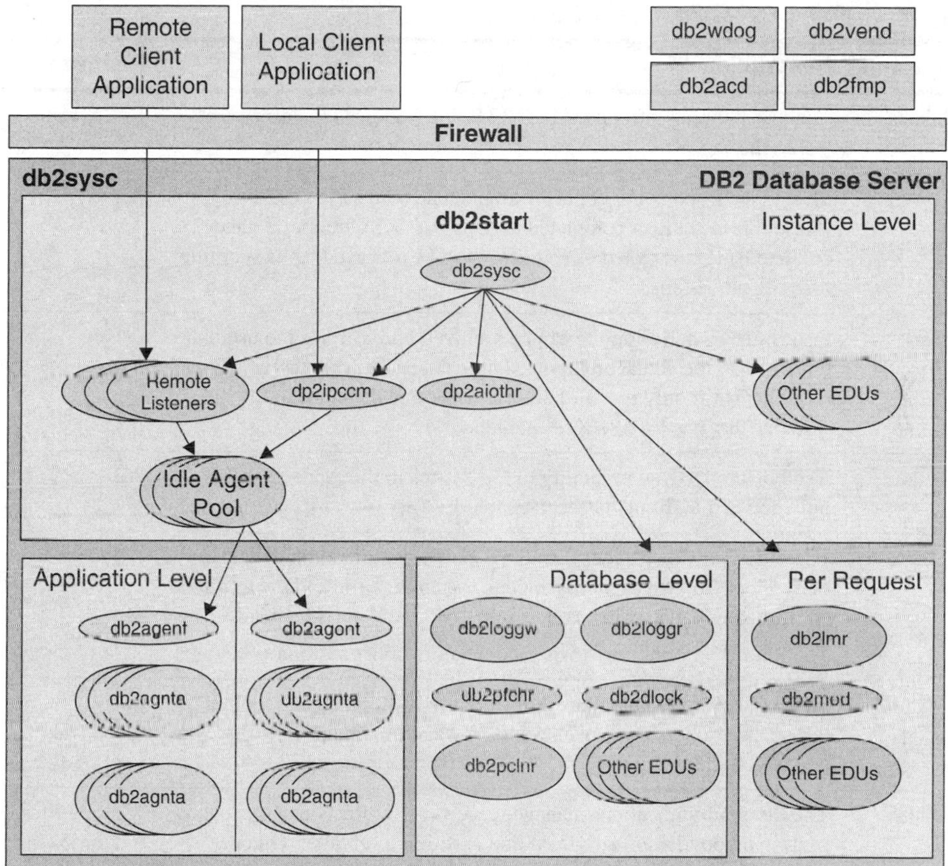

Figure 15.3 The main DB2 EDUs

overwrite DB2 internal buffers, causing DB2 to crash. This is why stored procedures and user functions should never run unfenced unless tested thoroughly.

In Figure 15.3, the EDUs are grouped in different levels. Let's look at what role each of them plays.

15.3.1 The DB2 Instance-Level EDUs

The core engine process is the DB2 system-controller process, *db2sysc*. The *db2sysc* process runs the entire DB2 engine infrastructure. This is the first process created when the instance starts. The *db2sysc* process then spawns an initial set of threads to perform various tasks, such as the listeners, which listen for client connections.

Table 15.2 lists and describes the DB2 instance-level EDUs.

Table 15.2 The DB2 Instance-Level EDUs

EDU Name	Description	Platform
db2alarm	The alarm thread introduced in DB2 9.5. It handles all alarm events inside the engine.	UNIX/Linux
db2aiothr	The Asynchronous I/O collector threads introduced in DB2 9.5. These threads collect completed asynchronous I/O requests. Once collected, the completed I/O requests will be retrieved by its submitter for post-processing.	All
db2cart	Determines when a log file can be archived and invokes the userexit thread to do the actual archiving. There is one *db2cart* thread per instance, but it only runs if there is at least one database in the instance that has USEREXIT enabled.	All
db2chkau	Used by the DB2 audit facility to log entries to the Audit log. It is only active if auditing has been enabled.	All
db2disp	The DB2 agent dispatcher thread. Dispatches application connections between the logical agent assigned to the application and the available coordinating agents when connection concentration is enabled. This thread will only exist when connection concentration is enabled.	All
db2extev	The External Event handlers introduced in DB2 9.5. These helper threads wait on external post events to wake up the listeners that wait on the completion queue.	All
db2fcmr	The fast communications manager-receiver daemon is responsible for routing inbound messages from one partition to another. One per server, per partition.	Multipartitioned database environment only
db2fcms	The fast communications manager-sender daemon is responsible for routing outbound messages from one partition to another. One per server, per partition.	Multipartitioned database environment only
db2fmtlg	Preallocates log files in the log path when the database is configured with LOGRETAIN ON and USEREXIT OFF. This is done so the engine process does not need to wait while switching from one log file to the next during normal processing.	All
db2glock	Global deadlock detector. Coordinates the information gathered from the *db2dlock* thread on each database partition to check for deadlock conditions that exist between database partitions. The *db2glock* thread runs on the catalog partition of a multi-partitioned database.	Multipartitioned database environment only

Table 15.2 The DB2 Instance-Level EDUs

EDU Name	Description	Platform
db2govd	The DB2 Governor daemon, a reactive governing thread that takes snapshots at the interval specified in the governor configuration file and checks the snapshot against all configured rules. If a rule is broken, the specified action is taken. This thread only exists when the DB2 governor is enabled.	All
db2licc	The license controller.	All
db2panic	The panic agent. Handles urgent requests after agent limits have been reached on any of the database's partitions.	Multipartitioned database environment only
db2pdbc	The Parallel Database (PDB) Controller. Handles parallel requests from remote nodes.	Multipartitioned database environment only
db2rebal	The rebalancer thread. Called when containers are added to an existing table space and a rebalance of the existing data is required. This thread performs the rebalance asynchronously.	All
db2resync	The resync manager thread. Supports applications that are using two-phase commit.	All
db2srvlst	Manages lists of addresses for systems such as DB2 for z/OS.	All
db2syslog	The system-logger thread. Writes to the operating system error log facility. On UNIX, this must be enabled by editing the file syslog.conf. On Windows, DB2 will automatically write the Windows event log.	All
db2ipccm	IPC communication manager. One per database partition. This is the interprocess communication listener for local client connections. A local client connection is a connection made from an application or the CLP within the same computer where the DB2 server is running.	All
db2sysc	The system controller thread. This thread is responsible for the start up and shut down and the management of the running instance. Its EDU name is the same as the process name of the main db2sysc process, which spawned this thread.	All
db2tcpcm	TCP communication manager. It works as a communication listener for TCP/IP connection requests. When a connection request is received, the listener associates the connection with an agent and then resumes listening for more connection requests.	All

(continues)

Table 15.2 The DB2 Instance-Level EDUs *(Continued)*

EDU Name	Description	Platform
db2tcpdm	Communication listener for TCP/IP discovery requests. Discovery requests are made by the Configuration Assistant when it is searching the network for remote DB2 servers and their databases.	All
db2thcln	The stack cleanup thread introduced in DB2 9.5. It waits for any EDU to exit and frees the stack memory.	UNIX / Linux

DB2 9.5 maintains the list of EDU names and their EDU IDs inside the database manager engine. A new option for the **db2pd** tool, **db2pd-edus,** is used to list all EDUs and their names and thread IDs to faciliate problem determination. See Chapter 4, Using the DB2 Tools, for more information about the **db2pd** tool.

In a Database Partitioning Feature (DPF) environment, each partition has the same set of DB2 EDUs. Figure 15.4 shows the list of DB2 EDUs after an instance is started by **db2start.** The instance has two database partitions. The last column indicates the partition with which the EDU is associated.

```
$ db2pd -edus —alldbpartitionnums

>>>> List of all EDUs for database partition 0 <<<<

db2sysc PID: 282730
db2wdog PID: 778382
db2acd  PID: 794864

EDU ID      TID          Kernel TID      EDU Name
===============================================================================
4627        4627         1601541         db2agent (idle) 0
4370        4370         1712235         db2agent (idle) 0
4113        4113         1564777         db2agent (idle) 0
3856        3856         1536007         db2agent (idle) 0
3599        3599         1175745         db2resync 0
3342        3342         1708049         db2tcpcm 0
3085        3085         1339579         db2tcpcm 0
2828        2828         1097901         db2tcpcm 0
2571        2571         1863791         db2ipccm 0
2314        2314         1597663         db2licc 0
2057        2057         1146939         db2pdbc 0
1800        1800         921613          db2extev 0
1543        1543         1908915         db2fcmr 0
1286        1286         663803          db2extev 0
1029        1029         1241275         db2fcms 0
772         772          1667131         db2thcln 0
515         515          1843227         db2aiothr 0
2           2            1835129         db2alarm 0
258         258          1826883         db2sysc 0
```

Figure 15.4 DB2 EDUs after an instance is started

```
>>>> List of all EDUs for database partition 1 <<<<

db2sysc PID: 184562
db2wdog PID: 340050
db2acd  PID: 475244

EDU ID      TID           Kernel TID     EDU Name
==============================================================================
3856        3856          1880227        db2agent (idle) 1
3599        3599          1896545        db2agent (idle) 1
3342        3342          1871907        db2agent (idle) 1
3085        3085          1589379        db2agent (idle) 1
2828        2828          1867995        db2resync 1
2571        2571          950405         db2ipccm 1
2314        2314          1114333        db2licc 1
2057        2057          1757315        db2pdbc 1
1800        1800          1187963        db2extev 1
1543        1543          1429759        db2fcmr 1
1286        1286          1110031        db2extev 1
1029        1029          1802471        db2fcms 1
772         772           1704093        db2thcln 1
515         515           1622169        db2aiothr 1
2           2             1839135        db2alarm 1
258         258           872579         db2sysc 1
```

Figure 15.4 DB2 EDUs after an instance is started *(Continued)*

15.3.2 The DB2 Database-Level EDUs

When a database becomes active, it starts several threads to handle database-level tasks such as prefetching, logging, and page cleaning. These threads are also spawned by the main engine process, *db2sysc*.

Table 15.3 shows the DB2 EDUs at the database level.

Table 15.3 The DB2 Database-Level EDUs

EDU Name	Description	Applicability
db2dlock	Local deadlock detector. One per database partition. Scans the lock list and looks for deadlock conditions. When a deadlock condition is encountered, one of the applications/transactions involved is chosen as the victim and rolled back.	All
db2glock	In a multipartitioned database environment, an additional EDU called db2glock is used to coordinate the information gathered from the db2dlock EDU on each partition. db2glock runs only on the catalog partition.	Multipartitioned database environment only

(continues)

Table 15.3 The DB2 Database-Level EDUs *(Continued)*

EDU Name	Description	Applicability
db2evm<p1><p2>(<p3>)	The event monitor thread, where <p1> can be • g—global file event monitor • l—local file event monitor • t—table event monitor • gp—global piped event monitor • lp—local piped event monitor where <p2> can be • i—coordinator • p—not coordinator and <p3> is the event monitor name. There is one *db2 event* thread per active event monitor, per active database. These threads capture the defined "events" and write to the output file specified for the Event Monitor.	All
db2hadrp	The HADR primary server thread. If HADR is enabled, controls the synchronization and heartbeat monitoring.	All
db2hadrs	The HADR secondary server thread. If HADR is enabled, controls the synchronization and heartbeat monitoring.	All
db2lfr	The log file reader thread. It processes individual log files.	All
db2loggr	The database log reader. Reads the database log files during transaction processing (i.e., roll back and roll forward operations) and restart recovery.	All
db2loggw	The database log writer. Flushes log records from the log buffer to the log files on disk.	All
db2logmgr	The DB2 log manager. Manages log files for a recoverable database. Controls the event-monitor threads and backup and restore threads.	All
db2logts	Collects historical information about which logs are active when a table space is modified. This information is recorded in the DB2TSCHG.HIS file in the database directory. It speeds up table space roll forward recovery by enabling the skipping of log files that are not needed for the roll-forward operation.	All

Table 15.3 The DB2 Database-Level EDUs *(Continued)*

EDU Name	Description	Applicability
db2pclnr	The buffer pool page cleaners. Asynchronously writes dirty pages from the buffer pool(s) back to disk. (A dirty page is one that was changed after it was read into the buffer pool, and the image on disk is no longer the same as the image in the buffer pool.) Works to ensure that there is room in the buffer pools for new pages being retrieved for applications. When the page cleaners are "triggered," they all run at the same time. Once they complete their assigned work they sleep until triggered again. The number of page cleaners per database is configured by the NUM_IOCLEANERS database configuration parameter.	All
db2pfchr	The buffer pool prefetchers. Reads data and index information from disk and into the database buffer pool(s) before it is read on behalf of applications. Prefetchers perform this "read-ahead" asynchronously. The DB2 agents, acting on behalf of the applications, send prefetch requests which are serviced by the prefetchers. The prefetchers perform big-block I/O to read the data more efficiently. The number of prefetchers per database is configured by the NUM_IOSERVERS database configuration parameter.	All
db2redom	The redo master. During recovery, processes redo log records and assigns log records to redo workers for processing.	All
db2redow	The redo worker. During recovery, processes redo log records at the request of the redo master.	All
db2stmm	The self-tuning memory manager thread. The db2stmm agent is part of the new self-tuning memory feature added in DB2 9. This agent remains connected to the database at all times and is not active if the database is activated in exclusive mode.	All
db2taskd	The background task daemon. The db2taskd agent is an internal daemon that distributes background database tasks introduced in DB2 9. This agent remains connected to the database at all times and is not active if the database is activated in exclusive mode.	All
db2wlmd	The workload manager daemon new in DB2 9.5. It is responsible for synchronizing time intervals for Workload Manager data collection. It starts when the database comes up.	All

As an example, Figure 15.5 shows the list of database-level EDUs after the *SAMPLE* database is started by a connection to the database. You can see that a set of database-level EDUs is created for each partition. For example, each partition has one db2loggr EDU, one db2loggw EDU, one db2dlock EDU, and three db2pfchr EDUs.

```
$ db2pd -edus -alldbpartitionnums

>>>> List of all EDUs for database partition 0 <<<<

db2sysc PID: 282730
db2wdog PID: 778382
db2acd  PID: 794864

EDU ID      TID          Kernel TID      EDU Name
================================================================================
7970        7970         1654893         db2agnta (SAMPLE) 0
4897        4897         1474725         db2agntp (SAMPLE) 0
7712        7712         1335315         db2pfchr (SAMPLE) 0
7455        7455         1638629         db2pfchr (SAMPLE) 0
7198        7198         1781763         db2pfchr (SAMPLE) 0
6941        6941         1548451         db2pclnr (SAMPLE) 0
6684        6684         1925329         db2pclnr (SAMPLE) 0
6427        6427         1556687         db2pclnr (SAMPLE) 0
6170        6170         1777817         db2dlock (SAMPLE) 0
5913        5913         1454093         db2glock (SAMPLE) 0
5656        5656         1634479         db2lfr (SAMPLE) 0
5399        5399         1470467         db2loggw (SAMPLE) 0
5142        5142         139497          db2loggr (SAMPLE) 0
4627        4627         1601541         db2taskd (SAMPLE) 0
4370        4370         1712235         db2wlmd (SAMPLE) 0
4113        4113         1564777         db2evmgi (DB2DETAILDEADLOCK) 0
3856        3856         1536007         db2agent (SAMPLE) 0
3599        3599         1175745         db2resync 0
3342        3342         1708049         db2tcpcm 0
3085        3085         1339579         db2tcpcm 0
2828        2828         1097901         db2tcpcm 0
2571        2571         1863791         db2ipccm 0
2314        2314         1597663         db2licc 0
2057        2057         1146939         db2pdbc 0
1800        1800         921613          db2extev 0
1543        1543         1908915         db2fcmr 0
1286        1286         663803          db2extev 0
1029        1029         1241275         db2fcms 0
772         772          1667131         db2thcln 0
515         515          1843227         db2aiothr 0
2           2            1835129         db2alarm 0
258         258          1826883         db2sysc 0

>>>> List of all EDUs for database partition 1 <<<<

db2sysc PID: 184562
db2wdog PID: 340050
db2acd  PID: 475244

EDU ID      TID          Kernel TID      EDU Name
================================================================================
6684        6684         1618173         db2pfchr (SAMPLE) 1
6427        6427         835637          db2pfchr (SAMPLE) 1
6170        6170         1531907         db2pfchr (SAMPLE) 1
```

Figure 15.5 The database-level DB2 EDUs after the SAMPLE database is started

```
5913        5913        884801        db2pclnr (SAMPLE) 1
5656        5656        1900713       db2pclnr (SAMPLE) 1
5399        5399        1675265       db2pclnr (SAMPLE) 1
5142        5142        1142921       db2agntp (SAMPLE) 1
4885        4885        1069245       db2dlock (SAMPLE) 1
4628        4628        909533        db2lfr (SAMPLE) 1
4371        4371        1699949       db2loggw (SAMPLE) 1
4114        4114        1421545       db2loggr (SAMPLE) 1
3856        3856        1880227       db2agent (SAMPLE) 1
3599        3599        1896545       db2agent (idle) 1
3342        3342        1871907       db2agent (idle) 1
3085        3085        1589379       db2agent (idle) 1
2828        2828        1867995       db2resync 1
2571        2571        950405        db2ipccm 1
2314        2314        1114333       db2licc 1
2057        2057        1757315       db2pdbc 1
1800        1800        1187963       db2extev 1
1543        1543        1429759       db2fcmr 1
1286        1286        1110031       db2extev 1
1029        1029        1802471       db2fcms 1
772         772         1704093       db2thcln 1
515         515         1622169       db2aiothr 1
2           2           1839135       db2alarm 1
258         258         872579        db2sysc 1
```

Figure 15.5 The database-level DB2 EDUs after the SAMPLE database is started *(Continued)*

15.3.3 The Application-Level EDUs

Application-level EDUs are also known as **worker agents.** After the listener thread accepts a client connection, it takes a free agent, *db2agent*, from the idle agent pool. If no free agent is available, a new db2agent will be created. The db2agent becomes the coordinator agent for the application, and it will perform all database operations on behalf of the application. There are four types of worker agents.

- Coordinator agents
- Active subagents
- Associated subagents
- Unassociated agents

A **coordinator agent** (db2agent) coordinates the work on behalf of an application and communicates to other agents using the interprocess communication (IPC) protocol (for local connections) or remote-communication protocol (for remote connections). Each connection request from client applications is allocated a coordinator agent.

Figure 15.5 shows that the db2agent EDU

```
3856        3856        1536007       db2agent (SAMPLE) 0
```

is assigned to a connection to the SAMPLE database. The SAMPLE in parenthesis indicates the database name that the db2agent is associated with.

There is one coordinator agent (i.e., the db2agent process) per connection, unless the connection concentrator is enabled. (We discuss the connection concentrator in Section 15.6, The Connection Concentrator.) In a partitioned database environment, the coordinator agent exists on the partition that the application is connected to. In this example, it exists on partition 0 (this is indicated by the 0 beside *SAMPLE*), because this is the partition from where the connection request was issued.

In a DPF environment, or when the INTRA_PARALLEL Database Manager Configuration parameter is enabled, the coordinator agent distributes the database requests to an **active subagent,** *db2agntp*. These subagents perform the work and return the result set to the coordinator agent to return to the application.

In Figure 15.5, one subagent, *db2agntp*, is shown:

```
4897        4897          1474725        db2agntp (SAMPLE) 0
```

This is because it is a multi-partition instance with two database partitions. This subagent works for the coordinator agent on database partition 0.

When a subagent completes its work it becomes an idle and **associated subagent.** It changes its name from *db2agntp* to *db2agnta*, and it is returned to the application's agent pool. However, it is still associated with the application. When needed, it is called by the coordinator agent or the active subagents to service the same application again. Or it can be stolen by another application, if that application cannot find an idle agent or no more agents can be created (i.e., the system memory limit is reached). This improves performance by minimizing the creation and destruction of EDUs.

The idle db2agnta agents remain associated with the application as long as the total number of idle agents in the instance does not exceed the value of the NUM_POOLAGENTS Database Manager Configuration parameter. If the number of NUM_POOLAGENTS has already been reached, then the db2agnta process disassociates itself from the application and terminates. If subagents must be constantly created and reassociated to applications, performance suffers. (See Chapter 17, Database Performance Considerations, for a discussion on tuning of the NUM_POOLAGENTS parameter.)

Unassociated agents are idle agents (db2agent) not associated with any existing applications. They are ready for use by any incoming client connections, and can be called by any coordinator agents or active subagents to perform work.

Figure 15.5 shows an idle db2agent:

```
3599        3599          1896545        db2agent (idle) 1
```

The number of idle agents is determined by the NUM_POOLAGENTS Database Manager Configuration parameter. The DB2 agent pool is shared by all databases in an instance, not just one database.

Table 15.4 lists the DB2 EDUs at the application level.

Table 15.4 The DB2 Application-Level EDUs

EDU Name	Description	Applicability
db2agent	DB2 coordinator/coordinating agent that performs all database requests on behalf of an application. There is one db2agent EDU per connected application, unless the connection concentrator is enabled. If intrapartition parallelism is enabled, the db2agent EDU calls the DB2 subagents to perform the work, and they return the result set to the coordinator agent to return to the application. In a partitioned database, the coordinator agent exists on the partition that the application connected to.	All
db2agentg	The gateway agent for DRDA application requesters.	All
db2agnsc	The parallel recovery agent. During roll forward and restart recovery, performs the actions from the logs in parallel. This can improve recovery time in comparison to a serial recovery. **Note:** This thread enables parallelism within logged transactions as well as between parallel transactions.	All
db2agnta	An idle subagent used in the past by a coordinating agent and still associated to that coordinating agent thread. Appears when the INTRA_PARALLEL dbm cfg parameter is set to YES or in a partitioned database environment.	All
db2agntdp	The database pooled agent.	All
db2agntgp	The gateway pooled agent.	All
db2agnti	The independent coordinator agent. It is used to perform tasks driven by the DB2 engine itself, not requiring actual connection from a client.	All
db2agntp	A subagent that is currently performing work on behalf of the coordinating agent it is associated with. These EDUs provide intrapartition parallelism, that is, the ability to execute a query in parallel within a database instance/partition. Appears when the INTRA_PARALLEL dbm cfg parameter is set to YES or in a partitioned database environment.	All

15.3.4 Per-Request EDUs

Table 15.5 lists the per-request DB2 EDUs.

As an example, Figure 15.6 shows the EDUs created during a database backup operation.

Table 15.5 The DB2 Per-Request EDUs

EDU Name	Description	Applicability
db2bm	The Backup/Restore buffer manipulator. Reads from a table space during a backup operation and writes to a table space during a restore operation. One db2bm EDU per backup/restore buffer is configured on the **`backup`** or **`restore`** command.	All
db2lbs	LOAD LOB scanner. Only used when the load tool is loading into a table with LOB columns. These threads scan the LOB object of the table and read the information back in.	All
db2lbm*X*	LOAD buffer manipulator. The last character (*X*) is a numeric identifier for the thread. Writes loaded data to the database and can be involved in asynchronous I/O. There is always one, and often more, depending on a heuristic, which is based on the number of CPUs on the system and the number of containers being written to. This "intelligent default" may be overridden by the DISK_PARALLELISM modifier to the load command. **Note:** This asynchronous I/O is *not* the asynchronous file I/O supported by some operating systems; it just means there are separate threads writing the I/O—that other threads are formatting the data and are not tied up on I/O waits.	All
db2lfrm*X*	LOAD formatter thread. The last character (*X*) is a numeric identifier. This thread formats the input data into internal form. It is always present in a LOAD. An intelligent default is used, but can be overridden by the CPU_PARALLELISM modifier to choose the optimum number of CPUs.	All
db2lfs	Used when the table being loaded has long varchar columns. These are used to read and format the long varchar columns in the table.	All
db2lmr	The LOAD media reader thread. Reads the load input file(s) and disappears once the input file(s) have been read completely—even before the entire load operation has completed.	All

Table 15.5 The DB2 Per-Request EDUs *(Continued)*

EDU Name	Description	Applicability
db2lmwX	The LOAD media writer threads. The last character (*X*) is a numeric identifier. These threads make the "load copy" if this option is specified for the **load** command. The load copy is essentially a backup of the data that was loaded into the table. These are the same as the media writers used by the **backup** and **restore** commands. There is one media writer invoked per copy session as described on the command line (you can create a load copy to multiple files). If there is no load copy, there is no media writer. They get input from the other threads in load depending on what the data type is, but typically every bit of data that gets written by a buffer manipulator will be passed on to the media writer. As with all the other threads they are controlled by the load agent.	All
db2lrid	Performs the index sort and builds the index RIDs during the LOAD. This thread is not present in a nonparallel database instance, that is, if INTRA_PARALLEL is disabled. The tasks performed by this thread are done by the formatter EDU in a nonparallel instance. This thread performs four functions: synchronizes SMP, allocates Record IDs (RIDs), builds the indexes, and controls the synchronization of the LOAD formatter threads.	All
db2ltsc	The Load table scanner. Scans the data object for the table being loaded and reads the information for the Load tool. These are used during a Load append operation.	All
db2linit	The Load initialization subagent. Acquires the resources required on the database partitions and serializes the reply back to the load catalog subagent.	Multipartitioned database environment only
db2lcata	The Load catalog subagent. Is executed only on the catalog partition and is responsible for spawning the initialization subagents and processing their replies, and storing the lock information at the catalog partition. The catalog subagent also queries the system catalog tables to determine which partitions to use for data splitting and partitioning. There is only one catalog subagent for a normal load job. The exception is when loads fail to acquire loading resources on some partitions. If setup errors are isolated on database partitions, the coordinator will remove the failed partitions from load's internal partition list and spawn a new catalog subagent. This thread is repeated until resources are successfully acquired on all partitions, or failures are encountered on all partitions.	Multipartitioned database environment only

(continues)

Table 15.5 The DB2 Per-Request EDUs *(Continued)*

EDU Name	Description	Applicability
db2lpprt	Load prepartition subagent. This subagent prepartitions the input data from one input stream into multiple output streams, one for each partitioning subagent. There is one prepartitioning subagent per each input stream.	Multipartitioned database environment only
db2lpart	The Load partition subagent. This subagent partitions the input data into multiple output streams, one for each database partition where the data will be written. You can configure the number of partitioning subagents with the PARTITIONING_DBPARTNUMS load option. The default number depends on the total number of output database partitions.	Multipartitioned database environment only
db2lmibm	The Load mini-buffer manipulator subagent threads. Writes the partitioned output file if the PARTITION_ONLY mode is used for the load. There is one mini-buffer manipulator subagent per output database partition.	Multipartitioned database environment only
db2lload	The Load subagent threads. Carries out the loading on each database partition, and spawns the formatters, ridder, buffer manipulators, and media writer EDUs and oversees their work. There is one load subagent for each output database partition.	Multipartitioned database environment only
db2lrdfl	The Load read-file subagent threads. Reads the message file on a given database partition and sends the data back to the client. There will be a read-file subagent for each output partition, partitioning partition, and prepartitioning partition.	Multipartitioned database environment only
db2llqcl	The Load query cleanup subagent threads. Removes all of the load temporary files from a given partition. There is one cleanup subagent for each output partition, partitioning partition, and prepartitioning partition.	Multipartitioned database environment only
db2lmitk	The Load mini-task subagent threads. Frees all LOB locators used in a load from cursor call or a CLI load. There is one mini-task subagent per cursor/CLI load running on the coordinator partition.	Multipartitioned database environment only
db2lurex	The Load user-exit subagent threads. Runs the user's file transfer command. There is one user-exit subagent for each load job using the **FILE_TRANSFER_CMD** option of the **load** command.	Multipartitioned database environment only
db2lmctk	Holds, releases, or downgrades locks held on the catalog partition as a result of the load.	Multipartitioned database environment only

Table 15.5 The DB2 Per-Request EDUs *(Continued)*

EDU Name	Description	Applicability
db2med	Handles the reading from and/or writing to the database table spaces for the **load**, **backup**, and **restore** commands, and writes the data in formatted pages to the table space containers.	All
db2reorg	Performs asynchronous table reorganzation operations on the database. This works similar to a disk defrag tool; it places the data rows in the specified order.	All

```
8117        8117        1499183     db2med.10841.0 (SAMPLE) 0
7860        7860        962591      db2bm.10841.0 (SAMPLE) 0
7091        7091        987271      db2bm.10841.2 (SAMPLE) 0
6834        6834        1019957     db2bm.10841.1 (SAMPLE) 0
```

Figure 15.6 The DB2 EDUs responsible for backing up a database

V9 15.4 Tuning the Number of EDUs

DB2 controls the instance-level EDUs: db2sysc, db2fcms, db2fcmr, and the listeners. You can control some but not all of the EDUs at the database level. For example, you can tune the number of page cleaners (db2pclnr) and prefetchers (db2pfchr) with the database configuration parameters NUM_IOCLEANERS and NUM_IOSERVERS respectively. Starting in DB2 9, the settings for the num_iocleaners and num_ioservers configuration parameters are set to *AUTOMATIC* by default if it is a new installation. This means that the number of prefetchers and page cleaners started will be based on your environmental characteristics, such as the number of CPUs, database partitions, and the parallelism settings of the table spaces in the database.

> **NOTE** If you are migrating your existing DB2 Version 8 database to DB2 9, these parameters will not change to AUTOMATIC. You can take advantage of this feature by manually setting the values of num_iocleaners and num_ioservers to AUTOMATIC.

At the application level, you can only tune the DB2 agents. The following Database Manager Configuration parameters control the number of different types of agents,

- MAX_CONNECTIONS controls the maximum number of concurrent connections allowed to all the databases that share the same instance. These connections can be either active or inactive. An active connection means the application is doing a unit of work.
- MAX_COORDAGENTS indicates the maximum number of coordinator agents that can exist at any time. In DB2 9.5, the default for both MAX_COORDAGENTS and MAX_CONNECTIONS is AUTOMATIC, with MAX_COORDAGENTS set to 200

and MAX_CONNECTIONS set to -1 (that is, set to the value of MAX_COORDAGENTS). This means that each connection has a coordinator agent assigned to it. When MAX_COORDAGENTS is set less than MAX_CONNECTIONS, the connection concentrator is enabled (the connection concentrator is discussed in Section 15.6, The Connection Concentrator).

- NUM_POOLAGENTS determines the maximum size of the idle agent pool. In DB2 9.5, it is set to AUTOMATIC with a value of 100 as the default. When this parameter is set to AUTOMATIC, an agent is first returned to the pool upon the completion of its work, even when more idle agents are created than are indicated by the value of this parameter. Depending on the workload, it might be terminated after a certain amount of time. The automatic setting allows additional idle agents to be pooled for times of heavier system activity.
- NUM_INITAGENTS determines the initial number of idle db2agents that are created in the agent pool at db2start time.

V9.5

NOTE MAXAGENT and MAXCAGENTS are deprecated in DB2 9.5. Any value specified for these configuration parameters will be ignored by DB2.

Version 9.5 provides a more flexible mechanism for configuring DB2 agents. You can now set MAX_CONNECTIONS, MAX_COORDAGENTS, and NUM_POOLAGENTS to AUTOMATIC or configure them dynamically (online). This simplified configuration eliminates the need for regular DBA intervention to make adjustments to those paramaters, and the need to recycle DB2 instances to have the new settings take effect.

For example, assume the Database Manager Configuration file has these settings:

```
Agent pool size                    (NUM_POOLAGENTS) = AUTOMATIC
Initial number of agents in pool   (NUM_INITAGENTS) = 0
```

Because **NUM_INITAGENTS** is zero, there will be no **db2agent (idle)** EDUs displayed at db2start time. If **NUM_INITAGENTS** had been set to 4 before the db2start time, then these EDUs would have shown after issuing a **db2start**:

```
4627      4627      1187855      db2agent (idle)
4370      4370      1130615      db2agent (idle)
4113      4113      1036433      db2agent (idle)
3856      3856      1396927      db2agent (idle)
```

After connecting to the SAMPLE database, the **db2agent (SAMPLE)** EDU appears. This EDU indicates there is in fact a connection to the SAMPLE database. If you issued the command

```
db2 connect reset
```

db2agent (SAMPLE) would become **db2agent (idle).** This is because **NUM_POOLAGENTS** is set to AUTOMATIC, which means the agent will remain allocated in the pool even though it is idle. If **NUM_POOLAGENTS** had been set to zero, then after the **connect reset** command was issued, there would have been no db2agent EDU running.

15.5 Monitoring and Tuning the DB2 Agents

In DB2 9.5, several agent-related database manager configuration parameters are set to AUTOMATIC by default. This means that DB2 no longer artificially limits the number of agents as long as there is enough memory to support them. For a database with workload characteristics you don't know, use the database monitoring tools to get a sense of what the workload is like.

The database manager Snapshot Monitor will give you the most information on DB2 agent usage (use the **GET SNAPSHOT FOR DBM** command). Figure 15.7 shows a snippet of the database manager snapshot output.

```
            Database Manager Snapshot

Node type                                       = Enterprise Server Edition with
local and remote clients
Instance name                                   = db2inst1
Number of database partitions in DB2 instance   = 2
Database manager status                         = Active

Product name                                    = DB2 v9.5.0.0
Service level                                   = s070426

Start Database Manager timestamp                = 04/22/2007
19:49:39.258796
Last reset timestamp                            =
Snapshot timestamp                              = 05/12/2007
15:04:29.606269

Remote connections to db manager                = 2
Remote connections executing in db manager      = 0
Local connections                               = 1
Local connections executing in db manager       = 0
Active local databases                          = 1

High water mark for agents registered           = 6
Agents registered                               = 5
Idle agents                                     = 0

Agents assigned from pool                       = 7
Agents created from empty pool                  = 7
Agents stolen from another application          = 0
High water mark for coordinating agents         = 6
```

Figure 15.7 Example of database manager snapshot output

Remote connections to db manager and *Remote connections executing in db manager* indicate the number of remote connections and the number of remote connections that are currently active (i.e., they are processing a unit of work) respectively. If the number of remote connections is much larger than the number of active connections, most of the remote connections are idle.

This also applies to *Local connections* and *Local connections executing in db manager.* In this case, you may consider using the connection concentrator, which is explained in the next section.

The sum of *Remote connections to db manager* and *Local connections* gives you the total number of connections to the instance at the time the snapshot was taken.

The *High water marks for agents registered* indicates the highest number of coordinator agents and subagents being used concurrently, at some point in time.

Agents assigned from pool indicates the number of agents taken from the idle agents pool. *Agents created from empty pool* indicates the number of agents created because the idle agents pool was empty. If the ratio of *Agents created from empty pool* to the *Agents assigned from pool* is high, then you should increase NUM_POOLAGENTS if it is not set to AUTOMATIC.

The snapshot also shows the number of Idle agents and the High water mark for coordinating agents.

> **NOTE** The *Max agents overflow* monitor element is deprecated in DB2 9.5.

Use snapshots frequently to analyze and get familiar with the type of workload on the instance. Setting the agents appropriately will save system resources and increase performance.

15.6 The Connection Concentrator

By default, each application is assigned a coordinator agent (MAX_CONNECTIONS = MAX_COORDAGENTS). Each agent operates within its own private memory and shares other memory sets with other agents. If an application connects to the database and does nothing, the resources associated with its coordinator agent are wasted. You can use the **connection concentrator** to avoid this.

The connection concentrator is enabled when MAX_CONNECTIONS is greater than MAX_COORDAGENTS. This means you can have more connections than the number of available coordinator agents. Each coordinator agent will service more than one connection.

When the connection concentrator is enabled, an application is in an active state only if there is a coordinator agent servicing it. Otherwise, the application is in an inactive state. Requests from an active application will be serviced by the database coordinator agent (and subagents in SMP or MPP configurations). Requests from an inactive application will be queued until a database coordinator agent is assigned to service the application (when the application becomes active). You can use the connection concentrator to control the load on the system.

For Internet applications with many relatively transient connections or any other applications with many relatively small transactions, the connection concentrator improves performance by allowing many more client applications to be connected. It also reduces system resource use for each connection.

When the connection concentrator is enabled, idle agents will always be returned to the idle agent pool, regardless of the value of the NUM_POOLAGENTS parameter. Therefore, more agents might be in the agent pool at any given time. Based on the system load and the time agents remain idle in the pool, agents might terminate themselves, as necessary, to reduce the size of the idle pool to the configured value.

15.7 Commonly Seen DB2 Executables

When you are running DB2, you will also see some additional executables on your server. Table 15.6 lists these executables.

Table 15.6 Commonly Used Executables

Process Name	Description	Applicability
db2	The DB2 Command Line Processor (CLP) foreground process. It is the interactive component of the DB2 CLP and parses DB2 commands and SQL statements. This front-end/back-end configuration does have some advantages for command line performance: The front-end handles the connection to the user, and the back-end interfaces with the database. You can use CTRL+C/CTRL+Break to stop processing (i.e., when too many records are returned) without killing the connection to the database.	All
db2bp	The persistent background process for the DB2 CLP; it is the process that actually connects to the database. Since the DB2 CLP allows OS as well as DB2 commands/statements, this background process is required.	All
db2cmd	Similar to the db2 executable, but for Windows. Invokes a Windows command window. On Windows, parent threads cannot terminate their child processes when they are terminated. The DB2 CLP has a front-end and back-end process/thread; a cookie (launched from DB2CMD.EXE) ties these threads together on Windows so that the back-end process is terminated if the user exits or kills the front-end process.	Windows only
db2start	User command to start up the DB2 engine.	All
db2star2	The real db2start program.	All

(continues)

Table 15.6 Commonly Used Executables *(Continued)*

Process Name	Description	Applicability
db2stop	User command to stop the DB2 engine.	All
db2stop2	The real db2stop program.	All

15.8 Additional Services/Processes on Windows

Because of the different architectures between Linux, UNIX, and Windows, you do see some slight differences among these operating systems. There are some extra services that you will likely see on your DB2 server if you are running on Windows (see Table 15.7).

Table 15.7 Other Windows Services/Processes

Process Name	Description
db2dasrrm.exe	The DB2 Admin Server process. Supports both local and remote administration requests using the DB2 Control Center.
db2dasstm.exe	The DB2 Administration Server tools database manager process. Stores and retrieves information from the tools database, if it has been set up on the DB2 server.
db2fmp.exe	Handles/executes all fenced stored procedures and user-defined functions.
db2rcmd.exe	DB2 Remote Command Service. Automatically handles interpartition administrative communications.
db2licd.exe	The DB2 License daemon. Verifies that a correct DB2 license is installed on the server when DB2 is started.
db2mgmtsvc.exe	DB2 Management Service. Manages DB2 registry entries for backward compatibility purposes for the DB2 copy.
db2sec.exe	Checks the user ID and password on the DB2 server on Windows. Since DB2 relies on operating system-level authentication, this process verifies the user ID and password when a user or application connects to a database on the server. This authentication will occur when authentication is set to SERVER or when a connection is made from a nonsecure operating system.
db2syscs.exe	The main DB2 system controller or engine on Windows. The EDUs are threads within this process. Note the *s* at the end for a Windows service.
db2systray.exe	Starts the DB2 system tray tool. It is a Windows operating system notify icon which monitors the status of a DB2 database service. db2systray provides a visual indication of when the service is started and stopped, as well as the ability to start and stop the service. It also provides a launch point for the DB2 Control Center.

15.9 Case Study

Diagnosing a Problem with the Help of DB2 EDUs

The following real-life example shows how you can solve problems by reviewing the running DB2 EDUs of a system.

One afternoon, a DB2 server on AIX machine encountered a general slow-down in query response time. A DB2 list applications command did not show anything out of the ordinary running at the time. Before taking DB2 snapshots, we looked at the DB2 EDUs running on this AIX machine and found that the *db2rebal* EDU was running. This EDU performs a rebalancing of the data across containers when a container is added to a DMS table space. The DBA realized that earlier that day he had added one container to a table space containing a 40GB table. No action was required; when the rebalancing finished, the queries went back to their regular good response time.

Control the Number of Connections by Setting the Number of DB2 Agents

Example 1

Consider a DB2 Enterprise environment with a single database partition in which 1,000 users on average are connected to the database concurrently. The number of connections that are actually active, however, is 250 at the maximum. The transactions are short.

For this workload, you can enable the connection concentrator such that the database manager can allow up to 1,000 concurrent connections. You can set a maximum of 250 coordinator agents to handle the active connections at any one time. Without the connection concentrator, 1,000 coordinator agents are required to be created, one for each connection.

The following Database Manager Configuration parameters need to be set.

- Set **MAX_CONNECTIONS** as AUTOMATIC with a value of 1,000 to ensure support for any number of connections. In fact, any value greater than 250 will be sufficient in this example, which is used only to enable connection concentrator.
- Set **MAX_COORDAGENTS** to 250 to support the maximum number of concurrent transactions.
- Set **NUM_POOLAGENTS** at the default (that is, AUTOMATIC with a value of 100), which should ensure database agents are available to service incoming client requests with little overhead of creating new ones.

Example 2

In a system for which you do not want to enable the connection concentrator but want to allow for 250 connected users at one time, set the Database Manager Configuration parameters as follows:

MAX_CONNECTIONS to 250
MAX_COORDAGENTS to 250

Example 3

In a system for which you do not want to enable the connection concentrator and you do not want to limit the number of connected users, set the Database Manager Configuration parameters as follows:

MAX_CONNECTIONS to AUTOMATIC
MAX_COORDAGENTS to AUTOMATIC

15.10 Summary

In this chapter you learned about a number of topics related to the DB2 process model. A connection is first accepted by an agent called a listener, and there are different listeners for different communication protocols. After an application connects to a database, a new agent is created and assigned to do work on behalf of the application. This agent is called a coordinator agent (db2agent). In a partitioned database environment, or if intrapartition parallelism is enabled, the coordinator agent distributes work to subagents (db2agntp). These subagents perform the work and return the result to the coordinator agent to return to the application.

Since DB2 threads live within the DB2 engine, threads are also called DB2 Engine Dispatchable Units (EDUs). A coordinator agent, a subagent, a page cleaner, and a listener agent are all examples of EDUs. EDUs are implemented as threads within the DB2 system controller process (db2sysc) across all server platforms.

The DB2 system controller process (db2sysc) is the first process created when an instance starts. The db2sysc process will then spawn critical instance-level EDUs, such as the db2resyn, db2pdbc, db2cart, and others.

There are four different types of DB2 agents: coordinator agents (db2agent), active subagents (db2agntp), associated idle subagents (db2agnta), and unassociated idle agents (db2agent (idle). Coordinator agents work on behalf of the application by communicating with other agents. Subagents are created in a DPF environment or when the INTRA_PARALLEL parameter is enabled. Associated subagents are nonactive agents (returned to the agent pool) that are still under the application coordinator agent's control. Unassociated idle agents are agents that are released by an application's coordinator agent (released to the agent pool) and thus can be used by any other application.

The number that the four types of agents can have is controlled by various Database Manager Configuration parameters, such as MAX_COORDAGENTS, NUM_POOLAGENTS and NUM_INITAGENTS. Tuning these parameters properly helps increase database performance. You can use the database manager Snapshot Monitor to check the usage of these agents, and then you can tune them accordingly.

Connection concentrator is enabled when MAX_CONNECTIONS is greater than MAX_COORDAGENTS. When enabled, an application has to wait for a coordinator agent to become available to service it. Otherwise, it remains in an inactive state. This feature is useful when you want to limit the resources used by each connection, especially when you know these connections are often idle.

15.11 Review Questions

1. What command should you use to display the names of DB2 EDUs on Linux and UNIX platforms?
2. What is the db2fmp process, and why is it executed outside of the address space of the DB2 engine?
3. What DB2 EDU flushes the data in the buffer pool to disk?
4. What kind of environment do DB2 subagents exist in?
5. What happens to a subagent when it completes its work?
6. What are the four types of DB2 agents?
7. What tool can you use to monitor the DB2 agent usage?
8. If NUM_INITAGENTS=3 and NUM_POOLAGENTS=5, how many db2agntp EDUs will be created when an instance is started?
   A. 3
   B. 5
   C. 0
   D. 8
9. Which of the following configuration parameters can NOT be set to AUTOMATIC?
   A. NUM_POOLAGENTS
   B. NUM_INITAGENTS
   C. MAX_COORDAGENTS
   D. MAX_CONNECTIONS
10. In a partitioned environment with four partitions, how many DB2 system controller processes are started when the instance starts?
    A. 1
    B. 2
    C. 3
    D. 4
11. Which of the following parameters controls the number of idle agents?
    A. MAX_CONNECTIONS
    B. NUM_POOLAGENTS
    C. NUM_INITAGENTS
    D. MAX_COORDAGENTS
12. With the connection concentrator disabled, how many db2agent threads are assigned to serve an application that is connected to a database with four partitions?
    A. 1
    B. 2

C. 3
D. 4

13. Which of the following database configuration parameters controls the number of prefetchers?
A. NUM_IOCLEANERS
B. NUM_IOSERVERS
C. NUM_INITAGENTS
D. NUM_PREFETCHERS

14. Which of the following is the DB2 system controller process?
A. db2wdog
B. db2acd
C. db2sys
D. db2sysc

15. Which of the following is responsible for handling local client connections?
A. db2ipccm
B. db2tcpdm
C. db2tcpcm
D. db2local

16. Given the following Database Manager Configuration information:

```
Agent pool size                        (NUM_POOLAGENTS) = 20
Initial number of agents in pool       (NUM_INITAGENTS) = 10
Max number of coordinating agents     (MAX_COORDAGENTS) = 100
Max number of client connections      (MAX_CONNECTIONS) = MAX_COORDAGENTS
```

what is the maximum number of concurrent connections possible to all databases in this instance?
A. 10
B. 20
C. 100
D. 200

17. Which of the following is not a DB2 agent EDU?
A. db2agent
B. db2agntp
C. db2agnta
D. db2agntb

18. In which of the following cases will the connection concentrator be enabled?
A. MAX_CONNECTIONS = 10 and MAX_COORDAGENTS = 10
B. MAX_CONNECTIONS = 10 and MAX_COORDAGENTS = 100
C. MAX_CONNECTIONS = 100 and MAX_COORDAGENTS = 10
D. MAX_CONNECTIONS = MAX_COORDAGENTS and MAX_COORDAGENTS = 1000

19. Which of the following EDUs will be seen when you enable the DB2 governor?

A. db2gov
B. db2govd
C. Governor
D. db2governor

20. Which of the following is a DB2 thread spawned by the db2sysc process?

A. db2fmp
B. db2acd
C. db2ckpwd
D. db2aiothr

CHAPTER 16

The DB2 Memory Model

It is important that you understand how and when DB2 allocates and utilizes its memory to enable you to design and set up your applications optimally so they won't interfere with the database on the server.

In this chapter you will learn about:

- How and when DB2 allocates memory
- DB2's use of shared and private memory

16.1 DB2 Memory Allocation: The Big Picture

DB2 allocates memory for three different types of operations.

- **Instance-level operations:** DB2 allocates memory for instance-level operations such as accepting connection requests, for starting up support to activate a database, and for interpartition communication if you have a multi-partition system. This is known as **instance-level shared memory** since it is shared by all databases in the instance and by all applications connecting to databases in the instance. Figure 16.1 shows the components that make up the instance-level shared memory in the top-left corner (Per Instance Global Control Block).
- **Database-level operations:** DB2 also allocates a piece of shared memory for every database that has been activated or that has one or more connections. This memory is used for all access to the database, concurrency control on the database, and logging related to the database. This is known as **database-level shared memory** since it is shared by all applications that are connected to the database. The components that make up the database-level shared memory are shown in the bottom-left corner of Figure 16.1 (Per DB).
- **Application/Agent-level operations:** For each connection to a database, the agents responsible for handling the requests for the application also need some memory. They

need some shared memory for application heap structures, access-plan generation, and database statistics, and some private memory for sorting, and so on. These memory areas are known as **application shared memory** and **agent private memory.** The components that make up the application shared memory are shown in the top-right corner of Figure 16.1 (Per DB), and those for agent private memory are on the bottom-right side of the figure (Per DB2 Agent).

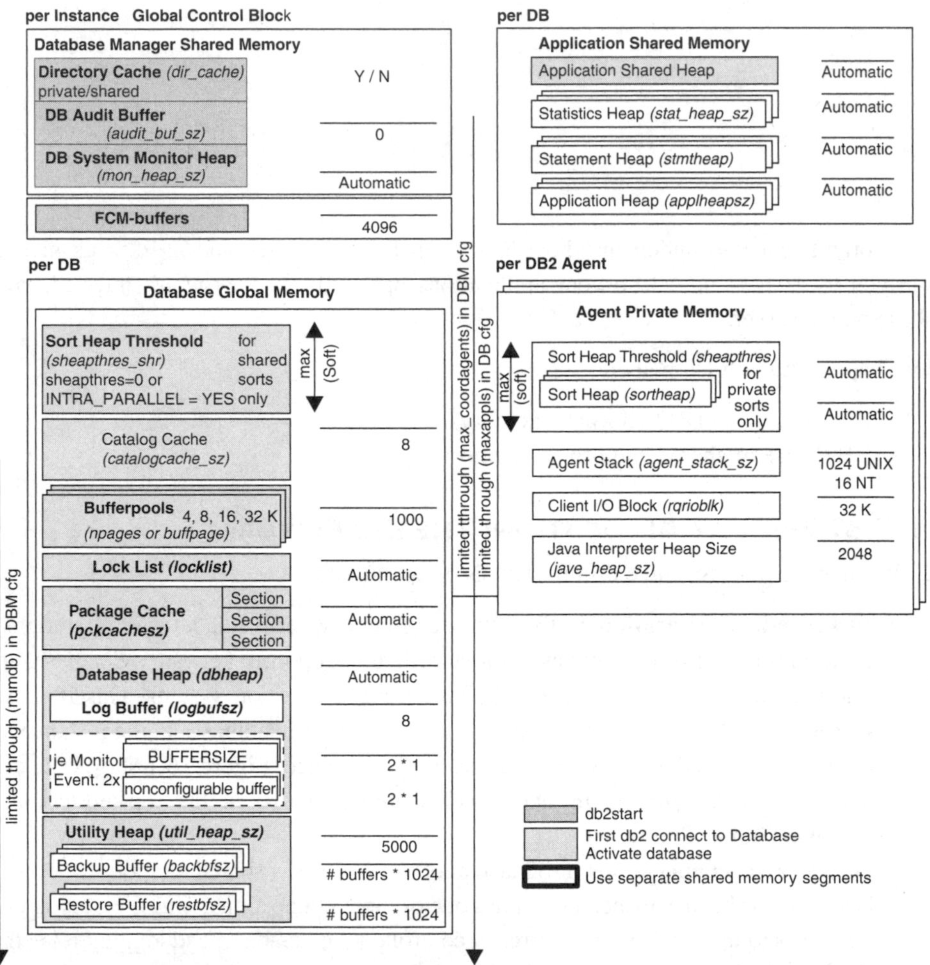

Figure 16.1 The DB2 memory model: the big picture

V9.5 DB2 allocates its instance-level shared memory for each instance that you start. This is the area on the top-left side of Figure 16.1. For every database in the instance that has been activated or that has at least one connection, DB2 will allocate the database-level shared memory, including both database global memory shown on the bottom-left side of Figure 16.1 and application shared memory in the top-right corner of the figure.

For every application connecting to the database, DB2 will allocate and maintain an application heap out of the application shared memory. Every DB2 agent that is either working or in the idle agent pool will have its own agent private memory. Figure 16.1 illustrates this (application shared memory and agent private memory).

16.2 INSTANCE-LEVEL SHARED MEMORY

When you start a DB2 instance using the **db2start** command, DB2 allocates the instance-level shared memory for the instance, and this remains allocated until you stop the instance using the **db2stop** command. The instance-level shared memory for the instance is shown in the top-left corner of Figure 16.2. DB2 uses this memory to manage and coordinate database and agent activity for all applications running against all databases in the instance.

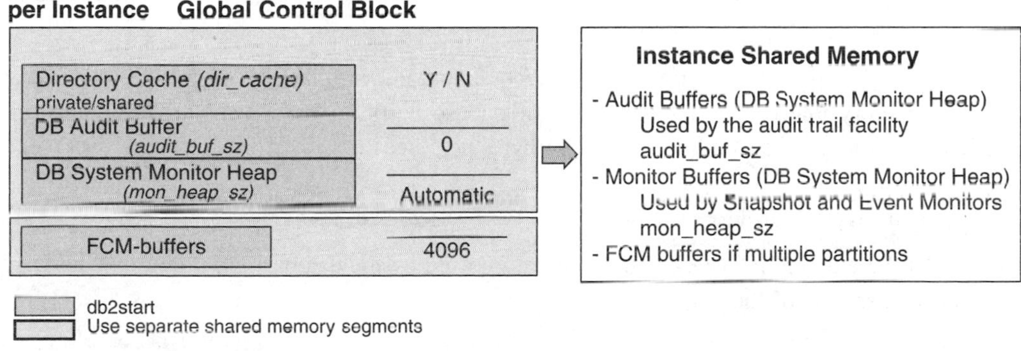

Figure 16.2 Instance-level shared memory

In a nonpartitioned DB2 instance, this memory contains information used by:

- The Snapshot and Event Monitors
- The audit-logging facility
- The DB2 trace facility

In a partitioned DB2 instance, this memory also contains information used by the **Fast Communications Manager** (FCM), which is used for interpartition communication. The amount of memory required for FCM communications depends on how you set up your multi-partition database system. If you have one partition per server, DB2 requires less memory for FCM since all communications use the TCP/IP interconnect. If you have more than one database partition within a server (also known as **logical partitions**), DB2 uses a segment of shared memory for FCM communications; this can greatly increase the amount of memory consumed at the instance level.

The Database Manager Configuration parameter *INSTANCE_MEMORY* controls how much memory can be allocated for a database partition. By default this is set to automatic, which allows DB2 to calculate how much memory is required. The actual value used is between 75 percent and 95 percent of the physical RAM on the system, divided by the number of configured local database partitions in the instance. This value should be suitable for dedicated database server systems. If the system is shared with many applications, or multiple DB2 instances, you can set this to a specific value to limit or control the amount of memory that can be allocated. However, you need to be aware that this can impact performance, especially for a multi-partitioned database with logical partitions: setting too large a value can cause excessive paging, and too low a value can restrict the memory that DB2 can allocate.

If INSTANCE_MEMORY is set to AUTOMATIC, you can determine its effective upper-bound value using the command:

```
db2 get dbm cfg show detail
```

If the instance is not started, this will only show the value AUTOMATIC, so remember to start the instance before running this command.

The following output of the **get dbm cfg** command shows that the maximum amount of instance memory that can be allocated for a database partition is set to 3,498,659 pages, or 1.33GB of memory (3,498,659 pages x 4,096 bytes per page).

```
Size of instance shared memory (4KB)
(INSTANCE_MEMORY) = AUTOMATIC(3498659)          AUTOMATIC(3498659)
```

To find out the amount of instance shared memory used by the database partition, use the DB2 memory tracker tool, **db2mtrk:**

```
db2mtrk –i –v
Tracking Memory on: 2007/05/21 at 19:41:06

Memory for instance
  Other Memory is of size 12255232 bytes
  Database Monitor Heap is of size 65536 bytes
  FCMBP Heap is of size 786432 bytes
  Total: 13107200 bytes
```

This example shows that 13MB is being used for the instance shared memory set at the time **db2mtrk** is run. If the instance is not started, **db2mtrk** returns that no memory is being used.

16.3 Database-Level Shared Memory

When you issue the **activate database** command or connect to a database for the first time, DB2 automatically allocates the database-level shared memory (see Figure 16.3). This memory caches the object pages that are being manipulated to control concurrency on the rows of data, ensure transactional integrity for all operations on the database, and so on.

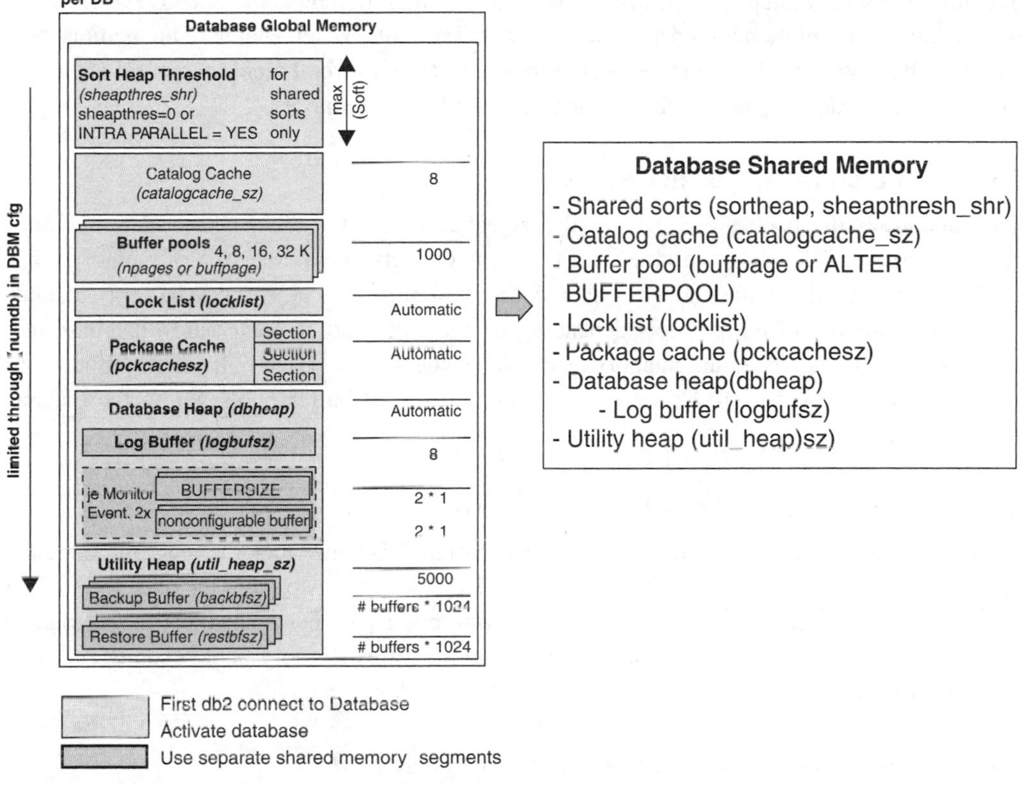

Figure 16.3 Database shared memory

The components of database shared memory include:

- The database buffer pool(s)
- The catalog cache
- The lock list
- The shared sort area if intrapartition parallelism is enabled, or if sheapthres is set to zero (0)
    - In order to use self-tuning of the sort memory, the sort-heap threshold (sheapthres) must be set to zero, so in this case all sorts will be in shared memory.
- The database heap, which also includes the log buffer
- The package cache
- The utility heap, which is used by agents such as backup and restore

> **NOTE** Self-Tuning Memory Management (STMM) automatically sets values for most memory configuration parameters and sizing buffer pools. It greatly simplifies the task of memory configuration. Please refer to Chapter 17, Database Performance Considerations to see STMM in action.

Self-tuning memory simplifies the task of memory configuration by automatically setting values for memory configuration parameters and sizing buffer pools. When enabled, the memory tuner dynamically distributes available memory resources between several memory consumers including the sort, package cache, and lock list areas, as well as buffer pools.

16.3.1 The Database Buffer Pools

The database buffer pools area is usually the largest component of the database shared memory. As discussed in Chapter 7, Working with Database Objects, this is the area of memory where DB2 manipulates all regular and index data. A database must have at least one buffer pool, and it can have a number of buffer pools depending on the workload characteristics, database page sizes used in the database, and memory available on the system. Each individual buffer pool is sized independently, but DB2 allocates the total size of all buffer pools within the database shared memory area.

16.3.2 The Database Lock List

To control access to rows that are being read and written, DB2 must lock the rows until the operation completes. Information about each lock that DB2 obtains is stored in the database lock list until the lock is released. The LOCKLIST configuration parameter specifies the amount of memory that can be used to store the lock information. If this memory pool becomes full, DB2 performs **lock escalation** to free up some space in the lock list.

16.3.3 The Database Shared Sort Heap Threshold

Starting in DB2 9, when the SHEAPTHRES database manager configuration parameter is set to 0 (which is the default behavior), all sorts are shared. Otherwise, when you enable intrapartition parallelism, DB2 may also choose to perform a shared sort if it thinks using that method will be more efficient than a private sort. If DB2 performs a shared sort, it allocates the sort heap for the sort in database shared memory. The SHEAPTHRES_SHR configuration parameter limits the amount of shared sort memory that can be allocated for the database. Starting in DB2 9, the SHEAPTHRES_SHR parameter represents a soft limit. If a new shared-sort request is made, and the allocation of the sort heap would exceed the shared sort heap threshold (SHEAPTHRES_SHR), DB2 will allocate additional unreserved database shared memory if needed.

16.3.4 The Package Cache

For dynamic SQL, performance can be greatly improved if DB2 is able to reuse an already compiled access plan rather than having to perform the access-plan generation. The **package cache** stores already compiled access plans so that they can be reused. Since multiple users can run the same applications, and therefore the same SQL statements, DB2 uses a shared package cache so that you can reuse an access plan even if it was originally compiled for another user. The size of the package cache is specified by the PCKCACHESZ configuration parameter.

16.3.5 The Utility Heap Size

DB2 allocates the utility heap when you first connect to or activate the database. Internal buffers are allocated out of the utility heap when you perform a backup, restore or load operation. You need to be aware of this and plan for this. If the value is set too low, you might not be able to run these utilities concurrently.

16.3.6 The Catalog Cache

The catalog cache is used to store previously accessed information such as object descriptions and privileges. In a multi-partitioned database, the catalog cache will be allocated on all partitions, but the information is not replicated. Each partition's catalog cache will contain information that has been previously accessed on that partition. In addition, when the Just-in-time Statistics feature is enabled in DB2 9.5, it will increase the requirement on the catalog cache size by around 25 percent to store entries for the system table object.

16.3.7 Database Logging Parameters

As you change data in your database, DB2 needs to log the changes so that it can:

- Roll back the changes if you issue the ROLLBACK statement
- Perform recovery operations if the server fails for any reason

To be able to perform well, DB2 cannot log the work that it is doing directly to disk, so DB2 uses a write-ahead logging algorithm to ensure that the changes are written to the log buffer (LOGBUFSZ) before they are made to the underlying index and data pages. DB2 also ensures that the log buffer is flushed to disk whenever a commit (or MINCOMMIT commits) occurs so that it is able to reapply any committed changes and can undo any uncommitted changes. This is discussed in more detail in Chapter 14, Developing Database Backup and Recovery Solutions.

The log buffer is allocated within the database heap along with some other database-level control information. In addition, for every page in the buffer pools, DB2 uses 12 bytes of memory in the database heap to store information about the state of the page.

16.3.8 Database Memory

The total amount of database shared memory allocated at a given time is the sum of all of these components. The amount of memory that is reserved for the database shared memory region is determined by the DATABASE_MEMORY configuration parameter. In DB2 9.5, the DATABASE_MEMORY configuration parameter can be configured dynamically across all platforms. It's recommended to set the parameter to AUTOMATIC (which is the default for a new database). So DB2 will automatically determine a suitable initial size. And if self-tuning memory is enabled, DB2 will further tune that size based on the memory requirement during the database run time. For environments that do not support the AUTOMATIC setting, set it to COMPUTED.

As discussed earlier for instance-level memory, you can use the **db2mtrk** tool to display the database shared memory used for your databases:

```
db2mtrk –d –v

Tracking Memory on: 2007/05/21 at 20:27:34
Memory for database: SAMPLE

Backup/Restore/Util Heap is of size 65536 bytes
Package Cache is of size 983040 bytes
Other Memory is of size 196608 bytes
Catalog Cache Heap is of size 393216 bytes
Buffer Pool Heap (1) is of size 8650752 bytes
Buffer Pool Heap (System 32k buffer pool) is of size 851968 bytes
Buffer Pool Heap (System 16k buffer pool) is of size 589824 bytes
Buffer Pool Heap (System 8k buffer pool) is of size 458752 bytes
Buffer Pool Heap (System 4k buffer pool) is of size 393216 bytes
Shared Sort Heap is of size 65536 bytes
Lock Manager Heap is of size 655360 bytes
Database Heap is of size 17956864 bytes
Application Heap (3384) is of size 65536 bytes
Application Heap (3383) is of size 65536 bytes
Application Heap (3382) is of size 65536 bytes
Application Heap (3381) is of size 65536 bytes
Application Heap (3380) is of size 65536 bytes
Applications Shared Heap is of size 524288 bytes
Total: 32112640 bytes
```

Notice there are five buffer pool heaps allocated; the following are the four hidden buffer pools:

```
Buffer Pool Heap (System 32k buffer pool) is of size 851968 bytes
Buffer Pool Heap (System 16k buffer pool) is of size 589824 bytes
Buffer Pool Heap (System 8k buffer pool) is of size 458752 bytes
Buffer Pool Heap (System 4k buffer pool) is of size 393216 bytes
```

In this case if you run the statement

```
select * from syscat.bufferpools
```

you will get only one row returned, because the hidden buffer pools do not have entries in the system buffer pool table.

> **NOTE** In DB2 V9.5, a single application shared memory set is created for a database (on each partition), which is separate from the database-shared memory set. **db2mtrk –d** displays the memory usage in both memory sets.

16.4 Application-Level Shared Memory

When a database is activated, or during the first connection to the database, DB2 allocates the database-level application shared memory set used by all applications connected to the database, as shown in Figure 16.4. DB2 uses the application shared memory:

- For coordinating and sending messages between the DB2 agents that are working on behalf of an application
- To store copies of currently executing sections of access plans
- For handling compilation of an SQL or XQuery statement
- For collecting statistics by the **runstats** command

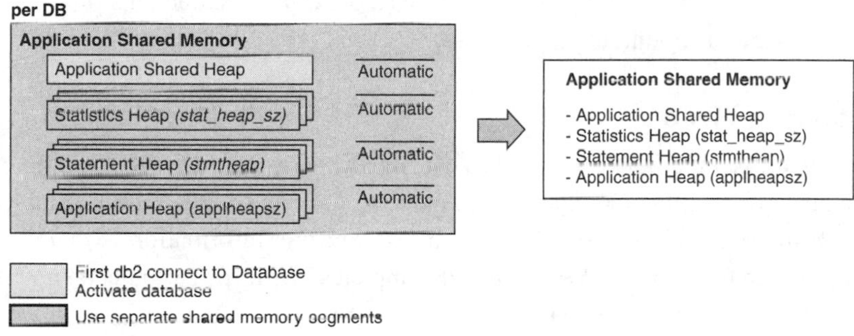

Figure 16.4 Application shared memory

The components of application shared memory in DB2 9.5 include

- The application shared heap
- The application heaps
- The statement heaps
- The statistics heaps

V9.5 16.4.1 Application Shared Heap

The **application shared heap** stores runtime sections of access plans for applications associated with the database. A single application shared heap is allocated during the database activation, and freed during the database deactivation. It is used by all applications running against the database. You cannot directly configure the application shared heap. Instead DB2 automatically sizes this heap based on the current application workload. The application shared heap cannot grow beyond the maximum size of the application shared memory set determined by the APPL_MEMORY configuration parameter that will be discussed shortly.

V9.5 16.4.2 Application Heap

The **application heap** is the working memory area accessed by all DB2 agents working for a database application. One application heap is allocated per application when the application first connects to a database. The amount of memory allocated will be only what is needed to process the application. In DB2 9.5, the application heap size (APPLHEAPSZ) has a default value of AUTOMATIC, meaning that DB2 will allocate additional memory as needed until either the APPL_MEMORY limit or the INSTANCE_MEMORY limit is reached. In addition, the heap size can be changed dynamically. After it is changed online, currently connected applications still use the old value, but all newly connected applications will use the new value.

16.4.3 Statement Heap

The DB2 optimizer uses the **statement heap** as a work space as it examines and builds the access plan for an SQL or XQuery statement. The statement heap is allocated when optimizing an SQL or XQuery statement, and released once the access plan for the statement has been built. For applications using dynamic SQL or XQuery statements, this work area is used during execution of the application. Applications using static SQL or XQuery statements only use this work area when the program is bound to the database.

16.4.4 Statistics Heap

The **statistics heap** is a memory area used by the **`runstats`** command to maintain and calculate the statistical information about tables and indexes. As **`runstats`** scans the table, it counts items, builds histograms for data distribution, and so on; this information is maintained in the statistics heap. When the **`runstats`** command completes, the information is then written to the catalog tables, and the statistics heap is freed.

NOTE In DB2 9.5, the application heap, statement heap, and statistics heap are part of the application shared memory instead of the agent-private memory in previous versions.

V9.5

16.4.5 Application Memory

All of these heaps are allocated in application shared memory used by all applications connected to a database. The maximum amount of application shared memory is defined by a new database configuration parameter introduced in DB2 9.5 called APPL_MEMORY. By default APPL_MEMORY is set to AUTOMATIC. So the initial application shared memory allocation at database activation time is minimal, and increases (or decreases) as needed, up to the INSTANCE_MEMORY limit.

To figure out the value used by the APPL_MEMORY configuration parameter, you can connect to the database and run the command:

```
get db cfg for dbname show detail
```

This command will show you how much maximum memory is defined for the application shared memory area. The following is a partial output of this command:

```
Application Memory Size (4KB)(APPL_MEMORY) = AUTOMATIC(40016)   AUTOMATIC(40000)
```

This shows that the maximum size of 40,016 pages is defined for the application shared memory area.

You can also use the **`db2mtrk`** tool to display the application shared memory currently used for your database:

```
db2mtrk -a -v
Tracking Memory on: 2007/05/22 at 09:45:54

Application Memory for database: SAMPLE

   Applications Shared Heap is of size 327680 bytes
   Total: 327680 bytes

  Memory for application 177

   Application Heap is of size 65536 bytes
   Other Memory is of size 65536 bytes
   Total: 131072 bytes

  Memory for application 176

   Application Heap is of size 65536 bytes
   Other Memory is of size 65536 bytes
   Total: 131072 bytes
  Memory for application 175

   Application Heap is of size 65536 bytes
   Other Memory is of size 196608 bytes
   Total: 262144 bytes
  Memory for application 174

   Application Heap is of size 65536 bytes
   Other Memory is of size 458752 bytes
   Total: 524288 bytes
   Total: 1376256 bytes
```

V9.5

> **NOTE** Under the simplified application memory model in DB2 9.5, application groups are eliminated. Moreover, instead of using APPL_CTL_HEAP_SZ, APPGROUP_MEMORY_SZ, and GROUPHEAP_RATIO to determine how many applications can fit in each application group, these three configuration parameters are deprecated and replaced by the new APPL_MEMORY configuration parameter to set the maximum limit on total application-memory consumption.

16.5 Agent Private Memory

Each DB2 agent also needs to acquire memory to perform its work. As you can see in Figure 16.5, agents use memory to perform sorts, to record cursor information such as location and state, and so on.

When a DB2 agent is created, it allocates the minimum amount of memory that is required to do some basic work. As it works, it may allocate more memory depending on the statements that are being processed, the number of cursors the application uses, and other functions.

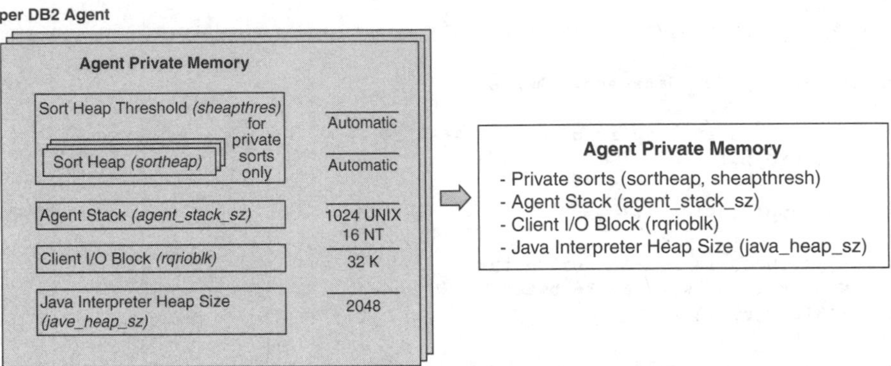

Figure 16.5 Agent private memory

16.5.1 The Sort Heap and Sort Heap Threshold

The **sort heap** (SORTHEAP) size specifies the maximum number of private memory pages to be used for private sorts, or the maximum number of shared memory pages to be used for shared sorts. If the DB2 optimizer chooses to perform a private sort, the sort heap size affects agent private memory. If the DB2 optimizer chooses to perform a shared sort, the sort heap size affects the database-level shared memory.

Each sort operation has a separate sort heap that is allocated as needed by DB2 where the underlying data is sorted. Normally DB2 will allocate a full sort heap; however, if directed by the optimizer, a smaller amount of memory than specified by the sort heap size may be allocated using the information provided by the optimizer and the database statistics.

For private sorts, the **sort heap threshold** parameter (SHEAPTHRES) is an instance-wide soft limit on the total amount of memory that can be used at any given time. When the total usage of private sort memory for a DB2 instance reaches this limit, the memory allocated for new private sort requests will be reduced by a factor of one half. Each time this happens, you will receive the following message in the db2diag.log:

```
Not enough memory available for a (private) sort heap of size <size of sortheap>.
Trying smaller size...
```

Chapter 18, Diagnosing Problems, discusses the db2diag.log file.

> **NOTE** In order to use the self-tuning feature of the sort memory, sheapthres must be set to zero (0). In this case all sorts will be shared sorts, and performed in the database shared memory.

16.5.2 Agent Stack

Each agent uses the **agent stack** to process SQL statements. When an SQL statement is running, its sections are copied to the agent stack to be processed. Large, complex queries need a larger agent stack as they typically have much larger access plans with a large number of sections. The default value of the agent stack size is suitable for most workloads.

16.5.3 Client I/O Block Size

The maximum requester **I/O block size** is the maximum amount of data that can be sent back and forth between a DB2 client and server. Each agent allocates the communication block in agent private memory for a DB2 instance; however, DB2 only uses what it needs up to this maximum size. If the application request or the output from DB2 is larger than the block size, the data will be split into multiple pieces and sent in multiple communication packets. The default maximum requester I/O block size is 32KB; the maximum size is 64KB.

16.5.4 Java Interpreter Heap

The **Java Interpreter Heap** parameter determines the maximum size of the heap used by the Java interpreter started to service Java DB2 stored procedures and UDFs. This heap is used as a work area for the Java interpreter as it processes actions for the DB2 agent.

> **NOTE** In Version 9.5, Query Heap (query_heap_sz) previously allocated out of agent private memory is deprecated. It is no longer needed to support DB2 for Linux, UNIX and Windows Version 7 (or earlier) clients using DB2RA protocol as the protocol is not supported any more.

16.6 The Memory Model

You can now look at all of these memory areas together to see how they are related. Within each instance you can create more than one database, so for every active database there will be a database shared memory area and an application shared memory area that are allocated in memory. Each application connected to the database has its own application heap in application shared memory. In addition, each DB2 agent will have its own private memory area, as summarized in Figure 16.6.

The **db2mtrk** tool is used to monitor the memory usage of those heaps that have been allocated. However, the actual memory consumed by the DB2 engine can also include the memory caches that are currently not allocated to any specific heap. The DB2 memory manager uses those caches in various memory areas (i.e., database global memory and application shared memory) for improved performance. To query overall memory consumption for a given instance, the ADMIN_GET_BP_MEM_USAGE() table function in DB2 9.5 provides an easy

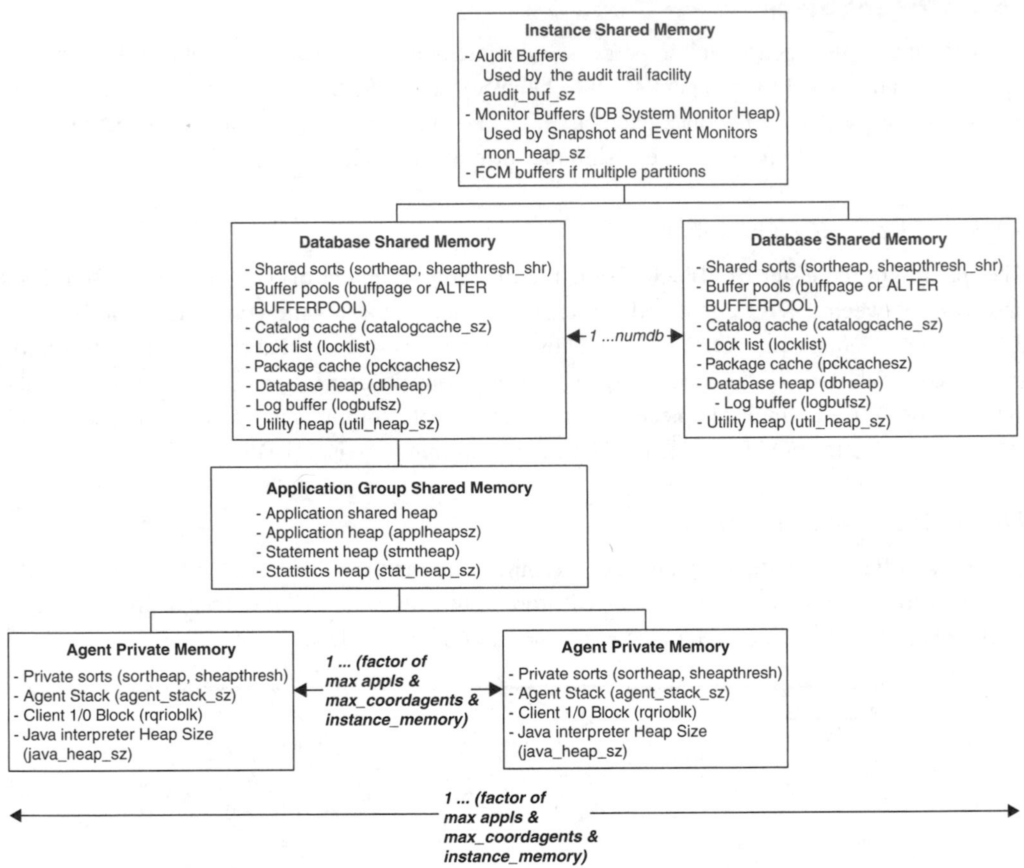

Figure 16.6 The memory model

way to do so. This table function takes an optional input argument *dbpartitionnum* (INTEGER type), which specifies a valid database partition number, and returns memory-consumption statistics for that single-database partition only. If the argument is omitted, statistics are returned for all active-database partitions. When using the Database Partitioning Feature (DPF), if you specify -1 or a NULL value for *dbpartitionnum*, data is returned from the currently connected partition as shown below.

```
db2 "select * from table (sysproc.admin_get_dbp_mem_usage(-1)) as t"
DBPARTITIONNUM MAX_PARTITION_MEM    CURRENT_PARTITION_MEM PEAK_PARTITION_MEM
-------------- -------------------- --------------------- --------------------
             0          14330507264             319422464            478347264

  1 record(s) selected.
```

The CURRENT_PARTITION_MEM column in the above example shows that 319,422,464 bytes (304.6MB) are being used by the DB2 engine in the given database partition when the query is issued.

16.7 Case Study

You can use the tools available in DB2 to examine how much memory is being used by different DB2 operations.

To get the most useful information, start with a stopped DB2 instance. Running the memory tracker tool, **db2mtrk,** will indicate whether or not the instance is running as shown below.

```
$db2stop
05/22/2007 15:07:02     0   0   SQL1064N  DB2STOP processing was successful.
SQL1064N  DB2STOP processing was successful.

$db2mtrk -i -p -v
Tracking Memory on: 2007/05/22 at 15:07:19

Instance not started
```

Start the instance and see how much memory it will use.

```
$db2start
05/22/2007 15:08:39     0   0   SQL1063N  DB2START processing was successful.
SQL1063N  DB2START processing was successful.

$db2mtrk -i -p -v
Tracking Memory on: 2007/05/22 at 15:09:28

Memory for instance

   Other Memory is of size 11993088 bytes
   Database Monitor Heap is of size 65536 bytes
   FCMBP Heap is of size 786432 bytes
   Total: 12845056 bytes

No active agents
```

The output above shows that this particular instance consumes 12,845,056 bytes (10.4MB) when it is started.

If you activate a database, all of its shared memory, such as the lock list and buffer pool, will be allocated as can be seen below.

```
$db2 activate db sample
DB20000I  The ACTIVATE DATABASE command completed successfully.

$db2mtrk -i -p –d -v
Tracking Memory on: 2007/05/22 at 15:14:00

Memory for instance

   Other Memory is of size 12451840 bytes
   Database Monitor Heap is of size 65536 bytes
   FCMBP Heap is of size 786432 bytes
   Total: 13303808 bytes

Memory for database: SAMPLE
```

```
   Backup/Restore/Util Heap is of size 65536 bytes
   Package Cache is of size 196608 bytes
   Other Memory is of size 196608 bytes
   Catalog Cache Heap is of size 196608 bytes
   Buffer Pool Heap (1) is of size 8650752 bytes
   Buffer Pool Heap (System 32k buffer pool) is of size 851968 bytes
   Buffer Pool Heap (System 16k buffer pool) is of size 589824 bytes
   Buffer Pool Heap (System 8k buffer pool) is of size 458752 bytes
   Buffer Pool Heap (System 4k buffer pool) is of size 393216 bytes
   Shared Sort Heap is of size 0 bytes
   Lock Manager Heap is of size 655360 bytes
   Database Heap is of size 17760256 bytes
   Application Heap (13) is of size 65536 bytes
   Application Heap (12) is of size 65536 bytes
   Application Heap (11) is of size 65536 bytes
   Application Heap (10) is of size 65536 bytes
   Applications Shared Heap is of size 65536 bytes
   Total: 30343168 bytes

Memory for agent 2571

   Other Memory is of size 65536 bytes
   Total: 65536 bytes

Memory for agent 2828

   Other Memory is of size 65536 bytes
   Total: 65536 bytes

Memory for agent 3085

   Other Memory is of size 196608 bytes
   Total: 196608 bytes
```

The output above shows that when the database is activated a total of about 41.9MB of memory is consumed. Let's execute some SQL statements and see how that affects the agent private memory allocation.

```
$db2mtrk -i –p –d –v
Tracking Memory on: 2007/05/22 at 17:10:31

Memory for instance

   Other Memory is of size 13565952 bytes
   Database Monitor Heap is of size 65536 bytes
   FCMBP Heap is of size 786432 bytes
   Total: 14417920 bytes

Memory for database: SAMPLE

   Backup/Restore/Util Heap is of size 65536 bytes
   Package Cache is of size 851968 bytes
   Other Memory is of size 196608 bytes
   Catalog Cache Heap is of size 393216 bytes
   Buffer Pool Heap (1) is of size 8650752 bytes
   Buffer Pool Heap (System 32k buffer pool) is of size 851968 bytes
```

```
    Buffer Pool Heap (System 16k buffer pool) is of size 589824 bytes
    Buffer Pool Heap (System 8k buffer pool) is of size 458752 bytes
    Buffer Pool Heap (System 4k buffer pool) is of size 393216 bytes
    Shared Sort Heap is of size 65536 bytes
    Lock Manager Heap is of size 655360 bytes
    Database Heap is of size 17825792 bytes
    Application Heap (154) is of size 65536 bytes
    Application Heap (13) is of size 65536 bytes
    Application Heap (12) is of size 65536 bytes
    Application Heap (11) is of size 65536 bytes
    Application Heap (10) is of size 65536 bytes
    Applications Shared Heap is of size 262144 bytes
    Total: 31588352 bytes

Memory for agent 2571

    Other Memory is of size 65536 bytes
    Total: 65536 bytes

Memory for agent 2828

    Other Memory is of size 65536 bytes
    Total: 65536 bytes

Memory for agent 3085

    Other Memory is of size 196608 bytes
    Total: 196608 bytes

Memory for agent 17478

    Other Memory is of size 458752 bytes
    Total: 458752 bytes
```

As shown above, the memory tracker tool shows the new agent that was created when the connection was established to the database, and also shows that the agent's memory has grown to 458,752 bytes (458KB). This is an increase of almost 262KB from the other agents due to an increase in the private working memory area. In the meantime the application shared heap has an increase of 196,608 bytes (196KB) in its memory usage. Since the statements would have been optimized to be run, their access plans would have been copied into the application shared heap as they were run.

Let's back up the database and see how that affects the memory used. During the backup operation you can see that the backup/restore buffer is allocated. Below is the db2mtrk output before the backup was run, while it is running, and after the backup has completed.

```
$db2start
05/22/2007 17:13:43     0   0   SQL1063N  DB2START processing was successful.
SQL1063N  DB2START processing was successful.

$db2mtrk -i -v -d
```

```
Tracking Memory on: 2007/05/22 at 17:14:06

Memory for instance

   Other Memory is of size 11993088 bytes
   Database Monitor Heap is of size 65536 bytes
   FCMBP Heap is of size 786432 bytes
   Total: 12845056 bytes

No active databases

$db2mtrk -i -v -d
Tracking Memory on: 2007/05/22 at 17:17:07

Memory for instance

   Other Memory is of size 12517376 bytes
   Database Monitor Heap is of size 65536 bytes
   FCMBP Heap is of size 786432 bytes
   Total: 13369344 bytes

Memory for database: SAMPLE

   Backup/Restore/Util Heap is of size 17563648 bytes
   Package Cache is of size 196608 bytes
   Other Memory is of size 196608 bytes
   Catalog Cache Heap is of size 196608 bytes
   Buffer Pool Heap (1) is of size 8650752 bytes
   Buffer Pool Heap (System 32k buffer pool) is of size 851968 bytes
   Buffer Pool Heap (System 16k buffer pool) is of size 589824 bytes
   Buffer Pool Heap (System 8k buffer pool) is of size 458752 bytes
   Buffer Pool Heap (System 4k buffer pool) is of size 393216 bytes
   Shared Sort Heap is of size 0 bytes
   Lock Manager Heap is of size 655360 bytes
   Database Heap is of size 17760256 bytes
   Application Heap (11) is of size 65536 bytes
   Applications Shared Heap is of size 65536 bytes
   Total: 47644672 bytes

$db2mtrk -i -v -d
Tracking Memory on: 2007/05/22 at 17:17:27

Memory for instance

   Other Memory is of size 11993088 bytes
   Database Monitor Heap is of size 65536 bytes
   FCMBP Heap is of size 786432 bytes
   Total: 12845056 bytes

No active databases
```

Once the backup completes, the backup/restore buffer gets released. Since this was an offline backup, it also releases the connection to the database, so the buffer pools, database heap, lock list, and other memory areas are also released.

16.8 Summary

DB2 provides you with a very flexible way to configure your databases for optimal performance. By understanding how and when DB2 uses and allocates memory, you can tune your system to handle any workload.

For each instance you can control the instance-level memory for such things as the agents that work on behalf of your applications, the overall memory available for private sorts to ensure that you do not overwhelm your server, and for the memory available for interpartition communications.

For each database you can control the size of each individual sort, the amount of space available for such things as locking and logging, as well as the size of the buffer pools available to retrieve data and index pages that need to be read and/or updated.

Now that you understand when and how these memory areas are allocated, and how they work together, you can better understand how changes to particular configuration parameters will impact the overall memory used on the system as well as how the configuration parameters will interact with each other. Starting in DB2 9, DB2 can automatically tune most of the memory areas by itself. It's a good practice to run sample workloads with Self-Tuning Memory Management (STMM) enabled for a long enough period of time (i.e., an hour or two) to get a solid set of initial configurations. You can then either fine tune individual memory areas as needed, or allow STMM to continue tuning those areas based on the workload characteristics during the run time.

16.9 Review Questions

1. Which tools can be used to display the memory used by DB2, and how are they associated with the DB2 configuration parameters?
2. What table function in DB2 9.5 can be used to query the total memory consumption for a given instance?
3. Which parameter can be increased in a dynamic SQL environment to allow applications to reuse the compiled statements of other applications?
4. What is the maximum amount of time that can elapse between one flush of the log buffer to disk and the next one?
5. How can you tell the current total amount of shared memory used by a database?
6. What is the largest client I/O block allowed by DB2?
7. What memory is allocated when you start your DB2 instance?
8. When is the database-level shared memory allocated?
9. When is the application shared heap allocated?
10. For what purpose are the FCM buffers used?

11. How many buffer pools will a database have by default immediately after it is created?
    - A. 1
    - B. 2
    - C. 3
    - D. 4
    - E. 5
12. Which of the following stores the runtime sections used by an application?
    - A. Application Heap
    - B. Statement Heap
    - C. Agent Stack
    - D. Application Shared Heap
13. Which of the following is not part of the database shared memory?
    - A. Lock list
    - B. Shared sort heap threshold
    - C. Package cache
    - D. Statistics heap
14. Which of the following is used to control the maximum size of the application shared memory?
    - A. DATABASE_MEMORY
    - B. APPL_CTL_HEAP_SZ
    - C. APPL_MEMORY
    - D. APPGROUP_MEMORY_SZ
15. Which of the following is used to list the memory usage in database shared memory?
    - A. db2mtrk –p
    - B. db2mtrk –d
    - C. db2mtrk –i
    - D. db2mtrk –a
16. Given the following configuration information:
    ```
    Sort heap thres for shared sorts (4KB) (SHEAPTHRES_SHR) = 2000
    Sort list heap (4KB)                         (SORTHEAP) = 256
    ```
    how many concurrent shared sorts can occur within memory for this database?
    - A. 1
    - B. 5
    - C. 7
    - D. 8
    - E. Unlimited
17. Given the following configuration information:
    ```
    Sort heap threshold (4KB)                  (SHEAPTHRES) = 2000
    Sort list heap (4KB)                         (SORTHEAP) = 256
    ```

how many concurrent private sorts can occur within memory for this database?

A. 1

B. 5

C. 7

D. 8

E. Unlimited

18. Which of the following is not part of the database manager shared memory?

A. DB2 trace

B. Event Monitors

C. DB2 audit facility

D. Buffer pools

19. Given the following output of the **`get db cfg`** command on a 32-bit DB2 instance:

```
Size of database shared memory (4KB) (DATABASE_MEMORY) = AUTOMATIC(75264)
```

how large would the DATABASE MEMORY be after a new 16K page size buffer pool, with a size of 10,000 pages, is allocated?

A. 75264

B. 85264

C. 100000

D. 125000

20. Which of the following is part of the agent private memory?

A. Statement heap

B. Statistics heap

C. Java interpret heap

D. Query heap

CHAPTER 17

Database Performance Considerations

Performance is probably the most important factor in databases and database applications. If performance was not important, people would simply create applications that store their data in flat files rather than purchase highly optimized relational database management systems.

Tuning a DB2 system to obtain optimal performance can be a lengthy process. Poor performance is usually a result of:

- Inefficient SQL
- Suboptimal system (hardware) design
- Suboptimal instance configuration
- Suboptimal database configuration
- Lack of proper maintenance
- No Workload Management

While you may not have a lot of control over the server and disks that are used for the database server, especially in a large UNIX shop, the hardware does have a big impact on the overall performance of the database system.

In this chapter you will learn about:

- The Database Manager (i.e., instance-level) Configuration parameters
- Database configuration parameters that have the largest impact on the performance of the system
- DB2 registry variables

- Maintenance operations that you must perform to ensure that the system continues to perform optimally once you have it running

> **NOTE** XML performance topics are mainly discussed in Chapter 10, Mastering the DB2 pureXML Support.

17.1 Relation Data Performance Fundamentals

When you start designing, building, and tuning your database system, you need to try to balance the three main areas that affect your performance:

- CPU usage
- I/O utilization
- Memory usage

At least one of these three areas is affected by any change that you make, either in designing the system or tuning the system using the registry variables or DB2 configuration parameters. For example, increasing the size of one or more of your buffer pools will increase the memory consumption on the server, but it may then decrease the I/O that is required. By understanding how the various registry variables and configuration parameters impact the CPU usage, I/O, and memory usage, you will be better prepared to judge whether the changes will help the performance of the system.

Let's take another example. If you have a system that is already paging (or swapping) but is not doing a lot of I/O operations, increasing the size of the buffer pools will not be a good idea since this will further increase the paging operations but will not likely reduce the I/O much less than the current level. This change might actually reduce the overall performance of the system, so by thinking this through you can save time and effort in the tuning process.

17.2 System/Server Configuration

The three commandments in designing your database server are

1. Ensure there is enough memory available.
2. Ensure there are enough physical disks to handle the I/O requirements.
3. Ensure there are enough CPUs to handle the workload.

17.2.1 Ensuring There Is Enough Memory Available

As discussed earlier in the book, all DB2 data and indexes are manipulated in the database buffer pools. The buffer pools are allocated in memory, so you need to ensure that you have enough real memory to hold the buffer pools that you have defined. If you have more buffer pool space defined than real memory, your system has to perform a lot of paging operations that have a very large negative effect on performance. While the buffer pools are normally the largest piece of DB2 memory used, there are other memory segments that DB2 also allocates, such as:

- Sort space
- The lock list
- Package cache
- Catalog cache
- Log buffer

Depending on your workload, allocate the available memory to different DB2 components. For a Decision Support System (DSS) or OLAP workload with large reports that scan vast amounts of data, the overall effect of the buffer pool is not as significant since DB2 typically has to scan a lot of data. In this type of workload, DB2 usually also needs to perform a number of sorts to help join and/or order the data. Therefore, in a DSS-type workload, try to divide your available memory evenly between the buffer pools and sort heaps.

Online Transaction Processing (OLTP) applications have traditionally read and written a single row in the database, and therefore get a very big benefit if the data is already in the buffer pool. This type of workload is also good at keeping "hot" or often-accessed pages in the buffer pool for reuse. In addition, if you make the sort heap space too large, DB2 can sometimes favor a sort over an index scan, which has a negative affect on overall performance. Therefore, in an OLTP-type workload, dedicate approximately 75 percent of your available memory to the buffer pool and divide the rest among the sort heaps.

Starting with DB2 9, you can also enable self tuning memory so that DB2 will automatically sample the workload, and performance characteristics of your database, and then adapt the sort heap, locklist, package cache, buffer pool(s), and total database memory to improve performance and throughput. In fact, in many tests self tuning memory can outperform a very optimized hand tuned system since it can adapt to changes in the workload, something that a hand tuned system cannot do. You can enable a buffer pool to be self tuning in the Control Center by checking the "enable self tuning" check box from the CREATE BUFFERPOOL or ALTER BUFFERPOOL Wizard as seen below in Figure 17.1.

To enable the sort heap to be tuned automatically by DB2, check the "Set automatically by DB2" check box in the configure database panel as shown in Figure 17.2 below.

17.2.2 Ensuring There Are Enough Disks to Handle I/O

Do *not* size your disk requirements based on the disk capacity! In other words, if you have a 500GB database, do not buy only 500GB of disk. I/O performance comes from having enough physical disk drives to provide and sustain the throughput required for your workload. With the advent of 100GB and 200GB disks, it is easy to think that you simply need five disks to store a 1TB database. But when you want to read and scan your data, you have only five disks trying to supply all of the data to the processors to be read.

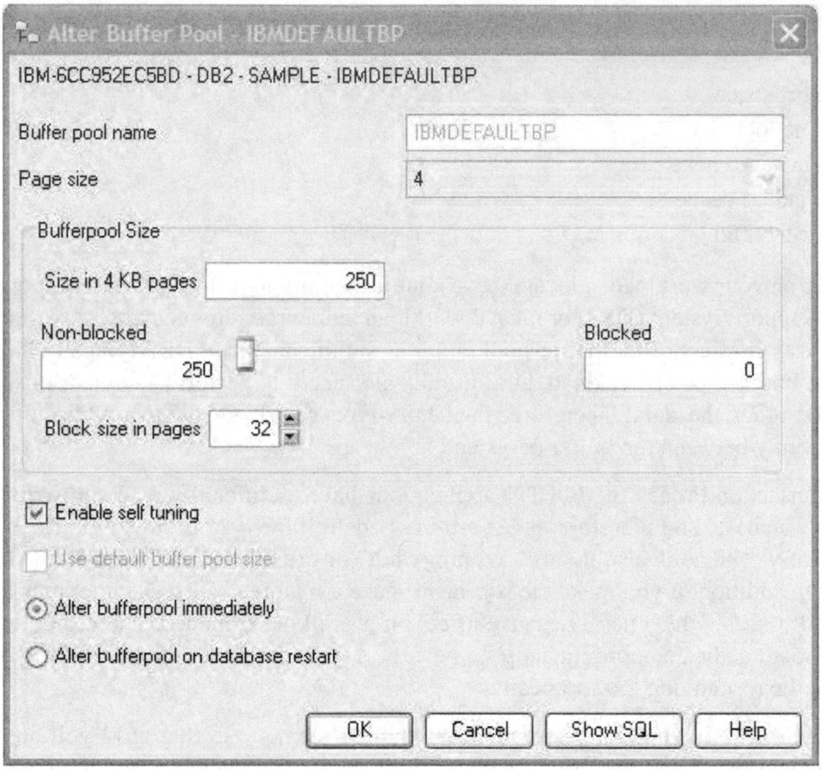

Figure 17.1 Enabling self tuning for a bufferpool

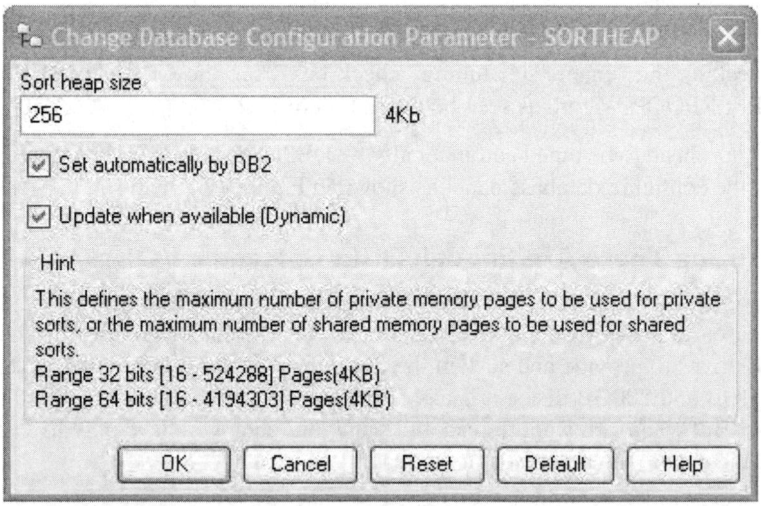

Figure 17.2 Setting Sort heap to be self tuning

Having too few physical disks is the number one source of poor database performance, so do not get caught in this trap. Make sure that you have at least six to ten physical disks per CPU in your server; otherwise, you very likely will be building a system that will be I/O-starved, constantly waiting for I/O, and not working on processing your requests.

17.2.3 Ensuring There Are Enough CPUs to Handle the Workload

Just like a car, the bigger the engine, the faster it can go. In a computer the CPUs are the engine, and the power of the system depends on the number and speed of the CPUs. To handle a large amount of data and a number of concurrent users, you need to be sure that the system has enough CPUs so that you are not constantly utilizing 100 percent of the available CPUs.

It is important to strive for a balanced system that under normal operations is only consuming at most 80 percent of the available CPUs, so that you have room for spikes in activity such as month-end processing and morning application sign-ons.

17.3 The DB2 Configuration Advisor

The Configuration Advisor is a tool that can be used to obtain an initial set of database configuration parameters. This tool can be run in either a graphical mode via the Control Center, or via the command line.

Let's begin by covering how to use the Configuration Advisor via the command line, and follow with the graphical version.

17.3.1 Invoking the Configuration Advisor from the Command Line

You can invoke the Configuration Advisor from the command line using the command **autoconfigure** as shown in Figure 17.3.

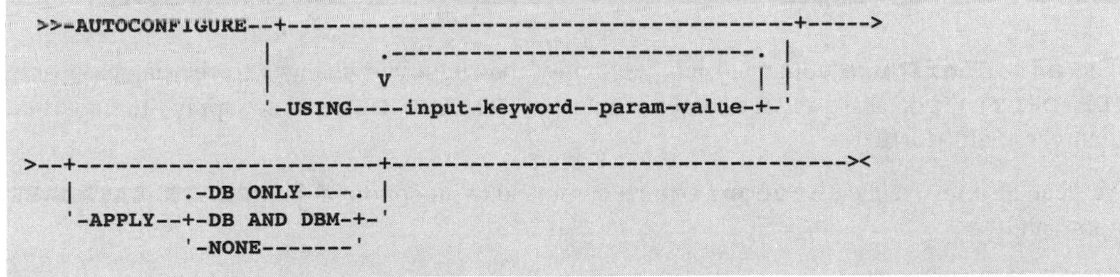

```
>>-AUTOCONFIGURE--+---------------------------------------+----->
                  |                                       |
                  |          .---------------------------.  |
                  |          V                           |  |
                  '-USING----input-keyword--param-value-+-'

>--+---------------------+----------------------------------><
   |        .-DB ONLY----. |
   '-APPLY--+-DB AND DBM-+-'
            '-NONE-------'
```

Figure 17.3 The autoconfigure command

Table 17.1 lists and describes the input keywords.

Table 17.1 Autoconfigure keywords

Keyword	Valid Values [default]	Explanation
mem_percent	1–100 [80]	Percentage of memory to dedicate. If applications other than the operating system are running on this server, set this to less than 100.
Workload_type	simple, mixed, complex [mixed]	Simple workloads tend to be I/O intensive and mostly transactions, whereas complex workloads tend to be CPU-intensive and mostly queries.
num_stmts	1–1000000 [10]	Number of statements per unit of work.
Tpm	1–50000 [60]	Transactions per minute.
admin_priority	performance, recovery, both [both]	Optimize for better performance (more transactions per minute) or better recovery time.
is_populated	yes, no [yes]	Whether the database is populated with data.
num_local_apps	0–5000 [0]	Number of connected local applications.
num_remote_apps	0–5000 [10]	Number of connected remote applications.
Isolation	RR, RS, CS, UR [CS]	Isolation level of applications connecting to this database (Repeatable Read, Read Stability, Cursor Stability, Uncommitted Read).
bp_resizeable	yes, no [yes]	Whether the buffer pools are resizable.

The **autoconfigure** command lets you apply the suggested changes to the database only (**DB ONLY**), the database and the database manager (**DB AND DBM**), or not apply the suggested changes at all (**NONE**).

You can also invoke the **autoconfigure** command as an option of the **CREATE DATABASE** command:

```
CREATE DATABASE mydb
      AUTOCONFIGURE using mem_percent 75 APPLY DB AND DBM
```

Note: The **autoconfigure** command can also be invoked using the **ADMIN_CMD** procedure.

17.3.2 Invoking the Configuration Advisor from the Control Center

The Configuration Advisor asks you a series of questions about the database server, the nature of the workload, transactions, priority, connections, and isolation level to determine a starting set of database configuration parameter values. You can modify these parameters later to suit the production workload and for additional fine-tuning.

The following are the general steps for configuring a database for optimal performance using the Configuration Advisor.

1. Open the DB2 Control Center.
2. Select the database to be configured.
3. Choose the Configuration Advisor.
4. Complete each of the applicable wizard pages. Discussion of each page follows.
5. The *Finish* button is available once enough information has been supplied for the Configuration Advisor to configure performance parameters for the database.

Click *Finish* to get a list of suggested configuration parameters for the database.

As you can see in Figure 17.4, the Configuration Advisor takes you through step by step.

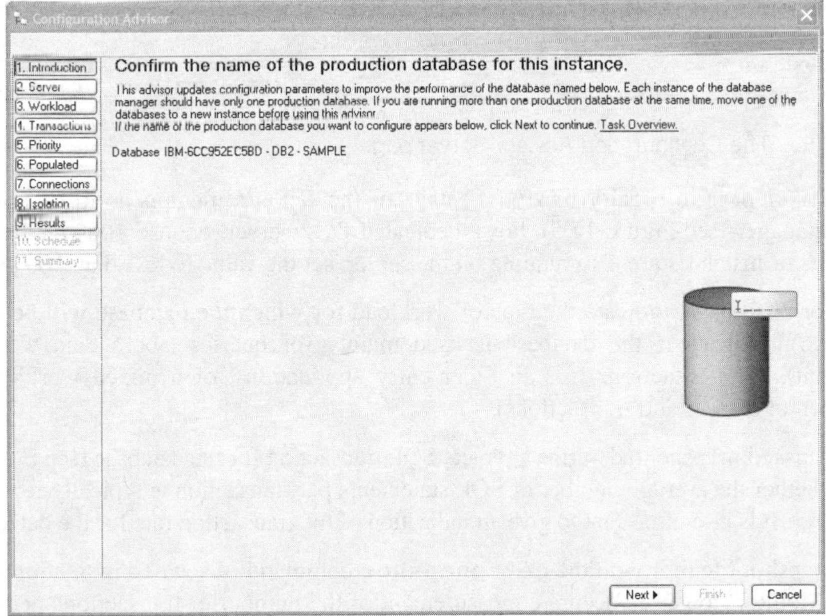

Figure 17.4 The Configuration Advisor Introduction page

The Introduction page lists the database that is currently being examined (see Figure 17.4). Verify that the correct database is shown. If the correct database is not listed, you might have selected a different database by mistake. Close the Configuration Advisor by selecting *Cancel* and start again.

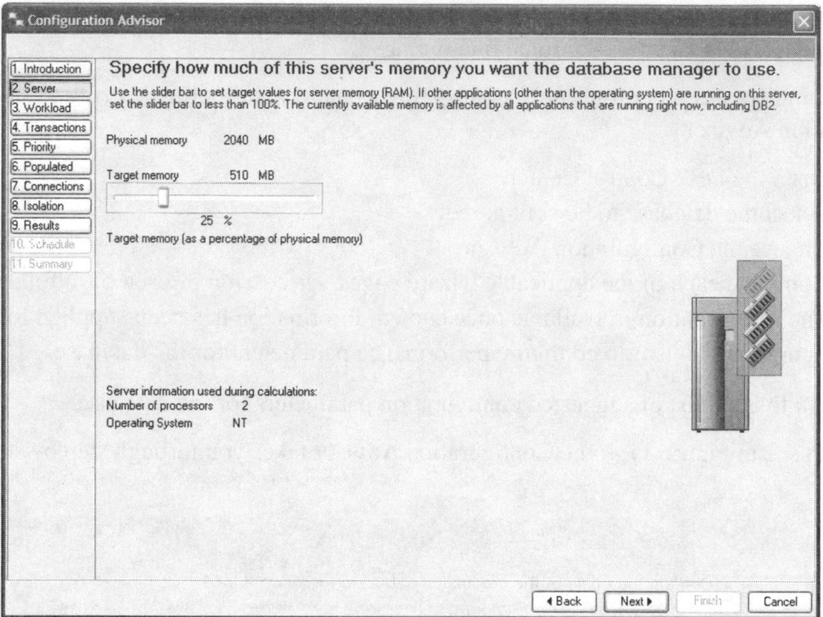

Figure 17.5 The Configuration Advisor Server page

Use the Server page to specify what percentage of the server's memory is to be used by the database manager (see Figure 17.5). For a dedicated DB2 server, choose 100 percent; if other applications or instances are also running on the server, set the value to less than 100 percent.

On the Workload page, indicate the type of workload for which the database will be used (see Figure 17.6). Indicate if the database is used mainly for queries (for a data warehousing environment), for transactions (for an order entry application), or a mixed workload (for a combination of queries and transactions).

Use the Transactions page to describe a typical SQL transaction for the database (see Figure 17.7). Indicate whether the average number of SQL statements per transaction is typically fewer than or more than 10. It is also important to give an indication of the transaction rate for the database.

Use the Snapshot Monitor with the **`get snapshot`** command (discussed in Section 17.8, The Snapshot Monitor) to get an accurate measurement of the number of transactions per minute if the database is already operational.

Specify the priority for the selected database on the Priority page (see Figure 17.8). If the database is optimized for fast transaction processing, the database may take longer to recover in the event of an error. If the database is optimized for fast recovery time, transaction performance normally will be slower. If it is equally important to optimize both, choose to balance the optimization of the two.

Indicate whether the database has been populated with data on the Populated page (see Figure 17.9). This is important because if the database has already been populated, the Configuration Advisor can use database statistics as input to its suggestions.

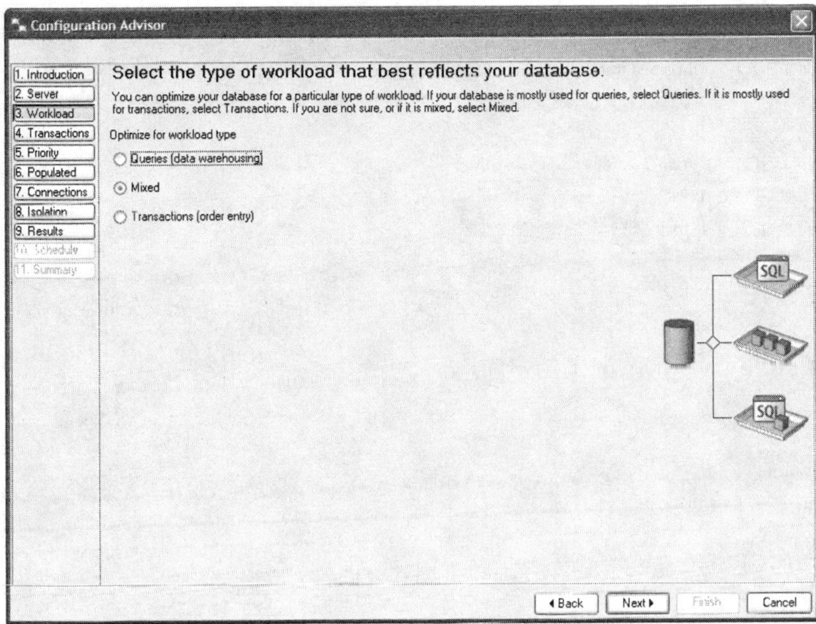

Figure 17.6 The Configuration Advisor Workload page

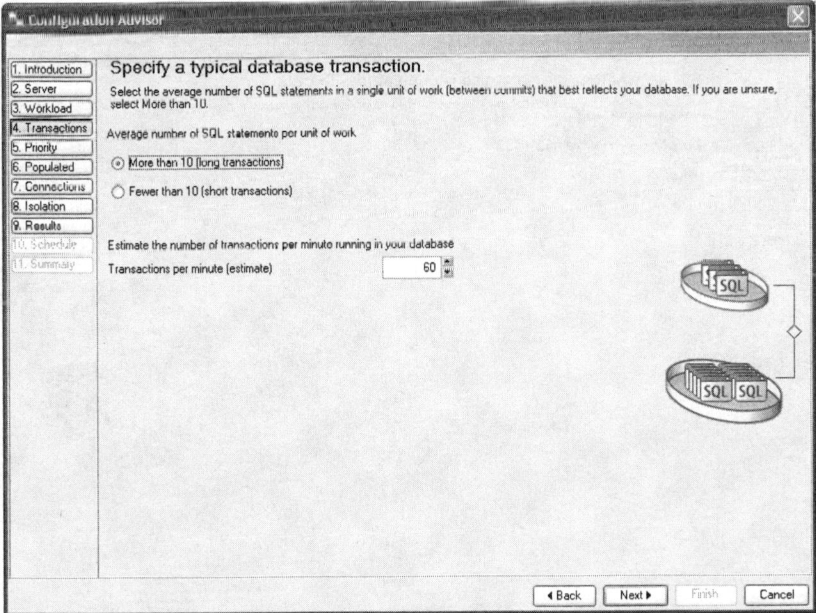

Figure 17.7 The Configuration Advisor Transactions page

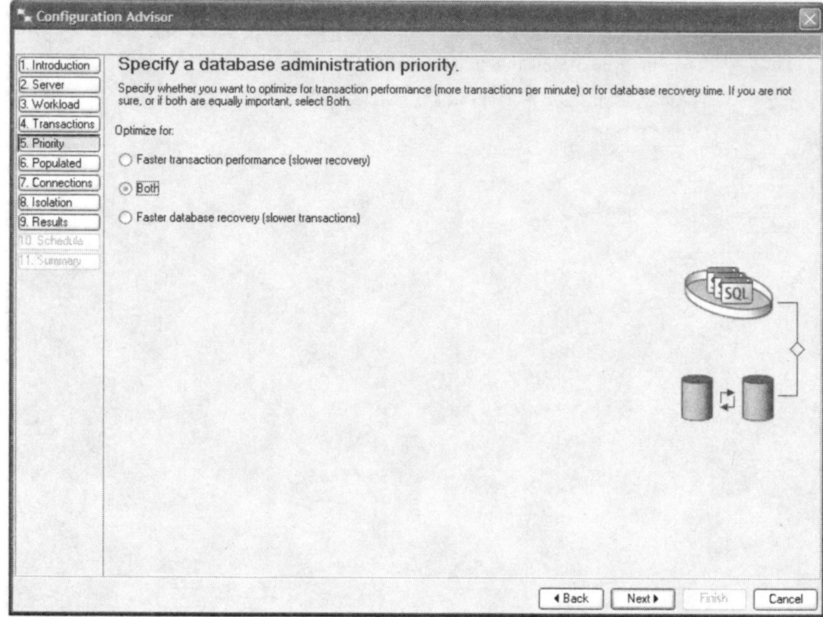

Figure 17.8 The Configuration Advisor Priority page

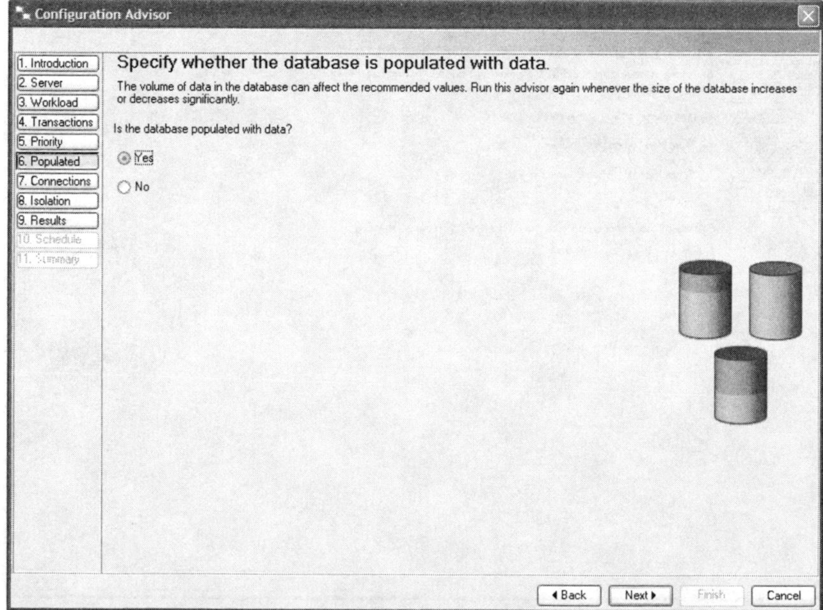

Figure 17.9 The Configuration Advisor Populated page

Indicate the average number of local applications and the average number of remote applications that will connect to the database on the Connections page (see Figure 17.10). If these numbers are not available and you don't have a good estimate, use the default values.

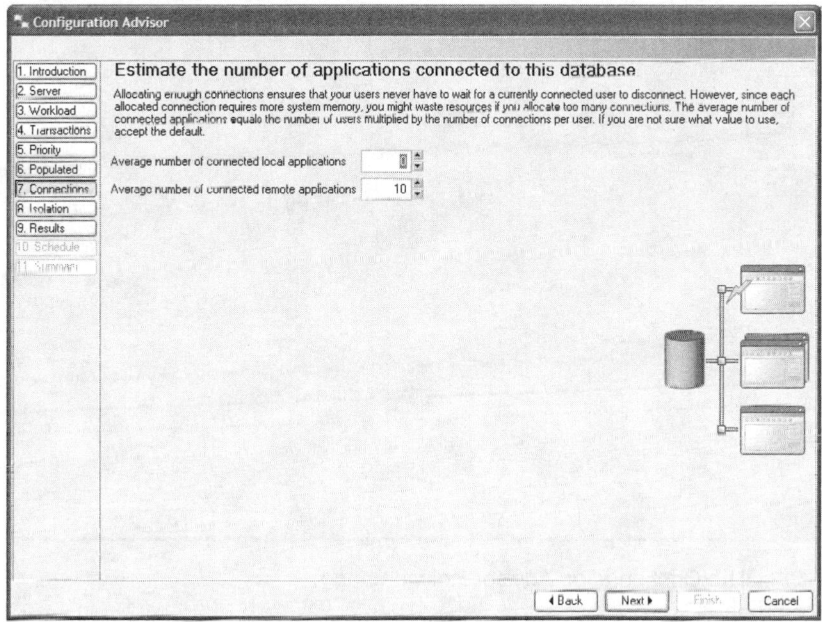

Figure 17.10 The Configuration Advisor Connections page

Use the Snapshot Monitor to get an accurate measurement of the number of remote and local applications that connect to the database.

Specify the isolation level that the applications will use to access the database on the Isolation page (see Figure 17.11). If you use multiple isolation levels, specify the one that is used most frequently in the applications, or the one used by the most important application. Refer to Chapter 12, Understanding Concurrency and Locking, for more information about isolation levels.

Specify whether a tools catalog database should be created to store information about scheduled tasks on the Schedule page (see Figure 17.12). The Task Center is required for the DB2 scheduling function to be enabled, and it requires the tools catalog (see Section 4.4.5, The Task Center).

The Results page displays the Configuration Advisor's recommended configuration parameter settings based on the information provided (see Figure 17.13). You can choose to apply the suggestions immediately, or save them to a script so you can apply the changes later.

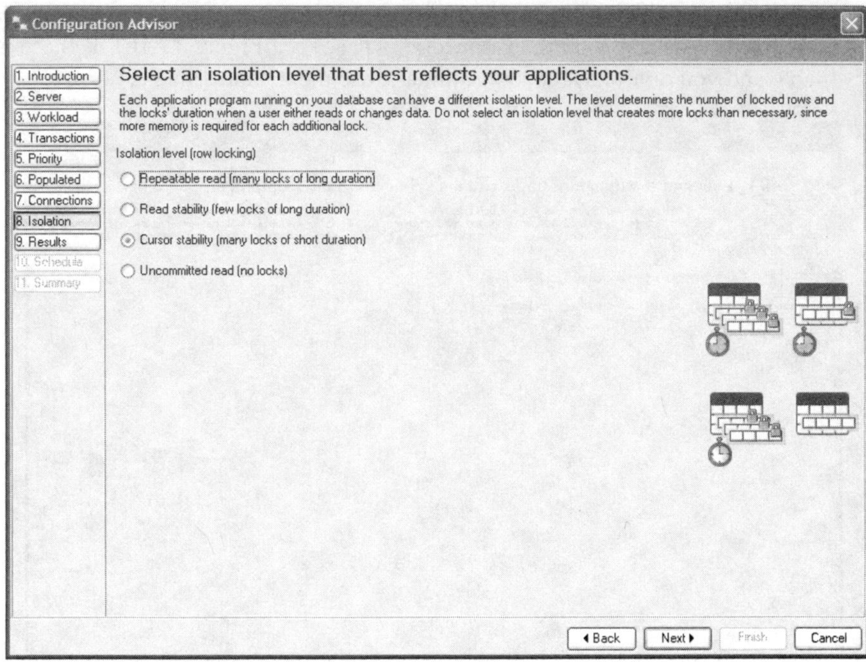

Figure 17.11 The Configuration Advisor Isolation page

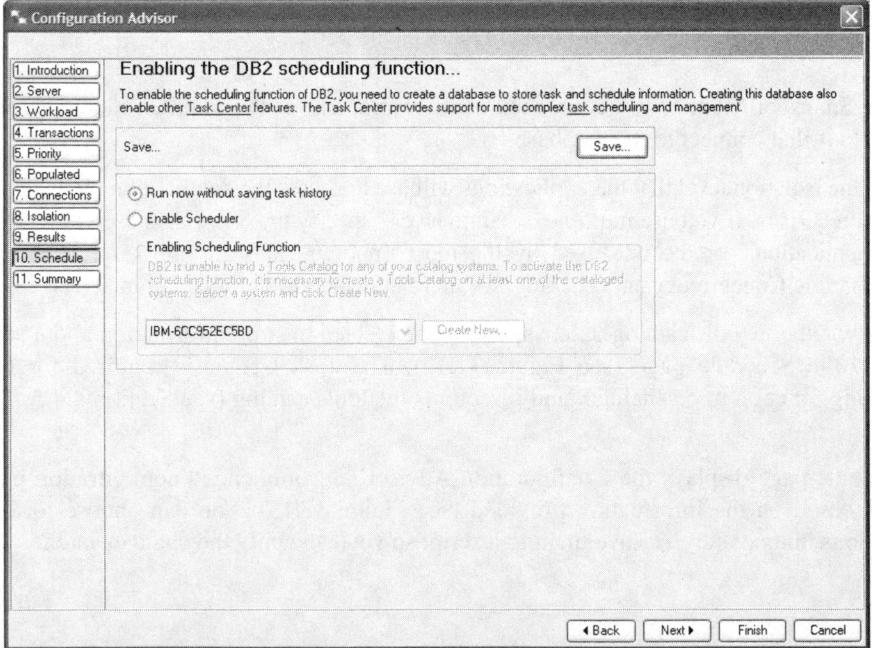

Figure 17.12 The Configuration Advisor Schedule page

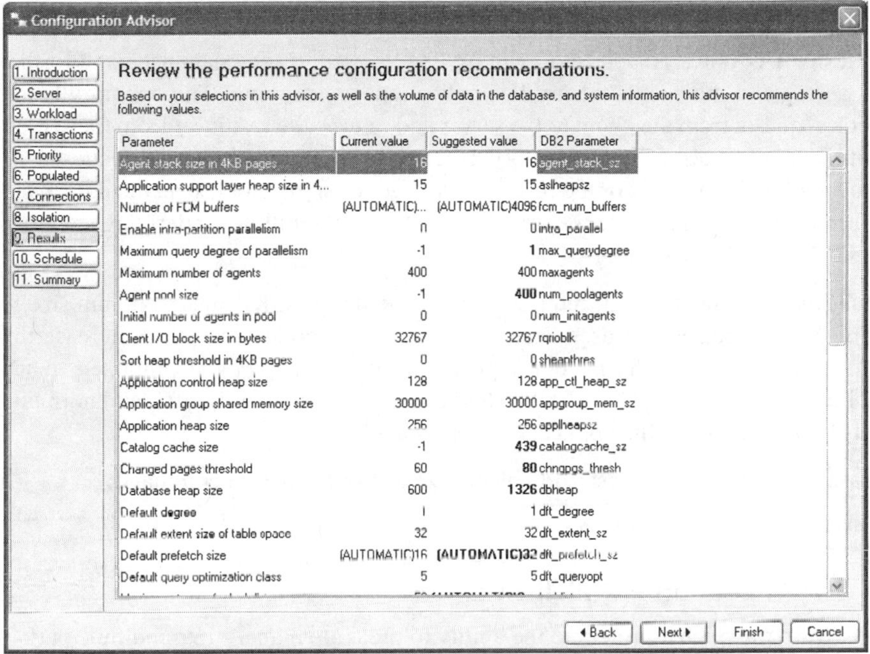

Figure 17.13 The Configuration Advisor Results page

17.4 Configuring the DB2 Instance

The Database Manager (instance-level) Configuration parameters affect the performance of all databases in the instance and all applications that access databases in the instance. This section examines the parameters that have the biggest impact on the system performance and gives suggestions on how to choose the right value for the parameter.

Table 17.2 lists the parameters with the biggest impact on system performance.

Table 17.2 Parameters with the Most Impact on System Performance for Configuring a DB2 Instance

Parameter Name	Description
RQRIOBLK	Maximum requester I/O block size.
INTRA_PARALLEL	Enables intra-partition parallelism.
SHEAPTHRES	Sort heap threshold.
NUM_INITAGENTS	Initial number of agents in pool.
NUM_POOLAGENTS	Agent pool size.

17.4.1 Maximum Requester I/O Block Size

The **requester I/O block** is a piece of memory that is used to send data back and forth between the DB2 server and the clients where the applications are running. This memory block passes application requests from the client to the server and returns the result set from the server back to the client. DB2 allocates as much memory as it needs, up to the maximum requester I/O block size. If the application request or the result set is larger than the block size, the data must be split into multiple blocks. These blocks are then sent using multiple underlying communication packets.

By default, the maximum size of requester I/O block size is 32KB; its maximum size is 64KB. Since DB2 only allocates and uses what is required, it is good practice to increase this to the maximum of 64KB, especially if your application requests and/or the result sets generated by your applications are greater than 32KB. This results in less network traffic and normally allows result sets to be returned to the application more quickly.

To increase the maximum requester I/O block size to 64KB, use the command:

```
update dbm cfg using rqrioblk 64
```

17.4.2 Intra-Partition Parallelism

Intra-partition parallelism refers to the ability to break up a query into multiple parts within a single database partition and execute these parts at the same time. This type of parallelism subdivides what is usually considered a single database operation, such as index creation, database load, or SQL queries, into multiple parts, many or all of which can be executed in parallel within a single database partition. You can use intra-partition parallelism to take advantage of multiple processors of a symmetric multiprocessor (SMP) server.

It is important to note that intra-partition parallelism is not recommended for all workloads, even if you are running DB2 on an SMP server. In general, if your workload is mostly OLTP and is composed of a large number of simple SQL statements, you will get better overall performance by disabling intra-partition parallelism. If you are running mostly large, complex queries on an SMP server, you likely will gain from enabling intra-partition parallelism.

You can enable or disable intra-partition parallelism using the instance-level configuration parameter INTRA_PARALLEL as follows:

```
update dbm cfg using intra_parallel yes
```

or

```
update dbm cfg using intra_parallel no
```

17.4.3 Sort Heap Threshold

If you issue an SQL statement that includes an ORDER BY, GROUP BY, or DISTINCT clause, DB2 must either use an index to sort the data or perform a sort operation. DB2 will need to sort the data if you have not defined an appropriate index on one or more of the tables you are querying.

DB2 can perform either a private sort or a shared sort. If you have not enabled intra-partition parallelism, then DB2 can perform private sorts only. If you have enabled intra-partition parallelism, DB2 then can choose private or shared sorts, depending on which is more optimal.

DB2 creates and assigns each individual sort its own sort heap space. The sort heap threshold specifies the maximum amount of memory that can be simultaneously used for private sorts across all databases in the DB2 instance. When the total amount of private sort memory in use reaches the sort heap threshold, DB2 reduces the amount of memory that is assigned to subsequent sort operations. So in effect, the sort heap threshold is a soft limit, since DB2 can allocate more total sort space than the sort heap threshold specifies.

Set the sort heap threshold based on the size of your database sort heaps and the average number of concurrently executing applications. For example, if:

- The sort heap for your database is set to 256 pages
  and
- Database monitor snapshots show an average of 20 concurrently executing applications

you should set the sort heap threshold to at least 5,120 pages (20 × 256 = 5,120). Since some access plans do more than one sort operation, you may want to set the sort heap threshold to 10,240 pages. To set the sort heap threshold to this value, use the command:

```
update dbm cfg using sheapthres 10240
```

17.4.4 The DB2 Agent Pool

In DB2 9.5 the number of agents in the agent pool (NUM_POOLAGENTS) is set to AUTOMATIC. By default DB2 will create 100 agent threads and will automatically manage the number of idle agents in the pool. This used to be an important parameter in previous version of DB2, but DB2 9.5 removes the work and worry involved in determing how to set this parameter.

17.5 Configuring Your Databases

The database configuration parameters affect all aspects of your database performance and all applications that access the database. This section examines the parameters that have the biggest impact on system performance and provides suggestions on how to choose the right value for the parameter.

Table 17.3 lists the parameters with the biggest impact on system performance.

Table 17.3 Parameters with the Most Impact on System Performance for Configuring Your Database

Parameter Name	Description
AVG_APPLS	Average number of active applications.
MINCOMMIT	Number of commits to group.
LOGBUFSZ	Size of the log buffer.

(continues)

Table 17.3 Parameters with the Most Impact on System Performance for Configuring Your Database *(Continued)*

Parameter Name	Description
SORTHEAP	Memory available for sorts.
SHEAPTHRES_SHR	Shared sort heap threshold.
LOCKLIST	Memory available to store lock information.
MAXLOCKS	Percent of lock list per application.
NUM_IOSERVERS	Number of I/O servers.
NUM_IOCLEANERS	Number of asynchronous page cleaners.
CHNGPGS_THRESH	Changed pages threshold before soft checkpoint.
SOFTMAX	Percent of log file before soft checkpoint.

The database buffer pools also have a very big impact on the performance of the database and its applications. You can choose the size of your buffer pools based on the default buffer pool size (BUFFPAGE), or you can size each buffer pool individually using the **create bufferpool** or **alter bufferpool** statements. (See Section 8.5, Buffer Pools, for a detailed discussion of buffer pool usage.)

17.5.1 Average Number of Active Applications

The DB2 optimizer uses the value you set for the average number of active applications when it is determining the optimal access plans for statements in your applications. This number is used to determine the percentage of total system resources that each application can use.

Examine your current workload to determine the best setting for the average number of active applications. You can do this by taking database monitor snapshots at various times throughout the day and averaging the *Average number of concurrently executing applications* snapshot element. You can get this information for the sample database using either of the following commands:

```
GET SNAPSHOT FOR DATABASE
ON sample | grep -i 'Appls. executing in db manager currently'
```

or

```
SELECT appls_in_db2
FROM table(snapshot_database('sample', -1)) as snapshot_database
```

You can then set the average number of active applications for the database sample based on the snapshot information as follows:

```
update db cfg for sample using avg_appls 10
```

17.5.2 Database Logging

The log buffer is an area of memory that helps speed up the database logging process. DB2 writes information about all transactions to the log buffer and then flushes this buffer to disk periodically. This improves database performance since DB2 does not have to write every change to disk immediately, before making the changes in the database. This process is known as **write-ahead logging.** Remember that writing log records to disk is different from writing database changes to disk. Database changes are written (flushed) to disk either during buffer pool cleaning or when the buffer pool is full.

To ensure the integrity of your database, DB2 writes the log buffers to disk when:

- One or more transactions commit
- The log buffer is full
- One second has elapsed since the last log buffer flush

By default the log buffer is flushed to disk after every commit statement. However, for a database with a lot of concurrent applications, you can tell DB2 to wait to flush the log buffer until a specific number of commits occur. This number is known as the **number of commits to group** and is controlled by the MINCOMMIT database configuration parameter. When you set this parameter to a value greater than one, the applications that issue a commit may not return immediately because DB2 must ensure that the log buffer is written to disk before returning to the application. If you have many applications running very small, short transactions, you may see a slow down in the applications since they may wait up to one second for the commits to return. You can increase the number of commits to group for the sample database to a value of 5 using the command:

```
update db cfg for sample using mincommit 5
```

Since the log buffer is also flushed to disk when it becomes full, it is important to have a log buffer that is large enough that it is not constantly being written to disk. To increase the size of the log buffer for the *sample* database to 250 pages, use the command:

```
update db cfg for sample using logbufsz 250
```

17.5.3 Sorting

There are two database configuration parameters that affect sorting in your database applications: sort heap (SORTHEAP) and shared sort heap threshold (SHEAPTHRES_SHR).

The database sort heap (SORTHEAP) specifies the maximum amount of memory that each individual sort can use. You will not be able to have a large enough sort heap so that all sorts can occur in memory, especially for a large data warehouse. Therefore, you need to estimate the sort heap requirements for your system based on the EXPLAIN information for the queries being executed. The EXPLAIN output tells you if the optimizer has chosen to perform a sort to build the result set for your query. If there is a sort in the access plan, then in the sort portion of the access plan, there are two pieces of information:

- The average row size
- The estimated number of rows to be sorted

You can multiply these two values together to get a rough estimate of the memory required for the sort operation.

NOTE Each row that is being sorted uses some extra space in the sort heap, so there is some overhead required to perform the sort.

You can set the sort heap threshold for the *sample* database as follows:

```
update db cfg for sample using sortheap 6400
```

As discussed earlier, private and shared sorts use memory from two different memory areas. The maximum amount of memory available for shared sorts (the shared sort heap threshold, SHEAPTHRES_SHR) within a database is allocated when the database is activated or when your first application connects to the database. When any shared sort occurs within the database it uses memory within this area. If there are already a number of shared sorts in process, and your application attempts to perform another shared sort, DB2 checks to make sure there is enough memory within this shared sort area. If there is enough memory available, the sort will be done as normal; if there is not enough memory available, the sort will be overflowed and DB2 creates a temporary table to perform the sort.

NOTE Unlike the sort heap threshold, the shared sort heap threshold is a hard limit.

You can set the shared sort heap threshold for the *sample* database using the following command:

```
update db cfg for sample using sheapthres_shr 120000
```

17.5.4 Locking

When you are accessing data in a database, DB2 acquires locks as it is reading the data. The mode of the lock and the object that the lock is obtained on are determined by the isolation level of the application. No matter on which object the lock is held, DB2 needs to store and manage the information about all locks in the database. This information is stored in the database lock list. The lock list size (LOCKLIST) specifies the amount of memory that is available to store the lock information for the database. You can set the size of the lock list for the *sample* database using the command:

```
update db cfg for sample using locklist 2048
```

If the lock list becomes full, DB2 will perform **lock escalation:** the process where DB2 replaces a number of row-level locks with a single table lock. This can drastically reduce the amount of free space in the lock list for future lock requests.

Lock escalation can also occur when the number of locks held by a single application reaches or exceeds the maximum percent of lock list before escalation (MAXLOCKS). When an application reaches or exceeds this value, DB2 performs lock escalation by:

1. Examining the lock list for all locks held by the application to determine which database object has the most row-level locks held on it by this application,
2. Requesting a table-level lock on this table, and
3. Releasing the row-level locks once the table lock is granted.

The default setting for the maximum percent of lock list before escalation is 10 percent on UNIX and 22 percent on Windows and Linux. You may want to increase this, especially for databases with few applications, as this can cause premature escalation. To increase the maximum percent of lock list before escalation to 35 percent, use the command:

```
update db cfg for sample using maxlocks 35
```

17.5.5 Buffer Pool Prefetching and Cleaning

When DB2 agents are working to service your applications, they need to read and manipulate data within the database buffer pools. If the page that DB2 needs is not already in the buffer pool, it has to be read from disk and placed into the buffer pool before DB2 can scan or update the page.

DB2 can detect when your applications are reading pages and can read them into the buffer pool before your applications need them, saving the time the applications must wait to get its result set from DB2. This is known as **prefetching.** You can control the amount of prefetching that your system can perform by using the number of I/O servers (NUM_IOSERVERS) configuration parameter.

In the previous example the buffer pool is full, so when DB2 tries to read a page from disk into the buffer pool, DB2 must choose a spot in the buffer pool to place the new page. If there is a page already in this spot, DB2 will check the page to see if it has changed since it was placed into the buffer pool. If it has not changed, DB2 can simply replace this page with the new page. If it has changed, DB2 must first write the page back to disk since it cannot lose these changes. Only after the page has been written to disk can the new page replace it in the buffer pool.

To try to eliminate these wait conditions, DB2 periodically—and asynchronously—writes changed pages in the buffer pool back to disk. This is known as **buffer pool page cleaning.** You can control the amount of buffer pool page cleaning that your system can perform using the number of asynchronous page cleaners (NUM_IOCLEANERS) configuration parameter.

Prefetching is most efficient if your table spaces have more than one container, allowing DB2 to take advantage of parallel I/O. Base the number of prefetchers on the number of physical disks on which you have created table spaces for your database. If your database named *sample* has table space containers on 32 different physical disks, you can set the number of prefetchers for the database to 32 using the command:

```
update db cfg for sample using num_ioservers 32
```

If your applications perform a lot of update operations, increasing the number of asynchronous page cleaners will help to improve the overall performance of your database applications. If a system crashes due to a power failure or some other reason, this also helps to reduce the database recovery time because it keeps writing changes to disk instead of having a buffer pool full of a large number of changes.

Since all the page cleaners are triggered at the same time, having too many can overwhelm your system. As a general rule of thumb, do not configure more asynchronous page cleaners than there are CPUs in your DB2 server. For an 8-way SMP server, you can set the number of asynchronous page cleaners for the *sample* database to 8 using the command:

```
update db cfg for sample using num_iocleaners 8
```

There are two different configuration parameters that let you control how frequently the page cleaners are triggered.

- The changed page threshold (CHNGPGS_THRESH) tells DB2 to trigger the page cleaners after any of the database's buffer pools is this percent used by pages that have changed since they were read into the buffer pool.
- The percent of the log file reclaimed before the soft checkpoint database configuration parameter (SOFTMAX) tells DB2 to trigger the page cleaners after this percent of any of the database log files has been filled by your transactions.

> **NOTE** DB2 also triggers the page cleaners if a DB2 agent is attempting to place a page into the buffer pool and needs to write a changed page to disk before it can place the page in the buffer pool.

17.6 Lack of Proper Maintenance

There are two important database maintenance operations that you need to perform on a regular basis.

- Reorganize your tables and indexes as they become unclustered due to INSERT, UPDATE, and DELETE statements.
- Keep the statistics on your tables and indexes current, especially as you add, change, or remove data from your tables.

The DB2 optimizer uses the statistics about your tables and indexes when it is building the access plan for the statements executed by your applications. If the statistics are out of date or show that the data is not clustered according to the indexes you have defined on the tables, the optimizer cannot choose the most efficient access plan.

Statistics about your database objects are stored in the database's system catalog tables. DB2 reads this information when the optimizer is building the access plan for one of your SQL statements. You can update this information with the current statistics by using one of these methods:

- Running the **RUNSTATS** utility
- Using the **LOAD** utility to load data into one of your tables
- Running the **REORGCHK** command

Use the **RUNSTATS** utility to gather new, updated statistics for tables and indexes after you have done any of the following:

- Reorganized a table or index
- Added a large number of rows to a table using the **LOAD** or **IMPORT** utilities
- Made a large number of changes to the data in the table using **INSERT, UPDATE,** or **DELETE** statements
- Changed a table space's prefetch size

The reorganize utility clusters the data in the table so that it is in the same order as the index you specify. Be sure to specify the index that is most often used to join this table with other tables, and/or to access data in this table as a result of the SQL you are executing. To reorganize the table named *org* so that it is clustered in the same order as the index *orgx* on the table, use the command:

```
reorg table org index orgx
```

You can also reorganize a table using the Control Center by opening the tables list, selecting the table you want to reorganize, and then right clicking on the table and choosing the **Reorganize** option. This displays the dialog shown in Figure 17.14.

You can choose the index on which you want to cluster the data, and also choose whether you want to perform an online or offline load. You can then open the *Schedule* tab and choose to either schedule the reorganization for a later time or run the reorganization immediately (see Figure 17.15). You can then select *OK*.

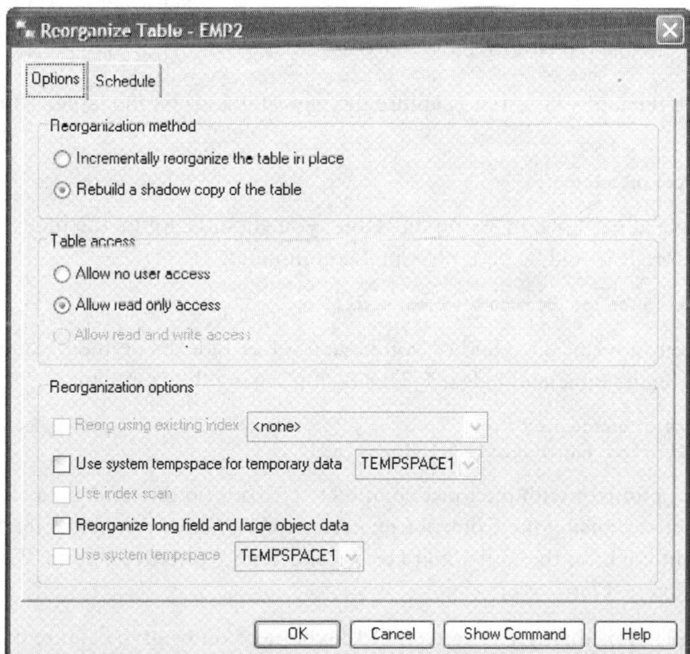

Figure 17.14 REORG utility options

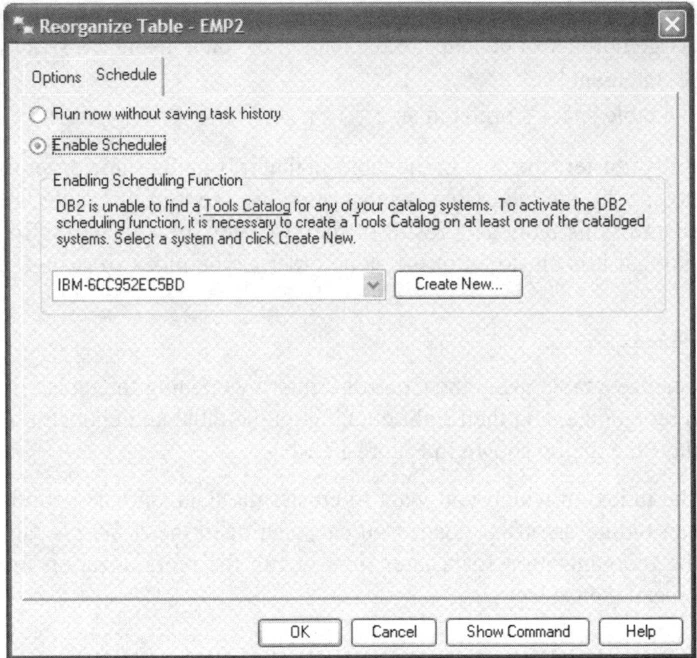

Figure 17.15 Scheduling a REORG

After reorganizing the table, be sure to capture the new statistics on the table. This is done using the command:

```
runstats on table johndoe.org
```

Since you also have at least one index on this table, you should capture the index statistics at the same time. Therefore it would be better to run the command:

```
runstats on table johndoe.org and indexes all
```

If this table contains a lot of data, and/or you have a lot of indexes defined, you should capture detailed statistics on the table and indexes. This is done using the command:

```
runstats on table johndoe.org
     with distribution and detailed indexes all
```

This provides the optimizer with the most complete statistics on the table data and indexes. You can also gather statistics using the Control Center. Open the tables list, select the table you want to reorganize, right click on the table, and choose the **Run Statistics** option. This displays the dialog shown in Figure 17.16.

On the *Column* tab in this dialog you can tell DB2 whether you want to capture basic statistics or if you want to capture distribution statistics on the table. You can then go to the *Index* tab to choose the index on which you want the data clustered (see Figure 17.17).

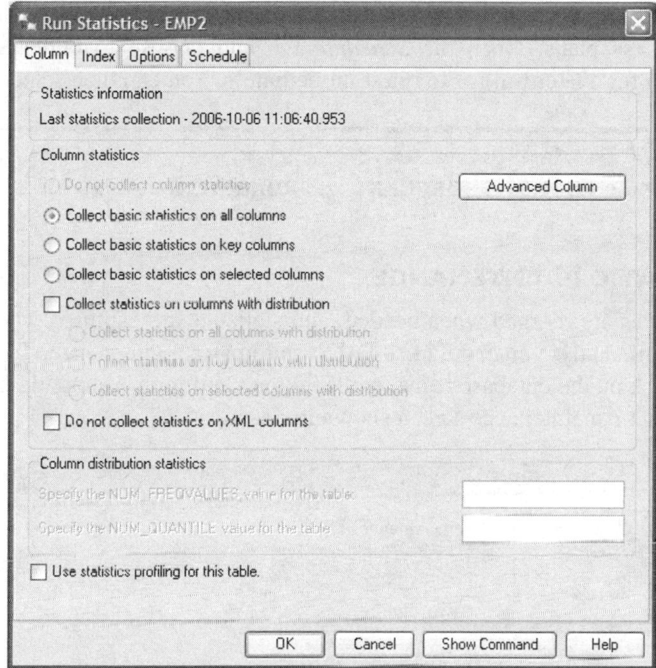

Figure 17.16 The RUNSTATS utility: Column tab

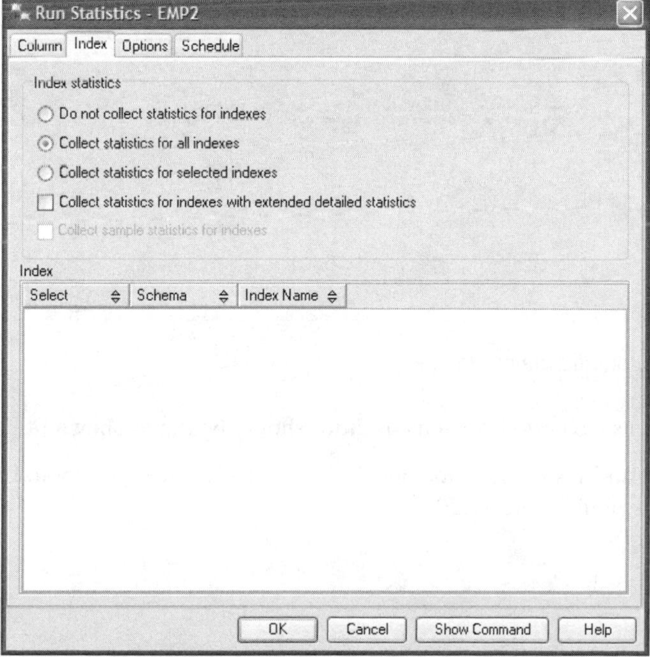

Figure 17.17 The RUNSTATS utility: Index tab

You can also specify if you want to capture detailed statistics that help the optimizer choose the most efficient access plans. Open the *Schedule* tab and choose to either schedule the run statistics operation for a later time or to run it immediately. You can then select *OK*.

> **NOTE** Refer to Chapter 13, Maintaining Data, for more details about the **REORG**, **REORGCHK**, and **RUNSTATS** utilities.

17.7 Automatic Maintenance

To ensure that tables are reorged when needed, and statistics are captured when the data in the table changes significantly, you should use DB2's automatic maintenance. To use this, select a database, right click on the database name, and click on Configure Automatic maintenance. You will see the automatic maintenance screen shown in Figure 17.18.

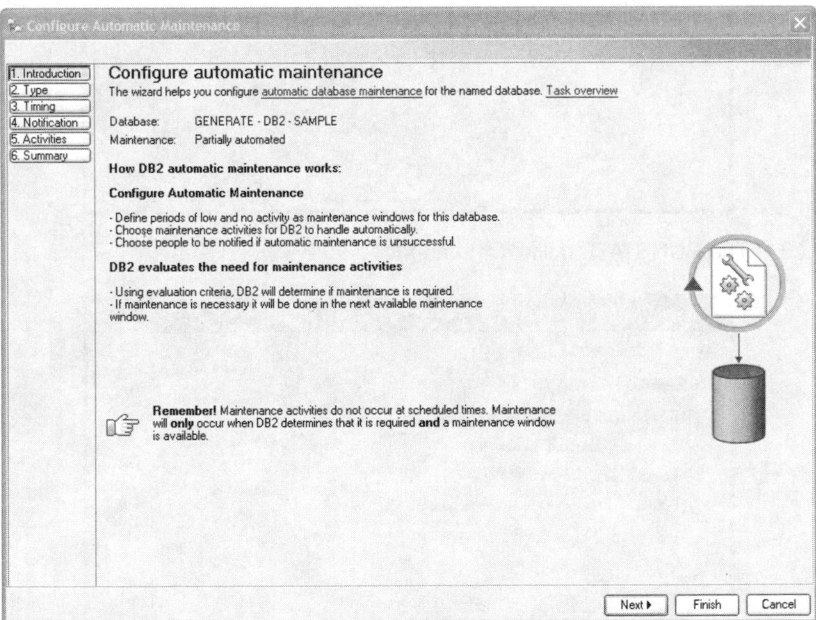

Figure 17.18 Automatic maintenance

Specify the maintenance period when the utilities should be run as shown in Figure 17.19.

Then choose what utilities to run automatically. For performance, you should select **REORG** and **RUNSTATS** as shown in Figure 17.20.

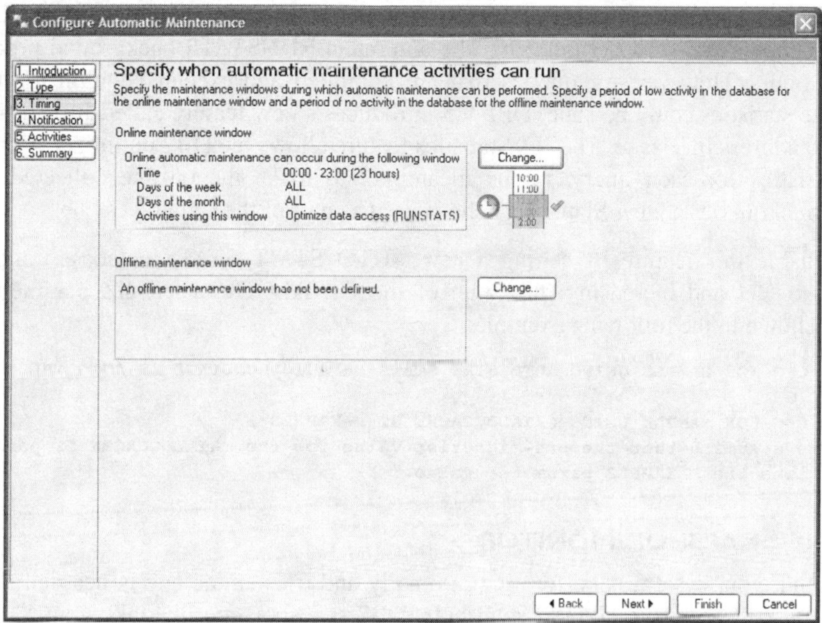

Figure 17.19 Scheduling Automatic maintenance

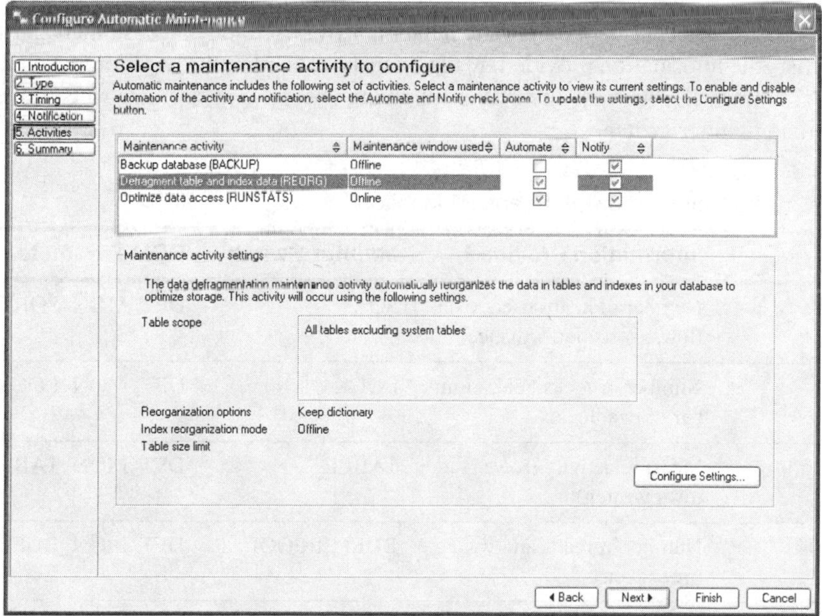

Figure 17.20 Enabling REORG and RUNSTATS to run automatically

The automatic RUNSTATS feature discussed previously has been implemented in DB2 8.2 to collect and update statistics periodically. The automatic RUNSTATS background process runs every two hours. However, for queries that are compiled and executed within the two-hour window, the statistics could be stale. DB2 9.5 introduces a new feature called Just-in-time (JIT) Statistics to address this issue. The JIT Statistics feature allows the DB2 optimizer to collect up-to-date statistics for each query. In the meantime, to make the on-line collected statistics available to all queries, a new Statistic Cache is used as part of the Catalog Cache.

You can enable this feature by setting a new AUTO_STMT_STATS database configuration parameter to ON and increasing the value of the CATALOGCACHE_SZ parameter by 25 percent as shown in the following example:

```
UPDATE DB CFG FOR SAMPLE USING AUTO_STMT_STATS ON AUTO_RUNSTATS ON AUTO_TBL_MAINT ON
AUTO_MAINT ON
UPDATE DB CFG FOR SAMPLE USING CATALOGCACHE_SZ MAXAPPLS*5
Where it is assuming that the pre-migration value for the CATALOGCACHE_SZ parameter
was four times the MAXAPPLS parameter value.
```

17.8 The Snapshot Monitor

To ensure that your system is performing optimally and to examine any issues that may arise, you normally will need to take DB2 snapshots. DB2 snapshots are like taking an X-ray of the various performance indicators within the DB2 engine, and just like doctors examine X-rays, you will examine the snapshot information.

Before capturing a snapshot, first determine what data you need the database manager to gather. Table 17.4 lists the information provided by the Snapshot Monitor, the monitor switch name, and the DBM parameter. If you want any of the following special types of data to be collected, set the appropriate monitor switches.

Table 17.4 Data Returned by the Snapshot Monitor

Group	Information Provided	Monitor Switch	DBM Parameter
Sorts	Number of heaps used, overflows, sorts performance	SORT	DFT_MON_SORT
Locks	Number of locks held, number of deadlocks	LOCK	DFT_MON_LOCK
Tables	Measure activity (rows read, rows written)	TABLE	DFT_MON_TABLE
Buffer pools	Number of reads and writes, time taken	BUFFERPOOL	DFT_MON_BUFPOOL
Unit of work	Start times, end times, completion status	UOW	DFT_MON_UOW

Table 17.4 Data Returned by the Snapshot Monitor *(Continued)*

Group	Information Provided	Monitor Switch	DBM Parameter
SQL statements	Start time, stop time, statement identification	STATEMENT	DFT_MON_STMT
Timestamp	Timestamps for operations	TIMESTAMP	DFT_MON_TIMESTAMP

The switches corresponding to the information provided in Table 17.4 are all OFF by default, except for the switch corresponding to times and timestamp information, which is ON by default.

You can take a snapshot using either:

- The **`get snapshot`** command

  or
- SQL SELECT statements against table functions

The SQL table functions are very powerful: You can use the power of the SQL language to gather only the information that you are interested in, and you can examine changes in the output over time.

Table 17.5 lists the different levels at which you can take snapshots.

Table 17.5 Levels for Taking Monitoring Snapshots

Level	Information Captured
Application	Applications.
Buffer Pool	Buffer pool activity.
Database	Databases.
Database Manager (Instance)	For an active instance.
Dynamic SQL	Point-in-time statement from the SQL statement cache for the database.
Lock	For locks held by applications against a database.
Table	For tables within a database.
Table Space	For table spaces within a database.

17.8.1 Setting the Monitor Switches

To capture snapshot information, the Snapshot Monitors must be enabled. You can enable them at either the instance or session level.

To enable the monitors at the instance level, you need to update the database configuration and set the monitor switch to ON:

```
update dbm cfg using DFT_MON_BUFPOOL ON
```

To enable the monitors at the session level, you can update the monitor switch directly:

```
update monitor switches using BUFFERPOOL ON
```

When you have set monitor switches at the session level, you can only take snapshots in the same session. Snapshots taken in one session will not pick up the monitor switch settings for other sessions. If you have set the instance-level monitor switch and stopped and restarted DB2, you can take snapshots in any session attached to the DB2 instance.

17.8.2 Capturing Snapshot Information

Since Version 8, you can capture snapshot information in two ways:

- Using the **GET SNAPSHOT** command
- Selecting from a snapshot table function

The **GET SNAPSHOT** command captures the requested snapshot information and writes the information to the screen or to an ASCII file. You then need to examine the output of the snapshot for the information that you are looking for. Since you access the snapshot table functions using SQL, you can select only the data you are interested in, store the data quickly into a history table, and so on.

To get a snapshot for all of the activity on the database *sample*, you would issue the command:

```
get snapshot for all on sample
```

To get the same information using the snapshot table function, you would use the statement:

```
SELECT *
  FROM TABLE(SNAPSHOT_DATABASE('SAMPLE',-1 )) as SNAPSHOT_DATABASE
```

For a complete list of the snapshot table functions, refer to the *DB2 SQL Reference*.

17.8.3 Resetting the Snapshot Monitor Switches

The data returned by a Snapshot Monitor is based primarily on counters, and the counters are associated with a monitor switch. Monitor switches are initialized or reset when one of the following occurs.

- Application-level monitoring is used, and the application connects to the database.
- Database-level monitoring is used, and the first application connects.
- Table-level monitoring is used, and the table is first accessed.
- Table space-level monitoring is used, and the table space is first accessed.
- Issuing the **RESET MONITOR** command.
- Turning on a particular monitor switch.

You can reset monitor switches for the entire instance by issuing the command **reset monitor all,** and for a database by issuing the command **reset monitor for database database_name.**

17.9 Event Monitors

While Snapshot Monitors let you "take a picture" of your system at a given time, Event Monitors allow you to collect information based on an event. A typical example is the case of deadlocks. Since it is very difficult to determine when a deadlock is going to happen, taking a snapshot at the right time is almost impossible. Instead, you can use an Event Monitor, which will automatically collect the deadlock information when it occurs. Event Monitors can also be used to collect static and dynamic SQL statements.

The following example shows a sequence of statements that illustrate how to collect Event Monitor information using commands.

```
(1) create event monitor mymon1 for database, statements write to file 'e:\temp'
(2) set event monitor mymon1 STATE=1
(3) select * from employee
(4) set event monitor mymon1 STATE=0
(5) drop event monitor mymon1
(6) db2evmon -path e:\temp
```

In the example, (1) is the statement used to create the Event Monitor *mymon1*, which specifically collects DATABASE and STATEMENTS events. Other events that can be collected are DEADLOCKS, TABLESPACES, BUFFERPOOLS, CONNECTIONS and TRANSACTIONS.

In (2), the Event Monitor is turned on. (3) is used as an example of an SQL statement that should be captured by the Event Monitor. In (4) the Event Monitor is turned off. In (5) the Event Monitor is dropped or deleted, and in (6) the collected information is analyzed with the command **db2evmon,** the command-line version of the Event Analyzer.

Table 17.6 shows part of the output of the **db2evmon** command after the previous sequence of statements was performed.

Table 17.6 Output of the db2evmon command

```
--------------------------------------------------------------------------
                              EVENT LOG HEADER
  Event Monitor name: MYMON1
  Server Product ID: SQL09010
  Version of event monitor data: 7
  Byte order: LITTLE ENDIAN
  Number of nodes in db2 instance: 1
  Codepage of database: 1252
  Territory code of database: 1
  Server instance name: DB2
--------------------------------------------------------------------------
```

(continues)

Table 17.6 Output of the db2evmon command *(Continued)*

```
--------------------------------------------------------------------------
  Database Name: SAMPLE
  Database Path: H:\DB2\NODE0000\SQL00003\
  First connection timestamp: 06/06/2006 03:10:25.965440
  Event Monitor Start time:   06/08/2006 02:49:26.271226
--------------------------------------------------------------------------

3) Connection Header Event ...
  Appl Handle: 249
  Appl Id: *LOCAL.DB2.016DC5204042
  Appl Seq number: 0014
  DRDA AS Correlation Token: *LOCAL.DB2.016DC5204042
  Program Name    : db2bp.exe
  Authorization Id: DB2ADMIN
  Execution Id    : DB2ADMIN
  Codepage Id: 1252
  Territory code: 1
  Client Process Id: 3048
  Client Database Alias: SAMPLE
  Client Product Id: SQL09010
  Client Platform: Unknown
  Client Communication Protocol: Local
  Client Network Name:
  Connect timestamp: 06/06/2006 03:11:27.082303

4) Statement Event ...
  Appl Handle: 249
  Appl Id: *LOCAL.DB2.016DC5204042
  Appl Seq number: 0014
  Record is the result of a flush: FALSE
  -------------------------------------------
  Operation: Static Commit
  Package  :
  Consistency Token  :
  Package Version ID  :
  Cursor   :
  Cursor was blocking: FALSE
  -------------------------------------------
  Start Time: 06/08/2006 02:49:26.367666
  Stop Time:  06/08/2006 02:49:26.379876
  Exec Time:  0.012210 seconds
  Number of Agents created: 1
  User CPU: 0.000000 seconds
  System CPU: 0.000000 seconds
  Fetch Count: 0
  Sorts: 0
  Total sort time: 0

  Sort overflows: 0
  Rows read: 0
  Rows written: 0
  Internal rows deleted: 0
  Internal rows updated: 0
  Internal rows inserted: 0
  Bufferpool data logical reads: 0
  Bufferpool data physical reads: 0
  Bufferpool temporary data logical reads: 0
```

Table 17.6 Output of the db2evmon command *(Continued)*

```
  Bufferpool temporary data physical reads: 0
  Bufferpool index logical reads: 0
  Bufferpool index physical reads: 0
  Bufferpool temporary index logical reads: 0
  Bufferpool temporary index physical reads: 0
  SQLCA:
   sqlcode: 0
   sqlstate: 00000

5) Statement Event ...
  Appl Handle: 249
  Appl Id: *LOCAL.DB2.016DC5204042
  Appl Seq number: 0015

  Record is the result of a flush: FALSE
  -------------------------------------------
  Type     : Dynamic
  Operation: Prepare
  Section  : 201
  Creator  : NULLID
  Package  : SQLC2E03
  Consistency Token  : AAAAAJHR
  Package Version ID  :
  Cursor    : SQLCUR201
  Cursor was blocking: FALSE
  Text     : select * from employee
  -------------------------------------------
  Start Time: 06/08/2005 02:49:37.126020
  Stop Time:  06/08/2005 02:49:37.163379
  Exec Time:  0.037359 seconds
  Number of Agents created: 1
  User CPU: 0.000000 seconds
  System CPU: 0.010014 seconds
  Fetch Count: 0
  Sorts: 0
  Total sort time: 0
  Sort overflows: 0
  Rows read: 0
  Rows written: 0
  Internal rows deleted: 0
  Internal rows updated: 0
  Internal rows inserted: 0
  Bufferpool data logical reads: 0
  Bufferpool data physical reads: 0
  Bufferpool temporary data logical reads: 0
  Bufferpool temporary data physical reads: 0
  Bufferpool index logical reads: 0
  Bufferpool index physical reads: 0
  Bufferpool temporary index logical reads: 0
  Bufferpool temporary index physical reads: 0
  SQLCA:
   sqlcode: 0
   sqlstate: 00000

...
```

You can also create Event Monitors through the Control Center.

17.10 The DB2 Optimizer

The DB2 optimizer, as stated in previous chapters, is the brain of DB2. The optimizer is a sophisticated and complex set of algorithms whose main objective is to calculate the fastest way to retrieve your data based on your database statistics.

The DB2 optimizer performs a number of tasks during the creation of the internal-compiled form of your SQL statements.

1. **Parse the query.** The optimizer's first task is to analyze the SQL query to validate the syntax. If it detects any syntax errors, the optimizer stops processing, and the appropriate SQL error is returned to the application attempting to compile the SQL statement. When parsing is complete, an internal representation of the query is created.
2. **Check the query semantics.** The second task of the optimizer is to further validate the SQL statement by checking to ensure that the parts of the statement make sense given the other parts, for example, ensuring that the data types of the columns input into scalar functions are correct for those functions. Also during this stage, the optimizer adds the behavioral semantics to the query graph model, such as the effects of referential constraints, table check constraints, triggers, and views.
3. **Rewrite the query.** The optimizer uses global semantics provided in the query graph model to transform the query into a form that can be optimized more easily. For example, the compiler might move a predicate, altering the level at which it is applied, in an attempt to improve query performance. This particular process is called **general predicate pushdown.** Any changes made to the query are rewritten back to the query graph model.
4. **Optimize the access plan.** The SQL optimizer portion of the optimizer uses the query graph model as input and generates many alternative execution plans for satisfying the user's request. It estimates the execution cost of each alternative plan using the statistics for tables, indexes, columns, and functions, and chooses the plan with the smallest estimated execution cost.

   The optimizer uses the query graph model to analyze the query semantics and to obtain information about a wide variety of factors, including indexes, base tables, derived tables, subqueries, correlation, and recursion.

   The output from this step of the optimizer is an **access plan,** which provides the basis for the information captured in the **explain tables.** The information used to generate the access plan can be captured with an **explain snapshot.**
5. **Generate the executable code.** The optimizer's final step uses the access plan and the query graph model to create an executable access plan, or section, for the query. This code generation step uses information from the query graph model to avoid repetitive execution of expressions that only need to be computed once for a query. Examples for which this optimization is possible include code page conversions and the use of host variables.

Information about access plans for static SQL is stored in the system catalog tables. When the package is executed, DB2 will use the information stored in the system catalog tables to determine how to access the data and provide results for the query. It is this information that is used by the db2expln tool.

It is recommended that you run the **RUNSTATS** command periodically on the tables used in queries where you need optimal performance. The optimizer will then be better equipped with relevant statistical information on the nature of the data. If the **RUNSTATS** command is not run, or the optimizer determines that **RUNSTATS** was run on empty or near-empty tables, the optimizer may either use defaults or attempt to derive certain statistics based upon the number of file pages used to store the table on disk.

17.11 The Explain Tool and Explain Tables

The **explain** tool examines the access plan chosen by the DB2 optimizer for your SQL statements. Explain information must be captured before you can review it using one of DB2's explain tools. While the query is being compiled, the information can be captured into a file or special tables known as **explain tables.** DB2 uses explain tables to store access plan information so that users can see the decisions that the optimizer has made. These explain tables are listed in Table 17.7.

Table 17.7 Explain Tables

Table Name	Description
EXPLAIN_ARGUMENT	Represents the unique characteristics for each individual operator.
EXPLAIN_INSTANCE	Main control table for all explain information. Each row of data in the explain tables is explicitly linked to one unique row in this table. Basic information about the source of the SQL statements being explained and environment information is kept in this table.
EXPLAIN_OBJECT	Contains data objects required by the access plan generated to satisfy the SQL statement.
EXPLAIN_OPERATOR	Contains all the operators needed to satisfy the SQL statement.
EXPLAIN_PREDICATE	Identifies which predicates are applied by a specific operator.
EXPLAIN_STATEMENT	Contains the text of the SQL statement in two forms. The original version entered by the user is stored in addition to the rewritten version that is the result of the compilation process.
EXPLAIN_STREAM	Represents the input and output data streams between individual operators and data objects. The data objects themselves are represented in the EXPLAIN_OBJECT table. The operators involved in a data stream are represented in the EXPLAIN_OPERATOR table.

The explain tables have to be created before any explain information can be gathered. This is normally done automatically the first time you invoke Visual Explain from the Command Editor. If you need to create the tables manually, use the script file **EXPLAIN.DDL** located in the *misc* subdirectory of the SQLLIB directory. This file contains the definition of the explain tables. To create the explain tables, you can connect to the database and then run the following command:

```
db2 –tvf explain.ddl
```

The explain tool can be invoked with the EXPLAIN statement, which has the following syntax:

```
>>-EXPLAIN--+-PLAN SELECTION-+--+--------------------+---------->
            +-ALL------------+  '-+-FOR--+--SNAPSHOT-'
            '-PLAN-----------'    '-WITH-'

>--+-----------------+--+----------------------+-------------->
   '-WITH REOPT ONCE-'  '-SET QUERYNO =--integer-'

>--+--------------------------------+------------------------->
   '-SET QUERYTAG =--string-constant-'

>--FOR--explainable-sql-statement-----------------------------><
```

Note that:

- Specifying PLAN SELECTION, ALL, or PLAN are all equivalent.
- The WITH SNAPSHOT option captures snapshot and EXPLAIN data. Using this option, Visual Explain can create a graph of the access path, and you can also query the appropriate tables for EXPLAIN data.
- The FOR SNAPSHOT option captures only snapshot data that can be used by Visual Explain. EXPLAIN data is not stored in any table.

If you don't specify any of these options, which is the default, only EXPLAIN data is collected. This will provide EXPLAIN data, but not snapshot data required by the Visual Explain tool. For example, the following statement populates the EXPLAIN tables with EXPLAIN and snapshot data for the query *select * from employee*:

```
EXPLAIN PLAN WITH SNAPSHOT FOR "select * from employee"
```

17.12 Using Visual Explain to Examine Access Plans

Once the EXPLAIN data has been stored in the explain tables, it can be queried or displayed using Visual Explain or other explain tools. This section describes how to use the Visual Explain tool to review and analyze an access plan.

Visual Explain is a graphical utility that gives the database administrator or application developer the ability to examine the access plan determined by the optimizer. Visual Explain can only be used with access plans explained using the snapshot option.

You can use Visual Explain to analyze previously generated explain snapshots or to gather explain data and explain dynamic SQL statements. If the explain tables have not been created when you start Visual Explain, it will create them for you. You can invoke Visual Explain either from the Command Center or Control Center.

From the Control Center interface, right-click on the database where your explain snapshots are stored.

The **Explain SQL...** option lets you gather explain data and show the graphical representation of a dynamic SQL statement. This is the easiest way to explain a single SQL statement.

Choosing the option **Show Explained Statements History** opens a window that lists all of the explained statements. In this view you will see the SQL statements and their cost in **timerons** (an estimate of database resources).

To examine an access plan in detail, double-click on the explained statement or highlight the entry of interest and use the menu to select **Statement Show access plan** in the Explained Statements History window.

All of the explain statements will be displayed in the Explained Statements History list, but only the explained statements with EXPLAIN SNAPSHOT information can be examined using Visual Explain.

The Visual Explain output displays a hierarchical graph representing the components of an SQL statement. Each part of the query is represented as a graphical object. These objects are known as **nodes.** There are two basic types of nodes:

- **OPERATOR** nodes indicate an action that is performed on a group of data.
- **OPERAND** nodes show the database objects where an operator action takes place. An operand is an object that the operators act upon. These database objects are usually tables and indexes.

There are many operators that can be used by the DB2 optimizer to determine the best access plan. These operators indicate how data is accessed (IXSCAN, TBSCAN, RIDSCN, IXAND), how tables are joined internally (MSJOIN, NLJOIN), and other factors, such as if a sort will be required (SORT). You can find more information about the operators in the Visual Explain online help. The objects shown in a Visual Explain graphic output are connected by arrows showing the flow of data from one node to another. The end of an access plan is always a RETURN operator.

If your application is an OLTP-type application, and the explain plan for one or more of your queries indicates that DB2 is choosing a table scan, you should analyze the EXPLAIN data to determine the reasons why an index scan was not used. If you are administering a data warehouse, the most important thing to look for in the access plans is the type of join used. If you see that you are not using the optimal joins methods, examine the SQL statement and perhaps the partitioning keys and indexes to determine if you can change anything to allow collocation to occur in the joins.

17.13 Workload Management

More and more you are consolidating databases or applications into a single database to reduce the duplication of data and administration of the environment. When you do this, the DB2 server is being stressed like never before. For example, consider a grocery chain that consolidates its transactional and reporting databases. In this case you will have the cash registers sending hundreds or thousands of INSERTs per second (depending on how large the chain is). At the same time, reports will be running that scan the database to be sure you are meeting sales targets, looking for hit and cold items, and so on. Each store will also be sending in batch updates as they restock their shelves at night, or if they reprice items to reflect sales. This will all be happening on the same server, in the same database.

To maintain control of the database and ensure that the applications can respond "in time," an efficient workload management system is critical. We used the term "in time" since the different applications will have different response time requirements. The cash registers will need to respond instantaneously, while the reports will take seconds or minutes to run. If a large report is running it cannot impact the performance and response time of the cash register application.

To ensure that the different applications and users are able to maintain their response times, DB2 has two forms of workload management, preemptive workload management and reactive workload management. The difference between these is implied by their names, one works before the query is run, and the other works on running queries.

17.13.1 Preemptive Workload Management

In the past some of you have used DB2 Query Patroller as your preemptive workload management tool. In DB2 9.5 we are making the integration of workload management deeper into the DB2 engine, and also integrating it with the workload management facilities in the operating system. DB2 WLM provides three main functions: identification, management, and monitoring.

The first function of WLM is to identify the queries that are running, who is running them and what roles and groups that person belongs to, what applications they belong to, and any accounting string that might have been specified along with the query or user. Once a query has been identified, and all of its information captured, it can then be managed as it run in the database.

When a query is being managed, it is assigned to a service class based on the query's identification. When you create a service class, you can specify the following resource controls to provide control over the following:

Control	Description
Agent Priority	This control will set a priority level for the agent processes and threads running within the service class.
Prefetch Priority	For I/O intensive work that uses a lot of prefetching, this control will map work to one of three prefetch queues, which have different priorities: high, medium, and low.
External Operating System Workload Management tag	This control allows a workload to have some of its resource management controlled by the operating system WLM features.

A workload class can also have subclasses, so that applications can be assigned a class, but in the WLM configuration, you can combine the classes assigned to the three HR applications into one larger class for management within the database.

You can define thresholds for these classes based on the following:

- Elapsed Time
- Idle Time
- Estimated Cost
- Rows returned
- Temporary Space Usage
- Number of concurrent queries in the class
- Number of database partition connections
- Number of concurrent queries in the database

As the queries are running, they are monitored to ensure that none of these thresholds are breached. When a threshold is breached, data on the query will be captured, and then one of the following actions will take place on the query:

- Stop the query
- Let the query run, but capture data on the query to find the source of the problem so it will not happen in the future
- Queue the query until a later time

Workload management monitoring provides you with access to real-time operational statistics for your database. You can retrience a list of running applications and queries, the queries running within each service class, average query response times, and so on using table functions similar to the snapshot table function introduced in DB2 8.

Some of these table functions include:

- WLM_GET_WORKLOAD_STATS
- WLM_GET_WORK_ACTION_SET_STATS
- WLM_GET_QUEUE_STATS

17.13.2 Reactive Workload Management

The governor allows you to set threshold and actions in a configuration file. In addition you also specify the governor interval, which indicates how frequently the governor runs. When the governor runs, it monitors the behavior of the applications that are running against the database, and if these applications have breached any of the specified thresholds, it will take the action associated with that threshold. The thresholds are typically set on the CPU time, number of rows read or the idle time, and the action can be to reduce its priority, force it, or schedule it to run at a later time.

The following is an example of a governor configuration file showing these threshold and actions.

```
desc "Allow no UOW to run for more than an hour"
setlimit uowtime 3600 action force;

desc "Slow down the db2 CLP after reading 250K rows "
applname db2bp.exe
setlimit rowssel 2500000;
```

17.14 Case Study

In this case study assume that your database *POSDB* is supporting a point-of-sale system. Since you will be processing simple, single row selects, updates, and deletes, do not enable intra-partition parallelism. Check the INTRA_PARALLEL instance-level parameter to ensure it is disabled.

On Linux and UNIX you can use the **grep** tool to retrieve the intra-partition parallelism line as follows:

```
get dbm cfg | grep –I intra_parallel
```

The **-I** option after the **grep** command is used to ignore the case.

On Windows you should redirect the output to a text file so you can open it with notepad and search for the string INTRA_PARALLEL.

If intra-partition parallelism is enabled, disable it using

```
update dbm cfg using intra_parallel off
```

Although you know there are 100 cash registers in your store, you do not know how many are normally active at the same time. To determine this information, capture some database manager snapshots over a period of time using the following statement:

```
SELECT rem_cons_in_exec , local_cons_in_exec,
   (rem_cons_in_exec + local_cons_in_exec) as total_executing
   FROM TABLE(SNAPSHOT_DBM(-1 ))
   as SNAPSHOT_DBM;
```

After capturing these snapshots over a period of time, calculate the average for the **total_executing** column in the output. If this average turns out to be 17, you can set the average number of active applications for your database to 17:

```
update db cfg for POSDB using avg_appls 17
```

You then notice that the performance of the system seems to slow down when there are a number of users using the application. Take a snapshot of the important performance-related information using this statement:

```
SELECT
   db_name,
   rows_read,
   rows_selected,
   lock_waits,
   lock_wait_time,
   deadlocks,
   lock_escals,
```

```
    total_sorts,
    total_sort_overflows
    FROM table (snapshot_database ('POSDB ', -1) ) as snapshot_database
```

If this statement shows that a large percentage of the sorts are causing sort overflows, you need to examine the setting for your sort heap and sort heap threshold. Since intra-partition parallelism is disabled, there is no need to worry about the sort heap threshold for shared sorts.

```
get db cfg for posdb | grep –I sort
get dbm cfg  | grep –I sort
```

From the output of the above commands, look at the following lines in particular:

```
Sort list heap (4KB)                          (SORTHEAP) = 256
Sort heap threshold (4KB)                   (SHEAPTHRES) = 1000
```

In this case you can see that the sort heap threshold is less than four times the value of the sort heap, so if there are more than three concurrent sorts, any subsequent sorts will have their sort heap reduced and are much more likely to overflow. Since the average number of concurrently executing applications you found earlier was 17, you should set the sort heap threshold to at least 17 times the sort heap. In this case you can choose 20 times the sort heap for ease of calculation ($20 \times 256 = 5120$).

```
update dbm cfg using sheapthres 5120
```

Assume that you then retest the application and recapture the snapshots. In the snapshot you see that this did improve the percentage of overflowed sorts, but the percentage is still too high. Therefore, the sort heap itself is likely too small for the amount of data that is being sorted. If you then increase the sort heap, you should also increase the sort heap threshold accordingly to keep it at 20 times the sort heap.

NOTE Having an excessively large sort heap makes sorts cost less to the DB2 optimizer, so do not increase the sort heap too much. Make this change iteratively, increasing the sort heap and sort heap threshold by small increments until you see the desired change in the percentage of overflow sorts and performance.

```
update db cfg for posdb using sortheap 400
update dbm cfg using sheapthres 8000
```

After retesting and recapturing the snapshots, you see that although this has improved the overall performance of your server, one of your applications still appears to be sluggish. Since this is specific to one application, it may be caused by poorly performing statements within the application. If the application is an embedded static SQL application, you can get the statements from your developers. If it is a dynamic SQL application, you can capture the SQL statements using the Snapshot Monitor or the Event Monitor.

You can run the application and then examine the performance of the SQL statements:

```
SELECT
(case
  when num_executions >0  then (rows_read / num_executions)
  else 0
end) as avg_rows_read,
(case
  when num_executions >0  then (rows_written / num_executions)
  else 0
end) as avg_rows_written,
(case
  when num_executions >0  then (stmt_sorts / num_executions)
  else 0
end) as avg_sorts,
(case
  when num_executions >0  then (total_exec_time / num_executions)
  else 0
end) as avg_exec_time,
substr(stmt_text,1,200) as SQL_Stmt
   FROM table (snapshot_dyn_sql ('sample', -1) ) as snapshot_dyn_sql
```

If you notice that there is one particular statement in the output of this SQL that has a long average execution time and performs three sorts per execution, you can use the Design Advisor to help tune this statement. If you extract the statement text from the output above, and put it into the file *bad.sql*, you can run the Design Advisor from the command line using:

```
db2advis –d posdb –i bad.sql
```

If an index will help the performance of the query, the Index Advisor will tell you the definition of the index or indexes it recommends, as well as the new cost of the query and the percent improvement in the cost.

```
C:\temp>db2advis -d posdb -i bad.sql
Using user id as default schema name. Use -n option to specify schema
execution started at timestamp 2006-03-28-12.51.39.570001
found [1] SQL statements from the input file

Recommending indexes...
total disk space needed for initial set [    0.009] MB
total disk space constrained to          [  33.322] MB

Trying variations of the solution set.
Optimization finished.
  2  indexes in current solution
 [ 13.0000] timerons  (without recommendations)
 [  0.1983] timerons  (with current solution)
[98.47%] improvement
--
--
-- LIST OF RECOMMENDED INDEXES
-- ===========================
-- index[1],    0.009MB
   CREATE INDEX "DSNOW    "."IDX403281751440000" ON "DSNOW    "."ORGX" ("C1" ASC) ALLOW
   REVERSE SCANS ;
   COMMIT WORK ;
   RUNSTATS ON TABLE "DSNOW    "."ORGX" FOR INDEX "DSNOW    "."IDX403281751440000";
   COMMIT WORK ;
```

```
-- RECOMMENDED EXISTING INDEXES
-- ============================
-- ==========================
--
11 solutions were evaluated by the advisor
DB2 Workload Performance Advisor tool is finished.
```

You can run the **create index** and **runstats** statements from the Design Advisor output, and rerun your tests to make sure that this does improve you application's performance.

17.15 SUMMARY

This chapter covered the main factors that affect the performance of your database system: CPU usage, I/O utilization, and memory usage.

To configure DB2 for optimal performance, you need to understand how the database and Database Manager Configuration parameters impact your applications and the overall system. The Configuration Advisor can facilitate your tuning efforts with respect to parameter configuration.

Examining maintenance operations like **REORG** and **RUNSTATS** help keep the database running optimally, but you will also need to monitor your system using either the Snapshot Monitor or the Event Monitor to be sure it is running efficiently. If the snapshots indicate that a particular SQL statement is performing poorly, you can examine its access plan using the Explain tool.

17.16 REVIEW QUESTIONS

1. What isolation level acquires no row-level locks?
2. What is the maximum requester I/O block size?
3. How can you eliminate the need for the first connections to a database to create their own agent?
4. When will a database's log buffer be written to disk?
5. When does lock escalation occur?
6. When can you capture the statistics about your tables and indexes?
7. What command can be used to remove overflow records from your tables?
8. What monitor switch is enabled by default in Version 8?
9. What command resets the counters reported by the database snapshot command?
10. What objects must exist in your database in order to use the visual explain tool?
11. Which of the following commands cannot update the statistical information about tables and indexes in your database?

    A. runstats

    B. load

    C. reorgchk

    D. import

12. Which of the following does not cause the log buffer to be written to disk?
A. When the log buffer becomes full
B. One second since the last time the log buffer was written to disk
C. When applications issue MINCOMMIT commit statements
D. When the percentage of the log buffer reaches SOFTMAX

13. When lock escalation occurs, row-level locks are converted to which of the following?
A. Page-level locks
B. Extent-level locks
C. Table-level locks
D. Table space-level locks

14. Which of the following configuration parameters allows DB2 to detect that pages are being read in order and automatically trigger prefetching?
A. DETECT_PREFETCH
B. SEQ_DETECT
C. ENABLE_PREFETCH
D. SCAN_DETECT

15. Which two of the following configuration parameters control when the page cleaners will be triggered to write dirty pages from the buffer pool to disk?
A. NUM_IOCLEANERS
B. SOFTMAX
C. DIRTY_THRESH
D. CHNGPGS_THRESH
E. MAX_LOG

16. Which of the following commands will indicate that you need to reorganize your tables because they contain too many overflow records?
A. reorgchk
B. runstats
C. inspect
D. check

17. Which of the following SQL statements can cause an overflow record to be created by DB2?
A. insert
B. update
C. delete
D. reorg

18. Which of the following steps is not performed by the optimizer when building the access plan for an SQL statement?
A. Query rewrite
B. Check query semantics
C. Parse the query
D. Apply hints

19. Which of the following is not an operator that you will see in a DB2 access plan?
   A. IXSCAN
   B. TBSCAN
   C. RIDSCN
   D. DTSCAN
20. Given the following database configuration information:
```
Sort heap thres for shared sorts (4KB) (SHEAPTHRES_SHR) = 1000
Sort list heap (4KB)                         (SORTHEAP) = 256
```
   what is the maximum number of concurrent shared sorts than can occur without causing the sort to overflow?
   A. 1
   B. 2
   C. 3
   D. 4

CHAPTER 18

Diagnosing Problems

This chapter describes how to investigate issues you may encounter while working with DB2 and how to isolate them using the diagnostic information that is provided by DB2. Once you isolate the problem, you can determine its root cause, and search for possible solutions and workarounds including previously reported problems.

In this chapter you will learn about:

- The big picture of DB2 problem diagnosis
- Obtaining more information about an error message
- Collecting diagnostic information: First Failure Data Capture (FFDC)
- The db2support tool
- The trace facility

18.1 Problem Diagnosis: The Big Picture

Figure 18.1 provides an overview of the actions that you should perform to investigate any issues you encounter when working with DB2. The following sections describe the items in the figure in detail.

18.2 How DB2 Reports Issues

Typically when working with DB2, a problem is manifested by an error message. The error message may be reported immediately to the user, or it may be written to some diagnostic file like the administration notification log or the db2diag.log (refer to Section 18.4, DB2 First Failure Data Capture for more details on these diagnostic files).

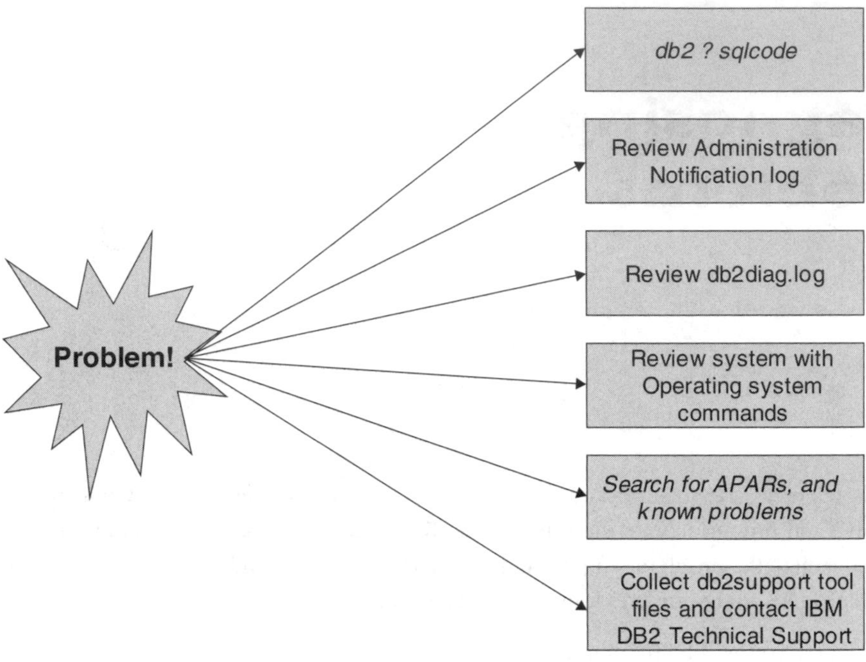

Figure 18.1 The big picture of problem source identification and resolution

Figures 18.2 and 18.3 show examples of DB2 reporting problems immediately after executing an operation. In the case shown in Figure 18.2, after clicking on the instance *MYINST* in the object tree of the Control Center, the user received the DB2 message SQL1032N indicating that the instance has not been started.

Figure 18.3 shows a DB2 error message SQL0104N after executing the SQL statement **`select from employee`** in the DB2 CLP. SQL0104N indicates that there is a syntax error in the statement (column names have not been specified).

Some problems may not report an error message. For example, if the DB2 instance abnormally hangs or the response time is very slow, you may need to run the db2pd tool or DB2 traces to further troubleshoot the problem.

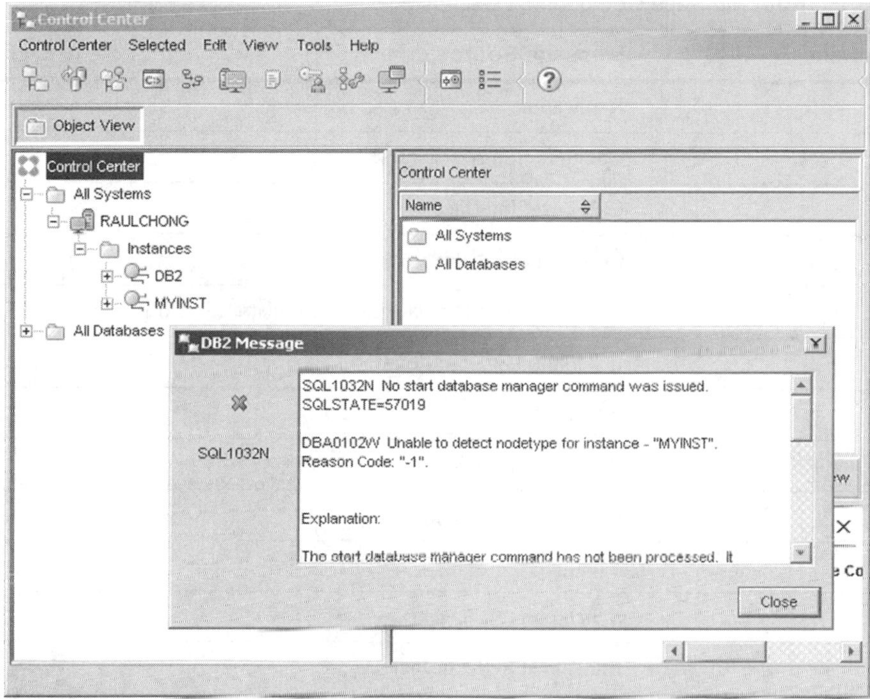

Figure 18.2 A DB2 error message reported by the Control Center

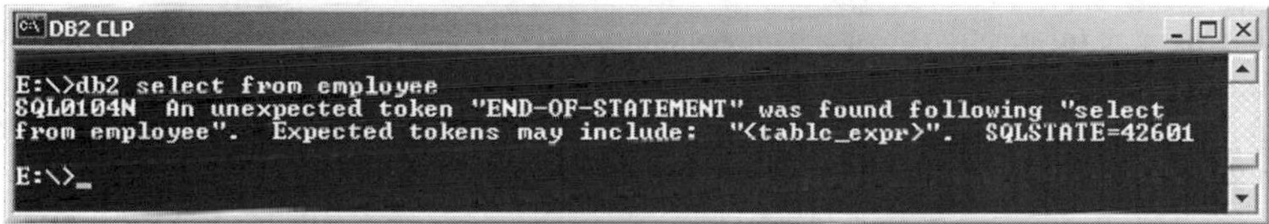

Figure 18.3 An error message reported by DB2 from the CLP

18.3 DB2 Error Message Description

DB2 error messages are structured as follows:

CCCnnnnnS

where:

- *CCC* identifies the DB2 component returning the message. See Table 18.1 for a list of all components.
- *nnnnn* is a three- to five-digit error code.
- *S* is the severity indicator. When *S* has a value *W*, it indicates a warning. When *S* has a value of *N*, it indicates an error (i.e. a negative SQL code).

Table 18.1 Error Message Component Description

Component	Message Source
ASN	Replication
CCA	Configuration Assistant
CLI	Call-Level Interface
DB2	Command Line Processor
DBA	Control Center and Database Administration Utility
DBI	Installation or Configuration
EXP	Explain utility
FLG	Information catalog manager
LIC	DB2 license manager
SAT	Satellite
SPM	Synch point manager
SQJ	Embedded SQLJ in Java
SQL	Database manager

To obtain more information about a message returned by DB2, you can use the message help (**?**) command from the CLP as discussed in Chapter 4, Using the DB2 Tools. The message help command lets you enter the SQL message code in different ways. For example, if you want to get more information about SQL0104N, you can use any of the following:

```
db2 ? SQL0104N
db2 ? SQL104N
db2 ? SQL-0104
db2 ? SQL-104
db2 ? SQL-104N
db2 ? sql0104
```

The component keyword, in this case **SQL,** needs to prefix the message code. Negative numbers can be suffixed with the letter *N.* Figure 18.4 shows the output that is displayed when you use any of the above help commands.

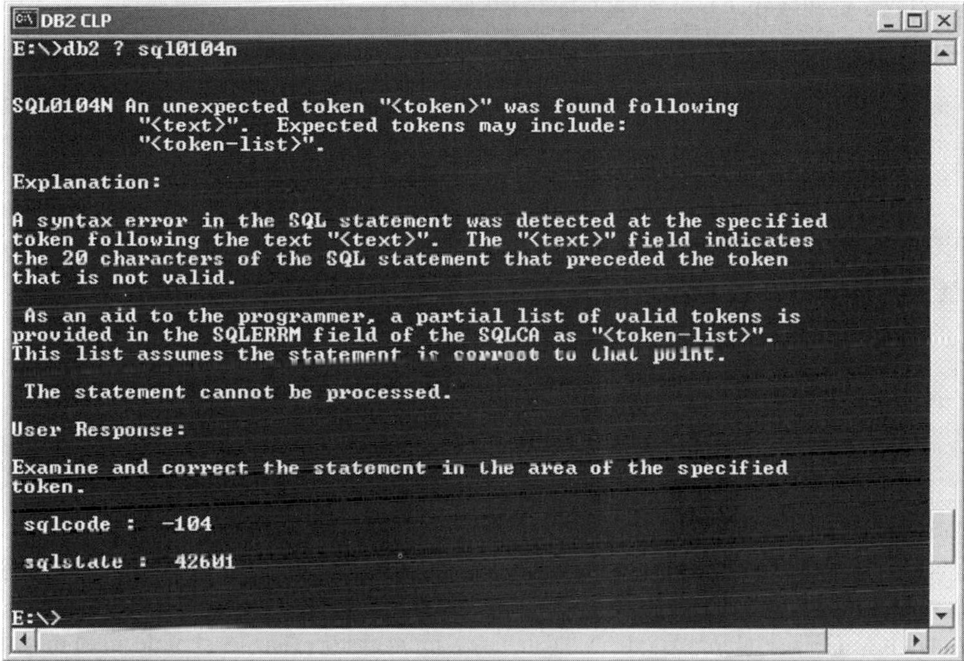

Figure 18.4 Using the help (?) command

18.4 DB2 First Failure Data Capture

First Failure Data Capture (FFDC) is a general term applied to the diagnostic information that DB2 captures automatically when messages occur. This information reduces the need to reproduce errors to get diagnostic information. The information captured by FFDC is stored in the following files.

- Administration Notification log or Windows Event log
- db2diag.log
- DB2 Dump files
- Trap files
- **Core files** (Linux/UNIX only)

The DIAGPATH Database Manager Configuration parameter specifies the location of these files.

> **NOTE** When we discuss DB2 messages, they can refer to error, warning, or informational messages.

The following will explain some important facts about these files:

Administration Notification log

When significant events occur, DB2 writes information to the administration notification log. The information is intended for use by database and system administrators. Many notification messages provide additional information to supplement the SQLCODE that is provided. The type of event and the level of detail of the information gathered are determined by the NOTIFYLEVEL Database Manager configuration parameter. (The NOTIFYLEVEL parameter is discussed in the next section.)

- On Windows systems, the DB2 administration notification log is not created as a separate file; instead, its entries are incorporated into the Windows event log and can be viewed using the Windows Event Viewer.
- On Linux and UNIX, the administration notification log for the instance is called *instance_name*.nfy.

db2diag.log

Diagnostic information about messages is recorded in the db2diag.log text file. This information is more detailed than the administration notification log and is intended for DB2 technical support, but it can be useful for experienced database administrators. The level of detail of the information is determined by the DIAGLEVEL Database Manager configuration parameter. (The DIAGLEVEL parameter is discussed in the next section.)

Trap files

The database manager generates a trap file if it cannot continue processing because of a trap, segmentation violation, or exception.

On Linux and UNIX, trap file names begin with the letter *t* followed by the thread ID (TID) that caused the trap. They have the file extension *nnn*, where *nnn* is the partition number.

On Windows systems, trap files begin with the letter *P* followed by the TID and the file extension *TRP*.

For example:
Linux/UNIX: t<tid>.nnn (t023945.000)
Windows: p<tid>.nnn (P023945.TRP)

The trap file contains the funtion sequence that was running when the error or exception occurred. This is sometimes called the *function call stack* or *stack trace back*. These files are intended for use by DB2 technical support only.

Dump files

For some error conditions, extra information is logged in external binary files named after the failing process ID or thread ID. These files have the file extension *nnn*, where *nnn* is the partition number. For single-partitioned environments, this extension is always *000*. Dump files are intended for use by DB2 technical support only.

Core files (Linux/UNIX only)

When DB2 terminates abnormally, the operating system generates a core file. The core file is a binary file that contains information similar to the DB2 trap files. Core files may also contain the entire memory image of the terminated process. These files are intended for use by DB2 technical support only.

18.4.1 DB2 Instance-Level Configuration Parameters Related to FFDC

The following Database Manager Configuration parameters are related to FFDC:

- DIAGPATH
- DIAGLEVEL
- NOTIFYLEVEL

18.4.1.1 The DIAGPATH Parameter

The DIAGPATH parameter specifies the fully qualified path in which DB2 puts the FFDC information. The default value for DIAGPATH is a null string. We recommend that you keep this default value. If you choose to change the value, we recommend that you use a centralized location, especially if there are multiple database instances.

When the value of DIAGPATH is a null string, the diagnostic log information is placed in the following locations.

- For Windows systems:

  If the DB2INSTPROF environment variable is *not* set, the information is placed in the folder DB2PATH*instance_name*, where DB2PATH is the environment variable that indicates where DB2 is installed on a Windows system.

  If the DB2INSTPROF environment variable *is* set, the information is placed in DB2INSTPROF*instance_name*, where DB2INSTPROF is the environment variable that indicates the location of the instance owner's home directory. The DB2INSTPROF variable is normally not set; therefore, instances on Windows are created under the directory specified in DB2PATH.
- For Linux/UNIX operating systems:

  The information is placed in *$HOME*/sqllib/db2dump, where *$HOME* is the home directory of the instance owner.

  We recommend that you compress or clean out the DIAGPATH directory files periodically to keep them from becoming too large.

18.4.1.2 The DIAGLEVEL Parameter

The DIAGLEVEL parameter specifies the type of diagnostic messages that will be recorded in the db2diag.log file. Table 18.2 lists the valid values for this parameter. The default level is 3. DB2 support may request that you set your diaglevel to level 4 when they are helping you troubleshoot a problem. Level 4 will produce additional informational messages that may provide a clue to identify the problem. It is not recommended to run your steady-state environment at level 4 because the additional informational messages can grow the size of the db2diag.log file quickly.

Table 18.2 Values for the DIAGLEVEL Parameter

Value	What It Captures
0	No diagnostic data.
1	Only severe errors.
2	All errors.
3	All errors and warnings (this is the default).
4	All errors, warnings, and informational messages.

18.4.1.3 The NOTIFYLEVEL Parameter

The NOTIFYLEVEL parameter specifies the type of notification messages that are written to the administration notification log. On Linux/UNIX platforms, the administration notification log is a text file called *instance.nfy*. On Windows, all administration notification messages are written to the Event Log. These messages can be written by DB2, the Health Monitor, or the SQL Replication's Capture and Apply programs. User applications can cause DB2 to write messages on its behalf. Table 18.3 lists the valid values for this parameter. You might want to increase the value of this parameter to gather additional problem-determination data to help resolve a problem.

Table 18.3 Values for the NOTIFYLEVEL Parameter

Value	What It Captures
0	No administration notification messages (this setting is not recommended).
1	Only fatal and unrecoverable errors.
2	Everything captured at NOTIFYLEVEL 1, plus conditions that require immediate attention from the system administrator or the database administrator. If the condition is not resolved, it could lead to a fatal error. Notification of very significant, non-error activities (for example, recovery) might also be logged at this level. This level captures Health Monitor alarms.

Table 18.3 Values for the NOTIFYLEVEL Parameter *(Continued)*

Value	What It Captures
3	Everything captured at NOTIFYLEVEL 2, plus conditions that are nonthreatening and do not require immediate action but might indicate the system is not optimal. This level captures Health Monitor alarms, Health Monitor warnings, and Health Monitor attentions. This is the default.
4	Everything captured at NOTIFYLEVEL 3, plus informational messages.

18.4.2 db2diag.log Example

The following is an example of a db2diag.log entry at a diagnostic level of 3:

```
2006-10-07-18.22.40.663000-240 I6636H441          LEVEL: Error
PID     : 2268                 TID  : 5124        PROC : db2syscs.exe
INSTANCE: DB2                  NODE : 000
APPHDL  : 0-665                APPID: *LOCAL.DB2.061007222240
AUTHID  : MDANG
FUNCTION: DB2 UDB, buffer pool services, sqlbDMSDoContainerOp, probe:810
MESSAGE : ZRC=0x8402001E=-2080243682=SQLB_CONTAINER_NOT_ACCESSIBLE
          "Container not accessible"
```

Figure 18.5 Example of a db2diag.log entry

Here is a breakdown of the entries in this db2diag.log:

- The message was generated at 2006-10-07-18.22.40.673000.
- The process ID (PID) is 2268.
- The thread ID (TID) is 5124.
- The process name is db2syscs.exe.
- The instance name is db2.
- The partition number is 0 as indicated by the field NODE: 000.
- The component identifier is buffer pool services.
- The DB2 function identifier is sqlbDMSStartPool.
- The unique error identifier (probe ID) within the function is 800. This indicates where in the DB2 source code the error or warning is logged. This information is used only by DB2 Technical Support.

The last part of the message entry is a message that often includes error codes, page dumps, or other detailed information. Sometimes this information will be complex, but usually it will give you an idea of the type of operation that is causing the failure, along with some supporting information to help the investigation. In this example, we can see that a table space container is not accessible. If we look at the next entry in the db2diag.log (see Figure 18.6), we will find the reason why the tablespace container is not accessible. An error occurred when DB2 was trying to check container 0 for table space 2. In fact, we changed the permissions of the container file to create this error message. Notice that the path to the container file was provided. In this case, you should have enough information from the error entry to investigate and resolve this error message.

```
2006-10-07-18.22.40.663000-240 I7079H466          LEVEL: Error
PID     : 2268                 TID  : 5124        PROC : db2syscs.exe
INSTANCE: DB2                  NODE : 000
APPHDL  : 0-665                APPID: *LOCAL.DB2.061007222240
AUTHID  : MDANG
FUNCTION: DB2 UDB, buffer pool services, sqlbDMSDoContainerOp, probe:810
DATA #1 : String, 100 bytes
Error checking container 0 (C:\DB2\NODE0000\SAMPLE\T0000002\C0000000.LRG) for tb
sp 2.  Rc = 860F000A
```

Figure 18.6 Useful db2diag.log entry

18.4.3 Administration Notification Log Examples

The following is a sample administration notification log entry in the notification log on a UNIX system:

```
2006-10-22-02.05.48.322796   Instance:db2inst1 █ Node:000
PID:25692(db2star2)    TID:1    Appid:none
base sys utilities  DB2StartMain Probe:911

ADM7513W  Database manager has started.
```

Figure 18.7 Example of administration notification log

You interpret these entries the same way as you do the entries in the db2diag.log. This message is logged when the Database Manager Configuration parameter NOTIFYLEVEL is set at 3 and indicates that the instance has started.

On Windows, you need to open the Windows Event Viewer to view the DB2 administration notification log entries. The method to launch the Event Viewer will differ will depend on the type of Windows operating system you are running. For example, to open the Event Viewer on Windows XP, from the Windows **Start** menu, choose **Control Panel > Administrative Tools > Event Viewer.** Figure 18.8 shows the Windows Event Viewer. The DB2 messages are displayed along with messages from other applications. The DB2 messages in the figure are displayed as *DB2-0* (where *DB2* is the instance name and *0* represents the partition number) in the Source column.

The entry highlighted is a DB2 message indicating it is a DB2 warning. Double click on it to display the entire message, as shown in Figure 18.9.

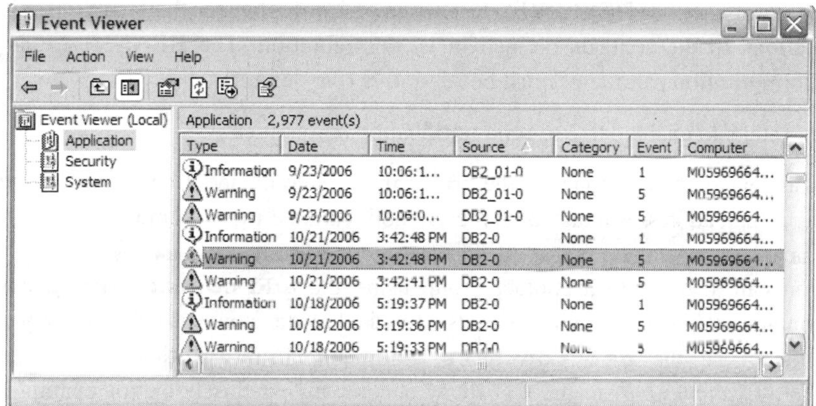

Figure 18.8 The Windows Event Viewer

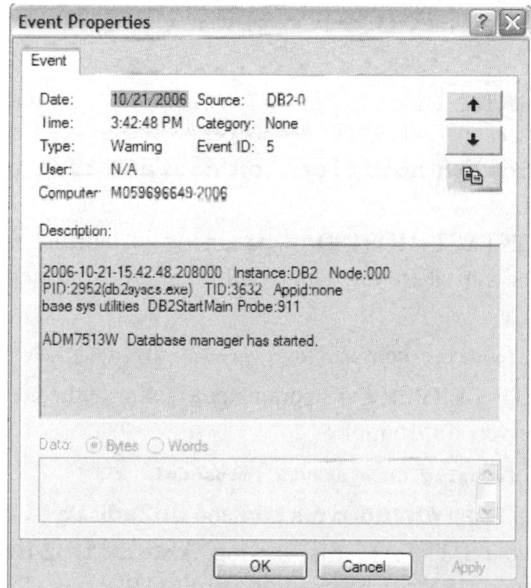

Figure 18.9 DB2 administration notification log entry on Windows

18.5 Receiving E-mail Notifications

If there is an SMTP server in your network, you can configure DB2 to send e-mail notifications to you (or any other administrator) automatically through it. This way, you do not have to monitor the administration notification log all the time: You will receive an e-mail when a problem occurs.

Note that you must set NOTIFYLEVEL to a value of 2 or higher for the Health Monitor to send any notifications to the contacts defined in its configuration. The HEALTH_MON Database Manager Configuration parameter must be set to ON (the default).

Follow these steps to enable DB2 to send notification automatically.

1. Add contact information with the **add contact** command. Use this command to add all the e-mail addresses that should receive notification e-mails from DB2. For example:

   ```
   add contact michael type email address michaela@youracme.com
   ```

   You can also create a contact group using the **add contactgroup** command to contain all the individual contacts. To display the contacts who already have been added, use the **get contacts** command. Refer to the file *Command_and_SQL_Examples.pdf* on the CD-ROM accompanying this book for examples showing how to use these commands.
2. Update the health notification contact list using

   ```
   update notification list
          add contact contact_name_from_step_1
   ```

   or

   ```
   update notification list
          add group contact_group_name_from_step_1
   ```

   Use the **get health notification contact list** command to display the contact list.
3. Update the CONTACT_HOST DAS parameter to indicate the host name or the IP address of the server where the contact information (from steps 1 and 2) is stored, for example:

   ```
   update admin cfg using CONTACT_HOST prodserv1
   ```
4. Update the SMTP_SERVER DAS parameter to indicate the host name or the IP address of the SMTP server; for example:

   ```
   update admin cfg using SMTP_SERVER smtpserv1
   ```
5. Restart the DAS using **db2admin stop** and **db2admin start**.
6. Make sure that the SMTP server is working. Also, the DB2 Health Monitor uses TCP/IP port 25, so port 25 must be open on the SMTP server. To test whether port 25 is open, from the DB2 server perform a telnet test as follows:

   ```
   telnet SMTP_SERVER 25
   ```

   If you get output similar to the following, then port 25 is enabled.

   ```
   Trying...
   Connected to <SMTP_SERVER>.
   Escape character is '^]'.
   220 <SMTP_SERVER> ESMTP Service (Lotus Domino Release 5.0.8) ready at Thu, 29
   Apr 2007 13:21:49 -0400
   ```

   If you do not get output like this or your session hangs, contact your network administrator to enable this port.

18.6 Tools for Troubleshooting

There are a host of DB2 problem-determination and analysis tools available for you to use to troubleshoot any abnormality within your database and/or database manager. These tools can be used separately for specific conditions or used in conjunction to troubleshoot complicated issues.

18.6.1 The db2support tool

The **db2support** tool is a **Problem Analysis and Environment Collection** tool. The **db2support** tool collects all diagnostic information, including the db2diag.log, dumps, and traps in one single compressed archive file called *db2support.zip*. DB2 Technical Support usually requests this zip file for problem-determination and troubleshooting purposes. With this handy tool, you do not have to look for the diagnostic files manually. It also has an optional interactive "Question and Answer" session, which poses questions about the circumstances of your problem.

The syntax of the **db2support** command is

```
db2support output_path -d db_alias options
```

This creates the file *db2support.zip* under *output_path* for the database *db_alias* after the command completes. The following options are usually required when running the **db2support** command:

- **-g** collects all files under the DIAGPATH directory. This includes the db2diag.log, dump files, trap files, and the DB2 administration notification log.
- **-s** collects detailed hardware and operating system information.
- **-c** attempts to connect to the specified database (default is no).

Type **db2support –h** to get all the supported options.

The db2support tool collects the following information under all conditions:

- db2diag.log
- All trap files
- locklist files
- Dump files
- Various system related files
- Output from various system commands
- db2cli.ini

Depending on the circumstances, the db2support utility might also collect

- Active log files
- Buffer pool and table space (SQLSPCS.1 and SQLSPCS.2) control files (with the **-d** option)
- Contents of the db2dump directory

- Core files (the **-a** option collects all core files, the **-r** option only collects the most recent core file)
- Extended system information (with the **-s** option)
- Database configuration settings (with the **-d** option)
- Database manager configuration settings files
- Log File Header file (with the **-d** option)
- Recovery History File (with the **-d** option)

One particular file of interest in the compressed .ZIP file is the db2support.html file. It can be looked at in any brower, and provides an excellent summary of your environment.

> **NOTE** The **db2support** utility should be run by a user with SYSADM authority, such as an instance owner, so that the utility can collect all of the necessary information without an error. If a user without SYSADM authority runs **db2support,** SQL errors (for example, SQL1092N) might result when the utility runs commands such as **QUERY CLIENT** or **LIST ACTIVE DATABASES.**

18.6.2 The DB2 Trace Facility

Sometimes the information in the FFDC files is not enough to determine the cause of a problem. Under normal circumstances, you should only take a trace if asked by DB2 Technical Support. The DB2 trace utility is useful when debugging reproducible problems. The process of taking a trace entails setting up the trace facility, reproducing the error, collecting the data, and turning off the trace facility.

The command to turn on the DB2 trace is

```
db2trc on options
```

Use **db2trc –h** to display all the available options. DB2 Technical Support usually requires you to perform the following steps to collect a trace.

- Turn on the DB2 trace to collect the last 8MB of information in the trace
  ```
  db2trc on –l 8M
  ```
- Re-create the error.
- Dump the trace information into a binary file:
  ```
  db2trc dmp db2trc.dmp
  ```
- Turn off DB2 trace:
  ```
  db2trc off
  ```
- Format the trace dump file into a text file that sorts the records by process/thread:
  ```
  db2trc fmt db2trc.dmp filename.fmt
  ```
- Format the trace dump file into a text file that sorts the records chronologically:
  ```
  db2trc flw db2trc.dmp filename.flw
  ```

You will then be asked to send the files named filename.fmt and filename.flw to DB2 Technical Support for analysis.

> **NOTE** Be aware that tracing will slow down the DB2 instance. The amount of performance degradation will depend on the type of problem, your current workload, and how busy your system is during the trace operation.

18.6.3 The db2dart Tool

You can use **db2dart** to inspect the whole database, a table space in the database, or a single table. When the inspection ends, it presents the results in a nicely organized report, deposited in the directory where the **db2dart** command was issued (on Linux/UNIX), or the *db2_install_dir**instance_name*\DART0000 directory (on Windows). The report has the name *dbalias.RPT.*

You can only use the **db2dart** tool when the database is offline, so no connections are allowed while the database is being inspected.

The syntax for the command is

```
db2dart DBALIAS [OPTIONS]
```

Type **db2dart** from the command line to see the list of all available options.

The following are some ways you can use **db2dart**.

- To perform an inspection on all objects in the *sample* database, issue

  ```
  db2dart sample
  ```

- To inspect table space USERSPACE1 in the *sample* database, issue

  ```
  db2dart sample /TSI 2
  ```

  where **2** is the table space ID for table space *USERSPACE1*. Table space IDs can be found in the **LIST TABLESPACES** command output.
- To inspect the *sales* table in the *sample* database, issue

  ```
  db2dart sample /TSI 2 /TN "sales"
  ```

If **db2dart** reports some data pages being corrupted, restore the database using a good backup image.

If **db2dart** reports some index pages being corrupted, you can fix this instead of having to restore from a backup.

If **db2dart** reports an index is corrupted, take the following steps to fix it:

1. Mark the index invalid using

   ```
   db2dart dbalias /MI /OI objectID of the index /TSI tablespaceID
   ```

   where both the **objectID** and **tablespaceID** can be found in the **db2dart** report.

2. Let DB2 automatically rebuild the index. When DB2 actually rebuilds this index depends on the INDEXREC database configuration parameter setting. Its values can be ACCESS, RESTART, or SYSTEM.
   - **ACCESS:** DB2 rebuilds invalid indexes when they are accessed again for the first time, after they have been invalidated by **db2dart.** With this method, the first user who accesses this index will experience a longer wait while the index is re-created.
   - **RESTART:** DB2 rebuilds invalid indexes when the database is restarted. With this method, the time taken to restart the database will be longer due to index re-creation, but normal processing is not impacted once the database has been brought back online.
   - **SYSTEM:** DB2 uses the setting in the INDEXREC at the database manager level.

> **NOTE** INDEXREC is available as a database configuration parameter and a Database Manager Configuration parameter. As a Database Manager Configuration parameter, the value of INDEXREC affects all databases that have INDEXREC set to SYSTEM. With this dual-level setting, you can choose to control the index re-creation at instance level or at individual database levels.

18.6.4 The INSPECT Tool

The **INSPECT** tool is the online equivalent of the db2dart tool, which can run while the database is online. The **INSPECT** tool inspects databases for architectural integrity and checks the pages of the database for page consistency. The inspection checks that the structures of table objects and table spaces are valid. However, it cannot be used to mark an index invalid or fix possible data corruptions like the **db2dart** tool can.

The results file of the inspection is generated in the DB2 diagnostic data directory (i.e., where the db2diag.log file is). It is a binary file that needs to be formatted with the **DB2INSPF** command. If no errors are found, by default, the results file is erased after the inspect operation is complete, unless the **KEEP** option is used.

- To inspect the SAMPLE database and write the results to a file called *inspect.out*, issue

```
CONNECT TO sample
INSPECT CHECK DATABASE RESULTS inspect.out
```

- To inspect the table space with table space ID *2* and keep the results and write it to the file *inspect.out*, issue

```
CONNECT TO sample
INSPECT CHECK TABLSPACE TBSPACEID 2 RESULTS KEEP inspect.out
```

- To format the results file, issue

```
DB2INSPF results_file output_file
```

where results_file is from the **inspect** command and output_file is the name of the output file generated.

The following tables list the differences between the tests that are performed by the db2dart and INSPECT commands:

Table 18.4 Feature Comparison of db2dart and INSPECT for Table Spaces

Tests Performed	db2dart	INSPECT
On SMS table spaces		
Check table space files	YES	NO
Validate contents of internal page header fields	YES	YES
On DMS tablespaces		
Check for extent maps pointed at by more than one object	YES	NO
Check every extent map page for consistency bit errors	NO	YES
Check every space map page for consistency bit errors	NO	YES
Validate contents of internal page header fields	YES	YES
Verify that extent maps agree with table space maps	YES	NO

Table 18.5 Feature Comparison of db2dart and INSPECT for Data Objects

Tests Performed	db2dart	INSPECT
Check data objects for consistency bit errors	YES	YES
Check the contents of special control rows	YES	NO
Check the length and position of variable length columns	YES	NO
Check the LONG VARCHAR, LONG VARGRAPHIC, and large object (LOB) descriptors in table rows	YES	NO
Check the summary total pages, used pages, and free space percentage	NO	YES
Validate contents of internal page header fields	YES	YES
Verify each row record type and its length	YES	YES
Verify that rows are not overlapping	YES	YES

Table 18.6 Feature Comparison of db2dart and INSPECT for Index Objects

Tests Performed	db2dart	INSPECT
Check for consistency bit errors	YES	YES
Check the location and length of the index key and whether there is overlapping	YES	YES
Check the ordering of keys in the index	YES	NO
Determine the summary total pages and used pages	NO	YES
Validate contents of internal page header fields	YES	YES
Verify the uniqueness of unique keys	YES	NO

V9 18.6.5 DB2COS (DB2 Call Out Script)

DB2 9 introduced improvements to the FFDC facility that will allow you to have increased control over the diagnostic information produced in case of a DB2 software failure. The **db2cos** script, which stands for "DB2 call out script" is invoked automatically when the database manager cannot continue processing due to a panic, trap, segmentation violation, or exception that causes the database manager to stop executing. By default, the **db2cos** script runs the **db2pd** tool to collect information in an unlatched manner, which means that it will not affect the performance of your database system while the script is running. Refer to Chapter 4, Using the DB2 Tools, for more information about the **db2pd** tool. You can edit the **db2cos** script to collect more or less information. If you want to capture a complete picture of what was happening when the DB2 software failed, you can simply put in the db2cos script **`db2pd –everything`** and DB2 will dump every option available to the db2pd tool. The **db2cos** script is located in the DB2PATH\bin directory on Windows and $INSTHOME/sqllib/bin directory on UNIX/Linux platforms.

When the default **db2cos** script is called, it will produce an output file called *db2cosXXXYYY.ZZZ,* where *XXX* is the process ID (PID) relating to the process that is failing, *YYY* is the thread ID (TID) identifier, and the *ZZZ* is the database partition number (000 for single partition databases). You can turn on db2cos to run automatically (on by default) or invoke it manually, during a DB2 hang condition for example. The default path is specified by the *DIAGPATH* database manager configuration parameter.

For example, Figure 18.10 shows a db2diag.log entry where db2cos is invoked:

The output file will be called *db2cos843287000001.000*. Figure 18.11 shows a sample **db2cos** excerpt using the default **db2cos script.** Additional **db2pd output** information is available, but is not shown. The output information will depend on the commands specified in the **db2cos** script.

```
2006-12-14-08.38.11.19952-300  I19441A349        LEVEL: Event
PID       : 843287             TID  : 1          PROC : db2sysc
INSTANCE: db2inst1             NODE : 000
FUNCTION: DB2 UDB, trace services, pdInvokeCalloutScript, probe:10
START     : Invoking /home/db2inst1/sqllib/bin/db2cos from oper system
Services sqloEDUCodeTrapHandler
```

Figure 18.10 Sample entry with db2cos in db2diag.log

```
2006-12-14-08.38.11.19952
PID       : 782348             TID  : 1          PROC : db2cos
INSTANCE: db2inst1             NODE : 0          DB   : SAMPLE
APPHDL    :                    APPID: *LOCAL.db2inst1.025714167819
FUNCTION: oper system services, sqloEDUCodeTrapHandler, probe:999
EVENT     : Invoking /home/db2inst1/sqllib/bin/db2cos from
oper system services sqloEDUCodeTrapHandler
Trap Caught
Instance db2inst1 uses 64 bits and DB2 code release SQL09010
...
Operating System Information:
OSName:    AIX
NodeName: n1
Version:   5
Release:   2
Machine:   000966594C00
```

Figure 18.11 DB2 administration notification log entry on Windows

V9 18.6.6 DB2PDCFG Command

In addition to db2cos, DB2 9 introduced the **db2pdcfg** (short for DB2 problem determination configure) command, which allows you to influence the detail of information collected during a DB2 software failure. You can use **db2dbcfg** with the **-cos** option to set the **db2cos** options, such as turning on or off the automatic call by the database manager during a database manager trap. The **db2pdcfg** command can also be used to "catch" particular SQLCODEs and perform specific actions based on those codes. Figure 18.12 presents a simplified version of the **db2pdcfg** syntax diagram.

As you can see, there are many options available to customize your problem-determination requirements. The following are a couple of examples of how to use the db2pdcfg command.

If you wanted to call **db2cos** whenever a deadlock condition arises, you can use the command:

```
db2pdcfg —CATCH -911, 2 DB2COS
```

If you wanted to catch a lock timeout condition caused by a particular lock name, use the following command:

```
db2pdcfg -911,68 LOCKNAME=000200030000001F0000000052
```

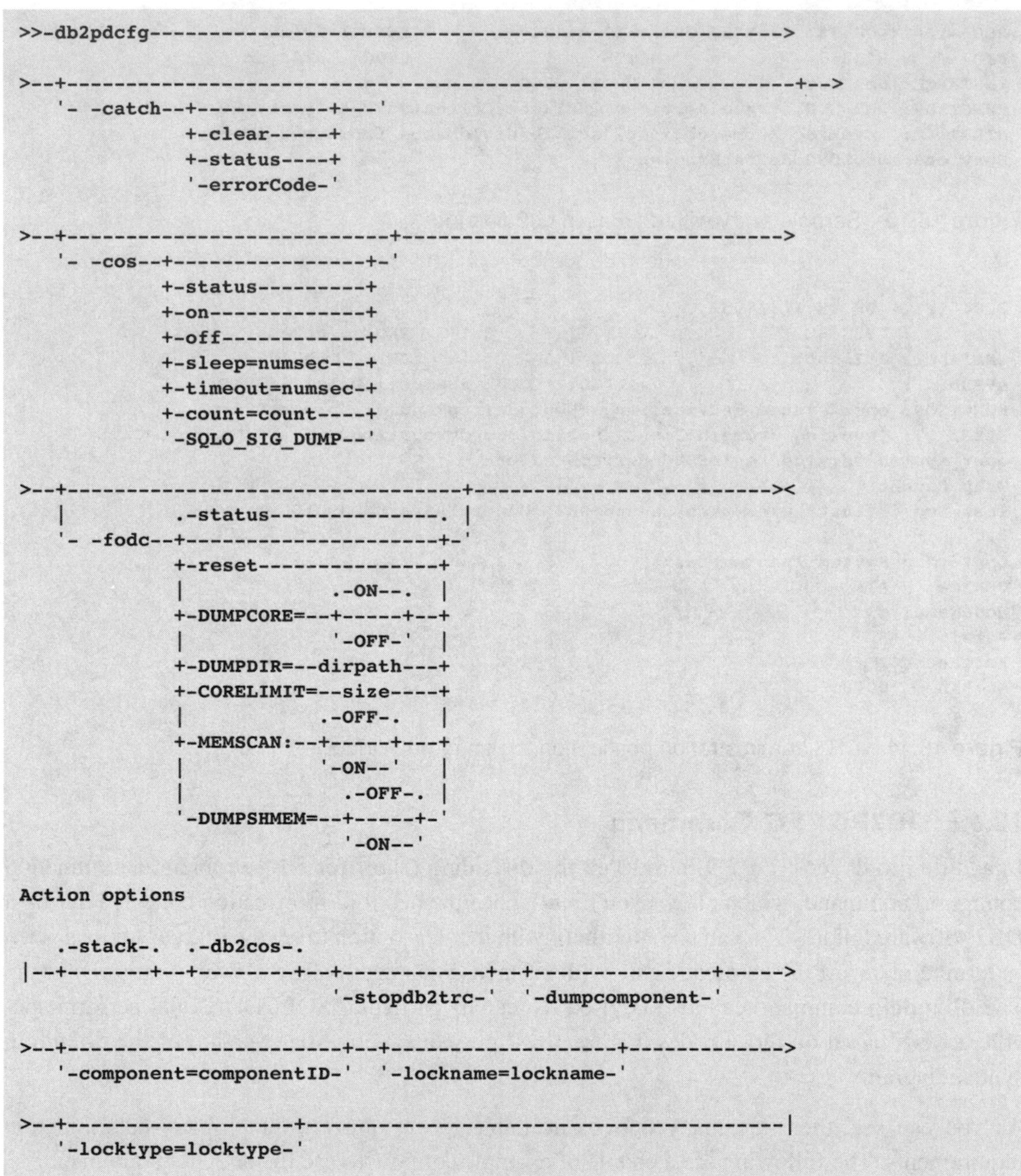

```
>>-db2pdcfg----------------------------------------------------->

>--+-------------------------------------------------------------+-->
   '- -catch--+-----------+---'
              +-clear-----+
              +-status----+
              '-errorCode-'

>--+---------------------------+-------------------------------->
   '- -cos--+----------------+-'
            +-status---------+
            +-on-------------+
            +-off------------+
            +-sleep=numsec---+
            +-timeout=numsec-+
            +-count=count----+
            '-SQLO_SIG_DUMP--'

>--+---------------------------------+-------------------------><
   |         .-status--------------. |
   '- -fodc--+---------------------+-'
             +-reset---------------+
             |            .-ON--.  |
             +-DUMPCORE=--+-----+--+
             |            '-OFF-'  |
             +-DUMPDIR=--dirpath---+
             +-CORELIMIT=--size----+
             |           .-OFF-.   |
             +-MEMSCAN:--+-----+---+
             |           '-ON--'   |
             |             .-OFF-. |
             '-DUMPSHMEM=--+-----+-'
                           '-ON--'
Action options

   .-stack-.  .-db2cos-.
|--+-------+--+--------+--+-----------+--+---------------+----->
                          '-stopdb2trc-'  '-dumpcomponent-'

>--+-----------------------+--+-------------------+------------>
   '-component=componentID-'  '-lockname=lockname-'

>--+-------------------+----------------------------------------|
   '-locktype=locktype-'
```

Figure 18.12 Syntax diagram of db2pdcfg command

To dump out all available information when a table space full condition is encountered, specify the following:

```
db2pdcfg -CATCH -289
```

V9.5 18.6.7 First Occurrence Data Capture (FODC)

In an effort to provide more detailed information to enhance the efficiency of the problem-determination process, DB2 9.5 has introduced a new tool, **db2fodc** (First Occurrence Data Capture), to collect and capture data when an outage or error condition is detected.

The **db2fodc** utility can be initiated either automatically or manually. Outages involving traps, panics, or data corruptions will invoke an automatic FODC call. You can initiate a manual FODC call during a hang condition where the database and DB2 commands are unresponsive. Once invoked, the **db2fodc** utility will capture symptom-based data about the outage or error condition and write the information to a FODC package. The FODC package is a set of diagnostic information collected into a specific location during a manual or automatic FODC invocation. The diagnostic information, such as log, trace, trap or dump files will be stored into a new subdirectory under the DB2 instances' diagnostic path (for example, $INSTHOME/sqllib/db2dump on UNIX/Linux). The new subdirectory path will have a name like *FODC_<outage type>_<timestamp>*; for example, *FODC_Trap_2007-05-12-17.34.50.171938*, where the outage type is a trap, and the timestamp is indicated as 2007-05-12-17.34.50.171938. The four outage types available include TRAP, PANIC, DATA CORRUPTION, and HANG.

Additional data that is collected by the **db2fodc** utility is controlled by the **db2pdcfg** utility's FODC options. For example, you may want to dump the shared memory data, which includes Database Manager (instance) shared memory, Fast Communication Manager's buffers, Fenced Mode Process memory set, Database memory, and Application memory, if you suspect a memory corruption in your recent database crash. You can set this option with the following command:

```
db2pdcfg -FODC DUMPSHMEM=ON
```

Figure 18.13 shows the syntax diagram for the db2fodc utility.

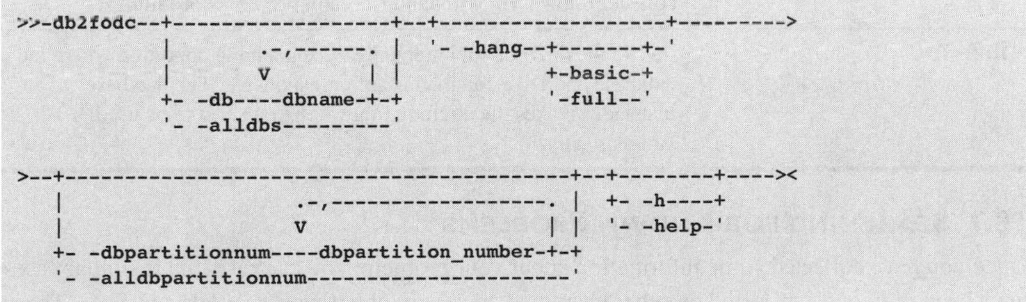

```
>>-db2fodc--+------------------+--+------------------+---------->
            |     .-,------.   |  '- -hang--+-------+-'
            |     V        |   |            +-basic-+
            +- -db----dbname-+-+            '-full--'
            '- -alldbs---------'

>--+------------------------------------------+--+--------+----><
   |                  .-,-----------------.   |  +- -h----+
   |                  V                   |   |  '- -help-'
   +- -dbpartitionnum----dbpartition_number-+-+
   '- -alldbpartitionnum----------------------'
```

Figure 18.13 Syntax diagram of db2fodc command

For example, you can collect data during a potential hang condition for all databases without stopping the database manager by specifying the following:

```
db2fodc –HANG –ALLDBS
```

If you want full details for a potential hang condition on the SAMPLE database, specify:

```
db2fodc -DB sample -HANG FULL
```

Once execution of the **db2fodc** command completes, the **db2support** tool must be run to prepare and collect the resulting diagnostic files and prepare the package for submission to IBM support for further analysis. By default, **db2support** will collect all *FODC_<outage type>_<timestamp>* directories found under the diagnostics data directory path. This is done to avoid additional requests, from IBM Support, for diagnostic information.

The following table summarizes the major tools used for problem determination discussed in this chapter:

Table 18.7 Summary of Problem-Determination Tools

Problem-Determination Tool	When to Use It
DB2SUPPORT	Invoke the db2support utility to automatically collect all DB2 and system diagnostic information available.
DB2 Trace Facility	Invoke the db2 trace facility to acquire detailed information about a reproducible problem operation that you are investigating.
DB2DART	Use the db2dart tool to determine AND fix possible data corruptions.
INSPECT	Use the INSPECT tool to determine possible data corruption.
DB2COS	The db2cos script is invoked by default when the database manager cannot continue processing due to a panic, trap, segmentation violation, or exception.
DB2PDCFG	Use the db2pdcfg command to configure how much information to collect or how DB2 will handle certain problems or failures.
DB2FODC	Invoke the db2fodc tool manually during a hang condition where the database and DB2 commands are unresponsive. The database manager invokes the db2fodc tool when you set it to be used automatically.

18.7 Searching for Known Problems

Once you have collected some information about your problem, you can research if similar cases have been previously reported by other customers and learn about workarounds and fixes. These are the steps you can follow to resolve your problem.

1. First confirm if the product is working as designed by reviewing the DB2 documentation using the DB2 9 Information Center (http://publib.boulder.ibm.com/infocenter/db2luw/v9/index.jsp).
   The DB2 Version 8 Information Center is still avalible at http://publib.boulder.ibm.com/infocenter/db2luw/v8/index.jsp.

2. Search the Internet for problems reported by other DB2 users.
3. If your environment allows it, apply the latest Fix Pack, which you can download for free from the DB2 for Linux, UNIX, and Windows Technical Support site (http://www-306.ibm.com/software/data/support/). The Fix Packs are cumulative, and they also come with an aparlist.txt file describing the authorized program analysis reports (APARs) that were fixed with the Fix Pack. (An APAR is simply the official method that IBM uses to acknowledge a defect in the product.)
4. If you cannot apply the Fix Pack in your environment at the moment, besides reviewing the aparlist.txt file, you can also research for related problems in the DB2 Technical Support site. This site includes FAQs, technical notes, flashes, and you can also search for specific APARs.
5. The DB2 for Linux, UNIX and Windows DeveloperWorks forum be found at http://www-128.ibm.com/developerworks/db2/zones/db2udb/
6. Ask in DB2 forums or newsgroups like **comp.databases.ibm-db2** for problems similar to the one you are encountering. Also try DB2 Blog sites such as http://www.planetdb2.com/ for hints and tips.
7. If your research doesn't lead to any hits, and you suspect it is a product defect issue, contact DB2 Technical support at **1-800-IBM-SERV.**

18.8 Case Study

You want to enable your DB2 database server running on Linux to accept client connections using TCP/IP. (This process is covered in Chapter 6, Configuring Client and Server Connectivity.) The first thing you need to do is to set the DB2COMM registry variable to TCPIP, for example:

```
db2set db2comm=tcpip
```

Then you stop and restart the instance for the setting of DB2COMM to take effect. However, when you start the instance again, you get the following message:

```
SQL5043N Support for one or more communications protocols failed to start
successfully. However, core database manager functionality started successfully.
```

You are not sure why this error would occur. You decide to look for more information about this error in the administration notification log, which is under the *$HOME*/sqllib/db2dump directory on Linux/UNIX systems. You open the file and the last entry in this file shows:

```
2007-07-07-16.24.57.229642   Instance:mdang     Node:000
PID:264502(db2sysc)    TID:1   Appid:none
common communication   sqlcctcpconnmgr Probe:50

ADM7006E The SVCENAME DBM configuration parameter was not configured. Update the
SVCENAME configuration parameter using the service name defined in the TCP/IP services
file.

2007-07-07-16.24.58.747410   Instance:mdang     Node:000
```

```
PID:442506(db2star2)    TID:1    Appid:none
base sys utilities  DB2StartMain Probe:911

ADM7513W Database manager has started.
```

The first message indicates that the SVCENAME parameter needs to be updated. The second message indicates that although the TCP/IP support failed to start, the instance is started regardless. This corresponds to the SQL5043N message.

You remember from Chapter 6 that to enable TCP/IP support on a DB2 server, you must also update the SVCENAME parameter to indicate the TCP/IP port number the DB2 instance is going to use. You execute the following command:

```
db2 update dbm cfg using svcename 50000
```

When you restart the instance, the error goes away. The message you get is

```
SQL1063N DB2START processing was successful.
```

You run your production DB2 instance with one database without any problems for over four months, but suddenly this morning, you notice that the database isn't responsive. Your applications appear to hang, and when you try to run a few DB2 commands such as:

```
db2 connect to proddb1
db2 list applications show detail
```

all your commands will not return. In the past, you have tried to force down the DB2 instance and restart it. However, now you would like to find out what may be causing this problem. You remember that there is a new tool in DB2 9 that can help with diagnostic information during hang conditions. You open the "Understanding DB2" book and find the section about the db2fodc tool. You issue the following command:

```
db2fodc –HANG –ALLDBS
```

After the command successfully completes, you invoke the db2suppport utility to generate a dump of all the neccesary diagnositic information.

```
db2support . -d <proddb1> -c –s
```

You call DB2 Support to report the problem, and FTP the db2support output file for further investigation.

You are now happy with your DB2 environment and everything is running smoothly. However, you have been contacted a couple of times by your users regarding the fact that their connection seems to be timing out occasionally. You decide to investigate this issue further. You look up the db2pdcfg command and find the error catch setting. You issue the following command to invoke db2pdcfg to catch all lock timeouts:

```
db2pdcfg -catch locktimeout count=1
Error Catch #1
Sqlcode: 0
ReasonCode: 0
ZRC: -2146435004
```

```
ECF: 0
Component ID: 0
LockName: Not Set
LockType: Not Set
Current Count: 0
Max Count: 1
Bitmap: 0x4A1
Action: Error code catch flag enabled
Action: Execute sqllib/db2cos callout script
Action: Produce stack trace in db2diag.log
```

Days go by without any issues, until today, you rcceive a call from your user. He is complaining about the following error message he received from his application:

```
SQL0911N  The current transaction has been rolled back because of a deadlock or
timeout.
Reason code "68".  SQLSTATE=40001
```

You find the corresponding message in the db2diag.log:

```
2007-06-17-01.28.41.803000-300 I22649H285         LEVEL: Event
PID      : 940                 TID  : 3136        PROC : db2syscs.exe
INSTANCE: DB2                  NODE : 000
FUNCTION: DB2 UDB, RAS/PD component, pdErrorCatch, probe:30
START    : Error catch set for ZRC -2146435004

...

2007-06-17-01.40.04.091000-300 I23330H309         LEVEL: Event
PID      : 940                 TID  : 2136        PROC : db2syscs.exe
INSTANCE: DB2                  NODE : 000         DB   : SAMPLE
APPHDL   : 0-251               APPID: *LOCAL.DB2.060217064002
FUNCTION: DB2 UDB, lock manager, sqlplnfd, probe:999
DATA #1 : preformatted
Caught rc -2146435004.  Dumping stack trace.

2007-06-17-01.40.04.106000-300 I23721H416         LEVEL: Event
PID      : 940                 TID  : 2136        PROC : db2syscs.exe
INSTANCE: DB2                  NODE : 000         DB   : SAMPLE
APPHDL   : 0-251               APPID: *LOCAL.DB2.060217064002
FUNCTION: DB2 UDB, trace services, pdInvokeCalloutScript, probe:10
START    : Invoking C:\PROGRA~1\IBM\SQLLIB\bin\db2cos.bat from lock manager sqlplnfd

...

2007-06-17-01.40.07.715000-300 I25489H399         LEVEL: Event
PID      : 940                 TID  : 2136        PROC : db2syscs.exe
INSTANCE: DB2                  NODE : 000         DB   : SAMPLE
APPHDL   : 0-251               APPID: *LOCAL.DB2.060217064002
FUNCTION: DB2 UDB, trace services, pdInvokeCalloutScript, probe:20
STOP     : Completed invoking C:\PROGRA~1\IBM\SQLLIB\bin\db2cos.bat
```

You look for the db2cos output files. The location of the files is controlled by the database manager configuration parameter DIAGPATH. You look there and find the following:

```
Lock Timeout Caught
Thu Feb 17 01:40:04 EST 2006
Instance DB2
Datbase: SAMPLE
Partition Number: 0
PID: 940
TID: 2136
Function: sqlplnfd
Component: lock manager
Probe: 999
Timestamp: 2006-02-17-01.40.04.106000
AppID: *LOCAL.DB2...
AppHdl:
...
Database Partition 0 -- Database SAMPLE -- Active -- Up 0 days 00:06:53
Locks:
Address TranHdl Lockname Type Mode Sts Owner Dur HldCnt Att Rlse
0x402C6B30 3 00020003000000040000000052 Row ..X W* 3 1 0 0 0x40
```

Look for the "`W*`" as this is the lock that experienced the timeout. You can map this to a transaction, application, agent, and even SQL statement with all of the output provided by the db2pd command. You then need to change the SQL statement or application logic to prevent future lock timeouts.

18.9 Summary

This chapter discussed how to diagnose problems encountered while working with DB2. DB2 reports problems using error messages and codes. The message help (?) command is a quick way to obtain more information about a DB2 message code.

The First Failure Data Capture (FFDC) is a generic term that refers to several diagnostic files that are generated or updated automatically by DB2, like the administration notification log or the file db2diag.log. Use the db2support tool to collect these diagnostic files automatically in a zip file called db2support.zip. For some types of problems, like hangs or crashes, DB2 Technical Support may ask you to collect a DB2 trace.

DB2 provides two tools to inspect your database. The db2dart tool is an offline database analysis and report tool. In addition to inspecting a database, it can be used to mark an index invalid so it can be rebuilt. If your database is a 24×7 database, an inspection by db2dart is not recommended. In this case, use the INSPECT tool, which can be used while the database is online.

New enhancements to troubleshooting and problem-determination tools were introduced. These tools, including the db2cos script, db2pdbcfg command and db2fodc tool, will simplify error tracking and logging.

Always check the DB2 documentation; it usually provides the answers to most problems. Otherwise, search for known problems on the DB2 Technical Support Web site.

18.10 Review Questions

1. What does the **?** command do?
2. An application developer tells you that he received an SQLCODE of -805. What command can you use to obtain more information about it?
3. What does FFDC stand for?
4. What is the name of the administration notification file in Windows?
5. What is the name of the administration notification file in Linux/UNIX?
6. How can you ensure the file db2diag.log captures the most information possible?
7. What does the db2support tool do?
8. What command is used to create a DB2 trace?
9. Where is the db2diag.log file placed by default for Linux and UNIX platforms?
10. What is the minimum NOTIFYLEVEL value required to receive e-mail messages?
11. Which of the following Database Manager configuration parameters is used to determine where the administration notification log file will reside on UNIX?
    A. path
    B. adminpath
    C. diagpath
    D. notifypath
12. Which of the following is *not* a Database Manager Configuration parameter used for FFDC?
    A. NOTIFYME
    B. NOTIFYLEVEL
    C. DIAGLEVEL
    D. DIAGPATH
13. Which of the following levels for NOTIFYLEVEL only logs fatal and unrecoverable errors?
    A. 0
    B. 1
    C. 2
    D. 3
14. Which of the following commands can be used to update the DB2 Administration Server parameter to indicate the host name of the SMTP server?
    A. update admin cfg using SMTP *hostname*
    B. update dbm cfg using SMTP *hostname*
    C. update admin cfg using SMTP_SERVER *hostname*
    D. update admin cfg using SMTP_SRV *hostname*
15. Which of the following is not a problem-determination tool?
    A. db2diag.log
    B. db2fodc
    C. db2cos
    D. Inspect

16. Which of the following is not collected with the db2support tool?
   A. db2diag.log
   B. Adminstration notification file
   C. Application log file
   D. Trap files

17. Which is the default value for DIAGLEVEL?
   A. 0
   B. 1
   C. 2
   D. 3

18. Which command should be used to configure how much information to collect or how DB2 will handle certain problems or failures?
   A. db2pdcfg
   B. db2diag
   C. db2pd
   D. db2diagcfg

19. Which is the default value for DIAGPATH?
   A. SQLLIB
   B. DB2DUMP
   C. DUMP
   D. NULL

20. Which of the following actions is not needed to enable e-mail notification?
   A. Add contact information using the ADD CONTACT command.
   B. Update the health notification contact list.
   C. Update the CONTACT_HOST DAS parameter.
   D. Update the CONTACT_LIST_GROUP DAS parameter.

APPENDIX A

Solutions to the Review Questions

Chapter 1

1. IBM added the term "Universal" to reflect DB2's capability to store all kinds of electronic data including traditional relational data, as well as audio, video, text, and so on, and the support of a range of operating systems and hardware architectures.
2. Rational, Information Management, WebSphere, Tivoli, and Lotus.
3. Yes. All the DB2 editions other than DB2 Everyplace have a set of core modules that are the same; therefore, an application that works with DB2 Personal will work against DB2 Enterprise.
4. No. DB2 Connect is required only in one direction: when connecting from a DB2 LUW to DB2 for z/OS or other host server like DB2 for i5/OS, DB2 for VM, and VSE or DB2 for OS/390.
5. pureXML
6. No. Federation support is built into the DB2 product for RDBMSs that are part of the IBM family, like IBM Informix.
7. A company migrating their production database from Oracle to DB2 may set up DB2 replication to replicate the data from the Oracle production server to the DB2 server. This approach lets developers at the company test their applications against the DB2 server with "real" data before switching completely to DB2.
8. No. Even though more than 90 percent of the code is common among these platforms, each platform has its own file used for installation for the appropriate platform.
9. The database partitioning feature (DPF) allows you to partition your data within a single server or across multiple servers running the same operating system. This provides for scalability.
10. Contact your IBM marketing representative, or call 1-800-IBM-SERV and indicate that you would like to buy a permanent license for your DB2 product.

11. **D.** The minimum software required on the Windows client is the IBM Data Server runtime client. This is required to *run* any application, other than an application using the JDBC type 4 driver.
12. **C.** The Data Server Driver for JDBC and SQLJ
13. **B.** DB2 Personal is a fully functional server that is designed for personal use only. As such, it does not support connections from remote clients.
14. **C.** DB2 Personal is not considered a DB2 server since it cannot accept inbound (remote) connections from clients.
15. **B.** The IBM Data Server client includes everything the IBM Data Server runtime client has plus the graphical administration tools.
16. **C.** DB2 Everyplace is a fully functional database that can be stored in mobile devices like PDAs. DB2 Everywhere is not a DB2 Edition, and DB2 Satellite Edition was merged with DB2 Personal Edition in Version 8.
17. **D.** Database Enterprise Developer's Edition (DEDE) includes DB2 Connect Enterprise Edition, which allows the connection to host servers. It also includes all the DB2 LUW clients. Because this is a software development company, DEDE is more convenient than DB2 Enterprise.
18. **A.** A System z server with a LPAR running the Linux operating system can run DB2 for Linux, UNIX, and Windows. Some of the other products mentioned are not data servers. Also, IBM Websphere Information Integrator has been split into two products: IBM Websphere Federation Server, and IBM Websphere Replication Server.
19. **A.** Database Enterprise Developer's Edition.
20. **B.** DB2 Warehouse Manager is one of the products under the Business Intelligence umbrella and can be used to help you understand your data to make better business decisions.

Chapter 2

1. They are classified in two categories: DB2 system commands and DB2 CLP commands.
2. For DB2 system commands use **`command -h.`** For DB2 CLP commands use **`db2 ? command.`**
3. The Information Center provides a fast search engine that lets you search all the manuals based on a keyword.
4. The **`db2icrt`** command creates a DB2 instance on the server where the command is run.
5. Every database has three default table spaces created automatically by DB2. These table spaces are:
   - SYSCATSPACE
   - TEMPSPACE1
   - USERSPACE1
6. The **`db2ilist`** command lists all instances that exist on a server, whether they are active or not.

7. When you install DB2 on a Windows server, the installation program will automatically create an instance named *DB2* on the server.
8. No. The DAS is required only to allow the use of graphical tools for remote administration. The DAS is not required when working with the DSAC.
9. The DB2 environment can be configured by changing values of parameters in different areas:
   - Environment variables
   - DB2 registry variables
   - The Database Manager Configuration (dbm cfg) file and database configuration (db cfg) file
10. The local database directory is populated with the **`CREATE DATABASE`** command (not with the **catalog** command). The system database directory can be populated with the **`CREATE DATABASE`** command, and with the **catalog** command.
11. **C.** The **`db2start`** command starts the current DB2 instance.
12. **B.** The **`db2set –all`** command lists all of the currently configured registry variables.
13. **D.** The command **`list db directory on C:`** will examine the local database directory, which is not removed when the instance is dropped, and list all of the databases on that *drive/filesystem*.
14. **D.** You must catalog the database before you can connect to it. To catalog the database in this situation, you must specify the drive or directory where the local database directory exists. In this case it is C:, so use the command **`catalog db sample on C:.`**
15. **C.** You must set the DB2INSTANCE environment variable to the instance you want to work with, in this case *inst2*, so the command is **`export db2instance=inst2.`**
16. **D.** The DB2_FORCE_FCM_BP registry variable tells DB2 to use shared memory for interpartition communication (FCM) and not to use the network. Note that this question does not apply to DB2 9.5 since this parameter is discontinued in that release because only 64-bit kernels of AIX® operating systems are supported, and they do not have shared memory segment size restrictions.
17. **B.** The **`db2_all`** command runs the specified command on all database partitions in the database.
18. **B.** Federated support is turned on using the dbm cfg parameter FEDERATED.
19. **C.** DB2NODE.
20. **A.** The CURRENT DBPARTITIONNUM special register provides this information.

Chapter 3

1. Two methods for Windows are available: the DB2 Setup Wizard and Silent install. Four methods for Linux and UNIX are available: the DB2 Setup Wizard, Silent install, the db2_install script, and manual installation of DB2 payload files.
2. No. DB2 image is always placed in the $HOME/sqllib directory, where $HOME represents the non-root user's home directory.

3. The default instance name is *db2inst1*. The user owner ID *db2inst1* is created as well. If *db2inst1* already exists, DB2 will try *db2inst2*, *db2inst3*, and so on.
4. An alternate FixPak contains all fixes, as does a regular FixPak, but the fixes are built into the product. Moreover, it is installed under a different directory, so DB2 treats it as a different product. This way you can have different DB2 FixPak levels for the same version on the same computer.
5. By default, three logs are generated under the /tmp directory: db2setup.his, db2setup.log, and db2setup.err. To redirect the logs to a different location, run the **`db2setup`** program with the **`–l`** option.
6. By default, two logs are generated under the My Documents\DB2LOG directory: db2.log and db2wi.log. To redirect them to a different location, run the **`setup`** program (from the DB2 installation media) with the **`–l`** option.
7. DB2ADMNS and DB2USERS.
8. You need to run the **`db2iupdt`** command for all of your DB2 instances after you install a DB2 FixPak to update the instance with the new libraries and to update the logical links to the installed libraries.
9. The following user rights are granted to the instance owner:
   - Act as part of the operating system
   - Debug programs
   - Create token objects
   - Increase quotas
   - Lock pages in memory
   - Log on as a service
   - Replace a process-level token
10. The user who is installing DB2 must have Local Administrator authority. If you want to have the DB2 Setup Wizard create a domain user account for the Instance owner or the DAS user, the installation ID must have the authority to create domain user accounts.
11. **B.** The DB2 Setup Wizard and the Silent install are the only two methods available on Windows.
12. **C.** A response file is a text file containing all the options to be used during the install process. Use this file as input during a silent install.
13. **C.** 50000 is the default
14. **D.** You need root authority.
15. **A.** The DAS User ID.
16. **B.** The db2_install script is not a valid method of installation on Windows.
17. **C.** The db2_install script.
18. **A.** **`db2setup –r response_file`**
19. **D.** The db2_install script.
20. **C.** The db2ls command can list the DB2 products and features installed on your Linux and UNIX systems, including the DB2 9 HTML documentation.

CHAPTER 4

1. The Task Center lets you schedule scripts containing SQL statements, XQuery statements, and/or DB2 commands to be run at specific times.
2. There is no equivalent DB2 tool in the Linux/UNIX platforms. The Linux/UNIX *shell* would be equivalent to the DB2 Command Window.
3. The registry variable is DB2OPTIONS.
4. When you plan to copy a command or statement that has carriage returns and then paste it into the CLP, it is best to use this method.
5. The **`terminate`** command.
6. You can invoke Visual Explain from the Command Editor. Type a query, and then choose either the *Execute and Access plan* or *Access Plan* button.
7. The IBM Data Studio tool.
8. No. The DSAC cannot currently be used to administer DB2 for i5/OS; however it can be used to administer DB2 for z/OS, IDS, and of course, DB2 for LUW. The support for all of these is at the same level of service and features.
9. The Journal keeps track of DB2 messages; therefore, review the Journal messages tab.
10. Access the Information Center from the Internet:
    For DB2 9: http://publib.boulder.ibm.com/infocenter/db2luw/v9/index.jsp
    For DB2 9.5: http://publib.boulder.ibm.com/infocenter/db2luw/v9r5/index.jsp
11. **B** and **C**. You can enter SQL statements and DB2 CLP commands in the Command Line Processor (CLP) or in the Command Editor.
12. **B.** The default termination character is a semi-colon (;).
13. **E.** By default the CLP has autocommit enabled, and this causes the CLP to issue a commit statement automatically after every statement. Therefore, in this case, the CLP will issue a commit four times—after each entry in the input file.
14. **C.** The Health Center will alert you when actions in the database exceed thresholds for performance-related characteristics that you have defined.
15. **B** and **E**. The Memory Visualizer will track the memory used by DB2 on your system and will plot/graph this memory usage for you automatically if you desire. The **`db2mtrk`** tool is the command-line interface to the same information, and it will provide the same information in a text-based report.
16. **A.** By default the CLP has autocommit enabled, which causes the CLP to issue a commit automatically after every statement. However, the **+c** flag tells the CLP to disable autocommit; therefore, in this case, the CLP will not issue a commit. Since there is no explicit commit statement, there will be no commits during the processing of this file.
17. **B.** To set a termination character you need to use the **`-td`** option, and to set the input file you need to use the **`-f`** option. However, if you specify a value for an option, you cannot string the options together. Therefore the correct answer is B.
18. **C and D. `db2 ? SQL-911`** is not commonly used, but it works. **`db2 ? SQL911N`** is most often used. Note that the *N* after the 911 is optional.

19. **D.** Repeat is not a DB2 CLP command and can't be run in interactive mode.
20. B, C and D are allowed from the CLP in interactive mode. A is not allowed since you cannot prefix the command with db2 when in interactive mode. B is a DB2 system command, and it can only be executed from the Command Window or the Linux/UNIX shell; however, the db2stop and the db2start system commands are exceptions to this rule.

Chapter 5

1. The DB2INSTANCE environment variable determines the current active instance, that is, the instance for your current session to which your commands would apply.
2. You can set up your DB2 environment in Linux/UNIX by adding the db2profile (for the Bourne and Korn shells) or db2cshrc (for the C shell) in the .login or .profile initialization files. You should also modify the db2profile file to set the DB2INSTANCE variable to the name of the instance you want active by default.
3. db2set DB2COMM= -g
4. db2ilist
5. To create a new instance with the **`db2icrt`** command on Linux or UNIX you must have root authority.
6. To create a new instance with the **`db2icrt`** command on Windows you must have Administrator authority.
7. The **`db2idrop`** command will remove the DB2 instance from the list, and remove all DB2-related executables and libraries from the instance owner's home directory.
8. No. Executing the command once from any database partition will start all of the other database partitions.
9. Issue the **`db2start`** command with the **`ADMIN MODE USER userID`** option.
10. An attachment is required to perform operations at the instance level, while a connection is required to perform operations at the database level.
11. **C.** The **`db2set –lr`** command lists all of the registry variables that DB2 recognizes.
12. **A** and **D**. Sort heap threshold (SHEAPTHRES) and maximum query degree of parallelism (MAX_QUERYDEGREE) are both database manager (instance)-level configuration parameters.
13. **D.** Each instance is a separate DB2 operating environment, so errors in one instance cannot affect the other instances. Therefore, to ensure that problems that you normally encounter in development do not affect your production system, put these databases in separate instances.
14. **B.** To get the current, effective setting for each configuration parameter along with the value of the parameter the next time the instance is stopped and restarted, use the **`show detail`** option of the **`get dbm cfg`** command.
15. **D.** To update the DAS configuration use the command **`db2 update admin cfg.`**
16. **D.** To change the DAS configuration back to its default values, use the command **`db2 reset admin cfg.`**

17. **C.** **`db2stop force`** forces all applications off the databases and prevents new connections from happening. Then it stops the active instance.
18. **A.** The **`list applications`** command requires an instance attachment.
19. **D.** The **`db2 get db cfg`** command is used to review the contents of the database configuration (db cfg) file. If you are not connected to the database, you need to specify the name of the database in the command.
20. **B** and **D**. The values of YES and ON are equivalent, but a *1* is not allowed. Also, INTRA_PARALLEL is a Database Manager Configuration parameter; therefore, **D** is incorrect.

Chapter 6

1. The system database directory contains all the databases you can connect to from a DB2 client machine.
2. To view the content of the database directory on the H: drive, you use the command **`list db directory on H:.`**
3. An entry type of *indirect* means that this entry corresponds to a local database.
4. To determine which port is being used, look for the string **`db2_cDB2`** in the *services* file.
5. APPC or TCPIP can be used as the communication protocol to connect from a DB2 Connect gateway to a DB2 for z/OS server.
6. DB2 Connect Enterprise Edition can be installed once on a gateway machine to allow all 1,000 clients to connect to the DB2 for iSeries server, while DB2 Connect Personal Edition is licensed only to be installed at the DB2 client machine.
7. To remove an entry from the DCS directory, you can use the command **`uncatalog dcs db dbname.`**
8. To remove an entry from the node directory, you can use the command **`uncatalog node nodename.`**
9. You should check the db2comm registry variable by issuing **`db2set -all`** to verify that the communication protocol is set correctly.
10. When you have a huge network with many hubs, the "Search the network" method will take a long time, and it may not find the database you want because this method will only search your local network.
11. **D.** This command puts an entry into the node directory that points to the remote server and port that the instance will use for inbound connections.
12. **C.** DB2 ESE has built-in DB2 Connect functionality, so it can use the DCS directory along with the DB2 Connect products. Therefore, DB2 Personal Edition is the one that cannot use the DCS directory.
13. **B.** You should use the value specified in the SVCENAME parameter in the command as shown in B.

14. **C.** When a database is created, an entry of type *indirect* is inserted into the system database directory.
15. **A** and **B** are required. **A** specifies the port number used by the instance. **B** turns on the TCP/IP listener.
16. **D.** *Unknown discovery* is not a valid method. Search the network can be done using *known discovery* and *search discovery.*
17. **A.** At the DAS level at the server machine, you can prevent Discover for the DB2 server.
18. **D.** To disable a certain database to be discovered, you can disable the DISCOVER_DB database configuration parameter.
19. **B.** This is the only catalog statement that is correct.
20. **B.** **`DISCOVER=disable`** is used to prevent a client machine from using the discovery method. In this case, the DB2 server is working as a DB2 client for other DB2 servers.

Chapter 7

1. **C.** Since no schema is explicitly specified, the schema will be the authorization ID for the connection. The authorization ID, also known as the connection ID, is the user ID used to connect to the database. Therefore, the table name will be *foo.t1*.
2. **B.** There is no object named IBMDEFAULTSPACE. When a database is created, DB2 creates the table spaces SYSCATSPACE, USERSPACE1, and TEMPSPACE1; the partition groups IBMCATGROUP, IBMTEMPGROUP, and IBMDEFAULTGROUP; and the buffer pool IBMDEFAULTBP.
3. **C.** An identity column ensures uniqueness, but only within a table. A sequence generates a unique value that is across the whole database and can therefore be used with multiple tables.
4. **D.** The statement **`alter table t1 activate not logged initially with empty table`** will delete all rows from the table and not log the deletions for the fastest response time. Table *t1* must have been created with the **`activate not logged initially`** clause for the **`alter table`** to work.
5. **B.** While you can enforce this by specifying the T or F constraint by creating a view (if all inserts are done using a view), this will not prevent you from inserting a different value if you insert into the table directly. To ensure that no other values are entered into this column, you need to define a check constraint.
6. **B.** The **`CASCADE`** option will delete all referenced rows in the child tables.
7. **B** and **D**. Both a unique constraint and a primary key constraint can be referenced by a foreign key constraint.
8. **C.** The statement inserting a value of 300 into the *productno* column will fail as this is an identity column GENERATED ALWAYS, so there will be two rows successfully inserted into the table.

9. **C.** The default precision and scale are 5, 0 if not explicitly specified in the **CREATE TABLE** statement.
10. **A.** INBETWEEN is not a type of trigger.
11. **C.** Each database has its own set of logs and system catalogs, and a schema is created within a database. However, the registry variables are set for all instances or at the instance level and control all databases in the instance.
12. **B.** The **CREATE TABLE** statement creates the table/data object for the database. Since there is a primary key clause in this statement, an index will also be created to support the primary key. This statement creates two objects.
13. **B.** There are two server names in the *db2nodes.cfg* file; therefore, the database is partitioned across two servers.
14. **D.** Distribute by. This is used for the Database Partitioning Feature (DPF).
15. **D.** You need to connect to the database and create the buffer pool with a 16K page size before you can create a table space with a 16K page size.
16. **A.** Only a table can be altered using the **ALTER TABLE** statement. You must drop and re-create an index, view, or schema to change its definition.
17. **A** and **B**. A package is stored in a database and contains the executable SQL statements and the access path the DB2 optimizer will choose to retrieve the data.
18. **D.** Object names must be unique within a schema, but since the schema is the high-level qualifier for the object name, objects can have the same name as long as they are in different schemas.
19. **B** and **C**. seq1.next and seq1.nextValue are not valid options.
20. **D.** A user temporary table space created with the **CREATE USER TEMPORARY TABLESPACE** statement is needed before global temporary tables can be declared. Global temporary tables are created with the **DECLARE GLOBAL TEMPORARY TABLE** statement.
21. **D** and **E**. CREATE TABLE and ALTER TABLE will enable compression, but actual compression of the rows will not occur until a REORG or INSPECT is run.
22. **A.** DETACH. After issuing a DETACH followed by a COMMIT, changes will take place immediately where the partition (a.k.a range) will become a stand-alone table.

Chapter 8

1. DB2 supports a database with up to 1,000 partitions.
2. The IBMDEFAULTBP buffer pool is created automatically in every database.
3. Since the row width is over 9,000 bytes, the table must be created in a table space with at least a 16K page size.
4. A table's data object in an SMS table space will be placed in a file with a .DAT extension.
5. The command **LIST TABLESPACES SHOW DETAIL** will display the number of used and free pages in each table space.

6. DMS table spaces are completely allocated when they are created.
7. SMS table spaces grow and shrink as the tables and indexes within them grow and shrink.
8. When a table has been defined with its data, index, and large objects in different table spaces, you cannot drop one of the table spaces without dropping the table first.
9. The block-based area of a buffer pool is used to improve performance of prefetching by allowing DB2 to read entire extents into contiguous pieces of the buffer pool.
10. The **`get snapshot for tablespaces`** command will show if and when a rebalance is occurring. It will show when the rebalance started and how many extents in the table space still need to be moved as part of the rebalance process.
11. **A.** DB2 supports 4K, 8K, 16K, and 32K page sizes.
12. **B.** Since the table spaces all use an 8K page size, they can all share a buffer pool with an 8K page size. However, since the system catalogs are created in a table space with a 4K page size, there must also be a buffer pool with a 4K page size. Therefore, the answer is 2.
13. **D.** Since there are 4 partitions, and with a 32K page size the maximum table space size is 512GB, the largest table could be 4 × 512GB or 2TB in size.
14. **D.** Under the /data directory, DB2 creates a directory with the instance name. The SQL*xxxxx* directories are created under the instance directory. Therefore, in this case, DB2 will create the directory *inst1* under the /data directory.
15. **A.** DB2 creates a directory with the partition number for that server under the /data/inst1 directory. Since partitions 2 and 3 are on server *mysrv2*, the directories will be NODE0002 and NODE0003.
16. **E.** By default DB2 Version 8 creates five subdirectories for the following:
    - The catalog table space
    - The temporary table space
    - Userspace1
    - The log directory
    - Event Monitor output
17. **B.** In this case, the database *sample* would use SQL00001. Sales would be placed in the directory SQL00002 and test in SQL00003. When the sales database is dropped, the SQL00002 directory is also dropped, and is then available in case other databases are created on the same drive or path. When the database *my_sales* is created, DB2 will reuse the SQL00002 directory.
18. **C.** Since the **`create database`** command was run on server *mysrv2*, the catalog partition will be on the partition with port number 0 on that server, in this case, partition 2.
19. **D.** You need to connect to the database and create the buffer pool with a 16K page size before you can create a table space with a 16K page size. Therefore, the correct answer is **D**.

20. **C.** The correct syntax is

```
CREATE BUFFERPOOL BP1
SIZE 150MB
        except on DBPARTITIONNUMS 1,2,3,4,5 size 100MB
```

CHAPTER 9

1. **A.** The condition of having *lastname* starting with the letter *P* returns two rows. However, the result set is further reduced to one row to obtain the only record that has a salary greater than $38,500.
2. **D.** Unknown values are identified by **NULL.** You verify the nullability of a value by checking **IS NULL.** The values ' ' and " " are known values of empty strings.
3. **C.** Selecting from an **UPDATE**, **DELETE**, or **INSERT** statement is an SQL enhancement available in DB2 Version 8.1 FixPak 4 or later. If the statement is executed on DB2 Version 8.1 with an earlier FixPak, it will fail. With FixPak 4 or later, the statement will execute the **DELETE** statement and return the number of rows removed.
4. **C.** An **INTERSECT** operation retrieves the matching set of distinct values (there are three distinct values) from the two columns. On the other hand, the **INTERSECT ALL** operator will return four rows because it returns all of the matching rows.
5. **C.** The UNIX command interpreter processes the * character, so to pass this character to DB2, you must enclose the command in quotes. To select all rows from a table you use the **SELECT *** syntax.
6. **D. FETCH FIRST n ROWS ONLY** limits the number of rows returned from a query. Use of the **OPTIMIZE FOR n ROWS** clause influences query optimization, based on the assumption that *n* rows will be retrieved. However, all rows of the result table will be retrieved.
7. **A.** % is used as a wildcard character in a **LIKE** clause of a **SELECT** statement.
8. **C** and **D.** Values to be inserted into the *employee* table must provide an *id* value in **INTEGER** data type, optionally provide a *name*, and *dept* must not be **NULL.** If no value is specified for *dept*, a default value *A00* will be used. You can choose to use the keyword **DEFAULT** to indicate that the default value defined in the table definition is used (in this case *A00*). Alternatively, simply do not specify a value for the column (as demonstrated in answers C and D).
9. **A.** Data is stored in no particular order. If data should be returned in certain order, the **ORDER BY** clause must be used.
10. **B.** The DB2 special register CURRENT DATE stores the date based on the time-of-day clock at the DB2 server. To perform date and time calculations, simply add or subtract the number of years, months, days, hours, minutes, or seconds; for example:

    ```
    CURRENT DATE + 3 YEARS + 2 MONTHS – 3 MINUTES
    ```
11. **B.**
12. **B.** The special register CURRENT DATE can be used to retrieve the current system date.

13. **A.**
14. **D.** There will be six rows:

```
col 1                col2
-------              ------
      2              Susan
      4              Mary
      5              Clara
      6              Jenny
      8              Tom
      9              Luisa
```

15. **C.** There will be two rows:

```
COL1        COL2                 COL1        COL2
----------- -------------------- ----------- --------------------
          2 Raul                           2 Susan
          9 Glenn                          9 Luisa
```

16. **D.** There will be six rows:

```
COL1        COL2                 COL1        COL2
----------- -------------------- ----------- --------------------
          2 Raul                           2 Susan
          - -                              5 Clara
          - -                              6 Jenny
          9 Glenn                          9 Luisa
          4 Mary                           - -
          8 Tom                            - -
```

17. **C.** There will be four rows:

```
COL1        COL2                 COL1        COL2
----------- -------------------- ----------- --------------------
          2 Raul                           2 Susan
          4 Mary                           - -
          8 Tom                            - -
          9 Glenn                          9 Luisa
```

18. **C.** There will be four rows:

```
COL1        COL2                 COL1        COL2
----------- -------------------- ----------- --------------------
          2 Raul                           2 Susan
          - -                              5 Clara
          - -                              6 Jenny
          9 Glenn                          9 Luisa
```

19. **B.** There will be two records successfully inserted into the employee table:

```
EMPNO  SALARY
------ -----------
000999           -
001000           -

  2 record(s) selected.
```

20. **E.** There were 10 records and 2 more were inserted, so there will be 12 records after executing the statement.

CHAPTER 10

1. The key characteristic of pureXML is that the storage format is the same as the processing format. XML documents are internally stored as trees (hierarchical data model), and processed using SQL/XML or XQuery, which work on the hierarchical model.
2. Because with pureXML, the XML document is parsed at INSERT time, and stored like this in disk. The tree is persisted, so it does not need to be built at query time. In addition, internal indexes are created, and you can also create user-defined indexes, which would allow DB2 not to bring the entire tree to memory, but only the parts pointed by the index.
3. A well-formed XML document implies that the document follows all the syntax rules as specified by W3C, for example, the fact that there should be a starting and an ending tag. A validated XML document means that the document is well-formed and that it is validated against an XML schema document or a DTD document, which contains the document structure definition.
4. Annotated XML Schema decomposition allows you to store XML documents using the shredding method where the XML document is decomposed in parts that are stored in tables. By using annotations, the XML Schema stores the mapping information between the XML document and tables.
5. Yes. And this allows for flexibility. DB2 leaves it up to the user to decide exactly how he/she would like to enforce validation. You can insert a row with the XMLVALIDATE function according to one schema, and can insert another row using the XMLVALIDATE function according to another schema.
6.
   - The query predicate must match the XML index data type.
   - The XMLPATTERN specified in the index is equally or less restrictive than the query predicate.
   - The text node and text() function must be used consistently in the query predicate and the index definitions.
7. The answer of choosing to store data as XML or relational should not be based solely on performance, but mainly on three things:
   - Will your schema change constantly?
   - Are you storing semi-structure type of information?
   - Will you be using your data mainly for exchange of information with other applications or businesses?

   If the answer to any of these questions is YES, then you should consider XML. If you feel these three questions are not applicable to your case, and would like to make a decision solely on performance, we would recommend you store the data in relational format given that SQL and relational databases are robust technology spanning more than 30 years.

8. Yes, but you would have to use the DB2 XML Extender. You cannot use pureXML as this is not currently supported with the Database Partitioning Feature.
9. Prior to version 9.5, the answer would be "No": Row compression does not apply to XML data; however, as illustrated in section 10.2.1 pureXML Storage in DB2, the tags and attributes are actually stored as integers, and a dictionary (a table in the Catalog) stores the mapping between the strings used for tags and attributes, and the integers. With DB2 9.5, the answer is "yes" if you choose to store XML inlined in the base table.
10. Yes! pureXML is new technology, so mass adoption has not yet taken place; however, you can go to this Web site for a list of IBM Business partners and a description of their solution using pureXML:
http://www-03.ibm.com/developerworks/wikis/pages/viewpage.action?pageId=6641
Moreover, if you want to try pureXML for free, you can download DB2 Express-C which is the free version of DB2 and includes pureXML technology. Here is the link: www.ibm.com/db2/express
11. **B.** XMLNODE
12. **A.** 901
902
13. **B.** 902
14. **D.**

```
<EmpList>
  101<name>John Doe</name>
  101<name>Peter Pan</name>
</EmpList>
```

15. **A.** (I), (II), (IV)
16. **A.** <name>Peter</name>
17. **C.** db2-fn:sqlquery
18. **D.** XMLJOIN. This operator doesn't exist.
19. **A.**

```
SELECT XMLQUERY ('$d/geneX' passing DNA as "d" )
  FROM patients
 WHERE XMLEXISTS ('$d/geneX[pattern="ABC"]'
                  passing DNA as "d");
```

The second one has "genex" instead of "geneX".
The third one is less restrictive than the index by using //geneX.
20. **A.** II, III, IV

Chapter 11

1. DB2 relies on operating system security and does not store user IDs and passwords in the database.
2. DB2 also supports Kerberos security service. Starting with DB2 Version 8.2, you can also write your own security service as plug-in. The plug-in will be loaded at instance startup.

3. When a new package is bound to the database, for example, when creating an SQL stored procedure, BINDADD is required.
4. He must have CONNECT privileges to connect to the database and CREATETAB privileges to create a new table in the database. Because he is trying to create a table that has a different schema than the authorization ID (i.e., *bob*), he must have IMPLICIT_SCHEMA privileges if schema *mary* does not already exist. If it does exist, then CREATEIN privileges on the schema *mary* is needed. In addition to all of the above, *bob* also needs to have USE privileges on the table space *ts1*.
5. DB2 SYS* authorities must be set to a user group. The command will be executed successfully, but *bob* will not receive the authority. It must be set to the group *dba* like this:

```
update dbm cfg using sysctrl dba
```

6. First, a local group, for example, called *db2dba*, defined on the DB2 server is required. Second, add the global group *glbgrp* as a member of the local group *db2dba*. Third, update the Database Manager Configuration parameter to set SYSADM to *db2dba*.
7. The first type is called untrusted clients, which do not have a reliable security facility. The second type is called trusted clients, which have a reliable security facility. The third type is called DRDA clients, which are clients on host systems with reliable security facility.
8. CREATETAB is granted to PUBLIC implicitly when a database is created. To allow only *bob* to create tables in the database, you must first revoke CREATETAB from PUBLIC and GRANT CREATETAB to *bob*.

```
REVOKE CREATETAB FROM PUBLIC;
GRANT CREATETAB TO USER bob;
```

9. Regardless of the SQL statements performed in the program, *bob* only needs EXECUTE privileges on the package. *Mary* needs the associated privileges to perform all the SQL statements in the program. In addition, BINDADD is required to bind the new package to the database.
10. Since TRUST_ALLCLNTS is set to NO, only trusted clients can be authenticated on the client. Windows ME is not a trusted client, so users from this OS must be authenticated on the server.
11. **B.** The default authentication takes place on the server, so in this case the user ID will be authenticated on the DBX1 server.
12. **C.** The SERVER_ENCRYPT authentication type encrypts only the user ID and password that is sent during an authentication request; it does not encrypt the data.
13. **A.** Since TRUST_ALLCLNTS is set to YES, users are authenticated on the client to see if they do exist.
14. **A** and **D.** Both SYSADM and DBADM authorities allow read/write access to tables.
15. **D.** If you choose, you can encrypt the user ID and password as it is passed from the client to the server. In Version 8.2 you can also encrypt the data for more security.
16. **A.** The user who wants to create or drop an event monitor must hold either SYSADM or DBADM authority.

17. **B.** Only SYSMON does not have the ability to take a DB2 trace.
18. **C.** When a privilege is revoked from a user, it does not cascade to users who received privileges from this user. Therefore, be careful who you give WITH GRANT OPTION permission to. In this example, Barney, Wilma, and Betty will have the privileges.
19. **D.** By default, PUBLIC is granted use of a table space when it is created. Therefore, to ensure only the group *grp1* can use the table space you must revoke use of the table space from PUBLIC.
20. **C.** CREATETAB is a database level privilege; therefore, information about its grantee is stored in the SYSCAT.DBAUTH table.

Chapter 12

1. Increasing MAXLOCKS (the percentage of the lock list that an application can use before escalation occurs) and increasing LOCKLIST can reduce the chances of getting lock escalations.
2. When a user performs a read operation, by default DB2 attempts to lock the rows with share locks. Once a share lock is acquired, concurrent users will not be able to make changes to the rows. However, concurrent read is allowed. In this example, Sam may have set the isolation level as UR, so DB2 will not acquire any row lock. This may result in uncommitted data within the same transaction as described here.
3. Databases: **`CONNECT TO dbname IN EXCLUSIVE MODE`**
   Table spaces: **`QUIESCE TABLESPACE FOR TABLE tabname INTENT FOR UPDATE`**
   Tables: **`LOCK TABLE tabname IN EXCLUSIVE MODE`**
4. U lock is compatible with S and NS lock only. (Refer to the Row lock mode compatibility chart in Figure 11.23.)
5. It means that the current transaction has been rolled back because of a lock timeout.
6. It means that the current transaction has been rolled back because of a deadlock.
7. There are two database configuration parameters that can cause locks to be escalated. Make sure LOCKLIST is sufficiently large. If LOCKLIST is full, lock escalation will occur. Next check if MAXLOCKS is set appropriately. This value defines the percentage of the total LOCKLIST permitted to be allocated to a single application. If any application holds locks more than this percentage, lock escalation will also occur. If both values are set appropriately, you may want to check the isolation level used in the application or maybe the application design.
8. DB2 comes with various troubleshooting and diagnosing tools. Those that are particularly useful for locking-related information are the **`list applications`** command, the Snapshot Monitor, snapshot table functions, Event Monitors, Activity Monitors, and the Health Center.

9. Application handle 14 is currently in a lock-wait status. It has been waiting for locks for 6507 ms. The dynamic SQL statement that this application is executing is **SELECT * FROM org.** It is requesting an IS lock on the table *org*.
10. By default, DB2 acquires row-level locking. Unless a lock escalation is required, table lock will not be requested. In this case, it is most likely that the table *employee* was altered to perform table-level locking rather than row-level locking. If row-level locking is the desired behavior, Mike can issue the following statement:
    ```
    ALTER TABLE employee LOCKSIZE ROW
    ```
11. **D.** Cursor With Hold is not a DB2 isolation level.
12. **B.** DB2 does not obtain page-level locks. If lock escalation occurs, a number of row-level locks will be turned into a table-level lock.
13. **B.** If you do not specify the isolation level for your application, DB2 defaults to cursor stability.
14. **D.** Since repeatable read must guarantee the same result set within the same unit of work, it retains locks on all rows required to build the result sets. Therefore, this typically causes many more locks to be held than the other isolation levels.
15. **A.** Uncommitted read obtains an intent none (IN) table-level lock, but does not obtain row-level locks while scanning your data. This allows DB2 to return uncommitted changes since it does not have to wait for locks on rows.
16. **A.** Uncommitted read allows access to changed data that has not been committed.
17. **C.** The read stability isolation level allows new rows to become part of the result set, but does not allow rows to be deleted that are part of the result set until the transaction completes.
18. **B.** The **WITH** isolation clause will change the isolation level for the statement to the specified value.
19. **C** and **E.** You can set the lock size for a table to be either an individual row or the whole table. For batch operations that update a large number of rows in a table, it is sometimes beneficial to set the lock size to the table level first.
20. **B.** The option **NOT WAIT** specifies that the application will not wait for locks that cannot be obtained immediately.

Chapter 13

1. The load utility supports CURSOR as the input. The cursor must be already declared before the load utility is invoked. The entire result of the query associated with the specified cursor will be processed by the load utility.
2. When the load utility is invoked in INSERT mode, one needs INSERT privileges on the target table. If REPLACE mode is used, INSERT and DELETE privileges on the target table are also required.
3. Rows that do not comply with the table definition will not be loaded and placed in the dump file. Therefore *stockdump.dmp* contains:
    ```
    20, "BBB", -
    40, "EEE", x
    ```

4. Rows that violated the unique constraint will be deleted and inserted into the exception table. Therefore *stockexp* has the following row:

```
30, "DDD", 4
```

5. The table will be in CHECK PENDING state because only unique constraints are validated during the load operation. If a constraint is defined in the table like the CHECK constraint in the example, the utility will place the table in CHECK PENDING statement. You need to issue the **SET INTEGRITY** command to validate the data before the table is available for further processing.
6. The table will be accessible after the **import** command is successfully executed. No other command is required because data is already validated during the import operation.
7. The command will generate the DDL for all objects in the database *department*, the **UPDATE** statements to replicate the statistics on all tables and indexes in the database, the **GRANT** authorization statements, the **UPDATE** statements for the Database Manager Configuration and database configuration parameters, and the **db2set** statements for the registry variables. The output will be stored in the file *db2look.sql*.
8. The step that Bob missed is to REBIND the packages. Packages for static and SQL stored procedures are created at compile time. When the packages are bound to the database, data access plans are determined. Since the large amount of data is inserted into the database and database statistics have been updated, data access plans for these packages are still based on the outdated statistics. A REBIND of all packages that already exist will ensure that the latest statistics are used, hence more optimal data access paths.
9. He can either increase the size of the log files (or the number of logs) sufficiently large enough to hold all the changes made during the import. Alternatively, he could include the **commitcount** option:

```
import from largeinputfile.ixf of ixf
    commitcount 1000
    messages import.out
    create into newtable in datats index in indexts
```

10. The option **insert_update** means that the utility will add imported data to the target table or update existing rows with matching primary keys. Therefore, the table must already exist with primary keys. Otherwise, the import will fail.
11. **C** and **E.** The load and import tools can read ASCII data from an input file and then insert them in a table in your database.
12. **E.** Only the import tool can insert records from an input file into a view. The load tool can only add data to a table, not a view.
13. **D.** DB2 does not support the XLS format. For column delimited data, use the WSF format.
14. **D.** The default column delimiter is a comma, so you need to modify the column delimiter as in answer D to import this data successfully.

15. **D.** The **REORG** utility builds a data dictionary used to compress and expand the rows in the table enabled with row compression.
16. **B.** **db2relocatedb** can be used to rename a database.
17. **C.** The load utility can capture statistics on all data added to the table during a load operation.
18. **B** and **D.** By default, the load utility locks the target table for exclusive access until the load completes. If the **allow read access** option is specified, it allows read access to data already existing in the table before the load was run. However, you cannot see the newly loaded data until the load completes.
19. **C.** With Version 9.5, both the import and load utilities support populating XML data into a target table.
20. **B.** PCTFREE = –1 means PCTFREE value for a table page is 0. With this setting, the import utility will not leave free space on the data pages. However, the load utility can do so by specifying the options **INDEXFREESPACE, PAGEFREESPACE,** and **TOTALFREESPACE.** The REORG utility will leave free space on the data and/or index pages based on the value of PCTFREE of the tables and indexes. This is especially important for tables with a clustering index.

CHAPTER 14

1. Besides crash recovery, DB2 also supports version recovery and roll forward recovery.
2. You can back up the transaction logs along with the database by using the **INCLUDE LOGS** option in the **BACKUP DATABASE** command.
3. Secondary logs are created when needed and are destroyed when the database is restarted.
4. Log buffer is flushed to log files when the log buffer is full or when the MINCOMMIT number of commits has been issued. Note that MINCOMMIT is a database configuration parameter.
5. False. Automatic Client Reroute can be used and set up for situations to reconnect a loss of communication between the client application and DB2 data server outside of a HADR environment.
6. Takeover by force is undesirable because it may result in both the old primary and new primary databases becoming active. Existing applications may continue to process transactions on the old primary, while new applications may access the new primary.
7. You can either restore from a good database backup or use the **db2dart** tool to mark the index invalid. Depending on the value of the INDEXREC database parameter, the index will be re-created either when the database is restarted or when the index is being accessed for the first time.
8. You can find out the minimum recovery time for a table space by using the **LIST TABLSPACES SHOW DETAIL** command. The time is shown in UTC time.

9. **C.** The LOGRETAIN database configuration parameter can be used to enable archival logging. When a log file is no longer active, it should be manually archived to a backup device to avoid the log path being filled up. In addition, you also need to manually retrieve those archived log files when they are required in case of recovery.
10. **A.** COMMIT or ROLLBACK (one word) can be used to complete or rollback a unit of work.
11. **B.** Circular logging is the default logging method used by DB2.
12. **C.** Log mirroring allows you to specify a secondary path for the database to manage copies of the active logs.
13. **D.** You must use the db2inidb command to restore the split mirrored image. For example ***`DB2INIDB sample AS MIRROR.`***
14. **C.** Roll forward recovery replays the transactions in the database logs to recover any transactions after the backup was performed.
15. **A.** DB2 does not allocate the secondary logs until they are needed, so they would *not* be allocated immediately after activating the database. DB2 also starts numbering the logs using the number 0, so the correct answer is A.
16. **C.** Infinite active logging is activated by setting log second to –1.
17. **C.** Archival logging must be enabled in order to perform online backups. Archival logging is enabled by setting LOGARCHMETH1 to a value other than OFF.
18. **B.** You cannot change from DMS to SMS or SMS to DMS using a redirected restore.
19. **B.** When using local time, it is always local relative to the server.
20. **D.** Backup is not a valid option of the db2inidb command.

Chapter 15

1. The **`db2pd –edus`** command.
2. The db2fmp EDU is the fenced-mode process for fenced UDFs and stored procedures. **Fenced** means it is executed outside of the address space of the DB2 engine. Should it misbehave, it is not able to overwrite DB2 internal buffers.
3. It is the DB2 page cleaner EDU, db2pclnr.
4. Subagents exist in partitioned database environment, or the database manager parameter intra-parallel = ON.
5. If the total number of idle agents in the instance is less than NUM_POOLAGENTS, then the subagent changes its name from db2agntp to db2agnta and it is returned to the idle agent pool. However, it is still associated with the application. When needed, it is called by the coordinator agent, or the active subagents, to service the same application again. Or it can be stolen by another application, if that application cannot find an idle agent or no more agents can be created.
6. The four types of agents are: coordinator agents (db2agent), active subagents (db2agntp), associated idle agents (db2agnta), and idle agents (db2agent (idle).
7. You can use **`dbm snapshot.`**

8. **C.** The NUM_INITAGENTS parameter controls how many db2agent EDUs are created at instance startup time, not the db2agntp EDUs.
9. **B.** The NUM_INITAGENTS parameter cannot be configured by the system automatically.
10. **D.** There is one db2sysc process per partition.
11. **B.** NUM_POOLAGENTS controls the number of idle agents.
12. **A.** There is one coordinator agent (db2agent) per connection, and it exists on the partition where the application is connected to. The other partitions have the db2agntp EDUs.
13. **B.** NUM_IOSERVERS controls the number of prefetches.
14. **D.** db2sysc is the DB2 system controller process.
15. **A.** The db2ipccm handles local client connections.
16. **C.** Since MAX_COORDAGENTS is set to 100, the maximum number of concurrent connections for this instance is 100.
17. **D.** Coordinating agents are named db2agent, active agents are named db2agntp, and idle agents are named db2agnta or db2agent, depending on whether they are associated with a coordinating agent. The EDU db2agntb does not exist.
18. **C.** The connection concentrator is enabled when MAX_CONNECTIONS is greater than MAX_COORDAGENTS. This means you can have more connections than there are the number of available coordinator agents.
19. **B.** The governor uses the db2govd EDU.
20. **D.** The db2aiothr EDU is the asychronous I/O collector thread spawned by the db2sysc process.

Chapter 16

1. The memory tracker and memory visualizer tools display DB2's memory usage at the instance, database, and agent levels.
2. The ADMIN_GET_BP_MEM_USAGE() table function in DB2 9.5 provides an easy way to query overall memory consumption for a given instance.
3. The package cache allows for the sharing and reuse of packages between applications.
4. The log buffer is flushed to disk:
   - When it is filled
   - When MINCOMMIT commits occur
   - Or every one second

   depending on which occurs first. Therefore, the longest time period between flushes of the log buffer is one second.
5. If the DATABASE_MEMORY configuration parameter is set to AUTOMATIC, you can connect to the database and at any time issue the **`GET DB CFG FOR dbname SHOW DETAIL`** command. It will show AUTOMATIC(*nnnnnn*), and *nnnnnn* will be the actual amount of used memory.

6. The largest size you can set for the client requester I/O block is 64KB.
7. The instance-level (database manager) shared memory is allocated when you run the **db2start** command.
8. The database shared memory is allocated when the database is activated or when the first connection to the database is made.
9. A single application shared heap is allocated during the database activation.
10. The Fast Communications Manager (FCM) buffers are used for inter-partition communication.
11. **E.** There will be the IBMDEFAULTBP, plus the four hidden buffer pools for a total of five buffer pools.
12. **D.** The application shared heap stores the runtime sections of access plans.
13. **D.** The statistics heap is allocated in agent private memory.
14. **C.** APPL_MEMORY controls the maximum amount of application memory that is allocated by DB2 database agents to service application requests.
15. **B.**
16. **C.** Since 2000 / 256 = 7.81, there can be a maximum of 7 concurrent shred sorts within this database.
17. **E.** DB2 does not limit the number of concurrent private sorts in memory; it reduces the sort heap allocated once the sort heap threshold is reached, so there is no limit.
18. **D.** The buffer pools are database specific, and therefore are not part of the database manager shared memory.
19. **D.** Since the 10,000 16K pages would use an additional 40,000 4K pages, the minimum size for the shared memory would be 115,264 pages, but of the options given, you would need to set the database memory to 125,000 pages for the CREATE BUFFERPOOL statement to be successful.
20. **C.** In DB2 9.5 the statement heap and statistics heap have moved from the agent private memory to the application shared memory; and the query heap previously allocated out of Agent Private Memory is deprecated.

Chapter 17

1. Uncommitted read applications acquire an IN lock on the table but no row-level locks.
2. The maximum requester I/O block size is 64K.
3. You can configure DB2 to create some agent processes when DB2 is started by setting the NUM_INITAGENTS parameter to a value greater than zero.
4. To ensure the integrity of your database, DB2 writes the log buffers to disk when:
   - One or more transactions commit
   - The log buffer is full
   - One second has elapsed since the last log buffer flush

5. Lock escalation will occur when:
   - The database lock list becomes full
   - Any one application uses more than the MAXLOCKS percent of the lock list
6. You can capture table and index statistics:
   - By running the **runstats** utility
   - When loading data into one of your tables
   - By running the **reorgchk** utility
7. The **reorg** command not only reclusters the data in the table, but it also removes embedded free space by deleting rows and eliminating overflow records.
8. The timestamp monitor switch is enabled by default (it is used by the health monitor).
9. The **reset monitor all** command will reset all of the database monitor counters.
10. You need to create the explain tables to use the Visual Explain tool.
11. **D.** The **import** command cannot capture statistics.
12. **D.** The SOFTMAX configuration parameter controls the percentage of a log file that is filled before the page cleaners are triggered to write dirty pages from the buffer pool(s) to disk.
13. **C.** When DB2 performs lock escalation, it converts row-level locks to a table level lock.
14. **B.** The configuration parameter sequential detection (SEQ_DETECT) allows DB2 to detect sequential page reads and trigger prefetching.
15. **B** and **D**. The page cleaners are triggered when the percentage of dirty pages in any one buffer pool reaches CHNGPGS_THRESH, or when applications write enough information to the logs to reach SOFTMAX percentage of any log file.
16. **A. reorgchk** will indicate if a reorg is suggested based on a number of conditions. One of these conditions is the number of overflow records in the table.
17. **B.** An overflow record is created when a row in a table is updated, a varchar column is updated, and its length increases so much that it can no longer fit on the same page.
18. **D.** DB2 does not support hints, as they are not needed due to the efficiency of the DB2 optimizer.
19. **D.** DTSCAN is not an operator used by DB2.
20. **C.** The shared sort heap threshold is a hard limit, and an attempt to start the fourth concurrent shared sort would cause that sort to overflow; therefore, the answer is C.

Chapter 18

1. The **?** is the help command that can be issued from the CLP. It provides a description of the error.
2. You use the command **db2 ? sql0805n** to get more information.
3. FFDC stands for first failure data capture.
4. There is no administration notification file in Windows. Administration notification logs are provided as part of the Windows Event Viewer.

5. The administration notification file in Linux/UNIX is *instance_name*.nfy.
6. To capture the most information possible, set the DIAGLEVEL Database Manager Configuration parameter to 4.
7. The db2support tool captures all the necessary information that DB2 Technical Support needs to research a problem.
8. The command **`db2trc`** is used to capture DB2 traces.
9. db2diag.log is located in the directory *$HOME*/sqllib/db2dump, where *$HOME* is the home directory of the instance owner.
10. To receive e-mail notification messages, you must use NOTIFYLEVEL 2 at least.
11. **C.** All FFDC information, including the administration notification log, is kept in the path specified by the Database Manager Configuration parameter DIAGPATH.
12. **A.** NOTIFYME is not a database manager configuration parameter.
13. **B.** NOTIFYLEVEL = 1 only logs fatal and unrecoverable errors.
14. **C.** SMTP hostname is defined in the database manager configuration file.
15. **A.** db2diag.log is a DB2 diagnostic file, not a tool.
16. **C.** Application log file is not collected with the db2support tool.
17. **D.** 3 is the default DIAGLEVEL.
18. **A.** db2pdcfg can be used to configure how DB2 will handle certain problems or failures.
19. **D.** DIAGPATH is set to NULL by default.
20. **D.** CONTACT_LIST_GROUP is not a DAS parameter.

APPENDIX B

Use of Uppercase versus Lowercase in DB2

Table B.1 identifies which kinds of statements, commands, parameters, objects, and data are case-sensitive in DB2 for Linux, UNIX, and Windows and gives examples.

Table B.1 Case-Sensitivity Requirements in DB2

Category	Description	Examples
DB2 system commands (including the *db2* executable)	You can treat DB2 system commands like any other program or application launched from the operating system. On Windows, the case does *not* matter. On Linux and UNIX, the case *does* matter, and since all DB2 system commands are named in lowercase, you need to issue the commands in lowercase.	These work in Linux, UNIX, and Windows: **`db2`** **`db2start`** **`db2ilist`** These only work in Windows: **`dB2`** **`db2STARt`** **`DB2ILIST`**
CLP commands	You can invoke CLP commands from the DB2 Command Line Processor, the DB2 Command Window (Windows only) and the Command Editor. These tools do *not* care about the case of the command.	These work in Linux, UNIX, and Windows: **`list applications`** **`LIST apPLicatIONs`** Or if working with the CLP in non-interactive mode: **`db2 list applications`** **`db2 LIST apPLicatIONs`**

(continues)

Table B.1 Case-Sensitivity Requirements in DB2 *(Continued)*

Category	Description	Examples

SQL statements	You can invoke SQL statements within an application or tool like the CLP. DB2 tools do *not* care about the case of the SQL statement.	These work in Linux, UNIX, and Windows:
		`select * from employee`
		`SELECT * frOM emPLOYee`

	When you create database objects, you can specify the object name in any case. However, DB2 usually stores names in the DB2 catalog in uppercase unless you use double quotes enclosing the object name when you create the object.[1]	These work in Linux, UNIX, and Windows:
		`create table Tab1 ...`
		`create table taB1 ...`
		(*TAB1* will be stored in the DB2 catalog tables.)
		`create table "taB1"`
		(*taB1* will be stored in the DB2 catalog tables.)

XQuery statements	All XQuery statements start with the keyword "xquery", which can be written in any case.	These works in Linux, UNIX, and Windows:
		`XqueRy db2-`
		`fn:xmlcolumn('CUSTOMER.INFO')`

	Column and table names inside the XQuery statement must be in uppercase.	These works in Linux, UNIX, and Windows:
		`xquery db2-`
		`fn:xmlcolumn('CUSTOMER.INFO')`
		This will return an error saying the table cannot be found:
		`xquery db2-`
		`fn:xmlcolumn('CustOMER.InfO')`

	Any XQuery or XPath expression is case sensitive.	This will return an error because the clauses in the FLWOR expression must be lowercase, and in this example, "fOr" uses mixed case. xquery **fOr** $i in … The following will not return an error, but an incorrect output if the actual XPath is /customerinfo/phone: **SELECT XMLQUERY (** **$d/CustomerInfo/Phone' passing INFO as "d") FROM CUSTOMER** This will return the correct output. Note that the SQL part of the statement is not case sensitive, but the XPath part of the statement is: **SelEcT XMLQUERY (** **$d/customerinfo/phone' passing INFO as "d") FROM cuSToMer**

Table B.1 Case-Sensitivity Requirements in DB2 *(Continued)*

Category	Description	Examples
DB2 registry variables	Case-insensitive on all platforms.	These work in Linux, UNIX, and Windows: db2options DB2optIOns
DB2 configuration parameters	Case-insensitive on all platforms.	These work in Linux, UNIX, and Windows: INTRA_PARALLEL intra_PARAllel
User data stored in the database	DB2 stores the data in your database exactly the way you inserted it.	In Linux, UNIX, and Windows, if you issue: insert into mytable (col2) values ('RAul') Then column *col2* in table *mytable* will have the value *RAul*, just as it was inserted.
Database object names or any system data already stored in DB2 catalog tables	Typically any database object names or system-related data stored implicitly by DB2 itself is in uppercase. However, the object name can be in mixed case if it was created using double quotes. Keep this in mind when you refer to these objects in a query.	In Linux, UNIX, and Windows if you issue: create table t1 (col2 integer) *t1* will be stored as *T1* and *col2* will be stored as *COL2* in DB2 catalog tables. If double quotes enclose the object: create table "t1" (col2 integer) *t1* will be stored as *t1* and *col2* will be stored as *COL2* in DB2 catalog tables.

1. Using the CLP in Windows to create an object in mixed case by using double quotes will not work. Use the Command Editor instead.

Appendix C

IBM Servers

Table C.1 provides a simplified overview of the servers that IBM offers. For detailed information, refer to the IBM Servers Web site at www.ibm.com/servers/.

Table C.1 IBM Servers

	Server Name	Operating System	Processor
Distributed Platform Servers	System x	Windows, Linux, Sun Solaris	Intel
	AMD processor-based servers	Windows, Linux, Sun Solaris	AMD
	System p	AIX, Linux	POWER
Mid-Range Servers	System i	i5/OS, OS/400, Windows, AIX 5L, Linux (on a separate LPAR)	POWER
Mainframe Servers	System z	z/OS, z/OS.e, z/VSE, TPF, Linux on System z and the z/VM hypervisor	zSeries Application Assist Processor (zAAP)

APPENDIX 

Using the DB2 System Catalog Tables

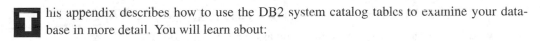

This appendix describes how to use the DB2 system catalog tables to examine your database in more detail. You will learn about:

- The different types of system catalog tables
- How to find useful information in the system catalog tables
- How to perform *what-if* analysis on query performance

DB2 System Catalog Tables

Each DB2 database has a set of tables called the **system catalog tables**. DB2 creates these tables when a database is created. They contain definitions of database objects (for example, tables, views, indexes, and packages), security information about the type of access that users have to these objects, and statistical information about the tables in the database.

DB2 automatically updates these tables when SQL Data Definition Language (DDL) statements are issued. For example, when you create a table, DB2 enters the definition of the table into the SYSIBM.SYSTABLES table. When you create an index, DB2 enters the index definition into the SYSIBM.SYSINDEXES table. DB2 uses these catalog tables to keep track of what exists in the database and their statistics. You cannot explicitly create or drop these tables, but you can query and view their contents.

DB2 creates the system catalog base tables under the SYSIBM schema. All of the table names have the prefix *SYS*, for example, SYSTABLES, SYSVIEWS, and SYSTABLESPACES. DB2 also creates a set of read-only views for the SYSIBM tables under the SYSCAT schema. These views contain the same or a subset of the information in the SYSIBM base tables, but the view names do not have the *SYS* prefix. For example, SYSCAT.TABLES is a view defined for the SYSIBM.SYSTABLES table, SYSCAT.VIEWS is a view defined for the SYSIBM.SYSVIEWS table, and SYSCAT.TABLESPACES is a view defined for the SYSIBM.SYSTABLESPACES table.

In addition to the SYSIBM tables and the SYSCAT views, DB2 defines the following database objects in the system catalog.

- A set of routines (functions and procedures) in the schemas SYSFUN and SYSPROC.
- A set of updatable catalog views in the SYSSTAT schema. The updatable views contain statistical information that is used by the optimizer. The values in some columns in these views can be changed to test query performance (see the section How to Use the SYSSTAT Tables to Perform What-If Modeling and Analysis).

To display the names of all the system catalog tables and views along with their creation time, use the **`LIST TABLES FOR SYSTEM`** command. To display tables or views by their schema names, use the **`LIST TABLES FOR SCHEMA`** ***`schemaname`*** command, where ***`schemaname`*** is any valid schema, for example, SYSIBM, SYSCAT, SYSFUN, SYSPROC, or SYSSTAT.

How to Find Information in the System Catalog Tables

When working with a database, sometimes you ask the following questions.

- How many buffer pools are there in the database and what table spaces use them?
- Are there any Event Monitors and are they active?
- What are the privileges given to users of this database?

You can answer all of these questions and more by querying the system catalog tables or views. In general, there is at least one system catalog table, and therefore one system catalog view, for each database object type. Table D.1 lists some of the system catalog views. For example, if you want to know about all the tables in the database, query the SYSCAT.TABLES view. If you want to know about all the indexes, query the SYSCAT.INDEXES view.

Table D.1 System Catalog Views

Database Object	SYSCAT System Catalog View
Table	TABLES
View	VIEWS
Index	INDEXES
Data type	DATATYPES
Column	COLUMNS
Table space	TABLESPACES
Buffer pool	BUFFERPOOLS

(continues)

Table D.1 System Catalog Views *(Continued)*

Database Object	SYSCAT System Catalog View
Package	PACKAGES
Constraints	CHECKS
Referential integrity	REFERENCES
Partition groups	NODEGROUPS
Partition group definitions	NODEGROUPDEF
XML values index	INDEXXMLPATTERNS
Stored procedures	PROCEDURES
Sequences	SEQUENCES
Event Monitors	EVENTMONITORS

The following examples show how you can extract useful information from the SYSCAT views. A database connection is required.

Example 1: Extracting Buffer Pool Data

To find out how many buffer pools are in the database and their information, issue the statement:

```
SELECT * FROM SYSCAT.BUFFERPOOLS
```

Figure D.1 shows sample output for this command. In this database, only one buffer pool is defined, IBMDEFAULTBP. This is the default buffer pool DB2 creates when the database is created. The buffer pool has an ID of 1. Its size is 1MB (250 pages × 4096 bytes per page).

BPNAME	BUFFERPOOLID	DBPGNAME	NPAGES	PAGESIZE	ESTORE	. . .
IBMDEFAULTBP	1	-	250	4096	N	

Figure D.1 Sample buffer pool information

> **NOTE** For detailed descriptions of all the columns in system catalog tables and views, search for the table/view name in the DB2 Information Center or refer to the *SQL Reference Manual*, Volume 1.

You can get the same information using the Control Center, as shown in Figures D.2 and D.3.

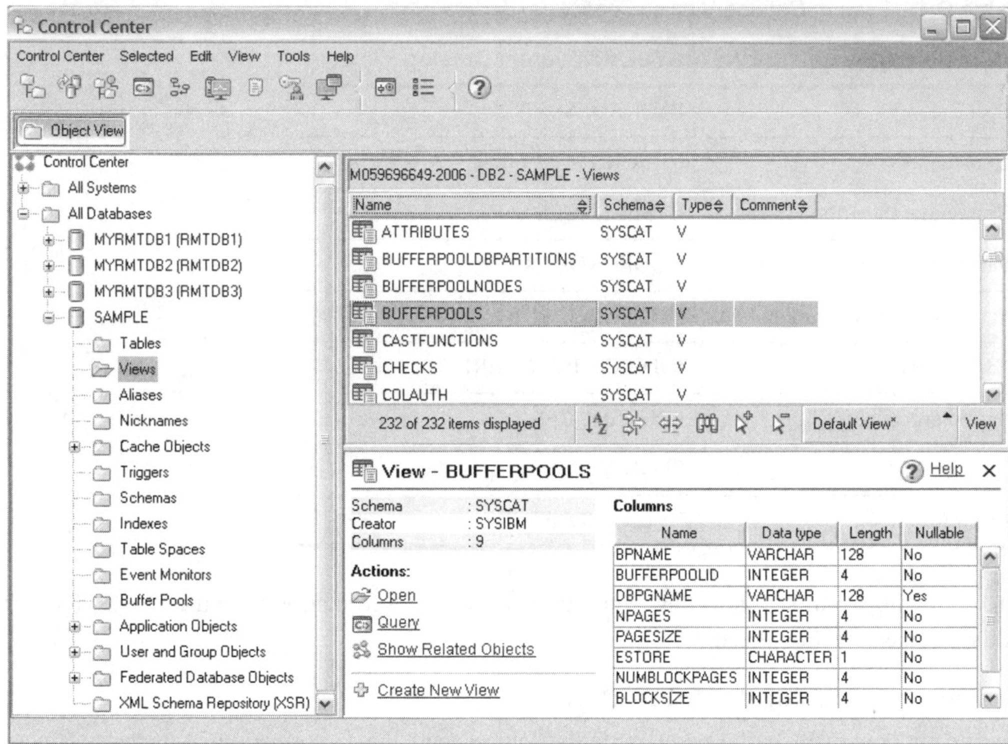

Figure D.2 The SYSCAT.BUFFERPOOLS view in the Control Center

From the Control Center, expand the *All Systems* folder until you find the database you want. All system catalogs tables (the SYSIBM tables) and user tables are stored in the *Tables* folder. All system catalog views (the SYSCAT views) and user-defined views are stored in the *Views* folder. Open the *Views* folder to display all the views. The contents of the selected folder in the left pane are displayed in the top-right pane.

In the top-right pane, click on the view you are interested in. The definition of the view is displayed in the bottom-right pane of Figure D.2. In this example, it is the SYSCAT.BUFFERPOOLS view.

Double click on the view name to display its contents (or right click on the view name and select **Open**). Figure D.3 shows the contents of the SYSCAT.BUFFERPOOLS view.

Note that the information in Figure D.3 is the same as the output of the **SELECT * FROM SYSCAT.BUFFERPOOLS** statement (see Figure D.1).

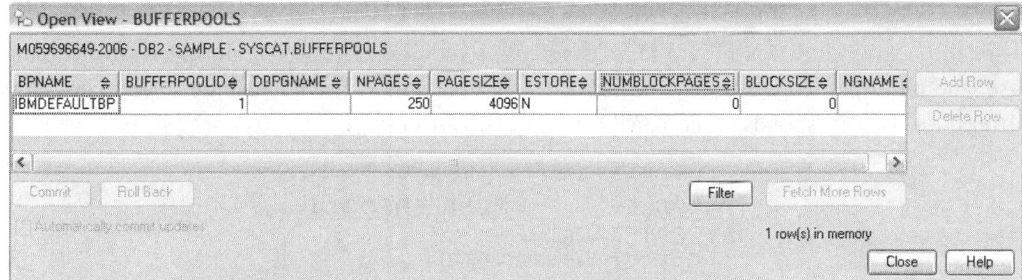

Figure D.3 Contents of the SYSCAT.BUFFERPOOLS view

Example 2: Determining Which Table Spaces Use the Buffer Pool

To find out which table spaces use the buffer pool found in Example 1, you need to query the SYSCAT.TABLESPACES view. Use the **DESCRIBE TABLE** command to display the columns defined in the view; then you can issue queries to display the contents of the columns you are really interested in. For example, the **DESCRIBE TABLE SYSCAT.TABLESPACES** statement displays the output shown in Figure D.4.

In Figure D.4, the columns you really need are the TBSPACE and BUFFERPOOLID columns. Issue the following:

Column name	Type Scema	Type name	Length	Scale	Null
TBSPACE	SYSIBM	VARCHAR	128	0	No
OWNER	SYSIBM	VARCHAR	128	0	No
CREATE_TIME	SYSIBM	TIMESTAMP	10	0	No
TBSPACEID	SYSIBM	INTEGER	4	0	No
TBSPACETYPE	SYSIBM	CHARACTER	1	0	No
DATATYPE	SYSIBM	CHARACTER	1	0	No
EXTENTSIZE	SYSIBM	INTEGER	4	0	No
PREFETCHSIZE	SYSIBM	INTEGER	4	0	No
OVERHEAD	SYSIBM	DOUBLE	8	0	No
TRANSFERRATE	SYSIBM	DOUBLE	8	0	No
PAGESIZE	SYSIBM	INTEGER	4	0	No
DBPGNAME	SYSIBM	VARCHAR	128	0	No
BUFFERPOOLID	SYSIBM	INTEGER	4	0	No
DROP_RECOVERY	SYSIBM	CHARACTER	1	0	No
NGNAME	SYSIBM	VARCHAR	128	0	No
DEFINER	SYSIBM	VARCHAR	128	0	No
REMARKS	SYSIBM	VARCHAR	254	0	Yes

Figure D.4 Output of the DESCRIBE TABLE command for SYSCAT.TABLESPACES

```
SELECT TBSPACE, BUFFERPOOLID FROM SYSCAT.TABLESPACES
```

to see the results shown in Figure D.5. You can see that there are five table spaces in the database, and all of them are using the buffer pool with an ID of 1. From Example 1, you know this buffer pool ID corresponds to the IBMDEFAULTBP buffer pool.

TBSPACE	BUFFERPOOLID
SYSCATSPACE	1
TEMPSPACE1	1
USERSPACE1	1
IBMDB2SAMPLEREL	1
IBMDB2SAMPLEXML	1

Figure D.5 Contents of the TBSPACE and BUFFERPOOLID columns

You can obtain the same information by displaying the contents of the SYSCAT.TABLESPACES view in the Control Center.

Example 3: Checking for Privileges and Authorizations

A user with user ID *user1* complains that he is not able to insert any rows into a table called MDANG.TABLE1. The first thing you need to know is whether the user *user1* has the authority to insert into MDANG.TABLE1.

You are not sure which SYSCAT view contains the table privilege information. Therefore, you issue the **LIST TABLES FOR SCHEMA SYSCAT** statement to display all available SYSCAT views and hope to see one that might give you the table privilege information.

You browse through the output and find a table called TABAUTH. This might be the table you are looking for. You issue

```
DESCRIBE TABLE SYSCAT.TABAUTH
```

to display its contents. Figure D.6 shows the output.

Figure D.6 displays the contents of the SYSCAT.TABAUTH view. The view contains 13 columns: GRANTOR, GRANTEE, GRANTEETYPE…UPDATEAUTH. The DELETEAUTH column contains information about whether a user has DELETE privileges. Likewise, the INSERTAUTH column contains information about whether a user has INSERT privileges. You issue the following statement to find out what privileges the user *user1* has on MDANG.TABLE1:

```
SELECT * FROM SYSCAT.TABAUTH WHERE GRANTEE = 'USER1'
```

As you can see in Figure D.7, the INSERTAUTH column has a value *N*. This means that the user *user1* does not have insert privileges; therefore, he cannot insert any rows. Note the

Column name	Type Schema	Type name	Length	Scale	Null
GRANTOR	SYSIBM	VARCHAR	128	0	No
GRANTEE	SYSIBM	VARCHAR	128	0	No
GRANTEETYPE	SYSIBM	CHARACTER	1	0	No
TABSCHEMA	SYSIBM	VARCHAR	128	0	No
TABNAME	SYSIBM	VARCHAR	128	0	No
CONTROLAUTH	SYSIBM	CHARACTER	1	0	No
ALTERAUTH	SYSIBM	CHARACTER	1	0	No
DELETEAUTH	SYSIBM	CHARACTER	1	0	No
INDEXAUTH	SYSIBM	CHARACTER	1	0	No
INSERTAUTH	SYSIBM	CHARACTER	1	0	No
REFAUTH	SYSIBM	CHARACTER	1	0	No
SELECTAUTH	SYSIBM	CHARACTER	1	0	No
UPDATEAUTH	SYSIBM	CHARACTER	1	0	No

Figure D.6 Output of the DESCRIBE TABLE command for SYSCAT.TABAUTH

SELECTAUTH column has a value *Y*. This means the user has SELECT privileges for the table MDANG.TABLE1.

GRANTOR	GRANTEE	...	TABSCHEMA	TABNAME	CONTROLAUTH	...	INSERTAUTH	...	SELECTAUTH	UPDATEAUTH
MDANG	USER1	...	MDANG	TABLE1	N	...	N	...	Y	N

Figure D.7 User privileges in a table

You can get the same information using the Control Center. First, browse through all the views in the *Views* folder, and then identify the SYSCAT.TABAUTH view and display its contents.

Now you know how to query the system catalog tables to get the information you need. If you prefer, you can use the Control Center to display the contents of the system catalog tables without having to issue any SQL statements.

How to Use the SYSSTAT Tables to Perform What-If Modeling and Analysis

DB2 maintains the SYSIBM and SYSCAT system catalog tables and views, so they are read-only. However, you can update the SYSSTAT views. This is a special set of views that you can use to update database statistics. The information contained in these views affects how the DB2 optimizer chooses access plans when executing a query.

For planning purposes, you can change the statistical information in the SYSSTAT tables so that they do not reflect the actual state of tables and indexes. This lets you:

- Model query performance on a development system using production system statistics.
- Perform what-if query performance analysis by examining various possible changes to the query access plan.

You must have explicit DBADM authority for the database to modify statistics for tables and indexes and their components. That is, your user ID must have DBADM authority in the SYSCAT.DBAUTH table.

Table D.2 provides information about the system catalog tables that contain catalog statistics and the RUNSTATS options that collect specific statistics.

Table D.2 Table Statistics (SYSCAT.TABLES and SYSSTAT.TABLES)

		RUNSTATS Option	
Statistic	**Description**	**Table**	**Indexes**
FPAGES	Number of pages being used by a table.	Yes	Yes
NPAGES	Number of pages containing rows.	Yes	Yes
OVERFLOW	Number of rows that overflow.	Yes	No
CARD	Number of rows in a table (cardinality).	Yes	Yes[1]
ACTIVE_BLOCKS	For MDC tables, the total number of occupied blocks.	Yes	No

1. If the table does not have any indexes defined and you request statistics for indexes, no new CARD statistics are updated. The previous CARD statistics are retained.

The Yes or No in the RUNSTATS Option column indicates whether you need to execute the **RUNSTATS** command on the table, the indexes, or both to collect the statistics specified in the Statistic column. For example, if you want to collect the statistics on FPAGES, you must execute the **RUNSTATS** command on both the table and indexes. On the other hand, if you want to collect the statistics for OVERFLOW, you need to execute the **RUNSTATS** command on the table only.

Let's walk through a what-if scenario: If the EMPLOYEE table had a lot more rows than it has now, which access plan would the DB2 optimizer choose?

First, collect the statistics on the EMPLOYEE table using the **RUNSTATS** command:

```
RUNSTATS ON TABLE MDANG.EMPLOYEE
```

After it is completed, obtain the statistics by querying the SYSSTAT.TABLES view:

```
SELECT * FROM SYSSTAT.TABLES
WHERE TABSCHEMA = 'MDANG' AND TABNAME = 'EMPLOYEE'
```

Figure D.8 shows the output.

TABSCHEMA	TABNAME	CARD	NPAGES	FPAGES	OVERFLOW	CLUSTERED ...
MDANG	EMPLOYEE	32	2	2	0	

Figure D.8 Statistics for the EMPLOYEE table

In Figure D.8, the CARD column indicates that the EMPLOYEE table currently has 32 rows. To update the statistics for the EMPLOYEE table to reflect a bigger table, issue the following:

```
UPDATE SYSSTAT.TABLES
       SET CARD = 10000,
       NPAGES = 1000,
       FPAGES = 1000,
       OVERFLOW = 2
   WHERE TABSCHEMA = 'MDANG' AND TABNAME = 'EMPLOYEE'
```

After this is completed, you can run your query against the EMPLOYEE table and get the access plan in text-based format using the **db2exfmt** command, or in graphic format using the Visual Explain GUI tool (see Chapter 4, Using the DB2 Tools).

You must be careful when manually updating catalog statistics: Arbitrary changes can seriously affect the performance of subsequent queries. You can use any of the following methods to revert your changes back.

- **ROLLBACK** the unit of work in which the changes have been made (assuming the unit of work has not been committed).
- Use the **RUNSTATS** utility to recalculate and refresh the catalog statistics.
- Update the catalog statistics to indicate that statistics have not been gathered. (For example, setting column NPAGES to –1 indicates that the number-of-pages statistic has not been collected.)
- Replace the catalog statistics with the data they contained before you made any changes. This method is possible only if you used the **db2look** command to capture the statistics before you made any changes.

In some cases, the optimizer may determine that some particular statistical value or combination of values is not valid, it will then use the default values and issue a warning. Such circumstances are rare, however, since most of the validation is done when updating the statistics.

Tables D.3 through D.9 briefly describe the rest of the updatable SYSSTAT views.

Table D.3 Column Statistics (SYSCAT.COLUMNS and SYSSTAT.COLUMNS)

		RUNSTATS Option	
Statistic	**Description**	**Table**	**Indexes**
COLCARD	Column cardinality.	Yes	Yes[1]
AVGCOLLEN	Average length of a column.	Yes	Yes[1]
HIGH2KEY	Second highest value in a column.	Yes	Yes[1]
LOW2KEY	Second lowest value in a column.	Yes	Yes[1]
NUMNULLS	Number of NULLs in a column.	Yes	Yes[1]
SUB_COUNT	Average number of subelements.	Yes	No[2]
SUB_DELIM_LENGTH	Average length of each delimiter separating each subelement.	Yes	No[2]

1. Column statistics are gathered for the first column in the index key.
2. These statistics provide information about data in columns that contain a series of subfields or subelements that are delimited by blanks. The SUB_COUNT and SUB_DELIM_LENGTH statistics are collected only for single-byte character set string columns of type CHAR, VARCHAR, GRAPHIC, and VARGRAPHIC.

Table D.4 Multicolumn Statistics (SYSCAT.COLGROUPS and SYSSTAT.COLGROUPS)

		RUNSTATS Option	
Statistic	**Description**	**Table**	**Indexes**
COLGROUPCARD	Cardinality of the column group.	Yes	No

The multicolumn distribution statistics listed in Tables D.5 and D.6 are not collected by **RUNSTATS.** You can update them manually, however.

Table D.5 Multicolumn Distribution Statistics (SYSCAT.COLGROUPDIST and SYSSTAT.COLGROUPDIST)

		RUNSTATS Option	
Statistic	**Description**	**Table**	**Indexes**
TYPE	F = Frequency value. Q = Quantile value.	Yes	No
ORDINAL	Ordinal number of the column in the group.	Yes	No
SEQNO	Sequence number *n* that represents the *n*th TYPE value.	Yes	No
COLVALUE	The data value as a character literal or a null value.	Yes	No

Table D.6 Multicolumn Distribution Statistics 2 (SYSCAT.COLGROUPDISTCOUNTS and SYSSTAT.COLGROUPDISTCOUNTS)

		RUNSTATS Option	
Statistic	**Description**	**Table**	**Indexes**
TYPE	F = Frequency value. Q = Quantile value.	Yes	No
SEQNO	Sequence number *n* that represents the *n*th TYPE value.	Yes	No
VALCOUNT	If TYPE = F, VALCOUNT is the number of occurrences of COLVALUEs for the column group identified by this SEQNO. If TYPE = Q, VALCOUNT is the number of rows whose value is less than or equal to COLVALUEs for the column group with this SEQNO.	Yes	No
DISTCOUNT	If TYPE = Q, this column contains the number of distinct values that are less than or equal to COLVALUEs for the column group with this SEQNO. Null if unavailable.	Yes	No

Table D.7 Index Statistics (SYSCAT.INDEXES and SYSSTAT.INDEXES)

		RUNSTATS Option	
Statistic	**Description**	**Table**	**Indexes**
NLEAF	Number of index leaf pages.	No	Yes
NLEVELS	Number of index levels.	No	Yes
CLUSTERRATIO	Degree of clustering of table data.	No	Yes[2]
CLUSTERFACTOR	Finer degree of clustering.	No	See [1,2]
DENSITY	Ratio (percentage) of SEQUENTIAL_ PAGES to the number of pages in the range of pages occupied by the index.[3]	No	Yes
FIRSTKEYCARD	Number of distinct values in the first column of the index.	No	Yes
FIRST2KEYCARD	Number of distinct values in the first two columns of the index.	No	Yes
FIRST3KEYCARD	Number of distinct values in the first three columns of the index.	No	Yes

(continues)

Table D.7 Index Statistics (SYSCAT.INDEXES and SYSSTAT.INDEXES) *(Continued)*

		RUNSTATS Option	
Statistic	**Description**	**Table**	**Indexes**
FIRST4KEYCARD	Number of distinct values in the first four columns of the index.	No	Yes
FULLKEYCARD	Number of distinct values in all columns of the index, excluding any key value in a type-2 index for which all record identifiers (RIDs) are marked deleted.	No	Yes
PAGE_FETCH_PAIRS	Page fetch estimates for different buffer sizes.	No	See [1, 2]
SEQUENTIAL_PAGES	Number of leaf pages located on disk in index key order, with few or no large gaps between them.	No	Yes
AVERAGE_SEQUENCE_PAGES	Average number of index pages accessible in sequence. This is the number of index pages that the prefetchers can detect as being in sequence.	No	Yes
AVERAGE_RANDOM_PAGES	Average number of random index pages between sequential page accesses.	No	Yes
AVERAGE_SEQUENCE_GAP	Gap between sequences.	No	Yes
AVERAGE_SEQUENCE_FETCH_PAGES	Average number of table pages accessible in sequence. This is the number of table pages that the prefetchers can detect as being in sequence when they fetch table rows using the index.	No	Yes[4]
AVERAGE_RANDOM_FETCH_PAGES	Average number of random table pages between sequential page accesses when fetching table rows using the index.	No	Yes[4]
AVERAGE_SEQUENCE_FETCH_GAP	Gap between sequences when fetching table rows using the index.	No	Yes[4]
NUMRIDS	Number of record identifiers (RIDs) in the index, including deleted RIDs in type-2 indexes.	No	Yes

Table D.7 Index Statistics (SYSCAT.INDEXES and SYSSTAT.INDEXES) *(Continued)*

Statistic	Description	RUNSTATS Option Table	RUNSTATS Option Indexes
NUMRIDS_DELETED	Total number of RIDs marked deleted in the index, except RIDs on leaf pages on which all record identifiers are marked deleted.	No	Yes
NUM_EMPTY_LEAFS	Total number of leaf pages on which all record identifiers are marked deleted.	No	Yes

1. Detailed index statistics are gathered by specifying the DETAILED clause on the RUNSTATS command.
2. CLUSTERFACTOR and PAGE_FETCH_PAIRS are not collected with the DETAILED clause unless the table is of a respectable size. If the table is greater than about 25 pages, then CLUSTERFACTOR and PAGE_FETCH_PAIRS statistics are collected. In this case, CLUSTERRATIO is –1 (not collected). If the table is a relatively small table, only CLUSTERRATIO is filled in by RUNSTATS while CLUSTERFACTOR and PAGE_FETCH_PAIRS are not. If the DETAILED clause is not specified, only the CLUSTERRATIO statistic is collected.
3. This statistic measures the percentage of pages in the file containing the index that belongs to that table. For a table having only one defined index, DENSITY should normally be 100. DENSITY is used by the optimizer to estimate how many irrelevant pages from other indexes might be read, on average, if the index pages were prefetched.
4. These statistics cannot be computed when this table is in a DMS table space.

Column distribution statistics (listed in Table D.8) are gathered by specifying the WITH DISTRIBUTION clause on the **RUNSTATS** command. Note that distribution statistics *cannot* be gathered unless there is a sufficient lack of uniformity in the column values.

Table D.8 Column Distribution Statistics (SYSCAT.COLDIST and SYSSTAT.COLDIST)

Statistic	Description	RUNSTATS Option Table	RUNSTATS Option Indexes
DISTCOUNT	If TYPE = Q, the number of distinct values that are less than or equal to COLVALUE statistics.	Distribution[1]	No
TYPE	Indicator of whether row provides frequent-value or quantile statistics.	Distribution	No
SEQNO	Frequency ranking of a sequence number to help uniquely identify the row in the table.	Distribution	No
COLVALUE	Data value for which frequency or quantile statistics is collected.	Distribution	No
VALCOUNT	Frequency with which the data value occurs in columns. For quantiles, the number of values is less than or equal to the data value (COLVALUE).	Distribution	No

1. DISTCOUNT is collected only for columns that are the first key column in an index.

Table D.9 Function Statistics (SYSCAT.FUNCTIONS and SYSSTAT.FUNCTIONS)

Statistic	Description
IOS_PER_INVOC	Estimated number of read/write requests executed each time a function is executed.
INSTS_PER_INVOC	Estimated number of machine instructions executed each time a function is executed.
IOS_PER_ARGBYTE	Estimated number of read/write requests executed per input argument byte.
INSTS_PER_ARGBYTES	Estimated number of machine instructions executed per input argument byte.
PERCENT_ARGBYTES	Estimated average percent of input argument bytes that the function will actually process.
INITIAL_IOS	Estimated number of read/write requests executed only the first/last time the function is invoked.
INITIAL_INSTS	Estimated number of machine instructions executed only the first/last time the function is invoked.
CARDINALITY	Estimated number of rows generated by a table function.

Resources

This section lists the Web site resources referenced in this book as well as additional resources, including traditional course offerings, computer-based training courses, free tutorials, and other information. The document WebsiteResources.txt provided on the Web site of this book (www.ibmpressbooks.com/title/0131580183) contains all the Web sites listed in this section so that you can copy and paste the URLs directly into your browser.

Table R.1 lists the Web site resources referenced in this book. It provides a brief description of the Web site and notes the chapter where it was referenced.

Table R.1 Web Sites Referenced in This Book

Resource Name	Description	URL	Chapter
Information On Demand	Main page for IBM's Information On Demand strategy	www.ibm.com/software/data/information-on-demand	1
DB2 for Linux, UNIX, and Windows main Web page	Information about DB2 products	www.ibm.com/db2	1
IBM DB2 Support Web site—FixPaks	Place to obtain DB2 clients and FixPaks and to search for APARS, fixes, and whitepapers	www.ibm.com/software/data/db2/support/db2_9	1
The DB2 Information Center	Search engine for searching in the DB2 manuals	**Version 9:** http://publib.boulder.ibm.com/infocenter/db2luw/v9/index.jsp **Version 9.5:** https://publib.boulder.ibm.com/infocenter/db2luw/v9r5/index.jsp	4
DB2 Documentation (on the DB2 Technical Support Web site)	PDF versions of the DB2 manuals	http://www-1.ibm.com/support/docview.wss?rs=71&uid=swg27009474	18
Search for DB2 known problems (within DB2 Technical Support Web site)		www.ibm.com/software/data/db2/udb/support.html	18

Table R.2 lists other books of interest we have mentioned in this book.

Table R.2 Other Books Referenced

Book Information	Chapter
Zamil, Janmohamed, Clara Liu, Drew Bradstock, Raul Chong, Michael Gao, Fraser McArthur, and Paul Yip. *DB2 SQL PL: Essential Guide for DB2 UDB on Linux, UNIX, Windows, i5/OS, and z/OS*. Boston: Prentice Hall. 2004.	7
Snow, Dwaine R. and Thomas X. Phan. *Advanced DBA Certification Guide and Reference* for DB2 Universal Database V8 for Linux, UNIX, and Windows. Boston: Prentice Hall. 2004.	17

In addition to reading this book to prepare for the DB2 database administration certification exams, there are free tutorials you can take. Table R.3 lists the IBM Professional Certification program Web site and the tutorial Web sites for all available certification exams.

Table R.3 IBM Certification Program and Tutorials Web Site

Web Site Name	URL
IBM's Professional Certification Program	www.ibm.com/certify
DB2 9 Fundamentals Certification (Exam 730) Tutorial	http://www.ibm.com/developerworks/offers/lp/db2cert/db2-cert730.html
DB2 9 DBA Certification (Exam 731) Tutorial	http://www.ibm.com/developerworks/offers/lp/db2cert/db2-cert731.html
DB2 9 Application Development Certification (Exam 733) Tutorial	http://www.ibm.com/developerworks/offers/lp/db2cert/db2-cert733.html
DB2 9 Advanced DBA Cerfitication (Exam 734)	Tutorials not yet available

Table R.4 lists some of the traditional classroom courses for DB2 database administration and performance tuning offered by IBM Learning Services. For more information, see the DB2 Education Web site at www.ibm.com/software/data/education.html.

Table R.4 Course Offerings

Course Number	Course Name
CF202	DB2 9 Database Administration Workshop for Linux
CF212	DB2 9 Database Administration Workshop for UNIX

Table R.4 Course Offerings

Course Number	Course Name
CF232	DB2 9 Database Administration Workshop for Windows
CF241	DB2 UDB Multi Partition Database Administration Workshop for UNIX
CF413	DB2 9 for Linux, UNIX, and Windows Performance Tuning and Monitoring Workshop
CF443	DB2 UDB for UNIX Multi Partition Performance Workshop
CF460	DB2 UDB Advanced Database Administration for Experts Workshop
CF491	DB2 UDB Advanced Recovery for Single Partition Databases

Table R.5 lists resources that provide articles, books, whitepapers, brochures, and so on about DB2. It also includes information about news groups.

Table R.5 DB2 Technical Resources, Magazines, and News Groups

Resource Name	Description	URL
IBM Software Support	One-stop shop for any software support resources	www.ibm.com/software/support
DeveloperWorks	DB2 articles of interest	www.ibm.com/developerworks/db2
IBM Redbooks	Free books about IBM technology	www.redbooks.ibm.com
DB2 Technical Materials Library	Books, whitepapers, brochures, consultant reports, technology overviews, and so on	www.ibm.com/software/data/pubs/
DB2 Forums	A list of all the IBM DB2 forums hosted by developerWorks	http://www-128.ibm.com/developerworks/forums/db2_forums.jsp
DB2 News Group	News, forums about DB2	comp.databases.ibm-db2
	comp.databases.ibm-db2 Google Newsgroup	http://groups.google.ca/group/comp.databases.ibm-db2/about
DB2 on CompuServe	News, forums about DB2	Go ibmdb2

(continues)

Table R.5 DB2 Technical Resources, Magazines, and News Groups *(Continued)*

Resource Name	Description	URL
DB2 Magazine	A magazine about DB2. Each issue contains a variety of features on technical and business topics for the DB2 community, plus columns with tips and techniques on data mining, programming, system administration, content management, and more. The magazine is available in print as well as on the Web.	www.db2mag.com

You can participate in user groups and DB2 conferences to keep up to date with the latest new features or version of DB2. Table R.6 lists the two most popular resources.

Table R.6 DB2 User Groups and Conferences

Resource Name	Description	URL
International DB2 Users Group (IDUG)	DB2 user group organization	www.idug.org/
DB2 and other IBM Technical Conferences	Technical conference with sessions of interest about DB2 and other products	www.ibm.com/services/learning/conf/us/index.html

For IBM Business Partners, Table R.7 lists the relevant Web site.

Table R.7 IBM Business Partners Information

Resource Name	Description	URL
IBM PartnerWorld Home Page	Home page for IBM Business Partners support	www.ibm.com/partnerworld

For blogs about DB2, Table R.8 lists the relevant Web sites.

Table R.8 Blogs about DB2

Resource Name	URL
Blogs about DB2	http://blogs.ittoolbox.com/database/db2luw
Blog aggregator about DB2 worldwide	http://planetdb2.com/

Other interesting resources can be found in Table R.9

Table R.9 Other Resources about DB2

Resource Name	URL
The DB2ZONE	http://www.gunningts.com/db2zone
LAZYDBA Listserver	http://www.lazydba.com/

Index

D

DB2

maintenance performance

E

F

G

H

I

J

K

L

M

N

O

P

Q

R

T

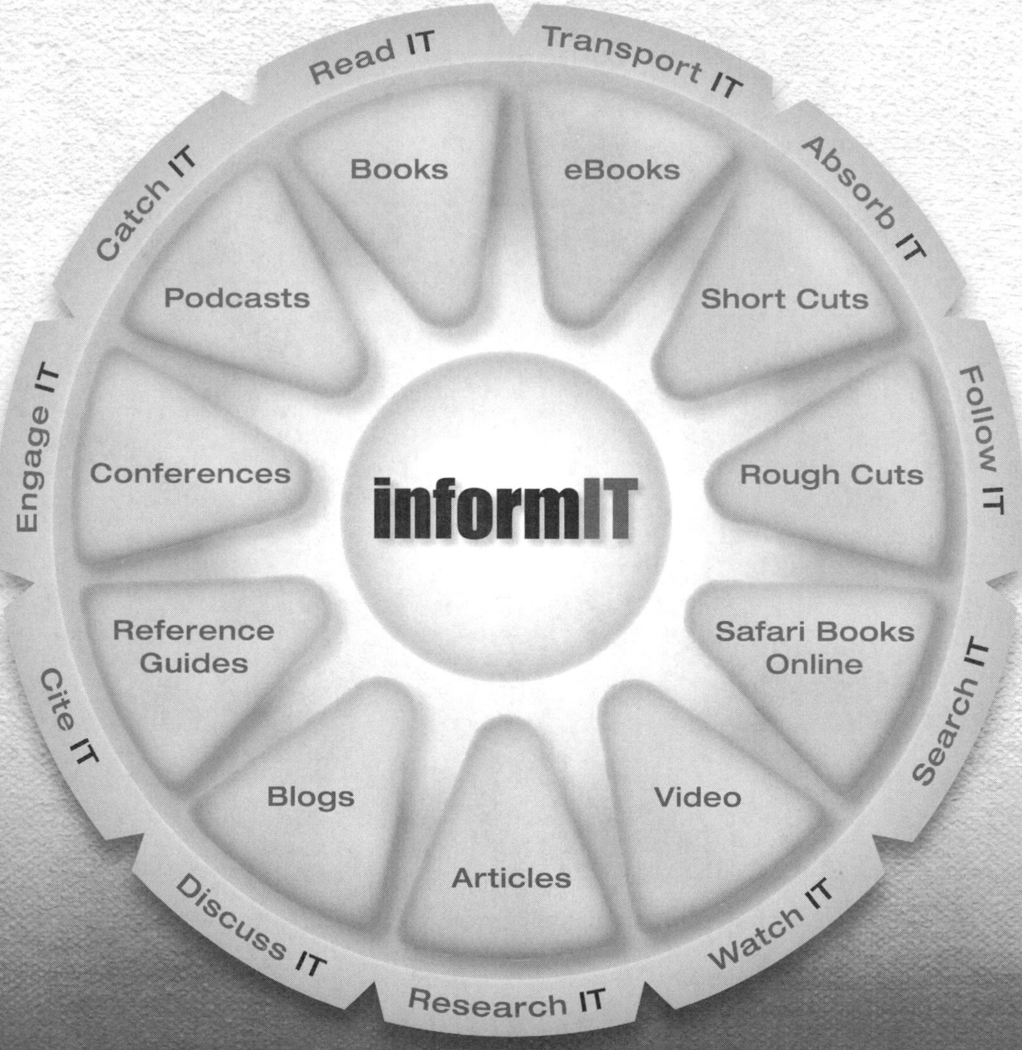